11th International Natural Language Generation Conference (INLG 2018)

Tilburg, The Netherlands
5 - 8 November 2018

ISBN: 978-1-5108-7431-2

INLG 2018

The 11th International
Natural Language Generation Conference

Proceedings of the Conference

November 5-8, 2018
Tilburg, The Netherlands

Order copies of this and other ACL proceedings from:

Association for Computational Linguistics (ACL)
209 N. Eighth Street
Stroudsburg, PA 18360
USA
Tel: +1-570-476-8006
Fax: +1-570-476-0860
acl@aclweb.org

Preface

We are proud to present the Proceedings of the 11th International Natural Language Generation Conference (INLG 2018)!

INLG 2018 was organised by the Tilburg University Language Production (TULP) research group, part of the Department of Communication and Cognition (DCC) of the Tilburg School of Humanities and Digital Sciences (TSHD). The event took place under the auspices of the Special Interest Group on Natural Language Generation (SIGGEN) of the Association for Computational Linguistics (ACL) as well as the International Speech Communication Association (ISCA).

In view of the long Dutch tradition of automatically generating soccer reports (e.g., Theune et al., 2001; van der Lee et al., 2017), we felt it was wholly appropriate that the conference was organised in the Willem II stadium, home of the best soccer team in The Netherlands (in 1916, 1952 and 1955).

The INLG conference is the main international forum for the presentation and discussion of all aspects of Natural Language Generation (NLG), including data-to-text, concept-to-text, text-to-text and vision-to-text approaches. Special topics of interest for the 2018 edition included:

- Generating Text with Affect, Style and Personality,

- Conversational Interfaces, Chatbots and NLG, and

- Data-driven NLG (including the E2E Generation Challenge).

Related to these three topics, we invited three international experts to contribute to the conference:

- Lillian Lee (Cornell University, Ithaca, USA)

- Piek Vossen (Vrije Universiteit Amsterdam, The Netherlands)

- Yoav Goldberg (Bar Ilan University, Israel)

The latter opened the conference with an invited tutorial on Neural NLG. In addition to the main conference, five workshops were accepted following a Call for Workshop Proposals:

- 3rd Workshop on Computational Creativity in Language Generation (CC-NLG 2018),

- Workshop on Intelligent Interactive Systems and Language Generation (2IS&NLG),

- MyNLG: 1st Workshop on Style, Affect and Character,

- Workshop on Natural Language Generation for Human-Robot Interaction and

- Workshop on Text adaptation.

Additionally, the conference hosted the third SIGGEN Hackathon which, for the first time, is a full day event.

For the main conference, we received a record number of 102 submissions, of which 20 were accepted for oral presentation, 4 as demo presentations and 38 as posters (including 5 related to the E2E challenge). All accepted papers are included in these proceedings.

We received financial support from the Netherlands Organisation for Scientific Research (NWO), via grant Grant PR-14-87 (Producing Affective Language: Content Selection, Message Formulation and Computational Modelling). Additionally, the conference was sponsored by (in alphabetical order):

- Arria NLG;

- flow.ai;

- Microsoft Research; and

- Philips.

We would like to thank all our sponsors for their support, and want to extend our gratitude to all speakers and reviewers for their excellent work.

Emiel Krahmer
Albert Gatt
Martijn Goudbeek

INLG 2018 PC Chairs

General and Programme Chairs:

> Emiel Krahmer (Tilburg University, The Netherlands)
> Martijn Goudbeek (Tilburg University, The Netherlands)
> Albert Gatt (University of Malta, Malta)

Invited Speakers:

> Yoav Goldberg (Bar Ilan University, Israel)
> Lillian Lee (Cornell University, Ithaca, USA)
> Piek Vossen (Vrije Universiteit Amsterdam, The Netherlands)

Workshop Chairs:

> Mariët Theune (University of Twente, The Netherlands)
> Sina Zarrieß (Universität Bielefeld, Germany)

Hackathon Chair:

> Somayajulu Sripada (University of Aberdeen/Arria NLG, UK)

Local Organization Committee:

> Nadine Braun (Tilburg University, The Netherlands)
> Thiago Castro Ferreira (Tilburg University, The Netherlands)
> Ákos Kádár (Tilburg University, The Netherlands)
> Ruud Koolen (Tilburg University, The Netherlands)
> Chris van der Lee (Tilburg University, The Netherlands)
> Lauraine de Lima (Tilburg University, The Netherlands)
> Fons Maes (Tilburg University, The Netherlands)
> Emiel van Miltenburg (Tilburg University, The Netherlands)
> Charlotte Out (Tilburg University, The Netherlands)
> Steffen Pauws (Tilburg University, The Netherlands)
> Ruben Vromans (Tilburg University, The Netherlands)
> Bram Willemsen (Tilburg University, The Netherlands)
> Jan de Wit (Tilburg University, The Netherlands)

Program Committee:

> Jose Alonso (CiTIUS-USC, Spain)
> Anja Belz (University of Brighton, UK)
> Alberto Bugarín Diz (CiTIUS-USC, Spain)
> Thiago Castro Ferreira (Tilburg University, The Netherlands)
> Robert Dale (Macquarie University, Australia)
> Kees van Deemter (Utrecht University, The Netherlands)
> Nina Dethlefs (University of Hull, UK)
> Ondřej Dušek (Heriot-Watt University, Edinburgh, UK)

Nikos Engonopoulos (University of Saarland, Germany)
Claire Gardent (LORIA-CNRS, France)
Albert Gatt (University of Malta, Malta)
Lorenzo Gatti (University of Twente, The Netherlands)
Pablo Gervás (UCM, Spain)
Dimitra Gkatzia (Edinburgh Napier University, UK)
Martijn Goudbeek (Tilburg University, The Netherlands)
Aki Harma (Philips Research, The Netherlands)
Helen Hastie (Heriot Watt University, UK)
David M. Howcroft (Universität des Saarlandes, Germany)
Amy Isard (University of Edinburgh, UK)
Ákos Kádár (Tilburg University, The Netherlands)
John Kelleher (Dublin Institute of Technology, Ireland)
Ioannis Konstas (University of Washington, USA)
Emiel Krahmer (Tilburg University, The Netherlands)
Cyril Labbe (Université Joseph Fourier, France)
Gerasimos Lampouras (University of Sheffield, UK)
Guy Lapalme (Université de Montréal, Canada)
Elena Lloret (University of Alicante, Spain)
Saad Mahamood (Arria NLG, UK)
David McDonald (SIFT, USA)
Simon Mille (Universitat Pompeu Fabra, Spain)
Emiel van Miltenburg (Vrije Universiteit Amsterdam, The Netherlands)
Diego Moussallem (Universität Leipzig, Germany)
Steffen Pauws (Philips Research/Tilburg University, The Netherlands)
Paul Piwek (The Open University, UK)
François Portet (University Grenoble, France)
Alejandro Ramos Soto (CiTIUS-USC, Spain)
Ehud Reiter (Arria NLG/University of Aberdeen, UK)
Alexander M. Rush (Harvard University, Cambridge, USA)
Daniel Sanchez (University of Granada, Spain)
David Schlangen (Universität Bielefeld, Germany)
Advaith Siddharthan (The Open University, UK)
Somayajulu Sripada (University of Aberdeen/Arria NLG, UK)
Kristina Striegnitz (Union College, USA)
Marc Tanti (University of Malta, Malta)
Mariët Theune (University of Twente, The Netherlands)
Keith Vander Linden (Calvin College, USA)
Marilyn Walker (UC Santa Cruz, USA)
Leo Wanner (Universitat Pompeu Fabra, Spain)
Michael White (Ohio State University, USA)
Sander Wubben (Flow.ai/Tilburg University, The Netherlands)
Sina Zarrieß (Universität Bielefeld, Germany)

Table of Contents

Conference Program

Monday, November 5, 2018

08:30–09:00 **Registration at Tilburg University Campus**

09:00–10:30 **Workshop 1: 3rd Workshop on Computational Creativity in Language Generation (CC-NLG)**

09:00–10:30 **Workshop 2: Workshop on Intelligent Interactive Systems and Language Generation (2IS&NLG)**

09:00–10:30 **Workshop 3: MyNLG: 1st Workshop on Style, Affect and Character**

10:30–11:00 **Coffee/Tea Break**

11:00–12:30 **Workshop 1 (cont.)**

11:00–12:30 **Workshop 2 (cont.)**

11:00–12:30 **Workshop 3 (cont.)**

12:30–13:30 **Lunch**

14:00–15:00 **Registration at Willem II Stadium**

15:00–15:15 **Opening of INLG 2018**

15:15–16:15 **Tutorial: Yoav Goldberg**, *Neural Natural Language Generation (Part 1)*

16:15–16:30 **Coffee/Tea Break**

16:30–17:30 **Tutorial: Yoav Goldberg**, *Neural Natural Language Generation (Part 2)*

17:30–19:00 **Welcome Reception**

Tuesday, November 6, 2018

08:30–09:00	**Registration**

09:00–09:05 Welcoming address

09:05–10:45 Oral Session 1: Knowledge Representation and Text Generation

09:05–09:25 *Deep Graph Convolutional Encoders for Structured Data to Text Generation*
Diego Marcheggiani and Laura Perez-Beltrachini

09:25–09:45 *Describing a Knowledge Base*
Qingyun Wang, Xiaoman Pan, Lifu Huang, Boliang Zhang, Zhiying Jiang, Heng Ji
and Kevin Knight

09;45–10:05 *Syntactic Manipulation for Generating more Diverse and Interesting Texts*
Jan Milan Deriu and Mark Cieliebak

10:05–10:25 *Automated Learning of Templates for Data-to-Text Generation: Comparing Rule-Based, Statistical and Neural Methods*
Chris van der Lee, Emiel Krahmer and Sander Wubben

10:25–10:45 *End-to-End Content and Plan Selection for Data-to-Text Generation*
Sebastian Gehrmann, Falcon Dai, Henry Elder and Alexander Rush

10:45–11:15 Coffee/Tea Break

11:15–12:15 Keynote 1: Piek Vossen
Don't Believe Everything You See, Hear or Read: A Theory of Mind that Drives Robot-Human Communication

12:15–12:30 3rd SIGGEN Hackathon: Introduction

Automatic Opinion Question Generation
Yllias Chali and Tina Baghaee

Modelling Pro-Drop with the Rational Speech Acts Model
Guanyi Chen, Kees van Deemter and Chenghua Lin

Self-Learning Architecture for Natural Language Generation
Hyungtak Choi, Siddarth KM, Haehun Yang, Heesik Jeon, Inchul Hwang and Jihie
Kim

Enriching the WebNLG Corpus
Thiago Castro Ferreira, Diego Moussallem, Emiel Krahmer and Sander Wubben

Towards Making NLG a Voice for Interpretable Machine Learning
James Forrest, Somayajulu Sripada, Wei Pang and George Coghill

*Template-Based Multilingual Football Reports Generation Using Wikidata as a
Knowledge Base*
Lorenzo Gatti, Chris van der Lee and Mariët Theune

Automatic Evaluation of Neural Personality-Based Chatbots
Yujie Xing and Raquel Fernández

12:30–14:30   Demo Session 1 (including lunch)

Poem Machine: A Co-creative NLG Web Application for Poem Writing
Mika Hämäläinen

Japanese Advertising Slogan Generator Using Case Frame and Word Vector
Kango Iwama and Yoshinobu Kano

14:30–15:30   Oral Session 2: Syntactic Realisation

14:30–14:50   *Underspecified Universal Dependency Structures as Inputs for Multilingual Surface
Realisation*
Simon Mille, Anja Belz, Bernd Bohnet and Leo Wanner

14:50–15:10   *LSTM Hypertagging*
Reid Fu and Michael White

15:10–15:30   *Sequence-to-Sequence Models for Data-to-Text Natural Language Generation:
Word- vs. Character-Based Processing and Output Diversity*
Glorianna Jagfeld, Sabrina Jenne and Ngoc Thang Vu

15:30–16:00   **Coffee/Tea Break**

16:00–17:00   **Oral Session 3: Applications of Automatic Text Generation**

16:00–16:20   *Generating E-Commerce Product Titles and Predicting their Quality*
José G. C. de Souza, Michael Kozielski, Prashant Mathur, Ernie Chang, Marco Guerini, Matteo Negri, Marco Turchi and Evgeny Matusov

16:20–16:40   *Designing and Testing the Messages Produced by a Virtual Dietitian*
Luca Anselma and Alessandro Mazzei

16:40–17:00   *Generation of Company Descriptions Using Concept-to-Text and Text-to-Text Deep Models: Dataset Collection and Systems Evaluation*
Raheel Qader, Khoder Jneid, François Portet and Cyril Labbé

18:00–20:00   **Social Event**

Wednesday, November 7, 2018

08:30–09:00 **Registration**

09:00–10:40 **Oral Session 4: Questions and Dialogue**

09:00–09:20 *Automatically Generating Questions about Novel Metaphors in Literature*
Natalie Parde and Rodney Nielsen

09:20–09:40 *A Master-Apprentice Approach to Automatic Creation of Culturally Satirical Movie Titles*
Khalid Alnajjar and Mika Hämäläinen

09:40–10:00 *Can Neural Generators for Dialogue Learn Sentence Planning and Discourse Structuring?*
Lena Reed, Shereen Oraby and Marilyn Walker

10:00–10:20 *Neural Generation of Diverse Questions using Answer Focus, Contextual and Linguistic Features*
Vrindavan Harrison and Marilyn Walker

10:20–10:40 *Evaluation Methodologies in Automatic Question Generation 2013-2018*
Jacopo Amidei, Paul Piwek and Alistair Willis

10:40–11:15 **Coffee/Tea Break**

11:15–12:30 **Generation Challenges Special Session**

11:15–11:35 *Task Proposal: The TL;DR Challenge*
Shahbaz Syed, Michael Völske, Martin Potthast, Nedim Lipka, Benno Stein and Hinrich Schütze

11:35–11:55 *Report on the Multilingual Surface Realization Challenge*
Simon Mille

11:55–12:15 *Findings of the E2E NLG Challenge*
Ondřej Dušek, Jekaterina Novikova and Verena Rieser

12:30–14:30   Poster Session 2 (including lunch)

Adapting Descriptions of People to the Point of View of a Moving Observer
Gonzalo Méndez, Raquel Hervas, Pablo Gervás, Ricardo de la Rosa and Daniel
Ruiz

BENGAL: An Automatic Benchmark Generator for Entity Recognition and Linking
Axel-Cyrille Ngonga Ngomo, Michael Röder, Diego Moussallem, Ricardo Usbeck
and René Speck

Sentence Packaging in Text Generation from Semantic Graphs as a Community De-tection Problem
Alexander Shvets, Simon Mille and Leo Wanner

Handling Rare Items in Data-to-Text Generation
Anastasia Shimorina and Claire Gardent

Comprehension Driven Document Planning in Natural Language Generation Sys-tems
Craig Thomson, Ehud Reiter and Somayajulu Sripada

Adapting Neural Single-Document Summarization Model for Abstractive Multi-Document Summarization: A Pilot Study
Jianmin Zhang, Jiwei Tan and Xiaojun Wan

Toward Bayesian Synchronous Tree Substitution Grammars for Sentence Planning
David M. Howcroft, Dietrich Klakow and Vera Demberg

The Task Matters: Comparing Image Captioning and Task-Based Dialogical Image Description
Nikolai Ilinykh, Sina Zarrieß and David Schlangen

Generating Summaries of Sets of Consumer Products: Learning from Experiments
Kittipitch Kuptavanich, Ehud Reiter, Kees van Deemter and Advaith Siddharthan

Neural Sentence Generation from Formal Semantics
Kana Manome, Masashi Yoshikawa, Hitomi Yanaka, Pascual Martínez-Gómez,
Koji Mineshima and Daisuke Bekki

Talking about Other People: An Endless Range of Possibilities
Emiel van Miltenburg, Desmond Elliott and Piek Vossen

Meteorologists and Students: A Resource for Language Grounding of Geographical Descriptors
Alejandro Ramos Soto, Ehud Reiter, Kees van Deemter, Jose Alonso and Albert
Gatt

Cyclegen: Cyclic Consistency Based Product Review Generator from Attributes
Vasu Sharma, Harsh Sharma, Ankita Bishnu and Labhesh Patel

Neural Transition-Based Syntactic Linearization
Linfeng Song, Yue Zhang and Daniel Gildea

12:30–14:30   **E2E Challenge Posters (including lunch)**

Characterizing Variation in Crowd-Sourced Data for Training Neural Language Generators to Produce Stylistically Varied Outputs
Juraj Juraska and Marilyn Walker

Char2char Generation with Reranking for the E2E NLG Challenge
Shubham Agarwal, Marc Dymetman and Eric Gaussier

E2E NLG Challenge Submission: Towards Controllable Generation of Diverse Natural Language
Henry Elder, Sebastian Gehrmann, Alexander O'Connor and Qun Liu

E2E NLG Challenge: Neural Models vs. Templates
Yevgeniy Puzikov and Iryna Gurevych

The E2E NLG Challenge: A Tale of Two Systems
Charese Smiley, Elnaz Davoodi, Dezhao Song and Frank Schilder

12:30–14:30   **Demo Session 2 (including lunch)**

Interactive Health Insight Miner: An Adaptive, Semantic-Based Approach
Isabel Funke, Rim Helaoui and Aki Harma

Multi-Language Surface Realisation as REST API Based NLG Microservice
Andreas Madsack, Johanna Heininger, Nyamsuren Davaasambuu, Vitaliia Voronik, Michael Käufl and Robert Weißgraeber

14:30–15:30 Keynote 2: Lillian Lee
Analyzing Phrasing Effects via Found Conversations: "Parallel Universes" in Movies, Twitter and ChangeMyView

15:30–16:00 Coffee/Tea Break

16:00–17:00 Oral Session 5: Referring Expression Generation

16:00–16:20 *Statistical NLG for Generating the Content and Form of Referring Expressions*
Xiao Li, Kees van Deemter and Chenghua Lin

16:20–16:40 *Specificity Measures and Reference*
Albert Gatt, Nicolás Marín, Gustavo Rivas-Gervilla and Daniél Sánchez

16:40–17:00 *Decoding Strategies for Neural Referring Expression Generation*
Sina Zarrieß and David Schlangen

18:30–23:00 Conference Dinner

Thursday, November 8, 2018

08:30–09:00	**Registration at Tilburg University Campus**

09:00–10:30   **Workshop 4: Workshop on Natural Language Generation for Human-Robot Interaction**

09:00–10:30   **Workshop 5: Workshop on Text Adaptation**

09:00–10:30   **3rd SIGGEN Hackathon**

10:30–11:00   **Coffee/Tea Break**

11:00–12:30   **Workshop 4 (cont.)**

11:00–12:30   **Workshop 5 (cont.)**

11:00–12:30   **3rd SIGGEN Hackathon (cont.)**

12:30–13:30   **Lunch**

13:30–15:00   **Workshop 4 (cont.)**

13:30–15:00   **3rd SIGGEN Hackathon (cont.)**

15:30–17:00   **Coffee/Tea Break**

15:30–17:00   **Workshop 4 (cont.)**

15:30–17:00   **3rd SIGGEN Hackathon (cont.)**

17:00   **End of Conference, Workshops and Hackathon**

Deep Graph Convolutional Encoders for Structured Data to Text Generation

Diego Marcheggiani[1,2]   **Laura Perez-Beltrachini**[1]
[1]ILCC, School of Informatics, University of Edinburgh
[2]ILLC, University of Amsterdam
marcheggiani@uva.nl   lperez@inf.ed.ac.uk

Abstract

Most previous work on neural text generation from graph-structured data relies on standard sequence-to-sequence methods. These approaches linearise the input graph to be fed to a recurrent neural network. In this paper, we propose an alternative encoder based on graph convolutional networks that directly exploits the input structure. We report results on two graph-to-sequence datasets that empirically show the benefits of explicitly encoding the input graph structure.[1]

1 Introduction

Data-to-text generators produce a target natural language text from a source data representation. Recent neural generation approaches (Mei et al., 2016; Lebret et al., 2016; Wiseman et al., 2017; Gardent et al., 2017b; Ferreira et al., 2017; Konstas et al., 2017) build on encoder-decoder architectures proposed for machine translation (Sutskever et al., 2014; Bahdanau et al., 2015).

The source data, differently from the machine translation task, is a structured representation of the content to be conveyed. Generally, it describes attributes and events about entities and relations among them. In this work we focus on two generation scenarios where the source data is graph structured. One is the generation of multi-sentence descriptions of Knowledge Base (KB) entities from RDF graphs (Perez-Beltrachini et al., 2016; Gardent et al., 2017a,b), namely the WebNLG task.[2] The number of KB relations modelled in this scenario is potentially large and generation involves solving various subtasks (e.g. lexicalisation and aggregation). Figure (1a) shows and example of source RDF graph and target natural language description. The other is the linguistic realisation of the meaning expressed by a source dependency graph (Belz et al., 2011), namely the SR11Deep generation task. In this task, the semantic relations are linguistically motivated and their number is smaller. Figure (1b) illustrates a source dependency graph and the corresponding target text.

Most previous work casts the graph structured data to text generation task as a sequence-to-sequence problem (Gardent et al., 2017b; Ferreira et al., 2017; Konstas et al., 2017). They rely on recurrent data encoders with memory and gating mechanisms (LSTM; (Hochreiter and Schmidhuber, 1997)). Models based on these sequential encoders have shown good results although they do not directly exploit the input structure but rather rely on a separate linearisation step. In this work, we compare with a model that explicitly encodes structure and is trained end-to-end. Concretely, we use a Graph Convolutional Network (GCN; (Kipf and Welling, 2016; Marcheggiani and Titov, 2017)) as our encoder.

GCNs are a flexible architecture that allows explicit encoding of graph data into neural networks. Given their simplicity and expressiveness they have been used to encode dependency syntax and predicate-argument structures in neural machine translation (Bastings et al., 2017; Marcheggiani et al., 2018). In contrast to previous work, we do not exploit the sequential information of the input (i.e., with an LSTM), but we solely rely on a GCN for encoding the source graph structure.[3]

The main contribution of this work is showing that explicitly encoding structured data with

---

[1]Code and data available at github.com/diegma/graph-2-text.

[2]Resource Description Framework https://www.w3.org/RDF/

[3]Concurrently with this work, Beck et al. (2018) also encoded input structures without relying on sequential encoders.

1

Proceedings of The 11th International Natural Language Generation Conference, pages 1–9,
Tilburg, The Netherlands, November 5-8, 2018. ©2018 Association for Computational Linguistics

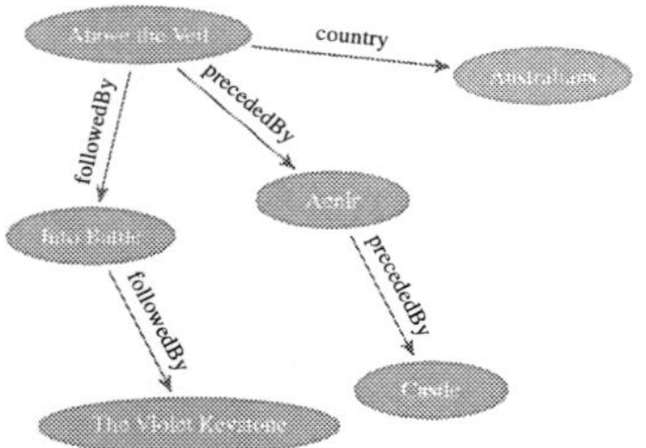

(a) *Above the Veil is an Australian novel and the sequel to Aenir and Castle . It was followed by Into the Battle and The Violet Keystone .*

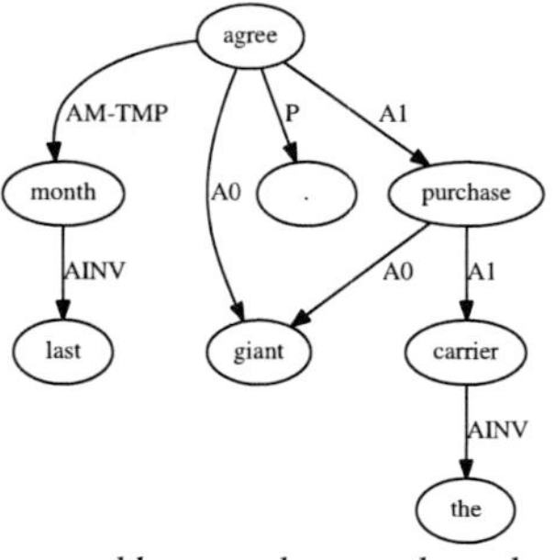

(b) *Giant agreed last month to purchase the carrier .*

Figure 1: Source RDF graph - target description (a). Source dependency graph - target sentence (b).

GCNs is more effective than encoding a linearized version of the structure with LSTMs. We evaluate the GCN-based generator on two graph-to-sequence tasks, with different level of source content specification. In both cases, the results we obtain show that GCNs encoders outperforms standard LSTM encoders.

2 Graph Convolutional-based Generator

Formally, we address the task of text generation from graph-structured data considering as input a directed labeled graph $X = (\mathcal{V}, \mathcal{E})$ where $\mathcal{V}$ is a set of nodes and $\mathcal{E}$ is a set of edges between nodes in $\mathcal{V}$. The specific semantics of X depends on the task at hand. The output Y is a natural language text verbalising the content expressed by X. Our generation model follows the standard attention-based encoder-decoder architecture (Bahdanau et al., 2015; Luong et al., 2015) and predicts Y conditioned on X as $P(Y|X) = \prod_{t=1}^{|Y|} P(y_t|y_{1:t-1}, X)$.

Graph Convolutional Encoder In order to explicitly encode structural information we adopt graph convolutional networks (GCNs). GCNs are a variant of graph neural networks (Scarselli et al., 2009) that has been recently proposed by Kipf and Welling (2016). The goal of GCNs is to calculate the representation of each node in a graph considering the graph structure. In this paper we adopt the parametrization proposed by Marcheggiani and Titov (2017) where edge labels and directions are explicitly modeled. Formally, given a directed graph $X = (\mathcal{V}, \mathcal{E})$, where $\mathcal{V}$ is a set of nodes, and $\mathcal{E}$ is a set of edges. We represent each node $v \in \mathcal{V}$ with a feature vector $\mathbf{x}_v \in \mathbb{R}^d$. The GCN calculates the representation of each node $\mathbf{h}'_v$ in a graph using the following update rule:

$$\mathbf{h}'_v = \rho\left(\sum_{u \in \mathcal{N}(v)} g_{u,v}\left(W_{dir(u,v)}\, \mathbf{h}_u + \mathbf{b}_{lab(u,v)}\right)\right),$$

where $\mathcal{N}(v)$ is the set of neighbours of v, $W_{dir(u,v)} \in \mathbb{R}^{d \times d}$ is a direction-specific parameter matrix. As Marcheggiani and Titov (2017); Bastings et al. (2017) we assume there are three possible directions ($dir(u,v) \in \{in, out, loop\}$): self-loop edges ensure that the initial representation of node $\mathbf{h}_v$ affects the new representation $\mathbf{h}'_v$. The vector $\mathbf{b}_{lab(u,v)} \in \mathbb{R}^d$ is an embedding of the label of the edge (u,v) . ρ is a non-linearity (ReLU). $g_{u,v}$ are learned scalar gates which weight the importance of each edge. Although the main aim of gates is to down weight erroneous edges in predicted graphs, they also add flexibility when several GCN layers are stacked. As with standard convolutional neural networks (CNNs, (LeCun et al., 2001)), GCN layers can be stacked to consider non-immediate neighbours.[4]

Skip Connections Between GCN layers we add skip connections. Skip connections let the gradient flows more efficiently through stacked hidden layers thus making possible the creation of deeper GCN encoders. We use two kinds of skip connections: residual connections (He et al., 2016) and dense connections (Huang et al., 2017). Residual connections consist in summing input and output representations of a GCN layer $\mathbf{h}^r_v = \mathbf{h}'_v + \mathbf{h}_v$. Whilst, dense connections consist in the concatenation of the input and output representations $\mathbf{h}^d_v = [\mathbf{h}'_v; \mathbf{h}_v]$. In this way, each GCN layer is directly fed with the output of every layer before itself.

Decoder The decoder uses an LSTM and a soft attention mechanism (Luong et al., 2015) over

---

[4] We discovered during preliminary experiments that without scalar gates the model ends up in poor local minima, especially when several GCN layers are used.

the representation induced by the GCN encoder to generate one word y at the time. The prediction of word y_{t+1} is conditioned on the previously predicted words $y_{1:t}$ encoded in the vector $\mathbf{w}_t$ and a context vector $\mathbf{c}_t$ dynamically created attending to the graph representation induced by the GCN encoder as $P(y_{t+1}|y_{1:t}, X) = softmax(g(\mathbf{w}_t, \mathbf{c}_t))$, where $g(\cdot)$ is a neural network with one hidden layer. The model is trained to optimize negative log likelihood: $\mathcal{L}_{NLL} = -\sum_{t=1}^{|Y|} log\, P(y_t|y_{1:t-1}, X)$

3 Generation Tasks

In this section, we describe the instantiation of the input graph X for the generation tasks we address.

3.1 WebNLG Task

The WebNLG task (Gardent et al., 2017a,b) aims at the generation of entity descriptions from a set of RDF triples related to an entity of a given category (Perez-Beltrachini et al., 2016). RDF triples are of the form (subject relation object), e.g., (Aenir precededBy Castle), and form a graph in which edges are labelled with relations and vertices with subject and object entities. For instance, Figure (1a) shows a set of RDF triples related to the book *Above the Veil* and its verbalisation. The generation task involves several micro-planning decisions such as lexicalisation (followedBy is verbalised as *sequel to*), aggregation (*sequel to Aenir and Castle*), referring expressions (subject of the second sentence verbalised as pronoun) and segmentation (content organised in two sentences).

Reification We formulate this task as the generation of a target description Y from a source graph $X = (\mathcal{V}, \mathcal{E})$ where X is build from a set of RDF triples as follows. We reify the relations (Baader, 2003) from the RDF set of triples. That is, we see the relation as a concept in the KB and introduce a new relation node for each relation of each RDF triple. The new relation node is connected to the subject and object entities by two new binary relations A0 and A1 respectively. For instance, (precededBy A0 Aenir) and (precededBy A1 Castle). Thus, $\mathcal{E}$ is the set of entities including reified relations and $\mathcal{V}$ a set of labelled edges with labels $\{A0, A1\}$. The reification of relations is useful in two ways. The encoder is able to produce a hidden state for each relation in the input; and it permits to model an arbitrary number of KB relations efficiently.

3.2 SR11Deep Task

The surface realisation shared task (Belz et al., 2011) proposed two generation tasks, namely shallow and deep realisation. Here we focus on the deep task where the input is a semantic dependency graph that represents a target sentence using predicate-argument structures (NomBank; (Meyers et al., 2004), PropBank; (Palmer et al., 2005)). This task covers a more complex semantic representation of language meaning; on the other hand, the representation is closer to surface form. Nodes in the graph are lemmas of the target sentence. Only complementizers *that*, commas, and *to* infinitive nodes are removed. Edges are labelled with NomBank and PropBank labels.[5] Each node is also associated with morphological (e.g. num=sg) and punctuation features (e.g. bracket=r).

The source graph $X = (\mathcal{V}, \mathcal{E})$ is a semantic dependency graph. We extend this representation to model morphological information, i.e. each node in $\mathcal{V}$ is of the form (lemma, features). For this task we modify the encoder, Section 2, to represent each input node as $\mathbf{h}_v = [\mathbf{h}_l; \mathbf{h}_f]$, where each input node is the concatenation of the lemma and the sum of feature vectors.

4 Experiments

We tested our models on the WebNLG and SR11Deep datasets. The WebNLG dataset contains 18102 training and 871 development datatext pairs. The test dataset is split in two sets, test *Seen* (971 pairs) and a test set with new unseen categories for KB entities. As here we are interested only in the modelling aspects of the structured input data we focus on our evaluation only on the test partition with seen categories. The dataset covers 373 distinct relations from DBPedia. The SR11Deep dataset contains 39279, 1034 and 2398 examples in the training, development and test partitions, respectively. It covers 117 distinct dependency relations.[6]

Sequential Encoders For both WebNLG and SR11Deep tasks we used a standard sequence-to-sequence model (Bahdanau et al., 2015; Luong et al., 2015) with an LSTM encoder as baseline. Both take as input a linearised version of

---

[5]There are also some cases where syntactic labels appear in the graphs, this is due to the creation process (see (Belz et al., 2011)) and done to connect graphs when there were disconnected parts.

[6] In both datasets we exclude pairs with >50 target words.

the source graph. For the WebNLG baseline, we use the linearisation scripts provided by (Gardent et al., 2017b). For the SR11Deep baseline we follow a similar linearisation procedure as proposed for AMR graphs (Konstas et al., 2017). We built a linearisation based on a depth first traversal of the input graph. Siblings are traversed in random order (they are anyway shuffled in the given dataset). We repeat a child node when a node is revisited by a cycle or has more than one parent. The baseline model for the WebNLG task uses one layer bidirectional LSTM encoder and one layer LSTM decoder with embeddings and hidden units set to 256 dimensions . For the SR11Deep task we used the same architecture with 500-dimensional hidden states and embeddings. All hyperparameters tuned on the development set.

GCN Encoders The GCN models consist of a GCN encoder and LSTM decoder. For the WebNLG task, all encoder and decoder embeddings and hidden units use 256 dimensions. We obtained the best results with an encoder with four GCN layers with residual connections. For the SR11Deep task, we set the encoder and decoder to use 500-dimensional embeddings and hidden units of size 500. In this task, we obtained the best development performance by stacking seven GCN layers with dense connections.

We use delexicalisation for the WebNLG dataset and apply the procedure provided for the baseline in (Gardent et al., 2017b). For the SR11Deep dataset, we performed entity anonymisation. First, we compacted nodes in the tree corresponding to a single named entity (see (Belz et al., 2011) for details). Next, we used a name entity recogniser (Stanford CoreNLP; (Manning et al., 2014)) to tag entities in the input with type information (e.g. person, location, date). Two entities of the same type in a given input will be given a numerical suffix, e.g. PER_0 and PER_1.

A GCN-based Generator For the WebNLG task, we extended the GCN-based model to use pre-trained word **E**mbeddings (GloVe (Pennington et al., 2014)) and **C**opy mechanism (See et al., 2017), we name this variant GCN_{EC}. To this end, we did not use delexicalisation but rather represent multi-word subject (object) entities with each word as a separate node connected with special Named Entity (NE) labelled edges. For instance, the book entity *Into Battle* is represented as (Into

Encoder	BLEU	METEOR	TER
LSTM	.526±.010	.38±.00	.43±.01
GCN	.535±.004	.39±.00	.44±.02
ADAPT	.606	.44	.37
GCN_{EC}	.559±.017	.39±.01	0.41±.01
Melbourne	.545	.41	.40
PKUWriter	.512	.37	.45

Table 1: Test results WebNLG task.

Encoder	BLEU	METEOR	TER
LSTM	.377±.007	.65±.00	.44±.01
GCN	.647±.005	.77±.00	.24±.01
GCN+feat	.666±.027	.76±.01	.25±.01

Table 2: Test results SR11Deep task.

NE Battle). Encoder (decoder) embeddings and hidden dimensions were set to 300. The model stacks six GCN layers and uses a single layer LSTM decoder.

Evaluation metrics As previous works in these tasks, we evaluated our models using BLEU (Papineni et al., 2002), METEOR (Denkowski and Lavie, 2014) and TER (Snover et al., 2006) automatic metrics. During preliminary experiments we noticed considerable variance from different model initialisations; we thus run 3 experiments for each model and report average and standard deviation for each metric.

5   Results

WebNLG task In Table 1 we report results on the WebNLG test data. In this setting, the model with GCN encoder outperforms a strong baseline that employs the LSTM encoder, with .009 BLEU points. The GCN model is also more stable than the baseline with a standard deviation of .004 vs .010. We also compared the GCN_{EC} model with the neural models submitted to the WebNLG shared task. The GCN_{EC} model outperforms PKUWriter that uses an ensemble of 7 models and a further reinforcement learning step by .047 BLEU points; and Melbourne by .014 BLEU points. GCN_{EC} is behind ADAPT which relies on sub-word encoding.

SR11Deep task In this more challenging task, the GCN encoder is able to better capture the structure of the input graph than the LSTM encoder, resulting in .647 BLEU for the GCN vs. .377 BLEU of the LSTM encoder as reported in Table 2. When we add linguistic features to the GCN encoding we get .666 BLEU points. We also

WebNLG	(William Anders dateOfRetirement 1969 - 09 - 01) (Apollo 8 commander Frank Borman) (William Anders was a crew member of Apollo 8) (Apollo 8 backup pilot Buzz Aldrin)
LSTM	William Anders was a crew member of the OPERATOR operated Apollo 8 and retired on September 1st 1969 .
GCN	William Anders was a crew member of OPERATOR ' s Apollo 8 alongside backup pilot Buzz Aldrin and backup pilot Buzz Aldrin .
GCN_{EC}	william anders , who retired on the 1st of september 1969 , was a crew member on apollo 8 along with commander frank borman and backup pilot buzz aldrin .
SR11Deep	(SROOT SROOT will) (will P .) (will SBJ temperature) (temperature A1 economy) (economy AINV the) (economy SUFFIX 's) (will VC be) (be VC take) (take A1 temperature) (take A2 from) (from A1 point) (point A1 vantage) (point AINV several) (take AM-ADV with) (with A1 reading) (reading A1 on) (on A1 trade) (trade COORD output) (output COORD housing) (housing COORD and) (and CONJ inflation) (take AM-MOD will) (take AM-TMP week) (week AINV this)
Gold	The economy 's temperature will be taken from several vantage points this week , with readings on trade , output , housing and inflation .
Baseline	the economy 's accords will be taken from several phases this week , housing and inflation readings on trade , housing and inflation .
GCN	the economy 's temperatures will be taken from several vantage points this week , with reading on trades output , housing and inflation .

Table 3: Examples of system output.

Model	BLEU			SIZE		
	none	res	den	none	res	den
LSTM	.543±.003	-	-	4.3	-	-
GCN						
1L	.537±.006	-	-	4.3	-	-
2L	.545±.016	.553±.005	.552±.013	4.5	4.5	4.7
3L	.548±.012	.560±.013	.557±.001	4.7	4.7	5.2
4L	.537±.005	.569±.003	.558±.005	4.9	4.9	6.0
5L	.516±.022	.561±.016	.559±.003	5.1	5.1	7.0
6L	.508±.022	.561±.007	.558±.018	5.3	5.3	8.2
7L	.492±.024	.546±.023	.564±.012	5.5	5.5	9.6

Table 4: GCN ablation study (layers (L) and skip-connections: none, residual(res) and dense(den)). Average and standard deviation of BLEU scores over three runs on the WebNLG dev. set. Number of parameters (millions) including embeddings.

compare the neural models with upper bound results on the same dataset by the pipeline model of Bohnet et al. (2011) (STUMBA-D) and transition-based joint model of Zhang et al. (2017) (TBDIL). The STUMBA-D and TBDIL model obtains respectively .794 and .805 BLUE, outperforming the GCN-based model. It is worth noting that these models rely on separate modules for syntax prediction, tree linearisation and morphology generation. In a multi-lingual setting (Mille et al., 2017), our model will not need to re-train some modules for different languages, but rather it can exploit them for multi-task training. Moreover, our model could also exploit other supervision signals at training time, such as gold POS tags and gold syntactic trees as used in Bohnet et al. (2011).

5.1 Qualitative Analysis of Generated Text

We manually inspected the outputs of the LSTM and GCN models. Table 3 shows examples of source graphs and generated texts (we included more examples in Section A). Both models suffer from repeated and missing source content (i.e. source units are not verbalised in the output text (under-generation)). However, these phenomena are less evident with GCN-based models. We also observed that the LSTM output sometimes presents hallucination (over-generation) cases. Our intuition is that the strong relational inductive bias of GCNs (Battaglia et al., 2018) helps the GCN encoder to produce a more informative representation of the input; while the LSTM-based encoder has to learn to produce useful representations by going through multiple different sequences over the source data.

5.2 Ablation Study

In Table 4 (BLEU) we report an ablation study on the impact of the number of layers and the type of skip connections on the WebNLG dataset. The first thing we notice is the importance of skip connections between GCN layers. Residual and dense connections lead to similar results. Dense connections (Table 4 (SIZE)) produce models bigger, but slightly less accurate, than residual connections. The best GCN model has slightly more parameters than the baseline model (4.9M vs.4.3M).

6 Conclusion

We compared LSTM sequential encoders with a structured data encoder based on GCNs on the task of structured data to text generation. On two different tasks, WebNLG and SR11Deep, we show that explicitly encoding structural information with GCNs is beneficial with respect to sequential encoding. In future work, we plan to apply the approach to other input graph representations like Abstract Meaning Representations (AMR; (Banarescu et al., 2013)) and scoped semantic representations (Van Noord et al., 2018).

Acknowledgments

We want to thank Ivan Titov and Mirella Lapata for their help and suggestions. We also gratefully acknowledge the financial support of the European Research Council (award number 681760) and the Dutch National Science Foundation (NWO VIDI 639.022.518). We thank NVIDIA for donating the GPU used for this research.

References

Franz Baader. 2003. *The description logic handbook: Theory, implementation and applications.* Cambridge university press.

Dzmitry Bahdanau, Kyunghyun Cho, and Yoshua Bengio. 2015. Neural Machine Translation by Jointly Learning to Align and Translate. In *Proceedings of the International Conference on Learning Representations, ICLR.*

Laura Banarescu, Claire Bonial, Shu Cai, Madalina Georgescu, Kira Griffitt, Ulf Hermjakob, Kevin Knight, Philipp Koehn, Martha Palmer, and Nathan Schneider. 2013. Abstract meaning representation for sembanking. In *Proceedings of the 7th Linguistic Annotation Workshop and Interoperability with Discourse*, pages 178–186.

Joost Bastings, Ivan Titov, Wilker Aziz, Diego Marcheggiani, and Khalil Simaan. 2017. Graph convolutional encoders for syntax-aware neural machine translation. In *Proceedings of the 2017 Conference on Empirical Methods in Natural Language Processing, EMNLP*, pages 1957–1967.

Peter W. Battaglia, Jessica B. Hamrick, Victor Bapst, Alvaro Sanchez-Gonzalez, Vinícius Flores Zambaldi, Mateusz Malinowski, Andrea Tacchetti, David Raposo, Adam Santoro, Ryan Faulkner, Çaglar Gülçehre, Francis Song, Andrew J. Ballard, Justin Gilmer, George E. Dahl, Ashish Vaswani, Kelsey Allen, Charles Nash, Victoria Langston, Chris Dyer, Nicolas Heess, Daan Wierstra, Pushmeet Kohli, Matthew Botvinick, Oriol Vinyals, Yujia Li, and Razvan Pascanu. 2018. Relational inductive biases, deep learning, and graph networks. *CoRR*, abs/1806.01261.

Daniel Beck, Gholamreza Haffari, and Trevor Cohn. 2018. Graph-to-sequence learning using gated graph neural networks. In *Proceedings of the 56th Annual Meeting of the Association for Computational Linguistics (Volume 1: Long Papers)*, pages 273–283.

Anja Belz, Michael White, Dominic Espinosa, Eric Kow, Deirdre Hogan, and Amanda Stent. 2011. The first surface realisation shared task: Overview and evaluation results. In *Proceedings of the 13th European workshop on natural language generation*, pages 217–226.

Bernd Bohnet, Simon Mille, Benoît Favre, and Leo Wanner. 2011. Stumaba : From deep representation to surface. In *ENLG 2011 - Proceedings of the 13th European Workshop on Natural Language Generation*, pages 232–235.

Michael Denkowski and Alon Lavie. 2014. Meteor universal: Language specific translation evaluation for any target language. In *Proceedings of the ninth workshop on statistical machine translation*, pages 376–380.

Thiago Castro Ferreira, Iacer Calixto, Sander Wubben, and Emiel Krahmer. 2017. Linguistic realisation as machine translation: Comparing different mt models for amr-to-text generation. In *Proceedings of the 10th International Conference on Natural Language Generation*, pages 1–10.

Claire Gardent, Anastasia Shimorina, Shashi Narayan, and Laura Perez-Beltrachini. 2017a. Creating training corpora for nlg micro-planners. In *Proceedings of the 55th Annual Meeting of the Association for Computational Linguistics (Volume 1: Long Papers)*, pages 179–188. (ACL 2017).

Claire Gardent, Anastasia Shimorina, Shashi Narayan, and Laura Perez-Beltrachini. 2017b. The WebNLG challenge: Generating text from rdf data. In *Proceedings of the 10th International Conference on Natural Language Generation*, pages 124–133. (INLG 2017).

Kaiming He, Xiangyu Zhang, Shaoqing Ren, and Jian Sun. 2016. Deep residual learning for image recognition. In *Proceedings of the IEEE Conference on Computer Vision and Pattern Recognition, CVPR*, pages 770–778.

Sepp Hochreiter and Jürgen Schmidhuber. 1997. Long Short-Term Memory. *Neural Computation*, 9(8):1735–1780.

Gao Huang, Zhuang Liu, Laurens van der Maaten, and Kilian Q. Weinberger. 2017. Densely connected convolutional networks. In *2017 IEEE Conference on Computer Vision and Pattern Recognition, CVPR 2017*, pages 2261–2269.

Diederik P. Kingma and Jimmy Ba. 2015. Adam: A method for stochastic optimization. In *Proceedings of the International Conference on Learning Representations, ICLR.*

Thomas N. Kipf and Max Welling. 2016. Semi-supervised classification with graph convolutional networks. In *Proceedings of the International Conference on Learning Representations, ICLR.*

Guillaume Klein, Yoon Kim, Yuntian Deng, Jean Senellart, and Alexander M. Rush. 2017. Opennmt: Open-source toolkit for neural machine translation. In *Proceedings of the 55th Annual Meeting of the Association for Computational Linguistics, ACL 2017*, pages 67–72.

Ioannis Konstas, Srinivasan Iyer, Mark Yatskar, Yejin Choi, and Luke Zettlemoyer. 2017. Neural amr: Sequence-to-sequence models for parsing and generation. In *Proceedings of the 55th Annual Meeting of the Association for Computational Linguistics (Volume 1: Long Papers)*, pages 146–157.

Rémi Lebret, David Grangier, and Michael Auli. 2016. Neural text generation from structured data with application to the biography domain. In *Proceedings of the 2016 Conference on Empirical Methods in Natural Language Processing*, pages 1203–1213.

Yann LeCun, Leon Bottou, Yoshua Bengio, and Patrick Haffner. 2001. Gradient-based learning applied to document recognition. In *Proceedings of Intelligent Signal Processing*.

Thang Luong, Hieu Pham, and Christopher D. Manning. 2015. Effective approaches to attention-based neural machine translation. In *Proceedings of the 2015 Conference on Empirical Methods in Natural Language Processing*, pages 1412–1421.

Christopher Manning, Mihai Surdeanu, John Bauer, Jenny Finkel, Steven Bethard, and David McClosky. 2014. The Stanford CoreNLP natural language processing toolkit. In *Proceedings of the 52nd Annual Meeting of the Association for Computational Linguistics: System Demonstrations*, pages 55–60.

Diego Marcheggiani, Joost Bastings, and Ivan Titov. 2018. Exploiting semantics in neural machine translation with graph convolutional networks. In *Proceedings of NAACL-HLT*.

Diego Marcheggiani and Ivan Titov. 2017. Encoding sentences with graph convolutional networks for semantic role labeling. In *Proceedings of the 2017 Conference on Empirical Methods in Natural Language Processing, EMNLP*, pages 1506–1515.

Hongyuan Mei, Mohit Bansal, and Matthew R. Walter. 2016. What to talk about and how? selective generation using lstms with coarse-to-fine alignment. In *Proceedings of the 2016 Conference of the North American Chapter of the Association for Computational Linguistics: Human Language Technologies*, pages 720–730.

Adam Meyers, Ruth Reeves, Catherine Macleod, Rachel Szekely, Veronika Zielinska, Brian Young, and Ralph Grishman. 2004. Annotating noun argument structure for nombank. In *Proceedings of the Fourth International Conference on Language Resources and Evaluation, LREC 2004*.

Simon Mille, Bernd Bohnet, Leo Wanner, and Anja Belz. 2017. Shared task proposal: Multilingual surface realization using universal dependency trees. In *Proceedings of the 10th International Conference on Natural Language Generation*, pages 120–123.

Martha Palmer, Daniel Gildea, and Paul Kingsbury. 2005. The proposition bank: An annotated corpus of semantic roles. *Computational linguistics*, 31(1):71–106.

Kishore Papineni, Salim Roukos, Todd Ward, and Wei-Jing Zhu. 2002. Bleu: a method for automatic evaluation of machine translation. In *Proceedings of 40th Annual Meeting of the Association for Computational Linguistics*, pages 311–318.

Jeffrey Pennington, Richard Socher, and Christopher Manning. 2014. Glove: Global vectors for word representation. In *Proceedings of the 2014 conference on empirical methods in natural language processing (EMNLP)*, pages 1532–1543.

Laura Perez-Beltrachini, Rania SAYED, and Claire Gardent. 2016. Building RDF Content for Data-to-Text Generation. In *Proceedings of COLING 2016, the 26th International Conference on Computational Linguistics: Technical Papers*, pages 1493–1502.

Franco Scarselli, Marco Gori, Ah Chung Tsoi, Markus Hagenbuchner, and Gabriele Monfardini. 2009. The graph neural network model. *IEEE Trans. Neural Networks*, 20(1):61–80.

Abigail See, Peter J. Liu, and Christopher D. Manning. 2017. Get to the point: Summarization with pointer-generator networks. In *Proceedings of the 55th Annual Meeting of the Association for Computational Linguistics (Volume 1: Long Papers)*, pages 1073–1083.

Matthew Snover, Bonnie Dorr, Richard Schwartz, Linnea Micciulla, and John Makhoul. 2006. A study of translation edit rate with targeted human annotation. In *Proceedings of association for machine translation in the Americas*, volume 200.

Nitish Srivastava, Geoffrey E. Hinton, Alex Krizhevsky, Ilya Sutskever, and Ruslan Salakhutdinov. 2014. Dropout: a simple way to prevent neural networks from overfitting. *Journal of Machine Learning Research*, 15(1):1929–1958.

Ilya Sutskever, Oriol Vinyals, and Quoc V Le. 2014. Sequence to sequence learning with neural networks. In *Advances in neural information processing systems*, pages 3104–3112.

Rik Van Noord, Lasha Abzianidze, Hessel Haagsma, and Johan Bos. 2018. Evaluating scoped meaning representations. In *Proceedings of the Eleventh International Conference on Language Resources and Evaluation (LREC 2018)*.

Sam Wiseman, Stuart Shieber, and Alexander Rush. 2017. Challenges in data-to-document generation. In *Proceedings of the 2017 Conference on Empirical Methods in Natural Language Processing*, pages 2243–2253.

Yue Zhang, Manish Shrivastava, and Ratish Puduppully. 2017. Transition-based deep input linearization. In *Proceedings of the 15th Conference of the European Chapter of the Association for Computational Linguistics, EACL 2017, Volume 1: Long Papers*, pages 643–654.

A Supplemental Material

A.1 Training details

We implemented all our models using OpenNMT-py (Klein et al., 2017). For all experiments we used a batch size of 64 and Adam (Kingma and Ba, 2015) as the optimizer with an initial learning rate of 0.001. For GCN models and baselines we used a one-layer LSTM decoder, we used dropout (Srivastava et al., 2014) in both encoder and decoder with a rate of 0.3. We adopt early stopping on the development set using BLEU scores and we trained for a maximum of 30 epochs.

A.2 More example outputs

Table 5 shows additional examples of generated texts for source WebNLG and SR11Deep graphs.

WebNLG	(Acharya Institute of Technology sportsOffered Tennis) (Acharya Institute of Technology established 2000) (Tennis sportsGoverningBody International Tennis Federation)
LSTM	The Acharya Institute of Technology was established in 2000 and is governed by the International Tennis Federation .
GCN	The sport of tennis , governed by the International Tennis Federation , is offered at the Acharya Institute of Technology which was established in 2000 .
GCN$_{EC}$	the acharya institute of technology was established in 2000 and is governed by the international tennis federation .
WebNLG	(Acharya Institute of Technology officialSchoolColour Blue , White and Orange) (Acharya Institute of Technology was given the ' Technical Campus ' status by All India Council for Technical Education)
LSTM	The Archarya Institute of Technology are blue , white and was given the Acharya Institute of Technology .
GCN	The Acharya Institute of Technology was given the ' Technical Campus ' status by the All India Council for Technical Education in LOCATION . The Institute was given the " Technical Campus " status by the Acharya Institute of Technology .
GCN$_{EC}$	acharya institute of technology was given the ' technical campus ' status by the all india council for technical education which has blue , white and orange .
WebNLG	(Saranac Lake , New York isPartOf Harrietstown , New York) (Saranac Lake , New York isPartOf Essex County , New York) (Adirondack Regional Airport cityServed Lake Placid , New York) (Adirondack Regional Airport cityServed Saranac Lake , New York) (Saranac Lake , New York country United States)
LSTM	Adirondack Regional Airport serves the cities of Lake Placid and Saranac Lake (Harrietstown) in the United States .
GCN	Adirondack Regional Airport serves the city of Saranac Lake , which is part of Harrietstown , Essex County , New York , United States .
GCN$_{EC}$	adirondack regional airport serves the cities of lake placid and saranac lake , essex county , new york , united states . adirondack regional airport serves the city of saranac lake , essex county , new york , united states .
WebNLG	(Adisham Hall location Sri Lanka) (Adisham Hall architecturalStyle Tudor Revival architecture) (Adisham Hall completionDate 1931) (Adisham Hall buildingStartDate 1927)
LSTM	Adisham Hall was built in 1927 and completed in 1931 . It was built in the Tudor Revival architecture style and is located in Sri Lanka .
GCN	Construction of Adisham Hall , Sri Lanka began in 1927 and was completed in 1931 .
GCN$_{EC}$	adisham hall , sri lanka , constructed in 1931 , is located in sri lanka . the hall has the architectural style ' tudor revival ' .
SR11Deep	(SROOT SROOT say) (say A0 economist) (say A1 be) (be SBJ export) (be VC think) (think A1 export) (think C-A1 have) (have VC rise) (rise A1 export) (rise A2 strongly) (strongly COORD but) (but CONJ not) (not AINV enough) (not AINV offset) (offset A1 jump) (jump A1 in) (in A1 import) (jump AINV the) (offset A2 export) (not AINV probably) (strongly TMP in) (in A1 august) (say P .)
Gold	Exports are thought to have risen strongly in August , but probably not enough to offset the jump in imports , economists said .
LSTM	exports said exports are thought to have rising strongly , but not enough to offset exports in the imports in august .
GCN	exports was thought to have risen strongly in august but not probably to offset the jump in imports , economists said .
SR11Deep	(SROOT SROOT be) (be P ?) (be SBJ we) (be TMP be) (be SBJ project) (project A1 research) (be VC curtail) (curtail A1 project) (curtail AM-CAU to) (to A1 cut) (cut A0 government) (cut A1 funding) (funding A0 government) (to DEP due) (to R-AM-TMP when) (be VC catch) (catch A1 we) (catch A2 with) (with SUB down) (down SBJ grant) (grant AINV our) (catch P ") (catch P ")
Gold	When research projects are curtailed due to government funding cuts , are we " caught with our grants down " ?
LSTM	is when research projects is supposed to cut " due " projects is caught with the grant down .
GCN	when research projects are curtailed to government funding cuts due to government funding cuts , were we caught " caught " with our grant down ?

Table 5: Examples of system output.

Describing a Knowledge Base

Qingyun Wang[1], Xiaoman Pan[1], Lifu Huang[1], Boliang Zhang[1], Zhiying Jiang[1],
Heng Ji[1], Kevin Knight[2]
[1] Rensselaer Polytechnic Institute
`jih@rpi.edu`
[2] DiDi Labs and University of Southern California
`knight@isi.edu`

Abstract

We aim to automatically generate natural language descriptions about an input structured knowledge base (KB). We build our generation framework based on a pointer network which can copy facts from the input KB, and add two attention mechanisms: (i) *slot-aware attention* to capture the association between a slot type and its corresponding slot value; and (ii) a new *table position self-attention* to capture the inter-dependencies among related slots. For evaluation, besides standard metrics including BLEU, METEOR, and ROUGE, we propose a *KB reconstruction* based metric by extracting a KB from the generation output and comparing it with the input KB. We also create a new data set which includes 106,216 pairs of structured KBs and their corresponding natural language descriptions for two distinct entity types. Experiments show that our approach significantly outperforms state-of-the-art methods. The reconstructed KB achieves 68.8% - 72.6% F-score.[1]

1 Introduction

Show and tell, showing an audience something and telling them about it, is a common classroom activity for early elementary school kids. As a similar practice for knowledge propagation, we often need to describe and/or explain the information in a structured knowledge base (KB) in natural language, in order to make the knowledge elements and their connections easier to comprehend.

---

[1]We make all data sets and programs of various models publicly available for research purposes at `https://github.com/EagleW/Describing_a_Knowledge_Base`.

For example, (Cawsey et al., 1997) presents a natural language generation system to convert structured medical records to natural language text descriptions, which enables more effective communication between health care providers and their patients and among health care providers themselves.

Moreover, 51% of entity attributes in the current English Wikipedia Infoboxes are not described in English articles in the Wikipedia dump of April 1, 2018. The availability of vast amounts of Linked Open Data (LOD) and Wikipedia derived resources such as DBPedia, WikiData and YAGO encourages pursuing a new direction of knowledge-driven (Whitehead et al., 2018; Lu et al., 2018) or semantically oriented (Bouayad-Agha et al., 2013) Natural Language Generation (NLG). We aim to fill in this knowledge gap by developing a system that can take a KB (consisted of a set of slot types and their values) about an entity as input (see example in Table 1), and automatically generate a natural language description (Table 2).

Slot Type	Row	Slot Value		
Name	1	Silvi Jan		
Member of Sports team	2	ASA Tel Aviv University		
	3	Hapoel Tel Aviv F.C.(women)		
	4	Maccabi Holon F.C. (women)		
	5	Israel women's national football team	Matches	22
			Goals	29
Date of Birth	6	27 October 1973		
Country of Citizenship	7	Israel		
Position	8	Forward (association football)		

Table 1: Input: Structured Knowledge Base

Neural generation to generalize linguistic expressions. One major challenge lies in generalizing a wide variety of expressions, patterns, tem-

10

Proceedings of The 11th International Natural Language Generation Conference, pages 10–21,
Tilburg, The Netherlands, November 5-8, 2018. ©2018 Association for Computational Linguistics

Reference	Silvi Jan (born 27 October 1973) is a retired female Israeli . Silvi Jan has been a Forward (association football) for the Israel women's national football team for many years appearing in 22 matches and scoring 29 goals. After Hapoel Tel Aviv F.C.(women) folded, Jan signed with Maccabi Holon F.C. (women) where she played until her retirement in 2007. In January 2009, Jan returned to league action and joined ASA Tel Aviv University . In 1999, with the establishment of the Israeli Women's League, Jan returned to Israel and signed with Hapoel Tel Aviv F.C.(women) .
Seq2seq	(born 23 April 1981) is a retired Israeli footballer. He played for the Thailand 's (scoring one goal) and was a member of the team that won the first ever player in the history of the National Basketball League. She played for the team from 1997 to 2001 scoring 29 goals. She played for the team from 1997 to 2001 scoring 29 goals. She played for the team from 1999 to 2001 and played for the team in the 1997 and 2003 seasons.
Pointer	Silvi Jan the fourth past the Maccabi Holon F.C. (women). On 27 October 1973 in 29 2014) (born 22) is a former Israel . She was a Forward (association football) and currently plays for Hapoel Tel Aviv F.C.(women) in the Swedish league. She played for the ASA Tel Aviv University in the Swedish league. She was a member of the Israel women's national football team at the beginning of the 2008 season.
+ Type	Silvi Jan (born 27 October 1973) is a former Israeli footballer. He played for Hapoel Tel Aviv F.C.(women) and ASA Tel Aviv University .
+ Type & Position	Silvi Jan (born 27 October 1973) is a former Israel . He played for Israel women's national football team , Hapoel Tel Aviv F.C.(women) , ASA Tel Aviv University and Maccabi Holon F.C. (women) . He was capped 22 times for the Israel women's national football team .

Table 2: Human and System Generated Descriptions about the KB in Table 1

plates and styles which human use to describe the same slot type. For example, to describe a football player's membership with a team, we can use various phrases including *member of*, *traded to*, *drafted by*, *played for*, *face of*, *loaned to* and *signed for*. Instead of manually crafting patterns for each slot type, we leverage the existing pairs of structured slots from Wikipedia infoboxes and Wikidata (Vrandečić and Krötzsch, 2014) and the corresponding sentences describing these slots in Wikipedia articles as our training data, to learn a deep neural network based generator.

Pointer network to copy over facts. The previous work (Liu et al., 2018) considers the slot type and slot value as two sequences and applies a sequence to sequence (seq2seq) framework (Cho et al., 2014) for generation. However, the task of describing structured knowledge is fundamentally different from creative writing, because we need to cover the knowledge elements contained in the input KB, and the goal of generation is mainly to clearly describe the semantic connections among these knowledge elements in an accurate and coherent way. The seq2seq model fails to capture such connections and tends to generate wrong information (e.g., *Thailand* in Table 2). To address this challenge, we choose a pointer network (See et al., 2017) to copy slot values directly from the

input KB.

Slot type attention. However, the copying mechanism in the pointer network is not able to capture the alignment between a slot type and its slot value, and thus it often assigns facts to wrong slots. For example, *22* in Table 2 should be the number of matches instead of birth date. It also tends to repeat the same slot value based on language model, e.g., *"Uroplatus ebenaui is a of gecko endemic to **Madagascar**. The Uroplatus is a member of the species of the genus **Madagascar**."*. We propose a **Slot-aware Attention** mechanism to compute slot type attention and slot value attention simultaneously and capture their correlation. Attention mechanism in deep neural networks (Denil et al., 2012) is inspired from human visual attention, which refers to human's capability to focus on a certain region of an image with high resolution while perceiving the surrounding image in low resolution. It allows the neural network to have access to the hidden state of the encoder, and thus learn what to attend to. For example, for a *Date of Birth* slot type, words such as *born* may receive higher attention than *female*. As we can see in Table 2 (*+Type*), the output with slot type attention contains more precise slots.

Table position attention. Multiple slots are often interdependent. For example, a football player may join multiple teams, with each team associated with a certain number of points, goals, scores and games participated. We design a new table position based self-attention to capture correlations among interdependent slots and put them in the same sentence. For example, our model successfully associates the number of matches *22* with the *Israel women's national football team* as shown in Table 2.

The major contributions of this paper are:

- For the first time, we propose a new table position attention which proves to be effective at capturing inter-dependencies among facts. This new approach achieves 2.5%-7.8% F-score gain at KB reconstruction.

- We propose a *KB reconstruction based metric* to evaluate how many facts are correctly expressed in the generation output.

- We create a large dataset of KBs paired with natural language descriptions for 106,216 entities, which can serve as a new benchmark.

2 Model

We formulate the input structured KB to the model as a list of triples: $L = [(s_1, v_1, (r_1, \hat{r_1})), ..., (s_n, v_n, (r_n, \hat{r_n}))]$, where s_i denotes a slot type (e.g., *Country of Citizenship*), v_i denotes the corresponding slot value (e.g., *Israel*), and $(r_i, \hat{r_i})$ denotes the position of the triple in the input list and consists of the forward position r_i and the backward position $\hat{r_i} = n - r_i + 1$. The outcome of the model is a paragraph $Y = [y_1, y_2, ..., y_m]$. The training instances for the generator are provided in the form of: $T = [(L_1, Y_1), ..., (L_k, Y_k)]$.

2.1 Sequence-to-Sequence with Slot-aware Attention

Following previous studies on describing structured knowledge (Lebret et al., 2016; Sha et al., 2018; Liu et al., 2018), we apply a sequence-to-sequence based approach, and incorporate a slot-aware attention to generate the descriptions.

Encoder Given a structured KB input: $L = [(s_1, v_1, (r_1, \hat{r_1})), ..., (s_n, v_n, (r_n, \hat{r_n}))]$, where s_i, v_i, r_i, $\hat{r_i}$[2] are randomly embedded as vectors $\mathbf{s}_i$, $\mathbf{v}_i$, $\mathbf{r}_i$, $\hat{\mathbf{r}}_i$ respectively, we concatenate the vector representations of these fields as $\mathbf{l}_i = [\mathbf{s}_i, \mathbf{v}_i, \mathbf{r}_1, \hat{\mathbf{r}}_1]$, and obtain $\mathbf{L} = [\mathbf{l}_1, \mathbf{l}_2, ..., \mathbf{l}_n]$.

We attempted to apply the average of $\mathbf{L}$ as the representation for the input KB. However, such flat representation vectors fail to capture the structured contextual information in the entire KB. Therefore, we apply a bi-directional Gated Recurrent Unit (GRU) encoder (Cho et al., 2014) on $\mathbf{L}$ to produce the encoder hidden states $\mathbf{H} = [\mathbf{h}_1, \mathbf{h}_2, ..., \mathbf{h}_n]$, where $\mathbf{h}_i$ is a hidden state for $\mathbf{l}_i$.

Decoder with Slot-aware Attention The decoder is a forward GRU network with an initial hidden state $\mathbf{h}_n$, which is the encoder hidden state of the last token. In order to capture the association between a slot type and its slot value, we design a **Slot-aware Attention**. At each step t, we compute the attention distribution over the sequence of input triples. For each triple i, we assign it an attention weight:

$$e_i^t = v^\top \tanh\left(W_h \tilde{\mathbf{h}}^t + W_s \mathbf{s}_i + W_v \mathbf{v}_i + W_c c_i^t + b_e\right)$$
$$\alpha^t = \text{Softmax}\left(e^t\right)$$

where $\tilde{\mathbf{h}}^t$ is the decoder hidden state at step t. $\mathbf{s}_i$ and $\mathbf{v}_i$ denote the embedding representations of slot type s_i and slot value v_i respectively. $c_i^t = \sum_{k=0}^{t-1} \alpha_i^k$ is a coverage vector, which is the sum of attention distributions over all previous decoder time steps and can be used to reduce repetition (See et al., 2017).

The source attention distribution α^t can be considered as the contribution of each source triple to the generation of the target word. Next we use α^t to compute two context vectors $\mathbf{L}_s^*$ and $\mathbf{L}_v^*$ as the representation of the slot types and values respectively:

$$\mathbf{L}_s^* = \sum_{i=1}^{n} \alpha_i^t \mathbf{s}_i$$
$$\mathbf{L}_v^* = \sum_{i=1}^{n} \alpha_i^t \mathbf{v}_i \tag{1}$$

At step t, the vocabulary distribution P_{vocab} is computed with the context vectors $\mathbf{L}_s^*$, $\mathbf{L}_v^*$ and the decoder hidden state $\tilde{\mathbf{h}}^t$, using an affine-Softmax layer:

$$P_{vocab} = \text{Softmax}\left(V[\tilde{\mathbf{h}}^t; \mathbf{L}_s^*; \mathbf{L}_v^*] + b_{vocab}\right)$$

The loss function is computed as:

$$Loss = \sum_t \left\{ -\log P_{vocab}(y_t) + \lambda \sum_i \min\left(\alpha_i^t, c_i^t\right) \right\}$$

where $P_{vocab}(y^t)$ is the prediction probability of the ground truth token y_t. λ is a hyperparameter.

---

[2] We use bold mathematical symbols to denote vector representations for the whole paper.

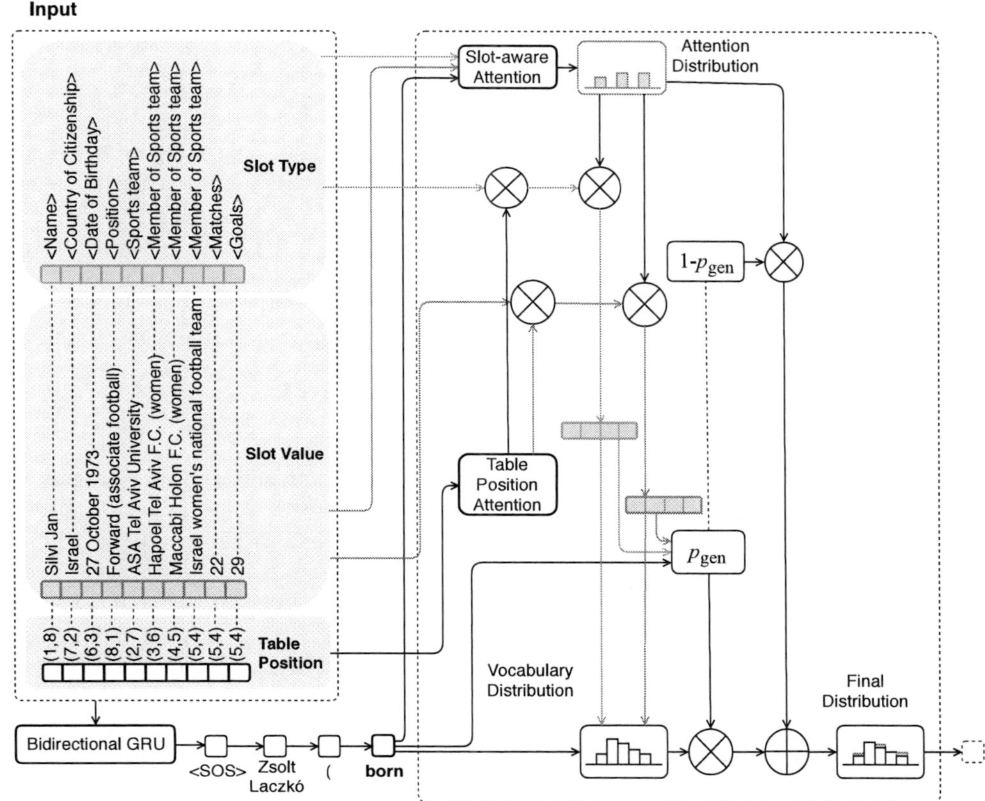

Figure 1: KB-to-Language Generation Model Overview

2.2 Table Position Self-attention

Although the sequence-to-sequence attention model takes into account the information of input triples, it still encodes the structured knowledge as sequential facts while ignoring the correlations between facts. In our task, multiple inter-dependent slots should be described within one sentence. For example, in Table 1, the sport team *Israel women's national football team* should be described together with *22* matches and *29* goals. Previous studies (Lin et al., 2017; Vaswani et al., 2017) applied self-attention on sentence level to capture the correlation between continuous tokens. Inspired by these approaches, we design a new table position based self-attention and incorporate it into the slot-aware attention.

In our task, since most triples are organized in temporal order, we use the row index r and the reverse row index $\hat{r}$ to denote the position information of each triple in the input KB. Given a structured KB as input: $L = [(s_1, v_1, (r_1, \hat{r}_1)), ..., (s_n, v_n, (r_n, \hat{r}_n))]$, we obtain

a sequence of row index embeddings $R = [\mathbf{r}_1', \mathbf{r}_2', ..., \mathbf{r}_n']$ with random initialization, where $\mathbf{r}_i' = [\mathbf{r}_i; \hat{\mathbf{r}}_i]$. We model the inter-dependencies among slots as a latent structure, where for each position i we assume it has a latent in-link and an out-link to denote where it is linked to or from. This assumption is similar to the structure attention applied in Liu and Lapata (2018), which assumes each word within a sentence can be a parent node or a child node in a latent tree structure. For each pair of slots i and j, we compute the attention score f_{ij} as follows:

$$g_{in} = \tanh\left(W_{in}\mathbf{r}_i'\right)$$

$$g_{out} = \tanh\left(W_{out}\mathbf{r}_j'\right)$$

$$f_{ij} = \text{Softmax}\left(g_{in}^\top W_g g_{out}\right)$$

where W_{in}, W_{out}, and W_g are learnable parameters. The attention score will not change during the decoding process.

13

f_{ij} can be viewed as the contribution from a context triple j to triple i. For each slot $\mathbf{s}_i$ and value $\mathbf{v}_i$, we obtain a context vector by collecting information from other slot types and their values:

$$\mathbf{s}_i^* = \sum\nolimits_{k=1}^{n} f_{ik}\mathbf{s}_k$$

$$\mathbf{v}_i^* = \sum\nolimits_{k=1}^{n} f_{ik}\mathbf{v}_k$$

We further encode position-aware representation of each slot type and value, and update their context vectors $\mathbf{L}_t^*$ and $\mathbf{L}_v^*$ in Equation 1 as:

$$\mathbf{L}_s^* = \sum\nolimits_{i=1}^{n} \alpha_i^t \mathbf{s}_i^*$$

$$\mathbf{L}_v^* = \sum\nolimits_{i=1}^{n} \alpha_i^t \mathbf{v}_i^*$$

2.3 Structure Generator

Traditional sequence-to-sequence models predict a target sequence by only selecting words from a vocabulary with a fixed size. However, in our task, we regard the slot value as a single information unit. Therefore, there is a certain amount of out-of-vocabulary (OOV) words during the test phase. Inspired by the pointer-generator (Gu et al., 2016; See et al., 2017), which is designed to automatically locate particular source words and directly copy them into the target sequence, we design a structure-aware generator as follows.

We first obtain a source attention distribution of all unique input slot values. Since one particular slot value may occur in the structure input for many times, we aggregate the attention weights for each unique slot value v_j from α_t and obtain its aggregated source attention distribution P_{source}^j by

$$P_{source}^j = \sum_{m|v_m=v_j} \alpha_m^t$$

The *gates* in neural networks act on the signals they receive, and block or pass on information based on its strength. In order to combine two types of attention distribution P_{source} and P_{vocab}, we compute a structure-aware gate $p_{gen} \in [0,1]$ as a soft switch between generating a word from the fixed vocabulary and copying a slot value from the structured input:

$$p_{gen} = \sigma\left(W_s^\top \mathbf{L}_s^* + W_v^\top \mathbf{L}_v^* + W_h^\top \tilde{\mathbf{h}}^t + W_y^\top \mathbf{y}^{t-1} + b_{gen}\right)$$

where $\mathbf{y}^{t-1}$ is the embedding of the previous generated token at time $t-1$, and σ is a Sigmoid function.

The final probability of a token y at time t can be computed by p_{gen}, P_{vocab} and P_{source}:

$$P(y_t) = p_{gen}P_{vocab} + (1 - p_{gen})P_{source}$$

The loss function, combining with the coverage loss (See et al., 2017), is presented as:

$$Loss = \sum_t \left\{ -\log P(y^t) + \lambda \sum_i \min\left(\alpha_i^t, c_i^t\right) \right\}$$

where $P(y^t)$ is the prediction probability of the ground truth token y. λ is a hyperparameter.

3 Experiments

3.1 Data

Using person and animal entities as case studies, we create a new dataset based on Wikipedia dump (2018/04/01) and Wikidata (2018/04/12) as follows: (1). Extract Wikipedia pages and Wikidata tables about person and animal entities, and align them according to their unique KB IDs. (2). For each Wikidata table, filter out the slot types of which frequency is less than 3. For each Wikipedia article, use its anchor links (clickable texts in hyperlinks) to locate all the entities and determine their KB IDs. (3). For each Wikidata table, search each value (including Number, Date) and entity contained in the table in the corresponding Wikipedia article according to its KB ID, and remove the values and entities which cannot be found in the corresponding Wikipedia article. (4). For each Wikipedia article, remove the sentences which contain no values, and remove sentences which only contain entities that do not exist in the Wikidata table. The remaining sentences will be taken as ground-truth reference descriptions. (5). Index the row numbers for each slot type according to their orders in the Wikidata table. The ground-truth structured KB is then created. (6). Build a fixed vocabulary for the whole corpus of ground-truth descriptions and label the words with frequency < 5 as OOV.

We further randomly shuffle and split the dataset into training (80%), development (10%) and test (10%) subsets for person and animal entities respectively. Table 3 shows the detailed statistics. Compared with the Wikibio dataset used in previous studies (Lebret et al., 2016; Sha et al., 2018; Liu et al., 2018), which contains one sentence only as the ground-truth description, our dataset contains multiple sentences to cover as many facts as possible in the input structured KB.

Entity type	# entity	# types before filtering	# types after filtering	# slots / sentence	# words / sentence	# slots / table	# words / entity	# sentence / entity
Person	100,000	109	76	1.9	16.8	8.0	70.9	4.2
Animal	6,216	30	12	1.3	17.1	3.2	42.2	2.5

Table 3: Data Statistics

Input KB:

Slot Type	Slot Value				
Name	Kim Da-som				
Date of Birth	6 May 1993				
Place of Birth	Gwangju				
Occupation	Singer				
Occupation	Actress				
Genres	K-pop				
Start Active Year	3 June 2010	Start Active Place	Seoul	Start Active Song	PUSH PUSH
Agent	King Kong by Starship				
Associated acts	Sistar				

Generate →

Kim Da-som (born 6 May 1993 in Seoul) is a singer. She is a member of Sistar under King Kong by Starship. On 3 June 2010, she made her debut.

→ *Reconstruct*

Reconstructed KB:

Slot Type	Slot Value
Name	Kim Da-som
Date of Birth	6 May 1993
Place of Birth	Seoul
Occupation	Singer
Associated acts	Sistar
Agent	King Kong by Starship
Start Active Year	3 June 2010

Figure 2: KB Reconstruction based Evaluation (Scores for the example: Overall Slot Filling P=$\frac{6}{7}$=85.7%, R=$\frac{6}{11}$=54.5%, F1=66.7%; Inter-dependent Slot Filling P=$\frac{5}{7}$=71.4%, R=$\frac{5}{9}$=55.6%, F1=62.5%)

It makes the generation task more challenging, practical and interesting.

3.2 Evaluation Metrics

We apply the standard BLEU (Papineni et al., 2002), METEOR (Denkowski and Lavie, 2014), and ROUGE (Lin, 2004) metrics to evaluate the generation performance, because they can measure the content overlap between system output and ground-truth and also check whether the system output is written in sufficiently good English.

In addition, we can also consider natural language as the most expressive way for knowledge transmission via a *noisy channel*. If we are able to reconstruct the input KB from the generated description, our generator achieves a 100% success rate at knowledge propagation. We propose a *KB reconstruction based metric* as follows: for each entity, construct a KB from the generated paragraph, and compute precision, recall and F-score by comparing it with the input KB from two aspects: (1). **Overall Slot Filling**: If a pair of slot type and its slot value exists in both of the reconstructed KB and the input KB, it's considered as a correct slot. (2). **Inter-dependent Slot Filling**: If a row that consists one or multiple slot types and their slot values exist in both of the reconstructed KB and the input KB, it's considered as a correct row.

If the same slot/row is correctly described multiple times in the system generation output, it's only counted as correct once, i.e., redundant descriptions will be penalized. This metric is further illustrated in Figure 2. It's similar to the relation extraction based generation evaluation metric proposed by (Wiseman et al., 2017) and entity/event extraction based metric proposed by (Whitehead et al., 2018; Lu et al., 2018). They compared automatic Information Extraction results from the reference description and the system generation output. However, the performance of state-of-the-art open-domain slot filling (Wu and Weld, 2010; Fader et al., 2011; Min et al., 2012; Xu et al., 2013; Angeli et al., 2015; Bhutani et al., 2016; Yu et al., 2017) is still far from satisfactory to serve as an automatic extraction tool for evaluating generation results. Therefore for the pilot study in this paper we manually reconstruct KBs from the generation output for evaluation. Notably none of the above automatic metrics is sufficient to capture adequacy, grammaticality and fluency of the generated descriptions. However extrinsic metrics such as system purpose and user task are expensive, while cheaper metrics such as human rating do not correlate with extrinsic metrics (Gkatzia and Mahamood, 2015). Moreover the task we address in this paper requires essential domain knowledge for a human user to assess the generated descriptions.

3.3 Baseline Models

We compare our approach with the following models: (1). **Seq2seq attention model** (Bahdanau et al., 2015). We concatenate slot types and values as a sequence, e.g., {*Name, Silvi Jan, Sports team, ASA Tel Aviv University, Hapoel Tel Aviv F.C. ...*} for Table 1, and apply the sequence to sequence with attention model to generate a description. (2). **Pointer-generator** (See et al., 2017) which introduces a soft switch to choose between generating a word from the fixed vocabulary and copying a word from the input sequence. Here, we concatenate all slot values as the input sequence, e.g., {*Silvi Jan, ASA Tel Aviv University, Hapoel Tel Aviv F.C. ...*} for Table 1. (3). **Pointer-generator + slot type attention** which incorporates the slot type attention (Section 2.1) into the pointer-generator. We use the sequence of (slot type, slot value) pairs as input, e.g., {*(Name, Silvi Jan), (Sports team, ASA Tel Aviv University), (Sports team, Hapoel Tel Aviv F.C.) ...*} for Table 1.

3.4 Hyperparameters

Table 4 shows the hyperparameters of our model.

Parameter	Value
Vocabulary size (|s|+|v|)	46,776
Value\type embedding size	256
Position embedding size	5
Slot embedding size	522
Decoder hidden size	256
Coverage loss λ	1.5
Optimization	Adam (Hu et al., 2009)
Learning rate	0.001

Table 4: Hyperparameters

3.5 Results and Analysis

Table 5 shows the performance of various models with standard metrics. We can see that our attention mechanisms achieve consistent improvement. We conduct paired t-test between our proposed model and all the other baselines on 10 randomly sampled subsets. The differences are statistically significant with $p \leq 0.016$ for all settings.

As shown in Table 6 and Table 7, the KBs reconstructed from models with these two attention mechanisms achieve much higher quality.

Figure 3 and Figure 4 visualize the attentions applied to the walk-through example in Table 1.

Impact of Slot-aware Attention. The same string can be filled into various slots of multiple types. For example, dates, ages, the number of matches and goals can all be presented as numbers. The pointer network often mistakenly mixes them up. For example, it produces "*24 September 1979 was born 3 October 1903 in 17 on 33 October 1906*", where *33* should be the number

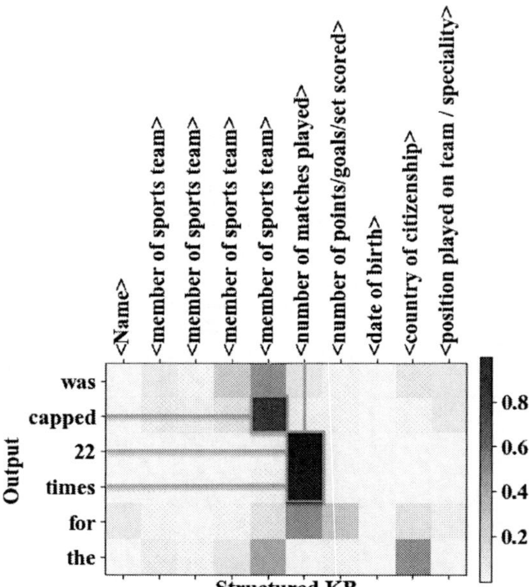

Figure 3: Slot Type Attention Visualization (Context words strongly associated with certain slot types receive high weights, e.g., *capped* to describe *member of sports team*, and *times* to describe *the number of matches played.*)

of matches and *17* should be the number of goals. In contrast our model with slot type attention correctly generates "*he made 33 appearances and scored 17 goals*". In addition, as mentioned earlier, the pointer network often produces redundant slot values because it loses control of slot types, e.g., "*He was born in the city of Association football. In the late 1990s he was appointed manager of the Association football team of the team.*".

Impact of Table Position Attention. The table position attention successfully captures interdependent slots, such as a membership with a sports team and its corresponding number of matches and games: "*Bill Sampy ... who played for Sheffield United F.C. 41 times.*"; "*Giancarlo Antognoni ... he was also a member of the Italy national football team at the 1982 FIFA World Cup.*".

Remaining Challenges. Some remaining errors are trivial to fix, such as fixing a country name to its adjective form when it appears right before a position slot (e.g., *Italian professional Association football player* instead of *Italy professional Association football player*). The KB reconstruction recall of person entities is relatively low mainly

Model	Person			Animal		
	BLEU	**METEOR**	**ROUGE**	**BLEU**	**METEOR**	**ROUGE**
Seq2seq	11.3	16.9	28.8	5.8	11.5	20.5
Pointer	17.2	21.1	37.4	6.6	13.7	37.8
+Type	23.1	22.2	39.5	**17.2**	**17.3**	42.8
+Type & Position	**23.2**	**23.4**	**42.0**	14.8	17.2	**45.0**

Table 5: Generation Performance based on Standard Metrics %)

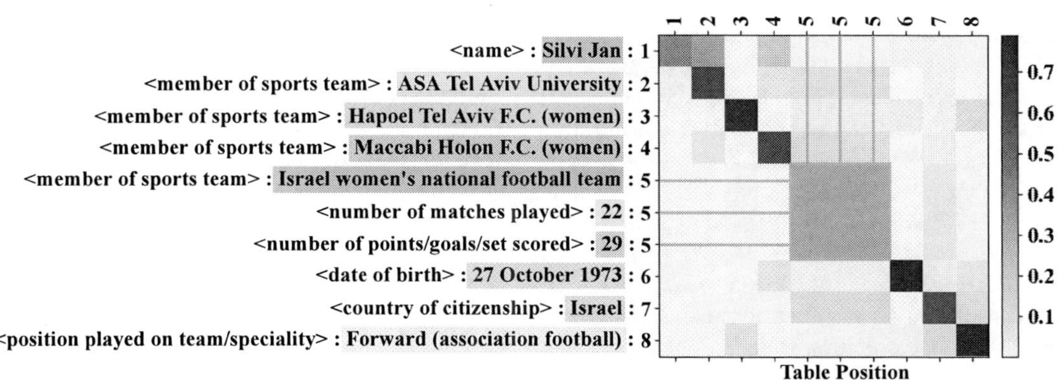

Figure 4: Table Position Self Attention Visualization (the highlighted inter-dependent slots appear in the same row and the same sentences, and thus they receive the same high weight.)

Model	Person			Animal		
	P	**R**	**F1**	**P**	**R**	**F1**
Seq2seq	74.6	29.3	42.0	82.5	27.8	41.6
Pointer	72.6	56.4	62.8	58.5	37.5	45.7
+Type	75.9	58.8	66.3	65.9	63.8	64.8
+Type & Position	**76.3**	**62.7**	**68.8**	**73.4**	**71.8**	**72.6**

Table 6: Overall Slot Filling Precision (P), Recall (R), F-score (F1) (%)

Model	Person			Animal		
	P	**R**	**F1**	**P**	**R**	**F1**
Seq2seq	74.7	30.0	43.4	82.5	27.9	41.7
Pointer	73.0	56.4	63.6	57.7	37.2	45.2
+Type	75.8	58.9	66.3	66.3	64.2	65.2
+Type & Position	**77.2**	**63.5**	**69.7**	**72.6**	**71.0**	**71.8**

Table 7: Inter-dependent Slot Filling Precision (P), Recall (R), F-score (F1) (%)

because we don't have enough training data for some rare slot types.

Contextual words generated by the LM introduces some incorrect facts, especially temporal expressions. For example, the generator does not have the commonsense knowledge that football players could not play before they were born: *"Aleksei Gasilin (born* **1 March 1996** *) is a Russian Association football Forward (association football). He made his professional debut in the Russian Second Division in* **1992** *for Russia national under-19 football team. "*. Similarly, a football player would probably not be still active when he was already 72 years old: *"Basil Rigg (born* **12 August 1926** *) is a former Australian rules football Rigg played for the Perth Football Club in the Western Australia cricket team from* **1998** *to* **1998**.".

Our approach sometimes fails to detect person gender so as to generate incorrect pronouns. For animal entities, human writers are able to elaborate more details. For example, human writes the specific endemic places for *Brown treecreeper*: *"The bird endemic to eastern Australia has a broad distribution occupying areas from* **Cape York Queensland** *throughout* **New South Wales** *and* **Victoria** *to* **Port Augusta** *and the* **Flinders Ranges South Australia**." while our system is only able to cover the generic location information *"It is endemic to* **Australia**." from the input KB.

4 Related work

Our task is similar to the WebNLG challenge generating text from DBPedia data (Gardent et al., 2017a). Previous approaches on generating natural language sentences from structured input KB can be divided into two categories: the first is to induce templates and then fill appropriate content into slots (Kukich, 1983; Cawsey et al., 1997; Angeli et al., 2010; Duma and Klein, 2013; Konstas and Lapata, 2013a; Flanigan et al., 2016a). These methods can generate high-quality descriptions but heavily rely on information redundancy to create templates. The second category is to directly generate a sequence of words using language model (Belz, 2008; Chen and Mooney, 2008; Liang et al., 2009; Angeli et al., 2010; Konstas and Lapata, 2012a,b, 2013a,b; Mahapatra et al., 2016) or deep neural networks (Sutskever et al., 2011; Wen et al., 2015; Kiddon et al., 2016; Mei et al., 2016; Gardent et al., 2017b; Wiseman et al., 2017; Wang et al., 2018; Song et al., 2018). Several studies (Lebret et al., 2016; Chisholm et al., 2017; Kaffee et al., 2018a,b; Liu et al., 2018; Sha et al., 2018) generate a person's biography from an input structure, which are closely related to our task. However, instead of modeling the input structure as a sequence of facts and generating one sentence only, we introduce a table position self-attention, inspired from structure attention (Lin et al., 2017; Kim et al., 2017; Vaswani et al., 2017; Shen et al., 2018a,b), to capture the dependencies among facts and generate a paragraph to describe all facts.

In contrast to some recent work on converting structured Abstract Meaning Representation (Banarescu et al., 2013) into natural language (Pourdamghani et al., 2016; Flanigan et al., 2016b), our task requires us to capture inter-dependent relation links in a knowledge base and use them to generate multiple sentences in most cases. Our work is also related to attention mechanisms for sequence-to-sequence generation (Bahdanau et al., 2015; Mei et al., 2016; Ma et al., 2017). Different from previous studies, our task requires the slot type and slot value to appear in the generated sentences in pairs. Thus we design a slot-aware attention to obtain two context vectors for both slot type and slot value simultaneously. To deal with OOV words, we use a structure generator, which is similar to the pointer-generator networks (Vinyals et al., 2015; Luong et al., 2015; Gulcehre et al., 2016; See et al., 2017) and copy mechanism (Gu et al., 2016).

5   Conclusions and Future Work

We develop an effective generator to produce a natural language description about an input knowl-edge base. Our experiments show that two attention mechanisms focusing on slot type and table position advance state-of-the-art on this task, and provide a KB reconstruction F-score up to 73%. We propose a new KB reconstruction based evaluation metric which can be used for other knowledge-driven NLG tasks such as news image/video captioning. In the future, we aim to address the remaining challenges as summarized in Section 3.5, and tackle the setting where multiple facts of the same slot type are not presented in temporal order in the input KB. We also plan to extend the framework to cross-lingual cross-media generation, namely to produce a foreign language description or an image/video about the KB.

Acknowledgments

This work was supported by the U.S. DARPA AIDA Program No. FA8750-18-2-0014 and U.S. ARL NS-CTA No. W911NF-09-2-0053. The views and conclusions contained in this document are those of the authors and should not be interpreted as representing the official policies, either expressed or implied, of the U.S. Government. The U.S. Government is authorized to reproduce and distribute reprints for Government purposes notwithstanding any copyright notation here on.

References

Gabor Angeli, Percy Liang, and Dan Klein. 2010. A simple domain-independent probabilistic approach to generation. In *Proceedings of the 2010 Conference on Empirical Methods in Natural Language Processing*.

Gabor Angeli, Melvin Jose Johnson Premkumar, and Christopher D Manning. 2015. Leveraging linguistic structure for open domain information extraction. In *Proceedings of the 53rd Annual Meeting of the Association for Computational Linguistics and the 7th International Joint Conference on Natural Language Processing*.

Dzmitry Bahdanau, Kyunghyun Cho, and Yoshua Bengio. 2015. Neural machine translation by jointly learning to align and translate. In *International Conference on Learning Representations*.

Laura Banarescu, Claire Bonial, Shu Cai, Madalina Georgescu, Kira Griffitt, Ulf Hermjakob, Kevin Knight, Philipp Koehn, Martha Palmer, and Nathan Schneider. 2013. Abstract meaning representation for sembanking. In *Proceedings of the 7th Linguistic Annotation Workshop and Interoperability with Discourse*.

Anja Belz. 2008. Automatic generation of weather forecast texts using comprehensive probabilistic generation-space models. *Natural Language Engineering*, 14(4):431–455.

Nikita Bhutani, HV Jagadish, and Dragomir Radev. 2016. Nested propositions in open information extraction. In *Proceedings of the 2016 Conference on Empirical Methods in Natural Language Processing*.

Nadjet Bouayad-Agha, Gerard Casamayor, and Leo Wanner. 2013. Natural language generation in the context of the semantic web. *Semantic Web Journal*.

Alison J Cawsey, Bonnie L Webber, and Ray B Jones. 1997. Natural language generation in health care. *Journal of the American Medical Informatics Association*, 4.

David L Chen and Raymond J Mooney. 2008. Learning to sportscast: a test of grounded language acquisition. In *Proceedings of the 25th international conference on Machine learning*.

Andrew Chisholm, Will Radford, and Ben Hachey. 2017. Learning to generate one-sentence biographies from wikidata. In *Proceedings of the 15th Conference of the European Chapter of the Association for Computational Linguistics*.

Kyunghyun Cho, Bart Van Merriënboer, Caglar Gulcehre, Dzmitry Bahdanau, Fethi Bougares, Holger Schwenk, and Yoshua Bengio. 2014. Learning phrase representations using rnn encoder-decoder for statistical machine translation. In *Proceedings of the 2014 Conference on Empirical Methods in Natural Language Processing*.

Misha Denil, Loris Bazzani, Hugo Larochelle, and Nando de Freitas. 2012. Learning where to attend with deep architectures for image tracking. *Neural Computation*, 24(8):2151–2184.

Michael Denkowski and Alon Lavie. 2014. Meteor universal: Language specific translation evaluation for any target language. In *Proceedings of the Ninth Workshop on Statistical Machine Translation*.

Daniel Duma and Ewan Klein. 2013. Generating natural language from linked data: Unsupervised template extraction. In *Proceedings of the 10th International Conference on Computational Semantics*.

Anthony Fader, Stephen Soderland, and Oren Etzioni. 2011. Identifying relations for open information extraction. In *Proceedings of the 2011 Conference on Empirical Methods in Natural Language Processing*.

Jeffrey Flanigan, Chris Dyer, Noah A Smith, and Jaime Carbonell. 2016a. Generation from abstract meaning representation using tree transducers. In *Proceedings of the 2016 Conference of the North American Chapter of the Association for Computational Linguistics: Human Language Technologies*.

Jeffrey Flanigan, Chris Dyer, Noah A. Smith, and Jaime Carbonell. 2016b. Generation from abstract meaning representation using tree transducers. In *Proc. the 15th Annual Conference of the North American Chapter of the Association for Computational Linguistics: Human Language Technologies (NAACL-HLT2016)*.

Claire Gardent, Anastasia Shimorina, Shashi Narayan, and Laura Perez-Beltrachini. 2017a. Creating training corpora for micro-planners. In *Proceedings of the 55th Annual Meeting of the Association for Computational Linguistics (Volume 1: Long Papers)*, Vancouver, Canada. Association for Computational Linguistics.

Claire Gardent, Anastasia Shimorina, Shashi Narayan, and Laura Perez-Beltrachini. 2017b. Creating training corpora for nlg micro-planners. In *Proceedings of the 55th Annual Meeting of the Association for Computational Linguistics*.

Dimitra Gkatzia and Saad Mahamood. 2015. A snapshot of nlg evaluation practices 2005 - 2014. In *Proceedings of the 15th European Workshop on Natural Language Generation (ENLG)*.

Jiatao Gu, Zhengdong Lu, Hang Li, and Victor O.K. Li. 2016. Incorporating copying mechanism in sequence-to-sequence learning. In *Proceedings of the 54th Annual Meeting of the Association for Computational Linguistics*.

Caglar Gulcehre, Sungjin Ahn, Ramesh Nallapati, Bowen Zhou, and Yoshua Bengio. 2016. Pointing the unknown words. In *Proceedings of the 54th Annual Meeting of the Association for Computational Linguistics*.

Chonghai Hu, Weike Pan, and James T. Kwok. 2009. Accelerated gradient methods for stochastic optimization and online learning. In *Advances in Neural Information Processing Systems 22*, pages 781–789.

Lucie-Aimée Kaffee, Hady Elsahar, Pavlos Vougiouklis, Christophe Gravier, Frédérique Laforest, Jonathon Hare, and Elena Simperl. 2018a. Learning to generate wikipedia summaries for underserved languages from wikidata. *arXiv preprint arXiv:1803.07116*.

Lucie-Aimée Kaffee, Hady Elsahar, Pavlos Vougiouklis, Christophe Gravier, Frédérique Laforest, Jonathon Hare, and Elena Simperl. 2018b. Mind the (language) gap: Generation of multilingual wikipedia summaries from wikidata for articleplaceholders. In *Proceedings of the 15th European Semantic Web Conference*.

Chloé Kiddon, Luke Zettlemoyer, and Yejin Choi. 2016. Globally coherent text generation with neural checklist models. In *Proceedings of the 2016 Conference on Empirical Methods in Natural Language Processing*.

Yoon Kim, Carl Denton, Luong Hoang, and Alexander M Rush. 2017. Structured attention networks. In *International Conference on Learning Representations*.

Ioannis Konstas and Mirella Lapata. 2012a. Concept-to-text generation via discriminative reranking. In *Proceedings of the 50th Annual Meeting of the Association for Computational Linguistics*.

Ioannis Konstas and Mirella Lapata. 2012b. Unsupervised concept-to-text generation with hypergraphs. In *Proceedings of the 2012 Conference of the North American Chapter of the Association for Computational Linguistics: Human Language Technologies*.

Ioannis Konstas and Mirella Lapata. 2013a. A global model for concept-to-text generation. *Journal of Artificial Intelligence Research*, 48:305–346.

Ioannis Konstas and Mirella Lapata. 2013b. Inducing document plans for concept-to-text generation. In *Proceedings of the 2013 Conference on Empirical Methods in Natural Language Processing*.

Karen Kukich. 1983. Design of a knowledge-based report generator. In *Proceedings of the 21st annual meeting on Association for Computational Linguistics*.

Rémi Lebret, David Grangier, and Michael Auli. 2016. Neural text generation from structured data with application to the biography domain. In *Proceedings of the 2016 Conference on Empirical Methods in Natural Language Processing*.

Percy Liang, Michael I Jordan, and Dan Klein. 2009. Learning semantic correspondences with less supervision. In *Proceedings of the Joint Conference of the 47th Annual Meeting of the ACL and the 4th International Joint Conference on Natural Language Processing of the AFNLP*.

Chin-Yew Lin. 2004. Rouge: A package for automatic evaluation of summaries. In *Proceedings of Text Summarization Branches Out*.

Zhouhan Lin, Minwei Feng, Cicero Nogueira dos Santos, Mo Yu, Bing Xiang, Bowen Zhou, and Yoshua Bengio. 2017. A structured self-attentive sentence embedding. In *International Conference on Learning Representations*.

Tianyu Liu, Kexiang Wang, Lei Sha, Baobao Chang, and Zhifang Sui. 2018. Table-to-text generation by structure-aware seq2seq learning. In *Proceedings of the 32nd AAAI Conference on Artificial Intelligence*.

Yang Liu and Mirella Lapata. 2018. Learning structured text representations. *Transactions of the Association for Computational Linguistics*, 6:63–75.

Di Lu, Spencer Whitehead, Lifu Huang, Heng Ji, and Shih-Fu Chang. 2018. Entity-aware image caption generation. In *Proc. 2018 Conference on Empirical Methods in Natural Language Processing (EMNLP2018)*.

Thang Luong, Ilya Sutskever, Quoc Le, Oriol Vinyals, and Wojciech Zaremba. 2015. Addressing the rare word problem in neural machine translation. In *Proceedings of the 53rd Annual Meeting of the Association for Computational Linguistics and the 7th International Joint Conference on Natural Language Processing*.

Shuming Ma, Xu Sun, Jingjing Xu, Houfeng Wang, Wenjie Li, and Qi Su. 2017. Improving semantic relevance for sequence-to-sequence learning of chinese social media text summarization. In *Proceedings of the 55th Annual Meeting of the Association for Computational Linguistics*.

Joy Mahapatra, Sudip Kumar Naskar, and Sivaji Bandyopadhyay. 2016. Statistical natural language generation from tabular non-textual data. In *Proceedings of the 9th International Natural Language Generation conference*.

Hongyuan Mei, Mohit Bansal, and Matthew R. Walter. 2016. What to talk about and how? selective generation using lstms with coarse-to-fine alignment. In *Proceedings of the 2016 Conference of the North American Chapter of the Association for Computational Linguistics: Human Language Technologies*.

Bonan Min, Shuming Shi, Ralph Grishman, and Chin-Yew Lin. 2012. Ensemble semantics for large-scale unsupervised relation extraction. In *Proceedings Joint Conference on Empirical Methods in Natural Language Processing and Computational Natural Language Learning*.

Kishore Papineni, Salim Roukos, Todd Ward, and Wei-Jing Zhu. 2002. Bleu: a method for automatic evaluation of machine translation. In *Proceedings of the 40th Annual Meeting of the Association for Computational Linguistics*.

Nima Pourdamghani, Kevin Knight, and Ulf Hermjakob. 2016. Generating english from abstract meaning representations. In *Proc. The International Natural Language Generation conference (INLG2016)*.

Abigail See, Peter J. Liu, and Christopher D. Manning. 2017. Get to the point: Summarization with pointer-generator networks. In *Proceedings of the 55th Annual Meeting of the Association for Computational Linguistics*.

Lei Sha, Lili Mou, Tianyu Liu, Pascal Poupart, Sujian Li, Baobao Chang, and Zhifang Sui. 2018. Order-planning neural text generation from structured data. In *Proceedings of the 32nd AAAI Conference on Artificial Intelligence*.

Tao Shen, Tianyi Zhou, Guodong Long, Jing Jiang, Shirui Pan, and Chengqi Zhang. 2018a. Disan: Directional self-attention network for rnn/cnn-free language understanding. In *Proceedings of the 32nd AAAI Conference on Artificial Intelligence*.

Tao Shen, Tianyi Zhou, Guodong Long, Jing Jiang, and Chengqi Zhang. 2018b. Bi-directional block self-attention for fast and memory-efficient sequence modeling. In *International Conference on Learning Representations*.

Linfeng Song, Yue Zhang, Zhiguo Wang, and Daniel Gildea. 2018. A graph-to-sequence model for amr-to-text generation. *arXiv preprint arXiv:1805.02473*.

Ilya Sutskever, James Martens, and Geoffrey E Hinton. 2011. Generating text with recurrent neural networks. In *Proceedings of the 28th International Conference on Machine Learning*.

Ashish Vaswani, Noam Shazeer, Niki Parmar, Jakob Uszkoreit, Llion Jones, Aidan N Gomez, Łukasz Kaiser, and Illia Polosukhin. 2017. Attention is all you need. In *Advances in Neural Information Processing Systems 22*.

Oriol Vinyals, Meire Fortunato, and Navdeep Jaitly. 2015. Pointer networks. In C. Cortes, N. D. Lawrence, D. D. Lee, M. Sugiyama, and R. Garnett, editors, *Advances in Neural Information Processing Systems 28*, pages 2692–2700.

Denny Vrandečić and Markus Krötzsch. 2014. Wikidata: a free collaborative knowledgebase. *Communications of the ACM*, 57(10):78–85.

Qingyun Wang, Zhihao Zhou, Lifu Huang, Spencer Whitehead, Boliang Zhang, Heng Ji, and Kevin Knight. 2018. Paper abstract writing through editing mechanism. In *Proceedings of the 56th Annual Meeting of the Association for Computational Linguistics*.

Tsung-Hsien Wen, Milica Gašić, Nikola Mrkšić, Pei-Hao Su, David Vandyke, and Steve Young. 2015. Semantically conditioned lstm-based natural language generation for spoken dialogue systems. In *Proceedings of the 2015 Conference on Empirical Methods in Natural Language Processing*.

Spencer Whitehead, Heng Ji, Mohit Bansal, Shih-Fu Chang, and Clare Voss. 2018. Incorporating background knowledge into video description generation. In *Proc. 2018 Conference on Empirical Methods in Natural Language Processing (EMNLP2018)*.

Sam Wiseman, Stuart Shieber, and Alexander Rush. 2017. Challenges in data-to-document generation. In *Proceedings of the 2017 Conference on Empirical Methods in Natural Language Processing*.

Fei Wu and Daniel S. Weld. 2010. Open information extraction using wikipedia. In *Proceedings of the 48th Annual Meeting of the Association for Computational Linguistics*.

Ying Xu, Mi-Young Kim, Kevin Quinn, Randy Goebel, and Denilson Barbosa. 2013. Open information extraction with tree kernels. In *Proceedings of the 2013 Conference of the North American Chapter of the Association for Computational Linguistics: Human Language Technologies*.

Dian Yu, Lifu Huang, and Heng Ji. 2017. Open relation extraction and grounding. In *Proceedings of the 8th International Joint Conference on Natural Language Processing*.

Syntactic Manipulation for Generating More Diverse and Interesting Texts

Jan Deriu
Zurich University of Applied Sciences
jan.deriu@zhaw.ch

Mark Cieliebak
Zurich University of Applied Sciences
mark.cieliebak@zhaw.ch

Abstract

Natural Language Generation plays an important role in the domain of dialogue systems as it determines how users perceive the system. Recently, deep-learning based systems have been proposed to tackle this task, as they generalize better and require less amounts of manual effort to implement them for new domains. However, deep learning systems usually adapt a very homogeneous sounding writing style which expresses little variation.

In this work, we present our system for Natural Language Generation where we control various aspects of the surface realization in order to increase the lexical variability of the utterances, such that they sound more diverse and interesting. For this, we use a Semantically Controlled Long Short-term Memory Network (SC-LSTM), and apply its specialized cell to control various syntactic features of the generated texts. We present an in-depth human evaluation where we show the effects of these surface manipulation on the perception of potential users.

1 Introduction

In this paper, we describe our end-to-end trainable neural network for producing natural language descriptions of restaurants from meaning representations (MR). Recently, data-driven natural language generation (NLG) systems have shown great promise, especially as they can be easily adapted to new data or domains. End-to-end systems based on deep learning can jointly learn sentence planning and sentence realization from unaligned data. However, a recurrent problem, which we found with the existing solutions

for NLG, is that the generated utterances express a very homogeneous writing style. More precisely, most utterances start by using the restaurant name, the follow-up sentences usually begin with the pronoun "It", and each attribute-value pair is expressed using the same formulation across different utterances (see Table 1).

Green Man is a family friendly japanese restaurant in riverside near Express by Holiday Inn.
Clowns is a pub near Crowne Plaza Hotel with a customer rating of 5 out of 5.
Wildwood is an italian pub located near Raja Indian Cuisine in the city centre. It is not family-friendly.
The Cricketers provides chinese food in the 20-25 price range. It is located in the riverside. It is near All Bar One. Its customer rating is high.

Table 1: Examples to highlight the homogeneity of the utterances generated by state-of-the-art systems.

The publicly available E2E dataset by (Novikova et al., 2017) provides pairs of Meaning Representations (MR's) and several human generated reference utterances for the restaurant-domain. It is the first dataset to provide large amounts of training data with an open vocabulary, complex syntactic structures, and more variabilty in expressing the attributes. In this work, we exploit these characteristics of the dataset to generate utterances which express a higher diversity in their writing style. For this, we extend the Semantically Conditioned Long Short-term Memory Network (SC-LSTM) proposed by (Wen et al., 2015b) with surface features to control the manipulation of the surface realization.

Since the data contains a large variety of formulations for an attribute-value pair, a simple delexicalization of the utterance is not possible. This fact also increases the difficulty of evaluating the utterances for their correctness. Thus, we introduce a semantic reranking procedure based on classification algorithms trained to rate whether

Proceedings of The 11th International Natural Language Generation Conference, pages 22–34,
Tilburg, The Netherlands, November 5-8, 2018. ©2018 Association for Computational Linguistics

the attributes are rendered correctly.

We evaluate our model on the E2E dataset and report the BLEU, NIST, METEOR, ROUGE-L and CIDEr scores. We measure the diversity of the generated utterances by counting the number of different uni- and bi-grams. Further, to evaluate the correctness of the generated utterances, we employ a soft metric based on the aforementioned classifiers. Finally, we present an in-depth human evaluation where we measured the effects of these more diverse utterances on the perceptions of potential users. More precisely, humans evaluated the quality and naturalness of an utterance, which of the attributes comprehensible, concise, elegant, and professional fits to the text, and which of the different systems generated the most preferred outputs. We release the code and all the scripts.[1]

2 Related Work

The task of NLG is usually divided into separate subtasks such as content selection, sentence planning, and surface realization (Stent et al., 2004). Traditionally, the task has been solved by relying on rule-based methods, but these methods do not scale and are hardly adaptable to new domains. Recently, deep learning techniques have become more prominent for NLG. With these techniques, there now exists a large variety of different network architectures, each tackling a different aspect of NLG: (Wen et al., 2015b) propose an extension to the vanilla LSTM (Hochreiter and Schmidhuber, 1997) to control the semantic properties of an utterance, whereas (Hu et al., 2017) use variational autoencoder (VAE) and generative adversarial networks to control the generation of texts by manipulating the latent space; (Mei et al., 2016) employ an encoder-decoder architecture extended by a coarse-to-fine aligner to solve the problem of content selection; (Wen et al., 2016) apply data counter-fitting to generate out-of-domain training data for pretraining a model where there is little in-domain data available; (Semeniuta et al., 2017; Bowman et al., 2015) use a VAE trained in an unsupervised fashion on large amounts of data to sample texts from the latent space; and (Dušek and Jurcicek, 2016) use a sequence-to-sequence model with attention to generate natural language strings as well as deep syntax dependency trees from dialogue acts. All these approaches solve different aspects of the NLG task.

In our work, we tackle the aspect of generating texts that display more complex and diverse syntactic structures. The dialogue system community has proposed most work on this topic, as the end-to-end trainable algorithms tend to produce the same universal answer to each input. In (Li et al., 2016a) the authors develop a new loss function based on mutual information, (Li et al., 2016b) propose a new decoding algorithm based on a modified beam search, which favors hypotheses from different parent nodes. In (Li et al., 2017) the authors aim to increase the diversity by removing training examples, which are similar to the most commonly used utterances. In (Shao et al., 2017) the authors propose a sequence-to-sequence model with an augmented attention mechanism, which takes into account parts of the target sentence. Finally, the authors adapt the beam-search ranking to work at a segment level and, thus, injecting diversity earlier during the decoding.

3 Task Definition

Natural language generation for dialogue systems describes the task of converting a meaning representation (MR) into an utterance in a natural language. The E2E training data consist of 50k instances in the restaurant domain, where one instance is a pair of a MR and an example utterance or reference. The data is split into training, development and test in a 76.5%-8.5%-15%-ratio. Each MR consists of 3-8 attributes and their values, see Table 2 for the domain ontology. The split ensures that the MRs in the different dataset-splits are distinct. The dataset contains an open vocabulary and more complex syntactic structures than other similar datasets, as shown in the dataset definition (Novikova et al., 2017). Especially, it contains various ways of expressing a single value of an attribute: for instance, the value *1 of 5* is expressed in the data as "one star rated", "rated with 1 of 5 stars", or "rated one out of five". In this work, we exploit this variety of formulation to produce utterances that express a more varied writing style.

4 Model

The goal of our model is to generate a text while providing the ability of controlling various semantic and syntactic properties of this text. Our model has two components: i) the generator and ii) semantic classifiers that rate the correctness of an ut-

Attribute	Type	Example Values
name	verbatim string	Alimentum, ..
eatType	dictionary	restaurant, pub, coffee shop
familyFriendly	boolean	yes, no
food	dictionary	Italian, French, English, ...
near	verbatim string	Burger King
area	dictionary	riverside, city center
customerRating	dictionary	1 of 5, 3 of 5, 5 of 5, low, average, high
priceRange	dictionary	<£20, £20-25, >£30 cheap, moderate, high

Table 2: Domain ontology of the E2E dataset.

terance.

We use the Semantically Conditioned Long Short-term Memory Network (SC-LSTM) proposed by (Wen et al., 2015b) as our generator, which has a specialized cell to process the one-hot encoded MR-vector. The semantic classifiers (SC) are trained for each attribute separately: they classify which value the generator rendered. With this, the correctness of an utterance can be determined, which is relevant when dealing with contradictory constraints during the generation of more diverse texts.

4.1 Semantically Conditioned LSTM

The SC-LSTM (Wen et al., 2015b) extends the original LSTM (Hochreiter and Schmidhuber, 1997) cell with a specialized cell, which processes the MR. The MR is represented as a one-hot encoded MR-vector d_0, which represents the value for each attribute. This cell assumes the task of the sentence planner, as it treats the MR-vector as a checklist to ensure that the information is fully represented in the utterance. The cell acts as a forget gate, keeping track of which information has already been consumed.

We briefly introduce the SC-LSTM as defined in (Wen et al., 2015b), which we will later on modify to meet our needs. Let $w_t \in \mathbb{R}^M$ be the input vector at time t, $d_t \in \mathbb{R}^D$ the MR-vector at time t, and N be the number of units of an SC-LSTM cell, then the formulation of the forward pass is defined as:

$$\begin{pmatrix} i_t \\ f_t \\ o_t \\ r_t \\ g_t \end{pmatrix} = \begin{pmatrix} \sigma \\ \sigma \\ \sigma \\ \sigma \\ \tanh \end{pmatrix} \mathbf{W}_{5n,2n} \begin{pmatrix} w_t \\ h_{t-1} \end{pmatrix}$$

$$d_t = r_t * d_{t-1}$$
$$c_t = i_t * g_t + f_t * c_{t-1} + \tanh(W_d d_t)$$
$$h_t = o_t * \tanh(c_t)$$

where σ is the sigmoid function, and $i_t, f_t, o_t, r_t \in [0,1]^N$ are the input, forget, output, and MR-reading gates, and $h_t, c_t \in [0,1]^N$ are the hidden state and the cell state. The weights $\mathbf{W}_{5n,2n}$ and $W_d \in \mathbb{R}^{D \times M}$ are the model parameters to be learned.

The prediction of the next token is performed by sampling from the probability distribution:

$$w_t \sim P(w_t | w_{0:t-1}, d_t) = \text{softmax}(W_s h_t)$$

where $W_s \in \mathbb{R}^{N \times M}$ is a weight matrix to be learned during training. During the training procedure the inputs to the SC-LSTM are the original tokens w_t from the training set. On the other hand, when generating new utterances we use the previously generated token as input to generate the next token.

Loss   To ensure that the SC-LSTM consumes the MR correctly, two conditions are defined: i) the MR-vector at the last time step d_T has to be zero, which ensures that all the required information has been rendered, and ii) the gate should not consume too much of the dialogue act in one time step, i.e. the difference $\|d_t - d_{t-1}\|$ should be minimised. From these criteria, the reconstruction loss is adapted to:

$$F(\theta) = \sum_t p_t^T log(y_t) + \|d_T\| + \sum_{t=0}^{T-1} \eta \xi^{\|d_t - d_{t-1}\|}$$

where the first term is the reconstruction error, which sums the cross-entropy loss for each time step and the following two terms ensure the two criteria defined above.

Semantic Classifiers   For each attribute a we train a CNN-based classifier D_a. Each classifier is trained to detect which of the possible values for the attribute a is rendered in the utterance or if the attribute is present in the utterance at all. We train the classifiers on the training set, where the input is the utterance and the output is the value for the attribute a, which is defined in the MR. These classifiers measure the semantic correctness of the produced utterances by comparing the output of the classifier to the MR. If the classifier output corresponds to the value defined in the MR then we regard the attribute as being rendered correctly.

5 Syntactic Control

The utterances produced by the basic model described in Section 4 lack syntactic variety, they all follow the trivial structure. To control the syntactic expressions of an utterance we expand the MR-vector with syntax specific features. More specifically, in this work we control three different surface features: i) the first word of the utterance, ii) the first word of each follow-up sentence in the utterance, and iii) for each attribute-value pair the formulation used to express it. For each of these control mechanisms, we produce one-hot encoded vectors and append these vectors to the MR-vector d_0. Through this mechanism, we provide the SC-LSTM with more prior information on the structure of the utterance. Thus, it learns to correlate how to render the surface based on the surface information provided. In the following, we describe the three control mechanisms in detail.

First Word Control Most utterances generated by the vanilla SC-LSTM begin by using the restaurant name. The main reason for this behaviour is that 59% of all utterances in the dataset have this characteristic. All the other starting words are used much less frequently: e.g. only 7% of all utterances start with the word "There", which is the second most used word. The model optimizes to generate the utterance, which yields the lowest average loss. Without additional information, this equates to the most common structure of utterances found in the training set. The first word used in an utterance greatly impacts how the rest of the utterance is rendered. Thus, using different first words increases the diversity of the rendered utterances. To generate more uncommon utterances, we provide the model with the information about the first word in the utterance during training. For this, we select all the words that appear more than $t = 60$ times as first word in the training data, which results in a set of $n = 20$ different words[2]. We then extend the MR-vector by adding a one-hot encoded vector $u_0 \in \mathbb{R}^{n+1}$, where the vector is set to '1' at the index of the first word in the utterance of the training sample. During the training, we use a dummy-index at $n + 1$ in case the first word of the utterance is not present in the list of first words. During test-time the first word is sampled from the set of n first words. To improve

the semantic correctness we use the sampling procedure to over-generate, i.e. m different words are sampled to generate m different utterances. Using the semantic classifiers, the produced utterances are ranked by their correctness score.

Follow-up First Word Control We observe that the follow-up sentences in an utterance, which are produced by the vanilla SC-LSTM also follow the same pattern. More precisely, in cases where the utterance uses multiple sentences, the follow-up sentences usually begin with the pronoun 'It' which refers to the restaurant name mentioned in the first sentence. Similarly, to the First-Word-Control, we control the first word of follow-up sentences by using one-hot encoded vectors. The encoding states which word is used as first word of each follow-up sentence. As most utterances are composed between one and four sentences, we use three vectors to encode the first word of the first three follow-up sentences.
There are $n = 22$ different first words used in follow-up sentences, thus, each vector f_i is of length $n + 1$, where $i \in \{2, 3, 4\}$ denotes the sentence enumeration. We add an extra dimension to denote the case where the number of sentences is less than i. This representation provides the ability to control the first word used in each follow-up sentence as well as the number of sentences rendered.

Attribute-Value Formulation Control We observe that the vanilla SC-LSTM learns to use the most common formulation for an attribute-value pair. On average over all the attribute-value pairs, the most common formulation is used in 76% of the cases in the training set. It turns out that the most used formulation for most attribute-value pairs is equivalent to the surface form of the value itself. For example, the value "5 out of 5" is mostly expressed using the formulation: "... with a customer rating of 5 out of 5", instead of "It has an excellent customer rating" or other formulations.
To extract the different formulations of an attribute-value pair, we use a simple TF-IDF approach based on unigrams. For the complete list of formulations refer to Table 11 in Appendix A. For each attribute, we treat the utterances for each value as one document, thus, the corpus is made of as many documents as there are values for this attribute. The score is computed as $1 + \log(\text{tf}_{iv}^a) * \log(1 + \frac{N}{\text{df}_i^a})$ where tf_{iv}^a is the term frequency of

---

[2] \$Name, Located, For, In, A, \$Near, An, Near, There, On, \$Food,The ,With ,Serving , If, At, Riverside, By, You, Family

term i for value v and df_i^a is the document frequency of term i in the documents of attribute a. We keep only those terms whose score is higher than 3. We apply manual filtering to clean the list from terms, which do not describe the attribute-value pair. With this method, we get on average 4.2 terms per attribute-value pair. We extend the MR-vector with one one-hot encoded vector for each attribute-value pair.

System	BLEU	NIST	METEOR	ROUGE_L	CIDEr
vanilla	0.634	8.270	0.428	0.653	1.9281
tgen	**0.661**	**8.550**	**0.446**	**0.687**	**2.201**
utt-fw	0.581	7.983	0.427	0.591	1.810
follow-fw	0.572	7.665	0.436	0.643	1.819
form	0.623	8.161	0.432	0.657	1.992
full	0.505	7.455	0.422	0.558	1.616

Table 3: Scores achieved for the corpus-based metrics by the different systems. The value of the best system for each score is highlighted in bold.

6 Experimental Setting

The goal for our application is to generate descriptions for restaurants. The dataset from (Novikova et al., 2017) contains 50k utterances for 5,751 different MRs. On average, each MR is composed of 5.43 attributes and there are 8.1 different references for each MR on average. For the evaluation, we report various corpus-based metrics: BLEU-4 (Papineni et al., 2002), NIST (Doddington, 2002) METEOR (Lavie and Agarwal, 2007), ROUGE-L (Lin, 2004), and CIDEr (Vedantam et al., 2015). Furthermore, we report various measures for lexical diversity: number of different tokens (#tokens), the type-token ratio (TTR) (Chotlos, 1944), the moving average type-token ratio (MSTTR) (Covington and McFall, 2010), and the measure of lexical diversity(MLTD) (McCarthy, 2005). Finally, we perform a human evaluation to measure the effect of the proposed manipulations on the user's perception.

Preprocessing Each utterance is treated as a string of characters, where each character is represented as a one-hot encoded vector. We replace the *name* and *near* values with the tokens 'X-name" and "X-near" respectively. The high diversity of the various formulations found for the attribute-value pairs, impedes us from replacing other attributes with placeholders. To generate the lexical features, we apply the Spacy-API[3] for word and sentence tokenization.

System Setup We train the SC-LSTM and the classifiers using AdaDelta (Zeiler, 2012) to optimize the loss function. We apply a softmax with decreasing temperature as proposed in (Hu et al., 2017) to approximate the discrete representation, which is used as input to the LSTM during the decoding stage. For the LSTM cell we use a hidden state of size 1024 and apply dropout as suggested

---
[3]https://spacy.io/

in (Yarin and Ghahramani, 2016). For the classifiers we use a 2-layer CNN with 256 kernels of length 3.

We use our character-based version of the SC-LSTM (*vanilla*) as well as the sequence-to-sequence model by (Dušek and Jurcicek, 2016) (*tgen*) as baseline. We evaluate different versions of our model: the model where we control only the first word of the utterance (*utt-fw*), the model where we only control the first words of the follow-up sentences (*follow-fw*), the model where we only control the formulations of the attribute-value pairs (*form*), and the model where we control all three factors (*full*).

Output Generation The input to the system is a meaning representation (MR) which is converted into the MR-vector d_0. For each MR, the system samples the syntactic control values at random, i.e. it samples the first word of the utterance, the first words of each of the follow-up sentences and the formulation for each attribute-value pair randomly from the list of their respective possibilities. Then, these syntactic features are encoded into the one-hot format as described above. The input to the SC-LSTM is composed of both the MR-vector and the syntactic control vector. To ensure that the sampling of the syntactic features did not introduce semantic error, the system samples 10 different values for each of the three control types and produces one utterance for each combination, e.g. the *full* system produces 1000 sentences for each MR. We then use the classifiers (previously trained to evaluate if the utterance rendered the MR correctly) to rank the 1000 utterances w.r.t. their correctness. Finally, the system samples the final utterance from the set of utterances with the highest score (as there can be multiple utterances with the same score).

name	eatType	price	rating	near	food	area	fam.
1.0	0.97	0.90	0.84	0.99	0.95	0.94	0.91

Table 4: Validation Accuracy scores for each classifier.

System	vanilla	tgen	utt-fw	follow-fw	form	full
$\mathbf{ERR}_{sc}$	0.158	0.192	0.093	0.100	0.100	**0.056**
$\mathbf{ERR}_{rule}$	0.086	0.059	0.028	0.054	0.040	**0.015**

Table 5: Error Rate for each system, best system is highlighted in bold. The *sc* subscript denotes the scores computed by the classifiers.

7 Results

7.1 Evaluation Metrics

We report the scores for the automatic evaluation. This includes the metrics BLEU, ROUGE-L, METEOR, NIST, and CIDEr score, which rely on the comparison between the predicted utterance and multiple reference utterances. Table 3 shows that the surface manipulation leads to a decrease in all of these scores. The best scores for each metric is achieved by the *tgen* system. Its BLEU score is 3 points above the score achieved by *vanilla*. The *full* system achieved the lowest scores in each metric. Generally speaking, the deeper the impact of the syntactic manipulation the lower the word-overlap based score. This behaviour is explained by the fact that the baseline systems generate utterances which are syntactically similar to the most used structure in the gold-standard. The other systems generate sentences whose style and structure is much rarer in the gold-standard. For example, 59% of the reference utterances start with the standard pattern, whereas only 3% of the sentences generated by the *full* system follow this pattern. Although there are multiple reference utterances, it is not likely that one of these follows the syntactic choices of the syntactically controlled systems. Table 6 displays the various lexical diversity scores for each system as well as for the human-written text for reference. As expected, the

System	#tokens	TTR	MATTR	MTLD
vanilla	106	0.0070	0.5410	31.4811
tgen	120	0.0081	0.5175	30.5444
utt-fw	131	0.0082	0.5980	34.2865
follow-fw	141	0.0084	0.5745	33.5055
form	155	0.0098	0.5748	33.4892
full	**224**	**0.0134**	**0.6310**	**35.7831**
human	425	0.0280	0.6373	36.4466

Table 6: Diversity scores for each system and the human texts. The highest score of a system is marked in bold.

human-written texts display the highest diversity across all scores. The *full* system achieves the highest scores out of all systems. Furthermore, both the *vanilla* and the *tgen* system obtain the lowest scores, thus, showing that the syntactic control mechanisms generate more diverse texts.

7.2 Classifier Performance

Since we use semantic classifiers to evaluate the correctness of the generated sentences, it is important to assess the quality of these classifiers. Table 4 shows the accuracy score for each of the classifiers on the testset. We note that all classifiers have a score greater than 0.9 except for the *customer rating*. The errors of the *customer rating* and the *price* classifiers stem from the semantic equivalence between the numerical and the verbal values which were used interchangeably in the references, e.g. when "price range is over £30" is expressed as "high-priced".

7.3 Correctness

We evaluate the correctness using a rule based system. We report the average error rate achieved by a system, as proposed by (Wen et al., 2015a), in Table 5, line $\mathbf{ERR}_{rule}$. The best error-rate is achieved by the *full* system, followed by *utt-fw* and *form*. This shows that our approach to rerank the utterances with the semantic classifiers works very well. For comparison, we also report the error-rates when using the semantic classifiers themselves to determine the correctness of an utterance $\mathbf{ERR}_{sc}$. It turns out that there is a mismatch between the scores achieved by the two metrics, especially for the *tgen* and *vanilla* system. This is due to the fact that the classifiers are used to filter the incorrect utterances, which leads the scores to be biased. Thus, it shows that the classifiers themselves are not suitable to compute a correctness score.

7.4 Qualitative Evaluation

In Table 8 two representative (cherry picked) examples are shown. For one MR we compare the outputs of all systems. In both examples the *tgen* and *vanilla* system produce utterances which follow the trivial pattern. The *uff-fw* and *full* systems produce a different style of utterance by starting the sentence with a preposition. The *follow-fw* system adds more variability to the utterance by starting the follow-up sentences with verbs (e.g.

"Located") or nouns ("Children") instead of pronouns referring to the restaurant name. The *form* system adds more variability by using different ways of phrasing an attribute-value pair (e.g. replacing "high price range" with "expensive"). We added a list of randomly sampled (non-cherry-picked) examples in Appendix B.

System	Quality	Naturalness
vanilla	3.979	**2.732**[*]
tgen	4.013	2.591
utt-fw	4.007	2.605
follow-fw	3.992	2.576
form	**4.035**	2.577
full	4.033	2.540

Table 7: Quality and naturalness results from the user study. Here, * implies a statistical significant difference between a system and the *tgen* system, measured with two-tailed Student's t-test with $p < 0.05$

7.5 Human Evaluation

To measure the effectiveness of our approach, we performed an extensive human evaluation. For this, we recruited judges from the Figure-Eight[4] platform. For each experiment the sentence is rated by three different judges.

Quality and Naturalness To show that the syntactic manipulations do not deteriorate the utterances, we evaluated the *quality* and *naturalness* of the utterances produced by the different systems. Here, *quality* is defined to measure the grammatical correctness, the fluency and the correctness of the content, whereas *naturalness* measures the likelihood that the utterance was written by a human. For this, we sampled 250 MR's and generated the respective utterances for each system. The judges rated all utterances on a Likert scale from 1 to 5 for *quality* and on a scale from 1 to 3 for *naturalness*[5]. Table 7 shows the results for both the *quality* and *naturalness* evaluation. Statistical significance is measured by means of a two-tailed Student's t-test between the *tgen* system and the other systems. For *quality* there is no statistically significant difference between the *tgen* system and any other system. For *naturalness* there is no statistically significant between *tgen* and the syntactically controlled systems. However, there is a

---

[4]www.figure-eight.com

[5]For naturalness we asked if the utterance is likely to be written by a human, by a machine or if it is not clear

significant difference between *tgen* and *vanilla*. In fact, the *vanilla* system is rated significantly higher in terms of *naturalness* than any other system. For both metrics, the scores of all systems are very high, thus, we conclude that the syntactical control mechanisms do not deteriorate the utterances.

Subjective Analysis The main goal of the human evaluation is to understand how humans *perceive* the new utterances. For this, we compare the utterances of *tgen* and the *full* system by first sampling a MR, generate the utterance for each system, and let the human judges decide which of the two utterances they prefer. Since preference is a very subjective measure that might not give complete insight, we asked the judges to also state which utterance they find more *comprehensible* (is the utterance easier to understand), more *concise* (does the utterance convey the information clearly with as little text as possible), more *elegant* (is the utterance more nicely written, more poetic, display higher variability) and more *professional* (could this text be written by an experienced and well trained writer). Table 9 shows the ratio at which the system was selected for each of the five aforementioned categories alongside the inter-annotator agreement computed with the Fleiss' κ. The results show that none of the two systems is significantly preferred by the judges, nor is any of the two systems rated as being more comprehensible. However, the judges perceive the *full* system to produce significantly more elegant and professional utterances, i.e. in 71.6% of the comparisons the utterances by the *full* system were rated as more elegant and in 66.6% as being more professional. On the other hand, the judges rate the utterances of the *tgen* system as being significantly more concise (75%).

There is a moderate correlation between the preference of an utterance and the elegance (Spearman's Rho $\rho = 0.557$) or professionalism ($\rho = 0.569$). Furthermore, there is a weak correlation between comprehensibility of a system and the professionalism ($\rho = 0.468$). However, we found that there is a strong correlation between the preference and the comprehensibility of an utterance ($\rho = 0.719$). The evaluation shows that although the utterances by the *full* system are rated as being more elegant and professional, they are not necessarily preferred. The strongest indicator for preference is, thus, the comprehensibility.

#	System	Utterance
1	MR	name=The Punter, eatType=pub, food=English, priceRange=high, area=city-centre, familyFriendly=no, near=Raja Indian Cuisine
	vanilla	The Punter is a pub that serves English food in the high price range and is located in the city centre near Raja Indian Cuisine.
	tgen	The Punter is an english pub in the city centre near Raja Indian Cuisine. It has a high price range and is not child friendly.
	utt-fw	In the city centre near Raja Indian Cuisine is a pub called The Punter. It serves English food and is not children friendly. The price range is high.
	follow-fw	The Punter is a pub that serves English food. Located in the city centre near Raja Indian Cuisine, it is not children friendly and has a high price range.
	form	The Punter is an expensive English Pub near Raja Indian Cuisine in the city centre. It is not child friendly.
	full	If you are looking for a pub serving English food, try The Punter. It is located in the city centre near Raja Indian Cuisine. Prices are on the higher end and it is not child friendly.
2	MR	name=Giraffe, eatType=restaurant, food=French, area=riverside, familyFriendly=yes, near=Raja Indian Cuisine
	vanilla	Giraffe is a family friendly restaurant that serves French food. It is located near Raja Indian Cuisine.
	tgen	Giraffe is a family friendly french restaurant near Raja Indian Cuisine in riverside.
	utt-fw	A French restaurant called Giraffe is located in the riverside area near Raja Indian Cuisine. It is child friendly.
	follow-fw	Giraffe is a restaurant that serves French food. The restaurant is located near Raja Indian Cuisine in the riverside area. Children are welcome.
	form	Giraffe is a French restaurant in the riverside area near Raja Indian Cuisine. It is family friendly.
	full	In the riverside area there is a French restaurant called Giraffe. You will find it near Raja Indian Cuisine. Yes, it is family friendly.

Table 8: Sample output of the vanilla SC-LSTM (V) and the First Word Control (F) for four different MRs where one attribute-value is changed.

Question	tgen	full	κ
Preference	0.476	0.523	0.587
Comprehensibility	0.476	0.523	0.555
Conciseness	0.750*	0.250	0.545
Elegance	0.283	0.716*	0.545
Professional	0.333	0.666*	0.529

Table 9: Results of the native speaking preference test. Significance is computed using a two-tailed binomial test. Where * denotes $p < 0.005$ and $N = 200$

Question	tgen	full	κ
Preference	0.593	0.406	0.456
Comprehensibility	0.682*	0.317	0.453
Conciseness	0.949**	0.050	0.312
Elegance	0.424	0.575	0.497
Professional	0.740**	0.259	0.342

Table 10: Results of the non-native speaking preference test. Significance is computed using a two-tailed binomial test, here * denotes $p < 0.05$ and ** denotes $p < 0.005$ and $N = 200$

Native vs. non-native speakers We observed that depending on whether the judges were native speaker or not the results were different. Thus, we repeated the same experiment by recruiting judges from non-native speaking countries[6]. Table 10 shows the results of the evaluation performed by the non-native speaking group. The differences of the ratings are significant. The non-native speakers rate the *tgen* system as significantly more comprehensible, more concise as well as more professional. There is still a high correlation between the preference and the comprehensibility of an utterance (Spearman's Rho $\rho = 0.709$). However, for the non-native group there is a significantly higher correlation between the comprehensibility and the professionalism of an utterance (Spearman's Rho $\rho = 0.628$) and a very high correlation between the preference and the professionalism (Spearman's Rho $\rho = 0.714$). This shows that the non-native speaking group finds it easier to understand the utterances produced by *tgen* and rates them as more preferable and more professional.

The evaluation shows that the two groups have different preferences and perceptions of the utterances. An in-depth analysis on the reasons behind these differences is left to future work. Our experiments indicate that the differences are due to the differences in language proficiency, as there is

---

[6]Judges were mostly recruited from eastern European countries and Asia.

a high correlation between the preference and the comprehensibility. However, to test this assumption, more characteristics about the judges need to be known.

8 Conclusion

In this work, we presented an end-to-end trainable deep-learning based system for the natural language generation task. With a simple control mechanism the utterances can be rendered more diverse and interesting. The human evaluation revealed that this control mechanism does not deteriorate the quality of the utterances in terms of semantic or grammatical errors. It further revealed that more diverse utterances are perceived as being more elegant and professional sounding to native speakers. Not surprisingly, the corpus-based metrics deteriorate when a more diverse vocabulary is used. One major challenge of this approach is the fact that during the generation the syntactic control features have to be sampled randomly to generate many utterances which have to be ranked and filtered. The solution to this inefficiency is part of future work.

References

Samuel R Bowman, Luke Vilnis, Oriol Vinyals, Andrew M Dai, Rafal Jozefowicz, and Samy Bengio. 2015. Generating sentences from a continuous space. *arXiv preprint arXiv:1511.06349*.

John W Chotlos. 1944. Iv. a statistical and comparative analysis of individual written language samples. *Psychological Monographs*, 56(2):75.

Michael A. Covington and Joe D. McFall. 2010. Cutting the gordian knot: The moving-average typetoken ratio (mattr). *Journal of Quantitative Linguistics*, 17(2):94–100.

George Doddington. 2002. Automatic evaluation of machine translation quality using n-gram cooccurrence statistics. In *Proceedings of the Second International Conference on Human Language Technology Research*, HLT '02, pages 138–145, San Francisco, CA, USA. Morgan Kaufmann Publishers Inc.

Ondřej Dušek and Filip Jurcicek. 2016. Sequence-to-sequence generation for spoken dialogue via deep syntax trees and strings. In *Proceedings of the 54th Annual Meeting of the Association for Computational Linguistics (Volume 2: Short Papers)*, pages 45–51. Association for Computational Linguistics.

Sepp Hochreiter and Jürgen Schmidhuber. 1997. Long short-term memory. *Neural computation*, pages 1735–1780.

Zhiting Hu, Zichao Yang, Xiaodan Liang, Ruslan Salakhutdinov, and Eric P. Xing. 2017. Toward controlled generation of tex. *International Conference on Machine Learning*, pages 1587–1596.

Alon Lavie and Abhaya Agarwal. 2007. Meteor: An automatic metric for mt evaluation with high levels of correlation with human judgments. In *Proceedings of the Second Workshop on Statistical Machine Translation*, StatMT '07, pages 228–231, Stroudsburg, PA, USA. Association for Computational Linguistics.

Jiwei Li, Michel Galley, Chris Brockett, Jianfeng Gao, and Bill Dolan. 2016a. A diversity-promoting objective function for neural conversation models. In *Proceedings of the 2016 Conference of the North American Chapter of the Association for Computational Linguistics: Human Language Technologies*, pages 110–119. Association for Computational Linguistics.

Jiwei Li, Will Monroe, and Dan Jurafsky. 2016b. A simple, fast diverse decoding algorithm for neural generation. *CoRR*, abs/1611.08562.

Jiwei Li, Will Monroe, and Dan Jurafsky. 2017. Data distillation for controlling specificity in dialogue generation. *CoRR*, abs/1702.06703.

Chin-Yew Lin. 2004. Rouge: A package for automatic evaluation of summaries. In *Text Summarization Branches Out: Proceedings of the ACL-04 Workshop*, pages 74–81, Barcelona, Spain. Association for Computational Linguistics.

Philip M McCarthy. 2005. An assessment of the range and usefulness of lexical diversity measures and the potential of the measure of textual, lexical diversity (mtld). *Dissertation Abstracts International*, 66(12).

Hongyuan Mei, TTI UChicago, Mohit Bansal, and Matthew R Walter. 2016. What to talk about and how? selective generation using lstms with coarse-to-fine alignment. In *Proceedings of NAACL-HLT*, pages 720–730.

Jekaterina Novikova, Ondrej Dušek, and Verena Rieser. 2017. The E2E dataset: New challenges for end-to-end generation. In *Proceedings of the 18th Annual Meeting of the Special Interest Group on Discourse and Dialogue*, Saarbrücken, Germany. ArXiv:1706.09254.

Kishore Papineni, Salim Roukos, Todd Ward, and Wei-Jing Zhu. 2002. Bleu: A method for automatic evaluation of machine translation. In *Proceedings of the 40th Annual Meeting on Association for Computational Linguistics*, ACL '02, pages 311–318, Stroudsburg, PA, USA. Association for Computational Linguistics.

Stanislau Semeniuta, Aliaksei Severyn, and Erhardt Barth. 2017. A hybrid convolutional variational autoencoder for text generation. *arXiv preprint arXiv:1702.02390*.

Yuanlong Shao, Stephan Gouws, Denny Britz, Anna Goldie, Brian Strope, and Ray Kurzweil. 2017. Generating high-quality and informative conversation responses with sequence-to-sequence models. In *Proceedings of the 2017 Conference on Empirical Methods in Natural Language Processing*, pages 2210–2219. Association for Computational Linguistics.

Amanda Stent, Rashmi Prasad, and Marilyn Walker. 2004. Trainable sentence planning for complex information presentation in spoken dialog systems. In *Proceedings of the 42Nd Annual Meeting on Association for Computational Linguistics*, ACL '04, Stroudsburg, PA, USA. Association for Computational Linguistics.

Ramakrishna Vedantam, C. Lawrence Zitnick, and Devi Parikh. 2015. Cider: Consensus-based image description evaluation. In *The IEEE Conference on Computer Vision and Pattern Recognition (CVPR)*.

Tsung-Hsien Wen, Milica Gasic, Dongho Kim, Nikola Mrksic, Pei-Hao Su, David Vandyke, and Steve Young. 2015a. Stochastic language generation in dialogue using recurrent neural networks with convolutional sentence reranking. pages 275–284. Association for Computational Linguistics.

Tsung-Hsien Wen, Milica Gašić, Nikola Mrkšić, Lina M. Rojas-Barahona, Pei-Hao Su, David Vandyke, and Steve Young. 2016. Multi-domain neural network language generation for spoken dialogue systems. In *Proceedings of the 2016 Conference of the North American Chapter of the Association for Computational Linguistics: Human Language Technologies*, pages 120–129. Association for Computational Linguistics.

Tsung-Hsien Wen, Milica Gašić, Nikola Mrkšić, Pei-Hao Su, David Vandyke, and Steve Young. 2015b. Semantically conditioned lstm-based natural language generation for spoken dialogue systems. In *Proceedings of the 2015 Conference on Empirical Methods in Natural Language Processing (EMNLP)*. Association for Computational Linguistics.

Gal Yarin and Zoubin Ghahramani. 2016. A theoretically grounded application of dropout in recurrent neural networks. *Advances in neural information processing systems*, pages 1019–1027.

Matthew D Zeiler. 2012. Adadelta: an adaptive learning rate method. *arXiv preprint arXiv:1212.5701*.

A Formulations of Attribute-Values

Attribute	Value	Formulations
customer rating	1 out of 5	1, one, poor
	3 out of 5	3, three
	low	low, one, poor, poorly
	5 out of 5	5, five, excellent
	average	average, an, three, averagely
	high	high, highly, between, ranging
familyFriendly	no	not, non, adult, adults, no, allowed, allow
food	English	English, British, breakfast, traditional
	Fast food	fast, fries, joint, American, burger
	French	French, wine, cheese, fine, drinks
	Italian	Italian, pasta
	Japanese	Japanese, sushi, bar
priceRange	cheap	cheap, inexpensive
	high	high, expensive, higher, end
	moderate	moderate, moderately, mid, medium, pricing
	less than £20	20, less, than, under, pounds, inexpensive, below, lower
	£20-25	20, from, between, mid, 20-25, ranging, around
	more than £30	30, more, than, expensive, over, higher, above, costs, euros, costing

Table 11: The most important formulations that appear in the training set for each attribute-value pair. Pairs with just a single formulation were omitted.

B Sampled Utterances

#	System	Utterance
1	**MR**	name=The Wrestlers, eatType=restaurant, food=Italian, priceRange=moderate, area=riverside, familyFriendly=no, near=Raja Indian Cuisine,
	vanilla	The Wrestlers is a moderately priced Italian restaurant near Raja Indian Cuisine that is not kid friendly.
	tgen	The Wrestlers is a moderately priced italian restaurant in riverside near Raja Indian Cuisine. It is not kid friendly.
	utt	There is a moderately priced Italian restaurant called The Wrestlers in the riverside area near Raja Indian Cuisine. It is not kid friendly.
	follow	The Wrestlers is a restaurant providing Italian food in the moderate price range. The are located in the riverside area near Raja Indian Cuisine. The restaurant is not kid friendly.
	form	The Wrestlers is a restaurant that serves Italian food at a moderate price range. It is located in riverside near Raja Indian Cuisine and is not kid friendly.
	full	With a moderate price range, The Wrestlers is a restaurant that serves Italian food. It is located near Raja Indian Cuisine in the riverside area. No children allowed.
	human	The Wrestlers is a restaurant that serves Italian food. Has a moderate price range, and is kids friendly. Located in the riverside area near Raja Indian Cuisine.
2	**MR**	name=Zizzi, eatType=coffee shop, customer rating=average, near=Burger King,
	vanilla	Zizzi is a coffee shop near Burger King with an average customer rating.
	tgen	Zizzi is a coffee shop near Burger King. It has an average customer rating.
	utt	If you are looking for a coffee shop near Burger King, try Zizzi. It has an average customer rating.
	follow	Zizzi is a coffee shop near Burger King. Zizzi has an average customer rating.
	form	Zizzi is a coffee shop near Burger King. It has an average customer rating.
	full	If you are looking for a coffee shop near Burger King, then you could try Zizzi. It has an average customer rating.
	human	Customers rate Zizzi coffee shop, near Burger King, average.
3	**MR**	name=The Punter, eatType=restaurant, food=Italian, priceRange=cheap, customer rating=average, area=city centre, familyFriendly=yes, near=Rainbow Vegetarian Café,
	vanilla	The Punter is a family-friendly restaurant located in the city centre near Rainbow Vegetarian Café. It is cheap and has an average customer rating.
	tgen	The Punter is an italian restaurant near Rainbow Vegetarian Café in the city centre. It is family-friendly and has a cheap price range and an average customer rating.
	utt	Rainbow Vegetarian Café is a family-friendly restaurant called The Punter that serves Italian food and has an average customer rating. It is located in the city centre.
	follow	The Punter is a cheap Italian restaurant in the city centre near Rainbow Vegetarian Café. The Punter is family friendly and has an average customer rating.
	form	The Punter is an inexpensive Italian restaurant in the city centre near Rainbow Vegetarian Café. It is family friendly and has an average customer rating.
	full	In the city centre is a family-friendly restaurant called The Punter. This is a cheap Italian restaurant near Rainbow Vegetarian Café. It has an average customer rating.
	human	There is a cheap, restaurant that serves Italian, named The Punter, in the city centre near Rainbow Vegetarian Café. It has an average customer rating and is family friendly

Table 12: Randomly sampled output. A meaning representation is sampled at random, the respective utterance from each system is displayed.

#	System	Utterance
1	**MR**	name=The Cricketers, eatType=coffee shop, customer rating=average, familyFriendly=yes, near=Café Sicilia,
	vanilla	The Cricketers is a coffee shop near Café Sicilia. It is family friendly and has an average customer rating.
	tgen	The Cricketers is a family friendly coffee shop near Café Sicilia with an average customer rating.
	utt	If you are looking for a child friendly coffee shop near Café Sicilia, try The Cricketers. It has an average customer rating.
	follow	The Cricketers is a coffee shop near Café Sicilia that is family friendly and has an average customer rating.
	form	The Cricketers is a coffee shop near Café Sicilia. It is family friendly and has an average customer rating.
	full	For a family friendly coffee shop near Café Sicilia, try The Cricketers. Customers have rated it as average.
	human	Near Café Sicilia there is a coffee shop named The Cricketers. It's family friendly with an average rating.
2	**MR**	name=The Waterman, eatType=restaurant, food=Italian, priceRange=less than 20, area=riverside, familyFriendly=no, near=Raja Indian Cuisine,
	vanilla	The Waterman is a restaurant providing Italian food in the less than 20 price range. It is located in the riverside. It is near Raja Indian Cuisine.
	tgen	The Waterman is an italian restaurant in the riverside area near Raja Indian Cuisine. It is not family-friendly and has a price range of less than 20.
	utt	Italian restaurant The Waterman is located in the riverside area near Raja Indian Cuisine. It is not family-friendly and has a price range of less than 20.
	follow	The Waterman is a restaurant located near Raja Indian Cuisine in the riverside area. The price range is less than 20. They serve Italian food and are not family-friendly.
	form	The Waterman is a restaurant providing Italian food in the low price range. It is located in the riverside area near Raja Indian Cuisine. It is not family friendly.
	full	Italian food is served at The Waterman restaurant in the riverside area near Raja Indian Cuisine. Prices are under 20. Not family-friendly.
	human	The Waterman is a mature Italian restaurant near the riverside with a competitive menu for under 20, near the Raja Indian Cuisine.
3	**MR**	name=The Wrestlers, eatType=pub, food=Italian, priceRange=less than 20, area=riverside, familyFriendly=yes, near=Raja Indian Cuisine,
	vanilla	The Wrestlers is a family friendly pub near Raja Indian Cuisine in the riverside area that serves Italian food for less than 20.
	tgen	The Wrestlers is a family-friendly pub near Raja Indian Cuisine in the riverside area. It serves italian food for less than 20.
	utt	Italian food is served at The Wrestlers pub located near Raja Indian Cuisine in the riverside area. It is family friendly and has a price range of less than 20.
	follow	The Wrestlers is a pub that serves Italian food. They are located in the riverside area near Raja Indian Cuisine. They are family friendly and the price range is less than 20.
	form	The Wrestlers is a family friendly pub serving Italian food in the low price range. It is located in the riverside area near Raja Indian Cuisine.
	full	On the riverside near Raja Indian Cuisine is a family friendly pub called The Wrestlers. The price range is less than 20 and they serve Italian food.
	human	The Wrestlers is a pub in the low price range that serves pasta. It is located near Raja Indian Cuisine and has a public restroom.

Table 13: Randomly sampled output. A meaning representation is sampled at random, the respective utterance from each system is displayed.

Automated learning of templates for data-to-text generation: comparing rule-based, statistical and neural methods

Chris van der Lee
Tilburg University
c.vdrlee@tilburguniversity.edu

Emiel Krahmer
Tilburg University
e.j.krahmer@tilburguniversity.edu

Sander Wubben
Tilburg University
s.wubben@tilburguniversity.edu

Abstract

The current study investigated novel techniques and methods for trainable approaches to data-to-text generation. Neural Machine Translation was explored for the conversion from data to text as well as the addition of extra templatization steps of the data input and text output in the conversion process. Evaluation using BLEU did not find the Neural Machine Translation technique to perform any better compared to rule-based or Statistical Machine Translation, and the templatization method seemed to perform similarly or sometimes worse compared to direct data-to-text conversion. However, the human evaluation metrics indicated that Neural Machine Translation yielded the highest quality output and that the templatization method was able to increase text quality in multiple situations.

1 Introduction

Most approaches to data-to-text generation fall into one of two broad categories: rule-based or trainable (Gatt and Krahmer, 2018). Rule-based systems are often characterised by a template-based design: texts with gaps that can be filled with information. The application of these templates generally results in high quality text (e.g. van Deemter et al., 2005). The text quality of trainable systems — e.g. statistical models that select content based on what is the most likely realization according to probability — is generally lower (Reiter, 1995) and their development slower (Sanby et al., 2016). However, trainable systems use data-driven algorithms and do not rely on manually written resources for text generation, while most template systems require manually written templates and rules for text generation. This makes trainable systems potentially more adaptable and maintainable. Different approaches have been tried to decrease the building time and cost of data-to-text systems associated with trainable approaches, while limiting the drop in output quality compared to rule-based data-to-text systems (e.g. Adeyanju, 2012; Liang et al., 2009; Mahapatra et al., 2016) by experimenting with the trainable method.

The goal of the current study was to explore the combination of template and trainable approaches by giving statistical and deep learning-based systems templatized input to create templatized output. The more homogeneous nature of this templatized form was expected to make production of output that is fluent and clear as well as an accurate representation of the data more feasible compared to their untemplatized counterpart, generally used for trainable approaches. Furthermore, the usage of statistical and deep learning methods reduces the reliance on manually written resources that is associated with most template based systems. The approach of the current study was tested on four corpora in the sports and weather domain, each with divergent characteristics, to assess the usefulness in different situations. The output of these systems is compared using automated metrics (i.e. BLEU) as well as human evaluation.

2 Background

2.1 Data-to-text

Historically, most data-to-text systems use rule-based approaches which select and fill templates in order to produce a natural language text (e.g. Goldberg et al., 1994; van der Lee et al., 2017) and these approaches are still the most widely used in practical applications (Gkatzia, 2016). This is partly because rule-based approaches are robust

Proceedings of The 11th International Natural Language Generation Conference, pages 35–45,
Tilburg, The Netherlands, November 5-8, 2018. ©2018 Association for Computational Linguistics

and can produce high quality output given sufficient development time and cost. In addition, the output of these approaches is fully controlled by humans, which make them generally accurate in their representation of the data (e.g. van der Lee et al., 2018). However, capturing data using rules may be feasible for simple situations, but reports in several domains often describe more complex situations which would require an extensive set of rules. Writing these rules is time intensive and covering all distinct rules is nearly impossible for many situations. Furthermore, developing and maintaining these systems is cost intensive and most systems are difficult to extend to other domains. Statistical approaches may provide a solution for these shortcomings. These approaches are trained using a parallel corpus, thus require no handcrafted rules. This also makes conversion to other domains less time-intensive compared to rule-based approaches.

2.2 Trainable approaches

Producing output by using such trainable approaches can be exercised in different ways. Retrieval-based models (e.g. Adeyanju, 2012), statistical approaches, such as Hidden Markov Models (e.g. Barzilay and Lee, 2004; Liang et al., 2009), and classification methods (Duboue and McKeown, 2002; Barzilay and Lapata, 2005) have all been successfully implemented. Another way of approaching the problem is by treating it as a translation challenge, where a machine translation system translates a data representation string into a target language string. Several authors have implemented Statistical Machine Translation (SMT) methods to generate natural language using aligned data-text test sets (e.g. Wong and Mooney, 2007; Belz and Kow, 2009, 2010; Langner et al., 2010; Pereira et al., 2015) all obtaining promising results. Furthermore, an SMT model was consistently among the higher scores in the WEB NLG Challenge, where the goal is to convert RDF data to text (Castro Ferreira et al., 2017; Gardent et al., 2017), thus showing the potential of SMT-based methods as a viable approach to data-to-text NLG. However, this SMT approach was less successful in other studies in which the SMT-based method was often outscored by other statistical approaches according to automated metrics as well as human evaluation (Belz and Kow, 2010).

The impressive performance of deep learning methods on various tasks such as text summarization and machine translation suggests that Neural Machine Translation methods (NMT) might have the potential to outperform its SMT counterpart. This is also supported by results in the WEB NLG Challenge where NMT approaches obtained the highest scores on automated metrics and among the highest on human evaluation. Wiseman et al. (2017) found that various Neural data-to-Text models performed relatively well on automated metrics as well as human evaluations, although they still noted a significant performance gap between these models and their baselines.

One possible reason for this performance difference Wiseman et al. (2017) found might be the nature of the datasets used. The authors noted that their data for one corpus was noisy and that many texts contained information that was not captured in the data. Other authors have also noted that the dataset is often a bottleneck of most trainable approaches, since many aligned data-text corpora are relatively small (Richardson et al., 2017). Furthermore, several data-text aligned corpora used for these tasks are the input and output of a (rule-based) data-to-text system, which means that experiments using these corpora are performing reverse-engineering and that these results may not reflect performance on human-written datasets (Reiter, 2017).

2.3 Current work

The current work investigated the potential limitations of automatically generated corpora by using several corpora with differing characteristics, but also attempted to address the issue of small datasets by exploring *templatization* as a possible solution. Templatization is similar to what others call a delexicalization step, which means that an extra step was added in the conversion from data to text: using simple rules, gaps were added in place of the data points in the aligned data and text documents. After this step, SMT and NMT techniques were trained on the aligned data-text set and new templates were produced. Finally, these templates were filled based on a similar ruleset that was responsible for templatizing the data and texts. By using such an approach, the data and texts are likely to become more homogeneous, which could help trainable approaches to find data-text connections more quickly. This means that the trainable approaches could be more robust on smaller datasets and datasets with high variety in language. Whether this hypothesis holds true is also investigated using BLEU scores as well as human assessment on clarity, fluency and correctness.

Combining trainable approaches with a template representation has been done previously, but such systems are scarce. Kondadadi et al. (2013) are one of the first and only researchers that have attempted this combination. However, their research experimented with automated sentence templatization and sentence aggregation rather than automatically generated sentences from data points. The aim of the current work can be seen as an exploratory first step in building a system that integrates these other automation techniques to generate text from data in a fully unsupervised fashion.

	Weather.gov	Prodigy-METEO	Robocup	Dutch Soccer
Lines	29,792	601	1,699	6,414
Words	258,856	6,813	9,607	116,796
Tokens	955,959	32,448	45,491	524,196
Domain	Weather	Weather	Sports	Sports
Writer type	Computer	Human	Computer	Human

Table 1: Characteristics of the (text-part of the) corpora used in this study.

3 Datasets and approaches

3.1 Datasets

A total of four different datasets were used in the current study, two datasets contain weather reports and two contain sports reports. Furthermore, one weather dataset and one sports dataset contain texts that resulted from (mainly) rule-based data-to-text generation, while the other weather and sports datasets contain human-written texts. Characteristics of these datasets are described in Table 1 and below.

3.1.1 Weather.gov

For this dataset, Liang et al. (2009) collected weather forecasts from `http://www.weather.gov`. These weather forecasts contain information on weather aspects, such as temperature, wind speed, and cloudiness. The original data representation was modified to reduce noise and to ensure that the data input representation and text documents both represented the same data. Furthermore, tags were added since previous research found this to be the representation resulting in the highest quality output (Belz and Kow, 2010). The complete forecast texts were reduced

Data type	Example
Original input representation	temperature.time:17-30 temperature.min:24 temperature.mean:28 temperature.max:38 (...) sleetChance.mode:–
Tagged input representation	skyCover_mode: 0-25 temperature_minmeanmax temperature_mode: 24-28-38
Templatized tagged input representation	skyCover_mode: <cloud_data> temperature_minmeanmax temperature_mode: <temperature>
Retrieval (direct)	mostly clear , with a low around 21 .
Retrieval (templatized)	<cloud_data> , with a <high_near_low_around_steady_temperature> <temperature> .
Retrieval (filled)	sunny , with a high near 38 .
SMT (direct)	mostly clear , with a low around 22 .
SMT (templatized)	<cloud_data> , with a <high_near_low_around_steady_temperature> <temperature> .
SMT (filled)	sunny , with a high near 38 .
NMT (direct)	mostly clear , with a low around 22 .
NMT (templatized)	<cloud_data> , with a <high_near_low_around_steady_temperature> <temperature> .
NMT (filled)	sunny , with a high near 38 .

Table 2: Examples of the (original and applied) data representation and text output examples for the Weather.gov corpus

to the first sentence to enable equal sentence-based data-to-text generation across all domains. This resulted in a total of 29,792 data-text pairs. The texts were most likely computer-generated, with possibly some human post-processing (Reiter, 2017).

3.1.2 Prodigy-METEO

Data type	Example
Original input representation	[[1,_SSW,10,14,-,-,0600],[2,_WSW,14,18,-,-,1200], [3,_W,10,14,-,-,0000]]
Tagged input representation	WindDir.1: SSW WindSpeedMin.1: 10 WindSpeedMax.1: 14 Time.1: 0600 (...) Time.3: 0000
Templatized tagged input representation	WindDir.1: <wind_direction> WindSpeed.1: <wind_speed_min> WindSpeed.1: <wind_speed_max> (...) Time.3: <time>
Retrieval (direct)	ssw 10-14 veering wsw 14-18 by midday easing w'ly 10-14 by late evening
Retrieval (templatized)	<wind_direction> <wind_speed> <wind_direction_change> <wind_direction> <wind_speed> <time> , <wind_speed_change> <wind_direction> <wind_speed> <time>
Retrieval (filled)	ssw 10-14 veering wsw 14-18 by midday, rising w 10-14 by late evening
SMT (direct)	ssw 10-14 veering wsw 14-18 by midday easing w'ly 10-14 by late evening
SMT (templatized)	<wind_direction> <wind_speed> <wind_direction_change> <wind_direction> <wind_speed> <time> <wind_direction_change> <wind_direction> <wind_speed> <time>
SMT (filled)	ssw 10-14 veering wsw 14-18 by midday veering w 10-14 later
NMT (direct)	ssw 10-14 veering wsw 14-18 by midday easing w'ly 10-14 by late evening
NMT (templatized	<wind_direction> <wind_speed> <wind_direction_change> <wind_direction> <wind_speed> <time> then <wind_direction_change> <wind_direction> <wind_speed> <time>
NMT (filled)	ssw 10-14 veering wsw 14-18 by afternoon then veering w 10-14 later

Table 3: Examples of the (original and applied) data representation and text output examples for the Prodigy-METEO corpus

Prodigy-METEO — a dataset derived from SumTime-Meteo — was used as the second weather dataset (Belz, 2008; Sripada et al., 2002). This dataset contains human-written texts on wind data. The dataset contains a total of 601 lines. The original input vector representation was also modified to a tagged input representation inspired by the tagged input vector of Belz and Kow (2010).

Data type	Example
Original input representation	badPass.arg1: purple11 badPass.arg2: pink9 turnover.arg1: purple11 turnover.arg2: pink9
Tagged input representation	turnover.arg1: purple11 turnover.arg2: pink9 badPass
Templatized tagged	turnover.arg1: <player_1_team_1> turnover.arg2: <player_1_team_2> badPass
Retrieval (direct)	purple11 tries to pass to purple10 but was picked off by pink3
Retrieval (templatized)	<player_1_team_1> turned the ball over to <player_1_team_2>
Retrieval (filled)	purple11 makes a bad pass that picked off by pink9
SMT (direct)	purple11 makes a bad pass that was intercepted by pink9
SMT (templatized)	<player_1_team_1> makes a bad pass that was picked off by <player_1_team_2>
SMT (filled)	purple11 makes a bad pass that was picked off by pink9
NMT (direct)	purple11 loses the ball to pink9
NMT (templatized)	<player_1_team_1> makes a bad pass that was picked off by <player_1_team_2>
NMT (filled)	purple11 makes a bad pass that was picked off by pink9

Table 4: Examples of the (original and applied) data representation and text output examples for the Robocup Sportscasting corpus

3.1.3 Robocup Sportscasting

This dataset — created by Chen and Mooney (2008) — provides data and texts on the 2001-2004 Robocup finals. Each sentence represents one match event and commentary fragment of the game. These sentences were created using a data-to-text system. The original dataset was slightly altered by removing data-text lines where the data did not (fully) represent the content of the text and a tagged input representation similar to the other datasets was added, resulting in 1699 aligned data-text lines. These lines represent match events such as passes, goals, interceptions, tackles, and possession.

3.1.4 Dutch Soccer

In addition to the other corpora, an aligned data-text corpus was created for this work. Dutch soccer reports on Eredivisie matches from the 15/16 and 16/17 season were scraped from ten news websites. Additionally, texts from the Dutch part of the MeMo FC corpus (Braun et al., in press) were added, which are soccer texts scraped from Eredivisie club websites (season 15/16). Data was scraped from Squawka for these Eredivisie seasons.[1] After collecting the data, a script was written to tokenize the soccer reports, align the match data and soccer matches, and connect match sentences to specific match events in the data input using data-text overlap and simple word occurrence heuristics. After running this alignment script, a total of 6,414 sentences were found that described goals (regular, penalty and own goals), yellow cards and red cards.

---

[1] https://github.com/emanjavacas/
squawka-scraper

Data type	Example
Original input representation	–
Tagged input representation	CardPlayer_Name: Jurgen Mattheij CardPlayer_Surname: Mattheij (...) OtherTeam: Roda JC Kerkrade ; home
Templatized tagged input representation	CardPlayer_Name: <card_player> CardPlayer_Surname: <card_player> (...) OtherTeam: <other_team>
Retrieval (direct)	rood voor jurgen mattheij , die wel knuffels van zijn ploeggenoten ontvangt *red card for jurgen mattheij, who does receive hugs from his teammates*
Retrieval (templatized)	<team> speelden <time> met tien man na een rode kaart voor <card_player> en bezitten momenteel de twaalfde positie in de eredivisie . *<team> played with ten men <time> after a red card for <card_player> and posses the twelfth place in the eredivisie .*
Retrieval (filled)	excelsior speelden vlak voor tijd met tien man na een rode kaart voor Jurgen Mattheij en bezitten momenteel de twaalfde positie in de eredivisie . *excelsior played with ten men at the end after a red card for Jurgen Mattheij and posses the twelfth place in the eredivisie .*
SMT (direct)	na een rode kaart voor een Jurgen Mattheij Mattheij ook bij de eerste rode kaart kreeg , maar zijn roda jc . *after a red card for Jurgen Mattheij Mattheij also received with the first red card , but his roda jc .*
SMT (templatized)	na <time> minuten met tien man verder nadat <card_player> met zijn eerste doelpunt voor <team> *continue with ten men after <time> minutes after <card_player> with his first goal for <team>*
SMT (filled)	na zeventien minuten met tien man verder nadat Jurgen Mattheij met zijn eerste doelpunt voor excelsior
NMT (direct)	tien minuten voor tijd kreeg milot rashica zijn tweede gele kaart . *milot rashica received his second yellow card ten minutes before the end .*
NMT (templatized)	<card_player> kreeg zijn tweede gele kaart . *<card_player> received his second yellow card .*
NMT (filled)	Jurgen Mattheij kreeg zijn tweede gele kaart . *Jurgen Mattheij received his second yellow card .*

Table 5: Examples of the (original and applied) data representation and text output examples for the Dutch Soccer corpus

3.2 Applied methods

Texts and data from the aforementioned datasets served as input and as training (80%), development (10%) and test (10%) set for three forms of trainable data-to-text approaches. Two of them are translation based (NMT and SMT), while the third was a retrieval-based method that served as a baseline. These methods are described in more detail below.

3.2.1 Sentence retrieval

The first method used was a retrieval-based method. Lines from the data representation in the test-set were matched with lines from the data representation in the train-set and assigned a score based on cosine similarity. Cosine similarity scores were obtained by converting the data representation of the target sentence into a bag of words, and doing the same for the data representations in the training set. Subsequently, the (normalized) similarity between the unweighted target data representation and the data representations in the training set is calculated. The line from the train-set with the highest score was chosen and the aligned text sentence was produced as output. A random choice was made between sentences if there were multiple sentences with the highest

Corpus	Distortion	LM	Word Penalty	Phrase Penalty	Translation Model	Unknown Word Penalty
Weather.gov	0.6	0.8	-1	1e-4	0.6, 1e-4 0.6, 1e-4	2
Prodigy-METEO	0.19	0.69	0	0.29	0.2 0.13, 0.36	0.13
Robocup	0.3	0.5	-1	0.2	0.2, 0.2 0.2, 0.2	0
Dutch Soccer	1e-4	0.8	-3	1e-4	1e-4, 0.6 0.6, 0.6	3

Table 6: MOSES parameters per corpus.

Corpus	Layers	RNN Size	Word Vec Size	Drop-out	Learning Rate	Learning Rate Decay	Batch Size	Beam Size
Weather.gov	1	850	1000	0.15	0.4	0.51	32	5
Prodigy-METEO	1	440	620	0.6	0.4	0.6	1	15
Robocup	1	1230	770	0.39	1	0.6	32	15
Dutch Soccer	2	520	1000	0.15	0.72	0.44	41	14

Table 7: OpenNMT parameters per corpus.

score.

3.2.2 Statistical Machine Translation

The MOSES toolkit (Koehn et al., 2007) was used for SMT. This Statistical Machine Translation system uses Bayes's rule to translate a source language string into a target language string. For this, it needs a translation model and a language model. The translation model was obtained from the parallel corpora described above, while the language model used in the current work is obtained from the text part of the aligned corpora. Translation in the MOSES toolkit is based on a set of heuristics. Parameters of these heuristics were tuned for each corpus using Bayesian Optimization[2] (Snoek et al., 2012). The parameters that returned the highest BLEU score for the non-templatized data were chosen as default parameters for the non-templatized as well as the templatized SMT model. See Table 6 for parameter information.

3.2.3 Neural Machine Translation

Besides Statistical Machine Translation, a Neural Machine Translation approach was explored as well for the current work. These models were trained using the OpenNMT-py toolkit (Klein et al., 2017). Parameters were chosen using the same Bayesian optimization method as was used for SMT. For the smaller corpora (i.e. Prodigy-METEO and Robocup), pre-trained word embeddings were also added to the train model, since these are known to boost performance in low-resource scenarios (Qi et al., 2018). The detailed parameter settings are in Table 7.

[2] https://github.com/fmfn/
BayesianOptimization

4 Templatization and lexicalization

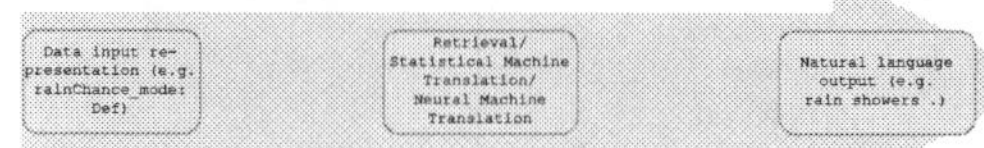

Figure 1: Direct method of data-to-text conversion.

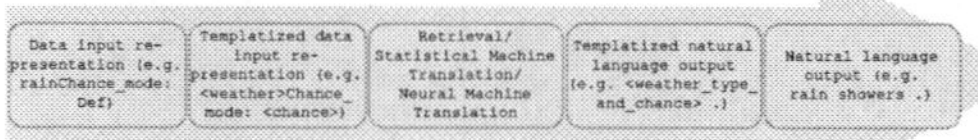

Figure 2: Templatization method of data-to-text conversion.

The current work investigated differences in output quality for data-to-text generation using 'direct' data-to-text conversion and extended models (see figure 1). For this extended model, the input representation and the text examples in the train and development set were 'templatized'. This means that the natural language sentences were converted to templates by replacing (sets of) words that directly represent (pieces of) data with slots. This replacement was done using a simple set of rules derived from consistencies in the text and data. After this templatization step the data-to-template generation was performed using the methods described in section 3.2, thus generating template sentence texts similar to the ones obtained with the templatization of the text. These obtained templates were finally lexicalized again using similar rules used for the templatization step. Using the original data, gaps were filled with the appropriate information. If multiple options were available to fill the gaps, a weighted random choice was made based on the occurrences of the possibilities in the training set (see figure 2). Thus, after these steps full natural language sentences were created based on a set of (templatized) data.[3]

5 Results automated evaluation

The quality of the generated sentences was assessed using NLTK's *corpus_bleu* that calculates BLEU scores based on 1-grams to 4-grams with equal weights and accounts for a micro-average precision score based on Papineni et al. (2002). Automated metrics such as BLEU have been criticized over the last few years (e.g. Reiter, 2018; Novikova et al., 2017). Especially in the context of NLG. However, Reiter (2018) also suggested that the metric can be used — albeit with caution

[3]Code for, and examples of, these steps can be found at https://github.com/TallChris91/
Automated-Template-Learning

Corpus	Retrieval			SMT			NMT		
	Templates (unfilled)	Templates (filled)	Direct	Templates (unfilled)	Templates (filled)	Direct	Templates (unfilled)	Templates (filled)	Direct
Weather.gov	63.94	34.52	69.57	89.29	36.56	61.92	89.85	36.93	78.90
Prodigy-METEO	44.47	27.65	23.66	39.32	26.15	30.37	45.03	26.52	27.82
Robocup	31.39	30.73	22.38	40.77	38.18	39.04	38.98	36.62	37.50
Dutch Soccer	2.49	1.65	4.99	1.64	0.90	2.10	1.95	1.23	1.70

Table 8: BLEU scores obtained for the different corpora with the techniques used in this study.

— for translation tasks, which the current task is in some way. Furthermore, correlations have been found between automated metrics and human ratings (e.g. Belz and Reiter, 2006). Therefore, the BLEU scores were seen as a first step to investigate differences between methods and corpora.

The BLEU scores show that the computer-generated corpora yielded the best results, with Weather.gov showing the best performance compared to the other corpora with BLEU scores for the lexicalized output varying from 34.52 (retrieval using the templatization method) to 78.90 (NMT using the direct method). This seems intuitively logical since the Weather.gov corpus is relatively large, and the sentences are also the most homogeneous out of the corpora, which makes producing output similar to the training data a feasible task. Results for the smaller Robocup soccer corpus are decent, but not as good as Weather.gov with BLEU scores for the lexicalized output ranging from 22.38 (retrieval using the direct method) to 39.04 (SMT using the direct method). While Prodigy-METEO is human-written, its sentence structure is still quite consistent, which might explain why its BLEU scores are not that far removed from those for computer-generated corpora with scores for the lexicalized output between 23.66 (retrieval using the direct method) and 30.37 (SMT using the direct method). Low BLEU scores were obtained for sentences from the Dutch Soccer corpus, with lexicalized output ranging from 0.90 (SMT using the templatization method) to 4.99 (Retrieval using the direct method). The low BLEU scores might indicate two things. First, it is possible that the systems struggle with the heterogeneous nature of the Dutch Soccer texts which results in low text quality output. However, the same heterogeneous nature might also make it difficult to use BLEU scores as an indication for text quality, since it is known to be difficult to find a good gold standard for corpora with diverse language.

BLEU scores for techniques do not show large differences: especially the sentences generated by SMT and NMT obtained close BLEU scores. Interestingly, the sentences produced using cosine similarity based retrieval seems to be consistently outperformed by the translation methods, with the exception of the Dutch Soccer corpus, which suggests that text generation is preferred over simple retrieval. The templatized (filled) and direct methods also scored roughly equal. The exception involves the Weather.gov corpus, where the direct method resulted in much higher BLEU scores compared to its templatized counterpart. Although the results are equal, the metrics show a large decrease in BLEU scores when lexicalizing the templates. This means that the templatization method has the potential to significantly outperform the direct method if the quality of the lexicalization step is improved. See Table 8.

6 Results human evaluation

6.1 Method

Besides an automated metric, a human evaluation was carried out to measure the perceived text quality of sentences from the investigated corpora, techniques and methods. A total of 24 people — all native Dutch students and (junior) colleagues not involved in this research — participated by filling out an online *Qualtrics* survey. Participants were asked to rate sentences generated by the previously described techniques and methods on the aforementioned corpora. For this, a 4 (Corpus: DutchSoccer, Weather.gov, Robocup, Prodigy-METEO) x 3 (Technique: Retrieval, SMT, NMT) x 2 (Method: Templatized, Direct) within-subjects design was implemented. The participants rated 4 sentences per condition — each connected to different data — resulting in a total of 96 sentences that were rated by humans (Krippendorff's $\alpha = 0.39$; Weighted $\kappa = 0.07$).

The participants judged the quality of the sentences on seven-point Likert-scales. These scales measured fluency: how fluent and easy to read the report is ('This text is written in proper Dutch', 'This text is easily readable'), clarity: how clear

	Corpus	Retrieval		SMT		NMT	
		Templates	Direct	Templates	Direct	Templates	Direct
Fluency	Weather.gov	4.08 (1.04)	5.32 (0.88)	5.24 (0.95)	4.76 (0.79)	5.00 (0.97)	5.50 (1.02)
	Prodigy-METEO	3.27 (1.13)	2.81 (1.14)	2.99 (1.16)	3.02 (1.13)	3.31 (1.47)	3.27 (1.43)
	Robocup	5.21 (0.99)	5.46 (1.05)	5.70 (0.99)	4.82 (1.20)	5.59 (1.04)	5.67 (1.11)
	Dutch Soccer	4.12 (0.99)	5.33 (0.91)	2.11 (0.97)	1.78 (0.85)	6.10 (0.84)	5.73 (0.84)
Clarity	Weather.gov	4.36 (1.14)	5.52 (0.99)	5.45 (1.02)	5.24 (1.02)	5.13 (1.26)	5.69 (1.04)
	Prodigy-METEO	2.94 (1.24)	2.73 (1.26)	2.82 (1.27)	2.96 (1.16)	3.25 (1.57)	3.29 (1.47)
	Robocup	5.59 (0.96)	5.73 (1.03)	5.96 (0.92)	5.11 (1.22)	5.84 (0.98)	5.78 (1.37)
	Dutch Soccer	4.85 (1.16)	5.52 (0.90)	2.43 (0.99)	1.94 (0.90)	6.10 (0.92)	5.74 (0.83)
Correctness	Weather.gov	3.34 (0.91)	3.92 (0.90)	2.55 (0.90)	2.70 (1.04)	4.03 (1.04)	3.22 (1.26)
	Prodigy-METEO	4.17 (1.22)	3.21 (0.97)	3.88 (1.23)	3.72 (1.20)	3.99 (1.18)	3.56 (0.88)
	Robocup	5.06 (1.14)	3.83 (1.08)	5.78 (1.08)	5.23 (1.13)	5.70 (1.09)	5.68 (0.92)
	Dutch Soccer	3.34 (0.91)	3.92 (0.90)	2.55 (0.90)	2.70 (1.04)	4.03 (1.04)	3.22 (1.26)

Table 9: Mean fluency, clarity, and correctness scores for the different corpora, techniques and methods. SD is represented between brackets

and understandable the report is ('While reading, I immediately understood the text'), and correctness: how well the information the report is based on is represented in the report itself ('This report does not include extraneous or incorrect information', 'This report does not omit important information'). In order to give ratings on the latter category, participants were provided with a table containing the information used to generate the sentences, followed by six sentences that were generated by the total of six different techniques and methods used in this study. The results were then analyzed using a repeated measures analysis of variance to investigate the effects of the corpus, techniques and methods on text perceptions of fluency, clarity and correctness. Post hoc effects were subsequently measured with a simple effects analysis using the Least Significant Difference test.[4]

6.2 Fluency

For fluency, a main effect was found for corpus ($F(1.89, 43.57) = 56.82$, $p < .001$), as well as technique ($F(2, 46) = 107.13$, $p < .001$), but not for method ($F(1, 23) = 2.22$, $p = .15$). Sentences based on Robocup data resulted in the highest fluency scores ($M = 5.41$, $SD = 0.90$), followed by the Weather.gov corpus ($M = 4.98$, $SD = 0.75$), Dutch Soccer corpus ($M = 4.20$, $SD = 0.50$), and Prodigy-METEO corpus ($M = 3.11$, $SD = 1.12$). Furthermore, sentences generated with NMT generation returned the highest scores on fluency ($M = 5.02$, $SD = 0.76$), followed by Retrieval ($M = 4.45$, SD

---

[4] Mauchlys Test of Sphericity showed that the sphericity assumption was violated for corpus, corpus x technique, and corpus x technique x method in the case of fluency, as well as clarity. Also for technique, corpus x technique, corpus x method, and technique x method in the case of correctness. Therefore, the Greenhouse-Geisser correction was used for the analyses of these effects.

$= 0.70$), and SMT ($M = 3.80$, $SD = 0.55$) (see table 9).

A significant interaction was also found for corpus x technique ($F(3.07, 70.61) = 87.85$, $p < .001$). NMT resulted in the highest fluency scores for most corpora, except for the Prodigy-METEO corpus where all techniques performed similarly on fluency. A significant interaction was also found for corpus x method ($F(3, 69) = 8.08$, $p < .001$), where the templatization method returned higher fluency scores for the Dutch Soccer and the direct method resulted in higher fluency scores for the Weather.gov corpus. Furthermore, a significant interaction was found for technique x method ($F(2, 46) = 29.76$, $p < .001$): the fluency scores for the retrieval method were higher when the direct method was used, while the templatization method resulted in higher scores for SMT. A further nuance in this finding can be given with the significant three-way interaction for corpus x technique x method ($F(2.83, 65.08) = 13.89$, $p < .001$). The templatization method combined with NMT resulted in higher fluency scores for the soccer corpus, but lower scores for the Weather.gov corpus. The same method combined with SMT resulted in higher scores compared to its direct counterpart for all corpora except Prodigy-METEO. For retrieval, the direct method gave higher fluency scores for all corpora.

These scores show that, in general, NMT produces the most fluent sentences. Whether the templatization method or direct method returns the most fluent output depends on the corpus and technique used. For SMT, the templatization method seems the clear winner, but for retrieval and NMT effectiveness of the templatization method differs per corpus. Interestingly, out of all the conditions, the highest fluency scores were obtained for the

Dutch Soccer corpus (NMT with the templatization method), while the BLEU scores for this category were fairly low.

6.3 Clarity

The overall scores for clarity look similar to those of fluency. A main effect for corpus was found ($F(2.08, 47.72) = 69.90$, $p < .001$), as well as technique ($F(2, 46) = 69.21$, $p < .001$), but not for method ($F(1, 23) = 1.64$, $p = .21$). Sentences based on Robocup ($M = 5.67$, $SD = 0.89$) were considered the clearest, followed by Weather.gov ($M = 5.23$, $SD = 0.89$), Dutch Soccer ($M = 4.43$, $SD = 0.48$), and Prodigy-METEO ($M = 3.00$, $SD = 1.23$). For technique, the lowest clarity scores were found for SMT generated sentences ($M = 3.99$, $SD = 0.61$), Retrieval-based sentences ($M = 4.66$, $SD = 0.76$) did slightly better, and sentences generated by NMT received the highest clarity scores ($M = 5.10$, $SD = 0.83$) (see table 9).[4]

All investigated interactions for clarity were significant (Corpus x technique: $F(3.26, 74.89) = 57.936$, $p < .001$; Corpus x method: $F(3, 69) = 11.18$, $p < .001$; Technique x method: $F(2, 46) = 23.01$, $p < .001$; Corpus x technique x method: $F(3.81, 87.56) = 6.03$, $p < .001$). The corpus x technique analysis shows that NMT generated sentences produce the most clear sentences for the Dutch Soccer corpus and the Prodigy-METEO corpus, and NMT and SMT had the shared highest clarity scores for the Weather.gov corpus. No differences in clarity were found for Robocup. Corpus x method results showed no significant difference for the Dutch Soccer and Prodigy-METEO corpus. The direct method resulted in significantly higher scores for the Weather.gov corpus, while sentences generated with the templatization method resulted in higher clarity scores for Robocup sentences. From the technique x method interaction it was observed that Retrieval combined with the direct method resulted in higher clarity scores compared to its templatization counterpart. The opposite is the case for SMT generated sentences, where templatization resulted in higher clarity scores. The three-way interaction of corpus x technique x method showed that NMT produces more clear sentences using the templatization method for the Dutch Soccer corpus and less clear sentences with templatization for the Weather.gov corpus compared to its direct counterpart. Retrieval combined with the direct method scored higher on these corpora with the direct method (vs. templatized), and SMT obtains higher clarity scores for the Dutch Soccer and Robosoccer corpus if the templatization method is applied (vs. templatized).

Overall, models trained on the computer-generated corpora gave the clearest output and, similar to fluency, sentences produced with NMT resulted in the highest clarity scores. Templatization was also overall more effective for SMT compared to the direct method, while templatization for NMT was mostly effective for the Dutch Soccer corpus. The clarity scores for the NMT with templatization method for the Dutch Soccer corpus resulted in the overall highest clarity scores, besides fluency scores as well.

6.4 Correctness

Significant main effects of correctness were found for corpus ($F(3, 69) = 32.86$, $p < .001$), technique ($F(1.58, 36.37) = 9.25$, $p = .001$), and method ($F(1, 23) = 9.77$, $p = .005$). Sentences from the Robocup corpus were deemed the most correct ($M = 5.21$, $SD = 0.92$), followed by Weather.gov ($M = 4.04$, $SD = 0.84$), with Prodigy-METEO ($M = 3.76$, $SD = 0.88$) and Dutch Soccer ($M = 3.29$, $SD = 0.76$) in shared last place. For technique, NMT generated sentences were perceived as the most correct ($M = 4.27$, $SD = 0.63$). SMT ($M = 4.01$, $SD = 0.72$) and Retrieval ($M = 3.94$, $SD = 0.61$) did not score significantly different. The results for method showed that templatization resulted in higher correctness scores ($M = 4.19$, $SD = 0.69$) than the direct method ($M = 3.96$, $SD = 0.59$) (see table 9).

Significant interactions were found for corpus x technique ($F(3.64, 83.77) = 20.22$, $p < .001$), corpus x method ($F(2.23, 51.29) = 9.24$, $p < .001$), and corpus x technique x method ($F(6, 138) = 15.00$, $p < .001$), but not for technique x method ($F(1.31, 30.12) = 0.18$, $p = .84$). The corpus x technique interaction shows that SMT generated sentences were perceived as significantly less correct for the Dutch Soccer corpus (vs. Retrieval and NMT), and Retrieval based sentences deemed less correct for Robocup sentences (vs. SMT and NMT). Corpus x method shows that the templatization method resulted in higher perceived correctness for the Robocup and Prodigy-METEO corpora compared to its direct counterpart. Finally, the three way corpus x technique x method interaction shows that templatization combined with NMT resulted in higher correctness scores for Dutch Soccer but lower for Prodigy-METEO (vs. direct). Direct was superior for all corpora when used with a retrieval technique, and the templatization method combined with SMT gives higher scores for the Robocup corpus (vs. direct).

In general, the models trained on the computer-generated corpora produced the most correct sentences. Furthermore, NMT and the templatization method were found to be effective techniques/methods to increase correctness. The fact that templatization increases correctness makes sense since the separate lexicalization step for information ensures that correct information is added to a sentence that is based on the data. This is not necessarily the case with the direct method.

7 Discussion and conclusion

This paper investigated ways to reduce the reliance on rule-based systems when converting data to natural language text. The use of deep learning methods in the form of NMT, and a method where input and output forms were templatized before converting the output template sentences to natural language text were explored. This (relatively) novel NMT approach was compared to more established approaches (i.e. Retrieval and SMT). Furthermore, the templatization method was compared to its direct counterpart that directly converts a data input representation to a natural language text. Sentences were generated for four corpora (two human-written, two computer-generated; two in the sports domain, two in the weather domain). Results of these different forms of generation were then compared using BLEU scores as well as human metrics.

Results of the BLEU scores suggested that the different techniques and approaches obtain the highest text quality when trained on computer-generated corpora, with techniques and approaches trained on the Dutch Soccer corpus generating the lowest text quality output. Furthermore, the Retrieval approach seemed to perform the best in general, and SMT and NMT obtained similar scores to each other. Finally, based on the BLEU scores, the templatization method did not seem to improve output quality when compared to its direct counterpart: similar or higher BLEU scores were found for the direct method.

However, the BLEU results were not corroborated by the results from human evaluation. While the output quality differed per technique, sentences for the Dutch Soccer corpus achieved scores similar or higher than sentences based on other corpora on both fluency, clarity and correctness. Furthermore, the performance of NMT seemed to be good compared to SMT and Retrieval. NMT generated sentences obtained the highest scores on both fluency, clarity and correctness. Also, the templatization method has the potential to increase output quality. Both the SMT and NMT method achieved higher fluency, clarity and correctness scores on sevaral corpora with the templatization method (vs. direct). This method especially seemed to boost performance on the Dutch Soccer corpus: this corpus is the most noisy out of the corpora and contains the most heterogeneous language. Therefore, the templatization method seems to be a useful step for human-written corpora.

The current paper should be seen as a first exploratory step in automating data-to-text systems: the investigated methods could save time and resources compared to a fully rule-based approach, but the steps to templatize data and text for the current article were still rule-based, which still takes manual effort and turned out to decrease output quality based on the BLEU scores. A system that does these conversions automatically would be an interesting avenue for further research. It would also be interesting to extend the current approach to (templated) sentence learning by comparing the translation method to statistical generation techniques such as HMM (e.g. Barzilay and Lee, 2004; Liang et al., 2009) or LSTM (Wen et al., 2015). Other steps in the data-to-text conversion process would be worth investigating as well. For instance automated alignment of data and text, or methods that convert data into the optimal data input representation format, or automated sentence aggregation methods to produce full texts. Further research can also focus on making the output more diverse by adding strategies for lexical variation (Guerini et al., 2011; Gatti et al., 2014). The current results would suggest that combining these steps with the described templatization method, and with NMT, has the potential to further approach the text quality of rule-based systems, and increase overall performance of trainable data-to-text approaches. Especially with noisy human-written corpora containing diverse language.

Acknowledgements

We received support from RAAK-PRO SIA (2014-01-51PRO) and The Netherlands Organization for Scientific Research (NWO 360-89-050), which is gratefully acknowledged. We would also like to thank Abelardo Vieira Mota, and the anonymous reviewers for their comments; Nadine Braun for providing us with the MeMo FC corpus; Chris Emmery, Lieke Gelderloos, and Bram Willemsen for their technical support; and all the people that were willing to participate in the human evaluation study.

References

Ibrahim Adeyanju. 2012. Generating weather forecast texts with case based reasoning. *International Journal of Computer Applications*, 45(10):35–40.

Regina Barzilay and Mirella Lapata. 2005. Collective content selection for concept-to-text generation. In *Proceedings of the Conference on Human Language Technology and Empirical Methods in Natural Language Processing (EMNLP)*, pages 331–338, Vancouver, Canada.

Regina Barzilay and Lillian Lee. 2004. Catching the drift: Probabilistic content models with applications to generation and summarization. In *Proceedings of the Human Language Technology Conference of the North American Chapter of the Association for Computational Linguistics (HLT-NAACL)*, pages 113–120, Boston, United States.

Anja Belz. 2008. Automatic generation of weather forecast texts using comprehensive probabilistic generation-space models. *Natural Language Engineering*, 14(4):431–455.

Anja Belz and Eric Kow. 2009. System building cost vs. output quality in data-to-text generation. In *Proceedings of the 12th European Workshop on Natural Language Generation*, pages 16–24, Athens, Greece.

Anja Belz and Eric Kow. 2010. Assessing the trade-off between system building cost and output quality in data-to-text generation. In *Empirical methods in natural language generation*, pages 180–200. Springer.

Anja Belz and Ehud Reiter. 2006. Comparing automatic and human evaluation of NLG systems. In *11th Conference of the European Chapter of the Association for Computational Linguistics*, pages 313–320, Trento, Italy. Association for Computational Linguistics.

Thiago Castro Ferreira, Chris van der Lee, Emiel Krahmer, and Sander Wubben. 2017. Tilburg University models for the WebNLG challenge. In *Proceedings of the 10th International Conference on Natural Language Generation*, Santiago de Compostella, Spain.

David L Chen and Raymond J Mooney. 2008. Learning to sportscast: a test of grounded language acquisition. In *Proceedings of the 25th International Conference on Machine learning*, pages 128–135, Montreal, Canada.

Kees van Deemter, Emiel Krahmer, and Mariët Theune. 2005. Real vs. template-based Natural Language Generation. *Computational Linguistics*, 31(1):15–23.

Pablo Duboue and Kathleen McKeown. 2002. Content planner construction via evolutionary algorithms and a corpus-based fitness function. In *Proceedings of the International Natural Language Generation Conference*, pages 89–96, Harriman, United States.

Claire Gardent, Anastasia Shimorina, Shashi Narayan, and Laura Perez-Beltrachini. 2017. The WebNLG challenge: Generating text from RDF data. In *Proceedings of the 10th International Conference on Natural Language Generation*, pages 124–133, Santiago de Compostella, Spain.

Albert Gatt and Emiel Krahmer. 2018. Survey of the state of the art in natural language generation: Core tasks, applications and evaluation. *Journal of Artificial Intelligence Research*, 61:65–170.

Lorenzo Gatti, Marco Guerini, Oliviero Stock, and Carlo Strapparava. 2014. Sentiment variations in text for persuasion technology. In *International Conference on Persuasive Technology (PERSUASIVE 2014)*.

Dimitra Gkatzia. 2016. Content selection in data-to-text systems: A survey. *arXiv preprint arXiv:1610.08375*.

Eli Goldberg, Norbert Driedger, and Richard I Kittredge. 1994. Using natural-language processing to produce weather forecasts. *IEEE Intelligent Systems*, 2:45–53.

Marco Guerini, Carlo Strapparava, and Oliviero Stock. 2011. Slanting existing text with Valentino. In *Proceedings of the 16th International Conference on Intelligent User Interfaces*, pages 439–440.

Guillaume Klein, Yoon Kim, Yuntian Deng, Jean Senellart, and Alexander Rush. 2017. OpenNMT: Open-source toolkit for Neural Machine Translation. *Proceedings of ACL 2017, System Demonstrations*, pages 67–72.

Philipp Koehn, Hieu Hoang, Alexandra Birch, and Chris Callison-Burch. 2007. MOSES: Open source toolkit for statistical machine translation. In *Proceedings of the 45th annual meeting of the ACL on interactive poster and demonstration sessions*, pages 177–180, Prague, Czech Republic.

Ravi Kondadadi, Blake Howald, and Frank Schilder. 2013. A statistical NLG framework for aggregated planning and realization. In *Proceedings of the 51st Annual Meeting of the Association for Computational Linguistics*, pages 1406–1415, Sofia, Bulgaria.

Brian Langner, Stephan Vogel, and Alan W Black. 2010. Evaluating a dialog language generation system: Comparing the MOUNTAIN system to other NLG approaches. In *Eleventh Annual Conference of the International Speech Communication Association (INTERSPEECH)*, pages 1109–1112, Makuhari, Japan.

Chris van der Lee, Emiel Krahmer, and Sander Wubben. 2017. PASS: A Dutch data-to-text system for soccer, targeted towards specific audiences. In *Proceedings of the 10th International Conference on Natural Language Generation*, pages 95–104, Santiago de Compostella, Spain.

Chris van der Lee, Bart Verduijn, Emiel Krahmer, and Sander Wubben. 2018. Evaluating the text quality, human likeness and tailoring component of PASS: A Dutch data-to-text system for soccer. In *Proceedings of the 27th International Conference on Computational Linguistics (COLING)*, Santa Fe, United States.

Percy Liang, Michael I Jordan, and Dan Klein. 2009. Learning semantic correspondences with less supervision. In *Proceedings of the Joint Conference of the 47th Annual Meeting of the ACL and the 4th International Joint Conference on Natural Language Processing of the AFNLP*, pages 91–99, Suntec, Singapore. Association for Computational Linguistics.

Joy Mahapatra, Sudip Kumar Naskar, and Sivaji Bandyopadhyay. 2016. Statistical natural language generation from tabular non-textual data. In *Proceedings of the 9th International Natural Language Generation conference*, pages 143–152, Edinburgh, Scotland.

Jekaterina Novikova, Ondřej Dušek, Amanda Cercas Curry, and Verena Rieser. 2017. Why we need new evaluation metrics for NLG. In *Proceedings of the 2017 Conference on Empirical Methods in Natural Language Processing (EMNLP)*, pages 2241–2252, Copenhagen, Denmark.

Kishore Papineni, Salim Roukos, Todd Ward, and Wei-Jing Zhu. 2002. BLEU: A method for automatic evaluation of machine translation. In *Proceedings of the 40th Annual Meeting on Association for Computational Linguistics*, pages 311–318, Philadelphia, United States.

José Casimiro Pereira, António Teixeira, and Joaquim Sousa Pinto. 2015. Towards a hybrid nlg system for data2text in portuguese. In *Proceedings da 10a Conferência Ibérica de Sistemas e Tecnologias de Informaçao (CISTI)*, pages 679–684, Lisbon, Portugal.

Ye Qi, Devendra Sachan, Matthieu Felix, Sarguna Padmanabhan, and Graham Neubig. 2018. When and why are pre-trained word embeddings useful for neural machine translation? In *Proceedings of the 2018 Conference of the North American Chapter of the Association for Computational Linguistics: Human Language Technologies (NAACL HLT)*, volume 2, pages 529–535, New Orleans, United States.

Ehud Reiter. 1995. NLG vs. templates. In *Proceedings of the 5th European Workshop on Natural Language Generation (EWNGL)*, pages 95–106, Leiden, The Netherlands.

Ehud Reiter. 2017. You need to understand your corpora! The Weathergov example.

Ehud Reiter. 2018. A structured review of the validity of BLEU. *Computational Linguistics*, pages 1–12.

Kyle Richardson, Sina Zarrieß, and Jonas Kuhn. 2017. The code2text challenge: Text generation in source code libraries. In *The 10th International Natural Language Generation conference*, pages 115–119, Santiago de Compostella, Spain.

Lauren Sanby, Ion Todd, and Maria C Keet. 2016. Comparing the template-based approach to GF: the case of Afrikaans. In *Proceedings of the 2nd International Workshop on Natural Language Generation and the Semantic Web (WebNLG)*, pages 50–53, Edinburgh, Scotland.

Jasper Snoek, Hugo Larochelle, and Ryan P Adams. 2012. Practical Bayesian optimization of machine learning algorithms. In *Advances in Neural Information Processing Systems*, pages 2951–2959.

Somayajulu Sripada, Ehud Reiter, Jim Hunter, and Jin Yu. 2002. Sumtime-meteo: Parallel corpus of naturally occurring forecast texts and weather data. *Technical Report AUCS/TR0201*.

Tsung-Hsien Wen, Milica Gašic, Nikola Mrkšic, Pei-Hao Su, David Vandyke, and Steve Young. 2015. Semantically conditioned lstm-based natural language generation for spoken dialogue systems. In *Proceedings of the 2015 Conference on Empirical Methods in Natural Language Processing (EMNLP)*, pages 1711–1721, Lisbon, Portugal.

Sam Wiseman, Stuart Shieber, and Alexander Rush. 2017. Challenges in data-to-document generation. In *Proceedings of the 2017 Conference on Empirical Methods in Natural Language Processing (EMNLP)*, pages 2253–2263, Copenhagen, Denmark.

Yuk Wah Wong and Raymond Mooney. 2007. Generation by inverting a semantic parser that uses statistical machine translation. In *Human Language Technologies 2007: The Conference of the North American Chapter of the Association for Computational Linguistics; Proceedings of the Main Conference (NAACL HLT)*, pages 172–179, Rochester, USA.

End-to-End Content and Plan Selection for Data-to-Text Generation

Sebastian Gehrmann
Harvard SEAS
gehrmann@seas.harvard.edu

Falcon Z. Dai
TTI-Chicago
dai@ttic.edu

Henry Elder
ADAPT
henry.elder@adaptcentre.ie

Alexander M. Rush
Harvard SEAS
srush@seas.harvard.edu

Abstract

Learning to generate fluent natural language from structured data with neural networks has become an common approach for NLG. This problem can be challenging when the form of the structured data varies between examples. This paper presents a survey of several extensions to sequence-to-sequence models to account for the latent content selection process, particularly variants of copy attention and coverage decoding. We further propose a training method based on diverse ensembling to encourage models to learn distinct sentence templates during training. An empirical evaluation of these techniques shows an increase in the quality of generated text across five automated metrics, as well as human evaluation.

1 Introduction

Recent developments in end-to-end learning with neural networks have enabled methods to generate textual output from complex structured inputs such as images and tables. These methods may also enable the creation of text-generation models that are conditioned on multiple key-value attribute pairs. The conditional generation of fluent text poses multiple challenges since a model has to select content appropriate for an utterance, develop a sentence layout that fits all selected information, and finally generate fluent language that incorporates the content. End-to-end methods have already been applied to increasingly complex data to simultaneously learn sentence planning and surface realization but were often restricted by the limited data availability (Wen et al., 2015; Mei et al., 2015; Dušek and Jurčíček, 2016; Lampouras and Vlachos, 2016). The re-

MR	name: The Golden Palace, eatType: coffee shop, food: Fast food, priceRange: cheap, customer rating: 5 out of 5, area: riverside
Reference	A coffee shop located on the riverside called The Golden Palace, has a 5 out of 5 customer rating. Its price range are fairly cheap for its excellent Fast food.

Figure 1: An example of a meaning representation and utterance pair from the E2E NLG dataset. Each example comprises a set of key-value pairs and a natural language description.

cent creation of datasets such as the E2E NLG dataset (Novikova et al., 2017) provides an opportunity to further advance methods for text generation. In this work, we focus on the generation of language from meaning representations (MR), as shown in Figure 1. This task requires learning a semantic alignment from MR to utterance, wherein the MR can comprise a variable number of attributes.

Recently, end-to-end generation has been handled primarily by Sequence-to-sequence (S2S) models (Sutskever et al., 2014; Bahdanau et al., 2014) that encode some information and decode it into a desired format. Extensions for summarization and other tasks have developed a mechanism to copy words from the input into a generated text (Vinyals et al., 2015; See et al., 2017).

We begin with a strong S2S model with copy-mechanism for the E2E NLG task and include methods that can help to control the length of a generated text and how many inputs a model uses (Tu et al., 2016; Wu et al., 2016). Finally,

Proceedings of The 11th International Natural Language Generation Conference, pages 46–56,
Tilburg, The Netherlands, November 5-8, 2018. ©2018 Association for Computational Linguistics

we also present results of the Transformer architecture (Vaswani et al., 2017) as an alternative S2S variant. We show that these extensions lead to improved text generation and content selection.

We further propose a training approach based on the diverse ensembling technique (Guzman-Rivera et al., 2012). In this technique, multiple models are trained to partition the training data during the process of training the model itself, thus leading to models that follow distinct sentence templates. We show that this approach improves the quality of generated text, but also the robustness of the training process to outliers in the training data.

Experiments are run on the E2E NLG challenge[1]. We show that the application of this technique increases the quality of generated text across five different automated metrics (BLEU, NIST, METEOR, ROUGE, and CIDEr) over the multiple strong S2S baseline models (Dušek and Jurčíček, 2016; Vaswani et al., 2017; Su et al., 2018; Freitag and Roy, 2018). Among 60 submissions to the challenge, our approach ranked first in METEOR, ROUGE, and CIDEr scores, third in BLEU, and sixth in NIST.

2 Related Work

Traditional approaches to natural language generation separate the generation of a sentence plan from the surface realization. First, an input is mapped into a format that represents the layout of the output sentence, for example, an adequate pre-defined template. Then, the surface realization transforms the intermediary structure into text (Stent et al., 2004). These representations often model the hierarchical structure of discourse relations (Walker et al., 2007). Early data-driven approach used phrase-based language models for generation (Oh and Rudnicky, 2000; Mairesse and Young, 2014), or aimed to predict the best fitting cluster of semantically similar templates (Kondadadi et al., 2013). More recent work combines both steps by learning plan and realization jointly using end-to-end trained models (e.g. Wen et al., 2015). Several approaches have looked at generation from abstract meaning representations (AMR), and Peng et al. (2017) apply S2S models to the problem. However, Ferreira et al. (2017) show that S2S models are outperformed by

phrase-based machine translation models in small datasets. To address this issue, Konstas et al. (2017) propose a semi-supervised training method that can utilize English sentences outside of the training set to train parts of the model. We address the issue by using copy-attention to enable the model to copy words from the source, which helps to generate out of vocabulary and rare words. We note that end-to-end trained models, including our approach, often do not explicitly model the sentence planning stage, and are thus not directly comparable to previous work on sentence planning. This is especially limiting for generation of complex argument structures that rely on hierarchical structure.

For the task of text generation from simple key-value pairs, as in the E2E task, Juraska et al. (2018) describe a heuristic based on word-overlap that provides unsupervised slot alignment between meaning representations and open slots in sentence plans. This method allows a model to operate with a smaller vocabulary and to be agnostic to actual values in the meaning representations. To account for syntactic structure in templates, Su et al. (2018) describe a hierarchical decoding strategy that generates different part of speech at different steps, filling in slots between previously generated tokens. In contrast, our model uses copy-attention to fill in latent slots inside of learned templates. Juraska et al. (2018) also describe a data selection process in which they use heuristics to filter a dataset to the most natural sounding examples according to a set of rules. Our work aims at the unsupervised segmentation of data such that one model learns the most natural sounding sentence plans.

3 Background: Sequence-to-Sequence Generation

We start by introducing the standard a text-to-text problem and discuss how to map structured data into a sequential form. Let $(\mathbf{x}^{(0)}, \mathbf{y}^{(0)}), \ldots (\mathbf{x}^{(N)}, \mathbf{y}^{(N)}) \in (\mathcal{X}, \mathcal{Y})$ be a set of N aligned source and target sequence pairs, with $(\mathbf{x}^{(i)}, \mathbf{y}^{(i)})$ denoting the ith element in $(\mathcal{X}, \mathcal{Y})$ pairs. Further, let $\mathbf{x} = x_1, \ldots, x_m$ be the sequence of m tokens in the source, and $\mathbf{y} = y_1, \ldots, y_n$ the target sequence of length n. Let $\mathcal{V}$ be the vocabulary of possible tokens, and $[n]$ the list of integers up to n, $[1, \ldots, n]$.

S2S aims to learn a distribution parametrized

---

[1] http://www.macs.hw.ac.uk/ InteractionLab/E2E/

by θ to maximize the conditional probability of $p_\theta(\mathbf{y}|\mathbf{x})$. We assume that the target is generated from left to right, such that $p_\theta(\mathbf{y}|\mathbf{x}) = \prod_{t=1}^{n} p_\theta(y_t|\mathbf{y}_{[t-1]}, \mathbf{x})$, and that $p_\theta(y_t|\mathbf{y}_{[t-1]}, \mathbf{x})$ takes the form of an encoder-decoder architecture with attention. The training aims to maximize the log-likelihood of the observed training data.

We evaluate the performance of both the LSTM (Hochreiter and Schmidhuber, 1997) and Transformer (Vaswani et al., 2017) architecture. We additionally experiment with two attention formulations. The first uses a dot-product between the hidden states of the encoder and decoder (Luong et al., 2015). The second uses a multi-layer perceptron with the hidden states as inputs (Bahdanau et al., 2014). We refer to them as *dot* and *MLP* respectively. Since *dot* attention does not require additional parameters, we hypothesize that it performs well in a limited data environment.

In order to apply S2S models, a list of attributes in an MR has to be linearized into a sequence of tokens (Konstas et al., 2017; Ferreira et al., 2017). Not all attributes have to appear for all inputs, and each attribute might have multi-token values, such as *area: city centre*. We use special start and stop tokens for each possible attribute to mark value boundaries; for example, an attribute *area: city centre* becomes _start_area_ *city centre* _end_area_. These fragments are concatenated into a single sequence to represent the original MR as an input sequence to our models. In this approach, no values are delexicalized, in contrast to Juraska et al. (2018) and others who delexicalize a subset of attributes. An alternative approach by Freitag and Roy (2018) treats the attribute type as an additional feature and learn embeddings for words and types separately.

4 Learning Content Selection

We extend the vanilla S2S system with methods that address the related problem of text summarization. In particular, we implement the pointer-generator network similar to that introduced by Nallapati et al. (2016) and See et al. (2017), which can generate content by copying tokens from an input during the generation process.

Copy Model The copy model introduces a binary variable z_t for each decoding step t that acts as a switch between copying from the source and generating words. We model the joint probability following the procedure described by Gulcehre

et al. (2016) as

$$p(y_t, z_t|y_{[t-1]}, \mathbf{x}) = \sum_{z \in \{0,1\}} p(y_t, z_t = z|\mathbf{y}_{[t-1]}, \mathbf{x})$$

To calculate the switching probability $p(z_t|\mathbf{y}_{[t-1]}, \mathbf{x})$, let $v \in \mathbb{R}^{d_{\mathrm{hid}}}$ be a trainable parameter. The hidden state of the decoder h_t is used to compute $p(z_t) = \sigma(h_t^T v)$ and decompose the joint distribution into two parts:

$$p(y_t|y_{[t-1]}, \mathbf{x}) = p(z_t = 1) \times p(y_t|z_t = 1) \\ + p(z_t = 0) \times p(y_t|z_t = 0),$$

where every term is conditioned on $\mathbf{x}$ and $\mathbf{y}_{[t-1]}$. $p(y_t|z_t = 0)$ is the distribution generated by the previously described S2S model, and $p(y_t|z_t = 1)$ is a distribution over $\mathbf{x}$ that is computed using the same attention mechanism with separate parameters.

In our problem, all values in the MR's should occur in the generated text and are typically words that would not be generated by a language model. This allows us to use an assumption by Gulcehre et al. (2016) that every word that occurs in both source and target was copied, which avoids having to marginalize over z. Then, the log-likelihood of y_t and z_t is maximized during training. This approach has the further advantage that it can handle previously unseen input by learning to copy these words into the correct position.

Coverage and Length Penalty We observed that generated text using vanilla S2S models with and without copy mechanism commonly omits some of the values in their inputs. To mitigate this effect, we use two penalty terms during inference; a length and a coverage penalty. We are using a coverage penalty during inference only, opposed to Tu et al. (2016) who introduced a coverage penalty term into the attention of an S2S model for neural machine translation and See et al. (2017) who used the same idea for abstractive summarization. Instead, we use the penalty term cp defined by Wu et al. (2016) as

$$cp(\mathbf{x}, \mathbf{y}) = \beta \cdot \sum_{i=1}^{|\mathbf{x}|} \log(\min(\sum_{t=1}^{|\mathbf{y}|} a_i^t, 1.0))).$$

Here, β is a parameter to control the strength of the penalty. This penalty term increases when too many generated words attend to the same input. We typically do not want to repeat the name of the

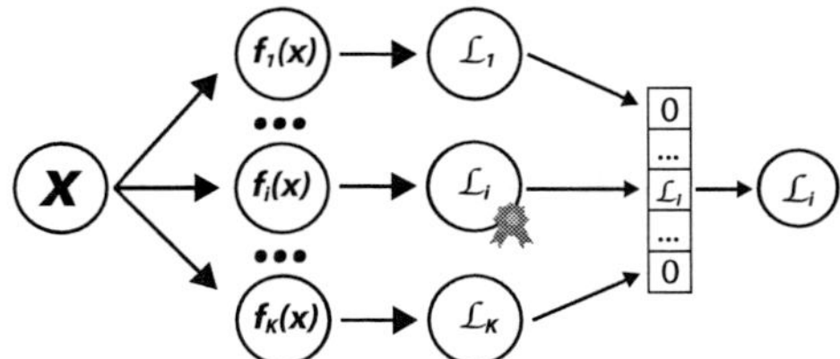

Figure 2: The multiple-choice loss for a single training example. $\mathcal{L}_i$ has the smallest loss and receives parameter updates.

restaurant or the type of food it serves. Thus, we only want to attend to the restaurant name once when we actually generate it. We also use the length penalty lp by Wu et al. (2016), defined as

$$lp(\mathbf{y}) = \frac{(5 + |\mathbf{y}|)^\alpha}{(5 + 1)^\alpha},$$

where α is a tunable parameter that controls how much the likelihoods of longer generated texts are discounted. The penalties are used to re-rank beams during the inference procedure such that the full score function s becomes

$$s(\mathbf{x}, \mathbf{y}, z) = \frac{\log p(\mathbf{y}, z|\mathbf{x})}{lp(\mathbf{y})} + cp(\mathbf{x}, \mathbf{y}).$$

A final inference time restriction of our model is the blocking of repeat sentence beginnings. Automatic metrics do not punish a strong parallelism between sentences, but repeat sentence beginnings interrupt the flow of a text and make it look unnatural. We found that since each model follows a strict latent template during generation, the generated text would often begin every sentence with the same words. Therefore, we encourage syntactic variation by pruning beams during beam search that start two sentences with the same bigram. Paulus et al. (2017) use similar restrictions for summarization by blocking repeated trigrams across the entire generated text. Since automated evaluation does not punish repeat sentences, we only enable this restriction when generating text for the human evaluation.

5 Learning Latent Sentence Templates

Each generated text follows a latent sentence template to describe the attributes in its MR. The model has to associate each attribute with its location in a sentence template. However, S2S models can learn wrong associations between inputs and

targets with limited data, which was also shown by Ferreira et al. (2017). Additionally, consider that we may see the generated texts for similar inputs: *There is an expensive British Restaurant called the Eagle.* and *The Eagle is an expensive, British Restaurant.*. Both incorporate the same information but have a different structure. A model that is trained on both styles simultaneously might struggle to generate a single output sentence. To address this issue and to learn a set of diverse generation styles, we train a mixture of models where every sequence is still generated by a single model. The method aims to force each model to learn a distinct sentence template.

The mixture aims to split the training data between the models such that each model trains only on a subset of a data, and can learn a different template structure. Thus, one model does not have to fit all the underlying template structures simultaneously. Moreover, it implicitly removes outlier training examples from all but one part of the mixture. Let $f_1, \ldots, f_K$ be the K models in the mixture. These models can either be completely disjoint or share a subset of their parameters (e.g. the word embeddings, the encoder, or both encoder and decoder). Following Guzman-Rivera et al. (2012), we introduce an unobserved random variable $w \sim \text{Cat}(1/K)$ that assigns a weight to each model for each input. Let $p_\theta(\mathbf{y}|\mathbf{x}, w)$ denote the probability of an output $\mathbf{y}$ for an input $\mathbf{x}$ with a given segmentation w. The likelihood for each point is defined as a mixture of the individual likelihoods,

$$\begin{aligned} \log p(\mathbf{y}|\mathbf{x}) &= \log \sum_w p(\mathbf{y}, w|\mathbf{x}) \\ &= \log \sum_w p(w) \times p(\mathbf{y}|w, \mathbf{x}). \end{aligned}$$

By constraining w to assume either 0 or 1, the optimization problem over the whole dataset becomes a joint optimization of assignments of models to data points and parameters to models.

To maximize the target, Guzman-Rivera et al. (2012) propose a multiple-choice loss (MCL) to segment training data similar to a hard EM algorithm or k-Means clustering. With MCL, after each training epoch, each training point is assigned to the model that predicts it with the minimal loss. After this segmentation, each model is trained for a further epoch using only its assigned

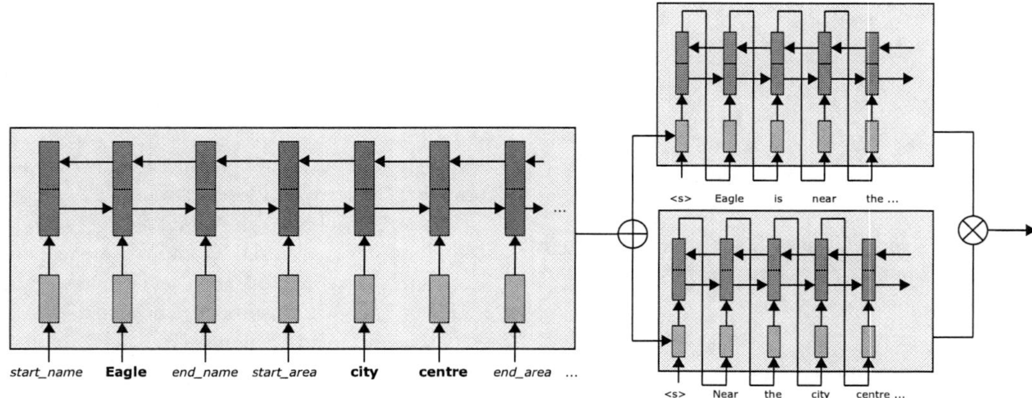

Figure 3: An illustration of the diverse ensembling method with $K = 2$ and a shared encoder. The encoder, shown on the left, reads the meaning representation and generates the contextual representations of the input tokens. The context is then used in parallel by the two separate decoders. Here, $\oplus$ represents the duplication of the input representation. The two decoders generate text independently from each other. Finally, only the decoder with the better generated text receives a parameter update. The exclusive choice is illustrated by the $\otimes$ operation.

data points. This process repeats until the point assignments converge. Related work by Kondadadi et al. (2013) has shown that models compute clusters of templates

Further work by Lee et al. (2016) reduce the computational overhead by introducing a stochastic MCL (sMCL) variant that does not require retraining. They compute the posterior over $p(w|\mathbf{x}, \mathbf{y})$ in the E-Step by choosing the best model for an example $\hat{k} = \mathrm{argmax}_{k \in [K]} p_\theta(\mathbf{y}|\mathbf{x}, w_k = 1, w_{\neg k} = 0)$. Setting $w_{\hat{k}}$ to 1 and all other entries in w to 0 achieves a hard segmentation for this point. After this assignment, only the model $\hat{k}$ with the minimal negative log-likelihood is updated in the M-Step. A potential downside of this approach is the linear increase in complexity since a forward pass has to be repeated for each model.

We illustrate the process of a single forward-pass in Figure 2, in which a model f_i has the smallest loss $\mathcal{L}_\rangle$ and is thus updated. Figure 3 demonstrates an example with $K = 2$ in which the two models generate text according to two different sentence layouts. We find that averaging predictions of multiple models during inference, a technique commonly used with traditional ensembling approaches, does not lead to increased performance. We further confirm findings by Lee et al. (2017) who state that these models overestimate their confidence when generating text. Since it is our goal to train a model that learns the best

Attribute	Value
area	city centre, riverside, ...
customerRating	1 out of 5, average, ...
eatType	coffee shop, restaurant, ...
familyFriendly	yes / no
food	Chinese, English, ...
name	Wildwood, The Wrestlers, ...
near	Café Sicilia, Clare Hall, ...
priceRange	less than £20, cheap, ...

Table 1: A list of all possible attributes and some example values for the E2E NLG dataset.

underlying template instead of generating diverse predictions, we instead generate text using only the model in the ensemble with the best perplexity on the validation set.

6 Experiments

We apply our method to the crowd-sourced E2E NLG dataset of Novikova et al. (2017) that comprises 50,000 examples of dialogue act-based MRs and reference pairs in the restaurant domain. Each input is a meaning representation of on average 5.43 attribute-value pairs, and the target a corresponding natural language utterance. A list of possible attributes is shown in Table 1. The dataset is split into 76% training, and 9% validation, and 15% test data. The validation and test data are

#	Setup	BLEU	NIST	METEOR	ROUGE	CIDEr
	TGEN (Dušek and Jurčíček, 2016)	69.3	8.47	47.0	72.6	2.39
	Ensemble with Slot Filling (Juraska et al., 2018)	69.3	8.41	43.8	70.1	/
	Hierarchical Decoding (Su et al., 2018)	44.1	/	/	53.8	/
	S2S with Slot Embeddings (Freitag and Roy, 2018)	72.7	8.3	/	75.1	/
(1)	*mlp*	70.6	8.35	47.3	73.8	2.38
(2)	*dot*	71.1	8.43	47.4	73.7	2.35
(3)	*mlp*, copy	71.4	8.44	47.0	74.1	2.43
(4)	*dot*, copy	69.8	8.20	47.8	74.3	2.51
(5)	*mlp*, $K = 2$	72.6	8.70	48.5	74.8	2.52
(6)	*dot*, $K = 2$	73.3	8.68	**49.2**	**76.3**	2.61
(7)	*mlp*, copy, $K = 2$	73.6	8.74	48.5	75.5	**2.62**
(8)	*dot*, copy, $K = 2$	**74.3**	**8.76**	48.1	75.3	2.55
(9)	Transformer	69.0	8.22	47.8	74.9	2.45
(10)	Transformer, $K = 2$	73.7	8.75	48.9	**76.3**	2.56

Table 2: Results of different S2S approaches and published baseline models on the E2E NLG validation set. The second section shows models without diverse ensembling, the third section with it. The fourth section shows results of the Transformer model. / indicates that numbers were not reported.

multi-reference; the validation set has on average 8.1 references for each MR. A separate test set with previously unseen combinations of attributes contains 630 MR's and its references are unseen and used for evaluation in the E2E NLG challenge.

For all LSTM-based S2S models, we use a two-layer bidirectional LSTM encoder, and hidden and embedding sizes of 750. During training, we apply dropout with probability 0.2 and train models with Adam (Kingma and Ba, 2014) and an initial learning rate of 0.002. We evaluate both *mlp* and *dot* attention types. The Transformer model has 4 layers with hidden and embedding sizes 512. We use the training rate schedule described by Vaswani et al. (2017), using Adam and a maximum learning rate of 0.1 after 2,000 warm-up steps. The diverse ensembling technique is applied to all approaches, pre-training all models for 4 epochs and then activating the sMCL loss. All models are implemented in OpenNMT-py (Klein et al., 2017)[2]. The parameters were found by grid search starting from the parameters used in the TGEN model by Dušek and Jurčíček (2016). Unless stated otherwise, models do not block repeat sentence beginnings, since it results in worse performance in automated met-

rics. We show results on the multi-reference validation and the blind test sets for the five metrics BLEU (Papineni et al., 2002), NIST (Doddington, 2002), METEOR (Denkowski and Lavie, 2014), ROUGE (Lin, 2004), and CIDEr (Vedantam et al., 2015).

7 Results

7.1 Results on the Validation Set

Table 2 shows the results of different models on the validation set. During inference, we set the length penalty parameter α to 0.4, the coverage penalty parameter β to 0.1, and use beam search with a beam size of 10. Our models outperform all shown baselines, which represent all published results on this dataset to date. Except for the copy-only condition, the data-efficient *dot* outperforms *mlp*. Both copy-attention and diverse ensembling increase performance, and combining the two methods yields the highest BLEU and NIST scores across all conditions. The Transformer performs similarly to the vanilla S2S models, with a lower BLEU but higher ROUGE score. Diverse ensembling also increases the performance with the Transformer model, leading to the highest ROUGE score across all model configurations. Table 3 shows generated text from different models. We can observe that the model without copy attention omits the rating, and without ensem-

[2]Code and documentation can be found at `https://github.com/sebastianGehrmann/diverse_ensembling`

bling, the sentence structure repeats and thus looks unnatural. With ensembling, both models produce sensible output with different sentence layouts. We note that often, only the better of the two models in the ensemble produces output better than the baselines. We further analyze how many attributes are omitted by the systems in Section 7.3.

To analyze the effect of length and coverage penalties, we show the average relative change across all metrics for model (8) while varying α and β in Figure 4. Both penalties increase average performance slightly, with an average increase of the scores by up to 0.82%. We find that recall-based metrics increase while the precision-based metrics decrease when applying the penalty, which can be explained by an increase in the average length of the generated text by up to 2.4 words. Results for ensembling variations of model (8) are shown in Table 4. While increasing K can lead to better template representations, every individual model will be trained on fewer data points. This can result in an increased generalization error. Therefore, we evaluate updating the top 2 models during the M-step and setting K=3. While increasing K from 2 to 3 does not show a major increase in performance when updating only one model, the K=3 approach slightly outperforms the K=2 one with the top 2 updates.

Having the K models model completely disjoint data sets and use a disjoint set of parameters could be too strong of a separation. Therefore, we investigate the effect of sharing a subset of the parameters between individual models. Our results in rows (5)-(7) of Table 4 show only a minor improvement in recall-based approaches when sharing the word embeddings between models but at the cost of a much lower BLEU and NIST score. Sharing more parameters further harms the model's performance.

7.2 Results on the Blind Test Set

We next report results of experiments on a held-out test set, conducted by the E2E NLG challenge organizers (Dušek et al., 2018), shown in Table 5. The results show the validity of the approach, as our systems outperform competing systems in these; ranking first in ROUGE and CIDEr and sharing the first rank in METEOR. The first row of the table shows the results with blocked repeat sentence beginnings. While this modification leads to slightly reduced scores on the automated

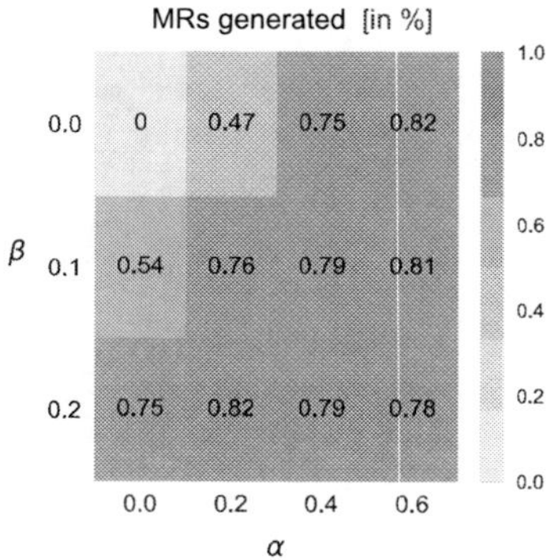

Figure 4: Relative change of performance averaged over all five metrics when varying inference parameters for model (8). Length penalty parameter α controls length, and coverage penalty parameter β penalizes source values with no attention.

MR	name: Wildwood; eatType: coffee shop; food: English; priceRange: moderate; customerRating: 3 out of 5; near: Ranch
(1)	Wildwood is a coffee shop providing English food in the moderate price range. It is located near Ranch.
(4)	Wildwood is a coffee shop providing English food in the moderate price range. It is near Ranch. Its customer rating is 3 out of 5.
(8).1	Wildwood is a moderately priced English coffee shop near Ranch. It has a customer rating of 3 out of 5.
(8).2	Wildwood is an English coffee shop near Ranch. It has a moderate price range and a customer rating of 3 out of 5.

Table 3: Examples of generated text by different systems for the same MR, shown in the first line. Numbers correspond to model configurations in Table 2.

metrics, it makes the text look more natural, and we thus use this output in the human evaluation.

The human evaluation compared the output to 19 other systems. For a single meaning representation, crowd workers were asked to rank output from five systems at a time. Separate ranks were collected for the *quality* and *naturalness* of the generations. The ranks for quality aim to reflect the grammatical correctness, fluency, and adequacy of the texts with respect to the structured input. In order to gather ranks for the naturalness, generations were shown without the meaning representation and rated based on how likely an utterance could have been produced by a na-

#	Setup	BLEU	NIST	METEOR	ROUGE	CIDEr
(1)	$K = 1$	69.8	8.20	47.8	74.3	2.51
(2)	$K = 2$	**74.3**	8.76	48.1	75.3	2.55
(3)	$K = 3$	73.6	8.73	48.8	75.5	**2.64**
(4)	$K = 3$, top 2	74.2	**8.81**	**48.6**	**76.1**	2.56
(5)	$K = 2$, share embedding	73.1	8.61	48.6	75.4	2.58
(6)	$K = 2$, share encoder	72.2	8.56	47.8	74.4	2.50
(7)	$K = 2$, share encoder + decoder	72.4	8.43	47.3	74.6	2.50

Table 4: Variants of diverse ensembling. The top section shows results of varying the number of models in a diverse ensemble on the validation set. The bottom section shows results with different numbers of shared parameters between two models in a diverse ensemble. All results are generated with setup (8) from Table 2.

Setup	BLEU	NIST	METEOR	ROUGE	CIDEr
TGEN (Dušek and Jurčíček, 2016)	65.9	8.61	44.8	68.5	2.23
Slot Filling (Juraska et al., 2018)	66.2	8.31	44.5	67.7	2.26
dot, $K = 3$, top 2, block repeats	65.0	8.53	43.9	68.7	2.09
dot, $K = 3$, top 2	65.8	8.57 (8)	44.1	68.9 (9)	2.11
Transformer, $K = 2$	66.2 (8)	8.60 (7)	**45.7 (1)**	70.4 (3)	**2.34 (1)**
dot, copy, $K = 2$	67.4 (3)	8.61 (6)	45.2 (4)	**70.8 (1)**	2.31 (3)

Table 5: The results of our model on the blind E2E NLG test set. Notable rankings within the 60 submitted systems are shown in parentheses. Systems by Freitag and Roy (2018) and Su et al. (2018) were not evaluated on this set.

tive speaker. The results were then analyzed using the TrueSkill algorithm by Sakaguchi et al. (2014). The algorithm produced 5 clusters of systems for both quality and naturalness. Within clusters, no statistically significant difference between systems can be found. In both evaluations, our main system was placed in the second best cluster. One difference between our and the system ranked first in quality by Juraska et al. (2018) is that our model frequently fails to generate text about inputs despite the coverage penalty.

7.3 Which Attributes do the Models Generate?

Vanilla S2S models frequently miss to include attributes of an MR, even though almost all the training examples use all of them. While Juraska et al. (2018) adds an explicit penalty for each attribute that is not part of a generated text, we aim to implicitly reduce this number with the coverage penalty. To investigate the effectiveness of the model extensions, we apply a heuristic that matches an input with exact word matches in the generated text. This provides a lower bound to the number of generated attributes since paraphrases are not captured. We omit the *familyFriendly* category from this figure since it does not work with this heuristic.

In Figure 5 (a) we show the cumulative effect of model extensions on generated attributes across all categories. Copy attention and the coverage penalty have a major effect on this number, while the ensembling only slightly improves it. In Figure 5 (b), we show a breakdown of the generated attributes per category. The base model struggles with *area*, *price range*, and *customer rating*. Price range and customer rating are frequently paraphrased, for example by stating that a restaurant with a 4 out of 5 rating has a good rating, while the area cannot be rephrased. While customer rating is one of the most prevalent attributes in the data set, the other two are more uncommon. The full model improves across almost all of the categories but also has problems with the price range. The only category in which it performs worse is the name category, which could be a side effect of the particular split of the data that the model learned. Despite the decrease in mistakenly omit-

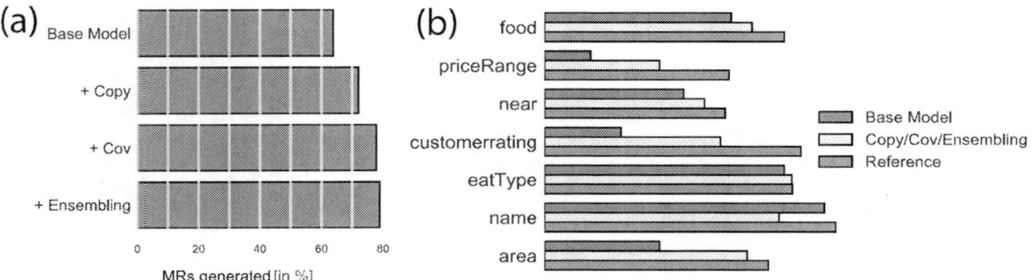

Figure 5: (a): The figure shows a lower bound on the percentage of all attributes the model is generating for each model type. The base model is missing almost 40% of all inputs. (b) The figure shows a breakdown per attribute how many the model is generating compared to the reference.

ted attributes, the model still misses up to 20% of attributes. We hope to address this issue in future work by explicitly modeling the underlying slots and penalizing models when they ignore them.

8   Conclusion

In this paper, we have shown three contributions toward end-to-end models for data-to-text problems. We surveyed existing S2S modeling methods and extensions to improve content selection in the NLG problem. We further showed that applying diverse ensembling to model different underlying generation styles in the data can lead to a more robust learning process for noisy data. Finally, an empirical evaluation of the investigated methods showed that they lead to improvements across multiple automatic evaluation metrics. In future work, we aim to extend the shown methods to address generation from more complex inputs, and for challenging domains such as data-to-document generation.

9   Acknowledgements

We thank the three anonymous reviewers for their valuable feedback. This work was supported by a Samsung Research Award.

References

Dzmitry Bahdanau, Kyunghyun Cho, and Yoshua Bengio. 2014. Neural machine translation by jointly learning to align and translate. *arXiv preprint arXiv:1409.0473*.

Michael Denkowski and Alon Lavie. 2014. Meteor universal: Language specific translation evaluation for any target language. In *Proceedings of the ninth workshop on statistical machine translation*, pages 376–380.

George Doddington. 2002. Automatic evaluation of machine translation quality using n-gram co-occurrence statistics. In *Proceedings of the second international conference on Human Language Technology Research*, pages 138–145. Morgan Kaufmann Publishers Inc.

Ondřej Dušek and Filip Jurčíček. 2016. Sequence-to-sequence generation for spoken dialogue via deep syntax trees and strings. *arXiv preprint arXiv:1606.05491*.

Ondrej Dušek, Jekaterina Novikova, and Verena Rieser. 2018. Findings of the E2E NLG challenge. In *(in prep.)*.

Thiago Castro Ferreira, Iacer Calixto, Sander Wubben, and Emiel Krahmer. 2017. Linguistic realisation as machine translation: Comparing different mt models for amr-to-text generation. In *Proceedings of the 10th International Conference on Natural Language Generation*, pages 1–10.

Markus Freitag and Scott Roy. 2018. Unsupervised natural language generation with denoising autoencoders. *arXiv preprint arXiv:1804.07899*.

Caglar Gulcehre, Sungjin Ahn, Ramesh Nallapati, Bowen Zhou, and Yoshua Bengio. 2016. Pointing the unknown words. *arXiv preprint arXiv:1603.08148*.

Abner Guzman-Rivera, Dhruv Batra, and Pushmeet Kohli. 2012. Multiple choice learning: Learning to produce multiple structured outputs. In *Advances in Neural Information Processing Systems*, pages 1799–1807.

Sepp Hochreiter and Jürgen Schmidhuber. 1997. Long short-term memory. *Neural computation*, 9(8):1735–1780.

Juraj Juraska, Panagiotis Karagiannis, Kevin Bowden, and Marilyn Walker. 2018. A deep ensemble model with slot alignment for sequence-to-sequence natural language generation. In *Proceedings of the 2018 Conference of the North American Chapter of the Association for Computational Linguistics: Human Language Technologies, Volume 1 (Long Papers)*, volume 1, pages 152–162.

Diederik Kingma and Jimmy Ba. 2014. Adam: A method for stochastic optimization. *arXiv preprint arXiv:1412.6980*.

Guillaume Klein, Yoon Kim, Yuntian Deng, Jean Senellart, and Alexander M Rush. 2017. Opennmt: Open-source toolkit for neural machine translation. *arXiv preprint arXiv:1701.02810*.

Ravi Kondadadi, Blake Howald, and Frank Schilder. 2013. A statistical nlg framework for aggregated planning and realization. In *Proceedings of the 51st Annual Meeting of the Association for Computational Linguistics (Volume 1: Long Papers)*, volume 1, pages 1406–1415.

Ioannis Konstas, Srinivasan Iyer, Mark Yatskar, Yejin Choi, and Luke Zettlemoyer. 2017. Neural amr: Sequence-to-sequence models for parsing and generation. In *Proceedings of the 55th Annual Meeting of the Association for Computational Linguistics (Volume 1: Long Papers)*, volume 1, pages 146–157.

Gerasimos Lampouras and Andreas Vlachos. 2016. Imitation learning for language generation from unaligned data. In *Proceedings of COLING 2016, the 26th International Conference on Computational Linguistics: Technical Papers*, pages 1101–1112. The COLING 2016 Organizing Committee.

Kimin Lee, Changho Hwang, KyoungSoo Park, and Jinwoo Shin. 2017. Confident multiple choice learning. *arXiv preprint arXiv:1706.03475*.

Stefan Lee, Senthil Purushwalkam Shiva Prakash, Michael Cogswell, Viresh Ranjan, David Crandall, and Dhruv Batra. 2016. Stochastic multiple choice learning for training diverse deep ensembles. In *Advances in Neural Information Processing Systems*, pages 2119–2127.

Chin-Yew Lin. 2004. Rouge: A package for automatic evaluation of summaries. In *Text summarization branches out: Proceedings of the ACL-04 workshop*, volume 8. Barcelona, Spain.

Minh-Thang Luong, Hieu Pham, and Christopher D Manning. 2015. Effective approaches to attention-based neural machine translation. *arXiv preprint arXiv:1508.04025*.

François Mairesse and Steve Young. 2014. Stochastic language generation in dialogue using factored language models. *Computational Linguistics*.

Hongyuan Mei, Mohit Bansal, and Matthew R Walter. 2015. What to talk about and how? selective generation using lstms with coarse-to-fine alignment. *arXiv preprint arXiv:1509.00838*.

Ramesh Nallapati, Bowen Zhou, Caglar Gulcehre, Bing Xiang, et al. 2016. Abstractive text summarization using sequence-to-sequence rnns and beyond. *arXiv preprint arXiv:1602.06023*.

Jekaterina Novikova, Ondrej Dušek, and Verena Rieser. 2017. The E2E dataset: New challenges for end-to-end generation. In *Proceedings of the 18th Annual Meeting of the Special Interest Group on Discourse and Dialogue*, Saarbrücken, Germany. ArXiv:1706.09254.

Alice H Oh and Alexander I Rudnicky. 2000. Stochastic language generation for spoken dialogue systems. In *Proceedings of the 2000 ANLP/NAACL Workshop on Conversational systems-Volume 3*, pages 27–32. Association for Computational Linguistics.

Kishore Papineni, Salim Roukos, Todd Ward, and Wei-Jing Zhu. 2002. Bleu: a method for automatic evaluation of machine translation. In *Proceedings of the 40th annual meeting on association for computational linguistics*, pages 311–318. Association for Computational Linguistics.

Romain Paulus, Caiming Xiong, and Richard Socher. 2017. A deep reinforced model for abstractive summarization. *arXiv preprint arXiv:1705.04304*.

Xiaochang Peng, Chuan Wang, Daniel Gildea, and Nianwen Xue. 2017. Addressing the data sparsity issue in neural amr parsing. In *Proceedings of the 15th Conference of the European Chapter of the Association for Computational Linguistics: Volume 1, Long Papers*, volume 1, pages 366–375.

Keisuke Sakaguchi, Matt Post, and Benjamin Van Durme. 2014. Efficient elicitation of annotations for human evaluation of machine translation. In *WMT@ ACL*, pages 1–11.

Abigail See, Peter J Liu, and Christopher D Manning. 2017. Get to the point: Summarization with pointer-generator networks. *Proceedings of the 55th Annual Meeting of the Association for Computational Linguistics, ACL 2017, Vancouver, Canada, July 30 - August 4, Volume 1: Long Papers*.

Amanda Stent, Rashmi Prasad, and Marilyn Walker. 2004. Trainable sentence planning for complex information presentation in spoken dialog systems. In *Proceedings of the 42nd annual meeting on association for computational linguistics*, page 79. Association for Computational Linguistics.

Shang-Yu Su, Kai-Ling Lo, Yi Ting Yeh, and Yun-Nung Chen. 2018. Natural language generation by hierarchical decoding with linguistic patterns. In *Proceedings of the 2018 Conference of the North American Chapter of the Association for Computational Linguistics: Human Language Technologies, Volume 2 (Short Papers)*, volume 2, pages 61–66.

Ilya Sutskever, Oriol Vinyals, and Quoc V Le. 2014. Sequence to sequence learning with neural networks. In *Advances in neural information processing systems*, pages 3104–3112.

Zhaopeng Tu, Zhengdong Lu, Yang Liu, Xiaohua Liu, and Hang Li. 2016. Modeling coverage for neural machine translation. *arXiv preprint arXiv:1601.04811*.

Ashish Vaswani, Noam Shazeer, Niki Parmar, Jakob Uszkoreit, Llion Jones, Aidan N. Gomez, Lukasz Kaiser, and Illia Polosukhin. 2017. Attention is all you need. *CoRR*, abs/1706.03762.

Ramakrishna Vedantam, C Lawrence Zitnick, and Devi Parikh. 2015. Cider: Consensus-based image description evaluation. In *Proceedings of the IEEE conference on computer vision and pattern recognition*, pages 4566–4575.

Oriol Vinyals, Meire Fortunato, and Navdeep Jaitly. 2015. Pointer networks. In *Advances in Neural Information Processing Systems*, pages 2692–2700.

Marilyn A Walker, Amanda Stent, François Mairesse, and Rashmi Prasad. 2007. Individual and domain adaptation in sentence planning for dialogue. *Journal of Artificial Intelligence Research*, 30:413–456.

Tsung-Hsien Wen, Milica Gasic, Nikola Mrksic, Pei-Hao Su, David Vandyke, and Steve Young. 2015. Semantically conditioned lstm-based natural language generation for spoken dialogue systems. *arXiv preprint arXiv:1508.01745*.

Yonghui Wu, Mike Schuster, Zhifeng Chen, Quoc V. Le, Mohammad Norouzi, Wolfgang Macherey, Maxim Krikun, Yuan Cao, Qin Gao, Klaus Macherey, Jeff Klingner, Apurva Shah, Melvin Johnson, Xiaobing Liu, Lukasz Kaiser, Stephan Gouws, Yoshikiyo Kato, Taku Kudo, Hideto Kazawa, Keith Stevens, George Kurian, Nishant Patil, Wei Wang, Cliff Young, Jason Smith, Jason Riesa, Alex Rudnick, Oriol Vinyals, Greg Corrado, Macduff Hughes, and Jeffrey Dean. 2016. Google's neural machine translation system: Bridging the gap between human and machine translation. *CoRR*, abs/1609.08144.

SimpleNLG-ZH: a Linguistic Realisation Engine for Mandarin

Guanyi Chen[1]**, Kees van Deemter**[12]**, Chenghua Lin**[2]
[1]Department of Information and Computing Sciences, Utrecht University
[2]Department of Computing Science, University of Aberdeen
{g.chen, c.j.vandeemter}@uu.nl, chenghua.lin@abdn.ac.uk

Abstract

We introduce SimpleNLG-ZH, a realisation engine for Mandarin that follows the software design paradigm of SimpleNLG (Gatt and Reiter, 2009). We explain the core grammar (morphology and syntax) and the lexicon of SimpleNLG-ZH, which is very different from English and other languages for which SimpleNLG engines have been built. The system was evaluated by regenerating expressions from a body of test sentences and a corpus of human-authored expressions. Human evaluation was conducted to estimate the quality of regenerated sentences.

1 Introduction

A classic natural language generation (NLG) system (Reiter and Dale, 2000) is a pipeline consisting of document planning, sentence planning and surface realisation (in that order). Surface realisation maps information produced by earlier components to well-formed output strings in the target language. A (surface) realiser employs language-specific morpho-syntactic constraints to achieve proper word ordering, inflection, and selection of function words. Different types of realisers exist (Gatt and Krahmer, 2018). Unlike approaches that aim primarily for linguistic depth and coverage (White et al., 2007), realisers in the SimpleNLG tradition aim primarily for ease of use and extendibility (Gatt and Reiter, 2009), and have become the realisation method of choice in many practical NLG applications, such as BabyTalk (Portet et al., 2009) and Absum (Lapalme, 2013).

SimpleNLG, as a human-crafted grammar-based realisation engine, performs linearisation and morphological inflection. Another realisation strategy uses statistical methods for acquiring probabilistic grammar from large corpora. For example, OpenCCG (White et al., 2007) built a grammar bank based on Combinatorial Categorial Grammar, extracted from the Penn Treebank (Marcus et al., 1993). When realising, OpenCCG applies a chart-based algorithm to generate all possible surface forms, which are then re-ranked by language models. Such an approach tends to have broader coverage, but less controllability and extendibility, which may explain why SimpleNLG is more popular in practical applications.

To date, the original English SimpleNLG has been adapted to German (Bollmann, 2011), French (Vaudry and Lapalme, 2013), Portuguese (De Oliveira and Sripada, 2014), Italian (Mazzei et al., 2016), Spanish (Soto et al., 2017), Filipino (Ong et al., 2011) and Telugu (Dokkara et al., 2015). There is no such adaptation work yet for Sino-Tibetan languages, whose morpho-syntactic structure is very different from the above languages. Mandarin, a Sino-Tibetan language with nearly 1 billion first-language speakers, offers huge opportunities for natural language generation, yet only a limited amount of work has focused on Mandarin realisation. KPML, a large-scale multilingual generation and development, supports limited sentence structures in Mandarin (Yang and Bateman, 2009). He et al. (2009) introduced a data-driven generator, with dependency trees as input. They used divide-and-conquer to break the dependency tree into sub-trees, realising each sub-tree using a log-linear model recursively. However, their system needs a large amount of fully inflected dependency trees as training data.

This paper describes a realisation engine fol-

Proceedings of The 11th International Natural Language Generation Conference, pages 57–66,
Tilburg, The Netherlands, November 5-8, 2018. ©2018 Association for Computational Linguistics

lowing the design principles of SimpleNLG, i.e., keeping a clear separation between morphological and syntactic operations (Gatt and Reiter, 2009). Although we took existing SimpleNLG systems as a source of inspiration, the system is, in many ways, a re-design[1]. For example, Mandarin, as a highly *analytical* language, needs far fewer morphological operations but many more syntactic constraints than English (Huang et al., 2009). SimpleNLG-ZH[2] ("Zhongwen" is Mandarin for "Chinese") was firstly built as a realiser for generating referring expressions in Mandarin (van Deemter et al., 2017; Van Deemter, 2016) which are mostly noun phrases together with simple verb phrases, and then extended to coverage other constructions and phenomena in Mandarin. It was developed as an adaptation from V4.4.8 of the original SimpleNLG[3] (SimpleNLG-EN). We show that SimpleNLG-ZH has wide coverage on test-sentences, and on the human authored corpus MTuna (van Deemter et al., 2017) as well.

2   The idea of SimpleNLG

SimpleNLG is a realisation engine designed for practical use. The input format of SimpleNLG is similar to a simplified dependency tree where the user should determine the specifiers, modifiers and complements of each input phrase using a set of features. SimpleNLG encodes different constraints, regarding lexicon, morphology, syntax and orthography, as a feature set (combining the features from the input) and passes the resulting structure onto the next stage. Figure 1 shows examples of an input for SimpleNLG-EN and SimpleNLG-ZH, respectively. To construct a sentence using SimpleNLG, we need to establish a verb phrase object and set its object(s) and subject.

SimpleNLG follows good software engineering design principles, clearly separating the modules for lexical and syntactic operations. The lexical component provides interfaces that handle the lexical features and apply morphological rules. Vital features such as `person`, `number` and `tense` are appended to target constituents or words for further realisation processes. The syntactic component takes over at the phrase and clause level, and provides `Java` classes for each phrasal sub-

type (`PhraseSpecs`), where `SPhraseSpec` stands for the class that model clauses.

SimpleNLG-EN offers significant coverage of English morphology and syntax, and provides easy-to-use APIs with which the realisation process is programmatically controllable. It provides a well established lexicon, the repository of the relevant items and their properties. The lexicon was constructed from the NIH specialist lexicon[4], which contains more than 300,000 entries. Each lexical entry was tagged with detailed lexical features as initial features of words. Simple shallow semantic features, like `COLOUR` and `QUANTITATIVE`, are appended for deciding word order.

3   Morphology

Morphology in Mandarin is usually thought to be extremely simple (Jensen, 1990). Packard (2000) has challenged this view, arguing that more morphological operations are involved in the construction of Chinese words than is usually thought. However, key mechanisms such as subject-verb agreement (which SimpleNLG-EN treated as part of morphology operations) are absent from Mandarin. We have therefore sided with mainstream linguistic opinion and kept our morphology component relatively simple. We use only two main rules for morphology: mapping pronouns to their surface forms and appending the collective marker "们" (mén).

3.1   Pronoun

Realising the surface forms of pronouns in SimpleNLG-ZH is similar to SimpleNLG-EN in its use of the features `gender` (masculine, feminine or neuter), `number` (singular or plural), and `person` (first, second or third). However, written Mandarin has different *third person plural* forms for all three different genders, i.e., "他们" (masculine), "她们" (feminine) and "它们" (neuter) (all of them have the same pronunciation: *tāmén*) rather than the one plural form *they* in English.

3.2   Collective Marker

In Mandarin, to say how many entities there are in a set, *classifiers* must be used. This is typically done in a *number phrase* of the form [number + classifier + noun], for instance "一把椅子" (yì bǎ

```
Phrase s1 = new SPhraseSpec('leave');
s1.setTense(PAST);
s1.setObject(new NPPhraseSpec('the', 'house'));
Phrase s2 = new StringPhraseSpec('the⌴boys');
s1.setSubject(s2);
```

```
Phrase s1 = new SPhraseSpec('离开');
s1.setParticle('了');
s1.setObject(new NPPhraseSpec('房子'));
Phrase s2 = new NPPhraseSpec('男孩');
s1.setSubject(s2);
```

Figure 1: Input code for generating the sentence "男孩离开了房子" (nánhái líkāile fángzi; *The boys left the house*) using SimpleNLG-EN (left) and SimpleNLG-ZH (right).

yǐzi; *a chair*), "两张桌子" (liǎng zhāng zhuōzi; *two tables*). Since number phrases are typically used referentially (not as quantifiers), they have generally been regarded as indefinite expressions, and these cannot be placed in subject or topic position in Mandarin (Huang et al., 2009).

Unlike English, Mandarin bare nouns and number phrases with numbers larger than 1 can express plural meaning without the help of inflected plural markers. The morpheme "们" in plural nouns serves as a "collective" marker rather than a traditionally plural marker (Li, 2006); here a "plurality" is a number of individuals, whereas a "collective" is a group (of individuals) as a whole. Under that definition, adding a morpheme "们" makes a nominal phrase definite, which results the morpheme "们" incompatible with a number phrases, so "们" cannot co-occur with number phrases. For example, the phrase "三个人们" (sān gè rénmén; *three people*) is not acceptable in Mandarin. Note that the rules discussed above do not apply to pronouns which follow the rules defined in §3.1.

It is hard to determine automatically whether a user wants to talk about a number of individuals or about a group as a whole. Moreover, "们" is always only optional. Therefore, in SimpleNLG-ZH, "们" is only added if the feature MEN is set to true. In addition, the system will refuse to add a "们" to a number phrase. The way of constructing number phrases is discussed in §4.

4 Syntax

The syntax module inherits the basic structure of SimpleNLG-EN, dividing the syntactic operations into processors that handle noun phrases, adjective phrases, verb phrases, verb phrases, and clauses. Each processor is enriched based on the grammar of Mandarin.

4.1 Noun Phrase

The Noun Phrase (NP) module is the most complex phrase module in SimpleNLG-ZH. Each noun phrase in SimpleNLG-ZH contains multiple specifiers, pre-modifiers, post-modifiers, complements, and a head noun.

4.1.1 Number Phrase

Each number phrase is constructed by a number, a classifier and a head noun; both the numeral and the classifier function as *specifiers* of the NP (for more about specifiers, please see §4.1.2).

As Number Phrases are very common in Mandarin, we designed a new constructor specifically for them. For instance, the number phrase "一本书" (yì běn shū; *a book*) can be constructed using this input:

```
NPPhraseSpec book = this.
    phraseFactory.createNounPhrase
    ("一", "本", "书");
```

The choice of classifiers depends mainly on the head noun. Additionally, for a given noun, the choice of classifiers may depend on its meaning. For example, the classifier of "房子" (fángzi; *house*) can be "座", "幢", "间", and many other possible classifiers based on the size or the shape of the house. The current SimpleNLG-ZH requires classifiers to be specified "by hand". By introducing a language model in the future, this process might be automated.

4.1.2 Specifier

SimpleNLG-ZH allows multiple specifiers (compared to a single specifier in SimpleNLG-EN) within one NP. For example, a number phrase needs two specifiers: a numeral and a classifier. All the following categories can be placed in specifier position: pronouns (with or without the collective marker "men"), proper names, classifiers, numerals and demonstratives. These specifiers appear in the following order (the $A > B$ means A should appear before B): proper name > pronoun > demonstrative > numeral > classifier. The decision of whether or not to realize each of these specifiers is subject to a number of constraints (Huang et al., 2009).

1. Suppose the input specification asks for a pronoun in the specifier position. This pronoun must have a collective marker except in a structure that includes [demonstrative/numeral + classifier] For instance, "他们学生" (tāmén xuéshēng; *them students*) contains the collective marker, but "他一个学生" (tā yígè xuéshēng; *them students*) does not;

2. Proper names in specifier position can only be realised if the structure includes [pronoun + numeral + classifier], [demonstrative + classifier] or [demonstrative + numeral + classifier]: "张三那个学生" (zhāngsān nàgè xuéshēng; *the student called Zhangsan*);

3. A demonstrative or a numeral will only be realised if there is a classifier in the same NP and vise versa: "(那/一)个学生" (nà/yí gè xuéshēng; *that/a student*).

As discussed in §3.2, number phrases are often seen as indefinite phrase but not always. When they are for quantification they can be placed in the subject/topic position. Therefore, SimpleNLG-ZH permits a number phrase in the subject/topic position, e.g., the sentence "三个人吃两块蛋糕" (sān gè rén chī liǎng kuài dàngāo; *three people eat two cakes*)

For nouns (including bare nouns, pronouns and proper nouns), the feature `possessive` is also realised in the specifier position: SimpleNLG-ZH adds a particle "的" (de) as an associative marker after the noun.

4.1.3 Localiser

Localisers (corresponding to English words such as "on", "above", etc.) form a special syntactic category. They are used in *location phrases*, which is a particular type of preposition phrases. The location information in a location phrase is expressed in the localiser rather than the head preposition, for example: [PP 在 [NP 桌子 上]] (zài zhuōzi shàng; *on the table*). The localiser "上" (on) works as a supplement of the noun phrase in the proposition phrase (i.e., location phrase).

In SimpleNLG-ZH, the localiser itself is defined as a normal noun with a lexical feature LOCATIVE in the lexicon. When constructing a location phrase, if the localiser is a disyllabic word, such as "上面" (shàngmiàn), then a particle "的" is inserted before the localiser to construct the phrase: "在桌子的上面" (zài zhuōzi shàngmiàn; *on the table*). However, if such a prepositional phrase works as a pre-modifier of another noun, then that inserted particle will be disregarded, for example: "在桌子上面的书" (zài zhuōzi shàngmiàn de shū; *the book on the table*).

4.1.4 Pre-modifier

SimpleNLG-EN handles the orders of multiple pre-modifiers based on their meanings, where the meanings are acquired from a huge lexicon that contains a series of tags (e.g., COLOUR, QUANTITATIVE) indicating the meaning of words. It adds pre-modifiers in the order of quantitative adjectives, colour adjectives, classifying adjectives and nouns. For SimpleNLG-ZH, more categories of words can be placed in the pre-modifier position, other than just adjectives and nouns. It performs re-ordering based on pre-modifiers' part-of-speech and lexical features set by the users.

Our system handles two different types of adjectives, namely, normal adjectives and non-predicate adjectives. For normal adjectives, the system will automatically add a "的" (de) between the adjectives and the head noun, such as "绿的椅子" (lǜ de yǐzi; *green chair*). "的" can be omitted by setting the feature NO_DE to TRUE, which results in the phrase "绿椅子" (*green chair*). Non-predicate adjectives, in contrast to normal adjectives, are a special type of adjectives that cannot function as predicate on their own (e.g., "男" (ná; *male*) and "女" (nǔ; *female*)), in which the particle "的" (de) is always omitted. Thus, the particle "的" will not be appended if the adjective is non-predicate, such as "男人" (nánrén; *man*). The feature is set based on the information of the lexicon loaded into SimpleNLG-ZH (details see §5).

Nouns and noun phrases, as pre-modifiers, can play two different roles: they can be concatenated with the head noun to construct a compound noun: for example, "大学教育" (dàxuē jiàoyù; *university education*); or, they can be connected by means of a particle "的", which works as an associative marker: for example, "黑头发的人" (hēitóufà de rén; *the man with black hair*). To construct the latter, the feature ASSOCIATIVE should be set to TRUE. The order of the pre-modifiers is localisers > verbs/clauses > adjectives with de > nouns with associative marker > adjectives without de > non-predicate adjectives > nouns.

4.2 Adjective Phrase

Adjective phrases in Mandarin differ from those in the languages for which previous SimpleNLG engines were built. Most adjectives in Mandarin can act as the predicate of a clause without the help of a copula verb (see below). Such adjectives are called predicate adjectives.

4.2.1 Predicate Adjective

Although adjectives can act as predicates, it is necessary to distinguish them from verbs (Huang et al., 2009). We implemented realisation of a clause like "他很高" (tā hěngāo; *he is very tall*) by specifying an empty copula. This is achieved by creating a new constructor which accepts a subject noun and a predicate adjective.

Predicate adjectives in SimpleNLG-ZH also accept negative words and modal words. For example, the sentence "他应该不高" (tā yīnggāi bùgāo; *he couldn't be tall*) has both a negative word "不", and a modal word "应该".

4.2.2 Non-predicate Adjective

As discussed in §4.1.4, non-predicate adjectives always omit the particle "的" between the adjective and the head noun. However, when a non-predicate adjective functions as a predicate (with the help of a copula), such as "他是男的" (tā shì nánde; *he is a man*), the copula "是" (shì) and the particle "的" (de) are obligatory (Paul, 2010).

4.2.3 "比" construction

In English, degree adjectives have comparative and superlative degrees, whose realisation is implemented in the morphology processor. In Mandarin, realisation is performed by modifying the syntax. The superlative degree is realised by adding an adverb pre-modifier "最" (zuì; *most*); the comparative through the "比" construction.

SimpleNLG-ZH implements the "比" (bǐ) construction as a prepositional phrase. For example, for the sentence "他比小明高" (tā bǐ xiǎomíng gāo; *he is taller than xiaoming*), the word "比" (bǐ) itself is seen as the head of a preposition phrase, which is a pre-modifier of a adjective phrase. Such a construction (i.e., as an adjective phrase), can act as the pre-modifier of a noun phrase, for example, "他们班没有比他更高的人" (tāmén bān méi-yǒu bǐ tā gènggāode rén; *none of his classmates is taller than he*). Note that the head of this noun phrase can be omitted, but the particle "的" (de) should be maintained as a sentence-final marker,

i.e. "他们班没有比他更高的" (tāmén bān méi-yǒu bǐ tā gènggāode).

4.3 Verb Phrase

4.3.1 Pre-modifier and Post-modifier

Verb phrases can contain the associative markers "得" and "地". The latter is appended to the pre-modifier if it is disyllabic, for example, "快速地跑" (kuàisù de pǎo; *fast run*). If the pre-modifier is monosyllabic, "快跑" (kuàipǎo) is constructed instead, with the particle "地" (de) disregarded. The particle "得" (de) connects head verbs with their complements: "跑得快" (pǎodekuài; *running fast*).

4.3.2 Aspect

KPML (Yang and Bateman, 2009) used templates with particles like "过", "了" or "着" (zhe)to model aspect. However, KPML's coverage of language variation is limited because it uses a limited number of templates. Since aspect in Mandarin is realised using post-verbal or post-clause particles, we took a more flexible strategy that enables users to add particles based on their need.

Particles can be in two positions: post-verbal and post-clausal. In "他吃着饭" (tā chīzhe fàn; *he is eating*), the particle "着" (zhe), which expresses the present continuous tense, is appended to a VPPhraseSpec object. Similarly, the class SPhraseSpec, which represents a clause, has the capability to append a particle to its end. For example, in "他吃饭了" (tā chī fànle; *he has eaten*), the particle "了" is appended to the clause "他吃饭" (tāchīfàn; *he eats*).

4.4 Clause

At the Clause level, apart from the issues related to negative and interrogative sentences inherited from SimpleNLG-EN, we considered "把" (bǎ) and "被" (bèi) constructions which are two common constructions in Mandarin. We also discuss how topicalised sentences are realised using SimpleNLG-ZH.

4.4.1 Negative Sentence

Negative sentences in SimpleNLG-ZH are realised by inserting negative words before the predicate verb (or the predicate) and after a modal word. For example, the negation of "他应该去上学" (tā yīnggāi qù shàngxué; *he should go to school*) is the sentence with an inserted negative word "不" (bù; *not*) before "去" (qù; *go*) and after the modal word "应该" (yīngāi; *should*): "他应该不去上学" (tā yīnggāi bū qù shàngxué; *he should haven't gone to school*). SimpleNLG-ZH can also realise negative modal by viewing the negative modal as a merged word, much like *haven't* or *shouldn't* in English (Xu, 1997). For example,"他不应该去上学" (tā bū yīnggāi qù shàngxué; *he should not go to school*).

In addition, Mandarin has a number of different negative words, selected based on the head verb. For example, applied to the sentence "他有椅子" (tā yǒu yǐzi; *he has chairs*), instead of using "不" (bù), the word "没" (méi) should be used: "他没有椅子" (tā mēiyǒu yǐzi; *he doesn't have a chair*). SimpleNLG-ZH allows users to specify by hand what negation word should be chosen in a specific case by using the feature negative_word, thus overruling the system's default choice.

4.4.2 "把" Construction

The "把" construction is a common seen and useful structure for focusing on the result or influence of an action, which is not exist in English. For example, considering the sentence, "他把小明重重地打" (tā bǎ xiǎomíng zhòngzhòng de dǎ; *he beat xiaoming heavily*), with the "把" construction, the influence of "打" (dǎ; beat) is highlighted. The natural phrase order of this example is: "他重重地打小明" (tā zhòngzhòng de dǎ xiǎomíng; *he beat xiaoming heavily*), which is the basic structure that SimpleNLG-ZH can handle. i.e., [subject + predicate verb + object]. In the "把" construction, however, the marker adverb "把" is added after the subject, and the object is moved to the position right before the predicate verb phrase: [subject + "把" + object + predicate verb].

Note that the positions of modal words and negative words do not follow the movement of the verb phrases (Liu et al., 2001). In other words, in the resulting "把" construction, the modal words and negative words are placed before the object in their own order, as in "他应该没把小明重重地打" (tā yīnggāi méi bǎ xiǎomīng zhòngzhòng de dǎ; *he should haven't beaten xiaoming heavily*). SimpleNLG-ZH realises a sentence with the "把" construction if the user set the feature BA to TRUE.

4.4.3 "被" Construction

The "被" construction in Mandarin is one of the ways to express the passive, using the basic syntactic structure: [object + "被" + subject + predicate verb]. Using the same example as before in §4.4.2, the transformed sentence would be "小明被他重重地打" (xiǎomīng bèitā zhòngzhòng de dǎ; *Xiaoming is beaten heavily by him*). SimpleNLG-ZH chooses between active and passive based on the value of the feature PASSIVE, which is inherited from SimpleNLG-EN.

4.4.4 Interrogative

SimpleNLG-ZH inherits and adapts all its interrogative patterns from SimpleNLG-EN, including "有没有" (yǒuméiyǒu; *Yes-or-no*) and wh-questions: "怎么" (zěnmè; *How*), "什么" (shénmè; *What*), "哪里" (nǎlǐ; *Where*), "谁" (shuí; *Who*), "为什么" (wèishénmè; *Why*), "多少" (duōshǎo; *How Many*). SimpleNLG-ZH adds two further types, namely "哪个" (nǎgè; *Which*) and "什么时候" (shénmèshíshòu; *When*). For Yes-or-no sentences, SimpleNLG-ZH appends the interrogative particle "吗" at the end of a sentence; for instance, "你去上学吗？" (nǐ qù shàngxué ma; *Will you go to school?*).

In SimpleNLG-EN, for wh-questions, only *What* and *Who* made a difference between whether to place the interrogative marker in subject or object position. In SimpleNLG-ZH, however, nearly all wh-question markers can be placed in both positions. Here we use a "什么" (*What*) sentence as an example: For "台风摧毁了他的房子" (táifēng cuīhuǐ le fángzi; *the typhoon destroyed his house*), if we set the feature INTERROGATIVE_TYPE to what_object, then the sentence is changed to "台风摧毁了什么？" (táifēng cuīhuǐ le shénme; *what did the typhoon destroy?*). Setting the feature to what_subject results in "什么摧毁了他的房子？" (shénme cuīhuǐ le tādefángzi; *what destroyed his house?*). In interrogated "把" constructions and '被' constructions, the wh-question markers are placed *in situ*, i.e., replacing the phrases in the original subject or object position, according to the value of INTERROGATIVE_TYPE.

4.4.5 Topicalisation

Topic structures, especially gapped topic structures, are a very common syntactic structure in Mandarin (Xu and Langendoen, 1985). For example, "绿色的椅子，那把大号的" (lǜsè de yǐzi, nà bǎ dàhào de; *(As for) the green chair, it is the large one*) is a gapped topicalised sentence, in which the constituent after the "的" in the phrase "那把大号的" (nàbǎ dàhào de; *the large one*) moved into the topic position and left a gap.

In the current version of SimpleNLG-ZH, we realise a gapped topicalised sentence by viewing it as two coordinated noun phrases, in which the second noun phrase has an empty head noun. For the sentence above, the two noun phrases are "绿色的椅子" (lùsè de yǐzi; *the green chair*) and "那把大号的" (nàbǎ dàhào de; *the large one*). In the current version of our system, there is no guarantee that the empty head of the second clause is bounded by the first clause. We also consider orthography in topicalisation, i.e., a conjunction words between two phrases should be changed to a comma. In our system, the topicalised sentence, as a `CoordinatedPhraseElement` object, calls the `topicalise()` function to take care of the punctuation.

5 Lexicon

Unlike SimpleNLG-EN, we did not have a ready-to-use elaborate lexicon for SimpleNLG-ZH. Instead, we extracted a primary lexicon from the Chinese as a Foreign Language (CFL) corpus[5] (Lee et al., 2017), which is a sub-corpus of the Universal Dependencies corpus. The CFL corpus has 451 human tagged dependency trees and 7,256 tokens in total. Each word in CFL was primarily mapped to one of the lexical categories in SimpleNLG-ZH based on the relations in Table 1 as well as the following rules:

1. The tag `<proper/>` is appended for PROPNs;
2. The tag `<nonpredicate/>` is appended for non-predicate adjectives manually, which is based on the non-predicate adjective list in Liu et al. (2001);
3. The tag `<locative/>` is appended for localisers manually;
4. The words that serve as a dependent of a `clf` (classifier) dependency relation are given the category `classifier`.

The constructed lexicon has 1,639 lexical entries at in total.

6 Evaluation

We decided to evaluate SimpleNLG-ZH in two ways. Firstly, following Soto et al. (2017) and Bollmann (2011), we applied a set of unit test to each module of the system, using the test cases

[5]`https://github.com/UniversalDependencies/UD_Chinese-CFL/tree/master`

Lexical Category	Universal POS Tag
adverb	ADV, PART
noun	NOUN, PROPN
preposition	ADP
demonstrative	DET
conjunction	SCONJ, CCONJ
pronoun	PRONOUN
adjective	ADJ
modal	AUX
verb	VERB

Table 1: Relationship between Universal POS tags and lexical categories in SimpleNLG-ZH.

from SimpleNLG-EN plus a set of newly constructed test cases that address some of the peculiarities of Mandarin (e.g., the "把" construct).

Secondly, we evaluated the system using a set of expressions from a corpus of actual language use; this was reminiscent of Mazzei et al. (2016) and Bollmann (2011), but using a larger set of expressions. In all cases, when faced with an input expression (i.e., from a test set or corpus), we used this expression to construct a formatted input that was then passed to SimpleNLG-ZH to produce an output expression which was then compared to the input expression.

Evaluation with tests cases. The test cases consist of 144 sentences manually translated and adapted from SimpleNLG V4.4.8 `JUnit Tests` and two reference grammar books (Huang et al., 2009; Liu et al., 2001). The test cases cover all the linguistic features discussed in previous sections and all possible syntactic structures of referring expressions in Mandarin introduced in van Deemter et al. (2017). All the tests were passed by SimpleNLG-ZH, that is, the generated sentences were all identical *verbatim* to the inputs.

Corpus-based evaluation. We picked 100 noun phrases at random from the MTuna corpus (van Deemter et al., 2017), which is the corpus that first version of SimpleNLG-ZH focus on as stated in §1. MTuna is a corpus that has totally 1,650 referring expressions. We then re-generated these expressions using SimpleNLG-ZH. Not all re-generated NPs were identical verbatim to the original MTuna NPs. 35 noun phrases did not match completely (i.e., *verbatim*) with the original noun phrases. Table 2 lists some typical examples, showing differences in word ordering, punctuation, and so on. We ran a human evaluation to find out whether the realised sentences were acceptable (i.e., are they fluent and do they have the same meaning as their inputs). Two native speak-

Type	ID	Noun Phrases from MTuna	Realised Sentence	Acceptable
1	1	黑头发，络腮胡，黑西服，浅色衬衣 hēitóufà, luòsāihú, hēixīfú, qiǎnsèchènyī *a man with black hair, whiskers, black suit and light shirt*	黑头发 络腮 胡 黑 西服 浅色 衬衣 hēitóufà luòsāihú hēixīfú qiǎnsèchènyī	Yes
2	2	一张大的红色的沙发 yìzhāng dà de hóngsè de shāfā *the large red sofa*	一张 红色 的 大 的 沙发 yìzhāng hóngsè de dà de shāfā	Yes
	3	戴眼镜的两个人 dài yǎnjìng de liǎng gè rén *the people who wear glasses*	两 个 戴眼镜 的 人 liǎng gè dài yǎnjìng de rén	Yes
	4	红色正面朝向屏幕小椅子或者绿色背向屏幕的大风扇 hóngsè zhèngmiàn cháoxiàng píngmù xiǎo yǐzì huòzhě lǜsè bèixiàng píngmù de dà fēngshàn *the fronting small red chair and the backing large green fan*	正面 朝向 屏幕 小 红色 椅子 或者 背向 屏幕 的 绿色 大 风扇 zhèngmiàn cháoxiàng píngmù xiǎo hóngsè yǐzì huòzhě bèixiàng píngmù de lǜsè dà fēngshàn	No
	5	黑色头发戴眼镜的 hēisè tóufà dài yǎnjìng de *the person with black hair and glasses*	戴 眼镜 的 黑色 头发 dài yǎnjìng de hēisè tóufà	No
3	6	红色椅子，椅子背朝向右边，可以看到椅子背的正面 hóngsè yǐzì, yǐzìbèi cháo yòubiān, kěyǐ kàndào yǐzìbèi de zhèngmiàn *It is a red chair whose back is facing right and we could see the front of its back.*	(failed)	No
	7	正朝向我们的小的椅子和正朝向我们的大的风扇 zhèng cháoxiàng wǒmén de xiǎo de yǐzì hé zhèng cháoxiàng wǒmén de dà de fēngshàn *the fronting small chair and the fronting large fan*	正 朝向 我 的 小 的 椅子 和 正 朝向 我 的 大 的 风扇 zhèng cháoxiàng wǒ de xiǎo de yǐzì hé zhèng cháoxiàng wǒ de dà de fēngshàn	No

Table 2: Example sentences (with their Pinyin and translations) that were not identical to the inputs from MTuna *(unmatched sentences)*. The last column says whether the output was judged to be acceptable by our annotators.

ers annotated the outputs; they reached good inter-annotator agreement ($\kappa = 0.77$) and were asked to produce a consensus annotation, which was then used for our evaluation. It turned out that 90 out of 100 sentences were judged to be acceptable, which we consider a very encouraging result.

We classified the unmatched sentences into three types. The first one is where punctuation was different, as in Example 1 in Table 2. The reason is that some sentences used commas to separate modifiers but SimpleNLG-ZH does not. These cases were generally judged to be acceptable.

The second type is where the word order of the realised sentences was different from the input. There are three sub-types: a) The order of adjective pre-modifiers was different, as in Examples 2 and 4. Most of these deviations were judged to be acceptable, but sentence 4 shows an unacceptable example, where the word "红色" (hóngsè; *red*) before "小" (xiǎo; *little*) accidentally produced a new word, "小红色" (*light red*), which has differ-ent meaning; b) SimpleNLG-ZH enforces the pre-modifiers to appear following the specifiers. However, in the MTuna corpus, there are expressions, like Example 3, that switch the place of speci-fiers and pre-modifiers. All such re-orderings were judged to be acceptable; c) There is a special syn-tactic pattern of noun phrases in Mandarin, where a Noun is omitted that is recoverable from the con-text. For example, in Example 5, the head is omit-ted in the original sentence to construct a free rel-ative (Teng, 1979) where the particle "的" works as sentence-final marker. However, SimpleNLG-ZH cannot recognise the functionality of the par-ticle, thus it switches two pre-modifiers according to the orders defined in §4.1.4, which results in a noun phrase with different meaning. We found 6 unacceptable cases of the second type.

SimpleNLG-ZH failed to reproduce some types of language use that are highly colloquial and not strictly grammatical. We found 4 such cases, as in Example 6 in Table 2, and in Example 7, where the pronoun "我们" (*us*) in the sentence actually refers to the subject himself (but using the plural form); SimpleNLG-ZH realises this as a singular pronoun.

Comparing these results with earlier evaluations of SimpleNLG-like systems, our results on the tests sets were perfect (with system input constructed by hand from the input expressions), which was also the cases for most earlier studies (Soto et al., 2017; Bollmann, 2011). Only three of the previous evaluations involved a corpus. Bollmann (2011) and Dokkara et al. (2015) evaluated their system on 152 sentences from five Wikipedia articles and 738 sentences randomly picked from a book, respectively. The linguistic variation of their test set is greater than ours (which focussed on referring expressions), but the quality of their output may have been lower: Dokkara et al. (2015) reported 57% of exact matches, lower than our 65%. Bollmann (2011) reported 76% of the sentences "could be generated", though what this meant is not entirely clear. Mazzei et al. (2016) tested the coverage and scalability of their system by automatically mapping 20 dependency trees from the Universal Dependency corpus. They reported only 10% exact matching sentences (2/20) and their discussion suggests that their results for declarative and interrogative sentences may have been disappointing.

7 Conclusion and Future Work

We have introduced and evaluated a realisation engine for Mandarin in the tradition of SimpleNLG. We hope SimpleNLG-ZH can be a good starting point for work on other Sino-Tibetan languages, such as Tibetan and Cantonese.

Realisation has turned out to be non-trivial in all the languages addressed in the SimpleNLG tradition so far, but *where* the most challenging problems are (i.e., in which components of the system), and what the optimal balance between handcrafting and Machine learning should lie, is something that differs per language.

As for the former issue, we have seen that Mandarin appears to require only a small set of morphological operators, but a much enhanced set of syntactic processing rules.

As for the latter issue, our study of errors in SimpleNLG-ZH offers support for the idea that some issues in realisation are best handled using Machine Learning (Langkilde, 2000; White et al., 2007). As it stands, SimpleNLG-ZH makes all its decisions based on a combination of handcrafted rules and explicit stipulation. It would be preferable if the role of the developer in making these decisions could be reduced. This is true for the choice of classifiers (see §4.1.1), for the use of particles (such as "的" and "了"), for the choice between different negation words ("不" or "没"), and for ordering the modifiers and specifiers (as mentioned in §6). In all these cases, SimpleNLG-ZH assumes that the choice is made outside the system (i.e., by a person or by another component of the NLG system). It would be useful if these choices were made by SimpleNLG-ZH itself, but it is difficult to see how a rule-based approach could accomplish this. We therefore aim to experiment with statistical models (e.g., language models) to make these decisions. The result would be a hybrid realisation system that combines rules and Machine Learning.

Acknowledgements

As well as the anonymous reviewers, we thank Rint Sybesma, Xiwu Han, Ehud Reiter, Yaji Sripada, and others in the Aberdeen CLAN group for their comments on SimpleNLG-ZH and this paper.

References

Marcel Bollmann. 2011. Adapting SimpleNLG to German. In *Proceedings of the 13th European Workshop on Natural Language Generation*, pages 133–138. Association for Computational Linguistics.

Rodrigo De Oliveira and Somayajulu Sripada. 2014. Adapting SimpleNLG for Brazilian Portuguese realisation. In *INLG*, pages 93–94.

Kees van Deemter, Le Sun, Rint Sybesma, Xiao Li, Chen Bo, and Muyun Yang. 2017. Investigating the content and form of referring expressions in Mandarin: introducing the Mtuna corpus. In *Proceedings of the 10th International Conference on Natural Language Generation*, pages 213–217.

Sasi Raja Sekhar Dokkara, Suresh Verma Penumathsa, and Somayajulu Gowri Sripada. 2015. A simple surface realization engine for Telugu. In *ENLG*, pages 1–8.

Albert Gatt and Emiel Krahmer. 2018. Survey of the state of the art in Natural Language Generation: Core tasks, applications and evaluation. *Journal of Artificial Intelligence Research (JAIR)*, 61:65–170.

Albert Gatt and Ehud Reiter. 2009. SimpleNLG: A realisation engine for practical applications. In *Proceedings of the 12th European Workshop on Natural Language Generation*, pages 90–93. Association for Computational Linguistics.

Wei He, Haifeng Wang, Yuqing Guo, and Ting Liu. 2009. Dependency based Chinese sentence realization. In *Proceedings of the Joint Conference of the 47th Annual Meeting of the ACL and the 4th International Joint Conference on Natural Language Processing of the AFNLP: Volume 2-Volume 2*, pages 809–816. Association for Computational Linguistics.

Cheng-Teh James Huang, Yen-hui Audrey Li, and Yafei Li. 2009. *The syntax of Chinese*, volume 8. Cambridge University Press Cambridge.

John T Jensen. 1990. *Morphology: Word structure in generative grammar*, volume 70. John Benjamins Publishing.

Irene Langkilde. 2000. Forest-based statistical sentence generation. In *Proceedings of the 1st North American chapter of the Association for Computational Linguistics conference*, pages 170–177. Association for Computational Linguistics.

Guy Lapalme. 2013. Natural language generation and summarization at RALI. In *Proceedings of the 14th European Workshop on Natural Language Generation*, pages 92–93.

John Lee, Herman Leung, and Keying Li. 2017. Towards universal dependencies for learner Chinese. In *Proceedings of the NoDaLiDa 2017 Workshop on Universal Dependencies (UDW 2017)*, pages 67–71.

Yen-hui Audrey Li. 2006. Argument determiner phrases and number phrases. *Argument*, 29(4).

Yuehua Liu, Wei Gu, and Wenyu Pan. 2001. *Chinese Grammar*. The Commercial Press.

Mitchell P Marcus, Mary Ann Marcinkiewicz, and Beatrice Santorini. 1993. Building a large annotated corpus of English: The Penn Treebank. *Computational linguistics*, 19(2):313–330.

Alessandro Mazzei, Cristina Battaglino, and Cristina Bosco. 2016. SimpleNLG-IT: adapting SimpleNLG to Italian. In *INLG*, pages 184–192.

Ethel Ong, Stephanie Abella, Lawrence Santos, and Dennis Tiu. 2011. A simple surface realizer for Filipino. In *PACLIC*, pages 51–59.

Jerome L Packard. 2000. *The morphology of Chinese: A linguistic and cognitive approach*. Cambridge University Press.

Waltraud Paul. 2010. Adjectives in Mandarin Chinese: The rehabilitation of a much ostracized category. *Adjectives: Formal analyses in syntax and semantics, ed. Patricia Cabredo Hofherr and Ora Matushansky*, 1:15–151.

François Portet, Ehud Reiter, Albert Gatt, Jim Hunter, Somayajulu Sripada, Yvonne Freer, and Cindy Sykes. 2009. Automatic generation of textual summaries from neonatal intensive care data. *Artificial Intelligence*, 173(7-8):789–816.

Ehud Reiter and Robert Dale. 2000. *Building natural language generation systems*. Cambridge university press.

Alejandro Ramos Soto, Julio Janeiro Gallardo, and Alberto Bugarín Diz. 2017. Adapting SimpleNLG to Spanish. In *Proceedings of the 10th International Conference on Natural Language Generation*, pages 144–148.

Shou-hsin Teng. 1979. Remarks on cleft sentences in Chinese. *Journal of Chinese Linguistics*, 7(1):101–14.

Kees Van Deemter. 2016. *Computational models of referring: a study in cognitive science*. MIT Press.

Pierre-Luc Vaudry and Guy Lapalme. 2013. Adapting SimpleNLG for bilingual English-French realisation. In *ENLG*, pages 183–187.

Michael White, Rajakrishnan Rajkumar, and Scott Martin. 2007. Towards broad coverage surface realization with CCG. In *Proc. of the Workshop on Using Corpora for NLG: Language Generation and Machine Translation (UCNLG+ MT)*.

Ding Xu. 1997. *Functional Categories in Mandarin Chinese*, volume 26. Holland Academic Graphics.

Liejiong Xu and D. Terence Langendoen. 1985. Topic structures in Chinese. *Language*, pages 1–27.

Guowen Yang and John A Bateman. 2009. The Chinese aspect generation based on aspect selection functions. In *Proceedings of the Joint Conference of the 47th Annual Meeting of the ACL and the 4th International Joint Conference on Natural Language Processing of the AFNLP: Volume 2-Volume 2*, pages 629–637. Association for Computational Linguistics.

Adapting SimpleNLG to Galician language

Andrea Cascallar-Fuentes[1], Alejandro Ramos-Soto[1,2], and Alberto Bugarín[1]

[1]Centro Singular de Investigación en Tecnoloxías da Información (CiTIUS),
Universidade de Santiago de Compostela, Spain
{andrea.cascallar.fuentes,alejandro.ramos,alberto.bugarin.diz}@usc.es
[2]Department of Computing Science, University of Aberdeen
alejandro.soto@abdn.ac.uk

Abstract

In this paper, we describe SimpleNLG-GL, an adaptation of the linguistic realisation SimpleNLG library for the Galician language. This implementation is derived from SimpleNLG-ES, the English-Spanish version of this library. It has been tested using a battery of examples which covers the most common rules for Galician.

1 Introduction

Realisation is the final task in natural language generation. Its goal is to ensure that well-formed texts are generated according to the grammar rules of the output language. Consequently, having tools that facilitate this task is desirable for any developer of a NLG system. For instance, templates are a widely-used realisation mechanism which is appropriate for many application domains, where generated texts are rather static.

Templates, however, are harder to maintain as they grow, and ensuring consistency among the elements of a realised template might become more difficult as more dynamic components appear. To address this kind of issues, other realisation tools pack language rules and syntactic structures to provide a framework for building well-formed sentences. This is the case of SimpleNLG, a Java realiser for English presented in (Gatt and Reiter, 2009) to facilitate realisation tasks. Some versions of this library have been created to support different languages: English-French (Vaudry and Lapalme, 2013), Italian (Mazzei et al., 2016), Brazilian Portuguese (de Oliveira and Sripada, 2014), German (Bollmann, 2011) and English-Spanish (Ramos-Soto et al., 2017). Other realisers described in the literature are Alethgen (Coch, 1996), FUF/SURGE (Elhadad and Robin, 1996), Real-Pro (Lavoie and Rainbow, 1997), KPML (Bateman, 1997), YAG (McRoy et al., 2000), HALogen (Langkilde-Geary, 2002) and OpenCCG (White, 2006).

This paper describes SimpleNLG-GL, a trilingual realisation tool for English, Spanish and Galician, derived from SimpleNLG-ES (Ramos-Soto et al., 2017). The Galician language is mainly spoken by approximately a million people in Galicia, NW of Spain. It is also closely related to the Portuguese language, since until the Middle Ages both were a single linguistic unit.

Given the closeness of Spanish and Galician, we decided to base this adaptation of SimpleNLG on the dual English-Spanish version. Nevertheless, Galician has a rich variety of specific features that clearly demanded a new adaptation of the library. Thus, we will also show some examples of the necessary steps to translate a phrase from Spanish to Galician, in order to illustrate the higher complexity that the Galician language has with respect to Spanish, and how this influenced our implementation of SimpleNLG-GL.

2 Covered subset of Galician

The Galician grammar used as reference is *"Normas ortográficas e morfolóxicas do idioma galego"* (Galega, 2012), which was created by the *Real Academia Galega* (Royal Galician Language Academy, founded 1906), a scientific institution whose objective is studying the Galician culture and, in particular, its language. This grammar was created to define the orthographic and morphological rules of the Galician language.

2.1 Lexicon

To create the lexicon used to develop this version of SimpleNLG, we chose the Galician dictionary provided by the FreeLing Project (Padró and Stanilovsky, 2012), an open source language

Proceedings of The 11th International Natural Language Generation Conference, pages 67–72,
Tilburg, The Netherlands, November 5-8, 2018. ©2018 Association for Computational Linguistics

analysis tool suite which provides some language analysis capabilities for a wide range of languages. This dictionary cannot be used directly by SimpleNLG, so we produced a compatible XML dictionary generated from the original file.

3 Features of the Galician language

In this section, we describe the most interesting features of the Galician language covered by the library, including syntax, orthography and morphology.

3.1 Syntax

3.1.1 Noun phrases

The structure of noun phrases is composed by a determiner, zero or one possessive, a noun and optionally one or more adjectives. When a phrase contains a possessive, in most cases it also includes a determiner (before). For instance, *"o meu fogar"* is translated as *"my home"* when *"o"* means *"the"*, *"meu"* means *"my"* (masculine) and *"fogar"* means *"home"*. Therefore, the literal translation is *"the my home"*. In a phrase with adjectives, the meaning of the phrase can slightly change depending on where the adjectives are placed (before or after the noun). Adjectives after the noun refer to features which were previously unknown by the speaker. However, if the adjective goes before the noun, the referred feature was already known. For instance, *"o novo fogar"* or *"o fogar novo"* mean *"the new home"*. To say *"his new home"* we can express it as *"o seu novo fogar"* or *"o seu fogar novo"*.

A specific feature when noun phrases are used as indirect objects is that a preposition *"a"*, which means *"to"*, is utilised before the phrase and a contraction is generated formed by that preposition and the phrase's determiner if applicable. For instance, *"Eu vin a Victoria"* means *"I saw Victoria"*. An example with contraction is *"Eu vin ao teu gato"*, translated as *"I saw your (male) cat"* when the preposition *"a"* and the masculine determiner *"o"* are contracted forming *"ao"*. Other example, with a feminine noun is *Eu vin á túa gata"* which means *"I saw your cat (female)"*.

3.1.2 Verb phrases

A general structure of verb phrases is composed by a subject, a verb and zero or more objects. However, in Galician there are sentences without a subject using the verb *"haber"* in its third person singular conjugation in the simple tense form *"hai"*,

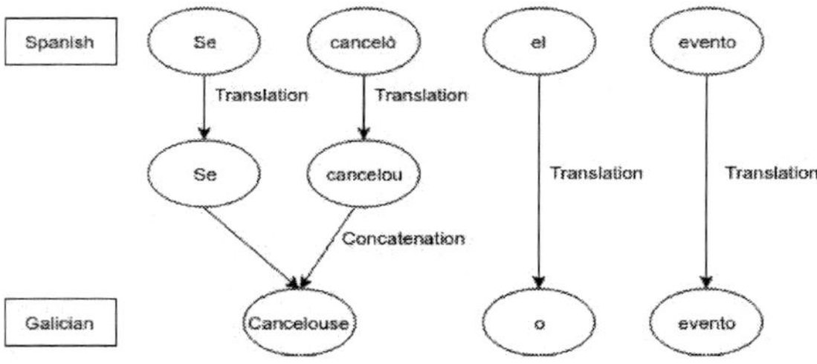

Figure 1: Steps to translate from Spanish to Galician language.

which means *"there is/are"*. For instance *"there is a cat on the tree"* would be expressed as *"hai un gato na árbore"*. Similarly, passive sentences are created adding the reflexive pronoun *"se"* connected to the verb and after it. For instance *"the event was cancelled"* can be expressed as *"cancelouse o evento"* (Figure 1).

A feature of the Galician language is the pronoun placement in relation to the verb when it is used as a direct or indirect object, either before or after the verb, appearing both combined in the latter case. This collocation depends on the sentence type, e.g., the pronoun is generally placed after the verb in affirmative sentences, whereas it is placed before it in negative sentences. For instance, *"el deume un regalo"* is translated as *"he gave me a present"*. In this case the verb is *"deu"* (*"gave"*) and the pronoun is *"me"*, which is combined with the verb. In a negative sentence, *"el non me deu un regalo"* translated as *"he did not give me a present"*, an the pronoun appears separately before the verb. To handle this feature, the library has to perform the following three tasks:

- Analyse the phrase type. The general rule is that pronouns are placed after the verb, however, we must analyse the phrase to determine its position. Some words change the verb's position as negation adverbs (*"non o vin"* which means *"I did not see it"*), doubt adverbs (*"quizais ela te chame mañá"* translated as *"maybe she calls you tomorrow"*), interrogative pronouns (*"que che pasou?"* which means *"what happened to you?"*).

- Split the verb into syllables. Adding the pronoun to the verb, its accentuation can change and an accent mark has to be added or moved if the verb has it. Therefore, we need to analyse the verb to find out its category according to where its strong syllable is. For instance,

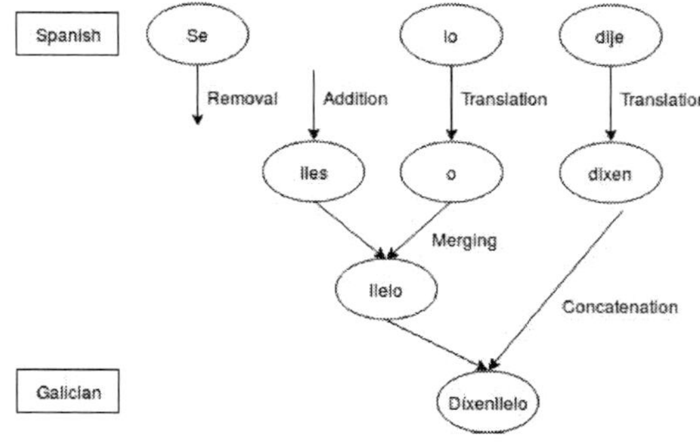

Figure 2: Steps to translate from Spanish to Galician language.

the form *"entendo"*, the first person singular conjugation in the present simple tense form of the verb *"understand"*, is split as *"en-ten-do"*.

- Accentuation. Once we know the verb's category, the last step is to concatenate the pronoun to the verb and to check the new word's accentuation, adding, moving or removing an accent mark. For instance, the first person singular conjugation in the past simple tense form *"dixen"* of the verb *"dicir"* (*"say"*) has the stress on its first syllable. If we add the pronoun *"lle"* expressed as *"to him"*, *"to her"* or *"to it"*, the composed word is *'díxenlle'*. If we add the contraction of pronouns (Table 6) *"llelo"*, composed by the pronoun *"lles"*, which means *"to them"*, and the pronoun *"o"*, which means *"it"*, the composed word is *"díxenllelo"* (Figure 2). The stress of the new words in these examples is also their first syllable. However, due to the Galician orthography rules, an accent mark (which is not present in the original word) has to be put on these first syllables.

More details about pronoun concatenation are given in Section 3.3.3.

3.1.3 Interrogative phrases

Interrogative phrases can be formed in many ways by simply adding the punctuation mark at the end of the sentence. For example, *"tes frío"* that means *"you are cold"* can be transformed into a question simply adding the punctuation mark *"tes frío?"* that means *"are you cold?"*.

When the interrogative pronouns *"what"* and *"who"* have the role of indirect objects, the preposition *"a"* is inserted in the beginning of the question. For instance, *"a quen chamaches?"* can be expressed as *"who did you call?"*.

3.2 Orthography

General Galician orthography rules (e.g. punctuation, capital letters at the beginning of sentences...) are like English and Spanish ones. This means that SimpleNLG already has them implemented.

As we mentioned before, Galician has special rules for word categorisation regarding their stress syllables. Besides, some words have accent marks on one vowel to stress the strong syllable. The entries in the lexicon we use contain accents according to the Galician orthography rules. However, it does not contain generated words formed by contractions, so we implemented the corresponding accentuation rules to handle these cases.

3.3 Morphology

3.3.1 Gender and number

Determiners, nouns and adjectives have to be inflected in gender and number. Our lexicon provides the base form of a word but not its gender and number variations so we had to implement some rules to generate them when they are regular.

3.3.2 Verb tenses

Verbs can be regular or irregular. We implemented some rules to generate regular forms, whereas irregular ones are provided by the lexicon.

3.3.3 Morphophonology

Galician is a very rich language in terms of its morphophonology rules. SimpleNLG-GL implements the contractions that exist between prepositions and articles, and also between pronouns when they function as direct and indirect objects.

Prepositions and articles: The prepositions shown in Table 1 can contract with definite articles, *"o"*, *"a"*, *"os"*, *"as"* which mean *"the"*, for instance *"o gato"* means *"the cat"*; and also indefinite articles, *"un"*, *"unha"*, *"uns"*, *"unhas"* which mean *"a"*, for instance, *"un gato"* means *"a cat"*. These contractions have the following meanings:

- *"a + definite article"* means *"to the"* whereas *"a + indefinite article"* means *"to a"*

Galician	English
a	to
con	with
de	of
en	in
por	by
tras	after

Table 1: Meaning of prepositions

		Articles			
		o	**a**	**os**	**as**
Prepositions	**a**	ao	á	aos	ás
	con	co	ca	cos	cas
	de	do	da	dos	das
	en	no	na	nos	nas
	por	polo	pola	polos	polas
	tras	tralo	trala	tralos	tralas

Table 2: Contractions between prepositions and definite articles

- *"con + definite article"* means *"with the"* whereas *"con + indefinite article"* means *"with a"*

- *"de + definite article"* means *"of the"* whereas *"de + indefinite article"* means *"of a"*

- *"en + definite article"* means *"in the"* whereas *"en + indefinite article"* means *"in a"*

- *"por + definite article"* can mean *"by the"* whereas *"por + indefinite article"* can mean *"by a"*

- *"tras + definite article"* can mean *"after the"* whereas *"tras + indefinite article"* can *"after a"*

In Tables 2 and 3 the contractions are shown.

Pronouns: The atonic pronouns having the role of indirect objects shown in Table 4 can also contract with others which have the role of direct objects which are shown in Table 5. For instance, the phrase *"El deumo"* (Figure 3) is expressed as *"He gave it to me"*, where *"deu"* means *"gave"* and

		Articles			
		un	**unha**	**uns**	**unhas**
Prepositions	**con**	cun	cunha	cuns	cunhas
	de	dun	dunha	duns	dunhas
	en	nun	nunha	nuns	nunhas

Table 3: Contractions between prepositions and indefinite articles

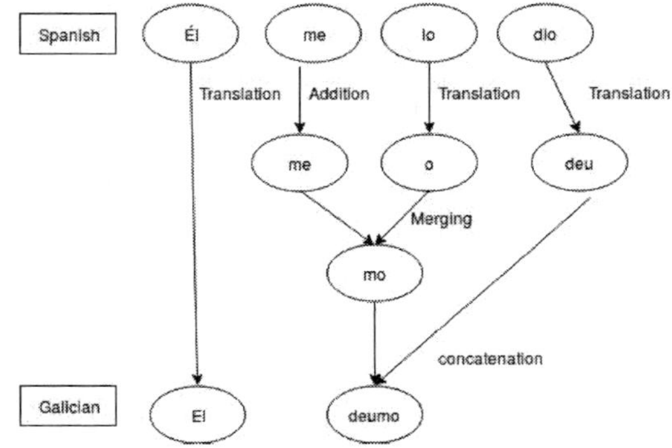

Figure 3: Steps to translate from Spanish to Galician language.

Galician	English
me	to me
che	to you (singular)
lle	to him/her/it
nos	to us
vos	to you (plural)
lles	to them

Table 4: Meaning of atonic pronouns with the role of indirect objects

"mo" is the contraction of *"me"* (*"to me"*) and *"o"* (*"it"*), respectively. In Table 6 all possible combinations are shown.

4 Availability, test and documentation

SimpleNLG-GL is available and fully downloadable at (Cascallar-Fuentes et al., 2018)

The documentation from SimpleNLG-ES has also been adapted to this version, and is also available at the library repository in the form of a wiki, as usual in SimpleNLG, which contains a tutorial with some examples.

SimpleNLG-GL has been tested using 180 unit tests adapted from SimpleNLG-ES. New tests have been generated to cover Galician language features not present in the Spanish language. We

Galician	English
o	him/it
a	her/it
os	them (masculine)
as	them (feminine)

Table 5: Meaning of atonic pronouns with the role of direct objects

	o	a	os	as
me	mo	ma	mos	mas
che	cho	cha	chos	chas
lle	llo	lla	llos	llas
nos	nolo	nola	nolos	nolas
vos	volo	vola	volos	volas
lles	llelo	llela	llelos	llelas

Table 6: Contractions between atonic pronouns

had to create new tests to cover the Galician language features previously described. For instance, we created 11 tests to cover contractions between all prepositions and articles, 4 tests to cover atonic pronouns collocation and 7 tests to cover contractions between atonic pronouns. Also, in some of the adapted tests from the Spanish version these features are present as well.

Besides, SimpleNLG-GL has been used in the real data-to-text service GALiWeather (Ramos-Soto et al., 2015), which generates daily weather forecasts for the Galician municipalities in the Website of the Galician Meteorological Agency (Agency). This service combines a template-based approach with the use of SimpleNLG-GL to generate correct sentences, in terms of the agreement between the elements of the phrase (for example, for choosing correct verb conjugations and ensuring gender and number coherence, among others).

5 Conclusions

We have described SimpleNLG-GL, an adaptation of the SimpleNLG Java realisation engine for Galician language, that provides a sophisticated covering of even the most complex rules found in this language. This library has been tested extensively using unit tests, 180 adapted from SimpleNLG-ES testing, whilst other 22 were newly developed for SimpleNLG-GL.

Acknowledgements

This research was supported by the Spanish Ministry of Economy and Competitiveness (grants TIN2014-56633-C3-1-R and TIN2017-84796-C2-1-R) and the Galician Ministry of Education (grants GRC2014/030 and "accreditation 2016-2019, ED431G/08"). All grants were co-funded by the European Regional Development Fund (ERDF/FEDER program). A. Ramos-Soto is funded by the "Consellería de Cultura, Educación e Ordenación Universitaria" (under the Postdoctoral Fellowship accreditation ED481B 2017/030).

References

Galician Meteorological Agency. Meteogalicia website. http://www.meteogalicia.gal. Accessed: 2018-09-26.

John A. Bateman. 1997. Enabling technology for multilingual natural language generation: the KPML development environment. *Natural Language Engineering*, 3(1):15–55.

Marcel Bollmann. 2011. Adapting SimpleNLG to German. In *Proceedings of the 13th European Workshop on Natural Language Generation*, pages 133–138. Association for Computational Linguistics.

Andrea Cascallar-Fuentes, Alejandro Ramos-Soto, and Alberto Bugarín. 2018. SimpleNLG-GL on CiTIUS GitHub. https://github.com/citiususc/SimpleNLG-GL. Accessed: 2018-09-26.

José Coch. 1996. Overview of AlethGen. In *Eighth International Natural Language Generation Workshop (Posters and Demonstrations)*, pages 25–28. Association for Computational Linguistics.

Michael Elhadad and Jacques Robin. 1996. An Overview of SURGE: a Reusable Comprehensive Syntactic Realization Component. In *Eighth International Natural Language Generation Workshop (Posters and Demonstrations)*, pages 1–4. Association for Computational Linguistics.

Real Academia Galega. 2012. Normas ortográficas e morfolóxicas do idioma galego. https://academia.gal/documents/10157/704901/Normas+ortogr%C3%A1ficas+e+morfol%C3%B3xicas+do+idioma+galego.pdf. Accessed: 2018-09-26.

Albert Gatt and Ehud Reiter. 2009. SimpleNLG: A Realisation Engine for Practical Applications. In *Proceedings of the 12th European Workshop on Natural Language Generation*, pages 90–93. Association for Computational Linguistics.

Irene Langkilde-Geary. 2002. An Empirical Verification of Coverage and Correctness for a General-Purpose Sentence Generator. In *Proceedings of the International Natural Language Generation Conference*, pages 17–24.

Benoit Lavoie and Owen Rainbow. 1997. A Fast and Portable Realizer for Text Generation Systems. In *Proceedings of the 15th conference on Applied natural language processing*, pages 265–268. Association for Computational Linguistics.

Alessandro Mazzei, Cristina Battaglino, and Cristina Bosco. 2016. SimpleNLG-IT: adapting SimpleNLG to Italian. In *Proceedings of the 9th International Natural Language Generation conference*, pages 184–192. Association for Computational Linguistics.

Susan Weber McRoy, Songsak Channarukul, and Syed S. Ali. 2000. YAG: A Template-Based Generator for Real-Time Systems. In *Proceedings of the 1st international conference on Natural language generation*, pages 264–267. Association for Computational Linguistics.

Rodrigo de Oliveira and Somayajulu Sripada. 2014. Adapting SimpleNLG for Brazilian Portuguese realisation. In *Proceedings of the 8th International Natural Language Generation Conference*, pages 93–94. Association for Computational Linguistics.

Lluís Padró and Evgeny Stanilovsky. 2012. Freeling 3.0: Towards wider multilinguality. In *Proceedings of the Eight International Conference on Language Resources and Evaluation (LREC'12)*, Istanbul, Turkey. European Language Resources Association (ELRA).

A. Ramos-Soto, J. Janeiro-Gallardo, and Alberto Bugarín. 2017. Adapting SimpleNLG to Spanish. In *10th International Conference on Natural Language Generation*, pages 144–148. Association for Computational Linguistics.

Alejandro Ramos-Soto, Alberto José Bugarín Diz, Senén Barro, and Juan Taboada. 2015. Linguistic descriptions for automatic generation of textual short-term weather forecasts on real prediction data. *IEEE Trans. Fuzzy Systems*, 23(1):44–57.

Pierre-Luc Vaudry and Guy Lapalme. 2013. Adapting simplenlg for bilingual english-french realisation. In *Proceedings of the 14th European Workshop on Natural Language Generation*, pages 183–187, Sofia, Bulgaria. Association for Computational Linguistics.

Michael White. 2006. CCG Chart Realization from Disjunctive Inputs. In *Proceedings of the Fourth International Natural Language Generation Conference*, pages 12–19. Association for Computational Linguistics.

Going Dutch: Creating SimpleNLG-NL

Ruud de Jong
Human Media Interaction
University of Twente
Enschede, The Netherlands
`r.f.dejong@utwente.nl`

Mariët Theune
Human Media Interaction
University of Twente
Enschede, The Netherlands
`m.theune@utwente.nl`

Abstract

This paper presents SimpleNLG-NL, an adaptation of the SimpleNLG surface realisation engine for the Dutch language. It describes a novel method for determining and testing the grammatical constructions to be implemented, using target sentences sampled from a treebank.

1 Introduction

SimpleNLG is a Java-based surface realisation library aimed at practical applications (Gatt and Reiter, 2009). It is meant to be simple to use, and in an architecture redesign in version 4 of the software it was also made easy for developers to alter its code. Over the years, SimpleNLG has been adapted for several languages other than English, such as German (Bollmann, 2011), Brazilian-Portuguese (De Oliveira and Sripada, 2014) and Italian (Mazzei et al., 2016).

In this paper we present a new version of SimpleNLG for surface realisation in Dutch, called SimpleNLG-NL. Like most adaptations for other languages, it is based on SimpleNLG-EnFr (Vaudry and Lapalme, 2013): a bilingual version of SimpleNLG that supports both English and French, based on SimpleNLG version 4.2. The architecture of SimpleNLG-EnFr was split into language independent and language dependent parts, making it relatively easy to add new languages.

As Dutch is closely related to German, Simple-NLG for German (Bollmann, 2011) might seem a more obvious starting point for SimpleNLG-NL. However, SimpleNLG for German is based on the differently structured version 3 of SimpleNLG, which made it unsuitable to build on.

This paper is structured as follows. In Section 2 we describe the method we used for developing SimpleNLG-NL, followed in Section 3 by an overview of the main characteristics of Dutch and how we implemented them. In Section 4 we present the current coverage of SimpleNLG-NL over a set of test sentences. We end with conclusions and directions for future work.

2 Method

Instead of following the structure of e.g., a grammar reference book for adapting the rules of SimpleNLG, we developed SimpleNLG-NL using target sentences sampled from a dependency treebank for Dutch. In SimpleNLG-IT (Mazzei et al., 2016) sentences from a dependency treebank were used as well, but only for evaluation purposes. For SimpleNLG-NL, we expanded their use to the development phase, using them in an iterative generate-evaluate-revise process.

For each sentence, the SimpleNLG input was written manually and the resulting realisation was compared with the target sentence. Differences between the realisation and the target sentence were analysed. Based on this, the relevant grammar rules were adapted for Dutch and missing lexicon entries were added. This process was repeated for each sentence, increasing the size of the covered grammar subset with each iteration.

The generate-evaluate-revise cycle was carried out in four rounds.

First round: In the first round we tried to reproduce 12 target sentences of increasingly higher word count. We assumed that increasing the word count would also increase the grammatical complexity of the sentence.

Second round: In the second round we applied unit tests to 37 short sentences that were manually written to test one feature of SimpleNLG-NL, or a combination of very few features. Features that were tested included basic verb inflec-

Proceedings of The 11th International Natural Language Generation Conference, pages 73–78,
Tilburg, The Netherlands, November 5-8, 2018. ©2018 Association for Computational Linguistics

tion, both regular and irregular, as well as adjectives and their inflection (10 sentences), morphology of different verb groups in multiple tenses (12 sentences) and syntax of negated sentences (5 sentences). Finally, 10 sentences were used to test interrogative sentence types.

Third round: In the third round we included two more sets of target sentences from the Dutch treebank. The first set consisted of 11 medium-length sentences (7-13 words). The second set consisted of 10 long sentences (14-20 words).

Fourth round: In the final round, 16 more unit tests were carried out. These were aimed at testing combinations of tenses, voices and verb form (perfect or simple). They were based on the same input sentence, which contained a subject, a verb and a direct object.

The test sentences for Rounds 1 and 3 were randomly selected from the Dutch Wikipedia corpus (100,000 sentences) available in Dact,[1] a viewer for Alpino corpora. Alpino is a dependency parser for Dutch (Bouma et al., 2001).[2] After a sentence was randomly picked, based on the word count needed for the current round, it was tested for two requirements: the sentence had to be grammatically correct and it should not contain direct speech. SimpleNLG does not support properly embedding direct speech in a sentence and neither would SimpleNLG-NL.

For each sentence that was selected, the input code for generation had to be written. We did this based on its dependency tree from the treebank, as generated by the Alpino parser. As the input for SimpleNLG is structured similar to a dependency tree, the Alpino trees could fairly easily be converted into input code. Similar to the conversion rules used in the evaluation of SimpleNLG-IT, when converting the dependency trees to SimpleNLG we kept the input isomorphic to the tree in terms of subject, object etc. We did not use canned text in the input (except for names and fixed multi-word expressions), and we did not provide information about word order or punctuation.

We started the creation of SimpleNLG-NL by cloning the French parts of SimpleNLG-EnFr. French was chosen because its features seemed more related to Dutch than the English features, in particular with respect to the more complex morphology of French and Dutch compared to English. Therefore, the first realisation results used French grammar rules. For the lexicon, we translated the closed classes from the French lexicon (106 entries). The open part of the lexicon started out empty; missing entries (for irregular word forms) were added as we went along. A full lexicon was created later, as described in Section 3.5.

3 Adaptations for Dutch

The main changes we made to SimpleNLG for surface realisation in Dutch are described in this section. As our main references for Dutch grammar and morphology we used the online linguistic resources Taalportaal[3] and e-ANS.[4]

3.1 Nouns

In Dutch, pluralisation of nouns almost always consists of adding either *-en* or *-s* as a suffix to the singular form. Which suffix to use is determined by the stress of the noun's last syllable: use *-en* when stressed; use *-s* when unstressed. However, since we do not have information on stress, and there are many exceptions to this rule, SimpleNLG-NL instead uses a set of word endings to determine when to use the *-s* suffix.[5] Other exceptions can be added to the lexicon. Dutch also has compound nouns. Compounds are currently treated as regular nouns. Because of that, pluralisation may result in an incorrect form if the compound is not in the lexicon and does not have one of the predetermined word endings described earlier. When adding plural suffixes, other morphological rules may apply to ensure the correct spelling of the surface form. Specifically, sometimes vowels need to be removed or consonants added to the noun stem.

3.2 Verbs

The following tenses have been implemented in SimpleNLG-NL: present simple, past simple, present perfect, past perfect, future and conditional. When inflecting verbs, SimpleNLG-NL first checks the lexicon for irregular verb forms. If none are found, it uses the rules for regular verbs. Inflections are based on the stem of the verb. For

---

[1]http://rug-compling.github.io/dact/
[2]http://www.let.rug.nl/~vannoord/alp/Alpino/

[3]http://www.taalportaal.org/
[4]http://ans.ruhosting.nl/e-ans/
[5]http://ans.ruhosting.nl/e-ans/03/05/03/body.html

example, past tense inflection involves adding the suffix *-te* if the stem ends in an unvoiced consonant; in all other cases *-de* is added. Similar to nouns, in some cases the spelling of the verb stem needs to be changed.

Auxiliary verbs have to be added in the future tense (*zullen* 'will') and the conditional tense (*zouden* 'would'). They are placed before the verb. The perfect form also requires one of two auxiliary verbs (*zijn* 'be' or *hebben* 'have'), which can be specified in the lexicon. Lastly, passive sentences require *zijn* 'be' to be added. When these features are combined, such as in a passive conditional perfect sentence, in the current version of the system this results in an incorrect order of auxiliary verbs. In some cases, one or more auxiliary verbs have to be placed after the main verb, but the system currently does not do this.

Separable Complex Verbs. In Dutch, a special group of verbs is that of the so-called *Separable Complex Verbs* (SCVs). An SCV is a verb that consists of a main verb and a prepended *preverb* (Booij and Audring, 2018). This preverb can be any word, but is often a preposition.

In the past and present simple tenses in main clauses, SCVs are split into their preverb and main verb, and their order is reversed. The main verb is inflected as it would if it were on its own. For example: *toekennen* in the third person present becomes *hij kent toe* ("he assigns"). The position of the preverb in the main clause is flexible: direct objects, indirect objects, prepositional phrases and even entire subclauses can be placed between the main verb and its preverb. In SimpleNLG-NL, we decided to position the preverb at the end of the sentence by default. In the perfect tenses and in subordinate clauses, the preverb attaches to the main verb. The main verb is inflected normally, and the preverb is prefixed to it after inflection. This results in, for example, *hij heeft toegekend* ("he has assigned") and *dat hij toekent* ("that he assigns").

The input for an SCV can be in either of two forms: *toe|kennen* or *toekennen*. The first input splits the verb *kennen* from the preverb *toe*. SimpleNLG-NL will then look for *kennen* in the lexicon and inflect it appropriately (either from lexicon data or regular verb rules). This is similar to how SimpleNLG for German deals with such verbs (Bollmann, 2011). In the second case, SimpleNLG-NL checks if the verb

is marked as an SCV in the lexicon using the `<preverb></preverb>` field. If it is not, SimpleNLG-NL tries to detect if the verb is an SCV based on a list of common SCV prefixes: *bij, in, na, uit, op, af, mee, tegen, tussen, terug, toe*. However, not all SCVs can be caught this way, as several verbs prefixed by a preposition are not SVCs, but look exactly like them with the difference being the stress. For example, *doorboren* (regular verb: 'pierce'; SVC: 'continue drilling') is only an SVC if the stress is on *door*.

3.3 Adjectives

Dutch adjectives can be used predicatively and attributively, with only the latter being supported by SimpleNLG and SimpleNLG-NL. Depending on the number and gender properties of the noun phrase, the adjective requires the suffix *-e*. Similar to nouns and verbs, in some cases the spelling of the stem needs to be changed.

Comparatives and superlatives are created with a suffix (*-er* or *-st*). In some cases, the adverbs *meer* ("more") or *meest* ("most") are used instead. In all cases, the adjective can be appended with the earlier mentioned *-e*. Comparative and superlative forms can be overwritten in the lexicon using the `<comparative></comparative>` and `<superlative></superlative>` fields.

3.4 Word order

SimpleNLG-NL uses the subject-verb-object order for main clauses and subject-object-verb for relative clauses and interrogative sentences. Exceptions are made for SCVs, as described in Section 3.2. The order of other constituents, specifically modifiers, can vary depending on many factors. Currently, SimpleNLG-NL allows for manipulating word order by specifying modifiers as 'premodifiers' or 'postmodifiers' in the input; otherwise, a default (and not always correct) word order is chosen.

3.5 Lexicon

A lexicon was created by parsing the Dutch pages of Wiktionary[6]. The content is licensed under the CC BY-SA 3.0 license[7], which makes it suitable for release with SimpleNLG-NL. This resulted in a lexicon containing 79437 entries (nouns, verbs, adverbs, adjectives and prepositions), including

---

[6]https://www.wiktionary.org/
[7]https://creativecommons.org/licenses/by-sa/3.0/deed

Sentence set	Sentences	Exact matches		Accepted as correct	
Round 1	12	8	66.7%	11	91.7%
Round 2	37	37	100.0%	37	100.0%
Round 3 (medium)	11	9	81.8%	9	81.8%
Round 3 (long)	10	5	50.0%	7	70.0%
Round 4	16	10	62.5%	10	62.5%
Total	86	69	80.2%	74	86.0%

Table 1: The final coverage of SimpleNLG-NL after development and testing. Generated sentences were "accepted as correct" if they met the criteria described in Section 4.

the closed part described in Section 2 and the entries added during the development rounds.

To accommodate making a choice in the trade-off between larger lexicons that take longer execution time and smaller lexicons that may miss required entries (cf. (De Oliveira and Sripada, 2014)), two smaller lexicons were generated based on subsets of the larger lexicon. The subsets were determined by matching the entries with word forms from a word frequency list based on Open-Subtitles.[8] Words in the frequency list can have multiple corresponding lexicon entries. The smallest lexicon, based on the top 1000 most frequent words, contains 3386 entries. The top 10,000 words result in 8600 entries. The full lexicon is over 10 MB, while the medium one is just over 1MB and the smallest is half of that. The choice of lexicon is based on scope and performance requirements. By default, SimpleNLG-NL uses the medium lexicon.

4 Evaluation

To determine the coverage of SimpleNLG-NL, each sentence generated in one of the four rounds described in Section 2 was judged on correctness. Since the number of sentences to be evaluated was small, using automated evaluation metrics such as BLEU (Papineni et al., 2002) would not have made much sense; moreover, these would not take into account that word order in Dutch is relatively free. Therefore we chose to manually evaluate the sentences.

We considered a sentence generated by SimpleNLG-NL to be generated "correctly" if the output met at least one of the following criteria:

- The output matched the target sentence exactly, including punctuation; or

[8]https://github.com/hermitdave/
FrequencyWords/

- The output only differed from the target in terms of punctuation (commas and quotation marks), with no change in meaning; or

- The output differed from the target in terms of word order, but without making the sentence unwellformed or causing a change in meaning.

The criteria are ordered by inclusiveness, with the first being the preferred outcome ("exact match"). The final coverage by SimpleNLG-NL of the test sentences according to these criteria, after all four rounds of generate-evaluate-revise, is shown in Table 1.

Results round 1: Out of 12 sentences, 11 were generated correctly (91.7%). The result counting only exact matches is 8 out of 12 (66.7%). Of the three accepted mismatches, one missed some non-mandatory commas, and two had acceptable differences in word order from their target sentences. (One lacked topicalisation, which is currently unsupported, and the other placed the past participle at the end of the sentence, a merely stylistic difference.) SimpleNLG-NL could not reproduce the longest sentence from Round 1 (26 words). This was due to several problems. First, SimpleNLG cannot handle clauses without verbs, in this case an enumeration ("tasks such as X, Y and Z"). Second, the sentence contained a verb cluster as well as an attributively used infinitive, neither of which SimpleNLG-NL could handle.

Results round 2: In Round 2, all 37 short test sentences were generated correctly, as exact matches (100%).

Results round 3: Of the 11 medium-length sentences, 9 were generated as exact matches (81.8%) and the same number were accepted as correct. The two incorrectly generated sentences both had problems with modifier ordering. Of the 10 long sentences, 7 were generated correctly (70.0%). This includes two sentences that did not match exactly. One accepted mismatch added an unnecessary (but acceptable) comma, the other positioned the preverb of an SCV at the end of the sentence. While that position is acceptable, it can be stylistically preferable to reduce the distance between the main verb and the preverb. However, SimpleNLG-NL does not yet support such a stylistic mechanism. The problems with the three incorrectly generated sentences involved incorrect ordering of modifiers and a verb cluster (*te gaan wonen*, lit. "to go live"), and lack of support for main clauses connected by a semi-colon.

Results round 4: Of the 16 varieties of the same sentence, 10 were generated as exact matches. There were no mismatches accepted as correct. The incorrect sentences all had an incorrect word order. Active sentences in the future perfect and the conditional tenses incorrectly positioned the auxiliary verb before the object. In passive sentences in the perfect form, the order of the verb and the two or three auxiliary verbs was incorrect (e.g., *zal zijn geweest gegooid* should be *zal gegooid zijn geweest* "will have been thrown").

Overall results: In total, 74 out of 86 test sentences (86.0%) were generated correctly. Of these, 69 (80.2%) are exact matches. If we only look at the 33 treebank sentences from Rounds 1 and 3, then 28 (84.8%) were generated correctly, with 22 (66,7%) exact matches. The open part of the lexicon gained 59 entries during the development rounds. Combined with the closed part, the final lexicon contained 165 entries. This lexicon was later replaced by a more extensive one, containing over 8000 entries (see Section 3.5).

5 Conclusions and Future Work

We have developed SimpleNLG-NL, a new version of SimpleNLG that is fit for surface realisation in Dutch. During the development process, the coverage of SimpleNLG-NL was gradually expanded by iteratively generating and testing on sentences from a Dutch treebank. Eventually, over 80% of the test sentences could be generated correctly, with a few acceptable differences in punctuation and word order. The issues with word order of auxiliary verbs will be addressed in future work.

Currently, word order can be altered with the use of premodifiers and postmodifiers. However, a better approach may be the one used in SimpleNLG for German, where Bollmann (2011) provided a feature to choose the desired word order. This also allows for easier sentence manipulation.

As the target sentences used for development and testing covered many different sentence structures, we believe the current grammatical coverage of SimpleNLG-NL is sufficient for simple surface realisation in Dutch. SimpleNLG-NL will be used in the POSTHCARD project[9] to realise (parts of) templates for dialogue generation, used to simulate conversations with patients suffering from Alzheimer's disease. The simulation aims to provide training for caregivers based on scenarios with a virtual Alzheimer's patient.

SimpleNLG is publicly available on Github.[10] Like SimpleNLG, SimpleNLG-NL is released under Mozilla Public License 1.1,[11] allowing for modification and commercial use. The SimpleNLG-NL code includes comments and Javadoc information that should make it easy to use and adapt. In addition, the SimpleNLG wiki[12] will be adapted for SimpleNLG-NL.

Acknowledgements

This research was carried out partially within the POSTHCARD project, funded by the European AAL programme (aal-call-2017-045). POSTHCARD is being made possible in The Netherlands by ZonMw, under project number 735170004.

References

Marcel Bollmann. 2011. Adapting SimpleNLG to German. In *Proceedings of the 13th European Workshop on Natural Language Generation (ENLG 2011)*, pages 133–138.

Geert Booij and Jenny Audring. 2018. Separable complex verbs (SCVs). Retrieved June 04, 2018 from http://www.taalportaal.org/taalportaal/topic/pid/topic-13998813296768009.

Gosse Bouma, Gertjan Van Noord, and Robert Malouf. 2001. Alpino: Wide-coverage computational analysis of Dutch. In *Computational Linguistics in the Netherlands 2000: Selected Papers from the Eleventh CLIN Meeting*, pages 45–59.

---

[9] `http://posthcard.eu`
[10] `https://github.com/rfdj/SimpleNLG-NL`
[11] `https://www.mozilla.org/en-US/MPL/`
[12] `https://github.com/simplenlg/simplenlg/wiki`

Rodrigo De Oliveira and Somayajulu Sripada. 2014. Adapting SimpleNLG for Brazilian Portuguese realisation. In *Proceedings of the 8th International Natural Language Generation Conference (INLG)*, pages 93–94.

Albert Gatt and Ehud Reiter. 2009. SimpleNLG: A realisation engine for practical applications. In *Proceedings of the 12th European Workshop on Natural Language Generation*, pages 90–93.

Alessandro Mazzei, Cristina Battaglino, and Cristina Bosco. 2016. SimpleNLG-IT: Adapting SimpleNLG to Italian. In *Proceedings of the 9th International Natural Language Generation conference*, pages 184–192.

Kishore Papineni, Salim Roukos, Todd Ward, and Wei-Jing Zhu. 2002. BLEU: a method for automatic evaluation of machine translation. In *Proceedings of the 40th annual meeting on association for computational linguistics*, pages 311–318.

Pierre-Luc Vaudry and Guy Lapalme. 2013. Adapting SimpleNLG for bilingual English-French realisation. In *Proceedings of the 14th European Workshop on Natural Language Generation*, pages 183–187.

Learning to Flip the Bias of News Headlines

Wei-Fan Chen[†]   **Henning Wachsmuth**[‡]   **Khalid Al-Khatib**[†]   **Benno Stein**[†]

[†] Bauhaus-Universität Weimar
Webis Group, Faculty of Media
<firstname>.<lastname>@uni-weimar.de

[‡] Paderborn University
Computational Social Science Group
henningw@upb.de

Abstract

This paper introduces the task of "flipping" the bias of news articles: Given an article with a political bias (left or right), generate an article with the same topic but opposite bias. To study this task, we create a corpus with bias-labeled articles from *allsides.com*. As a first step, we analyze the corpus and discuss intrinsic characteristics of bias. They point to the main challenges of bias flipping, which in turn lead to a specific setting in the generation process. The paper in hand narrows down the general bias flipping task to focus on bias flipping for news article *headlines*. A manual annotation of headlines from each side reveals that they are self-informative in general and often convey bias. We apply an autoencoder incorporating information from an article's content to learn how to automatically flip the bias. From 200 generated headlines, 73 are classified as understandable by annotators, and 83 maintain the topic while having opposite bias. Insights from our analysis shed light on how to solve the main challenges of bias flipping.

1 Introduction

News portals play a central role in our society in different ways: they keep people informed, bring essential topics into public discussions, and they gradually change the attitudes of communities. Noteworthily in this regard, recent studies have exposed various types of bias in the major media portals in the US (Groseclose and Milyo, 2005). For example, media is able to draw the attention to particular entities or events while ignoring others. Also, the selection of *what* to report about a specific entity (e.g., positive or negative facts) undoubtedly produces bias. And not least, the *way* in which news are phrased can emphasize a positive or a negative impression on certain entities and events.

Among these examples, one can argue that bias becomes more obvious when news articles discriminate against entities — particularly in political news. For illustration, consider the following two headlines on Trump recognizing Jerusalem as the capital of Israel, which have been taken from Fox News and New York Times respectively:

Why Trump is right in recognizing Jerusalem as Israel's capital

Trump is making a huge mistake on Jerusalem

While the two headlines describe the same event, they clearly convey a different stance on it. This difference in stance matches the observation that Fox News is considered to have a right-oriented bias, whereas the New York Times is rather seen as left in general.

To keep a news portal's bias uniform, copy editors possibly rewrite articles after receiving them from journalists or other sources (Einsohn, 2011). As a support of this process, but also as an element of the rhetorical machinery of forthcoming argumentation engines, an automatic "bias flipper" would be a very useful research tool. Moreover, a bias flipper would be helpful in practical application domains such as e-journalism, for instance, to automatically rewrite an article from Fox News and then report it on New York Times.

However, rewriting a text with an opposite bias is a challenging task. It requires to identify and to classify the bias (e.g., as left vs. right), which is anything but trivial. Taking a closer look into the example mentioned above, we also see that, without understanding how the bias is manifested in the texts and what the background of the event is, an automatic bias classifier and flipper will not achieve any reasonable performance.

Proceedings of The 11th International Natural Language Generation Conference, pages 79–88,
Tilburg, The Netherlands, November 5-8, 2018. ©2018 Association for Computational Linguistics

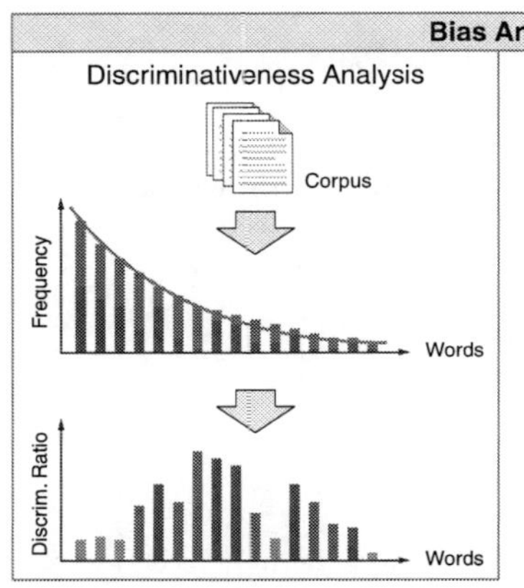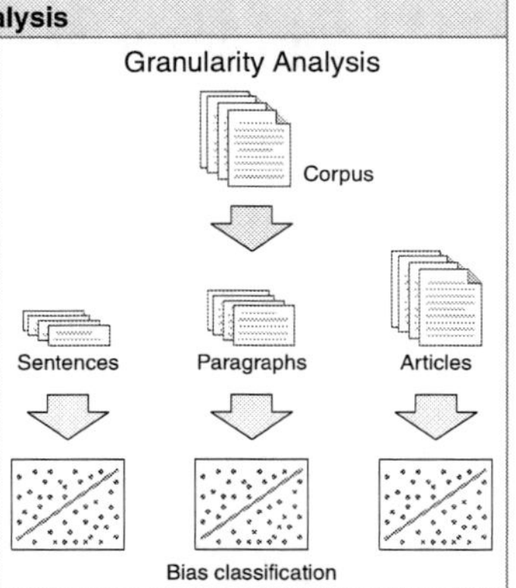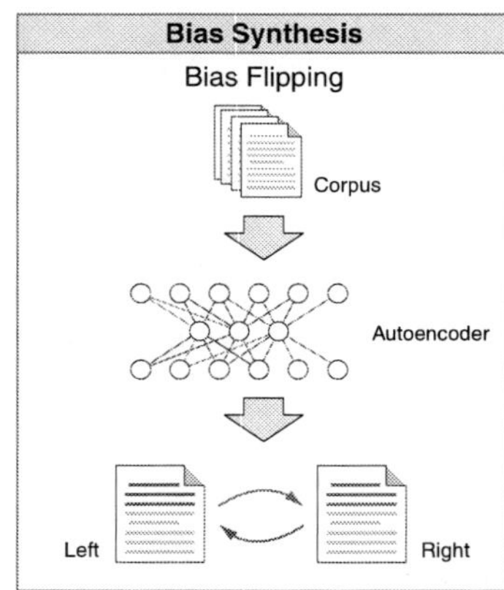

Figure 1: An overview of this paper. Left, we show the discriminativeness analysis of words in the biased text. In the middle, the granularity analysis trains three bias classifiers on different text segments. Right, we use biased articles to train a bias flipper based on autoencoder to flip the bias of headlines.

Accordingly, we approach the bias flipping task with a data-driven approach, addressing the following research questions: (1) How to acquire and sample a reasonable number of biased texts? (2) What kind of bias exists, and how is it manifested in the acquired texts? (3) Given biased texts and a mechanism to understand their bias, how far can we get using the current state-of-art text generation model in trying to flip the bias?

We tackle the first question by exploiting various sources on the web. In particular, we utilize the by-portal article-level bias labels found on *allsides.com*. This platform collects news articles that report on the same event while conveying different bias. Following the distant supervision paradigm, we build a new corpus of 2196 pairs of news article headlines, each of which addresses the same event and opposite bias (i.e., one headline is left-oriented, the other right-oriented).

Using the new corpus, we tackle the second question by analyzing the bias in several experiments (Section 4). Our analysis concentrates on the most discriminative words for identifying the bias, and on how bias is encoded along three granularities of text segments, i.e., in a full article, in a paragraph, and in a single sentence.

Our experiments yield insightful results: While sentimental words play a major role in identifying subjective texts, named entities are shown to be superior for distinguishing left-oriented from right-oriented texts. Moreover, bias often seems to be encoded at article or paragraph level only. In other words, it is hard to capture bias without reading at least a couple of sentences.

Our findings form the ground for tackling the third question, i.e., for developing the first "bias flipper" (Section 5). Considering the difficulty of the task, we focus on flipping news headlines, as a first substantial step in the direction of flipping complete articles. Accounting for recent advances on text generation using deep learning, we study the effectiveness of using autoencoders for flipping. An encoder conditioned on the source bias is used to encode the input text in the semantic representation, while a decoder conditioned on the target bias then decodes the representation into a new text.

We evaluate bias flipping automatically using the Rouge score and manually employing expert annotators. The results of both demonstrate the ability of our model to flip headlines successfully while maintaining the headlines' semantics.

An overview of all experiments carried out in this paper is shown in Figure 1. Our contribution is four-fold: We introduce a new natural language processing task, *bias flipping*; we develop a corpus for investigating this task; we analyze the bias in the developed corpus; and we apply an advanced deep learning model to flip the bias of news headlines. We observe that bias flipping and bias classification are still far from being solved. However, we believe that our bias analysis along with insights from the generation and evaluation experiments will shed light on how to deal with newspaper bias and possibly how to flip the bias of complete articles.

2 Related Work

This section reports on related work regarding the bias datasets, bias analysis, and bias flipping.

Bias Datasets To study the bias in the newspaper domain, several developed corpora include one or more label types related to bias. For example, the news quality corpus created by Arapakis et al. (2016) comprises 561 articles, each of which being labeled with 14 different quality aspects including article's subjectivity. Also, the MPQA corpus contains a label for the subjectivity of its 692 news articles (Wiebe et al., 2005). These two corpora were carefully developed with both article and sentence-level labels. However, they are not large enough to reliably train a supervised learning model.

Recently, a large-scale dataset has been released (Horne et al., 2018). The dataset allows for investigating the news based on various dimensions, including *bias* (the so-called "political impartiality prediction"). Although the dataset is pretty large, it has a major drawback concerning the bias dimension: The articles are not paired according to events, but such a pairing is essential for studying how different news sources report on the same event. To overcome this drawback, we develop a new corpus that aggregates pairs of articles from different news sources. The pairs report on the same event while their sources are said to have an opposite bias. We think that this event-controlled corpus will play a significant role in tackling the tasks of bias analysis and flipping.

Bias Analysis The analysis of media bias has been a subject of investigation for decades (Groseclose and Milyo, 2005; Fang et al., 2012; Arapakis et al., 2016). Various aspects of bias have been studied from different perspectives.

In particular, Groseclose and Milyo (2005) explored the bias on a sample of 20 news sources in the US. The bias was quantified based on the number of citations that were used by the think tanks and policy groups. Their work is one of the first that provided clear evidence of the presence of bias in media. Furthermore, Lin et al. (2011) proposed a scheme for bias categorization. The scheme includes the political party, frequently mentioned legislators, region, ideology, and gender. In a comparison study between the bias in news and blogs, the authors found blogs to be more sensitive to bursting events. In another related work, Yano et al. (2010) focused on liberal and conservative bias. Most notably, they conducted a manual annotation of the bias at the sentence-level. Their study showed that bias indicators usually include named entities of opposing bias. As for our work, we deal with right and left bias, e.g., the democrats' and republicans' bias, or conservative and liberal bias. Also, we conduct an analysis to find the terms that frequently indicate left or right bias.

Bias Flipping Over the few last years, several deep neural networks models have been proposed for text generation. In these models, a variational autoencoder (VAE) has often been used to impose a prior distribution on the hidden vector (Kingma and Welling, 2013; Rezende et al., 2014; Bowman et al., 2016; Yang et al., 2017).

A related research line that addresses rewriting texts is *controlled generation* (Guu et al., 2017; Mueller et al., 2017; Zhou and Neubig, 2017). Controlled generation studies how to rewrite a text with a given attribute. Examples of controlled models include the multi-space VAE of Zhou and Neubig (2017), which modifies a word for a given tense and a part-of-speech tag, and the model of Guu et al. (2017), which generates a sentence given a template vector and an edit vector. This model is shown to be able to paraphrase a given template instead of re-generating a sentence entirely.

Among the collection of VAE models, our work is most closely related to text style transfer (Shen et al., 2017; Hu et al., 2017; Li et al., 2018; Fu et al., 2018); The VAE of Hu et al. (2017) generates sentences with a given style aspect, such as a sentiment or tense. Moreover, the model of Shen et al. (2017) modifies the sentiment of restaurant reviews while aiming to preserve their meaning. However, none of these models has considered bias.

In contrast, this paper employs the cross-aligned autoencoder from Shen et al. (2017). The choice of this model was made based on the results we obtained in our analysis experiments. In particular, we "transfer" the bias of news article headlines using the content of the articles, i.e., we rewrite the headline while flipping the embedded bias from left to right or the other way round.

3 A Corpus of Biased News Articles

This section introduces our new corpus of news articles with different political bias, based on existing bias labels from a news aggregator. The corpus is freely available at `https://webis.de/data/corpus-webis-bias-flipper-18`.

3.1 The News Aggregator allsides.com

The news aggregation platform allsides.com lists news events as of June 1st, 2012; about two to three events per day, focusing on American politics. Each event comes with a title and a short summary, providing information to readers that is said to be free of bias. In addition, one selected news article is given for each of three biases: *left, center, right* (sometimes, only two articles are available).

The provided bias labels are not article-specific but portal-specific.[1] At the time we collected the data, 247 news portals were assigned one out of six labels each: *left, lean left, center, lean right, right,* and *mixed*. We see both the left and the lean left portals as left candidate news sources, and both the right and lean right portals as right candidate news sources. The center and mixed portals are preserved for future applications.

Since the labels are portal-specific, news articles with a particular bias are selected from all portals that have the respective label. Conversely, no portal contains articles with different biases.

3.2 Corpus Construction

We first collected all 2781 events available on the aggregator on February 10th, 2018 (spanning a period of about five and a half years).[2] For each event, the title, the summary, all news portals belonging to the event, and the links to the news portals with respective bias were recorded. After that, we crawled the news portals with the given links to retrieve their headlines and the content of all articles, because the content is not provided on allsides.com. Metadata such as an article's author and its publication time were also collected for future applications. Since some news articles were not available anymore, we retrieved 6447 news articles in the end.

3.3 Corpus

The distribution of news portals and articles in our corpus is shown in Table 1. To validate the accuracy of the by-portal bias, we asked one editing expert to label the bias of all headlines from major left-oriented (New York Times and Huffington Post) and right-oriented portals (Fox News and Townhall). The expert is familiar with American politics and he works as a news editor in the US. His labels are based on the headline only, and the

[1] https://www.allsides.com/media-bias/media-bias-ratings

[2] https://www.allsides.com/story-list

Bias	News Portals		News Articles	
	Most Common	Total	Most Common	Total
Left	Huffington Post	21	479	641
Lean left	NY Times	18	688	1747
Center	CNN (web)	24	776	1517
Lean right	Fox News	6	1061	1616
Right	Townhall	28	279	926

Table 1: News portals and articles in our corpus for each bias in total and in the most common portal.

judgments follow the notion of political bias from an American's point of view.

The expert assigned *left* to the headlines of left-oriented portals 3.4 times more than *right*, while the headlines from right-oriented portals have 1.9 times *right* more than *left*. Given that we only looked at the headlines, we conclude that the by-portal labels from the aggregator seem trustable.

The portal labels on allsides.com are created based on different methods including blind surveys, academic research, feedback from the community, and in-depth editorial reviews from allsides.com editors[3]. The final portal labels consider the strength and the consistency of the labels from the different methods. The most common portal contributes at least 30 percent of articles of each bias. The total number of right-oriented news slightly exceeds the number of left-oriented (2542 vs. 2388).

According to the community feedback on the website, the provided labels are agreed by the website's users in general. Thus, we argue that the labeling can be seen as being of high quality.

4 Bias Analysis

In this section, we describe experiments for analyzing biased text, whose results will later be discussed in Section 6. As in the example in Section 1, we observe that bias can be found if we can identify sentiment towards a given entity. Hence, it is worth studying whether the application of sentiment analysis techniques helps on biased text. We seek to identify words which discriminate either sentimental or biased text, and to classify the type of bias using standard features from sentiment analysis.

4.1 Discriminativeness Analysis

We capture the fundamental difference between biased and sentimental text based on the words that

[3] https://www.allsides.com/media-bias/media-bias-rating-methods

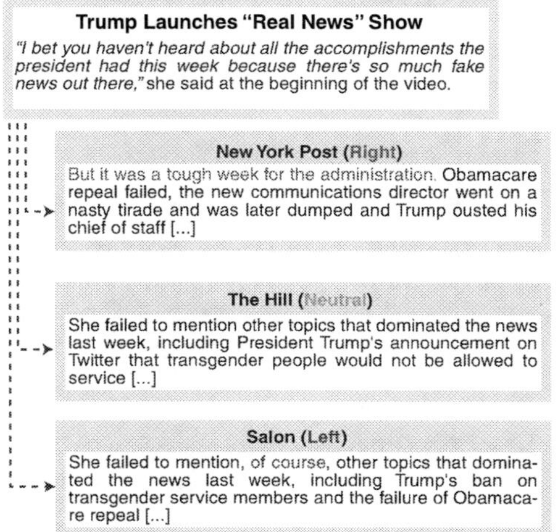

Figure 2: Three news articles on the event *Trump launches "real news" show*. Some bias indicators in the articles are highlighted. Representing three different points of view, the articles provide completely different interpretations of the event.

discriminate the two respective types best. Specifically, the discriminativeness of a word w can be measured in terms of the *discriminativeness ratio*

$$\frac{occ(w, D_t)}{occ(w, D_{\bar{t}})}, \tag{1}$$

where $occ(w, D)$ is the frequency of w in text D and t and $\bar{t}$ are the types of text. In biased text, t and $\bar{t}$ correspond to *right* and *left*. In sentimental text, t and $\bar{t}$ are *positive* and *negative* respectively. We normalize the occurrence by the total numbers of words of the respective type of texts.

The discriminativeness ratio will make function words and type-unrelated words have values close to one, because these words are expected to occur similarly often in both types. On the other hand, words that often appear in one type but rarely in the other will have a high value (in case of type t) or a low value (type $\bar{t}$). To demonstrate the differences in discriminativeness ratios, we analyze biased texts from the corpus introduced in the previous section and compare them to sentimental texts from the public yelp review corpus.[4]

4.2 Granularity Analysis

As in the example shown in Figure 2, we are also aware that some biased text segments can be identified just by looking at its preceding and/or following segments. In this figure, all three sources quote

---

[4]https://www.yelp.com/dataset

the same utterance, and later give three different interpretations in order to comment on why the woman referred to failed to mention some weakness points of the president during the show. The sentences by The Hill and by Salon are almost the same, but the phrase *of course* in the Salon article is an obvious clue of political bias in it. In contrast, the New York Post gives a reason to explain why the woman failed.

To account for such observations, we train bias models for classifying left and right, based on different lengths of text segments. For each model, we use a support vector machine with word trigram features—a standard yet powerful baseline in sentiment analysis (Liu and Zhang, 2012).

We use the left-right article pairs along with their label from the aggregator as the gold standard. To know whether bias is already recognizable in short text segments, we train and test the model on the article, the paragraph, and the sentence level (for uniform handling, a paragraph is approximated as a continuous sequence of 10 sentences). In case bias is less clear in smaller text segments, we should see a lower classification performance in the paragraph and sentence level results.

We point out, though, that other factors besides this *cross-segment* bias, can influence the performance as well. For example, the different writing style of portals may play an important role, because our dataset is dominated by certain portals (see Table 1). To account for this factor, we decided to upsample our data to balance sources. Since some portals appear only a few times in our dataset, we upsampled only the top-10 most frequent sources in both left and right text.

We expect the performance of classification after the conducted upsampling to be lower than before. However, we should be able to figure out that the performance of smaller text is lower.

5 Bias Flipping

In this section, we introduce a model from related work to generate right-biased headlines given left-biased headlines and vice versa. However, we observed that not all headlines in our corpus show bias. To enrich bias information in the training set, we added the content of each article, split into sentences. We use these sentences as supplemental information during learning. Since we do not have a "flipped" version of each sentence in the content, we do not use the content for the validation and test set, and we evaluate the results only based on the headlines. Knowing that two sentences in a training pair may have different semantics, we need a model that learns to flip bias, but at the same time infers the semantics of a sentence.

Formally, given a source sentence s_o along with its bias label b_o and its content z_o, during training, our goal is to generate the target sentence s_t with label b_t and content z_t, while z_o and z_t could be different. We are interested in flipping the bias from b_o to b_t and from b_t to b_o, so we train two encoders $E(s_k, b_k)$, $k \in \{o, t\}$, that learn to infer z_k:

$$z_k \sim E(s_k, b_k) \tag{2}$$

Analogously, we train two generators G to generate s_k given b_k and z_k:

$$\hat{s}_k \sim G(z_k, b_k) = p(s_k|b_k, z_k) \tag{3}$$

Given the parameters in E and G, θ_E and θ_G, the two autoencoders (one flips from source to target, the other from target to source) are then optimized to minimize the reconstruction error from s_k to $\hat{s}_k$:

$$\mathcal{L}_{rec}(\theta_E, \theta_G) = \mathbb{E}_{s_k \sim S_k}[-\log p(s_k|s_k, E(s_{\bar{k}}, b_{\bar{k}}))],$$

where $\bar{k}$ is o when k is s, and $\bar{k}$ is s when k is o.

As in other generative approaches, we also learn to maximize the loss of the adversarial discriminator as follows:

$$\mathcal{L}_{adv} = -\log D_k(s_k)] - \mathbb{E}[\log -D_k(\hat{s}_{\bar{k}}))], \tag{4}$$

where D_k is the discriminator used to distinguish s_k from the flipped version $s_{\bar{k}}$.

Finally, the loss function aims to minimize the loss from reconstruction and the adversarial discriminators from two directions:

$$\mathcal{L}_{rec_{o \to t}} + \mathcal{L}_{rec_{t \to o}} - (\mathcal{L}_{adv_{o \to t}} + \mathcal{L}_{adv_{t \to o}}),$$

where $o \to t$ means flipping from source to target and $t \to o$ from target to source. To train the model, the architecture of Shen et al. (2017) fits our needs (see Section 2). We thus replicate their cross-alignment setting: During training, we choose the same number of left and right sentences randomly and then train the autoencoder from two directions in one batch. Even though the pairing information is saved by this architecture, the results are promising: Modifying the sentiment while maintaining semantics worked correctly in 41.5% of all cases.

		Same Event (Q3)			
		Same	Changed	Not Sure	All
Bias (Q4)	Flipped	57	1	0	58
	Same	28	1	0	29
	Not Sure	10	1	2	13
	All	95	3	2	100

Table 2: Counts of all possible combinations in the manual evaluation of whether the ground-truth headlines capture the same event with flipped bias.

Besides, generative models are known to often produce *UNK* (the out-of-vocabulary word), which is especially harmful in understanding the meaning of short sentences, as given in our task. In order to reduce the frequency of *UNK* in the generated outputs, we set the size of beam search to 10, and keep the candidates with the fewest *UNK*.

6 Results and Discussion

In this section, we try to answer our three research questions from Section 1 by analyzing the results of our experiments. Firstly, to study the appropriateness of our corpus for the given task, we verify that the corpus headlines are informative and have the expected bias. Then, we discuss the result of bias analysis. Later, we evaluate headlines generated by the approach against this ground-truth, both automatically and manually. Finally, a general discussion of the bias flipping task is given.

6.1 Ground-truth Headlines

From our corpus, we took all 2196 opposite headline pairs *(left-oriented, right-oriented)*. Both headlines of a pair are about the same event. We randomly selected 100 pairs as the validation set, another 100 pairs as the test set, and the remaining as the training set. To verify the test set, we hired three experts in journalism editing to annotate all 100 test pairs. For each pair, the annotators had to answer four questions:

Q1. Do you understand headline 1?
{*yes* | *partially yes* | *no* | *not sure*}

Q2. Do you understand headline 2?
{*yes* | *partially yes* | *no* | *not sure*}

Q3. Do both headlines report on the same event?
{*same* | *mostly same* | *changed* | *not sure*}

Q4. Do the headlines have opposite bias?
{*flipped* | *partially flipped* | *same* | *not sure*}

Sentimental Text		Biased Text	
Word	**Ratio**	**Word**	**Ratio**
excellent	220.22	Chad	9.52
gem	183.99	Maduro	5.56
wonderful	183.66	purportedly	7.81
delicious	156.72	Chechnya	6.80
fantastic	142.52	Bethlehem	6.04
...	...	...	...
mushrooms	1.01	victorious	1.01
breadsticks	1.01	oppressive	1.01
dresser	0.99	tragedy	0.99
...	...	...	...
unfortunately	< 0.01	Shawn	0.04
terrible	< 0.01	incarceration	0.04
rude	< 0.01	album	0.03
horrible	< 0.01	valuable	0.03
worst	< 0.01	N.S.A	0.02

Table 3: The five words each with the highest and lowest discriminativeness ratio, and words with a ratio close to one, in sentimental and in biased text.

Text segment	Original	Source-normalized
Article	0.94	0.89
Paragraph	0.82	0.73
Sentence	0.76	0.59

Table 4: Bias classification accuracies on different size of text segments, once on the original data and once for normalized (upsampled) sources.

		Same Event (Q3)			
		Same	**Changed**	**Not Sure**	**All**
Bias (Q4)	**Flipped**	83	17	4	104
	Same	21	10	0	31
	Not Sure	23	33	9	65
	All	127	60	13	200

Table 5: Counts of all combinations in the manual evaluation of the generated compared to the ground-truth headlines in terms of event and bias.

The resulting Fleiss' κ values were 0.97 (Q1), 0.97 (Q2), 0.62 (Q3), and 0.30 (Q4). All annotators understood almost all headlines, except for one with only two words: "Lerner speaks". The agreement for Q3 was substantial and fair for Q4. Majority voting was used for the final decision.

Table 2 shows the annotations of Q3 and Q4, combining *same* and *mostly same* for Q3, and *flipped* and *partially flipped* for Q4. From the 100 pairs, 95 were labeled as being on the same event, while only five pairs confused the annotators. For the bias label, 58 headline pairs have opposite bias, while the rest did not show any clear difference.

6.2 Bias Analysis

In Table 3, we list the words having the highest and the lowest discriminativeness ratio in sentimental and in biased text respectively. We see that, the top-5 words in sentimental text are positive words and the bottom-5 words are negative words. Entities such as *mushrooms* or *dresser* have values close to one. The results fit the intuition that people usually use positive words in a positive review, such as "great breakfast place", and negative words in a negative review. While sometimes negative expressions use positive words by negating ("my experience here was not great at all"), the ratio of words clearly shows this tendency.

In contrast, we observe that this is not the case in biased text. There, both positive and negative sentiment words have a frequency ratio close to one. This is expected, because we observe that both sides use positive (negative) words to support

(oppose) some entities. Moreover, many of the top-5 and the bottom-5 words are named entities, such as *Maduro* and *N.S.A*. This indicates that articles with either bias tend to criticize or approve different entities, but that they do not use different sentiment words to do so. In line with this, a previous analysis on bias language showed that many bias indicators include named entities (Yano et al., 2010).

The results of bias classification is shown in Table 4, and the distribution of bias is balanced. In general, we observe that bias classification on the article level appears not to be very difficult. Even though we only employ rather simple models and features, we achieve a very high accuracy of 0.94. Also, the shorter the segments that we use for training and testing, the lower the classification performance we get (although it always remains higher than chance). As expected, when we upsample the sources, performance is reduced. However, our hypothesis is still supported: a part of bias is conveyed by longer text segments only.

6.3 Generated Headlines

Besides the model we propose in the paper, we also experimented with other approaches that generate a text given another text. Specifically, we tried (1) training our model only with headline pairs, (2) the pointer generator (See et al., 2017) trained only with headline pairs, and (3) the sentiment and style transfer from Li et al. (2018). The pointer generator originally focuses on abstractive summarization where it achieved high Rouge scores. It learns to copy words from the source to han-

Ground-truth headline pair		Generated versions of the headlines		Evaluation	
Headline	Bias	Headline	Bias	Event	Bias
John McCain urges republicans not to filibuster gun control.	left	*John McCain has elected to avoid gun control.*	right	same	flipped
White House looks to salvage gun-control legislation.	right	*White House got to get bipartisan change.*	neutral	mostly same	partially flipped
Obama accepts nomination, says his plan leads to a "better place".	left	*Obama blasted re-election, saying it a "very difficult" to go down.*	right	mostly same	flipped
Lackluster Obama: change is hard, give me more time.	right	*Real GOP: debate is right, and more Trump.*	left	changed	flipped

Table 6: Two left-right headline pairs, along with the rewritten versions generated by our approach. The bias of the ground-truth headlines is given in our corpus. The bias of the generated headlines is from the human annotators.

dle out-of-vocabulary issues. The sentiment and style transfer focuses on detecting the attribute (the sentiment words for instance), trying to alter it by looking for the best candidates in a corpus.

However, even when fine-tuning their parameters, neither of these approaches generated readable outputs. Mostly, they just repeated words or phrases, such as in "the the the" or "trump he same he for trump". So, without sufficient content in the training data, it seems hard to obtain a language model that generates meaningful sentences.

In particular, the pointer generator requires paired training samples, hence training with sentences from the content is not possible. The sentiment and style transfer does not require paired training samples, but its attribute detection mechanism requires an unequal distribution of sentiment words. From the experiment in bias analysis, we know that this assumption does not hold in our corpus. The model described in the approach section is an end-to-end model without any strong assumption. Although it has higher amount of parameters, it can produce more readable sentences.

For automatic evaluation, we measured the similarity between the generated and the ground-truth headlines via Rouge-1, Rouge-2, and Rouge-L, resulting in F-scores of 15, 3, and 12. In an additional manual evaluation, another three editing experts answered Q2 to Q4 by comparing the original and generated headlines, with a Fleiss' κ of 0.61 (Q2), 0.51 (Q3), and 0.29 (Q4). Out of 200 generated headlines (100 left-to-right, 100 right-to-left), 73 were seen as understandable (Q2), which we see as a good result for a generative model. For Q3 and Q4, Table 5 details the results. For those headlines, where the content was kept (127), the bias was flipped in 83 cases (65%). Even for those with changed meaning, 28% got the opposite bias.

6.4 Analysis

Table 6 shows selected pairs of ground-truth and generated headline. They demonstrate that our model keeps the event similar by using the same words, and flips bias by replacing or adding bias words. The generated headlines contain some grammar errors, but we see these as tolerable in machine-generated text on limited data.

In the first pair, the original headline states that McCain was pro gun control, while the rewritten one implies he was against — a successful flip. The ground-truth bias-flipped headline in the second row mostly uses other words while being pro gun control. The generated headline also keeps most words, but turns out rather neutral. In the second pair, the original headline shows a positive opinion on Obama, the generated headline a negative opinion on him. When rewriting the ground-truth bias-flipped headline (last row), the meaning is not kept. However, it is visible that the generated headlines is pro Trump.

We point out that there is a difference between bias flipping and fact changing. For example in the first pair, without knowing what John McCain stood for, we could neither guess his real opinion on gun control nor could we conclude what he supported or not. In fact, bias can be conveyed by emphasizing facts supporting a claim, as well as by hiding facts attacking a claim. In other words, we might see different facts about the same event with different types of bias. A news headline may be a conclusion, while the news content shows the facts supporting this conclusion. In such cases, no computational model will be able to flip the content only using the text itself, as it is hardly possible to simply generate new facts. Including more articles reporting on the same event will be useful to help the model learn the unseen information. We see this as future work on article-level bias flipping.

Finally, we found that an automatic evaluation of bias flipping is limited. In the discussed examples, we see that even for a successful flipping, the overlapping of generated and ground-truth headlines are very low. In fact, the successful cases have a mean Rouge-1 score of 17, unsuccessful ones of 15. Furthermore, if we divide the test pairs into those labeled as *same event* and *flipped bias* (57 pairs) and the rest (43), we find that the former are more often rewritten successfully (43% vs. 20%). This suggests that filtering out noisy cases with the help of experts will help improve the performance.

7 Conclusion

This paper has introduced the challenging task of rewriting news articles with flipped political bias as well as a bias-labeled corpus to study the task. As a first step, we have tackled the analysis of biased text and compared biased with sentimental text. We have found that (1) the types of discriminative words for biased and sentimental text are entirely different, and (2) some bias is visible on paragraph level only or even article level only. We have then applied a cross-aligned autoencoder to rewrite article headlines with flipped bias, incorporating content information from the article. Our experiments suggest that current state-of-the-art approaches struggle with this task. While our best tested model performed considerably well, there is still much room for improvement. Regarding the evaluation of the model, the Rouge score turned out insufficient to assess bias flipping quality.

In the future, we aim to employ the knowledge from bias analysis in the generation process, to rethink existing automatic evaluation metrics, and to study how to flip the bias of complete articles.

References

Ioannis Arapakis, Filipa Peleja, Barla Berkant, and Joao Magalhaes. 2016. Linguistic benchmarks of online news article quality. In *Proceedings of the 54th Annual Meeting of the Association for Computational Linguistics (Volume 1: Long Papers)*, volume 1, pages 1893–1902.

Samuel R. Bowman, Luke Vilnis, Oriol Vinyals, Andrew M. Dai, Rafal Józefowicz, and Samy Bengio. 2016. Generating sentences from a continuous space. In *CoNLL 2016*, pages 10–21.

Amy Einsohn. 2011. *The copyeditor's handbook: A guide for book publishing and corporate communications*. University of California.

Yi Fang, Luo Si, Naveen Somasundaram, and Zhengtao Yu. 2012. Mining contrastive opinions on political texts using cross-perspective topic model. In *Proceedings of the fifth ACM international conference on Web search and data mining*, pages 63–72. ACM.

Zhenxin Fu, Xiaoye Tan, Nanyun Peng, Dongyan Zhao, and Rui Yan. 2018. Style transfer in text: Exploration and evaluation. In *Proceedings of the Thirty-Second Conference on Artificial Intelligence*.

Tim Groseclose and Jeffrey Milyo. 2005. A measure of media bias. *The Quarterly Journal of Economics*, 120(4):1191–1237.

Kelvin Guu, Tatsunori B Hashimoto, Yonatan Oren, and Percy Liang. 2017. Generating sentences by editing prototypes. *arXiv preprint arXiv:1709.08878*.

Benjamin D Horne, William Dron, Sara Khedr, and Sibel Adali. 2018. Sampling the news producers: A large news and feature data set for the study of the complex media landscape. *arXiv preprint arXiv:1803.10124*.

Zhiting Hu, Zichao Yang, Xiaodan Liang, Ruslan Salakhutdinov, and Eric P Xing. 2017. Toward controlled generation of text. In *International Conference on Machine Learning*, pages 1587–1596.

Diederik P Kingma and Max Welling. 2013. Auto-encoding variational bayes. In *The 2nd International Conference on Learning Representations*.

Juncen Li, Robin Jia, He He, and Percy Liang. 2018. Delete, retrieve, generate: A simple approach to sentiment and style transfer. In *North American Association for Computational Linguistics*.

Yu-Ru Lin, James P. Bagrow, and David Lazer. 2011. More voices than ever? quantifying media bias in networks. In *Proceedings of the Fifth International Conference on Weblogs and Social Media*.

Bing Liu and Lei Zhang. 2012. A survey of opinion mining and sentiment analysis. In *Mining text data*, pages 415–463. Springer.

Jonas Mueller, David Gifford, and Tommi Jaakkola. 2017. Sequence to better sequence: continuous revision of combinatorial structures. In *International Conference on Machine Learning*, pages 2536–2544.

Danilo Jimenez Rezende, Shakir Mohamed, and Daan Wierstra. 2014. Stochastic backpropagation and approximate inference in deep generative models. In *Proceedings of the 31th International Conference on Machine Learning*, pages 1278–1286.

Abigail See, Peter J. Liu, and Christopher D. Manning. 2017. Get to the point: Summarization with pointer-generator networks. In *Proceedings of the 55th Annual Meeting of the Association for Computational Linguistics*, pages 1073–1083.

Tianxiao Shen, Tao Lei, Regina Barzilay, and Tommi Jaakkola. 2017. Style transfer from non-parallel text by cross-alignment. In *Advances in Neural Information Processing Systems*, pages 6833–6844.

Janyce Wiebe, Theresa Wilson, and Claire Cardie. 2005. Annotating expressions of opinions and emotions in language. *Language resources and evaluation*, 39(2-3):165–210.

Zichao Yang, Zhiting Hu, Ruslan Salakhutdinov, and Taylor Berg-Kirkpatrick. 2017. Improved variational autoencoders for text modeling using dilated convolutions. In *Proceedings of the 34th International Conference on Machine Learning*, pages 3881–3890.

Tae Yano, Philip Resnik, and Noah A Smith. 2010. Shedding (a thousand points of) light on biased language. In *Proceedings of the NAACL HLT 2010 Workshop on Creating Speech and Language Data with Amazon's Mechanical Turk*, pages 152–158. Association for Computational Linguistics.

Chunting Zhou and Graham Neubig. 2017. Multi-space variational encoder-decoders for semi-supervised labeled sequence transduction. In *Proceedings of the 55th Annual Meeting of the Association for Computational Linguistics*, pages 310–320.

Stylistically User-specific Response Generation

Abdurrisyad Fikri   **Hiroya Takamura**   **Manabu Okumura**
Department of Information and Communications Engineering
Tokyo Institute of Technology, Japan
`fikri@lr.pi.titech.ac.jp`, `{takamura, oku}@pi.titech.ac.jp`

Abstract

Recent neural models for response generation show good results in terms of general responses. In real conversations, however, depending on the speaker/responder, similar utterances should require different responses. In this study, we attempt to consider individual user's information in adjusting the notable sequence-to-sequence (seq2seq) model for more diverse, user-specific responses. We assume that we need user-specific features to adjust the response and we argue that some selected representative words from the users are suitable for this task. Furthermore, we prove that even for unseen or unknown users, our model can provide more diverse and interesting responses, while maintaining correlation with input utterances. Experimental results with human evaluation show that our model can generate more interesting responses than the popular seq2seqmodel and achieve higher relevance with input utterances than our baseline.

1   Introduction

Human-computer conversation is a challenging task in Natural Language Processing (NLP). The aim of conversation models is to generate fluent and relevant responses given an input in a free format, *i.e.,* not just in the form of a question. A large amount of available data on the Internet has sparked the shift in conversation models. Starting with Ritter et al. (2011), completely data-driven models are now commonly used to generate responses. Furthermore, the sequence-to-sequence (seq2seq) model initiated by Sutskever et al. (2014) has been adapted to many NLP tasks,

input	*how are you ?*
user1	*good morning how are you*
user2	*i'm doing ok*
user3	*i'm good ! ! !*
user4	*not really good*
input	*i am excited !*
user1	*are you sure ? !*
user2	*come to the party ?*
user3	*yay ! ! !*
user4	*are you gonna do it ?*

Table 1:   Sample responses from our proposed model involving four different users.

notably to machine translation (MT) and response generation.

Actual conversations involving humans would be more engaging and the responses are not always general and monotonic. However, neural conversation models tend to generate safe, general, and uninteresting responses, *e.g.,* *I don't know* or *I'm OK* (Sordoni et al., 2015; Vinyals and Le, 2015; Li et al., 2016b). We argue that, aside from adding or understanding the context of a conversation, speaking style and response diversity also play an important role in delivering a more interesting conversation.

Recent studies addressed the response diversity and engagement issues and have attempted to generate responses better than the common and general ones. Some tackled this issue by defining and emphasizing context; previous utterances are commonly used as context in a conversation (Sordoni et al., 2015; Li et al., 2016a). Other studies have attempted to diversify or manipulate responses using specific attributes such as user identification (Li et al., 2016b), profile information sets (Zhang et al., 2018; Wang et al., 2017; Herzig et al., 2017), topics (Xing et al., 2017), and speci-

Proceedings of The 11th International Natural Language Generation Conference, pages 89–98,
Tilburg, The Netherlands, November 5-8, 2018. ©2018 Association for Computational Linguistics

fied mechanisms (Zhou et al., 2017).

In this study, we focus on the issue of "response style." We intend to let the model learn to generate responses that resemble those of a real person. Given an input utterance and user-specific information, the model will generate a response relevant to the input utterance based on the given user-specific information.

The existing methods that exhibit the use of user-specific information (Li et al., 2016b; Zhang et al., 2018), usually require that the users appear in the training data. Therefore, these existing methods cannot handle the unseen users, *i.e.*, users that do not exist in the training data. This is a limitation that we want to address in this study. As we intend to make our model versatile, we want to cover also the users that are not present in the training data. Hence, in this study, we propose a model that also works with unseen users.

Since we need identifiers of users, we rely on Twitter as the source of datasets. The dataset used in this work was constructed by collecting tweets and replies, *i.e.*, responses to other tweets. Aside from the user identity, to construct user-specific information, we retrieved individual public tweets from each account that are not replies to other tweets. We assume that some selected representative words from the retrieved individual tweets are suitable as the user's information. Therefore, we use two types of user-specific information: user identities and collections of users' representative words.

Unlike other tasks that can assume a finite set of expected outputs, *e.g.*, machine translation, in response generation, an input utterance can elicit various responses. Thus, measuring the quality of the output becomes a formidable issue. To measure the quality of generated responses, we rely on human judgment. Three evaluation criteria are provided to the judges: *fluency*, *relevance*, and *style*. The results show that our model is significantly better than the baseline in *relevance* and *style*. Some examples of generated responses from our model are shown in Table 1.

2 Related Work

Attempts to develop neural response generation models have been increasing rapidly, providing several options to further improve neural conversation models. Some notable studies in this field (Vinyals and Le, 2015; Shang et al., 2015; Sordoni et al., 2015) follow the encoder-decoder framework of Sutskever et al. (2014). For response generation, the encoder-decoder models are usually supplemented by the attention mechanism, following the implementation of Bahdanau et al. (2015) or Luong et al. (2015).

As for response diversity, earlier researches have acknowledged that responses to one input utterance could be varied (Shang et al., 2015; Li et al., 2016a). To address this issue, several approaches have been proposed; some of these attempts incorporate style or a persona into the model while others focus only on increasing the variety.

Li et al. (2016b) proposed a persona-based model that uses a feature called *speaker embeddings* that are based on an individual user's identity. They have integrated these embeddings into the decoding phase. Despite showing positive results, this approach works only for the persona or user identity that appears in the training data. If a persona is absent from the training data, it would behave like the normal seq2seq model. Our work is similar to them in that we use the speaker identity in the decoding phase, but our work can generate user-specific responses even for unseen or unknown users.

Similar efforts have been made by Zhang et al. (2018), who attempted to personalize the output style using a set of introductory sentences as the user's profile. They combined the encoder-decoder model with the memory network, aiming to enhance the model's ability to "memorize" the profile. A study from Wang et al. (2017) has also attempted to "steer" the output style using additional information called *scenting datasets*. These *scenting datasets* consist of a corpus, or a collection of particular sentences, with each dataset being exclusive to one character. In their study, Wang et al. (2017) only focused on one character (*scenting dataset*) for each model. Hence, their model can only generate responses of one particular style at a time. We also use an additional dataset to control the style, but we differ from them in that we can deal with multiple characters in one model.

A model focusing on increasing diversity without using specific characteristic was devised by Zhou et al. (2017). They defined some mechanisms and generated latent features to divert the context of input utterances before feeding them to the decoder. They also presented some corresponding words to each mechanism.

3 Sequence-to-Sequence Setup

Following the popular approach in neural response generation, we base our encoder-decoder model on the seq2seq model with attention mechanism. Given the input sequence $X = (x_1, x_2, ..., x_{n_X})$, the model will attempt to produce the output sequence $Y = (y_1, y_2, ..., y_{n_Y})$ as a generated response. For the *encoder*, we adopt the LSTM (Hochreiter and Schmidhuber, 1997) unit to compute the representation of the input sequence. We keep all the hidden states produced by the encoder. Here, we use the notation $\bar{h}_s$ for each hidden state. Then, we adopt an attention-based model (Luong et al., 2015; Bahdanau et al., 2015) for the *decoder*. In general, the *decoding* process for each time step can be interpreted through the following equations:

$$p(y_t|y_{<t}, x) = \text{softmax}(W_s \tilde{h}_t), \quad (1)$$

$$\tilde{h}_t = \tanh(W_c[c_t; h_t]), \quad (2)$$

$$h_t = LSTM(y_{t-1}, h_{t-1}), \quad (3)$$

$$c_t = \sum_{s=1}^{S} a_t(s) \bar{h}_s, \quad (4)$$

$$a_t(s) = \text{softmax}(h_t^\top W_a \bar{h}_s), \quad (5)$$

$$= \frac{\exp(h_t^\top W_a \bar{h}_s)}{\sum_{s'} \exp(h_t^\top W_a \bar{h}_{s'})}.$$

The attention-based model used in this work is based on Luong et al. (2015). The weights W_s and W_c are the learned parameters of the decoder. With $a_t(s)$ as the vector containing the alignment score for each hidden state $\bar{h}_s$ of the encoder, c_t is the context for the current decoder at time step h_t. In addition to the attention-based model, we also apply the *input-feeding* approach by Luong et al. (2015) as an attempt to make the model capture the previous alignment. Input-feeding is done by concatenating the current attentional vector $\tilde{h}_t$ to the input to the decoder at the next time step. For both the encoder and the decoder, we employ two-layer LSTM architectures.

4 Response Generation with Attention to Speaker Information

As mentioned in Section 1, we argue for the importance of diversity in response style in creating a more compelling conversation. Our intention is to capture the characteristics of the users, *i.e.,* the responders, and to take them into account in response generation. Our work can be considered as an attempt to improve the persona-based model by Li et al. (2016b). Their model represents individual users, or in their term *speakers*, in the training data as a vector or embedding of speaker-specific information. Adapting their work, we pick usernames as one of the user-specific attributes, and then convert them to embeddings to allow the model to distinguish between users' characteristics. However, this approach can only accommodate users present in the training data. To overcome this issue, we suggest a small dataset for each user to serve as another characteristic feature.

4.1 User-Specific Information

In this study, we define two kinds of user-specific information: user embeddings and user-info embeddings. User embeddings are derived from usernames in the training data, while user-info embeddings are derived from separate collections of words used by the users. User embeddings are only useful for users present in the training data, while user-info embeddings are independent of the training data. The details about how these data are retrieved will be explained in Section 5.

Following the setup described in Section 3, let I_{train} denote the set of users (responders) in the training data, K_{word} the dimension of word embeddings, and K_{user} the dimension of user embeddings. We convert words in each input sequence X to embeddings with size K_{word}. Then, we define a user identity, embedding u_i with size K_{user} for each user $i \in I_{train}$. The user embedding u_i is shared to all conversations involving user i.

The second type of user information involves a collection of users' selected words. In order to capture the characteristic, especially the speaking style, of each user, we argue that we need to define a feature or a set of information that can let the model learn about the characteristic. Thus, we assume that a carefully selected set of words from each user's conversation history is suitable for this task.

Let I denote the set of users. Note that I_{train} is a subset of I. For each user in I, several sentences can be collected. From this collection of sentences, we then extract N words to represent the characteristics of the user. To select those N words, we need a particular approach to score the

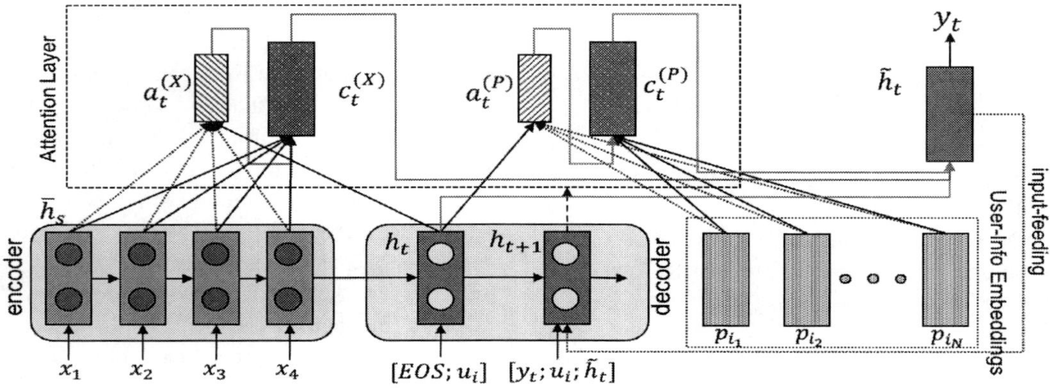

Figure 1: Overview of our neural conversation model with attention to user-specific information. We use two-layer LSTM for both the encoder and the decoder. The attention layer attends to source hidden states $\bar{h}_{s'}$ and user-info embeddings P_i for user i. User embeddings u_i are concatenated with the decoder input at every step.

words.

We compared several scoring methods that are simple enough to employ: word frequency, TF-IDF (Sparck Jones, 1988), and Pointwise Mutual Information (PMI). To compare them, we treated all the words in the selected sentences as the input for every method. Then we ranked the words according to the scores by every method and took N words with the highest ranks for each method. Hence, we have three sets of selected N words, and then deployed them in the training and evaluated the results preliminarily.

Two fluent speakers of English were asked to compare the quality of generated responses. We provided the two evaluators with three sets of generated responses using three different sets of N words, then asked them to evaluate the fluency and relevance to the input message. Based on their evaluation, we decided to choose TF-IDF as the scoring method to extract N words as the user-info dataset. Each of these words is further converted to an embedding of dimension K_{word}.

4.2 Attentional Conversation Model

Our attentional LSTM model takes three features as input: input word embeddings, user embeddings, and user-info embeddings. Both user embeddings and user-info embeddings are used in the decoder of the encoder-decoder model. Since our model also incorporates the *input-feeding* approach, the input for the decoding phase is the concatenation of the output of the previous time step

y_{t-1}, user embedding u_i, and input-feeding $\tilde{h}_{t-1}$. The user-info embeddings will be used later as the input for additional attention mechanism. Hence, the decoding process can be described as follows:

$$h_t = LSTM([y_{t-1}; u_i; \tilde{h}_{t-1}], h_{t-1}). \quad (6)$$

The user-info embeddings are constructed from the collection of top N ranked words uttered by intended users, where the users are not necessarily present in the training data. Using the same embeddings as input word embeddings, we compose $P_i = \{p_{i_1}, ..., p_{i_N}\}$ ($\forall k$, $p_{i_k} \in \mathbb{R}^{K_{word}}$) as user-info embeddings for user i.

The model is trained to attend not only to the input source, *i.e.*, the hidden states of the encoder, but also to the user-info embeddings. Therefore, since this model uses two contexts, we need to adjust Equation (3) to

$$\tilde{h}_t = \tanh(W_c[c_t^{(X)}; c_t^{(P)}; h_t]), \quad (7)$$

where we define $c_t^{(X)}$ as the context for input source and $c_t^{(P)}$ as the context for user-info embeddings. This proposed model is illustrated in Figure 1.

5 Datasets

Since our target is to incorporate and emphasize the response styles of actual human responders, we need to include user identification attributes in the datasets. Therefore, for datasets, we collected tweets from Twitter API. Then, we constructed two types of datasets: *conversation dataset* and *user-info dataset.*

5.1 Conversation Dataset

This dataset is designated to train the model to generate a response to a given input utterance in general. We extracted this dataset from Twitter, and retrieved only those tweets that satisfy the following conditions. We set a filter to select only reply tweets, *i.e.*, responses to other tweets, from users who had engaged in conversations with a minimum of three turns. We paired each reply with the tweet that it is a response of, as *response* and *input utterance*, respectively. We then used the responders' usernames as the user identification attribute, hence user embeddings. Note that the user embeddings can only be obtained from this conversation dataset.

To improve data quality, we further cleaned up the retrieved tweets to remove some noises, such as tweets with non-ASCII characters, duplications, and non-English tweets. We also removed URLs, hashtags, and mentions from tweets. The final conversation dataset consists of around 230,000 pairs of input utterances and responses.

5.2 User-Info Dataset

This dataset is an effort to capture more characteristic of the users and also to handle the unseen users in the training dataset. User-info embeddings mentioned in Section 4.1 are derived from this dataset. To construct user-info dataset, we retrieved tweets from the accounts of every username in the conversation dataset. To ensure that this dataset is independent from the conversation dataset, we retrieved only individual tweets, *i.e.,* non-replies as opposed to the reply tweets for conversation dataset. We retrieved all public tweets, via Twitter API, from each account and then applied TF-IDF to find the most important words for each user. For an individual user, we treated one tweet (sentence) as one document and hence computed the TF-IDF score for each word across all sentences. Then, we kept the top 50 words according to the TF-IDF scores.

The usage of this dataset is independent of the conversation dataset. We can pair the user information in the user-info dataset with the one, the same user, in the conversation dataset or we can disregard the relationship.

6 Experiments

6.1 Implementation Details

Both our encoder and decoder employed two-layer stacked LSTMs. Some hyper-parameter details are as follows:

- Each LSTM layer contains 300 hidden units.

- Embedding size is set to 300.

- Network parameters are initialized with uniform distribution $[-0.05, 0.05]$.

- Training batch size is set to 128.

- Learning rate for the encoder is set to 0.0001, multiplied by 2.5 for the decoder.

- Dropout rate is set to 0.1.

- Vocabulary size is 35,000.

We trained the model by using the Adam optimizer (Kingma and Ba, 2014) with different learning rates between the encoder and decoder. We conducted several procedures to determine the training stop condition. We observed the decrease in loss $H_{y'}(y) := -\sum_i y'_i \log(y_i)$. When the decrease was starting to converge, at around less than 7%, we asked two English fluent speakers to evaluate the generated responses. Finally, we stopped the training at the 47th epoch. We also limited the maximum length of an utterance to 15 words per sentence. The training was run on a single Titan X GPU for about three days.

The input utterance and user-info embeddings were initialized with GloVe embeddings (Pennington et al., 2014). We replaced the words not in the vocabulary with *UNK* tokens. The same treatment was applied to unseen users in user embeddings. We set the *UNK* token embeddings to a vector of all zeroes at the initial stage. To select the prediction, we opted to use the greedy approach.

6.2 Baseline and Comparison Models

We adopted the speaker model of Li et al. (2016b) to serve as the benchmark for our model. Their work used persona (user-identification attribute) in the decoding phase to let the model assimilate the style of that user, or "nearby" users, into the responses.

In terms of using user embeddings in the decoding phase, our model and theirs are similar. However, as mentioned in Section 5, user embeddings cannot cover unseen users. Our model overcomes that issue by using user-info embeddings. The decoder input of both the models can be represented by Equation (6). Since the baseline model does not have user-info embeddings, our model's attentional hidden $\tilde{h}_t$ is different from theirs. The attentional hidden of the baseline model would be the same as Equation (3), while our model's $\tilde{h}_t$ is represented by Equation (7).

We also prepare a variant of our proposed model, using unseen (*UNK*) users for user embeddings. The rationale for this setting is to investigate whether our model could generate better responses against our baseline's handicap. The last comparison model was a vanilla seq2seq model (without user and user-info embeddings). For simplicity, we labeled the four models as **User + Info** for our main model with *user embeddings* and *user-info embeddings*, **UserOnly** for baseline, **UNK + Info** for our variant model with *unseen users* and *user-info embeddings*, and **seq2seq** for vanilla seq2seq model.

Bio
Journalist. Writer. Broadcaster. For Hire. #AllBlackLivesMatter. Everything is wrestling. Header by @censored

Sample Tweets
- Breaking in a new pair of jeans today. Pray for yer boi.
- Nah it's asocial cold now. Don't invite me to any events. I'm not trekking. I'm not traveling unless there free food, booze or you paying me. It's blitz.
- Shouts to all my freelancers who are getting more work now the full time peeps are taking their winter/Christmas holiday time. Rumble workers, rumble.
- Nah someone needs to put you in the sin bin for 10 minutes. You are out of control today.
- Had creamed corned for the first time yesterday. Looked like sick, tasted alright

Figure 2: Example of a user's Twitter bio and sample tweets used in style evaluation. We censored any mentions of other accounts.

6.3 Evaluation Setup

Many previous studies on dialogue or response generation models (Li et al., 2016b,a; Sordoni et al., 2015; Xing et al., 2017) relied on BLEU (Papineni et al., 2002) as their automatic evaluation metric. To compute the score, BLEU measures the overlapping words or n-grams between the generated output (hypothesis) and the target output (reference). BLEU was initially intended for machine translation, which tends to have a finite target; therefore, it might not be suitable for evaluating conversation models.

According to Liu et al. (2016), BLEU is lowly correlated with human judgments of dialogue systems. Additionally, some other work on response generation (Shang et al., 2015; Li et al., 2016c; Wang et al., 2017; Zhou et al., 2017) did not use BLEU for their evaluation method, relying on human judgment instead. Thus, we opted to use only human evaluation in our work.

We hired judges from Amazon Mechanical Turk (AMT) to evaluate the quality of our generated responses. The following three judgment criteria were defined:

- *fluency* or **naturalness**: Whether the response could be produced by (an English speaking) human.

- *relevance* or **adequacy**: Whether the response could be accepted as a suitable answer or contained useful information regarding the input utterance.

- *style*: Whether the response could be produced by the same person if some profile information was provided.

The rationale behind measuring these criteria is as follows. Even though our goal is to integrate styles to the generated responses, we also want to assure that the generated responses are correct and useful to the input. Since we supposed that *style* is significantly harder to evaluate, the evaluation task was done in two stages: the first stage was for *fluency* and *relevance*, and the second stage was for *style*.

We randomly picked 12 users from the conversation dataset and retrieved tweets that they replied to. For each user, 5–10 tweets were obtained to be used as input utterances. In total, 100 tweets were collected, and each pair of an input utterance and its response was then evaluated by 10 judges.

Models	Fluency (%)			Relevance (%)		
	bad	enough	good	bad	enough	good
UserOnly (Baseline)	19.5	27.3	53.2	51.8	25.2	23.0
seq2seq	8.2	25.8	66.0	40.1	29.4	30.5
User + Info	17.5	26.4	56.1	44.9	28.2	26.9
UNK + Info (with unseen users)	9.0	23.7	**67.3**	37.4	31.2	**31.4**

Table 2: Human evaluation results for *fluency* and *relevance*, presented as raw score percentages. Our UNK + Info model with unseen users gains 26.5% more for fluency and 36.5% more for relevance compared to the baseline.

For the first stage, we provided the judges with only input utterance-response pairs. There were four models in total, so one utterance had four response alternatives. We employed a three-point Likert scale, labeled $\{bad, enough, good\}$, which were later converted to $\{-1, 0, +1\}$, respectively, and asked the judges to score every response alternative in terms of **fluency** and **relevance**.

In the second stage, the judges were provided with Twitter user bio, *i.e.*, a user's short biography or profile information that commonly contains keywords, and some sample tweets from the respective users. We asked the judges to evaluate the response alternatives on the basis of the provided information and to score them in the range from 1 to 5, where a smaller number is better. Since this time the judges have provided information to compare to, we assume that ranking is more appropriate to measure the similarity between response alternatives and provided samples. Ties in the score were permitted. For *style* evaluation, since we intended to investigate the influence of user-specific information to the response, we excluded the vanilla seq2seq model. An example of the provided information is shown in Figure 2.

7   Results and Analysis

7.1   Human Judgment

We first evaluated the *fluency* and *relevance* of the responses. In this stage, one utterance received four responses from all models. We let the judges score using three choices: bad, enough, and good.

To decide which model is the better one, first, we counted the number of each score label every model received. We call it raw scores. The summary of raw scores by the judges is shown in Table 2. According to these results, for both criteria, UNK + Info (with unseen users) received the highest *good* score, followed by the seq2seq

model. The UNK + Info gains 26.5% more *fluency* point compared to the baseline. To calculate this gain, we simply compared the percentage obtained by UNK + Info (67.3%) against UserOnly (53.2%).

While it is obvious that high *good* score is desirable, we also want to see if our model can generate more "good enough" response compared to other models. Then, we combined *enough* and *good* scores as *acceptable*. As shown in Table 4, seq2seq seems to achieve the highest score in terms of *fluency*, even though it only gains 0.87% more point than UNK + Info model. Therefore, we argue that our UNK + Info can be considered as fluent enough.

For *relevance*, the *bad* scores of all models are higher than the *good* scores. This implies that *relevance* is harder to achieve than *fluency*. Yet our variant model, UNK + Info, achieved the highest acceptable score in this criteria, gaining 36.5% compared to the baseline.

We calculated the average of the scores by converting them to $\{-1, 0, +1\}$ for each model and criteria, as seen in Table 5. In this table, our variant model, UNK + Info, wins in both criteria. Nevertheless, our model can get higher scores in both criteria than the baseline model, UserOnly. Using one-way ANOVA as significance test, we confirmed that our model is significantly better than the baseline in the *relevance* criteria.

In the second stage, we measured the similarity in style among generated responses and users' sample tweets. As in the first stage, each of the 100 input-response pairs was evaluated by 10 judges, resulting in 1,000 samples, from which we removed some results that did not show consistency, *e.g.*, the results with identical responses with a different score. As explained in Section 6.3, we evaluated only three models. This was done to

User	Input	Responses	
		User + Info	**UNK + Info**
User1	*i'm going to have a cardiac episode and my wife is not here*	*i love you*	*what if i do*
	hate to burst your bubble it snowed last night & this morning	*and now you get to the game*	*ahh ! ! ! i was so excited !*
	they cut so much out of the finale !	*i was thinking it was*	*it was a good season ! !*
User2	*if lebron loses this series does he leave and where does he go ?*	*he scored the house and got his back house*	*he was playing with his rb / 3*
	he was five for his last 50 you literally had to pound the middle of the zone three times	*are you saying that were no reason ?*	*he has a good draft ?*
	hey guess what ? the bills will draft a few football players this weekend	*lol you got that man ! ! ! ! ! !*	*you beat me ?*
User3	*this is such a mood and i can't even explain why*	*did you get braces or walmart ?*	*hello ! ! !*
	you can skip iron man 3	*do i get some rest ?*	*yeah i am*
	heard he cheated on her	*don't forget*	*she was a lesbian*

Table 3: Examples of responses from different users generated by our model, using known users and their user-info respectively, and its variant model, using unseen users and the same user-infos.

investigate the influence of user-specific information. Additionally, we intended to perform a comparison with a baseline with the same objective. The results can be observed in Table 6.

Based on the style evaluation results in Table 6, the average scores appear to be positioned in the middle of the range, *i.e.*, around rank three. It suggests that, in general all models only generate "good enough" responses in term of style. Nevertheless, our variant model is significantly better than the baseline, proved by the Friedman Test. Sample responses generated by our model are shown in Table 3.

Models	Fluency (%)	Relevance (%)
	acceptable	acceptable
UserOnly	80.5	48.2
seq2seq	**91.8**	59.9
User + Info	82.5	55.1
UNK + Info	91.0	**62.6**

Table 4: Acceptable or "Good enough" results with *good* and *enough* scores combined. seq2seq tops *fluency*, but our model with unseen users gets the highest *relevance* score.

Models	Fluency	Relevance
UserOnly	0.337 ± 0.06	-0.28 ± 0.06
seq2seq	0.578 ± 0.05	-0.09 ± 0.06
User + Info	0.386 ± 0.06	-0.18 ± 0.06
UNK + Info	$\mathbf{0.583 \pm 0.05}$	$\mathbf{-0.06 \pm 0.06}$

Table 5: Average scores for *fluency* and *relevance* criteria. For ***relevance***, our model achieved significantly better scores than the baseline (one-way ANOVA, $p < 0.05$).

Models	Style Rank
UserOnly	3.37 ± 0.09
User + Info	3.29 ± 0.09
UNK + Info	$\mathbf{3.16 \pm 0.09}$

Table 6: Results of style evaluation. Smaller values are better. Our variant model was significantly better than the baseline (Friedman Test, $p < 0.05$).

7.2 Analysis: External Resources and Response Style

Our main intention is to incorporate an individual user's characteristics to generated responses. We specifically attempted to incorporate more information to emphasize the response style of different users. Therefore, we conducted an experiment to incorporate additional information, and the evaluation we performed proved that the judges recognized a better change in style.

Furthermore, one aspect that distinguishes our model from others is the application of external resources. Usually, if a model was trained to pick up some specific traits or characteristics, such features should be included in the training. Our work also serves as an evidence of usability of external resources for response generation models. With simple mechanisms such as attention, our model can adjust the responses to be better with a small "plug and play" dataset.

An interesting finding is that the variant UNK + Info model achieved better scores than our User + Info model. Through manual observation, we conceived that a model with more injected information can become too "stylized" and lose some relevance to the input utterance. However, the baseline, with less information, still received lower scores. This indicates the strength of the attention mechanism.

In conclusion, a problem still persists in styling generated responses. Regardless of the results being better than the baseline for the previous work, generating fluent and relevant responses with an expected style is still challenging. It might be the common case that either the responses are good but general and timid, or they are interesting but lacking some relevance.

8 Conclusion and Future Work

In this study, we conducted experiments to address the response diversity issue, particularly in response style. We employed user-specific information to drive the generated responses to resemble real user's utterances. We considered usernames and the user-info dataset as user-specific information.

Evaluation through human judgment showed that the outputs of our model are better than the baseline overall, especially our variant model with unseen users. Our model also showed the potential of using external resources in encoder-decoder models. Although we cannot declare that our model architecture is sophisticated, our experiments can serve as the evidence that a simple but appropriate architecture can improve response quality.

The remaining challenge is how to properly emphasize the response style without damaging the content (context) or its relevance. If we can make a good compromise between response content and style and can control the use of these two elements, we argue that it would substantially increase the quality of conversation models.

Acknowledgements

This work is partially supported by JST PRESTO (Grant Number JPMJPR1655).

References

Dzmitry Bahdanau, Kyunghyun Cho, and Yoshua Bengio. 2015. Neural machine translation by jointly learning to align and translate. In *Proceedings of the International Conference on Learning Representations (ICLR)*.

Jonathan Herzig, Michal Shmueli-Scheuer, Tommy Sandbank, and David Konopnicki. 2017. Neural response generation for customer service based on personality traits. In *Proceedings of the 10th International Conference on Natural Language Generation*, pages 252–256. Association for Computational Linguistics.

Sepp Hochreiter and Jürgen Schmidhuber. 1997. Long short-term memory. *Neural Comput.*, 9(8):1735–1780.

Diederik P. Kingma and Jimmy Ba. 2014. Adam: A method for stochastic optimization. *CoRR*, abs/1412.6980.

Jiwei Li, Michel Galley, Chris Brockett, Jianfeng Gao, and Bill Dolan. 2016a. A diversity-promoting objective function for neural conversation models. In *Proceedings of the 2016 Conference of the North American Chapter of the Association for Computational Linguistics: Human Language Technologies*, pages 110–119. Association for Computational Linguistics.

Jiwei Li, Michel Galley, Chris Brockett, Georgios Spithourakis, Jianfeng Gao, and Bill Dolan. 2016b. A persona-based neural conversation model. In *Proceedings of the 54th Annual Meeting of the Association for Computational Linguistics (Volume 1: Long Papers)*, pages 994–1003, Berlin, Germany. Association for Computational Linguistics.

Jiwei Li, Will Monroe, Alan Ritter, Dan Jurafsky, Michel Galley, and Jianfeng Gao. 2016c. Deep reinforcement learning for dialogue generation. In *Proceedings of the 2016 Conference on Empirical Methods in Natural Language Processing*, pages 1192–1202. Association for Computational Linguistics.

Chia-Wei Liu, Ryan Lowe, Iulian Serban, Mike Noseworthy, Laurent Charlin, and Joelle Pineau. 2016. How not to evaluate your dialogue system: An empirical study of unsupervised evaluation metrics for dialogue response generation. In *Proceedings of the*

2016 Conference on Empirical Methods in Natural Language Processing, pages 2122–2132. Association for Computational Linguistics.

Thang Luong, Hieu Pham, and Christopher D. Manning. 2015. Effective approaches to attention-based neural machine translation. In *Proceedings of the 2015 Conference on Empirical Methods in Natural Language Processing*, pages 1412–1421. Association for Computational Linguistics.

Kishore Papineni, Salim Roukos, Todd Ward, and Wei-Jing Zhu. 2002. Bleu: A method for automatic evaluation of machine translation. In *Proceedings of the 40th Annual Meeting on Association for Computational Linguistics*, ACL '02, pages 311–318, Stroudsburg, PA, USA. Association for Computational Linguistics.

Jeffrey Pennington, Richard Socher, and Christopher Manning. 2014. Glove: Global vectors for word representation. In *Proceedings of the 2014 Conference on Empirical Methods in Natural Language Processing (EMNLP)*, pages 1532–1543, Doha, Qatar. Association for Computational Linguistics.

Alan Ritter, Colin Cherry, and William B. Dolan. 2011. Data-driven response generation in social media. In *Proceedings of the 2011 Conference on Empirical Methods in Natural Language Processing*, pages 583–593. Association for Computational Linguistics.

Lifeng Shang, Zhengdong Lu, and Hang Li. 2015. Neural responding machine for short-text conversation. In *Proceedings of the 53rd Annual Meeting of the Association for Computational Linguistics and the 7th International Joint Conference on Natural Language Processing (Volume 1: Long Papers)*, pages 1577–1586. Association for Computational Linguistics.

Alessandro Sordoni, Michel Galley, Michael Auli, Chris Brockett, Yangfeng Ji, Margaret Mitchell, Jian-Yun Nie, Jianfeng Gao, and Bill Dolan. 2015. A neural network approach to context-sensitive generation of conversational responses. In *Proceedings of the 2015 Conference of the North American Chapter of the Association for Computational Linguistics: Human Language Technologies*, pages 196–205, Denver, Colorado. Association for Computational Linguistics.

Karen Sparck Jones. 1988. Document retrieval systems. chapter A Statistical Interpretation of Term Specificity and Its Application in Retrieval, pages 132–142. Taylor Graham Publishing, London, UK, UK.

Ilya Sutskever, Oriol Vinyals, and Quoc V Le. 2014. Sequence to sequence learning with neural networks. In Z. Ghahramani, M. Welling, C. Cortes, N. D. Lawrence, and K. Q. Weinberger, editors, *Advances in Neural Information Processing Systems 27*, pages 3104–3112. Curran Associates, Inc.

Oriol Vinyals and Quoc V. Le. 2015. A neural conversation model. In *Proceedings of the 31th ICML Deep Learning Workshop*, Lille, France.

Di Wang, Nebojsa Jojic, Chris Brockett, and Eric Nyberg. 2017. Steering output style and topic in neural response generation. In *Proceedings of the 2017 Conference on Empirical Methods in Natural Language Processing*, pages 2140–2150. Association for Computational Linguistics.

Chen Xing, Wei Wu, Yu Wu, Jie Liu, Yalou Huang, Ming Zhou, and Wei-Ying Ma. 2017. Topic aware neural response generation. In *AAAI*.

Saizheng Zhang, Emily Dinan, Jack Urbanek, Arthur Szlam, Douwe Kiela, and Jason Weston. 2018. Personalizing dialogue agents: I have a dog, do you have pets too? *CoRR*, abs/1801.07243.

Ganbin Zhou, Ping Luo, Rongyu Cao, Fen Lin, Bo Chen, and Qing He. 2017. Mechanism-aware neural machine for dialogue response generation. In *AAAI*.

Explainable Autonomy: A Study of Explanation Styles for Building Clear Mental Models

Francisco J. Chiyah Garcia[1], David A. Robb[1], Xingkun Liu[1],
Atanas Laskov[2], Pedro Patron[2], Helen Hastie[1]
[1] Heriot-Watt University, Edinburgh, UK
[2] SeeByte Ltd, Edinburgh, UK
{fjc3, d.a.robb, x.liu, h.hastie}@hw.ac.uk
{atanas.laskov, pedro.patron}@seebyte.com

Abstract

As unmanned vehicles become more autonomous, it is important to maintain a high level of transparency regarding their behaviour and how they operate. This is particularly important in remote locations where they cannot be directly observed. Here, we describe a method for generating explanations in natural language of autonomous system behaviour and reasoning. Our method involves deriving an interpretable model of autonomy through having an expert 'speak aloud' and providing various levels of detail based on this model. Through an online evaluation study with operators, we show it is best to generate explanations with multiple possible reasons but tersely worded. This work has implications for designing interfaces for autonomy as well as for explainable AI and operator training.

1 Introduction

Robots and autonomous systems are increasingly being operated remotely in hazardous environments such as in the nuclear or energy sector domains (Hastie et al., 2018; Li et al., 2017; Kwon and Yi, 2012; Nagatani et al., 2013; Shukla and Karki, 2016; Wong et al., 2017). Typically, these remote robots instil less trust than those co-located (Bainbridge et al., 2008; Hastie et al., 2017b; Li, 2015). Thus, the interface between the operator and autonomous systems is key to maintaining situation awareness and understanding between the system and the human operator (Robb et al., 2018). It is this aspect of understanding that we examine here with respect to aligning the operator's mental model (Johnson-Laird, 1980), in terms of both *what* the system can do and *why* it is doing certain behaviours. We propose that this

type of explainability will increase trust and therefore adoption of remote autonomous systems.

According to Kulesza et al. (2013), varying the natural language generation of explanations in terms of verbosity (i.e. how many reasons to give or *completeness*) and the level of detail (*soundness*) changes the effectiveness of the explanations in terms of improving the user's mental model. It also affects whether the user thinks that it was "worth it" to read the explanation. It is these aspects of explanation generation that we explore here.

We focus on the natural language generation of explanations as a part of an interactive multimodal system called MIRIAM for situation awareness for autonomous underwater vehicles (AUVs). This interface was developed in conjunction with industry partner SeeByte Ltd (see Figure 1) and runs alongside their commercial UI called See-Track with a chat interface, which gives status and mission updates. This multimodal interface has been shown to increase situation awareness (Robb et al., 2018; Hastie et al., 2017a) both by using chat and graphical interface over just graphical interface alone.

We describe a method of explanation generation that is agnostic to the type of autonomy or vehicle. Our contribution is through the 'speak-aloud' method for deriving a model of autonomy for explanations and through the analysis of the forms that these explanations would take to maximally improve the user's mental model. The findings reported here can be used as heuristics for explaining behaviour of remote autonomous systems but also face-to-face robotics (Perera et al., 2016) and other explainable AI tasks such as explaining recommendations (Kulesza et al., 2013). Finally, they could be used to improve operator training.

Proceedings of The 11th International Natural Language Generation Conference, pages 99–108,
Tilburg, The Netherlands, November 5-8, 2018. ©2018 Association for Computational Linguistics

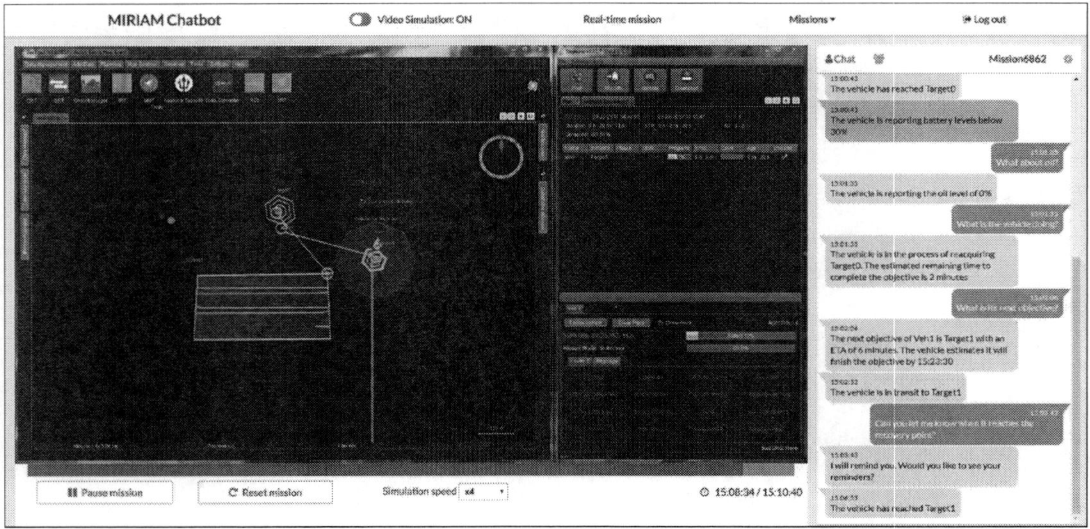

Figure 1: The multimodal interface with SeeTrack interface showing the predicted path of the vehicle on the left and the chat interface on the right where explanations appear.

2 Background

Explainability is an important facet of a transparent system (Wortham et al., 2017) as it can provide the user with a high fidelity mental model, along with increased confidence and performance (Bras et al., 2018; Lim et al., 2009). Mental models, in cognitive theory, provide one view on how humans reason either functionally (understanding what the robot does) or structurally (understanding how it works) (Johnson-Laird, 1980). Mental models are important as they strongly impact how and whether robots and systems are used. In previous work, explainability has been investigated for a variety of systems and users including: 1) explanation of deep learning models for developers, as in (Ribeiro et al., 2016) who showed that such explanations can increase trust; 2) explanations of planning systems (Tintarev and Kutlak, 2014; Chakraborti et al., 2017); and 3) verbalising robot (Rosenthal et al., 2016) or agent (Harrison et al., 2017) rationalisation. Here, we will be looking at verbalising rationalisation of behaviour of the autonomous system, in a similar way to 3). However, these explanations will not be in terms of a constant stream as in (Harrison et al., 2017), rather as part of a mixed-initiative conversational agent where explanations are available on request.

Gregor and Benbasat (1999) describe four types of explanation including *"Why"* and *"Why not"*, to explain the functionality and the structure of a system, respectively and *Justification* which includes general knowledge and *Terminological*. Lim et al. (2009) went on to investigate the first two of these and showed that explaining *why* a system behaved a certain way increased both understanding and trust, whilst *"Why not"* showed only an increase in understanding. Here, we will also be investigating these two types of explanations.

We compare our work to that of (Kulesza et al., 2013), who showed that high completeness and high soundness maximised understanding. However, their domain was different to ours (song recommendations) and their users required no specific training or domain knowledge to perform their task. In addition, given the cost of autonomous systems and effort to run missions, the stakes are considerably higher in our case. Adapting explanations to the various users and their existing mental models is touched upon here. Natural language generation has benefited from such personalisation to the user and this applies to explanation generation also. Previous studies in NLG have included adapting to style (Dethlefs et al., 2014), preferences (Walker et al., 2004), knowledge (Janarthanam and Lemon, 2014) and the context (Dethlefs, 2014) of the user. Whilst there has been much work on personalisation of explanations for recommender systems (Tintarev and Masthoff, 2012), there has been little done specifically for explainable AI/Autonomy.

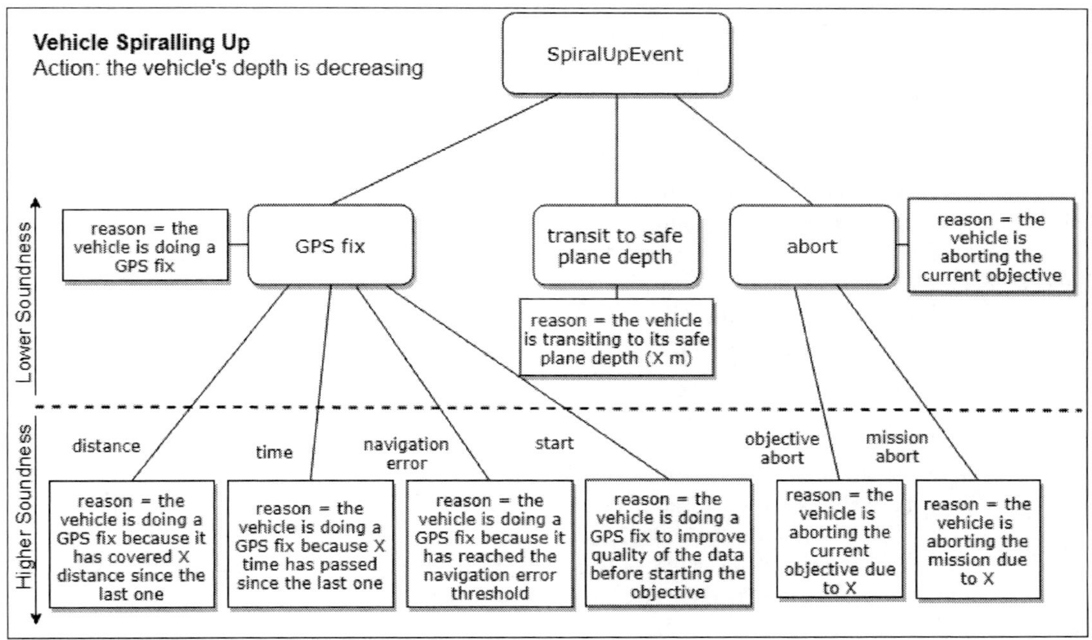

Figure 2: Part of the autonomy model, showing reasons for a vehicle spiralling up. Above/below the dashed line shows what part of the model is used for low/high soundness.

Finally, Gregor and Benbasat (1999) show, users will only take the time to process the explanation if the benefits are perceived to be worth it and do not adversely add to cognitive load (Mercado et al., 2016). Indeed, there needs to be a balance between the amount of information given and the cognitive effort needed to process it. Our evaluation investigates this aspect of explanation generation for our users, who will likely be cognitively loaded given the nature of the task.

3 MIRIAM: The Multimodal Interface

MIRIAM, (Multimodal Intelligent inteRactIon for Autonomous systeMs), as seen in Figure 1, allows for 'on-demand' queries for status and explanations of behaviour. MIRIAM interfaces with the Neptune autonomy software provided by SeeByte Ltd and runs alongside their SeeTrack interface.

MIRIAM uses a rule-based NLP Engine that contextualises and parses the user's input for intent, formalising it as a semantic representation. It is able to process both static and dynamic data, such as names and mission-specific words. For example, it is able to reference dynamic objects such as "auv1", the particular name given to a vehicle in the mission plan, without the requirement to hard-code this name into the system. It can han-

dle anaphoric references over multiple utterances e.g. "Where is Vehicle0?" ... "What is its estimated time to completion?". It also handles ellipsis e.g. "What is the battery level of vehicle0?" ..."What about vehicle1?". In this paper, we focus on explanations of behaviours and describe a method that is agnostic to the type of autonomy method. Please refer to (Hastie et al., 2017a) for further details of the MIRIAM system.

4 Method of Explanation Generation

As mentioned above, types of explanations investigated here include *why* (to provide a trace or reasoning) and *why not* (to elaborate on the system's control method or autonomy strategy), a subset of those described in (Gregor and Benbasat, 1999). Lim et al. (2009) show that both these explanations increase understanding and, therefore, are important with regards the user's mental model. We adopt here the 'speak-aloud' method whereby an expert provides rationalisation of the autonomous behaviours while watching videos of missions on the SeeTrack software. This has the advantage of being agnostic to the method of autonomy and could be used to describe rule-based autonomous behaviours but also complex deep learning models. Similar human-provided rationalisation has been used to generate explanations of deep neural models for game play (Harrison et al., 2017).

The interpretable model of autonomy derived from the expert is partially shown in Figure 2. If a *why* request is made, the decision tree is checked against the current mission status and history and the possible reasons are determined, along with a confidence value based on the information available at that point in the mission[1].

Whilst our explanation generation decides the *content* of the NLG output, the *surface representations* of the explanations are generated using template-based Natural Language Generation (NLG). Templates were picked over statistical surface realisation techniques (e.g. Dethlefs et al. (2014)) due to the fact that the end-user/customer prefers to avoid the variability that comes with statistical methods- these end-users/customers being e.g. the military and operators/technicians in the energy sector. In these domains, vocabulary and standard operating procedures lend themselves to the types of formulaic utterances that template-based systems afford.

The rationalisation of the autonomous behaviours into an intermediate interpretable model, as shown in Figure 2, assists with the uncertainty that remote autonomous systems entail. In our case, communications in the underwater domain are limited and often unreliable. The data received from the vehicles is used to steadily build a knowledge base and generate explanations on-demand. Furthermore, this rationalisation distances the reasoning from the low-level design of the autonomous vehicles to focus on what actually happens during a mission and allows for explanations in broader, high-level terms.

5 Soundness vs Completeness

As mentioned in the Introduction, Kulesza et al. (2013) explore how the level of *soundness* and *completeness* changes how explanations affect the user's mental model, as well as whether the user thinks that it was "worth it" to read the explanation. We adopt Kulesza's terminology here and similarly investigate this trade-off between soundness and completeness. For our domain, an agent that explains the autonomous system using a simpler model reduces soundness (i.e. the top layer

of the decision tree, above the line in Figure 2). In this case, the agent provides more general explanations with fewer details that may be easier to digest but may be too broad (see top left of Figure 3).

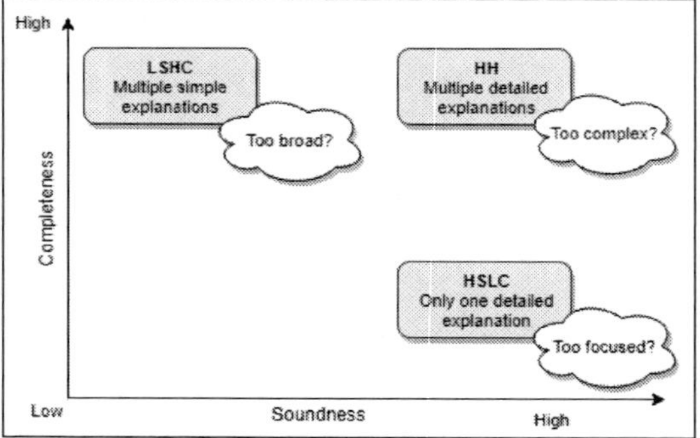

Figure 3: The three types of explanations used in the system, modified from Kulesza et al. (2013): Low Soundness High Completeness (LSHC), High Soundness High Completeness (HH) and High Soundness Low Completeness (HSLC).

High soundness here means that the explanation is taken from the the leaves of the decision tree, thus producing a focused and detailed explanation in Figure 2. An agent with high soundness that gives only one reason, reducing completeness but providing a more concise response, may be viewed as too focused (see bottom right Figure 3)[2]. Combining both high soundness and high completeness may result in too complex an explanation (see top right of Figure 3). We did not include a condition with low soundness and low completeness because it would omit too much data to be relevant or useful in our domain. We investigate these three combinations of varying soundness/completeness and measure their effect on Trust, User Satisfaction and a "worth it" score but primarily the evaluation study focuses on the effect on the user's mental model.

6 Evaluation Method

The experiment was a between-subjects experiment with three conditions, examples of which are given in Table 1. Specifically:

1. C1(HiSoundHiComp): High Soundness, High Completeness - multiple explanations,

---

[1]above 80% (high), 80% to 40% (medium) and below 40% (low) - levels were determined in consultation with the expert

[2]the one explanation that is presented is the one with the highest confidence at that time -if tied, an ordering that was recommended by the expert is applied

each explaining all of the autonomy model in detail;

2. C2(HiSoundLoComp): High Soundness, Low Completeness - one detailed explanation that explains all of the autonomy model;

3. C3(LoSoundHiComp): Low Soundness, High Completeness - multiple explanations each explaining just the top layer of the autonomy model.

6.1 Experimental Set-up

The experiment consisted of an on-line questionnaire with a pre-questionnaire to gather demographic data and two questions regarding the subjects' pre-existing mental model with regards AUVs: "I have a good understanding of how AUVs work" (Pre-MM-Q1) and "I have a good understanding of what AUVs can do" (Pre-MM-Q2). We were initially looking to investigate trust and so the users were asked to fill out a propensity to trust questionnaire (Rotter, 1967). After the pre-questionnaire, the participants watched 3 scenario videos. After each video, they answered 4 questions regarding the quality of the explanations (US-Q1-4). These questions were modified from the PARADISE-style questionnaire (Walker et al., 1997) for interactive systems and summed to create a User Satisfaction score. In addition, the participants were asked one question on whether the explanations were "worth it" and two questions on their post-explanation mental model (MM-Q1/2). All questions were on a Likert scale with 7 values: from strongly disagree (1) to strongly agree (7).

1. US-Q1: The system chat responses were easy to understand.

2. US-Q2: The system explanations were easy to understand.

3. US-Q3: The system explanations were useful.

4. US-Q4: The system explanations were as expected.

5. "Worth it" question: It would be worth reading the explanations to understand how the system is behaving.

6. MM-Q1: The system explanations in this video help me to increase my understanding of how AUVs work.

7. MM-Q2: The system explanations in this video help me to increase my understanding of what the AUVs were doing.

The mental model questions aim to capture two different dimensions of the user's mental model (Johnson-Laird, 1980): *structurally* so how AUVs work (MM-Q1) and *functionally* so what the AUVs were doing (MM-Q2). We will also refer to the mean of these two scores as the general mental model score, MM-G. After watching the 3 scenarios, a final questionnaire was administrated, which asked about trust and derived a general trust score using the Schaefer scale (Schaefer, 2013).

6.2 The Scenarios

There were three conditions, as discussed above, and for each condition the same three scenario videos were watched by the participants in the same order. Each video showed a mission as reflected in Figure 1 showing the same AUV mission but the text chat running alongside the mission varied depending on the condition. For example, the operator is able to observe in the SeeTrack interface that the vehicle has not done a GPS fix for some time. The operator in the video asks why it is not doing a GPS fix and the answer explains the relevant constraints on the vehicle, as captured in the interpretable autonomy model shown in Figure 2. The different scenarios and the questions are as follows:

1. **Scenario 1:** a *why* question about an event "Why is the vehicle spiralling down?". The system would answer with a few reasons (or only one if completeness was low) with medium confidence. The user would then repeat the question after some time and the system would give a concrete answer with high confidence. See Table 1 for the dialogue for this scenario. Note that in this scenario, the ranking of the most likely reasons does not change during the mission.

2. **Scenario 2:** a *why* question about an event "Why is the vehicle spiralling up?". Similar to Scenario 1 but, in this case, the most likely reason changes in the second answer. This scenario explores how not having all the information (low completeness) affects the user's mental model because the first system's response does not give all possible reasons for the event.

C1 (HiSoundHiComp)	C2 (HiSoundLoComp)	C3 (LoSoundHiComp)
User: Why is the vehicle spiralling up?	**User:** Why is the vehicle spiralling up?	**User:** Why is the vehicle spiralling up?
System: This could be due to the following reasons: - The vehicle is doing a GPS fix at the start of Survey0 to improve the quality of the data gathered (medium confidence) - The vehicle is transiting to its safe plane depth (5m) (medium confidence)	**System:** The vehicle is doing a GPS fix at the start of Survey0 to improve the quality of the data gathered (medium confidence)	**System:** This could be due to the following reasons: - The vehicle is doing a GPS fix (medium confidence) - The vehicle is transiting to its safe plane depth (medium confidence)
System: The vehicle has reached Survey0	**System:** The vehicle has reached Survey0	**System:** The vehicle has reached Survey0
User: Can you confirm now why the vehicle is spiralling up?	**User:** Can you confirm now why the vehicle is spiralling up?	**User:** Can you confirm now why the vehicle is spiralling up?
System: Yes, the vehicle is doing a GPS fix at the start of Survey0 to improve the quality of the data gathered (high confidence)	**System:** Yes, the vehicle is doing a GPS fix at the start of Survey0 to improve the quality of the data gathered (high confidence)	**System:** Yes, the vehicle is doing a GPS fix (high confidence)

Table 1: Example dialogue from Scenario 1 showing varying levels of soundness and completeness for a *why* question.

3. **Scenario 3:** a *why not* question "Why is the vehicle not doing Target0?". The system would compute a reason explaining the procedures of the vehicle in that situation. This scenario investigates how simple explanations (low soundness) about the vehicle's control strategies impact the user's mental model compared to more detailed explanations.

6.3 Participant Group

There were 21 participants (18 male and 3 female[3]). The 21 participants were distributed evenly across the conditions (7 in each). Participation was voluntary and remuneration was by a chance to win one of three £20 Amazon vouchers. The majority of participants were between 25-35 years old, educated to undergraduate, masters degree or PhD level and all worked in the field of software for AUVs, and include roles such as operators and development and software engineers.

For this study, it was important to get users of approximately the same prior mental model of AUVs. Therefore, participants were recruited from a pool of experts in AUVs from industry and academia. This allowed us to design the experiment at a certain level that did not require pre-training of subjects to get to the same expert level. Indeed, the pre-test scores reflect a high self-perceived ability within the participant group with regards their understanding of *how AUVs work* (Pre-MM-Q1 with mean/mode/median/stdev: 6.2/7/6/1) and *what AUVs can do* (Pre-MM-Q2: mean/mode/median/stdev 6.3/6/6/0.6). This approach, however, has the disadvantage of a small pool of users and results in an uneven gender balance. Note that expert levels were evenly spread between conditions.

6.4 Results

Table 2 gives results from the evaluation and shows that C3(LoSoundHiComp) results in higher User Satisfaction scores, "worth it" question and mental model scores. C1(HiSoundHiComp) has the highest level of user trust using the questionnaire from (Schaefer, 2013) with C2 (HiSoundLoComp) having the lowest level of trust, which we discuss below. As indicated in the table, only the mental model questions were found to be statistically significant.

---

[3]reflecting current gender proportions of employees in the engineering and technology sector, see https://www.theiet.org [accessed May 2018]

	C1 (HiSoundHiComp)		C2 (HiSoundLoComp)		C3 (LoSoundHiComp)	
	Mean **Median**	**SD** **Mode**	**Mean** **Median**	**SD** **Mode**	**Mean** **Median**	**SD** **Mode**
Human-Robot Trust	76.73% 79.29%	6.2% N/A	68.37% 74.29%	13.5% N/A	72.04% 70.00%	13.8% N/A
User Satisfaction	5.56 6	0.695 6	5.51 6	0.615 6	6.06 6	0.693 7
"Worth It" score	5.76 6	0.937 6	5.62 6	0.911 6	6.24 6	0.81 6
MM-Q1 for how work?	5.05 5	1.02 5	4.81 5	1.44 5	5.57* 6	1.66 6
MM-Q2 for what doing?	5.57 6	1.03 6	5.19 5	1.33 5	6.14* 6	1.11 6
MM-G for general MM	5.31 5.5	0.96 5	5 5	1.28 6	5.86* 6	1.23 6

Table 2: Overall descriptive statistics reporting Mean, SD, Median, and Mode. As described in the text, Human-Robot Trust is a score out of 100%. Scales were on a 7 point Likert Scale. User Satisfaction is a scale derived from the average of 4 Likert items. "Worth It" score, MM-Q1 and MM-Q2 are from single Likert scale items. MM-G for general MM is the average of the MM-Q1 and MM-Q2 per participant. N/A for some modes indicates there were no repeated values in that section of the data. We show modes mainly to help describe the sections of the data derived directly from Likert items, i.e. ordinal, but included them across all the data for completeness. These descriptive statistics are for the data aggregated across scenarios within each condition. The * symbols indicate the means of those conditions' distributions which were statistically significantly higher than those of the other two conditions by post hoc Mann-Whitney-U tests following Kruskal-Wallis tests for non-parametric data ($p < .05$) (see text).

Specifically, a Kruskal-Wallis test[4] found a statistically significant effect for these 3 dependant variables across conditions $p < .05$ with $\chi^2 = 9.3051$ for MM-Q1; $\chi^2 = 9.6836$ for MM-Q2, $\chi^2 = 17.846$ for MM-G rejecting the null hypothesis *"there is no difference in the participant's mental model scores between the conditions"*. Post-hoc Mann-Whitney-U one-tailed tests using Bonferroni's correction were able to show that C3 was significantly higher than the other two conditions for all three mental models scores at the 95% confidence level. C1 whilst higher than C2 was not significantly so (although there was a trend $p = .02$)[5].

We have also investigated how mental model scores vary across the scenarios during the experiment. We can see from Figure 4 that although C2(HiSoundLoComp) has significantly lower scores than C3(LoSoundHiComp), the user's mental model of how the system works (MM-Q1) builds over time, whereas in conditions C1(HiSoundHiComp) and C3(LoSoundHiComp), it remains steady for the first two scenarios with C2(HiSoundLoComp) actually ending up the highest score by the end of the experiment.

The graph on the bottom of Figure 4 reflects the user's mental model of what the vehicle is doing, which varies from scenario to scenario across conditions. As discussed in Section 6.1, there is a change in confidence in the explanation given in Scenario 2. The system predicts the AUV's action as normal for the first user query, yet in the second query, the system has more data and recomputes the most likely reason, which varies from the one originally presented. Perhaps unsurprisingly, this has a bigger impact on C2(HiSoundLoComp) than on C1(HiSoundHiComp) or C3(LoSoundHiComp) because in those last two conditions, all possible reasons are given so there is less of a surprise compared to the system seemingly 'chang-

---

[4]A Kruskal-Wallis test was used as MM-Q1/2 are non-parametric and MM-G was shown to be non-normally distributed via a KS Test

[5]$p < .0167$ for significance taking into account Bonferroni's correction

ing its mind' completely. This may also account for the lower general lack of trust for the vehicle in C2(HiSoundLoComp), as indicated in Table 2.

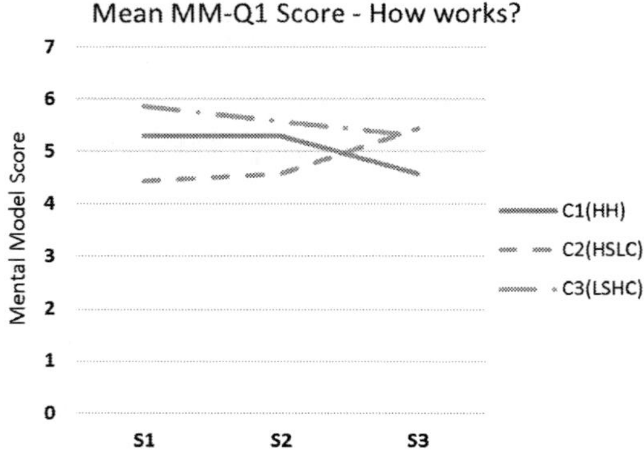

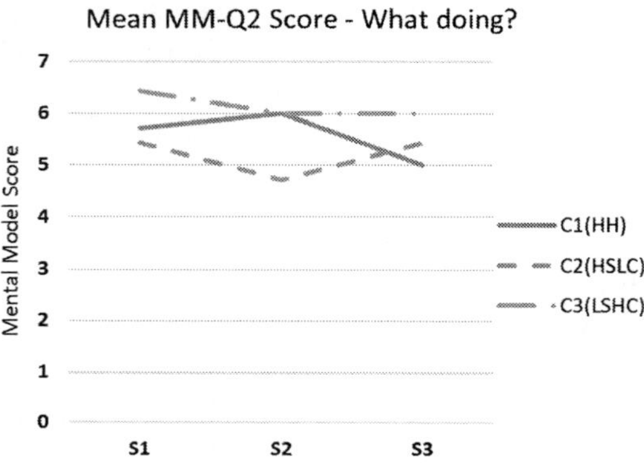

Figure 4: Mean mental model scores across scenarios: C1(HH)–High Soundness High Completeness, C2(HSLC)–High Soundness Low Completeness and C3(LSHC)–Low Soundness High Completeness. S1 to 3: Scenarios 1 to 3.

7 Discussion and Future Work

Kulesza et al. (2013) found that high soundness, high completeness (HiSoundHiComp) explanations performed the best[6]. They found that completeness was linked to better understanding of how the system worked and the highest average mental model scores. They also found that explanations with low completeness resulted in flawed mental models. This is similar to our study where the only condition with low completeness seemed

____
[6]although no statistical tests were performed due to the low number of subjects

to result in confusion as reflected by significantly lower mental model scores.

In our study, high completeness (i.e. giving all the reasons) is the consistent factor that is important for understanding *how a system works*. However, further investigation is needed to explore the effects of the mental model over longer missions and across missions and to see how the mental models build up in the various conditions, as suggested from Figure 4 where low completeness might be an appropriate presentation method if there is less urgency.

For understanding specific behaviours, i.e. *what the system is doing*, a high level of completeness is important, however a high level of soundness is not necessary (i.e. the reasons don't have to have a lot of detail). In fact, users have a clearer mental model if broader explanations with less details are used with C3(LoSoundHiComp) being statistically higher than the high soundness condition C1(HiSoundHiComp). The difference between our study and that of Kulesza et al. (2013) is that in our study the population have a high degree of pre-existing knowledge and therefore the high soundness may be redundant or even cause frustration or extra cognitive load (Lopes et al., 2018). In addition, according to (Gregor and Benbasat, 1999; Kulesza et al., 2013), "users will not expend effort to find explanations unless the expected benefit outweighs the mental effort". Thus, the system explanations with high soundness, high completeness (HiSoundHiComp) may be too convoluted or distracting in an already complex domain. Our results seem to reflect this trend as well with the "worth it" score, which is highest for C3(LoSoundHiComp). Investigating the cognitive load of processing these various types of explanations is part of future work.

In summary, we present here a method for monitoring and explaining behaviours of remote autonomous systems, which is agnostic to the autonomy model. The positive results from this study suggest that this method produces explanations that build on pre-existing mental models and improves users' understanding of how the systems work and why they are doing certain behaviours. This method, along with recommendations for how explanations should be presented to the user, informs design decisions for interfaces to manage remote autonomous vehicles, as well as explainable autonomy/AI in general.

Acknowledgements

This research was funded by EPSRC ORCA Hub (EP/R026173/1, 2017-2021); RAEng/ Leverhulme Trust Senior Research Fellowship Scheme (Hastie/ LTSRF1617/13/37).

References

Wilma A. Bainbridge, Justin Hart, Elizabeth S. Kim, and Brian Scassellati. 2008. The effect of presence on human-robot interaction. In *17th IEEE International Symposium on Robot and Human Interactive Communication (RO-MAN)*, pages 701–706, Munich, Germany. IEEE.

Pierre Le Bras, David A. Robb, Thomas S. Methven, Stefano Padilla, and Mike J. Chantler. 2018. Improving user confidence in concept maps: Exploring data driven explanations. In *Proceedings of the 2018 CHI Conference on Human Factors in Computing Systems*, pages 1–13. ACM.

Tathagata Chakraborti, Sarath Sreedharan, Yu Zhang, and Subbarao Kambhampati. 2017. Plan explanations as model reconciliation: Moving beyond explanation as soliloquy. In *Proceedings of the Twenty-Sixth International Joint Conference on Artificial Intelligence*, IJCAI'17, pages 156–163, Melbourne, Australia.

Nina Dethlefs. 2014. Context-sensitive natural language generation: From knowledge-driven to data-driven techniques. *Language and Linguistics Compass*, 8(3):99–115.

Nina Dethlefs, Heriberto Cuayáhuitl, Helen Hastie, Verena Rieser, and Oliver Lemon. 2014. Cluster-based prediction of user ratings for stylistic surface realisation. In *Proceedings of the 14th Conference of the European Chapter of the Association for Computational Linguistics, EACL 2014*, pages 702–711, Gothenburg, Sweden. Association for Computational Linguistics.

Shirley Gregor and Izak Benbasat. 1999. Explanations from intelligent systems: Theoretical foundations and implications for practice. *MIS Quarterly*, 23(4):497–530.

Brent Harrison, Upol Ehsan, and Mark O. Riedl. 2017. Rationalization: A neural machine translation approach to generating natural language explanations.

Helen Hastie, Francisco J. Chiyah Garcia, David A. Robb, Pedro Patron, and Atanas Laskov. 2017a. MIRIAM: A multimodal chat-based interface for autonomous systems. In *Proceedings of the 19th ACM International Conference on Multimodal Interaction, ICMI'17*, pages 495–496, Glasgow, UK. ACM.

Helen Hastie, Xingkun Liu, and Pedro Patron. 2017b. Trust triggers for multimodal command and control interfaces. In *Proceedings of the 19th ACM International Conference on Multimodal Interaction, ICMI'17*, pages 261–268, Glasgow, UK. ACM.

Helen Hastie, Katrin Solveig Lohan, Mike J. Chantler, David A. Robb, Subramanian Ramamoorthy, Ron Petrick, Sethu Vijayakumar, and David Lane. 2018. The ORCA hub: Explainable offshore robotics through intelligent interfaces. In *Proceedings of Explainable Robotic Systems Workshop, HRI'18*, Chicago, IL, USA.

Srinivasan Janarthanam and Oliver Lemon. 2014. Adaptive generation in dialogue systems using dynamic user modeling. *Comput. Linguist.*, 40(4):883–920.

Philip Nicholas Johnson-Laird. 1980. Mental models in cognitive science. *Cognitive science*, 4(1):71–115.

Todd Kulesza, Simone Stumpf, Margaret Burnett, Sherry Yang, Irwin Kwan, and Weng-Keen Wong. 2013. Too much, too little, or just right? Ways explanations impact end users' mental models. In *2013 IEEE Symposium on Visual Languages and Human Centric Computing*, pages 3–10, San Jose, CA, USA.

Young-Sik Kwon and Byung-Ju Yi. 2012. Design and motion planning of a two-module collaborative indoor pipeline inspection robot. *IEEE Transactions on Robotics*, 28(3):681–696.

Jamy Li. 2015. The benefit of being physically present: A survey of experimental works comparing copresent robots, telepresent robots and virtual agents. *International Journal of Human-Computer Studies*, 77:23–37.

Jinke Li, Xinyu Wu, Tiantian Xu, Huiwen Guo, Jianquan Sun, and Qingshi Gao. 2017. A novel inspection robot for nuclear station steam generator secondary side with self-localization. *Robotics and Biomimetics*, 4(1):26.

Brian Y. Lim, Anind K. Dey, and Daniel Avrahami. 2009. Why and why not explanations improve the intelligibility of context-aware intelligent systems. In *Proceedings of the SIGCHI Conference on Human Factors in Computing Systems*, CHI '09, pages 2119–2129.

José Lopes, Katrin Lohan, and Helen Hastie. 2018. Symptoms of cognitive load in interactions with a dialogue system. In *ICMI Workshop on Modeling Cognitive Processes from Multimodal Data*, Boulder, CO, USA.

Joseph E. Mercado, Michael A. Rupp, Jessie YC. Chen, Michael J. Barnes, Daniel Barber, and Katelyn Procci. 2016. Intelligent agent transparency in humanagent teaming for Multi-UxV management. *Human Factors: The Journal of Human Factors and Ergonomics Society*, 58(3):401–415.

Keiji Nagatani, Seiga Kiribayashi, Yoshito Okada, Kazuki Otake, Kazuya Yoshida, Satoshi Tadokoro, Takeshi Nishimura, Tomoaki Yoshida, Eiji Koyanagi, and Mineo Fukushima. 2013. Emergency response to the nuclear accident at the fukushima daiichi nuclear power plants using mobile rescue robots. *Journal of Field Robotics*, 30(1):44–63.

Vittorio Perera, Sai P. Selveraj, Stephanie Rosenthal, and Manuela Veloso. 2016. Dynamic generation and refinement of robot verbalization. In *25th IEEE International Symposium on Robot and Human Interactive Communication (RO-MAN)*, pages 212–218, New York, NY, USA. IEEE.

Marco Tulio Ribeiro, Sameer Singh, and Carlos Guestrin. 2016. "Why should I trust you?": Explaining the predictions of any classifier. In *Proceedings of the 22nd ACM SIGKDD International Conference on Knowledge Discovery and Data Mining*, KDD'16, pages 1135–1144, New York, NY, USA. ACM.

David A. Robb, Francisco J. Chiyah Garcia, Atanas Laskov, Xingkun Liu, Pedro Patron, and Helen Hastie. 2018. Keep me in the loop: Increasing operator situation awareness through a conversational multimodal interface. In *Proceedings of the 20th ACM International Conference on Multimodal Interaction*, ICMI'18, Boulder, Colorado, USA. ACM.

Stephanie Rosenthal, Sai P. Selvaraj, and Manuela Veloso. 2016. Verbalization: Narration of Autonomous Robot Experience. In *Proceedings of the Twenty-Fifth International Joint Conference on Artificial Intelligence*, IJCAI'16, pages 862–868, New York, NY, USA. AAAI Press.

Julian B. Rotter. 1967. A new scale for the measurement of interpersonal trust. *Journal of Personality*, 35(4):651–665.

Kristin E. Schaefer. 2013. *The Perception and Measurement of Human-Robot Trust*. Ph.D. thesis, College of Sciences at the University of Central Florida, Florida, USA.

Amit Shukla and Hamad Karki. 2016. Application of robotics in onshore oil and gas industry-A review part I. *Robotics and Autonomous Systems*, 75:490–507.

Nava Tintarev and Roman Kutlak. 2014. SAsSy–Making decisions transparent with argumentation and natural language generation. *Proceedings of IUI 2014 Workshop on Interacting with Smart Objects*, pages 1–4.

Nava Tintarev and Judith Masthoff. 2012. Evaluating the effectiveness of explanations for recommender systems. *User Modeling and User-Adapted Interaction*, 22(4):399–439.

Marilyn A. Walker, Diane J. Litman, Candace A. Kamm, and Alicia Abella. 1997. PARADISE: A framework for evaluating spoken dialogue agents. In *Proceedings of the Eighth Conference on European Chapter of the Association for Computational Linguistics*, EACL'97, pages 271–280, Madrid, Spain. Association for Computational Linguistics.

Marilyn A Walker, Stephen J Whittaker, Amanda Stent, Preetam Maloor, Johanna Moore, Michael Johnston, and Gunaranjan Vasireddy. 2004. Generation and evaluation of user tailored responses in multimodal dialogue. *Cognitive Science*, 28(5):811–840.

Cuebong Wong, Erfu Yang, Xiu-Tian T. Yan, and Dongbing Gu. 2017. An overview of robotics and autonomous systems for harsh environments. In *2017 23rd International Conference on Automation and Computing (ICAC)*, pages 1–6, Huddersfield, UK. IEEE.

Robert H. Wortham, Andreas Theodorou, and Joanna J. Bryson. 2017. Robot transparency: Improving understanding of intelligent behaviour for designers and users. In *Towards Autonomous Robotic Systems: 18th Annual Conference, TAROS 2017*, Lecture Notes in Artificial Intelligence, pages 274–289, Guildford, UK. Springer.

Treat the system like a human student: Automatic naturalness evaluation of generated text without reference texts

Ye Tian   **Ioannis Douratsos**   **Isabel Groves**

Amazon Research Cambridge

Cambridge, UK

`{yetiancl, ioannisd, isabeg}@amazon.co.uk`

Abstract

The current most popular method for automatic Natural Language Generation (NLG) evaluation is comparing generated text with human-written reference sentences using a metrics system, which has drawbacks around reliability and scalability. We draw inspiration from second language (L2) assessment and extract a set of linguistic features to predict human judgments of sentence naturalness. Our experiment using a small dataset showed that the feature-based approach yields promising results, with the added potential of providing interpretability into the source of the problems.

1 Introduction

More and more text is generated in Machine Translation, Text Summarization, Image Captioning, and Dialogue Systems. With this increased usage of Natural Language Generation (NLG) comes an increase in the importance of evaluating the language generated, and an increase in the difficulty of doing so as the quantity and variety of output increases. Automatic NLG evaluation focuses on two areas: accuracy and fluency. The former assesses how well the generated text conveys the desired meaning, while the latter assesses how well the language flows: the 'linguistic quality of the text' (Gatt and Krahmer, 2018) and whether it sounds like something a native speaker of the language would naturally produce. This paper focuses on the latter. We first review current approaches in metrics-based evaluation, in referenceless evaluation and in second language (L2) language assessment; we then present our experiment in section 3.

1.1 Metrics system using human reference set - the lion's share

NLG evaluation has traditionally relied on human judgments (Mellish and Dale, 1998). Beyond that, the predominant automated method is to compare generated text with one or more human-created reference texts using a metric-based system (Gatt and Krahmer, 2018). The more similar the system output is to the human authored text, the better the system is judged to be. Popular metrics include BLEU (Papineni et al., 2002), ROUGE (Lin and Hovy, 2003), NIST (Doddington, 2002), METEOR (Lavie and Agarwal, 2007) and CIDEr (Vedantam et al., 2015), among others. Up to 60% of NLG research published between 2012 and 2015 relied on such metrics (Gkatzia and Mahamood, 2015)

However, it has repeatedly been found that automated metrics do not correlate well with human evaluations of generated text (Stent et al., 2005; Belz and Reiter, 2006; Reiter and Belz, 2009) and that the correlation is weaker at sentence-level than when evaluating a system overall. (Novikova et al., 2017a; Shimorina, 2018). Novikova et al. (2017a) compared popular comparison metrics used to evaluate NLG systems, concluding that the current state-of-the-art metrics are insufficient and cannot replace human judgments. They demonstrated that all the aforementioned automated metrics based on word-overlap with reference texts were strongly correlated with each other and only weakly correlated with human judgments of naturalness and quality. Furthermore, the least weak correlation found between any metric and human naturalness judgments was on the least varied dataset that only expressed a limited set of attributes and had less lexical diversity as it was only partially lexicalised (all proper names were replaced by placeholder variables). Given that lex-

Proceedings of The 11th International Natural Language Generation Conference, pages 109–118,
Tilburg, The Netherlands, November 5-8, 2018. ©2018 Association for Computational Linguistics

icalisation is a source of ungrammaticality in NLG (Sharma et al., 2016), this dataset therefore does not fully represent the challenge of evaluating the final output of an NLG system.

In addition to accuracy concerns, using a metrics system with a human reference set has several practical limitations. Firstly, building reference sets tends to require experts (e.g. translators) and is thus costly to create. Secondly, an output that is different from a human-written reference is not necessarily a bad sentence for the task: there are often multiple valid ways to express a desired meaning. The evaluation therefore requires multiple reference sentences, which makes producing a reference set even harder and generates complexities in similarity calculation. Thirdly, creating a human gold standard is not suitable for fast or large scale assessment. For NLG systems that cover a large variety of topics, the quantity of reference sentences required can be prohibitive to using this approach during system development.

1.2 Moving away from human reference set

We should look beyond evaluation using human references and learn from research outside our immediate domain, since there has been more research into automatic evaluation of text without human references in tasks similar to NLG than there has been for NLG itself.

One such domain is second language learner (L2) language assessment. Here the target is not machine-generated text but human-produced text. Over the last decade, a large body of work has identified linguistic features that indicate language fluency and complexity (Hancke et al., 2012; Feng, 2010; Chen and Zechner, 2011; Lu, 2010; Vajjala and Meurers, 2012). The linguistic feature based models in L2 assessment seem to correlate more strongly with human judgments of naturalness than current NLG evaluation metrics (with the caveat that these are different tasks). Many of the features require syntactic and discourse parsing, and they capture linguistic knowledge of what makes sentences readable and natural, as reflected in psycholinguistic studies on reading and parsing effort. These features are often more interpretable than purely statistical metrics, so potentially they allow us to not only evaluate the naturalness of a sentence or document, but also to identify *why* it is good or bad.

Another relevant domain is automatic grammat-

icality judgment. Wagner et al. (2009) investigated grammaticality classification using features such as part-of-speech (POS) n-gram frequencies and the output of probabilistic parsers trained on corpora of grammatical and ungrammatical sentences. They found that parse probability is reduced by spelling, agreement and verb form errors. Heilman et al. (2014) also found linguistic feature based models to be effective when using spelling, language model and grammar features from different parsers. They found that n-gram frequencies and the ability to be parsed were the most influential features for indicating grammaticality. This feature-based method also proved effective in grammaticality evaluation when applied to grammatical error correction applications (Napoles et al., 2016).

In Machine Translation, quality estimation without reference texts has been the subject of multiple shared tasks (Bojar et al., 2017). The QuEst 2015 sentence level model (Specia et al., 2015)[1] that provided the baseline for the latest completed task uses features of the source and/or target sentences including features from language model scores, length, part-of-speech and dependency parsing The leading system (Kim et al., 2017) in the 2017 task used an end-to-end stacked neural model consisting of a bilingual neural word prediction model and neural quality estimator model. The next best performing team's submission (Martins et al., 2017) used a stacked combination of a linear feature-based model (with dependency, POS and syntactic features) with a neural network.

Within NLG evaluation, Novikova et al. (2017a) examined the correlation between human evaluations and grammar-based measures that indicate readability and grammaticality. To measure grammaticality, they used the number of misspellings and the Stanford parser parsing score. Using the Flesch Reading Ease score (Flesch, 1979) and various other measures of complexity such as character, word, syllable and sentence counts, they found that, at a system level, systems producing utterances of higher readability and shorter word length received higher naturalness and overall quality ratings from humans. However, at sentence level there was no strong correlation between such metrics and human ratings that could reliably identify generated sen-

---

[1]http://www.quest.dcs.shef.ac.uk

tences with low readability or low grammaticality. This evidence that the linguistic features of texts do correlate with human judgments in NLG but that no single feature does so with a strong correlation supports our proposal that combining multiple grammatical features could automatically identify the quality of generated sentences.

We apply the feature-based approach used elsewhere by trying to identify whether machine-generated sentences are fluent and natural, and compare the predictions with human produced labels. Unlike previous work on grammaticality prediction we focus on the notion of "naturalness" or "fluency" rather than just grammaticality. This is because 1) psycholinguistic studies have shown that human perception of grammaticality is gradient (Keller, 2001), and 2) for most systems involving NLG, it matters how easy it is for humans to understand the sentences, not just whether the sentences are grammatical. With this in mind, we use features to capture the ease of parsing (influenced by grammaticality and syntactic complexity) and semantic soundness (influenced by word collocations and frequency). One recent investigation into NLG evaluation without reference texts that we are aware of used a recurrent neural network to estimate quality using the meaning representation input and output sentence to estimate the overall quality (Dušek et al., 2017). Our work differs in the use of linguistic features, which have proved successful in other domains and offer the prospect of interpretability, and we maintain the separation between evaluating the adequacy of the semantic content and evaluating the fluency of the text as has been found to be advisable for NLG evaluation (Stent et al., 2005).

2 Deriving the linguistic feature set

Expanding on the literature on L2 language assessment, especially (Hancke et al., 2012), and on grammaticality evaluation, we derived five groups of features (see full list in Table 1).

2.1 Lexical features

Lexical features include counts and ratios of words, lemmas and Part-of-Speech (POS) tokens. Type-Token Ratio (TTR), the ratio of the number of word types (in terms of lemmas) to total number of word tokens in a text, and its variants are used to measure lexical variation in language acquisition studies. We adopted the variations described in (Vajjala and Meurers, 2012) and word counts by POS categories, extracted using spaCy[3].

2.2 Constituency parse features

We used the BLLIP reranking parser (Charniak and Johnson, 2005), which includes a generative constituent parser and a discriminative maximum entropy reranker, and the WSJ-Gigaword-v2 model which consists of the Wall Street Journal corpus from Penn Tree Bank and two million sentences from Gigaword. From the parser output we used as features the parser log probability and reranker log probability of the most likely parse after reranking the 50-best parses. The idea is that parse probability reflects parser confidence and correlates with sentence quality (Mutton et al., 2007). We also added features for kurtosis and skew of the log probabilities of the 50 most likely parses, based on the idea that the distribution reflects sentence grammaticality and readability (Wagner et al., 2006). Our intuition was that a well-formed grammatical sentence would have positive skew and high kurtosis dropping steeply from the highly probable best parse to other much less likely parses. Conversely, an ungrammatical sentence would have a flatter kurtosis as none of the parses are very probable. Other features include tree height (length of the longest path from the root), number of subtrees, proportion of non-terminal subtrees, the number and mean token length of Noun Phrase (NP), Verb Phrase (VP) and Adjective Phrase (AdjP) sub-trees.

2.3 Dependency parse features

Using the spaCy dependency parser, we extracted the root word of the dependency tree and its part of speech, the tree height and the subtree height to either side of the root. The part of speech of the root is an indicator of whether the sentence has a main verb. The size of the tree on either side of the root reflects whether a sentence is "top" or "tail" heavy, or more balanced. This feature is based on the principle that sentences are easier to process, and thus are judged to be natural and well worded, if the dependencies of the head are roughly evenly distributed on either side (Temperley, 2008), and that heavy noun phrases are hard to process at the beginning of the sentence (Stallings et al., 1998).

---

[3]https://github.com/explosion/spaCy

Lexical Features		Constituency Parse Features	
Type-Token Ratio(TTR)	Num nouns	Constituency Tree height	Num NPs
Root TTR*	Num verbs	Parser probability*	NP average length
Corrected TTR*	Num possessives	Reranker probability*	Num VPs
Bilogarithmic TTR	Num preposition	50-best reranker score kurtosis*	VP average length*
Uber Index	Num determiners	50-best reranker score skew*	Num PPs
Lexical Density	Num adjectives	Num subtrees	PP average length
Answer length	Num relative pronouns	Num non-terminal subtrees	
Lexical repetition*	Num digits	% of non-terminal subtrees	
Num tokens	Num conjunctions		
Dependency Parse Features		**Language Model Features**	
Dependency tree height	Left subtree height	POS LM - Unigram	POS LM - Bigram*
Right subtree height	Num words left of root	POS LM - Trigram	Words LM - Score*
Num words right of root	Root POS	Words LM - Perplexity*	
Grammar Checker	LanguageTool		

Table 1: Feature list. Highest contribution features indicated by *

Model	class "Not Perfect"		class "Perfect"		Weighted F1	Overall Accuracy
	Precision	Recall	Precision	Recall		
Baselines						
Baseline always predicting "Not Perfect"	.84	1	0	0	.76	.84
Deep Learning Baseline	.85	.97	.42	.12	.79	.83
Feature-based models						
Random Forest	.90	.97	.77	.45	.88	.89
Logistic Regression[2]	.91	.96	.70	.49	.87	.88
Feature ablation						
LM perplexity only - KNeighbors	.84	.1	.60	.02	.77	.84
Parser reranker probability only - KNeighbors	.87	.97	.63	.27	.86	.83
Top 11 ranked features - Random Forest	.90	.97	.75	.46	.88	.89

Table 2: Results of baselines, top two feature-based classifiers and models using subset of features.

2.4 Language Model based features

A Language Model (LM) represents the probability distribution of n-grams in a corpus and can measure how "surprised" the model is to see a sentence. We used both POS-based LMs and word-based LMs. For POS-LMs, the POS sequences of each sentence were evaluated against unigram, bigram and trigram POS-based LMs trained on the Wall Street Journal corpus made available in CoNLL2000 (Tjong Kim Sang and Buchholz, 2000). Word-based LMs were trained using the KenLM package (Heafield et al., 2013). We trained two models, one using an English news corpus (available at (Heafield et al., 2013)), and the other using WikiText (Merity et al., 2016). The score was calculated as $\log_{10} p(sentence\langle/s\rangle|\langle s\rangle)$ where $\langle s \rangle$ and $\langle/s\rangle$ are the symbols for beginning and end of sentence, respectively. This reflects, after seeing a start-of-sentence symbol, the probability of a sentence appearing and being followed by an end-of-sentence token. Perplexity of a sentence was calculated with $10.0^{\frac{-score(sentence)}{length(words)+1}}$.

2.5 Grammar checker

We used the open source rule-based grammar checker LanguageTool[4] (Naber, 2003) to output a binary label of whether a sentence violates any of the English grammatical rules encoded in this tool.

3 Experiment

3.1 Data description

We collected our ground-truth evaluations through Amazon Mechanical Turk, asking participants to read machine-generated sentences and judge whether or not they are "perfectly good" English sentences. We opted for a binary judgment task rather than a graded one to make the judgment task simple for participants. The sentences evaluated were 4000 machine-generated sentences from the data released in the 2007/2008 Workshops on Statistical Machine Translation[5]. We did not use the provided human evaluation results because these were evaluations of adequacy, i.e. a mixture of overall quality, content accuracy, and fluency, and the labels were system rankings. We

____

[4]https://languagetool.org/, "Grammar" category only.

[5]http://www.statmt.org/wmt08/shared-evaluation-task.html

randomly allocated 4000 generated sentences into 40 lists. Each participant read 100 sentences and judged whether each was a "perfectly good" sentence that would sound grammatical and natural to someone with a high proficiency in English. Each sentence was judged by at least 5 participants. Overall, most sentences received the "Not Perfect" rating (Figure 1). The Fleiss kappa on the whole data set is 0.3. We then categorized sentences into "Perfect" (more than 70% "Perfect" judgments), "Not Perfect" (less than 30% "Perfect" judgments), and "Not Sure" (the remainder). There were 603 "perfect" sentences and 2637 "Not Perfect" ones, which were used for model training and evaluation. The 929 "not sure" sentences were excluded.

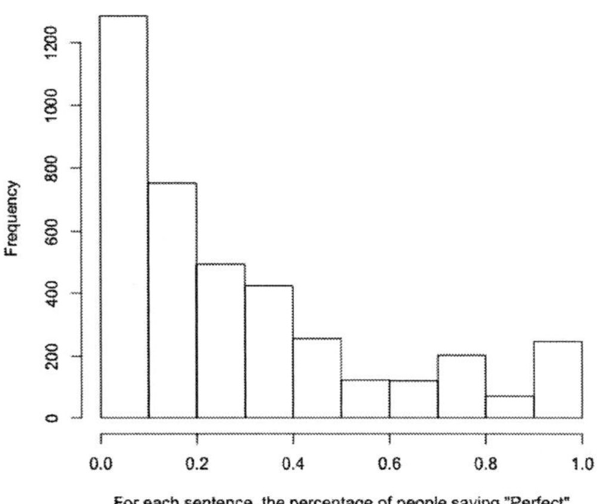

Figure 1: Percentage of "perfect" judgments per sentence

3.2 Training a classifier: Results

We trained "naturalness" classifiers in two ways: using a deep learning model on sentences represented by FastText word embeddings (Bojanowski et al., 2017), and using linguistic features. The deep learning model uses a pooled bidirectional Gated Recurrent Unit (GRU) architecture (Chung et al., 2014). After excluding data with missing feature values, there were 2934 observations for the models, 512 of which were "perfect". We split the data into three sets of equal size, two for training and one for testing.

Given the small dataset, the deep learning model serves as a baseline. It attained a marginally better weighted F1 than an "assume-all-not-perfect" baseline and a similar accuracy.

For the feature based models, we scaled numerical features to be centered around 0 with a standard deviation of 1. Categorical features were encoded in an 1-hot fashion so each level becomes a feature on its own. Using Scikit-learn (Pedregosa et al., 2011), we trained the following classifiers: Linear LVC with L1, L2 or combined penalty, Logistic Regression, KNeighbours Classifier, RandomForest, Perceptron, SGDClassifier and XGboost (Chen and Guestrin, 2016). We used the optimal hyper-parameters for each classifier acquired after running a 5-fold cross validation. We trained all classifiers 10 times and calculated the mean accuracy and F1 of the 10 sessions. The top six classifiers had very similar performances (Logistic Regression, LinearLVC with L1, L2 or combined penalty, RandomForest, SGD classifier). We report the mean results of the top two models in Table 2.

3.3 Error Analysis

When predicting the naturalness of 969 sentences, of which 158 were " Perfect", the top performing RandomForest model labeled 861 out of 969 (88.85%) correctly. It produced 87 incorrect "Not Perfect" labels, and 21 incorrect "Perfect" labels. The incorrect "Not Perfect" labels consisted of three main categories: long sentences (especially those with subordinate clauses), split sentences with inserts (e.g. "I shall, *of course*, inform the President of your comment.") and non-sentential segments that human judges deemed natural (e.g. "The Value of European Values."). Among the incorrect "Perfect" labels, some were assigned to sentences with isolated grammatical errors, such as incorrect verb agreement (e.g. "The Nobel laureate Gary Becker *disagree* with this view."), incorrect prepositions (e.g. "The journal Science *on* the issue last autumn published several contributions.", or word order errors (e.g. "What *now we can* do?"). The overall impression is that the sentences judged to be "Perfect" by the model are easier to read, and are less complex than ones judged to be "Not Perfect".

3.4 Feature Analysis

Different classifiers agreed on the top weighted features, but gave different rankings to features with lighter weight. The highest ranking feature for the top six classifiers is the parser-reranker probability, echoing previous findings that parse probability can be used to evaluate grammaticality

(Mutton et al., 2007). Other top features include number of tokens, number of verbs, constituency tree height and dependency tree height. The effectiveness of Language Model Perplexity and Score is sensitive to the corpora that the model is trained on. In this experiment, LM features trained on the Wikipedia data gave the whole model a .02% boost in F1 compared to LM scores trained on news corpora. We also tested a classifier that used the language model perplexity as the only feature in training and testing, and found this to be less accurate. This indicates that although a language model captures some notion of the likelihood of a sentence, it does not fully encapsulate all that is involved in making a sentence sound natural. Perhaps surprisingly, LanguageTool contributed very little. We realized that the rules it uses to detect grammatical errors are mostly linear and struggle with constituents involving longer dependencies. For example, LanguageTool judged the sentence "I represent a number of sugar beet growers and I am therefore very concerned." to violate the rule "MANY_NN_U", meaning that the quantifier "a number of" is followed by the uncountable noun "sugar", while the actual head noun is "growers".

For a feature ablation study, we used the Scikit-learn implementation of Recursive Feature Elimination to identify which features contributed most to the best performing model, the Random Forest Model. Retraining and testing on subsets of features found that using just the 11 best-performing features achieves the same F1 and accuracy as the model that used all the features. Adding additional lower-ranked features beyond that brought no significant additional benefit (Figure 2). These 11 features were: parser probability, reranker probability, reranker score kurtosis, reranker score skew, average length of verb phrases, the POS language model bigram score, root TTR, corrected TTR, lexical repetition, language model score and language model perplexity.

4 Model and Feature Set transferability

How well would our naturalness model trained on a small dataset in one domain - MT generated sentences about European politics - perform on an entirely different domain? To test the transferability, we used data provided by Novikova et al. (2017a)[6] of sentences produced by NLG systems participating in an end-to-end (E2E) NLG chal-

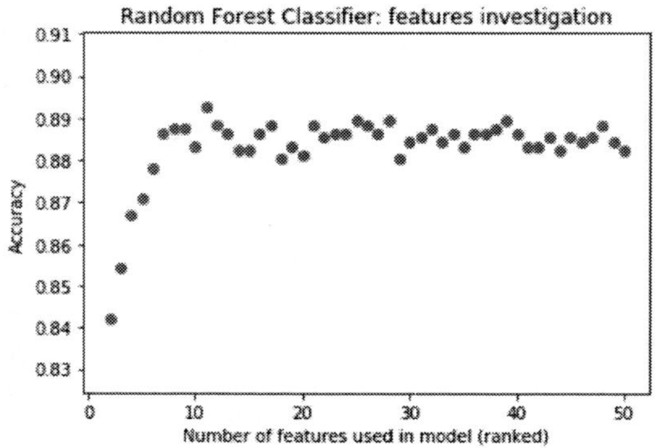

Figure 2: Accuracy results of Random Forest models using a subset of features, ranked by Recursive Feature Elimination

lenge[7] (Novikova et al., 2017b). We used the data from the lexicalised datasets SFRES and SFHOT datasets and the system outputs from the LOLS (Lampouras and Vlachos, 2016)[8] and RNNLG (Wen et al., 2015)[9] NLG systems. These sentences describe restaurant types, locations and categories to convey information given in a *slot+value* meaning representation. This provided 1954 unique sentences. We used the annotations for naturalness that human evaluators had provided on a 6-point Likert scale in response to the question '*Could the utterance have been produced by a native speaker?*'. For each unique system-generated response we took the mean naturalness score across the different annotators. As our model was trained for the task of identifying data as "perfect" versus "imperfect", we set a high threshold for naturalness: responses with a mean naturalness rating of greater than or equal to 5 and no single naturalness score below 5 were set with a ground-truth of perfect. This resulted in 426 "perfect" targets out of 1954 sentences. Using the model described above to predict the naturalness of this dataset resulted in an accuracy of .70 and a weighted F1 of .69. As a baseline for this dataset, always predicting 'imperfect' would have an accuracy of .78 and a weighted F1 of .68. Additionally, we used our classifier training and testing pipeline on this dataset, training on two thirds of the data (1309 sentences) and testing on the other third (645 sentences, of which 126 were 'perfect'). This surpassed the baseline for this dataset: across ten repetitions the mean weighted F1 was .73 and accuracy was .83. Repeating the exercise with just the top 11 features identified during the Feature Analysis above also

[6]https://github.com/jeknov/EMNLP_17_submission

[7]http://www.macs.hw.ac.uk/InteractionLab/E2E/
[8]https://github.com/glampouras/JLOLS_NLG
[9]https://github.com/shawnwun/RNNLG

Metric	Correlation with mean naturalness	p value
Our model	**0.23**	$p < 0.001$
METEOR	0.18	$p <0.001$
ROUGE L	0.17	$p <0.001$
Bleu 2	0.16	$p <0.001$
Bleu 1	0.15	$p <0.001$
CIDEr	0.15	$p <0.001$
Bleu 3	0.15	$p <0.001$
NIST	0.11	$p <0.01$
Bleu 4	0.11	$p <0.01$

Table 3: E2E NLG Challenge data: Spearman's ρ for mean fluency and grammaticality human judgments (model trained on E2E task data).

surpassed the baseline though was lower than the full feature set, resulting in a mean weighted F1 of .73 and an accuracy of .80. (always predicting 'imperfect' would achieve an F1 of .72 and accuracy of .80)

The model's predictions for this test set correlated weakly with the mean naturalness score with a Spearman's ρ of 0.23 ($p < 0.001$) (Table 3). Though this correlation is not very strong, it is notable that it is stronger than the correlation with all the other word-overlap metrics investigated by (Novikova et al., 2017a) and does not require a reference text to achieve this.

We also tested transferabiltiy with data from the WebNLG challenge[10] (Gardent et al., 2017) in order to test on more diverse content about different topics. The WebNLG data consists of sets of triples extracted from DBPedia across 15 different categories carefully designed to be varied. Utterances generated by WebNLG Challenge entrants underwent human annotation by participants from English-speaking countries. We used the annotations for fluency and grammaticality[11] which were graded separately, each on a three-point Likert scale. We set the ground truth of 'perfect' for those sentences which had a mean fluency and grammaticality annotation greater than or equal 2.6 with no single annotation lower than 2. This gave us 1959 unique sentences of which 624 were 'perfect'. Our original model's predictions resulted in an accuracy of 0.68 and a weighted F1 of 0.61. A baseline for this dataset that always predicted 'imperfect' would have an accuracy of 0.78 and an F1 of 0.55. As with the E2E set, performance

[10]http://webnlg.loria.fr/pages/challenge.html
[11]https://gitlab.com/shimorina/webnlg-human-evaluation/

	Correlation with fluency	Correlation with grammaticality
Our model	0.35	**0.46**
Bleu	0.33	0.28

Table 4: WebNLG Challenge data: Spearman's ρ correlation with mean fluency and grammaticality human judgments (model trained on WebNLG task data). All $p <0.001$

improved when trained on data from this task. We used our pipeline to train a model on this data, split two thirds/one third between training and testing giving a test set of 647 of which 433 were 'perfect'. This resulted in an accuracy of 0.71 and a weighted F1 of 0.69 (the mean over 10 iterations). A baseline for this test set that always predicted 'imperfect' would have an accuracy of 0.44 and an F1 of 0.55. This indicates that our feature set can capture some characteristics of what constitutes a well-worded response in these domains also.

We use the Bleu scores that had been calculated using the dataset's reference sentences to compare Bleu's correlation with fluency and grammaticality judgments and the correlation with our model's predictions. The original model correlates very weakly with mean fluency score (Spearman's ρ 0.08, $p <0.001$) and does not correlate significantly with mean grammaticality score $p >0.05$). However, when trained on this task, the model's predictions were moderately and significantly positively correlated with the mean fluency and grammaticality ratings (Table 4). The correlation with Bleu is weaker on this test set: trained on data from this task, we achieve better correlation with fluency and in particular grammaticality judgments than Bleu.

This exercise shows that while our model may have limited direct transferability when there are significant differences between the type of sentences seen in the training data domain versus the test, our feature-based method and feature set are more transferable than the model itself. When trained on data for a different task, different features from the set can contribute to identifying what constitutes a high quality sentence in this genre. This approach could be used to evaluate the naturalness of generated text for a particular task by using a small set of human-annotated data to train a model that can cheaply and easily be used over a larger quantity of data to given an indication of the naturalness.

5   Conclusions and Future Work

We presented a linguistic feature based approach to automatic naturalness evaluation of machine generated text, building on findings from L2 assessment research. Our experiment using a small dataset showed promising results suggesting that this is a viable path towards scalable naturalness evaluation of machine-generated text, with potential for interpretability which can help identify and prioritize improvements to an NLG system during development. In future work, we aim to extend this approach to outputs in multiple languages and multiple domains to further assess the transferability of the approach and of specific models. We will go beyond a binary classification of "perfect" versus "imperfect" to better account for cases where there is inter-speaker variation in naturalness judgments. We also plan to investigate improving deep neural models by adopting recent advancements in contextualized deep word and sentence embeddings (Peters et al., 2018; Perone et al., 2018) and transfer learning in sentence representation (Howard and Ruder, 2018; Radford et al., 2018).

References

Anja Belz and Ehud Reiter. 2006. Comparing automatic and human evaluation of NLG systems. In *11th Conference of the European Chapter of the Association for Computational Linguistics*.

Piotr Bojanowski, Edouard Grave, Armand Joulin, and Tomas Mikolov. 2017. Enriching word vectors with subword information. *Transactions of the Association of Computational Linguistics* 5(1):135–146.

Ondřej Bojar, Rajen Chatterjee, Christian Federmann, Yvette Graham, Barry Haddow, Shujian Huang, Matthias Huck, Philipp Koehn, Qun Liu, Varvara Logacheva, et al. 2017. Findings of the 2017 conference on machine translation (WMT17). In *Proceedings of the Second Conference on Machine Translation*. pages 169–214.

Eugene Charniak and Mark Johnson. 2005. Coarse-to-fine N-best parsing and maxent discriminative reranking. In *Proceedings of the 43rd Annual Meeting of the Association for Computational Linguistics (ACL'05)*. Association for Computational Linguistics, Ann Arbor, Michigan, pages 173–180. http://www.aclweb.org/anthology/P/P05/P05-1022.pdf.

Miao Chen and Klaus Zechner. 2011. Computing and evaluating syntactic complexity features for automated scoring of spontaneous non-native speech. In *Proceedings of the 49th Annual Meeting of the Association for Computational Linguistics: Human Language Technologies-Volume 1*. Association for Computational Linguistics, pages 722–731.

Tianqi Chen and Carlos Guestrin. 2016. Xgboost: A scalable tree boosting system. In *Proceedings of the 22nd acm sigkdd international conference on knowledge discovery and data mining*. ACM, pages 785–794.

Junyoung Chung, Çaglar Gülçehre, KyungHyun Cho, and Yoshua Bengio. 2014. Empirical evaluation of gated recurrent neural networks on sequence modeling. *CoRR* abs/1412.3555. http://arxiv.org/abs/1412.3555.

George Doddington. 2002. Automatic evaluation of machine translation quality using n-gram co-occurrence statistics. In *Proceedings of the Second International Conference on Human Language Technology Research*. Morgan Kaufmann Publishers Inc., San Francisco, CA, USA, HLT '02, pages 138–145. http://dl.acm.org/citation.cfm?id=1289189.1289273.

Ondřej Dušek, Jekaterina Novikova, and Verena Rieser. 2017. Referenceless quality estimation for natural language generation. *Proceedings of the 1st Workshop on Learning to Generate Natural Language, Sydney, Australia.* .

Lijun Feng. 2010. *Automatic readability assessment*.

Rudolf Franz Flesch. 1979. *How to write plain English: A book for lawyers and consumers*. Harpercollins.

Claire Gardent, Anastasia Shimorina, Shashi Narayan, and Laura Perez-Beltrachini. 2017. Creating training corpora for micro-planners. In *Proceedings of the 55th Annual Meeting of the Association for Computational Linguistics (Volume 1: Long Papers)*. Association for Computational Linguistics, Vancouver, Canada.

Albert Gatt and Emiel Krahmer. 2018. Survey of the state of the art in natural language generation: Core tasks, applications and evaluation. *Journal of Artificial Intelligence Research* 61:65–170.

Dimitra Gkatzia and Saad Mahamood. 2015. A snapshot of NLG evaluation practices 2005-2014. In *Proceedings of the 15th European Workshop on Natural Language Generation (ENLG)*. pages 57–60.

Julia Hancke, Sowmya Vajjala, and Detmar Meurers. 2012. Readability classification for german using lexical, syntactic, and morphological features. *Proceedings of COLING 2012* pages 1063–1080.

Kenneth Heafield, Ivan Pouzyrevsky, Jonathan H. Clark, and Philipp Koehn. 2013. Scalable modified Kneser-Ney language model estimation. In *Proceedings of the 51st Annual Meeting of the Association for Computational Linguistics*. Sofia, Bulgaria, pages 690–696.

Michael Heilman, Aoife Cahill, Nitin Madnani, Melissa Lopez, Matthew Mulholland, and Joel Tetreault. 2014. Predicting grammaticality on an ordinal scale. In *Proceedings of the 52nd Annual Meeting of the Association for Computational Linguistics (Volume 2: Short Papers)*. volume 2, pages 174–180.

Jeremy Howard and Sebastian Ruder. 2018. Universal language model fine-tuning for text classification. In *Proceedings of the 56th Annual Meeting of the Association for Computational Linguistics (Volume 1: Long Papers)*. volume 1, pages 328–339.

Frank Keller. 2001. *Gradience in grammar: Experimental and computational aspects of degrees of grammaticality*. Ph.D. thesis, University of Edinburgh.

Hyun Kim, Jong-Hyeok Lee, and Seung-Hoon Na. 2017. Predictor-estimator using multilevel task learning with stack propagation for neural quality estimation. In *Proceedings of the Second Conference on Machine Translation*. pages 562–568.

Gerasimos Lampouras and Andreas Vlachos. 2016. Imitation learning for language generation from unaligned data. In *Proceedings of COLING 2016, the 26th International Conference on Computational Linguistics: Technical Papers*. pages 1101–1112.

Alon Lavie and Abhaya Agarwal. 2007. METEOR: An automatic metric for MT evaluation with high levels of correlation with human judgments. In *Proceedings of the Second Workshop on Statistical Machine Translation*. Association for Computational Linguistics, pages 228–231.

Chin-Yew Lin and Eduard Hovy. 2003. Automatic evaluation of summaries using n-gram co-occurrence statistics pages 71–78.

Xiaofei Lu. 2010. Automatic analysis of syntactic complexity in second language writing. *International journal of corpus linguistics* 15(4):474–496.

André FT Martins, Fabio Kepler, and Jose Monteiro. 2017. Unbabel's participation in the WMT17 translation quality estimation shared task. In *Proceedings of the Second Conference on Machine Translation*. pages 569–574.

Chris Mellish and Robert Dale. 1998. Evaluation in the Context of Natural Language Generation. *Computer Speech & Language* 12(4):349–373. https://doi.org/10.1006/csla.1998.0106.

Stephen Merity, Caiming Xiong, James Bradbury, and Richard Socher. 2016. Pointer sentinel mixture models. *CoRR* abs/1609.07843. http://arxiv.org/abs/1609.07843.

Andrew Mutton, Mark Dras, Stephen Wan, and Robert Dale. 2007. GLEU: Automatic evaluation of sentence-level fluency. In *Proceedings of the 45th Annual Meeting of the Association of Computational Linguistics*. pages 344–351.

Daniel Naber. 2003. A rule-based style and grammar checker .

Courtney Napoles, Keisuke Sakaguchi, and Joel Tetreault. 2016. There's no comparison: Referenceless evaluation metrics in grammatical error correction. *arXiv preprint arXiv:1610.02124* .

Jekaterina Novikova, Ondřej Dušek, Amanda Cercas Curry, and Verena Rieser. 2017a. Why we need new evaluation metrics for NLG. In *Proceedings of the 2017 Conference on Empirical Methods in Natural Language Processing*. pages 2241–2252. http://arxiv.org/abs/1707.06875.

Jekaterina Novikova, Ondřej Dušek, and Verena Rieser. 2017b. The e2e dataset: New challenges for end-to-end generation. In *Proceedings of the 18th Annual SIGdial Meeting on Discourse and Dialogue*. pages 201–206.

Kishore Papineni, Salim Roukos, Todd Ward, and Wei-Jing Zhu. 2002. Bleu: a method for automatic evaluation of machine translation. In *Proceedings of the 40th annual meeting on association for computational linguistics*. Association for Computational Linguistics, pages 311–318.

F. Pedregosa, G. Varoquaux, A. Gramfort, V. Michel, B. Thirion, O. Grisel, M. Blondel, P. Prettenhofer, R. Weiss, V. Dubourg, J. Vanderplas, A. Passos, D. Cournapeau, M. Brucher, M. Perrot, and E. Duchesnay. 2011. Scikit-learn: Machine learning in Python. *Journal of Machine Learning Research* 12:2825–2830.

Christian S Perone, Roberto Silveira, and Thomas S Paula. 2018. Evaluation of sentence embeddings in downstream and linguistic probing tasks. *arXiv preprint arXiv:1806.06259* .

Matthew Peters, Mark Neumann, Mohit Iyyer, Matt Gardner, Christopher Clark, Kenton Lee, and Luke Zettlemoyer. 2018. Deep contextualized word representations. In *Proceedings of the 2018 Conference of the North American Chapter of the Association for Computational Linguistics: Human Language Technologies, Volume 1 (Long Papers)*. volume 1, pages 2227–2237.

Alec Radford, Karthik Narasimhan, Tim Salimans, and Ilya Sutskever. 2018. Improving language understanding by generative pre-training .

Ehud Reiter and Anja Belz. 2009. An investigation into the validity of some metrics for automatically evaluating natural language generation systems. *Computational Linguistics* 35(4):529–558.

Shikhar Sharma, Jing He, Kaheer Suleman, Hannes Schulz, and Philip Bachman. 2016. Natural language generation in dialogue using lexicalized and delexicalized data. *arXiv preprint arXiv:1606.03632* .

Anastasia Shimorina. 2018. Human vs automatic metrics: on the importance of correlation design. *arXiv preprint arXiv:1805.11474* .

Lucia Specia, Gustavo Paetzold, and Carolina Scarton. 2015. Multi-level translation quality prediction with QuEst++. *Proceedings of ACL-IJCNLP 2015 System Demonstrations* pages 115–120.

Lynne M Stallings, Maryellen C MacDonald, and Padraig G O'Seaghdha. 1998. Phrasal ordering constraints in sentence production: Phrase length and verb disposition in heavy-np shift. *Journal of Memory and Language* 39(3):392–417.

Amanda Stent, Matthew Marge, and Mohit Singhai. 2005. Evaluating evaluation methods for generation in the presence of variation. In *International Conference on Intelligent Text Processing and Computational Linguistics*. Springer, pages 341–351.

David Temperley. 2008. Dependency-length minimization in natural and artificial languages. *Journal of Quantitative Linguistics* 15(3):256–282.

Erik F. Tjong Kim Sang and Sabine Buchholz. 2000. Introduction to the CoNLL-2000 shared task: Chunking. In *Proceedings of the 2nd Workshop on Learning Language in Logic and the 4th Conference on Computational Natural Language Learning - Volume 7*. Association for Computational Linguistics, Stroudsburg, PA, USA, ConLL '00, pages 127–132. https://doi.org/10.3115/1117601.1117631.

Sowmya Vajjala and Detmar Meurers. 2012. On improving the accuracy of readability classification using insights from second language acquisition. In *Proceedings of the Seventh Workshop on Building Educational Applications Using NLP*. pages 163–173.

Ramakrishna Vedantam, C Lawrence Zitnick, and Devi Parikh. 2015. CIDEr: Consensus-based image description evaluation. In *Proceedings of the IEEE conference on computer vision and pattern recognition*. pages 4566–4575.

Joachim Wagner, Jennifer Foster, and Josef van Genabith. 2006. Detecting grammatical errors using probabilistic parsing. In *Workshop on Interfaces of Intelligent Computer-Assisted Language Learning*. pages 1–25. http://www.noe-kaleidoscope.org/group/idill/repository/iicall06.pdf.

Joachim Wagner, Jennifer Foster, and Josef van Genabith. 2009. Judging grammaticality: Experiments in sentence classification. *CALICO Journal* 26(3):474–490.

Tsung-Hsien Wen, Milica Gasic, Nikola Mrkšić, Pei-Hao Su, David Vandyke, and Steve Young. 2015. Semantically conditioned lstm-based natural language generation for spoken dialogue systems. In *Proceedings of the 2015 Conference on Empirical Methods in Natural Language Processing*. Association for Computational Linguistics, Lisbon, Portugal, pages 1711–1721. http://aclweb.org/anthology/D15-1199.

Content Aware Source Code Change Description Generation

Pablo Loyola[1*], Edison Marrese-Taylor[2*], Jorge A. Balazs[2]
Yutaka Matsuo[2] and Fumiko Satoh[1]
IBM Research, Tokyo, Japan[1]
{e57095, sfumiko}@jp.ibm.com
Graduate School of Engineering, The University of Tokyo, Japan[2]
{emarrese, jorge, matsuo}@weblab.t-utokyo.ac.jp
[*]Authors contributed equally to this work.

Abstract

We propose to study the generation of descriptions from source code changes by integrating the messages included on code commits and the intra-code documentation inside the source in the form of docstrings. Our hypothesis is that although both types of descriptions are not directly aligned in semantic terms —one explaining a change and the other the actual functionality of the code being modified— there could be certain common ground that is useful for the generation. To this end, we propose an architecture that uses the source code-docstring relationship to guide the description generation. We discuss the results of the approach comparing against a baseline based on a sequence-to-sequence model, using standard automatic natural language generation metrics as well as with a human study, thus offering a comprehensive view of the feasibility of the approach.

1 Introduction

Transferring the semantics from source code to natural language and vice-versa is at the core of several machine learning endeavors, as it could enable a direct communication between man and machine, improving the level of interpretability and comprehension between each other and easing their collaboration.

In that sense, source code can be conceived as an actual medium of communication from two perspectives, which have been explored separately in both computational linguistics and software engineering communities (Allamanis et al., 2017).

In the first place, from a *developer-program* perspective, source code encodes, in a set of human readable instructions, the requirements a developer commands a program to satisfy. This view has been operationalized as a machine translation problem, trying to learn efficient transitions between the dependencies that words and source code tokens exhibit. With this, recent approaches have been able to summarize source code snippets (Allamanis et al., 2016) or even synthesize natural language instructions into actual commands (Oda et al., 2015; Yin and Neubig, 2017).

In the second place, from a *developer-developer* perspective, the collaborative nature of software development has transformed source code into a common ground for human interaction. In that sense, every new code contribution takes into account the previous modifications, allowing developers to communicate indirectly. One of these applications is the generation of descriptions for source code changes (Loyola et al., 2017), which uses the information contained in a code commit – the *diff* representing the changed code and the message the developer provides at submission time – to train an encoder-decoder architecture. This problem has the particularity of containing certain elements of summarization, as most salient characteristics of the code change need to be extracted, and translation, as it is required to generate a natural language description from a code change.

In this work, we consider the generation of descriptions for source changes as a testing task to explore if the perspectives presented above can be integrated into a single learning architecture. That is, we want to learn to generate descriptions from changes exploiting the information in the source code commits, but incorporating the program functionality expressed through the *docstrings* contained within the source code.

Our hypothesis is that, while both perspectives point at different semantic directions, there should be a certain degree of dependency, since in order

Proceedings of The 11th International Natural Language Generation Conference, pages 119–128,
Tilburg, The Netherlands, November 5-8, 2018. ©2018 Association for Computational Linguistics

to perform a change on the code the developer first needs to understand its functionality. Moreover, we consider that integrating these two perspectives could contribute to alleviate the issues that current approaches for generating descriptions from source code change present, such as the hallucination in the generation, where generated descriptions are syntactically correct but that do not keep any semantic relationship with the actual code change, and also the inability of the model to produce descriptions with a relevant amount of detail.

We propose an approach that, given a code change, compresses the information associated to the docstrings within the file being modified and uses it as an additional context when selecting the next word from the output vocabulary. We also reported an exploratory approach that generates a mask to be used at decoding time that considers the inter-perspective distances based on a bilingual embedding.

In addition to integrating change descriptions and source code documentation, we also explore how to represent the code change itself. Previous work on description generation has relied on the output from the *diff* command, which provides a distinction between the portions of the source code that were added and removed. Such data source has been treated just as a sequence of source code tokens, such as in the case of Loyola et al. (2017). In contrast, we explore an architectural variation where we use two encoders to obtain a more expressive signal from the source code perspective, which can lead to a better natural language generation.

We constructed a dataset by merging both change history and docstring data from several real world open source projects to evaluate our approach. We reported the results on standard translation-based metrics as well through a user study using a crowd-sourcing, to get a more qualitative estimation of the performance of the model.

Our results show that, on average, incorporating a signal from the content of the source code file has a positive impact on the performance of the model. We consider these results could open the door to further research that considers the generation of descriptions from software artifacts from a more systemic perspective. The source code and data for this approach is available at: `https://github.com/epochx/py-commitgen`.

2 Related Work

The emergence of unifying paradigms that explicitly relate programming and natural languages in distributional terms (Hindle et al., 2012) and the availability of large corpus mainly from open source software opened the door for the use of language modeling for several tasks (Raychev et al., 2015). Examples of this are approaches for learning program representations (Mou et al., 2016), bug localization (Huo et al., 2016), API suggestion (Gu et al., 2016) and code completion (Raychev et al., 2014).

Source code summarization has received special attention, ranging from the use of information retrieval techniques to the addition of physiological features such as eye tracking (Rodeghero et al., 2014). In recent years several representation learning approaches have been proposed, such as (Allamanis et al., 2016), where the authors employ a convolutional architecture embedded inside an attention mechanism to learn an efficient mapping between source code tokens and natural language keywords. More recently, Iyer et al. (2016) proposed a encoder-decoder model that learns to summarize from Stackoverflow data, which contains snippets of code along with descriptions.

Both approaches share the use of attention mechanisms (Bahdanau et al., 2014) to overcome the natural disparity between the modalities when finding relevant token alignments. Although we also use an attention mechanism, we differ from them in the sense we are targeting the changes in the code rather than the description of a file.

In terms of specifically working on code change summarization, Cortés-Coy et al. (2014); Linares-Vásquez et al. (2015) propose a method based on a set of rules that considers the type and impact of the changes, and Buse and Weimer (2010) combines summarization with symbolic execution. The use of representation learning based models has been also explored recently, such as the work of Loyola et al. (2017) and Jiang et al. (2017). Both approaches make use of an encoder-decoder architecture, which receives code change, in the form of a *diff* output and the associated message submitted by the contributor.

In terms of ad-hoc datasets, we can mention Zhong et al. (2017) for questions, SQL queries, Oda et al. (2015) for pseudo code in Python, and more recently Barone and Sennrich (2017) for code-docstrings from Python projects on GitHub.

3 Proposed Approach

Our starting point is the code commit, understood as a pair conformed by (i) the differences in the source code obtained as the output of the *diff*[1] command and (ii) the associated message the committer provided to explain the action.

Therefore, for a given software project we can formalize our available data as the set of its T versions $v_1, \ldots, v_T$. Commits are well-defined for every pair of consecutive project versions $\Delta_{t-1}^{t}(v) \to Commit_t$, so we end up with a total of T commits, each associated to a project version. With this, we model each commit as a tuple (C_t, N_t), where C_t is a representation of the code changes associated to v in time t, and N_t is a representation of its corresponding natural language (NL) accompanying message. Concretely, C_t corresponds to the set of code tokens associated to the commit that was applied to a certain file F_{C_t}, based on the *atomicity* assumption. In principle, we do not assume this set of source code tokens is ordered in a sequential fashion, allowing us to also represent it as a bag of tokens.

Let $\mathcal{C}$ be the set of code changes and $\mathcal{N}$ be the set of all descriptions in NL. We consider a training corpus with T code snippets and message pairs (C_t, N_t), $1 \leq t \leq T$, $C_t \in \mathcal{C}$, $N_t \in \mathcal{N}$. Then, for a given code snippet $C_k \in \mathcal{C}$, our goal is to train a model to produce the most likely description $N^\star$.

Following Loyola et al. (2017), we start building our models upon a vanilla encoder-decoder model that at training time receives *(diff, message)* pairs. We use an attention-augmented architecture (Luong et al., 2015) with a bi-directional LSTM as encoder. Let $X_t = x_1, \ldots x_n$ be the embedded input code sequence $C_t = c_1, \ldots, c_n$ as extracted from the *diff*. After feeding these through our encoder, we have a set of vectors $H = h_1, \ldots h_n$ that represent the input. This is later given to the decoder, in our case also an LSTM, such that the probability of a description is modeled as the product of the conditional next-word probabilities, $p(n_i | n_1, \ldots, n_{i-1}) \propto W_c[s_i; a_i]$, where $N_t = n_1, \ldots, n_m$ corresponds to the message tokens, $\propto$ denotes a softmax operation, s_i represents the decoder hidden state and a_i is the contribution from the attention model on the input. W_c is a trainable combination matrix. The decoder repeats the recurrence until a fixed number of words or the special *EOS* token is generated.

The attention contribution a_i is defined as $a_i = \sum_{j=1}^{n} \alpha_{i,j} \cdot h_j$, where h_j is a hidden state associated to the input and $\alpha_{i,j}$ is a score obtained using the general attention scheme (Luong et al., 2015),
$$\alpha_{i,j} = \frac{\exp\left(h_i^\top W_a s_i\right)}{\sum_{j=1}^{n} \exp\left(h_j^\top W_a s_i\right)},$$
where W_a is a trainable scoring matrix.

During training, the decoder iterates until the end-of-sentence token is reached. For generation, we approximate $N^\star$ by performing a beam search on the space of all possible summaries using the model output, with a beam size of 10 and a maximum message length equal to the maximum length of the inputs of the dataset.

This model considers a direct transition between *diffs* and messages extracted from source code commits. However, programs usually provide an additional relationship between source code and natural language, in the form of intra-code documentation, commonly known as doc-strings.

This documentation appears in multiple locations inside a source code file, usually aligned with a specific line or block, explaining its functionality. The information contained in a *code, docstring* pair is intrinsically local, i.e. the docstring is used as an additional source to support the understanding of a portion of a program beyond the solely internalization of the available source code. Listing 1 presents an example of a real docstring associated to a class from the Pytorch library[2]. In this case we can see that the docstring provides an overall description of the functionality of the class and a summary of the required parameters.

```python
 1  class LambdaLR(_LRScheduler):
 2      """Sets the learning rate of each parameter group to the
            initial lr
 3      times a given function. When last_epoch=-1, sets initial
            lr as lr.
 4      Args:
 5          optimizer (Optimizer): Wrapped optimizer.
 6          lr_lambda (function or list): A function which
            computes a multiplicative
 7              factor given an integer parameter epoch, or a
            list of such
 8              functions, one for each group in optimizer.
            param_groups.
 9          last_epoch (int): The index of last epoch. Default:
            -1.
10      ...
11      """
12      def __init__(self, optimizer, lr_lambda, last_epoch=-1):
13      ...
```

Listing 1: Example of a docstring from a Pytorch module.

If we take a look at the changes committed to this specific class, we can find that most of the

---

[1] http://man7.org/linux/man-pages/man1/diff.1.html

commit messages associated keep certain relationship with the docstring. For example, a commit[3] from August 8th, 2018 states:

```
Changed serialization
mechanism of LambdaLR
scheduler
```

Therefore, we are in the presence of two sets of pairs that provide information about the characteristics of a program from two different perspectives. A *(diff, message)* pair set that allow us to understand *why* and *how* changes are conducted over a given file, and a *(code, docstring)* that allow us to understand *what* is the functionality of such file.

Our goal is then to integrate both sources, i.e., to study how the local source code - natural language feature representations learned from the *(code, docstring)* pair can be used to support the generation of natural language descriptions from code changes. Our hypothesis is that while the *(diff, message)* and *(code, docstring)* pairs associated to a file are not pointing at the same semantic direction, they should share certain representational components, as both are centered on the information contained on the file: one trying to explain the code itself *(code, docstring)* and the other trying to explain changes on such code *(diff, message)*.

3.1 Content-aware encoder

We noted that the comments contained within a source file are related to the local functionality of its adjacent source code lines or blocks. In contrast, the message associated to a commit is related to the actual action carried out on the given file. Such message, in theory, is indirectly associated to the functionality of the code, i.e. the code was modified in a given way because its previous functional state led triggered in a developer the need to change it.

Motivated by this idea, we propose an augmented encoder that allows us to capture these relations. Again, let $H = h_1, \ldots h_n$ be the result of embedding and processing the input content extracted from C_t. We extract the code and associated docstring of the total r lines of file F_{C_t}. With this, we model each code and docstring line as a sequence of tokens $L_k^c = x_1^c, \ldots, x_p^c$ and $L_k^d = x_1^d, \ldots, x_q^d$, of length p and q respectively. We use BiLSTMs to encode both sequences inde-

---

[3]https://bit.ly/2zx4041

pendently, as follows.

$$\vec{h}_i^c = \overrightarrow{\text{LSTM}}(x_i^c, \vec{h}_{i-1}^c) \tag{1}$$

$$\overleftarrow{h}_i^c = \overleftarrow{\text{LSTM}}(x_i^c, \overleftarrow{h}_{i+1}^c) \tag{2}$$

$$\vec{h}_i^d = \overrightarrow{\text{LSTM}}(x_i^d, \vec{h}_{i+1}^d) \tag{3}$$

$$\overleftarrow{h}_i^d = \overleftarrow{\text{LSTM}}(x_i^d, \overleftarrow{h}_{i+1}^d) \tag{4}$$

As Figure 1 shows, we concatenate the last hidden state corresponding to each code and docstring vector to obtain a representation for each line $h^k = [\vec{h}_p^c; \overleftarrow{h}_p^c; \vec{h}_q^d; \overleftarrow{h}_q^d]$, with $k = 1, \ldots, r$.

Finally, we use a standard LSTM to model the dependency across the r code/docstring line vectors and take the last hidden state as a means of aggregating and representing the content of both the code and docstring in F_{C_t}. This summarizing vector is concatenated to each h_i coming from the *diff*-level representation. The decoding phase works in a way analogous to the vanilla encoder-decoder model.

3.2 Content-aware decoder

During our feasibility study, we empirically observed that there was a significant overlap between the source code vocabularies coming from the *diffs* and from the code extracted from the files, which in some cases reaches up to 90%.

Our intuition based on such observation is that we can consider both source code vocabularies as a single vocabulary, which is used in two different contexts. In other words, a defined set of source code tokens is conforming a bridge between the messages from the code changes and the docstrings.

To exploit such bridge we explored incorporating the information contained in the *(code, doc-*

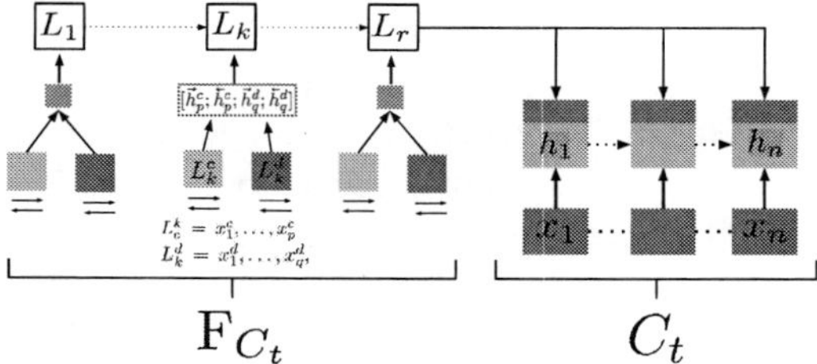

Figure 1: Diagram of our proposed content-aware encoder. It can be seen how the regular encoder hidden states $h_1, \ldots, h_n$ (in green) are augmented using the representation extracted from the content and docstring in F_{C_t} (in blue).

string) pairs into the code change description generation by building a mask to guide the decoder. This mask is built upon co-occurrence patterns between message and docstring words, which are used to re-weight the scores the decoder is generating on the output vocabulary. Concretely, during inference our goal was to re-weight the probabilities that are passed to the beam search module.

As stated before, for each project, we have a set of code changes represented as pairs (C_t, N_t), for $C_t \in \mathcal{C}$ the set of *diff* outputs, $N_t \in \mathcal{N}$ the set of messages submitted at commit time. On the other hand, for each commit-derived modified file associated to F_{C_t} $t = 1, \ldots, T$ we have a set of pairs *(code, docstring)*. We train bilingual word embeddings between the set of source code content and their associated docstring lines. The intuition behind this is that the docstring basically explains — or translates to natural language— the functionality of a source code block. While this intuition is arguably not entirely true from a machine translation perspective, at least it allows us to obtain a shared feature space between code and docstring tokens. We adapted the approach by Artetxe et al. (2017), calling the output embedding *C-DC*.

In the second place, we construct another embedding space to combine the set of messages from the commits, and the docstrings, such that this embedding only contains natural language tokens. In this case we do not expect a high overlap between the vocabularies of each set, as they are pointing at different semantic directions —their intent is different. To build this embedding space, we use a standard word2vec (Mikolov et al., 2013) implementation, and call the resulting embedding *M-DC*.

Using the above embedding spaces as mappings, the approach works as follows. Given an input sequence $C_t = c_1, \ldots, c_n$ from a *diff*, each of its tokens c_i used to query the *C-DC* embedding to obtain a set of k neighboring NL tokens K_t. For each NL token in K_t, we obtain its vector representation in *M-DC* and identify a medoid, med_{K_t}. We consider this medoid not only as the representative of K_t, but also indirectly of the associated source code token c_i. We then use this medoid vector and compute its distance to all the elements in the output message vocabulary OV present in *M-DC*, $d_{t,i} = dist(med_{K_t}, i)$ for $i \in OV$. We repeat this process for all the source code tokens from the input *diff* sequence obtaining a distance

matrix of $n \times |OV|$.

Finally, we compute the column-wise average distance, obtaining a vector d_s of size $1 \times |OV|$, which represents a compressed association between the input source code sequence C_t and the output vocabulary. This resulting vector is used during inference via a convex combination with the softmax vector l_{dec} output by the decoder $l_{dec} = \alpha * l_{dec} + (1 - \alpha) * d_{C_t}$. The modified vector is passed to the beam search, which selects the next tokens in a regular fashion. It should be noted that as the embedding training operations can be performed off-line, the inference overhead added by our mask is negligible, so there is almost no impact in terms of inference time.

3.3 Structure-aware encoder

Finally, we also explore a different take on the encoding phase. We note that the *diff* associated to a change has an inherent structure that allows us to distinguish the lines that were *added* and/or *removed*. In Loyola et al. (2017), the authors ignored such distinction and simply generated a single sequence by concatenating both added and removed parts. While this approach appears as a simple solution, we consider it limits the expressiveness of this input and introduce issues related to i) loss of the alignment between added and removed code within the source code file, and ii) source code token redundancy.

In order to overcome such issues, we propose to consider the *diff* explicitly as two inputs, one for the added tokens, and one for the removed tokens. We hypothesize that the quality and richness of the encoded input could be improved by comparing these two inputs in order to identify elements that may play a key semantic role in understanding the *diff*, both in terms of added or removed code chunks.

Concretely, let $X_t^+ = x_1^+, \ldots, x_n^+$ and $X_t^- = x_1^-, \ldots, x_m^-$ be the embedded sequences of the concatenated added and removed code lines, as extracted from the *diff* associated to example C_t. We use a single embedding matrix E and the same bidirectional LSTM to encode both sequences.

$$\vec{h}_i^+ = \overrightarrow{\mathrm{LSTM}}(x_i^+, \vec{h}_{i-1}^+) \tag{5}$$

$$\overleftarrow{h}_i^+ = \overleftarrow{\mathrm{LSTM}}(x_i^+, \overleftarrow{h}_{i+1}^+) \tag{6}$$

$$\vec{h}_i^- = \overrightarrow{\mathrm{LSTM}}(x_i^-, \vec{h}_{i-1}^-) \tag{7}$$

$$\overleftarrow{h}_i^- = \overleftarrow{\mathrm{LSTM}}(x_i^-, \overleftarrow{h}_{i+1}^-) \tag{8}$$

We later apply two matching strategies over the resulting vector sequences, which are based on the multi-perspective matching operation by Wang et al. (2017). The operation is built upon a cosine matching function f_m, which is used to compare two vectors, as follows.

$$m = f_m(v_1, v_2; W) \qquad (9)$$

where v_1 and v_2 are two d-dimensional vectors, $W \in \Re^{l \times d}$ is a trainable parameter with the shape $l \times d$, l is the number of perspectives, and the returned value m is a l-dimensional vector $m = [m_1, ..., m_k, ..., m_l]$. Each element $m_k \in m$ is a matching value from the k-th perspective, and it is calculated by the cosine similarity between two weighted vectors

$$m_k = cosine(W_k \circ v_1, W_k \circ v_2) \qquad (10)$$

where $\circ$ is the element-wise multiplication, and W_k is the k-th row of W, which controls the k-th perspective and assigns different weights to different dimensions of the d-dimensional space.

Full-Matching: In this strategy, each forward (or backward) vector $\vec{h}_i^+$ (or $\overleftarrow{h}_i^+$) is compared with the last time step of the forward (or backward) representation of the other sequence $\vec{h}_m^-$ (or $\overleftarrow{h}_m^-$).

$$\vec{m}_i^{full} = f_m(\vec{h}_i^+, \vec{h}_m^-; W^1)$$
$$\overleftarrow{m}_i^{full} = f_m(\overleftarrow{h}_i^+, \overleftarrow{h}_m^-; W^2) \qquad (11)$$

Maxpooling-Matching: In this strategy, each forward (or backward) vector $\vec{h}_i^+$ (or $\overleftarrow{h}_i^+$) is compared with every forward (or backward) vector of the other sequence $\vec{h}_j^-$ (or $\overleftarrow{h}_j^-$) for $j \in 1 \ldots m$, and only the maximum value of each dimension is retained.

$$\vec{m}_i^{max} = \max_{j \in (1...m)} f_m(\vec{h}_i^+, \vec{h}_j^-; W^3)$$
$$\overleftarrow{m}_i^{max} = \max_{j \in (1...m)} f_m(\overleftarrow{h}_i^+, \overleftarrow{h}_j^-; W^4) \qquad (12)$$

where $\max_{j \in (1...m)}$ is element-wise maximum.

These matching strategies are applied for both added and removed sequences. After, we concatenate each of the sequences of matching vectors and utilize another BiLSTM model to obtain a context-aware version each sequence. These two vector sequences are concatenated in the time dimension and provided to the decoder as context for the attention layer. Finally, to initialize the decoder, we concatenate the vectors from the last time-step of the BiLSTM models and aggregate them using an affine transformation. The decoder works analogously to the vanilla encoder-decoder case.

4 Empirical Study

Data: We consider real world open source Python projects. For our experiments using the content-augmented encoder, we resorted to the code-docstring-corpus (Barone and Sennrich, 2017). This dataset is a diverse parallel corpus of a hundred thousand Python functions with their docstrings, generated by scraping open source repositories on GitHub. In order to make our experiments comparable across settings, we only worked with projects that were also present in this dataset. We sorted the projects in the code-docstring-corpus according to their total number of commits in GitHub and chose the ones that contained at least 10,000 commits aiming at diversity in terms of topics. Specifically, in this paper we work with *Theano, astropy, nova, scikit-learn, mne-python, flocker* and *matplotlib*.

Following Loyola et al. (2017), we obtained all the *diff* files and the metadata associated to each commit, for a given project using the GitHub API. We also recovered information such as the author and message of each commit. The commit messages were processed using a modified version of the Penn Treebank tokenizer (Marcus et al., 1993). Besides using the rules defined by the original script, we replaced commit SHAs, commit author names and file names with generic tokens. In order to do so, we first collect the set of commit SHAs, committer names and project file names using the downloaded metadata for each commit. Each one of these lists is then matched against the words in the text to produce the output. Finally, we also removed certain repetitive patterns from the messages, such as the phrase *merge pull request*, keeping the rest of the content of each sequence, if any. Messages that solely contained these sequences were discarded as they provide no useful semantic information about the nature of the content of the commit. On the other hand, to obtain a representation of the source code content of each commit, we parsed the *diff* files and used a lexer (Brandl, 2016) to tokenize their contents in a per-line fashion. We ignored docstrings and code comment tokens, as well as tokens contained in literal strings. For our structure-aware encoder, when parsing the *diff* file we separately extract the added and removed lines, while the rest of the pre-processing remains the same.

We discarded commits that modify more than a single file, thus we consider only *atomic* commits. To combine the commit data with the code-docstring-corpus, we found the set of files modified by the commits and discarded all the ones that modify a file not present in the examples from the code-docstring-dataset. With this list, we extract all the source code and docstring lines from the corpus in a per-line fashion. In this manner, we create a mapping that allows us to recover, for each commit in our examples, the content and docstring lines of the file that commit modifies. Table 1 summarizes the size of our raw and pre-processed datasets.

Project	Total	Atomic	Content	Structure
Theano	22,995	15,814	7,708	15,210
astropy	19,599	12,195	4,708	11,896
nova	13,400	18,110	4,617	17,412
scikit-learn	15,575	12,885	3,965	12,482
mne-python	12,761	6,762	4,083	6,531
flocker	16,027	11,702	4,707	10,821
matplotlib	20,001	14,284	5,840	13,836

Table 1: Number of commits available on each dataset subset. Both the **Content** and **Structure** subsets are obtained using the **Atomic** subset.

Evaluation: As stated in the previous section, the problem of generating descriptions from source code changes does not yet have a formal way of evaluation. As the problem has certain elements from both translation and summarization, in principle metrics such as BLEU (Papineni et al., 2002) seem to appear as feasible alternatives for evaluation in our case. BLEU is based on n-gram overlap between the gold standard and the generated sequences. Smoothing techniques are also applied to deal with cases in which certain generated n-grams are not found on the gold standard. In particular, for this work we use BLEU-4 and for smoothing we simply add $\epsilon = 0.01$ to 0 counts.

On the other hand, we find METEOR (Lavie and Agarwal, 2007), a metric based on the alignment between hypothesis-reference pairs, which in turn is based on n-gram matching. Specifically, METEOR computes the alignment by comparing exact token matches, stemmed tokens and paraphrase matches. In addition to that, it also finds semantically similar tokens between hypotheses and references by using Word-Net synonyms. To obtain the final alignment, different overlap counts are combined using several free parameters that are tuned to emulate various human judgment tasks. Although this gives METEOR some extra flexibility, it makes it context dependent, specifically in terms of language. In our case, we work with the latest version available (1.5) with the model pre-trained for English, using the included scripts to tokenize and normalize punctuation.

Finally, we also considered MEANT (Lo and Wu, 2011). Our interest in this metric derives from the fact that it considers the verb as a key element when evaluating. More specifically, MEANT is based on semantic role labels and uses the Kuhn-Munkres algorithm to find matches in a bipartite graph built upon semantic frames. Thus, this metric aims at aligning the generated and gold standard sequences by finding semantically equivalent passages focusing on the main action in each passage. Compared to other metrics, the main drawback of standard MEANT is that it requires the inputs to have been annotated with their corresponding semantic role labels, while also requiring a notion of semantic distance to use for matching frames. To this end, we work with MEANT 2.0 (Lo, 2017), which is based on automatic SRL and word-embedding-based similarity for matching. For both requirements, we rely on SENNA (Collobert et al., 2011).

We trained our models using Adam (Kingma and Ba, 2014) with a learning rate of 0.001 with decay of 0.8 when there was no improvement in the validation loss. We used early stopping when the learning rate dropped below 10^{-4}. For evaluation on the test set, we used the three automatic metrics introduced before.

In addition, we conducted a crowd-sourced human evaluation. Concretely, we selected the best validation models on each case and relied on Amazon Mechanical Turk to evaluate the results on 50 randomly-chosen examples from the test sets. Each turker was presented with the gold standard and the generated message, and was asked to rate the level of correlation between them, from 1 (min) to 5 (max). We randomly swapped the order in which the messages appear, to avoid the turkers from easily locating each message. To ensure the quality of the evaluation, we filtered turkers using a quiz-based qualification in which users had to prove they had basic knowledge of Python and GitHub. In addition, each example was shown to 3 different turkers.

5 Results and Discussion

Table 2 summarizes our results in terms of all the evaluation metrics for both experiments, namely, i) the use of a content-aware encoder and ii) the use of the structure-aware encoder. In terms of notation, *Len* means the maximum length of the input sequence, *Use* refers to if content-aware and structure-aware was used (*No* means the standard baseline from Loyola et al. (2017)) . We see that in general, the usage of a context-aware encoder tends to increase performance, as the models with content perform better in 4 or 5 out of our 7 datasets, for each of the automatic evaluation metrics. These gains are also reflected in the average correlation scores from our human evaluation, where we can see that the content-aware models outperform the baseline in 4 datasets. In terms of sequence length, we observe that some content-aware models are able to outperform the baseline using shorter input-output pairs.

Regarding the usage of two linearized inputs, we see that the tendency is for the performance to decrease. This is evidenced in both automatic and human-based evaluation, where the majority of the structure-aware models perform worse than our baseline. We think this reinforces the urge for moving into a more ad-hoc representation in terms of structure, in which the code lines of the input *diff* are exploited thoroughly. Despite the fact that our current proposal goes in that direction, being designed to compare two sequential inputs, if these two inputs lack expressive power, still there is little the model can learn.

Comparing across models for a given automatic evaluation metric, we see a big difference in terms of their absolute values. In this sense, we note that MEANT offers scores that are arguably more lenient compared to BLEU and METEOR. We think the fact that these last two metrics are heavily based on n-gram overlap hinders their value. As MEANT essentially performs an action-based alignment between hypotheses and references, our intuition is that this could be a good direction in terms of evaluation, as the phenomenon to model is basically an action performed on a document, which is naturally articulated with a verb when summarizing the action performed (e.g. *Fix* a bug). Some empirical evidence about this was given by Jiang et al. (2017), who found that out of a sample of 1.6 M commit messages, roughly 47% of them begin with a verb and its direct object.

Regarding the mask-based approach, Table 3 presents some results associated to a initial exploratory study considering a subset of the projects. In this case, we can see that while the results are in the order of magnitude of the best results associated to the previous approach for content integration, there is still no clear pattern in terms of which metrics is more reliable as indicator of generative performance. In that sense, we consider it is critical to work towards obtaining an ad-hoc metric that is better aligned with the actual performance of the generation.

One known limitation of the current approach is that while the the data coming from the code changes in intrinsically time dependent, for the case of the code-docstring source, we are just using a static version, therefore we are not considering how docstring documentation could also change over time. While we were aware that such decision has direct implication on the vocabulary matching, it was a necessary simplification given the available dataset.

Additionally, given that the results associated to the use of two encoders did not produce a relevant improvement , we believe that even a two-encoder configuration does not produce a sufficiently expressive signal to be used by the decoder. That makes us conclude that treating a code change just a set of token sequences is not enough to obtain considerable increments and that it is necessary to obtain such input from a more flexible perspective, for example, by using an explicit dependency graph between changes, or even more complex constructs such as differences of execution traces or abstract syntax trees.

6 Conclusion and Future Work

We studied how to model the generation of description from source code changes by integrating the intra-code documentation as a guiding element to improve the quality of the descriptions. While the results from the empirical study are not completely conclusive, we consider that adding this extra information on average contribute positively, measured in terms of standard NLP metrics as well as through a human study. For future work, we consider necessary to focus on the expressiveness of the feature representations learned from the encoder. In that sense, we will explore other ways to treat the source code change, such as exploiting their abstract syntax tree representation.

126

Dataset	Content-aware encoder						Structure-aware encoder					
	Len.	Use	MEANT	METEOR	BLEU	Human	Len.	Use	MEANT	METEOR	BLEU	Human
Theano	200	No	0.1683	0.0505	0.0081	2.2533	100	No	0.1450	0.0310	0.0077	2.1667
	300	Yes	0.1600	0.0360	0.0080	2.0667	300	Yes	0.0080	0.0061	0.0053	1.4533
astropy	200	No	0.1942	0.1074	0.0292	2.5067	200	No	0.2586	0.0738	0.0220	2.8400
	300	Yes	0.2170	0.1100	0.0300	2.4867	200	Yes	0.2697	0.0555	0.0167	2.7133
flocker	300	No	0.0320	0.0405	0.0131	1.9133	300	No	0.1608	0.0668	0.0143	2.2267
	100	Yes	0.1100	0.0540	0.0110	2.0467	100	Yes	0.1186	0.0375	0.0054	2.1267
matplotlib	300	No	0.1944	0.0523	0.0126	2.3267	100	No	0.1687	0.0559	0.0139	2.3867
	100	Yes	0.1240	0.0830	0.0220	2.4067	300	Yes	0.1357	0.0542	0.0174	2.0000
mne-python	200	No	0.0147	0.0099	0.0052	2.2733	200	No	0.0568	0.0265	0.0171	2.4200
	200	Yes	0.0200	0.0250	0.0170	1.7667	300	Yes	0.0587	0.0250	0.0230	2.3933
nova	300	No	0.2798	0.0259	0.0275	2.4900	200	No	0.3151	0.0372	0.0187	2.4467
	100	Yes	0.3350	0.0410	0.0240	2.8066	300	Yes	0.2976	0.0477	0.0236	2.7000
scikit-learn	200	No	0.0669	0.1327	0.0276	2.0600	300	No	0.0547	0.0577	0.0170	2.0300
	100	Yes	0.0590	0.1010	0.0220	2.2200	300	Yes	0.0586	0.0341	0.0113	2.1267

Table 2: Best results using our context and structure aware architectures.

Dataset	Best Value		
	METEOR	MEANT	BLEU
Theano	0.1953	0.2103	0.0112
astropy	0.1077	0.2308	0.0302
matplotlib	0.0950	0.2397	0.0289

Table 3: Results of our content-based masking technique.

References

Miltiadis Allamanis, Earl T. Barr, Premkumar T. Devanbu, and Charles A. Sutton. 2017. A survey of machine learning for big code and naturalness. *CoRR*, abs/1709.06182.

Miltiadis Allamanis, Hao Peng, and Charles Sutton. 2016. A convolutional attention network for extreme summarization of source code. In *International Conference on Machine Learning*, pages 2091–2100.

Mikel Artetxe, Gorka Labaka, and Eneko Agirre. 2017. Learning bilingual word embeddings with (almost) no bilingual data. In *Proceedings of the 55th Annual Meeting of the Association for Computational Linguistics (Volume 1: Long Papers)*, volume 1, pages 451–462.

Dzmitry Bahdanau, Kyunghyun Cho, and Yoshua Bengio. 2014. Neural machine translation by jointly learning to align and translate. *arXiv preprint arXiv:1409.0473*.

Antonio Valerio Miceli Barone and Rico Sennrich. 2017. A parallel corpus of python functions and documentation strings for automated code documentation and code generation. *arXiv preprint arXiv:1707.02275*.

Georg Brandl. 2016. Pygments: Python syntax highlighter. http://pygments.org.

Raymond P.L. Buse and Westley R. Weimer. 2010. Automatically documenting program changes. In *Proceedings of the IEEE/ACM International Conference on Automated Software Engineering*, ASE '10, pages 33–42, New York, NY, USA. ACM.

Ronan Collobert, Jason Weston, Lon Bottou, Michael Karlen, Koray Kavukcuoglu, and Pavel Kuksa. 2011. Natural Language Processing (Almost) from Scratch. *Journal of Machine Learning Research*, 12:2493–2537.

Luis Fernando Cortés-Coy, Mario Linares Vásquez, Jairo Aponte, and Denys Poshyvanyk. 2014. On automatically generating commit messages via summarization of source code changes. In *SCAM*, volume 14, pages 275–284.

Xiaodong Gu, Hongyu Zhang, Dongmei Zhang, and Sunghun Kim. 2016. Deep api learning. In *Proceedings of the 2016 24th ACM SIGSOFT International Symposium on Foundations of Software Engineering*, FSE 2016, pages 631–642, New York, NY, USA. ACM.

Abram Hindle, Earl T Barr, Zhendong Su, Mark Gabel, and Premkumar Devanbu. 2012. On the naturalness of software. In *Software Engineering (ICSE), 2012 34th International Conference on*, pages 837–847. IEEE.

Xuan Huo, Ming Li, and Zhi-Hua Zhou. 2016. Learning unified features from natural and programming languages for locating buggy source code. In *Proceedings of the Twenty-Fifth International Joint Conference on Artificial Intelligence*, IJCAI'16, pages 1606–1612. AAAI Press.

Srinivasan Iyer, Ioannis Konstas, Alvin Cheung, and Luke Zettlemoyer. 2016. Summarizing source code using a neural attention model. In *Proceedings of the 54th Annual Meeting of the Association for Computational Linguistics (Volume 1: Long Papers)*, pages 2073–2083, Berlin, Germany. Association for Computational Linguistics.

Siyuan Jiang, Ameer Armaly, and Collin McMillan. 2017. Automatically generating commit messages from diffs using neural machine translation. In *Proceedings of the 32nd IEEE/ACM International Conference on Automated Software Engineering*, pages 135–146. IEEE Press.

Diederik P. Kingma and Jimmy Ba. 2014. Adam: A method for stochastic optimization. *CoRR*.

Alon Lavie and Abhaya Agarwal. 2007. Meteor: An automatic metric for mt evaluation with high levels of correlation with human judgments. In *Proceedings of the Second Workshop on Statistical Machine Translation*, StatMT '07, pages 228–231, Stroudsburg, PA, USA. Association for Computational Linguistics.

Mario Linares-Vásquez, Luis Fernando Cortés-Coy, Jairo Aponte, and Denys Poshyvanyk. 2015. Changescribe: A tool for automatically generating commit messages. In *Proceedings of the 37th International Conference on Software Engineering-Volume 2*, pages 709–712. IEEE Press.

Chi-kiu Lo. 2017. MEANT 2.0: Accurate semantic MT evaluation for any output language. In *Proceedings of the Second Conference on Machine Translation*, pages 589–597.

Chi-kiu Lo and Dekai Wu. 2011. MEANT: An inexpensive, high-accuracy, semi-automatic metric for evaluating translation utility based on semantic roles. In *Proceedings of the 49th Annual Meeting of the Association for Computational Linguistics: Human Language Technologies*, pages 220–229, Portland, Oregon, USA. Association for Computational Linguistics.

Pablo Loyola, Edison Marrese-Taylor, and Yutaka Matsuo. 2017. A neural architecture for generating natural language descriptions from source code changes. In *Proceedings of the 55th Annual Meeting of the Association for Computational Linguistics (Volume 2: Short Papers)*, pages 287–292. Association for Computational Linguistics.

Thang Luong, Hieu Pham, and Christopher D. Manning. 2015. Effective approaches to attention-based neural machine translation. In *Proceedings of the 2015 Conference on Empirical Methods in Natural Language Processing*, pages 1412–1421, Lisbon, Portugal. Association for Computational Linguistics.

Mitchell P Marcus, Mary Ann Marcinkiewicz, and Beatrice Santorini. 1993. Building a large annotated corpus of english: The penn treebank. *Computational linguistics*, 19(2):313–330.

Tomas Mikolov, Ilya Sutskever, Kai Chen, Greg S Corrado, and Jeff Dean. 2013. Distributed representations of words and phrases and their compositionality. In C. J. C. Burges, L. Bottou, M. Welling, Z. Ghahramani, and K. Q. Weinberger, editors, *Advances in Neural Information Processing Systems 26*, pages 3111–3119. Curran Associates, Inc.

Lili Mou, Ge Li, Lu Zhang, Tao Wang, and Zhi Jin. 2016. Convolutional neural networks over tree structures for programming language processing. In *Proc. AAAI*, pages 1287–1293. AAAI Press.

Yusuke Oda, Hiroyuki Fudaba, Graham Neubig, Hideaki Hata, Sakriani Sakti, Tomoki Toda, and Satoshi Nakamura. 2015. Learning to generate pseudo-code from source code using statistical machine translation (t). In *Automated Software Engineering (ASE), 2015 30th IEEE/ACM International Conference on*, pages 574–584. IEEE.

Kishore Papineni, Salim Roukos, Todd Ward, and Wei-Jing Zhu. 2002. Bleu: a method for automatic evaluation of machine translation. In *Proceedings of 40th Annual Meeting of the Association for Computational Linguistics*, pages 311–318, Philadelphia, Pennsylvania, USA. Association for Computational Linguistics.

Veselin Raychev, Martin Vechev, and Andreas Krause. 2015. Predicting program properties from big code. In *ACM SIGPLAN Notices*, volume 50, pages 111–124. ACM.

Veselin Raychev, Martin Vechev, and Eran Yahav. 2014. Code completion with statistical language models. In *Acm Sigplan Notices*, volume 49, pages 419–428. ACM.

Paige Rodeghero, Collin McMillan, Paul W McBurney, Nigel Bosch, and Sidney D'Mello. 2014. Improving automated source code summarization via an eye-tracking study of programmers. In *Proceedings of the 36th International Conference on Software Engineering*, pages 390–401. ACM.

Zhiguo Wang, Wael Hamza, and Radu Florian. 2017. Bilateral multi-perspective matching for natural language sentences. In *Proceedings of the 26th International Joint Conference on Artificial Intelligence*, IJCAI'17, pages 4144–4150. AAAI Press.

Pengcheng Yin and Graham Neubig. 2017. A syntactic neural model for general-purpose code generation. *arXiv preprint arXiv:1704.01696*.

Victor Zhong, Caiming Xiong, and Richard Socher. 2017. Seq2sql: Generating structured queries from natural language using reinforcement learning. *CoRR*, abs/1709.00103.

Improving Context Modelling in Multimodal Dialogue Generation

Shubham Agarwal,* **Ondřej Dušek, Ioannis Konstas and Verena Rieser**
The Interaction Lab, Department of Computer Science
Heriot-Watt University, Edinburgh, UK
*Adeptmind Scholar, Adeptmind Inc., Toronto, Canada
{sa201, o.dusek, i.konstas, v.t.rieser}@hw.ac.uk

Abstract

In this work, we investigate the task of textual response generation in a multimodal task-oriented dialogue system. Our work is based on the recently released Multimodal Dialogue (MMD) dataset (Saha et al., 2017) in the fashion domain. We introduce a multimodal extension to the Hierarchical Recurrent Encoder-Decoder (HRED) model and show that this extension outperforms strong baselines in terms of text-based similarity metrics. We also showcase the shortcomings of current vision and language models by performing an error analysis on our system's output.

1   Introduction

This work aims to learn strategies for textual response generation in a multimodal conversation directly from data. Conversational AI has great potential for online retail: It greatly enhances user experience and in turn directly affects user retention (Chai et al., 2000), especially if the interaction is multi-modal in nature. So far, most conversational agents are uni-modal – ranging from open-domain conversation (Ram et al., 2018; Papaioannou et al., 2017; Fang et al., 2017) to task oriented dialogue systems (Rieser and Lemon, 2010, 2011; Young et al., 2013; Singh et al., 2000; Wen et al., 2016). While recent progress in deep learning has unified research at the intersection of vision and language, the availability of open-source multimodal dialogue datasets still remains a bottleneck.

This research makes use of a recently released Multimodal Dialogue (MMD) dataset (Saha et al., 2017), which contains multiple dialogue sessions in the fashion domain. The MMD dataset provides an interesting new challenge, combining recent efforts on task-oriented dialogue systems, as well as visually grounded dialogue. In contrast to simple QA tasks in visually grounded dialogue, e.g. (Antol et al., 2015), it contains conversations with a clear end-goal. However, in contrast to previous slot-filling dialogue systems, e.g. (Rieser and Lemon, 2011; Young et al., 2013), it heavily relies on the extra visual modality to drive the conversation forward (see Figure 1).

In the following, we propose a fully data-driven response generation model for this task. Our work is able to ground the system's textual response with language and images by learning the semantic correspondence between them while modelling long-term dialogue context.

Figure 1: Example of a user-agent interaction in the fashion domain. In this work, we are interested in the textual response generation for a user query. Both user query and agent response can be multimodal in nature.

2   Model: Multimodal HRED over multiple images

Our model is an extension of the recently introduced Hierarchical Recurrent Encoder Decoder (HRED) architecture (Serban et al., 2016, 2017;

Proceedings of The 11th International Natural Language Generation Conference, pages 129–134,
Tilburg, The Netherlands, November 5-8, 2018. ©2018 Association for Computational Linguistics

Lu et al., 2016). In contrast to standard sequence-to-sequence models (Cho et al., 2014; Sutskever et al., 2014; Bahdanau et al., 2015), HREDs model the dialogue context by introducing a context Recurrent Neural Network (RNN) over the encoder RNN, thus forming a hierarchical encoder.

We build on top of the HRED architecture to include multimodality over multiple images. A simple HRED consists of three RNN modules: encoder, context and decoder. In multimodal HRED, we combine the output representations from the utterance encoder with concatenated multiple image representations and pass them as input to the context encoder (see Figure 2). A dialogue is modelled as a sequence of utterances (turns), which in turn are modelled as sequences of words and images. Formally, a dialogue is generated according to the following:

$$P_\theta(t_1, \ldots t_N) = \prod_{n=1}^{N} P_\theta(t_n | t_{<n}) \qquad (1)$$

where t_n is the n-th utterance in a dialogue. For each $m = 1, \ldots, M_n$, we have hidden states of each module defined as:

$$h_{n,m}^{text} = f_\theta^{text}(h_{n,m-1}^{text}, w_{m,n}) \qquad (2)$$

$$h_n^{img} = l^{img}([g_\theta^{enc}(img_1), \ldots g_\theta^{enc}(img_k)]) \qquad (3)$$

$$h_n^{cxt} = f_\theta^{cxt}(h_{n-1}^{cxt}, [h_{n,M_n}^{text}, h_n^{img}]) \qquad (4)$$

$$h_{n,m}^{dec} = f_\theta^{dec}(h_{n,m-1}^{dec}, w_{n,m}, h_{n-1}^{cxt}) \qquad (5)$$

$$h_{n,0}^{text} = 0; \quad h_0^{cxt} = 0; \quad h_{n,0}^{dec} = h_N^{cxt} \qquad (6)$$

where $f_\theta^{text}, f_\theta^{cxt}$ and f_θ^{dec} are GRU cells (Cho et al., 2014). θ represent model parameters, $w_{n,m}$ is the m-th word in the n-th utterance and g_θ^{enc} is a Convolutional Neural Network (CNN); here we use VGGnet (Simonyan and Zisserman, 2014). We pass multiple images in a context through the CNN in order to get encoded image representations $g_\theta^{enc}(img_k)$. Then these are combined together and passed through a linear layer l^{img} to get the aggregated image representation for one turn of context, denoted by h_n^{img} above. The textual representation h_{n,M_n}^{text} is given by the encoder RNN f_θ^{text}. Both h_{n,M_n}^{text} and h_n^{img} are subsequently concatenated and passed as input to the context RNN. h_N^{cxt}, the final hidden state of the context RNN, acts as the initial hidden state of the decoder RNN. Finally, output is generated by passing $h_{n,m}^{dec}$ through an affine transformation followed by a softmax activation. The model is trained using cross entropy on next-word prediction. During generation, the decoder conditions on the previous output token.

Saha et al. (2017) propose a similar baseline model for the MMD dataset, extending HREDs to include the visual modality. However, for simplicity's sake, they 'unroll' multiple images in a single utterance to include only one image per utterance. While computationally leaner, this approach ultimately loses the objective of capturing multimodality over the context of multiple images and text. In contrast, we combine all the image representations in the utterance using a linear layer. We argue that modelling all images is necessary to answer questions that address previous agent responses. For example in Figure 3, when the user asks "what about the 4th image?", it is impossible to give a correct response without reasoning over all images in the previous response. In the following, we empirically show that our extension leads to better results in terms of text-based similarity measures, as well as quality of generated dialogues.

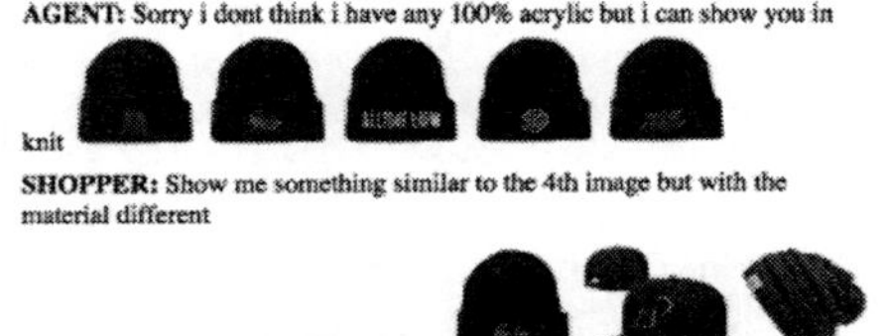

Our version of the dataset
Text Context: Sorry i don't think i have any 100 % acrylic but i can show you in knit | Show me something similar to the 4th image but with the material different
Image Context: [Img 1, Img 2, Img 3, Img 4, Img 5] | [0, 0, 0, 0, 0]
Target Response: The similar looking ones are
Saha et al. (Saha et al., 2017)
Text Context: |
Image Context: Img 4 | Img 5
Target Response: The similar looking ones are

Figure 3: Example contexts for a given system utterance; note the difference in our approach from Saha et al. (2017) when extracting the training data from the original chat logs. For simplicity, in this illustration we consider a context size of 2 previous utterances. '|' differentiates turns for a given context. We concatenate the representation vector of all images in one turn of a dialogue to form the image context. If there is no image in the utterance, we consider a 0_{4096} vector to form the image context. In this work, we focus only on the textual response of the agent.

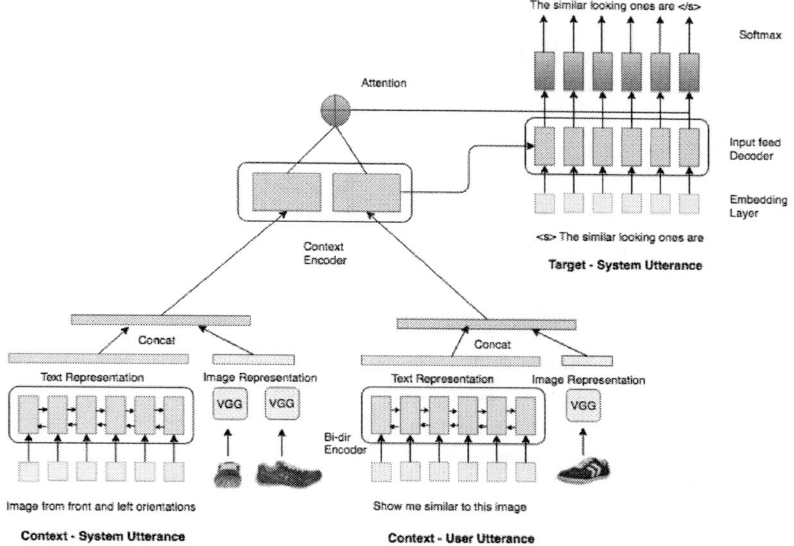

Figure 2: The Multimodal HRED architecture consists of four modules: utterance encoder, image encoder, context encoder and decoder. While Saha et al. (2017) 'rollout' images to encode only one image per context, we concatenate all the 'local' representations to form a 'global' image representation per turn. Next, we concatenate the encoded text representation and finally everything gets fed to the context encoder.

3 Experiments and Results

3.1 Dataset

The MMD dataset (Saha et al., 2017) consists of 100/11/11k train/validation/test chat sessions comprising 3.5M context-response pairs for the model. Each session contains an average of 40 dialogue turns (average of 8 words per textual response, 4 images per image response). The data contains complex user queries, which pose new challenges for multimodal, task-based dialogue, such as *quantitative inference (sorting, counting and filtering)*: "Show me more images of the 3rd product in some different directions", *inference using domain knowledge and long term context*: "Will the 5th result go well with a large sized messenger bag?", *inference over aggregate of images:* "List more in the upper material of the 5th image and style as the 3rd and the 5th", *co-reference resolution*. Note that we started with the raw transcripts of dialogue sessions to create our own version of the dataset for the model. This is done since the authors originally consider each image as a different context, while we consider all the images in a single turn as one concatenated context (cf. Figure 3).

3.2 Implementation

We use the PyTorch[1] framework (Paszke et al., 2017) for our implementation.[2] We used 512 as the word embedding size as well as hidden dimension for all the RNNs using GRUs (Cho et al., 2014) with tied embeddings for the (bidirectional) encoder and decoder. The decoder uses Luong-style attention mechanism (Luong et al., 2015) with input feeding. We trained our model with the Adam optimizer (Kingma and Ba, 2015), with a learning rate of 0.0004 and clipping gradient norm over 5. We perform early stopping by monitoring validation loss. For image representations, we use the FC6 layer representations of the VGG-19 (Simonyan and Zisserman, 2014), pre-trained on ImageNet.[3]

3.3 Analysis and Results

We report sentence-level BLEU-4 (Papineni et al., 2002), METEOR (Lavie and Agarwal, 2007) and ROUGE-L (Lin and Och, 2004) using the evaluation scripts provided by (Sharma et al., 2017).

---

[1] https://pytorch.org/

[2] Our code is freely available at:
https://github.com/shubhamagarwal92/mmd

[3] In future, we plan to exploit state-of-the-art frameworks such as ResNet or DenseNet and fine tune the image encoder jointly, during the training of the model.

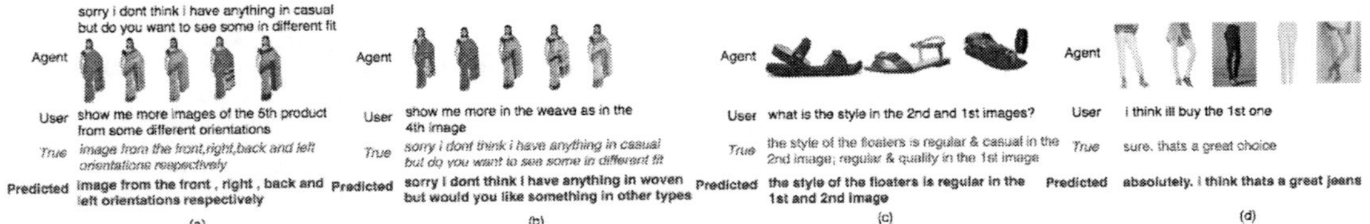

Figure 4: Examples of predictions using M-HRED–attn (5). Recall, we are focusing on generating textual responses. Our model predictions are shown in blue while the true gold target in red. We are showing only the previous user utterance for brevity's sake.

We compare our results against Saha et al. (2017) by using their code and data-generation scripts.[4] Note that the results reported in their paper are on a different version of the corpus, hence not directly comparable.

Model	Cxt	BLEU-4	METEOR	ROUGE-L
Saha et al. M-HRED*	2	0.3767	0.2847	0.6235
T-HRED	2	0.4292	0.3269	0.6692
M-HRED	2	0.4308	0.3288	0.6700
T-HRED–attn	2	0.4331	0.3298	0.6710
M-HRED–attn	2	0.4345	0.3315	0.6712
T-HRED–attn	5	0.4442	**0.3374**	0.6797
M-HRED–attn	5	**0.4451**	0.3371	**0.6799**

Table 1: Sentence-level BLEU-4, METEOR and ROUGE-L results for the response generation task on the MMD corpus. "Cxt" represents context size considered by the model. Our best performing model is M-HRED–attn over a context of 5 turns. *Saha et al. has been trained on a different version of the dataset.

Table 1 provides results for different configurations of our model ("T" stands for text-only in the encoder, "M" for multimodal, and "attn" for using attention in the decoder). We experimented with different context sizes and found that output quality improved with increased context size (models with 5-turn context perform better than those with a 2-turn context), confirming the observation by Serban et al. (2016, 2017).[5] Using attention clearly helps: even T-HRED–attn outperforms M-HRED (without attention) for the same context size. We also tested whether multimodal input has an impact on the generated outputs. However, there was only a slight increase in BLEU score (M-HRED–attn vs T-HRED–attn).

To summarize, our best performing model (M-HRED–attn) outperforms the model of Saha et al. by 7 BLEU points.[6] This can be primarily attributed to the way we created the input for our model from raw chat logs, as well as incorporating more information during decoding via attention. Figure 4 provides example output utterances using M-HRED–attn with a context size of 5. Our model is able to accurately map the response to previous textual context turns as shown in (a) and (c). In (c), it is able to capture that the user is asking about the style in the 1st and 2nd image. (d) shows an example where our model is able to relate that the corresponding product is 'jeans' from visual features, while it is not able to model fine-grained details like in (b) that the style is 'casual fit' but resorts to 'woven'.

4   Conclusion and Future Work

In this research, we address the novel task of response generation in search-based multimodal dialogue by learning from the recently released Multimodal Dialogue (MMD) dataset (Saha et al., 2017). We introduce a novel extension to the Hierarchical Recurrent Encoder-Decoder (HRED) model (Serban et al., 2016) and show that our implementation significantly outperforms the model of Saha et al. (2017) by modelling the full multimodal context. Contrary to their results, our generation outputs improved by adding attention and increasing context size. However, we also show that multimodal HRED does not improve significantly over text-only HRED, similar to observations by Agrawal et al. (2016) and Qian et al. (2018). Our model learns to handle textual correspondence between the questions and answers, while mostly ignoring the visual context. This indicates that we need better visual models to en-

---

[4]https://github.com/amritasaha1812/MMD_Code

[5]Using pairwise bootstrap resampling test (Koehn, 2004), we confirmed that the difference of M-HRED-attn (5) vs. M-HRED-attn (2) is statistically significant at 95% confidence level.

[6]The difference is statistically significant at 95% confidence level according to the pairwise bootstrap resampling test (Koehn, 2004).

code the image representations when he have multiple similar-looking images, e.g., black hats in Figure 3. We believe that the results should improve with a jointly trained or fine-tuned CNN for generating the image representations, which we plan to implement in future work.

Acknowledgments

This research received funding from Adeptmind Inc., Montreal, Canada and the MaDrIgAL EP-SRC project (EP/N017536/1). The Titan Xp used for this work was donated by the NVIDIA Corp.

References

Aishwarya Agrawal, Dhruv Batra, and Devi Parikh. 2016. Analyzing the behavior of visual question answering models. *Proceedings of EMNLP*.

Stanislaw Antol, Aishwarya Agrawal, Jiasen Lu, Margaret Mitchell, Dhruv Batra, C Lawrence Zitnick, and Devi Parikh. 2015. VQA: Visual question answering. In *Proceedings of ICCV*, pages 2425–2433.

Dzmitry Bahdanau, Kyunghyun Cho, and Yoshua Bengio. 2015. Neural machine translation by jointly learning to align and translate. In *Proceedings of ICLR*.

Joyce Yue Chai, Nanda Kambhatla, and Wlodek Zadrozny. 2000. Natural language sales assistant-a web-based dialog system for online sales. In *Proceedings of AAAI*.

Kyunghyun Cho, Bart Van Merriënboer, Caglar Gulcehre, Dzmitry Bahdanau, Fethi Bougares, Holger Schwenk, and Yoshua Bengio. 2014. Learning phrase representations using RNN encoder-decoder for statistical machine translation. In *Proceedings of EMNLP*.

Hao Fang, Hao Cheng, Elizabeth Clark, Ariel Holtzman, Maarten Sap, Mari Ostendorf, Yejin Choi, and Noah A Smith. 2017. Sounding board–university of washington's alexa prize submission. *Alexa Prize Proceedings*.

Diederik P Kingma and Jimmy Ba. 2015. Adam: A method for stochastic optimization. *CoRR abs/1412.6980*.

Philipp Koehn. 2004. Statistical significance tests for machine translation evaluation. In *Proceedings of EMNLP*.

Alon Lavie and Abhaya Agarwal. 2007. METEOR: An automatic metric for MT evaluation with high levels of correlation with human judgments. In *Proceedings of 2nd Workshop on Statistical Machine Translation*, pages 228–231.

Chin-Yew Lin and Franz Josef Och. 2004. Automatic evaluation of machine translation quality using longest common subsequence and skip-bigram statistics. In *Proceedings of ACL*, pages 605–612.

Jiasen Lu, Jianwei Yang, Dhruv Batra, and Devi Parikh. 2016. Hierarchical question-image co-attention for visual question answering. In *Proceedings of NIPS*, pages 289–297.

Minh-Thang Luong, Hieu Pham, and Christopher D Manning. 2015. Effective approaches to attention-based neural machine translation. *Proceedings of EMNLP*.

Ioannis Papaioannou, Amanda Cercas Curry, Jose L Part, Igor Shalyminov, Xinnuo Xu, Yanchao Yu, Ondrej Dušek, Verena Rieser, and Oliver Lemon. 2017. Alana: Social dialogue using an ensemble model and a ranker trained on user feedback. *Alexa Prize Proceedings*.

Kishore Papineni, Salim Roukos, Todd Ward, and Wei-Jing Zhu. 2002. BLEU: a method for automatic evaluation of machine translation. In *Proceedings of ACL*, pages 311–318.

Adam Paszke, Sam Gross, Soumith Chintala, Gregory Chanan, Edward Yang, Zachary DeVito, Zeming Lin, Alban Desmaison, Luca Antiga, and Adam Lerer. 2017. Automatic differentiation in pytorch. In *NIPS-W*.

Xin Qian, Ziyi Zhong, and Jieli Zhou. 2018. Multimodal machine translation with reinforcement learning. *CoRR abs/1805.02356*.

Ashwin Ram, Rohit Prasad, Chandra Khatri, Anu Venkatesh, Raefer Gabriel, Qing Liu, Jeff Nunn, Behnam Hedayatnia, Ming Cheng, Ashish Nagar, et al. 2018. Conversational AI: The science behind the alexa prize. *CoRR abs/1801.03604*.

Verena Rieser and Oliver Lemon. 2010. Natural language generation as planning under uncertainty for spoken dialogue systems. In *Empirical methods in natural language generation*, pages 105–120. Springer.

Verena Rieser and Oliver Lemon. 2011. *Reinforcement learning for adaptive dialogue systems: a data-driven methodology for dialogue management and natural language generation*. Springer.

Amrita Saha, Mitesh Khapra, and Karthik Sankaranarayanan. 2017. Multimodal dialogs (MMD): A large-scale dataset for studying multimodal domain-aware conversations. *CoRR abs/1704.00200*.

Iulian Vlad Serban, Alessandro Sordoni, Yoshua Bengio, Aaron C Courville, and Joelle Pineau. 2016. Building end-to-end dialogue systems using generative hierarchical neural network models. In *Proceedings of AAAI*.

Iulian Vlad Serban, Alessandro Sordoni, Ryan Lowe, Laurent Charlin, Joelle Pineau, Aaron C Courville, and Yoshua Bengio. 2017. A hierarchical latent variable encoder-decoder model for generating dialogues. In *Proceedings of AAAI*, pages 3295–3301.

Shikhar Sharma, Layla El Asri, Hannes Schulz, and Jeremie Zumer. 2017. Relevance of unsupervised metrics in task-oriented dialogue for evaluating natural language generation. *CoRR abs/1706.09799*.

Karen Simonyan and Andrew Zisserman. 2014. Very deep convolutional networks for large-scale image recognition. *CoRR abs/1409.1556*.

Satinder P Singh, Michael J Kearns, Diane J Litman, and Marilyn A Walker. 2000. Reinforcement learning for spoken dialogue systems. In *Proceedings of NIPS*, pages 956–962.

Ilya Sutskever, Oriol Vinyals, and Quoc V Le. 2014. Sequence to sequence learning with neural networks. In *Proceedings of NIPS*, pages 3104–3112.

Tsung-Hsien Wen, David Vandyke, Nikola Mrksic, Milica Gasic, Lina M Rojas-Barahona, Pei-Hao Su, Stefan Ultes, and Steve Young. 2016. A network-based end-to-end trainable task-oriented dialogue system. *CoRR abs/1604.04562*.

Steve Young, Milica Gašić, Blaise Thomson, and Jason D Williams. 2013. POMDP-based statistical spoken dialog systems: A review. *Proceedings of the IEEE*, 101(5):1160–1179.

Generating Market Comments Referring to External Resources

Tatsuya Aoki♠♣ **Akira Miyazawa**◇♡♣ **Tatsuya Ishigaki**♠♣ **Keiichi Goshima**♯♣
Kasumi Aoki♭♣ **Kobayashi Ichiro**♭♣ **Hiroya Takamura**♠♣ **Yusuke Miyao**♮♣

♠Tokyo Institute of Technology ◇The Graduate University for Advanced Studies
♡National Institute of Informatics ♯Bank of Japan* ♭Ochanomizu University
♣National Institute of Advanced Industrial Science and Technology ♮The University of Tokyo

```
{aoki, ishigaki}@lr.pi.titech.ac.jp miyazawa-a@nii.ac.jp
keiichi.goshima@boj.or.jp {g1120501, koba}@is.ocha.ac.jp
takamura@pi.titech.ac.jp yusuke@is.s.u-tokyo.ac.jp
```


Abstract

Comments on a stock market often include the reason or cause of changes in stock prices, such as *"Nikkei turns lower as yen's rise hits exporters."* Generating such informative sentences requires capturing the relationship between different resources, including a target stock price. In this paper, we propose a model for automatically generating such informative market comments that refer to external resources. We evaluated our model through an automatic metric in terms of BLEU and human evaluation done by an expert in finance. The results show that our model outperforms the existing model both in BLEU scores and human judgment.

1 Introduction

Nikkei Stock Average opens at a high price after Dow Jones Industrial Average closes at a high price.

This is an example of a comment on markets that describes the stock prices shown in Figure 1. The closing price of the Dow Jones Industrial Average at 5 am JST is represented as the right-most point in the figure on the top, while the opening price of the Nikkei Stock Average is represented as the left-most point in the figure at the bottom. While the comment describes the behavior of Nikkei Stock Average (henceforth, *Nikkei 225*), the main indicator of the Japanese stock market, it also refers to an external indicator, the Dow Jones Industrial Average, which represents the US stock market. Such

---

*Views expressed in this paper are those of the authors and do not necessarily reflect the official views of the Bank of Japan.

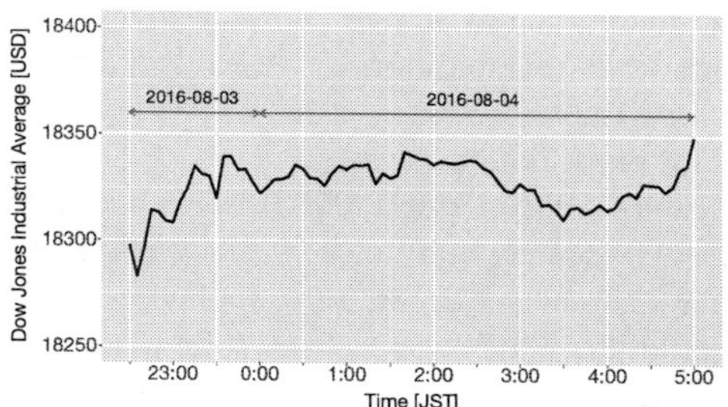

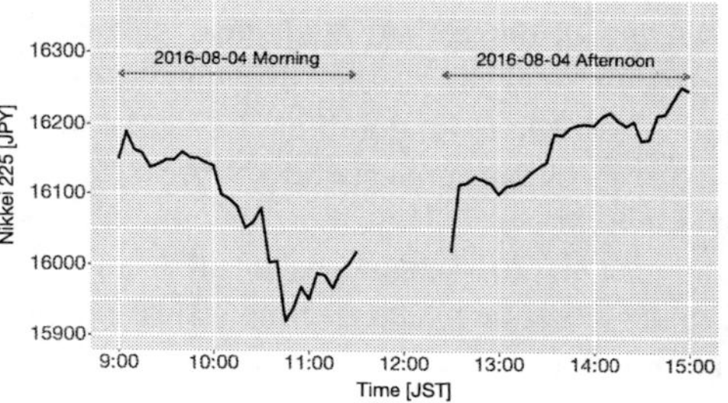

Figure 1: Relationship between Dow Jones Industrial Average and Nikkei 225 (Nikkei Stock Average).

mentions of external resources as a cause of the behavior of a target index are very common in market comments. Comments on the Japanese stock market can also refer to, for example, other stock market indices, foreign exchange rates, and oil prices, and comments that also describe causes will facilitate readers in understanding financial situations.

In this paper, we address the task of generating market comments that refer to external resources. Specifically, we extend the encoder in the encoder-decoder model proposed by Murakami et al. (2017) so that the model can take into account external resources related to the financial do-

135

Proceedings of The 11th International Natural Language Generation Conference, pages 135–139,
Tilburg, The Netherlands, November 5-8, 2018. ©2018 Association for Computational Linguistics

main. We encode each of the external resources in addition to the target index, i.e., Nikkei 225, and feed them to the decoder. The experimental results show that our proposed model outperforms the existing single-source model in terms of the fluency and informativeness of human evaluation, in addition to the BLEU score.

2 Related Work

There has been a lot of work on generating text from numerical time series or structured data including weather data (Belz, 2008), healthcare data (Portet et al., 2009), sports data (Liang et al., 2009), and market data (Kukich, 1983). Approaches to such tasks are traditionally dependent on hand-crafted rules (Goldberg et al., 1994; Dale et al., 2003) or are template-based.

Neural encoder-decoders (Sutskever et al., 2014; Bahdanau et al., 2015; Luong et al., 2015) have also been successfully applied to various data-to-text generation tasks. While many generate text from table data, such as reviews from product attributes (Dong et al., 2017) and biographies from the infoboxes of Wikipedia (Lebret et al., 2016), there is an attempt to generate text from numerical data (Murakami et al., 2017), in which market comments are generated from a time-series of stock prices. However, the model of Murakami et al. (2017), which is based on an encoder-decoder, takes only a target time series and ignores the fact that there are many mentions of external resources.

3 Generating Market Comments

We describe our model for generating comments. We extend the encoder part of the model proposed by Murakami et al. (2017), which had a limitation in generating informative market comments due to the lack of a capability to consider multiple data sources as input. We first explain the encoder used in the existing model and then show how we extend it.

3.1 Base Model (BASE)

The existing model by Murakami et al. (2017) takes only a single source of data, a sequence of prices of Nikkei 225, as input. Specifically, the prices are recorded every five minutes in the data. The model first converts the input data into two vectors: a short-term vector x_{short} and a long-term vector x_{long}. The vector x_{short} is N-dimensional

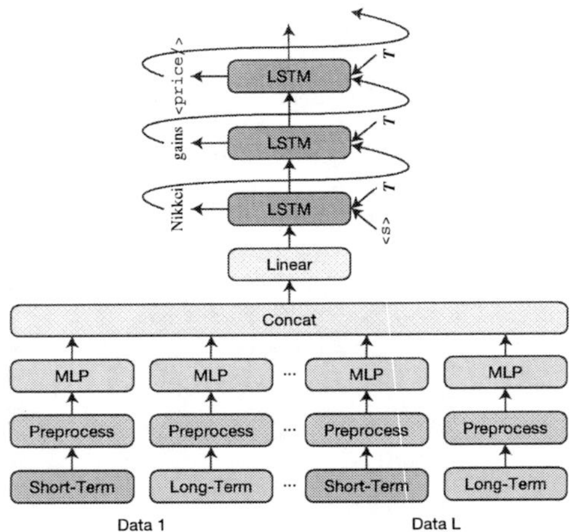

Figure 2: Neural-network architecture of our model. The symbol T denotes embedding of publishing time (see Murakami et al. (2017) for details).

and consists of the N previous stock prices, while x_{long} is M-dimensional and consists of the closing prices of the M preceding trading days. Thus, x_{short} contains short-term changes in the stock price, while x_{long} contains long-term changes.

In the encoding step, the vectors are passed to multilayer perceptrons (MLPs) with three layers and concatenated as

$$v_{\text{single}} = \left[\text{MLP}_{\text{short}} \left(x_{\text{short}} \right) ; \text{MLP}_{\text{long}} \left(x_{\text{long}} \right) \right],$$
$$(1)$$

where the semicolon represents the concatenation. The vector v_{single} is then transformed to a vector s_0 by an affine transformation $s_0 = W_s v_{\text{single}} + b_s$, where W_s is a weight matrix and b_s is a bias term.

In the decoding step, the hidden state of the decoder is initialized by s_0, and LSTM cells (Hochreiter and Schmidhuber, 1997) are used following the model by Murakami et al. (2017). Please refer to the original paper for more details on the decoder.

They also replaced numerical values in the training data with placeholders representing arithmetic operations, e.g., rounding down the difference between the latest price and the closing price of the previous day.

3.2 Multiple Source-Aware Model (MULTI)

The architecture of our model is shown in Figure 2. We extend the encoder part of the base model so that the model can take L different sources as input, including the Dow Jones Industrial Average, and US dollar/Japanese yen exchange rates in addition to Nikkei 225. We convert each input source to a continuous representation v^i ($1 \leq i \leq L$) as

$$v^i = \left[\mathrm{MLP}^i_{\mathrm{short}} \left(x^i_{\mathrm{short}} \right) ; \mathrm{MLP}^i_{\mathrm{long}} \left(x^i_{\mathrm{long}} \right) \right]. \tag{2}$$

Note that the model has $2L$ MLPs; L MLPs are for short-term data and the others are for long-term data. Each x^i_{short} is an N-dimensional short-term vector for the i-th data source generated with the same approach as Murakami et al. (2017). Each x^i_{long} is an M-dimensional long-term vector for the i-th data source.

The representations $v^1, \cdots, v^L$ are then concatenated to a representation v_{multi} as:

$$v_{\mathrm{multi}} = \left[v^1 ; \cdots ; v^L \right]. \tag{3}$$

It is then passed to an affine transform function as is done in the base model $s_0 = W_m v_{\mathrm{multi}} + b_m$, and s_0 is used for the initial state of the decoder.

Our model is clearly a straight extension of the model by Murakami et al. (2017). All the multiple input resources are treated equally with this architecture. The target resource to be described will be determined by the training data. For example, if the comments in the training data describe the behavior of Nikkei 225, the other resources are regarded as causes influencing Nikkei 225.

4 Experiments

4.1 Data

Training the model requires pairs consisting of a time series and a market comment aligned with it. As market comments, we used 20,093 headlines of Nikkei Quick News (NQN) that describe the behavior of Nikkei 225. They are provided by Nikkei, Inc. and written in Japanese. We divided them into three parts on the basis of the period of publication: 16,276 for training (Dec. 2010–Oct. 2015), 1,866 for validation (Oct. 2015–April 2016) and 1,951 for testing (April 2016–Oct. 2016). In addition, we retrieved the five-minute charts of 10 indices from Thomson Reuters DataScope Select[1]. They consist of seven stock market indices (Nikkei 225, TOPIX Price Index, S&P 500 Index, FTSE 100 Index, Hang Seng Index, Shanghai SE Composite Index, and Dow Jones Industrial Index),

a forward transaction index (Nikkei 225 Future), and two currency exchange rates, USD/JPY and EUR/JPY.

4.2 Preprocessing and Parameters

As a preprocessing procedure, we created short- and long-term sequences of each index from the five-minute charts in the same way as Murakami et al. (2017). The size N of a short-term vector was set to 62, and the size M of a long-term one was set to 7. We used Adam (Kingma and Ba, 2015) for optimization with a learning rate of 0.0001 and a mini-batch size of 100. The dimensions of the three hidden layers in MLPs were all set to 32.

4.3 Evaluation Settings

We compared our model with the model by Murakami et al. (2017). The latter was not provided with external resources as input, but could still refer to them groundlessly simply because mentions of external resources are found in the training data.

We conducted both an automatic evaluation in terms of BLEU scores and a manual evaluation done by a financial expert. The outputs from the proposed model were compared with reference market comments extracted from NQN and comments generated by the base model. In the automatic evaluation by BLEU score, we used the market comments collected from NQN as references. We calculated the BLEU scores for both the base model and our model. In the human evaluation, a human judge (an expert in finance) manually judged the outputs in terms of two criteria: *fluency* and *informativeness*. Specifically, we presented three market comments generated by a human (HUMAN), the base model (BASE), and our model (MULTI). For fluency, the human judge manually selected a label from two labels (`fluent` and `not_fluent`) for each comment. For informativeness, the judge was asked to evaluate whether a comment included a correct mention of an external resource. The human judge was asked to select one out of four labels: `no`, `correct`, `wrong`, and `subtle`. The label `no` means that a comment did not contain a mention of an external resource. The label `correct` means that the comment contained correct mentions of external resources, whereas the label `wrong` means that the comment contained a wrong mention of external resources. The label `subtle` corresponded to the other cases. For example, when a comment contained a mention of an external resource that was

---

[1] `https://hosted.datascope.reuters.com/DataScope/`

Method	BLEU (%)
BASE	21.88 ± 0.31
MULTI	23.66 ± 0.35

Table 1: Result of evaluation in terms of BLEU. Scores were macro-averaged over 5 runs. Each value after ± is standard deviation.

	fluent	not_fluent
HUMAN	98	2
BASE	95	5
MULTI	96	4

(a) Fluency.

	Mentions of Ext. Resources		
	no	yes	(cr / wr / sb)
HUMAN	54	46	(5 / 0 / 41)
BASE	51	49	(13 / 9 / 27)
MULTI	46	54	(11 / 2 / 41)

(b) Informativeness.

Table 2: Result of human evaluation. In (a), values are number of times that comments were judged `fluent` or `not_fluent`. In (b), `no` indicates number of comments that do not contain any mention of external resources. `yes` indicates number of comments that contain mention of external resources. `yes` is divided into `correct` (cr), `wrong` (wr), and `subtle` (sb), which respectively mean numbers of comments with correct, wrong, and subtle mentions.

not any of the L inputs, `subtle` was assigned. When evaluating the informativeness, the human judge does not simply measure the similarity between the generated comments and the reference comments; he referred to the input data to check the correctness of the generated comments.

5 Results

Table 1 shows the BLEU scores for each model. The scores were calculated by averaging the scores of five trials. By incorporating multiple resources as input, our model outperformed the base model with an improvement of 1.78 points in BLEU. This suggests that integrating multiple resources into the encoder helps to improve the ability to generate comments similar to human generated ones.

Table 2 shows the results of the human evaluation for each model. In terms of fluency, most of the comments generated by all of the methods were judged fluent. BASE and MULTI were slightly worse than HUMAN in fluency because they failed to output the correct placeholders representing arithmetic operations.

In terms of informativeness, our model referred to external resources more often than BASE. Specifically, our model outputs 54 comments with mentions of external resources, while 46 were without the mentions. The method BASE outputs only 49 comments with such a mention. In addition, the proportion of `wrong` was notably reduced by our model. The results suggest that our proposed model improved the ability to generate more informative sentences including correct mentions of external resources.

We show examples of the generated comments in Table 3. The method BASE erroneously mentioned external information, "US stock rise," due to the lack of input information. Our method, MULTI, tended to avoid generating clearly erroneous mentions such as "US stock rise." We also found that HUMAN often referred to important events as in the output example "easing Brexit concerns." Generating such comments requires yet other external resources such as news streams, which we leave for future work.

6 Conclusion

We proposed an encoder-decoder model for generating market comments that refer to external resources. Our automatic and manual evaluation showed that integrating multiple resources into the encoder improves the ability to include such information in the outputs and to generate more informative comments.

Our code is available at `https://github.com/aistairc/market-reporter`.

Acknowledgements

This paper is based on results obtained from a project commissioned by the New Energy and Industrial Technology Development Organization (NEDO). This work is partially supported by JST PRESTO (Grant Number JPMJPR1655).

Method	Output
HUMAN	*Toushou yoritsuki zokushin, agehaba 300 en koeru, ei EU ridatsu kenen-ga koutai* TSE opening continual_rise, gain 300 yen jump_over, UK EU leaving concern-NOM retreat "Tokyo stocks open 300 yen higher with a continual rise, due to easing Brexit concerns."
BASE	*Toushou yoritsuki zokushin, agehaba 300 en chou, bei-kabu-daka ya en-yasu-o koukan* TSE opening continual_rise, gain 300 yen over US-stock-high and yen-cheap-ACC good_feeling "Tokyo stocks open 300 yen higher with a continual rise, helped by a cheaper yen and US stocks rise."
MULTI	*Toushou yoritsuki zokushin, agehaba 300 en chou, en-yasu-de yushutsu-kabu-ni kai* TSE opening continual_rise, gain 300 yen over yen-cheap-INS exporting-stock-DAT purchase "Tokyo stocks open … a continual rise, thanks to demand for export-related shares boosted by a cheaper yen."

Table 3: Examples of generated comments. Each example is accompanied by original Japanese comment transliterated into English alphabet, its word-for-word translation, and the corresponding English sentence. TSE stands for Tokyo Stock Exchange. Abbreviations used in word-for-word translation are as follows. NOM: nominative, ACC: accusative, INS: instrumental, and DAT: dative.

References

Dzmitry Bahdanau, Kyunghyun Cho, and Yoshua Bengio. 2015. Neural machine translation by jointly learning to align and translate. In *Proceedings of International Conference on Learning Representations (ICLR)*.

Anja Belz. 2008. Automatic generation of weather forecast texts using comprehensive probabilistic generation-space models. *Natural Language Engineering*, 14(4):431–455.

Robert Dale, Sabine Geldof, and Jean-Philippe Prost. 2003. Coral: Using natural language generation for navigational assistance. In *Proceedings of the 26th Australasian computer science conference-Volume 16*, pages 35–44. Australian Computer Society, Inc.

Li Dong, Shaohan Huang, Furu Wei, Mirella Lapata, Ming Zhou, and Ke Xu. 2017. Learning to generate product reviews from attributes. In *Proceedings of the 15th Conference of the European Chapter of the Association for Computational Linguistics (EACL)*, volume 1, pages 623–632.

Eli Goldberg, Norbert Driedger, and Richard I Kittredge. 1994. Using natural-language processing to produce weather forecasts. *IEEE Intelligent Systems*, (2):45–53.

Sepp Hochreiter and Jürgen Schmidhuber. 1997. Long short-term memory. *Neural computation*, 9(8):1735–1780.

Diederik P. Kingma and Jimmy Ba. 2015. Adam: A method for stochastic optimization. In *Proceedings of International Conference on Learning Representations (ICLR)*.

Karen Kukich. 1983. Design of a knowledge-based report generator. In *Proceedings of Association for Computational Linguistics (ACL)*, pages 145–150.

Rémi Lebret, David Grangier, and Michael Auli. 2016. Neural text generation from structured data with application to the biography domain. In *Proceedings of Empirical Methods in Natural Language Processing (EMNLP)*, pages 1203–1213.

Percy Liang, Michael I. Jordan, and Dan Klein. 2009. Learning semantic correspondences with less supervision. In *Proceedings of the Joint Conference of the 47th Annual Meeting of the ACL (ACL2009)*, pages 91–99. Association for Computational Linguistics.

Thang Luong, Hieu Pham, and Christopher D. Manning. 2015. Effective approaches to attention-based neural machine translation. In *Proceedings of Empirical Methods in Natural Language Processing (EMNLP)*, pages 1412–1421.

Soichiro Murakami, Akihiko Watanabe, Akira Miyazawa, Keiichi Goshima, Toshihiko Yanase, Hiroya Takamura, and Yusuke Miyao. 2017. Learning to generate market comments from stock prices. In *Proceedings of Association for Computational Linguistics (ACL)*, pages 1374–1384.

François Portet, Ehud Reiter, Albert Gatt, Jim Hunter, Somayajulu Sripada, Yvonne Freer, and Cindy Sykes. 2009. Automatic generation of textual summaries from neonatal intensive care data. *Artificial Intelligence*, 173(7-8):789–816.

Ilya Sutskever, Oriol Vinyals, and Quoc V. Le. 2014. Sequence to sequence learning with neural networks. In *Advances in neural information processing systems (NIPS)*, pages 3104–3112.

SpatialVOC2K: A Multilingual Dataset of Images with Annotations and Features for Spatial Relations between Objects

Anja Belz
Computing, Engineering and Mathematics
University of Brighton
Lewes Road, Brighton BN2 4GJ, UK
a.s.belz@brighton.ac.uk

Adrian Muscat
Communications and Computer Engineering
University of Malta
Msida MSD 2080, Malta
adrian.muscat@um.edu.mt

Pierre Anguill   **Mouhamadou Sow**   **Gaétan Vincent**   **Yassine Zinessabah**
INSA Rouen Normandie
685 Avenue de l'Université
76800 Saint-Etienne-du-Rouvray, France

Abstract

We present SpatialVOC2K, the first multilingual image dataset with spatial relation annotations and object features for image-to-text generation, built using 2,026 images from the PASCAL VOC2008 dataset. The dataset incorporates (i) the labelled object bounding boxes from VOC2008, (ii) geometrical, language and depth features for each object, and (iii) for each pair of objects in both orders, (a) the single best preposition and (b) the set of possible prepositions in the given language that describe the spatial relationship between the two objects. Compared to previous versions of the dataset, we have roughly doubled the size for French, and completely reannotated as well as increased the size of the English portion, providing single best prepositions for English for the first time. Furthermore, we have added explicit 3D depth features for objects. We are releasing our dataset for free reuse, along with evaluation tools to enable comparative evaluation.

1 Introduction

Research in image labelling, description and understanding has a long tradition, but has recently seen explosive growth. Work in this area is most commonly motivated in terms of accessibility and data management, and has a range of different specific application tasks. One current research focus is detection of relations between objects, in particular for image description generation, and the research presented here contributes to this line of work with a new dataset, SpatialVOC2K,[1] in which object pairs in images have been annotated with spatial relations encoded as sets of prepositions, specifically for image-to-text generation. We start below with the source datasets from which we obtained the images, bounding boxes, and candidate prepositions (Section 2), followed by an overview of directory structure and file schemas (Section 3), and a summary of the annotation process (Section 4) and spatially relevant features (Section 5). We describe the two evaluation tools supplied with the dataset (Section 6), and finish with a survey of other datasets with object relation annotations (Section 7).

2 Source Data

Our main data source for SpatialVOC2K was the PASCAL VOC2008 image dataset (Everingham et al., 2010) in which every object belonging to one of 20 object classes is annotated with class label, bounding box (BB), viewpoint, truncation, occlusion, and identification difficulty (Everingham et al., 2010). Of these annotations we retain just the BB geometries and the class labels (aeroplane, bird, bicycle, boat, bottle, bus, car, cat, chair, cow, dining table, dog, horse, motorbike, person, potted plant, sheep, sofa, train, tv/monitor).

We also used Rashtchian et al.'s VOC'08 1K corpus (2010), which has 5 descriptions per im-

---

[1] https://github.com/muskata/SpatialVOC2K

Proceedings of The 11th International Natural Language Generation Conference, pages 140–145,
Tilburg, The Netherlands, November 5-8, 2018. ©2018 Association for Computational Linguistics

age obtained via Mechanical Turk for 50 images from each VOC2008 class, in order to determine an initial set of candidate prepositions for our annotations (for details see Section 4). Due to quality control measures, the VOC'08 1K descriptions are of relatively high quality with few errors.

For SpatialVOC2K, we selected all images from the VOC2008 data that had two or three object bounding boxes (BBs), meaning that images contained exactly two and three objects from the VOC2008 object classes, respectively. We also selected all images with four and five BBs where three were of normal size and the remainder very small (bearing the VOC2008 label 'difficult'). This selection process resulted in a set of 2,026 images with 9,804 unique object pairs. Numbers of BBs in images were distributed as follows:

Number of BBs	2	3	3+1	3+2
Number of images	1,020	534	357	141

For each image, we then (i) collected additional annotations (Section 4) which list, for each ordered object pair, (a) *the single best*, and (b) *all possible* prepositions that correctly describe the spatial relationship between the objects; and (ii) computed a range of spatially relevant features from the image and BB geometries, BB labels, and image depth maps (Section 1). All annotations and features are included in this dataset release.

3 SpatialVOC2K Structure and Schemas

The overall structure and file conventions of the SpatialVOC2K dataset mirror those of the VOC2008 dataset where possible:

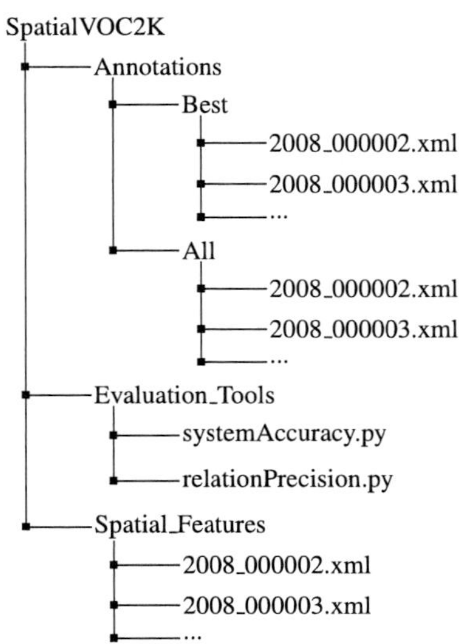

All files in the *Annotations* directory start with a line that is simply the original annotations from VOC2008. In the *Best* subdirectory, the remaining lines have the pattern $Object_1$ $Object_2$ Preposition, where $Object_1$ and $Object_2$ are the exact word strings, including any subscripts, of the object labels in the first line in the file, and Preposition is the single best preposition chosen by annotators for the two given objects presented in the given order (more about object order in Section 4 below). Each pair of annotated objects is thus associated with exactly two prepositions in the *Best* files, the best human-selected preposition for each order. The following is a simple example of a *Best* file:

```
1  VOC2012 2008_000008.jpg The VOC2008
   Database PASCAL VOC2008 flickr 500
   442 3 0 horse Left 0 1 53 87 471 420
   0 person Unspecified 1 0 158 44 289
   167 0
2  horse person under
3  person horse on
```

In the *All* directory, files have the same structure except that in the preposition lines, instead of a single preposition, there are as many prepositions as were selected by the human annotators as possible for a given ordered object pair.

The *Spatial_Features* files also have the same basic structure, except that instead of prepositions, there are 19 feature-value pairs (explained in Section 5) for each ordered object pair (some feature values differ depending on object order), e.g.:

```
1  VOC2012 2008_000008.jpg The VOC2008
   Database PASCAL VOC2008 flickr 500
   442 3 0 horse Left 0 1 53 87 471 420
   0 person Unspecified 1 0 158 44 289
   167 0
2  horse person F0 12 F1 14 F2 0.65 F3
   0.42 F4 1.54 ...
3  person horse F0 14 F1 12 F2 0.42 F3
   0.65 F4 0.65 ...
```

In the following three sections, we explain how we obtained the preposition annotations and spatial features, and how the metrics encoded by the evaluation tools are defined.

4 Preposition Annotations

We derived a set of candidate prepositions from the VOC2008 1K dataset (Section 2) by parsing the 5,000 descriptions in it with the Stanford Parser version 3.5.2[2] with the PCFG model, extracting the nmod:*prep* prepositional modifier relations, and manually removing the non-spatial

---

[2]http://nlp.stanford.edu/software/lex-parser.shtml#Download

ones. This gave us 38 English prepositions:

$\mathbf{V}_{\mathbf{E}}^{0} = \{$ *about, above, across, against, along, alongside, around, at, atop, behind, below, beneath, beside, beyond, by, close to, far from, in, in front of, inside, inside of, near, next to, on, on top of, opposite, outside, outside of, over, past, through, toward, towards, under, underneath, up, upon, within* $\}$

To obtain prepositions for French, we first asked two French native speakers to compile a list of possible translations of the English prepositions, and to check these against 200 sample images randomly selected from the complete set to be annotated. This produced 21 prepositions which were reduced to 19, based on evidence from previous work (Muscat and Belz, 2015), by eliminating prepositions that were used fewer than three times by annotators (*en haut de, parmi*). After the first batch of 1,020 images had been annotated, we furthermore merged prepositions which co-occur with another preposition more than 60%[3] of the times they occur in total (*á l'interieur de, en dessous de*), in accordance with the general sense of synonymity defined in previous work (Muscat and Belz, 2017). We found this kind of co-occurrence to be highly imbalanced, e.g. the likelihood of seeing *á l'interieur de* given *dans* is 0.43, whereas the likelihood of seeing *dans* given *á l'interieur de* is 0.91. We take this as justification for merging *á l'interieur de* into *dans*, rather than the other way around, and proceed in this way for all prepositions. The process leaves a final set of 17 French prepositions:

$\mathbf{V_F} = \{$ *à côté de, á l'éxterieur de, au dessus de, au niveau de, autour de, contre, dans, derrière, devant, en face de, en travers de, le long de, loin de, par delà, près de, sous, sur* $\}$

We also reduced the set of 38 English prepositions, using the same elimination process, starting with prepositions that occurred fewer than three times (*toward, towards, about, across, along, outside, outside of, through, up*). A further 12 prepositions were merged into others (*within, inside, inside of, beside, alongside, by, against, upon, atop, on top of, beneath, under*), yielding a final set of 17 English prepositions:

$\mathbf{V_E} = \{$ *above, around, at, behind, below, beyond, close to, far from, in, in front of, near, next to, on, opposite, over, past, underneath* $\}$

As discussed in more detail in previous work (Muscat and Belz, 2017), we make the domain-specific assumption that there is a one-to-one mapping from each preposition to the SR it denotes (whereas an SR can map to multiple prepositions). While our machine learning task is SR detection, we ask annotators to annotate our data with the corresponding prepositions (a more human-friendly task).

We used the above preposition sets in collecting annotations as follows. For each object pair O_i and O_j in each image, and for both orderings of the object labels, L_i, L_j and L_j, L_i, the task for annotators was to select (i) the single best preposition for the given pair (free text entry), and (ii) the possible prepositions for the given pair (selected from a given list) that accurately described the relationship between the two objects in the pair, given the template L_1 *is* ___ L_2 (*is* becomes *et* for French).

Even though in annotation task 1, annotators were not limited in their choice of preposition, they did not use any that were not in the list of prepositions offered in annotation task 2 (a few typos we corrected manually). As it would have been virtually impossible to remember the exact list of prepositions and only use those, we interpret this as meaning that annotators did not feel other prepositions were needed.

We used average pairwise kappa to assess inter-annotator and intra-annotator agreement as described in previous work (Muscat and Belz, 2017). First, figures for the first batch of French annotations (1,020 images with 2 or 3 objects in BBs[4]). For *single best* prepositions (annotation task 1), average inter-annotator agreement was 0.67, and average intra-annotator agreement was 0.81. For *all possible* prepositions (annotation task 2), average inter-annotator agreement was 0.63, and average intra-annotator agreement was 0.77.

For the second batch of French annotations (1,006 images with 3, 4 or 5 BBs), average inter-annotator agreement for *single best* prepositions (annotation task 1) was 0.33, and average intra-annotator agreement was 0.66. For *all possible* prepositions (annotation task 2), average inter-annotator agreement was 0.3, and average intra-annotator agreement was 0.62. A possible reason for the lower annotator agreement on batch 2 is that as the number of dominant objects in an im-

---

[3]This is a very high threshold and far above co-occurrence percentages for any other preposition pairs.

[4]Annotators were only ever shown images with 2 BBs in them.

$F0$:	Object label L_s — definition depends on learning method	NB, DT, RF: $\{0, 1, ..., 19\}$; others: 1-hot encoding (20 bits)
$F1$:	Object label L_o — definition depends on learning method	
$F2$:	Area of bounding box of Obj_s normalized by image size.	$[0, 1]$
$F3$:	Area of bounding box of Obj_o normalized by image size.	$[0, 1]$
$F4$:	Ratio of Obj_s bounding box area to that of Obj_o.	$[0,$ size of $Obj_s]$
$F5$:	Distance between bounding box centroids, normalized by image diagonal.	$[0, 1]$
$F6$:	Area of overlap of bounding boxes normalized by the area of the smaller bounding box.	$[0, 1]$
$F7$:	Distance between centroids divided by sum of square root of areas/2 (approximated average width of bounding boxes).	$[0, {\sim}20]$
$F8$:	Position of Obj_s relative to Obj_o expressed as one of 4 categories, depending on the angle with the vertical axis.	NB, DT, RF: $\{0, 1, 2, 3\}$; others: 1-hot encoding (4 bits)
$F9$–$F12$:	Let distance from image edge of left and right edges be $a1, b1$ for first box and $a2, b2$ for second box: $F9 = (a2-a1)/(b1-a1)$, $F10 = (b2-a1)/(b1-a1)$. Similarly for the top and bottom edges, giving $F11$ and $F12$.	$[{\sim}\text{-}40, {\sim}\text{+}40]$
$F13$:	Aspect ratio of box of Obj_s.	$[0, {\sim}10]$
$F14$:	Aspect ratio of box of Obj_o.	
$F15$:	GloVe word vector for L_s.	here: $\sim [-2, +3]$
$F16$:	GloVe word vector for L_o.	
$F17$:	Average depth in BB of Obj_s.	
$F18$:	Average depth in BB of Obj_o.	

Table 1: Spatially relevant features as included in SpatialVOC2K. Note that the 19 numbered features above correspond to feature vectors of length between 116 and 140, depending on conversion method for ML inputs.

age increases, the annotation task becomes more difficult; we also used different annotators for the second batch which may be a contributing factor.[5]

5 Spatially Relevant Features

Table 1 provides an overview of the 19 features included in SpatialVOC2K: F0, F1, F15 and F16 are language features. F0 is the class label of the first object, F1 of the second (e.g. *person*). F15 and F16 are GloVe word vectors of length 50 (Pennington et al., 2014) for the object labels.[6] F2–F14 are visual features measuring various aspects of the geometries of the image and two bounding boxes (BBs). Most features express a property of just one of the objects, but F4–F9 express a property of both objects jointly, e.g. F6 is the normalized BB overlap.

F17 and F18 are the average pixel-level depth value within the BB of Obj_s and Obj_o, respectively. Pixel-level depth values were computed via the method described in (Birmingham et al., 2018), which uses depth maps computed with monoDepth[7] (Godard et al., 2017) .

---

[5]Inter-AA/intra-AA for English and additional dataset statistics will be added to the project home on Github.

[6]GloVe is a count-based method for creating distributed word representations.

[7]https://github.com/mrharicot/monodepth

6 Evaluation Tools

SpatialVOC2K includes two evaluation tools which we have used in all previous work involving similar data. The two tools, `systemAccuracy` and `relationPrecision` implement the following two methods, respectively.

System-level Accuracy: There are four different variants of system-level Accuracy, denoted $Acc(n)$, $n \in \{1, 2, 3, 4\}$. Each variant returns Accuracy rates for the top n outputs returned by systems, in the sense that a system output is considered correct if at least one of the reference prepositions (the human-selected prepositions from the dataset annotations) can be found in the top n prepositions returned by the system (for $n = 1$ this yields standard Accuracy).

Weighted Average Per-preposition Precision: This measure, denoted Acc_P, computes the weighted mean of individual per-preposition precision scores. The individual per-preposition precision for a given system and a given preposition p is the proportion of times that p is among the corresponding human-selected prepositions out of all the times that p is returned as the top-ranked preposition by the system.

7 Related Datasets

A number of datasets are available that incorporate annotations representing relations between objects

Name	Authors	Task	Categories of relations	Annotated relations	Images
Visual Phrases	Sadeghi et al. 2011	Phrase Classification	action, verbal, spatial	1,796	2,769
Visual and Linguistic Treebank	Elliott and Keller, 2013	Image Description	action, verbal, spatial	5748	341 / 2424
Scene Graphs	Johnson et al. 2015	Image Retrieval	action, verbal, spatial, preposition	112,707	5K
ViSen	Ramisa et al. 2015	Preposition Prediction	spatial, preposition	78,317	33,262
VRD	Lu et al. 2016	Relation, Phrase Prediction	action, verbal, spatial, preposition, comparative	37,993	5K
Visual Genome	Krishna et al. 2016	Image Understanding	action, verbal, spatial, preposition, comparative	1.5M	108K

Table 2: Overview of related datasets. For explanation of relation categories see in text.

in images. Types of relationships that have been annotated include actions (e.g. *person kicks ball*), other verbal relations (*person wears shirt*), spatial relations (*person on horse*), and comparative relations (*one car bigger than another*). In this section, we provide a brief overview of available datasets with relation annotations, in terms of their stated purpose (application task), the types of relations included, the range of spatial prepositions included, as well as size and other properties of the dataset. Table 2 has a summary of the datasets.

Visual Phrases (Sadeghi and Farhadi, 2011) was the first image dataset with object relation annotations, and used the concept of a visual phrase (VP) which is defined as a bounding box that surrounds two objects in an image. Out of 17 different types of VPs annotated in the data set, 13 comprise 2 objects, and 4 comprise one object. However, there are 120 predicates per object category.

Visual and Linguistic Treebank (Elliott and Keller, 2013) contains 341 images that are annotated with regions (362 in total) and visual dependency representations, which unfold to a total of 5,748 spatial relations (from a set of 8) and are aligned to the dependency parse of the image description. This setup allows for the prediction of actions as well as spatial relations (using a set of 8 manual created rules).

Scene Graphs (Johnson et al., 2015) is a dataset of 5,000 human-generated scene graphs grounded to images; scene graphs describe objects and their relationships.

ViSen (Ramisa et al., 2015) associates sets of (object_1, preposition, object_2) triples with images, where the triples have been extracted from parses of the image descriptions in MSCOCO (Lin et al., 2014) and Flickr30k (Young et al., 2014). Prepositions covered include all those extracted from the image descriptions including non-spatial ones. By far not all descriptions contain prepositions so not all images have spatial relation annotations; the task addressed is preposition prediction, not spatial relation prediction.

Visual Relationships Dataset (VRD) (Lu et al., 2016) contains 5,000 images, 100 object categories, 6,672 unique relationships, and 24.25 relations per object category. Scant information is available about how the dataset was created other than that relations broadly fit into the categories action, verbal, spatial, preposition and comparative.

Visual Genome (Krishna et al., 2017) contains 108K images, split into 4M regions, corresponding to 108K scene graphs and about 4K region graphs, 1.5M object-object relations, 40K unique relations, and an average of 17 relations per image and 0.63 relations per region.

8 Future Work

We plan to expand the SpatialVOC2K dataset to other languages, and to more object pairs per language, in the future. Given the ever growing need for image description and labelling, and in combination with the image segmentation and description annotations that exist for the same VOC images, SpatialVOC2K can potentially be used in a range of different application tasks, including but not limited to image description generation.

References

B. Birmingham, A. Belz, and A. Muscat. 2018. Adding the third dimension to spatial relation detection in 2d images. In *Proceedings of INLG'18*.

D. Elliott and F. Keller. 2013. Image description using visual dependency representations. In *Proc. 18th Conf. on Empirical Methods in Natural Language Processing (EMNLP)*, pages 1292–1302, Seattle.

M. Everingham, L. Van Gool, C. K. Williams, J. Winn, and A. Zisserman. 2010. The pascal visual object classes (voc) challenge. *Int. J. of Computer Vision*, 88(2):303–338.

C. Godard, O. M. Aodha, and G. J. Brostow. 2017. Unsupervised monocular depth estimation with left-right consistency. In *2017 IEEE Conference on Computer Vision and Pattern Recognition (CVPR)*, pages 6602–6611.

J. Johnson, R. Krishna, M. Stark, L. Li, D. A. Shamma, M. S. Bernstein, and L. Fei-Fei. 2015. Image retrieval using scene graphs. In *2015 IEEE Conference on Computer Vision and Pattern Recognition (CVPR)*, pages 3668–3678.

Ranjay Krishna, Yuke Zhu, Oliver Groth, Justin Johnson, Kenji Hata, Joshua Kravitz, Stephanie Chen, Yannis Kalantidis, Li-Jia Li, David A. Shamma, Michael S. Bernstein, and Li Fei-Fei. 2017. Visual genome: Connecting language and vision using crowdsourced dense image annotations. *International Journal of Computer Vision*, pages 1–42.

Tsung-Yi Lin, Michael Maire, Serge Belongie, James Hays, Pietro Perona, Deva Ramanan, Piotr Dollár, and C Lawrence Zitnick. 2014. Microsoft Coco: Common objects in context. In *European conference on computer vision*, pages 740–755. Springer.

Cewu Lu, Ranjay Krishna, Michael Bernstein, and Li Fei-Fei. 2016. Visual relationship detection with language priors. In *Computer Vision – ECCV 2016*, pages 852–869, Cham. Springer International Publishing.

A. Muscat and A. Belz. 2015. Generating descriptions of spatial relations between objects in images. In *Proc. 15th European Workshop on Natural Language Generation (ENLG)*, pages 100–104, Brighton, UK.

Adrian Muscat and Anja Belz. 2017. Learning to generate descriptions of visual data anchored in spatial relations. *IEEE Computational Intelligence Magazine*, 12(3):29–42.

Jeffrey Pennington, Richard Socher, and Christopher Manning. 2014. Glove: Global vectors for word representation. In *Proc. 19th Conference on Empirical Methods in Natural Language Processing (EMNLP)*, pages 1532–1543, Doha, Qatar.

Arnau Ramisa, Josiah Wang, Ying Lu, Emmanuel Dellandrea, Francesc Moreno-Noguer, and Robert Gaizauskas. 2015. Combining geometric, textual and visual features for predicting prepositions in image descriptions. In *Proc. 20th Conf. on Empirical Methods in Natural Language Processing (EMNLP)*, pages 214–220, Lisbon, Portugal.

Cyrus Rashtchian, Peter Young, Micah Hodosh, and Julia Hockenmaier. 2010. Collecting image annotations using amazon's mechanical turk. In *Proc. NAACL HLT 2010 Workshop on Creating Speech and Language Data with Amazon's Mechanical Turk*, pages 139–147, Los Angeles, California.

Mohammad Amin Sadeghi and Ali Farhadi. 2011. Recognition using visual phrases. In *Computer Vision and Pattern Recognition (CVPR)*, pages 1745–1752. IEEE Computer Society.

Peter Young, Alice Lai, Micah Hodosh, and Julia Hockenmaier. 2014. From image descriptions to visual denotations: New similarity metrics for semantic inference over event descriptions. *Transactions of the Association for Computational Linguistics*, 2:67–78.

Adding the Third Dimension to Spatial Relation Detection in 2D Images

Brandon Birmingham   **Adrian Muscat**
Communications and Computer Engineering
University of Malta
Msida MSD 2080, Malta
adrian.muscat@um.edu.mt

Anja Belz
Computing, Engineering and Mathematics
University of Brighton
Lewes Road, Brighton BN2 4GJ, UK
a.s.belz@brighton.ac.uk

Abstract

Detection of spatial relations between objects in images is currently a popular subject in image description research. A range of different language and geometric object features have been used in this context, but methods have not so far used explicit information about the third dimension (depth), except when manually added to annotations. The lack of such information hampers detection of spatial relations that are inherently 3D. In this paper, we use a fully automatic method for creating a depth map of an image and derive several different object-level depth features from it which we add to an existing feature set to test the effect on spatial relation detection. We show that performance increases are obtained from adding depth features in all scenarios tested.

1 Introduction

Image description aims to produce a summarising description, in structured natural language, of an image (region), typically involving the prioritisation of more important elements and relationships between elements. Work in this area is most commonly motivated in terms of accessibility and data management, and has a range of distinct application tasks. Research in image description and understanding is booming, with relation detection currently a particular focus. The input to spatial relation detection is usually a set of secondary, abstract features derived from region boundaries and labels. A range of different language and geometric features have been used in existing work, but none that explicitly encode information about the third dimension (depth), except via manual annotations (Elliott, 2014). This is an issue for spatial relation detection, because many spatial relations involve three dimensions, some obviously so (e.g. in front of, behind), some less so (beyond, outside, across, etc.). Existing methods in effect try to guess 3D relations from 2D information.

In the experiments in this paper, we use a fully automatic method to generate a depth map from an image, derive different object-level abstract features from the depth values associated with pixels within object bounding boxes, and test the effect of adding such features on the performance of spatial relation detection methods. Below, we start by reviewing related research (Section 2) and describing the existing dataset and associated features we use in our experiments (Section 3). We next describe the depth map generation method we used, and the features we derive from depth maps (Section 4). We then describe the classifier methods we use in experiments (Section 5), and report results from experiments involving different classifier methods and combinations of depth features (Section 6). We conclude with some discussion and a look to the future (Section 7).

2 Related Research

Research on associating text with images goes back at least to the 1960s with early work focusing on object/region labelling (Rosenfeld, 1978). Image description proper starts where a summarising description of the whole image is aimed for. Some approaches measure the similarity of a new image with other images for which descriptions exist, and then use one or more of those descriptions to create a description for the new image (Socher et al., 2014; Karpathy and Fei-Fei, 2015; Ordonez et al., 2011). Our focus here is on methods that create a new description for a given image from scratch. Such methods can be said to involve three main steps: (1) identification of type and, optionally, location of objects and background/scene; (2) detection of attributes, relations and activities involving objects from Step 1; and (3) generation of

Proceedings of The 11th International Natural Language Generation Conference, pages 146–151,
Tilburg, The Netherlands, November 5-8, 2018. ©2018 Association for Computational Linguistics

a word string from the outputs from Steps 1 and 2. In Step 2, the focus of this paper, systems determine object attributes (Yatskar et al., 2014; Kulkarni et al., 2011), spatial relationships (Yang et al., 2011; Elliott and Keller, 2013), activities (Yatskar et al., 2014; Elliott and Keller, 2013), etc.

Identifying the spatial relationships between pairs of objects in images is an important part of Step 2, but overlaps into Step 3 if prepositions are selected directly. Methods that produce spatial prepositions sometimes do so as a side-effect of the overall method (Mitchell et al., 2012; Kulkarni et al., 2013); examples of preposition selection as a separate subtask include Elliott and Keller (2013) who base the mapping from features to spatial relations on manually composed rules, and Ramisa et al. (2015) and our own previous work (Muscat and Belz, 2017) where the mapping is learnt automatically. Elliott (2014) manually adds 3rd dimension annotations to images (e.g. whether objects are behind other objects).

There is a sizable literature on spatial relations and spatial language from cognitive and psycholinguistic perspectives, and the remainder of this section briefly surveys a selection of relevant results. Indications are that whether speakers use spatial relations in scene descriptions and referring expressions depends at least in part on individual preference and the context. E.g. when generating referring expressions, some people prefer not to use spatial relations at all (Viethen and Dale, 2008). Furthermore, speakers tend to make more use of spatial relations in domains unknown to them, whereas they use them comparatively less when the domain is known (Viethen and Dale, 2008). Kelleher and Kruiff (2005) categorise spatial relations as combinations of topological vs. projective, and contrastive vs. relative, the latter being dependent on context. Both studies (Viethen and Dale, 2008; Kelleher and Kruijff, 2005) agree that people are generally less likely to use projective spatial relations like *in front of* than topological relations like *on top of*. The former depend on a landmark whereas the latter depend on intersection, overlap and contiguity, which require less cognitive effort to process. For similar reasons, contrastive relations are used more than relative relations (Kelleher and Kruijff, 2005).

The comprehension and choice of spatial prepositions depend on function as well as context (Coventry et al., 2005), e.g. the choice of preposi-

tion in *person **at** a table*, depends on the functional relationship between the trajector object, *person*, and the landmark object, *table*. Dobnik and Kelleher (2014) derive functional semantic knowledge from corpora and use it to explore the dependency of spatial prepositions on functional knowledge.

Regier and Carlson (2001) show that projective spatial terms such as *above* are grounded in attention processes and vector-sum coding of overall direction, formalising these notions in their attentional vector-sum (AVS) model. The model is shown to predict linguistic acceptability judgments for spatial terms, for a variety of spatial configurations. Results indicate that spatial prepositions require more attention on the image compared to detecting an object, and geometric features based on the net vector sum over an area rather than the centre of mass are better predictors.

Kelleher et al. (2011) show that object occlusion degrades the performance of models that are based solely on geometric and functional features e.g. in the case of *in front of*, a projective preposition. Kelleher et al.'s occlusion-enabled regression-based model is shown to outperform Regier and Carlson's AVS model.

3   Data and Features

In the research reported here, we use a subset of the French part of the SpatialVOC2K dataset (Belz et al., 2018), referred to as 'DS-F-Best' below, for consistency with previous publications. Objects in this dataset are annotated with bounding boxes, object labels and spatial relations encoded as sets of prepositions. To create the spatial relation annotations, annotators were asked to (a) choose the single best preposition (free text entry), as well as (b) select all possible prepositions from a list of candidate spatial prepositions, such that the preposition(s) accurately describe(s) the spatial relationship between the given pair of objects.

In the experiments below, we are interested in studying the effect depth features have on recalling individual prepositions (especially the ones that have previously proven difficult to predict) in addition to the overall system-level recall. We therefore use the single *best* preposition for each object pair only, when training the single label classifiers.

In research involving this and similar datasets, sets of language and geometric features are normally computed from bounding boxes and object labels. Typical language features are label encoders (one hot vectors) and word2vec (Mikolov et al., 2013) vectors. Examples of geometric features are area of object bounding box normalised by combined area size for both objects, area of overlap between the two bounding boxes normalised by combined area, and Euclidean distance between two bounding boxes. Some of the feature functions are unary and others are binary. For the initial feature set in this paper, we used the union of geometric features from two previous lines of work, our own (Muscat and Belz, 2017) and Ramisa et al. (2015). This yielded a set of 18 geometric features, and although some of these are correlated, we left it to the classifier models to discriminate among the more useful ones. There are no 3D features in this initial set of features, although some features are intended as proxy features for depth, e.g. bounding box overlap.

4 Computing Depth Features

4.1 MonoDepth Features

We use *monoDepth*[1] (Godard et al., 2017), a convolutional neural network method trained on stereo image pairs which maps single images to depth maps where each pixel has a value assigned to it that represents the estimated distance from the viewer. More specifically we used the monodepth-cityscapes model, trained on the Cityscapes dataset (Cordts et al., 2016). Figure 1 shows an image from our dataset alongside the depth map generated for it by the monodepth-cityscapes model. The more towards the dark blue end of the colour spectrum an area is, the further away it is from the viewer, and the more towards the bright yellow end, the nearer. The model produces an impressively accurate rendering of the depths of the two trees, car, person, and road (not all depth maps are as good).

Once we have the depth map for a given image, we obtain depth values for the pixel grids inside the bounding boxes (BBs) of the pair of objects under consideration. We then compute the following object-level features for each BB:

- Average depth (AVG): simply the average depth value within each object BB.

- Radially weighted average (RWA) depth: starting from the central pixel(s), assign a weight to each pixel that is in inverse pro-

portion to its distance from the centre, then compute the weighted average.

Looking at the example in Figure 1, AVG is much lower in the red person BB than in the blue car BB, making 'person in front of car' a possibility. RWA is also less for the person BB, but the difference is less pronounced than would be the case if all of the car was further way than the person, thus making 'person next to car' an alternative possibility.

4.2 Human-estimated Depth Feature

We obtained human estimates of BB-level depth for 1,554 images and 3,642 objects as follows. Participants were shown an image with objects surrounded by BBs. Their task was to assign a number out of 100 to each bounding box, indicating the average depth of (just) the object inside the BB, where 100 is the maximum distance. The annotators were trained and mentored for some time before starting annotations proper. Three participants in total contributed to the annotations. Depth values were then normalised to range from 0 to 1 for each image.

We computed Pearson's correlation coefficients between the human estimated object depths and the corresponding AVG and RWA figures. Pearson's r between human and AVG depth values was 0.535 ($p < 0.0001$), and between human and RWA it was 0.523 ($p < 0.0001$). The correlation between AVG and RWA was 0.995($p < 0.0001$). We also converted the three sets of depth estimates to categorical values (foreground, background, neutral) and computed percentage agreement with human-estimated depth on these, which was 60.8% for AVG and 60.3% for RWA.

5 Methods

Using combinations of features from Section 3 and 4, we separately trained models of the six types below.[2] Where relevant, hyperparameters for the models were obtained by splitting the development data into separate training and validation sets, which were then recombined for training the final models and testing on a held-out test set. All models output the probability vector for the prepositions, from which results are calculated.

Naive Bayes (NB) models assume that each feature is conditionally independent of every other feature given the output class (preposition in our case). We use a prior computed from the output

---

[1] https://github.com/mrharicot/monodepth

[2] Using scikit-learn: http://scikit-learn.org

Figure 1: Example SpatialVOC2K image and depth map generated by monoDepth.

labels, and base the likelihood on the geometric features.

Decision Tree (DT): Decisions are based on conjunctions of features. Values for the maximum tree depth [2, 20] are determined by hyper-parameter optimisation (HPO).

Logistic Regression (LR): A linear classifier which models the SR probabilities with a logistic function. The value for the inverse of regularisation constant [0.1, 100.0] is determined by HPO. The regularisation is L1-norm, tolerance is 0.001 and one-versus-rest multi-class classification.

Support Vector Machine (SVM): A binary classifier solving the multiclass case via (here) one-versus-one classification. The RBF kernel parameters, C [0.1, 100.0] and gamma [0.001, 1.0] are determined by HPO.

Random Forests (RF): A meta-estimator comprising multiple decision-tree classifiers fitted to sub-samples of the data, using averaging to improve predictive accuracy and to control overfitting. The number of estimators [10, 150], maximum features [1, 156], maximum tree depth [2, 20], are determined by HPO.

6 Experiments and Results

We carried out experiments for all ML methods above, and for the following feature combinations: (i) the 18 geometrical features ('G' in results tables) from Section 3, (ii) the language features derived from the object labels ('L' in the tables), (iii) average depth ('avg' in tables), (iv) RWA ('rwa' in tables) and (V) human-estimated depth ('man' in tables). For each of (iii), (iv) and (v) we considered depth of object 1 ('d1' in tables), depth of object 2 ('d2' in tables), and the difference between the latter two depths ('dd' in tables).

Table 1 shows system-level weighted aver-

Features	RF	DT	LR	SVM	NB
G	0.45	0.36	0.4	0.38	0.24
+avg:d1,d2	0.45	0.36	0.4	0.39	0.25
+avg:dd	0.45	0.36	0.4	0.37	0.27
+avg:d1,d2,dd	**0.46**	0.36	0.39	0.37	0.27
+rwa:d1,d2	0.45	0.36	0.4	0.37	0.24
+rwa:dd	0.45	0.35	0.4	0.38	0.27
+rwa:d1,d2,dd	**0.46**	0.35	0.4	0.37	0.26
+man:d1,d2	0.47	0.36	0.4	0.4	0.24
+man:dd	0.47	0.39	0.41	0.4	0.27
+man:d1,d2,dd	**0.49**	0.39	0.4	0.4	0.27
L,G	0.48	0.4	0.46	0.43	0.26
+avg:d1,d2	0.5	0.4	0.46	0.46	0.27
+avg:dd	0.49	0.4	0.46	0.46	0.26
+avg:d1,d2,dd	0.5	0.4	0.46	0.45	0.27
+rwa:d1,d2	0.48	0.4	0.46	0.44	0.27
+rwa:dd	0.48	0.4	0.47	0.44	0.26
+rwa:d1,d2,dd	0.47	0.4	0.46	0.45	0.27
+man:d1,d2	0.49	0.4	0.48	0.46	0.27
+man:dd	**0.52**	0.42	0.47	0.44	0.26
+man:d1,d2,dd	0.51	0.42	0.48	0.44	0.27

Table 1: SpatialVOC2K: Weighted Average Recall for all feature combinations (for explanation of abbreviations, see in text).

age recall results. Depth features improved the weighted average recall results across the board. The highest increase is 8.9% when added to geometric features, and 8.3% when added to both language and geometric features. AVG and RWA features perform equally well, and less well than the human-estimated depths. Out of the three depth features, the difference in depth ($dd = d1 - d2$) has the most pronounced positive effect on scores individually; however, the overall highest scores are obtained when all three (d1, d2 and dd). Out of the different classifier modesl, the RF model resulted in the highest scores followed by LR, SVM, DT and NB. However, the NB model registered the highest increase in scores resulting from depth features: 12.5% when added to geometric features.

Features	a_cote_de	a_l'exterieur_de	au_dessus_de	au_niveau_de	autour_de	contre	dans	derriere	devant	en_face_de	loin_de	pres_de	sous	sur	wt_m	mean
G, avg:d1,d2	-4	-	-20	+8	0	-27	0	+10	+8	0	0	-24	-8	+5	0	-2
G, avg:dd	-4	-	-20	0	0	-27	0	+24	-5	0	+4	-24	-5	0	0	-2
G, avg:d1,d2,dd	-4	-	0	+8	0	0	0	+19	0	0	-6	0	-5	+5	+2	0
G, rwa:d1,d2	-4	-	-20	+8	0	0	0	+19	0	-16	-6	-36	-5	+8	0	-2
G, rwa:dd	0	-	+20	+8	0	+27	0	-5	-5	0	+4	-16	-8	+2	0	0
G, rwa:d1,d2,dd	0	-	-20	-8	0	+27	-25	+24	-5	0	-9	+20	-2	+5	+2	-2
G, man:d1,d2	-4	-	0	0	0	+27	0	+33	0	0	0	0	-2	-2	+4	+7
G, man:dd	0	-	0	+8	0	0	-25	+10	+32	-20	0	+28	0	+2	+4	0
G, man:d1,d2,dd	-4	-	0	+15	0	-27	0	+24	+12	0	+4	+4	+2	+8	+9	+9
G, L	+4	-	0	-15	+33	+73	+24	+5	+18	+20	-9	0	0	+11	+7	+7
G,L,avg:d1,d2	0	-	-20	+18	-25	0	0	+5	0	+7	+10	+20	-2	0	+4	+7
G,L,avg:dd	-4	-	-20	+18	-25	+15	0	+23	-15	0	0	0	0	0	+2	0
G,L,avg:d1,d2,dd	-4	-	-20	+27	-25	-27	0	+18	-9	0	+10	+12	0	+4	+4	+2
G,L,rwa:d1,d2	0	-	-20	+9	-25	+15	0	+5	+4	+7	+4	-16	-2	-2	0	0
G,L,rwa:dd	-4	-	-20	+27	-25	-15	0	+14	-4	-10	+10	-16	0	0	0	0
G,L,rwa:d1,d2,dd	0	-	-20	0	-25	-15	0	+9	-15	-17	+4	-8	0	-2	-2	0
G,L,man:d1,d2	0	-	-20	+18	-25	-15	0	+14	-9	+20	+14	-8	-2	0	+2	+2
G,L,man:dd	+4	-	-20	+55	0	0	0	+14	+9	0	+14	+12	0	0	+8	+7
G,L,man:d1,d2,dd	-4	-	-20	+36	0	-27	0	+23	+4	0	+27	0	+2	+2	+6	+9

Table 2: SpatialVOC2K: Percentage increase in recall per preposition for the RF model. Figures in top half relative to geometric features; lower half relative to both geometric and language features.

This could indicate that the other models are learning more about depth from the other features.

Table 2 shows per-preposition weighted average recall results. In this set of results we examine the effect of adding depth information on individual prepositions, looking at which combinations of features increase or decrease the recall per preposition. The table is split into two halves. The top half shows changes from adding depth features to (just) the geometric features (G), while the bottom half shows changes from adding depth features to the union of geometric and language features (G,L). Some prepositions fare better with depth information: *au niveau de* ("at the level of"), *derriere* ("behind"), *devant* ("in front of"), *sur* ("on"). Results for others worsen: *à côté de* ("next to"), *en face de* ("facing"), *sous* ("under"). For some, the results are inconclusive (*contre* ("against"), *dans* ("in"), *loin de* ("far from"), *près de* ("near")), while others are not affected (*au dessus de* ("above"), *autour de* ("around")).

The row labelled 'G,L' shows the effect of just adding language features to the geometric set. Some prepositions (most notably *autour de, contre* and *dans*) benefit substantially from language features while others benefit more from depth features. Some (*au niveau de, oin de*) fare worse when language features are added. The biggest improvement when depth information is added to geometric features is 33% for *derriere* ("behind"); the highest when depth is added to both geometrical and language is 55%, for *au niveau de* ("at the level of, at equal distance from the viewer").

Getting improvements for clearly 3D prepositions such as *derriere, devant* and *au niveau de* is as expected, but there are clear improvements for other prepositions too.

7   Conclusion

We have reported the first results for using object-level depth features computed from depth maps automatically generated for a given image with monoDepth as additional features in spatial relation prediction. We have shown that performance increases when depth features are added in all scenarios tested. However, automatically computed depth is still some way off manual toplines which resulted in bigger improvements.

References

A. Belz, A. Muscat, P. Anguill, M. Sow, G. Vincent, and Y. Zinessabah. 2018. Spatialvoc2k: A multilingual dataset of images with annotations and features for spatial relations between objects. In *Proceedings of INLG'18*.

Marius Cordts, Mohamed Omran, Sebastian Ramos, Timo Rehfeld, Markus Enzweiler, Rodrigo Benenson, Uwe Franke, Stefan Roth, and Bernt Schiele. 2016. The cityscapes dataset for semantic urban scene understanding. In *Proc. of the IEEE Conference on Computer Vision and Pattern Recognition (CVPR)*.

Kenny R. Coventry, Angelo Cangelosi, Rohanna Rajapakse, Alison Bacon, Stephen Newstead, Dan Joyce, and Lynn V. Richards. 2005. Spatial prepositions and vague quantifiers: Implementing the functional geometric framework. In *Spatial Cognition IV. Reasoning, Action, Interaction*, pages 98–110, Berlin, Heidelberg. Springer Berlin Heidelberg.

Simon Dobnik and John Kelleher. 2014. Exploration of functional semantics of prepositions from corpora of descriptions of visual scenes. In *Proceedings of the Third Workshop on Vision and Language*, pages 33–37. Dublin City University and the Association for Computational Linguistics.

D. Elliott and F. Keller. 2013. Image description using visual dependency representations. In *Proc. 18th Conf. on Empirical Methods in Natural Language Processing (EMNLP)*, pages 1292–1302, Seattle.

Desmond Elliott. 2014. *A Structured Representation of Images for Language Generation and Image Retrieval*. Ph.D. thesis, University of Edinburgh.

Clément Godard, Oisin Mac Aodha, and Gabriel J. Brostow. 2017. Unsupervised monocular depth estimation with left-right consistency. In *CVPR*.

A. Karpathy and L. Fei-Fei. 2015. Deep visual-semantic alignments for generating image descriptions. In *Proc. IEEE Conf. on Computer Vision and Pattern Recognition*, pages 3128–3137, Boston.

John Kelleher and Geert-Jan Kruijff. 2005. A context-dependent algorithm for generating locative expressions in physically situated environments. In *Proceedings of the Tenth European Workshop on Natural Language Generation (ENLG-05)*.

John D. Kelleher, Robert J. Ross, Colm Sloan, and Brian Mac Namee. 2011. The effect of occlusion on the semantics of projective spatial terms: a case study in grounding language in perception. *Cognitive Processing*, 12(1):95–108.

G. Kulkarni, V. Premraj, S. Dhar, S. Li, Y. Choi, A. C. Berg, and T. L. Berg. 2011. Baby talk: Understanding and generating simple image descriptions. In *Proc. IEEE Conf. on Computer Vision and Pattern Recognition*, pages 1601–1608, Colorado Springs.

G. Kulkarni, V. Premraj, V. Ordonez, S. Dhar, S. Li, Y. Choi, A. C. Berg, and T. Berg. 2013. Babytalk: Understanding and generating simple image descriptions. *IEEE Transactions on Pattern Analysis and Machine Intelligence*, 35(12):2891–2903.

Tomas Mikolov, Ilya Sutskever, Kai Chen, Greg Corrado, and Jeffrey Dean. 2013. Distributed representations of words and phrases and their compositionality. In *Proceedings of the 26th International Conference on Neural Information Processing Systems*, NIPS'13, pages 3111–3119, Lake Tahoe, Nevada. Curran Associates Inc.

Margaret Mitchell, Xufeng Han, Jesse Dodge, Alyssa Mensch, Amit Goyal, Alex Berg, Kota Yamaguchi, Tamara Berg, Karl Stratos, and Hal Daumé, III. 2012. Midge: Generating image descriptions from computer vision detections. In *Proc. of the 13th Conf. of the European Chapter of the Association for Computational Linguistics*, pages 747–756, Avignon, France.

A. Muscat and A. Belz. 2017. Learning to generate descriptions of visual data anchored in spatial relations. *IEEE Computational Intelligence Magazine*, 12(3):29–42.

V. Ordonez, G. Kulkarni, and T. L. Berg. 2011. Im2text: Describing images using 1 million captioned photographs. In *Advances in Neural Information Processing Systems*, pages 1143–1151, Granada, Spain.

Arnau Ramisa, Josiah Wang, Ying Lu, Emmanuel Dellandrea, Francesc Moreno-Noguer, and Robert Gaizauskas. 2015. Combining geometric, textual and visual features for predicting prepositions in image descriptions. In *Proc. 20th Conf. on Empirical Methods in Natural Language Processing (EMNLP)*, pages 214–220, Lisbon, Portugal.

Terry Regier and Laura A. Carlson. 2001. Grounding spatial language in perception: an empirical and computational investigation. *Journal of Experimental Psychology General*, 130(2):273–298.

A. Rosenfeld. 1978. Iterative methods in image analysis. *Pattern Recognition*, 10(3):181–187.

R. Socher, A. Karpathy, Q. V. Le, C. D. Manning, and A. Y. Ng. 2014. Grounded compositional semantics for finding and describing images with sentences. *Transactions of the Association for Computational Linguistics*, 2:27–218.

J. Viethen and R. Dale. 2008. The use of spatial relations in referring expression generation. In *Proc. 5th Int. Natural Language Generation Conf. (INLG)*, pages 59–67, Salt Fork, Ohio.

Y. Yang, C. L. Teo, H Daumé III, and Y. Aloimonos. 2011. Corpus-guided sentence generation of natural images. In *Proc. 16th Conf. on Empirical Methods in Natural Language Processing (EMNLP)*, pages 444–454, Edinburg, Scotland.

M. Yatskar, L. Vanderwende, and L. Zettlemoyer. 2014. See no evil, say no evil: Description generation from densely labeled images. In *Proc. 3rd Joint Conference on Lexical and Computational Semantics*, pages 110–120, Dublin, Ireland.

Automatic Opinion Question Generation

Yllias Chali
University of Lethbridge
4401 University Drive
Lethbridge, Alberta, T1K 3M4
chali@cs.uleth.ca

Tina Baghaee
University of Lethbridge
4401 University Drive
Lethbridge, Alberta, T1K 3M4
tina.baghaee@gmail.com

Abstract

We study the problem of opinion question generation from sentences with the help of community-based question answering systems. For this purpose, we use a sequence to sequence attentional model, and we adopt coverage mechanism to prevent sentences from repeating themselves. Experimental results on the Amazon question/answer dataset show an improvement in automatic evaluation metrics as well as human evaluations from the state-of-the-art question generation systems.

1 Introduction

Question generation (QG) can be considered as a task which affects many aspects of people's lives. One of the main significance of the question generation is its capability to improve one's learning ability. Studies have shown that asking questions can help students realize their knowledge deficits and encourages them to look for information to compensate for those deficits (Graesser and Person, 1994). Additionally, QG can be used as an aid to search engines by providing suggestions regarding the users' queries (Chali and Hasan, 2015). This way, the users can either choose one of those suggestions or obtain a better idea on how to modify their query to get better results. Moreover, QG can assist the reading comprehension task and the question answering community by providing a robust input for their systems (Serban et al., 2016; Rajpurkar et al., 2016; Yang et al., 2017).

In this work, we propose a sequence to sequence model that uses attention and coverage mechanisms for addressing the question generation problem at the sentence level. The attention and coverage mechanisms prevent language generation systems from generating the same word over and over

again, and have been shown to improve a system's output (See et al., 2017).

We benefit from the community-based question answering systems. Specifically, we use the Amazon question/answer dataset (McAuley and Yang, 2016). The sentences are mostly informal and sometimes do not follow the correct grammatical structure. We utilize the answers that people post on the community question answering system as inputs to our model; hence, proposing an **opinion question generation** system which could be used as an interface to online forums helping users in browsing and querying them by making questions as suggestions.

In the subsequent section, we describe the related works to QG. The next section is on the task definition, followed by the demonstration of the model structure. After that, we discuss the experimental settings and at the end provide a thorough discussion of our results.

2 Related Work

After the first question generation shared task evaluation challenge (Rus et al., 2010), the question generation task has received a huge attention from the natural language generation community. Many of the traditional approaches involve human resources to create robust templates and then employing them to generate questions. For instance, Heilman and Smith (2010) approach is to overgenerate questions by some hand-written rules and then rank them using a logistic regression model. Labutov et al. (2015) benefit from a low-dimensional ontology for document segments. They crowdsource a set of promising question templates that are matched with that representation and rank the results based on their relevance to the source. Lindberg et al. (2013) employed a template-based approach while taking

152

Proceedings of The 11th International Natural Language Generation Conference, pages 152–158,
Tilburg, The Netherlands, November 5-8, 2018. ©2018 Association for Computational Linguistics

advantage of semantic information to generate natural language questions for on-line learning support. Chali and Hasan (2015) consider the automatic generation of all possible questions from a topic of interest by exploiting the named entity information and the predicate argument structures of the sentences.

Lately, more approaches have been presented that utilize the neural encoder-decoder architecture. Serban et al. (2016) address the problem by transducing knowledge graph facts into questions. They created a factoid question and answer corpus by using the Recurrent Neural Network architecture.

QG can also be combined with its complementary task, Question Answering (QA) for further improvement. Tang et al. (2017) consider QG and QA as dual tasks and train their relative models simultaneously. Their training framework takes advantage of the probabilistic correlation between the two tasks. QG has also entered other communities such as computer vision. Mostafazadeh et al. (2016) introduced the visual question generation task where the goal of the system is to create a question given an image.

One of the latest studies on the QG task has been conducted by Du et al. (2017). Their task is a QG on both sentences and paragraphs for the reading comprehension task, and they adopt an attention-based sequence learning model. Another recent work is by Yuan et al. (2017), they generate questions from documents using supervised and reinforcement learning.

In our work, we generate questions using community questions and answers and apply the encoder-decoder structure. To boost the performance of our system, we use attention and coverage mechanisms as suggested in See et al. (2017).

3 Task Formulation

Given an answer $A = (a_1, a_2, ..., a_N)$, we are going to generate a natural language question $Q = (q_1, q_2, ..., q_M)$, where its answer is embedded in A. Our goal is to find Q such that the conditional probability $p(Q|A)$ is maximized. We model $p(Q|A)$ as a product of word predictions:

$$p(Q|A) = \prod_1^M p(q_t|q_{1:t-1}, A)$$

This indicates that the probability of each q_t relies on the previously generated words and the input sentence A.

4 Model Structure

For modeling $p(Q|A)$, we use the simple RNN encoder-decoder architecture (Cho et al., 2014) with the global attentional model (Luong et al., 2015), which lets the decoder learn to focus on a particular range of the input sequence during the generation task. To improve upon this model, we apply coverage mechanism (See et al., 2017), which prevents the word repetition problem.

4.1 Encoder

An encoder network maps an input sequence into word vectors and then converts them into hidden states $b_1, ..., b_N$. In our case, the encoder is a two layer bidirectional LSTM network (Hochreiter and Schmidhuber, 1997). We concatenate the output of the forward hidden states $\overrightarrow{b_j}$ and the backward hidden states $\overleftarrow{b_j}$, namely, $b_j = [\overrightarrow{b_j}; \overleftarrow{b_j}]$ for input token j. This b_j is used later by the decoder to calculate the context vector c_t, which stores the relevant source-side information and simplifies the prediction of the next target word. c_t is computed as a weighted sum of b_i:

$$c_t = \sum_{i=1}^N a_t(i)b_i \tag{1}$$

where a_t is an alignment vector and is calculated according to the general attention model:

$$a_t(i) = \frac{exp(h_t^T W_a b_i)}{\sum_j exp(h_t^T W_a b_j))} \tag{2}$$

To initialize the decoder's hidden state, we concatenate the hidden states of the forward and the backward pass of the encoder.

4.2 Decoder

The decoder is a two layer unidirectional LSTM. It keeps a coverage vector s, which is the sum of the previous alignment vectors:

$$s_t = \sum_{t'=0}^{t-1} a_{t'}$$

It shows how much coverage each input word has received from the attention mechanism so far and it helps the mechanism to avoid attending to the same words again once they have been attended to initially (See et al., 2017). It should be mentioned that s_0 is a zero vector since nothing has been covered on the first time step. This coverage vector will be added to the source hidden states b_i:

$$b_i = \tanh(b_i + w_s s_t(i))$$

This b_i will be substituted in equations (1) and (2) where w_s is a parameter to be learned. This way, with the help of s_t, the attention mechanism always has a memory of its past decisions.

The decoder predicts the next word q_t given the context vector c_t and all the previously predicted words $\{q_1, ..., q_{t-1}\}$. We use a softmax layer to produce the predictive distribution:

$$p(q_t | q_{1:t-1}, A) = softmax(W_s \widetilde{h}_t)$$

$\widetilde{h}_t$ is the attentional hidden state which is calculated given the target hidden state h_t and the source context vector c_t:

$$\widetilde{h}_t = \tanh(W_c[c_t; h_t])$$

where W_s and W_c are learnable parameters. The hidden state at time step t of the decoder is generated by:

$$h_t = LSTM(q_{t-1}, h_{t-1})$$

where q_{t-1} is the previously generated word and h_{t-1} is the former hidden state.

Moreover, we use the input feeding approach (Luong et al., 2015), which informs the decoder which words were considered for the past alignments. We do this by concatenating the attentional hidden state $\widetilde{h}_t$ with the inputs at the next time steps.

4.3 Training and Generation

The training objective is to minimize the negative log-likelihood of the training corpus. Considering $S = \{(a_i, q_i)\}_1^{|S|}$ as our whole training data, we define the objective as:

$$J_t = \sum_{i=1}^{|S|} -\log p(q_i | a_i) \tag{3}$$

In addition to this primary loss function, it is required to introduce a coverage loss to penalize an overlap between the coverage vector and the attention distribution, which means attending to the same location multiple times.

$$covloss_t = \sum_i \min(a_t(i), s_t(i))$$

After being reweigted by some hyperparameter λ, this amount is added to equation (3):

$$J_t = \sum_{i=1}^{|S|} -\log p(q_i | a_i) + \lambda covloss_t$$

In the generation step, we utilize the beam search for the inference to maximize the conditional probability.

Since the size of our vocabulary is limited to a small number, many unknown words (*UNK*) will be generated during the inference. We substitute the (*UNK*) tokens with the words with the highest attention weight from the source sentence.

5 Experiments

5.1 Dataset

We use the Amazon question/answer dataset (McAuley and Yang, 2016). We set the minimum length of the questions to 4 tokens, including the question mark to filter out poorly structured sentences. The answers must be at least 10 tokens long. Moreover, we set the maximum length of the questions and the answers to 20 and 35 tokens, respectively. As there are many URLs in the dataset, we replace them with a *URL* token to reduce the vocabulary size. We lower-case the entire dataset and use the NLTK toolkit [1] for sentence tokenization. There can be many examples where the questions are not grammatically correct. People may just ask: "Waterproof ?". The same problem occurs with the answers: the answer might be a single "Yes". We use 80% of the dataset as the training set, and the rest is divided between the validation set and the test set. Table 1 shows the total number of examples in each dataset after removing very long or very short sentences from the training and the validation datasets.

	Train	Validation	Test
# pairs	233729	28969	70648

Table 1: Statistics of the dataset

---

[1] http://www.nltk.org

5.2 Experimental Setting

Our base model is from OpenNMT system (Klein et al., 2017), and we use the PyTorch [2] library, a deep learning framework that provides maximum flexibility and speed. It accelerates the computation on both CPU and GPU by a great amount, and the memory usage is extremely efficient in PyTorch compared to other options. We fix the size of the answer and the question vocabularies to 50k. Only the most frequent words are kept, and the rest are replaced with the *UNK* token. We set the word embedding dimension to 300 and we use *glove.840B.300d* (Pennington et al., 2014) as the pre-trained word embedding on both the encoder and the decoder sides. These embeddings are updated during training. The LSTM hidden unit size is set to 600 and we set the number of layers to 2. We employ the stochastic gradient descent (SGD) as the optimization method with an initial learning rate of 1.0 and halve the learning rate after 10 epochs. The training continues for 20 epochs with the batch size of 64 and dropout probability of 0.3. The hyperparameter λ that is used for weighting the coverage loss is set to 1 [3]. The decoding is done using the beam search with the beam size of 5, and the generation is stopped when we reach the *EOS* token. In the end, we choose the model with the lowest perplexity on the validation set.

5.3 Baseline

We compare our model [4] to that of Du et al. (2017). We only experiment with their sentence-level model and run the same Amazon question and answer dataset on the system provided by the first author. We keep the source and target vocabulary size the same as ours, (i.e., 50k) and set the maximum and the minimum length of the questions and answers the same as our model. Everything else is left to the default values.

5.4 Automatic Evaluation Metrics

For evaluating our system automatically, we use three different evaluation metrics. The first one is BLEU (Papineni et al., 2002) that uses the n-gram similarity between a prediction and a set of references. We calculate BLEU score for unigrams and bigrams. The next one is METEOR

---

[2] http://pytorch.org
[3] We also experimented with $\lambda = 2$ but did not find it to be helpful.
[4] https://github.com/Tina-19/Question-Generation

(Denkowski and Lavie, 2014), which scores predictions by aligning them to ground truth sentences with the help of stemming, synonyms and paraphrases. The last evaluation metric is Rouge (Lin, 2004). It compares the generated sentences with the references based on n-gram. For this task, we use ROUGE$_\text{L}$, which reports the results based on the longest common subsequence. We use the evaluation package by Chen et al. (2015).

6 Results and Discussion

Table 2 shows the results of our system and the baseline. Our model improves the BLEU 1 score by at least 1.5 points. It also achieves a better result regarding the BLEU 2 and the METEOR whereas the ROUGE is lower than the baseline. If we consider the results reported in Du et al. (2017), we notice that the BLEU scores are much higher compared to our work. The reason is that they use the SQuAD dataset (Rajpurkar et al., 2016), which is a human-generated corpus. The sentences are well-structured, grammatically correct with fewer unnecessary punctuation and colloquialism. However, when working with the community-based question answering systems, the structure of sentences do not always follow the correct path. These sentences often contain useless information and symbols.

	Baseline	Our Model
BLEU 1	12.89	**14.67**
BLEU 2	6.95	**7.74**
METEOR	8.76	**9.43**
ROUGE$_\text{L}$	**25.91**	25.21

Table 2: BLEU 1-2, METEOR and ROUGE$_\text{L}$ scores on the test set. Bold numbers demonstrate the best performing system for each evaluation metric.

Another problem is that multiple questions can be generated from a single sentence. The system may generate a question which is correct both semantically and grammatically and also asks about accurate information in the sentence. However, if it is not the same as the ground-truth, the results will be affected.

Figure 1 shows some examples generated by our system and Du et al. (2017), where the coverage mechanism becomes useful and prevents the model from generating the same word 'material' twice.

Answer 1: I really don't know, I did full size cupcakes, mini ones it would hold a ton!
GT Question: How many mini-cupcakes will this hold?
DSC: what size is it?
Ours: how many cupcakes will it hold?
Answer 2: Nothing out of the ordinary. just a simple screw driver. if I recall correctly, I think it may have came with the tools needed to assemble. good luck and congratulations
GT Question: What tools are required to assemble unit?
DSC: What is the assembly required?
Ours: what tools do I need to assemble this?
Answer 3: You can definitely still do pushups with the wraps on. The wraps just give extra support, they really don't impact your range of motion at all.
GT Question: Can I do pushups while wearing these wraps, or is the material too stiff?
DSC: Can you still use the material while wearing the material?
Ours: Can I do pushups while wearing these wraps?
Answer 4: I would go with a medium it fits well and when you adjust it with the helmet it's tight to the chin.
GT Question: What size to buy for 14 yr old 125lb and 5'5?
DSC: I'm a woman with a small head, what size should I get?
Ours: What size should I get for a child who is 5'6"?
Answer 5: There's the ability to forward the bp measurement information via email to friends, family and doctors so I assume that once it's been sent an email you can print - it however I haven't tested this functionality yet. At the very least when you bring up the bp readings on your screen you can do a screen capture and then print that screen capture.
GT Question: Is it possible to print the BP readings?
DSC: What is the difference between the BP and the BP?
Ours: How do you print from the BP?

Figure 1: Examples of generated questions: ground truth (GT), Du et al. (2017) (DSC) and our model, with their answers.

7 Human Evaluations

To further assess the performance of our system, we performed human evaluations on the results. Three English-speaker students were asked to give a score from 1 (very poor) to 5 (very good) to the questions generated from both systems according to two criteria: **syntactic correctness** and **relevance**. Syntactic correctness indicates the grammaticality and the fluency and relevance demonstrates whether the question is meaningful and related to the sentence it is generated from. The three assessors performed the evaluations on 100 randomly selected question and answer pairs from the results. The comparison of human evaluations between our system and the Du et al. (2017) model is shown in Table 3. Bold numbers demonstrate the best performing system for each evaluation criteria, and we see that our system outperforms the Du et al. (2017) model on both criteria.

	Baseline	Our Model
Syntactic correctness	4.4	**4.52**
Relevance	2.93	**3.37**

Table 3: Human evaluation results for the syntactic correctness and relevance between our model and Du et al. (2017).

8 Conclusion

In this work, we presented a sequence to sequence learning model to address the opinion question generation task. We showed the training process using the global attention and applied the coverage mechanism to improve the model. We took advantage of community-based question answering systems which contain informal speech and its sentences do not always follow grammatical rules. Experimental results show an improvement in the automatic evaluation metrics as well as the human evaluations compared to the baseline system.

Acknowledgements

We would like to thank the anonymous reviewers for their useful comments. The research reported in this paper was conducted at the University of Lethbridge and supported by the Natural Sciences and Engineering Research Council (NSERC) of Canada discovery grant and the University of Lethbridge.

References

Yllias Chali and Sadid A. Hasan. 2015. Towards topic-to-question generation. *Computational Linguistics*, 41(1):1–20.

Xinlei Chen, Hao Fang, Tsung-Yi Lin, Ramakrishna Vedantam, Saurabh Gupta, Piotr Dollár, and C. Lawrence Zitnick. 2015. Microsoft COCO captions: Data collection and evaluation server. *arXiv preprint*, arXiv:1504.00325.

Kyunghyun Cho, Bart van Merrienboer, Caglar Gulcehre, Dzmitry nau, Fethi Bougares, Holger Schwenk, and Yoshua Bengio. 2014. Learning phrase representations using rnn encoder–decoder for statistical machine translation. In *Proceedings of the 2014 Conference on Empirical Methods in Natural Language Processing*, pages 1724–1734. Association for Computational Linguistics.

Michael Denkowski and Alon Lavie. 2014. Meteor universal: Language specific translation evaluation for any target language. In *Proceedings of the Ninth Workshop on Statistical Machine Translation*, pages 376–380, Baltimore, Maryland. Association for Computational Linguistics.

Xinya Du, Junru Shao, and Claire Cardie. 2017. Learning to ask: Neural question generation for reading comprehension. In *Proceedings of the 55th Annual Meeting of the Association for Computational Linguistics (Volume 1: Long Papers)*, pages 1342–1352, Vancouver, Canada. Association for Computational Linguistics.

Arthur C. Graesser and Natalie K. Person. 1994. Question asking during tutoring. *American Educational Research Journal*, 31(1):104–137.

Michael Heilman and Noah A. Smith. 2010. Good question! statistical ranking for question generation. In *Human Language Technologies: The 2010 Annual Conference of the North American Chapter of the Association for Computational Linguistics*, pages 609–617.

Sepp Hochreiter and Jürgen Schmidhuber. 1997. Long short-term memory. *Neural Computation*, 9:1735–1780.

G. Klein, Y. Kim, Y. Deng, J. Senellart, and A. M. Rush. 2017. OpenNMT: Open-Source Toolkit for Neural Machine Translation. *ArXiv e-prints*.

Igor Labutov, Sumit Basu, and Lucy Vanderwende. 2015. Deep questions without deep understanding. In *Proceedings of the 53rd Annual Meeting of the Association for Computational Linguistics and the 7th International Joint Conference on Natural Language Processing*, pages 889–898, Beijing, China. Association for Computational Linguistics.

Chin-Yew Lin. 2004. Rouge: a package for automatic evaluation of summaries. In *Text Summarization Branches Out: Proceedings of the ACL-04 Workshop*, pages 74–81, Barcelona, Spain. Association for Computational Linguistics.

David Lindberg, Fred Popowich, John C. Nesbit, and Philip H. Winne. 2013. Generating natural language questions to support learning on-line. In *Proceedings of the 14th European Workshop on Natural Language Generation*, pages 105–114, Sofia, Bulgaria. Association for Computational Linguistics.

Thang Luong, Hieu Pham, and Christopher D. Manning. 2015. Effective approaches to attention-based neural machine translation. In *Proceedings of the 2015 Conference on Empirical Methods in Natural Language Processing*, pages 1412–1421. Association for Computational Linguistics.

Julian McAuley and Alex Yang. 2016. Addressing complex and subjective product-related queries with customer reviews. In *Proceedings of the 25th International Conference on World Wide Web*, pages 625–635.

Nasrin Mostafazadeh, Ishan Misra, Jacob Devlin, Margaret Mitchell, Xiaodong He, and Lucy Vanderwende. 2016. Generating natural questions about an image. In *Proceedings of the 54th Annual Meeting of the Association for Computational Linguistics (Volume 1: Long Papers)*, pages 1802–1813. Association for Computational Linguistics.

Kishore Papineni, Salim Roukos, Todd Ward, and Wei-Jing Zhu. 2002. Bleu: a method for automatic evaluation of machine translation. In *Proceedings of the 40th Annual Meeting of the Association for Computational Linguistics*.

Jeffrey Pennington, Richard Socher, and Christopher Manning. 2014. Glove: Global vectors for word representation. In *Proceedings of the 2014 Conference on Empirical Methods in Natural Language Processing (EMNLP)*, pages 1532–1543. Association for Computational Linguistics.

Pranav Rajpurkar, Jian Zhang, Konstantin Lopyrev, and Percy Liang. 2016. Squad: 100,000+ questions for machine comprehension of text. In *Proceedings of the 2016 Conference on Empirical Methods in Natural Language Processing*, pages 2383–2392. Association for Computational Linguistics.

Vasile Rus, Brendan Wyse, Paul Piwek, Mihai Lintean, Svetlana Stoyanchev, and Cristian Moldovan. 2010. The first question generation shared task evaluation challenge. In *Proceedings of the 6th International Natural Language Generation Conference*, pages 251–257. Association for Computational Linguistics.

Abigail See, Peter J. Liu, and Christopher D. Manning. 2017. Get to the point: Summarization with pointer-generator networks. In *Proceedings of the 55th Annual Meeting of the Association for Computational Linguistics (Volume 1: Long Papers)*, pages 1073–1083. Association for Computational Linguistics.

Iulian V. Serban, Alberto García-Durán, Çalar Gülçehre, Sungjin Ahn, Sarath Chandar, Aaron Courville, and Yoshua Bengio. 2016. Generating factoid questions with recurrent neural networks: The 30m factoid question-answer corpus. In *Proceedings of the 54th Annual Meeting of the Association for Computational Linguistics*, pages 588–598, Berlin, Germany.

Duyu Tang, Nan Duan, Tao Qin, and Ming Zhou. 2017. Question answering and question generation as dual tasks. *arXiv preprint*, arXiv:1706.02027.

Zhilin Yang, Junjie Hu, Ruslan Salakhutdinov, and William Cohen. 2017. Semi-supervised qa with generative domain-adaptive nets. In *Proceedings of the 55th Annual Meeting of the Association for Computational Linguistics (Volume 1: Long Papers)*, pages 1040–1050, Vancouver, Canada. Association for Computational Linguistics.

Xingdi Yuan, Tong Wang, Caglar Gulcehre, Alessandro Sordoni, Philip Bachman, Saizheng Zhang, Sandeep Subramanian, and Adam Trischler. 2017. Machine comprehension by text-to-text neural question generation. In *Proceedings of the 2nd Workshop on Representation Learning for NLP*, pages 15–25, Vancouver, Canada. Association for Computational Linguistics.

Modelling Pro-drop with the Rational Speech Acts Model

Guanyi Chen[1], Kees van Deemter[12], Chenghua Lin[2]
[1]Department of Information and Computing Sciences, Utrecht University
[2]Department of Computing Science, University of Aberdeen
`{g.chen, c.j.vandeemter}@uu.nl, chenghua.lin@abdn.ac.uk`

Abstract

We extend the classic Referring Expressions Generation task by considering zero pronouns in "pro-drop" languages such as Chinese, modelling their use by means of the Bayesian Rational Speech Acts model (Frank and Goodman, 2012). By assuming that highly salient referents are most likely to be referred to by zero pronouns (i.e., pro-drop is more likely for salient referents than the less salient ones), the model offers an attractive explanation of a phenomenon not previously addressed probabilistically.

1 Introduction

Languages such as Chinese and Japanese make liberal use of zero pronouns (ZP) (Huang, 1984). The analysis of Wang et al. (2018) on a large Chinese-English parallel dialogue corpus shows that 26% of the English pronouns are dropped in Chinese. Such an abundant use of zero pronouns has been a key factor in linguist's idea (Huang, 1984, 1989) that Chinese is a *"cool"* language or a *discourse-oriented* language (Cao, 1979), i.e., one that relies heavily on context.

To exemplify zero pronouns in Chinese, consider the question "你今天看见比尔了吗?" (*Did you see Bill today?*). A Chinese speaker can respond in a variety of shorter expressions which are equivalent to "我看见他了" (*Yes, I saw him*), for example, "∅看见他了" (*Yes, ∅ saw him*), "我看见∅了" (*Yes, I saw ∅*), or even "∅看见∅了" (*Yes, ∅ saw ∅*). Here the ∅ symbol indicates the place from where a pronoun appears to have been "dropped" from a full sentence.

Generating zero pronouns (only) where they are appropriate is a difficult challenge for Referring Expression Generation (REG) (Van Deemter,

2016), and more specifically for the task of choosing *referential form*, a key step in the classic Natural Language Generation (NLG) architecture (Reiter and Dale, 2000). Traditionally, choosing referential form is framed as modelling speakers' behaviour of deciding whether entities are referred to using a pronoun, a proper name, or a description. However, for "cool" languages, an extra option, namely of choosing a zero pronoun, needs to be added (Yeh and Mellish, 1997) for fully simulating speakers' behaviour.

In this paper, we model the use of zero pronouns in Chinese with the Rational Speech Acts (RSA) model (Frank and Goodman, 2012) by assuming that speakers tend to choose a ZP if it is salient enough for successful communication (see §2). For computing discourse salience, we focus on ZPs that are *recoverable*, meaning that they either refer anaphorically to an entity mentioned earlier in the text (i.e., anaphoric ZPs, or AZPs for short), or to the speaker or hearer (i.e., deictic non-anaphoric ZPs or DNZPs for short) (Zhao and Ng, 2007); a ZP is *unrecoverable* if it cannot be linked to any referent, for example:

(1) ∅ 有　二十三　　项　　　高新技术
　　　∅ has　23　　CLASSFIER　high-tech
　　　项目　　进区　　　开发
　　　projects　in.the.zone　under.development

'there are 23 high-tech projects under development in the zone'

in which the ∅ cannot be recovered.

2 Related Work

Pro-drop raises challenges for a number of NLP tasks including, machine translation (MT), coreference resolution, and REG. When translating from a pro-drop language, recovering the dropped pronouns of the source language can improve the overall performance of MT (Wang et al., 2016,

159

Proceedings of The 11th International Natural Language Generation Conference, pages 159–164,
Tilburg, The Netherlands, November 5-8, 2018. ©2018 Association for Computational Linguistics

2018). Co-reference resolution of ZPs has been widely explored with a variety of techniques including the centring theory (Rao et al., 2015), statistical machine learning (Zhao and Ng, 2007; Chen and Ng, 2014, 2015), deep learning (Chen and Ng, 2016; Yin et al., 2016, 2017) and reinforcement learning (Yin et al., 2018). REG of ZPs for "cool" languages has been addressed through rule-based methods (Yeh and Mellish, 1997) including centring theory (Yamura-Takei et al., 2001) (for Japanese), but we are not aware of any testable computational account.[1] We offer such an account, along probabilistic lines.

Some discourse theories suggest that speakers choose referring expressions (REs) by considering discourse salience (Givón, 1983), i.e., speakers tend to choose pronouns if they believe the referent is highly salient. The intuition behind is that a highly salient referent tends to be highly prominent in the mind of the speaker and/or hearer. Orita et al. (2015) shared a similar view and argued that highly salient REs are highly *predictable*, so they are referred with pronouns (as opposed to full NPs) more often than the less salient ones.

A theory that is sometimes used for explaining the relation between discourse salience and human choice of referential forms is Uniform Information Density (UID) (Jaeger and Levy, 2007). UID asserts that speaker tends to optimise information density (quantity of information) of the utterances to achieve optimal communication. In other words, speakers tend to drop a RE when the referent of the RE is predictable (or recoverable), and vise versa.

Apart from salience, production cost (Rohde et al., 2012) and the listener models (Bard et al., 2004), meaning the models that how speakers model listeners' interpretation of the utterance, also have impact on language production. It suggests to us that the salience of the referent may not be enough for modelling speakers' choice. The RSA model (see §3) used in this paper is possible to take all these factors into consideration.

3 Methodology

3.1 The Rational Speech Acts Model

The Rational Speech Acts (RSA) model (Frank and Goodman, 2012) has been used for a variety

of tasks including modelling speakers' referential choice between pronouns and proper names (Orita et al., 2015), the selection of attributes for referring expressions (Monroe and Potts, 2015), and the generation of colour references (Monroe et al., 2017, 2018). The key idea of RSA is to model human communication by assuming that a rational listener P_L uses Bayesian inference to recover a speaker's intended referent r_s for word w under context C. In this way, RSA claims to offer not only accurate models, but highly explanatory ones as well. Formally, P_L is defined as

$$P_L(r_s|w, C) = \frac{P_S(w|r_s, C)P(r_s)}{\sum_{r' \in C} P_S(w|r', C)P(r')}, \quad (1)$$

where r' denotes a referent in context C, $P(r_s)$ represents the discourse salience of r_s, P_S is the speaker model defined by an exponential utility function:

$$P_S(w|r_s, C) = e^{\alpha(I(w;r_s,C) - C(w))}. \quad (2)$$

Here $I(w; r_s, C)$ is the informativeness of word w, $C(w)$ represents the speech cost.

Orita et al. (2015) extended the RSA by assuming that speakers estimate listener's interpretation of the (form of) RE w based on discourse information. The speaker chooses w by maximising the listener's belief in the speaker's intended referent r_s in relation to the speaker's speech cost $C(w)$, where the cost is estimated according to the complexity of the utterance, such as the length of w:

$$\begin{aligned} P_S(w|r_s) &\propto P_L(r_s|w) \cdot \frac{1}{C(w)} \\ &= \frac{P(w|r_s, C)P(r_s)}{\sum_{r'} P(w|r', C)P(r')} \cdot \frac{1}{C(w)} \end{aligned} \quad (3)$$

Here $P_L(r_s|w)$ estimates the informativeness of w, and $P(w|r_s, C)$ estimates the likelihood (according to the speaker) that the listener guesses that the speaker used w to refer to r_s.

3.2 Modelling Pro-drop with the RSA Model

We model the decision of whether to use a ZP-based on the formulation expressed in Eq. 3. The speaker model is $P_S(z|r_s)$, which is the probability that the speaker uses ZP (i.e., drops the RE). We assume that the speaker makes a binary choice (i.e., $z = \{1, 0\}$), with $z = 1$ indicating a ZP and $z = 0$ indicating a non-zero form of RE (NZRE). Note that whether the speaker uses a pronoun or

---

a proper name is not in the scope of this model. To simulate the speaker's choice, we need to estimate the dropping probability $P(z|r_s)$, the discourse salience of the referent $P(r_s)$, and the cost $C(z)$.

According to the UID theory (see §2), if a RE is recoverable, then the speaker prefers a ZP over a NZRE to maximise the information density since a ZP is shorter than any other referential form. In that sense, we follow Orita et al. (2015) to estimate the **cost function** $C(z)$ based on the length of the RE, i.e., the total number of words the RE contains. However, the length of the NZRE is not known in advance, thus we use the average length of a set of REs W instead:

$$C(z = 0) = \text{average\_length}(W) + 1 \quad (4)$$

We experimented with two ways of calculating the average length: (i) *global average length*, meaning that W is the set of all referring expressions in the corpus, and (ii) *local average length*, in which W is the set of expressions that can refer to referent r_s. For instance, if r_s is "*Barack Obama*", then given a corpus for computing local average length in which *he* is referred to, W might be the set {*Barack Obama, Obama, he, former president*}. The cost of a zero pronoun is always $C(z = 1) = 1$, which means no discount on $P(z = 1|w)$ and the plus 1 in Eq. 4 is to make the cost of choosing NZRE different from choosing ZP if W only contains pronouns (i.e., if length equals to 1).

We assume that the **dropping probability** $P(z|r_s)$ is dependent on whether the referent r_s is one of the participants in the dialogue (i.e., speaker or listener). For example, in the OntoNote 5.0 corpus, 30% of maximally salient entities are dropped, which is much higher than the 10% dropping rate of non-maximally salient entities. If r_s is one of the participants, we call it *maximally salient entity* (denoted as s). Otherwise, r_s is called *non-maximally salient entity* (denoted as ns). This assumption causes AZP and DNZP to have different proportions in the predicted results. Suppose $P(z = 1|r_s = \text{ns}) = a$ and $P(z = 1|r_s = \text{s}) = b$, then we have $a < b$, which implies that the speaker thinks the listener expects a maximally salient entity (i.e., speaker or listener).

Let $\alpha = \frac{a}{b}$ be the *dropping ratio*, then the probability of dropping a noun phrase that refers to the

speaker is:

$$P_S(\text{ZP}|\text{Speaker}) \propto P_L(\text{Speaker}|\text{ZP}) \cdot \frac{1}{C(z = 1)}$$
$$= \frac{P(\text{ZP}|\text{Speaker})P(\text{Speaker})}{\sum_{r'} P(\text{ZP}|r')P(r')} \cdot \frac{1}{C(z = 1)}$$
$$= \frac{N_{\text{Speaker}}}{\alpha \cdot N_{\text{NS}} + N_{\text{S}}} \cdot \frac{1}{C(z = 1)} \quad (5)$$

$P(\text{Speaker})$ is the **salience** of the speaker.[2] In general, we take the salience of a referent x to be in proportion to N_x, which is the number of times that x has been referred to in the preceding discourse, hence the use of N_{Speaker}, N_{S}, and N_{NS} in the equation. Note that $N_{\text{S}} + N_{\text{NS}}$ is the total number of REs in the preceding discourse.

Equation 5 shows that modelling the dropping probability for maximally salient entities and non-maximally salient entities differently acts as a discount for the number of referents that the ZP can refer to when predicting DNZP. Similarly, using the dropping ratio α, the dropping probability for AZPs is estimated as:

$$P_S(\text{AZP}|\text{Speaker}) = \frac{N_{\text{AZP}}}{N_{\text{NS}} + \frac{1}{\alpha}N_{\text{S}}} \quad (6)$$

which can be seen as adding a penalty.

The frequencies counted above are all based on the whole preceding discourse of a referent, which might not be reasonable for predicting ZPs. We hypothesise that the informativeness of a ZP depends on only a part of the preceding context. We tested two possible set-ups. One is setting a discourse window to limit the number of sentences that the simulator can look back to. The other uses recency (Chafe, 1994). Following Orita et al. (2015), we replace each count with: $Count(r_i, r_j) = e^{-d(r_i, r_j)/a}$, where r_j is the same referent as the r_i that has previously been referred to and d is the number of sentences between two REs. Instead of taking the direct raw count 1, $Count(r_i, r_j)$ decays exponentially with respect to how far it is from the predicting RE. The RE that has larger distance contributes less to the overall count of that referent.

For NZREs ($z = 0$), we assume that the number of times that the referent has been referred to is equal to the total number of referents referred to by that NZRE. Thus, the speaker believes that the listener can always resolve the reference by giving

---

[2]Our use of the term salience is similar to Hovy et al. (2006)'s use of "recoverability".

them a NZRE. In other words, their informativeness equals 1.

4 Experiments

4.1 The Dataset

We tested our model on the Chinese portion of OntoNotes Release 5.0 data[3] (Hovy et al., 2006), which has been widely used in (ZP) co-reference resolution tasks. The corpus contains 1,729 documents, including 143620 referring expressions. In Table 1, there is the basic statistics about the recoverable zero pronouns in OntoNotes corpus.

# of Recoverable Zero Pronouns	17,129
# of Anaphoric ZPs	14,675
# of Deictic Non-anaphoric ZPs	2,454

Table 1: Basic statistics of different types of recoverable ZPs in OntoNotes

Baseline. In this work, we used the modified rule 1 in Yeh and Mellish (1997), i.e., the RE in the subject position will be a ZP if it was referred to in the immediately preceding sentence, as the baseline. The modification is inspired by the fact that 99.2% ZPs in OntoNotes corpus are in the subject position.

4.2 Experiment Results

Table 2 shows the results (reported in accuracy) of various models on the OntoNote dataset. The dropping ratio α was empirically set to 0.1 and the decay parameter a of recency was set to 0.8. The window size was 1, so the simulator only looks at the current sentence and preceding sentence.

As expected, the models that look back to the whole preceding discourse perform badly on predicting ZPs (i.e., 8.35% of accuracy), especially DNZPs. They tend to predict all REs as NZREs, which even performs worse than the model using simple rule (i.e., the baseline). In contrast, limiting the discourse history by applying discourse windows or replacing frequency with recency have a negative impact on predicting NZREs, more specifically pronouns. Such an impact is caused by the idea that every NZRE can always be resolved by the listener, which is not correct for pronouns. However, so far, we cannot calculate the informativeness of pronouns properly since we do

[3]https://catalog.ldc.upenn.edu/ldc2013t19

not know which referent (speaker or listener) a deictic pronoun in the corpus refers to. For example, in the corpus, both the speaker and listener will use "I" to refer to themselves, so we don't know whether "I" refers to the speaker or the listener. This setting will lead to over-estimation of the informativeness of pronouns. On the other hand, computing cost by average length (as we do) overestimates the costs of pronouns, whose lengths are generally shorter than proper names.

The baseline model's performance is not bad, especially for predicting AZPs. This is partly because the rule predicts that all REs in object position are NZREs and this is nearly always correct. (Recall that 99.84% REs in object position are NZREs). At the same time, if the referent was referred to in the immediately preceding sentence (as the baseline model requires), then it is clearly more salient than if it wasn't. The baseline model is therefore quite similar to the model with discourse window, but its decisions are made in a simpler way (i.e., based on a simple "if-then" rule).

With respect to overall accuracy for predicting ZPs and NZREs, models with recency perform similarly to those that use a discourse window. However, recency offers better prediction on AZPs. Adding a dropping ratio could significantly improve the performance on predicting DNZPs without decreasing the accuracies of AZPs and NZREs very much (i.e., accuracy increase from 62.02% to 95.35%). For the choice of cost function, we found that using global average length is the best.

5 Conclusion and Future Work

This paper has explored the possibilities of using the RSA model for probabilistic simulation of speakers' use of ZPs (i.e., pro-drop), and investigated factors that influence speakers' choice.

Our model performs respectably yet, as mentioned in Section 4, it under-estimates the probability of choosing a pronoun. Solving this problem will require a more fine-grained annotation of the corpus, indicating which person each occurrence of the deictic pronouns "I" and "you" refers to. Once this has been done, we also hope to let the generator distinguish between ZP, pronoun, proper name, and full noun phrase.

When speakers are choosing between pronouns and full NPs, sentence position is known to be rel-

Discourse	Model	Cost	Total Acc.	ZP Acc.	AZP Acc.	DNZP Acc.	NZRE Acc.
-	baseline	-	78.57	40.88	42.90	28.81	83.67
Discourse Window	full	global	77.10	46.16	38.34	92.95	81.29
	full	local	81.79	22.53	25.50	4.81	89.81
	-dropping ratio	global	77.05	43.77	41.88	55.09	81.56
	-dropping ratio	local	81.44	23.67	27.09	3.19	89.26
Recency	full	global	75.64	**50.56**	43.08	**95.35**	79.03
	full	local	80.08	25.36	28.81	4.77	87.49
	-dropping ratio	global	74.04	50.26	**48.29**	62.02	78.04
	-dropping ratio	local	79.26	27.47	31.63	2.6	86.28
Whole	full	global	86.24	8.35	5.18	27.30	96.79
	full	local	**86.67**	3.67	4.27	0.08	**97.91**
	-dropping ratio	global	86.13	6.23	6.38	5.33	96.95
	-dropping ratio	local	86.61	3.84	4.47	0.04	97.81

Table 2: Accuracies of each model, recall that AZP and DNZP are two sub-categories of ZP.

evant. For example, pronouns are less common in object than in subject position Brennan (1995), which somehow dues to the fact that REs in subject position are more salient than in object position. In the OntoNotes corpus, 99.2% of ZPs appear in subject position; in Chinese, empty categories are acceptable in both subject and object (including the topic position (Huang, 1984)), but even there they are most frequent in subject position. The baseline model introduced in this paper has somehow proved that considering positions works in modelling pro-drop. In future we shall explore the way of combining that factor with the RSA for pro-drop model introduced in this paper.

In future, we will investigate alternative ways to estimate informativeness and costs. For example, it would be natural to use a co-reference resolver for calculating informativeness. Furthermore, one could follow on from (Yamura-Takei et al., 2001; Roh and Lee, 2003) by using elements of centring theory (Grosz et al., 1995) in the definition of cost (e.g., giving Rough Shifts a high cost). Alternatively, one could improve the model by adopting a trainable function for estimating both informativeness and costs.

Acknowledgements

We thank Ehud Reiter, people in the Aberdeen CLAN group and anonymous reviewers for their comments for earlier version of this paper. We also thank Qingyu Yin for his help on pre-processing the datasets.

References

Ellen Gurman Bard, Matthew P Aylett, J Trueswell, and M Tanenhaus. 2004. Referential form, word duration, and modeling the listener in spoken dialogue. *Approaches to studying world-situated language use: Bridging the language-as-product and language-as-action traditions*, pages 173–191.

Susan E Brennan. 1995. Centering attention in discourse. *Language and Cognitive processes*, 10(2):137–167.

Fengfu Cao. 1979. *A functional study of topic in Chinese: The first step towards discourse analysis*, volume 3. Student Book Co.

Wallace Chafe. 1994. Discourse, consciousness, and time. *Discourse*, 2(1).

Chen Chen and Vincent Ng. 2014. Chinese zero pronoun resolution: An unsupervised approach combining ranking and integer linear programming. In *AAAI*, pages 1622–1628.

Chen Chen and Vincent Ng. 2015. Chinese zero pronoun resolution: A joint unsupervised discourse-aware model rivaling state-of-the-art resolvers. In *Proceedings of the 53rd Annual Meeting of the Association for Computational Linguistics and the 7th International Joint Conference on Natural Language Processing (Volume 2: Short Papers)*, volume 2, pages 320–326.

Chen Chen and Vincent Ng. 2016. Chinese zero pronoun resolution with deep neural networks. In *Proceedings of the 54th Annual Meeting of the Association for Computational Linguistics (Volume 1: Long Papers)*, volume 1, pages 778–788.

Michael C Frank and Noah D Goodman. 2012. Predicting pragmatic reasoning in language games. *Science*, 336(6084):998–998.

Talmy Givón. 1983. *Topic continuity in discourse*. John Benjamins Publishing Company.

Barbara J Grosz, Scott Weinstein, and Aravind K Joshi. 1995. Centering: A framework for modeling the local coherence of discourse. *Computational linguistics*, 21(2):203–225.

Eduard Hovy, Mitchell Marcus, Martha Palmer, Lance Ramshaw, and Ralph Weischedel. 2006. Ontonotes: the 90% solution. In *Proceedings of the human language technology conference of the NAACL, Companion Volume: Short Papers*, pages 57–60. Association for Computational Linguistics.

C-T James Huang. 1984. On the distribution and reference of empty pronouns. *Linguistic inquiry*, pages 531–574.

C-T James Huang. 1989. Pro-drop in chinese: A generalized control theory. In *The null subject parameter*, pages 185–214. Springer.

T Florian Jaeger and Roger P Levy. 2007. Speakers optimize information density through syntactic reduction. In *Advances in neural information processing systems*, pages 849–856.

Will Monroe, Robert XD Hawkins, Noah D Goodman, and Christopher Potts. 2017. Colors in context: A pragmatic neural model for grounded language understanding. *arXiv preprint arXiv:1703.10186*.

Will Monroe, Jennifer Hu, Andrew Jong, and Christopher Potts. 2018. Generating bilingual pragmatic color references. *arXiv preprint arXiv:1803.03917*.

Will Monroe and Christopher Potts. 2015. Learning in the rational speech acts model. *arXiv preprint arXiv:1510.06807*.

Naho Orita, Eliana Vornov, Naomi Feldman, and Hal Daumé III. 2015. Why discourse affects speakers' choice of referring expressions. In *Proceedings of the 53rd Annual Meeting of the Association for Computational Linguistics and the 7th International Joint Conference on Natural Language Processing (Volume 1: Long Papers)*, volume 1, pages 1639–1649.

Sudha Rao, Allyson Ettinger, Hal Daumé III, and Philip Resnik. 2015. Dialogue focus tracking for zero pronoun resolution. In *Proceedings of the 2015 Conference of the North American Chapter of the Association for Computational Linguistics: Human Language Technologies*, pages 494–503.

Ehud Reiter and Robert Dale. 2000. *Building natural language generation systems*. Cambridge university press.

Ji-Eun Roh and Jong-Hyeok Lee. 2003. An empirical study for generating zero pronoun in korean based on cost-based centering model. In *Proceedings of the Australasian Language Technology Workshop 2003*, pages 30–37.

Hannah Rohde, Scott Seyfarth, Brady Clark, Gerhard Jäger, and Stefan Kaufmann. 2012. Communicating with cost-based implicature: A game-theoretic approach to ambiguity. In *Proceedings of the 16th Workshop on the Semantics and Pragmatics of Dialogue*, pages 107–116.

Kees Van Deemter. 2016. *Computational models of referring: a study in cognitive science*. MIT Press.

Longyue Wang, Zhaopeng Tu, Shuming Shi, Tong Zhang, Yvette Graham, and Qun Liu. 2018. Translating pro-drop languages with reconstruction models. *arXiv preprint arXiv:1801.03257*.

Longyue Wang, Zhaopeng Tu, Xiaojun Zhang, Hang Li, Andy Way, and Qun Liu. 2016. A novel approach to dropped pronoun translation. *arXiv preprint arXiv:1604.06285*.

Mitsuko Yamura-Takei, Miho Fujiwara, and Teruaki Aizawa. 2001. Centering as an anaphora generation algorithm: A language learning aid perspective. In *NLPRS*, volume 2001, pages 557–562.

Ching-Long Yeh and Chris Mellish. 1997. An empirical study on the generation of anaphora in chinese. *Computational Linguistics*, 23(1):171–190.

Qingyu Yin, Weinan Zhang, Yu Zhang, and Ting Liu. 2016. A deep neural network for chinese zero pronoun resolution. *arXiv preprint arXiv:1604.05800*.

Qingyu Yin, Yu Zhang, Weinan Zhang, and Ting Liu. 2017. Chinese zero pronoun resolution with deep memory network. In *Proceedings of the 2017 Conference on Empirical Methods in Natural Language Processing*, pages 1309–1318.

Qingyu Yin, Yu Zhang, Weinan Zhang, Ting Liu, and William Yang Wang. 2018. Deep reinforcement learning for chinese zero pronoun resolution. *arXiv preprint arXiv:1806.03711*.

Shanheng Zhao and Hwee Tou Ng. 2007. Identification and resolution of chinese zero pronouns: A machine learning approach. In *Proceedings of the 2007 Joint Conference on Empirical Methods in Natural Language Processing and Computational Natural Language Learning (EMNLP-CoNLL)*.

Self-Learning Architecture for Natural Language Generation

Hyungtak Choi, Siddarth K. M., Haehun Yang, Heesik Jeon, Inchul Hwang, Jihie Kim
Samsung Research, Samsung Electronics Co. Ltd., Seoul, Korea
`{ht777.choi, siddarth.km, haehun.yang, heesik.jeon,`
`inc.hwang, jihie.kim}@samsung.com`

Abstract

In this paper, we propose a self-learning architecture for generating natural language templates for conversational assistants. Generating templates to cover all the combinations of slots in an intent is time consuming and labor-intensive. We examine three different models based on our proposed architecture - Rule-based model, Sequence-to-Sequence (Seq2Seq) model and Semantically Conditioned LSTM (SC-LSTM) model for the IoT domain - to reduce the human labor required for template generation. We demonstrate the feasibility of template generation for the IoT domain using our self-learning architecture. In both automatic and human evaluation, the self-learning architecture outperforms previous works trained with a fully human-labeled dataset. This is promising for commercial conversational assistant solutions.

1 Introduction

Intelligent Conversational Assistants are prevalent now. They have been integrated into a wide range of IoT devices. Various recent studies on stochastic language generation have been conducted in NLG. Although these stochastic approaches outperform traditional LSTM language models, they have drawbacks including the requirement of large training datasets, low accuracy of trained models and lack of naturalness of generated sentences. Therefore, Most of commercial conversational assistant services adopt template-based approach (Cheyer and Guzzoni, 2014; Mirkovic and Cavedon, 2011) to implement natural language generation. This approach is robust and feasible for commercialization, but requires creating a large number of templates. In this approach, one needs to manually generate NLG templates that cover all the possible combinations of intents and slots.[1] There are statistical approaches for generating templates with 2, 3 and 4 slots (Narayan et al., 2011), but they suffer from exponential complexity as the number of slots increases. In addition, substitution-based implementation with SimpleNLG (Gatt and Reiter, 2009) can handle some of the cases, but this is not versatile enough. The number of templates required to cover all possible combinations of slots is:

$$\text{No. Templates}_n = 2^n - 1 \qquad (1)$$

where n is the total number of possible slots. The value is exponential as shown in equation 1. Manually generating an exponential number of templates is undesirable, especially when the intents get more complex.

We propose a self-learning architecture for NLG which solves the problem of generating an exponential number of templates. In order to generate informative and natural sentences, arguably, it is more important to generate consistent system responses with limited syntactic information than to generate error prone system responses with more variation in their grammatical form. In our proposed solution, we start with an initial training set containing less than or equal to 2 slots per intent, and iteratively build our model to increase its ability to cover more complex inputs. Thus, the re-

---

[1]Throughout this paper, **intent** denotes the intention of user utterance and **slot** denotes the variable part (slot value) and its name if any (slot name). Slot can be replaced by another phrase in user utterances or responses. NLG will be generated from **dialog act** and it will be written as $Intent($ $SlotName1 = SlotValue1; SlotName2 = SlotValue2$ $; \cdots)$. For example, from dialog act up(functionname=temperature;devicename='airconditioner';location='bedroom'), response "I turned up the temperature of the airconditioner in the bedroom" is generated.

165

Proceedings of The 11th International Natural Language Generation Conference, pages 165–170,
Tilburg, The Netherlands, November 5-8, 2018. ©2018 Association for Computational Linguistics

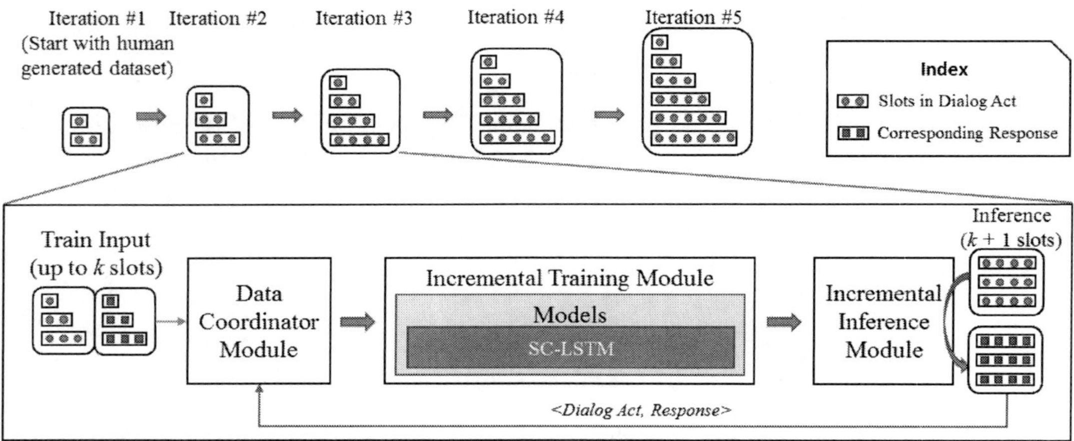

Figure 1: Proposed Self-Learning Architecture for NLG.

quired number of human generated templates decreases from $2^n - 1$ to $\binom{n}{1} + \binom{n}{2} = O(n^2)$.

2 Related Work

Several approaches have been studied for NLG systems. The template-based approach (McRoy et al., 2003; Channarukul et al., 2002) is most commonly used, because it guarantees the advantage of completely controlling the output quality. However, that approach has two main disadvantages. First, it is labor-intensive to generate and maintain templates (Galley et al., 2001). Second, it does not scale well when domains are changed or expanded (Channarukul et al., 2002; Reiter, 1996). Recently, various stochastic NLG methods such as Sequence to Sequence generation with attention (Seq2Seq w/ attn) (Dušek and Jurčíček, 2016) and Semantically Conditioned LSTM (SC-LSTM) (Wen et al., 2015) have been studied to overcome the disadvantages of template-based approaches. They also aim to remove the need for manual alignment of training dataset. They are directly trained on a data corpus and reduce the human effort required for producing templates. Other End-to-End deep learning approaches have been studied (Gehrmann et al., 2018), along with domain adaptation (Dethlefs, 2017), to solve the problem of domain specificity. Though they produce state-of-the-art results among stochastic approaches, the generated sentences are not natural enough for real-world conversational assistant services, where even the slightest mistakes can be detrimental. Another hurdle while training these models is the issue of finding the right dataset

for training (Gatt and Krahmer, 2018). We show that our proposed self-learning architecture can outperform existing neural models and greatly reduce human effort compared to template-based approaches without compromising much on output quality.

3 Self-Learning Architecture for NLG

In this section, we explain the proposed architecture to resolve the problem discussed above. We also briefly explain the models that we use for response generation, namely, Rule-based, Seq2Seq and SC-LSTM. Initially, all dialog acts in the training dataset contain all the combinations of slots with less than k^2 slots per training instance.

As a preparation step, we manually generate the initial training dataset as $\langle DialogAct, Response \rangle$ pairs for all the combinations of slots with up to two slots per instance. With the initial value of k as 2, see Algorithm 1.

Thus, we have successfully increased the size of our training dataset. Sample data for successive training steps is shown in Table 1. We experimented with three different models for response generation task using Dialog Acts: Rule-based model, Seq2Seq model and SC-LSTM model.

Figure 1 depicts the flow for the self-learning architecture.

3.1 Rule-Based Approach

This method was inspired by (Filippova, 2010), where shortest path finding algorithms are used

---

[2]All references to k in this paper denote the number of slots present in a training instance

Algorithm 1 Self Learning Architecture	**Algorithm 2** Rule-Based Generation

Algorithm 1 Self Learning Architecture

1: **while** $k <$ max_slots **do**
2:     Train a new language generation model that generates responses from dialog acts containing up to k slots
3:     Generate responses containing $k + 1$ slots using Dialog Acts containing $k + 1$ slots and the model trained above
4:     Augment the training dataset with the inferred sentences containing $k + 1$ slots from the previous step
5:     $k = k + 1$
6: **end while**

Algorithm 2 Rule-Based Generation

1: **procedure** PROTO_RULE_BASED(A, i, j)
2:     $A1 = $ GET_UTTERANCE$(A \setminus A[i])$
3:     $A2 = $ GET_UTTERANCE$(A \setminus A[j])$
4:     **return** $SCS(A1, A2)$
5: **end procedure**
6: **procedure** RULE_BASED(A)
7:     **for** $(0 \leq i < j < |A|)$ **do**
8:         $Y_{i,j} = $ PROTO_RULE_BASED(A, i, j)
9:     **end for**
10:     $\widehat{Y} = \arg \min_{Y_{i,j}} \{NUM_WORDS(Y_{i,j})\}$
11:     **return** $\widehat{Y}$
12: **end procedure**

to summarize multiple sentences. Although it is straightforward to understand and gives good scores on metrics such as longest common subsequence (LCS) metric used by (Zhao et al., 2002), the approach is different from our objective. We need to conserve all information from the source sentence. Consequently, we use the shortest common supersequence (SCS) for our task. Finding SCS of more than two sentences is an NP-complete problem (Räihä and Ukkonen, 1981), therefore we simplify it by considering SCS of two sentences.

Assumption 1: If sentence X is a good response for slot combination A and sentence Y is one for combination B, then their SCS Z will be a good response for slot combination $A \cup B$.
An example of A, B, X and Y is
A : up(functionname=temperature;devicename=' airconditioner'),
B : up(functionname=temperature;location='bedr oom'),
X : I will turn up the temperature for the airconditioner,
Y : I will turn up the temperature in the bedroom.
The SCS of X and Y is "I will turn up the temperature for the airconditioner in the bedroom", which is plausible response sentence for $A \cup B$.

Assumption 2: SCS Z will be an even better response if $|A \setminus B|$ and $|B \setminus A|$ are small.
Based on Assumptions 1 and 2 above, it is natural to think of a simple algorithm (see Algorithm 2) which generates natural response given slot combination A. There can be numerous candidates, so we opt for the shortest one.

3.2 Sequence to Sequence with Attention

Seq2Seq model (Sutskever et al., 2014) has been widely used in many machine learning tasks. For our task, we use an LSTM-based encoder and decoder model with Attention mechanism (Dušek and Jurčíček, 2016). The LSTM encoder takes a sequence of Dialog Acts as input, where each slot is a symbol in the vocabulary. While decoding, they use an LSTM-based re-ranker at the end to calculate slot errors and penalize responses that have wrong slots as compared to the input Dialog Act.

3.3 Semantically Conditioned LSTM

The SC-LSTM Model (Wen et al., 2015) deals with the issue of repetitive word generation in LSTM-based NLG. It receives the Dialog Act in the form of a bit vector, where each bit in the vector denotes whether a particular slot-value pair exists in the Dialog Act. This model tries to mitigate the issue by using additional control cell along with the standard LSTM cell. The control cell produces a surface realization which accurately encodes the input information and helps in cutting off repetitive words.

4 Experiments and Results

4.1 Dataset for Initial Training

We use a small domain-specific dataset for our experiment. Our dataset is derived from the one used by (Georgila et al., 2018), focused on the domain of IoT Home Appliances. We extract a subset of the system responses, and extend them for increased coverage, and generate $\langle DialogAct, Response \rangle$ pairs. The generated $\langle DialogAct, Response \rangle$ pairs are given to our

Phase	Data	# of slots	Sample training dataset
Phase 1	Training data	1	Dialog Act: up(functionname=temperature;devicename='airconditioner') Response: I turned up the temperature of the airconditioner
		2	Dialog Act: up(functionname=temperature;devicename='airconditioner';location='bedroom') Response: I turned up the temperature of the airconditioner in the bedroom
	Test data	3	Dialog Act: up(functionname=temperature;location='bedroom';date='saturday';time='7 am') Response: I will turn up the temperature in the bedroom on Saturday at 7 am
Phase 2	Training data	1	Dialog Act: up(functionname=temperature;devicename='airconditioner') Response: I turned up the temperature for the airconditioner
		2	Dialog Act: up(functionname=temperature;devicename='airconditioner';location='bedroom') Response: I turned up the temperature for the airconditioner in the bedroom
		3	Dialog Act: up(functionname=temperature;location='bedroom';date='saturday';time='7 am') Response: I will turn up the temperature in the bedroom on Saturday at 7 am
	Test data	4	Dialog Act: up(functionname=temperature;devicename='airconditioner';time='4 pm';date='saturday';location='living room') Response: I will turn up the temperature of the airconditioner in the living room on Saturday at 4 pm

Table 1: Sample data from IoT dataset. The first line of each example is Dialog Act and the next line is the corresponding response. For test data, the second line is inferred response. Notice that the inferred response is being reused in Phase 2.

Category	Model	BLEU Score (Slot count)			
		1~2 slots trainset / 3 slots testset	1~3 slots trainset / 4 slots testset	1~4 slots trainset / 5 slots testset	1~5 slots trainset / 6 slots testset
Fully Human Labeled	Seq2Seq w/ attn	70.3	72.3	77.2	82.9
	SC-LSTM	86.6	85.3	80.9	87.4
Self-Learning	Rule-Based	74.2	71.9	72.8	72.9
	Seq2Seq w/ attn	65.3	54.4	45.9	42.9
	SC-LSTM	**86.6**	**85.8**	**84.0**	**94.9**

Table 2: BLEU score Results. Test results for $k = 2$ to $k = 5$

Category	Model	Mean Human Ranking
Fully Human Labeled	Seq2Seq w/ attn	3.16
	SC-LSTM	2.02
Self-Learning	Rule-Based	2.39
	Seq2Seq w/ attn	3.6
	SC-LSTM	**1.55**

Table 3: Human Evaluation Results. For the human ranking, 1 is highest ranked and 5 is lowest ranked.

model as the training set. In the first training iteration, each $\langle DialogAct, Response \rangle$ pair in the dataset consists of a maximum of two slots. For each training iteration, we split the available training dataset into $4 : 1$ partitions for training and validation respectively. For testing, we use human generated $\langle DialogAct, Response \rangle$ pairs which contain one more slot compared to the dataset used in the training step. For comparison, we also trained our neural models using human generated test pairs with less than k slots combined with original train dataset. They are also evaluated using the test dataset which contains $k + 1$ slots per pair.

4.2 Evaluation Metrics

To evaluate our models, we measure BLEU scores and use a human evaluation. The BLEU score is the n-gram similarity between the reference response and the generated response. Higher BLEU scores indicate a better model. The whole test set was used to measure BLEU scores. For human rating, we asked 21 human evaluators to rank the outputs of all five models, considering the **grammatical correctness** and **informativeness** of the generated responses. Then we calculated the Mean Rank for each model. Lower Mean Rank indicates a better model. Randomly chosen 10 responses with 3 to 5 slots were used for human rating.

4.3 Results

The results can be found in Table 2 and Table 3. We were able to train both deep learning models using our self-learning architecture successfully, which can be trained from small amounts of data. The human labeled SC-LSTM model has better scores than the corresponding Seq2Seq model. When self-learning architecture is used, SC-LSTM outperforms all the other models. We think SC-LSTM model is more suitable for learning from structured data than the other models are. This is because SC-LSTM model uses an additional gated cell which plays the role of sentence planning to produce a surface realization which accurately encodes the input information. When the model encounters a Dialog Act with more slot-value pairs than those in the training dataset, it recognizes the extra slot and generates the response. The Seq2Seq model captures the same relation above using attention. However Seq2Seq-model could not outperform the SC-LSTM model, when it encounters a Dialog Act with more slots than the model was originally trained on. Therefore it fails on our self-learning task. The Rule-based model produces reasonable outputs, but its output heavily depends on the nature of input data and requires human effort. One interesting observation is that the BELU score was the highest when the maximum number of slots was used. We think the BLEU score can increase when the number of target slots rises above a certain level, because the dataset with more slots has more training responses and has responses about more complex combinations of slots.

5 Conclusion

This paper presents a self-learning architecture for NLG. We experimented with three different models: Rule-based, Seq2Seq and SC-LSTM models in the IoT domain. Our data-efficient architecture not only reduces human effort, but also outperforms models trained on the fully human labeled dataset. We think the proposed method can reduce the effort of building large-scale NLG systems for commercial conversational assistant solutions. In future work, we plan to apply other neural models to our architecture, and extend that architecture to cover multi-domain generation tasks.

Acknowledgments

We would like to thank Heriberto Cuayáhuitl and Seonghan Ryu for helpful discussions.

References

Songsak Channarukul, Susan McRoy, and Syed S. Ali. 2002. Jyag & idey: A template-based generator and its authoring tool. In *AAAI/IAAI*.

Adam Cheyer and Didier Guzzoni. 2014. Method and apparatus for building an intelligent automated assistant. US Patent 8,677,377.

Nina Dethlefs. 2017. Domain transfer for deep natural language generation from abstract meaning representations. *IEEE Computational Intelligence Magazine*, 12:18–28.

Ondřej Dušek and Filip Jurčíček. 2016. Sequence-to-sequence generation for spoken dialogue via deep syntax trees and strings.

Katja Filippova. 2010. Multi-sentence compression: Finding shortest paths in word graphs. In *COLING*.

Michel Galley, Eric Fosler-Lussier, and Alexandros Potamianos. 2001. Hybrid natural language generation for spoken dialogue systems. In *Proceedings of the 7th European Conference on Speech Communication and Technology (EUROSPEECH01)*, page 17351738, Aalborg, Denmark.

Albert Gatt and Emiel Krahmer. 2018. Survey of the state of the art in natural language generation: Core tasks, applications and evaluation. *J. Artif. Int. Res.*, 61(1):65–170.

Albert Gatt and Ehud Reiter. 2009. Simplenlg: A realisation engine for practical applications. In *Proceedings of the 12th European Workshop on Natural Language Generation*, ENLG '09, pages 90–93, Stroudsburg, PA, USA. Association for Computational Linguistics.

Sebastian Gehrmann, Falcon Dai, Henry Elder, and Alexander Rush. 2018. End-to-end content and plan selection for natural language generation.

Kallirroi Georgila, Carla Gordon, Hyungtak Choi, Jill Boberg, Heesik Jeon, and David Traum. 2018. Toward low-cost automated evaluation metrics for internet of things dialogues. In *Proceedings of the 9th International Workshop on Spoken Dialogue Systems Technology (IWSDS)*.

Susan McRoy, Songsak Channarukul, and Syed S. Ali. 2003. An augmented template-based approach to text realization. *Natural Language Engineering*, 9:381–420.

Danilo Mirkovic and Lawrence Cavedon. 2011. Dialogue management using scripts. US Patent 8,041,570.

Karthik Sankaran Narayan, Charles Lee Isbell, and David L. Roberts. 2011. Dextor: Reduced effort authoring for template-based natural language generation. In *AIIDE*.

Kari-Jouko Räihä and Esko Ukkonen. 1981. The shortest common supersequence problem over binary alphabet is np-complete. *Theor. Comput. Sci.*, 16:187–198.

Ehud Reiter. 1996. Building natural-language generation systems. *CoRR*, cmp-lg/9605002.

Ilya Sutskever, Oriol Vinyals, and Quoc V. Le. 2014. Sequence to sequence learning with neural networks. *CoRR*, abs/1409.3215.

Tsung-Hsien Wen, Milica Gasic, Nikola Mrksic, Pei-Hao Su, David Vandyke, and Steve Young. 2015. Semantically conditioned lstm-based natural language generation for spoken dialogue systems.

Li Zhao, Sung Sam Yuan, Sun Peng, and Tok Wang Ling. 2002. A new efficient data cleansing method. In *Proceedings of the 13th International Conference on Database and Expert Systems Applications*, DEXA '02, pages 484–493, London, UK, UK. Springer-Verlag.

Enriching the WebNLG corpus

Thiago Castro Ferreira[1]   **Diego Moussallem**[2,3]   **Sander Wubben**[1]   **Emiel Krahmer**[1]
[1]Tilburg center for Cognition and Communication (TiCC), Tilburg University, The Netherlands
[2]AKSW Research Group, University of Leipzig, Germany
[3]Data Science Group, University of Paderborn, Germany
`{tcastrof,s.wubben,e.j.krahmer}@tilburguniversity.edu`
`moussallem@informatik.uni-leipzig.de`

Abstract

This paper describes the enrichment of WebNLG corpus (Gardent et al., 2017a,b), with the aim to further extend its usefulness as a resource for evaluating common NLG tasks, including Discourse Ordering, Lexicalization and Referring Expression Generation. We also produce a silver-standard German translation of the corpus to enable the exploitation of NLG approaches to other languages than English. The enriched corpus is publicly available[1].

1 Introduction

Natural Language Generation (NLG) is the process of automatically converting non-linguistic data into a linguistic output format (Reiter and Dale, 2000; Gatt and Krahmer, 2018). Recently, the field has seen an increase in the number of available focused data resources as E2E (Novikova et al., 2017), ROTOWIRE (Wiseman et al., 2017) and WebNLG (Gardent et al., 2017a,b) corpora.

Although theses recent releases are highly valuable resources for the NLG community in general, all of them were designed to work with end-to-end NLG models. Hence, they consist of a collection of parallel raw representations and their corresponding textual realizations. No intermediate representations are available so researchers can straight-forwardly use them to develop or evaluate popular tasks in NLG pipelines (Reiter and Dale, 2000), such as Discourse Ordering, Lexicalization, Aggregation, Referring Expression Generation, among others. Moreover, these new corpora, like many other resources in Computational Linguistics more in general, are only available

in English, limiting the development of NLG-applications to other languages, which is currently an emerging theme in NLG research community – see, for instance, the increased availability of SimpleNLG tools to languages other than English (Mazzei et al., 2016; Bollmann, 2011; Vaudry and Lapalme, 2013; Ramos-Soto et al., 2017) and the recent Multilingual Surface Realization task (Mille et al., 2018).

This paper describes how we addressed the aforementioned issues by enriching the WebNLG corpus with intermediate representations and exploiting the possibilities of automatically translating the corpus to a second language (German). To this end, we first manually replaced all referring expressions in the WebNLG texts with general tags in a process called *Delexicalization*. The original texts and the delexicalized templates were then translated to the German language using an existing state-of-art English-German Neural Machine Translation (NMT) system (Sennrich et al., 2017), providing a silver-standard version of the corpus in another language. Finally, by automatically processing the original texts and the delexicalized templates for both English and (translated) German versions of the corpus, we obtained a collection of gold-standard referring expressions and discourse orderings. In sum, the main contributions of this study (all publicly available) are:

- A silver-standard version of the WebNLG corpus in German.

- A collection of 16,661 delexicalized templates in English and 16,292 in (silver-standard) German.

- A collection of 86,345 referring expressions to 1,771 Wikipedia entities and constants in English and (silver-standard) German.

---

[1]`https://github.com/ThiagoCF05/webnlg`

171

Proceedings of The 11th International Natural Language Generation Conference, pages 171–176,
Tilburg, The Netherlands, November 5-8, 2018. ©2018 Association for Computational Linguistics

- Discourse ordering information of 20,370 instances of the WebNLG corpus.

The paper is organized as follows: Section 2 briefly describes the WebNLG corpus, Section 3 depicts our delexicalization procedure in detail (briefly introduced in Castro Ferreira et al. 2018), Section 4 explains the process of translating the corpus texts to German, Section 5 introduces the intermediate representations automatically extracted from the corpus in its original and delexicalized forms, and, finally, Section 6 discusses the contributions and prospects of future work.

2   WebNLG corpus

The WebNLG corpus (Gardent et al., 2017a) is a parallel dataset initially released for the eponymous NLG challenge, where participants had to automatically convert non-linguistic data from the Semantic Web into a textual format (Gardent et al., 2017b). The source side of the corpus are sets of *Resource Description Framework* (RDF) triples, in which, each one of them is formed by a Subject, Predicate and Object. The Subject and Object are constants or Wikipedia entities, whereas predicates represent a binary relation between these two elements in the triple. The target side contains English texts, obtained by *crowdsourcing*, which describe the source triples.

The corpus consists of 25,298 texts describing 9,674 sets of up to 7 RDF triples (an average of 2.62 texts per set) in 15 domains: Astronaut, University, Monument, Building, Comics Character, Food, Airport, Sports Team, Written Work, City, Athlete, Artist, Means of Transportation, Celestial Body and Politician (last 5 were available only in the test set). Figure 1 shows an example of a set of 5 RDF triples and its corresponding English text.

3   Delexicalization

To account for data sparsity and unseen entities, many "end-to-end" NLG models work by first generating a *delexicalized* template, where references are represented by general tags (Konstas et al., 2017; Castro Ferreira et al., 2017). The referring expressions are only surface realized once the template is generated. Motivated by these studies, we manually delexicalized the training and development parts of the WebNLG corpus, generating gold-standard templates. The test part

of the corpus was not included in this study, since only its source RDF triples were publicly available at the time of writing.

We started the delexicalization process by automatically mapping each entity in the source representation to a general tag. All entities that appear on the left and right side of the triples were mapped to AGENTs and PATIENTs, respectively. Entities which appear on both sides in the relations of a set were represented as BRIDGEs. To distinguish different AGENTs, PATIENTs and BRIDGEs in a set, an ID was assigned to each entity of each kind (PATIENT-1, PATIENT-2, etc.).

Once all entities were mapped to different general tags in the text, the first two authors of this study manually replaced the referring expressions in the original target texts by their respective tags. Each annotator delexicalized half of the texts, and the few difficult cases were resolved in discussions with the co-authors. Figure 2 shows the entity mapping and the delexicalized template for the example in Figure 1.

In total, we delexicalized 20,370 different texts which describe 7,812 distinct sets of RDF triples, resulting in 16,661 distinct templates in English. Together with the original texts, we translated the delexicalized templates to German, and extracted a collection of referring expressions and discourse ordering information of the corpus as explained in the following sections.

4   Translation

We translated the original texts and the delexicalized templates by relying on the University of Edinburgh's Neural MT System for WMT17 (Sennrich et al., 2017; Bojar et al., 2017a). Not only are the training models publicly available[2], but this system is state-of-the-art in translating English-to-German at the time of writing[3], which guarantees we obtain arguably the best silver-standard resource currently feasible.

The University of Edinburgh system was modeled in a deep encoder attention-decoder architecture. Its translation model was trained on back-translated monolingual data (Sennrich et al., 2016a) in order to augment the training data. To have an open vocabulary, the rare words, which pose a well-known problem in NMT systems,

---

[2] http://data.statmt.org/wmt17_systems
[3] http://matrix.statmt.org/matrix/systems_list/1869

Subject	Predicate	Object
Appleton_International_Airport	location	Greenville,_Wisconsin
Greenville,_Wisconsin	isPartOf	Ellington,_Wisconsin
Greenville,_Wisconsin	isPartOf	Menasha_(town),_Wisconsin
Greenville,_Wisconsin	country	United_States
Appleton_International_Airport	cityServed	Appleton,_Wisconsin

↓

The Appleton International Airport is located in Greenville, Wisconsin, United States and serves the city of Appleton, Wisconsin. Greenville is part of the town of Menasha and Ellington, Wisconsin.

Figure 1: Example of a set of triples (top) and corresponding text (bottom).

Tag	Entity
AGENT-1	Appleton_International_Airport
BRIDGE-1	Greenville,_Wisconsin
PATIENT-1	United_States
PATIENT-2	Appleton,_Wisconsin
PATIENT-3	Menasha_(town),_Wisconsin
PATIENT-4	Ellington,_Wisconsin

↓

AGENT-1 is located in **BRIDGE-1** , **PATIENT-1** and serves the city of **PATIENT-2** . **BRIDGE-1** is part of **PATIENT-3** and **PATIENT-4** .

Figure 2: Mapping between tags and entities for the related delexicalized/wikified templates.

were segmented into sub-word units using Byte Pair Encoding (BPE) (Sennrich et al., 2016b).

To translate a sentence, the University of Edinburgh submission trained 4 left-to-right and 4 right-to-left models. The left-to-right models were ensembled to produce the 50 most likely translation hypotheses while the right-to-left models were then used to re-rank the outcomes from the left models. The process resulted in 20,370 texts and 16,292 delexicalized templates in German.

5   Automatic extraction process

In both English and (translated) German versions of the corpus, we used the original texts and the delexicalized templates to automatically extract a collection of referring expressions and discourse ordering information.

5.1   Referring expression collection

For both English and (translated) German versions, we automatically extracted a collection of referring expressions by tokenizing the original texts and delexicalized templates, and then finding the non-overlapping items. For instance, by processing the text in Figure 1 and its delexicalized template in Figure 2, we extracted referring expressions, for instance, "The Appleton International Airport" to ⟨ *AGENT-1, Appleton_International_Airport* ⟩, "Greenville, Wisconsin" and "Greenville" to ⟨ *BRIDGE-1, Greenville,_Wisconsin* ⟩, "the town of Menasha" to ⟨ *PATIENT-3, Menasha_(town),_Wisconsin* ⟩. In total, we obtained 86,345 referring expressions to 1,771 Wikipedia entities and constants, in which 72.6% (62,689) are proper names, 4.9% (4,230) pronouns, 22.13% (19,108) descriptions and 0.4% (318) demonstrative referring expressions.

5.2   Discourse Ordering

As depicted in Figure 1, each instance of the original WebNLG corpus consists of a set of triples and its respective text. However, in many cases, the order in which the triples are introduced in the set is not the same in which they are realized in the text. For instance, in Figure 1, the triple ⟨ *Appleton_International_Airport*, **cityServed**, *Appleton,_Wisconsin* ⟩ is the third argument expressed on the text, while it is represented as the 5th (last) one in the input set of triples. This is just a singular example of others that even exist in this instance. In order to solve the problem, we noticed that we could extract the order of the arguments in the text by looking into the order of the general tags in the delexicalized template, as Algorithm 1 shows.

The algorithm iterates over the words in a template (lines 4-16). If a word is a general tag (line

Algorithm 1 Discourse ordering pseudo-code

```
 1: function ORDER(tripleset, template)
 2:     orderedset ← ∅
 3:     prevTags ← ∅
 4:     for all word ∈ template do
 5:         if ISTAG(word) then
 6:             for all prevTag ∈ prevTags do
 7:                 triples ← tripleset[prevTag, word]
 8:                 if |triples| > 0 then
 9:                     triple ← triples[0]
10:                     orderedset ← orderedset ∪ triple
11:                     tripleset ← tripleset \ orderedset
12:                 end if
13:             end for
14:             prevTags ← prevTags ∪ word
15:         end if
16:     end for
17:     return orderedset
18: end function
```

5), the algorithm looks for a remaining instance on the triple set which relates the visited tag with a previous visited one (line 7). If a triple is found (line 8), this one is added on the ordering list (line 10) and removed from the input set (line 11).

6 Discussion

This study introduced an enriched version of the WebNLG corpus, easily usable on the evaluation of popular tasks of pipeline NLG models as Discourse Ordering, Lexicalization, Aggregation and Referring Expression Generation. Moreover, a silver-standard version of the corpus in German is provided, hopefully making it more useful for the exploration of NLG in other languages or for the study of Multilingual Surface Realization (Mille et al., 2018). We discuss below the main aspects of our results.

Delexicalization This process was applied to obtain 16,661 English templates and, after the translation process, 16,292 German templates. These representations can be used in the development of template-based NLG systems or Lexicalization models.

Automatic extraction process Using original texts and templates, we extracted important intermediate resources from the corpus, as a collection of referring expressions and discourse ordering information for English and (silver-standard) German. The former resource can be used to evaluate referring expression or wikification models, whereas the second may be a good resource for discourse ordering, content planning, and also for the aggregation task when combined with sentence tokenization information.

Translation While analyzing the translations from English to German, we could perceive that the NMT system did not face any big problem for translating the delexicalized templates. The main challenge was faced with transliterations and coreferences in the texts. The genitive case is an example, as in "Elliot See 's Besatzung war ein Testpilot.", where the apostrophe ('s) is placed wrongly. The same happens to the sentence "Bill Oddie Tochter ist Kate Hardie", where the name "Oddie" should have had the "s" in the end of this German sentence. In terms of transliterations, the preposition "von" played a key role in the challenge, as in the case of the reference "University of Texas", wrongly transliterated to "Universität von Texas" instead of the correct form "Universität Texas". These problems are well-known in WMT English-German tasks and still take a place even using the best NMT model (Koehn, 2009; Bojar et al., 2017b).

Conclusion This study aimed to enrich the WebNLG corpus, facilitating its use in popular tasks of pipeline NLG models as well as in other languages than English. In future work, we envision translating the corpus for other morphologically rich languages, as Brazilian Portuguese (Moussallem et al., 2018). Furthermore, we intend to experiment and come up with good automatic methods to improve the aforementioned challenges and generate useful silver-standard resources for NLG.

Acknowledgments

This work is part of the research program "Discussion Thread Summarization for Mobile Devices" which is financed by the Netherlands Organization for Scientific Research (NWO). It has also been supported by the National Council of Scientific and Technological Development from Brazil (CNPq) under the grants 203065/2014-0 and 206971/2014-1.

References

Ondřej Bojar, Rajen Chatterjee, Christian Federmann, Yvette Graham, Barry Haddow, Shujian Huang, Matthias Huck, Philipp Koehn, Qun Liu, Varvara Logacheva, Christof Monz, Matteo Negri, Matt Post, Raphael Rubino, Lucia Specia, and Marco Turchi. 2017a. Findings of the 2017 conference on machine translation (wmt17). In *Proceedings of the Second Conference on Machine Translation*, pages 169–214. Association for Computational Linguistics.

Ondřej Bojar, Rajen Chatterjee, Christian Federmann, Yvette Graham, Barry Haddow, Shujian Huang, Matthias Huck, Philipp Koehn, Qun Liu, Varvara Logacheva, et al. 2017b. Findings of the 2017 conference on machine translation (wmt17). In *Proceedings of the Second Conference on Machine Translation*, pages 169–214.

Marcel Bollmann. 2011. Adapting simplenlg to german. In *Proceedings of the 13th European Workshop on Natural Language Generation*, pages 133–138. Association for Computational Linguistics.

Thiago Castro Ferreira, Iacer Calixto, Sander Wubben, and Emiel Krahmer. 2017. Linguistic realisation as machine translation: Comparing different MT models for AMR-to-text generation. In *Proceedings of the 10th International Conference on Natural Language Generation*, INLG'17, pages 1–10, Santiago de Compostela, Spain. Association for Computational Linguistics.

Thiago Castro Ferreira, Diego Moussallem, Ákos Kádár, Sander Wubben, and Emiel Krahmer. 2018. Neuralreg: An end-to-end approach to referring expression generation. In *Proceedings of the 56th Annual Meeting of the Association for Computational Linguistics (Volume 1: Long Papers)*, pages 1959–1969. Association for Computational Linguistics.

Claire Gardent, Anastasia Shimorina, Shashi Narayan, and Laura Perez-Beltrachini. 2017a. Creating training corpora for NLG micro-planners. In *Proceedings of the 55th Annual Meeting of the Association for Computational Linguistics (Volume 1: Long Papers)*, ACL'17, pages 179–188, Vancouver, Canada. Association for Computational Linguistics.

Claire Gardent, Anastasia Shimorina, Shashi Narayan, and Laura Perez-Beltrachini. 2017b. The WebNLG challenge: Generating text from RDF data. In *Proceedings of the 10th International Conference on Natural Language Generation*, INLG'17, pages 124–133, Santiago de Compostela, Spain. Association for Computational Linguistics.

Albert Gatt and Emiel Krahmer. 2018. Survey of the state of the art in natural language generation: Core tasks, applications and evaluation. *Journal of Artificial Intelligence Research*, 61:65–170.

Philipp Koehn. 2009. *Statistical machine translation*. Cambridge University Press.

Ioannis Konstas, Srinivasan Iyer, Mark Yatskar, Yejin Choi, and Luke Zettlemoyer. 2017. Neural AMR: Sequence-to-sequence models for parsing and generation. In *Proceedings of the 55th Annual Meeting of the Association for Computational Linguistics (Volume 1: Long Papers)*, ACL'17, pages 146–157, Vancouver, Canada. Association for Computational Linguistics.

Alessandro Mazzei, Cristina Battaglino, and Cristina Bosco. 2016. Simplenlg-it: adapting simplenlg to italian. In *INLG*, pages 184–192.

Simon Mille, Anja Belz, Bernd Bohnet, Yvette Graham, Emily Pitler, and Leo Wanner. 2018. The First Multilingual Surface Realisation Shared Task (SR'18): Overview and Evaluation Results. In *Proceedings of the 1st Workshop on Multilingual Surface Realisation (MSR), 56th Annual Meeting of the Association for Computational Linguistics (ACL)*, pages 1–10, Melbourne, Australia.

Diego Moussallem, Thiago Ferreira, Marcos Zampieri, Maria Cláudia Cavalcanti, Geraldo Xexéo, Mariana Neves, and Axel-Cyrille Ngonga Ngomo. 2018. Rdf2pt: Generating brazilian portuguese texts from rdf data. In *Proceedings of the Eleventh International Conference on Language Resources and Evaluation (LREC 2018)*, Paris, France. European Language Resources Association (ELRA).

Jekaterina Novikova, Ondřej Dušek, and Verena Rieser. 2017. The e2e dataset: New challenges for end-to-end generation. In *Proceedings of the 18th Annual SIGdial Meeting on Discourse and Dialogue*, pages 201–206, Saarbrucken, Germany. Association for Computational Linguistics.

A. Ramos-Soto, J. Janeiro-Gallardo, and Alberto Bugarín. 2017. Adapting SimpleNLG to spanish. In *10th International Conference on Natural Language Generation*.

Ehud Reiter and Robert Dale. 2000. *Building natural language generation systems*. Cambridge University Press, New York, NY, USA.

Rico Sennrich, Alexandra Birch, Anna Currey, Ulrich Germann, Barry Haddow, Kenneth Heafield, Antonio Valerio Miceli Barone, and Philip Williams. 2017. The university of edinburgh's neural mt systems for wmt17. In *Proceedings of the Second Conference on Machine Translation*, pages 389–399. Association for Computational Linguistics.

Rico Sennrich, Barry Haddow, and Alexandra Birch. 2016a. Improving neural machine translation models with monolingual data. In *Proceedings of the 54th Annual Meeting of the Association for Computational Linguistics (Volume 1: Long Papers)*, pages 86–96. Association for Computational Linguistics.

Rico Sennrich, Barry Haddow, and Alexandra Birch. 2016b. Neural machine translation of rare words with subword units. In *Proceedings of the 54th Annual Meeting of the Association for Computational Linguistics (Volume 1: Long Papers)*, pages 1715–1725. Association for Computational Linguistics.

Pierre-Luc Vaudry and Guy Lapalme. 2013. Adapting simplenlg for bilingual english-french realisation. In *ENLG*, pages 183–187.

Sam Wiseman, Stuart Shieber, and Alexander Rush. 2017. Challenges in data-to-document generation. In *Proceedings of the 2017 Conference on Empirical Methods in Natural Language Processing*, pages 2253–2263, Copenhagen, Denmark. Association for Computational Linguistics.

Towards making NLG a voice for interpretable Machine Learning

James Forrest, Somayajulu Sripada, Wei Pang, George M. Coghill
University of Aberdeen, U.K.
`{j.forrest , yaji.sripada , pang.wei , g.coghill}`
`@abdn.ac.uk`

Abstract

This paper presents a study to understand the issues related to using NLG to humanise explanations from a popular interpretable machine learning framework called LIME. Our study shows that self-reported rating of NLG explanation was higher than that for a non-NLG explanation. However, when tested for comprehension, the results were not as clear-cut showing the need for performing more studies to uncover the factors responsible for high-quality NLG explanations.

1 Introduction

Machine Learning (ML) models are making ever greater numbers of decisions that affect user's lives. Many of these models are not interpretable and cannot be readily understood by the average person. This non-interpretability reduces user's acceptance of the models and their ability to make informed decisions, such as challenging an incorrect decision. Recently interpretable ML has been becoming an increasingly important field in ML (Chakraborty et al., 2017).

In this paper, we describe a small explanation system, where a Deep Neural Network is used to make a decision in the area of credit. Then an explanation of this decision is generated using the popular ML explanation framework LIME (Ribeiro et al., 2016). The explanation generated by LIME is only a list of features and their importance to the decision. The experiment in this paper compares people's understanding of this LIME explanation against an NLG interpretation of the same data, to test if NLG generates more interpretable explanations of ML decisions than uninterpreted output.

2 Related work - models & explanations

The number of decisions made by Machine Learning (ML) is increasing rapidly, due to the improvement in techniques, an increase in available data and the use of the Internet. Many of these ML decision models are black boxes (BB) whose workings cannot be easily understood. It has become essential that these ML decision models become interpretable for both deployers of BB models to be certain that they are working correctly and for consumers to trust that the BB are making correct decisions about them, and are doing so in a fair and accountable way. Recent changes in Data Protection laws, such as the E.U.'s GDPR have increased discussion about the 'right to explanation' about ML decisions. Because of these factors, the field of Interpretable ML has become increasingly important.

With the rapid growth of Interpretable ML a number of surveys of the field have been published recently. Biran and Cotton (2017) briefly survey the whole field of interpretable ML, whereas Chakraborty et al. (2017) take a narrower view only describing interpretable deep learning. Guidotti et al. (2018b) have a wide-ranging survey of the field of interpretable ML, while Abdul et al. (2018) survey the field of explanation through time, and how the field has evolved.

Interpretable Ml requires a solid, agreed definition of what 'Interpretability' is. 'Interpretability' according to Lipton (2016) is important but has no agreed definition concerning machine learning, in this paper we use the definition of interpretability from Guidotti et al. (2018b) that interpretability is the extent to which a person can understand a model and its predictions. Lipton states that an interpretable model is necessary when the output of the system (typically predictive performance) is mismatched with what is wanted in the real world outside of the model, e.g. fairness or accountabil-

Proceedings of The 11th International Natural Language Generation Conference, pages 177–182,
Tilburg, The Netherlands, November 5-8, 2018. ©2018 Association for Computational Linguistics

ity.

It has been noted in some surveys that cognitive science is under represented in explaining ML, a good understanding of how people interact with and understand ML is essential in making ML interpretable. Both people and machines understand the world by using models.

People use mental models to understand the world, these are conceptual in nature and are a simplify the part of the world being modelled to form the most parsimonious representation of the world possible (Johnson-Laird, 2010). Mental models struggle to represent modern ML decision models well because these decision models are mathematical (rather than conceptual) in nature and the decision models are too large for the mental model to contain all of the details of the decision model simultaneously.

The lack of understanding of the ML decision model by the users mental model is represented by a gap between the models in (Martens and Provost, 2014) . The more significant the difference between the two models, the lower the understanding of the mental model is and the larger gap between the models is. Martens and Provost (2014) propose that the mental models understanding of the decision model can be increased by providing explanations of the decision model, these explanations cause change in the mental model making it more similar to the decision model, increasing understanding and reducing the gap between them. Keil (2006) states explanations while capable of causing change in models are not models themselves but are shallower containing less information. Moreover, that a successful explanation that increases the recipients understanding.Hoffman and Klein (2017) state that a successful explanation can be used by people to perform causal reasoning, this enables them to understand current and past events, and predict future events, often using minimal amounts of information.

Many new tools for explaining ML decision models are becoming available these are of two types. The first are Decompositions that decompose the BB model into its constituent parts and generate an explanation from them, an example of this technique is the Layer-wise Relevance Propagation described in (Montavon et al., 2017) , these explanation techniques have the advantages of the explanation being generated directly from the decision model, but are not transferable from one decision model type to another. The second Model-agnostic or Pedagogic techniques use the BB model as an oracle to train a new interpretable model which have the advantage of being able to be used on any type BB model but have the disadvantage on explaining a proxy for the decision model rather than the decision model itself. Examples of these model-agnostic techniques are LIME (Ribeiro et al., 2016) and LORE (Guidotti et al., 2018a). The outputs of these techniques are claimed to be interpretable, but the interpretability of these techniques are not evaluated.

It is necessary to have to evaluate the effectiveness of explanations for users, to see which explanations are best. Lipton (2016) states that a claim of post-hoc interpretability should be clearly stated and provide evidence that the interpretability achieves it. Doshi-Velez and Kim (2017) provide guidelines for evaluating interpretability, and how to report findings of interpretability.

3 Explanation System

The system to create explanations for an ML decision, was a pipeline, starting with the data which was preprocessed and used to train the decision model. Then LIME was used to create a non-NLG explanation. Finally, the LIME output was used to create the NLG explanation, using a standard NLG pipeline as described by Reiter and Dale (1997).

3.1 Data

Because people are familiar with, and accepting of, credit applications being made by machines, the credit domain was chosen for creating explanations. The experiment used the German credit dataset; a publicly available (in the UCI data repository) anonymised dataset commonly used for creating machine learning models (Dheeru and Karra Taniskidou, 2017).

Because the dataset in over 20 years old, some attributes were removed for being irrelevant, due to their age. Some attributes were removed for being personal information. Because this dataset was also used with non-Deep Learning decision models attributes that did not correlate strongly with the output class or that were dependent on or correlated with each other attributes were removed. Despite this not being essential for Deep Learning models.

Figure 1: Non-NLG explanation

An automated explanation tool has been used to create the explanation below. It shows the influence each variable's value had on the algorithm. Positive numbers show the variable's value influenced the algorithm to give credit, negative numbers to refuse credit.

Input variable	Value	Influence on the decision
current account	in debit	-0.4091315961509456
assets	none known	-0.16429229114114663
savings account	less than 100	-0.1519065430658803
housing	free	0.08866542959656763
duration	24	-0.07703124519323554
credit history	delayed payments	0.06072233355420254
other credit	none	0.039698419547181805
credit value	4870	-0.03375140928142564
purpose	car(new)	0.0075587254522344096

3.2 Decision Model

A Deep Learning Neural Net was used as the classifier, because this type of model net is commonly used in credit decisions, and is a black box that is not interpretable without the use of an explanation tool. The model was implemented using the python scikit library, using the sklearn.neural_network.MLPClassifier using three hidden layers (Pedregosa et al., 2011). Before training the model, the first fifty instances were removed from the dataset to create a set of instances to be explained later, that the classifier had never seen. The remaining instances were used to train the classifier, by use of cross fold validation.

The classifier had an accuracy of 0.737, a precision of 0.781, a recall of 0.887 and an f-measure of 0.887.

3.3 LIME

LIME is a model-agnostic (or pedagogic) explanation module created by Ribeiro et al. (2016) that can give an explanation of the decisions of any black box classifier. The key intuition behind LIME is that a complex global decision boundary can be approximated to a linear model locally to the instance being explained.

LIME takes the instance to be explained, samples and weights instances close to it. Then uses the black box classifier as an oracle to relabel these local instances and generate a local linear model from them. The output of LIME is a list of tuples of attributes of the instance with a numeric importance value. The non-NLG explanation is the LIME output converted from an array of tuples to a table (Ribeiro et al., 2016). The non-NLG explanation is shown in figure 1 .

3.4 NLG

The NLG explanation is a textual interpretation generated using the values from the LIME explanation, using the NLG pipeline (Reiter and Dale, 1997). A template approach was used for the document planning and microplanning, this produced an ordered set of sentences. The ordering of the sentences was decided by describing the attributes from the most influential to the least, according to the ranking from LIME explainer.

In order to make the differences in understanding between the non-NLG and NLG explanations, only due to the presentation of the explanation, both the non-NLG and NLG explanations used all the attributes.

The sentences are realised and then formed into paragraphs by using SimpleNLG (Gatt and Reiter, 2009). The NLG explanation is shown in Figure 2 .

4 Experiment

An experiment was conducted to test if NLG or non-NLG explanations of algorithmic decision making are better at improving the understanding of their recipients. Participants were shown either NLG or non-NLG explanations, and then asked how well they understood the decision, while also asking questions that test specific parts of their understanding of the decision.

Figure 2: NLG explanation

An automated explanation tool has been used to create the explanation below. It shows the influence each variable had on the decision to give or refuse credit.

The decision reached by the algorithm is to refuse credit. The explanation tool has examined the values of the input variables. Their total influence on the algorithm was 81.0% to refuse credit, versus 19.0% to give credit.

The single greatest contribution to the decision is from the variable 'current account' with the value of 'in debit' this produced 40% of the whole decision, influencing the algorithm to refuse credit. Other important variables were 'assets' with the value 'none' and 'savings account' with the value 'less than 100', these influenced a decision to refuse credit.

Minor influences on the algorithm to refuse credit were 'duration' with the value '24' and 'credit value' with the value '4870'. Minor influences on the algorithm to give credit were 'housing' with the value 'free', 'credit history' with the value 'delayed payment', 'other credit' with the value 'none' and 'purpose' with the value 'car (new)'.

The experiment was conducted as an unsupervised web survey. 39 participants were recruited via social media and were split into two groups for a between groups study.

One group saw the non-NLG explanation (Tables 1), and the other saw the NLG interpretation (Table 2). There were 16 participants in the non-NLG group, and 23 participants in the NLG group. The reason for the imbalance in the groups was an error in the software used to run the experiment, that distributed the groups unevenly. Both groups were then asked the same questions.

The null hypothesis for this experiment is that *'There is no difference between the groups receiving the NLG and non-NLG explanations'*.

Ethical approval for the experiment was granted by the University of Aberdeen Physical Sciences and Engineering Ethics Board.

4.1 The Data Instance Explained

The type of decision that people will most want likely to want an explanation of, is a negative decision against the person, where they feel that their data merits a positive decision. To simulate this an instance was selected from the explanation set that was classified by the decision model as negative, but where in the decision set it was positive.

To keep the experiment time for the participants to around 10 minutes, the participants were tested on only one example.

4.2 Questions

The questions asked of the participants were of two types: Questions where the participants self-reported: the ease of reading (Q1), if they understood the decision (Q6) and if they would trust a decision with this explanation (Q7). Also, questions that tested the participants understanding of the explanation, by asking them which variable was the most important (Q2), which variables had a positive influence (Q3) or a negative influence (Q4) on the decision, or if the decision was close (Q5). The number of questions that test understanding was few, because of an aim to have the participants finish the experiment in around ten minutes. Both groups saw the same questions.

4.3 Demographic Information

The gender profile of the experiment skewed heavily towards males with of the 31 of the 39 participants, reporting as 'male'. The education profile of the experiment skewed towards the highly educated with only 4 participants not reporting as having at least a Bachelor's degree and 19 of 39 participants having at least a Master's degree.

5 Results

The results are shown in Table 1.

The participants self-reported understanding was significantly higher for the NLG group than for the non-NLG group. For the questions that tested the comprehension of the decision: For Q2 'Most influential variable' there is no significant difference between the groups. For Q3 & Q4 'Positive and negative variables', the non-NLG explanation group performed best, but only significantly better for Q3. A learning effect between Q3 and Q4 cannot be ruled out. For Q5 'Decision is close' the NLG explanation group performed significantly better.

Both groups of participants reported that they would trust a decision reached by the algorithm more if it came with the explanation provided(Q7). There was no significant difference between the groups. There was no significant difference be-

Table 1: Table of Questions & Results

Q#	Question	Answer Type	Test	non-NLG	NLG	p
1	Ease of reading	5 point Likert	Mann Whitney	3.13 (1.586)	3.96 (1.186)	0.399
2	Most influential variable	select one	χ^2	0.81 (0.403)	0.91 (0.288)	0.622
3	Positive variables	select all that apply	χ^2	**0.90 (0.303)**	0.64 (0.482)	p<0.0001
4	Negative Variables	select all that apply	χ^2	0.93 (0.262)	0.83 (0.374)	0.113
5	Decision is close	5 point Likert*	Mann Whitney	2.00 (0.765)	**1.30 (1.033)**	0.037
6	Understanding	5 point Likert	Mann Whitney	3.63(1.204)	**4.35 (0.885)**	0.043
7	Trust	5 point Likert	Mann Whitney	4.06(1.181)	4.35 (0.935)	0.471

* For this question the correct answer is 1 (Disagree Strongly). This means that unlike for other questions where high mean values are good, low mean values are good.

tween the groups for the ease of reading of the explanation and interpretation (Q1).

6 Discussion & further work

The group receiving the NLG explanation had a significantly greater self-reported understanding of the decision, compared to the non-NLG group. However, this was not clearly shown by the answers to the comprehension questions, with the explanations performing better for different questions.

The questions need to be improved, to be more precise and independent of each other. A good explanation would allow the participant to reason about the causes of the decision. However, the current questions do not test if the participants can use causal reasoning on the explanation well enough. Because Q2, Q3 and Q4 ask the participants to identify causes but not to reason about them. While Q5 does ask the participants to use causal reasoning more, a better example of a question to ask is 'should this decision be challenged ?', answering this would demonstrate if the explanation of the decision has given the participant enough understanding to reason about the decision.

The NLG treatment of the explanation needs improvement, the current text to be as similar to the non-NLG explanation as possible, mentions every variable. This overloads the participant with too much information. The NLG should be changed to only mention those variables that are important causes of the decision.

Because there is only one decision explained in this experiment there is a risk that the results of this experiment will not generalise to other decisions, further work should include more than one decision. The experiment should include other types of decision models such as Decision Trees. Also, the experiment should be extended to other types of explanations such as case-based or counterfactual explanations.

7 Conclusions

This paper is a scoping study into a method for evaluating explanations.

The NLG explanation produced a higher self-reported understanding than non-NLG explanation. However, this was not supported by testing the comprehension of participants understanding. Further work is required to produce questions that give a better test of the participants understanding and that make the participants use causal reasoning.

Acknowledgments

I would like to acknowledge the support given to me by the Engineering and Physical Sciences Research Council (EPSRC) DTP grant number EP/N509814/1.

References

Ashraf Abdul, Jo Vermeulen, Danding Wang, Brian Y Lim, and Mohan Kankanhalli. 2018. Trends and Trajectories for Explainable, Accountable and Intelligible Systems: An HCI Research Agenda. *Proceedings of the 2018 CHI Conference on Human Factors in Computing Systems* pages 1–18. https://doi.org/10.1145/3173574.3174156.

Or Biran and Courtenay Cotton. 2017. Explanation and Justification in Machine Learning : A Survey. *International Joint Conference on Artificial Intelligence Workshop on Explainable Artificial Intelligence (IJCAI-XAI)* pages 8–13.

Supriyo Chakraborty, Richard Tomsett, Ramya Raghavendra, Daniel Harborne, Moustafa Alzantot, Federico Cerutti, Mani Srivastava, Alun Preece, Simon Julier, Raghuveer M Rao, Troy D Kelley, Dave Braines, Murat Sensoy, Christopher J Willis, and Prudhvi Gurram. 2017. Interpretability of Deep Learning Models: A Survey of Results. *IEEE Smart World Congress 2017 Workshop: DAIS 2017* https://doi.org/10.1109/UIC-ATC.2017.8397411.

Dua Dheeru and Efi Karra Taniskidou. 2017. UCI machine learning repository. http:\\archive.ics.uci.edu\ml.

Finale Doshi-Velez and Been Kim. 2017. Towards A Rigorous Science of Interpretable Machine Learning (Ml):1–13. http://arxiv.org/abs/1702.08608.

Albert Gatt and Ehud Reiter. 2009. SimpleNLG : A realisation engine for practical applications. *Proceedings of the 12th European Workshop on Natural Language Generation* (March):90–93.

Riccardo Guidotti, Anna Monreale, Salvatore Ruggieri, Dino Pedreschi, Franco Turini, and Fosca Giannotti. 2018a. Local Rule-Based Explanations of Black Box Decision Systems (May). http://arxiv.org/abs/1805.10820.

Riccardo Guidotti, Anna Monreale, Salvatore Ruggieri, Franco Turini, Dino Pedreschi, and Fosca Giannotti. 2018b. A Survey Of Methods For Explaining Black Box Models 51(5). https://doi.org/10.1145/3236009.

Robert R. Hoffman and Gary Klein. 2017. Explaining explanation, Part 1: Theoretical foundations. *IEEE Intelligent Systems* 32(3):68–73. https://doi.org/10.1109/MIS.2017.54.

Phillip N. Johnson-Laird. 2010. Mental models and human reasoning. *Proceedings of the National Academy of Sciences* 107(43):18243–18250. https://doi.org/10.1073/pnas.1012933107.

Frank C Keil. 2006. Explaining and understanding. *Annual review of psychology* 57:227–254. https://doi.org/10.1146/annurev.psych.57.102904. 190100.Explanation.

Zachary C. Lipton. 2016. The Mythos of Model Interpretability (Whi). https://doi.org/10.1145/3236386.3241340.

David Martens and Foster Provost. 2014. Explaining Data-Driven Document Classifications. *Mis Quarterly* 38(1):73–+. https://doi.org/10.25300/MISQ/2014/38.1.04.

Grégoire Montavon, Wojciech Samek, and Klaus-Robert Müller. 2017. Methods for Interpreting and Understanding Deep Neural Networks. *Digital Signal Processing* https://doi.org/10.1016/j.dsp.2017.10.011.

Fabian Pedregosa, Gal Varoquaux, Alexandre Gramfort, Vincent Michel, Bertrand Thirion, Olivier Grisel, Mathieu Blondel, Peter Prettenhofer, Ron Weiss, Vincent Dubourg, Jake Vanderplas, Alexandre Passos, David Cournapeau, Matthieu Brucher, Matthieu Perrot, and Edouard Duchesnay. 2011. Scikit-learn: Machine learning in Python. *Journal of Machine Learning Research* 12:2825–2830.

Ehud Reiter and Robert Dale. 1997. Building applied natural language generation systems. *Journal of Natural Language Engineering* 3(1):57–87. https://doi.org/10.1017/S1351324997001502.

Marco Tulio Ribeiro, Sameer Singh, and Carlos Guestrin. 2016. "why should I trust you?": Explaining the predictions of any classifier. In *Proceedings of the 22nd ACM SIGKDD International Conference on Knowledge Discovery and Data Mining, San Francisco, CA, USA, August 13-17, 2016.* pages 1135–1144. https://doi.org/10.1145/1235.

Template-based multilingual football reports generation using Wikidata as a knowledge base

Lorenzo Gatti
Human Media Interaction
University of Twente
Enschede, The Netherlands
l.gatti@utwente.nl

Chris van der Lee
Tilburg center for Cognition and Communication
Tilburg University
Tillburg, The Netherlands
c.vdrlee@tilburguniversity.edu

Mariët Theune
Human Media Interaction
University of Twente
Enschede, The Netherlands
m.theune@utwente.nl

Abstract

This paper presents a new version of a football reports generation system called PASS. The original version generated Dutch text and relied on a limited hand-crafted knowledge base. We describe how, in a short amount of time, we extended PASS to produce English texts, exploiting machine translation and Wikidata as a large-scale source of multilingual knowledge.

1 Introduction

One of the advantages of natural language generation is the possibility of producing multilingual texts, e.g. for describing the same data in multiple languages that are familiar to different user groups. Within the extensive literature on NLG, however, relatively few systems have dealt with the problem of multilingual generation, despite the fact that NLG systems for many languages have been developed. It is telling that even the recent NLG survey by Gatt and Krahmer (2018) does not mention it directly.

One of the problems that hinder multilingual NLG research is the additional work required for generating text in different languages. In complex, grammar-based surface realizers such as KPML (Bateman, 1997) and FUF/SURGE (Elhadad and Robin, 1996), adding a new language requires developing a new grammar, a difficult and time-consuming step. Even statistical approaches to NLG, such as those used by OpenCCG (White and Rajkumar, 2009) or recent multilingual systems (Dušek and Jurčíček, 2013; Mille et al., 2016), require some kind of multilingual knowledge base,

or at least a large multilingual lexicon. For SimpleNLG, the simplest surface realisation system currently available, it took five months to create a bilingual English-French version (Vaudry and Lapalme, 2013).

Multilingual template-based systems often do not suffer from this problem. The domain is usually limited, such as in the case of reports on weather (Chevreau et al., 1999) or air quality (Busemann and Horacek, 1997), hence a small lexicon is sufficient; in many cases, even the knowledge base is unlikely to periodically need major revisions. The latter is not the case for sports report generation, however: in football, the composition of each team can vary from season to season, a new team can get promoted into a league from a lower one, or a new player might have a nickname in a language that is not used in another language (e.g. Gabriel Batistuta was known in Italy as "Batigol" or "Re Leone", while Spanish speakers nicknamed him "El Ángel Gabriel").

In this paper we present our efforts in dealing with these issues, that we have faced while adding a new language to PASS (van der Lee et al., 2017), a template-based generation system that produces football match reports in Dutch.

Our contribution is twofold. First, we added the possibility to generate English reports, while limiting the changes to the current architecture and without losing support for Dutch. Second, instead of using a hand-crafted local knowledge base, we have integrated the system with the knowledge present in Wikidata. Since the website where PASS collects game statistics reports data about most national leagues, this extension makes it possible to exploit the full potential of the system. That is, generating reports of consistent quality for

183

Proceedings of The 11th International Natural Language Generation Conference, pages 183–188,
Tilburg, The Netherlands, November 5-8, 2018. ©2018 Association for Computational Linguistics

```xml
<xml>
<MatchData>
  <Highlights>
    <League>Eerste Divisie</League>
    <StartDate>October 30, 2015</StartDate>
    <StartTime>19:00</StartTime>
    <Stadium>Mitsubishi Forklift-Stadion</Stadium>
    <City>Almere</City>
    <Attendees>906</Attendees>
    <Home>
      <Team>Almere City</Team>
      <GoalScorersList>
        <Goal GoalId="1" Minute="45" OwnGoal="n">
          K.Tadmine</Goal>
        <Goal GoalId="2" Minute="85" OwnGoal="n">
          R.Kip</Goal>
      </GoalScorersList>
      <FinalGoals>2</FinalGoals>
    </Home>
    <Away>
      <Team>Achilles '29</Team>
      <GoalScorersList>
        <Goal GoalId="1" Minute="19" OwnGoal="n">
          B.vandeBeek</Goal>
      </GoalScorersList>
      <FinalGoals>1</FinalGoals>
    </Away>
  </Highlights>
  <Events>
    <YellowCardList>
      <YellowCard YellowCardId="1" Minute="36">
        N. Mamedov</YellowCard>
    </YellowCardList>
    <YellowRedList/>
    <OwnGoalList/>
```

Figure 1: An excerpt from the XML files generated by scraping *Goal.com*.

potentially every match; with the original version, the system could not do that, as the information about teams was contained in a limited knowledge base created by the authors of PASS.

The paper is structured as follows. Section 2 gives an overview of the original PASS system and the reports it can generate. Sections 3 and 4 describe how the templates were translated, and other issues that needed to be addressed when expanding the system to generate a new language. In Section 5 we describe how Wikidata can be a useful resource for template-based NLG systems, and how we integrated it in our version of PASS. Finally, in Section 6 we present our conclusions and possible improvements for the system.

2   The PASS NLG system

The starting point for this work was PASS (van der Lee et al., 2017), a modular, open-source and publicly-available[1] natural language generation tool. PASS is based on templates, and generates football reports in Dutch, starting from match statistics. For each match, two reports are produced, one for the supporters of each club that played the match; the aim is generating a report that uses tailored emotional language, e.g. expressing disappointment for the loss or excitement for the victory. The templates were manually created, starting from an "affective soccer corpus" (Braun et al., 2016), i.e. summaries of the matches as published by the opposing teams, in which the emotional investment is clear.

PASS reports are composed of a title, summarizing the final result, a general introduction that gives information about the opponents or the team expectations, a summary of the game course and its events, and a final debriefing with the outcome for the team.

A brief overview of the general architecture of PASS follows.

Starting data.   First, the game statistics are scraped from Goal.com. Data about the match (final result and statistics for each team, who scored and when, who was given a card by the referee), the two teams, their players, the referee and the venue (such as location, name of stadium and number of attendees) is converted to XML (Figure 1).[2]

Governing module.   It controls the overall process, and shuffles data across the different modules, that are run in succession.

Lookup module.   It deals with the template database, providing to the following modules the templates that match the result of each team (i.e. templates for win, loss or tie).

Ruleset module.   It considers the game statistics, and depending on the results decides what templates are actually usable, for example discarding those mentioning an "equalizer goal" if the score was never even during the match.

Template selection module.   It selects the templates to be used among the possible templates, privileging those that are more descriptive of the match events.

Template filler module.   It replaces placeholders in templates (e.g. *<stadium>*) with the corresponding piece of information in the match data.

Topic collection module.   It decides what topics need to be reported for each team, and orders them chronologically according to the match data, thus ensuring that the second goal is not reported be-

---

[1] https://github.com/TallChris91/PASS

[2] For an exhaustive list of what is actually scraped and stored by the system, see (van der Lee et al., 2017, §3.1). The XML file of Figure 1 can be found at https://github.com/TallChris91/PASS/blob/master/InfoXMLs/AC_ACH_30102015_goal.xml

fore the first goal, for example.

Text collection module. It structures the text in the order previously mentioned, i.e. title, introduction, summary and debriefing.

Information variety module. It replaces templates that express the same information multiple times in the same report.

Reference variety module. It generates different referring expressions when repetitions are present, e.g. changing "Ajax" into "the club of manager Peter Bosz" if "Ajax" is mentioned in two subsequent sentences.

Between-text variety module. It keeps track of how the previous reports were generated, minimizing the repetition of templates across different reports.

3 Translating the templates

As mentioned in section 1, the version of PASS released by van der Lee et al. (2017) generates reports in Dutch only. To create the English version of PASS, we used Google Translate to translate the content of Dutch templates to English. After the automatic translation, each template was manually corrected, restoring garbled placeholders and fixing the mistakes that are inevitably introduced by the translation system. This allows even a person with limited knowledge of Dutch to translate the text of the templates, without requiring the intervention of a professional translator or of a bilingual person.

PASS templates consist of a string of text with one or more placeholders enclosed in angular brackets, such as "<*focus team*> verliest <*in eigen huis; home|op bezoek; away;; homeaway*> van <*final remaining players other team*> tal <*other team*>." Placeholders can be either "simple", such as <*focus team*>, where the template filler will simply insert a proper name or number, or they can contain a conditional statement (akin to a switch-case construct), such as in <*in eigen huis; home|op bezoek; away;; homeaway*>. In this case, the *homeaway* variable can contain either "home" or "away"; in the former case, this is replaced with "in eigen huis", while in the latter the text becomes "op bezoek". Some Dutch templates, their automatic translations and the revised versions are shown in Table 1. A sample report in English is shown in Figure 2.

Depending on the placeholder type and on the sentence, two problems can arise in translation:

In Amsterdam, PSV took three points thanks to goals from Gastón Pereiro. An eager Philips Sport Vereniging won Sunday with 1-2 against Ajax.
After 7 minutes the result was already written, thanks to Gastón Pereiro. After 10 minutes the equalizer from Amin Younes hit the net: 1-1. In the 79th minute, midfielder Gastón Pereiro decided the game by hitting the 1-2 with the help of midfielder Jorrit Hendrix.
Referee Nijhuis was forced to give 7 yellow cards to Jeffrey Bruma, Andrés Guardado, Kenny Tete, Jürgen Locadia, Joël Veltman, Mitchell Dijks and Gastón Pereiro.

Figure 2: A sample report targeted to PSV supporters .

either the brackets are incorrectly put in the translated sentence (e.g. one of the angular brackets is missing, or spaces are introduced between the placeholder text and the brackets, confusing the template-filler module), or they are unnecessary (as in the second example of Table 1). In both cases, the correction is trivial.

Often, however, the translation has to be reworked in a more substantial way. Examples of common errors are, for example, the order of adverbs or phrases (Table 1, third example), some gender-specific pronouns, or idiomatic expressions typical of football reporting (last example in Table 1). Mistakes are inevitable with current automatic translation systems (Hofstadter, 2018), and the presence of placeholders is likely to decrease the output quality of the machine translation software, hence the relatively poor quality of the translated output. Still, manually correcting an automatic translation is more time-efficient than producing a firsthand translation (Federico et al., 2012; Green et al., 2013), and it allowed a non-native speaker of Dutch to translate the templates.

4 Language-specific code

In addition to translating the templates from Dutch to English, the generation code also needed some changes.

A new placeholder had to be introduced in the templates, to solve the problem of ordinal numbers: in Dutch, ordinals are indicated with an "e" following the number (e.g. "na de <minute>e minuut", meaning "after the <minute>th minute"). In English templates, <th> was introduced, and the code was extended to replace this placeholder with "st", "nd", "rd" or "th", depending on the preceding number.

Still in the template filler, Dutch conjunctions,

Dutch template	*<focus team>* verslaat *<other team>*: *<final home goals>*-*<final away goals>*
Translation	*<focus team>* beats *<other team>*: *<final home goals>*-*<final away goals>*
Dutch template	*<focus team>* leed afgelopen *<day><ochtend; morning|middag; afternoon|avond; evening;; daytime>* een *<thuis; home|uit; away;; homeaway>* nederlaag tegen *<other team>*.
Translation	*<focus team>* suffered last *<day>* *<morning; morning | afternoon; afternoon | evening; evening ;; daytime>* a *<home; home | out; away ;; homeaway>* defeat against *<other team>*.
English template	*<focus team>* suffered last *<day>* *<daytime>* *<a home; home|an away; away;; homeaway>* defeat against *<other team>*.
Dutch template	*<red player>* zou na *<minute>* minuten met een rode kaart het veld moeten verlaten.
Translation	*<red player>* should leave the field after *<minute>* minutes with a red card.
English template	*<red player>* had to leave the field with a red card after *<minute>* minutes.
Dutch template	*<goal scorer>* ontvangt de bal van *<assist giver>* en jaagt het leer de winkelhaak in: *<home goals>*-*<away goals>*.
Translation	*<goal scorer>* receives the ball from *<assist giver>* and chases the leather into the square: *<home goals>* - *<away goals>*.
English template	*<goal scorer>* receives the ball from *<assist giver>* and gets the ball in the back of the net: *<home goals>*-*<away goals>*

Table 1: Samples of Dutch templates, their automatic translations and the corrected English templates.

weekdays and phrases such as "geen spelers" ("no players") were translated to English. Similarly, in the reference variety module, we had to translate multiple strings in the code that deals with referring expression generation.

These language-specific code changes are fairly limited due to the similarity between the Dutch and English grammar. The whole process of porting PASS to English took about a month and a half, with most of the time spent translating the templates. Languages with a richer morphology, or a complex grammatical case system, might instead require the insertion of grammatical information in the templates, an extensive lexicon, and the development of more extensive code for sentence realization.

5 Multilingual knowledge

Since the original version of PASS was generating reports in Dutch, its focus was on the Dutch first and second leagues. Given the limited number of teams that take part in these leagues, the system relied on a small local knowledge base, manually constructed by the authors, consisting of just 37 entries. For each team it contained name, league, city of provenance, and a list of nicknames.

This solution, however, seemed inadequate for a multilingual system. Toponyms are sometimes translated (e.g. The Hague is called "Den Haag" in Dutch, while "Londen" is the Dutch name of London), and nicknames are not necessarily shared

in different languages (e.g. the case of Batistuta mentioned in the Introduction). Furthermore, Goal.com is a comprehensive website, containing game results for most national leagues, so a limited hand-crafted knowledge base would cripple the potential of the system. To produce accurate reports, such a knowledge base would also need to be updated whenever a change in the leagues occurs, e.g. a team being promoted or demoted to a different league. To sidestep these issues, we decided to exploit Wikidata instead.

Wikidata[3] is a a free collaborative, multilingual database of structured data (in contrast to Wikipedia, which contains data in unstructured form). Wikidata is akin to DBpedia and similar projects. Wikidata can be seen as a collection of *items* (e.g. item $Q20110$, representing the Italian football player Francesco Totti), each consisting of a *label*, a *description* and a number of possible *aliases*. Each of these can have different language localizations; hence, while the label "Francesco Totti" will be the same for all languages,[4] the description will vary ("Italian footballer" for English, "Italiaanse voetballer" for Dutch), and so will the list of aliases (since in the Italian league nicknames are common, the list of aliases for Italian includes "il Capitano", "il Gladiatore", "er Pupone" and so on). Each item is also associ-

---

[3] https://www.wikidata.org
[4] That is, ignoring the transliterations for Arabic, Chinese and other alphabets and writing systems, which can also be present in Wikidata.

ated with a list of *statements*, i.e. *properties* and *values* that describe known facts about the item. Item Q20110 (Totti) has property P413 ("position played on team/speciality"), whose value is Q193592, i.e. the item "midfielder" (or "middenvelder", according to the Dutch label of entity Q193592).

The advantages of using Wikidata in a template-based system like PASS are many. It is multilingual, hence allowing the production of referring expressions such as "the club from The Hague" and "de club uit Den Haag", where every element including the city name is translated. It is a large-scale resource, containing structured knowledge that spans from major clubs, such as Ajax (Q81888), down to Cambridge United F.C. (Q18509) or NK Vinogradar (Q1348301), two teams playing in the third leagues of England and Croatia respectively. It is arguably more reliable and up-to-date than similar alternatives such as DBpedia, where content is automatically derived from Wikipedia instead of manually curated.[5] Last but not least, it seems that the football domain is among those with the most coverage (Fossati et al., 2017).

The integration of PASS and Wikidata is done in the Template Filler module; there, the MediaWiki API[6] is used to look for a string literal (e.g. "VVV"). This results in a list of items, such as Q25505492 (a student loan system), Q631778 (a magazine), Q1866807 (a women's football club from Venlo) and finally Q24689, the actual football club from the Dutch city of Venlo. To disambiguate between these entities, the algorithm looks for the first one whose property "instance of" (P31) has value "association football club" (Q476028). Once we have obtained an entity from Wikidata, information about that entity can be found in the system by looking at the relevant properties, and their label in the appropriate language -either Dutch or English- can be used to fill the template in.

For football clubs, the city of provenance, the name of the trainer and club nicknames can be found. For players, the nicknames and roles can be extracted. More information is available, and could potentially be used in future versions of the system, if the template placeholders or the referring expression generation module are extended.

---

[5] For an an extensive comparison between Wikidata and similar resources, see (Färber et al., 2016).

[6] WbSearchEntities and WbGetEntities in particular.

6 Conclusions and future work

The version of PASS presented in this paper is able to generate reports both in Dutch and English, and will soon be available online.

However, as described in Section 3, the current templates consist of a translation of the original Dutch templates, and hence may sometimes contain direct translations of idiomatic expressions that are not necessarily typical of English sports reporting.

In this perspective, better templates could be produced by repeating the same methodology used for creating the original PASS templates, i.e. starting from a corpus of English reports and manually annotating some sentences, replacing the entities therein contained with placeholders. The original corpus of PASS contains reports in Dutch, English and German (Braun et al., 2016), hence it would be appropriate for this task.

Moreover, as suggested by van der Lee et al. (2017), an automatic method of generating templates could be used to increase the number of templates, or to quickly introduce a new language.

Similarly, a more varied output could be obtained by adding strategies for lexical variations (Gatti et al., 2014): after generating the sentence from a template, the text is parsed and words are inserted, replaced or removed according to a language model. Hence, a template mentioning an "amazing goal" could result in a sentence describing a "great goal", or a "beautiful goal", without the need to add grammatical and semantic markers inside the templates.

In any case, an evaluation of the English generated texts should be performed, and the results compared with those of the Dutch version of PASS. As reported by van der Lee et al. (2017, 2018), readers were clearly able to distinguish the team for which a report was tailored, and found acceptable levels of clarity and fluency for the reports, while the correctness of the information given is even higher than in human-written reports. We expect the English version of PASS to obtain similar positive results.

We believe that the work here presented shows how Wikidata can be an useful resource, thanks to its extensive coverage - both in terms of knowledge and languages present - and its dynamic nature, and that it should be considered when developing multilingual NLG systems.

References

John A Bateman. 1997. Enabling technology for multilingual natural language generation: the KPML development environment. *Natural Language Engineering*, 3(1):15–55.

Nadine Braun, Martijn Goudbeek, and Emiel Krahmer. 2016. The Multilingual Affective Soccer Corpus (MASC): Compiling a biased parallel corpus on soccer reportage in English, German and Dutch. In *Proceedings of the 9th International Natural Language Generation Conference*, pages 74–78.

Stephan Busemann and Helmut Horacek. 1997. Generating air quality reports from environmental data. In *Proceedings of the DFKI Workshop on Natural Language Generation*, pages 15–21.

Karine Chevreau, José Coch, José A García-Moya, and Margarita Alonso. 1999. Generación multilingüe de boletines meteorológicos. *Procesamiento del lenguaje natural*, 25:51–58.

Ondřej Dušek and Filip Jurčíček. 2013. Robust multilingual statistical morphological generation models. In *Proceedings of the 51st Annual Meeting of the Association for Computational Linguistics, Student Research Workshop*, pages 158–164.

Michael Elhadad and Jacques Robin. 1996. An overview of SURGE: A reusable comprehensive syntactic realization component. In *Proceedings of the 8th International Natural Language Generation Workshop (Posters and Demonstrations)*.

Michael Färber, Frederic Bartscherer, Carsten Menne, and Achim Rettinger. 2016. Linked data quality of DBpedia, Freebase, OpenCyc, Wikidata, and YAGO. *Semantic Web*, 9(1):77–129.

Marcello Federico, Alessandro Cattelan, and Marco Trombetti. 2012. Measuring user productivity in machine translation enhanced computer assisted translation. In *Proceedings of the 10th Conference of the Association for Machine Translation in the Americas (AMTA)*, pages 44–56.

Marco Fossati, Emilio Dorigatti, and Claudio Giuliano. 2017. N-ary relation extraction for simultaneous t-box and a-box knowledge base augmentation. *Semantic Web*, 9(4):413–439.

Albert Gatt and Emiel Krahmer. 2018. Survey of the state of the art in natural language generation: Core tasks, applications and evaluation. *Journal of Artificial Intelligence Research*, 61:65–170.

Lorenzo Gatti, Marco Guerini, Oliviero Stock, and Carlo Strapparava. 2014. Sentiment variations in text for persuasion technology. In *International Conference on Persuasive Technology (PERSUASIVE 2014)*.

Spence Green, Jeffrey Heer, and Christopher D. Manning. 2013. The efficacy of human post-editing for language translation. In *Proceedings of the SIGCHI Conference on Human Factors in Computing Systems*, pages 439–448.

Douglas Hofstadter. 2018. The shallowness of Google Translate. *The Atlantic*.

Chris van der Lee, Emiel Krahmer, and Sander Wubben. 2017. PASS: A Dutch data-to-text system for soccer, targeted towards specific audiences. In *Proceedings of the 10th International Conference on Natural Language Generation*, pages 95–104.

Chris van der Lee, Bart Verduijn, Emiel Krahmer, and Sander Wubben. 2018. Evaluating the text quality, human likeness and tailoring component of PASS: A Dutch data-to-text system for soccer. In *Proceedings of the 27th International Conference on Computational Linguistics*.

Simon Mille, Miguel Ballesteros, Alicia Burga, Gerard Casamayor, and Leo Wanner. 2016. Multilingual natural language generation within abstractive summarization. In *Proceedings of the 1st International Workshop on Multimodal Media Data Analytics (in conjunction with ECAI)*, pages 33–38.

Pierre-Luc Vaudry and Guy Lapalme. 2013. Adapting SimpleNLG for bilingual English-French realisation. In *Proceedings of the 14th European Workshop on Natural Language Generation*, pages 183–187.

Michael White and Rajakrishnan Rajkumar. 2009. Perceptron reranking for CCG realization. In *Proceedings of the 2009 Conference on Empirical Methods in Natural Language Processing*, pages 410–419.

Automatic Evaluation of Neural Personality-based Chatbots

Yujie Xing and **Raquel Fernández**
Institute for Logic, Language and Computation
University of Amsterdam
`yujie.xing@outlook.com` `raquel.fernandez@uva.nl`

Abstract

Stylistic variation is critical to render the utterances generated by conversational agents natural and engaging. In this paper, we focus on sequence-to-sequence models for open-domain dialogue response generation and propose a new method to evaluate the extent to which such models are able to generate responses that reflect different personality traits.

1 Introduction

The advent of deep learning methods has led to the development of data-driven conversational agents for informal open-domain dialogue (see Serban et al., 2016a, for a review). These chatbot systems model conversation as a sequence-to-sequence (SEQ2SEQ) problem (Sutskever et al., 2014) and rely on large amounts of unannotated dialogue data for training. We investigate whether such models are able to generate responses that reflect different personality traits. We test two kinds of models: The speaker-based model by Li et al. (2016b), where response generation is conditioned on the individual speaker, and a personality-based model similar to Herzig et al. (2017), where generation is conditioned on a personality type.

Evaluating the output of chatbot systems is remarkably difficult (Liu et al., 2016). To make progress in this direction with regards to personality aspects, we propose a new statistical evaluation method that leverages an existing personality recogniser (Mairesse et al., 2007), thus avoiding the need for specialised corpora or manual annotations. We adopt the Big Five psychological model of personality (Norman, 1963), also called OCEAN for the initials of the five personality traits considered: Openness, Conscientiousness, Extraversion, Agreeableness, and Neuroti-

cism. Each of the traits is represented by a scalar value on a scale from 1 to 7.

In the remainder of the paper, we introduce the models we examine and describe our new evaluation method. Our results show that the models are able to generate output that reflects distinct personalities, over a baseline encoding chance personality variation. We conclude with a brief discussion on related work.

2 Dialogue Generation Models

The generation models we make use of are standard SEQ2SEQ models consisting of an encoder LSTM, an attention mechanism, and a decoder LSTM (Sutskever et al., 2014; Bahdanau et al., 2015). The model processes context-response pairs, where the context $X = x_1, x_2, \ldots, x_m$ corresponds to the latest utterance(s) in the dialogue and the response $Y = y_1, y_2, \ldots, y_n$ is the utterance to be generated next. The probability of the response Y given the context X is predicted as:

$$p(Y|X) = \prod_{t=1}^{n} p(y_t|y_1, \ldots, y_{t-1}, X) \quad (1)$$

The attention mechanism by Yao et al. (2015) is used over the hidden states of the encoder LSTM to generate a context vector c_t that determines the relative importance of the words in the context utterance at each decoding step t. Then the probability of each word w_k ($k \in |V|$, where V is the vocabulary) to be the next word at step t is predicted with a softmax function:

$$P_t(w_k) = \frac{exp((W)_k \cdot f(c_t, h_t))}{\sum_{k=1}^{|V|} exp((W)_k \cdot f(c_t, h_t))} \quad (2)$$

where h_t is the hidden state of the decoder LSTM and f is an activation function. The weights of matrix $W \in \mathbb{R}^{|V| \times d}$ are learned during training, with d being the number of hidden cells.

Both the Speaker Model and the Personality Model we describe below include 4-layer LSTMs with 1024 hidden cells per layer.

189

Proceedings of The 11th International Natural Language Generation Conference, pages 189–194,
Tilburg, The Netherlands, November 5-8, 2018. ©2018 Association for Computational Linguistics

2.1 Speaker Model

Our starting point is the persona-based model by Li et al. (2016b).[1] In this model, each speaker is associated with an embedding v_s learned during training. Whenever a response by speaker s is encountered during training, the corresponding embedding v_s is inserted into the first hidden layer of the decoder LSTM at each time step (i.e., conditioning each word in the utterance). The hidden states h_t of the decoder LSTM is thus calculated as follows (where y_t^* is the embedding of the response word at time t, and g stands for the LSTM cell operations):

$$h_t = g(h_{t-1}, y_t^*, c_{t-1}, v_s) \qquad (3)$$

Li et al. (2016b) evaluated their model regarding individual content (factual) consistency. Our goal is to evaluate whether the model preserves individual stylistic aspects related to personality traits.

2.2 Personality Model

We modify the Speaker Model to allow for the generation of responses reflecting different personality types. To this end, instead of leveraging speaker embeddings, we estimate the OCEAN scores for each speaker and insert a personality embedding v_o into the first layer of the LSTM decoder.[2]

OCEAN scores are 5-dimensional vectors o, where each dimension ranges from 1 to 7. We normalise them to the range $[-1, 1]$ and then embed them with a linear layer: $v_o = W_o \cdot \frac{o-4}{3}$, where $W_o \in \mathbb{R}^{5 \times d}$ is learned during training, thus learning relationships between OCEAN trait values and properties of the utterances. Whenever a response with personality traits o is encountered, we insert v_o into the first hidden layer of the decoder LSTM. Thus, the hidden states h_t are now calculated as:

$$h_t = g(h_{t-1}, y_t^*, c_{t-1}, v_o) \qquad (4)$$

This version of the model is similar to Herzig et al. (2017).[3] The authors focus on the customer service domain and evaluate the model output's style for only two personality traits with human evaluation. In contrast, we deal with open-domain chat and assess all OCEAN traits globally, using the automatic method we describe Section 4.

3 Experimental Setup

3.1 Dataset

We use transcripts from two American situation comedy television series: *Friends*[4] and *The Big Bang Theory*.[5] We consider only those characters who contribute a minimum of 2000 turns, which results in 13 characters (6 from *Friends* and 7 from *The Big Bang Theory*). We assign a unique speaker id to each character. In addition, we estimate the personality of each character as follows: for each character, we randomly select 50 samples of 500 utterances each, and estimate the OCEAN scores for each sample using the personality recogniser by Mairesse et al. (2007), which exploits linguistic features from 'Linguistic Inquiry and Word Count' (Pennebaker and King, 1999) and the MRC Psycholinguistic database (Coltheart, 1981).[6] We assign to each character the OCEAN score resulting from taking the arithmetic mean of the estimated scores for the corresponding 50 samples.

We consider every two consecutive turns in a scene to be a context-response pair and annotate each response with either the speaker id or the speaker's OCEAN scores. The resulting dataset contains ∼86k context-response pairs, of which around 2000 pairs were randomly selected and reserved for validation.

3.2 Training

Given the relatively small size of the TV-series dataset, following Li et al. (2016b) we use the OpenSubtitles dataset (Tiedemann, 2009) to pretrain the model. OpenSubtitles is a large open-domain repository containing over 50M lines from movie subtitles. Since this data does not include information on which character is the speaker of each line, we simply take each two consecutive lines to be a context-response pair. Due to limitations regarding computational power, we lever-

---

[1]See `http://github.com/jiweil/Neural-Dialogue-Generation`. We reimplemented the model in PyTorch.

[2]The procedure for assigning OCEAN scores to a given speaker is explained in the next section.

[3]Our personality model is a modified version of our reimplementation of the code by Li et al. (2016b) (see footnote 1). The code by Herzig et al. (2017) is not readily available.

[4]`https://sites.google.com/site/friendstvcorpus/`

[5]`https://bigbangtrans.wordpress.com/`

[6]We choose this recogniser because it can estimate numerical scores for each OCEAN trait, instead of binary classifications, and it's open source. For more details, we refer the reader to Mairesse et al. (2007).

age only a subset of the dataset: $\sim$1.8M pairs for training and $\sim$75k pairs for validation.

We train a standard SEQ2SEQ model for 15 iterations on the OpenSubtitles training set, until perplexity becomes stable in the validation set. We then initialise the Speaker and Personality models using the parameters learned with OpenSubtitles and train them on the TV-series training set for 30 more iterations, until the perplexity in the corresponding validation set stabilises.

We use the same settings as Li et al. (2016b) for training: We set the batch size to 128, the learning rate to 1.0 (halved after the 6th iteration), the threshold for clipping gradients to 5, and the dropout rate to 0.2. Vocabulary size is $25,000$ and the maximum length of an input sentence is 50. All parameters (including the speaker embeddings in the Speaker Model) are initialised sampling from the uniform distribution on $[-0.1, 0.1]$.

3.3 Testing

For testing, we again leverage OpenSubtitles to extract a large subset of $\sim$2.5M utterances not present in the training or validation sets. Using each of the utterances in this set as context, we let the trained Speaker and Personality models generate responses for each of the 13 characters, employing Stochastic Greedy Sampling (Li et al., 2017). Since general responses are a known problem in neural response generation chatbots (Sordoni et al., 2015; Serban et al., 2016b; Li et al., 2016a; Zhang et al., 2018) and our goal is to focus on personality-related stylistic differences, we remove the most frequent 100 responses common to all characters/personalities. After this cleaning step, we end up with $\sim$700k responses per character/personality. We refer to the clean set of generated responses as the evaluation set.

4   Evaluation Method

We propose a new evaluation method to measure whether persona-based neural dialogue generation models are able to produce responses with distinguishable personality traits for different characters and different personality types.

Using the evaluation set, for each character we randomly select 250 samples of 500 responses and calculate the OCEAN scores for each sample. Recall that the OCEAN scores correspond to 5-dimensional vectors. We label each of these 250 vectors with the corresponding character. This

gives us 13 gold classes—one for each character—with 250 datapoints each. We then use a support vector machine classifier[7] to test to what extent the OCEAN scores estimated from the generated responses allow us to recover the gold character classes. We compute results using 5-fold cross-validation (training on 80% of the set and testing on the remaining 20% once for each fold). We report average scores over ten iterations of this procedure (i.e., 5×10).

We consider a baseline obtained by randomising the gold character label in the set of generated responses, which indicates the level of performance we may expect by chance. In addition, we use the procedure described above to discriminate between characters using their original (gold) utterances from the transcripts, rather than model-generated responses. This serves as a sanity check for the personality recogniser used to estimate the OCEAN scores—if the recogniser cannot detect personality differences among the characters in the original transcripts, it is not reasonable to expect that the models will be able to generate responses with different personality styles—and provides an upper bound for the performance we can expect to achieve when evaluating generated responses.

Given that the particular personality recogniser we use (Mairesse et al., 2007) was not optimised for dialogues from TV-series transcripts, as an additional sanity check we compare its performance on the original (gold) utterances with a bag-of-words (BoW) approach. This allows us to test whether the recogniser may only be detecting trivial patterns of word usage.[8] We select the top 200 most frequent words over the original utterances as features, without removing words typically considered stop words such as pronouns or discourse markers, since they may be personality indicators. Then we run the same classification procedure using these BoW representations.

5   Results

In Table 1, we report average F1 score per character (including precision and recall) for the Speaker

---

[7]We use the SVM implementation in Python's `scikit-learn` library with radial basis function kernel. We tune the regularisation parameter C and use default settings for all other parameters. We tried a range of different algorithms, including k-means and agglomerative clustering as well as a multi-layer perceptron classifier, always obtaining the same trends in the results.

[8]We thank one of the anonymous reviewers for suggesting this additional test.

Friends	Precision	Recall	F1
Baseline	0.16 (σ=.01)	0.16 (σ=.01)	0.16
Gold	0.61 (σ=.12)	0.61 (σ=.16)	0.61
Speaker	0.32 (σ=.02)	0.32 (σ=.05)	0.32
Personality	0.22 (σ=.04)	0.23 (σ=.09)	0.23

Big Bang Theory	Precision	Recall	F1
Baseline	0.15 (σ=.01)	0.15 (σ=.02)	0.15
Gold	0.69 (σ=.11)	0.69 (σ=.16)	0.69
Speaker	0.46 (σ=.20)	0.47 (σ=.23)	0.47
Personality	0.29 (σ=.19)	0.31 (σ=.24)	0.30

Table 1: Average scores for 6 characters in *Friends* (left) and 7 characters in *The Big Bang Theory* (right)

and the Personality models, as well as the baseline and gold data. The results for these four conditions are all statistically significantly different from each other.[9]

5.1 Lower and Upper Bounds

The first thing to note is that the results on the gold transcripts are higher than the baseline, reaching 61% F1 score on *Friends* and 69% on *The Big Bang Theory*. This indicates that the evaluation method is able to distinguish between the different personalities in the data reasonably well. Apparently, *The Big Bang Theory* characters are more distinct from each other than those in *Friends*.

When we use the BoW approach on the gold transcripts instead of the representations by the personality recogniser, we obtain significantly lower results: 23% F1 score on *Friends* and 19% on *The Big Bang Theory*.[10] The personality recogniser thus detects patterns that go beyond what can be captured with BoW representations.

5.2 Speaker and Personality Models

We find that the responses generated by the Speaker model display consistent personality variation above baseline, although a significant level of the personality markers found in the original data seems to be lost (32% vs. 61% and 47% vs. 69%). The results obtained for the Personality model are significantly above baseline as well (23% vs. 16% and 30% vs. 15%). We also see that the personality traits found in the responses generated by the Personality model yield lower distinguishability than those by the Speaker model. This is to be expected, since the Personality model generates responses for a personality type, which

should be more varied (and hence less distinguishable) than those by an individual speaker.

An advantage of the Personality model, however, is that in principle it allows us to generate responses for novel, predefined personalities that have not been seen during training. To test this potential, we create five extreme personality types by setting up the score of one of the OCEAN traits to a high value (6.5) and all remaining four traits to an average value (3.5). We then let the model generate responses to all the utterances in the evaluation set for each of these extreme personalities and evaluate the extent to which the responses differ in style following the same procedure as in the previous experiment. Table 2 shows the results.

	Precision	Recall	F1
Baseline	0.19	0.19	0.19
Average	0.53 (σ=.07)	0.53 (σ=.09)	0.53
Open	0.46	0.46	0.46
Conscientious	0.59	0.62	0.61
Extravert	0.63	0.65	0.64
Agreeable	0.53	0.50	0.51
Neurotic	0.44	0.42	0.43

Table 2: Average scores for personality types with high value for different OCEAN personality traits

We find that the generated responses are distinguishable with 53% average F1 score. This indicates that the model has learned to generalise beyond the training data. Table 3 shows some examples of generated responses.

Joey (*Friends*):	*Oh, of course I love you, baby.*
Raj (*Big Bang*):	*I don't love you.*
Open:	*You are beautiful!*
Agreeable:	*Oh I, I love you too.*

Table 3: Responses to *Do you love me?* by the Personality model for personality types of given characters and extreme types not seen during training

---

[9]Significance is tested with a two-independent-sample t-test on the results of 10 iterations, first using Levene's test to assess the equality of variances and then applying Welch's or Student's t-test accordingly.

[10]We also run this experiment removing stop words (using the list of English stop words from `scikit-learn`), obtaining almost identical results: 22% F1 score on *Friends* and 18% on *The Big Bang Theory*.

6 Related Work and Conclusion

In recent years, there has been a surge of work on modelling different stylistic aspects, such as politeness and formality, in Natural Language Generation with deep learning methods (among others, Sennrich et al., 2016; Hu et al., 2017; Ficler and Goldberg, 2017; Niu and Bansal, 2018). Regarding generation in dialogue systems, besides the two response generation models we have tested, other recent approaches to open-domain dialogue have considered stylistic aspects. For example, Yang et al. (2017) leverage metadata about speakers' personal information, such as age and gender, to condition generation using domain adaptation methods; while Luan et al. (2017) use multi-task learning to incorporate an autoencoder that learns the speaker's language style from non-conversational data such as blog posts. The output of these models could also be assessed for personality differences using our method.

More recently, Oraby et al. (2018) have used the statistical rule-based generator PERSONAGE (Mairesse and Walker, 2010) to create a synthetic corpus with personality variation within the restaurant domain. They use the data to train and evaluate neural generation models that produce linguistic output given a dialogue act and a set of semantic slots, plus different degrees of personality information, and show that the generated output correlates reasonably well with the synthetic data generated by PERSONAGE. Our work differs from Oraby et al. (2018) in several respects: We focus on open-domain chit-chat dialogue, where the input to the model is surface text (rather than semantic representations such as dialogue acts) from naturally occurring dialogue data. Rather than relying on parallel data with systematic personality variation, we exploit a personality recogniser. In this respect, our approach has some similarities to Niu and Bansal (2018), who use a politeness classifier for stylistic dialogue generation. Here we have used the personality recogniser by Mairesse et al. (2007), which may not be ideal as it was originally trained on snippets of conversations combined with stream of consciousness essays. Our method, however, is not tied to this particular recogniser—any other personality recogniser that produces numerical scores may be used instead.

We think that the automatic evaluation method we have proposed can be a useful complement to qualitative human evaluation of chatbot models.

Our study shows that the models under investigation produce output that retains some stylistic features related to personality, and can learn surface patterns that generalise beyond the training data.

Acknowledgements

RF kindly acknowledges funding by the Netherlands Organisation for Scientific Research (NWO), under VIDI grant 276-89-008, *Asymmetry in Conversation*.

References

Dzmitry Bahdanau, Kyunghyun Cho, and Yoshua Bengio. 2015. Neural machine translation by jointly learning to align and translate. In *Proceedings of ICLR*.

Max Coltheart. 1981. The MRC psycholinguistic database. *The Quarterly Journal of Experimental Psychology Section A*, 33(4):497–505.

Jessica Ficler and Yoav Goldberg. 2017. Controlling linguistic style aspects in neural language generation. In *Proceedings of the Workshop on Stylistic Variation*, pages 94–104. Association for Computational Linguistics.

Jonathan Herzig, Michal Shmueli-Scheuer, Tommy Sandbank, and David Konopnicki. 2017. Neural response generation for customer service based on personality traits. In *Proceedings of The 10th International Natural Language Generation conference*, pages 252–256.

Zhiting Hu, Zichao Yang, Xiaodan Liang, Ruslan Salakhutdinov, and Eric P Xing. 2017. Controllable text generation. In *Proceedings of ICML*.

Jiwei Li, Michel Galley, Chris Brockett, Jianfeng Gao, and Bill Dolan. 2016a. A diversity-promoting objective function for neural conversation models. In *Proceedings of the 2016 Conference of the North American Chapter of the Association for Computational Linguistics: Human Language Technologies*, pages 110–119, San Diego, California. Association for Computational Linguistics.

Jiwei Li, Michel Galley, Chris Brockett, Georgios Spithourakis, Jianfeng Gao, and Bill Dolan. 2016b. A persona-based neural conversation model. In *Proceedings of the 54th Annual Meeting of the Association for Computational Linguistics (Volume 1: Long Papers)*, pages 994–1003. Association for Computational Linguistics.

Jiwei Li, Will Monroe, and Dan Jurafsky. 2017. Data distillation for controlling specificity in dialogue generation. *arXiv preprint arXiv:1702.06703*.

Chia-Wei Liu, Ryan Lowe, Iulian Serban, Mike Noseworthy, Laurent Charlin, and Joelle Pineau. 2016. How not to evaluate your dialogue system: An empirical study of unsupervised evaluation metrics for dialogue response generation. In *Proceedings of the 2016 Conference on Empirical Methods in Natural Language Processing (EMNLP)*.

Yi Luan, Chris Brockett, Bill Dolan, Jianfeng Gao, and Michel Galley. 2017. Multi-task learning for speaker-role adaptation in neural conversation models. In *Proceedings of the Eighth International Joint Conference on Natural Language Processing (Volume 1: Long Papers)*, pages 605–614.

François Mairesse and Marilyn A Walker. 2010. Towards personality-based user adaptation: psychologically informed stylistic language generation. *User Modeling and User-Adapted Interaction*, 20(3):227–278.

François Mairesse, Marilyn A Walker, Matthias R Mehl, and Roger K Moore. 2007. Using linguistic cues for the automatic recognition of personality in conversation and text. *Journal of artificial intelligence research*, 30:457–500.

Tong Niu and Mohit Bansal. 2018. Polite dialogue generation without parallel data. *Transactions of the Association for Computational Linguistics*, 6:273–389.

Warren T Norman. 1963. Toward an adequate taxonomy of personality attributes: Replicated factor structure in peer nomination personality ratings. *The Journal of Abnormal and Social Psychology*, 66(6):574.

Shereen Oraby, Lena Reed, Shubhangi Tandon, TS Sharath, Stephanie Lukin, and Marilyn Walker. 2018. Controlling personality-based stylistic variation with neural natural language generators. In *Proceedings of SIGdial*.

James W Pennebaker and Laura A King. 1999. Linguistic styles: Language use as an individual difference. *Journal of personality and social psychology*, 77(6):1296.

Rico Sennrich, Barry Haddow, and Alexandra Birch. 2016. Controlling politeness in neural machine translation via side constraints. In *Proceedings of the 2016 Conference of the North American Chapter of the Association for Computational Linguistics: Human Language Technologies*, pages 35–40.

Iulian V. Serban, Ryan Lowe, Laurent Charlin, and Joelle Pineau. 2016a. Generative deep neural networks for dialogue: A short review. In *30th Conference on Neural Information Processing Systems (NIPS 2016), Workshop on Learning Methods for Dialogue*.

Iulian V. Serban, Alessandro Sordoni, Yoshua Bengio, Aaron Courville, and Joelle Pineau. 2016b. Building end-to-end dialogue systems using generative hierarchical neural network models. In *Proceedings of the Thirtieth AAAI Conference on Artificial Intelligence*, AAAI'16, pages 3776–3783. AAAI Press.

Alessandro Sordoni, Michel Galley, Michael Auli, Chris Brockett, Yangfeng Ji, Margaret Mitchell, Jian-Yun Nie, Jianfeng Gao, and Bill Dolan. 2015. A neural network approach to context-sensitive generation of conversational responses. In *Proceedings of the 2015 Conference of the North American Chapter of the Association for Computational Linguistics: Human Language Technologies*, pages 196–205, Denver, Colorado. Association for Computational Linguistics.

Ilya Sutskever, Oriol Vinyals, and Quoc V Le. 2014. Sequence to sequence learning with neural networks. In *Advances in neural information processing systems*, pages 3104–3112.

Jörg Tiedemann. 2009. News from OPUS-A collection of multilingual parallel corpora with tools and interfaces. In *Recent Advances in Natural Language Processing*, volume 5, pages 237–248.

Min Yang, Zhou Zhao, Wei Zhao, Xiaojun Chen, Jia Zhu, Lianqiang Zhou, and Zigang Cao. 2017. Personalized response generation via domain adaptation. In *Proceedings of the 40th International ACM SIGIR Conference on Research and Development in Information Retrieval*, SIGIR '17, pages 1021–1024, New York, NY, USA. ACM.

Kaisheng Yao, Geoffrey Zweig, and Baolin Peng. 2015. Attention with intention for a neural network conversation model. *arXiv preprint arXiv:1510.08565*.

Saizheng Zhang, Emily Dinan, Jack Urbanek, Arthur Szlam, Douwe Kiela, and Jason Weston. 2018. Personalizing Dialogue Agents: I have a dog, do you have pets too? *ArXiv e-prints*.

Poem Machine - a Co-creative NLG Web Application for Poem Writing

Mika Hämäläinen
Department of Digital Humanities
University of Helsinki
`mika.hamalainen@helsinki.fi`

Abstract

We present Poem Machine, an interactive online tool for co-authoring Finnish poetry with a computationally creative agent. Poem Machine can produce poetry of its own and assist the user in authoring poems. The main target group for the system is primary school children, and its use as a part of teaching is currently under study.

1 Introduction

Automatic poem generation has received a fair share of attention in the recent years (Gervás, 2001; Colton et al., 2012; Bay et al., 2017). However, these generators can only seldom be interacted with by a user. Our system, Poem Machine[1], makes poem generation an interactive NLG task with full engagement from the user part.

In the field of computational creativity, the discourse has moved lately more and more towards human-computer co-creativity. The interest does not lie anymore on how a computer can generate creative artifacts on its own, but rather how such systems can be used together with human creativity to assist a person in a creative task.

Figure 1: Poem Machine poem editor.

Poem Machine works by creating a poem based on the user defined theme or a user provided URL.

[1] http://runokone.cs.helsinki.fi/

This poem is presented to the user in a user interface that is tailored towards co-creativity (see Figure 1). The user can edit the poem freely by natural gestures such as drag and drop. Furthermore, the user can consult Poem Machine's assisting functionalities to achieve his goals such as finding rhymes or following meter.

The primary user group of interest are primary school children, and it has been successfully used in schools to teach children about poetry (Kantosalo et al., 2015). The fact that the system can create a poem as a starting point removes the problem of not coming up with where to start when writing.

2 Poem Generator

The single most difficult NLG task the system has to tackle is the generation of the initial poem the user will then start to modify. The complex morphosyntax of Finnish does not make this task any less difficult.

For morphology, we use Omorfi (Pirinen et al., 2017), which is an FST based transducer to produce morphological forms. This tool is used by Syntax Maker (Hämäläinen and Rueter, 2018) which is a surface generation tool for Finnish. It resolves morphosyntax (agreement and government) based on an abstract syntactic structure filled with lemmas.

The poem generator in place is based on the one presented in (Hämäläinen, 2018). It uses SemFi (Hämäläinen, 2017) which is a semantic data set of relations of Finnish words based on their syntactic dependencies to produce poetry.

In order to initiate the poem generation, the user is provided with a list of themes such as *family* or *nature*. Each theme contains a list of seed nouns that are passed on to the poem generator for producing a novel poem. If the user provides a URL, the contents of the link are analyzed with TreeTag-

Proceedings of The 11th International Natural Language Generation Conference, pages 195–196,
Tilburg, The Netherlands, November 5-8, 2018. ©2018 Association for Computational Linguistics

ger (Schmid, Helmut, 1995) after removing boilerplate and the poem is generated by using those words instead of the ones originating from SemFi.

3 User Assisting Functionality

In addition to just a one way NLG interaction in producing the initial poem, Poem Machine sports a multitude of user assisting functionalities.

Poem Machine can suggest phonetically similar words for words the user drags into the rhymer tool. This tool will look up the Poem Machine database for rhyming or alliterating words, or words with assonance or consonance rhyme type. Additionally, Poem Machine can asses the meter of the poem the user is authoring. Selectable meters are haiku, tanka, kalevala and so on. Poem Machine uses Voikko [2] to divide verses into syllables to asses how well they follow the meter. For more complex meters such as the kalevala meter, Poem Machine provides additional stylistic feedback apart from syllabic count, such as the existence of alliterations and that longer words should be placed at the end of a verse.

The user can also reconsult the poem generator described earlier. This will generate a new verse at the end of the poem by following the same parameters that were set upon the creation of the poem.

Words can also be substituted by new ones by using the magic wand tool. Using the tool analyzes the verse syntactically and looks up for a suitable replacement for the word the wand was dragged on from SemFi. For easier replacement, Poem Machine will also inflect the word to match the original morphology with Omorfi.

4 Conclusions

Poem Machine is a complex computationally creative tool for helping people create poems of their own. The meter tool also helps people learn more about the poetic meter. Initial observations suggest that Poem Machine is successful in eliciting motivation and provoking more interest towards poetry in school kids.

It has been made publicly available for everyone to use it as an online service. Thus making it possible for the system to have more impact outside of the academia. Furthermore this has made it possible for technology enthusiastic teachers to use it as a part of their teaching without the need to participate in the scientific study on its use in classrooms.

Acknowledgments

This work has been supported by the Academy of Finland under grant 276897 (CLiC).

References

Benjamin Bay, Paul Bodily, and Dan Ventura. 2017. Text Transformation Via Constraints and Word Embedding. In *Proceedings of the Eighth International Conference on Computational Creativity*, pages 49–56.

Simon Colton, Jacob Goodwin, and Tony Veale. 2012. Full-FACE Poetry Generation. In *Proceedings of the Third International Conference on Computational Creativity*, pages 95–102.

Pablo Gervás. 2001. An Expert System for the Composition of Formal Spanish Poetry. *Knowledge-Based Systems*, 14(3):181–188.

Mika Hämäläinen. 2017. SemFi - Finnish Semantic Data for Poem Generation. Doi: 10.5281/zenodo.1137734.

Mika Hämäläinen. 2018. Harnessing NLG to Create Finnish Poetry Automatically. In *Proceedings of the Ninth International Conference on Computational Creativity*, pages 9–15.

Mika Hämäläinen and Jack Rueter. 2018. Development of an Open Source Natural Language Generation Tool for Finnish. In *Proceedings of the Fourth International Workshop on Computational Linguistics for Uralic Languages*, pages 51–58.

Anna Kantosalo, Jukka Toivanen, and Hannu Toivonen. 2015. Interaction Evaluation for Human-Computer Co-creativity: A Case Study. In *Proceedings of the Sixth International Conference on Computational Creativity*, pages 276–283.

Tommi A Pirinen, Inari Listenmaa, Ryan Johnson, Francis M. Tyers, and Juha Kuokkala. 2017. Open morphology of Finnish. LINDAT/CLARIN digital library at the Institute of Formal and Applied Linguistics, Charles University.

Schmid, Helmut. 1995. Improvements in Part-of-Speech Tagging with an Application to German. In *Proceedings of the ACL SIGDAT-Workshop*.

---

[2] https://voikko.puimula.org/

Japanese Advertising Slogan Generator using Case Frame and Word Vector

Kango Iwama
Department of Informatics, Graduate School of Integrated Science and Technology, Shizuoka University
Japan
kiwama@kanolab.net

Yoshinobu Kano
Faculty of Informatics, Shizuoka University
Japan
kano@inf.shizuoka.ac.jp

Abstract

There has been many works published for automatic sentence generation of a variety of domains. However, there would be still no single method available at present that can generate sentences for all of domains. Each domain will require a suitable generation method. We focus on automatic generation of Japanese advertisement slogans in this paper. We use our advertisement slogan database, case frame information, and word vector information. We employed our system to apply for a copy competition for human copywriters, where our advertisement slogan was left as a finalist. Our system could be regarded as the world first system that generates slogans in a practical level, as an advertising agency already employs our system in their business.

1 Introduction

There has been many works published on Japanese automatic sentence generation for a variety of domains. In literary works, generation of a short-short (short story) (Matsubara et al., 2013) (Sato et al., 2015), has become a hot topic. A wide variety of works have been published including business documents such as newspaper articles and financial summary[1], sports bulletins such as baseball inning breaking (Tagawa and Shimada, 2017), overview text of the weather forecast (Murakami et al., 2017), *haiku* (Wu et al., 2017), chat dialogue such as "high school girl AI *RINNA*." (Wu et al., 2016). However, these generation methods tend to be different for each case. For example, the short-short generation was performed with templates written manually; the inning bulletins generation was rule-based; the chat dialogue of the "high school girl AI *RINNA*" used RNN-GRU; the generation system of overview text of weather forecast incorporates neural networks, such as an encoder-decoder model. These variety of methods mean that there are still no single method available at present that is effective and unified for all of domains.

2 Advertisement Slogan Generator

Advertisement (ad) slogan itself is not a strict concept. There are many kinds of related types of phrases: copies of the ads, book titles and bands, headings of table of contents, headlines of newspapers and magazines, copies of the movie, titles of sales letters and blogs, e-mail magazines, the saying known in the world, impressive phrases that have heard or seen in the city (Kawakami 2016). Our target is automatic generation of practical ad slogans where professional copywriters would work for, rather than automatic creation support for amateur individuals. However, our system could be used e.g. for web ads in future to provide slogans in lower costs.

There are a couple of previous works as follows. Yamane and Hagiwara proposed a method for automatic generation of Japanese ad slogans with replacement of nouns (Yamane and Hagiwara, 2015). They used n-gram and search result information from the web. Baba et al. used Word2Vec to extend the number of candidates which are automatically generated from ad texts (Baba et al., 2015). However, no work reported in practical business level works yet.

Our automatic ad slogan generator uses case frames and word vectors, with ad slogans written by professional copy writers. Our system targets on Japanese language, but we will show input and output in English using a machine translation in our demonstration.

---

[1] http://pr.nikkei.com/qreports-ai/

Proceedings of The 11th International Natural Language Generation Conference, pages 197–198,
Tilburg, The Netherlands, November 5-8, 2018. ©2018 Association for Computational Linguistics

We applied our system to the 8th Shizuoka Copy Award[2], which is a competition of ad slogans for human copywriters. We submitted our generated slogans as humans, so the reviews did not know our slogans are by machine. Our submissions were manually selected from generated samples around ten times larger. Table 1 shows statistics of submissions and selections. Examples of generated slogans with selection results are shown in Table 2, also show slogans written by humans, a grand prize one and a part of finalists.

	Human	**System**
# of submissions	4060	228
Passed 1st review	584 (14.3%)	16 (7.0%)
Finalist	59 (1.4%)	1 (0.4%)

Table 1: Submission and selection statistics in the 8th Shizuoka Copy Award.

Finalist written by our system	親の意見と寄付は後で効く。 (Parents' opinions and donation will work later.)
Passed 1st review by our system	その朝、いちばんご機嫌なのは経済でした。 (This morning, it was the economy that seemed the best mood.)
	仲良しがはみ出てる。 (The chum is protruding.)
	可愛い子には U ターンをさせよ (Let your cute child to U-turn.)
Failed by our system	ふるさとを走ろう。 (Let's run in your hometown.)
	広告が、世界をつなぐ。 (The advertisement connects the world.)
	まだ見ぬお家に会いに行こう。 (Let's see a house you don't know.)
Grand Prize by human	変わらない味は、忘れない言葉で守られている。 (The unchanged taste is protected by unforgettable words.).
Finalist written by humans	好きな人にキスを。好きな街にキフを。 (Kiss the person you like, donate to the city you like.)
	「今」は、過去のだれかのやさしさでできている。 ("Now" is made of someone's kindness in the past.)
	分ければ分けるほど増えるもの。それは、幸せ。 (The more you divide, the more it increases. It is happiness.)

Table 2: Examples of ad slogans with selection results, by our system and human writers.

This system has already been used as a base of the *AICO* (AI COpywriter) system in Dentsu Inc., one of the five world largest advertising agency groups. Together with the competition results, our system could be regarded as the world first system that can generate ad slogans in the practical level.

Acknowledgments

We are grateful to the copywriters of Dentsu Inc.

References

Jun Baba, Yuki Iwazaki, Itsuki Sugio, Kosuke Kitade, Takeshi Fukushima. 2015. Automatic Generation of Title and Description Texts for Sponsored Search Ads. *The 29th Annual Conference of the Japanese Society for Artificial Intelligence*.

Tetsuya Kawakami. 2016. The basic of catch phrase power. Nippon Jitsugyo Publishing.

Hitoshi Matsubara, Satoshi Sato, Mina Akaishi, Kaoru Sumi, Kazushi Mukaiyama, Hideyuki Nakashima, Hideaki Sena, Hajime Murai, Yuko Otsuka. 2013. An attempt at automatic composition of Shin'ichi Hoshi-like short short stories. *The 27th Annual Conference of the Japanese Society for Artificial Intelligence*.

Soichiro Murakami, Ryohei Sasano, Hiroya Takamura, Manabu Okumura. 2017. Automatic generation of weather forecast comments from numerical forecast map. *2017 The Association for Natural Language Processing*.

Satoshi Sato. 2015. What is Automatic Story Generator? *The 29th Annual Conference of the Japanese Society for Artificial Intelligence*.

Yuki Tagawa, Kazutaka Shimada. 2017. Automatic generation of inning summary sentence by automatic generation of template. *2017 The Association for Natural Language Processing*.

Xianchao Wu, Kazushige Ito, Katsuya Iida, Kazuna Tsuboi, Momo Klyen. 2016. RINNA: high school girl Artificial Intelligence. *2016 The Association for Natural Language Processing*.

Xianchao Wu, Momo Klyen, Kazushige Ito, Zhan Chen. 2017. Haiku Generation Using Deep Neural Networks. *2017 The Association forNatural Language Processing*.

Hiroaki Yamane, Masafumi Hagiwara. 2015. Tag Line Generating System Using Information on the Web. *28th Fuzzy System Symposium*.

---

[2] http://shizuokacc.com/award/

Underspecified Universal Dependency Structures as Inputs for Multilingual Surface Realisation

Simon Mille
Universitat Pompeu Fabra
Barcelona, Spain
simon.mille@upf.edu

Anja Belz
University of Brighton
Brighton, UK
a.s.belz@brighton.ac.uk

Bernd Bohnet
Google Inc.
London, UK
bohnetbd@google.com

Leo Wanner
ICREA and Universitat Pompeu Fabra
Barcelona, Spain
leo.wanner@upf.edu

Abstract

In this paper, we present the datasets used in the Shallow and Deep Tracks of the First Multilingual Surface Realisation Shared Task (SR'18). For the Shallow Track, data in ten languages has been released: Arabic, Czech, Dutch, English, Finnish, French, Italian, Portuguese, Russian and Spanish. For the Deep Track, data in three languages is made available: English, French and Spanish. We describe in detail how the datasets were derived from the Universal Dependencies V2.0, and report on an evaluation of the Deep Track input quality. In addition, we examine the motivation for, and likely usefulness of, deriving NLG inputs from annotations in resources originally developed for Natural Language Understanding (NLU), and assess whether the resulting inputs supply enough information of the right kind for the final stage in the NLG process.

1 Introduction

There has long been an assumption in Natural Language Generation (NLG) that surface realisation can be treated as an independent subtask for which stand-alone, plug-and-play tools can, and should, be created. Early surface realisers such as KPML (Bateman, 1997) and FUF/Surge (Elhadad and Robin, 1996) were ambitious, independent surface realisation tools for English with wide grammatical coverage. However, the question of how the NLG components addressing the stage before surface realisation were supposed to put together inputs of the level of grammatical sophistication required by such tools was never quite

resolved. The success of SimpleNLG (Gatt and Reiter, 2009) which had much reduced grammatical coverage, but accepted radically simpler inputs demonstrated the importance of this issue.

The recently completed first Multilingual Surface Realisation Task (SR'18) (Mille et al., 2018) used for the first time inputs derived from the Universal Dependencies (UDs) (de Marneffe et al., 2014), a framework which was devised with the aim of facilitating cross-linguistically consistent grammatical annotation, and which has grown into a large-scale community effort involving more than 200 contributors, who have created over 100 treebanks in over 70 languages between them.[1] UDs provide a more general and potentially flexible input representation for surface realisation (SR). However, their use for NLG has not so far been demonstrated.

In this paper, we present the UD datasets used in the Shallow and Deep Tracks in SR'18, describe the precise conversion processes that were applied to them, and provide an assessment of their quality. Furthermore, we examine (a) the SR task in general, (b) the motivation for, and likely usefulness of, the derivation of NLG inputs from annotations in resources developed for Natural Language Understanding (NLU), (c) whether the resulting inputs supply enough information of the right kind for the final stage in the NLG process, and more tentatively, (d) what role SR is likely to play in the future in the NLG context.

Section 2 presents related work; Section 3 describes the datasets used in the two SR'18 tracks, and Section 4 provides a more procedural account of how the datasets were generated. Section 5 assesses the quality of the obtained representations,

---

[1] http://universaldependencies.org/

199

Proceedings of The 11th International Natural Language Generation Conference, pages 199–209,
Tilburg, The Netherlands, November 5-8, 2018. ©2018 Association for Computational Linguistics

while Section 6 discusses their suitability for SR and NLG more generally. Some conclusions are presented in Section 7.

2 Background

With the advent of large-scale treebanks and statistical NLG, surface realisation research turned to the use of treebank annotations, processed in various ways, as inputs to surface realisation. Annotation/sentence pairs constitute the training data, and similarity to the original sentences in the treebank is the main measure of success. A lot of this work used inputs derived from the Wall Street Journal corpus with varying amounts of information removed from the parse-tree annotations (Langkilde-Geary, 2002; Nakanishi et al., 2005; Zhong and Stent, 2005; Cahill and van Genabith, 2006; White and Rajkumar, 2009). Because of the variation among inputs, results were not entirely comparable. The first Surface Realisation Shared Task (SR'11) (Belz et al., 2011) was thus conceived with the aim of developing a common-ground input representation that would make different systems, for the first time, directly comparable. SR'11 used shallow and deep inputs for its two respective tracks, both derived from CoNLL'08 shared task data, which was in turn derived from the WSJ Corpus by automatically converting the corresponding Penn TreeBank parse trees to dependency structures (Surdeanu et al., 2008). While dependency structures offer a more flexible input structure and statistical systems, in principle, offer more robustness, the uptake of such systems as components in embedding NLG systems has been very limited.

Meanwhile, many of the more applied strands of NLG research have tended to bypass an explicit interface to surface realisation, instead mapping directly from more abstract representations of meaning to surface text. Recently, mostly under the aegis of the Generation Challenges series of shared tasks, several large-scale datasets have been made available that pair surface text with more abstract structured inputs, including:

- Weather forecast generation (Weather) dataset (Liang et al., 2009): time series from weather-related measurements;

- Abstract Meaning Representation (AMR) dataset (May and Priyadarshi, 2017): abstract predicate-argument graphs that cover several genres;

- WebNLG dataset (Gardent et al., 2017): DBpedia triples covering properties of 15 DBpedia categories;

- E2E dataset (Novikova et al., 2017): attribute-value pairs covering 8 properties related to the restaurant domain.

In all these datasets, the input structures are aligned with English sentences that match their contents. In the case of inputs coming from structured data (e.g. WebNLG, E2E, Weather, above), multiple sentences are generally paired with each input, whereas for the inputs coming from data initially annotated for Natural Language Understanding tasks (SR'11, AMR), only one reference per input is available. Both types of shared tasks (reusable surface realisation vs. task-specific generation) have been successful in terms of participation levels, and both have sizeable research communities behind them, but trainable surface realisation as a stand-alone subtask still has a way to go in terms of demonstrating its practical applicability.

3 The SR'18 Data

The First Multilingual Surface Realisation Shared Task (SR'18) ran from December 2017 to July 2018. As in SR'11, the shared task comprised two tracks with different levels of difficulty: a Shallow Track, starting from syntactic structures in which word order information has been removed and tokens have been lemmatised, and a Deep Track, which starts from more abstract structures from which, additionally, functional words (in particular, auxiliaries, functional prepositions and conjunctions) and surface-oriented morphological information have been removed.

Taking advantage of the growing availability of multilingual treebanks annotated with Universal Dependencies, the UD V2.0 treebank, as released in the context of the CoNLL 2017 shared task on multilingual dependency parsing (Zeman et al., 2017), was used. A subset of ten languages was selected that contains the necessary part-of-speech and morphological tags for the Shallow Track: Arabic, Czech, Dutch, English, Finnish, French, Italian, Portuguese, Russian and Spanish. Three of these languages, namely English, French and Spanish were used also for the Deep Track. Starting from UD structures as they appear in the treebanks, Shallow and Deep inputs

1	The	the	DET	DT	Definite=Def|PronType=Art	2	det
2	third	third	ADJ	JJ	Degree=Pos|NumType=Ord	5	nsubj_pass
3	was	be	AUX	VBD	Mood=Ind|Number=Sing|Person=3|Tense=Past|VerbForm=Fin	5	aux
4	being	be	AUX	VBG	VerbForm=Ger	5	aux_pass
5	run	run	VERB	VBN	Tense=Past|VerbForm=Part|Voice=Pass	0	root
6	by	by	ADP	IN	_	8	case
7	the	the	DET	DT	Definite=Def|PronType=Art	8	det
8	head	head	NOUN	NN	Number=Sing	5	obl
9	of	of	ADP	IN	_	12	case
10	an	a	DET	DT	Definite=Ind|PronType=Art	12	det
11	investment	investment	NOUN	NN	Number=Sing	12	compound
12	firm	firm	NOUN	NN	Number=Sing	8	nmod
13	.	.	PUNCT	.	_	5	punct

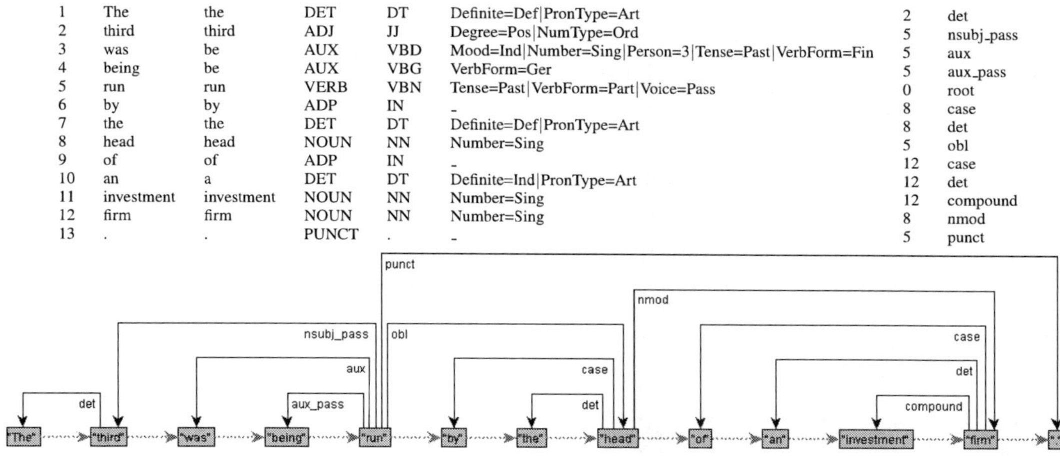

Figure 1: A sample UD structure in English (top: CoNLL-U, bottom: graphical)

1	the	_	DET	DT	Definite=Def|PronType=Art	2	det
2	third	_	ADJ	JJ	Degree=Pos|NumType=Ord	3	nsubj_pass
3	run	_	VERB	VBN	Tense=Past|VerbForm=Part|Voice=Pass	0	root
4	be	_	AUX	VBD	Mood=Ind|Number=Sing|Person=3|Tense=Past|VerbForm=Fin	3	aux
5	be	_	AUX	VBG	VerbForm=Ger	3	aux_pass
6	head	_	NOUN	NN	Number=Sing	3	obl
7	.	_	PUNCT	.	_	3	punct
8	by	_	ADP	IN	_	6	case
9	the	_	DET	DT	Definite=Def|PronType=Art	6	det
10	firm	_	NOUN	NN	Number=Sing	6	nmod
11	an	_	DET	DT	Definite=Ind|PronType=Art	10	det
12	investment	_	NOUN	NN	Number=Sing	10	compound
13	of	_	ADP	IN	_	10	case

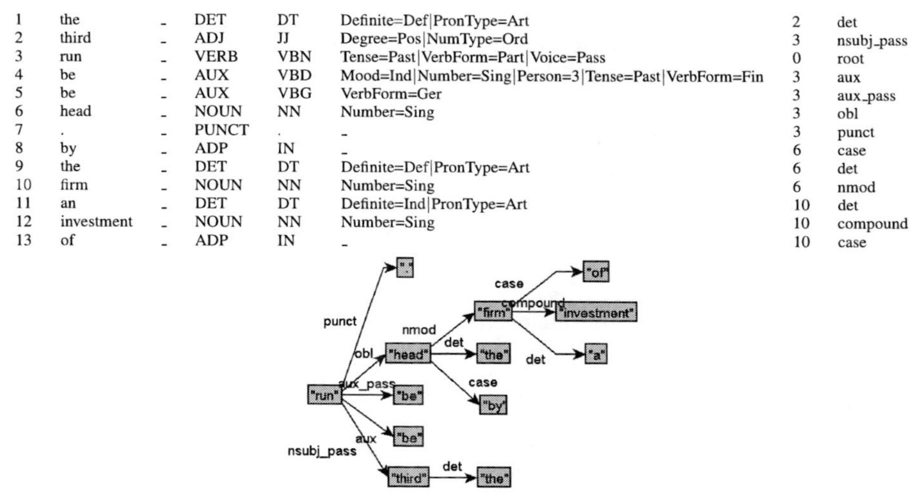

Figure 2: Shallow input (Track 1) derived from UD structure in Figure 1. (top: CoNLL-U, bottom: graphical)

were created automatically for the two tracks. The inputs for each language and track were released in the CoNLL-U format[2], together with parallel files that contain a reference sentence for each input. Figures 1, 2 and 3 show a sample original UD annotation for English, and the corresponding inputs for the Shallow and Deep Tracks, respectively, in the 10-column CoNLL-U format (the last two columns generally do not contain information and are thus omitted) and in graphical format. The training, development and test data are available at http://taln.upf.edu/pages/msr2018-ws/SRST.html#data.

[2]http://universaldependencies.org/format.html

3.1 Shallow inputs

The Shallow Track input structures are unordered syntactic trees with all the words of the sentence replaced with their lemmas, and labelled with their part-of-speech tags and the morphological information associated with each node. These structures are thus genuine UD structures, with only two differences: first, in the original CoNLL-U format, consecutive lines contain words that are also consecutive in the sentence, whereas in the SR'18 Shallow structures, no order information is available; second, original UD structures contain both lemmas and inflected forms, while only the former are available in the SR'18 structures. Fig-

1	third	_	ADJ	_	Degree=Pos	2	A2
2	run	_	VERB	_	Tense=Past|Aspect=Progr	0	ROOT
3	head	_	NOUN	_	Number=Sing|Definiteness=Def	2	A1
4	firm	_	NOUN	_	Number=Sing|Definiteness=Indef	3	A2
5	investment	_	NOUN	_	Number=Sing	4	AM

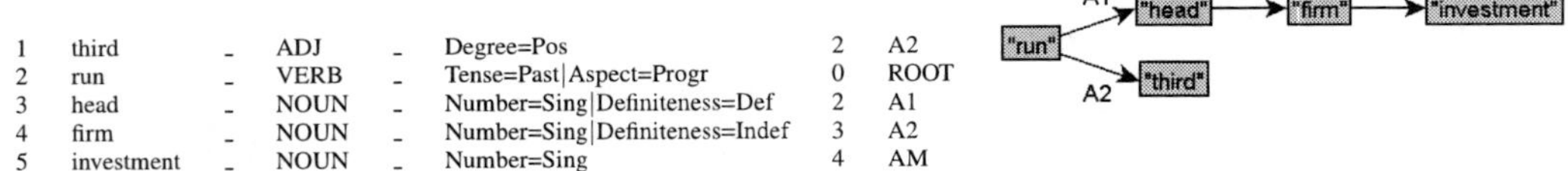

Figure 3: Deep input (Track 2) derived from UD structure in Figure 1. (left: CoNLL-U, righ: graphical)

ures 1 and 2 show an original UD structure and a SR'18 Shallow input, respectively.

3.2 Deep inputs

The Deep Track input structures are trees that contain only content words linked by predicate-argument edges, in the PropBank/NomBank (Palmer et al., 2005; Meyers et al., 2004) fashion.

The Deep inputs can be seen as closer to a realistic application context for NLG systems, in which the component that generates the inputs presumably would not have access to syntactic or language-specific information. At the same time, we used only information found in the UD structures to create the Deep inputs, and tried to keep their structure simple. In Deep inputs, words are not disambiguated, full (semantically loaded) prepositions may be missing, and some argument relations may be underspecified or missing. The next two subsections provide more details about the Deep nodes and edge labels.

3.2.1 Deep nodes

In contrast to the Shallow structures, which contain all the (lemmatised) words of the original sentence, the Deep structures do not contain functional words that can be inferred from another lexical unit or from the syntactic structure (such as bound prepositions and conjunctions), or can be represented as a feature on another node (such as auxiliaries, modals, or determiners). For instance (see also Figure 1 for the first four examples):

- the preposition *by* in the sentence *The third was being run by the head of an investment firm* is bound to the English agentive dependency in a passive construction;

- the preposition *of* in *the head of an investment firm* is bound to the noun *head*, and indicates the presence of its second argument;

- *being* in *was being run* is a passive voice marker, while *was* is part of the marker for the progressive aspect, associated with the verb *run*;

- *the* in *the head* can be seen as a marker for nominal definiteness;

- the conjunction (complementiser) *that* in, e.g., *I demand that you apologise*, appears because it connects a finite verb *apologise* as an argument of another verb *demand*.

Meaningful functional words such as auxiliaries and determiners are represented as attribute/value pairs associated with the relevant nodes, as, e.g., the *Aspect* feature on *run* in Figure 3.[3] Features are also used to encode information such as verbal tense or nominal number, which are needed for realisation. On the other hand, implicit nodes that have a role in the sentence are explicit in the Deep input: for instance, dummy pronoun nodes for the subject if an originally finite verb has no first argument and no available argument to build a passive or, for a pro-drop language such as Spanish, dummy pronouns when the first argument of a verb is missing.

3.2.2 Deep edge labels

In Deep inputs, content words are linked by predicate-argument labels in the PropBank/NomBank (Palmer et al., 2005; Meyers et al., 2004) fashion, that is, there are core (A1, A2, etc.) and non-core (AM) labels. Additional labels such as LIST or NAME have been added in order to connect all the elements within each sentence; see Table 1 for the inventory of relations. This subsection details the main features of the dependencies at this level.

First of all, the first argument is always labeled as A1, that is, there is no external argument A0, as can be found in PropBank and NomBank. For instance, both the verbs *fall* and *fancy* have a relation A1 with their first argument (*the ball*$_{A1}$ *falls*, *Martin*$_{A1}$ *fancies Chloe*), even though according to PropBank, the latter has an external argument (*Martin*$_{A0}$ *fancies Chloe*).

---

[3] For the available universal features set, see `http://universaldependencies.org/u/feat/index.html`.

Deep label	Description	Example
A1, A2, ..., A6	nth argument of a predicate	fall→ the ball
A1INV, ..., A6INV	nth inverted argument of a predicate	the ball→ fall
AM/AMINV	(i) none of governor or dependent are argument of the other (ii) unknown argument slot	fall→ last night
LIST	List of elements	fall→ [and] bounce
NAME	Part of a name	Tower→ Eiffel
DEP	Undefined dependent	N/A

Table 1: Deep labels

Second, in order to maintain the tree structure and account for some cases of shared arguments, there can be inverted argument relations. Consider, for instance, the difference between *the ball$_{A1}$ falls*, in which *ball* is the first argument of *fall*, and *the falling$_{A1INV}$ ball*, in which *fall* has the 'inverted first argument' label, which means that *ball* is actually the first argument of *fall*. Inverted relations are used also in relative clauses, as e.g., in *the ball that falls$_{A1INV}$*; in such a case, the subject (or object) relative pronoun does not appear in the structure, and the antecedent can thus be shared by two predicates, as An and AnINV.

Third, all modifier edges are assigned the same generic label AM. When an edge is underspecified, that is, when there is no predicate-argument relation between two connected nodes, or when there is a predicate-argument relation between two nodes, but it is not known which one specifically, the AM or AMINV label is used. For instance, in the case of nominal adverbials such as *last night*, the relation between the governing predicate and *night* is set as an AM. One of the most productive uses of the AM label is for prepositional groups or subordinate clauses, in which UD establishes a direct dependency between the content words that actually does not exist: *he will leave$_{Gov}$ after he finishes$_{Dep}$ his work*. In this case, *finish* is established as an AM of *leave*; note that this does not prevent the actual argumental structure from being recovered. Indeed, an edge AM that links a Governor with a Dependent and its A2INV preposition:

$$\overset{\text{AM}}{\frown}\quad\overset{\text{A2INV}}{\frown}$$
Gov Dep Prep

is equivalent to the preposition being a predicate and the Governor and Dependent being its first and second argument respectively:

$$\overset{\text{A1}}{\frown}\quad\overset{\text{A2}}{\frown}$$
Gov Prep Dep

Fourth, there are some edge labels that are not

related to predicate-argument relations: coordinated elements are linked by a dedicated edge LIST, compound named entities are linked by the edge NAME, and the edge label DEP is used in case of an unknown relation between two elements. Finally, each argument relation is unique for each predicate: if a predicate has an A2 dependent, it cannot have another A2 dependent, and it cannot be the A2INV dependent of another predicate.

In Section 4.2 below, we describe how the mapping between surface dependencies and predicate-argument labels was performed.

4 Generating the datasets

Following on from the more declarative description of Shallow and Deep inputs in the previous section, this section describes how those input were automatically created from the CoNLL'17 data.

4.1 Adaptation of the original UD structures

For the input to the Shallow Track, the UD structures were processed as follows:

1. the information on word order was removed by randomised scrambling;

2. the words were replaced by their lemmas.

For the Deep Track, additionally:

3. Functional prepositions and conjunctions in argument position, i.e. prepositions and conjunctions that can be inferred from other lexical units or from the syntactic structure, were removed; prepositions and conjunctions retained in the Deep representation can be found under an A2INV dependency;

4. Definite and indefinite determiners, auxiliaries and modals were converted into attribute/value pairs, as are definiteness features, and the universal aspect and mood features;

203

	ar	cs	en	es	fi	fr	it	nl	pt	ru
train	6,016	66,485	12,375	14,289	12,030	14,529	12,796	12,318	8,325	48,119
dev	897	9,016	1,978	1,651	1,336	1,473	562	720	559	6,441
test	676	9,876	2,061	1,719	1,525	416	480	685	476	6,366

Table 2: SR'18 dataset sizes for training, development and test sets.

5. copulas were removed and their two arguments connected with each other;

6. Subject and object relative pronouns directly linked to the main relative verb were removed (and instead, the verb is linked to the antecedent of the pronoun), and dummy pronouns were added.

7. Edge labels were generalised using the labels presented in Section 3.2.2;

8. Surface-level morphologically relevant information as prescribed by syntactic structure or agreement (such as verbal finiteness or verbal number) was removed, whereas semantic-level information such as nominal number and verbal tense was retained;

9. Fine-grained POS labels found in some treebanks (see e.g. column 5 in Figure 2) were removed, and only coarse-grained ones were retained (column 4 in Figures 2 and 3).

4.2 Generation of the inputs

Shallow Track inputs were generated with a Python script from the original UD structures, which were simply scrambled and their words replaced with lemmas. During the conversion, sentences that contained dependencies that only make sense in an analysis context were filtered out (e.g. *reparandum*, or *orphan*); this amounted to around 1.5% of sentences for all languages on average. Table 2 summarises the final size of the datasets.

Deep Track inputs were then generated by automatically processing the Shallow Track structures using a series of graph-transduction grammars (Bohnet and Wanner, 2010) that cover steps 3–9 above (in a similar fashion to Mille et al. (2017)), while ensuring a node-to-node correspondence between the Deep and Shallow structures.

The graph-transduction grammars are rules that apply to a subgraph of the input structure and produce a part of the output structure. During the application of the rules, both the input structure (covered by the left-hand side of the rule) and the current state of the output structure at the moment of application of a rule (i.e., the right-hand side of the

rule) are available as context. Figure 4 shows the rule that assigns deep dependency labels as found in the UD_lexicon dictionary; relative clause edges and adjectival modifiers are handled by different rules. The output structure in one transduction is built incrementally: the rules are all evaluated, the ones that have no right-hand side context and that match a part of the input graph are applied, and a first piece of the output graph is built; then the rules are evaluated again, this time with the right-hand side context as well, and another part of the output graph is built; and so on. The transduction is complete when no rule is left that matches the combination of the left-hand side and the right-hand side. At each iteration, the rules are first selected and then applied as a cluster, that is, the order in which they apply is not important. The only way to force a rule R2 to be applied after a rule R1 (for instance, for building edges after building the nodes) is to establish as R2's right-side condition elements built by R1: for instance, the rule shown in Figure 4 will apply only after the rules that build the nodes have applied, since the *?Xr* and *?Yr* are marked as right-side context (*rc:*). This allows the rules to be more generic and to combine with one another in an efficient way.

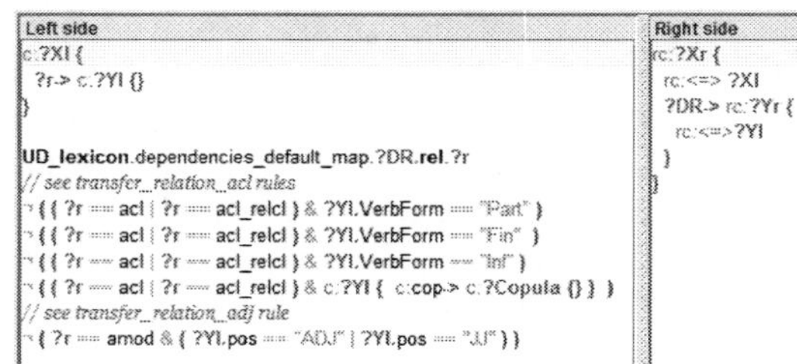

Figure 4: Sample graph transduction rule

Table 3 provides a summary of the graph-transduction grammars and rules for the mapping between surface-syntactic structures and UD-based semantic structures. The mapping is composed of three submodules. The pre-processing grammars are used to identify all nodes to be removed: it is easier and safer in the graph-transduction grammars to mark the nodes to be re-

Grammars	# rules	Description
Pre-processing	76	Identify nodes to be removed Identify verbal finiteness and tense
SSynt-Sem	120	Remove idiosyncratic nodes Establish correspondences with surface nodes Map UD labels to predicate-argument dependency labels (when possible) Predict predicate-argument dependency labels (when no direct mapping is available) Replace determiners, modality and aspect markers by attribute-value feature structures
Post-processing	60	Replace duplicated argument relations by best educated guess Identify remaining duplicated core dependency labels (for posterior debugging)

Table 3: Graph-transduction rules for producing the Deep inputs (counts include rules that simply copy node features, constituting about 40 per grammar).

moved (using solely positive conditions) and then to not generate them in the next step, than using rules that generate in one shot only the desired nodes, which would imply complex negative conditions. After this pre-processing, with the nodes that are to be removed marked, the core grammar (SSynt-Sem) takes care of establishing edge labels between the remaining nodes and associating the latter with attribute/value pairs. Most UD labels are mapped one-to-one to predicate-argument labels. In some cases only, the rules check the syntactic context of an edge in order to get a more precise label (e.g., a relative clause in which according to the structure and the UD label, we know that an argumental relation is holding: if the governor already has a first and a third arguments, the argumental relation is likely to be an A2). A post-processing grammar takes educated guesses in order to correct obvious labeling errors such as the duplication of an argument for a predicate. The unified cross-language annotation scheme of UD allows the large majority of the rules to be language-independent. Even though the annotations are not always consistent, adapting the grammars to a new language is relatively easy: most of the language-specific rules concern the processing of auxiliaries and modals, which have to be identified and mapped to the *Aspect* and *Mood* features.

5 Evaluation of the generated datasets

Since the processing applied to the Shallow inputs consists only in removing information and is very straightforward. It does not call for an evaluation. For the Deep Track, however, the changes are much more complex and the quality of the conversion needs to be assessed.

We evaluated the quality of the Deep inputs as follows. One of the authors manually annotated about 900 deep tokens ($\approx$75 sentences) in each language (English, French and Spanish), by post-editing the automatically converted structures correcting any mistakes. Since the same person post-edited all three datasets, the resulting gold-standard is consistent across the languages, even though it does not allow for calculating inter-annotator agreement. Note that the annotation remains quite open with respect to some phenomena, for which several annotations are considered correct. For instance, AM relations are left under-specified when it is not clear what argument slot is concerned (e.g., appositions, parentheticals, verbal/nominal adverbials, etc.); some argumental relations are ambiguous and left as such: $N \rightarrow ADJ$ is sometimes A1INV, and the adjective is sometimes an argument of the noun; numbers (e.g., *ten thousand people*) and hours are left as they are in the original annotations.

Once post-edited, the reference structures are compared to the ones produced by the automatic mapping from UD structures, using the LAS evaluation method of Ballesteros et al. (2015), specifically designed to handle the comparison between non-isomorphic trees. Since part of the mapping consists of adding and/or removing nodes, it often happens that the gold-standard and predicted structures end up with a different number of nodes, which makes evaluation scripts based on a strict node-to-node comparison unusable. Table 4 shows the results of the evaluation. Quality is not the same across languages: while English structures obtain an LAS of 79.83, French is more than 6 points lower, and Spanish more than 12. Since, as mentioned in the previous subsection, the mapping grammars are largely language-independent, and since roughly the same efforts have been dedicated to each language, it is likely that the LAS numbers reflect the quality of the original UD annotation.

Note that during the evaluation, POS and lemma-

	LAS
English	79.83
French	73.43
Spanish	67.28

Table 4: Evaluation of the quality of the output structures (Labeled Attachment Scores - LAS).

tisation[4] errors are not corrected, but structural errors due to original tagging/lemmatising errors are counted. In other words, what is being evaluated is how correct the outputs are in terms of dependencies and labeling, rather than how well the transduction grammars perform. An error analysis showed that most dependency errors come from the AM relation, which is usually A1, A2, A1INV or A2INV in the reference structures. The systematic replacement of AM by one of these four labels always results in a drop of the LAS score. That is, in order to improve the quality of the structures, an improvement of the UD structures or a more fine-grained processing (which would imply a large number of rules and the use of detailed lexicons) would be needed.

The mapping grammars were released together with the SR'18 datasets;[5] they can process about 39 sentences per second on an average laptop. The resulting mapping tool allows for automatically annotating large amounts of data. The tool has recently been used to convert about 600,000 English sentences that had been automatically parsed with an off-the-shelf UD parser. This tool is also currently being tested as part of conceptual relation extraction pipelines in the framework of several EU projects (see Acknowledgements).

6 Discussion

The UD-derived input structures described in this paper were successfully used in the SR'18 Shared Task, which attracted the participation of eight teams. In the Deep Track, an attempt was made to remove from inputs, as far as possible, the kind of information that cannot come from a deeper level of abstraction, such as, e.g., an ontological representation. For instance, where it was not possible, or too risky, to predict an argument slot, it was left undefined (AM label). If, because the annotation did not allow for the distinction be-

tween the two, there was a choice between leaving too many syntactic elements or removing meaningful words, the latter option was chosen. In this way, the Deep representations are much closer to the kind that might be used in a generation pipeline that starts from structured data,[6] and the tools trained on the present data can potentially be used in an applied NLG pipeline. On the other hand, the inputs can be considered less informative than those used in SR'11, in which only *that*-complementisers and *to*-infinitives were removed, and predicate-argument labels for nouns and verbs were fully specified (since they came from the NomBank and PropBank manually validated annotations). However, as is the case with the tectogrammatical layer of the Prague Dependency Treebank (Böhmová et al., 2005), in PropBank and NomBank no distinction is made between full and functional ('semantic') prepositions.[7] In contrast to AMRs, the Deep inputs do contain tense, number and definiteness information, but links to named entity databases or OntoNotes labels are not provided; in other words, the nodes are not disambiguated. The other difference to AMRs in terms of specificity is that the annotation of shared arguments is incomplete in SR'18 (an argument can only be shared by two predicates in SR'18 Deep inputs), and that the non-core relations are not typed. In terms of abstraction level, AMRs abstract the labels of nominal vs. verbal events, which is not done in the SR'18 dataset. In the SR'18 Shallow inputs, the removal of word order information is problematic for named entities, n-ary coordinations and punctuations, because it is not always possible to reconstruct the word order based on the dependencies. In order to cope with this, in SR'11, the components of named entities were numbered according to their original order, specific features encoded the bracketing information for punctuation signs, and coordinations were hierarchical, with each conjunct being a dependent of the previous conjunct.

As a result, the Deep input representation is a compromise between correctness and adequacy in a generation setup. Indeed, the conversion of the

---

[4]As in lexical reflexive verbs in French and Spanish; e.g. *aburrirse* 'to be bored' in Spanish, can end up with the lemma *aburrir*, that is, without the reflexive marker.

[5]http://taln.upf.edu/pages/msr2018-ws/SRST.html#data

[6]Note, however, that creating the Deep input structures from structured data would be far from trivial, since it would imply mapping given properties onto words as used in the UD datasets.

[7]This subcategorisation information can be partially derived from PropBank and NomBank, as done for the Deep Syntactic structures of Meaning-Text Theory (Ballesteros et al., 2015; Mille and Wanner, 2015).

UD structures into predicate-argument structures depends not only on the mapping process, but also on the availability of the information in the original annotation, even though it falls short in some cases: UD structures were not conceived for NLG applications, which is why using them in an NLG context presents considerable challenges. The underspecified UD structures created for the SR'18 Shared Task are perhaps as close as we can get to NLG-like meaning representations if all we have to construct inputs are parsing annotations from treebanks. To get even closer, the inputs would have to be enriched from additional sources of information, such as subcategorisation information, as found in PropBank or Ontonotes.

We may even be moving away from a situation where we have to rely on treebanks to obtain NLG inputs at reasonable cost, as the success of using fully automatically parsed data mentioned above shows. It is conceivable that a future shared task in NLG will involve paired (structured) data and text, plus an automatically created intermediate level of representation comprising underspecified UD (UUD) structures enriched with additional information obtained from the structured data level. This would correspond to three linked tracks (data-to-text, data-to-UUD, and UUD-to-text) where one track is the end-to-end task, and the other two tracks are subtasks that can be combined to solve the end-to-end task, similar to the GREC'10 shared task competition (Belz and Kow, 2010).

Or it could be argued, perhaps controversially still, that the days of structured linguistic representations in NLG are numbered anyway. The rapid development and spread of highly successful neural approaches to diverse NLG tasks, and the limited success so far of attempts to inject linguistic knowledge directly into neural networks, certainly lends some strength to this point of view. In the meantime, the above tripartite shared-task structure has the potential to accommodate both systems that map directly from data to text without structured representations, and two-component systems with a surface realiser as the second component.

7 Conclusion

In this paper, we have provided a detailed description of how the inputs to the Shallow and Deep Tracks at the First Multilingual Surface Re-

alisation Task were created by automatically converting annotated sentences from Universal Dependency treebanks V2.0 into Shallow and Deep Track inputs. The important contribution here is the process for creating Deep inputs, where we approximate the kind of abstract meaning representations used in native NLG tasks. This is not a simple matter of applying a few replacement rules (as it is for the Shallow inputs) with predictably correct results. To assess the quality of the Deep inputs, we conducted an evaluation that showed a labelled agreement score (LAS) of about 80 with human-corrected equivalents for English, displaying a high level of quality. However, future work will need to look at how to improve this quality further, especially for other languages, as well as to confirm what exactly the right extent of underspecification is for Deep inputs for surface realisation.

A separate question the field needs to address is to what extent *Shallow* underspecified UD inputs are suitable for surface realisation. More specifically, whether it is reasonable to expect other, content-determining, modules in an NLG system to generate such inputs. Finally, an overlapping question is whether inputs of either the Shallow or Deep type provide information that is sufficient for generating fully realised sentences, and if not, how such inputs can be enriched to provide it.

Acknowledgments

The work presented here has been supported in part by three projects funded by the European Commission: V4Design (H2020-779962-RIA), TENSOR (H2020-700024-RIA), and beAWARE (H2020-700475-RIA).

References

Miguel Ballesteros, Bernd Bohnet, Simon Mille, and Leo Wanner. 2015. Data-driven deep-syntactic dependency parsing. *Natural Language Engineering*, pages 1–36.

John Bateman. 1997. Enabling technology for multilingual natural language generation: The KPML development environment. *Natural Language Engineering Journal*, 3(1):15–55.

Anja Belz and Eric Kow. 2010. The GREC challenges 2010: Overview and evaluation results. In *Proceedings of the 6th International Natural Language Generation Conference*, INLG'10, pages 219–229, Stroudsburg, PA, USA. Association for Computational Linguistics.

Anja Belz, Michael White, Dominic Espinosa, Eric Kow, Deirdre Hogan, and Amanda Stent. 2011. The first surface realisation shared task: Overview and evaluation results. In *Proceedings of the 13th European Workshop on Natural Language Generation*, ENLG '11, pages 217–226, Stroudsburg, PA, USA. Association for Computational Linguistics.

Alena Böhmová, Silvie Cinková, and Eva Hajičová. 2005. A manual for tectogrammatical layer annotation of the Prague Dependency Treebank (English translation). Technical report, ÚFAL MFF UK, Prague, Czech Republic.

Bernd Bohnet and Leo Wanner. 2010. Open soucre graph transducer interpreter and grammar development environment. Valletta, Malta.

Aoife Cahill and Josef van Genabith. 2006. Robust PCFG-based generation using automatically acquired LFG approximations. In *Proceedings of the 21st International Conference on Computational Linguistics and the 44th annual meeting of the Association for Computational Linguistics*, pages 1033–1040. Association for Computational Linguistics.

M. Elhadad and J. Robin. 1996. An overview of SURGE: a reusable comprehensive syntactic realization component. Technical report, Ben Gurion University in the Negev.

Claire Gardent, Anastasia Shimorina, Shashi Narayan, and Laura Perez-Beltrachini. 2017. Creating training corpora for micro-planners. In *Proceedings of the 55th Annual Meeting of the Association for Computational Linguistics (Volume 1: Long Papers)*, Vancouver, Canada. Association for Computational Linguistics.

Albert Gatt and Ehud Reiter. 2009. Simplenlg: A realisation engine for practical applications. In *Proceedings of the 12th European Workshop on Natural Language Generation*, pages 90–93. Association for Computational Linguistics.

Irene Langkilde-Geary. 2002. An empirical verification of coverage and correctness for a general-purpose sentence generator. In *Proceedings of the International Natural Language Generation Conference (INLG'02)*.

Percy Liang, Michael I Jordan, and Dan Klein. 2009. Learning semantic correspondences with less supervision. In *Proceedings of the Joint Conference of the 47th Annual Meeting of the ACL and the 4th International Joint Conference on Natural Language Processing of the AFNLP: Volume 1-Volume 1*, pages 91–99. Association for Computational Linguistics.

Marie-Catherine de Marneffe, Timothy Dozat, Natalia Silveira, Katri Haverinen, Filip Ginter, Joakim Nivre, and Christopher D. Manning. 2014. Universal stanford dependencies: A cross-linguistic typology. pages 4585–4592, Reykjavik, Iceland. European Language Resources Association (ELRA). ACL Anthology Identifier: L14-1045.

Jonathan May and Jay Priyadarshi. 2017. Semeval-2017 task 9: Abstract meaning representation parsing and generation. In *Proceedings of the 11th International Workshop on Semantic Evaluation (SemEval-2017)*, pages 534–543, Vancouver, Canada. Association for Computational Linguistics.

Adam Meyers, R. Reeves, C. Macleod, R. Szekely, V. Zielinska, B. Young, and R. Grishman. 2004. The NomBank project: An interim report. In *HLT-NAACL 2004 Workshop: Frontiers in Corpus Annotation, Boston, MA, May 2004*, pages 24–31.

Simon Mille, Anja Belz, Bernd Bohnet, Yvette Graham, Emily Pitler, and Leo Wanner. 2018. The First Multilingual Surface Realisation Shared Task (SR'18): Overview and Evaluation Results. In *Proceedings of the 1st Workshop on Multilingual Surface Realisation (MSR), 56th Annual Meeting of the Association for Computational Linguistics (ACL)*, pages 1–12, Melbourne, Australia.

Simon Mille, Roberto Carlini, Ivan Latorre, and Leo Wanner. 2017. UPF at EPE 2017: Transduction-based deep analysis. In *Shared Task on Extrinsic Parser Evaluation (EPE 2017)*, pages 80–88, Pisa, Italy.

Simon Mille and Leo Wanner. 2015. Towards large-coverage detailed lexical resources for data-to-text generation. In *Proceedings of the First International Workshop on Data-to-text Generation*, Edinburgh, Scotland.

Hiroko Nakanishi, Ysuke Miyao, and Jun'ichi Tsujii. 2005. Probabilistic models for disambiguation of an HPSG-based chart generator. In *Proceedings of the International Workshop on Parsing Technologies*.

Jekaterina Novikova, Ondrej Dušek, and Verena Rieser. 2017. The E2E dataset: New challenges for end-to-end generation. In *Proceedings of the 18th Annual Meeting of the Special Interest Group on Discourse and Dialogue*, Saarbrücken, Germany. ArXiv:1706.09254.

Martha Palmer, Daniel Gildea, and Paul Kingsbury. 2005. The proposition bank: An annotated corpus of semantic roles. *Computational Linguistics*, 31(1):71–105.

Mihai Surdeanu, Richard Johansson, Adam Meyers, Lluís Màrquez, and Joakim Nivre. 2008. The CoNLL-2008 shared task on joint parsing of syntactic and semantic dependencies. In *Proceedings of the International Conference on Computational Linguistics and the Annual Meeting of the Association for Computational Linguistics (COLING-ACL'08)*.

Michael White and Rajakrishnan Rajkumar. 2009. Perceptron reranking for CCG realization. In *Proceedings of the Conference on Empirical Methods in Natural Language Processing (EMNLP'09)*.

Daniel Zeman, Martin Popel, Milan Straka, Jan Hajic, Joakim Nivre, Filip Ginter, Juhani Luotolahti, Sampo Pyysalo, Slav Petrov, Martin Potthast, et al. 2017. Conll 2017 shared task: multilingual parsing from raw text to universal dependencies. *Proceedings of the CoNLL 2017 Shared Task: Multilingual Parsing from Raw Text to Universal Dependencies*, pages 1–19.

Huayan Zhong and Amanda Stent. 2005. Building surface realizers automatically from corpora using general-purpose tools. In *Proceedings of the Workshop on Using Corpora for Natural Language Generation (UCNLG)*.

LSTM Hypertagging

Reid Fu
Department of Computer Science
The Ohio State University
`fu.349@buckeyemail.osu.edu`

Michael White
Department of Linguistics
The Ohio State University
`mwhite@ling.osu.edu`

Abstract

Hypertagging, or supertagging for surface realization, is the process of assigning lexical categories to nodes in an input semantic graph. Previous work has shown that hypertagging significantly increases realization speed and quality by reducing the search space of the realizer. Building on recent work using LSTMs to improve accuracy on supertagging for parsing, we develop an LSTM hypertagging method for OpenCCG, an open source NLP toolkit for CCG. Our results show significant improvements in both hypertagging accuracy and downstream realization performance.

1 Introduction

Hypertagging, or supertagging for surface realization, is the process of assigning lexical categories to nodes in a semantic graph as a step in grammar-based surface realization. It significantly increases realization speed and quality by reducing the search space of the realizer. Espinosa et al. (2008) built the original single-stage maximum entropy hypertagger for CCG in OpenCCG,[1] which obtained a single-best hypertagging accuracy of 93.6%. This hypertagger was later expanded into a two-stage model, which obtained a hypertagging accuracy of 95.1%.

Recent work has used neural networks to make significant improvements in supertagging for parsing (i.e., predicting lexical categories for a sequence of words), improving upon earlier work with maximum entropy supertagging (Curran et al., 2006). Lewis and Steedman (2014) used a feedforward neural network to obtain 91.3% category accuracy in the CCGBank (Hockenmaier

and Steedman, 2007) development section (Section 00). Lewis et al. (2016) improved on this result using an LSTM, obtaining 94.9% category accuracy on the development section and 94.7% on the test section (Section 23) of the CCGBank.

Our work uses techniques from Lewis et al. (2016) to implement an improved hypertagger. To do so, we first linearize the input graph using a method adapted from Konstas et al.'s (2017) approach to generating from Abstract Meaning Representations (AMRs).[2] Unlike in their work though, we found that the input ordering method substantially impacted hypertagging accuracy, with an English-like ordering yielding substantial improvements over random ordering while substantially trailing oracle ordering.

We evaluated the LSTM hypertagger on both tagging accuracy and its downstream effect on realization performance. Our results show significant improvement over the original hypertagger on both. We obtained 96.47% on tagging accuracy (up from 95.1%) and an increase in realization BLEU scores from 0.8429 with the original hypertagger to 0.8683 with the neural hypertagger. As expected, the LSTM hypertagger yielded large gains in accuracy on the difficult cases of unseen predicates and predicates not seen with the gold tag in training, helping to achieve a 7.8% increase in sentences with grammatically complete derivations. A human evaluation confirmed that using the LSTM hypertagger yielded significant improvements in adequacy and fluency, especially in cases where the LSTM hypertagger was essential for obtaining a complete derivation.

This paper is structured as follows. Section 2 provides background on surface realization with CCG, the maximum entropy hypertagger and LSTM supertagging. Section 3 describes our fea-

---

[1] `http://openccg.sf.net`

[2] `https://amr.isi.edu/`

Proceedings of The 11th International Natural Language Generation Conference, pages 210–220,
Tilburg, The Netherlands, November 5-8, 2018. ©2018 Association for Computational Linguistics

tures and model along with our approach to input linearization. The results and analysis appear in Section 4. Related work is discussed in Section 5, including where grammar-based realization stands in the current research landscape. Section 6 concludes.

2 Background

2.1 Surface Realization with OpenCCG

The OpenCCG realizer generates surface strings for input semantic dependency graphs (or logical forms) using a chart-based algorithm (White, 2006) for Combinatory Categorial Grammar (Steedman, 2000) together with a hypertagger for probabilistically assigning lexical categories to lexical predicates in the input, as noted above. An example input appears in Figure 1. In the figure, nodes correspond to discourse referents labeled with lexical predicates, and dependency relations between nodes encode argument structure; gold standard CCG lexical categories (i.e, what the hypertagger learns to predict) are also shown. Note that semantically empty function words such as infinitival-*to* are missing. Generally speaking, the semantic dependency graphs are more abstract than unordered dependency trees, but more detailed than AMRs. The grammar is extracted from a version of the CCGbank (Hockenmaier and Steedman, 2007) enhanced for realization, where the enhancements include: better analyses of punctuation (White and Rajkumar, 2008); less error prone handling of named entities (Rajkumar et al., 2009); re-inserting quotes into the CCGbank; and assignment of consistent semantic roles across diathesis alternations (Boxwell and White, 2008), using PropBank (Palmer et al., 2005).

As in other work with OpenCCG (e.g., Duan and White, 2014), we use OpenCCG's realization ranking model off the shelf in order to select preferred outputs from the chart; in particular, we use White & Rajkumar's (2009; 2012) averaged perceptron realization ranking model augmented with a large-scale 5-gram model based on the Gigaword corpus. The ranking model makes choices addressing all three interrelated sub-tasks traditionally considered part of the surface realization task in natural language generation research (Reiter and Dale, 2000): inflecting lemmas with grammatical word forms, inserting function words and linearizing the words in a grammatical and natural

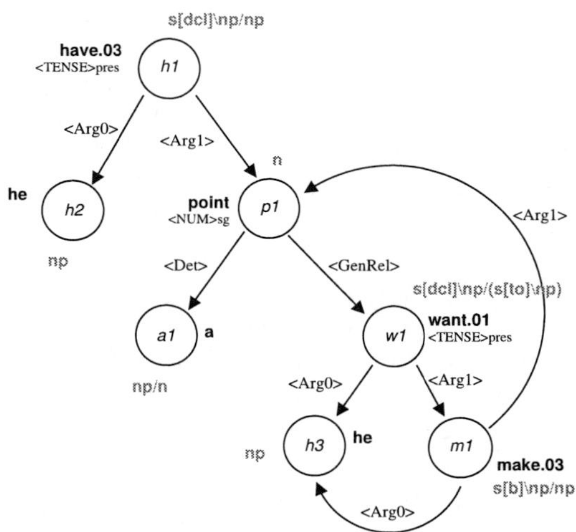

Figure 1: Example OpenCCG semantic dependency input for *he has a point he wants to make*, with gold standard lexical categories for each node

order.

Notably, to improve word ordering decisions, White & Rajkumar (2012) demonstrated that incorporating a feature into the ranker inspired by Gibson's (2000) **dependency locality theory** can deliver statistically significant improvements in automatic evaluation scores, better match the distributional characteristics of sentence orderings, and significantly reduce the number of serious ordering errors. With function words, Rajkumar and White (2011) showed that they could improve upon the earlier model's predictions for when to employ *that*-complementizers using features inspired by Jaeger's (2010) work on using the principle of **uniform information density**, which holds that human language use tends to keep information density relatively constant in order to optimize communicative efficiency.

Finally, to reduce the number of subject-verb agreement errors, Rajkumar and White (2010) extended the earlier model with features enabling it to make correct verb form choices in sentences involving complex coordinate constructions and with expressions such as *a lot of* where the correct choice is not determined solely by the head noun. They also improved animacy agreement with relativizers, reducing the number of errors where *that* or *which* was chosen to modify an animate noun rather than *who* or *whom* (and vice-versa), while also allowing both choices where corpus evidence was mixed.

211

2.2 Original Hypertagger

The original MaxEnt hypertagger uses three general types of features from logical forms: lexical features, graph structural features, and node attribute features. Lexical features are the words associated with the logical form nodes. Graph structural features are those pertaining to word dependency relations, and include the number of children (and argument children) of each node as well as the names of dependency relations. Node attribute features are those pertaining to semantic or syntactic features of words, and include tense and number.

The published single-stage MaxEnt hypertagger has an intermediate stage in which it predicts POS tags. These POS tags are then included in the feature set used to predict supertags. The two-stage hypertagger stacks on an additional stage in which predicted supertags in the local graph context are used as features for making final predictions.

The realizer uses the hypertagger in an iterative β-best algorithm in which the realizer repeatedly queries the hypertagger for β-best tags. The hypertagger has a list of β-values sorted from most restrictive to least. It first returns a β-best list of supertags for the most restrictive beta. If the realizer fails to find a complete realization with the returned supertags, it asks for the supertags associated with the next most restrictive beta, and so on until either a complete realization is found, time runs out, or there are no more betas in the list.

2.3 LSTM Supertagger

The model from Lewis et al. (2016) is summarized in Figure 2. Start and end tokens are added to each sentence. Each word in each sentence (including each start and end token) is mapped to a 50-element word embedding. Word embeddings are initialized using pre-trained word embeddings from Turian et al. (2010). Embeddings for features of the word are concatenated to the word's 50-element embedding. The concatenated embeddings are used as input to a stacked, bi-directional LSTM with depth 2. Lewis et al. used 1-4 character prefixes and suffixes as their features.

The LSTM cell used is a variant that has coupled input and forget gates. If a cell is at position t, we refer to the cell at t-1 as the *previous* cell and the cell at t+1 as the *next* cell. Each cell takes cell state c_{t-1} and hidden state h_{t-1} from the previous cell, and x_t from the previous layer, passing c_t

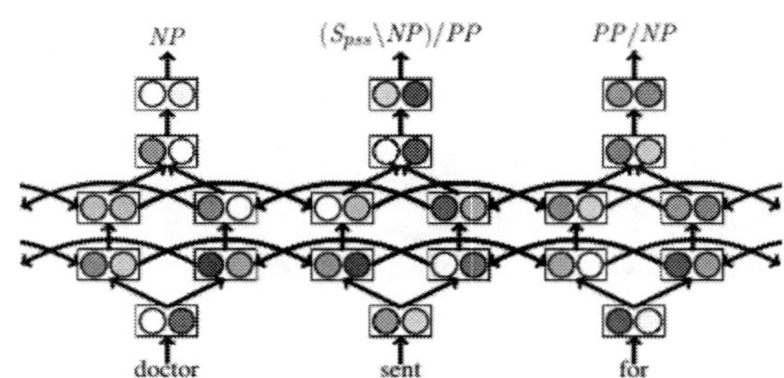

Figure 2: LSTM model used in Lewis et al. (2016) and our hypertagger (image from Lewis et al.). Concatenated embedding representations of each word are passed to stacked, bi-directional LSTM that reads sentence in both directions. Outputs of the directional LSTM's are combined. Applying a softmax over the combined outputs yields the probability distributions over supertags.

and h_t to the next cell, and h_t to the next layer. c_t and h_t are calculated as follows, with * indicating component-wise product:

$$i_t = \sigma(W_i[c_{t-1}, h_{t-1}, x_t] + b_i) \tag{1}$$

$$\tilde{c}_t = tanh(W_c[h_{t-1}, x_t] + b_{\tilde{c}}) \tag{2}$$

$$o_t = \sigma(W_o[\tilde{c}_t, h_{t-1}, x_t] + b_o) \tag{3}$$

$$c_t = i_t * \tilde{c}_t + (1 - i_t)c_{t-1} \tag{4}$$

$$h_t = o_t * tanh(c_t) \tag{5}$$

The model is trained using stochastic gradient descent with minibatch size of 1, learning rate of 0.01, and momentum of 0.7. The input layer has a dropout probability of 0.5. Order of sentences is shuffled after every epoch. We retained these settings for our hypertagger experiments.[3]

The outputs of the LSTM are passed to another hidden layer, a bias is added, and a rectified linear function is applied. The result is a set of logits that give the probability distributions over supertags for each word when passed to a softmax.

3 Approach

3.1 Features

We use a subset of the features from the original MaxEnt hypertagger (shown below). If a node has fewer than five parent or child relations, the val-

---

[3] As an anonymous reviewer points out, the training would be faster with a larger minibatch size, and inference would be faster using highly optimized implementations of standard LSTM cells.

ues of the missing relations were set to the empty string. This kept the size of the input constant.

- **Lexical Features**: Lemmatized words associated with elementary predication nodes

- **Node Attribute Features**: Named entity category, determiner, mood, number, particle, tense

- **Graph Structural Features**: Number of children, number of argument children, names of 5 parent relations, names of 5 child relations

Our hypertagger does not include a stage for predicting POS tags or for using the predicted supertags as features in a stacked model. The recurrent nature of the bi-LSTMs means that the node-level representations informing supertag prediction can be propagated to nearby nodes in the model.

Features were extracted from logical forms corresponding to Section 00 and Sections 02 to 21. Section 00 was used as the development set, and has 1883 sentences and 36,247 nodes. Sections 02 to 21 were used as the training set, and have a total of 35,765 sentences and 680,705 nodes.

3.2 Input Linearization

Each logical form was converted to a sequence of nodes, with each node containing all features discussed in the last sub-section. We refer to this conversion process as input linearization. Early experiments showed that the order of nodes in the linearized sequence made a significant difference in accuracy. Oracle linearization, in which nodes are ordered according to the order of words in the original sentence, outperformed random linearization by about 5%. Depth-first search linearization, in which the parent node came before all the child nodes and the child nodes were in random order relative to each other, improved over random linearization by about 2%. These experiments showed that more English-like input linearizations led to higher performance.

To approximate English ordering, we developed a heuristic of how nodes and their children should be ordered. The heuristic was applied recursively from the root node(s) of the logical form down to the leaves. The child ordering is shown below. The heuristic performed around 3% higher than random linearization, and around 2% lower than oracle linearization.

1. Determiner (Det) child

2. Possessor (GenOwn) child

3. First argument (Arg0)

4. One or two word modifiers

5. Parent node

6. Remaining arguments in order of argument number (Arg1, ..., Arg5)

7. Remaining children sorted ascending by subtree size. If two child subtrees have the same size, the one with a lesser sum of predicate name lengths comes before the other.

Konstas et al. (2017) were able to improve their model by adding parentheses and relation names into their AMR linearization sequence. We experimented with both. Adding parentheses around subsequences corresponding to subtrees of size five or more consistently resulted in an improvement of 0.2%. Adding relation names to the linearization sequence resulted in either no improvement or a slight decrease in accuracy.

3.3 Model

We adapted the bi-LSTM model from Lewis et al. (2016) to use our features and list of possible supertags. Each feature value was mapped to a feature embedding. Embeddings for lexical features were initialized using pre-trained word embeddings. Embeddings for other features were randomly initialized 8-element vectors. The embeddings for other features were concatenated onto the embeddings for lexical features, and the concatenated embeddings were used as input to the bi-LSTM.

We experimented with two sets of pre-trained word embeddings: those that were used in Lewis et al., which were of size 50, and a custom set, which were of size 100. Early experiments showed that performance was similar for both sets. Later experiments exclusively used the set used in Lewis et al.

Sentences with linearized sequences longer than 180 tokens (nodes and parentheses) were filtered out of the training and development sets. This filter removed one sentence from the development set, leaving it with 1882 sentences and 36,103 nodes.

Our list of possible supertags was originally of size 1210. We experimented with filtering the tags: tags that occurred fewer than 5 times in the training set were not listed as possible supertags. Instead, when a rare tag is encountered, it was replaced with the unknown tag and the associated word was counted as wrong in the accuracy. We found that filtering tags boosted performance. Our filtered list of possible supertags is of size 528. There were 1543 words in the training set and 88 words in the development set with gold tags filtered out.

The model was trained on the training set, and evaluated on the development set every 2 minutes during training. Training was run until either 7 hours had elapsed, or accuracy had not improved for 30 evaluations. Typically, training ran between 30 and 36 epochs.

3.4 Realization

The realizer is implemented in Java, while the LSTM model is implemented in Python. To establish communication between the realizer and the hypertagger, we used a server thread to run the LSTM model. The realizer got supertags from the hypertagger by running a client thread, then parsing the results returned by it. The LSTM hypertagger was otherwise used in the same way as the original MaxEnt hypertagger, with the realizer calling the hypertagger in an iterative β-best algorithm.

4 Results and Discussion

The LSTM hypertagger was tested against the original, baseline hypertagger on both tagging accuracy and downstream effect on realizer performance. Tagging accuracy was evaluated on Section 00, and realizer performance was evaluated on Sections 00 and 23. The lists of β-values for the LSTM hypertagger and baseline two-stage MaxEnt hypertagger were adjusted so that both would on average return about the same number of tags per word as the published single-stage MaxEnt hypertagger at each corresponding β-level. Section 00 was used to tune the list of β-values for the LSTM hypertagger.

4.1 Hypertagging Accuracy

The comparison in hypertagging accuracy is summarized in Table 1. In comparison to previously published results, the LSTM hypertagger achieves a nearly 3% absolute increase in single-best tagging accuracy, and achieves 99% accuracy at a multitagging level of only 1.2 tags per predicate, in comparison to 3.2 tags per predicate previously. Single-best tagging accuracy for the LSTM hypertagger had a mean of 96.384% and a variance of 0.031% (statistics taken over the six most recent runs). Figures in Table 1 are for one of the higher-performing runs.

We were interested in how the hypertaggers would perform on hard cases such as predicates that appeared in the development set but not in training, as well as predicates that appeared in training, but not with the correct tag in the development set. On these hard cases, our model obtained accuracies of 98.69% and 80.13%, respectively, while the two-stage MaxEnt hypertagger obtained accuracies of 94.58% and 69.96%, respectively. These improvements represent very large respective reductions in error of 76% and 34%. These results are summarized in Table 2.

The difference in accuracy between the LSTM hypertagger with English-like input linearization and the LSTM hypertagger with oracle input linearization is largely attributed to imperfections in the English-like linearization. There were many cases in which the English-like input linearization reversed the order between two phrases (e.g. *take these events place ago years, you but have to recognize*) or between two words in a phrase (e.g. *three times than more, among of us those*). In many of these cases, the hypertagger still predicted the correct tags despite the word order switches. For the words that the hypertagger did not tag correctly, when the word order switch was still grammatical, the assigned supertag was often similar enough to the gold tag to not significantly impact realization. By contrast, when the word order switch was ungrammatical, the assigned supertag was sometimes very different from the gold tag, which impacted realization negatively.

4.2 Realization Performance

The comparison in realization performance is summarized in Table 3. Using the LSTM hypertagger, the realizer obtained complete derivations for more than 6% more realizations (more than 100 more logical forms) in both the development and test sections. The increase in the number of complete derivations helped achieve a more than 2.5% absolute increase in BLEU scores for both

Tags/Pred	LSTM		MaxEnt1	
	β	Accuracy	β	Accuracy
1	1.0	96.5	1.0	93.6
1.1	0.13	98.5	0.16	95.8
1.2	0.04	99.0	0.05	96.6
1.5	7e-3	99.4	5.8e-3	97.9
1.8	2.8e-3	99.5	1.75e-3	98.4
2.2	1.27e-3	99.6	6.25e-4	98.7
3.2	3.65e-4	99.7	1.25e-4	99.0
3.9	2e-4	99.7	5.8e-5	99.1

Table 1: Comparison of tagging accuracies between LSTM hypertagger and published single-stage MaxEnt hypertagger on the development section (Section 00) of CCGBank. Results (in percentages) are for per-predicate tagging accuracies.

	LSTM	MaxEnt2
Unseen Predicates	98.69	94.58
Unseen Predicate-Tag Pairs	80.13	69.96

Table 2: Comparison of tagging accuracies between LSTM hypertagger and unpublished two-stage MaxEnt hypertagger on hard cases in the development set, namely predicates that are not seen in training and predicates that are seen in training but not with correct supertag.

sections.

Most of the incomplete or suboptimal realizations made with the LSTM hypertagger occurred due to one or more of the following reasons. Some sentences had several words in which the correct tag was in the list of β-best tags for the least restrictive beta, but had a low probability. This caused the realizer to time out due to the large size of the search space. Others had a single word in which the correct tag was not in the β-best tag list for the least restrictive beta. Instead there were many tags in the list that were similar to the gold tag, but that did not allow a complete realization. For example, the word *recognize* in the sentence *but you have to recognize that these events took place 35 years ago* had a gold tag of s[b]\np/s[em] (a bare verb subcategorizing for an embedded clause), but had a single-best assigned tag of s[b]\np (a bare intransitive verb), making it impossible to derive a constituent containing the embedded clause. These errors were likely caused by imperfections in the English-like input linearization. For the example above, the input linearization placed *recognize* at the end of the sequence, with no subsequent predicates to help predict the gold tag. Another reason for incomplete or suboptimal realizations is that the hyper-

tagger can't predict certain low-frequency tags, so some words will not have the correct tag in their β-best tag list regardless of the β value.

4.3 Human Evaluation

We also did a targeted human evaluation to determine whether the improvements in hypertagging accuracy generally led to noticeable improvements in realization quality, especially where it enabled a complete realization to be found.[4] Our procedure was as follows. We randomly chose 100 sentences from the devset where the realizations differed between using the LSTM hypertagger and the baseline two-stage MaxEnt hypertagger. 50 of the sentences were ones for which one system got a complete realization but the other did not—where we expected to find substantial differences—while the other 50 were ones for which either both systems got a complete realization or both did not get a complete realization. We generated a spreadsheet with the following columns: Reference sentence, Realization A, Realization B, Adequacy, and Fluency. Which system was A for each sentence was randomized,

---

[4]The complete set of examples and the evaluation script are available in the following supplement to the paper: https://osf.io/a4czs/?view_only= b7a0a49046a0408bb844ff7ea63c4e08

Section	LSTM			MaxEnt2		
	BLEU	Complete	Exact	BLEU	Complete	Exact
00	0.8783	90.38	49.36	0.8458	83.86	45.62
23	0.8683	87.75	48.35	0.8429	81.69	44.16

Table 3: Comparison in realization performance between systems using the LSTM and two-stage Max-Ent hypertaggers. The 'Complete' column indicates the percentage of logical forms realized with a complete (non-fragmentary) derivation, while the 'Exact' column indicates the percentage of realizations that exactly matched the reference sentence.

as was the order of sentences. A separate key file kept track of which system was A for each sentence, and which sentence belonged to which of the above sets of 50. Two linguists who had no familiarity with the research evaluated the realizations, marking in the Adequacy and Fluency columns whether they believed A or B was better in adequacy and fluency, respectively, or whether they were equally good for one or both measures. Raw agreement was relatively high, with the two judges agreeing on adequacy 70% of the time and fluency 73% of the time. However, nearly all the disagreements involved cases where only one judge found the pair of realizations to be the same on adequacy or fluency; on the subset of items where neither judge found the pair to be equal, agreement was 96% for adequacy and 95% for fluency.

The results of the human evaluations are summarized in Table 4. For the sentences where only one system produced a complete realization (Set 1), the LSTM hypertagger system outperformed the baseline one most of the time on both adequacy and fluency. For the other sentences (Set 2), the two systems were mostly tied on adequacy and fluency, but when the realizations were of distinct quality, the LSTM hypertagger system usually outperformed the original one. All differences in the counts of Better/Worse judgments were highly significant ($p < 0.001$, sign test).

Examples of the changes yielded by the LSTM hypertagger appear in Table 5, where the first two examples improve both adequacy and fluency, the next example makes adequacy and fluency worse, and the final one leaves adequacy and fluency the same. With wsj_0080.21, it seems that the two-stage MaxEnt system failed to match the subject with the verb, yielding a realization where *respond* doesn't have a subject and *them* is not clearly linked with its antecedent. With wsj_0004.8, the LSTM system switched *yields* and *nevertheless*,

making a realization that's different from the original sentence, but still grammatical. The two-stage MaxEnt system seemed to have trouble combining the words *yields*, *nevertheless*, and *may*, making a realization that gives an awkward order for these words and splits the sentence with the phrase *said Brenda Malizia Negus* at an awkward place; moreover, with *may* appearing initially, the sentence can be read as a wish rather than a declarative statement. With wsj_0097.19, the LSTM system incorrectly inverts the main subject and verb, and makes several other word order mistakes. Finally, wsj_0037.9 is an example where leaving out the complementizer *that* or the contraction does not substantially affect adequacy or fluency (though the reference sentence arguably makes the best choices here). More generally, while the choice whether to include a *that*-complementizer occasionally made a crucial difference, they were a frequent source of insubstantial differences, along with contractions and adverbial placement. There were also cases where both realizations made distinct but important mistakes that yielded equally bad realizations.

5 Related Work

Hypertagging can potentially benefit other grammar-based methods using lexicalized grammars, e.g. using HPSG (Velldal and Oepen, 2005; Carroll and Oepen, 2005; Nakanishi et al., 2005) or TAG (Gardent and Perez-Beltrachini, 2017). Much recent work in NLG (Wen et al., 2015; Dušek and Jurcicek, 2016; Mei et al., 2016; Kiddon et al., 2016; Konstas et al., 2017; Wiseman et al., 2017) has made use of neural sequence-to-sequence methods for generation rather than grammar-based methods. The learning flexibility of neural methods make it possible to develop very knowledge lean systems, but they continue to suffer from a tendency to hallucinate content and have not been used with texts exhibiting

216

Set	Adequacy			Fluency		
	Better	Same	Worse	Better	Same	Worse
1 ($\pm$complete)	84	12	4	88	7	5
2 (=complete)	31	62	7	37	52	11

Table 4: Results (counts of judgments) of human evaluations of realizations, which indicate how often the new system produced better, same, and worse realizations for the given aspect. Set 1 is the set of sentences in which one system had a complete realization while the other did not. Set 2 is the set of sentences in which either both systems had complete realizations or both did not.

wsj_0080.21	it was n't clear **how NL and Mr. Simmons would respond** if Georgia Gulf spurns them again .
LSTM	[same]
MAXENT2	it was n't clear **how to would respond** if Georgia Gulf spurns them again **NL and Mr. Simmons** .
wsj_0004.8	nevertheless , said Brenda Malizia Negus , editor of Money Fund Report , yields may blip up again before they blip down because of recent rises in short-term interest rates .
LSTM	**yields nevertheless may** blip up again before they blip down because of recent rises in short-term interest rates , said Brenda Malizia Negus , editor of Money Fund Report .
MAXENT2	**may nevertheless yields** , said Brenda Malizia Negus , editor of Money Fund Report , again blip up before they blip down because of recent rises in short-term interest rates .
wsj_0097.19	-lrb- Morgan Stanley last week joined a growing list of U.S. securities firms that have stopped doing index arbitrage for their own accounts . -rrb-
LSTM	**last week joined Morgan Stanley** . U.S. securities firms that growing a list of has stopped doing index arbitrage for their own accounts
MAXENT2	-lrb- **Morgan Stanley last week joined** a growing list of U.S. securities firms that have stopped doing index arbitrage for their own accounts .
wsj_0037.9	if " a Wild Sheep Chase " carries an implicit message for international relations , it 's that the Japanese are more like us than most of us think .
LSTM	if " a Wild Sheep Chase " carries an implicit message for international relations , **it 's the Japanese** are more like us than most of us think .
MAXENT2	if " a Wild Sheep Chase " carries an implicit message for international relations , **it is that the Japanese** are more like us than most of us think .

Table 5: Examples of devset sentences where the LSTM hypertagger improved adequacy/fluency (top), made it worse (middle) or left it the same (bottom).

the full complexity of genres such as news text. Approaches based on dependency grammar (Guo et al., 2008; Bohnet et al., 2010, 2011; Zhang and Clark, 2015; Liu et al., 2015; Puduppully et al., 2016, 2017; King and White, 2018) are also simpler than constraint-based grammar approaches, making them more robust to unexpected inputs and easier to deploy across languages, but it is difficult to determine whether they can fully substitute for precise grammars because these approaches have not used compatible inputs.

Although approaches using constraint-based grammars are clearly more difficult to implement and deploy, there is some evidence that they are beneficial for parsing, while for realization the question remains largely open. For parsing, Buys and Blunsom (2017) have recently shown that even though their incremental neural semantic graph parser substantially outperforms standard attentional sequence-to-sequence models, it still lags 4-6% behind an HPSG parser using a simple log-linear model (Toutanova et al., 2005) on a variety of parsing accuracy measures on DeepBank (Flickinger et al., 2012), a conversion of the Penn Treebank to Minimal Recursion Semantics (Copestake et al., 2005, MRS). The MRS representations in DeepBank are qualitatively similar to the OpenCCG semantic graphs used in this work, which are again qualitatively similar to the deep representations used in the First Surface Realization Shared Task (Belz et al., 2010, 2011). On the deep shared task representations, Bohnet et al. (2011) achieved a BLEU score of 0.7943, which Puduppully et al. (2017) later improved upon with a score of 0.8077. These scores are substantially lower than our BLEU score of 0.8683 reported here, though since the inputs are not exactly the same, the BLEU scores are of course not directly comparable.

Given the flexibility of neural methods, it would be interesting in future work to examine how well neural sequence-to-sequence generation methods would fare in a direct, head-to-head comparison using the kinds of detailed, deep inputs used with HPSG and CCG. To the extent that neural approaches continue to hallucinate content and fail to observe constraints and preferences implemented by grammar-based approaches in such a comparison, it would also be worthwhile to investigate additional ways of combining neural and grammar-based methods.

6   Conclusion

We have implemented a new LSTM hypertagger that significantly outperforms the existing OpenCCG hypertagger on both tagging accuracy and its downstream effect on realization performance. Since we have observed that the order in which input nodes are linearized substantially affects tagging accuracy, in future work we would like to explore whether graph-based neural tagging methods could yield further improvements in performance. Another direction of interest is exploring ways of incorporating hypertagging into architectures that synergistically combine grammar-based and neural generation methods.

Acknowledgments

We thank the OSU Clippers Group, Alan Ritter and the anonymous reviewers for helpful comments and discussion, and Sarah Ewing and Amad Hussain for their assistance with the evaluation. This work was supported in part by NSF grant IIS-1319318.

References

Anja Belz, Michael White, Dominic Espinosa, Eric Kow, Deirdre Hogan, and Amanda Stent. 2011. The first surface realisation shared task: Overview and evaluation results. In *Proceedings of the 13th European Workshop on Natural Language Generation*, pages 217–226. Association for Computational Linguistics.

Anja Belz, Mike White, Josef van Genabith, Deirdre Hogan, and Amanda Stent. 2010. Finding common ground: Towards a surface realisation shared task. In *Proceedings of INLG-10, Generation Challenges*, pages 267–272.

Bernd Bohnet, Simon Mille, Benoît Favre, and Leo Wanner. 2011. Stumaba : From deep representation to surface. In *Proceedings of the 13th European Workshop on Natural Language Generation*, pages 232–235. Association for Computational Linguistics.

Bernd Bohnet, Leo Wanner, Simon Mill, and Alicia Burga. 2010. Broad coverage multilingual deep sentence generation with a stochastic multi-level realizer. In *Proceedings of the 23rd International Conference on Computational Linguistics (Coling 2010)*, pages 98–106. Coling 2010 Organizing Committee.

Stephen Boxwell and Michael White. 2008. Projecting Propbank roles onto the CCGbank. In *Proc. LREC-08*.

Jan Buys and Phil Blunsom. 2017. Robust incremental neural semantic graph parsing. In *Proceedings of the 55th Annual Meeting of the Association for Computational Linguistics (Volume 1: Long Papers)*, pages 1215–1226. Association for Computational Linguistics.

John Carroll and Stefan Oepen. 2005. High efficiency realization for a wide-coverage unification grammar. In *Proc. IJCNLP-05*.

Ann Copestake, Dan Flickinger, Carl Pollard, and Ivan A Sag. 2005. Minimal recursion semantics: An introduction. *Research on language and computation*, 3(2-3):281–332.

James R. Curran, Stephen Clark, and David Vadas. 2006. Multi-tagging for lexicalized-grammar parsing. In *Proc. COLING-ACL '06*.

Manjuan Duan and Michael White. 2014. That's Not What I Meant! Using Parsers to Avoid Structural Ambiguities in Generated Text. In *Proceedings of the 52nd Annual Meeting of the Association for Computational Linguistics (Volume 1: Long Papers)*, pages 413–423, Baltimore, Maryland. Association for Computational Linguistics.

Ondřej Dušek and Filip Jurcicek. 2016. Sequence-to-sequence generation for spoken dialogue via deep syntax trees and strings. In *Proceedings of the 54th Annual Meeting of the Association for Computational Linguistics (Volume 2: Short Papers)*, pages 45–51. Association for Computational Linguistics.

Dominic Espinosa, Michael White, and Dennis Mehay. 2008. Hypertagging: Supertagging for surface realization with CCG. In *Proceedings of ACL-08: HLT*, pages 183–191, Columbus, Ohio. Association for Computational Linguistics.

Dan Flickinger, Yi Zhang, and Valia Kordoni. 2012. DeepBank. A dynamically annotated treebank of the Wall Street Journal. In *Proceedings of the 11th International Workshop on Treebanks and Linguistic Theories*, pages 85–96.

Claire Gardent and Laura Perez-Beltrachini. 2017. A statistical, grammar-based approach to microplanning. *Computational Linguistics*, 43(1).

Edward Gibson. 2000. Dependency locality theory: A distance-based theory of linguistic complexity. In Alec Marantz, Yasushi Miyashita, and Wayne O'Neil, editors, *Image, Language, brain: Papers from the First Mind Articulation Project Symposium*. MIT Press, Cambridge, MA.

Yuqing Guo, Josef van Genabith, and Haifeng Wang. 2008. Dependency-based n-gram models for general purpose sentence realisation. In *Proc. COLING-08*.

Julia Hockenmaier and Mark Steedman. 2007. CCGbank: A Corpus of CCG Derivations and Dependency Structures Extracted from the Penn Treebank. *Computational Linguistics*, 33(3):355–396.

T. Florian Jaeger. 2010. Redundancy and reduction: Speakers manage information density. *Cognitive Psychology*, 61(1):23–62.

Chloé Kiddon, Luke Zettlemoyer, and Yejin Choi. 2016. Globally coherent text generation with neural checklist models. In *Proceedings of the 2016 Conference on Empirical Methods in Natural Language Processing*, pages 329–339. Association for Computational Linguistics.

David King and Michael White. 2018. The osu realizer for srst '18: Neural sequence-to-sequence inflection and incremental locality-based linearization. In *Proceedings of the First Workshop on Multilingual Surface Realisation*, pages 39–48. Association for Computational Linguistics.

Ioannis Konstas, Srinivasan Iyer, Mark Yatskar, Yejin Choi, and Luke Zettlemoyer. 2017. Neural amr: Sequence-to-sequence models for parsing and generation. In *Proceedings of the 55th Annual Meeting of the Association for Computational Linguistics (Volume 1: Long Papers)*, pages 146–157. Association for Computational Linguistics.

Mike Lewis, Kenton Lee, and Luke Zettlemoyer. 2016. Lstm ccg parsing. In *Proceedings of the 2016 Conference of the North American Chapter of the Association for Computational Linguistics: Human Language Technologies*, pages 221–231. Association for Computational Linguistics.

Mike Lewis and Mark Steedman. 2014. Improved CCG parsing with semi-supervised supertagging. *TACL*.

Yijia Liu, Yue Zhang, Wanxiang Che, and Bing Qin. 2015. Transition-based syntactic linearization. In *Proceedings of NAACL*, Denver, Colorado, USA.

Hongyuan Mei, Mohit Bansal, and R. Matthew Walter. 2016. What to talk about and how? selective generation using lstms with coarse-to-fine alignment. In *Proceedings of the 2016 Conference of the North*

American Chapter of the Association for Computational Linguistics: Human Language Technologies, pages 720–730. Association for Computational Linguistics.

Hiroko Nakanishi, Yusuke Miyao, and Jun'ichi Tsujii. 2005. Probabilistic methods for disambiguation of an HPSG-based chart generator. In *Proc. IWPT-05*.

Martha Palmer, Dan Gildea, and Paul Kingsbury. 2005. The proposition bank: A corpus annotated with semantic roles. *Computational Linguistics*, 31(1).

Ratish Puduppully, Yue Zhang, and Manish Shrivastava. 2016. Transition-based syntactic linearization with lookahead features. In *Proceedings of the 2016 Conference of the North American Chapter of the Association for Computational Li nguistics: Human Language Technologies*, pages 488–493, San Diego, California. Association for Computational Linguistics.

Ratish Puduppully, Yue Zhang, and Manish Shrivastava. 2017. Transition-based deep input linearization. In *Proceedings of the 15th Conference of the European Chapter of the Association for Computational Linguistics: Volume 1, Long Papers*, pages 643–654. Association for Computational Linguistics.

Rajakrishnan Rajkumar and Michael White. 2010. Designing agreement features for realization ranking. In *Proc. Coling 2010: Posters*, pages 1032–1040, Beijing, China.

Rajakrishnan Rajkumar and Michael White. 2011. Linguistically motivated complementizer choice in surface realization. In *Proceedings of the UC-NLG+Eval: Language Generation and Evaluation Workshop*, pages 39–44, Edinburgh, Scotland. Association for Computational Linguistics.

Rajakrishnan Rajkumar, Michael White, and Dominic Espinosa. 2009. Exploiting named entity classes in CCG surface realization. In *Proc. NAACL HLT 2009 Short Papers*.

Ehud Reiter and Robert Dale. 2000. *Building Natural-Language Generation Systems*. Cambridge University Press.

Mark Steedman. 2000. *The syntactic process*. MIT Press, Cambridge, MA, USA.

Kristina Toutanova, Christopher D Manning, Dan Flickinger, and Stephan Oepen. 2005. Stochastic hpsg parse disambiguation using the redwoods corpus. *Research on Language and Computation*, 3(1):83–105.

Erik Velldal and Stefan Oepen. 2005. Maximum entropy models for realization ranking. In *Proc. MT-Summit X*.

Tsung-Hsien Wen, Milica Gasic, Nikola Mrkšić, Pei-Hao Su, David Vandyke, and Steve Young. 2015. Semantically conditioned lstm-based natural language generation for spoken dialogue systems. In *Proceedings of the 2015 Conference on Empirical Methods in Natural Language Processing*, pages 1711–1721. Association for Computational Linguistics.

Michael White. 2006. Efficient Realization of Coordinate Structures in Combinatory Categorial Grammar. *Research on Language & Computation*, 4(1):39–75.

Michael White and Rajakrishnan Rajkumar. 2008. A more precise analysis of punctuation for broad-coverage surface realization with CCG. In *Coling 2008: Proceedings of the workshop on Grammar Engineering Across Frameworks*, pages 17–24.

Michael White and Rajakrishnan Rajkumar. 2009. Perceptron reranking for CCG realization. In *Proceedings of the 2009 Conference on Empirical Methods in Natural Language Processing*, pages 410–419, Singapore. Association for Computational Linguistics.

Michael White and Rajakrishnan Rajkumar. 2012. Minimal dependency length in realization ranking. In *Proceedings of the 2012 Joint Conference on Empirical Methods in Natural Language Processing and Computational Natural Language Learning*, pages 244–255, Jeju Island, Korea. Association for Computational Linguistics.

Sam Wiseman, Stuart M. Shieber, and Alexander M. Rush. 2017. Challenges in data-to-document generation. In *Proceedings of the 2017 Conference on Empirical Methods in Natural Language Processing*. Association for Computational Linguistics.

Yue Zhang and Stephen Clark. 2015. Syntax-based word ordering using learning-guided search. *Computational Linguistics*, 41(3).

Sequence-to-Sequence Models for Data-to-Text Natural Language Generation: Word- vs. Character-based Processing and Output Diversity

Glorianna Jagfeld, Sabrina Jenne, Ngoc Thang Vu
Institute for Natural Language Processing (IMS)
Universität Stuttgart, Germany
{jagfelga,beersa,thangvu}@ims.uni-stuttgart.de

Abstract

We present a comparison of word-based and character-based sequence-to-sequence models for data-to-text natural language generation, which generate natural language descriptions for structured inputs. On the datasets of two recent generation challenges, our models achieve comparable or better automatic evaluation results than the best challenge submissions. Subsequent detailed statistical and human analyses shed light on the differences between the two input representations and the diversity of the generated texts. In a controlled experiment with synthetic training data generated from templates, we demonstrate the ability of neural models to learn novel combinations of the templates and thereby generalize beyond the linguistic structures they were trained on.

1 Introduction

Natural language generation (NLG) is an actively researched task, which according to Gatt and Krahmer (2018) can be divided into text-to-text generation, such as machine translation (Koehn, 2017), text summarization (See et al., 2017), or open-domain conversation response generation (Vinyals and Le, 2015) on the one hand, and data-to-text generation on the other hand. Here, we focus on the latter, the task of generating textual descriptions for structured data. Data-to-text generation comprises the generation of system responses based on dialog acts in task-oriented dialog systems (Wen et al., 2015b), sport games reports and weather forecasts (Angeli et al., 2010), and database entry descriptions (Gardent et al., 2017a). In this paper, we focus on sentence planning and surface realization. We build on data-to-

text datasets of two recent shared tasks for end-to-end NLG, namely the E2E challenge (Novikova et al., 2017b) and WebNLG challenge (Gardent et al., 2017b). Example input-text pairs for both datasets are shown in Figure 1.

Neural sequence to sequence (Seq2Seq) models (Graves, 2013; Sutskever et al., 2014) have shown promising results for this task, especially in combination with an attention mechanism (Bahdanau et al., 2014; Luong et al., 2015). Several recent NLG approaches (Dušek and Jurcícek, 2016; Mei et al., 2016; Kiddon et al., 2016; Agarwal and Dymetman, 2017), as well as most systems in the E2E and WebNLG challenge are based on this architecture. While most NLG models generate text word by word, promising results were also obtained by encoding the input and generating the output text character-by-character (Lipton et al., 2015; Goyal et al., 2016; Agarwal and Dymetman, 2017). Five out of 62 E2E challenge submissions operate on the character-level. However, it is difficult to draw conclusions from the challenge results with respect to this difference, since the submitted systems also differ in other aspects and were evaluated on a single dataset only.

Besides adequacy and fluency, variation is an important aspect in NLG (Stent et al., 2005). In addition to comparing the linguistic and content-wise correctness of word- and character-based Seq2Seq models through automatic and human evaluation, we investigate the variety of their outputs. While template-based systems can assure perfect content and linguistic quality, they often suffer from low diversity. Conversely, neural models might generalize beyond a limited amount of training texts or templates, thereby producing more diverse outputs. To test this hypothesis, we train Seq2Seq models on template-generated texts with a controlled amount of variation and show that they not only reproduce the templates, but also

Proceedings of The 11th International Natural Language Generation Conference, pages 221–232,
Tilburg, The Netherlands, November 5-8, 2018. ©2018 Association for Computational Linguistics

E2E input: name[Midsummer House], customer rating [average], near [The Bakers]
reference 1: Customers gave Midsummer House, near The Bakers, a 3 out of 5 rating.
reference 2: Midsummer house has an average customer rating and is near The Bakers.
delexicalized input: name[NAME], customer rating [average], near [NEAR]
delexicalized reference 1: Customers gave NAME, near NEAR, a 3 out of 5 rating.

WebNLG input: cityServed(Abilene Regional Airport[Abilene]), isPartOf(Abilene[Texas])
reference 1: Abilene is in Texas and is served by the Abilene regional airport.
reference 2: Abilene, part of Texas, is served by the Abilene regional airport.
delexicalized input: city served(AGENT-1[BRIDGE-1]), is part of(BRIDGE-1[PATIENT-1])
delexicalized reference 1: BRIDGE-1 is in PATIENT-1 and is served by the AGENT-1.

Figure 1: Example input-reference pairs from the E2E and WebNLG development set.

generate novel structures resulting from template combinations.

In sum, we make the following contribution:

- We compare word- and character-based Seq2Seq models for NLG on two datasets.

- We conduct an extensive automatic and manual analysis of the generated texts and compare them to human performance.

- In an experiment with synthetic training data generated from templates, we demonstrate the ability of neural NLG models to learn template combinations and thereby generalize beyond the linguistic structures they were trained on.

2 Related Work

This section reviews relevant related work according to the two main aspects of this paper: different input and output representations for data-to-text NLG as well as measuring and controlling the variation in the generated outputs.

2.1 Input and Output Representations

While the first NLG systems relied on hand-written rules or templates that were filled with the input information (Cheyer and Guzzoni, 2006; Mirkovic et al., 2006), the availability of larger datasets has accelerated the progress in statistical methods to train NLG systems from data-text pairs in the last twenty years (Oh and Rudnicky, 2000; Mairesse and Young, 2014). Generating output via language models based on recurrent neural networks (RNNs) conditioned on the input (Sutskever et al., 2011) proved to be an effective method for end-to-end NLG (Wen et al., 2015a,b, 2016).

The input can be represented in several ways: (1) In a discrete vector space via one-hot-vectors (Wen et al., 2015a,b), or in a continuous space either (2) by encoding fixed-size input information in a feed-forward neural network (Zhou et al., 2017; Wiseman et al., 2017) or (3) by the means of an encoder RNN, which processes variable-sized inputs sequentially, giving rise to the Seq2Seq architecture.

Character-based Seq2Seq models were first proposed for neural machine translation (Ling et al., 2015; Chung et al., 2016; Lee et al., 2017). Their main advantage over word-based models is that they can represent an unlimited word inventory with a small vocabulary. They can learn to copy any string from the input to the output, which is especially useful for data-to-text NLG, as information from the input such as the name of a restaurant or a database entity is often expected to appear verbatim in the generated text. Word-based models, in contrast, have to make use of delexicalization during pre- and postprocessing (Wen et al., 2015b; Dušek and Jurcícek, 2016) or have to apply dedicated copy mechanisms (Gu et al., 2016; See et al., 2017; Wiseman et al., 2017) to handle open vocabularies. The other side of the coin is that sequences are much longer in character-based processing, implying longer dependencies and more computation steps for encoding and decoding.

Subword-based representations (Sennrich et al., 2016; Wu et al., 2016) can offer a trade-off between word- and character-based processing and are a popular choice in NMT and summarization (See et al., 2017). Here, the vocabulary consists of subword units of different lengths, which are assigned by minimizing the entropy on the training set. We also experimented with such representations in preliminary experiments, but found them to perform much worse than word- or character-based representations. Our impression is that recurring entity names in the training data coming from multiple reference texts for the same input lead to overfitting on the training vocabulary and to poor generalization to novel inputs. This is also reflected by the rather unsatisfying performance of subword-based approaches in the E2E[1] and WebNLG challenge (ADAPT system (Gardent et al., 2017b)).

2.2 Output Diversity

Evaluation of data-to-text NLG has traditionally centered around semantic fidelity, grammaticality, and naturalness (Gatt and Krahmer, 2018; Oraby et al., 2018b). More recently, the controllability of the style of the outputs and their variation has moved into focus as well (Ficler and Goldberg, 2017; Herzig et al., 2017; Oraby et al., 2018b,a).

Oraby et al. (2018b) showed that the n-gram entropy of the outputs of a neural NLG system is significantly lower compared to its training data. This can be seen as evidence that the NLG system extracts only a few dominant patterns from the training data that it will generate over and over. Without explicit supervision signals, neural NLG models cannot distinguish linguistic or stylistic variation from noise. In the context of image caption generation Devlin et al. (2015) found Seq2Seq models to exactly reproduce sentences from their training data for 60% of the test instances.

Several approaches have been proposed to control NLG outputs with respect to certain stylistic aspects, e.g., mimicking a specific persona or character (Lin and Walker, 2011; Walker et al., 2011; Li et al., 2016), personality traits (Mairesse and Walker, 2008; Herzig et al., 2017; Oraby et al., 2018b,a), or various linguistic aspects such as formality, voice, descriptiveness (Ficler and Goldberg, 2017; Bawden, 2017; Niu et al., 2017). All share the feature that the NLG model is conditioned on a representation of the desired aspect in addition to the usual semantic input representation. While this approach makes it possible to successfully control particular, clearly defined aspects of the generated texts, further research is needed to grant more flexible and comprehensive NLG output control.

---

[1]The subword-based *bzhang_submit* system has the second best ROUGE-L score, but ranks poorly in terms of BLEU and quality in the human evaluation, see http://www.macs. hw.ac.uk/InteractionLab/E2E/#results.

3 Models

To encode variable-length inputs and generate variable-length texts, we implement a standard Seq2Seq model (Cho et al., 2014) with Long Short-Term Memory (LSTM) cells (Hochreiter and Schmidhuber, 1997) and attention. Given a training dataset of input-text pairs $D = \{(x^1, \bar{y^1}), (x^2, \bar{y^2}) \dots \}$, the model encodes an input sequence $x = \{x_1 \dots x_n\}$ of symbols x_i into a sequence of hidden states $\{h_1 \dots h_n\}$ by applying a recurrent neural network (RNN) with LSTM cells that can store and forget sequence information:

$$h_t = \text{LSTM}(X^{\text{in}}x_t, h_{t-1}) \tag{1}$$

The decoder generates the output sequence $y_1 \dots y_m$ one symbol y_t at a time by computing $p(y_t|y_1 \dots y_{t-1}, x) = \text{softmax}(W^{\text{out}}(c_t))$.

The decoder output c_t, also referred to as context vector, summarizes the input information in each decoding step as weighted sum of the encoder hidden states: $c_t = \sum_{i=1}^{n} \alpha_{ti} h_i$. The attention weights α_{ti} are computed with the general attention mechanism $\alpha_{ti} = \text{softmax}(s_t W^{\text{a}} h_i)$ (Luong et al., 2015). The decoder hidden states s_t are computed recursively based on the previous output token and decoder output:

$$s_t = \text{LSTM}((X^{\text{out}}(y_{t-1}) \circ c_{t-1}), s_{t-1}) \tag{2}$$

s_0 is initialized to the final encoder hidden state h_n, h_0, c_{-1} are initialized to 0; $\circ$ denotes concatenation. The parameters of the models are the input and output embedding matrices X^{in}, X^{out}, the encoder and decoder LSTM parameters, the attention matrix W^{a} and the output matrix W^{out}. They are optimized by minimizing the cross entropy of the generated texts y^j with the given references $\bar{y^j}$ for each example in the training set.

Instead of forcing the decoder to decide on a single output symbol in each decoding step, we apply beam search (Cho et al., 2014; Bahdanau et al., 2014) to explore n-best partial hypotheses in parallel.

In the word-based model, each input symbol x_t and output symbol y_t denotes a token. In contrast, in the character-based model, each input and output symbol denotes a single character. Our models learn separate encoder and decoder embedding matrices.

4 Data

We use two recently collected crowd-sourced data-to-text datasets since they are larger and offer more linguistic variety than previously available datasets (Novikova et al., 2017b; Gardent et al., 2017a). The E2E dataset (Novikova et al., 2017b) consists of 47K restaurant descriptions based on 5.7K distinct inputs of 3-8 attributes (*name, area, near, eat type, food, price range, family friendly, rating*), split into 4862 inputs for training, 547 for development and 630 for testing. The WebNLG dataset (Gardent et al., 2017a) contains 25K verbalizations of 9.6K inputs composed of 1-7 DBpedia triples from 15 categories such as *athletes, comic characters, food, sport teams*. It is divided into 6893 inputs for training, 872 for development and 1862 for testing. Both datasets have multiple verbalizations for each input. On average there are 8.3 (min. 1, max. 46) verbalizations per input in the E2E dataset and 2.63 (min. 1, max. 12) in the WebNLG dataset, respectively.

To preprocess both datasets, we lowercase all inputs and references and represent the inputs in the bracketed format as shown in Figure 1. For the word-based processing we additionally tokenize the texts with the nltk-tokenizer (Bird et al., 2009) and apply delexicalization, as also illustrated in Figure 1. For the E2E dataset we adopt the challenge's baseline delexicalization strategy (Dušek and Jurcícek, 2016), which replaces the values of the two open-class attributes *name* and *near* in the input and references by placeholders. For the WebNLG dataset, we adopt the delexicalization strategy of the TILBURG submissions to the challenge, since it performed well and does not require external information. They replaced the subject and object entities of the DBpedia triples in the input and text by numbered placeholders AGENT-N, PATIENT-N, BRIDGE-N, depending on whether they only appear as subject, object or in both roles in the input of an instance. Additionally, we split properties at the camel case in this dataset for both the word- and character-based models as proposed by the ADAPT and MELBOURNE submissions. Table 1 displays statistics for both datasets and processing types.

5 Experiments

We conduct our experiments with the OpenNMT toolkit (Klein et al., 2017), which we extend to also perform character-based processing. We

	E2E		WebNLG	
	word	char.	word	char.
avg. input length	28.5	106.0	24.8	139.8
avg. text length	20.0	109.3	18.8	117.1
input vocabulary	48	39	312	78
output vocabulary	2,721	53	4,264	83

Table 1: E2E and WebNLG training split statistics for word-based processing after delexicalization and character-based processing.

tuned the hyperparameters for each dataset and processing method to optimize the BLEU score on the development sets. The word-based model for the E2E dataset is trained by stochastic gradient descent (SGD) (Robbins and Monro, 1951) and an initial learning rate of 1.0. For all other models, we achieved better performance with the Adam optimizer (Kingma and Ba, 2015) with an initial learning rate of 0.001. If there is no improvement in the development perplexity, or in any case after the eighth epoch, we halve the learning rate. Also, we clip all gradients to a maximum of five. We use a batch size of 64. To prevent overfitting, we drop out units in the context vectors with a probability of 0.3. We keep the model with the lowest development perplexity in 13 training epochs.

The word-based E2E model has 64-dimensional word embeddings and a single encoder and decoder layer with 64 units each. All other models use 500-dimensional word- or character embeddings and two layers in the encoder and decoder with 500 dimensions each. While a unidirectional encoder was sufficient for the word-based models, bidirectional encoders were beneficial for the character-based models on both datasets.

We use a beam size of 15 for decoding with the word-based models, and found a smaller beam of five to yield better results for the character-based models. This is probably due to the much smaller vocabulary size of the character-based models.

For automatic evaluation, we report BLEU (Papineni et al., 2002), which measures the precision of the generated n-grams compared to the references, and recall-oriented ROUGE-L (Lin, 2004), which measures the longest common subsequence between the generated texts and the references. We compute these scores with the E2E challenge evaluation script[2].

---

[2]https://github.com/tuetschek/e2e-metrics

6 Results and Analysis

Table 2 and 3 display the results on the E2E and WebNLG test sets for models of the respective challenges and our own models[3]. Since the performance of neural models can vary considerably due to random parameter initialization and randomized training procedures (Reimers and Gurevych, 2017), we train ten models with different random seeds for each setting and report the average (avg) and standard deviation (SD).

On the E2E test set, our single best word- and character-based models reach comparable results to the best challenge submissions. The word-based models achieve significantly higher BLEU and ROUGE-L scores than the character-based models[4]. On the WebNLG test set, the BLEU score of our best word-based model outperforms the best challenge submission by a small margin. The character-based model achieves a significantly higher ROUGE-L score than the word-based model, whereas the BLEU score difference is not significant. In the following, we analyze our models in more detail.

6.1 Analysis of Within-Model Performance Differences

The large performance span of the character-based models on the E2E dataset is due to a single outlier model; the second worst model scores 64.5 BLEU points. The worst-scoring model had a lower accuracy of 91.8% on the development set, whereas all other models scored above 92.2%. To gain more insight on what might constitute the large performance difference, we manually compared the generated texts for ten randomly selected inputs for each number of attributes (60 inputs in total) of the character-based model with the best and worst BLEU score. We found that the worst model makes many mistakes on inputs with three to five attributes, often adding, modifying or removing information, whereas the outputs are mostly correct for inputs with six attributes or more. For these, the outputs of the model with the lowest BLEU score are occasionally even better than those of the best model, which often omits in-

---

[3]For an exact comparison, we recomputed the WebNLG challenge results with the E2E evaluation script. They are usually 1-2 points below the scores reported by Gardent et al. (2017b).

[4]All tests for significance in this paper are conducted with Wilcoxon rank sum tests with Bonferroni correction at a p-level of 0.05.

formation (mainly concerning the attribute *family friendly*). We conclude that the large performance difference might be caused by automatic evaluation measures punishing additions more severely than omissions.

We also observe a large performance span for the WebNLG word-based models. Here, we have two models that score exceptionally well with 57.4/58.4 BLEU points, whereas the remaining eight models only obtain BLEU scores in a range of 43.8-48.1. Again, we observe that better models in terms of BLEU score obtain higher accuracies on the development set. We manually compared the outputs of ten randomly chosen inputs for each number of input triples (75 inputs in total) for the model with the highest and lowest BLEU score. In this case, we found that the large difference in the automatic evaluation measures seems justified: The low-scoring model often hallucinates information not present in the input and generally produces many ungrammatical texts, which is not the case for the best model.

system	BLEU	ROUGE-L
challenge		
baseline	65.9	68.5
Thomson Reuters (np 3)	**68.1**	69.3
Thomson Reuters (np 4)	67.4	69.8
HarvardNLP & H. Elder	67.4	**70.8**
own		
word	67.8±0.8	70.4±0.6
character	64.6±6.0	67.9±4.7
word (best on dev.)	67.8	70.2
char. (best on dev.)	67.6	70.4

Table 2: E2E test set results. Own results correspond to avg±SD of ten runs and single result of best models on the development set.

6.2 Automatic Evaluation of Human Texts

To gain an impression of the expressiveness of the automatic evaluation scores for NLG, we computed the average scores that the human references would obtain. Table 4 shows the BLEU and ROUGE-L development set scores when treating each human reference as prediction once and evaluating it against the remaining references, compared to the scores of the word-based and

system	BLEU	ROUGE-L
challenge		
baseline	32.1	43.3
MELBOURNE	43.4	**61.0**
TILBURG-SMT	43.1	58.0
UPF-FORGE	37.5	58.8
own		
word (best on dev.)	**44.2**	60.9
char. (best on dev.)	41.3	58.4
word	37.0±3.8	56.3±2.6
character	39.7±1.7	58.4±0.7

Table 3: WebNLG test set results. Own results correspond to single best model on development set and avg±SD of ten runs.

metric	human	word	char.
E2E			
BLEU	55.5±0.7	68.2±1.4	65.8±2.6
ROUGE-L	62.0±0.4	72.1±0.7	69.8±2.6
WebNLG			
BLEU	48.3±0.7	40.6±4.2	43.7±2.4
ROUGE-L	62.4±0.3	58.5±3.0	63.1±0.8

Table 4: E2E and WebNLG development set results in the format avg±SD. Human results are averaged over using each human reference as prediction once.

	E2E		WebNLG	
	word	char.	word	char.
content errors				
info. dropped	40.0	30.0	42.9	66.7
info. added	0.0	0.0	6.7	1.9
info. modified	4.4	0.0	19.0	1.9
info. repeated	0.0	0.0	15.2	28.6
linguistic errors				
punctuation errors	5.6	5.6	8.6	3.8
grammatical errors	13.3	14.4	15.2	12.4
spelling mistakes	0.0	0.0	9.5	5.7
overall correctness				
content correct	55.6	70.0	46.7	31.4
language correct	83.3	81.1	69.5	79.0
all correct	48.9	61.1	33.3	26.7

Table 5: Percentage of affected instances in manual error analysis of 15 randomly selected development set instances for each input length.

character-based models[5]. Strikingly, on the E2E development set, both model variants significantly outperform human texts by far with respect to both automatic evaluation measures. While the human BLEU score is significantly higher than those of both systems on the WebNLG development set, there is no statistical difference between human and system ROUGE-L scores. This further demonstrates the limited utility of BLEU and ROUGLE-L scores to evaluate NLG outputs, which was previously suggested by weak correlations of such scores with human judgments (Scott and Moore, 2006; Reiter and Belz, 2009; Novikova et al., 2017a). Furthermore, the high scores on the E2E dataset imply that the models succeed in picking up patterns from the training data that transfer well to the similar development set, whereas human variation and creativity are punished by lexical overlap-based automatic evaluation scores.

6.3 Manual Error Analysis

Since the expressiveness of automatic evaluation measures for NLG is limited, as shown in the previous subsection, we performed a manual error analysis on inputs of each length. We define the input length as the number of input attributes for the E2E dataset, ranging from three to eight, and number of input triples for the WebNLG dataset, ranging from one to seven. We randomly selected 15 development instances for each input length, resulting in a total of 90 annotated E2E instances and 105 WebNLG instances.

One annotator (one of the authors of this paper) manually assessed the outputs of the models that obtained the best development set BLEU score as summarized in Table 5[6]. As we can see from the bottom part of the table, all models struggle more with getting the content right than with producing linguistically correct texts; 70-80% of the texts generated by all models are completely correct linguistically.

---

[5]For a fair comparison between human and model performance, we randomly removed one reference for each instance in the models' evaluation to ensure the same average number of references. We excluded 55 WebNLG instances that had only one reference.

[6]Although multiple annotators could increase the reliability of these results, the annotator reported that the task was very straightforward. We do not expect marking content and linguistic errors to lead to annotator disagreements, with the exception of accidentally missed errors.

	E2E			WebNLG		
	human	word	character	human	word	character
unique sents.	866.3±16.5	203.5±30.6	366.8±60.0	1,185.0±12.6	603.7±144.3	875.4±30.2
unique words	419.7±16.7	64.4±2.3	73.1±7.2	1447.3±7.4	620.3±35.5	881.5±26.0
word E	6.5±0.0	5.1±0.0	5.5±0.0	7.1±0.0	6.3±0.0	6.6±0.0
1-3-grams E	10.4±0.0	7.7±0.1	8.2±0.1	11.6±0.0	10.1±0.1	10.5±0.1
% new texts	99.7±0.2	98.2±0.3	98.8±0.2	91.1±0.3	69.8±4.8	87.5±0.6
% new sents.	85.1±1.1	61.8±6.4	71.4±4.7	87.4±0.4	57.2±5.8	82.1±1.2

Table 6: Linguistic diversity of development set references and generated texts as avg±SD. '% new' denotes the share of generated texts or sentences that do not appear in training references. Higher indicates more diversity for all measures.

Comparing the two datasets, we again observe that the WebNLG dataset is much more challenging than the E2E dataset, especially with respect to correctly verbalizing the content. This can be attributed to the increased diversity of the inputs and texts and to the limited availability of training data for this dataset (cf. Table 1). Moreover, spelling mistakes only appeared in WebNLG texts, mainly concerning omissions of accents or umlauts. This also indicates that there is too few and noisy data for the models to learn the correct spelling of all words. Notably, we did not observe any non-words generated by the character-based models.

The most frequent content error in both datasets concerns omission of information. For the E2E dataset, the *family friendly* attribute is most frequently dropped by both model types, indicating that the verbalization of this boolean attribute is more difficult to learn than other attributes, whose values mostly appear verbatim in the text. Information modification of the word-based model is mainly due to confusing *English* with *Italian* food. Information addition and repetition only occur in the WebNLG dataset. The latter is an especially frequent problem of the character-based model, affecting more than a quarter of all texts.

In comparison, character-based models reproduce the content more faithfully on the E2E dataset while offering the same level of linguistic quality as word-based models, leading to more correct outputs overall. On the WebNLG dataset, the word-based model is more faithful to the inputs, probably because of the effective delexicalization strategy, whereas the character-based model errs less on the linguistic side. Overall, the word-based model yields more correct texts, stressing the importance of delexicalization and data normalization in low resource settings.

6.4 Automatic Evaluation of Output Diversity

While correctness is a necessity in NLG, in many settings it is not sufficient. Often, variation of the generated texts is crucial to avoid repetitive and unnatural outputs. Table 6 shows automatically computed statistics on the diversity of the generated texts of both models and human texts and on the overlap of the (generated) texts with the training set. We measure diversity by the number of unique sentences and words in all development set references and generated texts, as done e.g. by Devlin et al. (2015). Additionally, we report the Shannon text entropy as measure of the amount of variation in the texts following (Oraby et al., 2018b). We compute the text entropy E for words (unigrams) and uni-, bi-, and trigrams as follows:

$$E = - \sum_{w \in V} \frac{f(w)}{\text{total}} * \log_2 \frac{f(w)}{\text{total}} \qquad (3)$$

where V is the set of all word types or uni-, bi- and trigrams, f denotes frequency and total is the token count or total number of uni-, bi- and trigrams in the texts, respectively.

To measure the extent by which the models generalize beyond plugging in restaurant or other entity names into templates extracted from the training data, we compute the results on the delexicalized outputs of the word-based models and delexicalize the character-based models' outputs. For the human scores, we generate n artificial prediction files, treating each n-th reference (42 for E2E, 8 for WebNLG) as reference, apply delexicalization, and average the scores for the n files.

On both datasets, our systems produce significantly less varied outputs and reproduce more

Template 1: NAME is a [FAMILY-FRIENDLY] EATTYPE which serves [FOOD] food [in the PRICE RANGE price range]. [It has a RATING rating] [and is located in the AREA area[, near NEAR]]. [It is not FAMILY-FRIENDLY.]

Example: NAME is a family-friendly coffee shop which serves Chinese food in the low price range. It has a high customer rating and is located in the city centre area, near NEAR.

Template 2: The [FAMILY-FRIENDLY] EATTYPE NAME serves [FOOD] food [in the PRICE RANGE price range]. [It is located in the AREA area[, near NEAR].] [It has a RATING rating.] [It is not FAMILY-FRIENDLY.]

Example: The family-friendly coffee shop NAME serves Chinese food in the low price range. It is located in the city centre area, near NEAR. It has a high customer rating.

Learned combinations of Template 1 and 2:
- NAME is a restaurant which serves English food in the moderate price range. It is located in the city centre area, near NEAR. It has a customer rating of 1 out of 5. It is not family friendly.
- The family-friendly pub NAME serves Indian food in the low price range. It has a customer rating of 5 out of 5 and is located in the riverside area, near NEAR.

Figure 2: Templates used for synthetic training data generation, parts in brackets are realized only if the input contains the corresponding attribute. Learned combinations are two template combinations produced by a model trained on data generated from both templates.

texts and sentences from the training data than the human texts. Interestingly, however, the character-based models generate significantly more unique sentences and copy significantly less from the training data than the word-based models, which copy about 40% of their generated sentences from the training data.

7 Generalizing from Templates

In search for empirical evidence that neural models are able to surpass the structures they were trained on, we train Seq2Seq models with synthetic training data created by templates. This enables us to control the variation in the training data and identify novel generations of the model (if any). We investigate two questions: (1) Do the neural NLG models indeed accurately learn the templates from the training data? (2) Do they learn to combine the training templates to produce more varied outputs than seen during training?

We generate synthetic training data based on two templates. Template 1 corresponds to UKP-TUDA's submission to the E2E challenge[7], where the order of describing the input information is fixed. Specifically, the restaurant's customer rating is always mentioned before its location. For Template 2, we change the the beginning of the template and switch the order of mentioning the

rating and location of the restaurant as shown in Figure 2. Potential combinations of the two templates are to combine the beginning of Template 1 with the ordering of rating and area of Template 2 or vice versa. We generate a single reference text for all 2261 training inputs of the E2E dataset where the NAME and EATTYPE attribute are present as these are the two obligatory attributes for the templates. We train word-based models on training data generated with Template 1, Template 2 and the concatenation of the training data from Template 1 and 2. To keep the amount of training data equal in all experiments, we once repeat the training corpus generated only with Template 1 or Template 2. The hyperparameters for the three models can be found in the appendix.

	c@1	c@2	c@5	c@30
template 1	0.8	0.8	0.9	1.7
template 2	1.0	1.2	1.3	1.9
template 1+2	0.9	1.6	2.2	3.3
+ reranker	0.9	1.9	2.7	3.3

Table 7: Manual evaluation of generated texts for 10 random test instances of a word-based model trained with synthetic training data from two templates. c@n: avg. number of correct texts (with respect to content and language) among the top n hypotheses.

---

[7]https://github.com/UKPLab/e2e-nlg-challenge-2017/blob/master/components/template-baseline.py

Table 7 shows our manual evaluation of the top 30 hypotheses for 10 random E2E test inputs generated by models trained with data synthesized from the two templates. As is evident from the first two rows, all models learned to generalize from the training data to produce correct texts for novel inputs consisting of unseen combinations of input attributes. It was verified in the manual evaluation that 100% of the texts generated by models trained on a single template adhered to this template. Yet, the picture is a bit different for the model trained on data generated by both templates. While the top two hypotheses are equally distributed between adhering to Template 1 and Template 2, more than 5% among the lower-ranked hypotheses constitute a template combination such as the example shown in the bottom part of Figure 2. For 60% of the examined inputs, there was at least one such hypothesis resulting from template combination, of which two thirds were actually correct verbalizations of the input.

Since we found that the models frequently ranked correct hypotheses below hypotheses with content errors, we implemented a simple rule-based reranker based on verbatim matches of attribute values. The reranker assigns an error point to each omission and addition of an attribute value. As can be seen in the final row of Table 7, this simple reranker successfully places correct hypotheses higher up in the ranking, improving the practical usability of the generation model by now offering almost three correct variants for each input among the top five hypotheses on average.

8 Conclusion

We compared word-based and character-based Seq2Seq models for data-to-text NLG on two datasets and analyzed their output diversity. Our main findings are as follows: Overall, Seq2Seq models can learn to verbalize structured inputs in a decent way; their success depends on the extent of the domain and available (clean) training data.

Second, in a comparison with texts produced by humans, we saw that neural NLG models can even surpass human performance in terms of automatic evaluation measures. On the one hand, this unveils the ability of the models to extract general patterns from the training data that approximate many reference texts, but on the other hand also once more stresses the limited utility of such measures to evaluate NLG systems.

Third, in light of the multi-faceted analysis we performed, it is difficult to draw a general conclusion on whether word- or character-based processing is more useful for data-to-text generation. Both models yielded comparable results with respect to automatic evaluation measures. In the manual error analysis, the character-based model performed better on the E2E dataset, whereas the word-based model generated more correct outputs on the WebNLG dataset. Character-based models were found to have a significantly higher output diversity.

Finally, in a controlled experiment with word-based Seq2Seq models trained on data synthesized from templates, we showed the capability of such models to perfectly reproduce the templates they were trained on. More importantly, models trained on two templates could generalize beyond their training data and come up with novel texts. In future work, we would like to extend this line of research and train more model variants on a higher number of templates.

References

Shubham Agarwal and Marc Dymetman. 2017. A surprisingly effective out-of-the-box char2char model on the e2e nlg challenge dataset. In *Proceedings of the 18th Annual SIGdial Meeting on Discourse and Dialogue*, pages 158–163, Saarbrücken, Germany.

Gabor Angeli, Percy Liang, and Dan Klein. 2010. A simple domain-independent probabilistic approach to generation. In *Proceedings of the 2010 Conference on Empirical Methods in Natural Language Processing*, EMNLP '10, pages 502–512, Stroudsburg, PA, USA.

Dzmitry Bahdanau, Kyunghyun Cho, and Yoshua Bengio. 2014. Neural Machine Translation by Jointly Learning to Align and Translate. *arXiv e-prints*, abs/1409.0473.

Rachel Bawden. 2017. Machine translation, it's a question of style, innit? the case of english tag questions. In *Proceedings of the 2017 Conference on Empirical Methods in Natural Language Processing, EMNLP 2017*, pages 2507–2512, Copenhagen, Denmark.

Steven Bird, Ewan Klein, and Edward Loper. 2009. *Natural Language Processing with Python*, 1st edition. O'Reilly Media, Inc.

Adam Cheyer and Didier Guzzoni. 2006. Method and apparatus for building an intelligent automated assistant. Patent US 11/518,292 (Patent pending).

Kyunghyun Cho, Bart Van Merriënboer, Çalar Gülçehre, Dzmitry Bahdanau, Fethi Bougares, Holger Schwenk, and Yoshua Bengio. 2014. Learning phrase representations using rnn encoder–decoder for statistical machine translation. In *Proceedings of the 2014 Conference on Empirical Methods in Natural Language Processing (EMNLP)*, pages 1724–1734, Doha, Qatar.

Junyoung Chung, Kyunghyun Cho, and Yoshua Bengio. 2016. A character-level decoder without explicit segmentation for neural machine translation. In *Proceedings of the 54th Annual Meeting of the Association for Computational Linguistics, ACL 2016, Volume 1: Long Papers*, pages 1693–1703, Berlin, Germany.

Jacob Devlin, Hao Cheng, Hao Fang, Saurabh Gupta, Li Deng, Xiaodong He, Geoffrey Zweig, and Margaret Mitchell. 2015. Language models for image captioning: The quirks and what works. In *Proceedings of the 53rd Annual Meeting of the Association for Computational Linguistics and the 7th International Joint Conference on Natural Language Processing of the Asian Federation of Natural Language Processing, ACL 2015, Volume 2: Short Papers*, pages 100–105, Beijing, China.

Ondřej Dušek and Filip Jurcícek. 2016. Sequence-to-sequence generation for spoken dialogue via deep syntax trees and strings. In *Proceedings of the 54th Annual Meeting of the Association for Computational Linguistics, ACL 2016, Volume 2: Short Papers*, pages 41–51, Berlin, Germany.

Jessica Ficler and Yoav Goldberg. 2017. Controlling linguistic style aspects in neural language generation. *CoRR*, abs/1707.02633.

Claire Gardent, Anastasia Shimorina, Shashi Narayan, and Laura Perez-Beltrachini. 2017a. Creating training corpora for NLG micro-planners. In *Proceedings of the 55th Annual Meeting of the Association for Computational Linguistics, ACL 2017, Volume 1: Long Papers*, pages 179–188, Vancouver, Canada.

Claire Gardent, Anastasia Shimorina, Shashi Narayan, and Laura Perez-Beltrachini. 2017b. The WebNLG Challenge: Generating Text from RDF Data. In *Proceedings of the 10th International Conference on Natural Language Generation*, pages 124–133, Santiago de Compostela, Spain.

Albert Gatt and Emiel Krahmer. 2018. Survey of the state of the art in natural language generation: Core tasks, applications and evaluation. *Journal of Artificial Intelligence Research (JAIR)*, 61:65–170.

Raghav Goyal, Marc Dymetman, and Éric Gaussier. 2016. Natural language generation through character-based rnns with finite-state prior knowledge. In *Proceedings of the 26th International Conference on Computational Linguistics, COLING 2016, Technical Papers*, pages 1083–1092, Osaka, Japan.

Alex Graves. 2013. Generating sequences with recurrent neural networks. *CoRR*, abs/1308.0850.

Jiatao Gu, Zhengdong Lu, Hang Li, and Victor O. K. Li. 2016. Incorporating copying mechanism in sequence-to-sequence learning. In *Proceedings of the 54th Annual Meeting of the Association for Computational Linguistics, ACL 2016, Volume 1: Long Papers*, pages 1631–1640, Berlin, Germany.

Jonathan Herzig, Michal Shmueli-Scheuer, Tommy Sandbank, and David Konopnicki. 2017. Neural response generation for customer service based on personality traits. In *Proceedings of the 10th International Conference on Natural Language Generation, INLG 2017*, pages 252–256, Santiago de Compostela, Spain.

Sepp Hochreiter and Jürgen Schmidhuber. 1997. Long Short-Term Memory. *Neural Computation*, 9(8).

Chloé Kiddon, Luke Zettlemoyer, and Yejin Choi. 2016. Globally coherent text generation with neural checklist models. In *Proceedings of the 2016 Conference on Empirical Methods in Natural Language Processing, EMNLP 2016*, pages 329–339, Austin, TX, USA.

Diederik Kingma and Jimmy Ba. 2015. Adam: A Method for Stochastic Optimization. In *International Conference on Learning Representations*, San Diego, CA, USA.

Guillaume Klein, Yoon Kim, Yuntian Deng, Jean Senellart, and Alexander M. Rush. 2017. Opennmt: Open-source toolkit for neural machine translation. *CoRR*, abs/1701.02810.

Philipp Koehn. 2017. Neural machine translation. *CoRR*, abs/1709.07809.

Jason Lee, Kyunghyun Cho, and Thomas Hofmann. 2017. Fully character-level neural machine translation without explicit segmentation. *TACL*, 5:365–378.

Jiwei Li, Michel Galley, Chris Brockett, Georgios Spithourakis, Jianfeng Gao, and William B. Dolan. 2016. A Persona-Based Neural Conversation Model. In *Proceedings of the 54th Annual Meeting of the Association for Computational Linguistics, ACL 2016, Volume 1: Long Papers*, pages 994–1003, Berlin, Germany.

Chin-Yew Lin. 2004. ROUGE: A Package for Automatic Evaluation of summaries. In *Proceedings of the ACL workshop on Text Summarization Branches Out*, pages 74–81, Barcelona, Spain.

Grace Lin and Marilyn Walker. 2011. All the worlds a stage: Learning character models from film. In *Proceedings of the Seventh AIIDE Conference*, pages 46–52, Palo Alto, CA, USA.

Wang Ling, Isabel Trancoso, Chris Dyer, and Alan Black. 2015. Character-based neural machine translation. *CoRR*, abs/1511.04586.

Zachary Chase Lipton, Sharad Vikram, and Julian McAuley. 2015. Capturing meaning in product reviews with character-level generative text models. *CoRR*, abs/1511.03683.

Thang Luong, Hieu Pham, and Christopher Manning. 2015. Effective approaches to attention-based neural machine translation. In *Proceedings of the 2015 Conference on Empirical Methods in Natural Language Processing, EMNLP 2015*, pages 1412–1421, Lisbon, Portugal.

François Mairesse and Steve J. Young. 2014. Stochastic language generation in dialogue using factored language models. *Computational Linguistics*, 40(4):763–799.

Francois Mairesse and Marilyn Walker. 2008. Trainable Generation of Big-Five Personality Styles through Data-driven Parameter Estimation. In *Proceedings of the 46th Annual Meeting of the Association for Computational Linguistics (ACL 2008)*, pages 165–173, Columbus, OH, USA.

Hongyuan Mei, Mohit Bansal, and Matthew Walter. 2016. What to talk about and how? selective generation using lstms with coarse-to-fine alignment. In *Proceedings of the Conference of the North American Chapter of the Association for Computational Linguistics Human Language Technologies (NAACL HLT)*, pages 720–730, San Diego, CA, USA.

Danilo Mirkovic, Lawrence Cavedon, Matthew Purver, Florin Ratiu, Tobias Scheideck, Fuliang Weng, Qi Zhang, and Kui Xu. 2006. Dialogue management using scripts and combined confidence scores. US Patent App. 11/298,765.

Xing Niu, Marianna Martindale, and Marine Carpuat. 2017. A study of style in machine translation: Controlling the formality of machine translation output. In *Proceedings of the 2017 Conference on Empirical Methods in Natural Language Processing, EMNLP 2017*, pages 2814–2819, Copenhagen, Denmark.

Jekaterina Novikova, Ondřej Dušek, Amanda Cercas Curry, and Verena Rieser. 2017a. Why we need new evaluation metrics for NLG. In *Proceedings of the 2017 Conference on Empirical Methods in Natural Language Processing, EMNLP 2017*, pages 2231–2242, Copenhagen, Denmark.

Jekaterina Novikova, Ondřej Dušek, and Verena Rieser. 2017b. The e2e dataset: New challenges for end-to-end generation. In *Proceedings of the 18th Annual SIGdial Meeting on Discourse and Dialogue*, pages 201–206, Saarbrücken, Germany.

Alice Oh and Alexander Rudnicky. 2000. Stochastic language generation for spoken dialogue systems. In *Proceedings of the 2000 ANLP/NAACL Workshop on Conversational Systems - Volume 3*, ANLP/NAACL-ConvSyst '00, pages 27–32, Stroudsburg, PA, USA.

Shereen Oraby, Lena Reed, Sharath T. S., Shubhangi Tandon, and Marilyn A. Walker. 2018a. Neural multivoice models for expressing novel personalities in dialog. In *Interspeech*, pages 3057–3061, Hyderabad, India. ISCA.

Shereen Oraby, Lena Reed, Shubhangi Tandon, Sharath T. S., Stephanie Lukin, and Marilyn Walker. 2018b. Controlling personality-based stylistic variation with neural natural language generators. In *Proceedings of the 19th Annual SIGdial Meeting on Discourse and Dialogue*, pages 180–190, Melbourne, Australia.

Kishore Papineni, Salim Roukos, Todd Ward, and Wei-Jing Zhu. 2002. Bleu: A method for automatic evaluation of machine translation. In *Proceedings of the 40th Annual Meeting on Association for Computational Linguistics*, ACL '02, pages 311–318, Stroudsburg, PA, USA.

Nils Reimers and Iryna Gurevych. 2017. Reporting score distributions makes a difference: Performance study of lstm-networks for sequence tagging. In *Proceedings of the 2017 Conference on Empirical Methods in Natural Language Processing*, pages 338–348, Copenhagen, Denmark.

Ehud Reiter and Anja Belz. 2009. An investigation into the validity of some metrics for automatically evaluating natural language generation systems. *Computational Linguistics*, 35(4):529–558.

Herbert Robbins and Sutton Monro. 1951. A stochastic approximation method. *Annals of Mathematical Statistics*, 22:400–407.

Donia Scott and Johanna Moore. 2006. An NLG evaluation competition? Eight Reasons to Be Cautious. In *Proceedings of the Fourth International Natural Language Generation Conference, INLG 2006, Special Session on Sharing Data and Comparative Evaluations*, Sydney, Australia.

Abigail See, Christopher Manning, and Peter Liu. 2017. Get to the point: Summarization with pointer-generator networks. In *Association for Computational Linguistics*.

Rico Sennrich, Barry Haddow, and Alexandra Birch. 2016. Neural machine translation of rare words with subword units. In *Proceedings of the 54th Annual Meeting of the Association for Computational Linguistics, ACL 2016, August 7-12, 2016, Berlin, Germany, Volume 1: Long Papers*.

Amanda Stent, Matthew Marge, and Mohit Singhai. 2005. Evaluating evaluation methods for generation in the presence of variation. In *Computational Linguistics and Intelligent Text Processing*, pages 341–351, Berlin, Heidelberg. Springer.

Ilya Sutskever, James Martens, and Geoffrey Hinton. 2011. Generating text with recurrent neural networks. In *Proceedings of the 28th International Conference on Machine Learning, ICML 2011*, pages 1017–1024, Bellevue, WA, USA.

Ilya Sutskever, Oriol Vinyals, and Quoc V. Le. 2014. Sequence to Sequence Learning with Neural Networks. In *Proceedings of the 27th International Conference on Neural Information Processing Systems*, NIPS'14, Cambridge, Massachusetts, USA. MIT Press.

Oriol Vinyals and Quoc V. Le. 2015. A neural conversational model. In *Proceedings of the International Conference on Machine Learning, Deep Learning Workshop*, Lille, France.

Marilyn A. Walker, Ricky Grant, Jennifer Sawyer, Grace I. Lin, Noah Wardrip-Fruin, and Michael Buell. 2011. Perceived or Not Perceived: Film Character Models for Expressive NLG. In *ICIDS*, volume 7069 of *Lecture Notes in Computer Science*. Springer.

Tsung-Hsien Wen, Milica Gasic, Dongho Kim, Nikola Mrksic, Pei-hao Su, David Vandyke, and Steve J. Young. 2015a. Stochastic language generation in dialogue using recurrent neural networks with convolutional sentence reranking. *CoRR*, abs/1508.01755.

Tsung-Hsien Wen, Milica Gasic, Nikola Mrksic, Lina Maria Rojas-Barahona, Pei-Hao Su, David Vandyke, and Steve J. Young. 2016. Multi-domain neural network language generation for spoken dialogue systems. In *NAACL HLT 2016, The 2016 Conference of the North American Chapter of the Association for Computational Linguistics: Human Language Technologies*, pages 120–129, San Diego, CA, USA.

Tsung-Hsien Wen, Milica Gasic, Nikola Mrksic, Pei-hao Su, David Vandyke, and Steve J. Young. 2015b. Semantically Conditioned LSTM-based Natural Language Generation for Spoken Dialogue Systems. In *Proceedings of the 2015 Conference on Empirical Methods in Natural Language Processing, EMNLP 2015*, pages 1711–1721, Lisbon, Portugal.

Sam Wiseman, Stuart Shieber, and Alexander Rush. 2017. Challenges in data-to-document generation. In *Proceedings of the 2017 Conference on Empirical Methods in Natural Language Processing, EMNLP 2017*, pages 2253–2263, Copenhagen, Denmark.

Yonghui Wu, Mike Schuster, Zhifeng Chen, Quoc V. Le, Mohammad Norouzi, Wolfgang Macherey, Maxim Krikun, Yuan Cao, Qin Gao, Klaus Macherey, Jeff Klingner, Apurva Shah, Melvin Johnson, Xiaobing Liu, ukasz Kaiser, Stephan Gouws, Yoshikiyo Kato, Taku Kudo, Hideto Kazawa, Keith Stevens, George Kurian, Nishant Patil, Wei Wang, Cliff Young, Jason Smith, Jason Riesa, Alex Rudnick, Oriol Vinyals, Greg Corrado, Macduff Hughes, and Jeffrey Dean. 2016. Google's neural machine translation system: Bridging the gap between human and machine translation. *CoRR*, abs/1609.08144.

Ming Zhou, Mirella Lapata, Furu Wei, Li Dong, Shaohan Huang, and Ke Xu. 2017. Learning to generate product reviews from attributes. In *Proceedings of the 15th Conference of the European Chapter of the Association for Computational Linguistics, EACL 2017, Volume 1: Long Papers*, pages 623–632, Valencia, Spain.

A Hyperparameters for Models Trained on Synthetic Training Data

For the model trained on template-generated data, we tune the hyperparameters to achieve 100% accuracy for their best hypotheses on template-generated references on the development set. All models have a single-layer LSTM with 64 hidden units in the encoder and decoder. We half the learning rate starting from the eighth training epoch or if the perplexity of the validation set does not improve. The gradient norm is capped at two. The decoder uses the general attention mechanism. For decoding, we set the beam size to 30. Table 8 shows hyperparameters which differ for the models.

hyperparameter	T 1	T 2	T 1+2
encoder	unidirectional		bidir.
embedding size	28	28	30
optimizer	Adam	SGD	SGD
init. learning rate	0.001	1.0	1.0
batch size	4	4	16
dropout	0.4	0.5	0.3
epochs	25	13	15

Table 8: Hyperparameters for the models trained on synthetic training data generated from Template 1 (T 1), Template 2 (T 2) and both (T 1+2).

Generating E-Commerce Product Titles and Predicting their Quality

José G. C. de Souza[1], Michael Kozielski[1], Prashant Mathur[1*], Ernie Chang[2],
Marco Guerini[3], Matteo Negri[3], Marco Turchi[3], and Evgeny Matusov[1†]

[1]eBay Inc., Core AI, Germany
{jgcdesouza,mkozielski}@ebay.com
[2]University of Washington, Seattle
cyc025@uw.edu
[3]Fondazione Bruno Kessler, Trento, Italy
{guerini,negri,turchi}@fbk.eu

Abstract

E-commerce platforms present products using titles that summarize product information. These titles cannot be created by hand, therefore an algorithmic solution is required. The task of automatically generating these titles given noisy user provided titles is one way to achieve the goal. The setting requires the generation process to be fast and the generated title to be both human-readable and concise. Furthermore, we need to understand if such generated titles are usable. As such, we propose approaches that (i) automatically generate product titles, (ii) predict their quality. Our approach scales to millions of products and both automatic and human evaluations performed on real-world data indicate our approaches are effective and applicable to existing e-commerce scenarios.

1 Introduction

E-Commerce websites are now an established way to buy and sell products using online platforms that have a vast and diverse catalog of products. A catalog is composed of a series of products that are unique and can broadly be identified by their brand, model and main features that vary according to the type of product (clothes, electronics, books). A product title is the realization of this information in a human-readable way so that users can understand the main features of the product.

Online platforms expose the products via product pages that condense the information for a product and can use the title as the product's main summary. A product page for "*ACME Model Smart-*

phone 64GB Black Unlocked" is shown in Figure 1. The product page also aggregates all the listings of the product being sold (bottom of the figure). A listing (or item) is an instance of a product sold in the platform by a seller. Its title might contain information such as condition of the item (used, new, among others), price, shipping and quantity tags, and other information specific to a particular item. Product titles cannot contain such information because they describe the product and not item-specific details like its price.

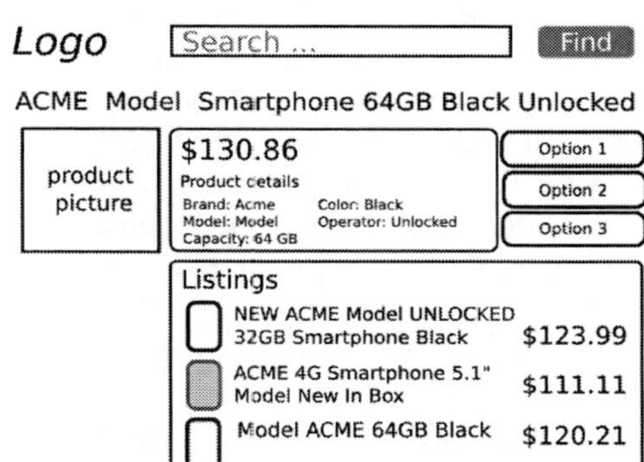

Figure 1: Example of product page.

Large e-commerce platforms have millions of products and manually creating titles for such products is not feasible. In order to scale the process of creating product titles, such platforms need to employ algorithms that automatically generate titles and are fast enough to scale. One possible way to generate text is to build a rule-based system that uses slot-value pairs to generate text, selecting the most important pairs in the output (Dale et al., 1998). Another possible way, that we propose in this study, is to leverage large amounts of seller-provided listing titles and recombine their n-grams to form hypotheses of product titles.

Observing the listing titles created by sellers, it

Proceedings of The 11th International Natural Language Generation Conference, pages 233–243,
Tilburg, The Netherlands, November 5-8, 2018. ©2018 Association for Computational Linguistics

*Now at AWS Inc.
†Now at Apptek Inc.

is noticeable that many of them contain a mix of irrelevant information (shipping, condition, price, information, among others) and relevant information (brand, model and features). The occurrence of ready-to-use product titles among listing titles is possible but not guaranteed. Based on this observation, one hypothesis that emerges is that a good product title could be formed by tokens that occur most frequently across listings aggregated for the product, and that combining these frequent expressions could yield a good product title.

The title generation approach presented here builds on top of this hypothesis. It is based on a statistical approach that first counts n-grams occurring in the titles aggregated into a product and then recombines them to form product title hypotheses. Furthermore, the available slot-value pairs can be used to enforce tokens that are important, ensuring that relevant product information is present in the generated output.

Though algorithms can scale the title generation process, often the quality of the output generated is not good, and some titles might not be adequate. This can happen due to several reasons, ranging from noisy input data (e.g. noisy aggregation of titles into a product) or bad hypothesis generation. Therefore, in addition to automatically generating titles, there should be a way to assess whether the generated titles are good enough for publishing, in order to avoid bad user experience. For example, in Figure 1, if a generated title has a brand other than "ACME", it would not be an appropriate title for that specific product.

In this paper we present approaches to both problems: (i) generating e-commerce product titles and (ii) predicting their quality. Our main contributions are:

- An approach that generates product titles taking seller-provided listing titles as input and that scales to millions of products. The method is based on a stack decoder search algorithm that recombines frequent n-grams observed in the listing titles to form a product title hypothesis.

- An approach to estimating the quality of titles based on supervised machine learning methods, in particular neural networks trained on human-annotated data.

- A thorough evaluation of the approaches on in-house data and a qualitative analysis of the system's outputs using human evaluation.

The remainder of the paper is organized as follows: Section 2 describes work in text generation related to the approaches described here; Section 3 describe the title generation approach; Section 4 presents the title quality prediction approach; Section 5 lays out the experimental settings used for evaluating the approaches described in the paper; Section 6 presents and discusses the results obtained and Section 7 summarizes the conclusions and lays out future work directions.

2   Related Work

Prior work on title generation for e-commerce focused on browse pages and has only explored a hybrid approach combining rule-based and statistical machine translation models (Mathur et al., 2017). The input to this approach consists of structured information about products in terms of slot/value pairs (e.g. `Watch_Type: wrist watch`). Although the task is similar to ours, hand-crafting and encoding product-specific rules is a time-consuming endeavour which does not scale to the hundreds of slot-value pairs and millions of products in the catalog. Below, we discuss three approaches that can either be directly applied or adapted to product title generation. The first approach is selection-based, while the last two are generation-based.

Hypothesis Selection. The most intuitive approach is to select, among the listing titles, the one that most "appropriately" describes the product. This can be achieved by applying diversity-based ranking techniques used in extractive summarization, such as Maximal Marginal Relevance (MMR), to prune and select from the set of titles (Carbonell and Goldstein, 1998; Gillick, 2011). Alternatively, systems can also learn how to pick the candidate title that is closest to the reference title. This approach can rely on ranking scores produced by models trained on listing titles and the corresponding human-curated reference product titles, with automatic metrics such as BLEU (Papineni et al., 2002) or TER (Snover et al., 2006) as labels. Some of these techniques are employed in system combination (Rosti et al., 2007; Barrault, 2010; Devlin and Matsoukas, 2012; Suzuki, 2011). However, this approach limits the number of possible generated titles and can potentially introduce seller-biases when a single seller's title is selected as the product title.

Re-decoding Approaches. Re-decoding is a

generative process that learns to predict the posterior probability $p(y|x)$ (in our case, the posterior probability of a generated title y given the initial list of user-created titles x), which can also be viewed as a sequence quality score. Since quality scores are used to rank the partial sequences, an accurate scoring function would yield the highest quality outputs. Decoding can be seen in Minimum Bayes' Risk Combination (González-Rubio et al., 2011; González-Rubio and Casacuberta, 2013), abstractive summarization (Rush et al., 2015; Chopra et al., 2016), and Neural Machine Translation (NMT) models (Bahdanau et al., 2014; Chen et al., 2016; Vaswani et al., 2017). State-of-the-art approaches utilize encoder-decoder models that extract a feature representation of a variable-length input sentence before generating an output. However, the bottleneck of this approach is its dependence on the size of quality data; it often performs poorly when annotated data is noisy and/or insufficient (Koehn, 2017).

Hypothesis Fusion. An alternative approach is neither to select nor to generate, but to 'fuse' already generated hypotheses. This, for instance, can be done using Confusion Network (CN) decoding (Ma, 2014). In this approach, a confusion network is generated by first selecting a listing title as backbone, and then by aligning it to all the other listings. The network is then traversed to obtain the product title with the highest consensus among the input hypotheses. This title can be decoded with decoding units that include either phrase-level (Feng et al., 2009; Du and Way, 2010) or word-level (Barrault, 2010; Rosti et al., 2007; Fiscus, 1997). Systems can choose between 1-to-1 mappings (Barrault, 2010; Rosti et al., 2007; Du and Way, 2010) or many-to-many mappings (lattice) (Feng et al., 2009; Ma and McKeown, 2015; Matusov et al., 2006) in hypothesis alignment. The main drawbacks of these solutions are: (1) final output quality is highly dependent on the quality of the selected backbone (aligning hypotheses to a poor-quality listing can result in outputs that are far from being usable in real industrial settings), and (2) lattice creation becomes computationally expensive as the number of initial hypotheses grows, potentially $\mathcal{O}(n^2)$. This makes approaches based on CN unsuitable for our working scenario where there is the need of generating titles for millions of products where each product consists of a potentially large number of listing ti-

tles. Our approach must generate product titles in linear time and must be robust to noises present in seller-created titles.

3 Title Generation

This system's purpose is to provide hypotheses of product titles. It receives as input a list of item titles for listings previously aggregated into one product (like the titles at the bottom of Figure 1) and product-related data in the form of slot-value pairs (as the name-value pairs shown under "Product Details" in Figure 1). In addition to these, a human-curated reference product title is required during training time.

The process of generating titles can be roughly summarized into two steps. The first is computing different statistics about the item titles: n-gram counts (in this implementation fixed to bi-grams), inverse document frequency (IDF) of each unigram, listing titles length, counts of tokens given the position of each unigram in the listings, and filtering of slot-value pairs. The slot-value pairs are defined a priori and they are based on the aggregation of titles into products, which means some of the pairs can present noise. In order to filter out noisy slot-value pairs and to understand which pairs are important, we derive an importance score for each pair. This score is computed by dividing the number of times a value appears at least once in the listing titles by the number of listing titles aggregated to the product. The top-k pairs according to this score are kept. The second step consists of performing the recombination of n-grams found in the titles using an heuristic stack-based search algorithm, also known as stack decoding (Wang and Waibel, 1997) using all the information computed in the first step.

3.1 Stack Decoding for Title Generation

The idea of stack decoding is to keep a list of multiple stacks, in which each stack represents a position of the title being generated. The search algorithm initiates with a start symbol (<s>) and expands the title hypotheses position-by-position (given the pre-computed bi-gram counts). The process is summarized in Algorithm 1.

The hypotheses are expanded by the `get_transitions` function. It consists of retrieving all the possible transitions from the current token (the last token of the hypothesis in hyp, that is the hypothesis being generated).

Algorithm 1: Stack decoder for title generation

Data: titles and SV_pairs preprocessed and
tokenized

Result: product_titles sorted by score

Initialize stacks with first stack with single
hypothesis <s> and max_stack_number- 1
empty stacks;

for *current stack in* stacks **do**

  while *previous stack in* stacks *is not*
empty **do**

    Get the top hypothesis hyp in the
previous stack;

    candidates ← `get_transitions`
(hyp, titles, SV_pairs);

    for *each* candidate *in* candidates **do**

      if candidate *token is not EOS*
symbol **then**

        create new_hyp out of
candidate;

        adds new_hyp to current stack
in stacks;

      end

    end

    `compute_scores` (candidates);

    order candidates by score;

    add `prune` (candidates) to current
stack in stacks;

  end

end

This is performed by looking up the most likely words to follow the current word as given by the bi-gram and token position counts (transformed into probabilities and represented by titles in Algorithm 1). For each hypothesis candidate token a new hypothesis is created and placed in the current position stack in stacks. If the candidate token of the new hypothesis is the end-of-sentence (EOS – </s>) symbol, the new hypothesis is not created. This whole process is repeated until the current stack is not empty, i.e., there are no hypotheses to expand.

The next step is to score all the hypotheses in candidates. Here, the approach taken is to build a regressor that predicts a score used to rank the hypotheses. This is implemented using an algorithm that induces a model that predicts BLEU scores (Papineni et al., 2002). The approach is simple: at training time, the scores are derived by computing the sentence-level BLEU score between each title hypothesis in candidates and the human-curated reference provided. At inference time, the score is the one predicted by the regressor.

For training the regressor we explore information computed during the search process. For each hypothesis (which can be a partial, not complete title), 13 features are extracted. The feature set contain features that are **global** and applied to every title under a product, such as: the number of listing titles of the product and average title length of the listings of the product. The other features are **local** to the hypotheses, such as: *1)* the cumulative bi-gram probability of the hypothesis; *2)* the cumulative position probability over all tokens in the hypothesis; *3)* the IDF score of the last token of the hypothesis; *4)* a ratio between the last token position and the average title length among all listings of the product; *5)* the hypothesis length; *6)* the number of irrelevant information matches in the hypothesis (computed based on lists of irrelevant condition-, shipping- or quantity-related tokens); *7)* coverage penalty: a slot-value pair coverage penalty that given the list of important slot-value pairs, computes a score that is a ratio of the importance score and the number of uncovered slots; *8)* language model (LM) score for the whole hypothesis string (4-gram LM trained with Kneser-Ney smoothing (Kneser and Ney, 1995) on a set of human-curated titles); *9)* number of values of slot-value pairs present in the hypothesis; *10)* length penalty: the absolute difference between the average title length and the current position of the candidate token divided by the average title length and *11)* gain function score: a log-linear combination of 1, 2, 6, 8 and 10. These features are descriptors that try to capture content and structure of the titles using information about what is important in a product title and what is not. They are language agnostic and can be applied to any language.

For training the regressor we use a least squares linear regression algorithm which is fast both during training and inference time. Before training, the feature matrix columns are normalized by removing the mean and scaling to unit variance.

After obtaining a score for each candidate in the current stack, the candidates are sorted in descending order and a pruning strategy is used to filter the hypothesis. The pruning approach that yielded best results during development was keeping the top-k candidates of the ordered list. This pruning is implemented in the `prune` function. After this step, the current stack is updated with the kept candidates and the process moves to the stack representing the next position in the generated title.

In the next section, we describe an approach that performs title quality prediction, similar to what the regressor used for ranking the hypotheses does. The main difference is that the quality prediction model is trained on tagged data with quality-oriented tags instead of BLEU scores. The quality tags are based on a pre-defined set of quality requirements which are a better proxy of quality than edit-distance referece-based metrics such as BLEU. Furthermore, the system can use a set of more diverse global information to incorporate during modeling as well as more complex learning algorithms, as there are no speed performance limiting issues. The regression model used in search, instead, needs to be fast enough to produce predictions at inference time during search without making the process slow.

4   Title Quality Prediction

The purpose of a title quality prediction system is to assess at real-time whether a title can be used or not, without relying on humans to perform the decision and independently of the system used to provide the title. Therefore, the system must be system/source-agnostic and work in an absolute notion of quality.

An important step of building a system that predicts the quality of automatically-generated output is the definition of quality itself. Here, we define what is a good product title and what are the main dimensions of this definition. Overall, a product title should provide a concise but accurate description of what the product is about. What is important to be in the title depends on different types of products (or categories). Cell phones for example require the brand, model, color and carrier, but not a shoe size.

The main dimensions used to determine whether a title is good or not are: absence of both important information issues and irrelevant information issues. The former refers to relevant information that is missing or incorrect in a title; for instance, the brand, model, and product type specification (what is the product) should be appropriate. The latter refers to information that is not required and should be omitted such as condition (e.g. *"new"*, *"used"*, *"in a box"*, etc), shipping

(e.g. *"free shipping"*, *"U.S shipping"*), marketing (e.g. *"amazing"*, *"best offer"*), quantity, and price expressions or any other kind of expressions that are not related to the product itself but to the listing. Furthermore, the latter also includes any kind of repetition (same surface word or related words). Next, we describe the approach to modeling title quality prediction using classification algorithms.

4.1   Learning Algorithms

We cast the title quality prediction problem as a classification problem in which the labels indicate whether the product title is good for usage. More details about the data used to train the classifier are given in Section 5.1. We have explored two different learning algorithms to induce classifiers for this task: random forests (Breiman, 2001) and Bidirectional Long Short-Term Memory models (LSTMs, Hochreiter and Schmidhuber (1997); Schuster and Paliwal (1997)). Random forests (RF) are ensemble classifiers that induce several decision trees using some source of randomness to form a diverse set of estimators (Breiman, 2001).

Recurrent neural networks (RNNs) are models well-suited to deal with variable-length input like natural language sentences. Though RNNs can cope with variable-length sequences, the optimization of the weight matrices in RNNs is hard: when the gradients are back-propagated, they decrease to the point of becoming so small that the weights cannot be updated, specially over long input sequences. Hochreiter and Schmidhuber (1997) proposed LSTMs, which are able to overcome the vanishing gradients problem by capturing long-range dependencies through the use of gated memory cell units that can sustain information across long input sequences. In this work, we use bidirectional LSTMs, which have an additional layer that receives the reversed sequence as input, thus keeping track of past and future states. For more details on RNNs, LSTMs and their bidirectional counterparts (biRNN and biLSTM) we refer the interested reader to Goldberg (2016).

4.2   Features and Architecture

For modelling the problem using the learning algorithms described in Section 4.1, we resort to several kinds of information. The RF models use as a basis a bag-of-words (BoW) representation of the titles whereas the biLSTM-based models use the embedded representation of the words. In addition to these, several features are extracted (total of 80 features) and they can be roughly grouped into: length features (e.g. length of the titles in tokens and chars, ratios of the title length and the aggregated average, max or min title length under a product), counts of repeated tokens (excluding punctuation and numbers), counts of encoding errors, and slot-value pairs coverage (counts and ratios of values matching the tokens of the title). All of these features are independent from the generation process and were designed to be agnostic with respect to the way the title has been obtained.

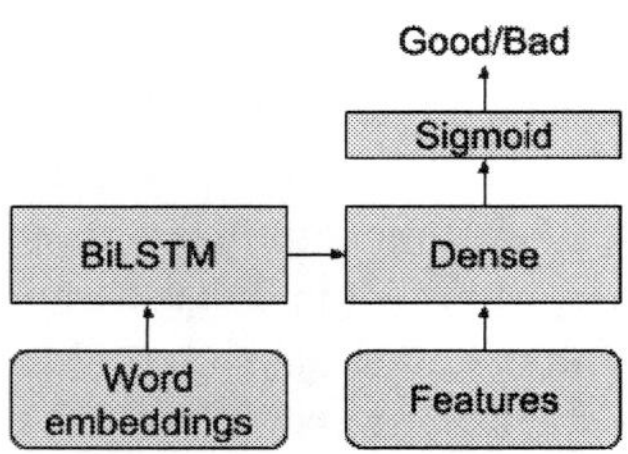

Figure 2: BiLSTM architecture with features concatenated in the hidden layer.

The feature extraction step for the RF models includes concatenating the BoW representation to the features extracted. The biLSTM-based models can also be used with features and the architecture is represented in Figure 4.2. The network has two inputs: the embedded representation of the words in the title and the features computed for the title. The word embeddings are used as input for the biLSTM network and the features are concatenated to the output representation of the biLSTM in a hidden layer. The output layer predicts the class using a sigmoid activation. When the features are not used, the only difference in Figure 4.2 is the concatenation of features.

5 Experimental Settings

In this section we describe relevant settings used in our experiments with the title generation and quality prediction systems.

5.1 Data

The input data for the systems consists of a series of listing titles aggregated into a product. In addition, we have access to slot-value pairs at the product-level. All the data used in our experiments is proprietary user-generated data containing different kinds of peculiarities and noise, such as spelling errors, emoticons and punctuation marks. In addition, the aggregation of the listing

titles into a specific product is not perfect, featuring noise due to the presence of items of other products. As an example, in Figure 1, one of the listing titles lists a smartphone with 32GB memory capacity while the product is of 64GB. Therefore, the challenges presented by the data are the same challenges posed by real-world contexts, in which noise is a constant. In order to alleviate some of these problems, we preprocess the data using an in-house modified version of the Stanford tokenizer that does not break certain tokens (e.g. model identifiers – "DM-234/5").

Generation Data. For training the generation model, we used about 1.4 million listing titles which are part of 16,733 products. The number of listings per product ranges from 1 to 500 with an average of 87.6 and a median of 6. About 62% of the products have 10 or less listings. There are about 1200 popular products which have 500 listings. In Addition we have on average 31.3 slot-values per product (median 27). The average length of a tile is 64.4 characters or 10.4 tokens. For each product we have one human-curated title as reference. As development data we use a set of 749 products with 51,441 listing titles which are sampled out of the same distribution of the training data. An important detail about the data splits is that they are performed at the product-level, i.e., listing titles of a product do not appear both in training and test splits. This is true for all the splits described in this section.

Quality Prediction Data. For the scoring model, a sub-sample of the generation data had each listing title annotated by humans, checking for quality problems related to irrelevant information or important missing information in the titles. The problems are organized in a hierarchy in which the main groups are: copyright issues (e.g. brand, model spelling problems); encoding issues; offensive wording issues; required data not present in the title (e.g. brand, or important features for some products such as color, capacity, among others); irrelevant data present in the title (e.g. condition, shipping, or marketing information, price tags, duplicated words and synonyms, among others); syntax/grammar problems (e.g. title not comprehensible because of word ordering or lack of words). This hierarchy has a total of 22 issues. By the end of this process we have a set of products with all the titles aggregated into it annotated with issues (there can be more than one issue per title or none if they are good titles).

The same annotation process and guidelines are used for evaluation. Since annotating each title requires effort, we used only 9,823 products with 52,050 titles, which are completely annotated. This sub-sample was created with a limited amount of listings per product to ensure a higher diversity in the data set. The evaluation process is carried out by several annotators (with no title overlap) and the quality of a sub-sample of their annotation has been assessed by a separate group of annotators.

We have on average 5.3 (median 5) titles and 37.2 (median 34) slot-values per product. The average title length is 63.7 characters and 10.6 tokens. The balance of positive and negative labels is 42.9/57.1. The development data consists of 1,000 products with 5,174 listing titles, which are sampled out of the same distribution of the scorer training data. The balance of positive and negative labels is 44.3/55.7.

Evaluation Data. In order to evaluate the generated output, human evaluation on an additional set of 2,000 products has been carried out. The evaluation is performed by analyzing the output of each system. The analysis process follows the same guidelines applied for annotating the title quality predictor training data described above, analyzing the different dimensions of a title that can lead to poor product titles (laid out in Section 4 and fine-grained in the quality prediction data description, above).

5.2 Baselines

For the **generation** task, a reasonable baseline is to have a rule-based system that combines the slot-value pairs while performing some content selection similar to the rule-based approach proposed by Mathur et al. (2017). For that, we built a simple system that concatenates the most important values of the product's slot-value pairs to form the product title. We derive the importance of a slot-value pair in the same way we obtain the score derived for filtering them, which is described in Section 3. After deriving the score, we order pairs by this value and select the top-10 to form a title. Another baseline is the selection of the most frequent listing title under a product. The fact that different sellers independently used it can in fact indicate that it represents a good title hypothesis.

For the **quality prediction** task the baseline is

the majority class of the training set.

5.3 Parameter Settings

The most important parameter of the **title generation** system is the beam size, which was set to 3 (the one giving the best performance in terms of BLEU score during the development of the model). We used sentence-level BLEU to compute the labels for training the regression model, set to 4-grams over cased titles and the smoothing mechanism described in (Chen and Cherry, 2014).

The hyper-parameters of the LSTM-based and RF-based **title quality prediction** models were respectively optimized with 300 and 600 iterations of random search with an inner 3-fold cross-validation over the training data. With RFs, we were able to explore the hyper-parameter search space more than with the neural-network-based models due to its faster training time.

6 Results and Discussion

In this Section, we report and discuss the results obtained for each task. We start with the quality prediction problem. It can work as a method for selecting good candidate product titles that complements the generation approach described in Section 3, working as a re-scorer. Next, we discuss the results of the generation task, from a quantitative and qualitative point of view.

6.1 Title Quality Prediction

The intrinsic evaluation of the quality prediction models is carried out on the development set described in Section 5.1. We use classification evaluation metrics to assess the performance of the models. One important remark about this task is that the most important class to predict correctly is the good class. In this problem, it is a bigger issue to have a false positive than a false negative. The metrics we use are the F1-score (harmonic mean of precision and recall for each class averaged), the F1-score for the positive (good) class and the Matthew's correlation coefficient (MCC). The latter is the main metric used in this evaluation because it takes into consideration the class imbalance of the data set.

The results of the experiments are summarized in Table 1. The simplest models trained were RF BoW and biLSTM which are both showing big improvements over the simple Majority baseline when looking at F1 only. When no features are involved, the best choice is to use biLSTM, which reaches a MCC of 34.6. An important trend observed in the results is the strength of the features developed for this problem. The RF trained with the features alone reaches the same performance of the biLSTM. Furthermore, both RF BoW and biLSTM models show large improvements when using the features (around 8 and 10 MCC absolute points, respectively). The best performance is achieved when concatenating the features to the biLSTM representation of the titles, yielding the best results in all metrics (in bold in Table 1). The quality prediction score could be used as a system that selects the best title out of the original listing titles or as a re-scorer mechanism for the stack decoder. We evaluate these in the next section.

6.2 Title Generation

In this section we report results of the title generation task and the human evaluation results. The numbers reported here and in Table 2 are sentence-level BLEU (sBLEU) scores on the development set (described in Section 5.1). The best performance of the generation approach was obtained with beam size 3 (60.1) after trying different values (a beam size of 5 yields 58.5 and performance is not improved with larger values). This is a large improvement over the slot-value pair concatenation baseline, which achieves only 17.1 sBLEU. The assumption that seller-provided titles could provide good hypothesis of titles is supported by the high sBLEU score achieved by the most frequent title baseline (58.8, 1.3 absolute points below generation). Leveraging the quality prediction to select the best title among the seller-provided titles also proves a very strong approach achieving the highest score (68.9). Using the quality prediction system as a re-scorer of the seller-provided and generated titles improves the generation approach by 6.3 absolute points but it does

System / Metric	MCC	F1	F1 good
Majority	0.0	35.8	0.0
RF BoW	31.5	61.1	66.8
RF feats	34.6	67	65.5
RF BoW + feats	40.8	69.9	69
biLSTM	34.6	64.1	67.8
biLSTM + feats	**44.7**	**71.7**	**71.2**

Table 1: Results for the title quality prediction models. MCC is Matthews correlation coefficient.

not match the performance of performing selection over seller titles only.

System	sBLEU
Slot-value pairs baseline	17.1
Most frequent title	58.8
(1) SD, beam = 3	60.1
(2) biLSTM + features	68.9
(1) + (2)	66.4

Table 2: Intrinsic evaluation of outputs of different approaches on development sent. Scores are sentence-level BLEU (sBLEU).

In addition, we performed a qualitative evaluation involving humans that inspected the outputs of the systems. The evaluation was performed to identify problems in the outputs that render them not useful, the same way the data for the quality prediction task is obtained (Section 5.1). We summarize the evaluation by reporting the number of outputs with no issues, represented by the number of good titles provided by each approach. The results of the human evaluation are summarized in Table 3, which shows that the approach with the highest number and proportion of produced outputs is the generation one (SD, beam = 3). It is followed by the combination of generation and quality prediction as re-scorer and last the quality prediction system over seller-provided titles only.

System	# good	% good
(1) SD, beam = 3	**754**	**37.7**
(2) biLSTM + feats	660	33
(1) + (2)	700	35

Table 3: Human evaluation results.

The human evaluation results contrasts with those obtained in the intrinsic evaluation using the BLEU metric over references. The main reason for this contrast is due to the fact that metrics based on string distances between outputs and references penalize very lightly crucial tokens that might render the output useless. For example, in our case, having an expression like *"new in a box"* makes the title not a good product title candidate anymore. Likewise, having a wrong brand or model, renders the title useless.

A few examples can be seen in Table 4, in which the third column lists issues found by the annotators during the qualitative evaluation of the sys-

System	Output	Comments
(1)	Edifier Studio R1280T 2.0 Channel Speaker	No issues
(2)	Edifier R1280T Wired Active	Missing product type
(1) + (2)	Edifier R1280T Wired Active	Missing product type
(1)	PLAYSTATION4 Bundle Sony Console-Uncharted 4 Slim 500GB	Casing of model, order of tokens
(2)	PLAYSTATION4 Slim 500GB Console-Uncharted 4 Bundle Sony	Casing of model, order of tokens
(1) + (2)	PLAYSTATION4 Slim 500GB Console-Uncharted 4 Bundle Sony	Casing of model, order of tokens
(1)	Quell Carbon Monoxide Detector Digital Display Alarm (No Wiring (Model PD04) Operated 130415	Unnecessary tokens and segmentation
(2)	Quell Carbon Monoxide Detector & Alarm	No issues
(1) + (2)	Quell Carbon Monoxide Detector & Alarm	No issues
(1)	Pioneer N-P01-K Compact Network Audio Player-Black but 2 Lines on Display	Unwanted tokens (but 2 Lines on Display)
(2)	Pioneer N-P01-K Network Audio Player-Black	No issues
(1) + (2)	Pioneer N-P01-K Compact Network Audio Player-Black Bluetooth Lines on Display	Unwanted tokens (Bluetooth Lines on Display)

Table 4: Output examples generated by the systems evaluated in the human evaluation. Third column lists the issues in each output.

tems outputs. In the first block of outputs, for example, some titles do not present the specification of the type of the product (what is the product). The observation that BLEU alone is not appropriate for evaluating natural language generation systems is not new and corroborates previous work on the field, most notably the recent work by Reiter (2018).

Another important trend observed in Table 3 is that using the quality prediction system as a re-scorer of the generated and seller titles does not improve over generation alone. We hypothesize this is due to the fact that both systems are trained separately and therefore do not leverage from the signals and features both systems explore. As future work we would like to experiment with joint training of the generation and quality prediction systems, in order to cope with this gap.

7 Conclusion

We present an approach that automatically generates e-commerce product titles out of seller-provided titles aggregated into a product. Furthermore, we devise an approach that automatically assesses the quality of a candidate product title without resorting to human references. We evaluate both approaches on a challenging real-world setting and perform quantitative and qualitative evaluation of the systems. Results show that the best generation approach is based on the stack decoder search algorithm followed by the combination of the search with the quality predictor as a re-scorer. Furthermore, both approaches presented in this work are robust enough to deal with real world user-generated data, i.e. they can produce good quality outputs even when the input data is noisy. Finally, this work sets a few interesting directions such as exploring ways of jointly training both the generation and quality prediction ap-

proach in order to improve the overall generation and quality prediction accuracy.

References

Dzmitry Bahdanau, Kyunghyun Cho, and Yoshua Bengio. 2014. Neural machine translation by jointly learning to align and translate. *arXiv preprint arXiv:1409.0473*.

Loïc Barrault. 2010. Many: Open source machine translation system combination. *The Prague Bulletin of Mathematical Linguistics*, 93:147–155.

Leo Breiman. 2001. Random forests. *Machine Learning*, 45(1):5–32.

Jaime Carbonell and Jade Goldstein. 1998. The use of mmr, diversity-based reranking for reordering documents and producing summaries. In *Proceedings of the 21st annual international ACM SIGIR conference on Research and development in information retrieval*, pages 335–336. ACM.

Boxing Chen and Colin Cherry. 2014. A systematic comparison of smoothing techniques for sentence-level bleu. In *Proceedings of the Ninth Workshop on Statistical Machine Translation*, pages 362–367, Baltimore, Maryland, USA. Association for Computational Linguistics.

Wenhu Chen, Evgeny Matusov, Shahram Khadivi, and Jan-Thorsten Peter. 2016. Guided alignment training for topic-aware neural machine translation. *arXiv preprint arXiv:1607.01628*.

Sumit Chopra, Michael Auli, Alexander M Rush, and SEAS Harvard. 2016. Abstractive sentence summarization with attentive recurrent neural networks. *Proceedings of NAACL-HLT16*, pages 93–98.

Robert Dale, Stephen J Green, Maria Milosavljevic, C Ecile Paris, Cornelia Verspoor, and Sandra Williams. 1998. The Realities of Generating Natural Language from Databases. In *Proceedings of the Applications Track of the 11th Australian Joint Conference on Artificial Intelligence*, pages 62–74.

Jacob Devlin and Spyros Matsoukas. 2012. Trait-based hypothesis selection for machine translation. In *Proceedings of the 2012 Conference of the North American Chapter of the Association for Computational Linguistics: Human Language Technologies*, pages 528–532, Montréal, Canada. Association for Computational Linguistics.

Jinhua Du and Andy Way. 2010. Using TERp to augment the system combination for SMT. In *Proceedings of the Ninth Conference of the Association for Machine Translation in the Americas*.

Yang Feng, Yang Liu, Haitao Mi, Qun Liu, and Yajuan Lü. 2009. Lattice-based system combination for statistical machine translation. In *Proceedings of the 2009 Conference on Empirical Methods in Natural Language Processing*, pages 1105–1113, Singapore. Association for Computational Linguistics.

Jonathan G Fiscus. 1997. A post-processing system to yield reduced word error rates: Recognizer output voting error reduction (rover). In *Automatic Speech Recognition and Understanding, 1997. Proceedings., 1997 IEEE Workshop on*, pages 347–354. IEEE.

Daniel Jacob Gillick. 2011. *The elements of automatic summarization*. Ph.D. thesis, UNIVERSITY OF CALIFORNIA, BERKELEY.

Yoav Goldberg. 2016. A primer on neural network models for natural language processing. *J. Artif. Int. Res.*, 57(1):345–420.

Jesús González-Rubio and Francisco Casacuberta. 2013. Improving the minimum Bayes' risk combination of machine translation systems. In *Proceedings of the International Workshop on Spoken Language Translation (IWSLT)*.

Jesús González-Rubio, Alfons Juan, and Francisco Casacuberta. 2011. Minimum bayes-risk system combination. In *Proceedings of the 49th Annual Meeting of the Association for Computational Linguistics: Human Language Technologies-Volume 1*, pages 1268–1277. Association for Computational Linguistics.

Sepp Hochreiter and Jürgen Schmidhuber. 1997. Lstm can solve hard long time lag problems. In *Advances in neural information processing systems*, pages 473–479.

Reinhard Kneser and Hermann Ney. 1995. Improved backing-off for m-gram language modeling. In *1995 International Conference on Acoustics, Speech, and Signal Processing, ICASSP '95, Detroit, Michigan, USA, May 08-12, 1995*, pages 181–184.

Philipp Koehn. 2017. Neural machine translation. *arXiv preprint arXiv:1709.07809*.

Wei-Yun Ma. 2014. *Hybrid System Combination for Machine Translation: An Integration of Phrase-level and Sentence-level Combination Approaches*. Columbia University.

Wei-Yun Ma and Kathleen McKeown. 2015. System combination for machine translation through paraphrasing. In *EMNLP*, pages 1053–1058.

Prashant Mathur, Nicola Ueffing, and Gregor Leusch. 2017. Generating titles for millions of browse pages on an e-commerce site. In *The 10th International Conference on Natural Language Generation*, pages 158–167. Association for Computational Linguistics.

Evgeny Matusov, Nicola Ueffing, and Hermann Ney. 2006. Computing consensus translation for multiple machine translation systems using enhanced hypothesis alignment. In *EACL*.

Kishore Papineni, Salim Roukos, Todd Ward, and Wei-Jing Zhu. 2002. Bleu: a method for automatic evaluation of machine translation. In *Proceedings of the 40th annual meeting on association for computational linguistics*, pages 311–318. Association for Computational Linguistics.

Ehud Reiter. 2018. BLEU Structured Review A Structured Review of the Validity of BLEU. *Computational Linguistics*.

Antti-Veikko I Rosti, Spyridon Matsoukas, and Richard Schwartz. 2007. Improved word-level system combination for machine translation. In *Annual Meeting-Association for Computational Linguistics*, volume 45, page 312.

Alexander M. Rush, Sumit Chopra, and Jason Weston. 2015. A neural attention model for abstractive sentence summarization. In *EMNLP*, pages 379–389. The Association for Computational Linguistics.

M. Schuster and K.K. Paliwal. 1997. Bidirectional recurrent neural networks. *Trans. Sig. Proc.*, 45(11):2673–2681.

Matthew Snover, Bonnie Dorr, Richard Schwartz, Linnea Micciulla, and John Makhoul. 2006. A Study of Translation Edit Rate with Targeted Human Annotation. In *Proceedings of Association for Machine Translation in the Americas*, pages 223–231, Cambridge, Massachusetts, USA.

Hirokazu Suzuki. 2011. Automatic post-editing based on SMT and its selective application by sentence-level automatic quality evaluation. In *Proceedings of the 13th Machine Translation Summit (MT Summit XIII)*, pages 156–163. International Association for Machine Translation.

Ashish Vaswani, Noam Shazeer, Niki Parmar, Jakob Uszkoreit, Llion Jones, Aidan N Gomez, Lukasz Kaiser, and Illia Polosukhin. 2017. Attention is all you need. *arXiv preprint arXiv:1706.03762*.

Ye-Yi Wang and Alex Waibel. 1997. Decoding algorithm in statistical machine translation. In *Proceedings of the 35th Annual Meeting of the Association for Computational Linguistics and Eighth Conference of the European Chapter of the Association for*

Computational Linguistics, ACL '98, pages 366–372, Stroudsburg, PA, USA. Association for Computational Linguistics.

Designing and testing the messages produced by a virtual dietitian

Luca Anselma
Dipartimento di Informatica
Università degli Studi di Torino
C.so Svizzera 185, 10149 Torino, Italy
anselma@di.unito.it

Alessandro Mazzei
Dipartimento di Informatica
Università degli Studi di Torino
C.so Svizzera 185, 10149 Torino, Italy
mazzei@di.unito.it

Abstract

This paper presents a project about the automatic generation of persuasive messages in the context of the diet management. In the first part of the paper we introduce the basic mechanisms related to data interpretation and content selection for a numerical data-to-text generation architecture. In the second part of the paper we discuss a number of factors influencing the design of the messages. In particular, we consider the design of the aggregation procedure. Finally, we present the results of a human-based evaluation concerning this design factor.

1 Introduction

The ubiquity of modern technologies allows computers to communicate anytime anywhere with humans. As a consequence, virtual assistant can give positive stimuli when it is really necessary, *kairos* in the Fogg's terminology (Fogg, 2002). In the context of the diet domain, the crucial moment is when people come into a restaurant and decide which dish or menu to order. Often people do not have a healthy diet since they do not know that a specific dish is in contrast to their diet. So, they do not have the correct information, that is the stimulus, at the right time. As a consequence, a *virtual dietitian*, that is a virtual assistant in the diet domain, needs to provide three specific facilities. First, the assistant needs to reason in order to enhance the users' computational abilities to recognize healthy dishes. Second, it needs to generate a persuasive stimulus when it is really necessary, i.e., when users have to decide what to eat. Third, the assistant has to support the user in devising the consequences of a diet transgression.

In this paper we consider the generation of persuasive natural language messages in the diet domain. We describe the actual implementation of the natural language generation (NLG) module of the diet management system called MADiMan (Multimedia Application for Diet Management) (Anselma and Mazzei, 2015). One of the main goals of this project is to investigate on the possibility to apply persuasive NLG for helping people to have a virtuous behavior (Reiter et al., 2003; Kaptein et al., 2012; Braun et al., 2015, 2018; Conde-Clemente et al., 2018). MADiMan performs numerical computation combining food energetic values with diet requirements and reports the result of the computation by using natural language. A crucial point in this process is the combination of information concerning the different macronutrients in the dish, that are carbohydrates, lipids and proteins.

The specific research questions which we want to investigate on in this paper concern the linguistic shape of the messages produced by MADiMan. As a first step towards the building of a complete persuasive system, we evaluate the appealing of the messages by varying two specific linguistic features, that are the aggregation strategy and the lexical choice procedure. We show the first results of a human-based experimentation, that is semantic aggregation increases the engaging of the messages. Moreover, we report some results on the desirability of lexical variability in the messages.

The paper is organized as follows. In Section 2 we give a brief introduction to MADiMan project. In Section 3, we describe the data interpretation and content selection process for converting the numerical output of the numeric reasoner into a symbolic form. In Section 4, we describe the design of the messages that are produced with a realization engine. In particular, in Section 4.1 we discuss two specific algorithms used to aggregate the

Proceedings of The 11th International Natural Language Generation Conference, pages 244–253,
Tilburg, The Netherlands, November 5-8, 2018. ©2018 Association for Computational Linguistics

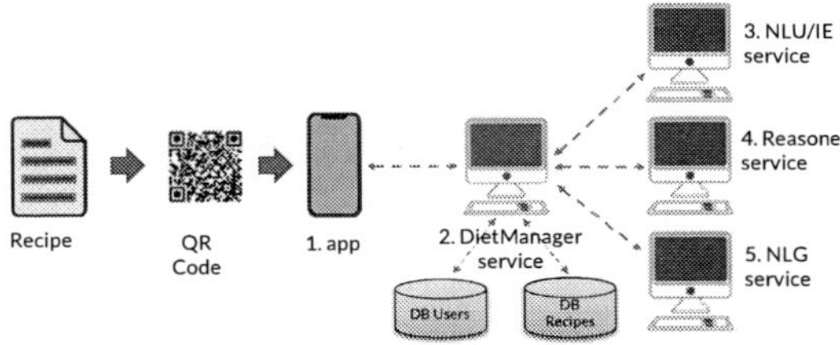

Figure 1: A schema of the MADiMan architecture.

messages. In Section 5, we discuss the experimental setting that we use to give a first human-based evaluation of the message generator. Finally, Section 6 closes the paper with some discussions and pointing on future work.

2   The MADiMan Architecture

The MADiMan system is a virtual dietitian designed: (1) to recover the nutritional information directly from a specific recipe, (2) to reason over recipes and diets by allowing some forms of diet disobedience, and (3) to persuade the user to minimize these acts of disobedience. MADiMan offers facilities to check the compatibility and to foresee the impact that a specific meal has with a specific diet.

In Figure 1 we depict the architecture of the system implementing the MADiMan virtual dietitian. The information flow is: (1) A user, by using an app, recovers the specific recipe of a dish which she wants to eat. (2) The app, communicating with the DietManager service, retrieves the user diet together with the list of the food that the user has eaten in the last days. (3) The NLU/IE module computes the salient nutrition information about the specific course. (4) The Reasoner, using the user diet and the list of the food that has been eaten in the last days, produces the final recommendation about the dish for the user. (5) The NLGenerator uses the recommendation given by the Reasoner, produces an explanation for the user in simple natural language. (6) The DietManager sends the result produced by the NLGenerator to the app: the user will see this final result on her smartphone. If the user decides to eat the dish, the app will send this information to the DietManager that will update the list of food eaten.

The reasoning module is a numeric reasoner based on Simple Temporal Problems (STPs) (Dechter et al., 1991). In a diet it is necessary to consider parameters such as energy require-

ments and amount of macronutrients. The medical literature (e.g., (LARN, 2014)) provides Dietary Reference Values (DRVs) that can be computed from user information such as weight, gender, age, lifestyle. For example, let us consider a 40-year-old male who is 1.80 m tall, weighs 71.3 kg and has a sedentary lifestyle; such a person has an energy requirement of 2450 kcal/day. Moreover, he is recommended to assume (LARN, 2014), e.g., 260 kcal/day of proteins, 735 kcal/day of lipids and 1455 kcal/day of carbohydrates. In MADiMan we represent the DRVs as STP constraints (Anselma et al., 2017). STP models a set of constraints as a conjunction of bounds on differences. $c \leq x - y \leq d$, i.e., the distance between the time points x and y is within c and d. In our setting, by substituting the temporal distance between temporal points of STP with the DRVs and the caloric values of a dish distributed on the three macronutrients. Thus, e.g., a constraint 500 kcal $\leq lunchE - lunchS \leq 600$ kcal imposes that the *distance* between the start and the end of lunch is between 500 and 600 kcal, i.e., that lunch provides 500-600 kcal. Thus, By using the ideal value for calories (see Fig. 2), MADiMan evaluates the compatibility of the specific dish with the actual status the diet. Moreover, in order to provide a user-friendly information not limited to "consistent/inconsistent" answer and to make it also useful for the sake of user persuasion, MADiMan converts the numeric reasoning into a symbolic form that is suitable for the generation of NL messages (Reiter, 2007).

In the next sections, we describe the detail of the algorithm designed to convert the numerical computation in symbols and to elaborate these symbols in order to produce messages.

3   Data interpretation: converting numbers into categories

In order to show to the user a meaningful feedback, it is necessary to interpret the data resulting from the STP. We consider the case where the user proposes to the system a dish, the system obtains its caloric value, translates it along with the user's diet and past meals into an STP and, by propagating the constraints, obtains the minimal network. For sake of clarity, we present the content selection algorithm by considering one single generic macronutrient, but the real suitability of a dish depends on the results of the three macronutrients (see Section 4).

Using the resulting STP it is possible to classify the proposed dish in one of the following five cases: *permanently inconsistent* (I_1), *occasionally inconsistent* (I_2), *consistent and not balanced* (C_1), *consistent and well-balanced* (C_2) and *consistent and perfectly balanced* (C_3). In the cases I_1 and I_2 the energy supply of the dish is inconsistent. In case I_1 the energy supply is inconsistent with regard to the user's diet as represented in the STP considering the tolerance values. The dish cannot be accepted even independently of the other food the user may possibly eat. This case is detected by considering whether the nutritional value of the dish violates a constraint in the STP. In case I_2 the dish per se does not violate the diet constraints, but – considering the past meals the user has eaten – it would preclude him to be consistent with the diet. Thus, it is inconsistent now, but in the future, e.g., next week, it could become possible to choose it. This case is detected by determining whether the energy supply, despite it satisfies the constraints in the initial STP, is inconsistent with the STP that contains also the constraints related to the food that the user has actually eaten so far.

In the cases C_1, C_2 and C_3 the value of the energy supply is consistent with the diet, also taking into account the other meals that the user has already eaten. It is possible to detect that a meal is consistent by exploiting the minimal network of the STP: if the value of the energy supply is included between the lower and upper bounds of the relative STP constraint, then the STP is certainly consistent and the meal is consistent with the diet. A consistent but not balanced choice of a meal will have consequences on the rest of the user's diet because the user will have to "compensate" it. Thus, we distinguish three cases depending on the level of the adequacy to the diet of the meal's energy supply. In order to discriminate between the cases C_1, C_2 and C_3, we consider how the value of the energy supply stacks upon the allowed range represented in the related STP constraint. We assume that the mean value is the "ideal" value according to the diet's goals and we consider two parametric user-adjustable thresholds relative to the mean: we classify the meal according to the distance from the ideal value as not balanced (C_1), well balanced (C_2) or perfectly balanced (C_3) (see Fig. 2). In particular, we distinguish between excess or lack

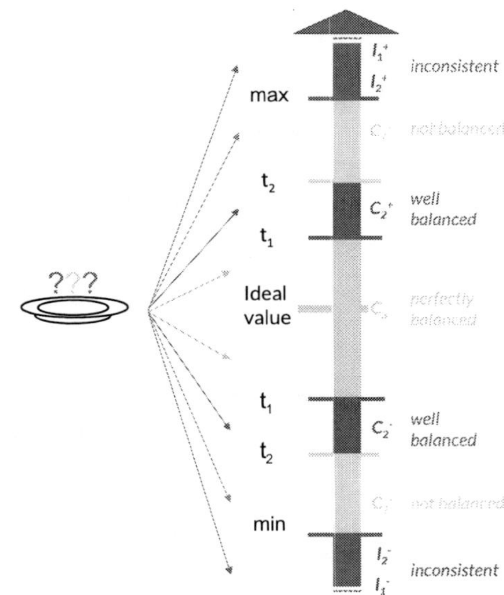

Figure 2: Classification of an inconsistent/consistent value of a meal's energy supply given the minimum and maximum value of an STP constraint.

of energy supply for a meal. If a meal is in excess with regard to the ideal value, we add a $+$ symbol to the category (e.g. C_2^+) to denote the deviation. In contrast, if a meal is lacking, we add a $-$ symbol to the category (e.g. C_1^-). This information is exploited in the generation of the messages.

4 Document/Sentence planning and realization

As a working hypothesis, in this stage of the project, MADiMan produces messages following a fixed rhetorical structure and the document plan follows a very simple fixed schema. The final message will be composed by two parts: an overall evaluation of the dish and three evaluations for the macronutrients (i.e., carbohydrates, lipids, proteins)[1]. For the sake of clarity, we now describe the message by assuming one single macronutrient and in Section 4.1 we discuss how to aggregate the three messages generated for the three different macronutrients.

The sentence generated for expressing the overall evaluation is a single declarative sentence. In order to give a little bit of variation flavor in the syntactic shapes of the messages, we decided to

---

[1] We plan to add a suggestion on the future dishes to eat to the final message in next work.

use a negative copula for I_1, a declarative for I_2, and a positive copula for C_1 or C_2 and C_3. In particular, the overall evaluation is *non buono* (*not good)* or *non va bene* (*not OK*) when there is at least one macronutrient classified as I_1 or I_2, respectively. In alternative, the global evaluation is *buono* (*good*) or *molto buono* (*very good*) when there is at least one macronutrient classified as C_1 or C_2 respectively. Finally, the global evaluation is a *ottima scelta* (*great choice*) (see Table 1).

The sentence generated for expressing the appropriateness of the specific macronutrient follows a fixed schema too. It is a positive copula sentence with a predicate expressing the deviation *ricco/povero/perfetto* (*rich/poor/perfect*), and a PP modifier specifying the macronutrient, e.g. *in lipidi* (*in lipids*). Moreover, an adverb, e.g. *leggermente* (*lightly*) distinguishes C_2 and C_2 cases (see Table 1).

Note that both the overall and the specific macronutrient messages do not use referring expressions. Indeed, at this stage of the project we did not yet account for this specific feature.

Given the persuasive intent of the system, a crucial point concerns the persuasiveness of the messages by considering psychological theories. Many works in literature considered the application of NLG for presenting the results of automated reasoning to the user, e.g., (Weiner, 1980; Barzilay et al., 1998; Lacave and Diez, 2004). Moreover, many theories on the design of persuasive textual (and multimedia) messages have been proposed in the last years. We can split these studies in two narrow categories. The first category includes the theories approaching the persuasion from an empirical point of view, by using strategies and methods typical of the psychology and of the interaction design (Fogg, 2002; Reiter et al., 2003; Cialdini, 2009; Kaptein et al., 2012). The second category includes the theories approaching the persuasion from a theoretical point of view, by using strategies and methods typical of cognitive science (Hovy, 1988; de Rosis and Grasso, 2000; Guerini et al., 2007). Similar to (Kaptein et al., 2012), the Cialdini's general theory of persuasion has inspired our design of the messages (Cialdini, 2009). Cialdini states that there are six patterns which are characteristic of human nature: (1) Reciprocity: *people feel obligated to return a favor*, (2) Scarcity: *people will value scarce products*, (3) Authority: *people value the opinion of ex-perts*, (4) Consistency: *people do as they said they would*, (5) Consensus: *people do as other people do*, (6) Liking: *we say yes to people we like*. Note that compared to the six Cialdini's persuasion patterns, all the messages in Table 1 belong to the patterns of authority and consistency. With respect to the low-level linguistic strategies, by following (de Rosis and Grasso, 2000), we used a number of adverbs, e.g. *davvero, molto, leggermente* (*really, very, lightly*) in order to enhance or mitigate a message. Furthermore, compared to Guerini et al. persuasive strategies taxonomy (Guerini et al., 2007), we can see that all the messages belong to one single category, called *action-inducement & goal-balance & positive-consequence*. This strategy induces an action (i.e. to choose a dish), by using the user's goal (i.e. a healthy diet) and by using the benefits deriving from this goal.

The sentences have been eventually realized by using the SimpleNLG-IT engine realizer, a porting of SimpleNLG for Italian language (Gatt and Reiter, 2009; Mazzei et al., 2016). So, the messages previously described have been primary encoded in the form of quasi-trees and secondary, after aggregation (Section 4.1) and word-lexicalization (Section 4.2), realized by using SimpleNLG-IT. There are several advantages to use SimpleNLG with respect to string templates in this specific project. The three majors advantages are: (i) we have a multilingual Italian/English version of the realiser, that allows to change language by simply switching from Italian to English lexicons, (ii) the design and implementation of the aggregation strategies are simpler, (iii) the diffusion of the Java language allows to integrate the generator into larger Java-based software platform.

In the next sections we describe the procedures of aggregation and lexicalization implemented by using the facilities exposed by SimpleNLG.

4.1 Aggregation strategies

The aggregation plays an important role to generate fluent and efficient texts (Reiter and Dale, 2000; Gatt and Krahmer, 2018). Moreover, in several domains, as healthcare or education, it has been proven that aggregation of the sentences improves the efficacy of the messages (McKeown et al., 1997; DiEugenio et al., 2005).

In the specific case of the MADiMan messages, aggregation can be performed in many ways since the messages concerning overall evaluation and

Category	Prototypical Message	English translation
I_1^+/I_1^-	Questo menù non è buono. Il menù è troppo *ricco/povero* in proteine.	This menu is not good. The menu is really *rich/poor* in proteins.
I_2^+/I_2^-	Questo menù non va bene. Il menù è *ricco/povero* in proteine.	This menu is not OK. The menu is *rich/poor* in proteins.
C_1^+/C_1^-	Questo menù è buono. Il menù è *ricco/povero* in proteine.	This menu is good. The menu is *rich/poor* in proteins.
C_2^+/C_2^-	Questo menù è molto buono. Il menù è leggermente *ricco/povero* in proteine.	This menu is very good. The menu is lightly *rich/poor* in proteins.
C_3	Questo menù è un'ottima scelta. Il menù è perfetto in proteine.	This menu is a great choice. The menu is perfect in proteins.

Table 1: The prototypical messages describing the STP reasoner classification for the caloric value for the proteins. The italicized text vary among $+/-$ deviation. The underlined text varies among the three macronutrients.

macronutrients often have very similar quasi-trees.

We write (O_C, O_L, O_P) to indicate the symbolic output for carbohydrates, lipids and proteins respectively, where $O_X \in \{I_1^-, I_1^+, I_2^-, I_2^+, C_1^-, C_1^+, C_2^-, C_2^+, C_3\}$. Indeed, a trivial aggregation strategy based on aggregation at the sentence level could merge only messages that belong to the same category, i.e. $O_x = O_y$: this trivial strategy corresponds to the *syntactic aggregation* in the classification of (Reape and Mellish, 1998). However, we design an aggregation strategy that accounts for a more sophisticated form of *conceptual aggregation*. The aggregation algorithm can be split in two parts, a *selection* and a *merging*.

Selection

In order to concentrate the focus on the most important information for the diet, the general idea of the selection is to give emphasis on the messages concerning incompatibility. So, during the selection step, if there are messages describing the incompatible value of a macronutrient, all the messages describing the compatible values will be removed. So, in the selection step there are three alternative cases:

A. There is a case of permanent inconsistence on one or more macronutrient: $\exists X \in \{C, L, P\} : O_X = I_1$

B. There is a case of occasional inconsistence on one or more macronutrient: $\forall X \in \{C, L, P\} : O_X \neq I_1 \land \exists Y \in \{C, L, P\} : O_Y = I_2$

C. All the three categories of macronutrients are consistent: $\forall X \in \{C, L, P\} \; \exists i \in \{1, 2, 3\} : O_X = C_i$

In the cases **A.** and **B.**, we aggregate the messages by exploiting the information about incompatibility, that is by removing the messages concerning the compatible macronutrients and by merging the messages about incompatible macronutrients. So, the final document will have one single overall sentence describing the inconsistence, and one merged message concerning the values of the inconsistent macronutrients. In the case **C.**, the final document will have one single overall sentence describing the minimal consistent value, and one merged message concerning the values of all the three macronutrients.

Merging

By taking into account the persuasive goals of the system, we decided to implement and test two different strategies to merge the specific messages concerning the macronutrients. In general there are many possible mechanisms to merge two sentences, i.e., simple conjunction, conjunction via shared participants, conjunction via shared structure, and syntactic embedding (Reiter and Dale, 2000). At this stage of the project, the system allows to use all these mechanisms but syntactic embedding. In particular, we decided to experimentally compare (see Section 5) the conjunction via shared structure on the VP constituent (VP-aggregation) and on the NP contained into prepositional phrase (set-aggregation). In other words, by considering the sentences (i) *The menu is perfect in proteins* and (ii) *The menu is perfect in lipids*, the VP-aggregation produces the sentence *The menu is perfect in proteins and is perfect in lipids* while the set-aggregation produces *The menu is perfect in proteins and lipids*.

We decided to use VP-aggregation and set-aggregation mechanisms since they have two specific features that could influence the persuasiveness of the final message. The VP-aggregation, by repeating the semantic predicate contained in the copula construction, could communicate in a more efficient way the (in)compatibility of a specific macronutrient. In contrast, the set-aggregation produces shorter messages that could be perceived as more natural and so more trustable. Note that VP-aggregation can be always applied independently by the compatibility values and the deviations expressed by the specific macronutrient messages. In contrast, we can apply set-aggregation only when the sentences have exactly the same syntactic shape, which corresponds to having the same value in compatibility and in deviation.

In Section 5 we will evaluate the appealing of messages built with two different aggregation strategies where the first (*all-VP* henceforth) always uses VP-aggregation and the second (*set+VP* henceforth) maximally uses set-aggregation in combination, in same cases, with VP-aggregation. In particular, in order to manage all the possible combinations of compatibility and deviations, for the *set+VP* strategy we follow this simple two-step algorithm:

1. Set-aggregate all the shape-equivalent sentences

2. VP-aggregate the sentence resulting from the first step (if any) with the remaining sentences.

For instance, the sentences *The menu is lightly rich in carbohydrates*, *The menu is rich in lipids*, *The menu is lightly rich in proteins*, will be aggregated in the *all-VP* strategy as *The menu is lightly rich in carbohydrates, is rich in lipids and is lightly rich in proteins*. In contrast, the same sentences will be aggregated in the *set+VP* strategy as *The menu is lightly rich in carbohydrates and proteins and is rich in lipids*.

Finally, note that in some cases we have a certain degree of freedom in the ordering of the aggregated sentences. We followed the idea to start with the most positive feedback, as suggested by some theories of persuasion (Steelman and Rutkowski, 2004; Dohrenwend, 2002). So, we decided to order the aggregated messages by considering their compatibility value. For instance, the sentences *The menu is poor in carbohydrates*, *The menu is lightly rich in lipids*, *The menu is lightly rich in proteins*, will be aggregated as *The menu*

is lightly rich in lipids and proteins and is poor in carbohydrates.

4.2 Choosing words

Another feature that we implemented in realization is a trivial treatment of lexical variations. Indeed, many studies showed the importance and the complexity of the lexicalization task, e.g. (Stede, 1994; Reiter et al., 2005). In particular, an acceptable lexicalization procedure should take into account the contextual and stylistic constraints arising from all the possible words combinations (Gatt and Krahmer, 2018).

We think that variability could play an important role in the persuasive goal of the system. Since a constant lexical choice could be perceived as boring or artificial, for open-class categories (that are nouns, verbs, adjectives and adverbs) we decided to implement two different versions of the lexicalization procedure. The first lexicalization procedure that always associated one single word for each concept, and an alternative second lexicalization procedure that randomly associated one word choosing from a set of three possible words. In particular, for the Italian version of the realizer, the synonymous set has been decided by searching in the default Italian lexicon, that is a *simple* lexicon, i.e., a lexicon studied to be perfectly understood by most Italian people (Mazzei, 2016). We are aware that this trivial lexicalization procedure could give a sort of *cognitive dissonance* in some cases, but we believe that it could also improve the trustability of the system.

Also if the main focus of the experimental part of the paper concerns the experimental evaluation of the aggregation strategies, in Section 5 we provide also some user feedback about lexicon variability.

5 Experimental setting: the CheckYourMeal! app

We describe a first human-based experimentation produced with a small group of 20 users. The main goal of this experimentation was to give a realistic feedback about the appealing and, in some form, the persuasion strength of the message aggregation strategies. So, we designed a *game of diet* simulation (see below). We are aware that a scientific evaluation about the real efficacy of the persuasion power of the NLG should follow the scientific standards of the medical research field (cf. (Reiter et al., 2003)). However, as pointed out by some research in the human computer interaction field, also pilot studies can give important feedbacks "especially when in the early stages of design or when evaluating novel technologies" (Klasnja et al., 2011; Hekler et al., 2013).

In order to create a realistic experimentation we designed and realized an app for mobile called *CheckYourMeal!* (Figure 3). In the current stage, *CheckYourMeal!* is still under development and it is used only for research purposes. So, it is not yet available as a commercial app.

CheckYourMeal! provides many standard functionalities of the *quantified self* domain app, as registration of username/password, log-in, insertion of personal and anthropometric data (e.g., age, weight, physical activity, etc.). The principal goal of the application is to help users in the management of their diets. The diet is considered as a number of constraints over the week (cf. Section 3). The week is scheduled as 21 slots to fill, i.e., breakfast, lunch and supper for each day from Monday to Sunday. For each slot of the week, a number of possible menus are presented to the user, and she can decide to eat one of them. The feedback about the compatibility of a specific menu is provided both in graphical and textual forms. The graphical feedbacks are (i) a cake-shaped diagram showing the caloric contents in carbohydrates, lipids and proteins, and (ii) three histograms showing their ideal values for that specific slot of the week. The textual feedbacks are two sentences automatically generated containing the overall evaluation and macronutrients evaluation respectively. In Figure 3 we report a screenshot of the app with the graphical (lower side) and textual (upper side) feedbacks. The experimentation was performed only in Italian.

We asked the users to interact with *CheckYourMeal!* by considering a simulation context. A user should imagine to eat for a period into a restaurant: for each slot of the week she has to choose only among the menus proposed in the app. In the simulation, the menus were randomly generated by considering the recipes of the Gedeone database, that is a collection of 500 Mediterranean recipes annotated with their caloric contents (Anselma et al., 2018).

Figure 3: A screenshot of the a message showed by CheckYourMeal! app.

Experimental protocol

We prepared an instruction sheet describing the game and the main goals of the experimentation. In particular, we explicitly informed the users that we wanted to compare two different versions of the NL message generator, the blue version and the violet version, but without any other information about the specific qualities that we wanted to test. The blue version corresponds to the *all-VP* aggregation strategy while the violet version corresponds to the *set+VP* aggregation strategy. We believe that with this briefing the testers could give more attention on the linguistic details of the textual feedback. Apart from the blue/violet version tests, we asked the testers to try also a feature called *variable lexicon* (see Section 4.2). We explicitly informed the testers that this feature was not our main experimental goal.

We asked the testers to play the diet game for a simulated period of two weeks, spending at least 15 minutes of their time. Moreover, we asked testers to play one week with the blue version and one week with the violet version. At the end of the experimentation, we asked the testers to compile a feedback form. The form was composed by 24 questions: 8 were multiple choices questions concerning personal data; 4 were Likert-scale questions concerning the app and the lexicon; 9 were Likert-scale questions concerning the blue and violet versions of the generator; finally, 3 were open general questions concerning suggestions for possible improvements of the app, the feeling perceived and the lexicon.

The main hypothesis that we tested was about the appealing of the violet version with respect to the blue version. In particular in the form we wanted to compare four specific properties of the messages, that are *Usefulness, Persuasiveness Boringness, Easiness*. These specific four questions are[2]:

QU: Usefulness perceived: *The text messages in the blue version are more useful than the text messages in the violet version in order to make the best choice.*

QP: Persuasiveness perceived: *The text messages in the blue version are more persuasive than the text messages in the violet version.*

QB: Boringness perceived: *The text messages in the blue version are more boring than the text messages in the violet version.*

QE: Easiness perceived: *The text messages in the blue version are easier to understand than the text messages in the violet version.*

We used a Likert scale from 1 to 5 where 1=*I totally disagree* and 5=*I totally agree.*

In order to evaluate the feasibility of the experimental setting, we first tried the game with a preliminary group of three people: this pre-test suggested us to prepare a more detailed instruction sheet. Successively, we conducted the main study with a group of 20 people. All of them were Italian mother tongue, have provided their real anthropometric data, and have completed the test in a silent ambient after reading the instructions. Most of them were students or faculties in computer science and used a smartphone provided by us. We are aware that the small size and the homogeneity of the test group in this study does not allow to discover possible correlations between subgroup features (e.g. demographics) and final results.

---

[2]Translated form the original Italian questions.

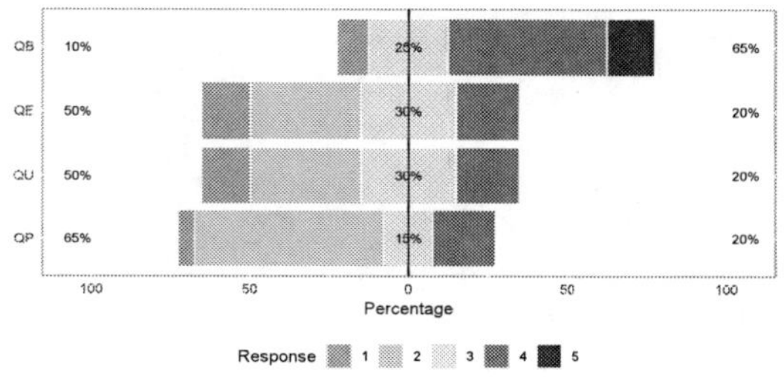

Figure 4: A plot showing the distribution of the answers to the questions QB, QE, QP, QU.

Results

In Figure 4 we report the distribution of the answers to the four questions which are the main goal of our experimentation[3].

The picture shows a quite clear preference for the violet version, which applies the *set+VP* aggregation strategy, with respect to the blue version, which applies the *all+VP* aggregation strategy. In other words, for all four properties, that are boringness (mean=3.60, s.d.=1.10), usefulness (mean=2.55, s.d.=1.00), persuasiveness (mean=2.50, s.d.=0.89), easiness (mean=2.55, s.d.=1.00), the shorter messages produced with the *set+VP* aggregation strategy are preferred with respect to the longer messages produced with the *all-VP* aggregation strategy. Indeed, we tested the statistical significance of the preference for the violet version with respect to the blue one (i.e., the answer has a numeric value < 3 for questions QE, QU, QP and > 3 for question QB). We obtained the (two-tailed) p-values 0.03, 0.03, 0.01, 0.01 for QE, QU, QP, QB respectively.

As post-hoc hypothesis we decided to analyze the result of the Likert-scale question concerning lexicon variability that is: *The "variable lexicon" option makes the use of the app more enjoyable.* (QV, 1=*I totally disagree* and 5=*I totally agree.*). In Figure 5 we report the distribution of the answers for QV (mean=3.40, s.d.=1.0). Also, if the distribution of the answers seems to show a preference for random lexical variations (the p-value for > 3 is 0.04), a specific experimentation is necessary to confirm this result.

An exploratory analysis of the responses given by the users gives us a feedback on the appealing of the app as a whole. In particular, we can infer

---

[3]The statistical analysis was performed by using the Likert package of R. We considered the points in the Likert scale as equidistant.

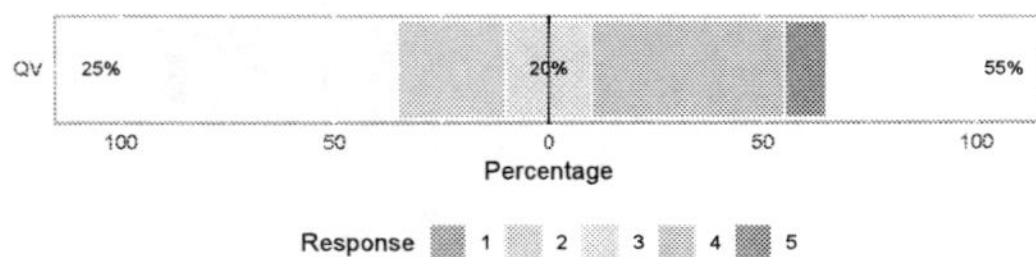

Figure 5: A plot showing the distribution of the answers for the questions QV.

from the distribution of the answers that (1) the user interface of the app is clear, (2) both graphics and text messages are perceived as useful to perform the best choice.

Finally, by reading the free comments section of the forms, an interesting speculation is that the two aggregation strategies have an appeal depending on the polarity of the messages. Indeed, some comments pointed out that the repetition of the predicate (*all-VP* strategy) gives a judgmental or blaming attitude to the virtual dietitian.

6 Conclusions and future work

In this paper we have presented a first human-based evaluation of a NL generator of persuasive messages in the diet management context. We have briefly described the main components of the MADiMan system and we have detailed the design and implementation system of the NLG module. Finally, we have described the details of a game-based simulation of the system by using the *CheckYourMeal!* app. By considering a number of perceived properties, the experimental results show preferences towards short messages obtained with a complex aggregation strategy.

In future work, we intend to perform the experimentation on a greater number of testers. In particular, in order to have more qualified feedback, we intend to evaluate the system with a group of undergraduate students in dietetics. Moreover, with more users we will be able to test several versions of the message generators, considering the variability of the lexicon too.

Another research question that we intend to follow regards the *explainability* of the answer. For tackling such issue, we intend to exploit the information regarding the past meals that the user has eaten during the week.

References

Luca Anselma and Alessandro Mazzei. 2015. Towards Diet Management with Automatic Reasoning and Persuasive Natural Language Generation. In *Progress in Artificial Intelligence - 17th Portuguese Conference on Artificial Intelligence, EPIA 2015, Coimbra, Portugal, September 8-11, 2015. Proceedings*, pages 79–90.

Luca Anselma, Alessandro Mazzei, and Franco De Michieli. 2017. An artificial intelligence framework for compensating transgressions and its application to diet management. *Journal of Biomedical Informatics*, 68:58–70.

Luca Anselma, Alessandro Mazzei, and Andrea Pirone. 2018. Automatic reasoning evaluation in diet management based on an italian cookbook. In *Proceedings of the Joint Workshop on Multimedia for Cooking and Eating Activities and Multimedia Assisted Dietary Management*, CEA/MADiMa '18, pages 59–62, New York, NY, USA. ACM.

Regina Barzilay, Daryl Mccullough, Owen Rambow, Jonathan Decristofaro, Tanya Korelsky, Benoit Lavoie, and Cogentex Inc. 1998. A new approach to expert system explanations. In *9th International Workshop on Natural Language Generation*, pages 78–87.

Daniel Braun, Ehud Reiter, and Advaith Siddharthan. 2015. Creating textual driver feedback from telemetric data. In *ENLG 2015 - Proceedings of the 15th European Workshop on Natural Language Generation, 10-11 September 2015, University of Brighton, Brighton, UK*, pages 156–165.

Daniel Braun, Ehud Reiter, and Advaith Siddharthan. 2018. Saferdrive: An nlg-based behaviour change support system for drivers. *Natural Language Engineering*, 24(4):551–588.

Robert B. Cialdini. 2009. *Influence: science and practice*. Pearson Education.

Patricia Conde-Clemente, Jose M. Alonso, and Gracian Trivino. 2018. Toward automatic generation of linguistic advice for saving energy at home. *Soft Computing*, 22(2):345–359.

Rina Dechter, Itay Meiri, and Judea Pearl. 1991. Temporal constraint networks. *Artif. Intell.*, 49(1-3):61–95.

Barbara DiEugenio, Davide Fossati, Dan Yu, Susan M. Haller, and Michael Glass. 2005. Aggregation Improves Learning: Experiments in Natural Language Generation for Intelligent Tutoring Systems. In *ACL 2005, 43rd Annual Meeting of the Association for Computational Linguistics, Proceedings of the Conference, 25-30 June 2005, University of Michigan, USA*, pages 50–57.

Anne Dohrenwend. 2002. Serving up the feedback sandwich. *Family practice management*, 9(10):43–50.

B.J. Fogg. 2002. *Persuasive Technology. Using computers to change what we think and do*. Morgan Kaufmann Publishers, Elsevier.

Albert Gatt and Emiel Krahmer. 2018. Survey of the state of the art in natural language generation: Core tasks, applications and evaluation. *J. Artif. Intell. Res.*, 61:65–170.

Albert Gatt and Ehud Reiter. 2009. SimpleNLG: A Realisation Engine for Practical Applications. In *Proceedings of the 12th European Workshop on Natural Language Generation*, ENLG '09, pages 90–93, Stroudsburg, PA, USA. Association for Computational Linguistics.

Marco Guerini, Oliviero Stock, and Massimo Zancanaro. 2007. A taxonomy of strategies for multimodal persuasive message generation. *Applied Artificial Intelligence*, 21(2):99–136.

Eric B. Hekler, Predrag Klasnja, Jon E. Froehlich, and Matthew P. Buman. 2013. Mind the theoretical gap: Interpreting, using, and developing behavioral theory in hci research. In *Proceedings of the SIGCHI Conference on Human Factors in Computing Systems*, CHI '13, pages 3307–3316, New York, NY, USA. ACM.

Eduard H. Hovy. 1988. *Generating Natural Language Under Pragmatic Constraints*. Lawrence Erlbaum, Hillsdale, NJ.

Maurits Kaptein, Boris E. R. de Ruyter, Panos Markopoulos, and Emile H. L. Aarts. 2012. Adaptive persuasive systems: A study of tailored persuasive text messages to reduce snacking. *TiiS*, 2(2):10.

Predrag Klasnja, Sunny Consolvo, and Wanda Pratt. 2011. How to evaluate technologies for health behavior change in hci research. In *Proceedings of the SIGCHI Conference on Human Factors in Computing Systems*, CHI '11, pages 3063–3072, New York, NY, USA. ACM.

Carmen Lacave and Francisco J. Diez. 2004. A review of explanation methods for heuristic expert systems. *Knowl. Eng. Rev.*, 19(2):133–146.

LARN. 2014. *LARN - Livelli di Assunzione di Riferimento di Nutrienti ed energia per la popolazione italiana - IV Revisione*. SICS Editore, Italy.

Alessandro Mazzei. 2016. Building a computational lexicon by using SQL. In *Proceedings of Third Italian Conference on Computational Linguistics (CLiC-it 2016) & Fifth Evaluation Campaign of Natural Language Processing and Speech Tools for Italian. Final Workshop (EVALITA 2016), Napoli, Italy, December 5-7, 2016.*, volume 1749, pages 1–5. CEUR-WS.org.

Alessandro Mazzei, Cristina Battaglino, and Cristina Bosco. 2016. SimpleNLG-IT: adapting SimpleNLG to Italian. In *Proceedings of the 9th International Natural Language Generation conference*, pages 184–192, Edinburgh, UK. Association for Computational Linguistics.

Kathleen R. McKeown, Shimei Pan, James Shaw, Desmond A. Jordan, and Barry A. Allen. 1997. Language generation for multimedia healthcare briefings. In *Proceedings of the Fifth Conference on Applied Natural Language Processing*, ANLC '97, pages 277–282, Stroudsburg, PA, USA. Association for Computational Linguistics.

Mike Reape and Chris Mellish. 1998. Just what is aggregation anyway? In *ENLG 1998 - Proceedings of the European Workshop on Natural Language Generation*.

E. Reiter, R. Robertson, and L. Osman. 2003. Lessons from a Failure: Generating Tailored Smoking Cessation Letters. *Artificial Intelligence*, 144:41–58.

Ehud Reiter. 2007. An architecture for data-to-text systems. In *Proc. of the 11th European Workshop on Natural Language Generation*, ENLG '07, pages 97–104, Stroudsburg, PA, USA. Association for Computational Linguistics.

Ehud Reiter and Robert Dale. 2000. *Building Natural Language Generation Systems*. Cambridge University Press, New York, NY, USA.

Ehud Reiter, Somayajulu Sripada, Jim Hunter, and Ian Davy. 2005. Choosing words in computer-generated weather forecasts. *Artificial Intelligence*, 167:137–169.

Fiorella de Rosis and Floriana Grasso. 2000. Affective interactions. chapter Affective Natural Language Generation, pages 204–218. Springer-Verlag, New York, NY, USA.

Manfred Stede. 1994. Lexicalization in natural language generation: A survey. *Artificial Intelligence Review*, 8(4):309–336.

Lisa A. Steelman and Kelly A. Rutkowski. 2004. Moderators of employee reactions to negative feedback. *Journal of Managerial Psychology*, 19(1):6–18.

J. L. Weiner. 1980. Blah, A system which explains its reasoning. *Artif. Intell.*, 15(1-2):19–48.

Generation of Company descriptions using concept-to-text and text-to-text deep models: dataset collection and systems evaluation

Raheel Qader[1]   **Khoder Jneid**[1]   **François Portet**[2]   **Cyril Labbé**[2]

Univ. Grenoble Alpes, LIG

38000 Grenoble, France

[1]`firstname.lastname@univ-grenoble-alpes.fr`

[2]`firstname.lastname@imag.fr`

Abstract

In this paper we study the performance of several state-of-the-art sequence-to-sequence models applied to generation of short company descriptions. The models are evaluated on a newly created and publicly available company dataset that has been collected from Wikipedia. The dataset consists of around 51K company descriptions that can be used for both concept-to-text and text-to-text generation tasks. Automatic metrics and human evaluation scores computed on the generated company descriptions show promising results despite the difficulty of the task as the dataset (like most available datasets) has not been originally designed for machine learning. In addition, we perform correlation analysis between automatic metrics and human evaluations and show that certain automatic metrics are more correlated to human judgments.

1 Introduction

Traditional approaches of Natural Language Generation (NLG) consist in creating specific algorithms in the consensual NLG pipeline (Reiter and Dale, 2000; Gatt and Krahmer, 2018). However, recently there has been a very quick and strong interest in End-to-End (E2E) NLG systems in particular in the Dialogue community (Mairesse and Young, 2014; Wen et al., 2015; Dusek and Jurcícek, 2016) which are data-driven NLG methods jointly learning sentence planning and surface realization. Probably the most well known current effort is the E2E NLG Challenge (Novikova et al., 2017) which has generated a high number of submissions and whose task was to perform sentence planing and realization from dialogue act-based Meaning Representation (MR) on *unaligned* data. This challenge was a great success as it gathered the community around this problem of data-driven NLG models and showed the diversity of techniques that has been proposed to deal with the proposed task. The challenge also revealed that sequence-to-sequence (seq2seq) attention models such as TGEN(Dusek and Jurcícek, 2016) are competitive, yet, other simpler template-based approaches can still be effective (Puzikov and Gurevych, 2018). It also showed that although automatic metrics are useful for learning, they cannot be blindly used to predict human performances in NLG (Reiter and Belz, 2009; Puzikov and Gurevych, 2018). Furthermore, the E2E data contained a lot of redundancy of structure and a limited amount of concepts plus a least 5 references for the same MR input. This is an ideal case for machine learning but is it the one that is encountered in all E2E NLG applications?

In this work, we are interested in applying E2E models in a real world application in which there is a low amount of resources and whose output quality must be at human-level. The task is to produce a short description of a company given either a semi-structured set of slots (MR) or a textual document. This work is performed in the context of a research project with the Skopai company whose aim is to use AI technique to support startup description for attracting investors. More precisely, the task will be to generate an abstract for the article that contains the main factual information about a company.

In this research, we focus on seq2seq models in order to generate a summary for an article for two approaches: **concept-to-text** and **text-to-text**. As emphasized by (Gatt and Krahmer, 2018), there seem to be a convergence of NLG and summarization techniques, that is why for both approaches were recently applied in the

Proceedings of The 11th International Natural Language Generation Conference, pages 254–263,
Tilburg, The Netherlands, November 5-8, 2018. ©2018 Association for Computational Linguistics

text-to-text domain. Furthermore, text-to-text approaches have to explicitly deal with content selection and document planning, tasks that were not the focus of the E2E challenge. In the literature, there has been few work related to our objective. For instance, in (Lebret et al., 2016), authors used a neural model to generate short biographical summaries from structured data (concepts) using a dataset collected from Wikipedia. Similarly, in (Chisholm et al., 2017) a sequence-to-sequence autoencoder with attention was used to generate biographies from Wikipedia. However, both of these work concentrate on generating mainly one sentence summaries, while our aim is to be able to generate longer summaries. In addition, since their generated summaries are extremely short, the information in the summaries is almost always is guaranteed to be present in the concepts, while in our dataset this is not the case. Finally, most Wikipedia biographies have very similar and repetitive writing styles which makes it easier for models to learn them, but in the case of company descriptions, the task is more challenging since most summaries are written in a different style.

The contribution of the paper can be summarized as follow:

- a collection of a realistic dataset for concept-to-text and text-to-text task that is made available to the community;

- the implementation and evaluation of several E2E models for the two tasks;

- an evaluation by naive human subjects and a comparison with the automatic metrics.

The paper starts by describing the dataset collection in Section 2 and then the seq2seq methods in Section 3. Corpus-based experiments and human evaluation are described in Section 4 and 5 respectively. The paper ends with a short discussion of the findings and an outlook for further work.

2 Dataset collection and Analysis

The task under study is to investigate the power of deep models on a specific task: the generation of company summaries. However, no large dataset corresponding to this task was available when the research started. Thus, a dataset about company descriptions has been collected, cleaned up, and organized for the task.

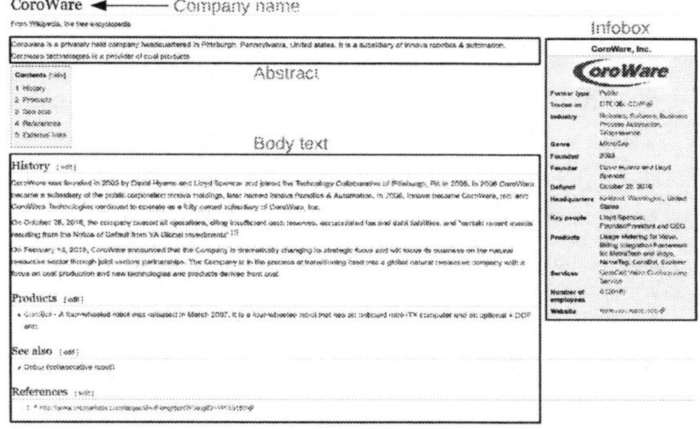

Figure 1: A Wikipedia page of a company. Abstract can be generated from the infobox (concept-to-text) or from the body text (text-to-txt).

2.1 Data source

Information about companies are typically be found in national company registers. However, they are not always accessible and are difficult to crawl. `dbpedia.org` also contains a semantically rich set of information about companies. However, the amount of companies is too small for a machine learning approach. A place were a large number of company descriptions can be found is Wikipedia. Wikipedia is a rich source of different types of data tackling a variety of topics, and the way articles are written in this source can be used for the task we address in this paper. As shown in Figure 1, an article contains an **abstract** followed by a table of content and then a **body** text. The abstract is a brief summary of the entire article containing the important ideas in the body text. Moreover, the top right side is the **infobox** (to be taken as MR), a panel containing semi-structured data about the company described in the article. As a result, English Wikipedia has been considered as a source for the dataset, and only articles about companies were collected.

2.2 Data collection method

The method to collect data was first to build a list of company name/id. This was performed from a dump of English Wikipedia (enwiki-20170820-pages-articles.xml.bz2) from which articles containing the terms "company" or "companies" in the "Category" section were retained. However a large number of articles were actually not company descriptions. Hence, we made use of the infobox attributes such as `Founded, Founder, Products,`

`Industry, Headquarters,` etc. which, in accordance to Wikipedia guidelines, should be found in company descriptions in Wikipedia. Then, articles which did not contain at least two company attributes in the infobox were dismissed from the list. At the end, we ended up with 64553 company links. The articles were then retrieved using the Wikipedia API. The abstract was directly extracted from the xml article as well as the infobox all stored into a json file as set of attribute value pairs. Articles that contained both an empty body and abstract were removed. Also those containing a too small amount of information were discarded leading to 51596 usable companies. Since the aim of the body text was to support single document summarization, information under the sections: `References, See also,` etc. were not needed. Thus the problem became to find out which section in each article indicates the end of the useful information. To do so, an analysis of the most frequent ending sections was performed. As a result, we end up with a list of 84 end headers (`reference, references, noteandreference,` etc.) chosen as a final maker of the body text. At the end of the process, 51k company were retrieved (excluded the empty articles).

For the infobox part, each attribute–value pair was represented as a sequence of string `attribute [value]`. Each attribute value which could contain a list was divided into at most 5 attributes (e.g., `attribute1 [value1] , attribute2 [value2] ... attribute5 [value5]`) using simple regex expression. Hence a string like *"Founder=[David Hyams and Lloyd Spencer]"* was converted into *"founder1[David Hyams], founder2[Lloyd Spencer]"*. At the end, the infobox is composed of 41 attributes with 4.5 attributes per article in average. The abstracts of the final dataset of 51k companies presents a vocabulary of size 158464 words.

2.3 Dataset characteristics

At the end of the process, although the dataset is faithful to the information found in Wikipedia, the dataset is not ideal for machine learning since the abstract, the body and the infobox are only loosely correlated. For instance, Figure 2 shows an abstract which is not based on information provided in the body text. Moreover, Figure 3 shows

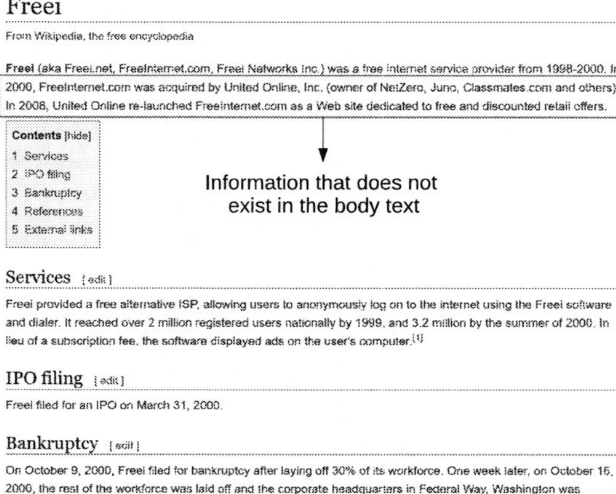

Figure 2: Body text information is not correlated with the summary

that most of the abstract length is between 1 to 5 sentences while the body text size is much more spread with a peak at 1 sentence. The Pearson's correlation between abstract and body length (sentences) is very low $r = 0.275$ even when the body data of size 1 is removed ($r = 0.327$).

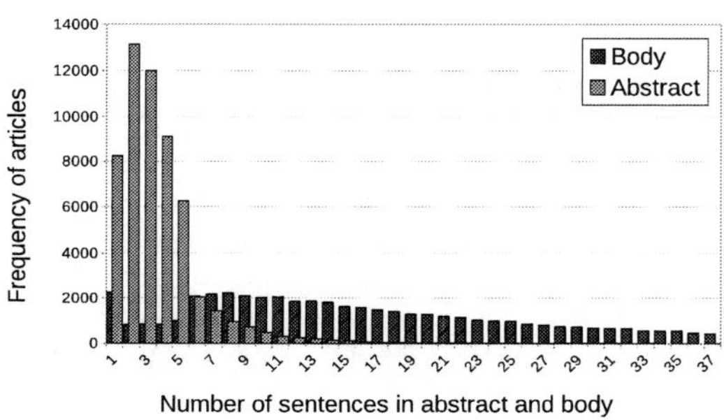

Figure 3: Distribution of abstract and body in terms of number of sentences.

In short, the problem found in the dataset can be summarized as follow. Given a article $a =< s, b, i >$ where s is the abstract b the body text, and i the infobox, the following problems exist:

- s is not guaranteed to be built from b.

- s and i does not always contains the same information.

- s, i and b vary greatly in terms of size and none of the size is correlated. Often, one or two of the sections are empty.

- there is only one version of s.

- there is no information about what was the objective of the writer(s) when producing s.

However, despites these problems, we believe this dataset represents a valuable resource since it represents the kind of data that can be found in real situations and that End2End systems must deal with in order to make a significant impact in society. The dataset is available for download[1].

3 E2E methods

3.1 Models

The basic model used for generating company description is based on the RNN seq2seq model architecture (Sutskever et al., 2014) which is divided into two main blocks: encoder which encodes the input sentence into fixed-length vector, and the decoder that decodes the vector into sequence of words. This model is able to treat sequence of words of variable size and has become the standard approach for many Natural Language Processing tasks. Briefly, a recurrent unit, at each step t takes an input x_t and a previous hidden state h_{t-1} and compute its hidden state and the output using:

$$h_t = \sigma_h(W_h x_t + U_h h_{t1} + b_h),$$

$$y_t = \sigma_y(W_y h_t + b_y),$$

where y_t is the output vector at each step; W, U, b are the parameters of the neural layer and σ_h and σ_y the activation functions of the neural layers. Once the encoder has read the entire input sequence of words (i.e., it read the special token $< EOS >$), the last hidden state h_t is passed to the decoder which begins to output a sequence of words using the previous hidden state and the previous predicted vector as input (using the special $< SOS >$ token as trigger) until it generates the end of a sequence (i.e., $< EOS >$). Numerous improvements have been made to this architecture such as using mono or multi layer of Long Short-Term Memory (LSTM) or Gated recurrent units (GRUs) to prevent the exploding/vanishing gradient problem and to model long dependencies in the sequence.

Another improvement is the attention mechanism introduced by (Bahdanau et al., 2014) which

enables the decoder to attend on specific information in the input (encoder) to predict the next output. In that case, the decoder uses another information during the decoding which is the context vector c. At each step i and based on the sequence length T_x:

$$c_i = \sum_{j=1}^{T_x} \alpha_{ij} h_j.$$

The weight α_{ij} is computed as follows:

$$\alpha_{ij} = \frac{\exp(e_{ij})}{\sum_{k=1}^{T_x} \exp(e_{ik})},$$

where e_{ij} is computed as follows:

$$e_{ij} = a(s_{i-1}, h_j).$$

e_{ij} represents an alignment or attention model that tells the decoder at step i which part of hidden state of the input sequence to attend. The alignment model a can be a simple feed-forward neural network jointly trained with the rest of the architecture. The probability α_{ij}, reflects the importance of h_j with respect to the previous hidden state $i - 1$ of the decoder in deciding the next state i and generating the output. Hence the decoder decides parts of the source sentence to pay attention to. This is particularly useful when the next word to output depends on an input word far apart in the input sequence. Note that this model, encoder-decoder with attention, is considered as a baseline model in almost all neural models in neural machine translation, text summarization, etc.

However, as pointed out by (See et al., 2017) the classical seq2seq models suffer from two commonly known problems: repetition of subsequences and wording off-topic (referred to as hallucination in the following).

Repetition is caused at the decoding stage, when the decoder relies too much on the previous output leading to infinite cycle. For instance if the decoder output 'to' then 'go' then 'to', it might happen that the next most probable word would be 'go' leading to an infinite 'to go to go to go to go to go...'. One way to deal with this problem is to use a coverage mechanism (Tu et al., 2016). This mechanism, used in machine translation, uses the attention weights to penalize the decoder for attending to input that has already been attended to previously. To do so, at each step t, the coverage vector $cov_t = \sum_{i=0}^{i=t-1} \alpha_i$ is computed, which is the sum of all the attention distributions until

$t - 1$. Which means that each source word coverage is the sum of the attentions it has received so far. Then, the coverage vector is added to the attention mechanism to have information of past attentions and then avoiding repetition. At the end, a new loss with a factor λ, specific to the coverage, can be computed and combined with the global loss

$$covloss = \lambda \sum_j min(\alpha_{ij}, cov_{i,j}).$$

Hallucination appears when some words are generated while there is no information related to these generated words in the input sequence. This can appear when the word to predict is infrequent in the training set and therefore has a poor word embedding making it close to a lot of other words. One way to deal with this problem would be to increase the training dataset but this is not always possible. Furthermore, any of such kind of systems will be likely to meet new unseen words such as company name and founder. Hence, a method to copy and past input word to the output has been developed in the translation domain and applied in the summarization community. The approach we have adopted is based on the Pointer-Generator Network (See et al., 2017) which computes a generation probability $p_{gen} \in [0, 1]$. This value evaluates the probability of 'generating' a word based on the vocabulary known by the model, versus copying a word from the source. The authors have implemented this pointing mechanism as:

$$P_{final}(w) = p_{gen}P_{vocab}(w) + (1 - p_{gen}) \sum_{i:w_i=w} a_i,$$

where $P_{final}(w)$ is the final probability of the word w, $P_{vocab}(w)$ is the probability of w as estimated by the model and $\sum_{i:w_i=w} a_i$ is the probability of w given the current attention it receives. In case w is the unknown word, then if the attention is high and p_{gen} sufficiently low then the input word will be used as output. It is important to note that in (See et al., 2017) p_{gen} is learned at the same time as the network.

3.2 concept-to-text approaches

The task of generating company description from a set of attribute–value pairs can be exemplified as going from the sequence

```
name [Bodyarmor SuperDrink], founded
[2011] , founder1 [Lance Collins] ,
```

```
founder2 [Mike Repole], headquarters
[Queens, New York, United States],
industry [Beverage manufacturing]
```
to the sequence
Bodyarmor SuperDrink is an independently owned drink manufacturing company based in Queens, New York. It was founded in 2011 by Lance Collins and Mike Repole.

However, the Wikipedia company dataset that was collected contains a rather low rate of attribute–value pairs per article. Indeed, as mentioned in section 2.3 the target descriptions were often written using pieces of information that were not present in the infobox section. For this reason, an attribute–value augmentation step was considered using Natural Language Understanding (NLU) technique. Thus, the concept-to-text was done in two processing steps:

NLU : extraction of attribute–value pair from textual company descriptions

NLG : generation of company descriptions from a set of attribute–value pairs

The strategy employed to deal with the NLU part was to first create a reversed dataset where the company abstract is considered as the source sequence and the infobox attribute–value pairs as the target sequence, using a 5-fold cross-validation. More specifically, at each of the 5 turns, a 4/5 of the data was used to train a seq2seq character NLU model to infer the missing attributes in the unseen 1/5 of the data. During training, since ground truth was only partially available, inferred attribute–value pair was classified correct if:

- it corresponds to an attribute–value pair in the infobox ;

- it corresponds to an attribute–value pair whose similarity in the input text is high.

The similarity was computed using "difflib" library[2] of Python, which is an extension of the Ratcliff and Obershelp algorithm (Ratcliff and Metzener, 1988).

Using this method the dataset went from 304475 total attributes to 328682 in the augmented dataset. This is this augmented dataset that was used in all the experiments.

---

[2]`https://docs.python.org/2/library/`
`difflib.html#difflib.SequenceMatcher`

For the NLG method, a basic seq2seq model with attention was used without any preprocessing. It is named C2T (Concept-to-Text). Also, a char to char model was used since it has been reported to be an effective model for the E2E challenge (Agarwal and Dymetman, 2017) despite a tendency to omit information or to repeat it on the E2E challenge data. The char to char model is an interesting way to deal with the rare word problem since the character vocabulary is very small and the network can learn to recompose unseen words. It is named C2T_char in the rest of the paper.

Another way to deal with rare word is to employ a pointing mechanism that is able to permit direct or indirect copy of input token in the output. Hence, the word seq2seq attention model was used with a pointer generator is called C2T+pg. Finally, to deal with repetitions, the coverage mechanism was added to the previous model to form the C2T+pg+cv system.

The recap of the systems under study:

1. C2T : the concept-to-text system word based seq2seq with attention model;

2. C2T_char : the concept-to-text system character based seq2seq with attention model;

3. C2T+pg : the concept-to-text system word based seq2seq with attention model with pointer generator;

4. C2T+pg+cv : same as above + coverage.

3.3 text-to-text approaches

Most text-to-text approaches require the ability to copy words or even sentences directly from the input to the output. Among the different models that we reviewed in Section 3, the Pointer-Generator Network has this capability, thus it was the only model used in the text-to-text experiments. The summary of the systems built to generate company description (abstract) from a source text (body text) are as the following :

5. Pointer-Generator Network (T2T+pg): deals with hallucination problem by having the ability to copy rare or unseen words during training while having the ability to generate words at the same time.

6. Coverage Model (T2T+pg+cv): deals with repetition problem by informing the decoder not to attend to input positions that have been repeatedly attended to. Note that this model is built on top of the Pointer-Generator Network.

4 Corpus based Experiment

4.1 Dataset formating

The original dataset has been through a limited amount of preprocessing for machine learning. For the C2T approaches, the dataset presented in Section 2 is filtered to contain only companies having abstracts of at least 7 words and at most 105 words. As a result of this process, 43681 companies are retained. Finally the dataset is partitioned to learning (35384), dev(3929) and test(4368) sets.

For the T2T approaches, the dataset is filtered at first to keep only the companies having abstracts with less than 105 tokens and bodies greater than 100 tokens while having the size of the abstract smaller than the size of the body text. As a result, 28034 are kept. The dataset is then splitted into three sets: training (21309), dev (2357) and test (4368).

In all the experiment the test set of 4368 companies is the same.

4.2 Corpus based evaluation

For the C2T and C2T_char experiments, we used the seq2seq model by Google[3], while for the C2T+pg, C2T+pg+cv, T2T+pg and T2T+pg+cv experiments, the Pointer-Generator Network implementation of (See et al., 2017)[4] was used. In addition, a baseline model called lead4 was also implemented. This baseline generates summaries by extracting the first 4 sentences from the article's body text.

The seq2seq model architecture has 2 layers of bidirectional LSTM trained using Adam optimization with learning rate of 0.001. As for the Pointer-Generator Network, it uses a single layer of bidirectional LSTM trained with AdaGrad and learning rate of 0.15. Both models have 256 hidden units for the encoder, decoders and embedding layers and a vocabulary size 50K (only for word models). The choice of hyper-parameters were determined by tunning the models on the dev set. Seq2seq models were trained until the loss on the dev set stops decreasing for several consecutive iterations. As for the Pointer-Generator Network

---

[3]https://github.com/google/seq2seq/
[4]https://github.com/abisee/pointer-generator

Table 1: Systems results on dev and test set using the E2E challenge metrics scripts provided with the baseline

	dev set					test set				
	BLEU	NIST	METEOR	ROUGE_L	CIDEr	BLEU	NIST	METEOR	ROUGE_L	CIDEr
lead4	0.0361	1.9599	**0.1282**	0.1645	0.0841	0.0364	2.0056	**0.1282**	0.1640	0.0908
C2T	0.0513	1.5784	0.0860	0.2032	0.1254	0.0608	1.9322	0.0906	0.2092	0.1872
C2T_char	**0.0648**	0.6390	0.1120	**0.2619**	**0.2351**	**0.0750**	1.0975	0.1159	0.2665	0.2731
C2T+pg	0.0327	0.0407	0.1014	0.2533	0.2198	0.0413	0.0893	0.1076	**0.2668**	**0.2836**
C2T+pg+cv	0.0400	0.2002	0.0975	0.2367	0.1888	0.0490	0.2349	0.1045	0.2589	0.2734
T2T+pg	0.0573	2.0101	0.1013	0.2232	0.2065	0.0567	1.9690	0.1002	0.2212	0.1992
T2T+pg+cv	0.0547	**2.1362**	0.1026	0.2214	0.1950	0.0558	**2.1188**	0.1024	0.2216	0.1974

and coverage models, we followed the strategy suggest in (See et al., 2017), i.e., to train the models with highly-truncated sequences then increase them during the training process until the maximum length is reached. Then the coverage mechanism is added and training is continued from the last training point of the Pointer-Generator Network.

Standard automatic measures BLEU (Papineni et al., 2002), ROUGE-L (Lin and Hovy, 2003), Meteor (Denkowski and Lavie, 2014) and CIDEr (Vedantam et al., 2015) were computed using the E2E challenge script. Table 1 shows evaluation results on both the dev and test sets for the lead4 (baseline), C2T and T2T tasks. The best system is difficult to extract from these results since there are close. However, C2T_char exhibits the best results for BLEU, ROUGE-L and CIDEr on the dev set while C2T+pg exhibits the best results for ROUGE-L and CIDEr on the test set. T2T+pg+cv shows the best NIST on both sets while lead4 is unbeatable from the METEOR perspective.

With respect to the results reported in the literature, such as the ones of the E2E challenge (for which the baseline system reaches: BLEU=0.6593; NIST=8.6094; METEOR=0.4483, ROUGE-L=0.6850, CIDEr=2.2338) these results are very low except for ROUGE-L. However, the main reason for such a large difference is that in the E2E challenge there are several references for each instance of the data. This leads to a higher ratio of match between the generated sentence words and the references ones, and thus, higher scores. In order to verify this, we conducted few tests using our C2T_char model on the E2E challenge data without any parameter tunning. The results showed that when only a single reference is counted, our model was able to achieve a score of 0.29 and 0.47 for BLEU and ROUGE-L respectively. However, when multiple references were included, the scores increased to 0.51 and 0.61 for BLEU and ROUGE-L. This clearly shows that the E2E challenge dataset is closer to the ideal case for machine learning than our case. Thus our results should not be directly compared with the E2E challenge.

However, we also computed the F1 of ROUGE 1, 2 and L score using the pyrouge package[5] and compared to recent summarization methods[6]. In that case C2T+pg exhibits the best results for ROUGE-1 (.3346) ROUGE-2 (.1701) and ROUGE-L (.3132) on the test set. These results are comparable to the abstractive method of (Nallapati et al., 2016) (ROUGE-1=.3546, ROUGE-2=.1330, ROUGE-L=.3265) and the pointer generation approach of (See et al., 2017) (ROUGE-1=.3644, ROUGE-2=.1728, ROUGE-L=.3342). However, they were both tested on the CNN/Daily Mail test set, for which no problem of content mismatch between documents and summaries were reported while it is a difficulty of our dataset. Furthermore, the difference with the E2E challenge is important since our dataset contains a large vocabulary, a large number of named entities and only one –not always reliable– reference summary. The few number of reference summaries give fewer opportunity for the models output to match n-grams in the references than when multiple references are available.

Although such metrics suggest our models are far from achieving satisfying results, they give in fact little insight about the actual weakness of the models. Moreover correlation between automatic and human-based metrics in NLG is still debatable (Gatt and Krahmer, 2018). That is why we conducted a human evaluation as well.

---

[5] https://pypi.python.org/pypi/pyrouge/0.1.0

[6] Also the ROUGE-L value given by the two scripts were not the same due to different parameters, we checked a very high (>.96) and significant Spearman correlation between all ROUGE value.

5 Human Evaluation

In order to gain more insight about the generation properties of each model a human evaluation with 19 human subjects was performed. We set up a web-based experiment which was circulated inside the lab but to people who were not involved in this project. The 4 questions below were asked on a 5-point Lickert scale:

Q1 How do you judge the Information Coverage of the company summary : 1 no information, 5 contains everything

Q2 How do you judge the Non-Redundancy of Information in the company summary. 1: means lots of repeated information, 5: no repetition.

Q3 How do you judge the Semantic Adequacy of the company summary? 1: lots of semantical mistakes, 5: semantically very correct.

Q4 How do you judge the Grammatical Correctness of the company summary? 1: very incorrect, 5: very good

We did not include fluency in the question since it is often correlated with grammar and because participants have difficulty to judge this property. Q1 to 4 were specifically designed to measure the recurrent weakness of seq2seq models: content selection, repetition, hallucination and bad segment connection.

Participants were exposed to a screen where a background (extract of the original Wikipedia body text, cut to 400 max), an infobox and a summary were visible all together in the screen. After reading the background, the infobox and the summary, the participant could answer the question by scrolling down. Not limit of time was imposed. A first example was given for training, then each participant had to treat 10 summaries. The participant could not go to the next step without explicitly answering all questions. In average one session last 15 minutes. At no time participants have been aware that one of the summary was human generated (i.e., the Wikipedia abstract).

30 companies were selected from the 4368 companies of the test set. They were selected based on the number of views during the month preceding the experiment. The less viewed one were retained to avoid participants judging well known companies.

Results of the human experiment are reported in Table 2. The first line report the result of the reference (i.e., the Wikipedia abstract) for comparison. It is clear from the coverage metric that no system nor the reference was seen as doing a good job at conveying the information. It is a known problem of the Wikipedia dataset and the systems were not able to do better than the reference. Non-redundancy metric gives a more contrasted view of the systems. C2T+pg was judged to be the least repetitive after the reference, while C2T_char to be the most repetitive. Regarding semantic correctness, C2T+pg is clearly above the others again including the reference. Same observation can be made for grammatical correctness.

Table 2: Results of the human evaluation per system.

	cover.	non-redun.	semant.	gramm.
reference	3.1	4.6	3.9	4.2
C2T	2.9	2.9	3.3	3.6
C2T_char	2.3	3.9	2.8	3.0
C2T+pg	2.3	4.5	4.0	4.3
C2T+pg+cv	2.7	3.9	3.6	4.2
T2T+pg	1.8	3.3	2.9	3.7
T2T+pg+cv	2.3	3.8	2.4	3.5

These results of human evaluation were compared to those of the automatic metrics (excluding the reference one). The correlation matrix is given in Figure 4. It can be seen that among automatic metrics, METEOR, ROUGE-L and CIDEr are highly correlated. When it comes to human vs automatic metrics, it is obvious that CIDEr has a highest correlation with semantic and grammar. It is worth noting that ROUGE-L is is also highly correlated to semantic and grammar.

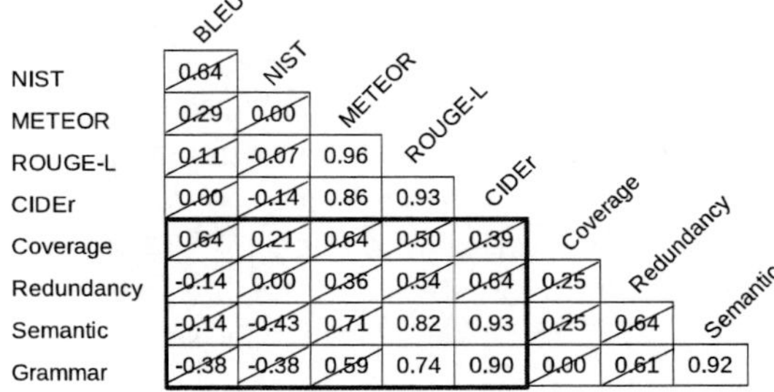

Figure 4: Correlation values based on Spearman's ρ. Human vs automatic metric correlations are in the black square. Crossed area are not significant correlation (p>.05).

Table 3: Sample of generated summaries from the test set using our systems along with the reference infobox, abstract and body text. Green color indicates repeated information and red color indicates factual errors.

Infobox: name1[rgb entertainment], headquarters1[argentina], founded1[2000], industry1[television production], type1[production company], owner1[gustavo yankelevich y victor gonzalez]
Body text (truncated): it was created in 2000 by gustavo yankelevich, former telefe director, and victor gonzalez, with headquarters in buenos aires, argentina and sao paulo, brazil. it include creation and production of television shows, films, cds, live events and multitudinous events. the company co-produces all cris morena productions...
Reference abstract: rgb entertainment is a production company from argentina. it was established in the year 2000.
C2T_char: rgb entertainment is an argentine television production company based in argentina. the company was founded in 2000 by gustavo yankelevich yankelevich yankelevich y victor gonzalez in 2000.
C2T+pg: rgb entertainment is a television production company in argentina .
T2T+pg: the argentine channel productions is an american film production and distribution company . the company was founded in 2000 by gustavo yankelevich and victor gonzalez in buenos , argentina . it is owned by ideas group.

6 Discussion and further work

Participants did not always understand the first question. They use English daily as working language but they were not native English speakers, that might have had an influence on the grammatical evaluation. However, English Wikipedia content is not always written by English natives and the level of English employed in the summary was quite standard.

C2T+pg capability is more emphasized by human evaluation than automatic metrics. Once again it shows that not all the automatic metrics are correlated with the human evaluation and that both evaluations are necessary to understand strengths and weaknesses of models. Despite this, some surprising correlation between semantics, grammar, CIDEr and ROUGE-L can be observed. However this findings are not in line with what was observed in (Shimorina, 2018), as they report only one significant correlation which is between semantics and METEOR. However, CIDEr and ROUGE-L are themselves highly correlated with METEOR. Nevertheless, this difference might be from the fact that our human evaluation questions are not exactly the same, thus, the answer of the subjects for certain questions might have been influenced by the other questions.

In order to better analyze the results, in Table 3 we show samples of generated summaries by some of our systems. The first remark that can be noticed is that the reference abstract does not contain some of the information given in the infobox, e.g., owners. This mismatch between the reference abstract and the infobox can be observed throughout all the corpus. This obviously poses a limitation on the models to learn to generate all the information given in the infobox. Then when it comes to our models, it can be seen that the C2T_char manages to generate all the infobox information but it has repetition problem. The T2T+pg, on the other hand, is not so behind when it comes to information coverage, however this models suffers from the problem of hallucination as it can be seen in its last sentence. Finally the C2T+pg manages to generate a correct but too short sentence which is lacking some information of the infobox.

Some weakness of the current C2T approaches may be due to the NLU model. A possible future work might be to deal with the weakness of the database and to perform more joined learning of NLU/NLG and to evaluate models on the real company database provided by the company that we are working with on a research project. In addition, we could also force the models to generate more guided summaries by taking both the infobox and the body text as input. In this way, the model can learn to do text-to-text and concept-to-text at the same time by giving more priority to sentences of the body text containing infobox values.

Acknowledgments

This project was partly funded by the IDEX Université Grenoble Alpes innovation grant (AI4I-2018-2019) and the Région Auvergne-Rhône-Alpes (AISUA-2018-2019).

References

Shubham Agarwal and Marc Dymetman. 2017. A surprisingly effective out-of-the-box char2char model on the E2E NLG challenge dataset. In *Proceedings of the Annual SIGdial Meeting on Discourse and Dialogue, Saarbrücken*, pages 158–163.

Dzmitry Bahdanau, Kyunghyun Cho, and Yoshua Bengio. 2014. Neural machine translation by jointly learning to align and translate. In *Proceedings of the International Conference on Learning Representations (ICLR)*.

Andrew Chisholm, Will Radford, and Ben Hachey. 2017. Learning to generate one-sentence biographies from wikidata. In *Proceedings of the Conference of the European Chapter of the Association for Computational Linguistics*, pages 633–642.

Michael Denkowski and Alon Lavie. 2014. Meteor universal: Language specific translation evaluation for any target language. In *Proceedings of the Ninth Workshop on Statistical Machine Translation*, pages 376–380.

Ondrej Dusek and Filip Jurcícek. 2016. Sequence-to-sequence generation for spoken dialogue via deep syntax trees and strings. In *Proceedings of the Annual Meeting of the Association for Computational Linguistics, (ACL)*, pages 45–51.

Albert Gatt and Emiel Krahmer. 2018. Survey of the state of the art in natural language generation: Core tasks, applications and evaluation. *Journal of AI Research*, pages 65–170.

Rémi Lebret, David Grangier, and Michael Auli. 2016. Neural text generation from structured data with application to the biography domain. In *Proceedings of the Empirical Methods in Natural Language Processing*, pages 1203–1213.

Chin-Yew Lin and Eduard Hovy. 2003. Automatic evaluation of summaries using n-gram co-occurrence statistics. In *Proceedings of the North American Chapter of the Association for Computational Linguistics on Human Language Technology*, pages 71–78.

François Mairesse and Steve J. Young. 2014. Stochastic language generation in dialogue using factored language models. *Computational Linguistics*, pages 763–799.

Ramesh Nallapati, Bowen Zhou, Cicero dos Santos, Ça glar Gulçehre, and Bing Xiang. 2016. Abstractive text summarization using sequence-to-sequence rnns and beyond. In *Proceedings of the SIGNLL Conference on Computational Natural Language Learning (CoNLL)*, pages 280–290.

Jekaterina Novikova, Ondrej Dušek, and Verena Rieser. 2017. The E2E dataset: New challenges for end-to-end generation. In *Proceedings of the Annual SIGdial Meeting on Discourse and Dialogue*, pages 201–206.

Kishore Papineni, Salim Roukos, Todd Ward, and Wei-Jing Zhu. 2002. Bleu: A method for automatic evaluation of machine translation. In *Proceedings of the Annual Meeting on Association for Computational Linguistics (ACL)*, pages 311–318.

Yevgeniy Puzikov and Iryna Gurevych. 2018. E2e nlg challenge: Neural models vs. templates.

John W Ratcliff and David E Metzener. 1988. Pattern-matching-the gestalt approach. *Dr Dobbs Journal*, pages 46–51.

Ehud Reiter and Anja Belz. 2009. An investigation into the validity of some metrics for automatically evaluating natural language generation systems. *Computational Linguistics*, pages 529–558.

Ehud Reiter and Robert Dale. 2000. *Building Natural Language Generation Systems*. Studies in Natural Language Processing. Cambridge University Press.

Abigail See, Peter J Liu, and Christopher D Manning. 2017. Get to the point: Summarization with pointer-generator networks. In *Proceedings of the Annual Meeting of the Association for Computational Linguistics (ACL)*, pages 1073–1083.

Anastasia Shimorina. 2018. Human vs automatic metrics: on the importance of correlation design. *CoRR*, abs/1805.11474.

Ilya Sutskever, Oriol Vinyals, and Quoc V Le. 2014. Sequence to sequence learning with neural networks. In *Proceedings of the Advances in Neural Information Processing Systems*, pages 3104–3112.

Zhaopeng Tu, Zhengdong Lu, Yang Liu, Xiaohua Liu, and Hang Li. 2016. Modeling coverage for neural machine translation. In *Proceedings of the Annual Meeting of the Association for Computational Linguistics, (ACL)*, pages 76–85.

Ramakrishna Vedantam, C. Lawrence Zitnick, and Devi Parikh. 2015. Cider: Consensus-based image description evaluation. In *Proceedings of IEEE Conference on Computer Vision and Pattern Recognition (CVPR)*, pages 4566–4575.

Tsung-Hsien Wen, Milica Gasic, Nikola Mrksic, Pei-hao Su, David Vandyke, and Steve J. Young. 2015. Semantically conditioned lstm-based natural language generation for spoken dialogue systems. In *Proceedings of the Empirical Methods in Natural Language Processing, EMNLP 2015, Lisbon, Portugal, September 17-21, 2015*, pages 1711–1721.

Automatically Generating Questions about Novel Metaphors in Literature

Natalie Parde
Computer Science
University of Illinois at Chicago
parde@uic.edu

Rodney D. Nielsen
Computer Science and Engineering
University of North Texas
rodney.nielsen@unt.edu

Abstract

The automatic generation of stimulating questions is crucial to the development of intelligent cognitive exercise applications. We developed an approach that generates appropriate *Questioning the Author* queries based on novel metaphors in diverse syntactic relations in literature. We show that the generated questions are comparable to human-generated questions in terms of naturalness, sensibility, and depth, and score slightly higher than human-generated questions in terms of clarity. We also show that questions generated about novel metaphors are rated as cognitively deeper than questions generated about non- or conventional metaphors, providing evidence that metaphor novelty can be leveraged to promote cognitive exercise.

1 Introduction

Automatic question generation is useful for a wide range of applications, including those providing educational and cognitive exercise support. Most question generation work to date has focused on generating *factoid* questions—that is, questions regarding factual content that is readily available in the source text. Factoid questions are well-suited to some contexts, such as quizzing for simple comprehension. However, answering them typically requires only shallow reasoning skills, rendering them unsuitable for situations in which deeper cognitive engagement is desired.

Less work has been conducted with the goal of generating deeper questions. We work toward filling that void by presenting an approach for automatically generating questions about *novel metaphors* from popular classic fiction using the *Questioning the Author* strategy. Metaphor novelty is defined here as the degree of likelihood with which one can expect to encounter a given metaphor on a regular basis. Consider the sentence:

I *spent* an *hour* on my homework.

The word pair, {*spent, hour*}, is a highly conventional metaphor—although one cannot literally spend time, phrases such as this are highly common in the English language. Alternately, consider:

The Queen was *frowning* like a *thunderstorm.*

The word pair, {*frowning, thunderstorm*}, is a highly novel metaphor. Novel metaphors reside at the opposite end of the continuum from conventional metaphors, and should strike one as being particularly interesting or creative. These are the metaphors of particular interest to us in this work.

The targeted focus on novel metaphors stems from prior work showing that novel metaphors are more difficult to process, both in young adults (Lai et al., 2009) and in older adults with and without dementia (Amanzio et al., 2008; Mashal et al., 2011). The latter are a key demographic for our use case, an elder-focused human-robot book discussion system (Parde, 2018). Here, we (1) introduce a method for generating deep questions about diverse novel metaphors following the Questioning the Author strategy. We (2) show that the resulting questions are comparable to or score slightly higher than questions generated by everyday users about the same topics in terms of naturalness, clarity, sensibility, and depth. Moreover, we (3) provide empirical evidence that questions automatically generated about novel metaphors are rated as having greater depth than questions

Proceedings of The 11th International Natural Language Generation Conference, pages 264–273,
Tilburg, The Netherlands, November 5-8, 2018. ©2018 Association for Computational Linguistics

automatically generated about non- or conventional metaphors. Finally, we (4) publicly release our source code and a corpus of question ratings and responses for both human- and automatically-generated questions to the research community to foster additional work in this area.

2   Related Work

Automatic question generation and its potential to facilitate learning has been of interest to researchers since at least the 1970s, when John Wolfe introduced the pattern-matching AUTO-QUEST question generation algorithm (Wolfe, 1977). Today, many question generation systems exist for educational applications, with most generating factoid questions about content found in expository text (Araki et al., 2016; Du et al., 2017; Gates, 2008; Heilman and Smith, 2010; Mazidi and Nielsen, 2014, 2015; Rus et al., 2007; Serban et al., 2016; Wyse and Piwek, 2009).

These systems achieve their goals in a number of ways, including templates (Araki et al., 2016; Mazidi and Nielsen, 2014, 2015; Rus et al., 2007; Wyse and Piwek, 2009), sentence transformations (Gates, 2008; Heilman and Smith, 2010), and recently, neural networks (Du et al., 2017; Serban et al., 2016). Template-based systems select templates based on syntactic structure, semantic role labels, dependency parses, and/or discourse cues to produce generally shallower questions (e.g., "Inflation is defined as an increase in the price level." → "How is inflation defined?" (Mazidi and Nielsen, 2015)). The template-based system developed by Araki et al. (2016) generated questions over multiple sentences to produce questions that required more inference steps than those generated from a single sentence, using event coreference, entity coreference, and paraphrases. However, the answers to these questions were still readily available in the original text passage (in fact, ensuring that this was the case was a goal of the system). Although shallower questions are suitable for quizzing comprehension of expository text (the most common scenario to which they are applied), they are inadequate for more involved discussions, such as those analyzing fiction narrative.

Deeper questions (or more aptly, writing prompts) were generated by Liu et al.'s (2012) system, designed to help students write better literature reviews. Sentences containing citations were classified as describing opinions, methods, results, or one of several other categories, and templates were selected based on those classifications to construct questions using content from the original sentence (e.g., "Cannon (1927) challenged this view mentioning that physiological changes were not sufficient to discriminate emotions." → "Why did Cannon challenge this view mentioning that physiological changes were not sufficient to discriminate emotions? (What evidence is provided by Cannon to prove the opinion?) Does any other scholar agree or disagree with Cannon?"). Lindberg et al.'s (2013) system prompted students for summaries, causal effects, and descriptions not expected to be answerable from the immediate sentence from which they were generated, using question templates selected based on semantic role patterns. The questions were then classified as having/not having learning value, allowing the system to automatically discard poor-quality questions. The learning value classifier was trained using length, language model, semantic role label, named entity, glossary, and syntax features.

The system developed by Becker et al. (2012) automatically identified question topics (i.e., the part of a sentence about which a question should be asked), and accordingly generated cloze (fill-in-the-blank) questions. However, cloze questions are shallow and have limited potential to stimulate deep reasoning. Olney et al. (2012) developed a system that automatically extracted concept maps from expository text, and generated questions based on those concept maps using templates associated with different types of start nodes, end nodes, and edge relations from the maps. Finally, Mostow and Chen (2009) developed a method for automatically generating self-questioning instruction for students reading children's stories. Although some stages of this instruction were scripted, others involved automatically generating example questions for students. The template-based generation approach resulted in "why" questions about mental states expressed in the stories (e.g., "And when the country mouse saw the cheese, cake, honey, jam and other goodies at the house, he was pleasantly surprised." → "Why was the country mouse surprised?"). Although these approaches for generating deeper questions are promising, none have specifically sought to implement the Questioning the Author paradigm, which revolves around building meaning from text rather than quizzing a reader's comprehension. Moreover, none focus on generating questions based on identified occurrences of highly novel metaphor in the source text.

2.1 Questioning the Author

The questions generated for the work described herein employ a questioning strategy commonly used in K-12 education known as *Questioning the Author (QtA)*. QtA seeks to encourage readers to consider the author's underlying intentions when crafting literary prose (Beck and McKeown, 2006). The strategy can be implemented with either expository text or fiction narrative. One of the key goals of QtA is to coax readers toward building meaning from and understanding the relationships between different elements or events present in the text, as opposed to focusing on isolated components as factoid questions are likely to do. Example QtA queries (Beck and McKeown, 2006) may include prompts such as:

- What is the author trying to say here?

- What do you think the author wants us to know?

- What is the author talking about?

- So what does the author mean right here?

- That's what the author said, but what did the author mean?

Such questions are open-ended, and typically elicit more detailed, free-form responses than factoid questions. They also typically encourage deeper analysis of the source text.

3 Template Development and Selection

We built templates based on sample questions from the book on QtA (Beck and McKeown, 2006), with slots to be filled using predicted novel metaphors that were automatically identified in literature. We describe the metaphor novelty scoring methodology in greater detail in Section 4.1. The identified metaphors were all syntactically-related pairs of words; we constructed different sets of templates for different syntactic relation types. The syntactic relation types for which questions could be generated included the *universal dependency relations* (McDonald et al., 2013) in Table 1. Some of the resulting templates are shown

Relation Type	Description	Example
nsubj	Nominal subject.	The *apple* is *red*.
nsubjpass	Nominal subject of a passive verb.	*Newton* was *hit* by an apple.
dobj	Direct object.	I *gave* him an *apple*.
iobj	Indirect object.	I *gave* him an apple.
csubj	Clausal subject.	What he *wanted* was an *apple*.
csubjpass	Clausal subject of a passive verb.	What he *wanted* as *taken* to be an apple.
xcomp	Open clausal component.	He *asked* to *eat* an apple.
nmod	Nominal modifier.	The *stem* of the *apple*.
acl	Clause that modifies a noun.	I need a *way* to *get* an apple.
appos	Appositional modifier.	The *fruit*, an *apple*, was red.
amod	Adjectival modifier.	It was a *red apple*.
advcl	Adverbial clause modifier.	He *got* is idea as the apple was *falling*.
dep	Dependency for which the parser cannot determine a finer-grained relation.	N/A
advmod	Adverbial modifier.	He *ate* the apple *quickly*.
compound	Multiword expression.	The apple had *polka dots*.

Table 1: Dependency relation types for which questions were generated.

in Table 2; the full list of 130+ templates can be found online.[1]

Templates were chosen randomly from among the pool of all relevant templates for a given dependency type. For example, if a question was to be generated about a metaphor formed by two words syntactically related to one another using an *nsubj* dependency, a random selection from all possible templates corresponding to the *nsubj* type would be made. Surface realizations were then constructed by fitting predicted novel metaphors into the selected templates. That process is described in the following section.

4 Surface Realization

Realization was performed based on the linguistic characteristics and syntactic parse details corresponding to the novel metaphors about which questions were generated. Our procedure for iden-

---

[1]http://natalieparde.com/papers/inlg_question_templates.pdf

Dependency	Template
nsubj	What is the author trying to say with the expression '<DEP (N/J/P)> <GOV (V)>'?
nsubjpass	What do you think the author wants us to know by figuratively saying '<DEP (N/J/P)>' <WAS/WERE> '<GOV (V)>'?
dobj/iobj	What is the author talking about when <HE/SHE> writes '<GOV (V)>' <? THE> '<DEP (N/J/P)>'?
csubj	What's the important message in the expression '<CLAUSE>'?
csubjpass	So what does the author mean when <HE/SHE> writes '<CLAUSE_PASS>'?
xcomp/nmod/acl	The author said '<STRING>,' but what did <HE/SHE> mean?
appos	Does the expression '<DEP>' with '<GOV>' make sense?
amod	How does the expression '<DEP> <GOV>' fit in with what the author told us?
advcl/dep	Does the author tell us why <HE/SHE> wrote '<PHRASE>'?
advmod	Why do you think the author tells us '<DEP (V/J/R)> <GOV (V/J/R)>'?
compound	What is the author telling us with the expression '<W1> <W2>'?

Table 2: Example question templates.

tifying particularly novel metaphors (Parde and Nielsen, 2018b) and our methods for incorporating the approach in this work are described in Subsection 4.1. Subsection 4.2 describes how template slots were subsequently filled using the identified novel metaphors.

4.1 Metaphor Novelty Scoring

Our metaphor novelty scoring approach predicts continuous scores for syntactically-related pairs of content words (nouns, verbs, adjectives, and adverbs), with higher scores reflecting greater novelty than lower scores (Parde and Nielsen, 2018b). It consists of a four-layer feedforward neural network trained using features based on psycholinguistic characteristics (concreteness, imageability, sentiment, and ambiguity), word co-occurrence, syntactic structure, semantic characteristics, and information from WordNet (Miller, 1995) regarding the words in the pair. For the work here, we trained our neural network model on a corpus of word pairs originally extracted from the VU Amsterdam Metaphor Corpus (Steen et al., 2010)

and labeled along a continuous scale for metaphor novelty (Parde and Nielsen, 2018a); the VU Amseterdam Metaphor Corpus is comprised of fiction, news articles, academic articles, and transcribed conversations. We then applied the learned model to all word pairs (52,279 total) extracted from a subset of sentences from 58 books that are publicly available on Project Gutenberg.[2] Finally, we randomly selected a small subset (457) of the word pairs having predicted scores greater than 1.0[3] as the identified novel metaphors about which to generate questions.

4.2 Slot Filling

As shown in Table 2, each template contains one or more slots: <GOV>, <DEP>, <WAS/WERE>, <HE/SHE>, <? THE>, <CLAUSE>, <CLAUSE_PASS>, <STRING>, <W1>, and <W2>. Filling the <GOV> and <DEP> slots is straightforward; the governor and modifier of the syntactic relation forming the predicted metaphor are merely substituted into the appropriate slots in the question template. The <HE/SHE> slot is the only slot requiring metadata about the source text being discussed (a gender was manually assigned to each book).

The token "was" or "were" is selected to fill the <WAS/WERE> slot based on the part-of-speech tags associated with the two words forming the predicted metaphor. Metaphors including plural nouns are given the verb "were," and all other metaphors are given the verb "was." The word "the" is optionally included in realizations of templates including the <? THE> slot based on the distance between the two words forming the predicted metaphor; if they are immediately next to one another, it is omitted, and otherwise it is included.

Filling the <CLAUSE> slot is more complex. A full dependency parse of the predicted metaphor's source sentence is first acquired using Stanford CoreNLP (Manning et al., 2014). A clause is then constructed using only tokens that are syntactically related to words forming the metaphor, in the order in which they occur in the source sentence. Consider the example sentence:

---

[2] https://www.gutenberg.org; the books selected included all books written in or translated to English and classified as fiction in the "Top 100 Books Over The Last 30 Days" list as of May 18, 2017.

[3] Across all word pairs, novelty predictions ranged from 0.24-1.41.

What he *tasted* on this dark and stormy night was a *dream.*

To fit {*tasted, dream*} into the template, "What's the important message in the expression '<CLAUSE>'?", the following words would be identified as syntactically related to *tasted* and *dream*: {What, he, *tasted*, was, a, *dream*}. The realized question, retaining the words in their original order, would thus be: "What's the important message in the expression 'What he tasted was a dream'?" <CLAUSE_PASS> is constructed similarly, but requires only words syntactically related to the modifier.

The <STRING> slot was filled by tokenizing the source sentence, and extracting the full span of text from one of the words in the metaphor up to and including the other. Consider the sentence:

She smelled a *melody* of *appetizers* and knew she had reached the networking event.

The word pair {*melody, appetizers*} would fit into the *nmod* template "The author said '<STRING>,' but what did <HE/SHE> mean?" as "The author said 'melody of appetizers,' but what did she mean?" The <PHRASE> slot was filled using a slightly broader window of text: the span reaching from the first word syntactically related to either of the words in the metaphor, to the last word syntactically related to either of those words, inclusive of the words forming the metaphor. Finally, <W1> and <W2> were filled simply by substituting the word from the metaphor that occurred first in the source sentence for <W1>, and the word that occurred second in the source sentence for <W2>.

5 Evaluation

The quality of the automatically-generated questions was evaluated relative to that of questions written by humans. The human-generated questions were comprised of two subsets: (1) those generated based on *sentences* containing predicted novel metaphors, and (2) those generated based on *pairs of words* predicted to be novel metaphors.

5.1 Data Collection

We crowdsourced human-generated questions based on a randomly-selected subset of the same

Source Sentence	Question Received
An icy horror of loneliness seized him; he saw himself standing apart and watching all the world fade away from him – a world of shadows, of fickle dreams.	What did he feel as he stood alone?
Perhaps, from the casement, standing hand-in-hand, they were watching the calm moonlight on the river, while from the distant halls the boisterous revelry floated in broken bursts of faint-heard din and tumult.	Do you think the people holding hands are supposed to be happy or sad?
I had crossed a marshy tract full of willows, bulrushes, and odd, outlandish, swampy trees; and I had now come out upon the skirts of an open piece of undulating, sandy country, about a mile long, dotted with a few pines and a great number of contorted trees, not unlike the oak in growth, but pale in the foliage, like willows.	Do you think the landscape reflects his inner feelings?
I quickly destroyed part of my sledge to construct oars, and by these means was enabled, with infinite fatigue, to move my ice raft in the direction of your ship.	If you were to make oars that way, how long do you think it would take?

Table 3: Sample questions generated by humans based on sentences.

457 predicted novel metaphors about which questions were automatically generated, using Amazon Mechanical Turk (AMT).[4] Workers were simply instructed to create "good" questions, such as what they might ask in a book discussion group if they came across the sentence (or the bolded word pair within that sentence) when reading. These instructions were purposely open-ended to foster diversity in the collected data. To that end, we also continued to collect questions until the human-generated question dataset included 35 unique question authors (180 questions; 90 of each type). Sample questions collected based on sentences and word pairs are shown in Tables 3 and 4.

The 180 human-generated and 457 automatically-generated questions were intermixed, and responses to the questions and ratings for four criteria for each question were also solicited using a separate pool of workers

Source Sentence	Question Received
Wavewhite wedded words shimmering on the **dim tide**.	what does dim tide mean?
All about me gathered the invisible terrors of the Martians; that **pitiless sword** of heat seemed whirling to and fro, flourishing overhead before it descended and smote me out of life.	Why would the martians kill him?
My father saw this change with pleasure, and he turned his thoughts towards the best method of eradicating the remains of my melancholy, which every now and then would return by fits, and with a **devouring blackness** overcast the approaching sunshine.	How is the image of mortality described with the weather?
But the **overflowing misery** I now felt, and the excess of agitation that I endured rendered me incapable of any exertion.	How did things get so bad that they essentially felt overflowing misery?

Table 4: Sample questions generated generated by humans based on word pairs.

from AMT. The criteria considered were as follows:

- **Naturalness:** The degree to which the question seems natural, or sounds "normal" to the reader.

- **Clarity:** The degree to which it is clear to the reader how he or she is supposed to respond to the question, regardless of whether he or she is sure of the answer.

- **Sensibility:** The degree to which the reader feels it makes sense to ask the question, given the source sentence upon which it is based.

- **Depth:** The degree to which the reader feels challenged in coming up with an answer to the question.

Two workers rated each criterion using a five-point scale. Small disagreements were adjudicated by averaging, and disagreements greater than a difference of 2.0 (e.g., a 1 and a 4) were forwarded to a third-party, native English speaking adjudicator (211 questions required adjudication for at least one of the four criteria). Overall, the crowd workers exhibited moderate agreement with one another, with Krippendorff's α=0.50, α=0.52, α=0.51, and α=0.52 for ratings of naturalness, clarity, sensibility, and depth, respectively. The collected question answers are not used in this

work, but they serve the plural purpose of making the dataset more broadly useful, lending insight regarding the types of answers expected to inform future work on question generation and response scaffolding, and providing a coarse-grained quantitative (time-based) measure of question depth.

5.2 Average Question Ratings

Average ratings for the question criteria, both overall and when only considering questions for a given criterion that had received above-midpoint (> 3.0) ratings for the previous criteria, are presented in Tables 5 and 6. The latter scenario was included to reduce the potential for confusion in interpreting the results (for instance, unclear questions that were also unnatural may have only been rated as such because they were unnatural; these questions are included in the average score reported in Table 5 but not in the average score reported in Table 6). To elaborate further, the constraints considered in the latter scenario (as well as for the results reported in Tables 7 and 8) were:

- Naturalness: All ratings were considered.

- Clarity: Only questions having a *Naturalness* score > 3.0 were considered.

- Sensibility: Only questions having *Naturalness* and *Clarity* scores > 3.0 were considered.

- Depth: Only questions having *Naturalness*, *Clarity*, and *Sensibility* scores > 3.0 were considered.

Significance values for both scenarios were determined via one-way ANOVA between the two groups. Not surprisingly, given the instructions to ask *good* questions, automatically-generated questions did not quite match the high bar set for depth by humans' questions, but this difference was not statistically significant. The only significant ($p < 0.05$) difference reported between the two groups in Table 6 was for ratings of *Clarity* (automatically-generated questions scored slightly higher). This finding was echoed when considering the overall averages (Table 5); again, the only statistically significant difference between groups was that ratings of *Clarity* were slightly higher for the automatically-generated questions than the human-generated questions.

	Human-Generated	Automatically-Generated	p
Naturalness	3.89	4.02	0.13
Clarity	3.78	4.04	0.00
Sensibility	3.83	4.00	0.06
Depth	3.78	3.67	0.24

Table 5: Average ratings across all question criteria, with significance values.

	Human-Generated	Automatically-Generated	p
Naturalness	3.89	4.02	0.13
Clarity	4.18	4.34	0.03
Sensibility	4.45	4.48	0.61
Depth	3.92	3.76	0.17

Table 6: Average ratings, considering only questions with above-average ratings for the preceding criteria.

	Human-Generated (Sentence)	Human-Generated (Word Pair)	Auto.-Generated
Nat.	3.92	3.85	4.02
Clar.	4.08	4.29	4.34
Sens.	4.30	4.42	4.48
Depth	3.91	4.03	3.76

Table 7: Average ratings for human-generated question subgroups and automatically-generated questions.

	TP	FP	p
Naturalness	3.99	4.06	0.42
Clarity	4.23	4.46	0.00
Sensibility	4.31	4.44	0.09
Depth	3.92	3.64	0.02

Table 8: Average ratings for true and false positives among automatically-generated questions.

5.3 Average Ratings for Question Subgroups

In addition to these broad comparisons of human- and automatically-generated questions, we examined the differences between different subgroups. Table 7 presents the average ratings for (1) human-generated questions based on sentences, (2) human-generated questions based on specified word pairs, and (3) automatically-generated questions. Statistical significance was computed using one-way ANOVAs beween each pair of groups: human-generated (sentence) and human-generated (word pair); human-generated (sentence) and automatically-generated; and human-generated (word pair) and automatically-generated. Only two statistically significant differences existed between the subgroups: the average ratings for *Clarity* and *Sensibility* were higher for automatically-generated questions than for human-generated questions based on sentences. These differences were not statistically significant when comparing human-generated questions based on word pairs and automatically-generated questions.

Table 8 presents average ratings for two subsets of automatically-generated questions: true positives (TP) for which the word pair about which the question was generated was both predicted to be a novel metaphor and actually was a novel metaphor, and false positives (FP) for which the word pair about which the question was generated was predicted to be a novel metaphor but was not actually a novel metaphor. We collected gold standard metaphor novelty scores for these word pairs in the same manner by which we built our previous VUAMC-based metaphor novelty dataset (Parde and Nielsen, 2018a), used to train the metaphor novelty prediction model in this work. Specifically, we crowdsourced five annotations for each word pair, and automatically aggregated them to continuous scores using a label aggregation model learned from features based on annotation distribution and presumed worker trustworthiness (Parde and Nielsen, 2017).

There were two statistically significant differences between the two groups: questions about false positives were rated as clearer than questions about true positives, and questions about true positives were rated as having more depth than questions about false positives. One hypothesis regarding the former finding is simply that non-metaphoric language is more clearly interpretable than metaphoric language. The finding that question depth is higher for questions about true positives (novel metaphors) than questions about other instances provides empirical support for the underlying motivations guiding this work—namely, that questions regarding novel metaphors are more cognitively challenging than similar questions about non-metaphors or conventional metaphors.

5.4 Correlations between Question Criteria

In addition to evaluating question quality on the basis of average ratings for each question criterion, we computed Pearson's correlation scores

	Nat.	Clar.	Sens.	Depth	Compl. Time
Nat.	-	0.55	0.48	0.03	-0.04
Clar.		-	0.65	0.05	-0.01
Sens.			-	0.05	-0.04
Depth				-	0.07
Compl. Time					-

Table 9: Correlations between categories of ratings for both automatically- and human-generated questions.

between the four criteria, as well as between those criteria and completion time (the amount of time workers took to complete each HIT, including rating the four criteria and writing a response to the question, on AMT) to examine which of these factors were correlated with one another. Questions rated as being natural, clear, and sensible (scores > 3.0) were included in this evaluation. Since a small number of HITs had outlier completion times far exceeding the average (indicating that the rater most likely left their browser open while taking a break, rather than actually spending that much time completing the HIT itself), we removed HITs with completion times +/- two standard deviations from the mean completion time from consideration.

Table 9 presents a matrix of overall correlation scores when considering ratings for both automatically-generated and human-generated questions. Overall, moderately strong positive correlations were found between naturalness and clarity ($r=0.55$), naturalness and sensibility ($r=0.48$), and clarity and sensibility ($r=0.65$). No strong correlations were found between these criteria and depth or completion time. When computing correlations only between ratings collected for human-generated questions or for only automatically-generated questions, these trends persisted. In addition to the correlations reported in Table 9, we computed the correlation between completion time and *metaphor novelty* for each set, finding correlations of $r=0.09$ across all questions, $r=0.19$ for human-generated questions, and $r=0.03$ for automatically-generated questions.

5.5 Discussion and Future Recommendations

The findings regarding the average ratings overall and for different subgroups, as well as regarding the correlations between types of ratings, provide interesting and in a few cases (such as the higher average *Clarity* score for automatically-generated questions rather than human-generated questions) slightly surprising observations. It is clear that the automatically-generated questions are very comparable with human-generated questions in terms of all criteria considered. **Across all comparisons, there were no cases in which an average rating associated with human-generated questions or a subset thereof statistically significantly outperformed an average rating for the same criterion with automatically-generated questions.** As such, it is reasonable to assume that the approach is capable of generating sufficiently natural, clear, sensible, and challenging questions relative to what the average person might generate.

That said, there are still some areas that could be improved upon. For example, the average depth rating for automatically-generated questions that were also rated as natural, clear, and sensible (as measured by having ratings greater than 3.0) was 3.76. Although this is above mid-range, it could certainly be higher (the maximum score allowed was a 5.0). Thus, additional work could be done to improve upon question depth in future work. This could perhaps be accomplished by introducing complementary strategies to QtA. Considerations could also be taken to identify optimal questioning *sequences*—that is, algorithmically deciding upon groups of questions most likely to challenge readers when asked in sequence, as opposed to simply selecting questions at the individual level.

Future work toward improved metaphor novelty scoring algorithms will result in a higher likelihood that the subjects of the automatically-generated questions are indeed novel metaphors. The evaluation indicates that improved identification of novel metaphors should lead to higher average ratings of question depth. Specifically, Table 8 shows that in a comparison of automatically-generated questions for true positives (instances predicted to be novel metaphors that were actually novel metaphors) versus false positives (instances predicted to be novel metaphors that were actually not), **questions generated for novel metaphors were rated as having more depth than similar questions generated for conventional or non-metaphors, and this difference was found to be statistically significant.**

Finally, many of the correlation scores observed between rating criteria were expected (it is difficult to think of questions that are, for instance, highly natural-sounding while also unclear). We had anticipated a slightly higher positive correlation than was observed between question depth and completion time, as a natural assumption is that if a question makes a reader think quite a bit before answering it, it will take longer to formulate an answer than if the question doesn't make a reader think at all. However, the measurement of completion time was coarse-grained; it only considered the overall amount of time that it took the worker to complete the full HIT including reading the instructions and a source sentence, rating four criteria, and finally constructing a written response to the question. Many variables outside of the question depth itself could therefore impact the overall completion time. In the future, work can be conducted to examine the correlation between completion time and question depth in a more controlled environment.

6 Conclusion

In this work, we introduced and evaluated a question generation approach to automatically construct QtA queries about predicted novel metaphors. We designed and validated question templates based on sample questions drawn directly from the book on QtA (Beck and McKeown, 2006), and demonstrated methods capable of producing high-quality question realizations. We evaluated the automatically-generated questions relative to human-generated questions based on the same source material, and discovered that the only statistically significant difference between the two groups with respect to four distinct criteria (naturalness, clarity, sensibility, and depth) was that the automatically-generated questions received slightly higher clarity scores. We analyzed the correlations among the four question criteria as well as between the question criteria and completion time, and found strong positive correlations between naturalness, clarity, and sensibility, but only weak correlations between each of those criteria and question depth.

All data and source code are publicly available. Ultimately, our evaluation proved that questions about novel metaphors in literature can be automatically generated at a quality level comparable to what the average human might generate. It also provided empirical support for an underlying motivation guiding this work: that questions about novel metaphors can be leveraged as a means for motivating cognitive exercise.

Acknowledgements

We thank the anonymous reviewers for their comments and suggestions. This material was based upon work supported by the National Science Foundation Graduate Research Fellowship Program under Grant 1144248, and the National Science Foundation under Grant 1262860. Any opinions, findings, and conclusions or recommendations expressed in this material are those of the author(s) and do not necessarily reflect the views of the National Science Foundation.

References

Martina Amanzio, Giuliano Geminiani, Daniela Leotta, and Stefano Cappa. 2008. Metaphor comprehension in alzheimers disease: Novelty matters. *Brain and Language*, 107(1):1 – 10.

Jun Araki, Dheeraj Rajagopal, Sreecharan Sankaranarayanan, Susan Holm, Yukari Yamakawa, and Teruko Mitamura. 2016. Generating questions and multiple-choice answers using semantic analysis of texts. In *Proceedings of COLING 2016, the 26th International Conference on Computational Linguistics: Technical Papers*, pages 1125–1136, Osaka, Japan. The COLING 2016 Organizing Committee.

Isabel L. Beck and Margaret G. McKeown. 2006. *Improving Comprehension with Questioning the Author: A Fresh and Expanded View of a Powerful Approach*. Theory and Practice. Scholastic.

Lee Becker, Sumit Basu, and Lucy Vanderwende. 2012. Mind the gap: Learning to choose gaps for question generation. In *Proceedings of the 2012 Conference of the North American Chapter of the Association for Computational Linguistics: Human Language Technologies*, pages 742–751, Montréal, Canada. Association for Computational Linguistics.

Xinya Du, Junru Shao, and Claire Cardie. 2017. Learning to ask: Neural question generation for reading comprehension. In *Proceedings of the 55th Annual Meeting of the Association for Computational Linguistics*.

Donna M. Gates. 2008. Generating look-back strategy questions from expository texts. In *Proceedings of the Workshop on the Question Generation Shared Task and Evaluation Challenge*.

Michael Heilman and Noah A. Smith. 2010. Good question! statistical ranking for question generation. In *Human Language Technologies: The 2010 Annual Conference of the North American Chapter of the Association for Computational Linguistics*, pages 609–617, Los Angeles, California. Association for Computational Linguistics.

Vicky Tzuyin Lai, Tim Curran, and Lise Menn. 2009. Comprehending conventional and novel metaphors: An ERP study. *Brain Research*, 1284:145 – 155.

David Lindberg, Fred Popowich, John Nesbit, and Phil Winne. 2013. Generating natural language questions to support learning on-line. In *Proceedings of the 14th European Workshop on Natural Language Generation*, pages 105–114, Sofia, Bulgaria. Association for Computational Linguistics.

Ming Liu, Rafael A Calvo, and Vasile Rus. 2012. G-asks: An intelligent automatic question generation system for academic writing support. *Dialogue & Discourse*, 3(2):101–124.

Christopher D. Manning, Mihai Surdeanu, John Bauer, Jenny Finkel, Steven J. Bethard, and David Mc-Closky. 2014. The Stanford CoreNLP natural language processing toolkit. In *Association for Computational Linguistics (ACL) System Demonstrations*, pages 55–60.

Nira Mashal, Ronit Gavrieli, and Gitit Kav. 2011. Age-related changes in the appreciation of novel metaphoric semantic relations. *Aging, Neuropsychology, and Cognition*, 18(5):527–543. PMID: 21819177.

Karen Mazidi and Rodney D. Nielsen. 2014. *Pedagogical Evaluation of Automatically Generated Questions*. Springer International Publishing.

Karen Mazidi and Rodney D. Nielsen. 2015. *Leveraging Multiple Views of Text for Automatic Question Generation*. Springer International Publishing.

Ryan McDonald, Joakim Nivre, Yvonne Quirmbach-Brundage, Yoav Goldberg, Dipanjan Das, Kuzman Ganchev, Keith Hall, Slav Petrov, Hao Zhang, Oscar Täckström, et al. 2013. Universal dependency annotation for multilingual parsing. In *Proceedings of the 51st Annual Meeting of the Association for Computational Linguistics*, volume 2, pages 92–97.

George A. Miller. 1995. Wordnet: A lexical database for english. *Commun. ACM*, 38(11):39–41.

Jack Mostow and Wei Chen. 2009. Generating instruction automatically for the reading strategy of self-questioning. In *Proceedings of the 2009 Conference on Artificial Intelligence in Education: Building Learning Systems That Care: From Knowledge Representation to Affective Modelling*, pages 465–472, Amsterdam, The Netherlands, The Netherlands. IOS Press.

Andrew M. Olney, Arthur C. Graesser, and Natalie K. Person. 2012. Question generation from concept maps. *Dialogue & Discourse*, 3(2):75–99.

Natalie Parde. 2018. Reading with robots: Towards a human-robot book discussion system for elderly adults. In *Proceedings of the Thirty-Second AAAI Conference on Artificial Intelligence (AAAI-18) Doctoral Consortium*, New Orleans, Louisiana.

Association for the Advancement of Artificial Intelligence.

Natalie Parde and Rodney D. Nielsen. 2017. Finding patterns in noisy crowds: Regression-based annotation aggregation for crowdsourced data. In *Proceedings of the 2017 Conference on Empirical Methods in Natural Language Processing*, pages 1908–1913, Copenhagen, Denmark. Association for Computational Linguistics.

Natalie Parde and Rodney D. Nielsen. 2018a. A corpus of metaphor novelty scores for syntactically-related word pairs. In *Proceedings of the 11th International Conference on Language Resources and Evaluation*, Miyazaki, Japan. European Language Resources Association.

Natalie Parde and Rodney D. Nielsen. 2018b. Exploring the terrain of metaphor novelty: A regression-based approach for automatically scoring metaphors. In *Proceedings of the Thirty-Second AAAI Conference on Artificial Intelligence (AAAI-18)*, New Orleans, Louisiana. Association for the Advancement of Artificial Intelligence.

Vasile Rus, Zhiqiang Cai, and Arthur C. Graesser. 2007. Experiments on generating questions about facts. In *Proceedings of the 8th International Conference on Computational Linguistics and Intelligent Text Processing*, CICLing '07, pages 444–455, Berlin, Heidelberg. Springer-Verlag.

Iulian Vlad Serban, Alberto García-Durán, Caglar Gulcehre, Sungjin Ahn, Sarath Chandar, Aaron Courville, and Yoshua Bengio. 2016. Generating factoid questions with recurrent neural networks: The 30m factoid question-answer corpus. In *Proceedings of the 54th Annual Meeting of the Association for Computational Linguistics (Volume 1: Long Papers)*, pages 588–598, Berlin, Germany. Association for Computational Linguistics.

Gerard J. Steen, Aletta G. Dorst, J. Berenike Herrmann, Anna Kaal, Tina Krennmayr, and Trijntje Pasma. 2010. *A method for linguistic metaphor identification: From MIP to MIPVU*, volume 14. John Benjamins Publishing.

John H. Wolfe. 1977. Reading retention as a function of method for generating interspersed questions. Technical report, San Diego: Navy Personnel Research and Development Center.

Brendan Wyse and Paul Piwek. 2009. Generating questions from openlearn study units. In *Proceedings of the AIED 2nd Workshop on Question Generation*, pages 66–73.

A Master-Apprentice Approach to Automatic Creation of Culturally Satirical Movie Titles

Khalid Alnajjar
Department of Computer Science
and Helsinki Institute for IT
Faculty of Science
University of Helsinki, Finland
alnajjar@cs.helsinki.fi

Mika Hämäläinen
Department of Digital Humanities
Faculty of Arts
University of Helsinki, Finland
mika.hamalainen@helsinki.fi

Abstract

Satire has played a role in indirectly expressing critique towards an authority or a person from time immemorial. We present an autonomously creative master-apprentice approach consisting of a genetic algorithm and an NMT model to produce humorous and culturally apt satire out of movie titles automatically. Furthermore, we evaluate the approach in terms of its creativity and its output. We provide a solid definition for creativity to maximize the objectiveness of the evaluation.

1 Introduction

Movie theaters used to be prohibited in Saudi Arabia by law, however in mid-December 2017, Saudi Arabia officially declared they would abolish the law by 2018[1]. This gave birth to a movement on Twitter by the hashtag *#SaudiMovieTitles* where people would post alternative movie titles meant to be satirical towards the Saudi Arabian legislative system. An example of such a title is *I Know What You Ate Last Ramadan* for *I Know What You Did Last Summer*.

In this paper, we present a novel master-apprentice approach to computational creativity for the generation of such humoristic movie titles automatically. Our system consists of two creative agents: a computationally creative master that is implemented with a genetic algorithm approach and a neural network based apprentice that will learn from the master along with its peers, namely real people writing satirical movie titles on Twitter. We are introducing the apprentice to achieve

creative autonomy, because of its nature of adjusting its standards by learning, a capability which is absent in the master.

Furthermore, we base our approach in terms of the design of its implementation and its evaluation on a solid definition of creativity that we build based on literature. This will make a reasoned evaluation of our system possible and set standards for future research in this topic.

For the purposes of our research, we understand cultural satire as a way of presenting critique towards a society in a humoristic fashion. The humoristic expression has to relate to Saudi Arabia in its expression - mostly by lexical choice. The relatedness has to be apparent when presented with the hashtag *#SaudiMovieTitles*.

Computational linguistic creativity of this nature poses a number of challenges, not only because it is a difficult NLG problem, but also because the generated output has to be humorous. Thus the goal of the system is very different from a more traditional NLG task where the system is to convey factual information such as timetables of a train or the current weather conditions in the form of natural language.

The message our system is to produce serves rather to convey emotion and provoke joy in the reader. Furthermore, the humor is to be delivered in a culture-specific way which combines cultural artifacts of the Western World, the Hollywood movie titles, with a Saudi Arabian cultural twist. The system will derive its satire from this juxtaposition of the two cultures following utterly conflicting norms.

2 Related Work

Automatic creation of humor has received some attention in the past. Valitutti et al. (2009) present a tool for interactive creation of puns. The sys-

---

[1]The press release of The Saudi Ministry of Culture and Information (MOCI) https://www.media.gov.sa/news/1101

Proceedings of The 11th International Natural Language Generation Conference, pages 274–283,
Tilburg, The Netherlands, November 5-8, 2018. ©2018 Association for Computational Linguistics

tem suggests funny replacement words for familiar expressions such as proverbs. The replacements are found by applying a phonetic similarity metric together with a Latent semantic analysis (LSA) based semantic similarity metric, which not only gives semantically related words but also semantically opposed ones.

A fully automated pun generator, presented in Valitutti et al. (2013), takes an English sentence as its input and changes one word in it based on three criteria: sound or spelling similarity, the replacement word has to be a taboo and that the word has to go well together with its immediate predecessor in the sentence. The system operates with a predefined set of taboo words and an n-gram model to assess how well the new words fit in the sentence.

A more recent take on the pun generation is that of Shah et al. (2016), which presents a template based approach on humor generation. The templates are filled by using WordNet relations for the input compound word. The system looks up a list of related words for the two words of the compound and forms a pun out of them.

Research has also been conducted in the vein of humoristic sarcasm generation, which is then served to the user as satire (Veale, 2018). The system generates sarcastic tweets that satirize a person with a knowledge-based approach and re-generative approach which regenerates sarcastic tweets giving the sarcasm a new contextual meaning. The system is online on Twitter and it actively engages into replying Tweets it has been mentioned in.

The related work, not unlike a great many publications in the field of computational creativity, overlooks an important aspect, which is a clear and motivated definition for creativity. This issue has been brought up in the past research as well (Jordanous, 2012), but yet a great many publications devote little to no comment on what creativity, the very thing that is computationally modeled, really means in the context of a creative system. This makes comparison to and building from previous research a difficult task. To provide an alleviation to this problem, we will provide a definition for creativity based on existing literature that we will follow in this paper.

3 Definition of Creativity

In order to say anything about the creativity of a computational system, it is important to define what creativity means in the context of the system. We do this by following the SPECS (Standardized Procedure for Evaluating Creative Systems) approach (Jordanous, 2012). In short, the approach requires us first to define what is needed for creativity in general and then what is needed for creativity in our case of producing cultural humorous movie titles in particular.

For the general definition, instead of undertaking defining something as abstract as creativity by ourselves, we opt for a well established definition in the field, namely the creative tripod (Colton, 2008). According to that definition, there are three indispensable components to creativity: *skill*, *imagination* and *appreciation*. All of them can come from the three different parties of the creative experience, the system, the programmer or the perceiver of the creative artifact. However, the system has to be perceived to exhibit all of them on its own to be considered creative.

To put the creative tripod in the context of our highly narrowed down task, we start by defining skill as an ability to produce a new title out of an existing one. To master this skill it is imperative that the original movie title still remain recognizable and that the new title deliver a humoristic joke that satirizes Saudi Arabia.

Imaginativeness requires that our system should at least achieve P-creativity. That is, according to Boden (2004), coming up with a surprising and valuable idea that is novel to the one who came up with it, as opposed to H-creativity which is novel in a more global context, i.e. no one else had thought of it before. What this means is that our system should come up with similar humorous titles as real people have in our dataset to achieve P-creativity, and preferably come up with humoristic titles nobody has ever tweeted about before to be H-creative.

Lastly, we define appreciation in this context as a computational capability of assessing various factors that affect on the quality of the created title. One of them is the ability of identifying puns by recognizing sound similarities on a phonetic level such as in *Sheikhs and the City* for *Sex and the City*. But a far more important requirement for appreciation is an automated assessment of the humorousness of the output. Two key components have been identified for humorousness in jokes: *surprise* and *coherence* (Brownell et al., 1983).

When the brain makes sense of the stimuli it

receives, it relies on prior experiences to predict what it is perceiving. When these predictions turn out to be wrong, surprise arises. This is even more clearly crystallized in the case of movie titles. When a title everyone has heard a plethora of times gets changed, it clearly breaks learned expectations of the brain of how the title should be, as it is the case for example with *How to Train Your Imam* from *How to Train Your Dragon*.

In the previous example, surprise arises from the fact that the brain was expecting to hear *dragon*, but got a wildly different word *imam*. This surprise, however, does not yet lead to humor if the surprising word is not interpreted in its context. This requires coherence; the word has to make sense in the context of the sentence, and also in the wider context of the movie the original title refers to. Part of the humoristic value comes from the thought of young Hiccup undertaking an adventurous task on training his imam, as he did in the original movie to train his dragon.

In addition to the requirements identified with the creative tripod framework, we also introduce the requirement of creative autonomy for our system. Creative autonomy (Jennings, 2010) requires *autonomous evaluation*, *autonomous change* and *non-randomness*. In other words, the system should be able to evaluate its output independently (this relates to the appreciation defined earlier) and change its standards on its own without instructions on how to do so. Neither of these two requirements can be based solely on a random choice.

We have defined the core requirements for our system to be considered to exhibit creative behavior. These requirements will be revisited in the Evaluation section of this paper to assess the extent to which they are met by the implementation. This is also required by the SPECS approach we have decided to follow in this paper.

4 Datasets

This section is devoted to the description of the datasets we have in use for the implementation of the system.

4.1 Movie Data

For our case, we are only interested in the popular movies people might have heard of, as one of our requirements is the original title to be recognizable after it has been turned into a humoristic form. No

matter how good the satire, the joke will not land, if the audience is unfamiliar with the original title.

To get indispensable information of the movies, we used the data dumps provided by the IMDB[2] to extract movie titles and their metadata. As the IMDB is a bit too extensive, sporting over a 5 million movies and TV shows in its database, we had to narrow it down to those that had got more than 100,000 votes from the IMDB. The number of votes does not tell anything about how well the movie was received by the audience, but it gives us a clue on its popularity. The more popular the movie, the more votes it will get. In total, we had a total of 1,661 movies.

As movies can be referred to without their episode name, we expand the list of movies by considering their titles without episode or sequel name. This is performed by stripping out words after the first dash or colon. For instance, the movie title *The Lord of the Rings: The Fellowship of the Ring* is converted into *The Lord of the Rings*.

4.2 Tweets

Another peculiar source of information are the tweets with the the hashtag *#SaudiMovieTitles*. We retrieved them by using the Twitter API, which resulted in a list of 2,445 tweets. However, the tweets are noisy because, more often than not, they contain other unrelated content (e.g. URLs, mentions and so on) in addition to the humoristic movie title. Moreover, the titles in the tweets might not be in the same format as the original movie title.

In order to serve us any use, the tweets needed to be processed so that what was left was just the humoristic title. This is done by converting the tweets into lowercase. Thereafter, the tokenization is applied, and any word starting with # or is filtered out to clean any hashtags and mentions, respectively. Any special characters and URLs are also deleted from the string. Finally, we remove all instances of the token "rt" from the string as it indicates a re-tweet.

Furthermore, we map the processed tweets to their original movie titles. The mapping phase is employed to backtrack any modifications performed on the original title for a humoristic effect. We achieve this by iterating over all tweets and calculating the edit distance on character and word level against all movie titles in the dataset. Movie

---

[2]https://datasets.imdbws.com/

titles with the least word edit distance, followed by character edit distance, are considered as the original title to tweets.

To reduce noise in the data (e.g. tweeted titles where all words have been changed), we keep the humoristic titles with at most 3 changed words, making still sure that not all the words have been changed in the tweeted title. Examples of mapped titles are *The Lord of the Thowbs* to *The Lord of the Rings* and *Gulf Fiction* to *Pulp Fiction*.

4.3 Saudi Arabia Related Vocabulary

We extract words, along with their part-of-speech tags that are related to Saudi Arabia from the tweets dataset. This is accomplished by parsing the tweeted titles and their mapped original counterparts with Spacy (Honnibal and Montani, 2017), followed by an analysis of their differences. We build the vocabulary by adding words that exist exclusively in the tweeted titles and not in the original ones. We also save the part-of-speech tags of the words.

Analyzing the vocabulary, it appears that all the added words, 1053 in total, are either nouns or adjectives. Examples of nouns are *thawab, imam* and *stone*, and adjectives are *saudi, shaytan* and *sunni*.

4.4 English Vocabulary of Arabic Origin

In order to produce titles relevant to the Saudi Arabian context, the system needs to have a list of English words related to the Arabian culture. The primary source of such words are the ones registered in the Oxford English Dictionary (OED, n.d.) as having Arabic as one of the languages in their etymology (514 in words in total). We have an access to the JSON files[3] of the OED, which made this task easier. The vocabulary also included the lexical categories of words.

5 Creating Movie Titles

In this section, we explain the method for creating movie titles. The method is divided into two submethods, (1) the master, which generates movie titles using genetic algorithms, and (2) the apprentice, which learns from the master and develops its own appreciation for generating movie titles.

5.1 The Master

The implementation of the master follows the one presented by Alnajjar et al. (2018) for slogan gen-

eration. The generator is a genetic algorithm that accepts an original movie title as an input and produces an entire population of satire movie titles based on the input.

The master operates on a semantic space of words related to Saudi Arabia to make the substitution of content words in the input with cultural words about Saudi Arabia possible. The semantic space is a combination of the vocabularies described in Section 4.3 and 4.4.

5.1.1 Evolutionary algorithm

Our algorithm starts by producing an initial population which undergoes an evolutionary process throughout a certain number of generations. The evolutionary algorithm in place is a standard (μ + λ)[4] which applies mutation and crossover on the current population to generate λ number of offspring. Subsequently, the algorithm evaluates the fitness of the individuals in the current population and their offspring, and selects μ number of the fittest individuals to survive to the next generation. Once the specified number of generations is reached, the evolutionary process terminates and returns the final population.

5.1.2 Initial Population

The method produces μ copies of the input movie title. For each copy, the method substitutes a randomly selected content word, i.e. not a stop word, with a random word from the semantic space. The substitution is done in such a fashion that the parts-of-speech of the original word and its substitute have to match. Furthermore, the word is inflected if necessary. The resulting titles form the initial population.

5.1.3 Mutation and Crossover

We define one type of mutation and crossover. The mutation procedure follows the same substitution approach performed during the construction of the initial population. The crossover employed in our function is a single-point crossover where words before and after a randomly selected point in two individuals are swapped.

5.1.4 Evaluation as Appreciation

The appreciation is implemented in the master by four internal evaluation dimensions, which are (1) prosody, (2) semantic relatedness to Saudi Arabia, (3) semantic similarity, and (4) number of al-

---

[3] We used the JSON files updated on the 14 of February in 2018

[4] We use the value 100 for both μ and λ

tered words. The first two dimensions are maximized, whereas the last two are minimized. Additionally, a dimension can be represented by the weighted sum of multiple sub-functions.

The prosody dimension assesses the sound similarity of the original word and its replacement. The dimension is composed of four prosody features, namely consonance, assonance, rhyme and alliteration. We utilize *espeak-ng tool*[5] to produce IPA transcriptions for words to better evaluate how they sound when pronounced. The tool is capable of producing IPA even for non-English words, such as *jahannam*.

To measure the semantic relatedness of words to Saudi Arabia, we build a semantic relatedness model following the model described in Xiao et al. (2016). Using the model, we measure the dimension as the maximum semantic relatedness of any content words in the generated title to the words "Saudi" and "saudi".

We employ a word2vec model trained on News dataset by Google (Mikolov et al., 2013) to measure the semantic similarity between two words. The dimension is represented as the mean of the semantic similarity of each introduced word to its original word. This dimension is minimized to increase surprise, with the idea that a lower semantic relatedness between the original word and its substitute would result in a bigger surprise.

The last dimension monitors the number of words altered in the input title. Minimizing this dimension motivates that less substitutions are made to the title, which makes it more recognizable.

These are the criteria based on which the fitness of individuals is evaluated at the end of each generation to let only the best ones survive to the next generation. Also, the master uses this exact same functionality when it is to show appreciation to titles outside of its own creations such as those created by the apprentice.

5.1.5 Selection and Filtering

To reduce having a dominating dimension and motivate generating titles with diverse and balanced scores on all four dimensions, we opt for a non-dominant sorting algorithm *–NSGA-II–* (Deb et al., 2002) as the selection algorithm.

During each iteration of the evolution, the current population and its offspring go through a filtering phase which filters out any duplicate titles.

---

[5]https://github.com/espeak-ng/
espeak-ng

5.2 The Apprentice

The apprentice is a sequence-to-sequence neural network model, which will be trained by the parallel data of the original titles and their humoristic counter-parts produced by the master. Furthermore, the apprentice is trained with the parallel titles extracted from the tweets. We use a general purpose NMT library called OpenNMT (Klein et al., 2017) for this task.

Similar sequence-to-sequence based approaches have been used in the past for text paraphrasing task (Brad and Rebedea, 2017; Sleimi and Gardent, 2016), which shares its similarities with the task we are set to solve. This gives us a reason to believe that sequence-to-sequence approach is a viable way of implementing the apprentice.

The apprentice was trained for 50 epochs with the titles the master had produced for a random set of the most popular IMDB movie titles. This set consisted of 6568 humoristic titles. After this, the model was trained for 50 additional epochs with the data from the 1,483 tweeted titles. This made it possible for the apprentice to learn to a set of standards for humoristic titles from its master and adjust those standards with the peer data. In both cases, we use a 25% of the data in validation. The high number of epochs together with a larger validation set seemed[6] to make the model learn more given the limitation imposed by the scarce training data.

5.3 The Symbiotic Nature

Currently, we cannot argument for the apprentice developing appreciation that matches the requirements we have set for it in the definition of creativity, albeit it will learn some kind of an appreciation because it is capable of giving a confidence score to its creations. However, as the nature of such appreciation is not assessed in this paper, we opt for a symbiotic approach in the appreciation of the full system.

The apprentice will only be allowed to learn from its peers if the master shows high enough appreciation towards the creations of its peers. Furthermore, when producing its creative output, the apprentice consults the master for its opinion on which output should be picked and presented to

---

[6]We tried training with fewer epochs and fewer titles in the validation, but the model failed to learn anything meaningful.

the audience.

The apprentice might be dependent on the master in terms of appreciation, but just as much the master is dependent on its apprentice. The master possesses no capability of adjusting its standards, because it exhibits no learning from others. This is where the apprentice can learn its own standards from its peers, and is thus the only one responsible of the creative autonomy of the entire system.

6 Evaluation

In this part, we are presenting an evaluation of the system from two points of view. Firstly, we will assess critically how the definition of creativity with its requirements is met in the implementation of the system. Secondly, we validate this assessment by having ordinary people evaluate the output of the system by answering to questions on a 5-point Likert scale. These questions are derived from the definition of creativity in our context by following the SPECS approach.

6.1 Evaluation of the Creative Process

The skill of converting a movie title into a humorous one can be shown on the implementation level of the master. It takes an existing title, uses it as a skeleton and outputs a new title. The apprentice model also clearly demonstrates this lowest level requirement for skill. By nature, the NMT model produces an output based on its input. However, we can say little about the fulfillment of the further criteria for skill just by looking at the creative process. Recognizability of the original title, humorousness and satire towards Saudi Arabia are highly subjective notions and thus they will be assessed by evaluators in the next section.

The system can be shown to achieve P-creativity with a rather easy test by looking at the output in relation to the data the systems were given initially. For example the master produced a title *The Hobbit: An Unexpected Desert* from *The Hobbit: An Unexpected Journey* even though the master was not given knowledge of such a possibility for a humoristic title. The apprentice was able to produce the title *The Amazing Spider Mosque* for *The Amazing Spiderman* even thought its training data did not provide it with this mapping.

In order to analyze the imagination any further, we have to assess also the H-creativity of the produced titles. We could perform a Google search with some of the generated titles and claim H-creativity if it did not return any hits. However, we feel that this is not quite enough as the same kind of a joke might have come up elsewhere with a slightly different context. This is the reason why we have to verify the H-creativity with evaluators.

Appreciation can be more easily assessed from the point of view of the master. The master has been programmed to look at sound similarity which covers the optional requirement for a pun. Surprise is modeled in the master by it minimizing the semantic similarity of the original word and the new replacement. If we define surprise as a failed prediction done by the brain, we can back the master's way of producing it in neuroscience. Research (Lau et al., 2008) has shown that words the brain expects to hear in a sentence cause a lower N400 response than unexpected words. This is because when the brain fails at its expectations, it has to activate the new surprising concepts together with those close to it semantically. This might not, however, be the only explanation for surprise nor a sufficient one. Therefore, the requirement for surprise, though met, has room for improvement.

The last requirement for appreciation was coherence. This has been implemented on the level of semantic coherence to Saudi Arabia. However, as some of the titles written by people, such as *Sheikhs and the City*, show, the contextual coherence is next to impossible to assess without the wider context of the movie itself. We feel that this kind of pragmatic coherence is such a wide task to tackle that it is deserving of a dedicated paper on its own right and thus is beyond the scope of this research. However, it is an important question for the future as it has been shown that humor of the kind we are focusing on in this paper derives its meaning greatly from its pragmatic context (Hämäläinen, 2016).

The appreciation will only be discussed here from the point of view of the master, as the design choice of the system was to give the master the responsibility of appreciation. However, an interesting question for the future is the appreciation learned by the apprentice. Since an NMT model can score its predictions, it has to have learned a kind of an appreciation, but the nature of it is not discussed here. Although this gives an interesting direction for the future research on the topic.

We can demonstrate that the system is capable

of achieving creative autonomy because it can appreciate autonomously its own creations and those of its peers. Furthermore, the changes it makes to its standards are guided by observations made on the artifacts of its peers that have received enough appreciation from the master. Even though the master will follow a limited way of generating humorous titles, its apprentice is liberated from such limits thanks to its neural network architecture.

6.2 Evaluation of the Output

The creative tripod, through which we have defined creativity, requires there to be perceivably skill, appreciation and imagination in the system. The existence of these in the output of the master and the apprentice is evaluated by formulating questions based on the requirements we set for this particular creative task.

6.2.1 Skill

Skill is probably the leg of the tripod that most vocally calls for evaluation from people. In the previous evaluation section, we could only clearly demonstrate that the system fills the most basic requirement, that is to produce a new title out of the existing one.

The further requirements, recognizability of the original title, whether the new title is humoristic and whether it satirizes Saudi Arabia, are beyond any justified assessment without resorting to people's opinion. Thus we need to asses them with the following questions.

1. The title is humorous

2. The original title is recognizable

3. The humor in the title relates to Saudi Arabia

4. The title is critical towards Saudi Arabia

The first question can be asked directly, there is no need to find a better way to ask whether the original title is still recognizable or not. It is important to note that when we are evaluating the skill, we only want to know whether the skill of producing humor exists. The quality of the humor is left for the evaluation of the appreciation.

As for the other questions we want to know whether humor is perceived and whether a relation to Saudi Arabia is perceived. Furthermore, we are curious to see whether criticism is perceived. We will not ask directly whether the title is satirical

for two reasons, firstly in order to understand anything as satire, further context is needed and secondly terms such as satire, sarcasm and irony are difficult for an ordinary person to grasp and get often mixed up with one another in people's minds.

6.2.2 Imagination

We took Boden's P- and H-creativity as the basis of the imagination quality of the system. We defined the system to be imaginative enough if it can come up with something new to itself and to exceed the expectations of its imagination if it can come up with something novel in a greater context.

The previous evaluation of the creativity in the system, we have showed that the system is capable of P-creativity and we have shown examples of its H-creativity. While P-creativity, as it is limited to the system itself, has been inarguably proven, the H-creativity calls for further validation. Therefore, we formulate the following evaluation questions to assess the imaginativeness of the system.

5. The joke in the title sounds familiar

6. The joke in the title is obvious

These questions get to the core of what is required from H-creativity, it has to be novel in a global context, i.e. it cannot sound familiar to another slightly different joke the evaluator might have heard before. Also, the joke cannot be too obvious, because if its perceived as an obvious one, people would likely come up with it easily and thus it can hardly be seen H-creative.

6.2.3 Appreciation

Appreciation is something we have discussed to a great extent in the previous evaluation section. As for appreciation, we are not interested to see whether the system gets a high grade from the people for each evaluation question. Instead, we are more interested in seeing the extent to which they are in line. Does the appreciation of the system predict human appreciation in the same variables?

The constituents of the appreciation we identified earlier were pun detection, and humorousness. The latter was then further divided into two appreciable features: surprise and coherence. To put these into the form of evaluation questions, we resulted in the following ones.

7. The title delivers a pun

8. The joke in the title is surprising

9. The joke of the title makes sense in the context of the original movie

The three evaluation questions are meant to evaluate the three requirements respectively. For coherence, we are interested in how coherent the humor is in the context of the movie. A title might be perfectly humoristic if it was in the context of one movie, where as it might make little to no sense in the case of another movie.

6.2.4 Results

The master was made to produce populations[7] for the most popular movie titles. Out of these, we picked at random 50 titles that exhibited appreciation based on the master's own standards. Furthermore, we picked another 50 titles at random that were produced by the apprentice and appreciated by the master.

The questions defined earlier were presented for each title produced by the master and the apprentice to evaluators on a platform called Figure-Eight. Due to the way the platform operates, every title was not presented to every evaluator, but they appeared at random in such a way that each individual title was evaluated by 20 different evaluators. All in all 48 evaluators participated. As knowledge of English is entailed by the system, we defined a further requirement for the evaluators' language to be Arabic. This way they should be familiar with the specialized cultural vocabulary exhibited by the humoristic titles and know enough English to understand the title.

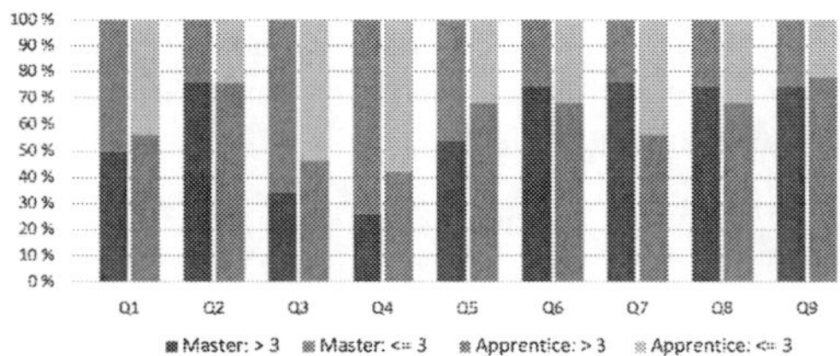

Figure 1: Results of the evaluation for the questions for both the master and the apprentice

For each evaluated title, we calculated the average of the judgments received on each question. Furthermore, judgments are considered agreeing if their average evaluation score is greater than 3, i.e.

above neutral. Figure 1 shows the percentage of agreements to neutral or disagreement judgments. Examples of the generated titles can be seen in Table 1,

From the results, it is evident that both methods, the master and the apprentice, were capable of producing humorous titles. Furthermore, it appears that the original movie titles were usually recognized, with 76%, form generated titles. Nevertheless, a low percentage, $\leq 45\%$, of the generated titles were perceived as related to or critical towards Saudi Arabia. In terms of the imagination questions, Q5 and Q6, statistics illustrate that the methods generated familiar and obvious jokes, most of the time; which suggests low H-creativity. Despite that, the methods have received high agreement on the appreciation questions. These results demonstrate that both methods have produced creative alternatives of original movies; however, further development and evaluation is needed to explore the methods and enhance their current state of creativity.

Comparing the results of the master and the apprentice, we notice that generated titles by the apprentice have received different judgments than the master, on most of the questions. Such distinction shows that the apprentice has developed its own internal appreciation. As a result, the apprentice exhibits characteristics of creative autonomy, and, with continuous data from the master and peers, the apprentice will adaptively adjust its appreciation.

7   Conclusions and Final Remarks

We have presented a novel approach for generating satirical humor. Evaluating it critically against the definition of the creativity we established, we identified two clear shortcomings of the approach: firstly a better definition for surprise is needed to better model it in the future, and secondly coherence calls for a better contextual model relating the coherence in the context of the original movie where the title has occurred. Both of these shortcomings require additional research and are worthy of own publications dedicated to the topics.

Our definition of creativity that has been built on top of existing theories gives us a good starting point to conduct any future research on the topic. Also the evaluation questions deriving from the definition provides us with a way of comparing the results of any future improvements to the ones

---

[7]The evaluated titles are the ones the apprentice was trained with. See Section 5.2

Question	High Scoring Ones	Low Scoring Ones
Q1	*The Lord of the Lambs: The Return of the King* *My Big Saudi Wedding*	*Iraqi of Arabia* *Empire of the State*
Q2	*Muslim League* *Captain Tanker*	*The Sunni: Part III* *Iraqi-man: Houthi*
Q3	*My Big Saudi Wedding* *The Good the Haram and the Saudi*	*Iraqi Buyers Club* *The Wedding Attack*
Q4	*Serabs of Saudi York* *Transformers Saudi of Extinction*	*La La Kill* *The Wedding Attack*
Q5	*Night at The Arabian* *My Big Saudi Wedding*	*La La Invasion* *Attack Powers: The Oil dependence Who Shagged Me*
Q6	*Night at the Arabian* *The Saudi Runner*	*The Sunni Life of Izars* *La La Invasion*
Q7	*Sunnah Squad* *The Twilight Bomb Eclipse*	*Muslim Story 3* *Harry Potter and the Revenge's Sulham*
Q8	*The Twilight Bomb Eclipse* *The Saudi Runner*	*The Imam Ultimatum* *Muslim Fu Panda*
Q9	*The Amazing Surah-man* *The Sound of Jihad*	*The Amazing Spider Mosque* *Harry Potter and the Revenge's Sulham*

Table 1: Examples of high and low scoring titles based on the evaluators' judgment

presented in this paper.

The master-apprentice approach makes it possible for us to study the creativity and its development in the apprentice from a multi-agent perspective. This evokes interesting questions such as: What if there were multiple master-apprentice pairs and they would function as each other's peers? What if an apprentice took classes of multiple masters simultaneously? What if the masters were experts on different fields such as humor and poetry? Would the apprentice then learn to generate based on both fields? We are also interested in diving into the black box of the NMT architecture of the apprentice to see what kind of an appreciation it can develop.

8 Acknowledgements

This work has been supported by the Academy of Finland under grants 276897 (CLiC) and 293009 (STRATAS).

References

Khalid Alnajjar, Hadaytullah Hadaytullah, and Hannu Toivonen. 2018. "Talent, Skill and Support." A method for automatic creation of slogans. In *Proceedings of the Ninth International Conference on Computational Creativity (ICCC 2018)*, pages 88–95, Salamanca, Spain. Association for Computational Creativity (ACC).

Margaret A Boden. 2004. *The creative mind: Myths and mechanisms*. Routledge.

Florin Brad and Traian Rebedea. 2017. Neural paraphrase generation using transfer learning. In *Proceedings of the 10th International Conference on Natural Language Generation*, pages 257–261, Santiago de Compostela, Spain. Association for Computational Linguistics.

Hiram H Brownell, Dee Michel, John Powelson, and Howard Gardner. 1983. Surprise but not coherence: Sensitivity to verbal humor in right-hemisphere patients. *Brain and Language*, 18(1):20 – 27.

Simon Colton. 2008. Creativity Versus the Perception of Creativity in Computational Systems. In *AAAI Spring Symposium: Creative Intelligent Systems*, Technical Report SS-08-03, pages 14–20, Stanford, California, USA.

K. Deb, A. Pratap, S. Agarwal, and T. Meyarivan. 2002. A fast and elitist multiobjective genetic algorithm: Nsga-ii. *IEEE Transactions on Evolutionary Computation*, 6(2):182–197.

Mika Hämäläinen. 2016. Reconocimiento automático del sarcasmo - ¡Esto va a funcionar bien! Master's thesis, University of Helsinki, Finland. URN:NBN:fi:hulib-201606011945.

Matthew Honnibal and Ines Montani. 2017. spaCy 2: Natural Language Understanding with Bloom Embeddings, Convolutional Neural Networks and Incremental Parsing. *To appear.*

Kyle E. Jennings. 2010. Developing Creativity: Artificial Barriers in Artificial Intelligence. *Minds and Machines*, 20(4):489–501.

Anna Jordanous. 2012. A standardised procedure for evaluating creative systems: Computational creativity evaluation based on what it is to be creative. *Cognitive Computation*, 4(3):246–279.

Guillaume Klein, Yoon Kim, Yuntian Deng, Jean Senellart, and Alexander M. Rush. 2017. OpenNMT: Open-Source Toolkit for Neural Machine Translation. In *Proceedings of the 55th Annual Meeting of the Association for Computational Linguistics-System Demonstrations*, pages 67–72, Vancouver, Canada. Association for Computational Linguistics.

Ellen F Lau, Colin Phillips, and David Poeppel. 2008. A Cortical Network for Semantics: (De)constructing the N400. *Nature Reviews Neuroscience*, 9:920–933.

Tomas Mikolov, Ilya Sutskever, Kai Chen, Greg Corrado, and Jeffrey Dean. 2013. Distributed representations of words and phrases and their compositionality. *CoRR*, abs/1310.4546.

OED. n.d. OED Online. Oxford University Press. Http://www.oed.com/.

Priyanshi R Shah, Chintan D Thakkar, and Swati Mali. 2016. Computational creativity: Automated pun generation. *International Journal of Computer Applications*, 140(10).

Amin Sleimi and Claire Gardent. 2016. Generating Paraphrases from DBPedia using Deep Learning. In *Proceedings of the 2nd International Workshop on Natural Language Generation and the Semantic Web (WebNLG 2016)*, pages 54–57.

Alessandro Valitutti, Oliviero Stock, and Carlo Strapparava. 2009. Graphlaugh: A tool for the interactive generation of humorous puns. pages 1 – 2.

Alessandro Valitutti, Hannu Toivonen, Antoine Doucet, and Jukka M Toivanen. 2013. "Let Everything Turn Well in Your Wife": Generation of Adult Humor Using Lexical Constraints. In *Proceedings of the 51st Annual Meeting of the Association for Computational Linguistics (Volume 2: Short Papers)*, volume 2, pages 243–248, Sofia, Bulgaria.

Tony Veale. 2018. A Massive Sarcastic Robot: What a Great Idea! - Two Approaches to the Computational Generation of Irony. In *Proceedings of the Ninth International Conference on Computational Creativity (ICCC 2018)*, pages 120–127, Salamanca, Spain. Association for Computational Creativity (ACC).

Ping Xiao, Khalid Alnajjar, Mark Granroth-Wilding, Kathleen Agres, and Hannu Toivonen. 2016. Meta4meaning: Automatic metaphor interpretation using corpus-derived word associations. In *Proceedings of the Seventh International Conference on Computational Creativity (ICCC 2016)*, Paris, France. Sony CSL, Sony CSL.

Can Neural Generators for Dialogue
Learn Sentence Planning and Discourse Structuring?

Lena Reed, Shereen Oraby and Marilyn Walker
Natural Language and Dialogue Systems Lab, University of California, Santa Cruz
{lireed,soraby,mawalker}@ucsc.edu

Abstract

Responses in task-oriented dialogue systems often realize multiple propositions whose ultimate form depends on the use of sentence planning and discourse structuring operations. For example a recommendation may consist of an explicitly evaluative utterance e.g. *Chanpen Thai is the best option*, along with content related by the justification discourse relation, e.g. *It has great food and service*, that combines multiple propositions into a single phrase. While neural generation methods integrate sentence planning and surface realization in one end-to-end learning framework, previous work has not shown that neural generators can: (1) perform common sentence planning and discourse structuring operations; (2) make decisions as to whether to realize content in a single sentence or over multiple sentences; (3) generalize sentence planning and discourse relation operations beyond what was seen in training. We systematically create large training corpora that exhibit particular sentence planning operations and then test neural models to see what they learn. We compare models without explicit latent variables for sentence planning with ones that provide explicit supervision during training. We show that only the models with additional supervision can reproduce sentence planning and discourse operations and generalize to situations unseen in training.

1 Introduction

Neural natural language generation (NNLG) promises to simplify the process of producing high quality responses for conversational agents by relying on the neural architecture to automatically learn how to map an input meaning representation (MR) from the dialogue manager to an output utterance (Gašić et al., 2017; Sutskever et al., 2014). For example, Table 1 shows sample training data for an NNLG with a MR for a restaurant named ZIZZI, along with three reference realizations, that should allow the NNLG to learn to realize the MR as either 1, 3, or 5 sentences.

#	Type	Example
		PRICERANGE[MODERATE], AREA[RIVERSIDE], NAME[ZIZZI], FOOD[ENGLISH], EATTYPE[PUB] NEAR[AVALON], FAMILYFRIENDLY[NO]
1	1 Sent	Zizzi is moderately priced in riverside, also it isn't family friendly, also it's a pub, and it is an English place near Avalon.
2	3 Sents	Moderately priced Zizzi isn't kid friendly, it's in riverside and it is near Avalon. It is a pub. It is an English place.
3	5 Sents	Zizzi is moderately priced near Avalon. It is a pub. It's in riverside. It isn't family friendly. It is an English place.

Table 1: Sentence Scoping: a sentence planning operation that decides what content to place in each sentence of an utterance.

In contrast, earlier models of statistical natural language generation (SNLG) for dialogue were based around the NLG architecture in Figure 1 (Rambow et al., 2001; Stent, 2002; Stent and Molina, 2009).

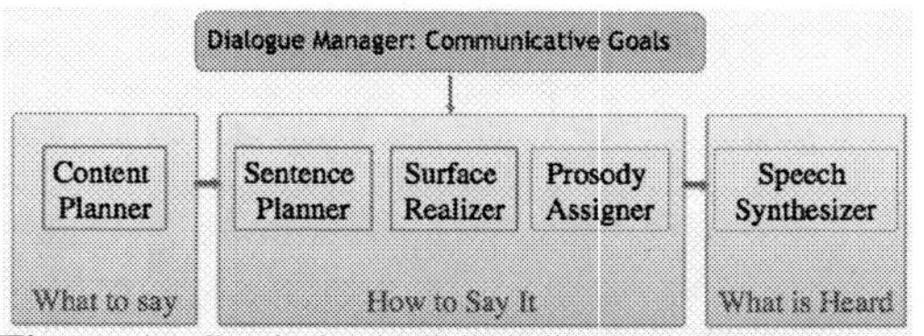

Figure 1: Statistical NLG Dialogue Architecture

Here the dialogue manager sends one or more dialogue acts and their arguments to the NLG en-

284

Proceedings of The 11th International Natural Language Generation Conference, pages 284–295,
Tilburg, The Netherlands, November 5-8, 2018. ©2018 Association for Computational Linguistics

gine, which then makes decisions how to render the utterance using separate modules for content planning and structuring, sentence planning and surface realization (Reiter and Dale, 2000). The sentence planner's job includes:

- **Sentence Scoping**: deciding how to allocate the content to be expressed across different sentences;
- **Aggregation**: implementing strategies for removing redundancy and constructing compact sentences;
- **Discourse Structuring**: deciding how to express discourse relations that hold between content items, such as causality, contrast, or justification.

Sentence scoping (Table 1) affects the complexity of the sentences that compose an utterance, allowing the NLG to produce simpler sentences when desired that might be easier for particular users to understand. Aggregation reduces redundancy, composing multiple content items into single sentences. Table 2 shows common aggregation operations (Cahill et al., 2001; Shaw, 1998). Discourse structuring is often critical in persuasive settings (Scott and de Souza, 1990; Moore and Paris, 1993), in order to express discourse relations that hold between content items. Table 3 shows how RECOMMEND dialogue acts can be included in the MR, and how content can be related with JUSTIFY and CONTRAST discourse relations (Stent et al., 2002).

Recent work in NNLG explicitly claims that training models end-to-end allows them to do **both** sentence planning and surface realization without the need for intermediate representations (Dusek and Jurcícek, 2016b; Lampouras and Vlachos, 2016; Mei et al., 2016; Wen et al., 2015; Nayak et al., 2017). To date, however, no-one has actually shown that an NNLG can faithfully produce outputs that exhibit the sentence planning and discourse operations in Tables 1, 2 and 3. Instead, NNLG evaluations focus on measuring the semantic correctness of the outputs and their fluency (Novikova et al., 2017; Nayak et al., 2017).

Here, we systematically perform a set of controlled experiments to test whether an NNLG can learn to do sentence planning operations. Section 2 describes our experimental setup and the NNLG architecture that allows us, during training, to vary the amount of supervision provided as to

#	Type	Example
		NAME[THE MILL], EATTYPE[COFFEE SHOP], FOOD[ITALIAN], PRICERANGE[LOW], CUSTOMERRATING[HIGH], NEAR[THE SORRENTO]
4	With, Also	The Mill is a coffee shop with a high rating with a low cost, also The Mill is an Italian place near The Sorrento.
5	With, And	The Mill is a coffee shop with a high rating with a high cost and it is an Italian restaurant near The Sorrento.
6	Distributive	The Mill is a coffee shop with a **high rating and cost**, also it is an Italian restaurant near The Sorrento.

Table 2: Aggregation Operation Examples

#	Discourse Rel'n	Example
		NAME[BABBO], RECOMMEND[YES], FOOD[ITALIAN], PRICE[CHEAP], QUAL[EXCELLENT], NEAR[THE SORRENTO], LOCATION[WEST VILLAGE], SERVICE[POOR]
7	JUSTIFY ([REC-OMMEND] [FOOD, PRICE, QUAL])	I would suggest Babbo **because it serves Italian food with excellent quality and it is inexpensive**. The service is poor and it is near the Sorrento in the West Village.
8	CONTRAST [PRICE, SERVICE]	I would suggest Babbo because it serves Italian food with excellent quality and **it is inexpensive. However the service is poor**. It is near the Sorrento in the West Village.

Table 3: Justify & Contrast Discourse Relations

which sentence planning operations appear in the outputs. To ensure that the training data contains enough examples of particular phenomena, we experiment with supplementing crowdsourced data with automatically generated stylistically-varied data from PERSONAGE (Mairesse and Walker, 2011). To achieve sufficient control for some experiments, we exclusively use Personage training data where we can specify exactly which sentence planning operations will be used and in what frequency. It is not possible to do this with crowdsourced data. While our expectation was that an NNLG can reproduce any sentence planning operation that appears frequently enough in the training data, the results in Sections 3, 4 and 5 show that explicit supervision improves the **semantic accuracy** of the NNLG, provides the capability to **control** variation in the output, and enables **generalizing** to unseen value combinations.

2 Model Architecture and Experimental Overview

Our experiments focus on sentence planning operations for: (1) sentence scoping, as in Table 1, where we experiment with controlling the number of sentences in the generated output; (2) distributive aggregation, as in Example 6 in Table 2, an aggregation operation that can compactly express a description when two attributes share the same value; and (3) discourse contrast, as in Example 8 in Table 3.

Distributive aggregation requires learning a proxy for the semantic property of **equality** along with the standard mathematical **distributive** operation, while discourse contrast requires learning a proxy for semantic comparison, i.e. that some attribute values are evaluated as positive (*inexpensive*) while others are evaluated negatively (*poor service*), and that a successful contrast can only be produced when two attributes are on opposite poles (in either order), as defined in Figure 2.[1]

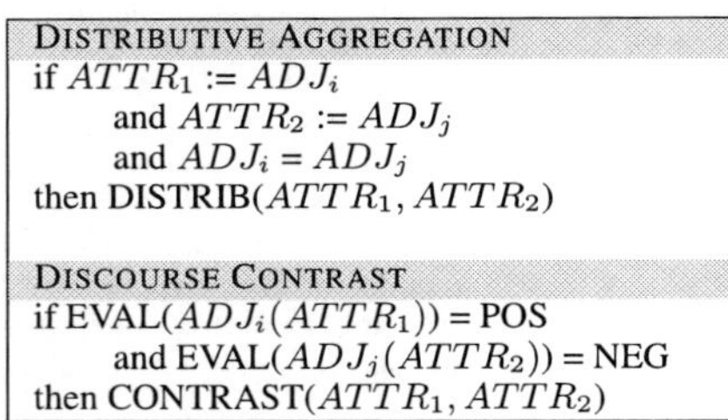

Figure 2: Semantic operations underlying distributive aggregation and contrast

Our goal is to test how well NNLG models can produce realizations of these sentence planning operations with varying levels of supervision, while simultaneously achieving high semantic fidelity. Figure 3 shows the general architecture, implemented in Tensorflow, based on TGen, an open-source sequence-to-sequence (seq2seq) neural generation framework (Abadi and others., 2015; Dusek and Jurcícek, 2016a).[2] The model uses seq2seq generation with attention (Bahdanau et al., 2014; Sutskever et al., 2014) with a sequence of LSTMs (Hochreiter and Schmidhuber, 1997) for encoding and decoding, along with beam-search and an n-best reranker.

The input to the sequence to sequence model is a sequence of tokens $x_t, t \in \{0, \ldots, n\}$ that represent the dialogue act and associated arguments. Each x_i is associated with an embedding vector w_i of some fixed length. Thus for each MR, TGen takes as input the dialogue acts represent-

---

[1] We also note that the evaluation of an attribute may come from the attribute itself, e.g. "kid friendly", or from its adjective, e.g. "excellent service".

[2] https://github.com/UFAL-DSG/tgen

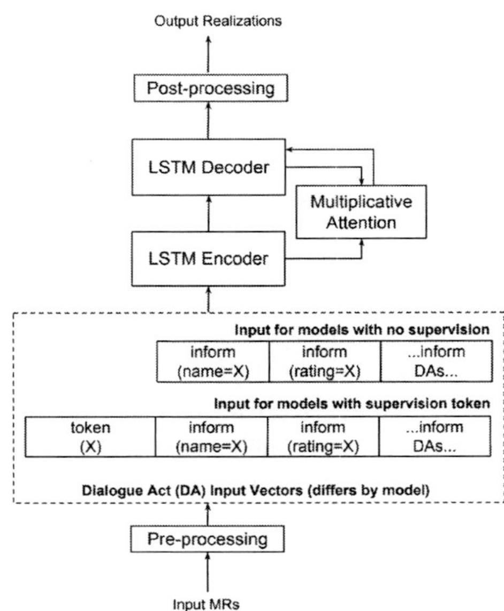

Figure 3: Neural Network Model Architecture, illustrating both the NO SUPERVISION baseline and models that add the TOKEN supervision

ing system actions (*recommend* and *inform* acts) and the attributes and their values (for example, an attribute might be *price range*, and its value might be *moderate*), as shown in Table 1. The MRs (and resultant embeddings) are sorted internally by dialogue act tag and attribute name. For every MR in training, we have a matching reference text, which we delexicalize in pre-processing, then re-lexicalize in the generated outputs. The encoder reads all the input vectors and encodes the sequence into a vector h_n. At each time step t, it computes the hidden layer h_t from the input w_t and hidden vector at the previous time step h_{t-1}, following:

$$h_t = (W_1.x_t + W_2.h_{t-1}) + b$$

All experiments use a standard LSTM decoder.

We test three different dialogue act and input vector representations, based on the level of supervision, as shown by the two input vectors in Figure 3: **(1) models with no supervision**, where the input vector simply consists of a set of *inform* or *recommend* tokens each specifying an attribute and value pair, and **(2) models with a supervision token**, where the input vector is supplemented with a new token (either *period* or *distribute* or *contrast*), to represent a latent variable to guide the NNLG to produce the correct type of sentence planning operation; **(3) models with semantic supervision**, tested only on distributive aggregation, where the input vector is supplemented with specific instructions of which attribute value to distribute over, e.g. *low*, *average* or *high*, in the DISTRIBUTE token. We describe the specific model variations for each experiment below.

Data Sets. One challenge is that NNLG models are highly sensitive to the distribution of phenomena in training data, and our previous work has shown that the outputs of NNLG models exhibit less stylistic variation than their training data (Oraby et al., 2018b). Moreover, even large corpora, such as the 50K E2E Generation Challenge corpus, may not contain particular stylistic variations. For example, out of 50K crowdsourced examples in the E2E corpus, there are 1,956 examples of contrast with the operator "but". There is only 1 instance of distributive aggregation because attribute values are rarely lexicalized identically in E2E. To ensure that the training data contains enough examples of particular phenomena, our experiments combine crowdsourced E2E data[3] with automatically generated data from PERSONAGE (Mairesse and Walker, 2011).[4] This allows us to systematically create training data that exhibits particular sentence planning operations, or combinations of them. The E2E dataset consists of pairs of reference utterances and their meaning representations (MRs), where each utterance contains up to 8 unique attributes, and each MR has multiple references. We populate PERSONAGE with the syntax/meaning mappings that it needs to produce output for the E2E meaning representations, and then automatically produce a very large (204,955 utterance/MR pairs) systematically varied sentence planning corpus.[5]

Evaluation metrics. It is well known that evaluation metrics used for translation such as BLEU are not well suited to evaluating generation outputs (Belz and Reiter, 2006; Liu et al., 2016; Novikova et al., 2017): they penalize stylistic variation, and don't account for the fact that different dialogue responses can be equally good, and can vary due to contextual factors (Jordan, 2000;

Krahmer et al., 2002). We also note that previous work on sentence planning has always assumed that sentence planning operations improve the quality of the output (Barzilay and Lapata, 2006; Shaw, 1998), while our primary focus here is to determine whether an NNLG can be trained to perform such operations while maintaining semantic fidelity. Moreover, due to the large size of our controlled training sets, we observe few problems with output quality and fluency.

Thus we leave an evaluation of fluency and naturalness to future work, and focus here on evaluating the multiple targets of semantic accuracy and sentence planning accuracy. Because the MR is clearly defined, we define scripts (information extraction patterns) to measure the occurrence of the MR attributes and their values in the outputs. We then compute Slot Error Rate (SER) using a variant of word error rate:

$$SER = \frac{S + D + I + H}{N}$$

where S is the number of substitutions, D is the number of deletions, I is the number of insertions, H is the number of hallucinations and N is the number of slots in the input MR.

We also define scripts for evaluating the accuracy of the sentence planner's operations. We check whether: (1) the output has the right number of sentences; (2) attributes with equal values are realized using distributive aggregation, and (3) discourse contrast is used when semantically appropriate. Descriptions of each experiment and the results are in Section 3, Section 4, and Section 5.

3 Sentence Scoping Experiment

To test whether it is possible to control basic sentence scoping with an NNLG, we experiment first with controlling the number of sentences in the generated output, as measured using the period operator. See Table 1. We experiment with two different models:

- **No Supervision:** no additional information in the MR (only attributes and their values)
- **Period Count Supervision:** has an additional supervision token, PERIOD, specifying the number of periods (i.e. the number of sentences) to be used in the output realization.

For sentence scoping, we construct a training set of 64,442 output/MR pairs and a test set of 398 output/MR pairs where the reference utterances

---

[3]http://www.macs.hw.ac.uk/ InteractionLab/E2E/

[4]Source code for PERSONAGE was provided by François Mairesse.

[5]We make available the sentence planning for NLG corpus at: nlds.soe.ucsc.edu/sentence-planning-NLG.

for the outputs are generated from PERSONAGE. Table 4 shows the number of training instances for each MR size for each period count. The right frontier of the table shows that there are low frequencies of training instances where each proposition in the MR is realized in its own sentence (Period = Number of MR attrs -1). The lower left hand side of the table shows that as the MRs get longer, there are lower frequencies of utterances with Period=1.

Attributes		Number of Periods						
		1	2	3	4	5	6	7
	3	3745	167	0	0	0	0	0
	4	5231	8355	333	0	0	0	0
	5	2948	9510	7367	225	0	0	0
	6	821	5002	7591	3448	102	0	0
	7	150	1207	2983	2764	910	15	0
	8	11	115	396	575	388	82	1

Table 4: Distribution of Training Data

We start with the default TGen parameters and monitor the losses on Tensorboard on a subset of 3,000 validation instances from the 64,000 training set. The best settings use a batch size of 20, with a minimum of 5 epochs and a maximum of 20 (with early-stopping based on validation loss). We generate outputs on the test set of 398 MRs.

Sentence Scoping Results. Table 5 shows the accuracy of both models in terms of the counts of the output utterances that realize the MR attributes in the specified number of sentences. In the case of NOSUP, we compare the number of sentences in the generated output to those in the corresponding test reference, and for PERIODCOUNT, we compare the number of sentences in the generated output to the number of sentences we *explicitly* encode in the MR. The table shows that the NOSUP setting fails to output the correct number of sentences in most cases (only a 22% accuracy), but the PERIODCOUNT setting makes only 2 mistakes (almost perfect accuracy), demonstrating almost perfect control of the number of output sentences with the single-token supervision. We also show correlation levels with the gold-standard references (all correlations significant at $p \leq 0.01$).

Model	Slot Error	Period Accuracy	Period Correlation
NOSUP	.06	0.216	0.455
PERIOD COUNT	.03	0.995	0.998

Table 5: Sentence Scoping Results

Generalization Test. We carry out an additional experiment to test generalization of the PERIODCOUNT model, where we randomly select a set of 31 MRs from the test set, then create a set instance for each possible PERIOD count value, from 1 to the N-1, where N is the number of attributes in that MR (i.e. PERIOD=1 means all attributes are realized in the same sentence, and PERIOD=N-1 means that each attribute is realized in its own sentence, except for the restaurant name which is never realized in its own sentence). This yields 196 MR and reference pairs.

This experiment results in an 84% accuracy (with correlation of 0.802 with the test refs, $p \leq 0.01$). When analyzing the mistakes, we observe that all of the scoping mistakes the model makes (31 in total) are the case of PERIOD=N-1. These cases correspond to the right frontier of Table 4 where there were fewer training instances. Thus while the period supervision improves the model, it still fails on cases where there were few instances in training.

Complexity Experiment. We performed an additional sentence scoping experiment where we specified a target sentence complexity instead of a target number of sentences, since this may more intuitively correspond to a notion of reading level or sentence complexity, where the assumption is that longer sentences are more complex (Howcroft et al., 2017; Siddharthan et al., 2004). We used the same training and test data, but labeled each reference as either high, medium or low complexity. The number of attributes in the MR does not include the name attribute, since that is the subject of the review. A reference was labeled high when there are > 2 attributes per sentence, medium when the number of attributes per sentence is > 1.5 and ≤ 2 and low when there are ≤ 1.5 attributes per sentence.

This experiment results in 89% accuracy. Most of the errors occur when the labeled complexity was medium. This is most likely because there is often only one sentence difference between the two complexity labels. This indicates that sentence scoping can be used to create references with either exactly the number of sentences requested or categories of sentence complexity.

4 Distributive Aggregation Experiment

Aggregation describes a set of sentence planning operations that combine multiple attributes into

Operation	Example
PERIOD	*X serves Y. It is in Z.*
"WITH" CUE	*X is in Y, with Z.*
CONJUNCTION	*X is Y and it is Z. & X is Y, it is Z.*
ALL MERGE	*X is Y, W and Z & X is Y in Z*
"ALSO" CUE	*X has Y, also it has Z.*
DISTRIB	*X has Y and Z.*

Table 6: Scoping and Aggregation Operations in PERSONAGE

single sentences or phrases. We focus here on distributive aggregation as defined in Figure 2 and illustrated in Row 6 of Table 2. In an SNLG setting, the generator achieves this type of aggregation by operating on syntactic trees (Shaw, 1998; Scott and de Souza, 1990; Stent et al., 2004; Walker et al., 2002b). In an NNLG setting, we hope the model will induce the syntactic structure and the mathematical operation underlying it, automatically, without explicit training supervision.

To prepare the training data, we limit the values for PRICE and RATING attributes to LOW, AVERAGE, and HIGH. We reserve the combination {PRICE=HIGH, RATING=HIGH} for test, leaving two combinations of values where distribution is possible ({PRICE=LOW, RATING=LOW} and {PRICE=AVERAGE, RATING=AVERAGE}). We then use all three values in MRs where the price and rating are not the same {PRICE=LOW, RATING=HIGH}. This ensures that the model *does* see the value HIGH in training, but never in a setting where distribution is possible. We always distribute when possible, so every MR where the values are the same uses distribution. All other opportunities for aggregation, in the same sentence or in other training sentences, use the other aggregation operations defined in PERSONAGE as specified in Table 6, with equal probability.

Model	Slot Error	Distrib Accuracy	Distrib Accuracy (on HIGH)
NOSUP	.12	0.29	0.00
BINARY	.07	0.99	0.98
SEMANTIC	.25	0.36	0.09

Table 7: Distributive Aggregation Results

The aggregation training set contains 63,690 total instances, with 19,107 instances for each of the two combinations that can distribute, and 4,246 instances for each of the six combinations that can't distribute. The test set contains 408 MRs, 288 specify distribution over HIGH (which we note is *not* a setting seen in train, and explicitly tests the

models' ability to generalize), 30 specify distribution over AVERAGE, 30 over LOW, and 60 are examples that do not require distribution (NONE). We test whether the model will learn the equality relation independent of the value (HIGH vs. LOW), and thus realize the aggregation with HIGH. The distributive aggregation experiment is based on three different models:

- **No Supervision:** no additional information in the MR (only attributes and their values)
- **Binary Supervision:** we add a supervision token, DISTRIBUTE, containing a binary 0 or 1 indicating whether or not the corresponding reference text contains an aggregation operation over attributes *price range* and *rating*.
- **Semantic Supervision:** we add a supervision token, DISTRIBUTE, containing a string that is either *none* if there is no aggregation over *price range* and *rating* in the corresponding reference text, or a value of LOW, AVERAGE, or HIGH for aggregation.

As above, we start with the default TGen parameters and monitor the losses on Tensorboard on subset of 3,000 validation instances from the 63,000 training set. The best settings use a batch size of 20, with a minimum of 5 epochs and a maximum of 20 epochs with early-stopping.

Distributive Aggregation Results. Table 7 shows the accuracy of each model overall on all 4 values, as well as the accuracy specifically on HIGH, the only distribution value unseen in train. Model NO-SUP has a low overall accuracy, and is completely unable to generalize to HIGH, which is unseen in training. It is frequently able to use the HIGH value, but is not able to distribute (generating output like *high cost and cost*). Model BINARY is by far the best performing model, with an almost perfect accuracy (it is able to distribute over LOW and AVERAGE perfectly), but makes some mistakes when trying to distribute over HIGH; specifically, while it is always able to distribute, it may use an incorrect value (LOW or AVERAGE). Whenever BINARY correctly distributes over HIGH, it interestingly always selects attribute RATING before COST, realizing the output as *high rating and price*. Also, BINARY is consistent even when it incorrectly uses the value LOW instead of HIGH: it always selects the attribute *price* before *rating*. To our surprise, Model SEMANTIC does poorly, with 36% overall accuracy, and only 9% accuracy

Source	MR	Realization
NYC	name[xname], recommend[no], cuisine[xcuisine], decor[bad], qual[acceptable], location[xlocation], price[affordable], service[bad]	I imagine xname isn't great because xname is affordable, but it provides bad ambiance and rude service. It is in xlocation. It's a xcuisine restaurant with acceptable food.
E2E	name[xname], cuisine[xcuisine], location[xlocation], familyFriendly[no]	It might be okay for lunch, but it's not a place for a family outing.
E2E	name[xname], eatType[coffee shop], cuisine[xcuisine], price[more than $30], customerRating[low], location[xlocation], familyFriendly[yes]	Xname is a low customer rated coffee shop offering xcuisine food in the xlocation. Yes, it is child friendly, but the price range is more than $30.

Table 8: Training examples of E2E and NYC Contrast sentences

Training Sets	NYC #N	E2E #N
3K	N/A	3,540 contrast
7K	3,500 contrast	3,540 contrast
11K	3,500 contrast	3,540 contrast + 4K random
21K	3,500 contrast	3,540 contrast + 14K random
21K CONTRAST	3,500 contrast	3,540 contrast + 14K random

Table 9: Overview of the training sets for contrast experiments

on HIGH, where most of the mistakes on HIGH include repeating the attribute *high rating and rating*, including examples where it does not distribute at all, e.g. *high rating and high rating*. We plan to explore alternative semantic encodings in future work.

5 Discourse Contrast Experiment

Persuasive settings such as recommending restaurants, hotels or travel options often have a critical discourse structure (Scott and de Souza, 1990; Moore and Paris, 1993; Nakatsu, 2008). For example a recommendation may consist of an explicitly evaluative utterance e.g. *Chanpen Thai is the best option*, along with content related by the justify discourse relation, e.g. *It has great food and service*, as in Table 3.

Our experiments focus on DISCOURSE-CONTRAST. We developed a script to find contrastive sentences in the 40K E2E training set by searching for any instance of a contrast cue word, such as *but, although,* and *even if*. This identified 3,540 instances. While this data size is comparable to the 3-4K instances used in prior work (Wen et al., 2015; Nayak et al., 2017), we anticipated that it might not be enough data to properly test whether an NNLG can learn to produce discourse contrast. We were also interested in testing whether synthetic data would improve the ability of the NNLG to produce contrastive utterances while maintaining semantic fidelity. Thus we used PERSONAGE with its native database of New York City restaurants (NYC) to generate an additional 3,500 examples of one form

of contrast using only the discourse marker *but*, which are most similar to the examples in the E2E data. Table 8 illustrates both PERSONAGE and E2E contrast examples. While PERSONAGE also contains JUSTIFICATIONS, which could possibly confuse the NNLG, it offers many more attributes that can be contrasted and thus more unique instances of contrast. We create 4 training datasets with contrast data in order to systematically test the effect of the combined training set. Table 9 provides an overview of the training sets, with their rationales below.

3K Training Set. This dataset consists of all instances of contrast in the E2E training data, i.e. 3,540 E2E references.

7K Training Set. We created a training set of 7k references by supplementing the E2E contrastive references with an equal number of PERSONAGE references.

11K Training Set. Since 7K is smaller than desirable for training an NNLG, we created several additional training sets with the aim of helping the model learn to correctly realize domain semantics while still being able to produce contrastive utterances. We thus added an additional 4K crowdsourced E2E data that was not contrastive to our training data, for a total of 11,065. See Table 9.

21K Training Set. We created an additional larger training set by adding more E2E data, again to test the effect of increasing the size of the training set on realization of domain semantics, without a significant decrease in our ability to produce contrastive utterances. We added an additional 14K E2E references, for a total of 21,065. See Table 9.

We perform two experiments with the 21K training set. First we trained on the MR and reference exactly as we had done for the 7K and 11K training sets. The second experiment added a contrast token during training time with values of either 1 (contrast) or 0 (no contrast) to test if that would achieve better control of contrast.

Contrast Test Sets. To have a potential for contrast there must be an attribute with a positive value and another attribute with a negative value in the same MR. We constructed 3 different test sets, two for E2E and one for NYC. We created a delexicalized version of the test set used in the E2E generation challenge. This resulted in a test of 82 MRs of which only 25 could support contrast (E2E TEST). In order to allow for a better test of contrast, we constructed an additional test set of 500 E2E MRs all of which could support contrast (E2E CONTRAST TEST). For the NYC test, which provides many opportunities for contrast, we created a dataset of 785 MRs that were different than those seen in training (NYC TEST). At test time, in the 21K contrast token experiment, we utilize the contrast token as we did in training.

Train	E2E Test (N = 82)		
	SLOT ERRORS	CONTRAST ATTEMPTS	CONTRAST CORRECT
3K	.38	13	.15
7K	.56	61	.41
11K	.31	24	.33
21K	.28	2	.50
21K CONTRAST	**.24**	25	**.84**

Table 10: Slot Error Rates and Contrast for E2E

Train	E2E Contrast Test (N=500)		
	SLOT ERRORS	CONTRAST ATTEMPTS	CONTRAST CORRECT
3K	.70	213	.19
7K	.45	325	.22
11K	.23	227	.70
21K	.17	13	.62
21K CONTRAST	**.16**	422	**.75**

Table 11: Slot Error Rates and Contrast for E2E, Contrast Only

Train	NYC Test (N = 785)		
	SLOT ERRORS	CONTRAST ATTEMPTS	CONTRAST CORRECT
3K	N/A	N/A	N/A
7K	.29	784	.65
11K	.26	696	.71
21K	.25	659	.82
21K CONTRAST	.24	566	**.85**

Table 12: Slot Error Rates and Contrast for NYC

Contrast Results. We present the results for both slot error rates and contrast for the E2E test set in Table 10, E2E Contrast in Table 11, and NYC test set in Table 12.

Table 10 shows the results for testing on the original E2E test set, where we only have 25 instances with the possibility for contrast. Overall, the table shows large performance improvements with the CONTRAST token supervision for 21K for both slot errors and correct contrast. On the E2E test set, the the 3K E2E training set gives a slot error rate of .38 and only 15% correct contrast. The 7K training set, supplemented with additional generated contrast examples gets a correct contrast of .41 but a much higher slot error rate. Interestinglyx, the 11K dataset is much better than the 3K for contrast correct, suggesting a positive effect for the automatically generated contrast examples along with more E2E training data. The 21K set without the contrast token does not attempt contrast since the frequency of contrast data is low, but with the CONTRAST token, it attempts contrast every time it is possible (25/25 instances).

In Table 11 with only contrast data, we see similar trends, with the lowest slot error rate (.16) and highest correct contrast (.75) ratios for the experiment with token supervision on 21K. Again, we see much better performance from the 11K set than the 3K and 7K in terms of slot error and correct contrast, indicating that more training data (even if that data does not contain contrast) helps the model. As before, we see very low contrast attempts with 21K without supervision, with a huge increase in the number of contrast attempts when using token supervision (422/500).

Table 12 also shows large performance improvements from the use of the CONTRAST token supervision for the NYC test set, again with improvements for the 21K CONTRAST in both slot error rate and in correct contrast. Interestingly, while we get the highest correct contrast ratio of .85 with 21K CONTRAST, we actually see *fewer* contrast attempts, showing that the most explicitly supervised model is becoming more selective when deciding when to do contrast. When training on the 7K dataset, the neural model **always** produces a contrastive utterance for the NYC MRs (all the NYC data is contrastive). Although it never sees any NYC non-contrastive MRs, the additional E2E training data allows it to improve its ability to decide when to contrast (Row 21K CONTRAST) as well as improving the slot error rate in the final experiment.

6 Related Work

Much of the previous work focused on sentence planning was done in the framework of statistical NLG, where each module was assumed to require training data that matched its representational requirements. Methods focused on training individual modules for content selection and linearization (Marcu, 1997; Lapata, 2003; Barzilay and Lapata, 2005), and trainable sentence planning for discourse structure and aggregation operations (Stent and Molina, 2009; Walker et al., 2007; Paiva and Evans, 2004; Sauper and Barzilay, 2009; H. Cheng and Mellish, 2001). Previous work also explored statistical and hybrid methods for surface realization (Langkilde and Knight, 1998; Bangalore and Rambow, 2000; Oh and Rudnicky, 2002). and text-to-speech realizations (Hitzeman et al., 1998; Bulyko and Ostendorf, 2001; Hirschberg, 1993).

Other work on NNLG also uses token supervision and modifications of the architecture in order to control stylistic aspects of the output in the context of text-to-text or paraphrase generation. Some types of stylistic variation correspond to sentence planning operations, e.g. to express a particular personality type (Oraby et al., 2018b; Mairesse and Walker, 2011; Oraby et al., 2018a), or to control sentiment and sentence theme (Ficler and Goldberg, 2017). Herzig et al. (2017) automatically label the personality of customer care agents and then control the personality during generation. Rao and Tetreault (2018) train a model to paraphrase from formal to informal style and Niu and Bansal (2018) use a high precision classifier and a blended language model to control utterance politness.

Previous work on contrast has explored how the user model determines which values should be contrasted, since people may have differing opinions about whether an attribute value is positive or negative (e.g. *family friendly*) (Carenini and Moore, 1993; Walker et al., 2002a; White et al., 2010). To our knowledge, no-one has yet trained an NNLG to use a model of user preferences for content selection. Here, values are treated as inherently good or bad, e.g. service is ranked from great to terrible.

7 Discussion and Conclusion

This paper presents detailed, systematic experiments to test the ability of NNLG models to produce complex sentence planning operations for response generation. We create new training and test sets designed specifically for testing sentence planning operations for sentence scoping, aggregation and discourse contrast, and train novel models with increasing levels of supervision to examine how much information is required to control neural sentence planning. The results show that the models benefit from extra latent variable supervision, which improves the **semantic accuracy** of the NNLG, provides the capability to **control** variation in the output, and enables **generalizing** to unseen value combinations.

In future work we plan to test these methods in different domains, e.g. the WebNLG challenge or WikiBio dataset (Wiseman et al., 2018; Colin et al., 2016). We also plan to experiment with more complex sentence planning operations and test whether an NNLG system can be endowed with fine-tuned control, e.g. controlling multiple aggregation operations. Another possibility is that hierarchical input representations representing the sentence plan might improve performance or allow finer-grained control (Moore et al., 2004; Su and Chen, 2018; Bangalore and Rambow, 2000). It may be desirable to control which attributes are aggregated together, distributed or contrasted, and to allow more than two values to be contrasted.

Here, our main goal was to test the ability of different neural architectures to learn particular sentence planning operations that have been used in previous work in SNLG. Because we don't make claims about fluency or naturalness, we did not evaluate these with human judgements. Instead, we focused our evaluation on automatic assessment of semantic fidelity, and the extent to which the neural architecture could reproduce the desired sentence planning operations. In future work, we hope to quantify the extent to which human subjects prefer the outputs where the sentence planning operations have been applied.

8 Acknowledgments

This work was supported by NSF Cyberlearning EAGER grant IIS 1748056 and NSF Robust Intelligence IIS 1302668-002 as well as an Amazon Alexa Prize Gift 2017 and Grant 2018 awarded to the Natural Language and Dialogue Systems Lab at UCSC.

References

Martín Abadi and others. 2015. TensorFlow: Large-scale machine learning on heterogeneous systems. Software available from tensorflow.org.

Dzmitry Bahdanau, Kyunghyun Cho, and Yoshua Bengio. 2014. Neural machine translation by jointly learning to align and translate. *CoRR*, abs/1409.0473.

S. Bangalore and O. Rambow. 2000. Exploiting a probabilistic hierarchical model for generation. In *Proc. of the 18th Conference on Computational Linguistics*, pages 42–48.

Regina Barzilay and Mirella Lapata. 2005. Collective content selection for concept-to-text generation. In *Proceedings of the conference on Human Language Technology and Empirical Methods in Natural Language Processing*, pages 331–338. Association for Computational Linguistics.

Regina Barzilay and Mirella Lapata. 2006. Aggregation via set partitioning for natural language generation. In *Proceedings of the main conference on Human Language Technology Conference of the North American Chapter of the Association of Computational Linguistics*, pages 359–366. Association for Computational Linguistics.

Anja Belz and Ehud Reiter. 2006. Comparing automatic and human evaluation of nlg systems. In *EACL*.

I. Bulyko and M. Ostendorf. 2001. Joint Prosody Prediction and Unit Selection for Concatenative Speech Synthesis. In *ICASSP*, volume II, pages 781–784.

Lynne Cahill, John Carroll, Roger Evans, Daniel Paiva, Richard Power, Donia Scott, and Kees van Deemter. 2001. From rags to riches: exploiting the potential of a flexible generation architecture. In *Meeting of the Association for Computational Linguistics*.

Giuseppe Carenini and Johanna Moore. 1993. Generating explanation in context. In *Proc. of the International Workshop on Intelligent User Interfaces*.

Emilie Colin, Claire Gardent, Yassine Mrabet, Shashi Narayan, and Laura Perez-Beltrachini. 2016. The webnlg challenge: Generating text from dbpedia data. In *Proceedings of the 9th International Natural Language Generation conference*, pages 163–167.

Ondrej Dusek and Filip Jurcícek. 2016a. A context-aware natural language generator for dialogue systems. volume abs/1608.07076.

Ondrej Dusek and Filip Jurcícek. 2016b. Sequence-to-sequence generation for spoken dialogue via deep syntax trees and strings. volume abs/1606.05491.

Jessica Ficler and Yoav Goldberg. 2017. Controlling linguistic style aspects in neural language generation. In *Proceedings of the EMNLP Workshop on Stylistic Variation*, pages 94–104.

Milica Gašić, Dilek Hakkani-Tür, and Asli Celikyilmaz. 2017. Spoken language understanding and interaction: machine learning for human-like conversational systems. *Computer Speech and Language 46*, pages 249 – 251.

Renate Henschel H. Cheng, Massimo Poesio and Chris Mellish. 2001. Corpus-based np modifier generation. In *Proc. of the NAACL*.

Jonathan Herzig, Michal Shmueli-Scheuer, Tommy Sandbank, and David Konopnicki. 2017. Neural response generation for customer service based on personality traits. In *Proceedings of the 10th International Conference on Natural Language Generation*, pages 252–256.

Julia B. Hirschberg. 1993. Pitch accent in context: predicting intonational prominence from text. *Artificial Intelligence Journal*, 63:305–340.

Janet Hitzeman, Alan W. Black, Paul Taylor, Chris Mellish, and Jon Oberlander. 1998. On the use of automatically generated discourse-level information in a concept-to-speech synthesis system. In *Proc. of the International Conference on Spoken Language Processing, ICSLP98*, pages 2763–2766.

Sepp Hochreiter and Jürgen Schmidhuber. 1997. Long short-term memory. *Neural computation*, 9(8):1735–1780.

David M. Howcroft, Dietrich Klakow, and Vera Demberg. 2017. The extended sparky restaurant corpus: Designing a corpus with variable information density. In *Proc. Interspeech 2017*, pages 3757–3761.

Pamela W. Jordan. 2000. Influences on attribute selection in redescriptions: A corpus study. In *Proc. of CogSci2000*.

Emiel Krahmer, André Verleg, and Sebastiaan van Erk. 2002. Graph-based generation of referring expressions. *Computational Linguistics*, page to appear.

Gerasimos Lampouras and Andreas Vlachos. 2016. Imitation learning for language generation from unaligned data. In *COLING*, pages 1101–1112. ACL.

I. Langkilde and K. Knight. 1998. Generation that exploits corpus-based statistical knowledge. In *Proc. of COLING-ACL*.

M. Lapata. 2003. Probabilistic text structuring: Experiments with sentence ordering. In *Proc. of the ACL*.

Chia-Wei Liu, Ryan Lowe, Iulian V Serban, Michael Noseworthy, Laurent Charlin, and Joelle Pineau. 2016. How not to evaluate your dialogue system: An empirical study of unsupervised evaluation metrics for dialogue response generation. In *Proc. of Empirical Methods in Natural Language Processing (EMNLP)*.

Francois Mairesse and Marilyn A. Walker. 2011. Controlling user perceptions of linguistic style: Trainable generation of personality traits. *Computational Linguistics*.

Daniel Marcu. 1997. From local to global coherence: A bottom-up approach to text planning. In *Proc. of the 14th National Conference on Artificial Intelligence and 9th Innovative Applications of Artificial Intelligence Conference (AAAI-97/IAAI-97)*, pages 629–636, Menlo Park. AAAI Press.

Hongyuan Mei, Mohit Bansal, and Matthew R. Walter. 2016. What to talk about and how? selective generation using lstms with coarse-to-fine alignment. In *Proceedings of NAACL-HLT*, pages 720–730.

J. D. Moore and C. L. Paris. 1993. Planning text for advisory dialogues: Capturing intentional and rhetorical information. *Computational Linguistics*, 19(4).

Johanna Moore, Mary Ellen Foster, Oliver Lemon, and Michael White. 2004. Generating tailored, comparative descriptions in spoken dialogue. In *Proc. FLAIRS-04*.

Crystal Nakatsu. 2008. Learning contrastive connectives in sentence realization ranking. In *Proceedings of the 9th SIGdial Workshop on Discourse and Dialogue*, pages 76–79, Columbus, Ohio. Association for Computational Linguistics.

Neha Nayak, Dilek Hakkani-Tur, Marilyn Walker, and Larry Heck. 2017. To plan or not to plan? discourse planning in slot-value informed sequence to sequence models for language generation. In *Proc. of Interspeech 2017*.

Tong Niu and Mohit Bansal. 2018. Polite dialogue generation without parallel data. *Transactions of the Association for Computational Linguistics*, 6:273–289.

Jekaterina Novikova, Ondej Duek, Amanda Cercas Curry, and Verena Rieser. 2017. Why we need new evaluation metrics for nlg. In *Proceedings of the 2017 Conference on Empirical Methods in Natural Language Processing*, pages 2241–2252.

Alice H. Oh and Alexander I. Rudnicky. 2002. Stochastic natural language generation for spoken dialog systems. *Computer Speech and Language: Special Issue on Spoken Language Generation*, 16(3-4):387–407.

Shereen Oraby, Lena Reed, TS Sharath, Shubhangi Tandon, and Marilyn Walker. 2018a. Neural multivoice models for expressing novel personalities in dialog. *Proc. Interspeech 2018*, pages 3057–3061.

Shereen Oraby, Lena Reed, Shubhangi Tandon, TS Sharath, Stephanie Lukin, and Marilyn Walker. 2018b. Controlling personality-based stylistic variation with neural natural language generators. In *SIGDIAL*.

Daniel S. Paiva and Roger Evans. 2004. A framework for stylistically controlled generation. In *Natural Language Generation, Third Internatonal Conference, INLG 2004*, number 3123 in LNAI, pages 120–129. Springer.

O. Rambow, M. Rogati, and M. Walker. 2001. Evaluating a trainable sentence planner for a spoken dialogue travel system. In *Proc. of the Meeting of the Association for Computational Lingustics, ACL 2001*.

Sudha Rao and Joel Tetreault. 2018. Dear sir or madam, may i introduce the gyafc dataset: Corpus, benchmarks and metrics for formality style transfer. In *North American Associatio of Computational Linguistics Conference, NAACL-18*.

Ehud Reiter and Robert Dale. 2000. *Building Natural Language Generation Systems*. Cambridge University Press.

Christina Sauper and Regina Barzilay. 2009. Automatically generating wikipedia articles: A structure-aware approach. In *Proceedings of the Joint Conference of the 47th Annual Meeting of the ACL and the 4th International Joint Conference on Natural Language Processing of the AFNLP: Volume 1-Volume 1*, pages 208–216. Association for Computational Linguistics.

Donia R. Scott and Clarisse Sieckenius de Souza. 1990. Getting the message across in RST-based text generation. In Robert Dale, Chris Mellish, and Michael Zock, editors, *Current Research in Natural Language Generation*. Academic Press, London.

James Shaw. 1998. Clause aggregation using linguistic knowledge. In *Proc. of the 8th International Workshop on Natural Language Generation*, Niagara-on-the-Lake, Ontario.

A. Siddharthan, A. Nenkova, and K. McKeown. 2004. Syntactic simplification for improving content selection in multi-document summarization. In *Proceedings of the 20th International Conference on Computational Linguistics (COLING 2004)*.

Amanda Stent. 2002. A conversation acts model for generating spoken dialogue contributions. *Computer Speech and Language: Special Issue on Spoken Language Generation*.

Amanda Stent and Martin Molina. 2009. Evaluating automatic extraction of rules for sentence plan construction. In *Proc. of the SIGDIAL 2009 Conference: The 10th Annual Meeting of the Special Interest Group on Discourse and Dialogue*, pages 290–297.

Amanda Stent, Rashmi Prasad, and Marilyn Walker. 2004. Trainable sentence planning for complex information presentation in spoken dialogue systems. In *Meeting of the Association for Computational Linguistics*.

Amanda Stent, Marilyn Walker, Steve Whittaker, and Preetam Maloor. 2002. User-tailored generation for spoken dialogue: An experiment. In *ICSLP*.

Shang-Yu Su and Yun-Nung Chen. 2018. Investigating linguistic pattern ordering in hierarchical natural language generation. In *7th IEEE Workshop on Spoken Language Technology (SLT 2018)*.

Ilya Sutskever, Oriol Vinyals, and Quoc V Le. 2014. Sequence to sequence learning with neural networks. In *Advances in neural information processing systems*, pages 3104–3112.

M. A. Walker, S. J. Whittaker, A. Stent, P. Maloor, J. D. Moore, M. Johnston, and G. Vasireddy. 2002a. Speech-Plans: Generating evaluative responses in spoken dialogue. In *In Proc. of INLG-02*.

Marilyn Walker, Owen Rambow, and Monica Rogati. 2002b. Training a sentence planner for spoken dialogue using boosting. *Computer Speech and Language: Special Issue on Spoken Language Generation*, 16(3-4):409–433.

Marilyn A. Walker, Amanda Stent, François Mairesse, and Rashmi Prasad. 2007. Individual and domain adaptation in sentence planning for dialogue. *Journal of Artificial Intelligence Research (JAIR)*, 30:413–456.

Tsung-Hsien Wen, Milica Gasic, Nikola Mrksic, Pei-Hao Su, David Vandyke, and Steve Young. 2015. Semantically conditioned lstm-based natural language generation for spoken dialogue systems. In *Proceedings of the 2015 Conference on Empirical Methods in Natural Language Processing*.

Michael White, Robert A. J. Clark, and Johanna D. Moore. 2010. Generating tailored, comparative descriptions with contextually appropriate intonation. *Computational Linguistics*, 36(2):159–201.

Sam Wiseman, Stuart M. Shieber, and Alexander M. Rush. 2018. Learning neural templates for text generation. *CoRR*, abs/1808.10122.

Neural Generation of Diverse Questions
using Answer Focus, Contextual and Linguistic Features

Vrindavan Harrison and **Marilyn Walker**
University of California Santa Cruz
Santa Cruz, CA, US
{vharriso, mawalker}@ucsc.edu

Abstract

Question Generation is the task of automatically creating questions from textual input. In this work we present a new Attentional Encoder–Decoder Recurrent Neural Network model for automatic question generation. Our model incorporates linguistic features and an additional sentence embedding to capture meaning at both sentence and word levels. The linguistic features are designed to capture information related to named entity recognition, word case, and entity coreference resolution. In addition our model uses a copying mechanism and a special answer signal that enables generation of numerous diverse questions on a given sentence. Our model achieves state of the art results of 19.98 Bleu_4 on a benchmark Question Generation dataset, outperforming all previously published results by a significant margin. A human evaluation also shows that the added features improve the quality of the generated questions.

1   Introduction

Question Generation (QG) is the task of automatically generating questions from textual input (Rus et al., 2010). There are a wide variety of question types and forms, e.g., short answer, open ended, multiple choice, and gap questions, each require a different approach to generate. One distinguishing aspect of a QG system is the type of questions that it produces. This paper focuses on the generation of factoid short answer questions, i.e., questions that can be answered by a single short phrase, usually appearing directly in the input text.

The work of a QG system typically consists of three conceptual subtasks: Target Selection, Question Representation Construction, and Question Realization. In Target Selection, important sentences and words within those sentences are identified. During Question Representation Construction, suitable question–type and syntactic form are determined based on the characteristics of the sentence at hand and the words it contains. An example of this can be seen in Agarwal et al. (2011) who define rules based on the discourse connectives in a sentence to decide which question–type is most appropriate. In the Question Realization step, the final surface form of the question is created.

It is common for QG systems to use a combination of semantic pattern matching, syntactic features, and template methods to create questions. Typically these systems look for patterns of syntax, keywords, or semantic roles that appear in the input sentence. Then they use these patterns to choose an appropriate question template, or use syntactic features to perform manipulations on the sentence to produce a question.

These rule-based systems have some strengths over Neural Network models: they are easier to interpret and allow developers greater control over model behavior. Furthermore, they typically require less data to develop than a complex Neural Network might need to achieve a similar level of performance. However, rule-based systems have some weaknesses as well. They tend to be laborious to develop, or domain specific. For example the system developed by Mostow and Chen (2009) relies on the presence of one of a set of 239 modal verbs in a sentence, and Olney et al. (2012) use 3000 keywords provided by the glossary of a Biology text book and a test-prep study guide. The system described in Chali and Hasan (2015) uses roughly 350 hand-crafted rules. Furthermore, these systems rely heavily on syntactic parsers, and may struggle to recover from parser inaccuracies.

Proceedings of The 11th International Natural Language Generation Conference, pages 296–306,
Tilburg, The Netherlands, November 5-8, 2018. ©2018 Association for Computational Linguistics

#	Sentence
S1	The character of midna has the most voice acting – her on-screen dialog is often accompanied by a babble of pseudo-speech , which was produced by scrambling the phonemes of english phrases [better source needed] sampled by japanese voice actress akiko komoto.
Gold Standard	
Q1	which person has the most spoken dialogue in the game?
Q2	who provided the basis for midna's voice?
Q3	what country does akiko komoto come from?
Baseline	
Q4	what is her ?
Our Model: FocusCR	
Q5	what character has the most voice acting in english?
Q6	what is the name of the japanese voice actress?
Q7	what is the nationality of akiko komoto?

Table 1: Sentence and associated questions generated from the baseline and our best model.

Among many different approaches to question generation, our work is most similar to recent work applying neural network models to the task of generating short answer factoid questions for SQUAD (Du et al., 2017; Yuan et al., 2017; Sachan and Xing, 2018). However these previous models have several limitations. As illustrated in Table 1, the SQUAD corpus (Rajpurkar et al., 2016) provides multiple gold standard references for each sentence (Q1, Q2, and Q3), but previous work to date can only generate one question for each sentence as represented by the baseline model (Q4), whereas our model can generate multiple questions as shown in Table 1.

In Section 2, we present our novel model that introduces additional token supervision representing features of the text as well as an additional lower dimensional word embedding. The features include a Named Entity Recognition (NER) feature, a word case feature, and a special answer signaling feature. The answer signaling feature allows our model to generate multiple questions for each sentence, illustrated with Q5, Q6 and Q7 in Table 1. We also introduce a coreference resolution model and supplement the sentence input representation with resolved coreferences, as well as a copying mechanism. Section 3 presents an evaluation of the final model on the benchmark SQuAD testset using automatic evaluation metrics and shows that it achieves state of the art results of 19.98 BLEU_4, 22.26 METEOR, and 48.23 ROUGE (Papineni et al., 2002; Banerjee and Lavie, 2005; Lin, 2004). To our knowledge this model outperforms all previously published results by a significant margin. A human evalu-

ation also shows that the introduced features and answer-specific sentence embedding improve the quality of the generated questions. We delay a more detailed review of previous work to Section 4 and conclude in Section 5.

2 Model

Our QG model follows a standard RNN Encoder–Decoder model (Sutskever et al., 2014) that maps a source sequence (declarative sentence) to a target sequence (question). The architecture of the baseline model is as follows: the encoder is a multi-layer bidirectional LSTM (Hochreiter and Schmidhuber, 1997) and the decoder is a unidirectional LSTM that uses global attention with input-feeding (Luong et al., 2015). This baseline model yields one question per sentence (Q4 in Table 1).

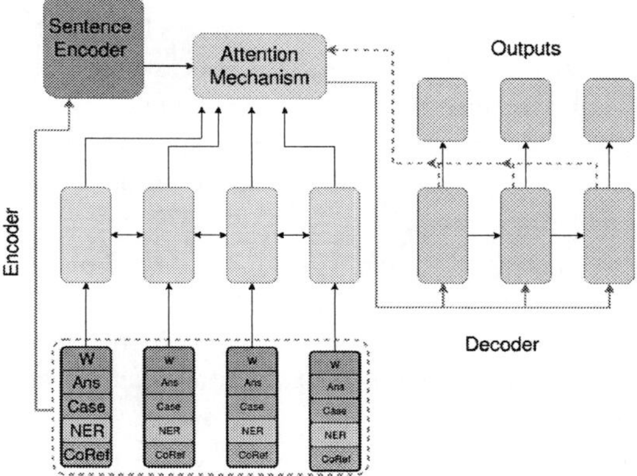

Figure 1: Diagram of our answer focus model.

We create our model by enhancing the baseline model in the following three ways:

- We add 4 different token level supervision features to the input. See Section 2.1.

- We add a sentence encoder that creates a question specific sentence embedding.

- We use a copy mechanism (See et al., 2017) to copy words from the sentence directly into the question.

2.1 Feature Supervision

A feature-rich encoding is constructed by concatenating several token level features onto the token's word-based embedding using a method similar to that described by Nallapati et al. (2016) for abstractive text summarization.

#	Sentence w/ Feature Additions
S1	the character of **midna**$_{a1}$(NE = LOCATION) has the most voice acting – her (COREF = THE CHARACTER OF MIDNA(NE = LOCATION)) on-screen dialog is often accompanied by a babble of pseudo-speech, which was produced by scrambling the phonemes of english(NE = NATIONALITY) phrases [better source needed] sampled by **japanese**$_{a3}$(NE = NATIONALITY) voice **actress**$_{a2}$(NE =TITLE) **akiko**$_{a2}$(NE = PERSON) **komoto**$_{a2}$(NE = PERSON) .

Table 2: Feature Markup on S1

Answer Signal Feature. It is usually the case that multiple questions can be asked about information contained within a single sentence. Therefore, a model that is capable of generating multiple questions for a single sentence has greater utility than a model such as the one described by Du et al. (2017) which is capable of generating only a single question per unique input sentence. This need to generate multiple questions for a sentence motivates our use of an answer signal. The model described by Yuan et al. (2017) also uses an answer signal feature. However, by combining it with additional features and the question specific sentence encoder our model achieves better results, as we show in Section 3.

The answer signal is equivalent to the output of the target selection module in a standard QG pipeline; this is provided as part of the SQUAD corpus, but is straightforward to calculate automatically.

The Answer Signal feature guides the model in deciding which information to focus on when reading the sentence. The signal being active in some location of the sentence indicates the answer to the question being generated. Then, modifying the location of the answer signal and keeping the rest of the sentence fixed enables the model to generate multiple answer specific questions per a given sentence.

The Answer Signal feature is implemented as a binary feature indicating whether or not a given token is part of the answer span. Table 2 illustrates the results of the answer signal feature on S1 from Table 1. The answer signals are shown in **bold** and annotated with an index. The indices $a1$, $a2$ and $a3$ correspond to Q5, Q6 and Q7, respectfully, from Table 1 (as generated by our best model). For the sake of brevity we have simultaneously accentuated three separate answer signals in Table 2. In actuality, the model sees only one answer signal series per sentence input. To gener-ate questions Q5, Q6, and Q7 the model was fed the same sentence three separate times, each time with only one of $a1$, $a2$ or $a3$ activated.

Case Feature. The case feature is a simple binary feature that represents whether or not the input token contains an upper case letter.

NER Feature. We use an NER feature that is designed in the same fashion as Nallapati et al. (2016), who have previously used an NER based feature embedding to improve performance of their sequence-to-sequence model used for Abstractive Text Summarization. Just as in Abstractive Text Summarization, identifying important entities that are central to the meaning of a sentence is an imperative component of the QG task.

The NER labels are computed in a pre-processing step. The result of NER labeling performed on a sentence is shown in Table 2. Similar to traditional word embeddings, we build a look-up based embedding for each NER label. During execution, the embedding associated with each token's NER label is retrieved using a table look-up and then concatenated onto the word embedding. The NER embeddings are a trainable parameter which get updated during the model's training process. Figure 1 shows a diagram depicting how the NER feature is incorporated into each token's feature rich encoding via concatenation.

Coreference Feature. Coreference labels are computed automatically in a pre-processing step. The coreference labels are calculated using all of the prior context for the input sentence text, but the input to the model is just the sentence augmented with the additional feature input. Table 2 shows how the NER and coreference features are expectedly noisy. Nevertheless, they improve the model as we show below.

Table 3 provides a detailed example for coreference showing context and the input sentence representation with and without the coreference feature, as well as the effect on the questions generated by the model. It is easy to see the benefits of the coreference representation qualititively on individual examples. For example, without coreference the model finds an entity *elizabeth* who is associated with *net worth* in the language model and uses that entity to generate the question rather than using *beyoncé*, the entity in context. In Section 3 we show that this qualitative difference affects the quantitative performance measures.

Coreference information is incorporated into

#	Partial Context
C1-33	In June 2014, Beyoncé ranked at #1 on the Forbes Celebrity 100 list, earning an estimated $115 million throughout June 2013 June 2014. This in turn was the first time she had topped the Celebrity 100 list as well as being her highest yearly earnings to date.
Sentence	
S2	As of May 2015, her net worth is estimated to be $250 million.
Model Input with Coreference	
S2 w/ coref	As of may(NE = DATE) 2015(NE = DATE), her (COREF = BEYONCÉ (NE = PERSON)'S) net worth is estimated to be $(NE = MONEY) 250(NE = MONEY) million(NE = MONEY).
Q8	what is beyoncé's net worth in 2015?
Model Input w/out Coreference	
S2 no coref	As of may(NE = DATE) 2015(NE = DATE), her net worth is estimated to be $(NE = MONEY) 250(NE = MONEY) million(NE = MONEY).
Q9	what is elizabeth's net worth in may 2015 ?

Table 3: Context, Sentence and Questions generated with and without coreference.

the model by augmenting the input text as shown in Table 3. The representative mention of each entity gets inserted into the sentence following its coreferent. This results in two phrases referencing the same entity appearing in the text one immediately following the other, the first being the one that appeared in the original text and the second being the entity's representative mention. Each token is assigned a binary feature indicating whether the token was in the original text or if it has been thus inserted. This way the model can learn to include or ignore the augmenting text as it deems necessary.

2.2 Answer Focused Sentence Embedding

The input sentence is encoded using a multi-layer bidirectional LSTM distinct from the token level encoder as illustrated in Figure 1. After completing the calculations of the last time step, the final state of the LSTM is taken as a sentence embedding. Then, this sentence embedding is concatenated on to the token level encoding for each time step. This allows the answer-specific sentence embedding to influence decoding decisions during each time step of the decoding process.

We experiment with pre-training the sentence encoder. The pre-training process is carried out in two steps. First, to facilitate training of the sentence encoder by itself, we need some ground truth sentence representation from which to measure similarity. Since this sentence encoder is used

in question generation, it would be helpful to encode the sentence in such a way as to maximize its benefit to the QG model. With this as motivation, we train an instance of the full QG encoder–decoder model with the sentence encoder, but the sentence encoder is given the target question as input instead of the sentence. As expected, in this setting the model learns to generate questions very well because it "cheats" by taking the target as input. Next, the trained sentence encoder — that was trained by encoding the target questions — is decoupled from the full model for use in the following step.

In the second step, the question embeddings produced by the earlier trained encoder are used as ground truth representations from which to maximize similarity. Now, a new sentence encoder is trained that takes as input a declarative sentence. The new sentence encoder is trained to maximize the similarity between the input sentence's embedding and the question embedding — produced by the earlier trained encoder — belonging to a specific question associated with the sentence. Specifically, loss is calculated between a sentence embedding s and a ground truth representation q using a Cosine Embedding Loss defined by:

$$\mathrm{loss}(s, q) = 1 - \cos(s, q) \qquad (1)$$

where $\cos(s, q)$ is traditional cosine distance.

The pre-trained sentence encoder is then used to initialize the sentence encoder used in training a new instance of the full QG model.

3 Experimental Setup and Results

We conduct experiments exploring the effects of each of our model enhancements and train and evaluate all the models using the SQuAD dataset (Rajpurkar et al., 2016). We evaluate the models using both automatic evaluation metrics and a human evaluation using crowd sourced workers. In addition, we perform ablation tests to experiment with different feature settings. We name our two best models Focus and FocusCR, where FocusCR uses the coreference feature, and Focus does not.

Dataset. SQuAD is a dataset of over one hundred thousand (document, question, answer) tuples. The documents are Wikipedia articles and the questions are created by crowd workers. Answers to the questions are subsequently created by a separate group of crowd workers who select as the question's answer a span of text from

# Model	Sentences and Examples
S3	West got his big break in the year 2000, when he began to produce for artists on Roc-A-Fella Records.
Q10 Copy	when did west got his big break?
Q11 No Copy	in what year did " big break " begin?
S4	A high-definition remaster of the game, The Legend of Zelda: Twilight Princess HD, is being developed by Tantalus Media for the Wii U.
Q12 Copy	who developed the legend of zelda?
Q13 No Copy	who is the creator of the soundtrack of mortal kombat?
S5	Both six- and seven-track versions of the game's soundtrack were released on November 19, 2006, as part of a Nintendo Power promotion and bundled with replicas of the Master Sword and the Hylian Shield.
Q14 Copy	What was released on november 19, 2006?
Q15 No Copy	What was released on september 17, 2006?
S6	At the age of 10, West moved with his mother to Nanjing, China, where she was teaching at Nanjing University as part of an exchange program.
Q16 Copy	at what age did west move with his mother to nanjing?
Q17 No Copy	at what age did von neumann teach at nanjing university?

Table 4: Question Generation with and without the Copy mechanism.

within the article. The creators of SQuAD keep part of the dataset private to be used as a hidden evaluation set in Question Answering tasks. For this work we use the roughly 92,000 examples that are publicly available. The 92,000 examples are partitioned into training (roughly 70k examples), development (roughly 10k examples), and test (roughly 11k examples) subsets. For the sake of comparison, we have used the same partitioning as Du et al. (2017) who have kindly made their data setting available on-line.

Using Stanford CoreNLP (Finkel et al., 2005; Manning et al., 2014) the data is tokenized, and NER and Coreference Resolution are performed. All the feature used by our model are calculated at this stage. Finally, the text is lowercased. We calculate separate source and target vocabularies of size 45,000 and 28,000, respectfully. Tokens that fall out of vocabulary (OOV) are represented with a special UNK token. In retrospect, separate vocabularies are not necessary for this task. We remove examples that have sentences or questions over 100 and 50 words long, respectfully.

Model Implementation. Our model is imple-

mented using PyTorch[1] and OpenNMT-py[2] which is a PyTorch port of OpenNMT(Klein et al., 2017). The encoder, decoder, and sentence encoder are multi-layer RNNs, each with two layers. We use bi-directional LSTM cells with 640 units. The model is trained using Dropout (Srivastava et al., 2014) of 0.3 between RNN layers. Word embeddings are initialized using Glove 300 dimensional word vectors (Pennington et al., 2014) that are not updated during training. The sentence encoder is initialized using the pre-training process described in Section 2.2. All other model parameters are initialized using Glorot initialization (Glorot and Bengio, 2010).

The model parameters are optimized using Stochastic Gradient Descent with mini-batches of size 64. Beam search with five beams is used during inference and OOV words are replaced using the token of highest attention weight in the source sentence. We tune our model with the development dataset and select the model of lowest Perplexity to evaluate on the test dataset.

3.1 Automatic Evaluation

We compare our system's results to that of several other QG systems. The rows of Table 5 with labels H&S, Yuan, Du, and S&X refer to the models presented in Heilman and Smith (2010a); Yuan et al. (2017); Du et al. (2017), and Sachan and Xing (2018), respectfully. Please refer to Section 4 Related Work for further details on each of these systems. The results of the H&S system are reported in this work for the sake of comparison. The actual experiments were performed by Du et al. (2017) who describe the specific configuration of H&S in greater detail.

Results. We use BLEU score (Papineni et al., 2002) as an automatic evaluation metric and compare directly to other work. BLEU measures the similarity between a generated text called a candidate and a set of human written texts called a reference set. The score is calculated by comparing the n-grams of the candidate with the n-grams of the reference texts and then counting the number of matches.

Unfortunately there are inconsistencies in the method by which previous works have used BLEU to evaluate QG models. Therefore, to accurately compare BLEU scores, we evaluate our model us-

---

[1] pytorch.org
[2] github.com/OpenNMT/OpenNMT-py

Model	BLEU_4	METEOR	ROUGE
baseline	11.53	15.93	39.57
H&S*	11.18	15.95	30.98
Du	12.28	16.62	39.75
S&X	14.37	18.57	42.73
FocusCR	19.86	21.96	**48.35**
Focus	**19.98**	**22.26**	48.23

Table 5: System performance in automatic evaluation.

Model	BLEU_4
baseline	8.45
Yuan	10.5
FocusCR	14.16
Focus	**14.39**

Table 6: BLEU-4 scores when using answer-specific ground-truth questions as reference texts.

ing two different setups. First, when calculating BLEU for a given hypothesis question, some publications have used a reference set containing all the ground-truth questions corresponding to the sentence from which the hypothesis was generated. Table 5 shows our model's results compared to previous work using this setup of BLEU and the same partitioning of the SQuAD dataset.

Each of our models outperform previously published results in each of the BLEU, METEOR, and ROUGE categories by a significant margin. FocusCR is the second highest performing system and achieves an impressive BLEU_4 score of 19.86, which greatly improves on the third highest BLEU_4 score of 14.37 belonging to S&X. Focus gets a BLEU_4 score of 19.98 and is the best performing system overall.

In the second setup, for a given hypothesis question, Yuan et al. (2017) used a reference set containing only a single ground-truth question that corresponds to the same sentence and answer span from which the hypothesis was generated. We use this setup to evaluate our Focus and FocusCR models. The results are shown in Table 6. Here, Focus and FocusCR are the same models as shown in Table 5, with the only difference being the setting under which they are evaluated. Again, FocusCR achieves the second highest score and Focus gets the highest BLEU_4 score at 14.39. While the datasets in aggregate are the same, our partitioning of training, development, and test datasets is different from that of Yuan et al. (2017).

We perform ablation experiments to study the effects of each feature incorporated into the model. The results of these experiments can be seen in Table 8. With the exception of the CoRef feature, each feature added produces an improvement in BLEU, with the answer feature producing the greatest improvement. The copy-mechanism and sentence embedding, which is called Focus in the

table, each increase performance further.

We also examine the effect of pre-training the sentence encoder as described in Section 2.2. In Table 8, the Focus and FocusCR models use a pre-trained sentence encoder. The sentence encoder used by FocusCR-npt is not pre-trained. We find that the pre-training has a positive effect on BLEU scores with FocusCR-npt getting BLEU 13.99, compared to the FocusCR getting BLEU 14.16.

Table 8 suggests that the coreference mechanism actually hurts performance as measured by BLEU but the example shown in Table 3 and the additional examples shown in Table 10 suggest that it is very effective.

Table 4 provides examples of the effect of the copy mechanism. Again, as with coreference, it is easy to see the benefits of the copying mechanism qualititively. For example, in Q14 and Q15 the model can effectively copy the right date into the question. In Q17, without copying, the model finds an entity *von neumann* who is associated with *teaching* and *university* in the model and uses that entity to generate the question rather than *west* the entity in context.

Question Diversity. We are interested in how the new features effect the quantity of unique questions produced by our model. Therefore, we counted the number of unique questions output by the model when considering the entire testing set as inputs. Here, we measure similarity using a strict character match comparison. Table 7 shows the results. We can see that the FocusCR model produces 10,194 unique questions, which is a 55%

Model	Unique Q's
Baseline	6,595
FocusCR	10,194
Human	11,801

Table 7: Amount of unique questions generated.

Model	BLEU_4	METEOR	ROUGE
baseline	7.62	13.41	34.19
+ Answer	11.15	16.64	40.39
+ NER	11.54	16.94	40.93
+ Case	11.56	16.98	40.96
+ CoRef	10.28	16.14	39.22
+ Copy	13.00	18.43	42.78
FocusCR-npt	13.99	-	-
FocusCR	14.16	19.24	43.07
Focus	14.39	19.54	43.00

Table 8: Results of ablation test.

increase over the 6,595 unique questions produced by the Baseline model. Although strict character matching is a crude method of measuring question similarity, we conclude that the features incorporated into the FocusCR model have a positive effect on the diversity of generated questions.

3.2 Human Evaluation

We perform human evaluation using crowd workers on Amazon Mechanical Turk[3]. The Turkers rate a pool of questions constructed by randomly selecting questions and their associated text passages from the test set. We select 114 questions each from the test dataset, the questions generated by the baseline model, and the questions generated by our FocusCR model. The questions are selected such that they all correspond to the same declarative sentence. In other words, we construct a set of 114 tuples where each tuple consists of one text passage, two model generated questions, and one human authored question.

We use a qualification criteria to restrict the participation of Turkers in our evaluation study. The Turkers must have above 95% HIT approval rate with at least 500 HITs previously approved. Furthermore, Turkers are required to be located in English speaking countries. Turkers recieved $0.1 for completing each HIT.

We closely follow the experiment design described by Heilman and Smith (2010b), who instruct Turkers to produce a single five-point quality rating per question. They provide Turkers with the following four reasons to downgrade a question: (Un)grammaticality, Incorrect Information, Vagueness, and Awkwardness. In our evaluation study, we use four categories of evaluation that resemble these criteria.

Turkers are asked to rate each question across four categories: Grammaticality, Correct Information, Answerability, and Naturalness. Grammaticality encompasses things like adherence to rules of syntax, use of the wrong *wh*-word, verb tense consistency, and overall legitimacy as an English sentence. The Correct Information category considers whether or not the question is related to the text passage (e.g., asking about Madonna when the passage is about Beyonce), implies something that is obviously incorrect, or contradicts information given in the text passage. The Answerability category reflects how much of the information required to correctly answer the question is contained within the text passage. Also, it considers whether or not the question has a clear answer, or is too vague (e.g., *"What is it?"*). The Naturalness category reflects how natural the question reads and considers whether or not it has some awkward phrasing. The Naturalness category also encompasses any other problems in the question that do not fall in the previous categories.

During evaluation, the Turker is presented with the text passage and its three corresponding questions in scrambled order. They are asked to give a rating from worst (1) to best (5) in each category for each question. Each HIT contains three text passages and a total of nine questions. Each HIT is assigned to three Turkers resulting in three ratings per question.

Results. Table 9 shows an average of the ratings assigned by the Turkers in each category. Answerability is the category in which the FocusCR model has the greatest improvement over the Baseline. In this category, FocusCR receives an average rating of 4.13, compared to the baseline's average rating of 3.73. FocusCR also outperforms the Baseline model in the Correct Information category with average ratings 4.13 and 3.78, respectfully. In the Grammaticality and Naturalness categories the Baseline model has average ratings of 4.23 and 4.10, respectfully. The FocusCR model has average ratings of 4.20 and 4.09 in the Grammaticality and Naturalness categories. The human authored questions outperform both models by a significant margin in all categories.

We note that there is only a slight difference between ratings achieved by the Baseline and FocusCR models in the Grammaticality and Naturalness categories. Yet, in both these categories the Baseline model slightly outperforms FocusCR.

---

[3]www.mturk.com

We suspect this is due to the brevity and generality of questions produced by the Baseline model. In contrast, FocusCR produces longer sentences with more information content and, at times, increasingly complex sentence structure.

Next, we observe that the average rating of the human-authored questions are surprisingly low across all categories, but particularly in Naturalness with a rating of 4.36. We attribute this to the crowd-sourcing methodology used to create the original SQuAD dataset. Nevertheless, we hypothesize that the average ratings of the gold questions will increase with larger sample sizes in subsequent human evaluation studies.

Inter-rater agreement was measured by comparing the Turkers' ratings to those of an expert annotator who is a native English speaking graduate student in Computational Linguistics. The expert annotator rated a random sample of 60 questions using a private version of the HIT created on Mechanical Turk. Then, the arithmetic mean of the three Turker ratings was calculated for each question and category of evaluation. The Pearson correlation coefficient between the expert annotator's rating and the means of the Turker ratings was $r = 0.47$ for the Correct Information category, $r = 0.38$ for the Answerability category, $r = 0.20$ for Grammaticality, and $r = 0.32$ for Naturalness. The significance of each correlation was calculated using a two-tailed test that resulted in $p < 0.01$ for each category. We observe a positive correlation between the expert annotator and the Turker ratings in each category, although some of the the correlation strengths are less than ideal, particularly in the Grammaticality category. The consistent positive correlation across each category and their statistical significance provide evidence that the rating scheme is well defined, and that the Turkers are able to judge the quality of questions with relative reliability.

Model	Grammar	Info.	Answer.	Natural
Baseline	4.23	3.78	3.73	4.10
FocusCR	4.20	4.13	4.13	4.09
Human	**4.40**	**4.40**	**4.47**	**4.36**

Table 9: Human Evaluation Results

4 Related Work

Much of the work on automatic question generation has been motivated by helping teachers in test creation (Mitkov and Ha, 2003; Heilman and Smith, 2010a; Labutov et al., 2015; Araki et al.,

# Model	Sentences and Examples
S7	she publicly endorsed same sex marriage on march 26, 2013, after the supreme court debate on california 's proposition 8.
Q18 FocusCR	what did beyonce publicly support?
Q19 Focus	what did madonna publicly endorsed on march 26, 2013?
S8	west is one of the best-selling artists of all time, having sold more than 32 million albums and 100 million digital downloads worldwide
Q20 FocusCR	how many grammy awards did he win?
Q21 Focus	how many grammy awards has madonna won?

Table 10: Additional Coreference Examples

2016; Chinkina and Meurers, 2017). Questions play an essential role in knowledge acquisition and assessment. It is standard practice for teachers to assess students' reading comprehension through question answering. Automatic question generation has the potential to assist teachers in the test creation process, thereby freeing teachers to spend more time on other aspects of the education process, and reducing the cost of receiving an education.

Automatic question generation has the potential to be useful in the areas of automatic Question Answering (QA) and Machine Comprehension of text. Recently, large datasets such as SQuAD (Rajpurkar et al., 2016), and MS MARCO (Nguyen et al., 2016) have facilitated advances in both areas. These datasets are expensive to create and consist of human authored (document, question, answer) triples with questions and answers either being collected from the web or created by crowd workers. Automatic Question Generation methods can be used to cheaply supplement resources available to QA models, further assisting in advancing QA capabilities. Indeed, Sachan and Xing (2018) have recently shown that a joint QA-QG model is able to achieve state-of-the art results on a variety of different QA related tasks.

Sequence-to-sequence Neural Network models have been shown to be effective at a variety of other NLP problems (Bahdanau et al., 2014; Rush et al., 2015; Juraska et al., 2018), and recent work has also applied them to QG (Du et al., 2017; Zhou et al., 2017; Yuan et al., 2017). As in other recent work on QG, we use an attentional Recurrent Neural Network encoder–decoder model that is similar to the model of Bahdanau et al. (2014). In this approach, the QG task is cast as a sequence-to-sequence language modeling task. The input sentence, represented as a series of words, is mapped to an output series of words representing a question. Sequence-to-sequence models have several advantages over previous rule-based approaches to QG. First, they eliminate the need for large hand-crafted rule sets – the model automatically learns how to perform the subtasks of Question Representation Construction and Question Realization. Another advantage is that the model does not rely on domain-specific keywords. In fact, in this approach the model is trained on examples from a variety of topics and then evaluated on examples from previously unseen topic domains.

Among the numerous approaches to question generation, our work is most similar to recent work applying neural network models to the task of generating short answer factoid questions.

Yuan et al. (2017) developed a Recurrent Neural Network (RNN) sequence-to-sequence model that generates questions from an input sentence. Their model is trained using supervised learning combined with reinforcement learning to maximize several auxiliary goals, including performance of a QA model on generated questions.

Du et al. (2017) present an attentional sequence-to-sequence model for question generation. Their model is similar to our baseline model but with one key difference: their model uses paragraph-level information in addition to sentence-level information. They use an RNN encoder to embed the paragraph surrounding the sentence that contains the answer. Then the decoder's hidden state is initialized with the concatenation of the encoder's outputs and the paragraph embedding.

Sachan and Xing (2018) present an ensemble model that jointly learns both QA and QG tasks. The QG model is an RNN sequence-to-sequence model similar to that proposed by Du et al. (2017). First the QA and QG models are trained independent of each other on the labeled corpus. Then the QG model is used to create more questions from unlabeled data that are then answered by the QA model. A question selection oracle selects — based on several heuristics — a subsample of questions upon which to stochastically update each model. This process is repeated until both models cease to show improvement.

Heilman and Smith (2010a) present a system that generates fact-based questions similar to those in SQuAD using an "overgenerate-and-rank" strategy. Their system generates questions through use of hand crafted rules that operate on declarative sentences, transforming them into questions. In order to control quality, the output questions are filtered through a logistic regression model that ranks the questions on acceptability.

5 Conclusion and Future Work

We propose an encoder–decoder model for automatic generation of factual questions. We create a novel Neural Network architecture that uses two source sequence encoders; the first encoder being at the token level, and the second being at the sentence level. This enables the decoder to take into account word meaning and sentence meaning information while making decoding decisions. Also, the encoders are able to produce diverse encodings based on an answer focus feature. We demonstrate that this new model greatly improves on the state of the art in Question Generation when evaluated using automatic methods. We show that incorporating linguistic features into our model improves question generation performance as well. Lastly, a human evaluation confirms the improvement in quality of generated questions.

Currently, our system generates only factual questions for expository text. In future work we plan to explore question generation on other categories of text such as narrative discourse. One limitation of our system is that it relies on the existence of previously created answer phrases. Therefore, we would like to investigate methods of automatically extracting answer candidates from text, thus facilitating QG experiments on other categories of text that do not currently have large question-answer datasets.

6 Acknowledgements

This work was supported by NSF Cyberlearning EAGER grant IIS-1748056, NSF Robust Intelligence grant IIS-1302668-002, and an Amazon Alexa Prize 2017 Gift and 2018 Grant awarded to the Natural Language and Dialogue Systems Lab at UC Santa Cruz.

References

Manish Agarwal, Rakshit Shah, and Prashanth Mannem. 2011. Automatic question generation using discourse cues. In *Proceedings of the 6th Workshop on Innovative Use of NLP for Building Educational Applications*, page 19. Association for Computational Linguistics.

Jun Araki, Dheeraj Rajagopal, Sreecharan Sankaranarayanan, Susan Holm, Yukari Yamakawa, and Teruko Mitamura. 2016. Generating questions and multiple-choice answers using semantic analysis of texts. In *Proceedings of COLING 2016, the 26th International Conference on Computational Linguistics: Technical Papers*, page 11251136.

Dzmitry Bahdanau, Kyunghyun Cho, and Yoshua Bengio. 2014. Neural machine translation by jointly learning to align and translate. *arXiv:1409.0473 [cs, stat]*. ArXiv: 1409.0473.

Satanjeev Banerjee and Alon Lavie. 2005. Meteor: An automatic metric for mt evaluation with improved correlation with human judgments. In *Proceedings of the acl workshop on intrinsic and extrinsic evaluation measures for machine translation and/or summarization*, pages 65–72.

Yllias Chali and Sadid A. Hasan. 2015. Towards topic-to-question generation. *Computational Linguistics*, 41(1):120.

Maria Chinkina and Detmar Meurers. 2017. Question generation for language learning: From ensuring texts are read to supporting learning. In *Proceedings of the 12th Workshop on Innovative Use of NLP for Building Educational Applications*, page 334344.

Xinya Du, Junru Shao, and Claire Cardie. 2017. Learning to ask: Neural question generation for reading comprehension. *arXiv:1705.00106 [cs]*. ArXiv: 1705.00106.

Jenny Rose Finkel, Trond Grenager, and Christopher D. Manning. 2005. Incorporating non-local information into information extraction systems by gibbs sampling. In *Proc. of the 43nd Annual Meeting of the Association for Computational Linguistics (ACL 2005)*, pages 363–370.

Xavier Glorot and Yoshua Bengio. 2010. Understanding the difficulty of training deep feedforward neural networks. In *Proceedings of the thirteenth international conference on artificial intelligence and statistics*, page 249256.

Michael Heilman and Noah A. Smith. 2010a. Good question! statistical ranking for question generation. In *Human Language Technologies: The 2010 Annual Conference of the North American Chapter of the Association for Computational Linguistics*, HLT 10, page 609617. Association for Computational Linguistics.

Michael Heilman and Noah A. Smith. 2010b. Rating computer-generated questions with mechanical turk. In *Proceedings of the NAACL HLT 2010 Workshop on Creating Speech and Language Data with Amazons Mechanical Turk*, CSLDAMT 10, page 3540. Association for Computational Linguistics.

Sepp Hochreiter and Jürgen Schmidhuber. 1997. Long short-term memory. *Neural computation*, 9(8):1735–1780.

Juraj Juraska, Panagiotis Karagiannis, Kevin Bowden, and Marilyn Walker. 2018. A deep ensemble model with slot alignment for sequence-to-sequence natural language generation. In *Proceedings of the 2018 Conference of the North American Chapter of the Association for Computational Linguistics: Human Language Technologies, Volume 1 (Long Papers)*, volume 1, pages 152–162.

Guillaume Klein, Yoon Kim, Yuntian Deng, Jean Senellart, and Alexander M. Rush. 2017. OpenNMT: Open-source toolkit for neural machine translation. In *Proc. ACL*.

Igor Labutov, Sumit Basu, and Lucy Vanderwende. 2015. Deep questions without deep understanding. In *Proceedings of the 53rd Annual Meeting of the Association for Computational Linguistics and the 7th International Joint Conference on Natural Language Processing (Volume 1: Long Papers)*, volume 1, page 889898.

Chin-Yew Lin. 2004. Rouge: A package for automatic evaluation of summaries. *Text Summarization Branches Out*.

Minh-Thang Luong, Hieu Pham, and Christopher D Manning. 2015. Effective approaches to attention-based neural machine translation. *arXiv preprint arXiv:1508.04025*.

Christopher D Manning, Mihai Surdeanu, John Bauer, Jenny Rose Finkel, Steven Bethard, and David McClosky. 2014. The Stanford CoreNLP natural language processing toolkit. In *ACL (System Demonstrations)*, pages 55–60.

Ruslan Mitkov and Le An Ha. 2003. Computer-aided generation of multiple-choice tests. In *Proceedings of the HLT-NAACL 03 Workshop on Building Educational Applications Using Natural Language Processing - Volume 2*, HLT-NAACL-EDUC 03, page 1722. Association for Computational Linguistics.

Jack Mostow and Wei Chen. 2009. Generating instruction automatically for the reading strategy of self-questioning. In *The 14th International Conference on Artificial Intelligence in Education*, page 8.

Ramesh Nallapati, Bowen Zhou, Cicero Nogueira dos santos, Caglar Gulcehre, and Bing Xiang. 2016. Abstractive text summarization using sequence-to-sequence rnns and beyond. *arXiv:1602.06023 [cs]*. ArXiv: 1602.06023.

Tri Nguyen, Mir Rosenberg, Xia Song, Jianfeng Gao, Saurabh Tiwary, Rangan Majumder, and Li Deng. 2016. Ms marco: A human generated machine reading comprehension dataset. *arXiv:1611.09268 [cs]*. ArXiv: 1611.09268.

Andrew M. Olney, Arthur C. Graesser, and Natalie K. Person. 2012. Question generation from concept maps. *Dialogue & Discourse*, 3(2):7599.

Kishore Papineni, Salim Roukos, Todd Ward, and Wei-Jing Zhu. 2002. Bleu: a method for automatic evaluation of machine translation. In *Proceedings of the 40th annual meeting on association for computational linguistics*, pages 311–318. Association for Computational Linguistics.

Jeffrey Pennington, Richard Socher, and Christopher Manning. 2014. Glove: Global vectors for word representation. In *Proceedings of the 2014 conference on empirical methods in natural language processing (EMNLP)*, page 15321543.

Pranav Rajpurkar, Jian Zhang, Konstantin Lopyrev, and Percy Liang. 2016. Squad: 100,000+ questions for machine comprehension of text. *arXiv:1606.05250 [cs]*. ArXiv: 1606.05250.

Vasile Rus, Brendan Wyse, Paul Piwek, Mihai Lintean, Svetlana Stoyanchev, and Cristian Moldovan. 2010. *The first question generation shared task evaluation challenge*. Association for Computational Linguistics.

Alexander M Rush, Sumit Chopra, and Jason Weston. 2015. A neural attention model for abstractive sentence summarization. *arXiv preprint arXiv:1509.00685*.

Mrinmaya Sachan and Eric Xing. 2018. Self-training for jointly learning to ask and answer questions. *Proceedings of the 2018 Conference of the North American Chapter of the Association for Computational Linguistics: Human Language Technologies, Volume 1 (Long Papers)*, 1:629640.

Abigail See, Peter J Liu, and Christopher D Manning. 2017. Get to the point: Summarization with pointer-generator networks. In *Proceedings of the 55th Annual Meeting of the Association for Computational Linguistics (Volume 1: Long Papers)*, volume 1, pages 1073–1083.

Nitish Srivastava, Geoffrey Hinton, Alex Krizhevsky, Ilya Sutskever, and Ruslan Salakhutdinov. 2014. Dropout: a simple way to prevent neural networks from overfitting. *The Journal of Machine Learning Research*, 15(1):19291958.

Ilya Sutskever, Oriol Vinyals, and Quoc V Le. 2014. Sequence to sequence learning with neural networks. In *Advances in neural information processing systems*, pages 3104–3112.

Xingdi Yuan, Tong Wang, Caglar Gulcehre, Alessandro Sordoni, Philip Bachman, Saizheng Zhang, Sandeep Subramanian, and Adam Trischler. 2017. Machine comprehension by text-to-text neural question generation. In *Proceedings of the 2nd Workshop on Representation Learning for NLP*, page 1525.

Qingyu Zhou, Nan Yang, Furu Wei, Chuanqi Tan, Hangbo Bao, and Ming Zhou. 2017. Neural question generation from text: A preliminary study. *arXiv:1704.01792 [cs]*. ArXiv: 1704.01792.

Evaluation methodologies in Automatic Question Generation 2013-2018

Jacopo Amidei and **Paul Piwek** and **Alistair Willis**
School of Computing and Communications
The Open University
Milton Keynes, UK
{jacopo.amidei, paul.piwek, alistair.willis}@open.ac.uk

Abstract

In the last few years Automatic Question Generation (AQG) has attracted increasing interest. In this paper we survey the evaluation methodologies used in AQG. Based on a sample of 37 papers, our research shows that the systems' development has not been accompanied by similar developments in the methodologies used for the systems' evaluation. Indeed, in the papers we examine here, we find a wide variety of both intrinsic and extrinsic evaluation methodologies. Such diverse evaluation practices make it difficult to reliably compare the quality of different generation systems. Our study suggests that, given the rapidly increasing level of research in the area, a common framework is urgently needed to compare the performance of AQG systems and NLG systems more generally.

1 Introduction

Evaluation is a critical phase for the development of Natural Language Generation (NLG) systems. It helps to improve performance by highlighting weaknesses, and to identify new tasks to which generation systems can be applied. Given that generation systems and evaluation methodologies should be developed hand in hand, a systematic study of evaluation methodologies for NLG should take a central role in the effort of building machines which are able to reach human-like levels of linguistic communication. Such a study should investigate the current evaluation practices used in various areas of NLG in order to see their weaknesses and suggest directions to improve them.

The aim of this paper is to analyze the evaluation methodologies used in Automatic Question Generation (AQG) as a representative subtask of NLG. To the best of our knowledge, since the introduction of the Question Generation Shared Task Evaluation Challenge (QG-STEC) (Rus et al., 2010), no attempts have been made to introduce a common framework for evaluation in AQG.

To approach this task, we examined the papers in the ACL anthology with a publication date between the years 2013-2018 (more precisely January 2013 to June 2018). Table 1 shows the distribution of the papers involved in the current study across this period. The ACL anthology website represents a resource of inestimable value[1] for this work.

Year of publication	# papers
2018 (Jan-June)	7 (so far)
2017	13
2016	9
2015	5
2014	1
2013	2

Table 1: Number of papers per year describing question generation systems.

We used the single term *question generation* as the search term with the search engine provided in the ACL Anthology website. From the papers that were returned by this query, we focussed only on those papers that were about question generation systems. This gave us 37 papers to analyze, of which 36 were published in conference proceedings and 1 was published in a journal. The number of papers by year is given in Table 1 and illustrated in Figure 1. Figure 1 indicates the rapid increase in publications in this area in recent years.

---

[1] http://aclweb.org/anthology/

Proceedings of The 11th International Natural Language Generation Conference, pages 307–317,
Tilburg, The Netherlands, November 5-8, 2018. ©2018 Association for Computational Linguistics

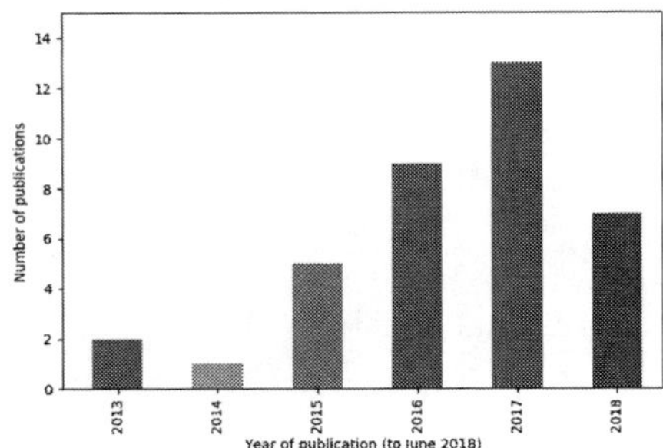

Figure 1: Number of papers on AQG published by year in the ACL anthology.

Note that this study of the literature was carried out in June 2018, and so several major conferences in this area (including ACL, INLG, EMNLP and COLING) had not taken place.[2]

Publication type	Journal or conference name	# of papers
Conference proceeding	INLG	7
	ACL	7
	NAACL-HLT	6
	Workshop on Innovative Use of NLP for Building Educational Application	6
	EMNLP	3
	IJCNLP	1
	EACL	1
	SIGDIAL	1
	COLING	1
	NLPTEA	1
	RANLP	1
	Workshop on Representation Learning for NLP	1
Journal	Computational Linguistics	1

Table 2: Number of papers per conference proceedings or journal.

Before looking more closely at the publications involved, let us introduce the AQG tasks studied in these papers. AQG is the task

> of automatically generating questions from various inputs such as raw text, database, or semantic representation (Rus et al., 2008).

The above definition, adopted by the AQG community, leaves room for researchers to decide what kind of questions and input work with. Following Piwek and Boyer (2012) a particular AQG task can be characterized by three aspects: the input, the

output, and finally the relationship between the input and the output. The 37 papers we analyzed can be divided into the following three categories:

1. *Input*: text;
   Output: text;
   Relation: the output question is answered by the input text or the output question asks a clarification question about the input text.

2. *Input*: knowledge base structured data (for example triples ⟨subject, object, subject/object relation⟩);
   Output: text;
   Relation: the output question is answered by the information structure in the input.

3. *Input*: image or image and text or image segmentation annotations;
   Output: text;
   Relation: the output question is answered by the information pictured in the input.

For the sake of simplicity we will denote with *Text2Text* the task expressed by category 1, *Kb2Text* the task expressed by category 2 and finally *Mm2Text* the task expressed by category 3, where *Mm* is short for "Multi-modal". Within each category, we find papers with different aims. We show these in the following list, where the number in brackets shows how many papers fall into that class:

1. *Text2Text* (30)
   - Web searching (1)
   - Chatbot component (1)
   - Creation of comparative questions related to the input topic (1)
   - Clarification questions (1)
   - Question Answering (5)
   - Dataset creation purpose (1)
   - Educational purpose (9)
   - AQG general purposes (11)

2. Kb2Text (4)
   - Question Answering (1)
   - Dataset creation purpose (1)
   - Educational purpose (1)
   - AQG general purposes (1)

3. Mm2Text (3)

---

[2]A complete list of papers used in this study, as well as useful information to reproduce the results presented in the present paper, can be found at the following link:

https://bit.ly/2IuPJIa

- Data augmentation Visual Question Answering (VQA) purpose (1)
- AQG general purposes (2)

Regarding the papers in the *Text2Text* category, we found some variety in the different types of output. Although in the majority of cases, the system's output was an interrogative sentence, there are 5 papers in which the output is a "fill the gap" question, 3 papers where output is a multiple choice question (with its associated set of distractors) and 3 papers in which the output is a question/answer pair. Also in both the *Kb2Text* and *Mm2Text* categories there is 1 paper each in which the output is a question/answer pair. We also note that one paper in the *Text2Text* category developed a question generator which takes a paragraph of text and an associated answer as input. In this case, the generated question must be answered by the answer given in the input. We conclude this section by specifying that *AQG general purposes* means that the system was not tied to a particular domain or task-dependent setting, whereas *Question Answering* means that the AQG system is developed in order to be used in the Question Answering task.

2   Related Work

Two of the key references for evaluation in NLG are Krahmer and Theune (2010) and Gatt and Krahmer (2018). Both devote an entire section to evaluation. In particular, Section 7 of Gatt and Krahmer's paper gives a helpful description of the methodologies used in NLG for the purpose of evaluation, alongside examples and a discussion of the relevant problems.

Another highly relevant work is that of Gkatzia and Mahamood (2014). Gkatzia and Mahamood studied the use of evaluation methodologies for NLG, performing a study which analyzed a corpus of 79 conference and journal papers published between the years 2005-2014. Their results show the increasing prevalence of automatic evaluation over human evaluation and the prevalence of intrinsic evaluation over extrinsic ones (we discuss intrinsic and extrinsic methods in Section 3). Gkatzia and Mahamood also report that the evaluation approaches are correlated with the publication venue, so that papers published in the same journal or conference tend to use the same evaluation methodologies. Our paper represents a continuation and refinement of the Gkatzia and Mahamood paper, with our specific focus on AQG.

Regarding more specific work on AQG we refer to Rakangor and Ghodasara (2015) and Le et al. (2014), both of which survey AQG, with the latter focussing specifically on educational applications of AQG. For each paper considered, Rakangor and Ghodasara present the methodology used, the generated question type, the language of the generated question, the evaluation methodologies and its results. In contrast, Le et al. report on the educational support type and the evaluation methodologies, in one table and the question type and evaluation results in the other table. Although Le et al. present these results in two tables, the tables in fact have only one paper in common. In comparison, in this paper we focus all our attention on the evaluation methodologies used. For this reason, we report neither the systems' specifications nor the systems' performance.

A final publication of importance to the current work is the report on the Question Generation Shared Task Evaluation Challenge (QG-STEC) (Rus et al., 2010). In the QG-STEC, two tasks, A and B, were defined. Although both tasks shared the same output type, task A took a paragraph and a target question type as input, whereas task B took a single sentence and a target question type as input. Both tasks were evaluated through a human evaluation methodology, based on the 5 criteria: *relevance, syntactic correctness and fluency, ambiguity, question type* and *variety*. However, the Inter Annotator Agreement (IAA) reached in the evaluation phase was low. An attempt to improve the IAA for task B is described in Godwin and Piwek (2016), in which the authors define an interactive process where the annotators discussed their opinions about the criteria used in the evaluation. Although their method improves the IAA, the reproducibility of their results is not guaranteed.

3   Evaluation methodologies for AQG

In this section we present the findings of our analysis. We focus our analysis on two dimensions: *intrinsic evaluation methodology* and *extrinsic evaluation methodology*.

Intrinsic evaluation methods measure the performance of a system by evaluating the system's output "in its own right, either against a reference corpus or by eliciting human judgements of quality" (Gatt and Belz, 2010, p. 264). For example, this could involve measuring the output's grammaticality and fluency. The prevailing intrinsic methods are *human evaluation* and *automatic evaluation*. In order to assess the quality of a generated sentence, the former method uses human judgements, while the latter applies an algorithm that automatically calculates a score, for example by checking the similarity between the generated sentence and a set of reference sentences.

Extrinsic methods measure the performance of a system by evaluating the system's output with respect to its ability to accomplish the task for which it was developed. An example of extrinsic evaluation methods is that used to evaluate the STOP system (Reiter et al., 2003). STOP generates "short tailored smoking cessation letters, based on responses to a four-page smoking questionnaire" (p. 41) with the aim of helping people to give up smoking. This system was evaluated "by recruiting 2553 smokers, sending 1/3 of them letters produced by STOP and the other 2/3 control letters, and then measuring how many people in each group managed to stop smoking"[3]. In this case the system was evaluated in the real world to see whether it has the desired effect, of helping people to quit smoking. The results showed that there were no relevant differences between the STOP letters and the control letters.

3.1 A general overview

Table 3 shows the evaluation methodologies used in the papers that we examined. With respect to

Evaluation methodologies	# of papers			
	Text2Text	Kb2Text	Mm2Text	Total
Intrinsic human only	13	1	-	14
Intrinsic automatic only	9	-	1	10
Extrinsic (human) only	2	-	-	2
Intrinsic human & Intrinsic automatic	3	2	2	7
Intrinsic human & Extrinsic (human)	2	-	-	2
Intrinsic automatic & Extrinsic (automatic)	1	-	-	1
Intrinsic human & Intrinsic automatic & Extrinsic (automatic)	-	1	-	1

Table 3: Evaluation methodologies used.

the frequency of use of intrinsic compared to extrinsic methods, Table 3 confirms the trend identified in Gkatzia and Mahamood (2014). Gkatzia and Mahamood found out that the 74.7% of the papers used the intrinsic evaluation method. In our analysis we found that 83% of the papers used

[3]See Ehud Reiter's blog https://ehudreiter.com/2017/01/19/types-of-nlg-evaluation/

this methodology. However, we note that with respect to Gkatzia and Mahamood's results, we have an inverted trend between the use of an extrinsic method compared to both intrinsic and extrinsic. Indeed, Gkatzia and Mahamood found that 15.2% of the papers used extrinsic methods, against the 6% we get in our analysis, and 10.1% of the papers used both methodologies, where our analysis shows that 11% of the papers use a combination of both.

Furthermore, our analysis confirms the trend between the use of automatic compared to human intrinsic evaluation methodologies. In Gkatzia and Mahamood (2014) the authors report that in 45.4% of the cases human evaluation is used, whereas in 38.2% of the cases automatic evaluation were adopted. Similarly, our analysis shows that between the papers that prefer intrinsic evaluation methods, 45% used human evaluation, 32% used automatic evaluation and 23% used both human and automatic evaluation.

Table 1 shows that in the period since 2016, there has been a considerable increase in the number of publications in this area. It therefore makes sense to ask whether this increase has been accompanied with a change in the evaluation methodologies used.

Evaluation methodologies	# of papers	
	2013-2015	2016-2018
Intrinsic human only	6	8
Intrinsic automatic only	1	9
Extrinsic (human) only	-	2
Intrinsic human & Intrinsic automatic	1	6
Intrinsic human & Extrinsic (human)	-	2
Intrinsic automatic & Extrinsic (automatic)	-	1
Intrinsic human & Intrinsic automatic & Extrinsic (automatic)	-	1

Table 4: Variation of the evaluation methodologies used between 2013 - 2015 and between 2016 - 2018.

Table 4 shows how the range of evaluation methodologies used has changed. Between the years 2013 - 2015 only intrinsic evaluation methodologies were used – with 75% of papers using human evaluation, 12.5% using automatic evaluation and 12.5% using both methodologies – for the years between 2016 - 2018 extrinsic evaluation methods have also been introduced. Indeed, although the majority of the papers in this period (79%) used intrinsic evaluation methods, 7% of papers used extrinsic evaluation methods and 14%

used both the methodologies. We can also see a change in the tendency to use intrinsic methods. Between the years 2016 - 2018, 35% of the papers used human evaluation (a decrease of 40% from the years between 2013 - 2015), 39% of the papers used automatic evaluation (a 26.5% increase on the years between 2013 - 2015) and 26% of the papers used both methodologies (a 13.5% increase on the years between 2013 - 2015).

3.2 Automatic evaluation

Table 5 presents a list of automatic metrics used in the papers studied in the present research. From our analysis it turns out that the most used automatic metric is BLEU followed by METEOR. Note that Table 5 only describes those that use the specified metrics; other papers use metrics that are defined for the specific aims described in the paper that introduces them.

Evaluation methodologies	# of papers			
	Text2Text	Kb2Text	Mm2Text	Total
BLEU (Papineni et al., 2002)	8	3	2	13
METEOR (Banerjee and Laviel, 2005)	4	2	1	7
ROUGE (Lin and Och, 2004)	3	1	-	4
Precision	4	-	-	4
Recall	4	-	-	4
F1	4	-	-	4
Accuracy	2	0	1	3
ΔBLEU (Galley et al., 2015)	-	-	1	1
Embedding Greedy (Rus and Lintean., 2012)	-	1	-	1
Others	5	-	-	5

Table 5: Automatic metrics used.

In our survey we found out that 31% of the papers used just a single metric, whereas the other 69% used more than one. The average is 2 metrics per paper, with a minimum of 1 metric (6 papers) and a maximum of 5 metrics (1 paper). In almost 50% of cases (9 papers), 3 metrics were used. We noticed that only a single paper used an embedding based metric (see Sharma et al. (2017)). In a majority of studies, word-overlap based metrics were used (see Sharma et al. (2017)).

In the last few years, many studies in NLG have shed light on the correlation between human judgement and automatic metrics. The results, which have shown how this correspondence is somewhat weak[4], shed doubt on the feasibility of using these metrics for evaluating the overall quality of a system.

To the best of our knowledge, the area of AQG is currently missing a study which aims to verify the correlation between human judgement and automatic metrics[5]. Such research would have two merits: on one hand, this kind of meta-evaluation study would give a better characterisation of the general problem. On the other hand, the research could provide guidance to researchers about which metric is most appropriate in evaluating a particular model or system.

In conclusion, we believe that research in AQG would benefit from a systematic study that aims to clarify the relation between different evaluation methodologies.

3.3 Human evaluation

Among the various human evaluation methodologies, eliciting *quality judgments* is most common: human annotators are asked to assess the quality of a question based on criteria such as question's grammaticality and fluency. Only two papers used a *preference judgement* methodology, in which the human annotators are asked either to assess pairwise preference between questions or given a couple of questions, one human generated and one automatically generated, assess which one is automatically generated (or which one is the the human generated). One of these papers also used the other methodology of eliciting quality judgements.

Quality judgment methodologies typically ask annotators to use Likert or rating scales to record their judgements. In our analysis, we found that 56% of the papers used some kind of numerical scale. For example, human annotators were often asked to assess the grammaticality of a question on a scale from 1 (worst) to 5 (best). On the other hand, 44% of the papers used a linguistic (or semantic) scale. In these cases, human annotators were typically asked to classify the questions in some category such as coherent, somewhat coherent or incoherent. The number of categories used in the Likert or rating scales by the papers that adopted quality judgment methodologies are shown in Table 6.

Only three papers used more than one scale in the evaluation. One of these uses a free scale in

---

[4]For an in depth discussion of this point we refer to Reiter and Belz (2009) and to Gatt and Krahmer (2018), especially section 7.4.1 and the references presented there.

[5]Yuan et al. (2017) raise some doubts about the capacity of BLEU to effectively measure the quality of systems used in *Text2Text* tasks.

which the annotators have to choose a positive integer to count the inference steps necessary for answer a question.

Number of categories	# of papers			
	Text2Text	Kb2Text	Mm2Text	Total
2	6	-	-	6
3	6	-	2	8
4	1	1	-	2
5	8	1	-	9
7	-	1	-	1

Table 6: Number of categories used in the Likert or rating scales.

Table 6 shows that the two most common number of categories used in the Likert or rating scales are 3 and 5. In a recent paper, Novikova et al. (2018) suggest that the use of a continuous scale and relative assessments can improve the quality of human judgments. Although in our study, we found 2 papers that used relative assessment, we did not find any papers that use a continuous scale.

Another interesting point is the number of annotators used in the evaluation. This number varies a lot from paper to paper. We found a minimum of 1 annotator (2 papers) to a maximum of 364 annotators (1 paper). Taking the papers which provided information on the number of annotators used (24 papers), and removing five papers that used 53, 63, 67, 81 and 364 annotators – these can be seen as outliers – we found out that the average number of annotators used was almost 4. The most common number was two annotators, used by 29% (7 papers) of the papers. 3 annotators were used by 17% (4 papers) and 4 annotators were used by 13% (3 papers). The others paper used 5, 7, 8 or 10 annotators.

There is a similar breadth in the number of output questions used (that is, the questions generated by the systems), and the criteria (that is, the question features to be checked) used in the evaluation. The number of questions ranged from a minimum of 60 questions (1 paper) to a maximum of 2186 (1 paper). Amongst those papers which actually provide this information (17 papers, or 65%), we found out that the average number of questions used per paper is almost 493. 7 papers (27%) did not report this information, whereas 2 papers (8%) report information about the amount of data from which the questions were generated, without giving the exact number of questions used for the evaluation.

Regarding the criteria used, we noticed that 35% of the papers (8 studies) used an overall qual-

ity criterion, that is, a single criterion which was used to evaluate the question's overall quality. On the other hand, 52% of the papers (12 studies) used specific criteria, for example, question grammaticality, question answerability, etc. A full list of these criteria is shown in Table 7. 13% of the papers (3 studies) used both specific criteria and an overall criterion. As Table 7 shows, there is a wide assortment of criteria used across the set of collected papers.

Criterion used	# of papers			
	Text2Text	Kb2Text	Mm2Text	Total
Grammaticality	7	-	-	7
Semantic correctness	4	-	-	4
Answer existence	3	-	-	3
Naturalness	2	1	-	3
Question type	3	-	-	3
Clarity	3	-	-	3
Discriminator quality	3	-	-	3
Relevance	2	-	-	2
Correctness	2	-	-	2
Well-formedness	1	-	-	1
Key selection accuracy	1	-	-	1
Corrected retrieval	1	-	-	1
Fluency	1	-	-	1
Coherence	1	-	-	1
Timing	1	-	-	1
Inference step	1	-	-	1
Question diversity	1	-	-	1
Importance	1	-	-	1
Specificity	1	-	-	1
Predicate identification	-	1	-	1
Difficulty	1	-	-	1
Overall criterion	7	2	2	11

Table 7: Criteria used.

As we can see from Table 7, the specific criteria are mainly used in the *Text2Text* task. Just two criteria are used in the *Kb2Text* task and none in the *Mm2Text*, where an overall quality criterion was preferred. We note that some criteria, for example timing or importance, are specific to one of the aims of the paper in which they are used. Indeed, as shown in the introduction, we can find different aims behind the papers' motivations. We note that among the papers analyzed here, often only little information is provided about the evaluation guidelines[6]. We cannot exclude that, given the evaluation guidelines, some of the criteria presented in Table 7 can be collapsed together. That is, it is possible that different researchers use different names in order to check the same question feature. In order to have a better way to check the quality across systems, we suggest that researchers should publish the evaluation guidelines used in the evaluation, as well as the quantitative results.

---

[6]Human evaluations are driven by some annotation guideline which is a direct manifestation of some annotation scheme. Whereas the latter characterize the criteria to be evaluated, the first strictly define such criteria and suggest how they should be evaluated.

Table 8 supplies an overview about the IAA reached in the human evaluations. We note that 54% of the papers (14 studies) did not supply this information. Only one of the two papers that used preference judgments reported the agreement between evaluators. In that paper, Fleiss' κ was used to measure the IAA reached between 3 to 5 evaluators. The results, for three batches with different evaluators and questions, were 0.242, 0.234 and 0.182. Table 8 presents the IAA results reported by the papers that used quality judgement methods. Between the papers that reported this information, we found that the IAA was measured in 26 cases and 9 of these were measured with two different coefficients, for a total of 35 IAA values. The agreements were measured for specific criteria or for the overall quality criterion. In one case the agreement over all the criteria was reported. It

Metric used for calculate IAA	# of criteria measured	Average	Min.	Max.
Cohen's κ	14	0.46	0.10	0.80
Krippendorff's α	2	0.143	0.05	0.236
Fleiss's κ	4	0.45	0.33	0.62
Pearson's r	4	0.71	0.47	0.89
Average measure	9	0.80	0.50	0.91
k no better specified	2	0.085	0.08	0.09

Table 8: Measures of Inter-Annotator Agreement.

is notable that the agreement reached in the various evaluations is generally quite low. Indeed, following Artstein and Poesio (2008), only agreement greater than or equal to 0.8 should be considered. Quoting Artstein and Poesio, p. 591:

> Both in our earlier work (Poesio and Vieira 1998; Poesio 2004a) and in the more recent (Poesio and Artstein 2005) efforts we found that only values above 0.8 ensures an annotation of reasonable quality. We therefore felt that if a threshold needs to be set, 0.8 is a good value.

Taking this as an appropriate quality threshold, among the papers that report IAA, very few evaluations should be considered appropriate. More specifically, we found that only 23% (8 over 35 values) of the evaluations reported IAA scores that were greater than or equal to 0.8.[7]

---

[7]Using the popular Krippendorff's Kappa scales of interpretation (Krippendorff, 1980) – where any data annotation with agreement in the interval [0.8, 1] should be considered good, agreement in the interval [0.67, 0.8) should be considered tentative, and data annotation with agreement below 0.67 should be discarded– we conclude that 43% (15 out of 35) of the evaluations should be considered tentative.

Checking the agreement for number of annotators we found that in the case with 364 annotators the IAA, measured for two criteria and a not better specified κ, was between 0.08 and 0.09. We found only 2 cases for 5 evaluators, which reported a value of 0.05 for Krippendorff's α and an average measure of 0.89. Two papers used 4 annotators altogether: one reported a value of Krippendorff's α of 0.236, with the other reporting a Pearson's r of 0.71. Another paper used 3 evaluators and the Fleiss's κ to measure the IAA for 4 criteria. The results are reported in Table 8.

All other papers reporting an IAA measure were in evaluations that used 2 annotators. The results of these cases are shown in Table 8 highlighting Cohen's κ, the Average measure and Pearson's r.[8]

There are sometimes attempts to design the experimental methodology to improve the level of IAA. In order to improve the agreement, one paper collapsed two score classes into one, whereas two papers allowed a difference of one score between the annotators rating. Two examples of the latter case are the maximum value for Cohen's κ and the maximum value for the average measure reported in Table 8.

We conclude this section by noting that the problem of a low IAA was present also in the Shared Task Evaluation Challenge (QG-STEC) (Rus et al., 2010). In that case, an attempt to improve the IAA for task B was carried out by Godwin and Piwek (2016). Godwin and Piwek define an interactive process in which the annotators can discuss their opinions about the criteria used in the evaluation. At the end of the evaluation process, repeated three times with three annotators on different data each time, they got high IAA with a peak of 0.94 for one of the five criteria used in the evaluation.

Although other papers (see for example Bayerl and Paul (2011), Lommel et al. (2014) and Hwee Tou Ng and Foo (1999)) propose techniques which aim to improve the IAA, in a recent paper (Amidei et al., 2018) we suggest thinking carefully about this practice in the case of NLG tasks. Indeed, if evaluation results have to inform generation sys-

---

[8]Regarding Pearson's r, we should clarify that in the case of 2 evaluators, IAA was measured for 3 criteria and not 4 as reported in table 8. However, because the Pearson's r measured for the fourth criterion was 0.71, that is the average value, the Pearson's r measure in the case of 2 evaluator is exactly the one shown in Table 8. Furthermore, for the average measure there is a case with 5 annotators. Removing that case, the average for 2 annotators is 0.79.

tems developers of the extent to which they can improve the communicative power of their systems, the aim of attaining a higher IAA runs the danger of biasing system developers towards ignoring important aspects of human language. An unchecked and unquestioned focus on the reduction of disagreement among annotators runs the danger of creating generation goals that reward output that is more distant from, rather than closer to, natural human-like language.

3.4 Extrinsic evaluation

As shown in Table 3, extrinsic evaluation methodologies are rare in the area. As reported by Gkatzia and Mahamood (2014) this is generally true for NLG tasks. Amongst the papers that have chosen to use this kind of evaluation technique, human judges were used in 4 times out of the 6. In the papers where human judges were not used, the Question Generation (QG) system was tested as a component of a Question Answering (QA) system. The performance was evaluated by checking the difference between the QA system without the use of the QG system against the performance of the QA system with the use of the QG system. The aim of those papers was to improve QA systems by creating more accurate question/answer pairs to be used for training purposes.

As a consequence of the different tasks in play, the other papers used humans in different ways. We can find tasks such as: answer the generated questions or use the generated questions in a web page and then answer a survey about the utility of those questions. Or also: engage in a conversation with a chatbot which involves a question-based dialogue, and then rate the conversations.

Also in this case, the number of humans involved in the evaluation varies from paper to paper, ranging from 2 to 81. In contrast to the case of intrinsic human evaluation, in this case the IAA is not reported. We note that human agreement in extrinsic evaluation is not as relevant as in the case of intrinsic evaluation. Indeed, for intrinsic evaluations, agreement is required to have a reliability and validity measure of the evaluation scheme and guidelines (Artstein and Poesio, 2008). The agreement measure should gather evidence that different humans can make similar judgements about the questions evaluated. This fact, following Krippendorff (2011) should allow us to answer the question of: *"how much the resulting data can be trusted to represent something real"?* (page 1). In human intrinsic evaluation, the agreement can be seen as a measure of the replicability of the results. For example, Carletta (1996, p. 1) wrote:

> At one time, it was considered sufficient...to show examples based on the authors' interpretation. Research was judged according to whether or not the reader found the explanation plausible. Now, researchers are beginning to require evidence that people besides the authors themselves can understand and make the judgments underlying the research reliably. This is a reasonable requirement because if researchers can't even show that different people can agree about the judgments on which their research is based, then there is no chance of replicating the research results.

In the case of extrinsic methods, the evaluation aim is to check if the generated sentences fulfil the task for which they were generated. To test this, humans need to use those sentences in real contexts. Now, humans make use of the same tools in different ways, and similarly they answer questions in different ways. For this reason, it is not expected that humans reach similar results in a real context of language use.

4 Discussion

Although systems and tools have been developed in the AQG area over the last few years, Table 1 illustrates that this has not been accompanied by similar improvements in evaluation methodologies. Indeed, with the exception of the Shared Task Evaluation Challenge (QG -STEC) (Rus et al., 2010), no attempts have been undertaken to introduce a common framework for evaluation that allows for comparisons between systems.

We have seen that in human evaluation, different criteria and scales/categories are used. To address this, we recommend that researchers share their evaluation guidelines, and work towards adopting common guidelines that can used to check quality across systems. Furthermore, out of the papers examined here, the problem of evaluation validity emerges. In those studies where it has actually been reported, the IAA is generally low. Also in this case we suggest researchers systematically determine the IAA and share their results, as well as ideas to attempt to understand and classify any divergences between annotators.

Automatic evaluation can be thought of as a technique to provide a way to standardize the evaluation. Unfortunately, a comparison of human and automatic evaluation is missing in the area. This makes it difficult to understand to what extent the automatic metrics capture the systems' quality. Lacking such comparison, and following Reiter (2018), we suggest considering metrics such as BLEU as tools for systems' diagnostic more than evaluation techniques able to measure the output quality of the systems.

There is scope for more extrinsic evaluation, which can *"provide useful insight of domains' need, and thus they provide better indications of the systems' usefulness and utility"* (Gkatzia and Mahamood, 2014, p. 60). Unfortunately, extrinsic evaluations are not yet widely used.

Though the QG-STEC evaluation scheme has only limited uptake, with the much increased popularity of AQG, it is timely to revisit and address the need for a shared evaluation scheme. The variety of evaluation methodologies, as brought to light by the present work, demonstrates how difficult it currently is to check question quality across generation systems. This prevents us from understanding the actual contributions that are made by new generation systems that are being introduced ever more frequently.

We conclude this section with the following observation. The problem of having a high degree of variation in methodologies is compounded by the use of different datasets in the evaluation phase (see Table 9). The use of a common dataset for evaluation – as suggested by the Shared Task Evaluation Campaign (STEC) (Gatt and Belz, 2010) – could remove bias coming from the training phase. This is particularly true for generation systems that use machine learning techniques. We note that the high variability in the dataset used in the evaluation phase is also due to the variation in the papers' motivations. However, Table 9 suggests that the aim of building a common framework for AQG tasks should involve creation of a dataset to be used only for evaluation purposes. If we want to understand the degree to which a system advances the state of the art, we need to compare different systems on the same dataset, or better, a set of datasets, of course, using the same evaluation methodologies.

Tasks	Dataset or source of test articles
Text2Text	SQuAD; MS-MARCO; WikiQA; TriviaQA; TrecQA; Wikinews; Penn Treebank; QG-STEC datasets; StackExchange; Wikipedia; OMG! website; Project Gutemberg; ReadWorks.org; Engarde corpus; CrunchBase; Newswire (PropBank); textbook from OpenStax and Saylor; not specify TOEFL book; not specify science text books; not specify course Web page; not specify news articles not specify teachers articles; 40 people's personal data.
Kb2Text	Ontology documenting K-12 Biology concepts; SimpleQuestions; Freebase; WikiAnswers.
Mm2Text	COCO-QA; COCO-VQA; IGC_{Crowd}; Bing; COCO; Flickr.

Table 9: Dataset used.

An open evaluation platform in which researchers share their evaluation methodologies and their results can be effective to compare the quality across systems. In such a platform, the shared evaluation methodologies, alongside some datasets used only for evaluation, can be used by researchers to test their systems' performance and the results can be recorded in the open platform. Another benefit of this platform could be to generate an evolutionary process which allows the community to select the evaluation methodologies that are considered more effective.

5 Conclusion

In this paper we have analysed 37 papers which were about AQG. The aim of our work was to study the evaluation methodologies used in the area. Our work confirms the conclusion of Gkatzia and Mahamood (2014) for NLG in general. In AQG we lack a standardised approach for evaluating generation systems. Indeed, our overview shows a quite variegated evaluation landscape which prevents comparison of question quality across generation systems. A careful look at the papers published in the AQG area in the last five years shows how little attention has been given to the evaluation methodology introduced in the QG-STEC. Given the ever-increasing number of publications in the area, a common framework for testing the performance of generation systems is urgently needed.

Acknowledgments

We warmly thanks the anonymous reviewers for their helpful suggestions.

References

Jacopo Amidei, Paul Piwek, and Alistair Willis. 2018. Rethinking the agreement in human evaluation tasks. In *Proceedings of the 27th International Conference on Computational Linguistics*, pages 3318–3329.

Ron Artstein and Massimo Poesio. 2008. Inter-coder agreement for computational linguistics. *Computational Linguistics*, 34(4):555–596.

Satanjeev Banerjee and Alon Laviel. 2005. Meteor: An automatic metric for MT evaluation with improved correlation with human judgments. In *Proceedings of the ACL Workshop on Intrinsic and Extrinsic Evaluation Measures for Machine Translation and/or Summarization*, pages 65–72.

Petra S. Bayerl and Karsten I. Paul. 2011. What determines inter-coder agreement in manual annotations? a meta-analytic investigation. *Computational Linguistics*, 37(4):699–725.

Jean Carletta. 1996. Assessing agreement on classification tasks: The kappa statistic. *Computational Linguistics*, 22(2):249–254.

Michel Galley, Chris Brockett, Alessandro Sordoni, Yangfeng Ji, Michael Auli, Chris Quirk, Margaret Mitchell, Jianfeng Gao, and Bill Dolan. 2015. δbleu: A discriminative metric for generation tasks with intrinsically diverse targets. In *Proceedings of the 53rd Annual Meeting of the Association for Computational Linguistics and the 7th International Joint Conference on Natural Language Processing*, pages 26–31.

Albert Gatt and Anja Belz. 2010. Introducing shared tasks to NLG: The TUNA shared task evaluation challenges. *in E. Krahmer and Mariët Theune (Eds.),* Empirical Methods in Natural Language Generation *Springer-Verlag, Berlin Heidelberg.*

Albert Gatt and Emiel Krahmer. 2018. Survey of the state of the art in natural language generation: Core tasks, applications and evaluation. *Journal of Artificial Intelligence Research*, 61(1):65–170.

Dimitra Gkatzia and Saad Mahamood. 2014. A snapshot of NLG evaluation practices 2005 - 2014. In *Proceedings of the 15th European Workshop on Natural Language Generation (ENLG)*, pages 57–60.

Keith Godwin and Paul Piwek. 2016. Collecting reliable human judgements on machine-generated language: The case of the qg-stec data. In *Proceedings INLG16*, pages 212–216.

Chung Yong Lim Hwee Tou Ng and Shou King Foo. 1999. A case study on inter-annotator agreement for word sense disambiguation. In *Proceedings of the ACL SIGLEX Workshop: Standardizing Lexical Resources*, pages 9–13.

Emiel Krahmer and Mariët Theune (Eds.). 2010. *Empirical Methods in Natural Language Generation.* Springer-Verlag, Berlin Heidelberg.

Klaus Krippendorff. 1980. *Content Analysis: An Introduction to Its Methodology.* Sage Publications, Beverly Hills, CA.

Klaus Krippendorff. 2011. Computing Krippendorff's alpha-reliability. Retrieved from `http://repository.upenn.edu`.

Nguyen-Thinh Le, Tomoko Kojiri, and Niels Pinkwart. 2014. *Automatic Question Generation for Educational Applications The State of Art. In: van Do T., Thi H., Nguyen N. (eds) Advanced Computational Methods for Knowledge Engineering.* Springer, Cham.

Chin-Yew Lin and Franz Josef Och. 2004. Automatic evaluation of machine translation quality using using longest common subsequence and skip-bigram statistics. In *Proceedings ACL'04*, pages 605–612.

Arle Lommel, Maja Popovic, and Aljoscha Burchardt. 2014. Assessing inter-annotator agreement for translation error annotation. In: MTE: Workshop on Automatic and Manual Metrics for Operational Translation Evaluation, Reykjavik, Iceland.

Jekaterina Novikova, Ondřej Dušek, and Verena Rieser. 2018. RankMe: Reliable human ratings for natural language generation. In *Proceedings of NAACL-HLT*, pages 72–78.

Kishore Papineni, Salim Roukos, Todd Ward, and Wei-Jing Zhu. 2002. BLEU: a method for automatic evaluation of machine translation. In *Proceedings of the 40th Annual meeting of the Association for Computational Linguistics.*, pages 311–318.

Paul Piwek and Kristy. E. Boyer. 2012. Varieties of question generation: Introduction to this special issue. dialogue and discourse. *Dialogue and Discourse*, 3(2):1–9.

Sheetal Rakangor and Y. R. Ghodasara. 2015. Literature review of automatic question generation systems. *International Journal of Scientific and Research Publications*, 5(1):1–5.

Ehud Reiter. 2018. A structured review of the validity of bleu. *Computational Linguistics*, 44(3):393–401.

Ehud Reiter and Anja Belz. 2009. An investigation into the validity of some metrics for automatically evaluating natural language generation systems. *Computational Linguistics*, 35(4):529–558.

Ehud Reiter, Roma Robertson, and Liesl M.Osman. 2003. Lessons from a failure: Generating tailored smoking cessation letters. *Artificial Intelligence*, 144(1-2):41–58.

Vasile Rus, Zhiqiang Cai, and Art Graesser. 2008. Question generation: Example of a multi-year evaluation campaign. In *Rus, V. and A. Graesser (eds.), online Proceedings of 1st Question Generation Workshop*, pages 25–26.

Vasile Rus and Mihai C. Lintean. 2012. A comparison of greedy and optimal assessment of natural language student input using word-to-word similarity metrics. In *In Proceedings of the Seventh Workshop on Building Educational Applications Using NLP*.

Vasile Rus, Brendan Wyse, Paul Piwek, Mihai Lintean, Svetlana Stoyanchev, and Cristian Moldovan. 2010. The first question generation shared task evaluation challenge. In *Proceedings of the Sixth International Natural Language Generation Conference (INLG)*, pages 7–9.

Shikhar Sharma, Layla El Asri, Hannes Schulz, and Jeremie Zumer. 2017. Relevance of unsupervised metrics in task-oriented dialogue for evaluating natural language generation. *arXiv:1706.09799*.

Xingdi Yuan, Tong Wang, Caglar Gulcehre, Alessandro Sordoni, Philip Bachman, and Saizheng Zhang. 2017. Machine comprehension by text-to-text neural question generation. In *Proceedings of the 2nd Workshop on Representation Learning for NLP*, pages 15–25.

Task Proposal - The TL;DR challenge

Shahbaz Syed[a]   Michael Völske[a]   Martin Potthast[b]   Nedim Lipka[c]

Benno Stein[a]   Hinrich Schütze[d]

[a]Bauhaus-Universität Weimar   [b]Leipzig University   [c]Adobe Research   [d]LMU Munich

Abstract

The TL;DR challenge fosters research in abstractive summarization of informal text, the largest and fastest-growing source of textual data on the web, which has been overlooked by summarization research so far. The challenge owes its name to the frequent practice of social media users to supplement long posts with a "TL;DR"—for "too long; didn't read"—followed by a short summary as a courtesy to those who would otherwise reply with the exact same abbreviation to indicate they did not care to read a post for its apparent length. Posts featuring TL;DR summaries form an excellent ground truth for summarization, and by tapping into this resource for the first time, we have mined millions of training examples from social media, opening the door to all kinds of generative models.

1   Task overview

The task of participants is straightforward: given a social media posting, generate a summary. Ours is to evaluate the participants' approaches quantitatively and qualitatively, which will include measures from the literature as well as manual review via crowdsourcing. For diversity, we intend to offer additional evaluation categories that further constrain a summary, e.g., summaries that include the topic of an underlying discussion, summaries in the form of questions, or, for fun sake, wacky summaries. To ensure reproducibility, we employ the cloud-based TIRA[1] evaluation platform, to which participants will deploy working prototypes of their summarizers for blind and semi-automated evaluation.

[1]www.tira.io

2   Motivation

Text summarization ranks among the oldest synthesis tasks of computer science, addressing the nowadays almost stereotypical problem of information overload. Traditionally, the task has been tackled within natural language processing and information retrieval by extracting phrases from a to-be-summarized text. However, the task draws increasing attention from the machine learning community. Owing to advances in theory, algorithms, and hardware, the training of complex models has become feasible that *abstract* over the to-be-summarized text. Here, deep generative models have delivered some impressive results (Chopra et al., 2016; Nallapati et al., 2016; See et al., 2017; Chen and Bansal, 2018). Since these models need substantially large amounts of training data in order to understand and generate natural language text, the availability of suitable corpora is important. The most commonly used datasets for abstractive summarization, namely the Gigaword corpus (Graff and Cieri, 2003) and the CNN Dailymail news dataset (Hermann et al., 2015), comprise short articles from the news domain, representing only one of the many genres of written text. Target summaries in both these corpora are extractive where either the first sentence or some key points are combined together to train the model. In particular, there have been no resources covering user-generated content until now, severely limiting the range of applications of summarization research and technology on the web.

Social media platforms and search engines alike rely on showcasing contents to their users in order to maintain and increase user engagement. Besides the intelligent, personalized recommendation and retrieval systems which retrieve the right content at the right time, they mostly resort to extractive summarization techniques for presentation. While con-

Proceedings of The 11th International Natural Language Generation Conference, pages 318–321,
Tilburg, The Netherlands, November 5-8, 2018. ©2018 Association for Computational Linguistics

tents with a high production value, such as news, regularly come with pre-produced summaries tailored to the most important platforms and search engines, this is not the case for user-generated content, which makes up for the vast majority of content on many platforms. At the same time, user-generated content, due to the informal nature of its writing, does not readily lend itself to extractive summarization techniques. Abstractive approaches may offer great value to these platforms by capturing the gist of a piece of user-generated content while harmonizing the style of presentation. This is particularly important in cases where the user interface is limited, such as that of mobile devices or the narrow audio-only interface of conversational AI agents.

Through our competition, we want to spur the development of novel model architectures and optimizations for generative models, in order to bridge the gap between the quality of automatic summaries and those written by humans. In accordance with the motto of INLG, we encourage discussions about a multitude of unsolved research questions related to text summarization and its evaluation. To the best of our knowledge, we are the first to tackle abstractive summarization of user-generated content at scale. As organizers of many previous shared tasks in the areas of natural language processing and machine learning, we look back on years of experience in provisioning and administering the infrastructure required.

3   Task Description

The task of participants is to provide a software that, given a text, generates an abstractive summary for it. This task is at the heart of modern summarization technology that may be used in the aforementioned scenarios. Participants are encouraged to perform any preprocessing/normalization of the provided training data as well as to incorporate third party data as they see fit. Their training process must accordingly be described in detail in the paper accompanying their final submissions.

The task is challenging, but—given recent advances in deep generative modeling—not impossible, anymore. Key to solving this task is to identify means that will allow for generating summaries that are short as well as self-explanatory, to work around the idiosyncratic usage in user-generated content, and to find levers to adjust summary quality. In this regard, a promising direction may also be the combination of traditional, extractive sum-

Table 1: Sample content-summary pair

Content: not necessarily my lucky day , but some kids this is how it went was sitting out on the dock at a local lake with a friend sharing some beers . little boy aged 2-3 yrs old walks up with a wooden stick and starts poking at the water . it was windy out and the dock was moving , and sure enough the kid leans over just enough to topple head first into the water . i had already pulled my phone out and wallet out just in case i was to accidentally fall in so i went straight over and hopped in . saw his little hand reaching up and tossed him straight back onto the dock . walked him to his dad who didn ' t speak any english and was very confused why i had his son soaking wet . left later that day and saw the kid back on the dock ! it blew my mind.

TL;DR: saved a 2 year old from drowning at a lake because i was drinking beers with a friend .

marization approaches with deep generative models as demonstrated by Liu et al. (Liu et al., 2018).

3.1   Data

The competition can be immediately started, since its training dataset is already available (Völske et al., 2017). We have mined Reddit for user postings that include a TL;DR summary, collecting a total of 4,044,501 content-summary pairs (see Table 1 for an example). In terms of size, our dataset matches the state-of-the-art Gigaword corpus. This dataset covers a wide range of everyday topics, drawing examples from 32,778 *subreddits*, each of which focuses on a particular topic. The mining process was carefully adjusted to include and extract the many syntactical variants of TL;DR summaries while excluding automatically generated postings and summaries by bots. To ensure high quality, we frequently reviewed large samples of the data, adjusting the mining process until at least 95% of the samples were of sufficient quality. Each item of the dataset is a pair of posting and summary written by the same author.

For the competition, we will use a subset of this dataset comprising 3,084,410 of the content-summary pairs to harmonize the length distributions. In this subset, the average length of a posting is 211 words, ranging from from 100 to 400 words, and that of a summary is 25 words, ranging from 10 to 200 words. Participants are free to split this into training and validation sets as deemed fit. The test dataset comprises 1000 items held out from the training data, each of which has been carefully reviewed by at least three human annotators for quality. Of these, 800 will be used in the initial automatic evaluation runs, and the remaining 200 in a final round of manual evaluation.

3.2   Protocol

The competition will comprise three phases: (1) participants will train summarization models using

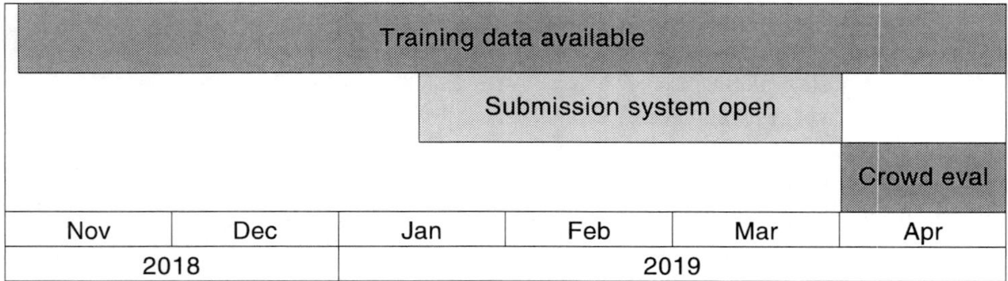

Figure 1: Planned timeline for the TL;DR challenge.

the provided training data on their own hardware; (2) with the submission system open, participants will deploy their trained models on the TIRA infrastructure; the systems will generate candidate summaries against the automatic evaluation test samples, without network access or direct involvement of the participants. (3) once the submission dates conclude, the candidate summaries generated by the submitted models will be evaluated by crowdsourcing workers against the private test set.

Phase (1) will begin two and a half months before Phase (2), from which point both will run in parallel until the submissions system closes. Participants will be able to train and submit models at their discretion. For the duration of Phase (2), submitted summaries will be automatically evaluated using the ROUGE measure against half of the test set samples. Automatic evaluation scores will populate the public leaderboard. The final portion of the test set will only be used in the manual evaluation round, so that overfitting against the leaderboard scores can be avoided.

To ensure blind evaluation, and reproducibility, the trained summarization models will be submitted as working *software* that performs summary inference given a set of input texts. Participants will deploy this software and all required dependencies on a virtual machine provided by the challenge organizers. The test dataset will not be accessible to participants while the competition is running; test set summaries will be generated offline on the aforementioned virtual machine, without direct input from the participants. All evaluation runs will be started from a clone of the participant's virtual machine, without network access, such that no test set data can be leaked. We operate the cloud infrastructure as well as the TIRA evaluation platform ourselves, so that no third party need be involved. TIRA has been successfully employed for various large-scale competitions since 2012; it is battle-

tested.

Finally, we will encourage participants to share their code bases in a central organization at GitHub as a kind of Open Source Proceedings.

3.3 Schedule

We envision the milestones shown in Figure 1 for scheduling the TL;DR challenge:

- **November 5th, 2018:** Challenge announced; training data available.

- **January 15th, 2019:** Submissions system and public leaderboard open. Challenge participants will be able to submit working summarizers to the TIRA infrastructure; the online leaderboard will be continuously updated to reflect the latest performance on the test set.

- **April 1st, 2019:** Deadline for final software submissions; crowd evaluation begins.

3.4 Evaluation

To determine the winners of the TL;DR challenge, we will deploy a two step process involving both automatic measures and a thorough human evaluation of the generated summaries. Content selection evaluation metrics such as ROUGE, BLEU, and METEOR, will be reported to provide participants with a first impression of the coherence and information capturing capabilities of their models. Additionally, embedding based metrics such as cosine similarity of word and sentence representations of the generated summaries will be reported against the reference summaries.

For qualitative evaluation, human annotators recruited via Amazon Mechanical Turk will read the candidate summaries and rate them based on the standard summary evaluation criteria established by the DUC competitions (Dang, 2005). Each generated summary will be judged by at least three annotators to ensure accuracy; annotators will rate individual summaries, as well as pairs of summaries from different participants to establish preference and break ties. The final ranking, and the winner of the TL;DR challenge, will be derived from the human annotators' quality judgments. The crowdsourcing evaluation phase will employ 200 test samples not used during the automatic evaluation phase. Based on the number of submitted summarization systems, participation in the crowd evaluation phase may be limited to the top performers on the automatic evaluation leaderboard—based on our projections, up to approximately thirty submissions will be considered for crowd evaluation.

Some time after the conclusion of the competition, all testing data and annotator decisions will be made available to the research community at large; we expect that the analysis of the resulting data, and how it correlates with automatically computed ROUGE scores, will benefit the development of better evaluation metrics.

Outside of the ranking, we intend to offer evaluation scenarios in constrained summarization, such as generating summaries that include the topic of the underlying discussion, summaries in the form of questions, or wacky summaries deliberately including off-color vocabulary. We envision such scenarios to gain interest as summarization technology becomes integrated into conversational agents.

4 Conclusion

We strongly believe that our shared task proposal will encourage creation of diverse datasets for neural summarization. The TL;DR dataset poses a different set of challenges for neural generation models compared to News corpora. By emphasizing on the effectiveness and limitations of exisiting models through our challenge, the NLG community can focus on novel models and evaluation measures for developing better summarization technology.

References

Yen-Chun Chen and Mohit Bansal. 2018. Fast abstractive summarization with reinforce-selected sentence rewriting. In *Proceedings of ACL*.

Sumit Chopra, Michael Auli, and Alexander M. Rush. 2016. Abstractive sentence summarization with attentive recurrent neural networks. In *NAACL HLT 2016, The 2016 Conference of the North American Chapter of the Association for Computational Linguistics: Human Language Technologies, San Diego California, USA, June 12-17, 2016*. pages 93–98. http://aclweb.org/anthology/N/N16/N16-1012.pdf.

Hoa T. Dang. 2005. Overview of DUC 2005. In *Proceedings of the Document Understanding Conference*.

David Graff and Christopher Cieri. 2003. English Gigaword LDC2003T05. Web Download. Philadelphia: Linguistic Data Consortium.

Karl Moritz Hermann, Tomáš Kočiský, Edward Grefenstette, Lasse Espeholt, Will Kay, Mustafa Suleyman, and Phil Blunsom. 2015. Teaching machines to read and comprehend. In *Advances in Neural Information Processing Systems (NIPS)*. http://arxiv.org/abs/1506.03340.

Peter J. Liu, Mohammad Saleh, Etienne Pot, Ben Goodrich, Ryan Sepassi, Lukasz Kaiser, and Noam Shazeer. 2018. Generating wikipedia by summarizing long sequences. *CoRR* abs/1801.10198. http://arxiv.org/abs/1801.10198.

Ramesh Nallapati, Bowen Zhou, Cícero Nogueira dos Santos, Çaglar Gülçehre, and Bing Xiang. 2016. Abstractive text summarization using sequence-to-sequence rnns and beyond. In *Proceedings of the 20th SIGNLL Conference on Computational Natural Language Learning, CoNLL 2016, Berlin, Germany, August 11-12, 2016*. pages 280–290. http://aclweb.org/anthology/K/K16/K16-1028.pdf.

Abigail See, Peter J. Liu, and Christopher D. Manning. 2017. Get to the point: Summarization with pointer-generator networks. In *Proceedings of the 55th Annual Meeting of the Association for Computational Linguistics, ACL 2017, Vancouver, Canada, July 30 - August 4, Volume 1: Long Papers*. pages 1073–1083. https://doi.org/10.18653/v1/P17-1099.

Michael Völske, Martin Potthast, Shahbaz Syed, and Benno Stein. 2017. Tl;dr: Mining reddit to learn automatic summarization. In *Proceedings of the Workshop on New Frontiers in Summarization, NFiS@EMNLP 2017, Copenhagen, Denmark, September 7, 2017*. pages 59–63. https://aclanthology.info/papers/W17-4508/w17-4508.

Findings of the E2E NLG Challenge

Ondřej Dušek, Jekaterina Novikova and **Verena Rieser**
The Interaction Lab, School of Mathematical and Computer Sciences
Heriot-Watt University
Edinburgh, Scotland, UK
{o.dusek, j.novikova, v.t.rieser}@hw.ac.uk

Abstract

This paper summarises the experimental setup and results of the first shared task on end-to-end (E2E) natural language generation (NLG) in spoken dialogue systems. Recent end-to-end generation systems are promising since they reduce the need for data annotation. However, they are currently limited to small, delexicalised datasets. The E2E NLG shared task aims to assess whether these novel approaches can generate better-quality output by learning from a dataset containing higher lexical richness, syntactic complexity and diverse discourse phenomena. We compare 62 systems submitted by 17 institutions, covering a wide range of approaches, including machine learning architectures – with the majority implementing sequence-to-sequence models (seq2seq) – as well as systems based on grammatical rules and templates.

1 Introduction

This paper summarises the first shared task on end-to-end (E2E) natural language generation (NLG) in spoken dialogue systems (SDSs). Shared tasks have become an established way of pushing research boundaries in the field of natural language processing, with NLG benchmarking tasks running since 2007 (Belz and Gatt, 2007). This task is novel in that it poses new challenges for recent end-to-end, data-driven NLG systems for SDSs which jointly learn sentence planning and surface realisation and do not require costly semantic alignment between meaning representations (MRs) and the corresponding natural language reference texts, e.g. (Dušek and Jurčíček, 2015; Wen et al., 2015b; Mei et al.,

2016; Wen et al., 2016; Sharma et al., 2016; Dušek and Jurčíček, 2016a; Lampouras and Vlachos, 2016).[1] So far, end-to-end approaches to NLG are limited to small, delexicalised datasets, e.g. BAGEL (Mairesse et al., 2010), SF Hotels/Restaurants (Wen et al., 2015b), or RoboCup (Chen and Mooney, 2008), whereas the E2E shared task is based on a new crowdsourced dataset of 50k instances in the restaurant domain, which is about 10 times larger and also more complex than previous datasets. For the shared challenge, we received 62 system submissions by 17 institutions from 11 countries, with about 1/3 of these submissions coming from industry. We assess the submitted systems by comparing them to a challenging baseline using automatic as well as human evaluation. We consider this level of participation an unexpected success, which underlines the timeliness of this task.[2] While there are previous studies comparing a limited number of end-to-end NLG approaches (Novikova et al., 2017a; Wiseman et al., 2017; Gardent et al., 2017), this is the first research to evaluate novel end-to-end generation at scale and using human assessment.

2 The E2E NLG dataset

2.1 Data Collection Procedure

In order to maximise the chances for data-driven end-to-end systems to produce high quality output, we aim to provide training data in high quality and large quantity. To collect data in large enough quantity, we use crowdsourcing with automatic

---

[1] Note that as opposed to the "classical" definition of NLG (Reiter and Dale, 2000; Gatt and Krahmer, 2018), generation for dialogue systems does not involve content selection and its sentence planning stage may be less complex.

[2] In comparison, the well established Conference in Machine Translation WMT'17 (running since 2006) received submissions from 31 institutions to a total of 8 tasks (Bojar et al., 2017a).

Proceedings of The 11th International Natural Language Generation Conference, pages 322–328,
Tilburg, The Netherlands, November 5-8, 2018. ©2018 Association for Computational Linguistics

MR	name[The Wrestlers], priceRange[cheap], customerRating[low]
Reference	The wrestlers offers competitive prices, but isn't highly rated by customers.

Figure 1: Example of an MR-reference pair.

Attribute	Data Type	Example value
name	verbatim string	*The Eagle, ...*
eatType	dictionary	*restaurant, pub, ...*
familyFriendly	boolean	*Yes / No*
priceRange	dictionary	*cheap, expensive, ...*
food	dictionary	*French, Italian, ...*
near	verbatim string	*Zizzi, Cafe Adriatic, ...*
area	dictionary	*riverside, city center, ...*
customerRating	dictionary	*1 of 5 (low), 4 of 5 (high), ...*

Table 1: Domain ontology of the E2E dataset.

quality checks. We use MRs consisting of an unordered set of *attributes* and their *values* and collect multiple corresponding natural language texts (references) – utterances consisting of one or several sentences. An example MR-reference pair is shown in Figure 1, Table 1 lists all the attributes in our domain.

In contrast to previous work (Mairesse et al., 2010; Wen et al., 2015a; Dušek and Jurčíček, 2016), we use different modalities of meaning representation for data collection: textual/logical and pictorial MRs. The textual/logical MRs (see Figure 1) take the form of a sequence with attribute-value pairs provided in a random order. The pictorial MRs (see Figure 2) are semi-automatically generated pictures with a combination of icons corresponding to the appropriate attributes. The icons are located on a background showing a map of a city, thus allowing to represent the meaning of attributes *area* and *near* (cf. Table 1).

In a pre-study (Novikova et al., 2016), we showed that pictorial MRs provide similar collection speed and utterance length, but are less likely to prime the crowd workers in their lexical choices. Utterances produced using pictorial MRs were considered to be more informative, natural and better phrased. However, while pictorial MRs provide more variety in the utterances, this also introduces noise. Therefore, we decided to use pictorial MRs to collect 20% of the dataset.

Our crowd workers were asked to verbalise all information from the MR; however, they were not

Figure 2: An example pictorial MR.

E2E data part	MRs	References
training set	4,862	42,061
development set	547	4,672
test set	630	4,693
full dataset	6,039	51,426

Table 2: Total number of MRs and human references in the E2E data sections.

penalised for skipping an attribute. This makes the dataset more challenging, as NLG systems need to account for noise in training data. On the other hand, the systems are helped by having multiple human references per MR at their disposal.

2.2 Data Statistics

The resulting dataset (Novikova et al., 2017b) contains over 50k references for 6k distinct MRs (cf. Table 2), which is 10 times bigger than previous sets in comparable domains (BAGEL, SF Hotels/Restaurants, RoboCup). The dataset contains more human references per MR (8.27 on average), which should make it more suitable for data-driven approaches. However, it is also more challenging as it uses a larger number of sentences in references (up to 6 compared to 1–2 in other sets) and more attributes in MRs.

For the E2E challenge, we split the data into training, development and test sets (in a roughly 82-9-9 ratio). MRs in the test set are all previously unseen, i.e. none of them overlaps with training/development sets, even if restaurant names are removed. MRs for the test set were only released to participants two weeks before the challenge submission deadline on October 31, 2017. Participants had no access to test reference texts. The whole dataset is now freely available at the E2E NLG Challenge website at:

```
http://www.macs.hw.ac.uk/
InteractionLab/E2E/
```

System	BLEU	NIST	METEOR	ROUGE-L	CIDEr	norm. avg.
TGEN baseline (Novikova et al., 2017b): seq2seq with MR classifier reranking	0.6593	8.6094	0.4483	0.6850	2.2338	0.5754
SLUG (Juraska et al., 2018): seq2seq-based ensemble (LSTM/CNN encoders, LSTM decoder), heuristic slot aligner reranking, data augmentation	**0.6619**	**8.6130**	0.4454	0.6772	**2.2615**	0.5744
TNT1 (Oraby et al., 2018): TGEN with data augmentation	0.6561	8.5105	**0.4517**	0.6839	2.2183	0.5729
NLE (Agarwal et al., 2018): fully lexicalised character-based seq2seq with MR classification reranking	0.6534	8.5300	0.4435	0.6829	2.1539	0.5696
TNT2 (Tandon et al., 2018): TGEN with data augmentation	0.6502	8.5211	0.4396	**0.6853**	2.1670	0.5688
HARV (Gehrmann et al., 2018): fully lexicalised seq2seq with copy mechanism, coverage penalty reranking, diverse ensembling	0.6496	8.5268	0.4386	**0.6872**	2.0850	0.5673
ZHANG (Zhang et al., 2018): fully lexicalised seq2seq over subword units, attention memory	0.6545	8.1840	0.4392	**0.7083**	2.1012	0.5661
GONG (Gong, 2018): TGEN fine-tuned using reinforcement learning	0.6422	8.3453	0.4469	0.6645	**2.2721**	0.5631
TR1 (Schilder et al., 2018): seq2seq with stronger delexicalization (incl. *priceRange* and *customerRating*)	0.6336	8.1848	0.4322	0.6828	2.1425	0.5563
SHEFF1 (Chen et al., 2018): 2-level linear classifiers deciding on next slot/token, trained using LOLS, training data filtering	0.6015	8.3075	0.4405	0.6778	2.1775	0.5537
DANGNT (Nguyen and Tran, 2018): rule-based two-step approach, selecting phrases for each slot + lexicalising	0.5990	7.9277	0.4346	0.6634	2.0783	0.5395
SLUG-ALT (*late submission,* Juraska et al., 2018): SLUG trained only using complex sentences from the training data	0.6035	8.3954	0.4369	0.5991	2.1019	0.5378
ZHAW2 (Deriu and Cieliebak, 2018): semantically conditioned LSTM RNN language model (Wen et al., 2015b) + controlling the first generated word	0.6004	8.1394	0.4388	0.6119	1.9188	0.5314
TUDA (Puzikov and Gurevych, 2018): handcrafted templates	0.5657	7.4544	**0.4529**	0.6614	1.8206	0.5215
ZHAW1 (Deriu and Cieliebak, 2018): ZHAW2 with MR classification loss + reranking	0.5864	8.0212	0.4322	0.5998	1.8173	0.5205
ADAPT (Elder et al., 2018): seq2seq with preprocessing that enriches the MR with desired target words	0.5092	7.1954	0.4025	0.5872	1.5039	0.4738
CHEN (Chen, 2018): fully lexicalised seq2seq with copy mechanism and attention memory	0.5859	5.4383	0.3836	0.6714	1.5790	0.4685
FORGE3 (Mille and Dasiopoulou, 2018): templates mined from training data	0.4599	7.1092	0.3858	0.5611	1.5586	0.4547
SHEFF2 (Chen et al., 2018): vanilla seq2seq	0.5436	5.7462	0.3561	0.6152	1.4130	0.4462
TR2 (Schilder et al., 2018): templates mined from training data	0.4202	6.7686	0.3968	0.5481	1.4389	0.4372
FORGE1 (Mille and Dasiopoulou, 2018): grammar-based	0.4207	6.5139	0.3685	0.5437	1.3106	0.4231

Table 3: A list of primary systems in the E2E NLG challenge, with word-overlap metric scores.

System architectures are coded with colours and symbols: seq2seq, other data-driven, rule-based, template-based. Unless noted otherwise, all data-driven systems use partial delexicalisation (with *name* and *near* attributes replaced by placeholders during generation), template- and rule-based systems delexicalise all attributes. In addition to word-overlap metrics (see Section 4.1), we show the average of all metrics' values normalised into the 0-1 range, and use this to sort the list. Any values higher than the baseline are marked in bold.

3 Systems in the Competition

The interest in the E2E Challenge has by far exceeded our expectations. We received a total of 62 submitted systems by 17 institutions (about 1/3 from industry). In accordance with ethical considerations for NLP shared tasks (Parra Escartín et al., 2017), we allowed researchers to withdraw or anonymise their results if their system performs in the lower 50% of submissions. Two groups from industry withdrew their submissions and one group asked to be anonymised after obtaining automatic evaluation results.

We asked each of the remaining teams to identify 1-2 primary systems, which resulted in 20 systems by 14 groups. Each primary system is described in a short technical paper (available on the challenge website) and was evaluated both by automatic metrics and human judges (see Sec-

tion 4). We compare the primary systems to a baseline based on the TGEN generator (Dušek and Jurčíček, 2016a). An overview of all primary systems is given in Table 3, including the main features of their architectures. A more detailed description and comparison of systems will be given in (Dušek et al., 2018).

4 Evaluation Results

4.1 Word-overlap Metrics

Following previous shared tasks in related fields (Bojar et al., 2017b; Chen et al., 2015), we selected a range of metrics measuring word-overlap between system output and references, including BLEU, NIST, METEOR, ROUGE-L, and CIDEr. Table 3 summarises the primary system scores. The TGEN baseline is very strong in terms of word-overlap metrics: No primary system is able

Quality					Naturalness			
#	TrueSkill	Rank	System		#	TrueSkill	Rank	System
1	0.300	1–1	SLUG		1	0.211	1–1	SHEFF2
2	0.228	2–4	TUDA		2	0.171	2–3	SLUG
	0.213	2–5	GONG			0.154	2–4	CHEN
	0.184	3–5	DANGNT			0.126	3–6	HARV
	0.184	3–6	TGEN			0.105	4–8	NLE
	0.136	5–7	SLUG-ALT *(late)*			0.101	4–8	TGEN
	0.117	6–8	ZHAW2			0.091	5–8	DANGNT
	0.084	7–10	TNT1			0.077	5–10	TUDA
	0.065	8–10	TNT2			0.060	7–11	TNT2
	0.048	8–12	NLE			0.046	9–12	GONG
	0.018	10–13	ZHAW1			0.027	9–12	TNT1
	0.014	10–14	FORGE1			0.027	10–12	ZHANG
	-0.012	11–14	SHEFF1		3	-0.053	13–16	TR1
	-0.012	11–14	HARV			-0.073	13–17	SLUG-ALT *(late)*
3	-0.078	15–16	TR2			-0.077	13–17	SHEFF1
	-0.083	15–16	FORGE3			-0.083	13–17	ZHAW2
4	-0.152	17–19	ADAPT			-0.104	15–17	ZHAW1
	-0.185	17–19	TR1		4	-0.144	18–19	FORGE1
	-0.186	17–19	ZHANG			-0.164	18–19	ADAPT
5	-0.426	20–21	CHEN		5	-0.243	20–21	TR2
	-0.457	20–21	SHEFF2			-0.255	20–21	FORGE3

Table 4: TrueSkill measurements of *quality* (left) and *naturalness* (right).
Significance cluster number, TrueSkill value, range of ranks where the system falls in 95% of cases or more, system name. Significance clusters are separated by a dotted line. Systems are colour-coded by architecture as in Table 3.

to beat it in terms of all metrics – only SLUG comes very close. Several other systems beat TGEN in one of the metrics but not in others.[3] Overall, seq2seq-based systems show the best word-based metric values, followed by SHEFF1, a data-driven system based on imitation learning. Template-based and rule-based systems mostly score at the bottom of the list.

4.2 Results of Human Evaluation

However, the human evaluation study provides a different picture. Rank-based Magnitude Estimation (RankME) (Novikova et al., 2018) was used for evaluation, where crowd workers compared outputs of 5 systems for the same MR and assigned scores on a continuous scale. We evaluated output naturalness and overall quality in separate tasks; for naturalness evaluation, the source MR was not shown to workers. We collected 4,239 5-way rankings for naturalness and 2,979 for quality, comparing 9.5 systems per MR on average.

The final evaluation results were produced using the TrueSkill algorithm (Herbrich et al., 2006; Sakaguchi et al., 2014), with partial ordering into significance clusters computed using bootstrap resampling (Bojar et al., 2013, 2014; Sakaguchi et al., 2014). For both criteria, this resulted in 5

clusters of systems with significantly different performance and showed a clear winner: SHEFF2 for *naturalness* and SLUG for *quality*. The 2nd clusters are quite large for both criteria – they contain 13 and 11 systems, respectively, and both include the baseline TGEN system.

The results indicate that seq2seq systems dominate in terms of *naturalness* of their outputs, while most systems of other architectures score lower. The bottom cluster is filled with template-based systems. The results for *quality* are, however, more mixed in terms of architectures, with none of them clearly prevailing. Here, seq2seq systems with reranking based on checking output correctness score high while seq2seq systems with no such mechanism occupy the bottom two clusters.

5 Conclusion

This paper presents the first shared task on end-to-end NLG. The aim of this challenge was to assess the capabilities of recent end-to-end, fully data-driven NLG systems, which can be trained from pairs of input MRs and texts, without the need for fine-grained semantic alignments. We created a novel dataset for the challenge, which is an order-of-magnitude bigger than any previous publicly available dataset for task-oriented NLG. We received 62 system submissions by 17 participating institutions, with a wide range of architectures, from seq2seq-based models to simple templates.

---

[3]Note, however, that several secondary system submissions perform better than the primary ones (and the baseline) with respect to word-overlap metrics.

We evaluated all the entries in terms of five different automatic metrics; 20 primary submissions (as identified by the 14 remaining participants) underwent crowdsourced human evaluation of naturalness and overall quality of their outputs.

We consider the SLUG system (Juraska et al., 2018), a seq2seq-based ensemble system with a reranker, as the overall winner of the E2E NLG challenge. SLUG scores best in human evaluations of quality, it is placed in the 2nd-best cluster of systems in terms of naturalness and reaches high automatic scores. While the SHEFF2 system (Chen et al., 2018), a vanilla seq2seq setup, won in terms of naturalness, it scores poorly on overall quality – it placed in the last cluster. The TGEN baseline system turned out hard to beat: It ranked highest on average in word-overlap-based automatic metrics and placed in the 2nd cluster in both quality and naturalness.

The results in general show the seq2seq architecture as very capable, but requiring reranking to reach high-quality results. On the other hand, while rule-based approaches are not able to beat data-driven systems in terms of automatic metrics, they often perform comparably or better in human evaluations.

We are preparing a detailed analysis of the results (Dušek et al., 2018) and a release of all system outputs with user ratings on the challenge website.[4] We plan to use this data for experiments in automatic NLG output quality estimation (Specia et al., 2010; Dušek et al., 2017), where the large amount of data obtained in this challenge allows a wider range of experiments than previously possible.

Acknowledgements

This research received funding from the EPSRC projects DILiGENt (EP/M005429/1) and MaDrIgAL (EP/N017536/1). The Titan Xp used for this research was donated by the NVIDIA Corporation.

References

Shubham Agarwal, Marc Dymetman, and Éric Gaussier. 2018. Char2char generation with reranking for the E2E NLG Challenge. In *Proceedings of INLG*.

Anja Belz and Albert Gatt. 2007. The attribute selection for GRE challenge: Overview and evaluation results. In *Proceedings of MT Summit*, pages 75–83, Copenhagen, Denmark.

Ondřej Bojar, Rajen Chatterjee, Christian Federmann, Yvette Graham, Barry Haddow, Shujian Huang, Matthias Huck, Philipp Koehn, Qun Liu, Varvara Logacheva, et al. 2017a. Findings of the 2017 conference on machine translation (WMT17). In *Proceedings of WMT*, pages 169–214, Copenhagen, Denmark.

Ondřej Bojar, Christian Buck, Chris Callison-Burch, Christian Federmann, Barry Haddow, Philipp Koehn, Christof Monz, Matt Post, Radu Soricut, and Lucia Specia. 2013. Findings of WMT. In *Proceedings of WMT*, pages 1–44, Sofia, Bulgaria.

Ondřej Bojar, Christian Buck, Christian Federmann, Barry Haddow, Philipp Koehn, Johannes Leveling, Christof Monz, Pavel Pecina, Matt Post, Herve Saint-Amand, Radu Soricut, Lucia Specia, and Aleš Tamchyna. 2014. Findings of the 2014 Workshop on Statistical Machine Translation. In *Proceedings of WMT*, pages 12–58, Baltimore, Maryland, USA.

Ondřej Bojar, Yvette Graham, and Amir Kamran. 2017b. Results of the WMT17 Metrics Shared Task. In *Proceedings of WMT*, pages 489–513, Copenhagen, Denmark.

David L. Chen and Raymond J. Mooney. 2008. Learning to sportscast: A test of grounded language acquisition. In *Proceedings of ICML*, pages 128–135, Helsinki, Finland.

Mingje Chen, Gerasimos Lampouras, and Andreas Vlachos. 2018. Sheffield at E2E: structured prediction approaches to end-to-end language generation. In *E2E NLG Challenge System Descriptions*.

Shuang Chen. 2018. A General Model for Neural Text Generation from Structured Data. In *E2E NLG Challenge System Descriptions*.

Xinlei Chen, Hao Fang, Tsung-Yi Lin, Ramakrishna Vedantam, Saurabh Gupta, Piotr Dollar, and C. Lawrence Zitnick. 2015. Microsoft COCO Captions: Data Collection and Evaluation Server. *CoRR*, abs/1504.00325.

Jan Deriu and Mark Cieliebak. 2018. End-to-End Trainable System for Enhancing Diversity in Natural Language Generation. In *E2E NLG Challenge System Descriptions*.

Ondřej Dušek, Jekaterina Novikova, and Verena Rieser. 2018. The E2E NLG Challenge. In *(in prep.)*.

Ondřej Dušek and Filip Jurčíček. 2015. Training a natural language generator from unaligned data. In *Proceedings of ACL-IJCNLP*, pages 451–461, Beijing, China.

---

[4] `http://www.macs.hw.ac.uk/ InteractionLab/E2E`

Ondřej Dušek and Filip Jurčíček. 2016. A Context-aware Natural Language Generator for Dialogue Systems. In *Proceedings of SIGDIAL*, pages 185–190, Los Angeles, CA, USA.

Ondřej Dušek and Filip Jurčíček. 2016a. Sequence-to-sequence generation for spoken dialogue via deep syntax trees and strings. In *Proceedings of the 54th Annual Meeting of the Association for Computational Linguistics*, pages 45–51, Berlin, Germany. arXiv:1606.05491.

Ondřej Dušek, Jekaterina Novikova, and Verena Rieser. 2017. Referenceless Quality Estimation for Natural Language Generation. In *Proceedings of the 1st Workshop on Learning to Generate Natural Language (LGNL)*, Sydney, Australia. ArXiv: 1708.01759.

Henry Elder, Sebastian Gehrmann, Alexander O'Connor, and Qun Liu. 2018. E2E NLG Challenge Submission: Towards Controllable Generation of Diverse Natural Language. In *Proceedings of INLG*.

Claire Gardent, Anastasia Shimorina, Shashi Narayan, and Laura Perez-Beltrachini. 2017. The WebNLG Challenge: Generating text from RDF data. In *Proceedings of INLG*, pages 124–133, Santiago de Compostela, Spain.

Albert Gatt and Emiel Krahmer. 2018. Survey of the State of the Art in Natural Language Generation: Core tasks, applications and evaluation. *Journal of Artificial Intelligence Research (JAIR)*, 61:65–170.

Sebastian Gehrmann, Falcon Z. Dai, Henry Elder, and Alexander M. Rush. 2018. End-to-End Content and Plan Selection for Natural Language Generation. In *E2E NLG Challenge System Descriptions*.

Heng Gong. 2018. Technical Report for E2E NLG Challenge. In *E2E NLG Challenge System Descriptions*.

Ralf Herbrich, Tom Minka, and Thore Graepel. 2006. TrueSkill™: a Bayesian skill rating system. In *Proceedings of NIPS*, pages 569–576, Vancouver, Canada.

Juraj Juraska, Panagiotis Karagiannis, Kevin K. Bowden, and Marilyn A. Walker. 2018. A Deep Ensemble Model with Slot Alignment for Sequence-to-Sequence Natural Language Generation. In *Proceedings of NAACL-HLT*, New Orleans, LA, USA.

Gerasimos Lampouras and Andreas Vlachos. 2016. Imitation learning for language generation from unaligned data. In *Proceedings of COLING*, pages 1101–1112, Osaka, Japan.

François Mairesse, Milica Gašić, Filip Jurčíček, Simon Keizer, Blaise Thomson, Kai Yu, and Steve Young. 2010. Phrase-based statistical language generation using graphical models and active learning. In *Proceedings of ACL*, pages 1552–1561, Uppsala, Sweden.

Hongyuan Mei, Mohit Bansal, and Matthew R. Walter. 2016. What to talk about and how? Selective generation using LSTMs with coarse-to-fine alignment. In *Proceedings of NAACL-HLT*, San Diego, CA, USA.

Simon Mille and Stamatia Dasiopoulou. 2018. FORGe at E2E 2017. In *E2E NLG Challenge System Descriptions*.

Dang Tuan Nguyen and Trung Tran. 2018. Structure-based Generation System for E2E NLG Challenge. In *E2E NLG Challenge System Descriptions*.

Jekaterina Novikova, Ondřej Dušek, Amanda Cercas Curry, and Verena Rieser. 2017a. Why we need new evaluation metrics for NLG. In *Proceedings of EMNLP*, pages 2231–2242.

Jekaterina Novikova, Ondrej Dušek, and Verena Rieser. 2017b. The E2E Dataset: New Challenges for End-to-End Generation. In *Proceedings of SIGDIAL*, pages 201–206, Saarbrücken, Germany.

Jekaterina Novikova, Ondřej Dušek, and Verena Rieser. 2018. RankME: Reliable Human Ratings for Natural Language Generation. In *Proceedings of NAACL-HLT*, pages 72–78, New Orleans, LA, USA.

Jekaterina Novikova, Oliver Lemon, and Verena Rieser. 2016. Crowd-sourcing NLG data: Pictures elicit better data. In *Proceedings of INLG*, pages 265–273, Edinburgh, UK. arXiv:1608.00339.

Shereen Oraby, Lena Reed, Shubhangi Tandon, Sharath T.S., Stephanie Lukin, and Marilyn Walker. 2018. TNT-NLG, System 1: Using a statistical NLG to massively augment crowd-sourced data for neural generation. In *E2E NLG Challenge System Descriptions*.

Carla Parra Escartín, Wessel Reijers, Teresa Lynn, Joss Moorkens, Andy Way, and Chao-Hong Liu. 2017. Ethical considerations in NLP shared tasks. In *Proceedings of the First ACL Workshop on Ethics in Natural Language Processing*, pages 66–73.

Yevgeniy Puzikov and Iryna Gurevych. 2018. E2E NLG Challenge: Neural Models vs. Templates. In *Proceedings of INLG*.

E. Reiter and R. Dale. 2000. *Building Natural Language Generation Systems*, studies in natural language processing edition. Cambridge University Press.

Keisuke Sakaguchi, Matt Post, and Benjamin Van Durme. 2014. Efficient elicitation of annotations for human evaluation of machine translation. In *Proceedings of WMT*, pages 1–11, Baltimore, MD, USA.

Frank Schilder, Charese Smiley, Elnaz Davoodi, and Dezhao Song. 2018. The E2E NLG Challenge: A tale of two systems. In *Proceedings of INLG*.

Shikhar Sharma, Jing He, Kaheer Suleman, Hannes Schulz, and Philip Bachman. 2016. Natural language generation in dialogue using lexicalized and delexicalized data. *CoRR*, abs/1606.03632.

Lucia Specia, Dhwaj Raj, and Marco Turchi. 2010. Machine translation evaluation versus quality estimation. *Machine translation*, 24(1):39–50.

Shubhangi Tandon, Sharath T.S., Shereen Oraby, Lena Reed, Stephanie Lukin, and Marilyn Walker. 2018. TNT-NLG, System 2: Data repetition and meaning representation manipulation to improve neural generation. In *E2E NLG Challenge System Descriptions*.

Tsung-Hsien Wen, Milica Gasić, Dongho Kim, Nikola Mrkšić, Pei-Hao Su, David Vandyke, and Steve Young. 2015a. Stochastic language generation in dialogue using recurrent neural networks with convolutional sentence reranking. In *Proceedings of SIGDIAL*, pages 275–284, Prague, Czech Republic.

Tsung-Hsien Wen, Milica Gašić, Nikola Mrkšić, Lina Maria Rojas-Barahona, Pei-hao Su, David Vandyke, and Steve J. Young. 2016. Multi-domain neural network language generation for spoken dialogue systems. In *Proceedings of NAACL-HLT*, pages 120–129, San Diego, CA, USA.

Tsung-Hsien Wen, Milica Gašić, Nikola Mrkšić, Pei-Hao Su, David Vandyke, and Steve Young. 2015b. Semantically conditioned LSTM-based natural language generation for spoken dialogue systems. In *Proceedings of EMNLP*, pages 1711–1721, Lisbon, Portugal.

Sam Wiseman, Stuart M. Shieber, and Alexander M. Rush. 2017. Challenges in data-to-document generation. In *Proceedings of EMNLP*, pages 2253–2263, Copenhagen, Denmark.

Biao Zhang, Jing Yang, Qian Lin, and Jinsong Su. 2018. Attention Regularized Sequence-to-Sequence Learning for E2E NLG Challenge. In *E2E NLG Challenge System Descriptions*.

Adapting Descriptions of People
to the Point of View of a Moving Observer

Gonzalo Méndez and **Raquel Hervás** and **Pablo Gervás**
Ricardo de la Rosa and **Daniel Ruiz**
Facultad de Informática - Instituto de Tecnología del Conocimiento
Universidad Complutense de Madrid (Spain)
{gmendez,raquelhb,pgervas}@fdi.ucm.es, {ricarosa,danruiz}@ucm.es

Abstract

This paper addresses the task of generating descriptions of people for an observer that is moving within a scene. As the observer moves, the descriptions of the people around him also change. A referring expression generation algorithm adapted to this task needs to continuously monitor the changes in the field of view of the observer, his relative position to the people being described, and the relative position of these people to any landmarks around them, and to take these changes into account in the referring expressions generated. This task presents two advantages: many of the mechanisms already available for static contexts may be applied with small adaptations, and it introduces the concept of changing conditions into the task of referring expression generation. In this paper we describe the design of an algorithm that takes these aspects into account in order to create descriptions of people within a 3D virtual environment. The evaluation of this algorithm has shown that, by changing the descriptions in real time according to the observers point of view, they are able to identify the described person quickly and effectively.

1 Introduction

The task of Referring Expression Generation (REG) has traditionally been considered in static contexts, where neither the properties of the objects being described nor their relation to the observer change over time. This is a good starting point to address the problem because it includes the elements that are involved in more complex situations. The case where the observer is moving along a static context is a slight departure from the basic static case, with two significant advantages: many of the mechanisms available for static contexts may be applied with small adaptations, and it introduces the concept of changing conditions into the task of referring expression generation. For this reason, it is a worthwhile problem to explore.

A challenge when trying to address this problem is the need to continuously gather data on the relevant conditions – the field of view of the observer, his relative position to the people being described, and the relative position of these people to any landmarks around them in terms of how they appear in the field of view of the observer.

Gathering these data in a real life context may be very difficult, but if the situation is modeled in a 3D environment that represents the chosen scene, with a camera following the observer in first person mode, the compilation of all these data becomes a feasible task, and the generation of descriptions in real time becomes possible.

We have studied different proposals to solve similar problems and have developed a meta-algorithm based on the work depicted in (Méndez et al., 2017), where the authors studied the behavior of classic REG algorithms applied to this problem (section 3). Then, we have built a 3D scene and have populated it with people in order to test this meta-algorithm when the observer can move around the scene (section 4). The results of this evaluation have shown that the descriptions can be improved in order for the observers to find the target person more easily, so we have extended the previous algorithm to include additional information to the descriptions (section 5). We have subsequently evaluated the new algorithm using the same scenes (section 6) and the results show that the observers are able to find the target person faster and with a much higher hit rate than before.

Proceedings of The 11th International Natural Language Generation Conference, pages 329–338,
Tilburg, The Netherlands, November 5-8, 2018. ©2018 Association for Computational Linguistics

2   Related Work

A Referring Expression (RE) is a description created with the intention of distinguishing a certain element (i.e. *referent*) from a number of other elements (i.e. *distractors*). It must identify the referent unambiguously, effectively ruling out all the distractors. Therefore, any expression that meets these criteria can be called a referring expression. However, not all of them can be considered equally good: they may be too long or too short, they may not contain enough information or they may have too many unhelpful details that hinder the listener.

The field of Referring Expression Generation (REG) has been widely explored for several decades (see (Krahmer and van Deemter, 2012) for an extensive survey), and there have been many studies for generating appropriate REs in different contexts. However, most of these solutions have approached the problem considering static contexts where neither the objects being described nor the point of view of the observer change over time.

In (Méndez et al., 2017) the authors assume that people and objects are described in different ways, since attributes such as size, shape or color, used to describe objects, are not so suitable for describing people. In order to identify what features are relevant for individuals when they have to describe other people, they conducted a number of surveys with human evaluators. These studies provided two important insights. The first one was that distance (from the viewer and to landmarks) influences the identification of referents, and REs that include information about nearby objects or people appeared to be easier to understand. The second insight obtained from the study was a list of preferred attributes when describing people in crowded environments. Based on these results, they proposed as future work the creation of a meta-algorithm that, depending on the particular circumstances pertaining to a given scene, selected a particular referring expression generation algorithm out of a set of the classic solutions studied.

Additionally, in recent years, computational approaches to REG have increasingly explored the task of adapting to dynamic contexts. The generation of appropriate referring expressions in the context of interactive dialogues is one of the problems that has received a lot of attention. Stoia et al. (2006) presented a REG system in dialogues that takes into account the current field of view of the speakers, how distant they are from the target, and the dialogue history. Similarly, Fang et al. (2014) describe two approaches to REG in situated dialog with artificial agents, both of which generate multiple small expressions that lead to the target object with the goal of minimizing the collaborative effort between the human and the agent. Janarthanam and Lemon (2009) explored a method for automatically adapting referring expressions to the lexical knowledge of users. Gatt et al. (2011) proposed a new model for interactive REG which incorporated both property preferences and priming effects and obtained good results in comparison with human experimental data. Garoufi and Koller (2014) presented a model of effective reference generation in situational contexts which distinguishes speaker helpfulness in a certain situation with the aim of modelling helpful speaker behaviour. Baltaretu et al. (2017) describe an approach that discusses the use of moving landmarks to generate route directions and how the listeners evaluate these instructions. The results show that listeners understand these instructions without much effort, but speakers tend to use stable landmarks more often. Unlike these approaches, which take advantage of situational dialogue and interaction with the user, the work described in this paper does not assume that the interaction with the user is possible or desirable, that is, we cope with the dynamics of the environment and try to provide the users with the best possible description, rather than requiring their collaboration to generate it.

Considering the physical context when generating REs, there are some works which have explored the REG problem in the context of 3D environments. The GIVE challenges (Byron et al., 2009; Koller et al., 2010; Striegnitz et al., 2011) focused on the generation of instructions in a virtual 3D environment to help a user solve a treasure-hunt task. One interesting aspect of using a virtual environment was that spatial and relational expressions played a bigger role than in other NLG tasks, and the necessary information to create the descriptions was already present in the environment. Garoufi et al. (2015) present an interesting work which has used the GIVE environment to study how a generation system that uses listener gaze to provide rapid feedback improves the generation of REs in comparison with two systems that do not consider the listener's gaze.

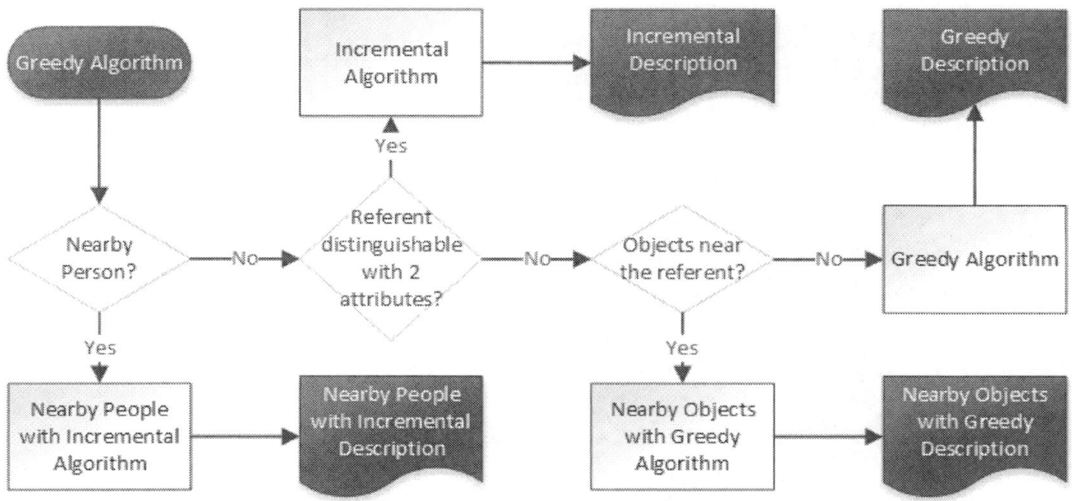

Figure 1: Design of the meta-algorithm

3 Design of a Meta-Algorithm for Character Descriptions

Based on the results and conclusions described in (Méndez et al., 2017), we decided to design and implement a meta-algorithm that, based on classic REG solutions, could dynamically decide which of them was more suitable to describe a given situation.

The classic algorithms considered were: *Incremental* (Reiter and Dale, 1992; Dale and Reiter, 1995), *Greedy* (Dale, 1989, 1992), *Nearby People with Incremental* – extend the description with relation to the nearest person, using the Incremental algorithm to describe that person –, and *Nearby Objects with Greedy* – extend the description with relation to nearest object, using the Greedy algorithm to describe the referent.

Taking into account the results obtained in the empirical evaluation of these algorithms in (Méndez et al., 2017), the meta-algorithm works as follows (see Figure 1 for a graphical description of the process).

First, the meta-algorithm tries to create a Nearby People with Incremental description. In order to do that, the meta-algorithm uses the Greedy algorithm to determine if there is a nearby person that is very easily identifiable (can be described by using only two attributes). If there is, the meta-algorithm returns the Incremental description of the referent plus the Greedy description of the nearby person.

If there is no other character near the target that is sufficiently distinguishable, the meta-algorithm goes on to find out if the referent stands out in the scene (can be referred to by using exactly two attributes). If this is the case, the meta-algorithm generates an Incremental description for the referent.

If the referent does not stand out, the meta-algorithm then tries to use the Nearby Objects with Greedy Algorithm. We use the Greedy Algorithm here only to describe the referent. Because of the low number and variation of objects in the scenes, we have considered the name of the object to be descriptive enough.

If there are no distinguishable objects near the referent, the meta-algorithm finishes by generating the description of the referent using the Greedy Algorithm.

The evaluation of this meta-algorithm with 38 users (15 women and 23 men) and 9 different scenes showed a total hit rate of 95% (324 correct answers out of 342). Even though in the evaluations used to design the meta-algorithm the users had shown a slight preference for the descriptions generated by the Nearby People with Incremental Algorithm, in this last evaluation the results were a little better when the descriptions were generated by the Nearby Objects with Greedy Algorithm, since all the users found the right target when this algorithm was used. In addition, after the evaluation some of the users reported that some of the mistakes they had made had to do with the difficulty to remember long descriptions.

Algorithm	Description	Hits	Scene
Greedy	The girl in the blue shirt standing, leaning on a table	96%	10
Nearby Objects	The boy in the red rolled up sleeves shirt near the window	89%	7
Nearby People	The girl in the blue sweater with black hair. She is near, next to the girl in the yellow tank top	89%	3
Nearby People	The girl in the green tank top who is standing up. She is near, next to the girl standing pointing at something	85%	6
Nearby Objects	The boy in the black shirt sitting near the window	85%	1
Nearby Objects	The boy in the blue t-shirt with black hair sitting near the window	67%	2
Greedy	The girl in the red shirt with redhead hair	63%	5
Nearby Objects	The boy in the green shirt with redhead hair sitting near the column	48%	9
Incremental	The boy in the red t-shirt with spike blond hair who is sitting down. He is far	48%	4
Incremental	The boy in the blue rolled up sleeves shirt with spike redhead hair. He is near	44%	8

Table 1: Results of the meta-algorithm evaluation

4 Perspective-Based Evaluation of the Meta-Algorithm

One of the difficulties when generating descriptions in changing environments is to decide when and how to change the referring expression we use to describe an element's situation, even more if we take into account that not everybody refers to an element in the same manner. In order to generate this kind of descriptions, the first step we took was to test the behavior of the meta-algorithm described in section 3 in dynamic conditions, in order to check the suitability of the generated descriptions as the user's viewpoint changed.

A survey was carried out in order to study how the changes in the user's point of view affected the perceived accuracy of the descriptions generated by algorithms thought to work in static conditions. The survey was completed by 27 people (45% of women and 55% of men), with ages from 20 to 45 years old. The users were shown ten scenes in a 3D virtual environment, together with the description of the target character they had to identify in each of them, generated by the meta-algorithm.

The description was presented to the users as a written message on the top part of the screen, and it was kept there until the users clicked on what they considered to be the target character. They were not told whether they could see the target character or not, and they could move around the environment in order to find the described person.

The users had to click on it once they thought they had found it, but the provided description did not change as they moved.

All the scenes were reproductions of pictures taken in our canteen (so they all represent real situations), and all of them included more than 30 characters, both male and female, most of them between 18 and 25 years old, with varied characteristics, and typical actions included people speaking, drinking or working together, either standing up or sitting down. The scenes and characters were selected so that they put to test some difficult situations, such as characters that were initially out of sight, other characters that might get out of sight as the users moved around the scene, or some others that were difficult to see from a long distance and that looked similar to other characters close to them.

Table 1 shows the description generated for each scene of the evaluation, along with the algorithm selected by the meta-algorithm to generate it and the percentage of users that found the described character. Most correct clicks were achieved when the descriptions were generated by the nearby objects or people algorithms to describe the target; some of these descriptions made reference to the posture of the target to describe it.

In contrast, the incremental algorithm has got low hit rates in the two scenes where it was selected by the meta-algorithm to generate the descriptions. The reason behind it is that this algorithm is selected when there are no salient objects or characters than can be used by other algorithms, and the incremental algorithm does not provide enough discriminating power when there are too many characters that look like the target one. This, in turn, has more to do with the difficulty to describe the characters in these scenes than with the algorithm itself, as it has been selected by the meta-algorithm precisely because it works better than the rest in these situations.

An advantage of the incremental algorithm is the inclusion of the distance between the user position and the target character as a descriptor. However, as the user moves around the scene, the meta-algorithm fails in updating this reference, thus making the description invalid. This points to the need of changing the description as the user moves, to keep it aligned with the user perspective of the scene, which will be included in the algorithm described in the next section.

Many users got some scenes wrong when they had to find easy to identify persons, because there was a character that looked like them in the users' field of view at the start. A way to fix this is to specify in the description if the target is in the user's field of view or not, and if it is near or far. Regarding the distance, the users were sometimes confused by the indication of the target being far, when they considered that it was not that far. Thus, a finer distinction of the distance to the target may also improve the quality of the descriptions.

5 Implementation of a Perspective-Based Algorithm to Describe People

With the results of the previous survey, and using the graphical engine Unity 3D, an extension to the meta-algorithm described in section 3 has been developed to generate descriptions of characters in real time that change according to the user's position within the environment.

The developed algorithm was implemented in a game where the user had to find the character that was being described, for which he could move around the environment and the provided description changed accordingly. The content of the description is based on the character's physical appearance, which does not change, its position within the environment, and its situation with respect to other relevant characters and objects that are present in the environment. Therefore, a complete description consists in the composition of two different parts:

- *attribute-based description*, which refers to the static characteristics of an individual and its environment, and they cannot change during the simulation. This part of the description is generated using the meta-algorithm;

- *perspective-based description*, which has to be generated in real time according to the situation of the user relative to the situation of the described character.

The perspective-based description of a character is composed of sub-descriptions, which are generated according to the data that is obtained from the scene. There are three possible types of sub-descriptions:

- *description of reference points*: this description contains information related to the reference points scattered all over the scene, such as the end of a corridor or a corner;

- *description of the visibility*: it contains the information about the visibility of the target from the user's point of view, such as the fact that the described person is behind a column or another person, or even behind the user;

- *distance between the described person and the user*: it contains a textual explanation of the distance between the described person and the user: near, a little far (i.e. medium distance) and far. This is a source of mismatch with the meta-algorithm, as it only considered that targets might be either near or far.

These sub-descriptions are generated and updated in real time, and they are shown to the users as soon as the conditions used to generate the current description change (e.g. the described character starts being visible, or the user gets close to the target character), according to the following rules:

1. First the algorithm checks the distance between the user and the reference points previously placed into the scene. If the distance from the user to one of these points is greater than a predefined constant (that depends on the dimensions of the scene), the generated description is updated with information about the proximity of the described character to

(a) Zoom of the initial situation of scene 3. The target person is a girl that is not near the observer, hidden behind a column. The provided initial description is *The girl in the blue sweater with black hair, next to the girl in the yellow tank top. The described person is behind a column. She is not far*

(b) Final situation of scene 3. The observer has moved closer to the target person and is looking at her from the other side. The provided description is *The girl in the blue sweater with black hair, next to the girl in the yellow tank top. She is near. You can see the described person*

Figure 2: Sample scene used in the evaluation. A red circle has been drawn around the described person

that point (e.g. *the described person is at the end of the corridor*, if the user is far from the end of the corridor).

2. Then, the algorithm checks if the target character is in the user's point of view (i.e. approximately in front of the user). If not, the generated description must contain the positional references of the described person to the user: it indicates whether the described person is to the left, right or behind the user.

3. If the described person is within the user's field of view, the algorithm checks the absolute distance between the target and the user and indicates the user whether he is near, not far or far from the described person.

Finally, the description that is shown to the user has to be composed. First, if the description provided by the meta-algorithm contains information about the distance from the user to the target character, it is removed, as the new algorithm may treat this information differently. Then, by combining sub-descriptions, and using the previous rules, the perspective-based descriptions are generated (e.g. *The boy in the black shirt sitting near the window. The described person is behind another person. He is not far*).

6 Evaluation of the Perspective-Based Algorithm

A second evaluation was carried out six months after the first one, using the same conditions and instructions as in the first one. The main objective of this evaluation was to test the improvements added to the meta-algorithm by comparing the obtained results with those of the first survey. Therefore, the people that had to be found by the observer, and the scenes used for it, were the same as in the previous one. This way, a reliable comparison could be made between both versions of the meta-algorithm in order to test their effectiveness. A sample scene used for this evaluation can be seen in Figure 2. The number of people that completed the survey was twenty seven, the same as in the first survey. 85% of them were between 20 and 30 years old, and the remaining 15% were between 30 and 40. 63% of the participants were male, and the remaining 37% were female. Five of the evaluators had also completed the first survey, but after six months they assured they did not notice the scenes and characters were the same as in the first one.

Table 2 shows the results obtained in this evaluation. The column corresponding to the description only shows the initial descriptions of the tar-

Algorithm	Initial Description	Hits	Scene
Greedy	The girl in the blue shirt standing, leaning on a table. You can see the described person. She is a little far	96%	10
Nearby Objects	The boy in the red rolled up sleeves shirt near the window. The described person is far from you	92%	7
Nearby People	The girl in the blue sweater with black hair, next to the the girl in the yellow tank top. The described person is behind a column. She is a little far	92%	3
Nearby People	The girl in the green tank top who is standing up. The described person is a little far from you	92%	6
Nearby Objects	The boy in the black shirt sitting near the window. The described person is behind another person. He is a little far.	89%	1
Nearby Objects	The boy in the blue t-shirt with black hair sitting near the window. The described person is far from you	89%	2
Nearby Objects	The boy in the red t-shirt near the column. He is at the back of the canteen	89%	4
Nearby Objects	The boy in the green shirt sitting near the column. The described person is far from you	85%	9
Incremental	The boy in the blue rolled up sleeves shirt with spike redhead hair. The described person is a little far from you	85%	8
Greedy	The girl in the red shirt with redhead hair. The described person is far from you	78%	5

Table 2: Results of the perspective-based meta-algorithm evaluation

get characters, so that they can be compared with the ones in Table 1. An example of the initial and final descriptions for scene 3 in shown in Figure 2.

All the scenes have obtained an increased hit rate, except for the first one, which scores the same as in the first evaluation (96%). The first five scenes in the first evaluation still occupy the same positions in the second one, but with higher hit rates, as we have mentioned. So does the sixth one, but with a much higher hit rate than before. The last four ones have also experienced improvements in their hit rates, with slight variations in their relative positions.

Some remarkable differences can be found between the descriptions in Tables 1 and 2. In scenes 6 and 8, the target is not described as being *near* any more, but *a little far*. This is due to the finer distinction that the new algorithm makes for describing distances. In addition, in scene 4, the algorithm used to generate the description is different in both evaluation. This is caused by the inclusion of a landmark in the scene (i.e. *the back of the canteen*) which causes the meta-algorithm to change the algorithm selected to generate the description.

On average, the new perspective-based meta-algorithm has a hit rate of 88% (240/270). Comparing it to the previous algorithm that got 71% (194/270), we can see an improvement in the algorithm's capabilities to adapt the descriptions to different points of view.

A lot of factors have influenced the overall improvement in the results. For example, the participants of the second survey who had also completed the first survey provided us with some feedback about the improvements they had perceived. One of their comments was that they felt more confident looking for the target character if they knew at the beginning where to start looking for it. This confirms that having the algorithm detail the distance of the observer to the target character and specifying if he/she was in the field of view of the observer has provided better indications for the users to find the described person.

The change of the description in real time has helped the observers in a more realistic way, mimicking how a real person would be providing the description. Again, the users' feedback shows that they get lost less frequently when the algorithm offers them clues about where the target person is.

In both evaluations, we measured the time it took the users to click on the person they though

Scene	First Eval	Second Eval
10	0.82	0.90
7	2.99	4.30
3	3.01	3.50
6	2.12	4.40
1	3.79	5.00
2	4.88	5.30
4	3.50	2.90
9	1.66	0.48
8	0.70	0.30
5	7.40	4.70

Table 3: Average response times (in seconds) for each scene

that was being described. Table 3 shows the average response times for each scene, sorted descendingly according to the hit rates obtained in the second evaluation. At first sight, it seems that the results obtained with the new version of the algorithm are slightly worse than those of the first version. However, a careful analysis of the collected data has shown that this is due to the increased hit rate of the second evaluation. In the first evaluation, the users who clicked on the wrong target answered much faster than the ones who tried to find the right one. Comparing the ones who took the right choice, the average response times are slightly better using the second version of the algorithm, although the difference is not significant and may be even due to the users ability to play in first person games.

Even though this evaluation is not statistically significant, provided that there were only 10 scenes and 27 evaluators, the improvement obtained using the perspective-based algorithm was quite consistent across all the scenes, so we can conclude that adding information regarding the location and visibility of the target character, along with updates in the descriptions when the user's point of view changes, allow the users to better find the person that is being described, very much in line with some the previous work described in section 2.

7   Discussion

The current work has focused on describing people in dynamic contexts in which the observer can move around the environment, while the rest of the people are static.

The first question that arises is whether the described approach only works for people or if it is possible to generalize it to describe other entities. As far as we can tell, the way in which people are described differs from the way in which other entities are. Previous results presented earlier in this paper suggest that, when describing people, the attributes and order in which they are used differ from those used to describe objects. The algorithms we have used to describe people are not specifically tailored for the situations and environments in which the experiments have been run, so it is certainly possible to adapt them to describe other entities. It is not the case, however, of the meta-algorithm and the perspective-based meta-algorithm, as their design is based on experimental results drawn exclusively from descriptions of people, so further study is required in order to figure out how the adaptation to describe objects or other entities might be carried out.

The second question that arises is whether the proposed approach should have been used to describe objects instead of people, as the environment is static, or whether we should have been immersed in a more realistic, dynamic environment where the rest of the characters could also move. The answer to the first part of the question is that our main interest was in describing people, as much less research work seems to have been carried out in this area. This links with the second part of the question, for which the answer is that describing characters that can move around the environment is a much more complicated problem, since they can change their position, posture, the way they dress or, more important for some of the algorithms we have used, they can become or stop being a reference element in the description (e.g. *Nearby People with Incremental*), which introduces a high degree of complexity in the descriptions and requires the algorithms to monitor many more variables when deciding which elements to include in the descriptions. This work provides a first approach to deal with more dynamic environments where not only the observer's point of view is to be considered, but also other elements that move around the environment.

There are other limitations to the current approach, such as the lack of references to groups of people (or even objects) doing something (e.g. *the boy in the red t-shirt sitting near the girls playing Scrabble*), which becomes even more complicated in dynamic contexts where groups may form and break, and which also leads us to evaluate under what conditions should we consider that some people are forming a group or not.

Some of the limitations of the proposed algorithm have not been studied yet, such as the results it would produce in environments where there is little variation in the aspect of the characters being described (e.g. all the characters are wearing a uniform). Another limitation is the fact that we have tested the algorithm in scenes where the number of relevant objects that may be included in the description is small, so just using the name of the objects in the descriptions was enough, but additional decisions on how to use object descriptions may be necessary if this situation changes.

8 Conclusions and Future Work

Throughout this work we have seen that the problem we have addressed – describing people when the observers can change their point of view – poses challenging issues that have been satisfactorily solved, although there is still space for improvement. He have shown that, by using the techniques that have been used traditionally to describe static situations, we can generate acceptable descriptions when we shift to more dynamic environments, closer to real life situations, in which the observer can move to get a better perspective of the person being described. In contrast with the works described in section 2, which assume that the users can interact and collaborate to let the system generate small bits of the description that takes them progressively closer to the target, we do not take that for granted, so we always provide users with a full description of the target from the current point of view, which is updated as the users move across the scene.

In addition, we have put forward that, if we take into account certain aspects that change as the observer moves, the descriptions we generate can be more accurate and can help the observer identify the target person more easily. The aspects we have taken into account in this work have been: the distance between the observer and the target subject; the visibility that the observer has of the described person; and the relative position among the observer, the referent and significant landmarks that can help locate the objective more easily.

The proposed solution to generate descriptions is based on the use of crisp values to determine thresholds in order to generate linguistic labels to refer, for example, to distances. However, this specific aspect can benefit from the use of fuzzy logic to generate descriptions of spatial relationships. Although we have not been able to find an approach of this kind in the reviewed literature, there have been some efforts to solve similar problems in the fields of image analysis and computer vision, as described by Bloch and Ralescu (2003), who have subsequently developed several methods to describe spatial relations between objects (Hudelot et al., 2008). Other authors have tackled the problem of automatic scene descriptions in image analysis using fuzzy rule-based systems (Keller and Wang, 2000) and fuzzy sets (Matsakis et al., 2001), through the use of histograms of angles and forces and a dictionary of labels.

In addition, the generation of descriptions in more realistic environments, where the elements of the scene can move and change, is another problem that still needs to be tackled and that poses even more challenging issues to solve.

Acknowledgements

The work presented in this paper has been partially funded by the projects IDiLyCo: Digital Inclusion, Language and Communication, Grant. No. TIN2015-66655-R (MINECO/FEDER) and InVITAR-IA: Infraestructuras para la Visibilización, Integración y Transferencia de Aplicaciones y Resultados de Inteligencia Artificial, UCM Grant. No. FEI-EU-17-23.

References

Adriana Baltaretu, Emiel Krahmer, and Alfons Maes. 2017. Landmarks on the move: Producing and understanding references to moving landmarks. *Spatial Cognition & Computation*, 17(3):199–221.

I. Bloch and A. Ralescu. 2003. Directional relative position between objects in image processing: a comparison between fuzzy approaches. *Pattern Recognition*, 36(7):1563–1582.

Donna Byron, Alexander Koller, Kristina Striegnitz, Justine Cassell, Robert Dale, Johanna Moore, and Jon Oberlander. 2009. Report on the First NLG Challenge on Generating Instructions in Virtual Environments (GIVE). In *Proceedings of the 12th European Workshop on Natural Language Generation (Special session on Generation Challenges)*.

Robert Dale. 1989. Cooking up referring expressions. In *Proc. of the 27th Annual Meeting of the Association for Computational Linguistics*, pages 68–75, University of British Columbia,Canada.

Robert Dale. 1992. *Generating Referring Expressions: Constructing Descriptions in a Domain of Objects and Processes*. MIT Press, Cambridge, MA, USA.

Robert Dale and Ehud Reiter. 1995. Computational interpretations of the gricean maxims in the generation of referring expressions. *Cognitive Science*, 19(2):233–263.

Rui Fang, Malcolm Doering, and Joyce Y. Chai. 2014. Collaborative models for referring expression generation in situated dialogue. In *Proceedings of the Twenty-Eighth AAAI Conference on Artificial Intelligence*, AAAI'14, pages 1544–1550. AAAI Press.

Konstantina Garoufi and Alexander Koller. 2014. Generation of effective referring expressions in situated context. *Language, Cognition and Neuroscience*, 29(8):986–1001.

Konstantina Garoufi, Maria Staudte, Alexander Koller, and Matthew Crocker. 2015. Exploiting listener gaze to improve situated communication in dynamic virtual environments. *Cognitive Science*.

Albert Gatt, Martijn Goudbeek, and Emiel Krahmer. 2011. Attribute preference and priming in reference production: Experimental evidence and computational modeling. In *Proc. of the 33rd Annual Meeting of the Cognitive Science Society (CogSci'11)*, Austin, TX. Cognitive Science Society.

C. Hudelot, J. Atif, and I. Bloch. 2008. Fuzzy spatial relation ontology for image interpretation. *Fuzzy Sets and Systems*, 159(15):1929–1951.

Srinivasan Janarthanam and Oliver Lemon. 2009. Learning lexical alignment policies for generating referring expressions in spoken dialogue systems. In *Proceedings of the 12th European Workshop on Natural Language Generation*, ENLG '09, pages 74–81, Stroudsburg, PA, USA. Association for Computational Linguistics.

J. M. Keller and X. Wang. 2000. A fuzzy rule-based approach to scene description involving spatial relationships. *Comp. Vision and Image Understanding*, 80(1):21–41.

Alexander Koller, Kristina Striegnitz, Andrew Gargett, Donna Byron, Justine Cassell, Robert Dale, Johanna Moore, and Jon Oberlander. 2010. Report on the Second NLG Challenge on Generating Instructions in Virtual Environments (GIVE-2). In *Proceedings of the Sixth International Natural Language Generation Conference (Special session on Generation Challenges)*, Dublin.

Emiel Krahmer and Kees van Deemter. 2012. Computational generation of referring expressions: A survey. *Computational Linguistics*, 38(1):173–218.

P. Matsakis, J.M. Keller, L. Wendling, J. Marjamaa, and O. Sjahputera. 2001. Linguistic description of relative positions in images. *IEEE Transactions on Systems, Man and Cybernetics*, 31(4):573–88.

Gonzalo Méndez, Raquel Hervás, Susana Bautista, Adrián Rabadán, and Teresa Rodríguez-Ferreira. 2017. Exploring the behavior of classic reg algorithms in the description of characters in 3d images. In *International Natural Language Generation Conference (INLG2017)*, Santiago de Compostela, Spain.

Ehud Reiter and Robert Dale. 1992. A fast algorithm for the generation of referring expressions. In *Proceedings of the 14th International Conference on Computational Linguistics*, pages 232–238, Nantes, France.

Laura Stoia, Darla Magdalene Shockley, Donna K. Byron, and Eric Fosler-Lussier. 2006. Noun phrase generation for situated dialogs. In *Proceedings of the Fourth International Natural Language Generation Conference*, pages 81–88, Stroudsburg, PA, USA. Association for Computational Linguistics.

Kristina Striegnitz, Alexandre Denis, Andrew Gargett, Konstantina Garoufi, Alexander Koller, and Mariet Theune. 2011. Report on the Second Second Challenge on Generating Instructions in Virtual Environments (GIVE-2.5). In *Proceedings of the 13th European Workshop on Natural Language Generation (Special session on Generation Challenges)*, Nancy.

BENGAL: An Automatic Benchmark Generator for Entity Recognition and Linking

Axel-Cyrille Ngoma Ngomo[1,2]   Michael Röder[1]   Diego Moussallem[1,2]   Ricardo Usbeck[1]   René Speck[1,2]
[1]Data Science Group, University of Paderborn, Germany
[2]AKSW Research Group, University of Leipzig, Germany
`{first.lastname}@upb.de`
`lastname@informatik.uni-leipzig.de`

Abstract

The manual creation of gold standards for named entity recognition and entity linking is time- and resource-intensive. Moreover, recent works show that such gold standards contain a large proportion of mistakes in addition to being difficult to maintain. We hence present BENGAL, a novel automatic generation of such gold standards as a complement to manually created benchmarks. The main advantage of our benchmarks is that they can be readily generated at any time. They are also cost-effective while being guaranteed to be free of annotation errors. We compare the performance of 11 tools on benchmarks in English generated by BENGAL and on 16 benchmarks created manually. We show that our approach can be ported easily across languages by presenting results achieved by 4 tools on both Brazilian Portuguese and Spanish. Overall, our results suggest that our automatic benchmark generation approach can create varied benchmarks that have characteristics similar to those of existing benchmarks. Our approach is open-source. Our experimental results are available at `http://faturl.com/bengalexpinlg` and the code at `https://github.com/dice-group/BENGAL`.

1 Introduction

The creating of gold standard is of central importance for the objective assessment and development of approaches all around computer science. For example, evaluation campaigns such as BioASQ (Tsatsaronis et al., 2012) have led to an improvement of the F-measure achieved by biomedical question answering systems by more than 5%. While the manual creation of Named Entity Recognition (NER) and Entity Linking (EL) gold standards (also called benchmarks) has the advantage of yielding resources which reflect human processing, it also exhibits significant disadvantages: **a)** *Annotation mistakes*: Human annotators have to read through every sentence in the corpus and often (a) miss annotations or (b) assign wrong resources to entities for reasons as various as fatigue or lack of background knowledge (and this even when supported with annotation tools). For example, Jha et al. (2017) was able to determine that up to 38,453 of the annotations in commonly used benchmarks (see GERBIL (Usbeck et al., 2015) for a list of these benchmarks) were erroneous. A manual evaluation of 25 documents from the ACE2004 benchmark revealed that 195 annotations were missing and 14 of 306 annotations were incorrect. Similar findings were reported for AIDA/CONLL (Tjong Kim Sang and De Meulder, 2003) and OKE2015 (Nuzzolese et al., 2015). **b)** *Volume*: Manually created benchmarks are usually small (commonly $< 2,500$ documents, see Table 2). Hence, they are of little help when aiming to benchmark the scalability of existing solutions (especially when these solutions use caching). **c)** *Lack of updates*: Manual benchmark generation approaches lead to static corpora which tend not to reflect the newest reference knowledge graphs (also called Knowledge Base (KB)s). For example, several of the benchmarks presented in GERBIL (Usbeck et al., 2015) link to outdated versions of Wikipedia or DBpedia. **d)** *Popularity bias*: van Erp et al. (2016) show that manual benchmarks are often biased towards popular resources. **e)** *Lack of availability*: The lack of benchmarks for resource-poor languages inhibits the development of corresponding

Proceedings of The 11th International Natural Language Generation Conference, pages 339–349,
Tilburg, The Netherlands, November 5-8, 2018. ©2018 Association for Computational Linguistics

NER and EL solutions.

Automatic methods are a *viable and supplementary* approach for the generation of gold standards for NER and EL, especially as they address some of the weaknesses of the manual benchmark creation process. *The main contribution of our paper is a novel approach for the automatic generation of benchmarks for NER and EL* dubbed BENGAL. Our approach relies on the abundance of structured data in Resource Description Framework (RDF) on the Web and is based on Natural Language Generation (NLG) techniques which verbalize such data to generate automatically annotated natural language statements. Our automatic benchmark creation method addresses the drawbacks of manual benchmark generation aforementioned as follows: **a)** It alleviates the human annotation error problem by relying on data in RDF which explicitly contain the entities to find. **b)** BENGAL is able to generate arbitrarily large benchmarks. Hence, it can enhance the measurement of both the accuracy and the scalability of approaches. **c)** BENGAL can be updated easily to reflect the newest terminology and reference KBs. Hence, it can generate corpora that reflect the newest KBs. **d)** BENGAL is not biased towards popular resources as it can choose entities to include in the benchmark generated following a uniform distribution. **e)** BENGAL can be ported to any token-based language. This is exemplified by porting BENGAL to Portuguese and Spanish.

2 Related Work

2.1 Gold Standards for NER and EL

According to GERBIL (Usbeck et al., 2015), the 2003 CoNLL shared task (Tjong Kim Sang and De Meulder, 2003) is the most used benchmark dataset for recognition and linking. The ACE2004 and MSNBC (Cucerzan, 2007) news datasets were used by Ratinov et al. (Ratinov et al., 2011) to evaluate their seminal work on linking to Wikipedia. Another often-used corpus is AQUAINT, e.g., used by Milne and Witten (Milne and Witten, 2008). Detailed dataset statistics on some of these benchmarks can be found in Table 2.

A recent uptake of publicly available corpora (Röder et al., 2014; Steinmetz et al., 2013) based on RDF has led to the creation of many new datasets. For example, the Spotlight corpus and the KORE 50 dataset were proposed to showcase the usability of RDF-based annotations (Mendes et al., 2011). The multilingual N3 collection (Röder et al., 2014) was introduced to widen the scope and diversity of NIF-based corpora. Another recent observation is the shift towards gold standards for micropost documents like tweets. For example, the Microposts2014 corpus (Cano Basave et al., 2014) was created to evaluate NER on smaller pieces of text.

Semi-automatic approaches to benchmark creation are commonly crowd-based. They use one or more recognizers to create a first set of annotations and then hand over the tasks of refinement and/or linking to crowd workers to improve the quality. Examples of such approaches include Voyer et al. (2010) and CALBC (Rebholz-Schuhmann et al., 2010). Oramas et al. (2016) introduced a voting-based algorithm which analyses the hyperlinks presented in the input texts retrieved from different disambiguation systems such as Babelfy (Moro et al., 2014). Each entity mention in the input text is linked based on the degree of agreement across three EL systems.

BENGAL is the first automatic approach that makes use of structured data and can be replicated on any RDF KB for EL benchmarks.

2.2 NLG for the Web of Data

A plethora of works have investigated the generation of Natural Language (NL) texts from Semantic Web Technologies (SWT) such as Staykova (2014); Bouayad-Agha et al. (2014). However, the generation of NL from RDF has only recently gained momentum. This attention comes from the great number of published works such as (Cimiano et al., 2013; Duma and Klein, 2013; Ell and Harth, 2014; Biran and McKeown, 2015) which used RDF as an input data and achieved promising results. Moreover, the works published in the WebNLG (Colin et al., 2016) challenge, which used deep learning techniques such as (Sleimi and Gardent, 2016; Mrabet et al., 2016), also contributed to this interest. RDF has also been showing promising benefits to the generation of benchmarks for evaluating NLG systems, e.g., (Gardent et al., 2017; Perez-Beltrachini et al., 2016; Mohammed et al., 2016; Schwitter et al., 2004; Hewlett et al., 2005; Sun and Mellish, 2006). However, RDF has never been used for creating NER and NEL benchmarks. BENGAL addresses this research gap.

340

3 The BENGAL approach

BENGAL is based on the observation that more than 150 billion facts pertaining to more than 3 billion entities are available in machine-readable form on the Web (i.e., as RDF triples).[1] The basic intuition behind our approach is hence as follows: *Given that NER and EL are often used in pipelines for the extraction of machine-readable facts from text, we can invert the pipeline and go from facts to text*, thereby using the information in the facts to produce a gold standard that is *guaranteed to contain no errors*. In the following, we begin by giving a brief formal overview of RDF. Thereafter, we present how we use RDF to generate NER and EL benchmarks automatically and at scale.

3.1 Preliminaries and Notation

3.1.1 RDF

The notation presented herein is based on the RDF 1.1 specification. An RDF graph G is a set of facts. Each fact is a triple $t = (s, p, o) \in (R \cup B) \times P \times (R \cup B \cup L)$ where R is the set of all resources (i.e., things of the real world), P is the set of all predicates (binary relations), B is the set of all blank nodes (which basically express existential quantification) and L is the set of all literals (i.e., of datatype values). We call the set $R \cup P \cup L \cup B$ our universe and call its elements entities. A fragment of DBpedia[2] is shown below. We will use this fragment in our examples. For the sake of space, our examples are in English. However, note that we ported BENGAL to Portuguese and Spanish so as to exemplify that it is not biased towards a particular language. Also, the morphological richness of both led us to choose them as languages.

```
:Albert_Einstein dbo:birthPlace :Ulm .
:Albert_Einstein dbo:deathPlace :
    Princeton .
:Albert_Einstein rdf:type dbo:Scientist
    .
:Albert_Einstein dbo:field :Physics .
:Ulm dbo:country :Germany.
:Albert_Einstein rdfs:label "Albert␣
    Einstein"@en.
```

Listing 1: Example RDF dataset.

3.1.2 Benchmarks

We define a benchmark as a set C of annotated documents D_i. Each document D_i is a sequence of characters $s_{i1} \ldots s_{in}$. Each subsequence $s_{ij} \ldots s_{ik}$ (with $j < k$) of the document D_i which stands for a resource $r \in R$ is assumed to be marked as such. We model the marking of resources by the function $m : C \times \mathbb{N} \times \mathbb{N} \to R$ and write $m(D_i, j, k) = r$ to signify that the substring $s_{ij} \ldots s_{ik}$ stands for the resource r. In case the substring $s_{ij} \ldots s_{ik}$ does not stand for a resource, we write $m(D_i, j, k) = \epsilon$. Let D_0 be the example shown in Listing 2. We would write $m(D_0, 0, 14) = $:AlbertEinstein.

```
Albert Einstein was born in Ulm.
```

Listing 2: Example sentence.

3.2 Verbalization

The notation and formal framework for verbalization in BENGAL are based on SPARQL2NL (Ngonga Ngomo et al., 2013). Let W be the set of all words in the dictionary of our target language (e.g., English). We define the realization function $\rho : R \cup P \cup L \to W^*$ as the function which maps each entity to a word or sequence of words from the dictionary. Formally, the goal of our NLG approach is to devise an extension of ρ to conjunctions of RDF triples. This extension maps all triples t to their realization $\rho(t)$ and defines how these atomic realizations are to be combined. We denote the extension of ρ by the same label ρ for the sake of simplicity. We adopt a rule-based approach to devise the extension of ρ, where the rules extending ρ to RDF triples are expressed in a conjunctive manner. This means that for premises $P_1, \ldots, P_n$ and consequences $K_1, \ldots, K_m$ we write $P_1 \wedge \ldots \wedge P_n \Rightarrow K_1 \wedge \ldots \wedge K_m$. The premises and consequences are explicated by using an extension of the Stanford dependencies.[3] We rely especially on the constructs explained in Table 1. For example, a possessive dependency between two phrase elements e_1 and e_2 is represented as $\mathrm{poss}(e_1, e_2)$. For the sake of simplicity, we sometimes reduce the construct $\mathrm{subj}(\mathtt{y}, \mathtt{x}) \wedge \mathrm{dobj}(\mathtt{y}, \mathtt{z})$ to the triple $(\mathtt{x}, \mathtt{y}, \mathtt{z}) \in W^3$.

3.3 Approach

BENGAL assumes that it is given (1) an RDF graph $G \subseteq (R \cup B) \times P \times (R \cup B \cup L)$, (2) a number of

---

[1] http://stats.lod2.eu
[2] http://dbpedia.org

[3] For a complete description of the vocabulary, see http://nlp.stanford.edu/software/dependencies_manual.pdf.

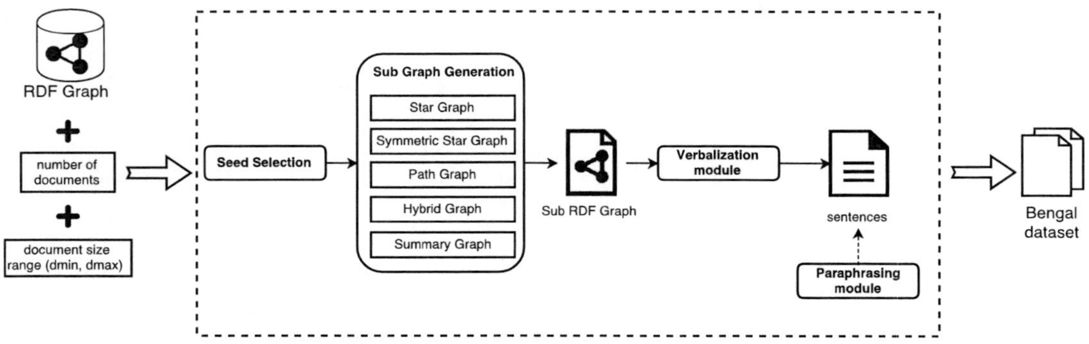

Figure 1: Overview of the BENGAL approach.

Table 1: Dependencies used by BENGAL.

Dependency	Explanation
cc	Stands for the relation between a conjunct and a given conjunction (in most cases and or or). For example in the sentence John eats an apple and a pear, cc(PEAR,AND) holds. We mainly use this construct to specify reduction and replacement rules.
conj*	Used to build the *conjunction* of two phrase elements, e.g. conj(subj(EAT,JOHN), subj(DRINK,MARY)) stands for John eats and Mary drinks. conj is not to be confused with the logical conjunction ∧, which we use to state that two dependencies hold in the same sentence. For example subj(EAT,JOHN) ∧ dobj(EAT,FISH) is to be read as John eats fish.
dobj	Dependency between a verb and its *direct object*, for example dobj(EAT,APPLE) expresses to eat an/the apple.
nn	The *noun compound modifier* is used to modify a head noun by the means of another noun. For instance nn(FARMER,JOHN) stands for farmer John.
poss	Expresses a possessive dependency between two lexical items, for example poss(JOHN,DOG) expresses John's dog.
subj	Relation between *subject* and verb, for example subj(BE,JOHN) expresses John is.

documents to generate, (3) a minimal resp. maximal document size (i.e., number of triples to use during the generation process) d_{min} resp. d_{max}, (4) a set of restrictions pertaining to the resources to generate and (5) a strategy for generating single documents. Given the graph G, BENGAL begins by selecting a set of *seed resources* from G based on the restrictions set using parameter (4). Thereafter, it uses the strategy defined via parameter (5) to select a subgraph of G. This subgraph contains a randomly selected number d of triples with $d_{min} \leq d \leq d_{max}$. The subgraph is then verbalized. The verbalization is annotated automatically and finally returned as a single document. Each single document then may be paraphrased if this option is chosen in the initial phase. This process is repeated as many times as necessary to reach the predefined number of documents. In the following, we present the details of each step underlying our benchmark generation process displayed in Figure 1.

3.3.1 Seed Selection

Given that we rely on RDF, we model the seed selection by means of a SPARQL SELECT query with one projection variable. Note that we can use the wealth of SPARQL to devise seed selection strategies of arbitrary complexity. However, given that NER and EL frameworks commonly focus on particular classes of resources, we are confronted with the condition that the seeds must be instances of a set of classes, e.g., :Person, :Organization or :Place. The SPARQL query for our example dataset would be as follows:

```
SELECT ?x WHERE { {?x a :Person.} UNION
    {?x a :Organization.} UNION {?x a :
    Place.} }
```

Listing 3: Example seed selection query.

3.3.2 Subgraph Generation

Our approach to generating subgraphs is reminiscent of SPARQL query topologies as available in SPARQL query benchmarks. As these queries (e.g., FEASIBLE[4] queries) describe real informa-

----
[4]http://aksw.org/Projects/Feasible

tion needs, their topology must stand for the type of information that is necessitated by applications and humans. We thus distinguish between three main types of subgraphs to be generated from RDF data: (1) *star graphs* provide information about a particular entity (e.g, the short biography of a person); (2) *path graphs* describe the relations between two entities (e.g., the relation between a gene and a side-effect); (3) *hybrid graphs* are a mix of both and commonly describe a specialized subject matter involving several actors (e.g., a description of the cast of a movie).

Star Graphs. For each $s_i \in S$, we gather all triples of the form $t = (s_i, p, o) \in R \times P \times (R \cup L)$.[5] The triples are then added to a list $L(s_i)$ sorted in descending order according to a hash function h. After randomly selecting a document size d between d_{min} and d_{max}, we select d random triples from $L(s_i)$. For the dataset shown in Listing 1 and $d = 2$, we would for example get Listing 4.

```
:AlbertEinstein :birthPlace :Ulm .
:AlbertEinstein :deathPlace :Princeton .
```

Listing 4: Example dataset generated by the star strategy.

Symmetric Star Graphs. As above with $t \in \{(s_i, p, o) \in G \vee (o, p, s_i) \in G\}$.

Path Graphs. For each $s_i \in S$, we begin by computing list $L(s_i)$ as in the symmetric star graph generation. Then, we pick a random triple (s_i, p, o) or (o, p, s_i) from $L(s_i)$ that is such that o is a resource. We then use o as seed and repeat the operation until we have generated d triples, where d is randomly generated as above. For the example dataset shown in Listing 1 and $d = 2$, we would for example get Listing 5.

```
:AlbertEinstein :birthPlace :Ulm .
:Ulm :country :Germany .
```

Listing 5: Example dataset generated by the path strategy.

Hybrid Graphs. This is a 50/50-mix of the star and path graph generation approaches. In each iteration, we choose and apply one of the two strategies above randomly. For example, the hybrid graph generation can generate:

```
:AlbertEinstein :birthPlace :Ulm .
:AlbertEinstein :deathPlace :Princeton .
```

---

[5]Note that we do not consider blank nodes as they cannot be verbalized due to the existential quantification they stand for.

```
:Ulm :country :Germany .
```

Listing 6: Example dataset generated by the hybrid strategy.

Summary Graph Generation. This last strategy is a specialization of the star graph generation where the set of triples to a resource is not chosen randomly. Instead, for each class (e.g., :Person) of the input KB, we begin by filtering the set of properties and only consider properties that (1) have the said class as domain and (2) achieve a coverage above a user-set threshold (60% in our experiments) (e.g., :birthPlace, :deathPlace, :spouse). We then build a property co-occurence graph for the said class in which the nodes are the properties selected in the preceding step and the co-occurence of two properties p_1 and p_2 is the instance r of the input class where $\exists o_1, o_2 : (r, p_1, o_1) \in K \wedge (r, p_2, o_2) \in K$. The resulting graph is then clustered (e.g., by using the approach presented by Ngonga Ngomo and Schumacher (2009)). We finally select the clusters which contain the properties with the highest frequencies in K that allow the selection of at least d triples from K. For example, if :birthPlace (frequency = 10), :deathPlace (frequency = 10) were in the same cluster while :spouse (frequency = 8) were in its own cluster, we would choose the pair (:birthPlace, :deathPlace) and return the corresponding triples for our input resource. Hence, we would return Listing 4 for our running example.

3.3.3 Verbalization module

The verbalization (micro-planning) strategy for the first four strategies consists of verbalizing each triple as a single sentence and is derived from SPARQL2NL (Ngonga Ngomo et al., 2013). To verbalize the subject of the triple $t = (s, p, o)$, we use one of its labels according to Ell et al. (2011) (e.g., the rdfs:label). If the object o is a resource, we follow the same approach as for the subject. Importantly, the verbalization of a triple $t = (s, p, o)$ depends mostly on the verbalization of the predicate p (see Table 1 for semantics). If p can be realized as a noun phrase, then a possessive clause can be used to express the semantics of (s, p, o). For example, if p can be verbalized as a nominal compound like birth place, then the verbalization $\rho(s, p, o)$ of the triple is as follows: $\text{poss}(\rho(p), \rho(s)) \wedge$

343

$\mathrm{subj}(\mathrm{BE},\rho(p)) \wedge \mathrm{dobj}(\mathrm{BE},\rho(o))$. In case p's realization is a verb, then the triple can be verbalized as $\mathrm{subj}(\rho(p),\rho(s)) \wedge \mathrm{dobj}(\rho(p),\rho(o))$. In our example, verbalizing (`:AlbertEinstein`, `dbo:birthPlace`, `:Ulm`) would thus lead to `Albert Einstein's birth place is Ulm.`, as `birth place` is a noun.

In the case of summary graphs, we go beyond the verbalization of single sentences and merge sentences that were derived from the same cluster. For example, if p_1 and p_2 can be verbalized as nouns, then we apply the following rule: $\rho(s,p_1,o_1) \wedge \rho(s,p_2,o_2) \Rightarrow \mathrm{conj}(\mathrm{poss}(\rho(p_1),\rho(s)) \wedge \mathrm{subj}(\mathrm{BE}_1,\rho(p_1)) \wedge \mathrm{dobj}(\mathrm{BE}_1,\rho(o_1)) \wedge \mathrm{poss}(\rho(p_2),\rho(\mathrm{pronoun}(s))) \wedge \mathrm{subj}(\mathrm{BE}_2,\rho(p_2)) \wedge \mathrm{dobj}(\mathrm{BE}_2,\rho(o_2))$. Note that `pronoun(s)` returns the correct pronoun for a resource based on its type and gender. Therewith, we can generate `Albert Einstein's birth place is Ulm and his death place is Princeton.`

3.3.4 Paraphrasing

With this step, BENGAL avoids the generation of a large number of sentences that share the same terms and the same structure. Additionally, this step makes the use of reverse engineering strategies for the generation more difficult as it increases the diversity of the text in the benchmarks. Our paraphrasing is largely based on Androutsopoulos and Malakasiotis (2010) and runs as follows:

1. Change the structure of the sentence: We use the location of verbs in each sentence to randomly change passive into active structures and vice-versa. Sentences which describe type information (e.g., `Einstein is a person`) are not altered.

2. Replace synonyms: We use POS tags to select alternative labels from the knowledge base and a reference dictionary to replace entity labels by a synonym.

An example of a paraphrase generated by BENGAL is shown in Listing 7.

```
Original: Edmund Pettus Bridge is a
    bridge. It crosses Alabama River.
    Its type is Through arch bridge. It
    was declared a National Historic
    Landmark on March 11, 2013.

Paraphrased: Edmund Pettus Bridge is a
    bridge. It crosses Alabama River.
```

```
Through arch bridge is its type.
Pettus was declared a National
Historic Landmark on March 11, 2013.
```

Listing 7: Example Paraphasing at Summary Generation

4 Experiments and Results

We generated 13 datasets in English (B1-B13), 4 datasets in Brazilian Portuguese and 4 datasets in Spanish to evaluate our approach.[6] B1 to B10 were generated by running our five sub-graph generation methods with and without paraphrasing. The number of documents was set to 100 while (d_{min}, d_{max}) was set to $(1,5)$. B11 shows how BENGAL can be used to evaluate the scalability of approaches.[7] Here, we used the hybrid generation strategy to generate 10,000 documents. B12 and B13 comprise 10 longer documents each with d_{min} set to 90. For B12, we focused on generating a high number of entities in the documents while B13 contains less entities but the same number of documents.

We compared B1-B13 with the 16 manually created gold standards for English found in GER-BIL. The comparison was carried out in two ways. First, we assessed the features of the datasets. Then, we compared the micro F-measure of 11 NER and EL frameworks on the manually and automatically generated datasets. We chose to use these 11 frameworks because they are included in GERBIL. This inclusion ensures that their interfaces are compatible and their results comparable. In addition, we assessed the performance of multilingual NER and EL systems on the datasets P1-P4 to show that BENGAL can be easily ported to languages other than English.

4.1 English Dataset features

The first aim of our evaluation was to quantify the variability of the datasets B1–B13 generated by BENGAL. To this end, we compared the distribution of the part of speech (POS) tags of the BENGAL datasets with those of the 16 benchmark datasets. An analysis of the Pearson correlation of these distributions revealed that the manually

---

[6]All BENGAL datasets can be found at `https://hobbitdata.informatik.uni-leipzig.de/bengal/`

[7]The scalability results are available at `https://goo.gl/9mnbwC` and cannot be presented herein due to space limitations.

created datasets (D1–D16) have a high correlation (0.88 on average) with a minimum of 0.61 (D10–D16). The correlation of the POS tag distributions between BENGAL datasets and a manually created dataset vary between 0.34 (D7–B11) and 0.89 (D14–B9) with an average of 0.67. This shows that BENGAL datasets can be generated to be similar to manually created datasets (D14–B9) as well as to be very different to them (D7–B11). Hence, BENGAL can be used for testing sentence structures that are not common in the current manually generated benchmarks.[8]

We also studied the distribution of entities and tokens across the datasets in our evaluation. Table 2 gives an overview of these distributions, where E is the set of entities in the corpus C. The distribution of values for the different features is very diverse across the different manually created datasets. This is mainly due to (1) different ways to annotate entities and (2) the domains of the datasets (news, description of entities, microposts). As shown in Table 2, BENGAL can be easily configured to generate a wide variety of datasets with similar quality and number of documents to those of real datasets. This is mainly due to our approach being able to generate benchmarks ranging from (1) benchmarks with sentences containing a large number of entities without any filler terms (high entity density) to (2) benchmarks which contain more information pertaining to entity types and literals (low entity density).

4.2 Annotator performance

We used GERBIL to evaluate the performance of 11 annotators on the manually created as well as the BENGAL datasets. We evaluated the annotators within an A2KB (annotation to knowledge base) experiment setting: Each document of the corpora was sent to each annotator. The annotator had to find and link all entities to a reference KB (here DBpedia). We measured both the performance of the NER and the EL steps.

Table 3 shows the micro F1-score of the different annotators on chosen datasets. The manually created datasets showed diverse results. We analyzed the results further by using the F1-scores of the annotators as features of the datasets. Based on these feature vectors, we calculated the Pearson correlations between the datasets to identify

datasets with similar characteristics.[9] The Pearson correlations of the F-measures achieved by the different annotators on the AIDA/CoNLL datasets (D2–D5) are very high (0.95–1.00) while the correlation between the results on the Spotlight corpus (D7) and N3-Reuters-128 (D13) is around -0.62. The results on D1 and D12–D15 have a correlation to the AIDA/CoNLL results (D2–D5) that is higher than 0.5. In contrast, the correlations of D7 and D8 to the AIDA/CoNLL datasets range from -0.54 to -0.36. These correlations highlight the diversity of the manually created datasets and suggest that creating an approach which emulates all datasets is non-trivial.

Like the correlations between the manually created datasets, the correlations between the results achieved on BENGAL datasets and hand-crafted datasets vary. The results on BENGAL correlate most with the results on the OKE 2015 data. The highest correlations were achieved with the OKE 2015 Task 1 dataset and range between 0.89 and 0.92. This suggests that our benchmark can emulate entity-centric benchmarks. The correlation of BENGAL with OKE is however reduced to 0.82 in D13, suggesting that BENGAL can be parametrized so as to diverge from such benchmarks. A similar observation can be made for the correlation D12 and ACE2004, where the correlation increased with the size of the documents in the benchmark. The correlation between the results across BENGAL datasets varies between 0.54 and 1, which further supports that BENGAL can generate a wide range of diverse datasets.

4.3 Annotator Performance on Spanish and Brazilian Portuguese

We implemented BENGAL for Brazilian Portuguese by using the RDF verbalizer presented in Moussallem et al. (2018) and ran four multilingual NER and EL (MAG (Moussallem et al., 2017), DBpedia Spotlight, Babelfy, and PBOH (Ganea et al., 2016)) frameworks thereon. We also evaluated the performance of these annotators on subsets of the HAREM datasets (Freitas et al., 2010)[10]. We then extended this verbalizer to Spanish using the adaption of SimpleNLG to Spanish (Soto et al., 2017). We generated Spanish BENGAL datasets and evaluated the aforemen-

---

[9]All values are at http://goo.gl/Mg3rE1.
[10]All Portuguese results at http://faturl.com/bengalpt.

345

Table 2: Excerpt of the features of the datasets used in our evaluation. The datasets B4, B6, B8 and B10 are paraphrased versions of B3, B5, B7 resp. B9 and share similar characteristics.

ID	Name	Doc. $|C|$	Tokens $|T|$	Entities $|E|$	$|T|/|C|$	$|E|/|C|$	$|E|/|T|$
D1	ACE2004	57	21312	306	373.9	5.4	0.01
D2	AIDA/CoNLL-Complete	1393	245008	34929	175.9	25.1	0.14
D8	IITB	104	66531	18308	639.7	176.0	0.28
D11	Microposts2014-Train	2340	40684	3822	17.4	1.6	0.09
D15	OKE 2015 Task 1 evaluation	101	3064	664	30.3	6.6	0.22
B1	BENGAL Path 100	100	1202	362	12.02	3.6	0.30
B2	BENGAL Path Para 100	100	1250	362	12.5	3.6	0.29
B3	BENGAL Star 100	100	3039	880	30.39	8.8	0.29
B5	BENGAL Sym 100	100	2718	725	27.18	7.25	0.26
B9	BENGAL Summary 100	100	2033	637	20.33	6.37	0.31
B11	BENGAL Hybrid 10000	10000	556483	165254	55.6	16.5	0.30
B12	BENGAL Hybrid Long 10	10	9162	2417	241.7	916.2	0.26
B13	BENGAL Star Long 10	10	7369	316	31.6	736.9	0.04

Table 3: Excerpt of micro F1-scores of the annotators for the A2KB experiments on chosen datasets. N/A means that the annotator stopped with an error.

Experiment	Dataset ID	AIDA	Babelfy	Spotlight	Dexter	E.eu	FOX	FRED	FREME	WAT	xLisa-NER	xLisa-NGRAM
A2KB	D1	0.26	0.13	0.18	0.21	0.14	0.13	N/A	0.19	0.25	0.36	0.27
	D2	0.68	0.45	0.54	0.47	0.39	0.51	N/A	0.34	0.67	0.43	0.36
	D8	0.14	0.13	0.26	0.21	0.15	0.10	N/A	0.07	0.14	0.07	0.23
	D11	0.38	0.31	0.45	0.39	0.36	0.32	0.07	0.25	0.40	0.36	0.32
	D15	0.57	0.41	0.46	0.47	0.28	0.55	0.33	0.27	0.53	0.53	0.47
	B1	0.65	0.47	0.69	0.70	0.39	0.50	0.45	0.49	0.61	0.45	0.61
	B2	0.67	0.49	0.68	0.70	0.38	0.54	0.41	0.47	0.61	0.44	0.62
	B3	0.62	0.48	0.57	0.65	0.27	0.47	0.35	0.38	0.53	0.36	0.43
	B5	0.42	0.40	0.42	0.44	0.17	0.34	0.29	0.30	0.35	0.24	0.33
	B9	0.51	0.39	0.57	0.52	0.26	0.43	0.39	0.30	0.46	0.44	0.51
	B11	0.68	0.68	0.69	0.74	0.24	0.49	0.41	0.47	0.65	0.44	0.51
	B12	0.83	N/A	0.79	0.84	0.40	0.73	N/A	0.50	0.79	0.23	0.28
	B13	0.33	0.38	0.33	0.40	0.11	0.17	N/A	0.22	0.45	0.44	0.50

tioned NER and EL systems on them. [11] We also included VoxEL (Rosales-Méndez et al., 2018), a recent gold standard for Spanish. While the extension of BENGAL to Portuguese is an important result in itself, our results also provide additional insights in the NER and EL performance of existing solutions. Our results suggest that existing solutions are mostly biased towards a high precision but often achieve a lower recall on this language. For example, both Spotlight's and Babelfy's recall remain below 0.6 in most cases while their precision goes up to 0.9. This clearly results from the lack of training data for these resource-poor languages. In contrast, the Spanish annotators presented low but consistent results, which confirms the lack of training data of these approaches on Spanish.

5 Discussion and Conclusion

We presented and evaluated BENGAL, an approach for the automatic generation of NER and EL benchmarks. Our results suggest that our approach can generate diverse benchmarks with characteristics similar to those of a large proportion of existing benchmarks in several languages.

Overall, our results suggest that BENGAL benchmarks can ease the development of NER and EL tools (especially for resource-poor languages) by providing developers with insights into their performance at virtually no cost. Hence, BENGAL can improve the push towards better NER and EL frameworks. In future work, we plan to extend the

---

[11] All Spanish results at http://faturl.com/bengales.

ability of BENGAL to generate longer and more complex sentences as well as the capability of generating different surface forms for a given entity by relying on referring expression models such as NeuralREG model (Castro Ferreira et al., 2018). We also intend to provide thorough evaluations of annotators across other resource-poor languages and create corresponding datasets to push the development of tools to process these languages.

Acknowledgements

This work has been supported by the H2020 project HOBBIT (GA no. 688227) as well as the BMVI projects LIMBO (project no. 19F2029C), OPAL (project no. 19F20284) and also supported by the German Federal Ministry of Education and Research (BMBF) within 'KMU-innovativ: Forschung für die zivile Sicherheit' in particular 'Forschung für die zivile Sicherheit' and the project SOLIDE (no. 13N14456). The authors gratefully acknowledge financial support from the German Federal Ministry of Education and Research within Eurostars, a joint programme of EUREKA and the European Community under the project E! 9367 DIESEL and E! 9725 QAMEL.

References

Ion Androutsopoulos and Prodromos Malakasiotis. 2010. A survey of paraphrasing and textual entailment methods. *Journal of Artificial Intelligence Research*, pages 135–187.

Or Biran and Kathleen McKeown. 2015. Discourse planning with an n-gram model of relations. In *EMNLP*, pages 1973–1977.

Nadjet Bouayad-Agha, Gerard Casamayor, and Leo Wanner. 2014. Natural language generation in the context of the semantic web. *Semantic Web*, 5(6):493–513.

Amparo Elizabeth Cano Basave, Giuseppe Rizzo, Andrea Varga, Matthew Rowe, Milan Stankovic, and Aba-Sah Dadzie. 2014. Making sense of microposts (#microposts2014) named entity extraction & linking challenge. In *Proceedings of 4th Workshop on Making Sense of Microposts*.

Thiago Castro Ferreira, Diego Moussallem, Ákos Kádár, Sander Wubben, and Emiel Krahmer. 2018. Neuralreg: An end-to-end approach to referring expression generation. In *Proceedings of the 56th Annual Meeting of the Association for Computational Linguistics (Volume 1: Long Papers)*, pages 1959–1969. Association for Computational Linguistics.

Philipp Cimiano, Janna Lüker, David Nagel, and Christina Unger. 2013. Exploiting ontology lexica for generating natural language texts from rdf data. In *Proceedings of the 14th European Workshop on Natural Language Generation*, pages 10–19, Sofia, Bulgaria. Association for Computational Linguistics.

Emilie Colin, Claire Gardent, Yassine Mrabet, Shashi Narayan, and Laura Perez-Beltrachini. 2016. The webnlg challenge: Generating text from dbpedia data. In *Proceedings of the 9th International Natural Language Generation conference*, pages 163–167.

Silviu Cucerzan. 2007. Large-scale named entity disambiguation based on wikipedia data. In *Conference on Empirical Methods in Natural Language Processing-CoNLL*.

Daniel Duma and Ewan Klein. 2013. Generating natural language from linked data: Unsupervised template extraction. In *IWCS*, pages 83–94.

Basil Ell and Andreas Harth. 2014. A language-independent method for the extraction of rdf verbalization templates. In *INLG*, pages 26–34.

Basil Ell, Denny Vrandečić, and Elena Simperl. 2011. Labels in the web of data. *ISWC*.

Marieke van Erp, Pablo Mendes, Heiko Paulheim, Filip Ilievski, Julien Plu, Giuseppe Rizzo, and Joerg Waitelonis. 2016. Evaluating entity linking: An analysis of current benchmark datasets and a roadmap for doing a better job. In *Proceedings of LREC*.

Cláudia Freitas, Paula Carvalho, Hugo Gonçalo Oliveira, Cristina Mota, and Diana Santos. 2010. Second harem: advancing the state of the art of named entity recognition in portuguese. In *quot; In Nicoletta Calzolari; Khalid Choukri; Bente Maegaard; Joseph Mariani; Jan Odijk; Stelios Piperidis; Mike Rosner; Daniel Tapias (ed) Proceedings of the International Conference on Language Resources and Evaluation (LREC 2010)(Valletta 17-23 May de 2010) European Language Resources Association*. European Language Resources Association.

Octavian-Eugen Ganea, Marina Ganea, Aurelien Lucchi, Carsten Eickhoff, and Thomas Hofmann. 2016. Probabilistic bag-of-hyperlinks model for entity linking. In *Proceedings of the 25th International Conference on World Wide Web*, WWW '16, pages 927–938, Republic and Canton of Geneva, Switzerland. International World Wide Web Conferences Steering Committee.

Claire Gardent, Anastasia Shimorina, Shashi Narayan, and Laura Perez-Beltrachini. 2017. Creating training corpora for nlg micro-planning. In *Proceedings of ACL*.

Daniel Hewlett, Aditya Kalyanpur, Vladimir Kolovski, and Christian Halaschek-Wiener. 2005. Effective nl paraphrasing of ontologies on the semantic web. In *Workshop on end-user semantic web interaction, 4th int. semantic web conference, galway, ireland*.

Kunal Jha, Michael Röder, and Axel-Cyrille Ngonga Ngomo. 2017. All that glitters is not gold–rule-based curation of reference datasets for named entity recognition and entity linking. In *ISWC*.

Pablo N. Mendes, Max Jakob, Andres Garcia-Silva, and Christian Bizer. 2011. DBpedia Spotlight: Shedding Light on the Web of Documents. In *7th International Conference on Semantic Systems (I-Semantics)*, pages 1–8.

David Milne and Ian H Witten. 2008. Learning to link with wikipedia. In *ACM CIKM*.

Rania Mohammed, Laura Perez-Beltrachini, and Claire Gardent. 2016. Category-driven content selection. In *Proceedings of the 9th International Natural Language Generation conference*, pages 94–98.

Andrea Moro, Francesco Cecconi, and Roberto Navigli. 2014. Multilingual word sense disambiguation and entity linking for everybody. In *Proceedings of the 2014 International Conference on Posters & Demonstrations Track-Volume 1272*, pages 25–28. CEUR-WS. org.

Diego Moussallem, Thiago Castro Ferreira, Marcos Zampieri, Maria Claudia Cavalcanti, Geraldo Xexeo, Mariana Neves, and Axel-Cyrille Ngonga Ngomo. 2018. RDF2PT: Generating Brazilian Portuguese Texts from RDF Data. In *LREC*.

Diego Moussallem, Ricardo Usbeck, Michael Röder, and Axel-Cyrille Ngonga Ngomo. 2017. MAG: A Multilingual, Knowledge-base Agnostic and Deterministic Entity Linking Approach. In *K-CAP: Knowledge Capture Conference*, page 8. ACM.

Yassine Mrabet, Pavlos Vougiouklis, Halil Kilicoglu, Claire Gardent, Dina Demner-Fushman, Jonathon Hare, and Elena Simperl. 2016. Aligning texts and knowledge bases with semantic sentence simplification. *WebNLG 2016*.

Axel-Cyrille Ngonga Ngomo, Lorenz Bühmann, Christina Unger, Jens Lehmann, and Daniel Gerber. 2013. Sorry, i don't speak sparql — translating sparql queries into natural language. In *Proceedings of WWW*, pages 977–988.

Axel-Cyrille Ngonga Ngomo and Frank Schumacher. 2009. Borderflow: A local graph clustering algorithm for natural language processing. In *Computational Linguistics and Intelligent Text Processing*, pages 547–558. Springer.

Andrea Giovanni Nuzzolese, Anna Lisa Gentile, Valentina Presutti, Aldo Gangemi, Darío Garigliotti, and Roberto Navigli. 2015. Open knowledge extraction challenge. In *Semantic Web Evaluation Challenge*.

Sergio Oramas, Luis Espinosa Anke, Mohamed Sordo, Horacio Saggion, and Xavier Serra. 2016. ELMD: an automatically generated entity linking gold standard dataset in the music domain. In *LREC*.

Laura Perez-Beltrachini, Rania Sayed, and Claire Gardent. 2016. Building rdf content for data-to-text generation. In *COLING*, pages 1493–1502.

Lev Ratinov, Dan Roth, Doug Downey, and Mike Anderson. 2011. Local and global algorithms for disambiguation to wikipedia. In *Proceedings of the 49th Annual Meeting of the Association for Computational Linguistics: Human Language Technologies*, pages 1375–1384.

Dietrich Rebholz-Schuhmann, Antonio José Jimeno Yepes, Erik M Van Mulligen, Ning Kang, Jan Kors, David Milward, Peter Corbett, Ekaterina Buyko, Elena Beisswanger, and Udo Hahn. 2010. Calbc silver standard corpus. *Journal of bioinformatics and computational biology*.

Michael Röder, Ricardo Usbeck, Daniel Gerber, Sebastian Hellmann, and Andreas Both. 2014. N^3 - A Collection of Datasets for Named Entity Recognition and Disambiguation in the NLP Interchange Format. In *LREC*.

Henry Rosales-Méndez, Aidan Hogan, and Barbara Poblete. 2018. Voxel: A benchmark dataset for multilingual entity linking. In *International Semantic Web Conference*. Springer.

Rolf Schwitter, Marc Tilbrook, et al. 2004. Controlled natural language meets the semantic web. In *Proceedings of the Australasian Language Technology Workshop*, volume 2, pages 55–62.

Amin Sleimi and Claire Gardent. 2016. Generating paraphrases from dbpedia using deep learning. *WebNLG 2016*, page 54.

Alejandro Ramos Soto, Julio Janeiro Gallardo, and Alberto Bugarín Diz. 2017. Adapting simplenlg to spanish. In *Proceedings of the 10th International Conference on Natural Language Generation*, pages 144–148.

Kamenka Staykova. 2014. Natural language generation and semantic technologies. *Cybernetics and Information Technologies*, 14(2):3–23.

Nadine Steinmetz, Magnus Knuth, and Harald Sack. 2013. Statistical analyses of named entity disambiguation benchmarks. In *1st Workshop on NLP&DBpedia 2013*, pages 91–102.

Xiantang Sun and Chris Mellish. 2006. Domain independent sentence generation from rdf representations for the semantic web. In *Combined Workshop on Language-Enabled Educational Technology and Development and Evaluation of Robust Spoken Dialogue Systems, European Conference on AI, Riva del Garda, Italy*.

Erik F. Tjong Kim Sang and Fien De Meulder. 2003. Introduction to the conll-2003 shared task: language-independent named entity recognition. In *Proceedings of the seventh conference on Natural language learning at HLT-NAACL 2003 - Volume 4*, pages 142–147.

George Tsatsaronis, Michael Schroeder, Georgios Paliouras, Yannis Almirantis, Ion Androutsopoulos, Eric Gaussier, Patrick Gallinari, Thierry Artieres, Michael R. Alvers, Matthias Zschunke, and Axel-Cyrille Ngonga Ngomo. 2012. BioASQ: A challenge on large-scale biomedical semantic indexing and question answering. In *AAAI Information Retrieval and Knowledge Discovery in Biomedical Text*.

Ricardo Usbeck, Michael Röder, Axel-Cyrille Ngonga Ngomo, Ciro Baron, Andreas Both, Martin Brümmer, Diego Ceccarelli, Marco Cornolti, Didier Cherix, Bernd Eickmann, Paolo Ferragina, Christiane Lemke, Andrea Moro, Roberto Navigli, Francesco Piccinno, Giuseppe Rizzo, Harald Sack, René Speck, Raphaël Troncy, Jörg Waitelonis, and Lars Wesemann. 2015. Gerbil: General entity annotator benchmarking framework. In *WWW '15*.

Robert Voyer, Valerie Nygaard, Will Fitzgerald, and Hannah Copperman. 2010. A hybrid model for annotating named entity training corpora. In *Proceedings of the 4th Linguistic Annotation Workshop*.

Sentence Packaging in Text Generation from Semantic Graphs as a Community Detection Problem

Alexander Shvets
DTIC, UPF
alexander.shvets@upf.edu

Simon Mille
DTIC, UPF
simon.mille@upf.edu

Leo Wanner
ICREA and DTIC, UPF
leo.wanner@upf.edu

Abstract

An increasing amount of research tackles the challenge of text generation from abstract ontological or semantic structures, which are in their very nature potentially large connected graphs. These graphs must be "packaged" into sentence-wise subgraphs. We interpret the problem of sentence packaging as a community detection problem with post optimization. Experiments on the texts of the VerbNet/FrameNet structure annotated-Penn Treebank, which have been converted into graphs by a coreference merge using Stanford CoreNLP, show a high F_1-score of 0.738.

1 Introduction

An increasing amount of research in Natural Language Text Generation (NLTG) tackles the challenge of generation from abstract ontological (Bontcheva and Wilks, 2004; Sun and Mellish, 2006; Bouayad-Agha et al., 2012; Banik et al., 2013; Franconi et al., 2014; Colin et al., 2016) or semantic (Ratnaparkhi, 2000; Varges and Mellish, 2001; Corston-Oliver et al., 2002; Kan and McKeown, 2002; Bohnet et al., 2010; Flanigan et al., 2016) structures. Unlike input structures to surface generation, which are syntactic trees, ontological and genuine semantic representations are predominantly connected graphs or collections of elementary statements (as, e.g., RDF-triples or minimal predicate-argument structures) in which re-occurring elements are duplicated (but which can be, again, considered to be a connected graph). In both cases, the problem of the division of the graph into sentential subgraphs, which we will refer henceforth to as "sentence packaging", arises. In the traditional generation task distribution, sen-tence packaging is largely avoided. It is assumed that the text planning module creates a *text plan* from selected elementary statements (*elementary discourse units*), establishing discourse relations between them. The sentence planning module then either *aggregates* the elementary statements contained in the text plan into more complex statements or keeps them as separate simple statements, depending on the language, style, preferences of the targeted reader, etc. (Shaw, 1998; Dalianis, 1999; Stone et al., 2003). Even if data-driven, as, e.g., in (Bayyarapu, 2011), this strat-egy may suggest itself mainly for input representations with a limited number of elementary elements and simple sentential structures as target. In the context of scalable report (or any other narration) generation, which can be assumed to start, for instance, from large RDF-graphs (i.e., RDF-triples with cross-referenced elements), or from large semantic graphs, the aggregation challenge is incomparably more complex. In the light of this challenge and the fact that in a narration the dis-course structure is, as a rule, defined over senten-tial structures rather than elementary statements, sentence packaging on semantic representations appears as an alternative that is worth to be ex-plored. More recent data-driven concept-to-text approaches to NLTG, e.g., (Konstas and Lapata, 2012), text simplification, e.g., (Narayan et al., 2017), dialogue act realization, e.g., (Mairesse and Young, 2014; Wen et al., 2015), deal with sentence packaging, but, as a rule, all of them concern in-puts of limited size, with at most 3 to 5 resulting sentence packages, while realistic large input se-mantic graphs may give rise to dozens. In what follows, we present a model for sentence packag-ing of large semantic graphs, which contain up to 75 sentences.

In general, the problem of sentence packaging consists in the optimal decomposition of a given

Proceedings of The 11th International Natural Language Generation Conference, pages 350–359,
Tilburg, The Netherlands, November 5-8, 2018. ©2018 Association for Computational Linguistics

graph into subgraphs, such that: (i) each subgraph is in itself a connected graph; (ii) the outgoing edges of the predicative vertices in a subgraph fulfil the valency conditions of these vertices (i.e., the obligatory arguments of a predicative vertice must be included in the subgraph); (iii) the appearance of a vertice in several subgraphs is subject to linguistic restrictions of co-reference.[1] In graph-theoretical terms, sentence packaging can be thus viewed as an approximation of *dense subgraph decomposition*, which is a very prominent area of research in graph theory. It has been also studied in the context of numerous applications, including biomedicine (e.g., for protein interaction network (Bader and Hogue, 2003) or brain connectivity analysis (Hagmann et al., 2008)), web mining (Sarıyuece et al., 2015), influence analysis (Ugander et al., 2012), community detection (Asim et al., 2017), etc. Our model is inspired by the work on community detection. The model has been validated in experiments on the VerbNet/FrameNet annotated version of the Penn TreeBank (Mille et al., 2017), in which coreferences in the individual texts of the corpus have been identified using the Stanford CoreNLP toolkit (Manning et al., 2014) and fused to obtain a graph representation. The experiments show that we achieve an F_1-score of 0.738 (with a precision of 0.792 and a recall of 0.73), which means that our model is able to cope with the problem of sentence packaging in NLTG.

The remainder of the paper is structured as follows. In Section 2, we introduce the semantic graphs that are assumed to be decomposed and analyze them. Section 3 outlines the experiments we carried out, and Section 4 discusses the outcome of these experiments. In Section 5, we briefly review the work that is related to ours. In Section 6, finally, we draw some conclusions and outline possible lines of future work.

2 Semantic Graphs

2.1 Overview

We assume a semantic graph to which the problem of sentence packaging is applied to be a labeled graph with *semantemes*, i.e., word sense disambiguated lexical items, as vertice labels and predicative argument relations as edge labels. The vertice labels are furthermore assumed to be typed in terms of semantic categories such as 'action',

'object', 'property', etc. A semantic graph of this kind can be a *Abstract Meaning Representation* (AMR) (Banarescu et al., 2013) obtained from the fusion of coreference vertices across individual sentential AMRs or a VerbNet or FrameNet structure obtained from the merge of sentential VerbNet respectively FrameNet structures that contain coreferences. An RDF-triple store which is annotated with semantic metadata, e.g., in OWL (https://www.w3.org/OWL/) can be equally converted into such a graph (Rodriguez-Garcia and Hoehndorf, 2018). Without loss of generality, we will assume, in what follows, that our semantic graphs are hybrid VerbNet / Framenet graphs in that we use first level VerbNet type ids / FrameNet type ids as vertice labels and VerbNet relations as edge labels.

As already mentioned in the Introduction, we use the VerbNet/FrameNet annotated version of the Penn TreeBank (henceforth *dataset*) to which we apply the co-reference resolution from Stanford OpenCore NLP to obtain a graph representation (and which we split into a development set and test set, with 85% and 15% texts that contained 78% and 22% of the sentences respectively). Consider the schematic representation of the semantic graph of one of the texts from the development set in Figure 1. It consists of two isolated subgraphs: one of them (to the left) comprises three sentences and the second (to the right) corresponds to a single sentence. The blue (dark) nodes correspond to verbal and nominal predicate tokens.

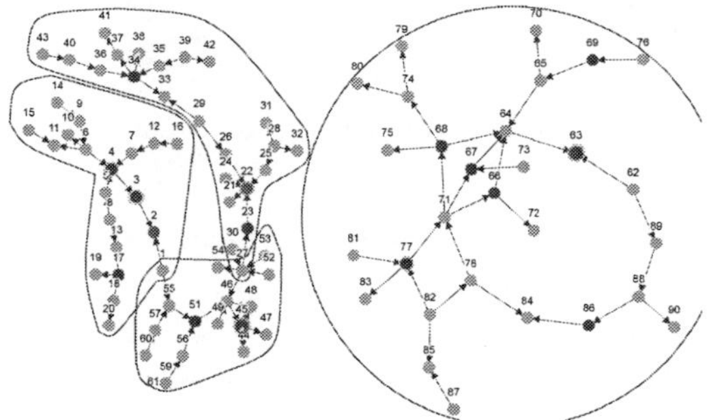

Figure 1: Example of a semantic graph of a text

As illustrated in Figure 2, a significant number (to be precise: 94%) of the text graphs obtained after the co-reference merge in the development set contain subgraphs which combine several sentences (in total, 77% of sentences were combined),

---

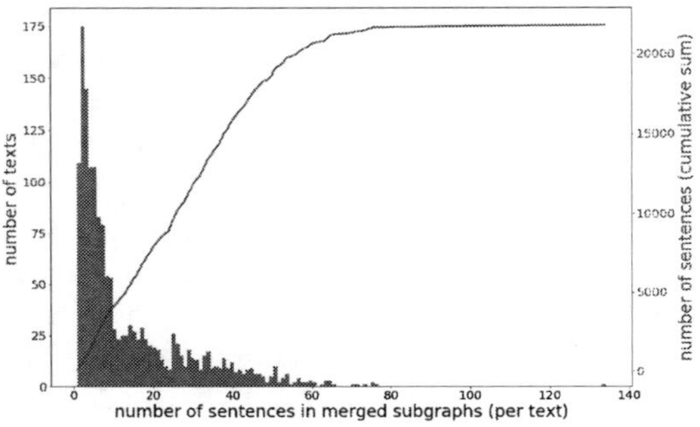

Figure 2: Sentence distribution in the graphs of the VerbNet/FrameNet annotated version of the Penn TreeBank

	min	Q_2	mean	max	N_1	N_2
# tokens	2	17	17.5	95	28253	1.0
# edges	1	21	21.7	130	28253	1.0
# predicate nodes	0	11	11.3	67	28189	0.99
# argument nodes	1	12	12.6	67	28253	1.0
# roots	1	4	5	37	28253	1.0
# VerbNet nodes	0	3	3.2	15	26355	0.93
# Argument1	0	6	5.9	40	27794	0.98
# Argument2	0	4	4.3	30	27024	0.96
# Elaboration	0	2	2.2	19	22247	0.79
# NonCore	0	0	0.7	8	13415	0.47
# Set	0	0	1.2	26	12680	0.45

Table 1: Statistics of the features in the development set used for building up the linear regression model

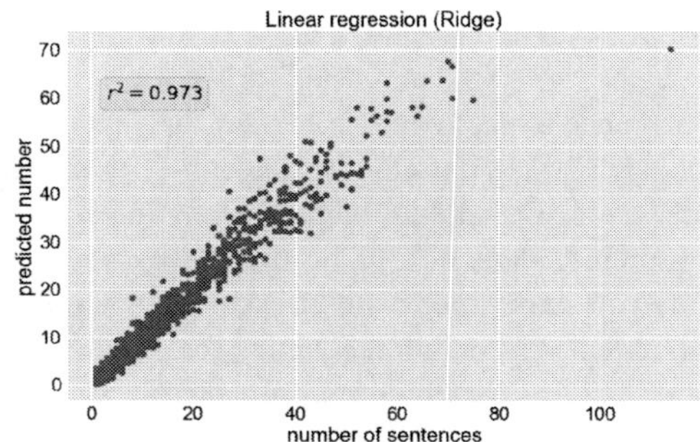

Figure 3: Predicting the number of sentences on the development set

such that the task of sentence packaging is a necessary task in the context of NLTG. Even if the number of texts with a large number of merged sentences is relatively small, we can observe in Figure 2 that the line corresponding to the cumulative sum has a constant slope for the majority of texts, which implies that the number of sentences per bin of texts of the same size is close to constant. This means that each bin contributes evenly when we evaluate the quality of obtained packaging since we focus on recovering the sentences and assessing each of them individually, without averaging within a text.

2.2 Graph Analysis for Sentence Packaging

The generation information that characterizes a graph in the context of sentence packaging concerns: (i) the optimal number of sentences into which this given graph can be divided, and (ii) the profile (in semantic or graph theory terms) of a typical sentence of this graph. We use this information in the subsequent stages of sentence packaging.

2.2.1 Estimation of the Number of Sentences

In order to estimate the number of sentences into which a given semantic graph is to be decomposed, we built up a linear regression model with Ridge regularization on the development set with the features listed in the first column of Table 1. The statistics on chosen features are shown in the other columns, where Q_2 is a median, N_1 is an absolute number of sentences with a non-zero value of a parameter, and N_2 is a corresponding relative number.

The highest R^2-value was reached with the combination of all features, including FrameNet and VerbNet classes of roots, which made R^2-value increase by 0.5 percentage point from 0.968 to 0.973; cf. Figure 3. The value is high, which means that the obtained model allows an accurate prediction of the number of sentences and can be used as an input parameter in community detection algorithms. We did not opt for using the number of predicates corresponding to different types for the regression since most of the types cover less than 7% of sentences from the development set.

2.2.2 Sentence Profiling

In order to obtain the prototypical profiles of the sentences in our dataset, we enriched the types of features used for the linear regression model above by features that play an important role in sentence formation: the type(s) of the parent node(s) of each node in the development set and the types of its arguments. With these enriched features at hand, we first built a multivariate normal distribution (MVN) of the most common non-correlated features of sentences chosen iteratively by cross-validation in such a way that a matrix of feature vectors is not singular for any set of folds. We

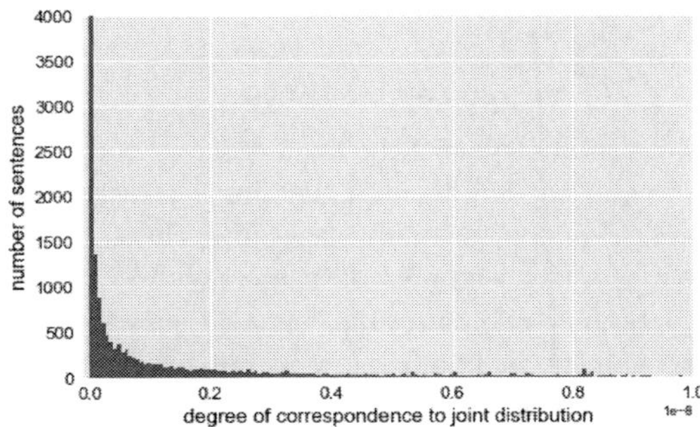

Figure 4: Correspondence of the sentences to the MVN distribution

ended up with the MVN distribution of 20 non-correlated features chosen from the top 100 features that appeared most frequently in sentences of 400 randomly chosen texts from the development set.

As an alternative to an iterative selection of the appropriate features, we applied Principal Component Analysis (PCA) (Jolliffe, 1986) to a space of the most common 100 features and selected principal vectors that describe 90% of the variance for building an MVN distribution. This step made the matrix of values of sentence features to be invertible, as required for the MVN distribution.

We assessed the proximity of the sentences of the development set to these initially obtained MVN distributions. As illustrated in Figure 4, the distribution of the degrees of correspondence to the joint distribution of 20 non-correlated features is right-skewed, with many sentences on the left that fit the distribution poorly. In order to remedy this, we implemented, for cases of a weak correspondence of a significant part of sentences (more than 15%) of the development set with the joint distribution, a clustering algorithm in a space of selected features (K-means, k=10) and built the distribution separately for each cluster. The proximity of the profile of the sentence being packaged has been assessed with respect to the joint distribution of each of the clusters – with success, as the results in Table 2, Subsection 3.2 below show.

3 Experiments

3.1 Background

Community detection aims to cluster a given social network (graph) into groups of tightly connected or similar vertices (Asim et al., 2017). The different algorithms which have been proposed are often adapted to the particular characteristics of the investigated network (Fortunato and Hric, 2016). Some algorithms take into account only the network structure (the mutual arrangement of vertices and the relationships between them) and are aimed at maximizing the modularity value (Blondel et al., 2008). Other algorithms consist in clustering the vertices by combining the most similar elements in terms of their attribute values without link analysis (Combe et al., 2015). Recently, the tendency has been to use both relationships between vertices and their characteristics and identify overlapping groups for optimal network decomposition (Yang et al., 2013). In our work, we experimented so far with algorithms which operate with links between vertices and allow for fast partitioning of huge graphs.

3.2 Setup of the Experiments

We first began to experiment with three community detection algorithms: LOUVAIN (Blondel et al., 2008), METIS (Karypis and Kumar, 2000), and COPRA (Gregory, 2010). However, already the first simple tests showed that COPRA performed poorly on our data in that it decomposed each graph into a small set of isolated subgraphs that did not include all the vertices of the original graph (see the exact figures below). Therefore, we discarded COPRA from further experiments, while LOUVAIN and METIS were taken to serve as baselines. Since METIS requires as input the number of communities (= sentences) into which a given graph is to be decomposed, we use linear regression presented in Subsection 2.2.1 as preprocessing stage.

To improve the quality of the initial decomposition made using community detection algorithms (i.e., our baselines) we carried out a local descent search, adding neighbour vertices to each subgraph one by one and keeping them if the correspondence of the subgraph to the multivariate distribution increased. The optimization is performed as a post-processing stage as follows:

1. for each $s \in S$, with S: = set of sentence subgraphs obtained by LOUVAIN / METIS

    (a) determine the degree of correspondence to the joint distribution (in case of several subgraphs, choose the most appropriate one) that is to be optimized.

    (b) apply local descent search, adding nodes from $s' \in S$ (with $s' \neq s$) iteratively each time when it leads to the increase of the optimized parameter (subgraphs can share common nodes, i.e., overlap)

2. stop local descent search when there is no node that improves s.

F_1-score was chosen as a measure for the comparison of the quality of decompositions obtained by different algorithms on the test set. It is calculated for each original sentence since we consider a sentence as a separate unit. Its value takes into account which part of the original sentence was covered by the obtained subgraph and how many nodes that did not belong to the original sentence were mistakenly appended. Each isolated subgraph corresponds to one unit only, although it can include several original sentences. For those original sentences that are not captured in the majority of their nodes in any individual subgraph, F_1-score is equal to 0. The macro-F_1, i.e. the average F_1-score over all sentences, is a final measure.

The results are displayed in Table 2. 'No decomposition' stands for the case when any graph in the test set is considered to be a sentence (it can be considered as an additional baseline); 'METIS$_{LR}$' for "METIS with linear regression as a preprocessing stage", 'DC$_K$' for "descent search with K-means", and 'DC$_{\neg K}$' "for descent search without K-means".

	Recall	Precision	F_1-score
No decomposition	0.313	0.264	0.274
LOUVAIN	0.69	0.726	0.68
METIS$_{LR}$	0.693	**0.814**	0.727
LOUVAIN+DC$_K$	0.707	0.709	0.681
LOUVAIN+DC$_{\neg K}$	0.705	0.704	0.678
LOUVAIN+PCA+ DC$_K$	0.701	0.714	0.681
METIS$_{LR}$+DC$_K$	0.73	0.792	**0.738**
METIS$_{LR}$+DC$_{\neg K}$	**0.731**	0.788	0.736
METIS$_{LR}$+PCA+ DC$_K$	0.714	0.795	0.731

Table 2: Results of testing the obtained models

As already mentioned above, COPRA showed a very poor performance on our data. The exact numbers were: mean recall = 0.113, mean precision = 0.088, and mean F_1-score = 0.084). Therefore, we did not include them into Table 2 and did not combine COPRA with other techniques.

4 Discussion

4.1 Performance Assessment

We can observe that the local descent search with the chosen optimization function leads to an increase of the mean F_1-score in each case. The use of a larger number of features with PCA leads to slightly poorer results, but still shows an improvement in comparison to the baseline community detection (LOUVAIN, and METIS$_{LR}$). However, METIS$_{LR}$ is somewhat better than our optimizations with respect to precision and METIS$_{LR}$+DC$_{\neg K}$ is the best (even if by only a very minor margin, compared to the best F_1-score reaching METIS$_{LR}$+DC$_K$).

The very low figures for 'No Decomposition', i.e., the interpretation of each single graph as a sentence, show us that the problem of sentence packaging (or, in other words, decomposition of textual semantic graphs into sentential subgraphs) is indeed a relevant problem in large scale semantics-to-text generation.

Carrying out the error analysis, we assessed several obtained subgraphs in detail and identified at least two causes of the low values of precision and recall. The first cause lies in a suboptimal performance of the coreference resolution related to the merge of co-referenced nodes. For example, for the entity 'Mr. Peladeau', which appeared in a given text ten times, the module generated a node labeled 'Peladeau' and ten nodes labeled 'Mr.', connecting the 'Peladeau' node to all ten 'Mr.' nodes. This decreased our precision. We fixed the erroneous graphs by combining non-root nodes that were connected to the same input and output nodes with the same types of arguments and recalculated the measures. Some sentences were significantly affected by this change. For instance, for the mentioned example, the precision increased from 0.35 to 0.44. However, the overall mean F_1-score increased only by 0.5% because this error affected a relatively small number of subgraphs.

Another cause for poor quality of some obtained subgraphs consisted in the creation of subgraphs that contained subgraphs of several ground truth sentences. This led to the low value of precision, even if the recall was relatively high. To account for this problem, we defined a procedure that allowed us to separate such compound graphs into a set of subgraphs. This procedure duplicates those nodes that have two or more non-overlapping input paths from roots which include a node with a defined VerbNet class. Since the output paths of duplicated nodes and the input paths without a node from VerbNet should not be necessarily assigned to all the copies of a node, we remove these paths to avoid overloading each single subgraph with redundant information.

The application of the node duplication procedure to the graphs obtained by LOUVAIN+PCA+DC$_K$ led to an increase of the overall mean precision (taking into account only covered ground truth sentences) from 0.85 to 0.96 and to a decrease of the recall from 0.86 to 0.67 since the procedure also affected some optimal sentence subgraphs by splitting them further into single clause subgraphs. At the same time, the coverage of the original sentences was improved (857 instead of 687 out of 908 were covered), which compensated the lower recall and led to an increase of the F_1-score by 10%. The potential values of precision and recall that could be reached if we combine subgraphs that belong to the same sentences are 0.91 and 0.77 respectively, which results in an F_1-score of 0.83. To tackle the problem of combining the subgraphs of clauses, full-text clustering could be used (Devyatkin et al., 2015). Adding back the removed paths linked to copied nodes will also contribute to the increase of overall quality of sentences.

4.2 Example

For illustration, consider in Figure 5 a subgraph obtained from a larger initial graph, which is shown in Figure 6 (the obtained subgraph is circled). The subgraph corresponds to the ground truth subgraph with a precision of 0.938 and a recall of 0.882. It might be seen that the obtained subgraph contains enough information to generate a sentence with a similar meaning as the original one.

The original sentence that corresponds to the subgraph in Figure 5 is *He said the company is experimenting with the technique on alfalfa, and plans to include cotton and corn, among other crops.*; cf. also Figure 7 for the text (with the corresponding sentence highlighted) captured by the initial graph. The text comprises 755 tokens of 41 sentences, which formed 10 isolated graphs after coreference resolution. The largest graph contains 578 vertices, which correspond to 32 sentences with 18 vertices that link sentences.

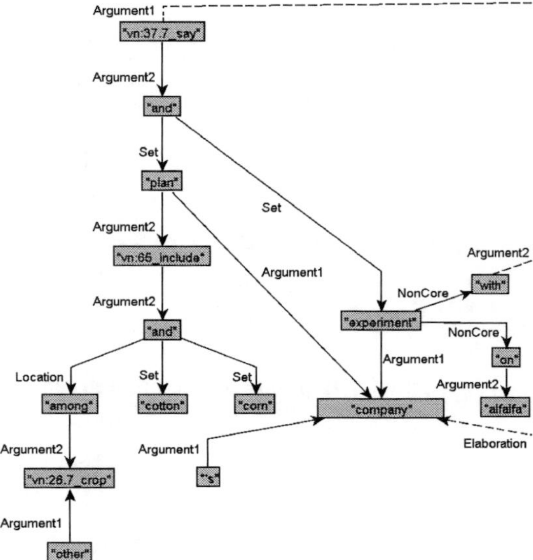

Figure 5: A sample subgraph extracted from a text graph

The LOUVAIN+PCA+DC$_K$ method applied to the whole graph detected 31 sentences out of 41. An additional separation of the obtained graphs by the procedure described above led to the detection of 9 extra sentences. Thus, the 98% of the ground truth sentences were recovered to a certain extent.

5   Related Work

A number of natural language text generators take as input sentence structures – for instance, sentence templates, as in the case of SimpleNLG generators (Gatt and Reiter, 2009), syntactic structures, as in the case of surface-oriented generators (Belz et al., 2011; Mille et al., 2018a), or more abstract semantic structures such as, e.g., AMRs; cf., e.g., (May and Priyadarshi, 2017; Song et al., 2018). For these generators, the problem of sentence packaging or aggregation is obviously obsolete. As already mentioned in the Introduction, in setups that start from input that is not yet cast into sentence structures, traditional NLTG foresees the task of (content) aggregation, which is dealt with as part of sentence planning (or *microplanning*): the elementary content elements, as assumed to be present in the text plan, are aggregated into more complex elements; see, among others, (Shaw, 1998; Dalianis, 1999; Stone et al., 2003; Gardent and Perez-Beltrachini, 2017).

Our work is more in line with Konstas and La-

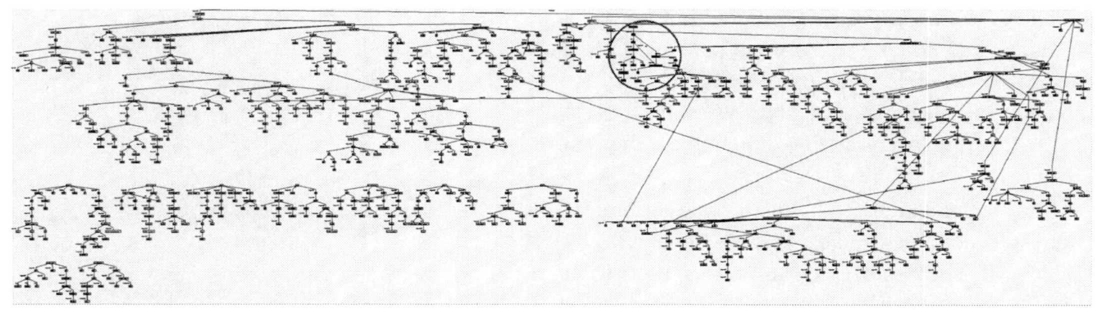

Figure 6: Example of the initial graph with one of the detected sentence subgraphs circled

116 - Researchers at Plant Genetic Systems N.V. in Belgium said they have developed a genetic engineering technique for creating hybrid plants for a number of key crops. 117 - The researchers said they have isolated a plant gene that prevents the production of pollen. 118 - The gene thus can prevent a plant from fertilizing itself. 119 - Such so - called male - sterile plants can then be fertilized by pollen from another strain of the plant , thereby producing hybrid seed. 120 - The new generation of plants will possess the flourishing , high - production trait known as `` hybrid vigor , '' similar to that now seen in hybrid corn. 121 - `` The development could have a dramatic effect on farm production , especially cotton , '' said Murray Robinson , president of Delta & Pine Land Co. , a Southwide Inc. subsidiary that is one of the largest cotton seed producers in the U.S.. 122 - On a commercial scale , the sterilization of the pollen - producing male part has only been achieved in corn and sorghum feed grains. 123 - That 's because the male part , the tassel , and the female , the ear , are some distance apart on the corn plant. 124 - In a labor - intensive process , the seed companies cut off the tassels of each plant , making it male sterile. 125 - They sow a row of male - fertile plants nearby , which then pollinate the male - sterile plants. 126 - The first hybrid corn seeds produced using this mechanical approach were introduced in the 1930s and they yielded as much as 20 % more corn than naturally pollinated plants. 127 - The vast majority of the U.S. corn crop now is grown from hybrid seeds produced by seed companies. 128 - A similar technique is almost impossible to apply to other crops , such as cotton , soybeans and rice. 129 - The male part , the anthers of the plant , and the female , the pistils , of the same plant are within a fraction of an inch or even attached to each other. 130 - The anthers in these plants are difficult to clip off. 131 - In China , a great number of workers are engaged in pulling out the male organs of rice plants using tweezers , and one - third of rice produced in that country is grown from hybrid seeds. 132 - At Plant Genetic Systems , researchers have isolated a pollen - inhibiting gene that can be inserted in a plant to confer male sterility. 133 - Jan Leemans , research director , said this gene was successfully introduced in oil - producing rapeseed plants , a major crop in Europe and Canada , using as a carrier a `` promoter gene '' developed by Robert Goldberg at the University of California in Los Angeles. 134 - The sterilizing gene is expressed just before the pollen is about to develop and it deactivates the anthers of every flower in the plant. 135 - Mr. Leemans said this genetic manipulation does n't hurt the growth of that plant. 136 - The researchers also pulled off a second genetic engineering trick in order to get male - sterile plants in large enough numbers to produce a commercial hybrid seed crop. 137 - They attached a second gene , for herbicide resistance , to the pollen - inhibiting gene. 138 - Both genes are then inserted into a few greenhouse plants , which are then pollinated and allowed to mature and produce seed. 139 - The laws of heredity dictate that half of the plants springing from these greenhouse - produced seeds will be male sterile and herbicide resistant and half will be male fertile and herbicide susceptible. 140 - The application of herbicide would kill off the male - fertile plants , leaving a large field of male - sterile plants that can be cross - pollinated to produce hybrid seed. 141 - Mr. Leemans said the hybrid rapeseeds created with this genetic engineering yield 15 % to 30 % more output than the commercial strains used currently. 142 - `` This technique is applicable to a wide variety of crops , '' he said , and added that some modifications may be necessary to accommodate the peculiarities of each type of crop. **143 - He said the company is experimenting with the technique on alfalfa , and plans to include cotton and corn , among other crops.** 144 - He said that even though virtually all corn seeds currently planted are hybrids , the genetic approach will obviate the need for mechanical emasculation of anthers , which costs U.S. seed producers about $ 70 million annually. 145 - In recent years , demand for hybrid seeds has spurred research at a number of chemical and biotechnology companies , including Monsanto Co. , Shell Oil Co. and Eli Lilly & Co. 146 - One technique developed by some of these companies involves a chemical spray supposed to kill only a plant 's pollen. 147 - But there have been problems with chemical sprays damaging plants ' female reproductive organs and concern for the toxicity of such chemical sprays to humans , animals and beneficial insects. 148 - However , Paul Johanson , Monsanto 's director of plant sciences , said the company 's chemical spray overcomes these problems and is `` gentle on the female organ. '' 149 - Biosource Genetics Corp. , Vacaville , Calif. , is developing a spray containing a gene that spreads from cell to cell and interferes with the genes that are responsible for producing pollen. 150 - This gene , called `` gametocide , '' is carried into the plant by a virus that remains active for a few days. 151 - Robert Erwin , president of Biosource , called Plant Genetic 's approach `` interesting '' and `` novel , '' and `` complementary rather than competitive. '' 152 - `` There is a large market out there hungry for hybrid seeds , '' he said. 153 - Mr. Robinson of Delta & Pine , the seed producer in Scott , Miss. , said Plant Genetic 's success in creating genetically engineered male steriles does n't automatically mean it would be simple to create hybrids in all crops. 154 - That 's because pollination , while easy in corn because the carrier is wind , is more complex and involves insects as carriers in crops such as cotton. 155 - `` It 's one thing to say you can sterilize , and another to then successfully pollinate the plant , '' he said. 156 - Nevertheless , he said , he is negotiating with Plant Genetic to acquire the technology to try breeding hybrid cotton.

Figure 7: Original plain text with the recovered sentence subgraph highlighted

pata (2012)'s data-driven concept-to-text model, which creates from the input database records hypergraphs that are then projected onto multiple sentence reports. We also depart from graphs (which we create from isolated semantic sentence structures by establishing coreference links between coinciding elements across different structures), only that we work with graphs that are considerably larger than those Konstas and Lapata work with (up to 75 resulting sentences per graph vs. >10 resulting sentences per graph). Furthermore, while we use community detection algorithms (and focus only on the problem of sentence packaging), they view the entire problem of the verbalization of a hypergraph as a graph traversal problem.

The difference in the size of the input data (and thus the number of the resulting sentences) is also a distinctive feature of our proposal when we compare it to other works that deal with sentence packaging. For instance, Narayan et al. (2017) split in their experiments on text simplification complex sentences into 2 to 3 more simple sentences. As content representation, they use the WebNLG dataset of RDF-triples (Gardent et al., 2017). To split a given set of RDF-triples into several subsets, they learn a probabilistic model. Wen et al. (2015) use LSTM-models to generate utterances from a given sequence of tokens in the context of a dialogue application.

Since for our experiments we apply coreference resolution to create from the VerbNet/Framenet annotated sentences of the Penn Treebank large connected graphs, our work could be also considered to be related to the recent efforts on the creation of datasets for NLTG; cf., e.g., (Gardent et al., 2017; Novikova et al., 2017; Mille et al., 2018b). However, so far, the coreference resolution has been entirely automatic, with no subsequent thorough validation and manual correction. Both would be needed to ensure high quality of the resulting dataset.

6 Conclusions and Future Work

We have presented a community detection-based strategy for packaging semantic (VerbNet/FrameNet) graphs into sentential subgraphs and tested it on a large dataset. We have shown that, in principle, sentence packaging can be interpreted as a community detection problem since community detection algorithms aim to identify densely connected subgraphs–which can be expected from sentential structures. The evaluation suggests that the subgraphs obtained by community detection can be further improved by a post-processing stage, e.g., by descent search or PCA.

The duplication of nodes for an additional decomposition of obtained graphs led to an increase of the performance. To avoid the unnecessary splitting of optimal subgraphs, as observed in some cases, the offered procedure might be furthermore restricted, for example, by duplicating only the nodes with high centrality measures.

In the future, we plan to explore community detection algorithms which will allow us to take the attributes of the vertices into account. For this purpose, the optimization function must be modified to take into account the mutual compatibility of vertices rather than their similarity, since vertices within one sentence usually have different properties and do not form homogeneous communities in a general sense. Furthermore, we plan to explore to what extent reinforcement learning-based graph partitioning algorithms that take the specifics of the semantic graphs into account in terms of features are suitable for the problem of sentence packaging.

Acknowledgments

The presented work was supported by the European Commission under the contract numbers H2020-645012-RIA, H2020-7000024-RIA, H2020-700475-IA, and H2020-779962-RIA and by the Russian Foundation for Basic Research under the contract number 18-37-00198. Many thanks to the three anonymous reviewers, whose insighful comments helped to improve the final version of the paper.

References

Yousra Asim, Abdul Majeed, Rubina Ghazal, Basit Raza, Wajeeha Naeem, and Ahmad Kamran Malik. 2017. Community detection in networks using node attributes and modularity. *Int J Adv Comput Sci Appl* 8(1):382–388.

G. Bader and C. Hogue. 2003. An automated method for finding molecular complexes in large protein interaction networks. *BMC Bioinformatics* 4(2).

L. Banarescu, C. Bonial, S. Cai, M. Georgescu, K. Griffitt, U. Hermjakob, K. Knight, P. Koehn, M. Palmer, and N. Schneider. 2013. Abstract meaning representation for sembanking. In *Proceedings of the Linguistic Annotation Workshop*.

Eva Banik, Claire Gardent, and Eric Kow. 2013. The KBGen challenge. In *Proceedings of ENLG*. pages 94–97.

H.S. Bayyarapu. 2011. Efficient Algorithm for Context Sensitive Aggregation in Natural Language Generation. In *Proceedings of the Recent Advances in Natural Language Processing Conference*. pages 84–89.

Anja Belz, Michael White, Dominic Espinosa, Eric Kow, Deirdre Hogan, and Amanda Stent. 2011. The First Surface Realisation Shared Task: Overview and Evaluation Results. In *Proceedings of the 13th European Workshop on Natural Language Generation*. pages 217–226.

Vincent D Blondel, Jean-Loup Guillaume, Renaud Lambiotte, and Etienne Lefebvre. 2008. Fast unfolding of communities in large networks. *Journal of statistical mechanics: theory and experiment* 2008(10):P10008.

Bernd Bohnet, Leo Wanner, Simon Mille, and Alicia Burga. 2010. Broad coverage multilingual deep sentence generation with a stochastic multi-level realizer. In *Proceedings of COLING*. Beijing, China, pages 98–106.

Kalina Bontcheva and Yorick Wilks. 2004. Automatic report generation from ontologies: the MIAKT approach. In *International conference on application of natural language to information systems*. Springer, pages 324–335.

Nadjet Bouayad-Agha, Gerard Casamayor, Simon Mille, and Leo Wanner. 2012. Perspective-oriented generation of football match summaries: Old tasks, new challenges. *ACM Trans. Speech Lang. Process.* 9(2):3:1–3:31. https://doi.org/10.1145/2287710.2287711.

Emilie Colin, Claire Gardent, Yassine Mrabet, Shashi Narayan, and Laura Perez-Beltrachini. 2016. The WebNLG challenge: Generating text from dbpedia data. In *Proceedings of INLG*. pages 163–167.

David Combe, Christine Largeron, Mathias Géry, and Előd Egyed-Zsigmond. 2015. I-louvain: An attributed graph clustering method. In *International Symposium on Intelligent Data Analysis*. Springer, pages 181–192.

Simon Corston-Oliver, Michael Gamon, Eric Ringger, and Robert Moore. 2002. An overview of Amalgam: A machine-learned generation module. In *Proceedings of INLG*. New-York, NY, USA, pages 33–40.

Hercules Dalianis. 1999. Aggregation in natural language generation. *Computational Intelligence* 15(4):384–414.

Dmitry Devyatkin, Ilya Tikhomirov, Alexander Shvets, Oleg Grigoriev, and Konstantin Popov. 2015. Full-text clustering methods for current research directions detection. In *DAMDID/RCDL*. pages 152–156.

Jeffrey Flanigan, Chris Dyer, Noah A Smith, and Jaime Carbonell. 2016. Generation from abstract meaning representation using tree transducers. In *Proceedings of NAACL:HLT*. pages 731–739.

Santo Fortunato and Darko Hric. 2016. Community detection in networks: A user guide. *Physics Reports* 659:1–44.

Enrico Franconi, Claire Gardent, Ximena Juarez-Castro, and Laura Perez-Beltrachini. 2014. Quelo natural language interface: Generating queries and answer descriptions. In *Natural Language Interfaces for Web of Data*.

Claire Gardent and Laura Perez-Beltrachini. 2017. A statistical, grammar-based approach to microplanning. *Computational Linguistics* 43(1):1–30.

Claire Gardent, Anastasia Shimorina, Shashi Narayan, and Laura Perez-Beltrachini. 2017. Creating Training Corpora for NLG Micro-planning. In *Proceedings of ACL*.

Albert Gatt and Ehud Reiter. 2009. SimpleNLG: A realisation engine for practical applications. In *Proceedings of the 12th European Workshop on Natural Language Generation*. pages 90–93.

Steve Gregory. 2010. Finding overlapping communities in networks by label propagation. *New Journal of Physics* 12(10):103018.

P. Hagmann, L. Cammoun, X. Gigandet, R. Meuli, C. J. Honey, V. J. Wedeen, and O. Sporns. 2008. Mapping the structural core of human cerebral cortex. *PLoS Biology* 6(7):888–893.

Ian T Jolliffe. 1986. Principal component analysis and factor analysis. In *Principal component analysis*, Springer, pages 115–128.

Min-Yen Kan and Kathleen McKeown. 2002. Corpus-trained text generation for summarization. In *Proceedings of INLG*. New-York, NY, USA, pages 1–8.

George Karypis and Vipin Kumar. 2000. Multi-level k-way hypergraph partitioning. *VLSI design* 11(3):285–300.

I. Konstas and M. Lapata. 2012. Unsupervised concept-to-text generation with hypergraphs. In *Proceedings of NAACL*. pages 752–761.

F. Mairesse and S. Young. 2014. Stochastic Language Generation in Dialogue Using FLMs. *Computational Linguistics* 40(4):763–799.

C.D. Manning, M. Surdeanu, J. Bauer, J. Finkel, S.J. Bethard, and D. McClosky. 2014. The Stanford CoreNLP Natural Language Processing Toolkit. In *Proceedings of the 52nd Annual Meeting of the Association for Computational Linguistics: System Demonstrations*. pages 55–60.

Jonathan May and Jay Priyadarshi. 2017. SemEval-2017 Task 9: Abstract Meaning Representation Parsing and Generation. In *Proceedings of the 11th International Workshop on Semantic Evaluations (SemEval-2017)*.

Simon Mille, Anja Belz, Bernd Bohnet, Yvette Graham, Emily Pitler, and Leo Wanner. 2018a. The First Multilingual Surface Realisation Shared Task (SR '18): Overview and Evaluation Results. In *Proceedings of the First Workshop on Multilingual Surface Realisation*. pages 1–12.

Simon Mille, Anja Belz, Bernd Bohnet, and Leo Wanner. 2018b. Underspecified Universal Dependency Structures, as Inputs for Multilingual Surface Realisation. In *Proceedings of the 11th International Conference on Natural Language Generation*.

Simon Mille, Roberto Carlini, Ivan Latorre, and Leo Wanner. 2017. UPF at EPE 2017: Transduction-based Deep Analysis. In *Shared Task on Extrinsic Parser Evaluation (EPE 2017)*. Pisa, Italy, pages 80–88.

Shashi Narayan, Claire Gardent, Shay B Cohen, and Anastasia Shimorina. 2017. Split and rephrase. *arXiv preprint arXiv:1707.06971* .

J. Novikova, O. Dušek, and Verena Rieser. 2017. The E2E dataset: New challenges for end-to-end generation. In *Proceedings of the 18th Annual Meeting of the Special Interest Group on Discourse and Dialogue (SIGDIAL)*.

Adwait Ratnaparkhi. 2000. Trainable methods for surface Natural Language Generation. In *Proceedings of NAACL:HLT*. Seattle, WA, USA, pages 194–201.

M.A. Rodriguez-Garcia and R. Hoehndorf. 2018. Inferring ontology graph structures using OWL reasoning. *BMC Bioinformatics* 19(7).

A.E. Sarıyuece, C. Seshadhri, A. Pinar, and Ue.V. Çatalyuek. 2015. Finding the hierarchy of dense subgraphs using nucleus decompositions. *arXiv:1411.3312v2* .

James Shaw. 1998. Clause Aggregation Using Linguistic Knowledge. In *Proceedings of INLG*. pages 138–148.

Linfeng Song, Yue Zhang, Zhiguo Wang, and Daniel Gildea. 2018. A Graph-to-Sequence Model for AMR-to-Text Generation. In *Proceedings of ACL*.

Matthew Stone, Christine Doran, Bonnie L. Webber, Tonia Bleam, and Martha Palmer. 2003. Microplanning with Communicative Intentions: The SPUD System. *Computational Intelligence* 19:311–381.

Xiantang Sun and Chris Mellish. 2006. Domain independent sentence generation from rdf representations for the semantic web. In *Combined Workshop on Language-Enabled Educational Technology and Development and Evaluation of Robust Spoken Dialogue Systems*. Riva del Garda, Italy.

J. Ugander, L. Backstrom, C. Marlow, and J. Kleinberg. 2012. Structural diversity in social contagion. *Proceedings of the National Academy of Sciences* 109(16):5962–5966.

Sebastian Varges and Chris Mellish. 2001. Instance-based Natural Language Generation. In *Proceedings of NAACL*. Pittsburgh, PA, USA, pages 1–8.

Tsung-Hsien Wen, Milica Gašć, Nikola Mrkšć, Pei-Hao Su, David Vandyke, and Steve Young. 2015. Semantically Conditioned LSTM-based Natural Language Generation for Spoken Dialogue Systems. In *Proceedings of EMNLP*. pages 1711–1721.

Jaewon Yang, Julian McAuley, and Jure Leskovec. 2013. Community detection in networks with node attributes. In *Data Mining (ICDM), 2013 IEEE 13th international conference on*. IEEE, pages 1151–1156.

Handling Rare Items in Data-to-Text Generation

Anastasia Shimorina
Lorraine University / LORIA, Nancy, France
anastasia.shimorina@loria.fr

Claire Gardent
CNRS / LORIA, Nancy, France
claire.gardent@loria.fr

Abstract

Neural approaches to data-to-text generation generally handle rare input items using either delexicalisation or a copy mechanism. We investigate the relative impact of these two methods on two datasets (E2E and WebNLG) and using two evaluation settings. We show (i) that rare items strongly impact performance; (ii) that combining delexicalisation and copying yields the strongest improvement; (iii) that copying underperforms for rare and unseen items and (iv) that the impact of these two mechanisms greatly varies depending on how the dataset is constructed and on how it is split into train, dev and test[1].

1 Introduction

The input to data-to-text generation often contains rare items, i.e. low frequency items such as names, locations and dates. This makes it difficult for neural models to predict their verbalisation. To address these issues, neural approaches to data-to-text generation typically resort either to delexicalisation (Wen et al., 2015; Dušek and Jurcicek, 2015; Trisedya et al., 2018; Chen et al., 2018) or to a copy mechanism (Chen, 2018; Elder et al., 2018; Gehrmann et al., 2018). Character-based encodings (Agarwal and Dymetman, 2017; Deriu and Cieliebak, 2018) and byte pair encodings have also been used (Elder, 2017; Zhang et al., 2018). However, when applying a character-based approach within a standard sequence-to-sequence model to the WebNLG and E2E datasets, the results were low. Hence we chose not to discuss them.

When using delexicalisation, the data is pre-processed to replace rare items with placeholders and the generated text is post-processed to replace these placeholders with appropriate values based on a mapping between placeholders and initial values built during preprocessing. While this method is often used, it has several drawbacks. It requires an additional pre- and post-processing step. These processing steps must be re-implemented for each new data-to-text application. The matching procedure needed to correctly match a rare input item (e.g., Barack Obama) with the corresponding part in the output text (e.g., the former President of the United States) may be quite complex which may result in incorrect or incomplete delexicalisations. In contrast, the copy mechanisms standardly used in neural approaches to summarisation (See et al., 2017; Gu et al., 2016; Cheng and Lapata, 2016), paraphrasing (Cao et al., 2017), answer generation (He et al., 2017) and data-to-text generation (Gehrmann et al., 2018; Chen et al., 2018) is a generic technique which is easy to integrate in the encoder-decoder framework and can be used independently of the particular domain and application.

In this paper, we investigate the impact of copying and delexicalisation on the quality of generated texts using two sequence-to-sequence models with attention: one using the copy and coverage mechanism of See et al. (2017), the other using delexicalisation. We evaluate their respective output on two data-to-text datasets, namely the E2E (Novikova et al., 2017) and the WebNLG (Gardent et al., 2017a) datasets. We also compare the two methods in two different settings: the original train/dev/test partition produced by the E2E and by the WebNLG challenge *vs.* a more constrained train/dev/test split which aims to further minimise the amount of redundancy between train, dev and test data. This latter experimental setting is in-

---

[1]All the data, scripts and evaluation results used in this study can be found at https://gitlab.com/shimorina/inlg-2018.

Proceedings of The 11th International Natural Language Generation Conference, pages 360–370,
Tilburg, The Netherlands, November 5-8, 2018. ©2018 Association for Computational Linguistics

MR	Reference
Original: name[The Cricketers], eatType[coffee shop], food[Chinese], customer rating[average], familyFriendly[no], near[The Portland Arms] **Delexicalised:** name[NAME], eatType[coffee shop], food[Chinese], customer rating[average], familyFriendly[no], near[NEAR]	**Original:** The Cricketers is a coffee shop that also has Chinese food, located near The Portland Arms. It is not family friendly, and has an average customer rating. **Delexicalised:** NAME is a coffee shop that also has Chinese food, located near NEAR. It is not family friendly, and has an average customer rating.
Original: (Bakewell pudding – region – Derbyshire Dales), (Bakewell pudding – dishVariation – Bakewell tart), (Bakewell pudding – servingTemperature – Warm or cold), (Bakewell pudding – course – Dessert), (Bakewell pudding – mainIngredients – Ground almond, jam, butter, eggs) **Delexicalised:** (FOOD – region – REGION), (FOOD – dishVariation – DISHVARIATION), (FOOD – servingTemperature – SERVINGTEMPERATURE), (FOOD – course – DESSERT), (FOOD – mainIngredients – MAININGREDIENTS)	**Original:** Bakewell pudding, also called bakewell tart, originates from the Derbyshire Dales. Classified as a dessert which can be served warm or cold, its main ingredients are ground almond, jam, butter and eggs. **Delexicalised:** FOOD, also called DISHVARIATION, originates from the REGION. Classified as a COURSE which can be served SERVINGTEMPERATURE, its main ingredients are MAININGREDIENTS.

Table 1: Entry examples of the E2E (first row) and WebNLG (second row) datasets with and without delexicalisation.

spired by a recent paper by Aharoni and Goldberg (2018), which shows that the train/dev/test split may have a strong impact on how much the model learns to generalise and how much it memorises.

Our study suggests the following.

- Rare items strongly impact the performance of Data-to-Text generation.
- Combining delexicalisation and copying yields the strongest improvements.
- Copying underperforms for items not, or rarely, seen in the training data.
- The content (e.g., distribution and number of named entities) and the partitioning (constraints on the test set) of the training data strongly affect the impact of both copying and delexicalisation.

2 Experiments

2.1 Datasets

Two recently released corpora for data-to-text generation served as experimental datasets for our study: the E2E (Novikova et al., 2017) and the WebNLG (Gardent et al., 2017a) datasets.

In the E2E dataset, the input to generation is a dialogue act consisting of three to eight slot-value pairs describing a restaurant, while the output is a restaurant recommendation verbalising this input. Table 1 shows an example with an input consisting of six slot-value pairs. In average, each input is associated with 8.1 references. The number of possible values for each slot ranges from two (binary slots) to 34 (restaurant name). Tables 2 and 3 summarise the statistics of the E2E dataset.

In WebNLG, the aim is to verbalise a set of RDF (Resource Description Framework) triples describing entities of different categories. An RDF triple is of the form *(subject, property, object)* where *subject* and *object* denotes entities or values and *property* denotes a binary relation holding between *subject* and *object*. The inputs consist of sets of (one to seven) triples and the entities belong to fifteen distinct DBpedia categories[2].

Both dataset releases gave rise to a shared task in NLG in 2017[3]. Note though that for WebNLG, the present study relies on the final release data (version 2)[4], which is a larger dataset than that used for the WebNLG Challenge 2017.

2.2 Delexicalising Datasets

We derive delexicalised datasets from the original E2E and WebNLG datasets as follows.

For each dataset, we replicated the delexicalisation procedure which was applied to the baseline systems developed for the E2E (Novikova et al., 2017) and for the WebNLG challenge (Gardent et al., 2017b) respectively[5]. As shown in Table 1, both input data and output text were delexicalised. In E2E, only the *name* and *near* slots were delexicalised (because contrary to the other slots,

---

[2]http://wiki.dbpedia.org/
dbpedia-dataset-version-2015-10

[3]http://www.macs.hw.ac.uk/
InteractionLab/E2E/, http://webnlg.loria.
fr/pages/results.html

[4]available at https://gitlab.com/shimorina/
webnlg-dataset

[5]For the full details of these delexicalisation procedures, see (Novikova et al., 2017; Gardent et al., 2017b) and the webpages of the two challenges mentioned above.

Attribute	Value Range	Example
area	2	city centre, riverside
customer rating	6	3 out of 5, low, high
eatType	3	restaurant, coffee shop, pub
familyFriendly	2	no, yes
food	7	English, Chinese, Fast food
name	34	The Plough, Alimentum, Zizzi
near	19	Café Sicilia, Crowne Plaza Hotel
priceRange	6	more than £30, cheap, moderate

	Count	Example
Properties	373	dateOfBirth, genre
Subjects	732	Buzz Aldrin
Objects	2,916	1932-03-15, jazz

Table 2: Statistics on attribute values in E2E (left) and on RDF-triple constituents in WebNLG (right).

	E2E Dataset					WebNLG Dataset			
	Unconstrained		*Constrained*			*Unconstrained*		*Constrained*	
	Instances	MRs	Instances	MRs		Instances	MRs	Instances	MRs
train	40,868	4,862	40,826	4,877	train	34,352	12,876	34,536	12,895
dev	4,521	547	3,946	547	dev	4,316	1,619	4,217	1,594
test	4,577	630	5,194	615	test	4,224	1,600	4,148	1,606

Table 3: Training/development/test sets statistics in E2E and WebNLG in original (unconstrained) and constrained splits. *Instances* count is a number of (data, text) pairs; *MRs* count is a number of unique data inputs.

they have a large number of distinct values). In WebNLG, delexicalisation was done on the subjects and objects of RDF triples.

While delexicalisation was flawless in E2E, WebNLG data poses additional challenges as the subject and object values in the input do not necessarily match the corresponding text fragment in the output. As a result, not all subjects and objects were delexicalised.

In the delexicalised E2E corpus, placeholders constitute 5.7% of all tokens, while they reach 15.7% in the WebNLG data.

2.3 The Copy Mechanism

The copy mechanism is widely used in text production approaches where it is relevant for handling rare input but also, for instance, in text summarisation, for copying input into the output. Thus, Cao et al. (2017) uses a copy mechanism to generate paraphrases, Gu et al. (2016), Cheng and Lapata (2016) for text summarisation and He et al. (2017) for answer generation.

Here we use the copy mechanism introduced by See et al. (2017). The decoder uses an extended vocabulary which consists of a predefined target vocabulary P_{vocab} which is dynamically extended at inference time with the tokens contained in the input. At each time step during decoding, the model then decides whether to copy from the input or to generate from the target vocabulary using a probability distribution over the extended vocabulary which is computed based on a generation probability (sampling from the target vocabulary) and on the attention distribution (sampling from the input).

The attention distribution a_t is calculated as in (Bahdanau et al., 2015):

$$e_i^t = v^T tanh(W_h h_i + W_s s_t + b_{attn})$$
$$a^t = softmax(e^t)$$

with v, W_h, W_s and b_{attn} parameters to be learned, s_t is the decoder state and h_i is a variable ranging over the encoder hidden states.

The generation probability p_{gen} is then defined as:

$$p_{gen} = \sigma(W_h^T.h_t + W_s^T.s_t + W_x^T.x_t + b_{ptr})$$

where W_h, W_s, W_x, b_{ptr} are parameters to be learned, x_t is the decoder input and h_t is the context vector produced by the attention mechanism as the weighted sum $\sum_1^E a_i^t h_i$ of the encoder states (with N the number of encoder states).

Finally, the probability distribution over the extended vocabulary is defined as:

$$P(w) = p_{gen} P_{vocab}(w) + (1 - p_{gen}) \sum_{i:w_i=w} a_i^t$$

2.4 Constraining Datasets

The train/dev/test split is often constrained to ensure that there is no overlap in terms of *input* between the training, the development and the test set. As Aharoni and Goldberg (2018) recently showed however, this may result in a setup where certain *input fragments* (in that case, subject and object entities present in the input set of RDF triples) are present so often in the test set that models built on this standard split, overfit and memorise rather than learn. Thus, in the split-and-rephrase application they studied, Aharoni and Goldberg (2018) observed that, given some input containing the entity e and some set of facts $T(e)$ about this entity, the model will regularly output a text which mentions e but is unrelated to the set of facts $T(e)$. That is, instead of learning to generate text from data, the model learns to associate a text with an entity.

To better assess the impact of delexicalisation and copying on the output of data-to-text generation models, we therefore consider two ways of partitioning the corpus into train, dev and test: the traditional way (*Unconstrained*) where the overlapping constraint applies to entire inputs (i.e., sets of RDF triples in WebNLG and dialogue moves in E2E) and a more challenging split (*Constrained*) where the no-overlap constraint applies to input fragments (i.e., RDF triples in WebNLG and slot-values in E2E). Table 3 shows the statistics for both splits for each dataset.

Unconstrained The unconstrained split is the original split provided by the challenge organisers.

The E2E dataset was split into training, validation and test sets following a 76.5/8.5/15 ratio. It was ensured that the input were distinct for all three sets and that a similar distribution of input and reference text lengths was kept. We found 1,430 identical (data, text) pairs in the original E2E data. They were deleted for the subsequent experiments.

In WebNLG, the original split follows an 80/10/10 ratio. As with the E2E dataset, there is a null intersection in terms of input between train, dev and test. In addition, sets of triples of different sizes and sets of triples of different categories were proportionally distributed between training, dev and test sets.

Constrained We consider a second partitioning where we aim to minimise the overlap between train, dev and test in terms of input fragments.

As shown in Table 2, in the E2E dataset, most of the slots have under eight possible values. As these few values appear with a large number of distinct slot-value combinations (49,966 input-text instances), they are unlikely to trigger fact memorisation. We therefore focus on those slots which have a higher number of values and restrict the test set using restaurant names, a slot with 34 possible values. Four restaurant names were selected to occur only in the test data and to support a distribution of inputs types and text length similar to that of the original train/dev/test (cf. Table 3).

Nonetheless, it is worth noting that the E2E dataset was constructed in such a way that a specific restaurant name may have mutually exclusive values in different inputs, such as *low customer rating* and *high customer rating*. This might result in weak association between restaurant names and specific inputs and therefore, in little risk of memorising facts related to a specific restaurant name. As we shall see in Section 3, this intuition is confirmed by the results which show little differences, for the E2E data, in terms of both automatic and human-based metrics between the *Constrained* and the *Unconstrained* setting. Note also that since the E2E *Constrained* split is defined with respect to a slot value (restaurant names) which is delexicalised, the constrained *vs.* unconstrained split distinction loses its impact in the delexicalised setting.

For the WebNLG dataset, the constraint on the train/dev/test partition is in terms of triples. In addition to the exclusion from the test set all inputs (set of RDF triples) which occur in either the dev or the train set, we require that no RDF triple occurs in two of these sets. Let $t = (s, p, o)$ be an RDF-triple, with p a property and s, o subject and object RDF resources. In the constrained dataset, if, t is in the test set, then t may not be in either the dev or the training set but variants such as (s', p, o), (s, p, o'), (s', p, o') or (s, p', o) may (with $s \neq s'$, $p \neq p'$ and $o \neq o'$). In this way, models can be trained which must learn to verbalise properties independently of their arguments. Again, care was taken to keep the distribution in terms of input length similar to that of the original split (cf. Table 3).

2.5 Model Parameters

We trained two types of models: a standard sequence-to-sequence model and the same model augmented with a copy and coverage mechanism (denoted as C in the tables). For the standard sequence-to-sequence model, we made use

E2E	name[Cocum], eatType[pub], customer rating[high], near[Burger King]
prediction	Cotto is a family-friendly pub with a high customer rating.
annotation	Cotto {*wrong*}, family-friendly {*added*}, pub {*right*}, high customer rating {*right*}, near Burger King {*missed*}
WebNLG	A Wizard of Mars – author – Diane Duane
prediction	A Wizard of Mars was written in the United States in 1995.
annotation	A Wizard of Mars {*right*}, was written {*right*}, in the United States {*wrong*}, in 1995 {*added*}.

Table 4: Manual annotation of text predictions for E2E and WebNLG data. Annotations are between curly braces.

of an LSTM encoder-decoder model with attention (Luong et al., 2015) from the OpenNMT-py toolkit[6], a PyTorch port of OpenNMT (Klein et al., 2017). The default parameters of OpenNMT-py were used for training and decoding. The encoder and decoder both have two layers. Models were trained for 13 epochs, with a mini-batch size of 64, a dropout rate of 0.3, and a word embedding size of 500. They were optimised with SGD with a starting learning rate of 1.0.

Data was not lowercased, nor was it truncated (the maximal sequence length was used in the source and target).

Special options available in OpenNMT-py were used to augment the standard model with the copy and the coverage mechanisms. The OpenNMT-py implementation of training additional copy and coverage attention layers follows See et al. (2017).

2.6 Evaluation

Automatic Evaluation Systems were evaluated using four automatic corpus-based metrics: BLEU (Papineni et al., 2002), NIST (Doddington, 2002), METEOR (Denkowski and Lavie, 2014), $ROUGE_L$ (Lin, 2004). We made use of the scripts used for the E2E Challenge evaluation[7]. The first three metrics were originally developed for machine translation, the last one for summarisation. Roughly speaking, BLEU calculates the n-gram precision; NIST is based on BLEU, but adds more weight to rarer n-grams; METEOR computes the harmonic mean of precision and recall, featuring also stem and synonymy matching; $ROUGE_L$ calculates recall for common longest subsequences in a reference and candidate text. Given our task— handling rare items (or named entities in the corpora in question)—we also applied the slot-error rate (SER) to evaluate outputs which seems to be more suitable for evaluating the presence of named entities. SER was calculated by exact matching slot values in the candidate texts,

$$SER = \frac{S + D + I}{N},$$

where S is a number of substitutions, D is a number of deletions, I is a number of insertions, and N is a total number of slots in the reference. The resulting SER is an average of SER for each prediction. While computing SER for the dialogue slot-based E2E corpus is straightforward (the binary slot *familyFriendly* was excluded), it results in some noise for WebNLG where subjects and objects are numerous (3,648 vs. 79 values in E2E) and where they were rephrased in references (cf. also Section 2.2).

Manual Annotation To allow comparisons between constrained and unconstrained settings, we intersected inputs of constrained and unconstrained test sets and gathered corresponding predictions from them for all the models. The intersection between the two test sets has 40 inputs in the E2E corpus and 153 in WebNLG. For E2E, we manually evaluated all 40 predictions available for each system (constrained and unconstrained); for WebNLG, we chose 44 predictions ensuring the presence of different sizes and categories. By manually assessing outputs for the same inputs for all the systems, contrasts between constrained and unconstrained settings are better highlighted.

Manual inspection of outputs revealed that most of generated predictions did not encounter issues with grammar or fluency. For this reason, we chose to focus on semantic adequacy of predicted texts. The evaluation was done by one human judge. After the evaluation was finished, the human annotator confirmed that, except for one system (see Section 3), all system outputs demonstrated fluent and grammatical English sentences.

Once presented with an input and a corresponding prediction text, a human judge was asked to evaluate semantic information present in the prediction. A minimal unit of analysis was a slot-value pair in E2E and an RDF triple element (sub-

---

[6]https://github.com/OpenNMT/OpenNMT-py
[7]https://github.com/tuetschek/e2e-metrics

	Unconstrained				Constrained			
	NIL	C	D	D+C	NIL	C	D	D+C
BLEU	0.56	**0.68**	0.67	**0.68**	0.52	0.57	**0.72**	**0.72**
NIST	7.54	8.67	8.60	**8.74**	7.12	7.67	**8.93**	8.90
METEOR	0.38	**0.46**	0.45	**0.46**	0.39	0.41	**0.47**	**0.47**
ROUGE$_L$	0.62	**0.71**	0.70	0.70	0.58	0.62	**0.74**	**0.74**
SER	26.07%	7.25%	**4.08%**	4.56%	29.6%	17.09%	5.18%	**4.2%**
right	81.72%	95.7%	96.24%	**96.77%**	72.04%	82.8%	**95.7%**	94.09%
wrong	16.13%	0%	0%	0%	27.96%	16.13%	0%	0%
missed	2.15%	4.3%	3.76%	3.23%	0%	1.08%	4.3%	5.91%
added	6.45%	0%	5.38%	2.15%	0%	4.84%	2.15%	0%

Table 5: E2E dataset (*D*: Delexicalisation, *D+C*: delexicalisation and copying, *C*: copy and coverage, *NIL*: Neither copy nor delexicalisation). The upper half of the table presents automatic evaluation results; the lower half—human evaluation results. Best scores are in bold.

ject, object, or property) in WebNLG. For each semantic unit, the judge indicated if it was rendered correctly (*right*) or incorrectly (*wrong*) in the text. If the unit was missing, it was noted as *missed*; new semantic content, not present in the source input, was labelled as *added*. Then, the number of each type of annotations was calculated for each input and converted to percentage with respect to the number of slot-value pairs (E2E) or number of triple constituents (WebNLG). Given the E2E example in Table 4, statistics about the example is the following: right: 2, wrong: 1, added: 1, missed: 1 (*near[Burger King]* was omitted). Total number of slots being 4, the performance in the percentage is then right: 50%, wrong: 25%, added: 25%, missed: 25%.

WebNLG example annotations were done taking into account the three parts of a triple. If a property was not translated correctly, we considered that a model missed out that information. While a subject or object was not rendered correctly, they were annotated as wrong. All the semantic information beyond the size of initial set of triples was evaluated as added. The WebNLG example in Table 4 received the following scores, the total number of constituents being three: right: 2 (66%), wrong: 1 (33%), missed: 0 (0%), added: 1 (33%). If semantic information was repeated, it was rated as added.

The human evaluation analysis presented above is modest due to the lack of resources. To justify it, we argue that our focus is solely on semantic adequacy which is a more objective parameter in evaluations than, say, fluency or grammaticality. Furthermore, human scores showed strong corre-

lations with most of automatic metrics. For example, *right* exhibits statistically significant correlations of 0.9, 0.55, 0.89, 0.85, −0.87 with BLEU, NIST, METEOR, ROUGE$_L$, SER respectively (Spearman's ρ; $p < 0.05$). *Wrong* has −0.91, −0.71, −0.88, −0.96, 0.78 correlation coefficients respectively.

With no intent to question the documented unreliability of automatic metrics in NLG, we attribute such high correlations to the design of our configurations which cover some extreme cases where models are supposed to show a drastic drop in performance.

3 Results and Discussion

We compared the output of the sequence-to-sequence model with attention described in Section 2.5 on two datasets (WebNLG and E2E) and considering eight different configurations depending on how rare words are handled (without delexicalisation, with delexicalisation, with a copy-and-coverage mechanism and with both delexicalisation and a copy-and-coverage mechanism) and on how the train/dev/test partition is constructed (unconstrained *vs.* constrained).

As pointed out in Section 2.6, automatic scores are reported using the whole test sets whereas human evaluation is based on shared MR instances between the non-constrained and constrained test sets (40 instances for E2E and 44 for WebNLG).

The results are summarised in Table 5 (E2E) and 6 (WebNLG). Some example predictions are shown in Tables 7 and 8.

	Unconstrained				Constrained			
	NIL	*C*	*D*	*D+C*	*NIL*	*C*	*D*	*D+C*
BLEU	0.54	**0.61**	0.56	0.56	0.09	0.34	0.44	**0.48**
NIST	9.70	**10.90**	10.19	10.11	2.37	6.81	7.37	**8.09**
METEOR	0.37	**0.42**	0.39	0.39	0.10	0.29	0.33	**0.36**
ROUGE$_L$	0.64	**0.71**	0.67	0.68	0.26	0.54	0.61	**0.65**
SER	43.66%	34.76%	34.93%	**31.83%**	92.5%	66.91%	50.48%	**45.45%**
right	69.26%	83.33%	83.70%	**87.04%**	10%	41.11%*	70.00%	**76.67%**
wrong	9.63%	5.56%	9.26%	7.78%	49.26%	32.59%	17.78%	15.93%
missed	21.11%	11.11%	7.04%	5.19%	40.74%	26.30%	12.22%	7.41%
added	0.37%	0%	0%	0%	1.11%	1.11%	0%	0%

Table 6: WebNLG dataset (*D*: Delexicalisation, *D+C*: delexicalisation and copying, *C*: copy and coverage, *NIL*: Neither copy nor delexicalisation). The upper half of the table presents automatic evaluation results; the lower half—human evaluation results. Best scores are in bold. * – word repetitions present in predictions.

Delexicalisation and Copying *vs.* Standard Encoding-Decoding A first observation is that, when neither delexicalisation nor copying is used, there is a strong drop in semantic adequacy. In the worst case, the SER increases by 25.4 for the E2E dataset (constrained setting, NIL *vs.* D+C) and by 47.05 points (constrained setting, NIL *vs.* D+C) in the WebNLG dataset. Similarly, the proportion of correcly predicted items (right) decreases by up to 23.66 points for the E2E dataset (constrained setting, NIL *vs.* D) and 60 points for the WebNLG dataset (constrained setting, NIL *vs.* D).

A similar, though weaker, trend can be observed for the other automatic metrics (e.g., ∆BLEU E2E, NIL *vs.* D+C, unconstrained: −0.12 points).

Delexicalisation, Copying or Both The results show two trends. First, combining copying and delexicalisation yields the best results across the board. Second, while in the unconstrained setting, there is not much difference in terms of results between copying and delexicalisation, in the constrained setting, copying yields lower results (∆BLEU E2E: −0.15, ∆BLEU WebNLG: −0.10, ∆right E2E: −12.9%, ∆right WebNLG: −28.89%, ∆SER E2E: +11.91, ∆SER WebNLG: +16.43; constrained setting, C *vs.* D). This suggests that copying only partially captures rare items. Looking at the outputs, copying seems to work better when the item to be copied has been seen in the training data. When an entity was not seen, the network often chooses to generate a frequent entity seen in the source, rather than copying. For instance, for the E2E data, restau-

rant names (which had not been seen in the training data) were not copied over in the constrained setting. In most cases, the input restaurant name was replaced by a restaurant name that is frequent in the training data. For example, given the MR *name[Cocum], eatType[coffee shop], near[The Rice Boat]*, the text *Near The Rice Boat there is a coffee shop called Fitzbillies* was generated, where *Fitzbillies*, a frequently occurring restaurant name in the training data (2,371 instances), was generated instead of the input restaurant name *Cocum*.

Constrained *vs.* Unconstrained Setting There is a clear difference in terms of relative performance in the constrained *vs.* the unconstrained setting between the two datasets.

For the E2E dataset, since the constrained dataset is defined with respect to slot values (name and near) which are delexicalised, the constrained setting is in fact similar to the unconstrained setting. And indeed the scores are similar (e.g., unconstrained *vs.* constrained, D, E2E: ∆BLEU: −0.05, ∆SER: −1.1 and ∆right: +0.54%). When using copying however, the results are lower in the constrained setting again suggesting that copying underperforms for items that have rarely been seen at training and development time (e.g., unconstrained *vs.* constrained, C, E2E: ∆BLEU: 0.11, ∆SER: −9.84 and ∆right: 12.9%).

For the WebNLG data, the difference between constrained and unconstrained setting is much stronger for both delexicalisation and copying. For instance, for copying the BLEU score in the unconstrained setting is 0.61 *vs.* 0.34 in the constrained setting. Semantic adequacy also drops noticeably (unconstrained: 83%, constrained: 41%). This is in line with Aharoni and Goldberg (2018)'s observation that in the unconstrained setting, the model learns to memorise association between facts and entities and thereby fails to generate text that adequately captures the meaning of the input data. The low scores for the copying mechanism also confirm the observation made above that copying underperforms for rare data fragments.

This difference between datasets is further discussed in the next paragraph.

Semantic Adequacy As mentioned above, the manual and automatic evaluation metrics we used to assess semantic adequacy strongly correlate. They both show that semantic adequacy is much lower for the WebNLG data (higher SER, higher proportion of wrong and missed items). This is not surprising, since the WebNLG dataset contains a much higher number of distinct values (3,648 against 79 in the E2E dataset) and exhibits a greater mismatch between input and output value names[8]. That is, the delta shows that the efficiency of copying and delexicalisation varies depending on the variety and content of the dataset.

The two datasets also differ with respect to the proportion of added slots which is higher for the E2E dataset and suggests an overfitting effect due to a skewed distribution in favour of inputs containing more than 3 attributes. Thus, the human evaluation shows that the majority of cases with added slots are cases where the input consists of three slots (the minimal number of attributes in E2E). The overgeneration can be explained by the restricted number of three-slot inputs in the E2E dataset (only 2.5% MRs out of the whole corpus). That claim is also supported by predictions produced by adversarial examples. While inputting dialogue moves consisting of 2 slots (the non-existent number of attributes in E2E), all eight E2E models tend to overgenerate by predicting texts with 3 or 4 slot-value pairs.

Fluency As mentioned in Section 2.6, while annotating the data for semantic adequacy, we found that almost all systems outputs were well-formed English sentences. The only exception

was the WebNLG model with copy mechanism where stutterings were spotted in half of the examined instances. Despite those repetitions, it was always possible to detect the subject-predicate-object structure (e.g., *1001 kelvins is an escape velocity of 1001 kelvins*; *Asterix was created by R. Goscinny and was created by R. Goscinny*), so the annotation was not hampered.

4 Related Work

Delexicalisation remains one of the most popular techniques for handling rare named entities. We analysed the submissions participating in the E2E and WebNLG challenges, which used a neural approach. Among them, six teams applied delexicalisation (Chen et al., 2018; Davoodi et al., 2018; Juraska et al., 2018; Puzikov and Gurevych, 2018; Trisedya et al., 2018; van der Lee et al., 2017), three resorted to the copy mechanism (Chen, 2018; Elder et al., 2018; Gehrmann et al., 2018), two developed character-based systems (Agarwal and Dymetman, 2017; Deriu and Cieliebak, 2018), and another two made use of byte pair encodings (Elder, 2017; Zhang et al., 2018).

A copy mechanism allows to detect a word in an input sequence and to copy it to an output sequence. The copy mechanism is widely used in text production approaches where it is relevant for handling rare input but also, for instance in text summarisation, for copying input into the output. See et al. (2017), Gu et al. (2016), Cheng and Lapata (2016) introduced pointer networks (Vinyals et al., 2015) extended with a copy mechanism for text summarisation. Similarly, Cao et al. (2017) uses a copy mechanism to generate paraphrases and He et al. (2017) to generate answers. The copy mechanism is often paired with coverage, which tries overcoming a common problem of repeated or omitted content in neural network outputs. It was used for instance in NMT (Tu et al., 2016) and summarisation (See et al., 2017).

Finally, some approaches apply neither copying nor delexicalisation. In particular, Nayak et al. (2017), working in the restaurant domain for dialogue systems, investigated ways of including slot values directly into the input representation of sequence-to-sequence models.

5 Conclusion

We investigated the impact of copying and delexicalisation on two datasets and using two different

---

[8]In the E2E dataset, the value name in the input is usually realised by the same string in the corresponding text while in WebNLG, they often differ, e.g., USA/the United States of America.

MR	name[Wildwood], eatType[pub], food[Italian], area[city centre], familyFriendly[no], near[Raja Indian Cuisine]
reference	Wildwood is an Italian pub situated in the city centre, near the Raja Indian Cuisine. It is not family-friendly.
unconstr., NIL	Wildwood is an Italian pub located in the city centre near **the Ranch**. It is not family-friendly.
unconstr., C	Wildwood is an Italian pub located in the city centre near Raja Indian Cuisine. It is not family-friendly.
unconstr., D	Wildwood is an Italian pub located in the city centre near Raja Indian Cuisine. It is not family-friendly.
unconstr., D+C	Wildwood is an Italian pub located near the Raja Indian Cuisine in the city centre. It is not family-friendly.
constr., NIL	In the city centre near Raja Indian Cuisine there is an Italian pub called the **Aromi**. It is not family-friendly.
constr., C	There is a pub near Raja Indian Cuisine in the city centre called **Aromi**. It serves Italian food and is not family-friendly.
constr., D	Wildwood is an Italian pub near Raja Indian Cuisine in the city centre. It is not family-friendly.
constr., D+C	Wildwood is an Italian pub located near the Raja Indian Cuisine in the city centre. It is not family-friendly.

Table 7: Example predictions for E2E. Mistakes are in bold.

MR	108 St Georges Terrace – floorCount – 50; 108 St Georges Terrace – completionDate – 1988
reference	108 St Georges Terrace has a floor count of 50 and was completed in 1988.
unconstr., NIL	108 St Georges Terrace **cost 120 million Australian dollars**.
unconstr., C	108 St Georges Terrace was completed in 1988 and has 50 floors.
unconstr., D	108 St Georges Terrace has 50 floors and was completed in 1988.
unconstr., D+C	108 St Georges Terrace has 50 floors and was completed in 1988.
constr., NIL	**The coach of the Democratic Party in the United States is the Conservative Party (UK).**
constr., C	108 Georges Terrace **completionDate were created by 108 Georges**.
constr., D	108 St Georges Terrace has 50 floors and was completed in 1988.
constr., D+C	108 St Georges Terrace has 50 floors and was completed in 1988.

Table 8: Example predictions for WebNLG. Mistakes are in bold.

ways of splitting the data into train, dev and test. The results show some regularities and highlight some interesting differences.

Overall, the results indicate that delexicalisation outperforms copying. Furthermore, they show that copying underperforms on rare items. Since delexicalisation is a somewhat ad hoc process, an interesting direction for future research would be to devise copying methods that are more accurate and that can better handle rare data items.

Another direction for future research would be to further investigate how the content and train/dev/test split of a dataset impact learning. Our results suggest two ways in which these may induce overfitting.

In the WebNLG dataset, strong associations between entities and facts seem to result in generation models that memorise facts with entities rather than generate a text that adequately verbalises the input. This is highlighted in the manual evaluation by the high number of wrong and missed data items observed both in the constrained and in the unconstrained setting.

In the E2E dataset, on the other hand, we saw that added facts are frequent and manual evaluation suggests that this is due to an overfitting effect whereby, because most inputs consists of more than three slot-value pairs, the models tend to overgenerate by predicting texts that verbalise four or more slot-value pairs.

In both cases, the copy-and-coverage mechanism does not suffice to ensure correct output and the results further decrease in the constrained setting. It would therefore be interesting to see to what extent better methods can be devised both for creating datasets and for devising train/dev/test splits that adequately test the ability of models to generalise.

Another direction for future work is to investigate the capability of byte pair encoding models and subword representations to handle rare input tokens in data-to-text generation.

Acknowledgments

The research presented in this paper was partially supported by the French National Research Agency (ANR) within the framework of the ANR-14-CE24-0033 WebNLG Project.

References

Shubham Agarwal and Marc Dymetman. 2017. A surprisingly effective out-of-the-box char2char model on the e2e nlg challenge dataset. In *Proceedings of the 18th Annual SIGdial Meeting on Discourse and Dialogue*, pages 158–163. Association for Computational Linguistics.

Roee Aharoni and Yoav Goldberg. 2018. Split and rephrase: Better evaluation and stronger baselines. In *Proceedings of the 56th Annual Meeting of the Association for Computational Linguistics (Volume 2: Short Papers)*, pages 719–724. Association for Computational Linguistics.

Dzmitry Bahdanau, Kyunghyun Cho, and Yoshua Bengio. 2015. Neural machine translation by jointly learning to align and translate. In *International Conference on Learning Representations*.

Ziqiang Cao, Chuwei Luo, Wenjie Li, and Sujian Li. 2017. Joint copying and restricted generation for paraphrase. In *AAAI*, pages 3152–3158.

Mingje Chen, Gerasimos Lampouras, and Andreas Vlachos. 2018. Sheffield at e2e: structured prediction approaches to end-to-end language generation. Technical report, E2E Challenge System Descriptions.

Shuang Chen. 2018. A general model for neural text generation from structured data. Technical report, E2E Challenge System Descriptions.

Jianpeng Cheng and Mirella Lapata. 2016. Neural summarization by extracting sentences and words. In *Proceedings of the 54th Annual Meeting of the Association for Computational Linguistics (Volume 1: Long Papers)*, pages 484–494. Association for Computational Linguistics.

Elnaz Davoodi, Charese Smiley, Dezhao Song, and Frank Schilder. 2018. The e2e nlg challenge: Training a sequence-to-sequence approach for meaning representation to natural language sentences. Technical report, E2E Challenge System Descriptions.

Michael Denkowski and Alon Lavie. 2014. Meteor universal: Language specific translation evaluation for any target language. In *Proceedings of the Ninth Workshop on Statistical Machine Translation*, pages 376–380. Association for Computational Linguistics.

Jan Deriu and Mark Cieliebak. 2018. End-to-end trainable system for enhancing diversity in natural language generation. Technical report, E2E Challenge System Descriptions.

George Doddington. 2002. Automatic evaluation of machine translation quality using n-gram co-occurrence statistics. In *Proceedings of the Second International Conference on Human Language Technology Research*, HLT '02, pages 138–145, San Francisco, CA, USA. Morgan Kaufmann Publishers Inc.

Ondřej Dušek and Filip Jurcicek. 2015. Training a natural language generator from unaligned data. In *Proceedings of the 53rd Annual Meeting of the Association for Computational Linguistics and the 7th International Joint Conference on Natural Language Processing (Volume 1: Long Papers)*, pages 451–461. Association for Computational Linguistics.

Henry Elder. 2017. Adapt centre submission for the webnlg challenge. Technical report, WebNLG Challenge System Descriptions.

Henry Elder, Sebastian Gehrmann, Alexander OConnor, and Qun Liu. 2018. E2e nlg challenge submission: Towards controllable generation of diverse natural language. Technical report, E2E Challenge System Descriptions.

Claire Gardent, Anastasia Shimorina, Shashi Narayan, and Laura Perez-Beltrachini. 2017a. Creating training corpora for nlg micro-planners. In *Proceedings of the 55th Annual Meeting of the Association for Computational Linguistics (Volume 1: Long Papers)*, pages 179–188. Association for Computational Linguistics.

Claire Gardent, Anastasia Shimorina, Shashi Narayan, and Laura Perez-Beltrachini. 2017b. The webnlg challenge: Generating text from rdf data. In *Proceedings of the 10th International Conference on Natural Language Generation*, pages 124–133. Association for Computational Linguistics.

Sebastian Gehrmann, Falcon Dai, Henry Elder, and Alexander Rush. 2018. End-to-end content and plan selection for natural language generation. Technical report, E2E Challenge System Descriptions.

Jiatao Gu, Zhengdong Lu, Hang Li, and Victor O.K. Li. 2016. Incorporating copying mechanism in sequence-to-sequence learning. In *Proceedings of the 54th Annual Meeting of the Association for Computational Linguistics (Volume 1: Long Papers)*, pages 1631–1640. Association for Computational Linguistics.

Shizhu He, Cao Liu, Kang Liu, and Jun Zhao. 2017. Generating natural answers by incorporating copying and retrieving mechanisms in sequence-to-sequence learning. In *Proceedings of the 55th Annual Meeting of the Association for Computational Linguistics (Volume 1: Long Papers)*, pages 199–208. Association for Computational Linguistics.

Juraj Juraska, Panagiotis Karagiannis, Kevin Bowden, and Marilyn Walker. 2018. A deep ensemble model with slot alignment for sequence-to-sequence natural language generation. In *Proceedings of the 2018 Conference of the North American Chapter of the Association for Computational Linguistics: Human Language Technologies, Volume 1 (Long Papers)*, pages 152–162. Association for Computational Linguistics.

Guillaume Klein, Yoon Kim, Yuntian Deng, Jean Senellart, and Alexander Rush. 2017. Opennmt: Open-source toolkit for neural machine translation. In *Proceedings of ACL 2017, System Demonstrations*, pages 67–72. Association for Computational Linguistics.

Chris van der Lee, Thiago Castro Ferreira, Emiel Krahmer, and Sander Wubben. 2017. Tilburg university models for the webnlg challenge. Technical report, WebNLG Challenge System Descriptions.

Chin-Yew Lin. 2004. Rouge: A package for automatic evaluation of summaries. In *Text Summarization Branches Out*.

Thang Luong, Hieu Pham, and Christopher D. Manning. 2015. Effective approaches to attention-based neural machine translation. In *Proceedings of the 2015 Conference on Empirical Methods in Natural Language Processing*, pages 1412–1421. Association for Computational Linguistics.

Neha Nayak, Dilek Hakkani-Tr, Marilyn Walker, and Larry Heck. 2017. To plan or not to plan? discourse planning in slot-value informed sequence to sequence models for language generation. In *Proc. Interspeech 2017*, pages 3339–3343.

Jekaterina Novikova, Ondřej Dušek, and Verena Rieser. 2017. The e2e dataset: New challenges for end-to-end generation. In *Proceedings of the 18th Annual SIGdial Meeting on Discourse and Dialogue*, pages 201–206. Association for Computational Linguistics.

Kishore Papineni, Salim Roukos, Todd Ward, and Wei-Jing Zhu. 2002. Bleu: a method for automatic evaluation of machine translation. In *Proceedings of the 40th Annual Meeting of the Association for Computational Linguistics*.

Yevgeniy Puzikov and Iryna Gurevych. 2018. E2e nlg challenge: Neural models vs. templates. Technical report, E2E Challenge System Descriptions.

Abigail See, Peter J. Liu, and Christopher D. Manning. 2017. Get to the point: Summarization with pointer-generator networks. In *Proceedings of the 55th Annual Meeting of the Association for Computational Linguistics (Volume 1: Long Papers)*, pages 1073–1083. Association for Computational Linguistics.

Bayu Distiawan Trisedya, Jianzhong Qi, Rui Zhang, and Wei Wang. 2018. Gtr-lstm: A triple encoder for sentence generation from rdf data. In *Proceedings of the 56th Annual Meeting of the Association for Computational Linguistics (Volume 1: Long Papers)*, pages 1627–1637. Association for Computational Linguistics.

Zhaopeng Tu, Zhengdong Lu, Yang Liu, Xiaohua Liu, and Hang Li. 2016. Modeling coverage for neural machine translation. In *Proceedings of the 54th Annual Meeting of the Association for Computational Linguistics (Volume 1: Long Papers)*, pages 76–85. Association for Computational Linguistics.

Oriol Vinyals, Meire Fortunato, and Navdeep Jaitly. 2015. Pointer networks. In *Advances in Neural Information Processing Systems*, pages 2692–2700.

Tsung-Hsien Wen, Milica Gasic, Nikola Mrkšić, Pei-Hao Su, David Vandyke, and Steve Young. 2015. Semantically conditioned lstm-based natural language generation for spoken dialogue systems. In *Proceedings of the 2015 Conference on Empirical Methods in Natural Language Processing*, pages 1711–1721. Association for Computational Linguistics.

Biao Zhang, Jing Yang, Qian Lin, and Jinsong Su. 2018. Attention regularized sequence-to-sequence learning for e2e nlg challenge. Technical report, E2E Challenge System Descriptions.

Comprehension Driven Document Planning in Natural Language Generation Systems

Craig Thomson, Ehud Reiter, and Somayajulu Sripada

Department of Computing Science, University of Aberdeen:
{c.thomson, e.reiter, yaji.sripada}@abdn.ac.uk

Abstract

This paper proposes an approach to NLG system design which focuses on generating output text which can be more easily processed by the reader. Ways in which cognitive theory might be combined with existing NLG techniques are discussed and two simple experiments in content ordering are presented.

1 Introduction

Document Planning is a difficult task for which there has been little research compared with other aspects of NLG. This is evident in the recent survey of NLG (Gatt and Krahmer, 2017) which devotes relatively little space to the problem. Existing approaches focus on human authored corpora as a gold standard, extracting relations from them in order to structure messages.

This paper proposes NLG system design with the guiding principle of producing output text which is optimal input for the human comprehension process. Comprehension in this context is the readers ability to process text. Construction-Integration (CI) theory (Kintsch, 1998) states that the cognitive process of reading is iterative. A highly interconnected knowledge graph based on both the text and the readers prior knowledge forms the readers mental model as text is processed.

A basic system is presented which orders messages using distributional semantics. The system uses a simple graph database to generate texts describing a products suitability for a task. An example generated text can be seen in Figure 1 with message ID's shown in parentheses.

The Nepal Extreme consists of an outsole, a rand, an upper and a lining (M0). It has a crampon rating which is required for mountaineering (M1). The outsole is stiff which is good (M3). The outsole and the rand consist of rubber which is durable, this suits mountaineering (M2,M4). The upper consists of synthetic leather and synthetic fabric which are both durable and water-resistant, this is good (M10,M8,M9,M11). The lining has insulation which suits mountaineering (M5). It also consists of Gore-Tex which is waterproof, this is required for mountaineering (M7). Gore-Tex is breathable as well which is good (M6).

Figure 1: Generated Product Description (message ID's in parenthesis)

2 NLG Document Planning

Document Planning within NLG is most often defined as the tasks of Content Determination and Document Structuring (Reiter and Dale, 1999). The system must decide what to say, how to say it and in what order. Further, if there is an optimal way to convey the input data such that the reader better comprehends it or is moved to action by it, then text should be generated in this way.

Approaches to Document Structuring generally focus on the relationships between messages. Schema based approaches (McKeown, 1985) and Rhetorical Structure Theory (RST) (Mann and Thompson, 1988), (Hovy, 1993) offer methods for generating text driven by the relations between messages or groups of messages. Whilst they have some limited success it is difficult to generalize

Proceedings of The 11th International Natural Language Generation Conference, pages 371–380,
Tilburg, The Netherlands, November 5-8, 2018. ©2018 Association for Computational Linguistics

them across domains. They also require much manual work and each relation needs to be defined by annotators who often do not agree even within a domain.

Machine Learning has been investigated as a method for both Content Determination and Document Structuring (Lapata, 2006), (Barzilay and Lee, 2004), (Liang et al., 2009). Such models rely on existing corpora within the domain and often paired data-corpus. If the domain is changed, or if there is disagreement as to what the correct corpus should be within a domain then such approaches experience difficulty.

3 The Construction-Integration Model

RST and Schemata focus on the relations between messages. Focus mechanisms can be used to check if different messages contain identical subjects or objects, utilizing this information when ordering messages. Focus (Sidner, 1979), Centering Theory (Grosz et al., 1995), (Poesio et al., 2004) and Scripts (Schank and Abelson, 1975) all offer appealing models for how people read and process text. It has been difficult however to implement any of them in an NLG context, especially in a general fashion. Perhaps this is because structuring a narrative is a complex task with many variables, of which individual approaches might only address a subset.

With the CI model (Kintsch, 1998) argues that a text is not in itself sufficient to account for the meaning acquired when the reader processes it. The reader's prior knowledge and experience add to the mental model which is established and iteratively modified as the text is processed. Whilst relations play a role, it is primarily the argument concepts of a proposition which activate and filter relevant concepts in the reader's mental model. This has some experimental backing, such as the work of (Schwanenflugel and White, 1991) which found that word priming from previous discourse altered the processing of words in future paragraphs.

Long-term memory (LTM) is the complete set of a readers knowledge. We do not have clearly indexed and direct access to this knowledge, even if it is relevant in the current context. Short-term memory (STM) contains our immediate thoughts although it is limited to a small number of concepts. The capacity of STM has a long history of study (Murdock Jr, 1960) and whilst estimates vary, they are often in the range of 10-15 terms. This is orders of magnitude lower than the number of terms and inferred concepts present in even short narratives, making STM an unsuitable mechanism to explain our ability to comprehend text (Ericsson and Kintsch, 1995). Kintsch describes human comprehension as loosely analogous to a computer system. Data is stored in both STM (registers / cache) as well as LTM (a large but slower access storage device). Working memory (WM) is the processor in this analogy. When a reader has expert knowledge of a domain they are able to use STM as an index to LTM, allowing for increased cognitive ability using WM. Expert readers can then create a rich set of inferences in their mental model which can then be used to better comprehend the text.

Kintsch suggests propositions as a suitable first class concept for modeling meaning in language. A proposition in the context of CI theory is a predicate-argument schema. This is a simplified view of propositions as conceived in formal logics. These simple propositions form complex ones, which in turn can be used to generate the text. CI theory adds additional nodes to this network which are not present in the text. These can be thought of as inferences based on the context of the propositions. Kintsch calls these 'knowledge elaborations' and relations between them and the proposition nodes from the text are added to form a complex highly interconnected network in the readers mental model.

4 Operationalization of the CI Model

Whilst a graph representation of data contains all the input information required to generate a given text, CI theory suggests this only forms a subset of the complete model of comprehension held by the reader. A system based on CI would require some method of simulating knowledge elaborations. This additional information would allow for the simulation of inferences, with the complete mental model being a combination of the propositional representation of the text and these inferences.

Distributional Semantic methods such as word embeddings created with word2vec (Mikolov et al., 2013) can provide indication of some kinds of relatedness between terms. Large data sets, such as Wikipedia, could be used as general knowledge. Domain specific corpora could also be used if available, either in place of or in some combination with general knowledge. By combining a graph representation of propositions with distributional semantics we would appear to have something which at a very basic level fits the CI model proposed by Kintsch. The angle between vector representations of arguments can be used to weight the system knowledge graph.

Knowledge elaborations are not added to the system knowledge base, this is not possible as there is no direct access to the users mental model. If distributional semantics can provide weights for the edges in our system graph, these can be considered when planning content. An assumption is made that when a path has short inter-message distances (lower angles between vectors), readers will be able to construct a richer interconnected network of propositions and knowledge elaborations than they would when inter-message distance is high.

Content would be selected from the system graph based on queries which return subsets of the graph. For example all paths between a start node and an end node. With the optional aid of content structuring rules, these subgraphs can be clustered and ordered based upon the edge weights as well as the connectivity of propositions, the latter being similar to implementations such as the WISHFUL system (Zukerman and McConachy, 1998). An optimization function would need to be implemented which finds the most appropriate representation of text given the graph data, input queries, distributional semantics and any imposed structural rules.

The bottom-up approach suggested here could be used in combination with existing top-down methods such as RST. A domain expert could inform the writer of the most important factors for a specific NLG system, providing an outline for the system. The comprehension driven techniques would then provide a sensible default where the narrative structure has not been defined. A convention-over-configuration approach.

5   System

The simple system used for exploratory investigation of NLG motivated by CI theory is outlined here. This is an early version of the system and further work is required to properly assess its capabilities. System input is in the form of messages which are extracted as paths from a knowledge graph. These messages are then ordered to form a Document Plan, before simple Micro Planning techniques are applied and the text is realized.

5.1   Vector Space Model

The Vector Space Model (VSM) was created using the Python Gensim implementation of Word2Vec. The corpus was stripped of all characters which were not within the alphabet for the given language. The corpus was lemmatized (using spaCy). The VSM is trained on English Wikipedia using Word2Vec. The training settings were skip-gram with 600 dimensions, a window of 5, negative sampling of 5 and all words with a lower total frequency than 5 were discarded.

Whilst Word2Vec has been used as a starting point, it is possible that models generated using systems such as GloVe (Pennington et al., 2014) and ELMo (Peters et al., 2018) would improve an NLG system which relies upon distributional semantics. Vector Space Specialisation (Mrksic et al., 2017) may also be useful.

5.1.1   System Input

Figure 2 shows nodes and relations from the graph database (Neo4j) for a Product which consists of Components, with each Component being made of Materials. All Products, Components and Materials (collectively Items) may have Attributes which have suitabilities for different Tasks. Items may also have a direct suitability for a Task.

The system will describe the suitability of a product for a task. The input to the system is an unordered list of proposition chains, with each proposition chain itself being an ordered list of proposition triples. All possible paths from the product to the task are extracted from the graph shown in Figure 2. Directionality of the edges is ignored at this stage. To generate the text shown in Figure 1 each unique path from the product (Nepal Extreme) to the task (mountaineering) is found and combined to form the list of proposition chains shown in Figure 3. In the special case where a task requires an attribute which is not present on the product or any of its child items, a chain is created to represent it. These proposition chains are messages in the NLG system.

5.1.2   Ordering to form the Document Plan

A vector representation for each message is calculated by combining the vectors for each argu-

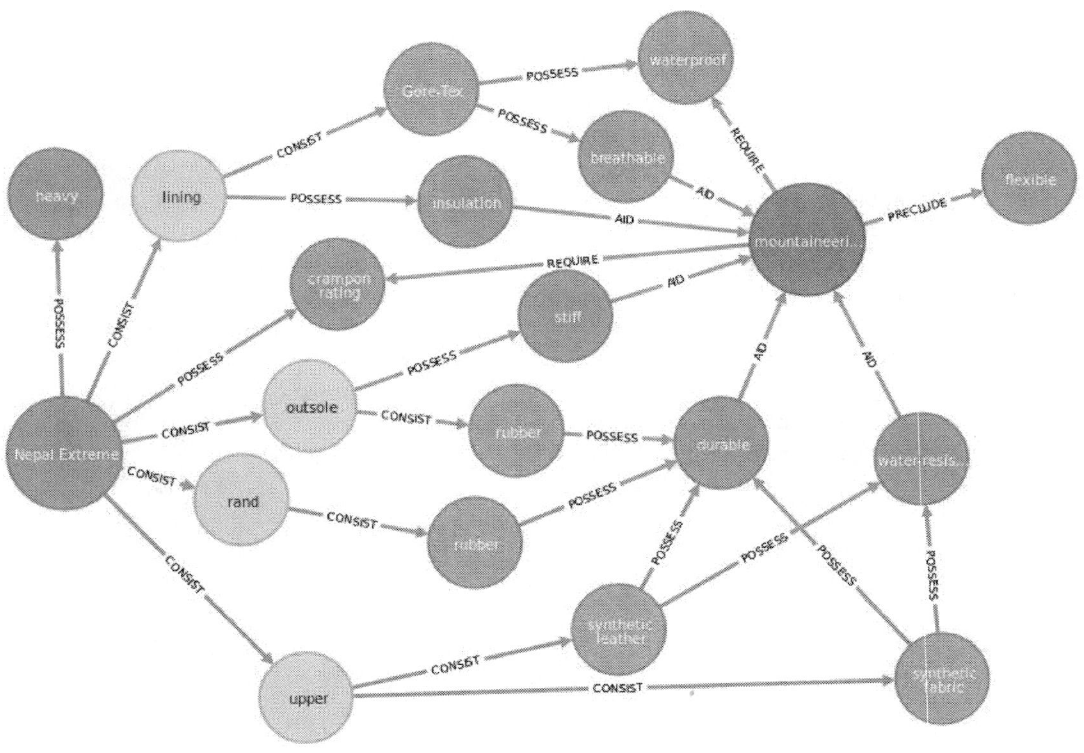

Figure 2: Product Composition, Attributes and Task.

ment. Vectors for individual arguments are taken from the VSM described in 5.1. The document plan is an ordered list of messages. To populate the document plan, messages are ordered using a greedy algorithm which minimizes inter-message distance. Inter-message distance is defined as the angle between the message vectors. The algorithm will stop once all input messages have been added to the document plan. The ordering of messages for the text example shown in Figure 1 can be seen, with inter-message distance in radians, in Figure 4.

5.2 Micro Planning

The focus of this paper is on content ordering at the Document Plan level. More advanced Micro Planning techniques could be used and would probably improve the quality of the text. The Aggregation and Referring Expression techniques (REG) used are far from state of the art and are meant only as a quick means to add variety and remove obvious repetition.

5.2.1 Aggregation

Functions were created to realize different patterns of proposition chains. The system iterates over the Document Plan, adding to a sublist of chains which are to be realized. If at any point the system determines it would be unable to realize this sublist, it reverts back to the last point at which it could and calls a suitable realizer function for the it. The system then starts from the chain which could not be realized, before continuing until all chains have been realized. It is always possible to realize a sublist of a single chain. Aggregation candidates can be seen on Figure 2 where paths diverge and re-converge, although the specific ordering means aggregation is not always possible.

Repeated propositions are removed at this stage. For example in Figure 3 the proposition triple at the beginning of both chains M3 and M4 describe how the 'Nepal Extreme CONSIST outsole'. This information was used for the purpose of ordering however it is only sent to be realized once, in the introductory sentence (M0) in Figure 1.

374

$$Q = \begin{vmatrix} A_{01} & \text{`Nepal Extreme'} & \text{NULL} & A_{03} & \text{`mountaineering'} \end{vmatrix}$$

$$M1 = \begin{vmatrix} A_{01} & \text{`Nepal Extreme'} & \text{POSSESS} & A_{02} & \text{`crampon rating'} \\ A_{02} & \text{`crampon rating'} & \text{REQUIRE} & A_{03} & \text{`mountaineering'} \end{vmatrix}$$

$$M2 = \begin{vmatrix} A_{01} & \text{`Nepal Extreme'} & \text{CONSIST} & A_{04} & \text{`rand'} \\ A_{04} & \text{`rand'} & \text{CONSIST} & A_{05} & \text{`rubber'} \\ A_{05} & \text{`rubber'} & \text{POSSESS} & A_{06} & \text{`durable'} \\ A_{06} & \text{`durable'} & \text{AID} & A_{03} & \text{`mountaineering'} \end{vmatrix}$$

$$M3 = \begin{vmatrix} A_{01} & \text{`Nepal Extreme'} & \text{CONSIST} & A_{07} & \text{`outsole'} \\ A_{07} & \text{`outsole'} & \text{POSSESS} & A_{08} & \text{`stiff'} \\ A_{08} & \text{`stiff'} & \text{AID} & A_{03} & \text{`mountaineering'} \end{vmatrix}$$

$$M4 = \begin{vmatrix} A_{01} & \text{`Nepal Extreme'} & \text{CONSIST} & A_{07} & \text{`outsole'} \\ A_{07} & \text{`outsole'} & \text{CONSIST} & A_{05} & \text{`rubber'} \\ A_{05} & \text{`rubber'} & \text{POSSESS} & A_{06} & \text{`durable'} \\ A_{06} & \text{`durable'} & \text{AID} & A_{03} & \text{`mountaineering'} \end{vmatrix}$$

$$M5 = \begin{vmatrix} A_{01} & \text{`Nepal Extreme'} & \text{CONSIST} & A_{09} & \text{`lining'} \\ A_{09} & \text{`lining'} & \text{POSSESS} & A_{10} & \text{`insulation'} \\ A_{10} & \text{`insulation'} & \text{AID} & A_{03} & \text{`mountaineering'} \end{vmatrix}$$

$$M6 = \begin{vmatrix} A_{01} & \text{`Nepal Extreme'} & \text{CONSIST} & A_{09} & \text{`lining'} \\ A_{09} & \text{`lining'} & \text{CONSIST} & A_{11} & \text{`Gore-Tex'} \\ A_{11} & \text{`Gore-Tex'} & \text{POSSESS} & A_{12} & \text{`breathable'} \\ A_{12} & \text{`breathable'} & \text{AID} & A_{03} & \text{`mountaineering'} \end{vmatrix}$$

$$M7 = \begin{vmatrix} A_{01} & \text{`Nepal Extreme'} & \text{CONSIST} & A_{09} & \text{`lining'} \\ A_{09} & \text{`lining'} & \text{CONSIST} & A_{11} & \text{`Gore-Tex'} \\ A_{11} & \text{`Gore-Tex'} & \text{POSSESS} & A_{13} & \text{`waterproof'} \\ A_{13} & \text{`waterproof'} & \text{REQUIRE} & A_{03} & \text{`mountaineering'} \end{vmatrix}$$

$$M8 = \begin{vmatrix} A_{01} & \text{`Nepal Extreme'} & \text{CONSIST} & A_{14} & \text{`upper'} \\ A_{14} & \text{`upper'} & \text{CONSIST} & A_{15} & \text{`synthetic fabric'} \\ A_{15} & \text{`synthetic fabric'} & \text{POSSESS} & A_{06} & \text{`durable'} \\ A_{06} & \text{`durable'} & \text{AID} & A_{03} & \text{`mountaineering'} \end{vmatrix}$$

$$M9 = \begin{vmatrix} A_{01} & \text{`Nepal Extreme'} & \text{CONSIST} & A_{14} & \text{`upper'} \\ A_{14} & \text{`upper'} & \text{CONSIST} & A_{15} & \text{`synthetic fabric'} \\ A_{15} & \text{`synthetic fabric'} & \text{POSSESS} & A_{16} & \text{`water-resistant'} \\ A_{16} & \text{`water-resistant'} & \text{AID} & A_{03} & \text{`mountaineering'} \end{vmatrix}$$

$$M10 = \begin{vmatrix} A_{01} & \text{`Nepal Extreme'} & \text{CONSIST} & A_{14} & \text{`upper'} \\ A_{14} & \text{`upper'} & \text{CONSIST} & A_{17} & \text{`synthetic leather'} \\ A_{17} & \text{`synthetic leather'} & \text{POSSESS} & A_{06} & \text{`durable'} \\ A_{06} & \text{`durable'} & \text{AID} & A_{03} & \text{`mountaineering'} \end{vmatrix}$$

$$M11 = \begin{vmatrix} A_{01} & \text{`Nepal Extreme'} & \text{CONSIST} & A_{14} & \text{`upper'} \\ A_{14} & \text{`upper'} & \text{CONSIST} & A_{17} & \text{`synthetic leather'} \\ A_{17} & \text{`synthetic leather'} & \text{POSSESS} & A_{16} & \text{`water-resistant'} \\ A_{16} & \text{`water-resistant'} & \text{AID} & A_{03} & \text{`mountaineering'} \end{vmatrix}$$

Figure 3: Input for text in Figure 1.

5.2.2 Referring Expression Generation

REG in the system is very simple. Pronouns are used only when the subject of the sentence is the same as that of the previous sentence. Whilst typically a Micro Planning task, this is done during realization, determined by the specific function which is called to realize the pattern of proposition chains.

5.3 Realization

Realization is performed using SimpleNLG (Gatt and Reiter, 2009). The realizer functions themselves use helper functions which construct commonly occurring patterns of text. An introductory sentence (labeled M0 in Figure 1) is included at the beginning of the output text detailing the product and its components. This is the only fixed ordering rule. The conjunction of components is realized in the order that the components would otherwise first be mentioned.

6 Experiments

6.1 Message Ordering

The first experiment evaluates the output of the simple product description system described in Section 5. The products within the system are all outdoor footwear. This domain was chosen because outdoor footwear can be broken down into a small number of components and attributes, then explained in broad terms. This would not hold true in a live system as there would be many ambiguity problems. It does however allow for a simple and contained preliminary test. The components of the product are parts of the boot/shoe such as upper, lining, rand and sole. Examples of materials are leather, suede and rubber. Attributes are most often adjectives such as durable or waterproof although they can also be concepts such as deep lugs. The tasks in this system are mountaineering, hiking and trail walking. With Item, Product, Component, Material, Attribute and Task being labels for nodes on the graph, the relations which are available are CONSIST, POSSESS, AID, HINDER, REQUIRE and PRECLUDE. These relationships can be seen on Figure 2. The experiment presented the below task descriptions to participants.

- Mountaineering - Walking and climbing in the mountains, often in the winter time when there is ice and snow.

- Hillwalking - Walking in the hills during every season except for winter. There may be some rough ground and it may be wet.

- Trail Walking - Walking on forest paths or other well kept trails. Usually in warmer weather although there may be some light rain.

In order to keep the system as simple as possible just four relations were used.

- AID - Attribute aids in the completion of the task, but is not essential. This is realized as 'is good for' or 'suits'.

- HINDER - Attribute hinders the completion of the task, but not to the point where it renders impossible. This is realized as 'is not good for' or 'does not suit'.

375

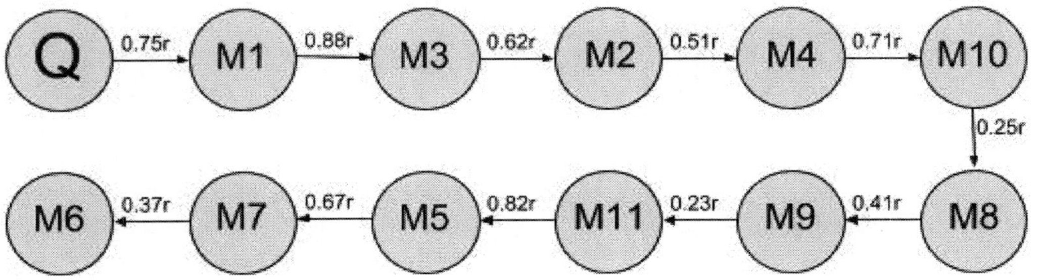

Figure 4: Ordering of Chains

- REQUIRE - Attribute is essential for the task. This is rendered as 'is essential for' or 'is required for'.

- PRECLUDE - Attribute precludes the item from the task. This was rendered as 'unsuitable for'. This was perhaps too close to 'does not suit'.

6.1.1 Experiment Setup

Participants were recruited for an online survey using email lists and social media. There were 37 respondents of which 28 stated English as their native language. Participants were shown 12 scenarios of which 6 were system generated narratives (like Figure 1) and 6 were hand crafted lists (like Figure 5 as might be seen on an online retail website. Each subset of 6 was equally divided such that participants received 3 product descriptions where the product was designed for the task (a match) and 3 descriptions where the product was not designed for the task (not a match). Participants were shown 4 statements and asked whether they agreed with each as it related to the current description using a five point Likert scale. The statements can be seen on Table 1

6.1.2 Hypothesis

Although this was exploratory research, the working hypothesis was that the ordering of the information would be evaluated as superior for the narrative descriptions, compared to list based descriptions. It was also suspected that narratives would outperform lists in the other categories although without a pilot experiment there was no real basis for this.

Attributes:

- Has a crampon rating.
- Upper - Made of synthetic leather and synthetic fabric. Is water-resistant and durable.
- Lining - Made of Gore-Tex. Is waterproof and breathable. Has insulation.
- Outsole - Made of durable rubber. Is stiff.
- Rand - Made of durable rubber.

Usefulness:

- Crampon rating and waterproof are essential for mountaineering.
- Water-resistant, durable, insulation, breathable and stiff are good for mountaineering.

Figure 5: List Based Description of Product Construction

6.1.3 Results and Evaluation

Table 1 shows the mean response for each question. Table 2 shows the results of the ANOVA test performed for each statement. The results show that several factors have an impact on the perceived quality of text. For all statements there was a statistically significant effect ($p < 0.005$) for whether the product being described was designed for the given task e.g. texts for mountaineering boots scored lower when being described for other tasks. There were also highly significant ($p < $ 3e-05) effects when comparing narrative to list structure for all statements except S2 (The description explains the suitability of the product for the task). Lists were more highly rated overall although whether this would hold as the number of propositions increases is unclear and worthy of further examination.

There is a lot of ambiguity with the definitions used for the relations, Items, Attributes and Tasks. The line between Components and Attributes can be blurred, with 'deep lugs' being a good example. This could be a Component of the outsole or an Attribute of it. Ultimately the distinction has little impact on the system as it is the path from the Product to the Task which is important and this is unaffected by a change to the label of a node. Further, it is the name of the node which is used for word embeddings, not the label itself. The only impact for the final text is that the relation (and therefore verb) used will be CONSIST for a Component and POSSESS for an Attribute.

Where ambiguity is more of a problem is in the relations and the Tasks. There is a lot of overlap between mountaineering, hiking and trail walking. It is not always the case that these tasks are carried out in isolation. A mountaineer might walk over easier terrain using footwear which is suboptimal in order to approach a technical climb for which the footwear is essential.

6.2 Ordering Different Languages

A second experiment was conducted using the same system, the only difference being that argument concepts were translated to different languages for the purposes of ordering. Vector space models were trained for French and Spanish Wikipedia using almost identical settings as the English model (Section 5.1). The only change in the training pipeline was to allow additional characters such as accented vowels. Arguments were translated into French and Spanish by a single native speaker for each language. The domain was explained to each annotator and they were asked to translate arguments to the semantically closest word or phrase, with annotators having the ability to translate from a single term to a short phrase or vice versa.

6.2.1 Results and Evaluation

There were some difficulties in translation. Only one annotator was used per language. Any further work involving the definition of terms based on semantics, whether within English or to another language, should be done with multiple annotators

and their agreement assessed.

Even with allowing annotators to translate into multiple terms, some did not directly translate. Hiking and Trail Walking were difficult to separate in French although ambiguity may exist in English as well. Trail Walking more often refers to walks at lower elevation on well maintained paths. Hiking includes walking off the path and on steeper, less stable terrain. A cursory Internet search for images based on these terms would appear to back this definition up, although exactly at which point Hiking becomes Trail Walking is ambiguous. The French annotator felt that 'randonnée' was the best term for both Hiking and Trail Walking although it was closer to Hiking. The phrase 'sentier de randonnée' is what Google translate returns for Trail Walking although this refers to the actual path which is walked upon, not the task. The concept could be expressed as a complex proposition although as this system only allows for simple lists of proposition triples, 'randonnée' was used for both tasks.

Table 3 shows the mean deviation of the ordering position of chains in Spanish and French when compared with the original English orderings. The overline indicates narratives where the stated product was not designed for the given task. It is difficult to evaluate the ordering based on translated proposition arguments as the English ordering makes for a poor gold standard. It is not clear if when using such a simple data source and such trivial propositions that there is a correct ordering.

Figure 6 shows the English realized text based on ordering using Spanish translations of graph nodes. The French example for the Nepal Extreme boot, used as an example throughout, was almost identical to the original English text in 1. Therefore, it has been omitted due to space restrictions.

7 Conclusion and Future Work

This paper describes a new approach to Document Planning based on the psychological model offered by Construction-Integration (CI) theory. It is interesting that CI suggests graph structure as a representation for human comprehension. Even if we cannot directly implement CI, the idea of manipulating graph data on the machine (speaker) end such that it might influence the 'graph data' on the human (hearer) end is worth pursuing. Investigation into this new approach is still in the early

	Statement	N	$\overline{N}$	L	$\overline{L}$
S1	The description is easy to read and understand	3.61	3.35	4.09	3.94
S2	The description explains the suitability of the product for the task	3.89	3.46	4.05	3.71
S3	The description is presented in a sensible order	3.63	3.29	4.05	3.75
S4	Overall, this is a good description	3.50	3.18	4.01	3.67

N : Narrative (matching Product)

L : List (matching Product)

$\overline{N}$: Narrative (non-matching Product)

$\overline{L}$: List (non-matching Product)

Table 1: Mean Response

Variable	S1		S2		S3		S4	
	F	p	F	p	F	p	F	p
Type	18.237	<0.001	2.135	0.145	18.43	<0.001	20.955	<0.001
Match	8.585	<0.01	22.685	<0.001	13.319	<0.001	15.003	<0.001
Participant	0.009	0.93	0.508	0.477	3.139	0.077	0.176	0.675
Product	1.001	0.44	1.503	0.129	1.376	0.183	1.615	0.093

Table 2: ANOVA Results

Task	French	Spanish	$French$	$Spanish$
Mountaineering	1.58	2.47	2.03	2.37
Hiking	2.60	2.27	2.96	1.67
Trail Walking	2.36	1.93	3.27	2.76

Table 3: Mean Order Variance per Language

stages and much remains to be done.

To fully test Comprehension Driven NLG, richer data sets and more comprehensive generation models will be required. Identifying and evaluating these are key prerequisites of future work. The qualitative evaluation of the first experiment presented in this paper only investigates the preferences of participants. *Evaluation of recall and deep understanding will also be required.* It is unclear as to whether the list based summary in its current form is a suitable gold standard to compare system generated narrative. Suitable methods of evaluating the Document Plan independently of the downstream system components will also be needed.

Existing approaches to Document Planning look at human authored corpora and attempt to construct narratives based upon patterns identified within them. This is either with hand crafted systems, ML/AI or a combination of the two. Whilst this corpus analysis is useful, it is a limitation of such methods that the text structure is insufficient to explain the comprehension process of reading

The Nepal Extreme consists of an upper, an outsole, a rand and a lining (M0). It has a crampon rating which is required for mountaineering (M1). The upper consists of synthetic fabric and synthetic leather which are both water-resistant and durable, this is good (M9,M11,M10,M8). The outsole and the rand consist of rubber which is durable, this suits mountaineering (M4,M2). It is also stiff which is good (M3). The lining consists of Gore-Tex which is waterproof (M7), this is required for mountaineering. Gore-Tex is breathable as well which suits mountaineering (M6). It has insulation which is good (M5).

Figure 6: Example Text (Spanish Order).

it.

Attempting to combine an NLG system's knowledge base with the mental knowledge base of the reader may appear highly impractical. Both however are processing systems, with the output from the former being the input to the latter. It therefore makes sense to optimize the writers output such that it can be more easily processed by the reader.

Future work will focus on identifying NLG techniques which generate output with this as a primary consideration. It is the use of the human comprehension process itself, almost as a specialist node in a heterogeneous system, which will frame the research.

The most important task is designing an experiment which can demonstrate that either recall or deep understanding has been improved using an NLG system designed following comprehension principles. Work is in progress towards a system which will attempt to select optimal paths through a distributional semantical weighted proposition graph to explain a concept. *The system will look for paths, with smaller individual edge weights, rather than shorter paths which may be available but have greater inter-message distance.* It is hoped this will increase the chance that connected inferences are generated in the reader's mental model. Continued work on sentence ordering as discussed in this paper will be used to order the content.

As with many NLG systems, what has been discussed so far only operates on a small number of messages which at most would constitute a single paragraph or short communication format. *Document Planning is not however restricted to short texts and more research in the planning of long form documents is required.* Whilst this is a very complex task, paragraphs could be identified by clustering based on distributional semantics content. The most prominent propositions within paragraphs could be identified and used to generate top and tail statements, bridging paragraphs and even chapters. All of these techniques would first and foremost be comprehension driven.

Acknowledgments

This work is funded by the Engineering and Physical Sciences Research Council (EPSRC), which funds Craig Thomson under a National Productivity Investment Fund Doctoral Studentship (EP/R512412/1).

The authors would also like to thank Théo Morel and Alejandro Ramos Soto for translating the Argument Concepts to French and Spanish respectively.

References

Regina Barzilay and Lillian Lee. 2004. Catching the drift: Probabilistic content models, with applications to generation and summarization. *CoRR*, cs.CL/0405039.

K Anders Ericsson and Walter Kintsch. 1995. Long-term working memory. *Psychological review*, 102(2):211.

Albert Gatt and Emiel Krahmer. 2017. Survey of the state of the art in natural language generation: Core tasks, applications and evaluation. *CoRR*, abs/1703.09902.

Albert Gatt and Ehud Reiter. 2009. Simplenlg: A realisation engine for practical applications. pages 90–93.

Barbara J. Grosz, Scott Weinstein, and Aravind K. Joshi. 1995. Centering: A framework for modeling the local coherence of discourse. *Comput. Linguist.*, 21(2):203–225.

Eduard H. Hovy. 1993. Automated discourse generation using discourse structure relations. *Artificial Intelligence*, 63(1):341 – 385.

Walter Kintsch. 1998. *Comprehension : a paradigm for cognition*, 1st edition. Cambridge University Press.

Mirella Lapata. 2006. Automatic evaluation of information ordering: Kendall's tau. *Comput. Linguist.*, 32(4):471–484.

Percy Liang, Michael I. Jordan, and Dan Klein. 2009. Learning semantic correspondences with less supervision. In *Proceedings of the Joint Conference of the 47th Annual Meeting of the ACL and the 4th International Joint Conference on Natural Language Processing of the AFNLP: Volume 1 - Volume 1*, ACL '09, pages 91–99, Stroudsburg, PA, USA. Association for Computational Linguistics.

W.C. Mann and S.A. Thompson. 1988. Rhetorical structure theory: Toward a functional theory of text organization. *Text*, 8(3):243–281. Cited By 820.

K.R. McKeown. 1985. Discourse strategies for generating natural-language text. *Artificial Intelligence*, 27(1):1–41. Cited By 112.

Tomas Mikolov, Kai Chen, Greg Corrado, and Jeffrey Dean. 2013. Efficient estimation of word representations in vector space. *CoRR*, abs/1301.3781.

Nikola Mrksic, Ivan Vulic, Diarmuid Ó Séaghdha, Ira Leviant, Roi Reichart, Milica Gasic, Anna Korhonen, and Steve J. Young. 2017. Semantic specialisation of distributional word vector spaces using monolingual and cross-lingual constraints. *CoRR*, abs/1706.00374.

Bennet B Murdock Jr. 1960. The immediate retention of unrelated words. *Journal of Experimental Psychology*, 60(4):222.

Jeffrey Pennington, Richard Socher, and Christopher D. Manning. 2014. Glove: Global vectors for word representation. In *Empirical Methods in Natural Language Processing (EMNLP)*, pages 1532–1543.

Matthew E. Peters, Mark Neumann, Mohit Iyyer, Matt Gardner, Christopher Clark, Kenton Lee, and Luke Zettlemoyer. 2018. Deep contextualized word representations. *CoRR*, abs/1802.05365.

Massimo Poesio, Rosemary Stevenson, Barbara Di Eugenio, and Janet Hitzeman. 2004. Centering: A parametric theory and its instantiations. *Comput. Linguist.*, 30(3):309–363.

Ehud Reiter and Robert Dale. 1999. *Building natural language generation systems*. Studies in natural language processing. Cambridge University Press, New York.

Roger C. Schank and Robert P. Abelson. 1975. Scripts, plans, and knowledge. In *Proceedings of the 4th International Joint Conference on Artificial Intelligence - Volume 1*, IJCAI'75, pages 151–157, San Francisco, CA, USA. Morgan Kaufmann Publishers Inc.

Paula J. Schwanenflugel and Calvin R. White. 1991. The influence of paragraph information on the processing of upcoming words. *Reading Research Quarterly*, 26(2):160–177.

Candace L Sidner. 1979. Towards a computational theory of definite anaphora comprehension in english discourse. Technical report, Cambridge, MA, USA.

Ingrid Zukerman and Richard McConachy. 1998. An optimizing method for structuring inferentially linked discourse.

Adapting Neural Single-Document Summarization Model for Abstractive Multi-Document Summarization: A Pilot Study

Jianmin Zhang and **Jiwei Tan** and **Xiaojun Wan**

Institute of Computer Science and Technology, Peking University

The MOE Key Laboratory of Computational Linguistics, Peking University

{zhangjianmin2015,tanjiwei,wanxiaojun}@pku.edu.cn

Abstract

Till now, neural abstractive summarization methods have achieved great success for single document summarization (SDS). However, due to the lack of large scale multi-document summaries, such methods can be hardly applied to multi-document summarization (MDS). In this paper, we investigate neural abstractive methods for MDS by adapting a state-of-the-art neural abstractive summarization model for SDS. We propose an approach to extend the neural abstractive model trained on large scale SDS data to the MDS task. Our approach only makes use of a small number of multi-document summaries for fine tuning. Experimental results on two benchmark DUC datasets demonstrate that our approach can outperform a variety of baseline neural models.

1 Introduction

Document summarization is a task of automatically producing a summary for given documents. Different from Single Document Summarization (SDS) which generates a summary for each given document, Multi-Document Summarization (MDS) aims to generate a summary for a set of topic-related documents. Previous approaches to document summarization can be generally categorized to extractive methods and abstractive methods. Extractive methods produce a summary by extracting and merging sentences from the original document(s), while abstractive methods generate a summary using arbitrary words and expressions based on understanding the document(s). Due to the difficulty of natural language understanding and generation, previous research on document summarization is more focused on extrac-

tive methods (Yao et al., 2017). However, extractive methods suffer from the inherent drawbacks of discourse incoherence and long, redundant sentences, which hampers its application in reality (Tan et al., 2017). Recently, with the success of sequence-to-sequence (seq2seq) models in natural language generation tasks including machine translation (Bahdanau et al., 2014) and dialog systems (Mou et al., 2016), abstractive summarization methods has received increasing attention. With the resource of large-scale corpus of human summaries, it is able to train an abstractive summarization model in an end-to-end framework. Neural abstractive summarization models (See et al., 2017; Tan et al., 2017) have surpass the performance of extractive methods on single document summarization task with abundant training data.

Unfortunately, the extension of seq2seq models to MDS is not straightforward. Neural abstractive summarization models are usually trained on about hundreds of thousands of gold summaries, but there are usually very few human summaries available for the MDS task. More specifically, in the news domain, there is only a few hundred multi-document summaries provided by DUC and TAC conferences in total, which are largely insufficient for training neural abstractive models. Apart from insufficient training data, neural models for abstractive MDS also face the challenge of much more input content, and the study is still in the primary stage.

In this study, we investigate applying seq2seq models to the MDS task. We attempt various ways of extending neural abstractive summarization models pre-trained on the SDS data to the MDS task, and reveal that neural abstractive summarization models do not transfer well on a different dataset. Then we study the factors which affect the transfer performance, and propose methods to

Proceedings of The 11th International Natural Language Generation Conference, pages 381–390,
Tilburg, The Netherlands, November 5-8, 2018. ©2018 Association for Computational Linguistics

adapt the pre-trained model to the MDS task. We also study leveraging the few MDS training data to further improve the pre-trained model. We conduct experiment on the benchmark DUC datasets, and experiment results demonstrate our approach is able to achieve considerable improvement over a variety of neural baselines.

The contributions of this study are summarized as follows:

- To the best of our knowledge, our work is one of the very few pioneering works to investigate adapting neural abstractive summarization models of single document summarization to the task of multi-document summarization.

- We propose a novel approach to adapt the neural model trained on the SDS data to the MDS task, and leverage the few MDS training data to further improve the pre-trained model.

- Evaluation results demonstrate the efficacy of our proposed approach, which outperforms a variety of neural baselines.

We organize the paper as follows. In Section 2 we introduce related work. In Section 3 we describe the previous neural abstractive summarization model. Then we introduce our proposed approach in Section 4. Experiment results and discussion are presented in Section 5. Finally, we conclude this paper in Section 6.

2 Related Work

2.1 Extractive Summarization Methods

The study of MDS is pioneered by (McKeown and Radev, 1995), and early notable works also include (McKeown et al., 1999; Radev et al., 2000). Extractive summarization systems that compose a summary from a number of important sentences from the source documents are by far the most popular solution for MDS (Avinesh and Meyer, 2017). Redundancy is one of the biggest problems for extractive methods (Gambhir and Gupta, 2017), and the Maximal Marginal Relevance (MRR) (Carbonell and Goldstein, 1998) is a well-known algorithm for reducing redundancy. In the past years various models under extractive framework have been proposed (Tao et al., 2008; Wan and Yang, 2008; Wang et al., 2011; Tan et al., 2015). One important architecture is

to model MDS as a budgeted maximum coverage problem, including the prior approach (McDonald, 2007) and improved models (Woodsend and Lapata, 2012; Li et al., 2013; Boudin et al., 2015). There are still recent studies under traditional extractive framework (Peyrard and Eckle-Kohler, 2017; Avinesh and Meyer, 2017).

2.2 Abstractive Summarization Methods

Abstractive summarization methods aim at generating the summary based on understanding the original documents. Sequence-to-sequence models with attention mechanism have been applied to the abstractive summarization task. Success attempts are on sentence summarization (Rush et al., 2015; Chopra et al., 2016; Nallapati et al., 2016) or single document summarization (Tan et al., 2017; See et al., 2017; Paulus et al., 2017), which have abundant gold summaries to train an end-to-end system.

Until very recently, there occurs attempt for abstractive multi-document summarization under the seq2seq framework. The lack of enough train examples is the major obstacle to this end. To address this, Liu et al. (2018) study the task of generating English Wikipedia under a viewpoint of multi-document summarization. They construct a large corpus with reference summaries, so that end-to-end training of a seq2seq is capable. Their study reveals that seq2seq model works when there are abundant training data for MDS. Very recently Baumel et al. (2018) try to apply pre-trained abstractive summarization model of SDS to the query-focused summarization task. They sort the input documents and then iteratively apply the SDS model to summarize each single document until the length limit is reached. Their major concern is incorporating query information into the abstractive model or using the query to filter the original documents, which is different from our work focusing on generic multi-document summarization. Moreover, the intuitive idea of using the SDS model for summarizing each single document in the multi-document set is adopted in the baseline models for comparison as well.

3 Preliminaries

In this work we investigate abstractive MDS approach based on the state-of-the-art neural abstractive model in Tan et al. (2017). Compared with another neural abstractive model in See et al. (2017),

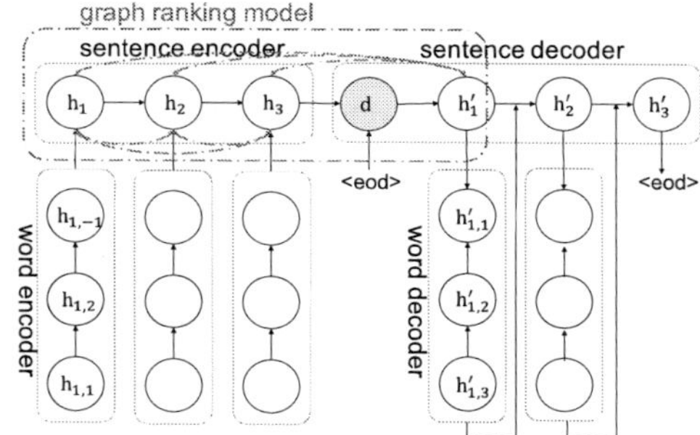

Figure 1: SinABS model. The figure is borrowed from Tan et al. (2017).

Tan et al. (2017) adopt a hierarchical encoder-decoder framework which we found is more scalable to more and longer input documents. The model is named **SinABS** in this paper. SinABS uses a hierarchical encoder-decoder framework like Li et al. (2015), where a PageRank (Page et al., 1999) based attention mechanism is proposed to identify salient sentences in the original documents. The SinABS model is illustrated in Figure 1.We introduce the SinABS model following Tan et al. (2017).

3.1 Encoder

The target of the encoder is to encode the input documents into vector representations. SinABS adopts a hierarchical encoder framework, where a word encoder enc_{word} is used for encoding a sentence into the sentence representation from its words, as $\mathbf{h}_{i,k} = enc_{\text{word}}(\mathbf{h}_{i,k-1}, \mathbf{e}_{i,k})$, where $\mathbf{h}_{i,k}$ represents the hidden state when LSTM receives word $\mathbf{e}_{i,k}$. Then a sentence encoder enc_{sent} is used for encoding an input document into the document representation from its sentences, as $\mathbf{h}_i = enc_{\text{sent}}(\mathbf{h}_{i-1}, \mathbf{x}_i)$, where $\mathbf{x}_i = \mathbf{h}_{i,-1}$ is the last hidden state when word encoder receives the whole sentence i. The input to the word encoder is the word sequence of a sentence, appended with an "<eos>" token indicating the end of a sentence. The last hidden state after the word encoder receives "<eos>" is used as the embedding representation of the sentence. A sentence encoder is used to sequentially receive the embeddings of the sentences. A pseudo sentence of an "<eod>" token is appended at the end of the document to indicate the end of the whole document. The hidden state after the sentence encoder receives "<eod>" is treated as the representation of the input doc-

ument, denoted as **c**. Long Short-Term Memory (LSTM) (Hochreiter and Schmidhuber, 1997) is used as the word encoder enc_{word} and also the sentence encoder enc_{sent}.

3.2 Decoder

Similar to the hierarchical encoder, The sentence decoder dec_{sent} receives the document representation **d** as the initial state $\mathbf{h}'_0 = \mathbf{d}$, and predicts the sentence representations sequentially, by $\mathbf{h}'_j = dec_{\text{sent}}(\mathbf{h}'_{j-1}, \mathbf{x}'_{j-1})$, where $\mathbf{x}'_{j-1}$ is the encoded representation of the previously generated sentence s'_{j-1}. The word decoder dec_{word} receives a sentence representation $\mathbf{h}'_j$ as the initial state $\mathbf{h}'_{j,0} = \mathbf{h}'_j$, and predicts the word representations sequentially, by $\mathbf{h}'_{j,k} = dec_{\text{word}}(\mathbf{h}'_{j,k-1}, \mathbf{e}_{j,k-1})$, where $\mathbf{e}_{j,k-1}$ is the embedding of the previously generated word. The predicted word representations are first concatenated with the context vector $\mathbf{c}_j$, and then mapped to vectors of the vocabulary size dimension by a projection layer, and finally normalized by a softmax layer as the probability distribution of generating the words in the vocabulary. A word decoder stops when it generates the "<eos>" token and similarly the sentence decoder stops when it generates the "<eod>" token.

3.3 Attention Mechanism

The attention mechanism used in SinABS sets a different context vector $\mathbf{c}_j$ when generating the words of sentence j, by $\mathbf{c}_j = \sum_i \alpha_i^j \mathbf{h}_i$. The graph-based attention mechanism in Tan et al. (2017) adopts the topic-sensitive PageRank algorithm to compute the attention weights, by

$$\mathbf{f} = (1 - \lambda)(I - \lambda W D^{-1})^{-1}\mathbf{y} \qquad (1)$$

where $\mathbf{f} = [f_1, \ldots, f_n] \in \mathcal{R}^n$ denotes the rank scores of the n original sentences. D is a diagonal matrix with its (i, i)-element equal to the sum of the i-th column of W. $W(i, j) = \mathbf{h}_i^T P \mathbf{h}_j$ where P is a parameter matrix to be learned. λ is a damping factor and set to 0.9. $\mathbf{y} \in \mathcal{R}^n$ is a one hot vector and only $y_0 = 1$. The ranked scores are then integrated with a distraction mechanism, and finally computed as:

$$\alpha_i^j = \frac{\max(f_i^j - f_i^{j-1}, 0)}{\sum_l \left(\max(f_l^j - f_l^{j-1}, 0) \right)} \qquad (2)$$

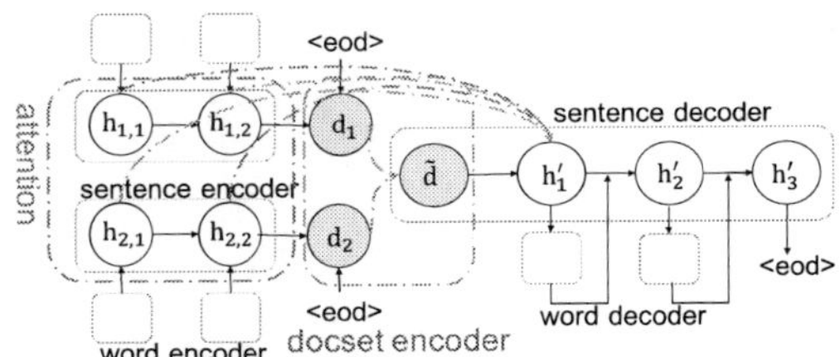

Figure 2: Framework of our model. The difference from Figure 1 is the docset encoder and the concentrated attention mechanism.

4 Our Approach

4.1 Overview

In this section we introduce our approach. Our abstractive MDS model is the extension of the single document summarization model SinABS. It is an encoder-decoder framework, which takes all the documents of a document set as input, then encodes the documents into a document set representation, and further generates the summary with a decoder. To adapt SinABS to the MDS task, our model is different from SinABS in the encoder model and the attention mechanism, and it will also be tuned on the MDS dataset to adapt to the MDS task. The framework of our model is illustrated in Figure 2.

4.2 Multi-Document Encoder

The major difference of MDS is that we need to generate a summary for multiple input documents. So our system needs to deal with the multiple input documents although SinABS is trained to generate a summary for one document. Considering that the decoder generates the summary from the representation vector encoded by the encoder, we can generate a summary for a document set if the document set is encoded to a representation vector containing its key information. In our approach, we achieve this by adding a document set encoder, to encode a set of document representation vectors into a document set representation. Thus the hierarchical encoder structure becomes three levels.

The document set encoder enc_{docset} takes document vectors $\{\mathbf{d}_m\}$, $m \in [1, M]$ where M is the number of documents in a document set as input, produces a new document set vector $\tilde{\mathbf{d}}$, and then $\tilde{\mathbf{d}}$ is provided to the decoder to generate the summary for the document set. The decoder will be a two-level hierarchical framework similar to that

in Tan et al. (2017). Since there is no order and dependency relationship between different documents in a document set, it is not reasonable to use LSTM as the document set encoder. Instead, we define the document set encoder as:

$$\tilde{\mathbf{d}} = enc_{\text{docset}}\left(\{\mathbf{d}_m\}\right) = \sum_m w_m \mathbf{d}_m \qquad (3)$$

where $\mathbf{w} = [w_1, \ldots, w_m] \in \mathcal{R}^m$ is a weight vector to merge the document vectors into a document set representation. The weight vector $\mathbf{w}$ can be a fixed one as $\mathbf{w} = [1/m, \ldots, 1/m]$, but in our system we hope to assign different w_m to different $\mathbf{d}_m$, since different documents may contribute differently to the overall summary. However, it is unreasonable to treat $\mathbf{w}$ as a parameter vector and learn it directly, because the weight w_m for $\mathbf{d}_m$ should be based on $\mathbf{d}_m$. The position of a document should not affect its weight since there is no order in a document set.

In our system the weight for a document is decided based on the document itself, and its contribution to the representation of the overall document set. Therefore, we define:

$$w_m = \frac{\mathbf{q}^T[\mathbf{d}_m; \mathbf{d}_\Sigma]}{\sum_{m'} \mathbf{q}^T[\mathbf{d}_{m'}; \mathbf{d}_\Sigma]} \qquad (4)$$

where $\mathbf{d}_\Sigma = \sum_m \mathbf{d}_m$ and $[\mathbf{d}_m; \mathbf{d}_\Sigma]$ is the concatenation of $\mathbf{d}_m$ and $\mathbf{d}_\Sigma$. The intuitive explanation of Eq. 4 is that the weight of $\mathbf{d}_m$ is decided by its relationship (modeled by parameterized dot product) with the representation of the whole document set $\mathbf{d}_\Sigma$. $\mathbf{q}$ is the parameter to be learned, whose dimension is twice the dimension of $\mathbf{d}_m$ or $\mathbf{d}_\Sigma$.

4.3 Attention

The decoder receives the document set vector $\tilde{\mathbf{d}}$ as initial state and generates the output summary from the document set representation. The difference of the decoder to SinABS is that when computing the attention distribution now it should be computed on all the sentences in a document set. Not only the amount of original sentences becomes larger, but also the original sentences come from different documents. Nevertheless, we believe the topic-sensitive PageRank attention mechanism is still able to identify salient sentences, since similar idea in LexRank and TextRank methods achieves good performance on MDS. Therefore, the attention distribution is now computed on all the input sentences, by conducting the topic-sensitive PageRank algorithm in Eq. 1 and Eq. 2 on all the original sentences.

However, a problem does occur because the amount of original sentences is much larger than that of single document summarization task. Even though the graph-based attention mechanism is still able to rank the relevance and salience of original sentences, the attention distribution will be too disperse and even. This results in that too many sentences are considered to produce the context vector, making the context vector contain too much information. We believe a more concentrated attention distribution will be better. Therefore, when computing the attention weights, only the top K ranked sentences can have attention weights. This can be easily realized by switching the rank scores of sentences not in largest K sentences to minimum value and re-normalizing the attention weights. K is a hyper-parameter.

4.4 Model Tuning

SinABS is trained on the single document summarization corpus - CNN/DailyMail. Although both the CNN/DailyMail corpus and DUC datasets are news data, the reference summaries of the datasets differ much. In order to better adapt the Sin-ABS model on the MDS task, we attempt to fine tune the pre-trained SinABS model, although we have only a few reference summaries for the MDS task. In our approach we tune the decoders of the model. The parameters are the LSTM parameters of the word and sentence decoders, and the weight vector $\mathbf{q}$ in the document set encoder. The loss function and the optimization algorithm are the same with those of the original SinABS model, and we use the cross-entropy loss and the Adam (Kingma and Ba, 2014) algorithm to train the model. To prevent overfitting the training is stopped when performance begins to decrease.

5 Experiments

5.1 Dataset

We conduct experiments on the DUC datasets which are widely used in document summarization. We use the MDS tasks of DUC 2002 and 2004 as test sets, which contain 50 document sets and 59 document sets, respectively. When evaluating on the DUC 2004 dataset, the DUC 2001-2003 and DUC 2005-2007 datasets are used for tuning the model, and DUC 2001, DUC 2003-2007

datasets are used when testing on the DUC 2002 dataset. The MDS tasks of DUC 2005-2007 are query focused summarization, but we ignore the query since these datasets are only used for training. There are on average 10 documents per set in DUC 2004 and 9.58 documents per set in DUC 2002. For the datasets of DUC 2005-2007 we use only the top 10 documents which are most similar to the topic of a document set.

5.2 Implementation

We implement our approach based on the source code and pre-trained model on the CNN/DailyMail corpus provided by Tan et al. (2017). We process the DUC datasets similar to Tan et al. (2017), including tokenizing and lower-casing the text, replacing all digit characters with the "#" symbol and label all name entities with CoreNLP toolkit[1]. The "#" symbols are mapped back to the original digits after decoding according to the context. We also implement our model in Theano[2] based on the SinABS model. K is set to 15 based on developing on the training set.

5.3 Evaluation Metric

ROUGE: We use ROUGE-1.5.5 (Lin and Hovy, 2003) toolkit and report the Rouge-1, Rouge-2 and Rouge-SU4 F1-scores, which has been widely adopted by DUC and TAC for automatic summary quality evaluation. It measured summary quality by counting overlapping units such as the n-gram, word sequences and word pairs between the candidate summary and the reference summary.

Edit distance: In order to test if our model is truly abstractive, instead of simply copying relevant fragments verbatim from the input documents, we compute the word edit-distance between each generated sentence s_i and the most similar original sentence of it, as ed_i, and report the average $ED = \frac{1}{n} \sum_{i=1}^{n} ed_i$.

Considering the significant difference of length between sentences, we also divide the word edit-distance for each generated sentence by its word number w_i as $ED/w = \frac{1}{n} \sum_{i=1}^{n} ed_i/w_i$.

5.4 Baselines

To verify the effectiveness of our approach, we investigate various strategies to adapt SinABS to MDS task for comparison. Since SinABS takes

---

[1] http://stanfordnlp.github.io/CoreNLP/
[2] https://github.com/Theano/Theano

one document as input but there are multiple input documents in the MDS task, we explore four possible approaches to address this ("ex." indicates extractive method and "ab." indicates abstractive method. SinABS is denoted as Δ).

Single-ab.: One representative document of every document set is selected as the input document to the SinABS model. This is the most straightforward way to adapt single document summarization model to the MDS task. The representative document is chosen by conducting the PageRank (Page et al., 1999) algorithm on every document set. This baseline is denoted as P.R.+Δ.

Single-ex.+Merge+Single-ab.: Different from selecting one representative document, we also investigate constructing a pseudo document as the input to SinABS. We achieve this by first using extractive single document summarization method to summarize every input document, and then concatenate these summaries to form a new document. The motivation of this strategy is to keep only the important content of original documents, so that the input is both the key information and suitable for SinABS to handle. The methods for extractive summarization are Lead, LexRank, TextRank and Centroid. These four baselines are denoted as Lead/Lex./Text./Cent.+Δ respectively.

Single-ab.+Merge+Single-ab.: Generate the abstractive summary for every original document with SinABS. Then the abstractive summaries are concatenated to form a pseudo document, as the input to SinABS again. The difference from Single-ex.+Merge+Single-ab. is that no extractive methods are required. This baseline his denoted as Δ+Δ.

Single-ab.+Multi-ex.: Generate the summary for every original document, then summarize these summaries using some extractive MDS method instead of SinABS to get the final summary. The extractive MDS methods used are Lead, LexRank, TextRank, Centroid and Coverage. Note that Coverage is specially designed for the MDS task, therefore it is not used in Single-ex.+Merge+Single-ab. baselines. These five baselines are denoted as Δ+Lex./Text./Cent./Cov./Lead.

We introduce the extractive MDS methods used in previous baselines as follows. These extractive methods themselves can also be the baselines for comparison.

Lead: This baseline method takes the first sentences one by one in single document or the first document in the document collection, where documents in the collection are assumed to be ordered by name.

Coverage: It takes the first sentence one by one from the first document to the last document in the document collection.

LexRank: LexRank (Erkan and Radev, 2004) computes sentence importance based on the concept of eigenvector centrality in a graph representation of sentences. In this model, a connectivity matrix based on intra-sentence cosine similarity is used as the adjacency matrix of the graph representation of sentences.

TextRank: TextRank (Mihalcea and Tarau, 2004) builds a graph and adds each sentence as vertices, the overlap of two sentences is treated as the relation that connects sentences. Then graph-based ranking algorithm is applied until convergence. Sentences are sorted based on their final score and a greedy algorithm is employed to impose diversity penalty on each sentence and select summary sentences.

Centroid: In centroid-based summarization (Radev et al., 2000) method, a pseudo-sentence of the document called centroid is calculated. The centroid consists of words with TF-IDF scores above a predefined threshold. The score of each sentence is defined by summing the scores based on different features including cosine similarity of sentences with the centroid, position weight and cosine similarity with the first sentence.

Method	R-1	R-2	R-SU4	ED	ED/w
P.R. +Δ	28.3	4.83	8.8	24	0.88
Lead+Δ	31.9	5.85	10.1	30	0.87
Lex. +Δ	31.0	5.52	9.8	25	0.87
Text.+Δ	32.3	5.68	10.4	34	0.89
Cent.+Δ	32.4	6.42	10.4	31	0.90
Δ+Lead	31.5	5.34	9.9	27	0.87
Δ+Cov.	32.4	5.65	10.3	29	0.88
Δ+Lex.	32.7	5.80	10.5	20	0.96
Δ+Text.	32.6	5.96	10.4	32	0.79
Δ+Cent.	31.7	5.44	10.0	43	0.80
Δ+Δ	31.5	5.30	10.0	48	0.88
Our Model	**34.0**	**6.96**	**11.4**	22	1.01

Table 1: Comparison results with abstractive baselines on the DUC 2002 test set.

5.5 Results

Method	R-1	R-2	R-SU4	ED	ED/w
P.R. +Δ	31.7	5.56	10.1	27	0.85
Lead+Δ	31.8	5.74	10.0	28	0.83
Lex. +Δ	32.9	6.28	10.8	33	0.89
Text.+Δ	33.3	6.10	10.7	41	0.90
Cent.+Δ	34.4	6.68	11.1	44	0.93
Δ+Lead	33.2	6.12	10.6	27	0.83
Δ+Cov.	34.4	6.84	11.2	27	0.84
Δ+Lex.	34.0	6.30	11.0	20	0.91
Δ+Text.	34.3	6.71	11.1	35	0.78
Δ+Cent.	32.8	5.77	10.3	44	0.80
Δ+Δ	31.3	4.70	9.6	52	0.88
Our Model	**36.7**	**7.83**	**12.4**	22	1.10

Table 2: Comparison results with abstractive baselines on the DUC 2004 test set.

The comparison results with abstractive baselines are presented in Table 1 and Table 2, respectively. As seen from Table 1 and Table 2, selecting one document as the representation of a document set (Single-ab.) performs poorly. This indicates considering the information of all documents is necessary for MDS task. Generally generating the abstractive summary for every document first and then merging these summaries with extractive MDS methods (i.e. Single-ab.+Multi-ex.) performs slightly better than constructing pseudo single document by extractive summarization methods (i.e. Single-ex.+Merge+Single-ab.). It may be explained that Single-ab.+Multi-ex. keeps the integrity of a document, thus the Sin-ABS model will perform better. Similarly Single-ab.+Merge+Single-ab. does not perform well because the constructed document is much different from a real one. Our system achieves the best performance on both datasets, since our model at the same time keeps the integrity of all original documents and takes into consideration only the salient sentences by ranking all original sentences in the attention mechanism.

The edit distance results verify that our method produces sentences that are quite different from original sentences, indicating the property of abstractive summarization.

Method	Encoder	Attention	Tuning
Model-1	fixed	raw	no
Model-2	fixed	concentrated	no
Model-3	fixed	concentrated	yes
Our Model	learned	concentrated	yes

Table 3: Details of model validation.

Method	R-1	R-2	R-SU4	ED	ED/w
Model-1	31.7	5.89	10.0	42	0.89
Model-2	32.2	6.16	10.3	43	0.90
Model-3	32.8	6.42	10.8	24	1.06
Our Model	**34.0**	**6.96**	**11.4**	22	1.01

Table 4: Model validation results on DUC 2002.

5.6 Model Validation

We conduct ablation experiments to verify the effectiveness of our model. Since we make three extensions to the SinABS model, namely the learned weights in the document set encoder, the attention mechanism and the tuning of the model. We validate their effect with three baseline models, by each changes one of the three parts. The difference of the three baselines are listed in Table 3. Model-1 is the simplest model without tuning, which uses a fixed weight vector $\mathbf{w} = [1/m, \ldots, 1/m]$, and uses the raw attention mechanism in Tan et al. (2017). Model-2 verifies the effectiveness of making the attention distribution more concentrated on the 15 most salient sentences. Model-3 verifies tuning the decoder but not the document set encoder. Compared with Model-3, our model further learns different weights for different documents in the document encoder. Results are presented in Table 4 and Table 5. As seen from Table 4 and Table 5, all the three strategies considerably improve the performance, validating how to better adapt single abstractive summarization model to the MDS task.

Method	R-1	R-2	R-SU4	ED	ED/w
Model-1	33.9	6.64	11.0	45	0.90
Model-2	34.1	7.10	11.2	49	0.91
Model-3	34.9	7.52	11.8	21	1.06
Our Model	**36.7**	**7.83**	**12.4**	22	1.10

Table 5: Model validation results on DUC 2004.

Method	Coherence	N.R.	Readability
Lead+Δ	2.32	2.74	2.71
Cent.+Δ	2.63	2.84	3.29
Δ+Cov.	2.30	3.53	2.92
Δ+Text.	3.18	3.75	3.34
Δ+Δ	2.23	2.57	2.57
Our Model	**3.76**	**3.92**	**4.08**

Table 6: Human evaluation results on 20 samples from the DUC 2002 and DUC 2004 datasets.

5.7 Human Evaluation

We also conduct human evaluation to evaluate the linguistic quality of the generated abstractive summaries, and compare with some significant baselines. We randomly sample 10 document sets from the DUC 2002 dataset and another 10 document sets from the DUC 2004 dataset for human evaluation. Three volunteers who are fluent in English were asked to perform manual ratings on three dimensions: Coherence, Non-Redundancy (N.R. for short) and Readability. The ratings are in the format of 1-5 numerical scores (not necessarily integral), with higher scores denote better quality. The average results are shown in Table 6. It can be observed that our system also outperforms other abstractive summarization approaches in human evaluation, achieving good coherence and readability.

5.8 Case Study

We show the abstractive summaries generated for an example from the DUC 2004 test set in Figure 3. It can be seen that the abstractive summaries generally read well, and has the potential to better convey the key information of original documents.

6 Conclusion and Future Work

Abstractive Multi-Document Summarization (MDS) is still a challenging and open problem. Although sequence-to-sequence models have achieved great progress in single document summarization, the demands of large amount of training data makes it hard to apply it to the MDS task. In this paper, we address this problem from another direction, that we investigate leveraging pre-trained successful single document summarization model to the MDS task. We propose a framework to realize this goal by adding a document set encoder into the hierarchical framework,

Lead+Δ:
politics , opposition leader hun sen and the prime minister were ousted <eos> in the u.s. khmer rouge , the government 's prime minister 's ruling party has had a lengthy majority of its leader in cambodia 's human rights record . <eos> of the country 's opposition party leaders and opposition members , the government have become prime minister <eos> of parliament with its prime minister , the presidency of the khmer rouge has been ruled out by the government 's leading opposition <eos> two political parties previously clashed with the government 's top two parties <eod>

Δ+Text:
king hun sen on tuesday praised by cambodia 's top two political parties, a coalition government led by prime minister <eos> in a short letter sent to news agencies, the king said he had received copies of fiscal and his cambodian people 's party in the government. <eos> cambodia 's leading opposition party ruled out sharing the top position in the presidency of parliament with its opposition <eos> in talks between the two party opposition bloc and the cambodian people 's party to form a new government. <eod>

Our System:
opposition leader cambodian people 's party won the election. <eos> in the u.s. , they were arrested in bangkok and charged with a lengthy coup of human rights . <eos> leading opposition party , the top position in parliament with its political rights , was arrested in bangkok , insisting it would lead to the presidency of thailand 's leading government . <eos> prime minister , political parties won a three - month agreement and agreed to a coalition government . <eos> the government would not end in a new coup vote and his arrest was rejected by the parties of parliament . <eod>

Figure 3: Example of generated abstractive summary by our system.

and we propose three strategies to further improve the model performance. Experimental results demonstrate our approach is able to achieve promising results on standard MDS datasets.

Our study is still primary effort towards abstractive MDS. Future work we can do includes alleviating the requirement of a good pre-trained abstractive summarization model, designing better attention mechanism for MDS, and investigating our approach based on other model architectures.

Acknowledgment

This work was supported by National Natural Science Foundation of China (61772036, 61331011) and Key Laboratory of Science, Technology and Standard in Press Industry (Key Laboratory of Intelligent Press Media Technology). We thank the anonymous reviewers for their helpful comments. Xiaojun Wan is the corresponding author.

References

P. V. S. Avinesh and Christian M. Meyer. 2017. Joint optimization of user-desired content in multi-document summaries by learning from user feedback. In *Proceedings of the 55th Annual Meeting of the Association for Computational Linguistics, ACL 2017, Vancouver, Canada, July 30 - August 4, Volume 1: Long Papers*, pages 1353–1363.

Dzmitry Bahdanau, Kyunghyun Cho, and Yoshua Bengio. 2014. Neural machine translation by jointly learning to align and translate. *arXiv preprint*, arXiv:1409.0473.

Tal Baumel, Matan Eyal, and Michael Elhadad. 2018. Query focused abstractive summarization: Incorporating query relevance, multi-document coverage, and summary length constraints into seq2seq models. *arXiv preprint*, arXiv:1801.07704.

Florian Boudin, Hugo Mougard, and Benoît Favre. 2015. Concept-based summarization using integer linear programming: From concept pruning to multiple optimal solutions. In *Proceedings of the 2015 Conference on Empirical Methods in Natural Language Processing, EMNLP 2015, Lisbon, Portugal, September 17-21, 2015*, pages 1914–1918.

Jaime G. Carbonell and Jade Goldstein. 1998. The use of mmr, diversity-based reranking for reordering documents and producing summaries. In *SIGIR '98: Proceedings of the 21st Annual International ACM SIGIR Conference on Research and Development in Information Retrieval, August 24-28 1998, Melbourne, Australia*, pages 335–336.

Sumit Chopra, Michael Auli, and M. Alexander Rush. 2016. Abstractive sentence summarization with attentive recurrent neural networks. In *Proceedings of the 2016 Conference of the North American Chapter of the Association for Computational Linguistics: Human Language Technologies*, pages 93–98.

Günes Erkan and Dragomir R Radev. 2004. Lexrank: Graph-based lexical centrality as salience in text summarization. *Journal of Artificial Intelligence Research*, 22:457–479.

Mahak Gambhir and Vishal Gupta. 2017. Recent automatic text summarization techniques: a survey. *Artif. Intell. Rev.*, 47(1):1–66.

Sepp Hochreiter and Jürgen Schmidhuber. 1997. Long short-term memory. *Neural computation*, 9(8):1735–1780.

Diederik P. Kingma and Jimmy Ba. 2014. Adam: A method for stochastic optimization. *arXiv preprint*, arXiv:1412.6980.

Chen Li, Xian Qian, and Yang Liu. 2013. Using supervised bigram-based ILP for extractive summarization. In *Proceedings of the 51st Annual Meeting of the Association for Computational Linguistics, ACL 2013, 4-9 August 2013, Sofia, Bulgaria, Volume 1: Long Papers*, pages 1004–1013.

Jiwei Li, Minh-Thang Luong, and Dan Jurafsky. 2015. A hierarchical neural autoencoder for paragraphs and documents. In *Proceedings of the 53rd Annual Meeting of the Association for Computational Linguistics and the 7th International Joint Conference on Natural Language Processing of the Asian Federation of Natural Language Processing, ACL 2015, July 26-31, 2015, Beijing, China, Volume 1: Long Papers*, pages 1106–1115.

Chin-Yew Lin and Eduard Hovy. 2003. Automatic evaluation of summaries using n-gram co-occurrence statistics. In *Proceedings of the 2003 Conference of the North American Chapter of the Association for Computational Linguistics on Human Language Technology-Volume 1*, pages 71–78.

Peter J. Liu, Mohammad Saleh, Etienne Pot, Ben Goodrich, Ryan Sepassi, Lukasz Kaiser, and Noam Shazeer. 2018. Generating wikipedia by summarizing long sequences. *arXiv preprint*, arXiv:1801.10198.

Ryan T. McDonald. 2007. A study of global inference algorithms in multi-document summarization. In *Advances in Information Retrieval, 29th European Conference on IR Research, ECIR 2007, Rome, Italy, April 2-5, 2007, Proceedings*, pages 557–564.

Kathleen McKeown, Judith Klavans, Vasileios Hatzivassiloglou, Regina Barzilay, and Eleazar Eskin. 1999. Towards multidocument summarization by reformulation: Progress and prospects. In *Proceedings of the Sixteenth National Conference on Artificial Intelligence and Eleventh Conference on Innovative Applications of Artificial Intelligence, July 18-22, 1999, Orlando, Florida, USA.*, pages 453–460.

Kathleen McKeown and Dragomir R. Radev. 1995. Generating summaries of multiple news articles. In *SIGIR'95, Proceedings of the 18th Annual International ACM SIGIR Conference on Research and Development in Information Retrieval. Seattle, Washington, USA, July 9-13, 1995 (Special Issue of the SIGIR Forum)*, pages 74–82.

Rada Mihalcea and Paul Tarau. 2004. Textrank: Bringing order into text. In *Proceedings of the 2004 conference on empirical methods in natural language processing*.

Lili Mou, Yiping Song, Rui Yan, Ge Li, Lu Zhang, and Zhi Jin. 2016. Sequence to backward and forward sequences: A content-introducing approach to generative short-text conversation. In *COLING 2016, 26th International Conference on Computational Linguistics, Proceedings of the Conference: Technical Papers, December 11-16, 2016, Osaka, Japan*, pages 3349–3358. ACL.

Ramesh Nallapati, Bowen Zhou, Cícero Nogueira dos Santos, Çaglar Gülçehre, and Bing Xiang. 2016. Abstractive text summarization using sequence-to-sequence rnns and beyond. In *Proceedings of the 20th SIGNLL Conference on Computational Natural Language Learning, CoNLL 2016, Berlin, Germany, August 11-12, 2016*, pages 280–290. ACL.

Lawrence Page, Sergey Brin, Rajeev Motwani, and Terry Winograd. 1999. The pagerank citation ranking: Bringing order to the web. Technical report, Stanford InfoLab.

Romain Paulus, Caiming Xiong, and Richard Socher. 2017. A deep reinforced model for abstractive summarization. *arXiv preprint*, arXiv:1705.04304.

Maxime Peyrard and Judith Eckle-Kohler. 2017. Supervised learning of automatic pyramid for optimization-based multi-document summarization. In *Proceedings of the 55th Annual Meeting of the Association for Computational Linguistics, ACL 2017, Vancouver, Canada, July 30 - August 4, Volume 1: Long Papers*, pages 1084–1094.

Dragomir R Radev, Hongyan Jing, and Malgorzata Budzikowska. 2000. Centroid-based summarization of multiple documents: sentence extraction, utility-based evaluation, and user studies. In *Proceedings of the 2000 NAACL-ANLPWorkshop on Automatic summarization-Volume 4*, pages 21–30. Association for Computational Linguistics.

Alexander M. Rush, Sumit Chopra, and Jason Weston. 2015. A neural attention model for abstractive sentence summarization. In *Proceedings of the 2015 Conference on Empirical Methods in Natural Language Processing, EMNLP 2015, Lisbon, Portugal, September 17-21, 2015*, pages 379–389.

Abigail See, Peter J. Liu, and Christopher D. Manning. 2017. Get to the point: Summarization with pointer-generator networks. In *Proceedings of the 55th Annual Meeting of the Association for Computational Linguistics, ACL 2017, Vancouver, Canada, July 30 - August 4, Volume 1: Long Papers*, pages 1073–1083.

Jiwei Tan, Xiaojun Wan, and Jianguo Xiao. 2015. Joint matrix factorization and manifold-ranking for topic-focused multi-document summarization. In *Proceedings of the 38th International ACM SIGIR Conference on Research and Development in Information Retrieval, Santiago, Chile, August 9-13, 2015*, pages 987–990. ACM.

Jiwei Tan, Xiaojun Wan, and Jianguo Xiao. 2017. Abstractive document summarization with a graph-based attentional neural model. In *Proceedings of the 55th Annual Meeting of the Association for Computational Linguistics, ACL 2017, Vancouver, Canada, July 30 - August 4, Volume 1: Long Papers*, pages 1171–1181. Association for Computational Linguistics.

Yuhui Tao, Shuigeng Zhou, Wai Lam, and Jihong Guan. 2008. Towards more effective text summarization based on textual association networks. In *Fourth International Conference on Semantics, Knowledge and Grid, SKG '08, Beijing, China, December 3-5, 2008*, pages 235–240.

Xiaojun Wan and Jianwu Yang. 2008. Multi-document summarization using cluster-based link analysis. In *Proceedings of the 31st Annual International ACM SIGIR Conference on Research and Development in Information Retrieval, SIGIR 2008, Singapore, July 20-24, 2008*, pages 299–306.

Dingding Wang, Shenghuo Zhu, Tao Li, Yun Chi, and Yihong Gong. 2011. Integrating document clustering and multidocument summarization. *TKDD*, 5(3):14:1–14:26.

Kristian Woodsend and Mirella Lapata. 2012. Multiple aspect summarization using integer linear programming. In *Proceedings of the 2012 Joint Conference on Empirical Methods in Natural Language Processing and Computational Natural Language Learning, EMNLP-CoNLL 2012, July 12-14, 2012, Jeju Island, Korea*, pages 233–243.

Jin-ge Yao, Xiaojun Wan, and Jianguo Xiao. 2017. Recent advances in document summarization. *Knowledge and Information Systems*, 53(2):297–336.

Toward Bayesian Synchronous Tree Substitution Grammars
for Sentence Planning

David M. Howcroft and **Dietrich Klakow** and **Vera Demberg**
Department of Language Science and Technology
Saarland Informatics Campus, Saarland University, Germany
`{howcroft,vera}@coli.uni-saarland.de`
`dietrich.klakow@lsv.uni-saarland.de`

Abstract

Developing conventional natural language generation systems requires extensive attention from human experts in order to craft complex sets of sentence planning rules. We propose a Bayesian nonparametric approach to learn sentence planning rules by inducing synchronous tree substitution grammars for pairs of text plans and morphosyntactically-specified dependency trees. Our system is able to learn rules which can be used to generate novel texts after training on small datasets.

1   Introduction

Developing and adapting natural language generation (NLG) systems for new domains requires substantial human effort and attention, even when using off-the-shelf systems for surface realization. This observation has spurred recent interest in automatically learning end-to-end generation systems (Mairesse et al., 2010; Konstas and Lapata, 2012; Wen et al., 2015; Dušek and Jurčíček, 2016); however, these approaches tend to use shallow meaning representations (Howcroft et al., 2017) and do not make effective use of prior work on surface realization to constrain the learning problem or to ensure grammaticality in the resulting texts.

Based on these observations, we propose a Bayesian nonparametric approach to learning sentence planning rules for a conventional NLG system. Making use of existing systems for surface realization along with more sophisticated meaning representations allows us to cast the problem as a grammar induction task. Our system induces synchronous tree substitution grammars for pairs of text plans and morphosyntactically-specified dependency trees. Manual inspection of the rules and texts currently produced by our system indicates that they are generally of good quality, encouraging further evaluation.

2   Overview

Whether using hand-crafted or end-to-end generation systems, the common starting point is collecting a corpus with semantic annotations in the target domain. Such a corpus should exhibit the range of linguistic variation that developers hope to achieve in their NLG system, while the semantic annotations should be aligned with the target input for the system, be that database records, flat 'dialogue act' meaning representations, or hierarchical discourse structures.

For our system (outlined in Figure 1) we focus on generating short paragraphs of text containing one or more discourse relations in addition to propositional content. To this end we use as input a *text plan* representation based on that used in the SPaRKy Restaurant Corpus (Walker et al., 2007). These text plans connect individual propositions under nodes representing relations drawn from Rhetorical Structure Theory (Mann and Thompson, 1988).

Rather than using a fully end-to-end approach to learn a tree-to-string mapping from our text plans to paragraphs of text, we constrain the learning problem by situating our work in the context of a conventional NLG pipeline (Reiter and Dale, 2000). In the pipeline approach, NLG is decomposed into three stages: document planning, sentence planning, and surface realization. Our approach assumes that the text plans we are working with are the product of document planning, and we use an existing parser-realizer for surface realization. This allows us to constrain the learning problem by limiting our search to the set of tree-to-tree mappings which produce valid input for the sur-

391

Proceedings of The 11th International Natural Language Generation Conference, pages 391–396,
Tilburg, The Netherlands, November 5-8, 2018. ©2018 Association for Computational Linguistics

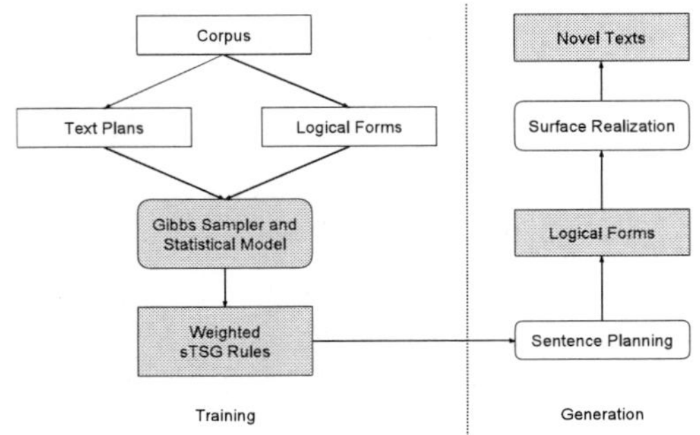

Figure 1: Overview of our pipeline. Square boxes represent data; rounded boxes represent programs. Blue boxes represent our system and the outputs dependent on it, while boxes with white background represent existing resources used by our system.

face realizer, leveraging the linguistic knowledge encoded in this system. Restricting the problem to sentence planning also means that our system needs to learn lexicalization, aggregation, and referring expression generation rules but not rules for content selection, linearization, or morphosyntactic agreement.

The input to our statistical model and sampling algorithm consists of pairs of text plans (TPs) and surface realizer input trees, here called *logical forms* (LFs). At a high level, our system uses heuristic alignments between individual nodes of these trees to initialize the model and then iteratively samples possible alternative and novel alignments to determine the best set of synchronous derivations for TP and LF trees. The synchronous tree substitution grammar rules induced in this way are then used for sentence planning as part of our NLG pipeline.

3   Synchronous TSGs

Synchronous tree substitution grammars (TSGs) are a subset of synchronous tree adjoining grammars, both of which represent the relationships between pairs of trees (Shieber and Schabes, 1990; Eisner, 2003). A tree substitution grammar consists of a set of *elementary trees* which can be used to expand non-terminal nodes into a complete tree.

Consider the example in Figure 2, which shows the text plan and logical form trees for the sentence, *Sonia Rose has very good food quality, but Bienvenue has excellent food quality.*

The logical form in this figure could be derived

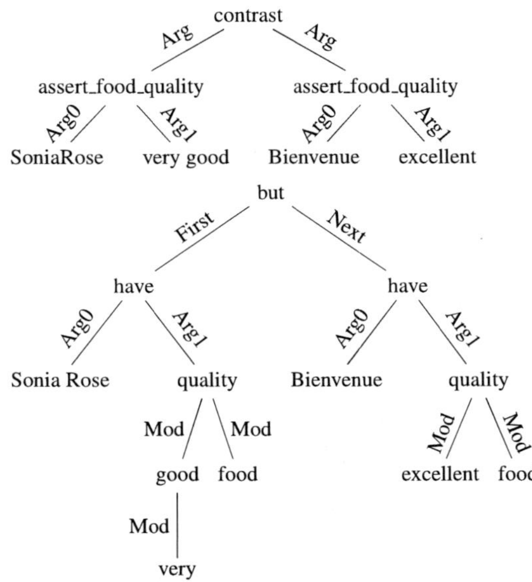

Figure 2: Text plan (top) & logical form (bottom) for the text *Sonia Rose has very good food quality but Bienvenue has excellent food quality.*

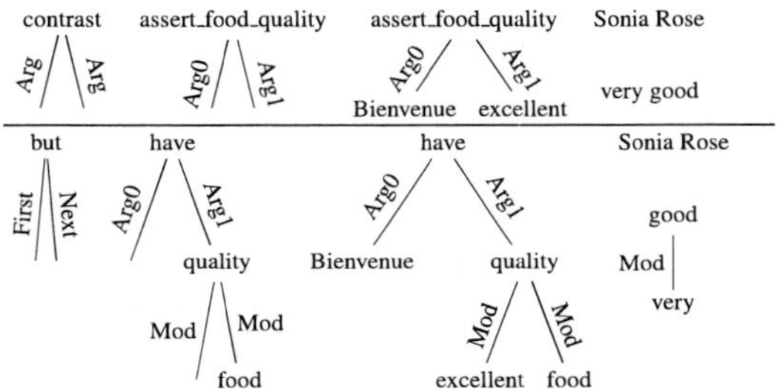

Figure 3: Possible elementary trees for the TP (top row) and LF (bottom row) in Figure 2, omitting some detail for simplicity.

in one of three ways. First, we could simply have this entire tree memorized in our grammar as an elementary tree. This would make the derivation trivial but would also result in a totally ungeneralizable rule. On the other hand, we could have the equivalent of a CFG derivation for the tree consisting of rules like *but → First Next, First → have, have → Arg0 Arg1*, and so on. These rules would be very general, but the derivation then requires many more steps. The third option, illustrating the appeal of using a tree substitution grammar, involves elementary trees of intermediate size, like those in Figure 3.

The rules in Figure 3 represent a combination

of small, CFG-like rules (e.g. the elementary tree rooted at *but*), larger trees representing memorized chunks (i.e. the rule involving *Bienvenue*), and intermediate trees, like the one including *have* → *quality* → *food*. In these elementary trees, the empty node sites at the end of an arc represent *substitution sites*, where another elementary tree must be expanded for a complete derivation. In typical applications of TSGs over phrase structure grammars, these substitution sites would be labeled with non-terminal categories which then correspond to the root node of the elementary tree to be expanded. In our (synchronous) TSGs over trees with labeled arcs, we consider the 'nonterminal label' at each substitution site to be the *tree location*, which we define as the label of the parent node paired with the label of the incoming arc.

A *synchronous* tree substitution grammar, then, consists of pairs of elementary trees along with an alignment between their substitution sites. For example, we can combine the TP elementary tree rooted at *contrast* with the LF elementary tree rooted at *but*, aligning each (*contrast*, *Arg*) substitution site in the TP to the (*but*, *First*) and (*but*, *Next*) sites in the LF.

4   Dirichlet Processes

The Dirichlet process (DP) provides a natural way to trade off between prior expectations and observations. For our purposes, this allows us to define prior distributions over the infinite, discrete space of all possible pairs of TP and LF elementary trees and to balance these priors against the full trees we observe in the corpus.

We follow the Chinese Restaurant Process formulation of DPs, with concentration parameter $\alpha = 1$.[1] Here, the probability of a particular elementary tree e being observed is given by:

$$P(e) = \frac{freq(e)}{\#obs + \alpha} + \frac{\alpha}{\#obs + \alpha} P_{prior}(e), \quad (1)$$

where $freq(e)$ is the number of times we have observed the elementary tree e, $\#obs$ is the total number of observations, and P_{prior} is our prior.

It is clear that when we have no observations, we estimate the probability of e entirely based on our prior expectations. As we observe more data, however, we rely less on our priors in general.

---

[1] Other concentration parameters are possible, but $\alpha = 1$ is the standard default value, and we do not perform any search for a more optimal value at this time.

5   Statistical Model

Our model uses Dirichlet processes with other DPs as priors (i.e. Hierarchical Dirichlet Processes, or HDPs). This allows us to learn more informative prior distributions (the lower-level DPs) to improve the quality of our predictions for higher-level DPs. Section 5.1 describes the HDPs used to model elementary trees for text plans and logical forms, which rely on prior distributions over possible node and arc labels. This model in turn serves as the prior for the synchronous TSG's pairs of elementary trees, as described in Section 5.2 along with the HDP over possible alignments between the frontier nodes of these pairs of elementary trees. A plate diagram of the model is presented in Figure 4.

5.1   HDP for TSG Derivations

We begin by defining TSG base distributions for text plans and logical forms independently. Our generative story begins with sampling an elementary tree for the root of the tree and then repeating this sampling procedure for each frontier node in the expanded tree.

Since the tree locations l corresponding to frontier nodes are completely determined by the current expansion of the tree, we only need to define a distribution over possible elementary trees conditioned on the tree location:

$$T|l \sim DP(1.0, P(e|l)) \quad (2)$$
$$P(e|l) = N(n(root(e))|l) \quad (3)$$
$$\Pi_{a \in a(root(e))} A(a|n(root(e)))$$
$$\Pi_{child \in children(root(e))} P(child|l(child)),$$

where N and A are Dirichlet processes over possible *node* labels and *arc* labels, we use $N(n|l)$ for the probability of node label n at tree location l according to DP N, and similarly for A. We further overload our notation to use $n(node)$ to indicate the node label for a given node, $a(node)$ to indicate the outward-going arc labels from *node*, and $l(e)$ or $l(node)$ to indicate the location of a given subtree or node within the tree as an (n, l) pair. $root(e)$ is a function selecting the root node of an elementary tree e and $children(node)$ indicates the child subtrees of a given node.

The distributions over node labels given tree locations $N|l$ and arc labels given source node labels $A|n$ are DPs over simple uniform priors:

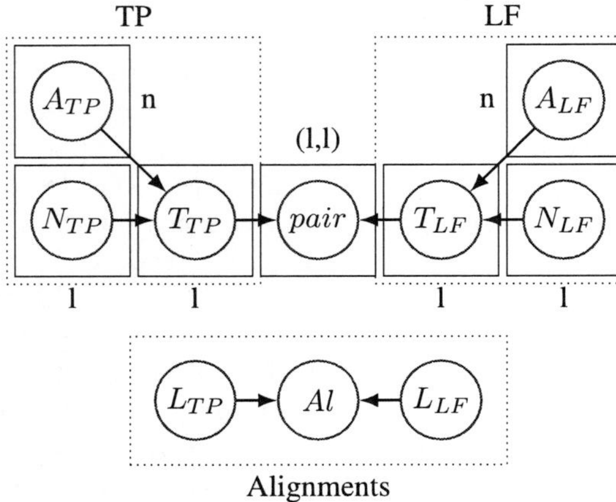

Figure 4: Dependencies in our statistical model, omitting parameters for clarity. Each node represents a Dirichlet process over base distributions (see Sec. 5) with $\alpha = 1$. n here indexes node labels for TPs or LFs as appropriate, while l similarly represents tree locations.

$$N|l \sim DP(1.0, Uniform(\{n \in corpus\})) \quad (4)$$
$$A|n \sim DP(1.0, Uniform(\{a \in corpus\})) \quad (5)$$

5.2 HDP for sTSG Derivations

Our synchronous TSG model has two additional distributions: (1) a distribution over pairs of TP and LF elementary trees; and (2) a distribution over pairs of tree locations representing the probability of those locations being aligned to each other.

Similarly to the generative story for a single TSG, we begin by sampling a pair of TP & LF elementary trees, a *TreePair*, for the root of the derivation. We then sample alignments for the frontier nodes of the TP to the frontier nodes of the LF. For each of these alignments, we then sample the next TreePair in the derivation and repeat this sampling procedure until no unfilled frontier nodes remain.

The distribution over TreePairs for a given pair of tree locations is given by a Dirichlet process with a simple prior which multiplies the probability of a given TP elementary tree by the probability of a given LF elementary tree:

$$pair|l_{TP}, l_{LF} \sim$$
$$DP(1.0, P(e_{TP}, e_{LF}|l_{TP}, l_{LF})) \quad (6)$$
$$P(e_{TP}, e_{LF}|l_{TP}, l_{LF}) =$$
$$T_{TP}(e_{TP}|l_{TP})T_{LF}(e_{LF}|l_{LF}) \quad (7)$$

The distribution over possible alignments is given by an DP whose prior is the product of the probabilities of pair of (TP and LF) tree locations in question. These probabilities are each modeled as a DP with a uniform prior over possible tree locations.

$$Al \sim DP(1.0, P(l_{TP}, l_{LF})) \quad (8)$$
$$P(l_{TP}, l_{LF}) = P(l_{TP})P(l_{LF}) \quad (9)$$
$$P(l_.) \sim DP(1.0, Uniform(\{l_.\})) \quad (10)$$

5.3 Sampling

Our Gibbs sampler adapts the blocked sampling approach of (Cohn et al., 2010) to synchronous grammars. For each text in the corpus, we resample a synchronous derivation for the entire text before updating the associated model parameters.

6 Generation

While our pipeline can in principle work with any reversible parser-realizer, our current implementation uses OpenCCG[2] (White, 2006; White and Rajkumar, 2012). We use the broad-coverage grammar for English based on CCGbank (Hockenmaier, 2006). The 'logical forms' associated with this grammar are more or less syntactic in nature, encoding the lemmas to be used, the dependencies among them, and morphosyntactic annotations in a dependency semantics. Parsing the corpus with OpenCCG provides the LFs we use for training.

After training the model, we have a collection of synchronous TSG rules which can be applied to (unseen) text plans to produce new LFs. For this rule application we use Alto[3] (Koller and Kuhlmann, 2012) because of its efficient implementation of parsing for synchronous grammars. The final stage in the generation pipeline is to realize these LFs using OpenCCG, optionally performing reranking on the resulting texts. Some examples of the resulting texts are provided in the next section.

---

[2] https://github.com/OpenCCG/openccg
[3] https://bitbucket.org/tclup/alto

7 Example output

As a testbed during development we used the SPaRKy Restaurant Corpus (2007), a corpus of restaurant recommendations and comparisons generated by a hand-crafted NLG system. While the controlled nature of this corpus is ideal for testing during development, our future evaluations will also use the more varied Extended SRC (Howcroft et al., 2017).[4]

After training on about 700 TP-LF pairs for 5k epochs, our system produces texts such as:

1. Chanpen Thai has the best overall quality among the selected restaurants. Its price is 24 dollars and it has good service. **This Thai restaurant** has good food quality, with decent decor.

2. **Since** Komodo's price is 29 dollars and it has good decor, it has the best overall quality among the selected restaurants.

3. Azuri Cafe, **which** is a **Vegetarian** restaurant has very good food quality. Its price is 14 dollars. It has the best overall quality among the selected restaurants.

4. Komodo has very good service. It has **food food quality, with very good food quality, it has very good food quality** and its price is 29 dollars.

Here we see examples of pronominalization throughout, as well as the deictic referring expression *this Thai restaurant* (in 1), which avoids repeating either the pronoun 'it' or the name of the restaurant again. The system also makes good use of discourse connectives (like 'since' in 2) as well as non-restrictive relative clauses (as in 3). However, the system does not always handle punctuation correctly (as in 3) and sometimes learns poor semantic alignments, aligning but ommitting part of the meaning in saying 'Vegetarian' for 'Kosher, Vegetarian' in 3 and completely misaligning 'good' to 'food' in (4) due to the frequent co-occurrence of these words in the corpus. Moreover, example 4 also demonstrates that some combinations of rules based on poor alignments can lead to repetition.

While there is clearly still room for improvement, the quality of the texts overall is encouraging, and we are currently preparing a systematic human evaluation of the system.

8 Related Work

While the present work aims to learn sentence planning rules in general, White and Howcroft (2015) focused on learning clause-combining rules, using a set of templates of possible rule types to extract a set of clause-combining operations based on pattern matching. The resulting rules were, like ours, tree-to-tree mappings; however, our rules proceed directly from text plans to final logical forms, while their approach assumed lexicalized text plans (i.e. logical forms without any aggregation operations applied) paired with logical forms as training input. In learning a synchronous TSG, the model presented here aims to avoid using hand-crafted rule templates, which are more dependent on the specific representation chosen for surface realizer input.

As mentioned in the introduction, there have been a number of attempts in recent years to learn end-to-end generation systems which produce text directly from database records (Konstas and Lapata, 2012), dialogue acts with slot-value pairs (Mairesse et al., 2010; Wen et al., 2015; Dušek and Jurčíček, 2016), or semantic triples like those used in the recent WebNLG challenge (Gardent et al., 2017). In contrast, we assume that content selection and discourse structuring are handled before sentence planning. In principle, however, our methods can be applied to any generation subtask involving tree-to-tree mappings.

9 Discussion and Conclusion

We have presented a Bayesian nonparametric approach to learning synchronous tree substitution grammars for sentence planning. This approach is designed to address specific weaknesses of end-to-end approaches with respect to discourse structure as well as grammaticality. Our preliminary analysis suggests that our approach can learn useful sentence planning rules from smaller datasets than those typically used for training neural models. We are currently preparing to launch an extensive human evaluation of our model compared to current neural approaches to text generation.

Acknowledgments

We would like to thank Leon Bergen for advice on Bayesian induction of TSGs, Jonas Groschwitz for assistance with Alto, and Sacha Beniamine & Meaghan Fowlie for proofreading and revision advice. This work was supported by DFG collaborative research center SFB 1102 'Information Density and Linguistic Encoding'.

---

[4]For details about differences between these two corpora, we refer the interested reader to Howcroft et al. (2017).

References

Trevor Cohn, Phil Blunsom, and Sharon Goldwater. 2010. Inducing Tree-Substitution Grammars. *Journal of Machine Learning Research* 11:3053–3096.

Ondřej Dušek and Filip Jurčíček. 2016. Sequence-to-Sequence Generation for Spoken Dialogue via Deep Syntax Trees and Strings. In *Proc. of the 54th Annual Meeting of the Association for Computational Linguistics (ACL; Volume 2: Short Papers)*. Association for Computational Linguistics, Berlin, Germany, pages 45–51. https://doi.org/10.18653/v1/P16-2008.

Jason Eisner. 2003. Learning non-isomorphic tree mappings for machine translation. In *Proc. of the 41st Annual Meeting on Association for Computational Linguistics (ACL): Short Papers*. Association for Computational Linguistics, volume 2, pages 205–208.

Claire Gardent, Anastasia Shimorina, Shashi Narayan, and Laura Perez-Beltrachini. 2017. The WebNLG Challenge: Generating Text from RDF Data. In *Proc. of the 10th International Conference on Natural Language Generation (INLG)*. Association for Computational Linguistics, Santiago de Compostela, Spain, pages 124–133. https://doi.org/10.18653/v1/W17-3518.

Julia Hockenmaier. 2006. Creating a CCGbank and a wide-coverage CCG lexicon for German. In *Proc. of the 21st International Conference on Computational Linguistics and 44th Annual Meeting of the Association for Computational Linguistics (COLING-ACL)*. Association for Computational Linguistics, Sydney, Australia, pages 505–512. https://doi.org/10.3115/1220175.1220239.

David M. Howcroft, Dietrich Klakow, and Vera Demberg. 2017. The Extended SPaRKy Restaurant Corpus: Designing a Corpus with Variable Information Density. In *Proc. of Interspeech 2017*. ISCA, Stockholm, Sweden, pages 3757–3761. https://doi.org/10.21437/Interspeech.2017-1555.

Alexander Koller and Marco Kuhlmann. 2012. Decomposing TAG algorithms using simple algebraizations. In *Proc. of the 11th International Workshop on Tree Adjoining Grammars and Related Formalisms (TAG+)*. Association for Computational Linguistics, Paris, France, pages 135–143.

Ioannis Konstas and Mirella Lapata. 2012. Unsupervised concept-to-text generation with hypergraphs. In *Proc. of the 2012 Conference of the North American Chapter of the Association for Computational Linguistics: Human Language Technologies (NAACL-HLT)*. Association for Computational Linguistics, Montréal, Canada, pages 752–761.

François Mairesse, Milica Gasic, Filip Jurčicek, Simon Keizer, Blaise Thomson, Kai Yu, and Steve Young. 2010. Phrase-based Statistical Language Generation using Graphical Models and Active Learning. In *Proceedings of the 48th Annual Meeting of the Association for Computational Linguistics (ACL)*. Association for Computational Linguistics, Uppsala, Sweden.

William C Mann and Sandra A Thompson. 1988. Rhetorical Structure Theory: Towards a functional theory of text organization. *TEXT* 8(3):243–281.

Ehud Reiter and Robert Dale. 2000. *Building Natural Language Generation Systems*. Cambridge University Press.

Stuart M. Shieber and Yves Schabes. 1990. Synchronous tree-adjoining grammars. In *Papers Presented to the 13th International Conference on Computational Linguistics*. Helsinki, Finland, volume 3, pages 253–258. https://doi.org/10.3115/991146.991191.

Marilyn A. Walker, Amanda Stent, François Mairesse, and Rashmi Prasad. 2007. Individual and domain adaptation in sentence planning for dialogue. *Journal of Artificial Intelligence Research* 30:413–456. https://doi.org/10.1613/jair.2329.

Tsung-Hsien "Shawn" Wen, Pei-hao Su, David Vandyke, Steve Young, and Trumpington Street. 2015. Semantically Conditioned LSTM-based Natural Language Generation for Spoken Dialogue Systems. In *Proc. of the 2015 Conference on Empirical Methods in Natural Language Processing (EMNLP)*. Association for Computational Linguistics, Lisbon, Portugal, pages 1711–1721. https://doi.org/10.18653/v1/D15-1199.

Michael White. 2006. CCG Chart Realization from Disjunctive Inputs. In *Proc. of the Fourth International Natural Language Generation Conference (INLG)*. Association for Computational Linguistics, Sydney, Australia, pages 12–19.

Michael White and David M. Howcroft. 2015. Inducing Clause-Combining Rules: A Case Study with the SPaRKy Restaurant Corpus. In *Proc. of the 15th European Workshop on Natural Language Generation (ENLG)*. Association for Computational Linguistics, Brighton, United Kingdom, pages 28–37. https://doi.org/10.18653/v1/W15-4704.

Michael White and Rajakrishnan Rajkumar. 2012. Minimal Dependency Length in Realization Ranking. In *Proc. of the 2012 Joint Conference on Empirical Methods in Natural Language Processing and Computational Natural Language Learning (EMNLP)*. Association for Computational Linguistics, Jeju Island, South Korea, pages 244–255.

The Task Matters: Comparing Image Captioning and Task-Based Dialogical Image Description

Nikolai Ilinykh, Sina Zarrieß, David Schlangen
Dialogue Systems Group
University of Bielefeld
Germany
`{first.last}@uni-bielefeld.de`

Abstract

Image captioning models are typically trained on data that is collected from people who are asked to describe an image, without being given any further task context. As we argue here, this context independence is likely to cause problems for transferring to task settings in which image description is bound by task demands. We demonstrate that careful design of data collection is required to obtain image descriptions which are contextually bounded to a particular meta-level task. As a task, we use MeetUp!, a text-based communication game where two players have the goal of finding each other in a visual environment. To reach this goal, the players need to describe images representing their current location. We analyse a dataset from this domain and show that the nature of image descriptions found in MeetUp! is diverse, dynamic and rich with phenomena that are not present in descriptions obtained through a simple image captioning task, which we ran for comparison.

1 Introduction

Automatic description generation from real-world images has emerged as a key task in vision & language in recent years (Fang et al., 2015; Devlin et al., 2015; Vinyals et al., 2015; Bernardi et al., 2016), and datasets like Flickr8k (Hodosh et al., 2013), Flickr30k (Young et al., 2014) or Microsoft CoCo (Lin et al., 2014; Chen et al., 2015) are typically considered to be general benchmarks for visual and linguistic image understanding. By exploiting these sizeable data collections and recent advances in computer vision (e.g. ConvNets, attention, etc.), image description models have

achieved impressive performance, at least for in-domain training and testing on existing benchmarks.

Nevertheless, the actual linguistic definition and foundation of image description as a task remains unclear and is a matter of ongoing debate, e.g. see (van Miltenburg et al., 2017) for a conceptual discussion of the task from a cross-lingual perspective. According to (Bernardi et al., 2016), image description generation involves *generating a textual description (typically a sentence) that verbalizes the most salient aspects of the image*. In practice, however, researchers have observed that eliciting descriptions from naive subjects (i.e. mostly crowd-workers) at a consistent level of quality is a non-trivial task (Rashtchian et al., 2010), as workers seem to interpret the task in different ways. Thus, previous works have developed relatively elaborate instructions and quality checking conventions for being able to systematically collect image descriptions.

In this paper, we argue that problems result from the fact that the task is typically put to the workers without providing any further context. This entirely monological setting essentially suggests that determining the salient aspects of an image (like highly important objects, object properties, scene properties) can be solved in a general, "neutral" way, by humans and systems. We present ongoing work on collecting image descriptions in task-oriented dialogue where descriptions are generated collaboratively by two players. Importantly, in our setting (which we call the MeetUp! environment), image descriptions serve the purpose of solving a higher-level task (meeting in a room, which in the game translates to determining whether an image that is seen is the same as the one that the partner sees). Hence, our participants need not be instructed explicitly to produce image descriptions. In this collaborative setting,

Proceedings of The 11th International Natural Language Generation Conference, pages 397–402,
Tilburg, The Netherlands, November 5-8, 2018. ©2018 Association for Computational Linguistics

we observe that the notion of saliency is non-static throughout a dialogue. Depending on the history of the interaction, and the current state, speakers seem to flexibly adjust their descriptions (ranging from short scene descriptions to specific object descriptions) to achieve their common goal. Moreover, the descriptions are more factual than those collected in a monological setting. We believe that this opens up new perspectives for image captioning models, which can be trained on data that is bounded to its contextual use.

2 Related Work

As described above, the fact that the seemingly simple task of image captioning can be interpreted differently by crowd-workers has already been recognised in the original publications describing the datasets (Hodosh et al., 2013; Young et al., 2014; Chen et al., 2015). However, it has been treated as a problem that can be addressed through the design of instructions (e.g., "do not give people names", "do not describe unimportant details", (Chen et al., 2015)). (van Miltenburg et al., 2016; van Miltenburg, 2017) later investigated the range of pragmatic phenomena to be found in such caption corpora, with the conclusion that the instructions do not sufficiently control for them and leave it to the labellers to make their own decisions. It is one contribution of the present paper to show that providing a task context results in more constrained descriptions.

Schlangen et al. (2016) similarly noted that referring expressions in a corpus that was collected in a (pseudo-)interactive setting (Kazemzadeh et al., 2014), where the describers were provided with immediate feedback about whether their expression was understood, were more concise than those collected in a monological setting (Mao et al., 2016).

Similar to MeetUp, the use of various dialogue game set-ups has lately been established for dialogue data collection. Das et al. (2017) designed the "Visual Dialog" task where a human asks an agent about the content of an image. De Vries et al. (2017) similarly collected the GuessWhat? corpus of dialogues in which one player has to ask polar questions in order to identify the correct referent in the pool of images. de Vries et al. (2018) also develop a new navigation task, where a "tourist" has to reach a target location via communication with a "guide" given 2D images of

various map locations. While similar in some respects, MeetUp is distinguished by being a symmetrical task (no instruction giver/follower) and broader concerning language data (more phenomena such as repairs, strategy negotiation).

3 Data collection

3.1 MeetUp image descriptions

The MeetUp game is a two-player text-based communication game set in a visual 2D environment.[1] The game starts with two players being placed in different 'rooms'. Rooms are represented to the players through images.[2] Each player only sees their own location. The objective of the game is to find each other; that is, to be in the same room. To solve this task, players can communicate via text messages and move freely (but unnoticed by the other player) to adjacent rooms. In the process of the game, the players naturally produce descriptions of what they currently see— and, interestingly, sometimes of what they have previously seen—to determine whether they have reached their goal or not. When they think that they have indeed achieved their goal, they indicate this via a particular command, and the dialogue ends.

The corpus we use here consists of 25 MeetUp (MU) games, collected via crowd-sourcing with Amazon Mechanical Turk. Workers were required to be native speakers of English. The dialogues all end with *a matching phase* where the players try to establish whether they are in the same room, by exchanging descriptions and come to the conclusion that they are (correctly in fact, in all but one dialogue). In some games, the players earlier already suspected to be in the same room and had such a "matching phase", but concluded that they weren't.

The complexity of the game board is likely to have an influence on the shape of the dialogue. For this data collection, we handcrafted a set of game boards to contain a certain degree of room type redundancy (e.g., more than one bed room per game board) and varying levels of overall complexity, as indicated in Table 2.

For our investigations here, we take these "matching phase" sub-dialogues and the images

---

[1]See `https://github.com/dsg-bielefeld/meetup` for more details.

[2]The images were taken from the ADE20k dataset (Zhou et al., 2016), which is a collection of images of indoor and outdoor scenes.

Figure 1: Example of a scene and corresponding monological captions

	Time	Private to A	Public	Private to B
31	(01:45)		A: I am now in a kitchen with **wood floors** and **a poster** that says **CON-TRATTO**	
59	(02:50)		B: Wait– I found the kitchen!	
60	(02:55)	$\xrightarrow{N}$ kitchen		
61	(02:55)	You can go [/n]orth [/e]ast [/s]outh [/w]est		
62	(03:13)		A: I am back in kitchen. It has **a white marble dining table** in center	
63	(03:29)		B: Yes. There are **four chairs** on **the island**.	
64	(03:35)		A: Exactly	
65	(03:37)		B: And **the big Contratto poster**.	
66	(03:48)		B: **Three lights** above **the island**?	
67	(03:53)		A: yep	
71	(04:05)			B: /done
72	(04:07)	A: /done		
73	(04:10)		Well done! You are all indeed in the same room!	

Table 1: Excerpt from a dialogue involving image description (of the image shown in Figure 1)

Gameboard	Rooms	Types	R/T Ratio
House	11	9	1.2
Airport	22	15	1.5
Hospital	13	12	1.08
Shopping Mall	15	14	1.07
School	17	14	1.2

Table 2: Description of gameboards

that they are about (note that for the non-matching situations, there are two images for one sub-dialogue), to give us a set of 33 images together with corresponding utterances. We will call these utterances *dialogical image descriptions (DDs)*, in contrast to the *monological image descriptions (MDs)* described in the next subsection.

An example of such a description is shown in Table 1. From left to right columns represent line number in a dialogue, timestamp of a message, messages private to player A, messages seen by both, private messages of player B. Lines 60-72 in the transcript contain part of the dialogue where players act on suspicion that they might be in the same location and start describing images presented to them individually. In earlier stages of the dialogue (lines 31 and 59), this room had already been referenced to. It indicates that the player keeps a memory of what has already been mentioned and can refer back to that.

3.2 Monological image descriptions

In order to compare dialogical descriptions with data produced in a typical non-context caption environment, we also collected MDs on Amazon Mechanical Turk (AMT). We presented workers with the 33 images and instructed them to produce captions for them. We adopted the instructions from the MS COCO collection (Chen et al., 2015), which ask workers to "describe the important parts" of the image, and, importantly, to provide at least eight (8) words per image description. We collected four captions per image; and thus 132 captions overall. An example of four monological image descriptions for one image is shown in Figure 1.

4 Analysis

An important task is to determine what types of referring expressions are present in the datasets. In order to identify and analyse referring expressions, we used the brat annotation tool (Stenetorp et al., 2012) to tokenise and annotate both DDs and MDs. The first author of the paper annotated whether an utterance contains descriptions of scene with objects (*a kitchen with wood floors*), or objects only (*a white marble dining table*), expresses players' actions (*moving north now*) or is

	MDs	DDs		
		DD_{roam}	DD_{match}	DD_{all}
Number of descr.	132	94	174	268
Number of tokens	1655	915	1400	2315
Average length	12.5	9.73	8.05	8.64
Type / Token ratio	0.30	0.38	0.34	0.29
Number of REXs	138	184	344	528
REX per description	1.0	1.96	1.98	1.97
Average length of REXs	1.82	2.26	2.23	2.24

Table 3: Analysis of image descriptions

related to players' beliefs about their current state (*I think we are in the same room*). For our analysis we define referring expressions (REXs) as nominal phrases that refer to the objects in the scene (*four chairs*) or to the scene itself (*a kitchen*).

Additionally, we identified parts of speech in both DDs and MDs using Stanford Log-linear Part-Of-Speech Tagger (Toutanova et al., 2003). Examples of REXs according to this definition are displayed in bold in Figure 1 for MDs and in Table 1 for DDs.

Table 3 gives some basic statistics about the two data sets. The goal is to look at the task dependence of image descriptions. Each MU dialogue can be divided into phases, two of which are exemplified in Table 1. The *roaming phase* (part of it are lines 31, 59) is typically filled with movements and players informing each other about their location. The *matching phase* (lines 60-72) ends the dialogue with the determination that the two players are present in the same place. In order to demonstrate dynamics of interactions in MeetUp, we look at all DDs as well as at their statistical characteristics in two phases. There were almost two times more DDs than MDs overall, with matching phase requiring a high number of descriptions as well. At the same time, MDs tend to be longer than all DDs, though both sets have nearly identical type/token ratio.

4.1 Referring expressions in MDs and DDs

When looking at the number of REXs in Table 3, in the MeetUp set-up players produced almost four times more overall referring expressions than the workers that produced the MD set. The majority of these occurred in the matching phases, which indicates that the different subgoals between phases have an influence. There were also nearly two times as many REXs per individual description in the MeetUp setting than in the monological descriptions. Additionally, given the fact

that MeetUp descriptions are generally more condensed than the MDs (8.64 vs. 12.5), it appears that MDs contain much material not directly relevant for reference to the scene or its objects. In particular we observed that there are on average 11 words in MDs (88%) which are not REXs and thus not related to an image, while there are nearly only 6 (70%) non-REX words in DDs. MeetUp players also produce longer REXs and this parameter is stable for all MeetUp phases. These observations show that the MeetUp descriptions are more focused on the task, less broad, contain much more referring expressions, which are longer then the ones in the non-task-driven set-up.

4.2 Adjectives in MD and DD

Table 4 displays the most frequent adjectives in both datasets in the spirit of (Baltaretu and Ferreira, 2016), who compared type and frequency of adjectives in a similar task design. It clearly shows a trend that seems to be present in the overall data: MDs cover a broader range of object properties or image attributes than the DDs.

Adj	Num	Adj	Num
clean	15	white	18
small	11	blue	11
large	9	red	11
empty	9	left	7
beautiful	8	small	6
white	7	same	5
nice	7	open	4
dark	5	yellow	4
old	5	black	4
many	5	right	3

Table 4: First 10 most frequent adjectives in both MDs (left) and DDs (right)

For example, evaluative adjectives (*beautiful, nice*) appear very often in MDs, while none of them is observed for the DDs. The latter ones seem to concentrate on attributes like colour, size, position, qualities of objects, while monological captions additionally have adjectives which refer to age, feelings, a number of objects in the scene. Furthermore, 78 adjectives occur only once among all words in MDs, while this number is almost half that for the DDs (38). It additionally supports the idea that absence of the task makes humans to produce broad image descriptions, which are not necessarily grounded in scene objects.

5 Conclusion

The task of collecting appropriate training data for image caption generation systems, and language & vision in general, is not a trivial one. We found that in a standard crowdsourcing-based collection procedure, annotators tend to produce interpretative, non-factual descriptions, leading to potentially unsystematic or noisy data. We have presented a task-oriented interactive set-up for data collection where image descriptions are naturally used by speakers to solve a higher level task. Our data collected in a small-scale pilot study indicates that dialogical image descriptions consistently lead to factual descriptions containing many more reasonable referring expressions than monological descriptions. The analysis presented here will be used to further control MeetUp! data collection in order to avoid data that is similar to non-task-drive monological captions.

References

Adriana Baltaretu and Thiago Castro Ferreira. 2016. Task demands and individual variation in referring expressions. In *INLG 2016 - Proceedings of the Ninth International Natural Language Generation Conference, September 5-8, 2016, Edinburgh, UK*, pages 89–93. The Association for Computer Linguistics.

Raffaella Bernardi, Ruket Cakici, Desmond Elliott, Aykut Erdem, Erkut Erdem, Nazli Ikizler-Cinbis, Frank Keller, Adrian Muscat, and Barbara Plank. 2016. Automatic description generation from images: A survey of models, datasets, and evaluation measures. *J. Artif. Int. Res.*, 55(1):409–442.

Xinlei Chen, Hao Fang, Tsung-Yi Lin, Ramakrishna Vedantam, Saurabh Gupta, Piotr Dollár, and C. Lawrence Zitnick. 2015. Microsoft COCO captions: Data collection and evaluation server. *CoRR*, abs/1504.00325.

Abhishek Das, Satwik Kottur, Khushi Gupta, Avi Singh, Deshraj Yadav, José MF Moura, Devi Parikh, and Dhruv Batra. 2017. Visual dialog. In *Proceedings of the IEEE Conference on Computer Vision and Pattern Recognition*, volume 2.

Harm De Vries, Florian Strub, Sarath Chandar, Olivier Pietquin, Hugo Larochelle, and Aaron Courville. 2017. Guesswhat?! visual object discovery through multi-modal dialogue. In *Proc. of CVPR*.

Jacob Devlin, Hao Cheng, Hao Fang, Saurabh Gupta, Li Deng, Xiaodong He, Geoffrey Zweig, and Margaret Mitchell. 2015. Language models for image captioning: The quirks and what works. In *Proceedings of the 53rd Annual Meeting of the Association for Computational Linguistics and the 7th International Joint Conference on Natural Language Processing (Volume 2: Short Papers)*, pages 100–105, Beijing, China. Association for Computational Linguistics.

Hao Fang, Saurabh Gupta, Forrest Iandola, Rupesh Srivastava, Li Deng, Piotr Dollar, Jianfeng Gao, Xiaodong He, Margaret Mitchell, John Platt, Lawrence Zitnick, and Geoffrey Zweig. 2015. From captions to visual concepts and back. In *Proceedings of CVPR*, Boston, MA, USA. IEEE.

Micah Hodosh, Peter Young, and Julia Hockenmaier. 2013. Framing image description as a ranking task: Data, models and evaluation metrics. *J. Artif. Int. Res.*, 47(1):853–899.

Sahar Kazemzadeh, Vicente Ordonez, Mark Matten, and Tamara L Berg. 2014. ReferItGame: Referring to Objects in Photographs of Natural Scenes. In *Proceedings of the Conference on Empirical Methods in Natural Language Processing (EMNLP 2014)*, pages 787–798, Doha, Qatar.

Tsung-Yi Lin, Michael Maire, Serge J. Belongie, Lubomir D. Bourdev, Ross B. Girshick, James Hays, Pietro Perona, Deva Ramanan, Piotr Dollár, and C. Lawrence Zitnick. 2014. Microsoft COCO: common objects in context. *CoRR*, abs/1405.0312.

Junhua Mao, Jonathan Huang, Alexander Toshev, Oana Camburu, Alan L. Yuille, and Kevin Murphy. 2016. Generation and comprehension of unambiguous object descriptions. In *Proceedings of CVPR 2016*, Las Vegas, USA.

Emiel van Miltenburg. 2017. Pragmatic descriptions of perceptual stimuli. In *Proceedings of the Student Research Workshop at the 15th Conference of the European Chapter of the Association for Computational Linguistics*, pages 1–10. Association for Computational Linguistics.

Emiel van Miltenburg, Desmond Elliott, and Piek Vossen. 2017. Cross-linguistic differences and similarities in image descriptions. *arXiv preprint arXiv:1707.01736*.

Emiel van Miltenburg, Roser Morante, and Desmond Elliott. 2016. Pragmatic factors in image description: The case of negations. In *Proceedings of the 5th Workshop on Vision and Language*, pages 54–59. Association for Computational Linguistics.

Cyrus Rashtchian, Peter Young, Micah Hodosh, and Julia Hockenmaier. 2010. Collecting image annotations using amazon's mechanical turk. In *Proceedings of the NAACL HLT 2010 Workshop on Creating Speech and Language Data with Amazon's Mechanical Turk*, CSLDAMT '10, pages 139–147, Stroudsburg, PA, USA. Association for Computational Linguistics.

David Schlangen, Sina Zarrieß, and Casey Kennington. 2016. Resolving references to objects in photographs using the words-as-classifiers model. In *Proceedings of ACL 2016*, Berlin, Germany.

P. Stenetorp, S. Pyysalo, G. Topić, T. Ohta, S. Ananiadou, and J. Tsujii. 2012. brat: a web-based tool for nlp-assisted text annotation. In *Proceedings of the Demonstrations at the 13th Conference of the European Chapter of the Association for Computational Linguistics*, pages 102–107. Association for Computational Linguistics.

Kristina Toutanova, Dan Klein, Christopher D. Manning, and Yoram Singer. 2003. Feature-rich part-of-speech tagging with a cyclic dependency network. In *Proceedings of the 2003 Conference of the North American Chapter of the Association for Computational Linguistics on Human Language Technology - Volume 1*, NAACL '03, pages 173–180, Stroudsburg, PA, USA. Association for Computational Linguistics.

Oriol Vinyals, Alexander Toshev, Samy Bengio, and Dumitru Erhan. 2015. Show and tell: A neural image caption generator. In *Computer Vision and Pattern Recognition*.

Harm de Vries, Kurt Shuster, Dhruv Batra, Devi Parikh, Jason Weston, and Douwe Kiela. 2018. Talk the walk: Navigating new york city through grounded dialogue. *CoRR*, abs/1807.03367.

Peter Young, Alice Lai, Micah Hodosh, and Julia Hockenmaier. 2014. From image descriptions to visual denotations: New similarity metrics for semantic inference over event descriptions. *Transactions of the Association for Computational Linguistics*, 2:67–78.

Bolei Zhou, Hang Zhao, Xavier Puig, Sanja Fidler, Adela Barriuso, and Antonio Torralba. 2016. Semantic understanding of scenes through the ade20k dataset. *arXiv preprint arXiv:1608.05442*.

Generating Summaries of Sets of Consumer Products:
Learning from Experiments

Kittipitch Kuptavanich
Department of Computing Science
University of Aberdeen
Aberdeen, UK
kittipitch.kuptavanich@abdn.ac.uk

Ehud Reiter
Department of Computing Science
University of Aberdeen
Aberdeen, UK
e.reiter@abdn.ac.uk

Kees Van Deemter
Utrecht University
Utrecht, NL
k.vandeemter@uu.nl

Advaith Siddharthan
Knowledge Media Institute
The Open University
Milton Keynes, UK
advaith.siddharthan@open.ac.uk

Abstract

We explored the task of creating a textual summary describing a large set of objects characterised by a small number of features using an e-commerce dataset. When a set of consumer products is large and varied, it can be difficult for a consumer to understand how the products in the set differ; consequently, it can be challenging to choose the most suitable product from the set. To assist consumers, we generated high-level summaries of product sets. Two generation algorithms are presented, discussed, and evaluated with human users. Our evaluation results suggest a positive contribution to consumers' understanding of the domain.

1 Introduction

When presented with a large amount of data in tabular form, an additional textual summary could aid a reader's comprehension of the otherwise overwhelming information at hand. The task of automatically creating a summary from numerical data is an ongoing research area within Natural Language Generation (NLG). We explored this task in the context of generating a textual summary describing a large set of objects [products] from a large database, where each object is characterised by several product features.

Product set overviews can be written by hand if the category is known beforehand. For example, manually written product reviews often start with an overview paragraph that discusses a wider set of products of which the product is a member. However, when a consumer searches for products

with keywords or through filters (e.g. on an e-commerce website), an overview of the returned set of search results would have to be automatically generated.

In this paper, we test the hypothesis that automatically generated textual summaries can be of benefit to customers. This can be seen as a specific instance of Shneiderman's Visual Information Seeking mantra (Shneiderman, 1996) of "Overview first, zoom and filter, then details-on-demand". One of the main ideas presented there is that it is beneficial for a reader to be exposed to an overview of the information before diving into specific details of interest.

There have been related NLG research about sets of objects, although with different goals or focuses. For example, to refer to or identify a set of objects within a larger set (Van Deemter, 2002), to perform a data-to-text analysis of tabularized data by records[1], to generate a page title for set items with shared characteristics from existing metadata (Mathur et al., 2017), or to address the issue of missing data encountered in summarisation (Inglis et al., 2017). In contrast, our work explores summaries that describe commonalities and differences within a set in order to help a user make informed decisions in selecting an object from the set. Our work focuses particularly on Content Determination step in the NLG pipe-line (Reiter and Dale, 2000), including selecting features and values to be presented.

2 Analysis of Hand-written Reviews

To inform our algorithms, we manually analysed 30 hand-written reviews gathered with the search term "best TV review" on Google. We used

---

[1]www.ax-semantics.com

Proceedings of The 11th International Natural Language Generation Conference, pages 403–407,
Tilburg, The Netherlands, November 5-8, 2018. ©2018 Association for Computational Linguistics

the 30 top ranked pages which contained a list of TVs (not just one single product). We then defined a per-clause tagging scheme to identify aspects that could be generated from product specifications and to systematically observe how reviewers described sets of products. In our scheme, a clause could have multiple tags. There was one annotator involved in the tagging (the first author). Our finding are summarised below.

Feature Selection: We analysed how often each product feature gets mentioned in the reviews. We found, as shown in Table 1, besides the price, the most frequent features (in descending order) are screen size, resolution, smart/internet feature, brand, backlight technology, ports, and contrast.

Feature	Frequency (%)
Screen Size	73
Resolution	60
Smart/Internet	43
Brand	40
Backlight Technology	30
Connectivity (Ports)	30
Contrast	30

Table 1: Frequency Count of Features in Reviews

Price Description: The product price in the reviews are typically mentioned only vaguely, using terms like "desirable price", "cheap", "expensive" or "premium". The description is vague even when numbers are involved e.g. "around £300". But when a crisp description is used it is more often found in the form of stating the starting point, e.g., "you can get a 1080p TV starting at £270" or the maximum e.g. "Discover the best 32 inch Smart TVs under £300 here".

Description of a Set of Items: Usually in a review, only a small number of sentences explicitly describe the set as a whole, for example "Most 32-inch TVs these days are labeled as *HD Ready*". When they do they uses quantifying words like "most". Numbers are described vaguely e.g. weight is mentioned as "light" or "response time" is either "fast" or "slow". Some features, for example the screen size, are mentioned both as exact numbers and vague description.

Price–Features Relationship: The relationship with price is used as a secondary justification to the features that the reviewers already think important, for example, "A TV with a 1920 × 1080

resolution [are] not even that much more expensive" or "good image quality and available smart features [...] carry a price premium."

Based on this analysis, we decided that our summaries should describe the shape of the price curve, the important features, and the effect of these features on price.

A large part of the reviews gathered included domain knowledge, for example, descriptions of technical terms and other insights. This part of the reviews clearly could not be produced from specification table. There were also mentions of features that can be, non trivially, derived from the table, e.g. picture quality (which can be based on columns like resolution and contrast).

3 The Algorithms

3.1 Alg1. Summarising a set of products

In our previous work (Kuptavanich, 2018), we presented an algorithm (called Alg1 here) to generate summaries consisting of (a) the shape of the price curve, (b) common features within the set and (c) features that influence price (Figure 1 gives an example of the generated text). The algorithm mainly used the influence of a feature on the product price to determine its importance.

> *As a result of your query for TVs, the price of most products in the result (432 out of 456 models) falls in the range of £275 - £1500 with a median price of about £630.*
> *Most TVs in this result have following features: 4K Ultra HD Display Resolution Max and FREE Shipping*
> *The features that have a strong impact on the price of TVs in this result are: Display Size, Image Aspect Ratio, Supported Content Service, Tuner Technology, Brand, Connectivity Technology, and Freeview Enabled.*

Figure 1: Alg1 Summary Example

3.2 Alg2. Dynamically summarising and contextualising a set of products

Alg1 only included content that could be generated from descriptions of items in a set being summarised. Following our analysis of the handwritten reviews, we adapted the algorithm. The resulting Alg2 allows for dynamic creation of sets through the use of feature filters and the contextualisation of these sets with respect to the unfiltered wider set as described below.

Shape of the Price Curve: Alg1 reports the median price and the price range of the set. [alg2] additionally compares the median price of the filtered set against the median price of the wider category. For instance, the first 3 lines of Figure 3 show a situation where the user has filtered the set of TVs to those that are 40–59 inches with 4K ultra high definition. The underlined portion is generated only by Alg2.

Description of Important Features: In the TV domain, the following features occurred most frequently: *display size, display resolution, smart/internet feature, support content service, brand, display technology, connectivity technology (ports) and HDR.* We therefore focussed on these features, but generated more detail about them than in Algo1. The description of each feature consisted of two parts. The first used quantifiers to describe the common values for the feature within the set. The second compared the median price of products with the said feature values against the median price of general products in this category and reported feature values that impacted on price (Figure 2).

Brand: Most products in the result are branded Samsung, Sony, LG Electronics, or Philips Brand. TVs with Samsung Brand are generally more expensive (£580 vs £450).

Figure 2: Our Description of Important Features

(a) Quantifiers. Here we generated expressions such as *"Most products in the result are..."* If the values of a feature are continuous numbers e.g. weight, we report them in the same fashion as the price (i.e. range and median value). Otherwise, we use the quantifiers "most" (more than 50%), "a large proportion" (more than 25%) and "some" (more than 10%).

(b) Comparatives and Qualifiers. In the second part, we also use phrases such as "more expensive" , "less expensive" or "about the same price" (when the difference is less than 5%). If the difference falls between 5 - 10%, we qualify this using the word "slightly". This generates texts such as *"TVs with Smart-Internet Feature are generally slightly more expensive (£475 vs £450)."* (Figured 3, in the next section).

The processes from document structuring through realization was carried out through template/schemata approach (McKeown, 1985). Also, the tone of the discourse is primarily to provide factual product overview without trying to be persuasive. Both algorithm were implemented using the Jinja2[2]template engine.

____

[2]jinja.pocoo.org

4   Evaluation Experiment

Our previous work (Kuptavanich, 2018) revealed difficulties designing a suitable task that reflected real consumer behaviours in the task based experiments, but a promising result with human rating. We therefore decided only to focus on human rating evaluation[3]. The scenario of interest is where a consumer is searching for products on an e-commerce website. Our Laboratory Human Ratings Evaluation experiment had three goals. First, we wanted to find out whether the text summaries generated by Alg2 were preferred over those generated by Alg1, and also over the static introductory text provided on the e-commerce site. Second, we asked the participants to identify parts of the summaries that were useful, parts that were unnecessary, and what they want to see added. Third, we wanted to also find out what product features are important in the decision-making process.

4.1   Method

Materials: We scraped TV product data from Amazon UK[4] during May - June 2018 to obtain 1478 products. We used this database to generate the summaries using both Alg1 and Alg2. As our baseline, we used Amazon's static text provided on their TV browsing page. An excerpt is shown in Figure 4. The full text can be found on Amazon UK TVs[5] page.

We used two product search scenarios on Amazon UK, based on its search filters. Each scenario produced a different set of search results and thus generated different summaries for Alg1 and Alg2.

Participants: Participants were 18 graduate students in Computing Science and Chemistry Department of University of Aberdeen recruited through the departments' internal student mailing lists.

Design and Procedure: In total, there were 2 pre-determined product search scenarios:

- Scenario 1: 40 – 59 inch TVs with Ultra HD
- Scenario 2: TVs of any size that are smart TVs

First, summaries [amz], [alg1], and [alg2] were presented in random order. To ensure that participants engaged with the task, each participant was asked to select one product. Then they were asked

____

[3]https://ehudreiter.com/2017/01/19/types-of-nlg-evaluation

[4]www.amazon.co.uk

[5]www.amazon.co.uk/LED-Smart-4K-TVs/b?node=560864

Size (inches): 40 - 49, or 50 - 59
Price:
Keyword(s): 4K Ultra HD
—

From your search result, the price of most products falls in the region between £275 and £1500, with many models around £630 price point, making it more expensive than TVs in all categories combined on average (£630 vs £450). Below we list a number of features that might be of interest to most people.

Display Size: Most products in the result either have 55, or 49" Display Size. Some have 43". TVs with 55" Display Size are generally more expensive (£770 vs £450).

Display Resolution Max: Most products in the result have 4K Ultra HD Display Resolution Max. TVs with 4K Ultra HD Display Resolution Max are generally more expensive (£660 vs £450).

Feature: Most products in the result have Smart-Internet Feature. TVs with Smart-Internet Feature are generally slightly more expensive (£475 vs £450).

Supported Content Service: Most products in the result either have Netflix or YouTube Supported Content Service. Some have Amazon Video. TVs with Netflix Supported Content Service are generally about the same price (£440 vs £450).

Brand: Most products in the result are branded Samsung, Sony, LG Electronics, or Philips Brand. TVs with Samsung Brand are generally more expensive (£580 vs £450).

Display Technology: Most products in the result have LED Display Technology. Some have unspecified. TVs with LED Display Technology are generally less expensive (£370 vs £450).

Connectivity Technology: Most products in the result either have USB, WiFi, HDMI, or Ethernet Connectivity Technology. TVs with USB Connectivity Technology are generally less expensive (£355 vs £450).

HDR: Most products in the result have no HDR. A large proportion have HDR. TVs with no HDR are generally less expensive (£310 vs £450).

Figure 3: [alg2] Summary Example

The TV is the heart of your home cinema system. It's often the focal point of gatherings with friends or family, where you can catch up on the news, cheer for a sports team, enjoy the latest episode of that drama you love, or re-watch your favorite film. ... When you're looking for a new television at a great price with convenient delivery options, Amazon.co.uk is the place for you. You'll find a wide array of TVs that will fit both your needs and your budget.

Figure 4: An Excerpt from the Baseline Summary

to rank the summaries; "Please rank the summaries (#1 being most useful)" Then, they were asked 3 free text questions:

[Q1]: "From the summaries above, which part do you think is most useful? (please quote)"

[Q2]: "What would you like to see added to the summaries?"

[Q3]: "Which part do you think is not necessary?"

After the 2nd scenario was completed, we asked the participants to select 3 products they liked. Then we asked:

[Q4]: "When buying a TV which feature do you think is most important?"

[Q5]: "What information do you think should be in a summary?"

[Q6]: "What kind of summary would help you choose a good TV?"

For [Q4], participants could choose from a list with the following choices: price, screen size, supported content service, smart/internet, resolution, Freeview, connectivity (ports) and also could specify their own features.

Hypotheses: Our research hypotheses were:

[Hyp1]: Participants prefer the [alg2] summary over the baseline [amz] summary

[Hyp2]: Participants prefer the [alg2] summary over the [alg1] summary

4.2 Results

Summary Preference: The number of times each summary was ranked first, second or third in the 36 trials is as shown in Figure 5. The average ranking of each algorithm 1.47 [alg2], 1.81 [alg1], and 2.72 [amz] respectively.

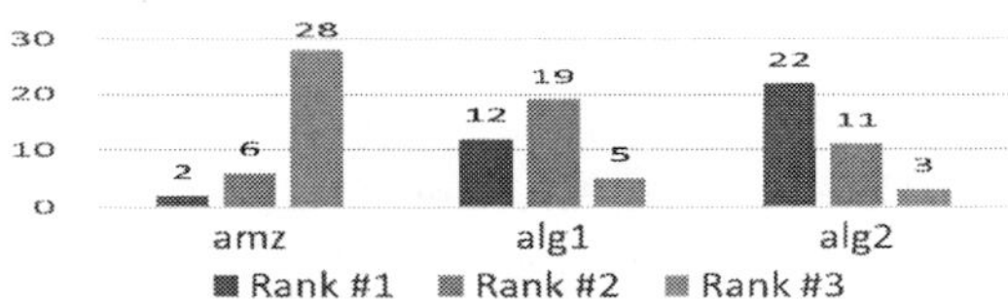

Figure 5: Ranking Counts of Each Algorithm

Out of all 36 trials, there were 31 (86.11%) where the participants preferred [alg2] over [amz] and 24 (66.67%) where the participants preferred [alg2] over [alg1].

A Friedman (1940) analysis of the rankings confirmed that the distributions of rankings were different for [amz], [alg1] and [alg2] (p-value of 2.8×10^{-7}). A post-hoc Friedman Aligned Ranks test (García et al., 2010) showed that [alg2] was significantly better than [amz] (p-value of 1.09×10^{-9}), thus confirming [Hyp1]. We could not confirm [Hyp2] as the p-value for [alg2] vs [alg1] was 0.104, though the numerical difference was in the expected direction.

Free Text Answer: Many responses (7 in total) asked for the summary to be short and precise or even bulleted. Furthermore, to [Q1] most participants found the price range and the relationship between price and features useful, which was supported by the data in the ranking. For [Q2], participants wanted to see product rating and other features, e.g. display frequency, model year or warranty added to the summary. They wanted to see some explanation of the technical terms and/or specification (e.g. what a smart TV is and what it can do). To [Q3], most participants did not find the Amazon summary useful and thought that it was not necessary. To [Q4], participants emphasized price (14 counts), screen size (11 counts), resolution (10 counts) and smart/internet feature (8 counts) when buying a TV. To the questions [Q5] and [Q6], participants thought that the features and their descriptions (including terminology explanations), how the features impact the price, user reviews, and information about warranty make a good summary.

5 Discussion and Future Work

Generalisation of our findings – which were based on only a very small set of scenarios – is tricky: we do not know whether they generalise to different kinds of products (e.g., groceries or paintings) and to product sets of different sizes (e.g. a set of just 3 products). However, our results suggest that customers find high-level product set summaries of the type we investigated more useful than Amazon's static product category overviews. This was further confirmed by the free text question where many participants quote substantial parts of [alg2] summary as being useful.

In future, we aim to experiment with refinements and extensions of [alg2]. For instance, in order to expand the algorithm work with various product domains, an automation of the analysis of hand-written reviews has to be implemented.

Additionally, based on participants' comments, technical information (as canned text) could also be included into the summary.

Since a number of readers pointed out that the summaries generated by [alg2] were too lengthy, the future version of the summary could be shorten (e.g., by omitting price comparisons in some cases). Some comments proposed that the summary should group together features that make the products different, separately from those the products have in common, this, as well, has a potential as a next feature to be experimented on.

In addition, to mimic more of human-written texts, approches to reduce the repetition in the generated text could be considered.

Finally, a more seamless integration of the summary to e-commerce websites could also be considered, maybe as a browser extension or a website wrapper.

Acknowledgment

The authors would like to thank the reviewers for their constructive comments and suggestions.

References

Milton Friedman. 1940. A comparison of alternative tests of significance for the problem of m rankings. *Ann. Math. Statist.*, 11(1):86–92.

Salvador García, Alberto Fernández, Julián Luengo, and Francisco Herrera. 2010. Advanced nonparametric tests for multiple comparisons in the design of experiments in computational intelligence and data mining: Experimental analysis of power. *Inf. Sci.*, 180(10):2044–2064.

Stephanie Inglis, Ehud Reiter, and Somayajulu Sripada. 2017. Textually summarising incomplete data. In *Proceedings of the 10th International Conference on Natural Language Generation*, pages 228–232, Santiago de Compostela, Spain. Association for Computational Linguistics.

Kittipitch Kuptavanich. 2018. Using textual summaries to describe a set of products. In *Proceedings of the 12th ACM Conference on Recommender Systems*, RecSys '18. ACM.

Prashant Mathur, Nicola Ueffing, and Gregor Leusch. 2017. Generating titles for millions of browse pages on an e-commerce site. In *Proceedings of the 10th International Conference on Natural Language Generation*, pages 158–167. Association for Computational Linguistics.

Kathleen R. McKeown. 1985. Discourse strategies for generating natural-language text. *Artificial Intelligence*, 27(1):1–41.

Ehud Reiter and Robert Dale. 2000. *Building Natural Language Generation Systems*. Cambridge University Press, New York, NY, USA.

B. Shneiderman. 1996. The eyes have it: a task by data type taxonomy for information visualizations. In *Proceedings 1996 IEEE Symposium on Visual Languages*, pages 336–343.

Kees Van Deemter. 2002. Generating Referring Expressions: Boolean Extensions of the Incremental Algorithm. *Computational Linguistics*, 28(1):37–52.

Neural sentence generation from formal semantics

Kana Manome[1]
manome.kana@is.ocha.ac.jp

Masashi Yoshikawa[2]
yoshikawa.masashi
.yh8@is.naist.jp

Hitomi Yanaka[3]
hitomi.yanaka@riken.jp

Pascual Martínez-Gómez[4]*
gomepasc@amazon.com

Koji Mineshima[1]
mineshima.koji@ocha.ac.jp

Daisuke Bekki[1]
bekki@is.ocha.ac.jp

[1]Ochanomizu University   [2]Nara Institute of Science and Technology
[3]RIKEN   [4]Amazon

Abstract

Sequence-to-sequence models have shown strong performance in a wide range of NLP tasks, yet their applications to sentence generation from logical representations are underdeveloped. In this paper, we present a sequence-to-sequence model for generating sentences from logical meaning representations based on event semantics. We use a semantic parsing system based on Combinatory Categorial Grammar (CCG) to obtain data annotated with logical formulas. We augment our sequence-to-sequence model with masking for predicates to constrain output sentences. We also propose a novel evaluation method for generation using Recognizing Textual Entailment (RTE). Combining parsing and generation, we test whether or not the output sentence entails the original text and vice versa. Experiments showed that our model outperformed a baseline with respect to both BLEU scores and accuracies in RTE.

1 Introduction

In recent years, syntactic and semantic parsing has been developed and improved significantly. Syntactic parsing based on syntactic theories has been accomplishing reasonable accuracy to support various application tasks (Clark and Curran, 2007; Lewis and Steedman, 2014; Yoshikawa et al., 2017). Mapping sentences to logical formulas automatically has also been studied in depth, so there are semantic parsing systems that can produce high quality formulas (Bos, 2008, 2015; Martínez-Gómez et al., 2016).

One advantage of using logical formulas in semantic parsing is that they have expressive power that goes beyond simple representations such as predicate-argument structures. More specifically, logical formulas can capture aspects of sentence meanings that arise from complex syntactic structures such as coordination, functional words such as negation and quantifiers, and the scope of interactions between them (Steedman, 2000, 2012). In combination with the restricted use of higher-order logic (HOL) developed in formal semantics, those logical formulas have recently been used for RTE (Mineshima et al., 2015; Abzianidze, 2015) and Semantic Textual Similarity (STS) (Yanaka et al., 2017) and achieved high accuracy.

Compared with these recent developments in syntactic and semantic parsing, automatic generation of sentences from expressive logical formulas has received relatively less attention, despite a long and venerable tradition of work on surface realization, including those based on Minimal Recursion Semantics (MRS) (Carroll et al., 1999; Carroll and Oepen, 2005) and CCG (White, 2006; White and Rajkumar, 2009). If one can generate sentences from formulas, it would be possible to perform other NLP tasks in combination with RTE, including those challenging tasks such as paraphrase extraction (Levy et al., 2016) and sentence splitting and rephrasing (Narayan et al., 2017; Aharoni and Goldberg, 2018).

Meanwhile, sequence-to-sequence models showed high performance in machine translation and many other areas in NLP (Sutskever et al., 2014), yet their applications to sentence generation from logical meaning representations are still underdeveloped, mainly due to a lack of data and the structural complexity of meaning representations (Konstas et al., 2017). To address this challenge, we introduce a first sequence-to-sequence model for sentence generation from

---

*This work was done prior to joining Amazon.

Proceedings of The 11th International Natural Language Generation Conference, pages 408–414,
Tilburg, The Netherlands, November 5-8, 2018. ©2018 Association for Computational Linguistics

logical formulas. We use the semantic parsing system ccg2lambda (Martínez-Gómez et al., 2016)[1] to obtain data annotated with logical formulas including higher-order ones. Since the distinction between content words and function words plays an important role in parsing and generation, we augment the sequence-to-sequence model with masking for predicates, so that content words in input logical formulas occur in output sentences with a list of function words utilized in the parsing system.

We also propose a novel evaluation method for sentence generation. BLEU (Papineni et al., 2002) is widely used to evaluate the quality of decoded sentences, but it has difficulties in assessing fine-grained meaning relations between sentences. Instead, we use an RTE system for evaluation. We test whether or not the output sentence entails the original text and vice versa. This idea is motivated by the assumption that unlike surface-based methods such as BLEU, textual entailment is sensitive to syntactic and semantic aspects of sentences, thus making it possible to distinguish fine-grained meaning relations between original and output sentences. RTE has also been shown to be effective for evaluation of machine translation (Padó et al., 2009). Experiments show that our model outperforms a baseline with respect to both BLEU scores and accuracy in RTE.

2 Background and Related Work

2.1 Input logical formula

For input, we use logical formulas obtained from ccg2lambda (Martínez-Gómez et al., 2016), a parsing and inference system that can be used for RTE. This system parses sentences into syntactic trees based on CCG (Steedman, 2000), a syntactic theory suitable for semantic composition from syntactic structures. The meaning of each word is specified using a lambda term. Logical formulas are obtained compositionally, by combining lambda terms in accordance with the meaning composition rules specified in the CCG tree and semantic templates. Semantic templates are defined manually based on formal semantics (Mineshima et al., 2015).

For logical formulas, we use standard Neo-Davidsonian event semantics (Parsons, 1990). For instance, the sentence *Eddy walked on the green grass* is represented as $\exists e.(\text{walk}(e) \wedge \text{subj}(e) =$

$\text{eddy} \wedge \exists x.(\text{green}(x) \wedge \text{grass}(x) \wedge \text{on}(e,x)))$. In this semantics, content words such as nouns and verbs are represented as predicates, and function words such as determiners, negation, and connectives are represented as logical operators with scope relations.

We decided not to include the following linguistic information in the input formulas: the definite–indefinite and singular–plural distinctions for NPs and tense and aspect for VPs. The intention is to normalize these semantic differences, so that the resulting formulas are easily usable in reasoning tasks based on RTE, where such fine-grained linguistic distinctions may sometimes make it more difficult to establish entailment relations between sentences. While more fine-grained linguistic information in logical formulas is readily obtainable by modifying semantic templates, we leave testing formulas with such additional semantic information for future work.

2.2 Related Work

A large amount of work has been done to convert meaning representations to their surface forms. In addition to those works mentioned in Section 1, there has been also a line of work on generating sentences from meaning representations used in semantic parsing systems (Wong and Mooney, 2007; Lu et al., 2009). Recently, Mei et al. (2016) has proposed an end-to-end neural sentence generation model from such meaning representations. These studies use datasets annotated with meaning representations, such as ROBOCUP (www.robocup.org) and GEOQUERY (Zelle and Mooney, 1996). However, these meaning representations are much simpler than logical formulas used in formal semantics in that they do not contain logical operators such as disjunction and quantifiers nor variable binding structures in standard first-order logic.

Recent rule-based approaches to generation using formal semantics and higher-order logic include a type-theoretic system based on Grammatical Framework (GF) (Ranta, 2011) and a system called Treebank Semantics based on event semantics (Butler, 2016).

Closest to our work is the one based on AMRs (Konstas et al., 2017), which has achieved high performance in sentence generation using neural networks from AMR-graphs (Banarescu et al., 2013). While AMR has been used as an

---

[1]https://github.com/mynlp/ccg2lambda

intermediate meaning representation for a wide range of tasks, it has less descriptive power than standard first-order logic (Bos, 2016). In addition, current AMRs do not support inference systems and thus cannot deal with logical inference as handled by RTE systems.

3 Method

We present a sequence-to-sequence model with attention for formula-to-sentence conversion.

3.1 Embedding

In using the sequence-to-sequence model, the point to address is how to linearize logical formulas. We test two ways of embedding: one is a token-based method where a formula is separated by each token (predicate and operator) and the other is based on graph representations converted from input logical formulas.

The token-based method tokenizes logical expressions. Below is an example of token-separated linearization:

$$[\texttt{exists}, e, (, \texttt{walk}, (, e,), \&, \texttt{Subj}, (, e,), ...]$$

On the other hand, a graph representation reflects the structure of a logical formula. We use the formula-to-graph conversion presented in Wang et al. (2017). This method converts a formula to a tree structure and then obtains its graph representation by identifying the nodes for a same variable and replacing edges of the tree accordingly. See Wang et al. (2017) for the detail.

3.2 Sequence-to-Sequence with Attention

Our baseline model is a sequence-to-sequence with attention mechanism. Let $\mathbf{x} = (x_1, \ldots, x_{|\mathbf{x}|})$ and $\mathbf{y} = (y_1, \ldots, y_{|\mathbf{y}|})$ be an input formula and an output sentence, respectively. Then, the probability of the sentence $\mathbf{y}$ given a formula $\mathbf{x}$ is

$$P_\Theta(\mathbf{y}|\mathbf{x}) = \prod_{i=1}^{|\mathbf{y}|} P_\Theta(y_i|\mathbf{y}_{<i}, \mathbf{x}),$$

$$y_i|\mathbf{y}_{<i}, \mathbf{x} \sim softmax(\mathbf{f}(\Theta, \mathbf{y}_{<i}, \mathbf{x})), \quad (1)$$

where $\mathbf{y}_{<i}$ denotes the previously generated sequence of words at step i, $\mathbf{x}$ is the input formula and Θ are the model parameters. The function $\mathbf{f}$ is defined as

$$\mathbf{f}(\Theta, \mathbf{y}_{<i}, \mathbf{x}) = W_o \, MLP\left(\begin{bmatrix} \mathbf{g}_i \\ \mathbf{c}_i \end{bmatrix}\right) + \mathbf{b}_o,$$

$$\mathbf{g}_i = LSTM_{dec}(\mathbf{v}_T(y_{i-1}), \mathbf{g}_{i-1}),$$

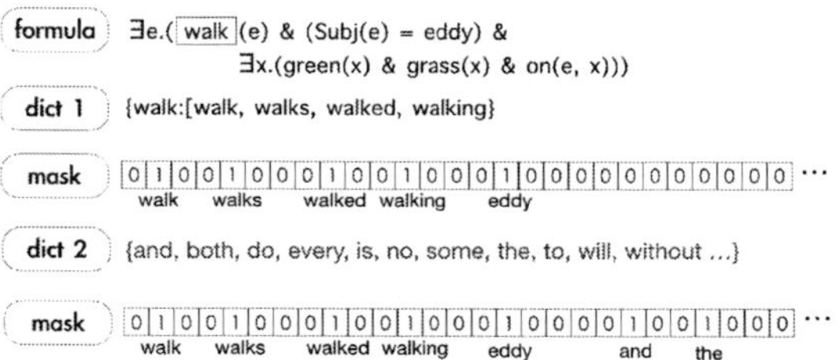

Figure 1: Masking

where MLP is a multi-layer perceptron with tanh activation, $\mathbf{v}_T(y)$ is an embedding vector of y, and $\mathbf{c}_i$ is a weighted average (attention) $\sum_{j=1}^{|\mathbf{x}|} \alpha_{ij}\mathbf{h}_j$ of the hidden vectors $\mathbf{h}_j$ for each x_j, where

$$\alpha_i = softmax(\mathbf{e}_i),$$
$$e_{ij} = MLP(\mathbf{g}_{i-1}, \mathbf{h}_j),$$
$$\mathbf{h}_j = LSTM_{enc}(\mathbf{v}_S(x_j), \mathbf{h}_{j-1}),$$

and $LSTM_{enc}$ is an LSTM encoder, which calculates a hidden state $\mathbf{h}_j$ using embedding vector $\mathbf{v}_S(x_j)$ and its previous hidden state.

We train the entire model by optimizing the log-likelihood with respect to the training data.

3.3 Masking

Logical formulas contain predicates for content words that should invariably appear in decoded sentences. For instance, in the sentence *Eddy walked on the green grass*, its content words are *Eddy, walked, green*, and *grass*, while *on* and *the* are function words. Using ccg2lambda, we obtain the following formula for this sentence:

```
exists e.(walk(e) & (Subj(e) = eddy) &
exists x.(green(x) & grass(x) & on(e, x))).
```

To utilize the information available in a logical formula, we use a masking vector $\mathbf{m} \in \{0,1\}^N$, where N is the size of the output vocabulary, which zeroes out the probabilities of words that do not appear in the formula (see Figure 1). Thus, instead of Eq. 1, we take the element-wise multiplication of the softmax probability and mask $\mathbf{m}$ as

$$y_i|\mathbf{y}_{<i} \sim \mathbf{m} \otimes softmax(\mathbf{f}(\Theta, \mathbf{y}_{<i}, \mathbf{x})).$$

To construct the masking vector, we use a dictionary that maps a lemma to a list of its inflected forms, since logical formulas contain only lemmatized forms of words. The idea of using a masking vector can be seen as a simplified method of employing a coverage vector, as has been widely used in a line of work on chart realization by Kay (1996). Our method provides a simple adaptation to sequence-to-sequence models. We obtained the dictionary by applying the lemmatizer implemented in C&C parser (Clark and Curran, 2007) to all training data used in the experiment.

In the previous example, there is a dictionary entry that maps *walk* to the list *walk*, *walks*, *walked* and *walking*. We set 1 in **m** at positions that correspond to these inflected forms (see dict1 in Figure 1). Additionally, we made functional words always available at decoding, by using a predefined list of those words (see dict2 in Figure 1).

4 Experiment

4.1 Dataset

We create a dataset annotated with logical formulas from the SNLI corpus (Bowman et al., 2015), a collection of 570,000 English sentence pairs manually labeled with an entailment relation. We use 50,000 hypothesis sentences from its training portion and split them into 42,000, 4,000, and 4,000 sentences for our training, development, and test sets, respectively. We map the sentences into logical formulas using ccg2lambda. We use C&C parser for converting tokenized sentences into CCG trees.

Table 1 shows the number of words in the constructed corpus (vocab), the max length (max-len) and average length (ave-len) of sequences obtained for the token-based (**token**) and graph-based methods (**graph**). Here **output** shows information on the output sentences.

As a baseline, we use Treebank Semantics (Butler, 2016)[2], a rule-based system for parsing and generation with logical formulas based on event semantics.

4.2 Evaluation

For evaluation, AMR generation tasks (Konstas et al., 2017) use BLEU, which does not directly consider the meaning and structure of a sentence. For instance, two sentences *No one visited the old man to greet him* and *Someone visited the old man to greet him* are similar but differ in meaning. To avoid this problem, we propose an evaluation method using parsing and RTE. Namely, we first

[2]http://www.compling.jp/ajb129/
generation.html

	vocab	max-len	ave-len
token	6,822	419	44
graph	6,747	145	17
output	8,875	40	8

Table 1: Information about sequences.

	BLEU	$S_1 \Rightarrow S_2$	$S_2 \Rightarrow S_1$	$S_1 \Leftrightarrow S_2$
token	43.0	87.3	87.3	87.3
+mask	**60.0**	92.3	90.8	89.8
graph	42.2	86.3	90.0	86.3
+mask	50.0	**92.5**	**92.3**	**90.8**
rule	38.3	61.5	62.3	58.8

Table 2: Evaluation results.

parse an input sentence S_1 to obtain a formula P and then generate a sentence S_2 from the formula P. Finally, we check whether S_1 entails S_2 and vice versa. Our method based on RTE can detect differences in meaning in cases like the above.

We measure the accuracy of RTE for unidirectional and bidirectional entailments: $S_1 \Rightarrow S_2$, $S_2 \Rightarrow S_1$ and $S_1 \Leftrightarrow S_2$. We use ccg2lambda for parsing original and generated sentences and proving entailment relations between them. We use 400 pairs of sentences taken from the test set for RTE experiments. The inference system outputs *yes* (entailment), *no* (contradiction) or *unknown*. The gold answer is set to *yes*. The parsing and inference system of ccg2lambda achieved high precision in RTE tasks; Martínez-Gómez et al. (2017) reported that the precision was nearly 100% for the SICK dataset (Marelli et al., 2014). Thus, a predicted entailment (*yes*) judgement can serve as a reliable measure for evaluating the entailment relation between S_1 and S_2.

4.3 Results

Table 2 shows BLEU scores and RTE accuracy. Here, **token** and **graph** show the results for a token-based model with attention and the graph-based model with attention, respectively, and **+mask** means the model with masking. The baseline is shown by **rule**, which is the performance of Treebank Semantics. As shown here, all the models outperformed the baseline with respect to both BLEU score and RTE accuracy. For the RTE accuracy, the increase in the score of the **graph + mask** model was slightly larger than the increase for the **token + mask** model.

Table 3 shows examples of decoded sentences

	Input sentence (S_1)	Decoded sentence (S_2)
(1)	the girls are swimming in the ocean.	the girls are swimming in the ocean.
(2)	a dog is playing fetch with his owner.	a dog is playing fetch with owner.
(3)	a man is sitting on the couch.	the men are sitting on a couch.
(4)	a tall man.	the man is tall.
(5)	a child is standing.	the children are standing together.
(6)	there are several people in this picture.	people are pictured in a picture.

Table 3: Examples of decoded sentences obtained from the **graph + mask** model

obtained from the **graph + mask** model. (1) and (2) are examples that preserve the form of input sentences. (3) is an example where singular form is changed to plural form, as well as articles *a* and *the*. This is because our semantics neutralizes these distinctions. The decoded sentence is grammatically correct, accommodating *be*-verbs. In (4), the input is a noun phrase, while the decoded result is a sentence. Example (5) contains an unnecessary word *together*, but the subject is also changed so that the decoded sentence is meaningful. In example (6), the *there*-construction in the input is removed while preserving the same content.

5   Conclusion

To our knowledge, this is the first study to describe a neural sentence generation model from logical formulas. We also proposed a new evaluation method based on RTE. In future work, we will refine our model for generation of longer sentences and test formulas with richer semantic information.

Acknowledgement   We would like to thank the reviewers for their helpful comments and suggestions. We are also grateful to Ribeka Tanaka, Yurina Ito, and Yukiko Yana for helpful discussion and Fadoua Ghourabi for reading an earlier draft of the paper. This work was partially supported by JST AIP-PRISM Grant Number JPMJCR18Y1, Japan.

References

Lasha Abzianidze. 2015. A Tableau Prover for Natural Logic and Language. In *Proceedings of the 2015 Conference on Empirical Methods in Natural Language Processing*, pages 2492–2502.

Roee Aharoni and Yoav Goldberg. 2018. Split and rephrase: Better evaluation and stronger baselines. In *Proceedings of the 56th Annual Meeting of the Association for Computational Linguistics*, pages 719–724.

Laura Banarescu, Claire Bonial, Shu Cai, Madalina Georgescu, Kira Griffitt, Ulf Hermjakob, Kevin Knight, Philipp Koehn, Martha Palmer, and Nathan Schneider. 2013. Abstract Meaning Representation for Sembanking. In *Proceedings of the 7th Linguistic Annotation Workshop and Interoperability with Discourse*, pages 178–186.

Johan Bos. 2008. Wide-coverage semantic analysis with Boxer. In *Proceedings of the 2008 Conference on Semantics in Text Processing*, pages 277–286.

Johan Bos. 2015. Open-domain semantic parsing with Boxer. In *Proceedings of the 20th Nordic Conference of Computational Linguistics*, pages 301–304.

Johan Bos. 2016. Expressive power of abstract meaning representations. *Computational Linguistics*, 42(3):527–535.

Samuel R. Bowman, Gabor Angeli, Christopher Potts, and Christopher D. Manning. 2015. A large annotated corpus for learning natural language inference. In *Proceedings of the 2015 Conference on Empirical Methods in Natural Language Processing*, pages 632–642.

Alastair Butler. 2016. Deterministic natural language generation from meaning representations for machine translation. In *Proceedings of the 2nd Workshop on Semantics-Driven Machine Translation*, pages 1–9.

John Carroll, Ann Copestake, Dan Flickinger, and Victor Poznański. 1999. An efficient chart generator for (semi-) lexicalist grammars. In *Proceedings of the 7th European Workshop on Natural Language Generation*, pages 86–95.

John Carroll and Stefan Oepen. 2005. High efficiency realization for a wide-coverage unification grammar. In *Proceedings of International Joint Conference on Natural Language Processing*, pages 165–176.

Stephen Clark and James R. Curran. 2007. Wide-coverage efficient statistical parsing with CCG and log-linear models. *Computational Linguistics*, 33(4):493–552.

Martin Kay. 1996. Chart generation. In *Proceedings of the 34th annual meeting on Association for Computational Linguistics*, pages 200–204.

Ioannis Konstas, Srinivasan Iyer, Mark Yatskar, Yejin Choi, and Luke Zettlemoyer. 2017. Neural AMR: Sequence-to-sequence models for parsing and generation. In *Proceedings of the 55th Annual Meeting of the Association for Computational Linguistics*, pages 146–157.

Omer Levy, Ido Dagan, Gabriel Stanovsky, Judith Eckle-Kohler, and Iryna Gurevych. 2016. Modeling extractive sentence intersection via subtree entailment. In *Proceedings of the 26th International Conference on Computational Linguistics*, pages 2891–2901.

Mike Lewis and Mark Steedman. 2014. A* CCG parsing with a supertag-factored model. In *Proceedings of the 2014 Conference on Empirical Methods in Natural Language Processing*, pages 990–1000.

Wei Lu, Hwee Tou Ng, and Wee Sun Lee. 2009. Natural language generation with tree conditional random fields. In *Proceedings of the 2009 Conference on Empirical Methods in Natural Language Processing*, pages 400–409.

Marco Marelli, Stefano Menini, Marco Baroni, Luisa Bentivogli, Raffaella Bernardi, and Roberto Zamparelli. 2014. A SICK cure for the evaluation of compositional distributional semantic models. In *Proceedings of LREC2014*, pages 216–223.

Pascual Martínez-Gómez, Koji Mineshima, Yusuke Miyao, and Daisuke Bekki. 2016. ccg2lambda: A Compositional Semantics System. In *Proceedings of ACL 2016 System Demonstrations*, pages 85–90.

Pascual Martínez-Gómez, Koji Mineshima, Yusuke Miyao, and Daisuke Bekki. 2017. On-demand injection of lexical knowledge for recognising textual entailment. In *Proceedings of the 15th Conference of the European Chapter of the Association for Computational Linguistics*, pages 710–720.

Hongyuan Mei, Mohit Bansal, and Matthew R. Walter. 2016. What to talk about and how? selective generation using LSTMs with coarse-to-fine alignment. In *Proceedings of the 2016 Conference of the North American Chapter of the Association for Computational Linguistics: Human Language Technologies*, pages 720–730.

Koji Mineshima, Pascual Martínez-Gómez, Yusuke Miyao, and Daisuke Bekki. 2015. Higher-order logical inference with compositional semantics. In *Proceedings of the 2015 Conference on Empirical Methods in Natural Language Processing*, pages 2055–2061.

Shashi Narayan, Claire Gardent, Shay Cohen, and Anastasia Shimorina. 2017. Split and rephrase. In *Proceedings of the 2014 Conference on Empirical Methods in Natural Language Processing*, pages 617–627.

Sebastian Padó, Michel Galley, Dan Jurafsky, and Chris Manning. 2009. Robust machine translation evaluation with entailment features. In *Proceedings of the Joint Conference of the 47th Annual Meeting of the ACL and the 4th International Joint Conference on Natural Language Processing of the AFNLP*, pages 297–305.

Kishore Papineni, Salim Roukos, Todd Ward, and Wei-Jing Zhu. 2002. BLEU: a method for automatic evaluation of machine translation. In *Proceedings of the 40th Annual Meeting on Association for Computational Linguistics*, pages 311–318.

Terence Parsons. 1990. *Events in the semantics of English: a study in subatomic semantics*. The MIT Press.

Aarne Ranta. 2011. *Grammatical framework: Programming with Multilingual Grammars*. CSLI Publications.

Mark Steedman. 2000. *The Syntactic Process*. The MIT Press.

Mark Steedman. 2012. *Taking scope: The natural semantics of quantifiers*. The MIT Press.

Ilya Sutskever, Oriol Vinyals, and Quoc V Le. 2014. Sequence to Sequence Learning with Neural Networks. In *Advances in neural information processing systems*, pages 3104–3112.

Mingzhe Wang, Yihe Tang, Jian Wang, and Jia Deng. 2017. Premise selection for theorem proving by deep graph embedding. In *Advances in Neural Information Processing Systems*, pages 2783–2793.

Michael White. 2006. Efficient Realization of Coordinate Structures in Combinatory Categorial Grammar. *Research on Language & Computation*, 4(1):39–75.

Michael White and Rajakrishnan Rajkumar. 2009. Perceptron reranking for CCG realization. In *Proceedings of the 2009 Conference on Empirical Methods in Natural Language Processing*, pages 410–419.

Yuk Wah Wong and Raymond Mooney. 2007. Generation by inverting a semantic parser that uses statistical machine translation. In *Human Language Technologies 2007: The Conference of the North American Chapter of the Association for Computational Linguistics*, pages 172–179.

Hitomi Yanaka, Koji Mineshima, Pascual Martínez-Gómez, and Daisuke Bekki. 2017. Determining Semantic Textual Similarity using Natural Deduction Proofs. In *Proceedings of the 2017 Conference on Empirical Methods in Natural Language Processing*, pages 692–702.

Masashi Yoshikawa, Hiroshi Noji, and Yuji Matsumoto. 2017. A* CCG parsing with a supertag and dependency factored model. In *Proceedings of the 55th Annual Meeting of the Association for Computational Linguistics*, pages 277–287.

John M. Zelle and Raymond J. Mooney. 1996. Learning to parse database queries using inductive logic programming. In *Proceedings of the Thirteenth National Conference on Artificial Intelligence*, pages 1050–1055.

Talking about other people: an endless range of possibilities

Emiel van Miltenburg
Tilburg University
C.W.J.vanMiltenburg@uvt.nl

Desmond Elliott
University of Copenhagen
de@di.ku.dk

Piek Vossen
Vrije Universiteit Amsterdam
piek.vossen@vu.nl

Abstract

Image description datasets, such as Flickr30K and MS COCO, show a high degree of variation in the ways that crowd-workers talk about the world. Although this gives us a rich and diverse collection of data to work with, it also introduces uncertainty about how the world should be described. This paper shows the extent of this uncertainty in the PEOPLE domain. We present a taxonomy of different ways to talk about other people. This taxonomy serves as a reference point to think about how other people should be described, and can be used to classify and compute statistics about labels applied to people.

1 Introduction

There are currently two major data sets used to train and evaluate automatic description systems: Flickr30K and MS COCO (Young et al., 2014; Lin et al., 2014). Both of these data sets contain images with multiple crowd-sourced descriptions per image. These datasets are typically used to train data-driven natural language generation systems to automatically learn to associate visual features with natural language descriptions (Bernardi et al., 2016). Following the training phase, image description systems are evaluated by comparing their output with human generated descriptions for the same image (using textual similarity metrics like BLEU or METEOR, Papineni et al. 2002; Denkowski and Lavie 2014). The standard for what the image descriptions should look like is implicit in the corpus. The only point at which any explicit guidelines are provided is during the crowd-sourcing task, where annotators are given general instructions about what their description should look like. Here are the Flickr30K instructions (the MS COCO instructions are similar):

1. Describe the image in one complete but simple sentence. 2. Provide an explicit description of prominent entities. 3. Do not make unfounded assumptions about what is occurring. 4. Only talk about entities that appear in the image. 5. Provide an accurate description of the activities, people, animals and objects you see depicted in the image. 6. Each description must be a single sentence under 100 characters.
(Hodosh et al., 2013, edited for brevity)

These guidelines leave much of the task open for interpretation by the annotator. For example, it is unclear how the descriptions will be used, or what the target audience is (as pointed out by van Miltenburg et al. 2017). Thus, the underspecified nature of the task invites *variation* and *creativity*. It is important for us to understand the extent of this variation because image description corpora currently set the standard for what an image description should look like.

Earlier work has looked at stereotyping behavior, reporting bias, and the use of negations in image descriptions (van Miltenburg, 2016; Misra et al., 2016; van Miltenburg et al., 2016, 2017), and recently Van Miltenburg et al. (2018) provided an overview of measures to quantify diversity. This paper looks at the variation in the labels used to refer to other people, and presents a taxonomy (based on the Flickr30K dataset) that shows the range of properties that crowd-workers consider in the description process. This taxonomy ranges from physical attributes, such as hair color, to attributes concerning socio-economic status (e.g. *unemployed*).

After discussing related work (§2), we present our method to select person-labels and to categorize (partial) labels into semantic categories (§3).

Proceedings of The 11th International Natural Language Generation Conference, pages 415–420,
Tilburg, The Netherlands, November 5-8, 2018. ©2018 Association for Computational Linguistics

Following this, Section 4 shows the resulting taxonomy, with examples from the Flickr30K dataset. Section 5 discusses our taxonomy in light of the recently published Face2Text dataset (Gatt et al., 2018), and considers the reliability of perceived attributes. We believe these contributions will be useful for practitioners interested in the generation of person-descriptions. Our code and data is publicly available online.[1]

2 Related work

Natural Language Generation researchers tasked with describing other people have mostly been concerned with generating referring expressions *without* visual context, usually for well-known entities (e.g. Castro Ferreira et al. 2016; Kutlak et al. 2016). The closest related work comes from Gatt et al. (2018) and Van Miltenburg (2016).

Gatt et al. (2018) present a dataset of images of human faces, with multiple elicited descriptions per image. They annotated a part of their dataset to estimate how many of the descriptions refer to physical (85%), emotional (44%), or inferred (46%) properties of the subjects depicted in the images. In contrast, the present paper presents a more precise taxonomy, and discusses Gatt et al.'s Face2Text dataset in light of this taxonomy.

Van Miltenburg (2016) used the Flickr30K-entities dataset (Plummer et al., 2015) to cluster entity mentions based on their co-reference to the same entities. We refer to these mentions as *labels*. Their clustering approach yields hundreds of groups of labels referring to similar entities. Here is one of those clusters, relating to FACIAL HAIR:

> beard, goatee, beard and mustache, gray beard, black beard, white beard, red beard, braided beard, gray braided beard, long, white beard, long brown beard, flaming red beard, big beard, short beard, bubble beard, large white beard, thick beard, neatly trimmed beard, scruffy beard, red facial hair

Van Miltenburg (2016) uses this example as anecdotal evidence for the richness of image description data, without further analysis. Our paper aims to provide a deeper analysis of the labels used to refer to other people, by manually categorizing the labels into semantically coherent sub-groups. For example, if we look more closely at the FACIAL HAIR cluster, we can see that these terms include references to the KIND OF HAIR (*beard,*

goatee, mustache), the COLOR (*gray, black, white*), LENGTH (*long, short*), SIZE (*big, large*), ORDERLINESS (*neatly trimmed, scruffy*), and PRESENTATION (*braided*). This means that, when asked to talk about an image, people consider at least six different variables just to describe facial hair.

3 Method

We created a taxonomy of the labels used to refer to other people by manually sorting the entity labels into different semantic categories, instead of clustering the labels (as in Van Miltenburg 2016). The advantage of manually sorting the labels is that we have full control over the categories. This makes it possible to make more fine-grained distinctions, and to show the breadth of the label distribution. In this paper, we use the English Flickr30K corpus, focusing on the different ways that crowd-workers describe other people.

3.1 Initial selection

The starting point for our categorization is a list of labels. We compiled this list using the Flickr30K-entities annotations provided by Plummer et al. (2015), and listed all labels that were classed as PEOPLE. After normalization, we found 19,634 unique labels, which is too much to categorize by hand.[2] (It is not possible to crowd-source our categorization task, because the categories are not known beforehand.) Hence we focus our efforts only on the 5,526 labels that end with any of the nouns *girl, boy, woman, man, female, male*, or any of their plural forms.[3] This makes the task more manageable, but it also potentially reduces the variation in the data because the selected labels are more homogeneous. Nevertheless, as we will see in Section 4, we still found a broad range of variation in the labels.

During the categorization task, we found several typing errors, and words unrelated to people-labeling. We addressed these issues by semi-automatically correcting the typing errors, and creating a list of stopwords that were automatically removed from the labels. This further reduced the number of unique labels-to-be-categorized from 5526 to 3401.

---

[1] https://github.com/evanmiltenburg/LabelingPeople

[2] We normalized the labels by lowercasing them, and removing the characters @ + , & ( ).

[3] We applied the same approach to the attributes in the Visual Genome dataset (Krishna et al., 2017), but for reasons of space we focus on Flickr30K. Results are available online.

Category	Examples
ABILITY	wheelchair bound, able-bodied, disabled, handicapped, blind, one-armed, legless, crippled
ACTIVITY	running, chasing, waving, speaking, parachuting, roller-skating, protesting, partying, hiking
AGE	young, old, middle-aged, adult, elderly, infant, twenty-something, teen-aged, adolescent
ATTRACTIVENESS	attractive, beautiful, pretty, sexy, cute, ugly, adorable, hot, handsome, nicé, good looking
BUILD	petite, muscular, slender, lanky, heavy chested, potbellied, well built, burly, stocky, potbellied
CLEANLINESS	dirty, shaggy, scruffy, muddy, disheveled, messy, well-groomed, grouchy looking, dirty faced
CLOTHING – AMOUNT	shirtless, topless, barefooted, scantily clad, nude, unclothed, undressed, semi-naked, shoe-less
– COLOR	green black uniformed, brightly dressed, red shirted, colorfully clothed, vibrantly colored
– KIND	uniformed, casually dressed, sari-garbed, leather-clad, robed, suited, kilted, gothic-dressed
ETHNICITY	african-american, asian, oriental, caucasian, chinese, foreign, middle-eastern, indian, tribal
EYES	blue-eyed, brown eyed, green eyed, bespectacled, glasses-wearing, sun-glassed
FITNESS	physically fit, healthy fit, in shape, healthy and fit, weak looking, out-of-shape
GROUP	cast, circle, audience, crowd, ensemble, couple, team, roomful, group, trio, bunch, gathering
HAIR – COLOR	blond, dark-haired, brown-haired, brunette, redheaded, fair, dark, ginger, dirty-blonde, graying
– FACIAL	bearded, goateed, shaved, white-bearded, mustachioed, stubbled, green bearded, clean-shaven
– LENGTH	bald, short-haired, long-haired, balding, nearly bald, partially bald, shaved head, bald-headed
– STYLE	curly-haired, frizzy-haired, pony-tailed, shaggy-haired, curly, dreadlocked, spiky haired
HEIGHT	tall, short, petite, taller, long, littler, tall looking, shorter, rather tall, slightly taller
JUDGMENT	stylish, tacky looking, strange, silly, odd looking, hip, comical, flamboyant, shady, shadowy
MOOD	happy, excited, curious, enthusiastic, tired, thoughtful, pensive, angry-looking, weary, sad
OCCUPATION	military, navy, photographer, coast guard, executive, cooking professional, bartender
RELIGION	muslim, hindu, amish, christian, islamic, religious, jewish, buddhist, catholic, mormon, hindi
SOCIAL GROUP	homeless, goth, hippie, rasta, peasant, unemployed, poor looking, trash, middle class, high class
STATE	drunk, extremely drunk, wet, bloody, pregnant, sweaty, cold, handcuffed, ill, injured, deceased
WEIGHT	overweight, fat, slim, skinny, obese, plump, heavyset, heftier, mildly overweight, heavy, hefty

Table 1: Taxonomy of labels referring to other people, with selected examples for each category. All examples are (partial) labels from the Flickr30K dataset.

3.2 Sorting procedure

We manually sorted (partial) labels into semantic categories, shown in Table 1. Nothing crucially hinges on these specific categories, but from our experience with image description datasets, we believe they provide a good first approximation, capturing the breadth of the labels used by the crowd. Our sorting procedure works as follows.

1. Start with a set of labels to be categorized.
2. Remove task-specific stopwords and unrelated phrases (e.g. *a picture of*) from the labels. This reduces the number of unique labels.
3. Select (partial) labels from the list, add them to an existing category file, or create a new category file with those labels.
4. Match the labels with the categories. We use a context-free grammar (CFG, see Figure 1; implemented using the NLTK, Bird et al. 2009) because each label may consist of multiple modifiers from different categories. For example: *African-American young man* has both ETHNICITY and AGE modifiers.
5. Remove matches from the set of labels to be categorized.
6. Either stop categorization, or go to 3.

```
LABEL → MOD, GENDEREDNOUN
LABEL → MOD, MOD, GENDEREDNOUN
MOD → ABILITY | ACTIVITY | AGE | ...
GENDEREDNOUN → woman | man | girl | boy | ...
AGE → young | old | middle-aged | adult | elderly | ...
ETHNICITY → African-American | Asian | oriental | ...
```

Figure 1: Subset of our Context-Free Grammar, designed to match labels with different categories of modifiers. Production rules are based on our category files (which are updated in step 3).

Our goal is to get an overview of the different kinds of labels used by the crowd-workers, not to achieve a perfect categorization of all labels. Thus, our stopping criterion is as follows. The sorting task is finished whenever there are no more examples matching existing categories, or warranting new categories. New categories are warranted if there are multiple (partial) labels that clearly fall under the same umbrella, but do not fit into any of the existing categories.

4 Results

We sorted the (partial) labels into 20 different categories, until we were left with only 341 labels

(10%) that could not be fully matched with our categories by the CFG matcher. Examples of uncategorized labels are *birthday girl* and *blood pressure of a man*. The former could be classed as a role associated with an event, but we did not find many such examples. The latter is an artifact of the automated label categorization process for the Flickr30K Entities dataset.

Table 1 shows the 20 different label categories, with examples for each category. With this table, we have an empirically derived taxonomy that provides an overview of the choices that crowd-workers make in order to describe other people. The different categories show the diversity and breadth of the label distribution. In future work, we hope to extend the coverage of our taxonomy (ideally to all 19,634 person-labels in Flickr30K-Entities), and present statistics about the proportion of person-labels from the Flickr30K dataset that fall into each category.

Our taxonomy also provides a reference point to think about the characteristics that we would and would *not* like image description systems to describe. For example, the automatic description of features like RELIGION, WEIGHT, or SOCIAL GROUP would probably do more harm than good. Table 1 also shows us what makes image description difficult. For this domain alone, to produce human-like descriptions, systems need to be able to predict 20 different kinds of features, and decide which feature values are relevant to mention. A further complication is that even after deciding which characteristics to describe, there are still within-category choices to be made. For example, when describing a game of basketball, one might choose to talk about a *man playing basketball* (seeing basketball-playing as a transient property), or *male basketball player* (seeing basketball-playing as an inherent property). These choices go beyond the scope of this paper, but see Beukeboom 2014; Fokkens et al. 2018 for a discussion.

5 Discussion and Future Research

5.1 Extending the taxonomy to Face2text

We obtained the Face2Text corpus (Gatt et al., 2018, v0.1) from the authors to see to what extent our taxonomy could be applied to their data. The main difference between the Flickr30K-Entities labels and the Face2Text descriptions is that the former are part of a larger description, whereas the latter are full-blown descriptions themselves. As a result, the Face2Text descriptions are much longer (a mean of 26.9 tokens versus 2.4 for the Flickr30k-entities labels). This leads to crowd-workers providing much more (and seemingly more specific) information about the people in the images. For example, there are 24 occurrences of 'jaw' in Face2Text, with modifiers such as *angular, pointy, traditional square* to denote the specific shape of the jaw. Such details do not seem relevant enough to mention in a short label, as in the Flickr30K-Entities dataset.

In future work, we hope to extend our taxonomy to cover the Face2Text data. This would make users more aware of the contents of the corpus, and enable them to make a conscious choice about the kinds of features they would like their face description systems to generate.

5.2 Consistency is no substitute for truth

In earlier research, Song et al. (2017) present a system that is able to predict (to varying degrees of success) perceived social attributes from faces. Human participants rated faces from a large database for their attractiveness, friendliness, familiarity, but also to what extent they thought the subjects were egotistical, emotionally stable, or responsible.[4]

It is important to stress that these ratings only indicate *perceived* characteristics, and do not necessarily reflect the actual characters of the individuals in the dataset. More generally, even though people may be able to consistently ascribe a particular property to an individual, this alone does not entail that the property actually applies (see Todorov et al. 2013; Agüera y Arcas et al. 2017 for a discussion). When considering different ways to label other people, we should ask ourselves: is it reasonable to predict this label category based on visual information alone?

5.3 Limitations

The approach taken in this paper has three main limitations, which we will discuss in turn.

First, our taxonomy is based on a subset of the person-labels in the Flickr30K-Entities dataset, and thus may overlook other relevant label categories.

---

[4]Song et al. (2017) list the following 20 pairs of social traits: (attractive, unattractive), (happy, unhappy), (friendly, unfriendly), (sociable, introverted), (kind, mean), (caring, cold), (calm, aggressive), (trustworthy, untrustworthy), (responsible, irresponsible), (confident, uncertain), (humble, egotistical),(emotionally stable, emotionally unstable), (normal, weird), (intelligent, unintelligent), (interesting, boring), (emotional, unemotional), (memorable, forgettable), (typical, atypical), (familiar, unfamiliar) and (common, uncommon).

We emphasize that our work is not meant to provide an exhaustive categorization of the labels used in the Flickr30K data. Rather, our goal is to highlight the breadth of the label distribution. The fact that the broad taxonomy developed in this paper is based on a subset of all the labels (less than a third of the Flickr30K data) only supports the main point of this paper, which is that humans use a wide array of terms to refer to other people.

Second, our taxonomy is constructed manually, and it is unclear whether replication would yield similar results. This is a natural result of a manual categorization of the person labels, and it would be interesting to see if we could automatically induce a similar taxonomy from the corpus data (for example using LDA; Blei et al. 2003). To facilitate future research in this area, we made all our code and data available online.[1]

Finally, our taxonomy is exclusively based on English, without any input from other languages. It may be the case that speakers of other languages highlight other features, in making reference to other people. This idea opens up another avenue of research, asking two related questions:

1. Do speakers of the same language tend to mention the same person-attributes for the same images?
2. Are there any cross-linguistic differences in what features are mentioned in reference to other people?

Although some work has *mentioned* cross-linguistic differences in how annotators refer to other people (e.g. Li et al. 2016; van Miltenburg et al. 2017), we are not aware of any systematic study that specifically looks at how speakers of different languages make reference to other people, and what features they tend to mention.

6   Conclusion

We have looked at the variation in the ways crowd-workers talk about other people in the Flickr30K dataset. Our main result is that this variation covers a wide range of variables, from appearance to socio-economic status. We formalized this variation in a taxonomy of person-labels, which should help us reflect on the image description task, and the kinds of descriptions that image description systems should produce. Future research should be aware that, even though crowd-workers may systematically produce particular labels, this does not mean that the label is true. We encourage the development of standards and guidelines, that tell us which kinds of labels to use in what kind of situations. Such guidelines may benefit system evaluation and help us avoid the inappropriate labeling of other people.

Acknowledgments

This paper was written while the first author was at the Vrije Universiteit Amsterdam, supported by the NWO Spinoza Prize awarded to Piek Vossen.

References

Blaise Agüera y Arcas, Margaret Mitchell, and Alexander Todorov. 2017. Physiognomy's new clothes. Medium.

Raffaella Bernardi, Ruket Cakici, Desmond Elliott, Aykut Erdem, Erkut Erdem, Nazli Ikizler-Cinbis, Frank Keller, Adrian Muscat, and Barbara Plank. 2016. Automatic description generation from images: A survey of models, datasets, and evaluation measures. *Journal of Artificial Intelligence Research*, 55:409–442.

Camiel J. Beukeboom. 2014. Mechanisms of linguistic bias: How words reflect and maintain stereotypic expectancies. In J. Laszlo, J. Forgas, and O. Vincze, editors, *Social cognition and communication*, volume 31, pages 313–330. Psychology Press. Author's pdf: http://dare.ubvu.vu.nl/handle/1871/47698.

Steven Bird, Ewan Klein, and Edward Loper. 2009. *Natural language processing with Python: analyzing text with the natural language toolkit.* " O'Reilly Media, Inc.".

David M Blei, Andrew Y Ng, and Michael I Jordan. 2003. Latent dirichlet allocation. *Journal of machine Learning research*, 3(Jan):993–1022.

Thiago Castro Ferreira, Emiel Krahmer, and Sander Wubben. 2016. Towards more variation in text generation: Developing and evaluating variation models for choice of referential form. In *Proceedings of the 54th Annual Meeting of the Association for Computational Linguistics (Volume 1: Long Papers)*, pages 568–577, Berlin, Germany.

Michael Denkowski and Alon Lavie. 2014. Meteor universal: Language specific translation evaluation for any target language. In *Proceedings of the EACL 2014 Workshop on Statistical Machine Translation*.

Antske Fokkens, Nel Ruigrok, Camiel Beukeboom, Gagestein Sarah, and Wouter Van Attveldt. 2018. Studying Muslim Stereotyping through Microportrait Extraction. In *Proceedings of the Eleventh International Conference on Language Resources and*

Evaluation (LREC 2018), Miyazaki, Japan. European Language Resources Association (ELRA).

Albert Gatt, Marc Tanti, Adrian Muscat, Patrizia Paggio, Reuben A Farrugia, Claudia Borg, Kenneth P Camilleri, Mike Rosner, and Lonneke van der Plas. 2018. Face2text: Collecting an annotated image description corpus for the generation of rich face descriptions. In *Proceedings of the 11th edition of the Language Resources and Evaluation Conference (LREC'18)*.

Micah Hodosh, Peter Young, and Julia Hockenmaier. 2013. Framing image description as a ranking task: Data, models and evaluation metrics. *Journal of Artificial Intelligence Research*, 47:853–899.

Ranjay Krishna, Yuke Zhu, Oliver Groth, Justin Johnson, Kenji Hata, Joshua Kravitz, Stephanie Chen, Yannis Kalantidis, Li-Jia Li, David A. Shamma, Michael S. Bernstein, and Li Fei-Fei. 2017. Visual genome: Connecting language and vision using crowdsourced dense image annotations. *Int. J. Comput. Vision*, 123(1):32–73.

Roman Kutlak, Kees van Deemter, and Chris Mellish. 2016. Production of referring expressions for an unknown audience: A computational model of communal common ground. *Frontiers in psychology*, 7:1275.

Xirong Li, Weiyu Lan, Jianfeng Dong, and Hailong Liu. 2016. Adding chinese captions to images. In *Proceedings of the 2016 ACM International Conference on Multimedia Retrieval*, pages 271–275. ACM.

Tsung-Yi Lin, Michael Maire, Serge Belongie, James Hays, Pietro Perona, Deva Ramanan, Piotr Dollár, and C Lawrence Zitnick. 2014. Microsoft coco: Common objects in context. In *European Conference on Computer Vision*, pages 740–755. Springer.

Emiel van Miltenburg. 2016. Stereotyping and bias in the flickr30k dataset. In *Proceedings of Multimodal Corpora: Computer vision and language processing (MMC 2016)*, pages 1–4.

Emiel van Miltenburg, Desmond Elliott, and Piek Vossen. 2017. Cross-linguistic differences and similarities in image descriptions. In *Proceedings of the 10th International Conference on Natural Language Generation*, pages 21–30, Santiago de Compostela, Spain. Association for Computational Linguistics.

Emiel van Miltenburg, Desmond Elliott, and Piek Vossen. 2018. Measuring the diversity of automatic image descriptions. In *Proceedings of the 27th International Conference on Computational Linguistics*, pages 1730–1741. Association for Computational Linguistics.

Emiel van Miltenburg, Roser Morante, and Desmond Elliott. 2016. Pragmatic factors in image description: The case of negations. In *Proceedings of the 5th Workshop on Vision and Language*, pages 54–59, Berlin, Germany. Association for Computational Linguistics.

Ishan Misra, C Lawrence Zitnick, Margaret Mitchell, and Ross Girshick. 2016. Seeing through the human reporting bias: Visual classifiers from noisy human-centric labels. In *2016 IEEE Conference on Computer Vision and Pattern Recognition (CVPR)*, pages 2930–2939.

Kishore Papineni, Salim Roukos, Todd Ward, and Wei-Jing Zhu. 2002. Bleu: a method for automatic evaluation of machine translation. In *Proceedings of 40th Annual Meeting of the Association for Computational Linguistics*, pages 311–318, Philadelphia, Pennsylvania, USA. Association for Computational Linguistics.

Bryan A Plummer, Liwei Wang, Chris M Cervantes, Juan C Caicedo, Julia Hockenmaier, and Svetlana Lazebnik. 2015. Flickr30k entities: Collecting region-to-phrase correspondences for richer image-to-sentence models. In *Proceedings of the IEEE International Conference on Computer Vision*, pages 2641–2649.

Amanda Song, Linjie Li, Chad Atalla, and Garrison Cottrell. 2017. Learning to see people like people: Predicting the social perception of faces. In *Proceedings of the 39th Annual Conference of the Cognitive Science Society*. Austin, TX: Cognitive Science Society.

Alexander Todorov, Peter Mende-Siedlecki, and Ron Dotsch. 2013. Social judgments from faces. *Current opinion in neurobiology*, 23(3):373–380.

Peter Young, Alice Lai, Micah Hodosh, and Julia Hockenmaier. 2014. From image descriptions to visual denotations: New similarity metrics for semantic inference over event descriptions. *Transactions of the Association for Computational Linguistics*, 2:67–78.

Meteorologists and Students:
A resource for language grounding of geographical descriptors

Alejandro Ramos-Soto[1,2], Ehud Reiter[2], Kees van Deemter[2,3], Jose M. Alonso[1], and Albert Gatt[4]

[1]Centro Singular de Investigación en Tecnoloxías da Información (CiTIUS), Universidade de Santiago de Compostela:
{alejandro.ramos,josemaria.alonso.moral}@usc.es

[2]Department of Computing Science, University of Aberdeen:
{alejandro.soto,e.reiter,k.vdeemter}@abdn.ac.uk

[3]Utrecht University: k.vandeemter@uu.nl

[4]Institute of Linguistics and Language Technology, University of Malta: albert.gatt@um.edu.mt

Abstract

We present a data resource which can be useful for research purposes on language grounding tasks in the context of geographical referring expression generation. The resource is composed of two data sets that encompass 25 different geographical descriptors and a set of associated graphical representations, drawn as polygons on a map by two groups of human subjects: teenage students and expert meteorologists.

1 Introduction

Language grounding, i.e., understanding how words and expressions are anchored in data, is one of the initial tasks that are essential for the conception of a data-to-text (D2T) system (Roy and Reiter, 2005; Reiter, 2007). This can be achieved through different means, such as using heuristics or machine learning algorithms on an available parallel corpora of text and data (Novikova et al., 2017) to obtain a mapping between the expressions of interest and the underlying data (Reiter et al., 2005), getting experts to provide these mappings, or running surveys on writers or readers that provide enough data for the application of mapping algorithms (Ramos-Soto et al., 2017).

Performing language grounding ensures that generated texts include words whose meaning is aligned with what writers understand or what readers would expect (Roy and Reiter, 2005), given the variation that is known to exist among writers and readers (Reiter and Sripada, 2002). Moreover, when contradictory data appears in corpora or any other resource that is used to create the data-to-words mapping, creating models that remove inconsistencies can also be a challenging part of lan-guage grounding which can influence the development of a successful system (Reiter et al., 2005).

This paper presents a resource for language grounding of geographical descriptors. The original purpose of this data collection is the creation of models of geographical descriptors whose meaning is modeled as graded or fuzzy (Fisher, 2000; Fisher et al., 2006), to be used for research on generation of geographical referring expressions, e.g., (Turner et al., 2010, 2008; de Oliveira et al., 2015; Ramos-Soto et al., 2016, 2017). However, we believe it can be useful for other related research purposes as well.

2 The resource and its interest

The resource is composed of data from two different surveys. In both surveys subjects were asked to draw on a map (displayed under a Mercator projection) a polygon representing a given geographical descriptor, in the context of the geography of Galicia in Northwestern Spain (see Fig. 1). However, the surveys were run with different purposes, and the subject groups that participated in each survey and the list of descriptors provided were accordingly different.

The first survey was run in order to obtain a high number of responses to be used as an evaluation testbed for modeling algorithms. It was answered by 15/16 year old students in a high school in Pontevedra (located in Western Galicia). 99 students provided answers for a list of 7 descriptors (including cardinal points, coast, inland, and a proper name). Figure 2 shows a representation of the answers given by the students for "Northern Galicia" and a contour map that illustrates the percentages of overlapping answers.

The second survey was addressed to meteorologists in the Galician Weather Agency (MeteoGalicia, 2018). Its purpose was to gather data to create

Proceedings of The 11th International Natural Language Generation Conference, pages 421–425,
Tilburg, The Netherlands, November 5-8, 2018. ©2018 Association for Computational Linguistics

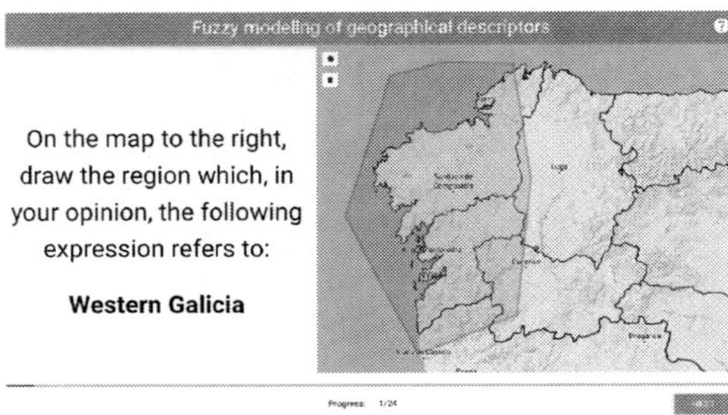

Figure 1: Snapshot of the version of the survey answered by the meteorologists (translated from Spanish).

fuzzy models that will be used in a future NLG system in the weather domain. Eight meteorologists completed the survey, which included a list of 24 descriptors. For instance, Figure 3 shows a representation of the answers given by the meteorologists for "Eastern Galicia" and a contour map that illustrates the percentage of overlapping answers.

Table 1 includes the complete list of descriptors for both groups of subjects. 20 out of the 24 descriptors are commonly used in the writing of weather forecasts by experts and include cardinal directions, proper names, and other kinds of references such as mountainous areas, parts of provinces, etc. The remaining four were added to study intersecting combinations of cardinal directions (e.g. exploring ways of combining "north" and "west" for obtaining a model that is similar to "northwest").

The data for the descriptors from the surveys is focused on a very specific geographical context. However, the conjunction of both data sets

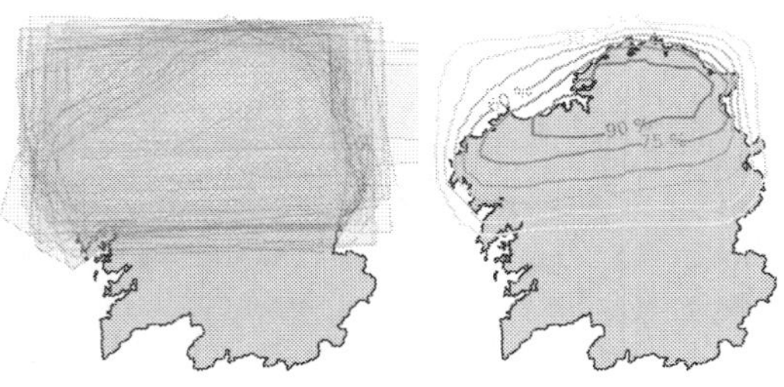

Figure 2: Representation of polygon drawings by students and associated contour plot showing the percentage of overlapping answers for "Northern Galicia".

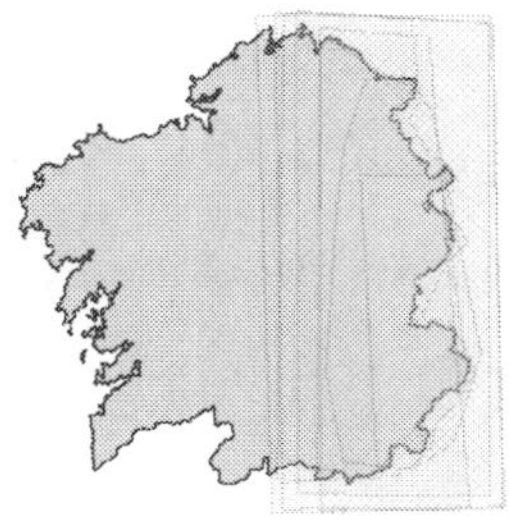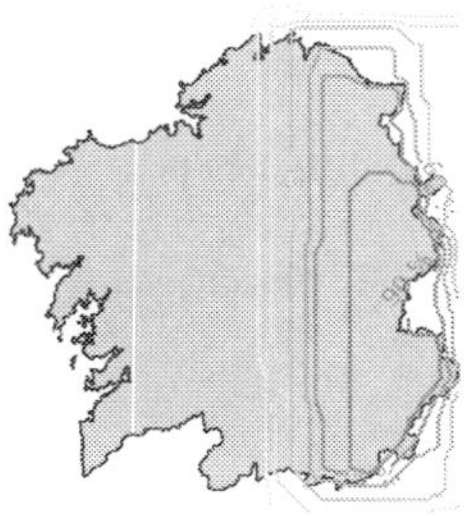

Figure 3: Representation of polygon drawings by experts and associated contour plot showing the percentage of overlapping answers for "Eastern Galicia".

provides a very interesting resource for performing a variety of more general language grounding-oriented and natural language generation research tasks, such as:

- Testing algorithms that create geographical models. These models would aggregate the answers from different subjects for each descriptor. The differences among the subjects can be interpreted from a probabilistic or fuzzy perspective that allows a richer characterization of the resulting models. For instance, in Fig. 2 the contour plots could be taken as the basis or support for the semantics of the expression "Northern Galicia", with a core region that is accepted by the majority, and a gradual decay as one moves to the outer periphery of the regions outlined.

- Analyzing differences between the expert and non-expert groups for the descriptors they have in common (as Table 1 shows, both groups share 6 descriptors).

- Studying how to combine models represent-

Subject Group	Spanish	English translation
Common	Norte de Galicia, Sur de Galicia, Oeste de Galicia, Este de Galicia, Interior de Galicia, Rías Baixas	Northern Galicia, Southern Galicia, Western Galicia, Eastern Galicia, Inland Galicia, Rías Baixas
Students	Costa de Galicia	Galician Coast
Experts	Tercio Norte, Extremo Norte, Áreas de montaña de Lugo, Áreas de montaña de Ourense, Oeste de A Coruña, Comarcas Atlánticas, Litoral Atlántico, Litoral Cantábrico, Litoral Norte, Interior de Coruña, Interior de Pontevedra, Oeste de Ourense, Sur de Ourense, Sur de Lugo, Noroeste de Galicia, Noreste de Galicia, Suroeste de Galicia, Sureste de Galicia	Northern Third, Extreme North, Mountainous areas in Lugo, Mountainous areas in Ourense, Western A Coruña, Atlantic Regions, Atlantic Coast, Cantabrian Coast, Northern Coast, Inland Coruña, Inland Pontevedra, Western Ourense, Southern Ourense, Southern Lugo, Northwestern Galicia, Northeastern Galicia, Southwestern Galicia, Southeastern Galicia

Table 1: List of geographical descriptors in the resource.

ing the semantics of different cardinal directions, such as "south" and "east" to obtain a representation of "southeast".

- Developing geographical referring expression generation algorithms based on the empirically created models.

3 Qualitative analysis of the data sets

The two data sets were gathered for different purposes and only coincide in a few descriptors, so providing a direct comparison is not feasible. However, we can discuss general qualitative insights and a more detailed analysis of the descriptors that both surveys share in common.

At a general level, we had hypothesized that experts would be much more consistent than students, given their professional training and the reduced number of meteorologists participating in the survey. Comparing the visualizations of both data sets we have observed that this is clearly the case; the polygons drawn by the experts are more concentrated and therefore there is a higher agreement among them. On top of these differences, some students provided unexpected drawings in terms of shape, size, or location of the polygon for several descriptors.

If we focus on single descriptors, one interesting outcome is that some of the answers for "Northern Galicia" and "Southern Galicia" overlap for both subject groups. Thus, although 'north' and 'south' are natural antonyms, if we take into account the opinion of each group as a whole, there exists a small area where points can be considered as belonging to both descriptors at the same time (see Fig. 4). In the case of "west" and "east", the drawings made by the experts were almost divergent and showed no overlapping between those two descriptors.

Regarding "Inland Galicia", the unions of the answers for each group occupy approximately the same area with a similar shape, but there is a very high overlapping among the answers of the meteorologists. A similar situation is found for the remaining descriptor "Rías Baixas", where both groups encompass a similar area. In this case, the students' answers cover a more extensive region and the experts coincide within a more restricted area.

3.1 A further analysis: apparent issues

As in any survey that involves a task-based collection of data, some of the answers provided by the subjects for the described data sets can be considered erroneous or misleading due to several reasons. Here we describe for each subject group some of the most relevant issues that any user of this resource should take into account.

In the case of the students, we have identified minor drawing errors appearing in most of the descriptors, which in general shouldn't have a negative impact in the long term thanks to the high number of participants in the original survey. For some descriptors, however, there exist polygons drawn by subjects that clearly deviate from what could be considered a proper answer. The clearest example of this problem involves the 'west' and 'east' descriptors, which were confused by some of the students who drew them inversely (see Fig. 5, around 10-15% of the answers).

In our case, given their background, some of the students may have actually confused the meaning of + "west" and "east". However, the most plausible explanation is that, unlike in English and other languages, in Spanish both descriptors are phonetically similar ("este" and "oeste") and can be easily mistaken for one another if read without atten-

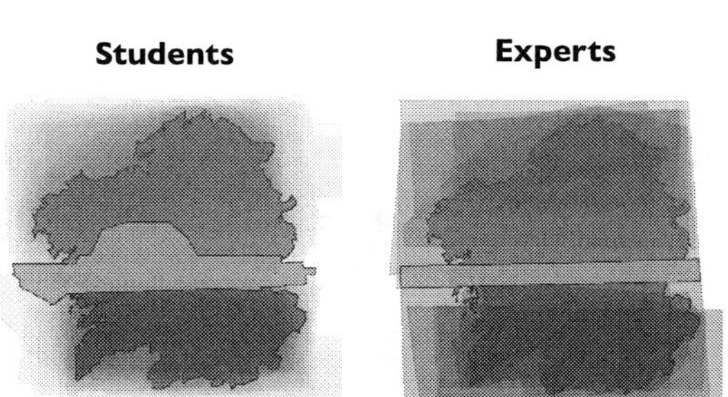

Figure 4: Areas overlapping "north" and "south" for both subject groups (in blue).

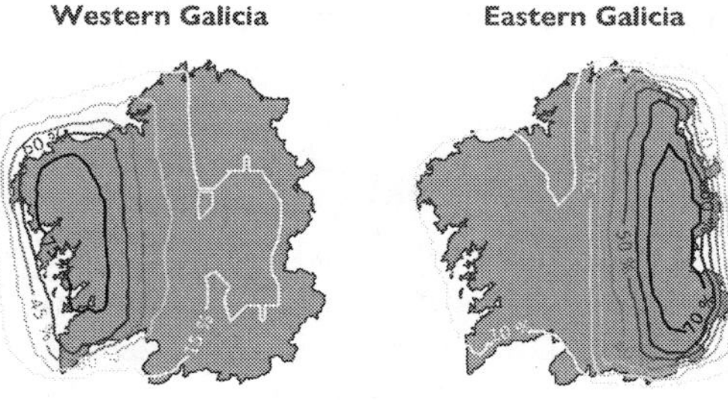

Figure 5: Contour maps of student answers for "Western Galicia" and "Eastern Galicia".

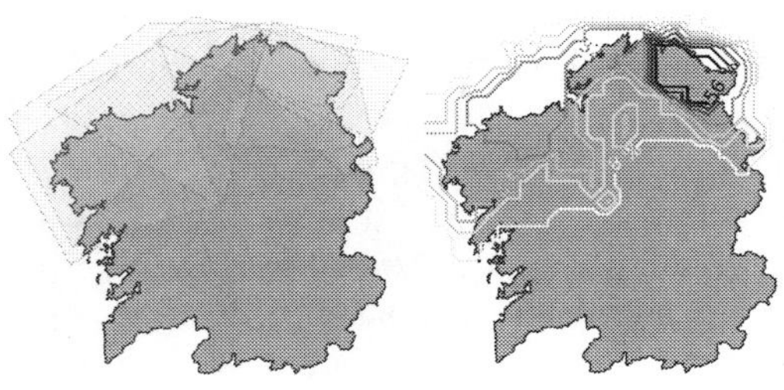

Figure 6: Representation of polygon drawings by experts and associated contour plots showing the percentage of overlapping answers for "Northeastern Galicia".

tion.

As for the expert group, a similar case is found for "Northeastern Galicia" (see Fig. 6), where some of the given answers (3/8) clearly correspond to "Northwestern Galicia". However, unlike the issue related to "west" and "east" found for the student group, this problem is not found reciprocally for the "northwestern" answers.

4 Resource materials

The resource is available at (Ramos-Soto et al., 2018) under a Creative Commons Attribution-NonCommercial-ShareAlike 4.0 International License. Both data sets are provided as SQLite databases which share the same table structure, and also in a compact JSON format. Polygon data is encoded in GeoJSON format (Butler et al., 2016). The data sets are well-documented in the repository's README, and several Python scripts are provided for data loading, using Shapely (Gillies et al., 2007–2018); and for visualization purposes, using Cartopy (Met Office, 2010–2015).

5 Concluding remarks

The data sets presented provide a means to perform different research tasks that can be useful from a natural language generation point of view. Among them, we can highlight the creation of models of geographical descriptors, comparing models between both subject groups, studying combinations of models of cardinal directions, and researching on geographical referring expression generation. Furthermore, insights about the semantics of geographical concepts could be inferred under a more thorough analysis.

One of the inconveniences that our data sets present is the appearance of the issues described in

Sec. 3.1. It could be necessary to filter some of the answers according to different criteria (e.g., deviation of the centroid location, deviation of size, etc.). For more applied cases, manually filtering can also be an option, but this would require a certain knowledge of the geography of Galicia. In any case, the squared-like shape of this region may allow researchers to become rapidly familiar with many of the descriptors listed in Table 1.

As future work, we believe it would be invaluable to perform similar data gathering tasks for other regions from different parts of the world. These should provide a variety of different shapes (both regular and irregular), so that it can be feasible to generalize (e.g., through data-driven approaches) the semantics of some of the more common descriptors, such as cardinal points, coastal areas, etc. The proposal of a shared task could help achieve this objective.

Acknowledgments

This research was supported by the Spanish Ministry of Economy and Competitiveness (grants TIN2014-56633-C3-1-R and TIN2017-84796-C2-1-R) and the Galician Ministry of Education (grants GRC2014/030 and "accreditation 2016-2019, ED431G/08"). All grants were co-funded by the European Regional Development Fund (ERDF/FEDER program). A. Ramos-Soto is funded by the "Consellería de Cultura, Educación e Ordenación Universitaria" (under the Postdoctoral Fellowship accreditation ED481B 2017/030). J.M. Alonso is supported by RYC-2016-19802 (Ramón y Cajal contract).

The authors would also like to thank Juan Taboada for providing the list of most frequently used geographical expressions by MeteoGalicia, and José Manuel Ramos for organizing the survey at the high school IES Xunqueira I in Pontevedra, Spain.

References

H. Butler, M. Daly, A. Doyle, S. Gillies, S. Hagen, and T. Schaub. 2016. *"The GeoJSON Format", RFC 7946*.

Peter Fisher. 2000. Sorites paradox and vague geographies. *Fuzzy Sets and Systems*, 113(1):7–18.

Peter Fisher, Alexis Comber, and Richard Wadsworth. 2006. Approaches to uncertainty in spatial data. *Fundamentals of Spatial Data Quality*, pages 43–59.

Sean Gillies et al. 2007–2018. Shapely: manipulation and analysis of geometric objects. `https://github.com/Toblerity/Shapely`.

Met Office. 2010–2015. Cartopy: a cartographic python library with a matplotlib interface. `http://scitools.org.uk/cartopy`.

MeteoGalicia. 2018. Meteogalicia's web site. `http://www.meteogalicia.es`.

Jekaterina Novikova, Ondrej Dušek, and Verena Rieser. 2017. The E2E dataset: New challenges for end-to-end generation. In *Proceedings of the 18th Annual Meeting of the Special Interest Group on Discourse and Dialogue*, Saarbrücken, Germany. ArXiv:1706.09254.

Rodrigo de Oliveira, Yaji Sripada, and Ehud Reiter. 2015. Designing an algorithm for generating named spatial references. In *Proceedings of the 15th European Workshop on Natural Language Generation (ENLG)*, pages 127–135. Association for Computational Linguistics.

Alejandro Ramos-Soto, Jose M Alonso, Ehud Reiter, Kees van Deemter, and Albert Gatt. 2017. An empirical approach for modeling fuzzy geographical descriptors. In *Fuzzy Systems (FUZZ-IEEE), 2017 IEEE International Conference on*, pages 1–6. IEEE.

Alejandro Ramos-Soto, Ehud Reiter, Kees van Deemter, Jose M. Alonso, and Albert Gatt. 2018. geodescriptors. `https://gitlab.citius.usc.es/alejandro.ramos/geodescriptors`. Accessed: 2018-07-09.

Alejandro Ramos-Soto, Nava Tintarev, Rodrigo de Oliveira, Ehud Reiter, and Kees van Deemter. 2016. Natural language generation and fuzzy sets: An exploratory study on geographical referring expression generation. In *2016 IEEE International Conference on Fuzzy Systems (FUZZ-IEEE)*, pages 587–594.

Ehud Reiter. 2007. An architecture for data-to-text systems. In *Proceedings of the 11th European Workshop on Natural Language Generation*, pages 97–104.

Ehud Reiter and Somayajulu Sripada. 2002. Should corpora texts be gold standards for NLG? In *Proceedings of the International Natural Language Generation Conference*, pages 97–104.

Ehud Reiter, Somayajulu Sripada, Jim Hunter, and Ian Davy. 2005. Choosing words in computer-generated weather forecasts. *Artificial Intelligence*, 167:137–169.

Deb Roy and Ehud Reiter. 2005. Connecting language to the world. *Artificial Intelligence*, 167(1-2):1–12.

Ross Turner, Somayajulu Sripada, and Ehud Reiter. 2010. Generating approximate geographic descriptions. In *Empirical Methods in Natural Language Generation*, volume 5790 of *Lecture Notes in Computer Science*, pages 121–140. Springer Berlin Heidelberg.

Ross Turner, Somayajulu Sripada, Ehud Reiter, and Ian P. Davy Davy. 2008. Using spatial reference frames to generate grounded textual summaries of georeferenced data. In *Proceedings of the 2008 International Conference on Natural Language Generation (INLG08)*, pages 16–24.

Cyclegen: Cyclic consistency based product review generator from attributes

Vasu Sharma
School of Computer Science,
Carnegie Mellon University
sharma.vasu55@gmail.com

Harsh Sharma
Robotics Institute
Carnegie Mellon University
harsh.sharma@gmail.com

Ankita Bishnu
Indian Institute of Technology, Kanpur
ankita.iitk@gmail.com

Labhesh Patel
Jumio Inc.
labhesh@gmail.com

Abstract

In this paper we present an automatic review generator system which can generate personalized reviews based on the user identity, product identity and designated rating the user wishes to allot to the review. We combine this with a sentiment analysis system which performs the complimentary task of assigning ratings to reviews based purely on the textual content of the review. We introduce an additional loss term to ensure cyclic consistency of the sentiment rating of the generated review with the conditioning rating used to generate the review. The introduction of this new loss term constraints the generation space while forcing it to generate reviews adhering better to the requested rating. The use of 'soft' generation and cyclic consistency allows us to train our model in an end to end fashion. We demonstrate the working of our model on product reviews from Amazon dataset.

1 Introduction

In this age of growing e-commerce markets, reviews are taken very seriously, however, manually writing these reviews has become an extremely laborious task. This leads us to work on systems which can automatically generate realistic looking reviews which can be automatically customized to the user writing it, the product being reviewed and the desired rating the generated review should express. This makes the reviewing process much easier which can potentially increase the number of reviews posted leading to a more informed choice for potential buyers.

Natural Language Generation has always been one of the most challenging task in the field of natural language processing. Most of the present day approaches very loosely constraint the generation process often leading to ill formed or meaningless generations. Ensuring semantic and syntactic coherence across the generated sentence is also an immensely challenging task. We explore enforcing additional constraints on the generation process which we hope will restrict the generation manifold and generate more meaningful and semantically consistent sentence also adhering to the desired ratings. In this paper we attempt to perform the following tasks:

- We implement an automatic review generator using Long Short Term Memory Networks (LSTM) (Hochreiter and Schmidhuber, 1997), which has proved useful in remembering context and modelling sentence syntax. We also incorporate a soft attention mechanism which helps the model to attend better to the relevant context and generate better reviews. Such a review generator system caters to each individual users reviewing style and would convert a user provided rating into a review personalized to the users writing style and based on their rating.

- Sentiment Analysis from reviews. This includes going through the reviews and trying to gauge user sentiment and assign a score based on it. Score parameters have been found to be much easier to go through and base ones decisions upon rather than manually going through hundreds of reviews.

- In this paper we propose an additional cyclic consistency loss term which allows for joint training of the generation network with the sentiment analysis network. This improves the generator network which is now more constrained and is forced to generate reviews which adhere to the provided rating.

Proceedings of The 11th International Natural Language Generation Conference, pages 426–430,
Tilburg, The Netherlands, November 5-8, 2018. ©2018 Association for Computational Linguistics

- The use of 'soft' generation instead of a sampling based generation allows end to end gradient propagation allowing us to train our models end to end.

2 Dataset

In this paper we validate our generation framework on the Amazon dataset which contains reviews and scores for products sold on amazon.com and is part of the dataset collected by McAuley and Leskovec (2013). We used the reviews in the books category. Specifically, we have 80,256 books and 19,675 users after using the same preprocessing as used in (Dong et al., 2017). The ratings are converted into 5 integer levels from 1-5.

3 Attribute Based Review generation

In this section we explain the network we used for the attribute based review generation. The network we implement uses an architecture similar to the one proposed by Dong et al (2017). The overview of the architecture is shown in Figure 1. The architecture consists of 3 parts i.e. Attribute Encoder, Sequence Generator and a soft attention mechanism. We now describe these parts in detail.

3.1 Attribute Encoder

Let us represent the attributes by a vector a where each element of a represents a specific attribute. In our case the attribute vector consists of user ID, product ID and the rating on a scale of 1-5 each represented as one hot vectors. The model begins by using a multi layer perceptron with a single hidden layer to learn the attribute embeddings.

$$g(a_i) = W_a^i \cdot (a_i)$$

Where a_i are the one hot representations of the various attributes. This allows each of the attributes to be encoded separately. We then combine the various attribute embeddings by concatenating them and passing them through another layer of a Multi Layer Perceptron.

$$e_a = tanh(W_g \cdot [g(a_1), ..., g(a_n)] + b_a)$$

Here e_a denotes the final joint representation of the attribute embeddings and n represents the number of attributes ($n = 3$ in our case). [.] represents the concatenation operator.
The weight matrix W_g here is chosen to generate

an output of size Ln where L is the number of layers in the generator network and n is the hidden state size of the LSTM units in the generator network. e_a is now used to initialize the hidden states of the multi layer LSTM based generator network.

3.2 Sequence Generator

The sequence generator network is based on a Multi Layer LSTM architecture. Unlike Dong et al, we initialize our word embeddings using a concatenation of the Glove (Pennington et al., 2014) and Cove embeddings (McCann et al., 2017). The word embeddings are fine tuned as the network trains. The attribute encodings defined in the previous section are used to initialize the hidden state of the generator network. The Ln dimensional attribute encoding is split into L parts of length n each which are used to initialize the hidden states of the L layers of the LSTM network. This basic model of the generator network without the soft attention mechanism is shown in Figure 2

3.3 Soft Attention Mechanism

Soft attention has recently been utilized to better utilize contextual information in a variety of tasks (Maas et al., 2011), (Wang and Manning, 2012). In this paper, we utilize the soft attention mechanism to make better use of the encoding information from the attributes. The architecture which implements the soft attention mechanism is shown in Figure 3. The attention is computed from the hidden vector of the LSTM over all the attribute embeddings we learned using the attribute encoder. This attention is then used to compute the attention weighted context vector c^t. This is represented by the equations:

$$r_t^i = exp(Tanh(W_h^s \cdot h_t^L + W_a^s \cdot g(a_i))$$

$$s_t^i = \frac{r_t^i}{\sum_{j=1}^n r_t^j}$$

$$c^t = \sum_{i=1}^n s_t^i \cdot g(a_i)$$

Here s_t^i is the attention weight of the ith attribute and n is the number of attributes. Here W_h and W_a are parameter matrices. We use this attention weighted context vector to predict the next word generated by the sequence generator as:

$$h_t^{att} = tanh(W_1 \cdot c_t + W_2 \cdot h_t^L)$$
$$o_t = (W_p \cdot h_t^{att})$$

Here W_1, W_2 and W_p are parameter matrices. The generation thus involves a sequence of discrete decision making which samples a token from a multinomial distribution parameterized using softmax function at each time step t:

$$\hat{x}_t \sim softmax(o_t/\tau)$$

where o_t is the logit vector as the inputs to the softmax function. The temperature τ is set to $\tau \to 0$ as training proceeds, yielding increasingly peaked distributions that finally emulate discrete case. The generation process ends when the EOS token is generated or when 3 complete sentences are generated, whichever happens first.

4 Training

The review network is initially pre-trained independently of the sentiment analysis network by maximizing the log likelihood of the generated sequence. After running a few epochs of training the generator alone, we enforce an additional cyclic consistency term in the loss function. The idea is the sentiment analysis score of the generated review should be consistent with the original rating provided as an attribute. Similar consistency terms can be applied to the other attributes as well, but here we explore only the consistency of the rating score term. A cross entropy loss between the predicted sentiment rating class and the ground truth rating class is used as the additional loss function to enforce cyclic consistency. Since sampling words from the generator will make the model non-differentiable preventing end to end training, hence we keep things in the probabilistic domain by resorting to a continuous approximation by using the probability vector instead of the sampled one hot vector. The probability vector is used as the output at the current step and the input to the next step along the sequence of decision making. This leads to a 'soft' predicted sequence $\widetilde{G}(a)$, which we use to compute the cyclic rating consistency loss term and this being fully probabilistic is differentiable allowing end to end training of the network. The cyclic consistency loss term can be denoted as:

$$L_{cyc} = \mathbb{E}_{(a,r) \in D} \, q_D(\widetilde{G}(a), r)$$

where q_D is the loss from the sentiment rating class predictor and r is the ground truth rating. Hence the joint loss function becomes:

$$L_{tot} = -L_{likelihood} + \lambda L_{cyc}$$

Adam optimizer (Kingma and Ba, 2014) with default parameters is used to train the model. NLTK tokenizer (Bird et al., 2009) is used to tokenize the sentences and all words which appear less than 10 times in the corpus are replaced by the $< UNK >$ token. All LSTM layers use 512 dimensional hidden units and 3 layers are used in the generator LSTM. The test time generations are generated using greedy search algorithms.

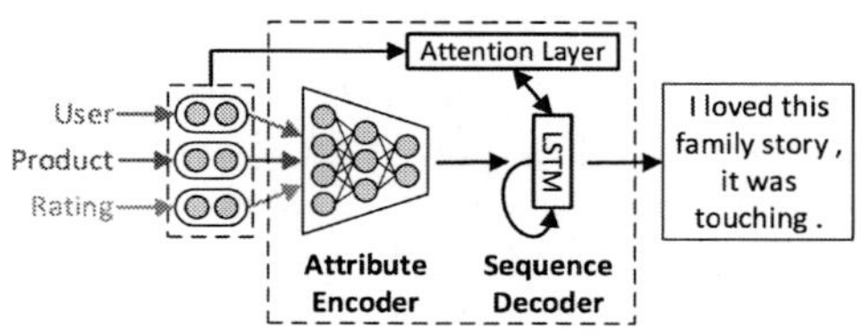

Figure 1: The model first learns attribute embeddings and then uses an LSTM network to generate the reviews one word at a time. A soft attention mechanism is used to learn alignments between attribute embeddings and the generated words.

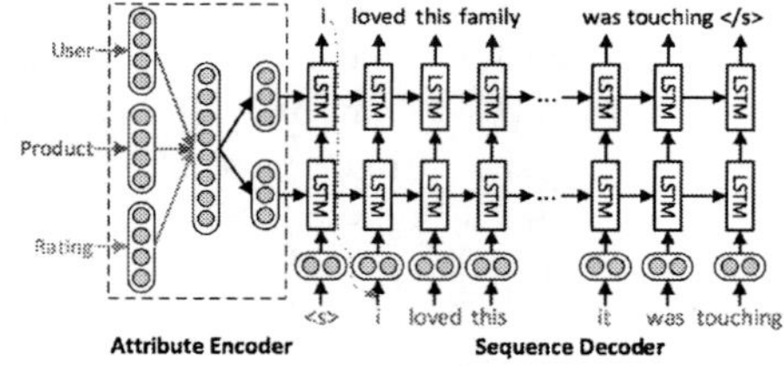

Figure 2: The basic setup of the generator network without attention

5 Sentiment Analysis Rating Predictor

For sentiment analysis we use a bidirectional RNN with Gated Recurrent Units (GRU) (Chung et al., 2014) pipeline which takes as input the generated review and generates a rating score at the end. The words are first embedded to vectors using an embedding layer which is initialized using

User	Product	Rating	Generated Review
A	X	1	the story was really boring. i was expecting much more. the ending was abrupt.
A	X	5	i loved the characters. the movie was thoroughly enjoyable. the plot was well written.
B	X	1	this book is not as good as the previous one. i was looking forward to reading this. i will not be reading the next one.
B	X	5	the books from this author just keep getting better. will highly recommend this book to everyone. looking forward to more books from the author.
A	Y	1	the plot of this book is really confusing. the book is not well written. i was unable to read the whole book.
A	Y	5	i really enjoyed reading this book. the characters are amazing.

Table 1: Some examples from the review generator network for various users, products and rating scores

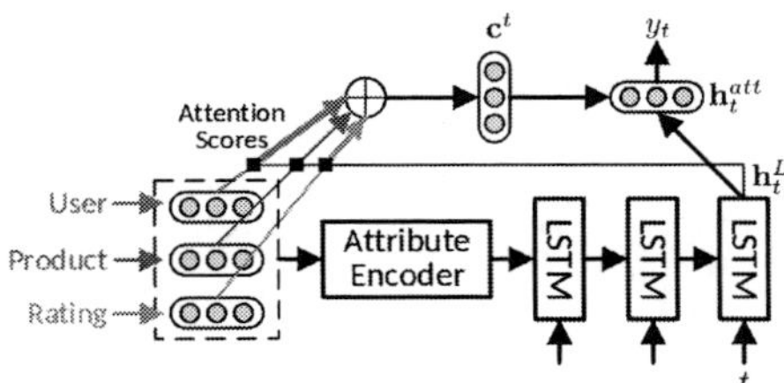

Figure 3: The soft attention is computed by using the present hidden state of the generator LSTM and the attribute vector. Attention weighted attribute vector embeddings are used as input to the generator along with the previous generated word to generate the review.

Method	BLEU-4 (%)	BLEU-1 (%)
Rand	0.86	20.36
MELM	1.28	21.59
NNpr	1.53	22.44
NNur	3.61	26.37
Att2Seq	4.51	30.24
Att2Seq+A	5.03	30.48
Cyclegen(Ours)	**5.46**	**30.63**

Table 2: Evaluation of our generated sentence quality using BLEU score and comparison with baseline systems (details in Appendix A) Baseline results as in (Dong et al., 2017)

Method	Att2seq	Att2seq+A	CycleGen
Accuracy(%)	82.3	85.6	87.5

Table 3: Accuracy of polarity (positive/negative) of the generated sentences by manual human comparison against input polarities (1-3 is considered negative and 4-5 is considered positive)

concatenations of Glove embeddings (Pennington et al., 2014) and CoVe embeddings (McCann et al., 2017). We noticed a substantial performance improvement by using the CoVe embeddings in addition to the Glove embeddings compared to the traditionally used Glove embeddings or word2vec embeddings (Mikolov et al., 2013). We also allow the embeddings to be fine tuned with training. The final hidden layer generated by the GRU is then passed onto a Multi Layer Perceptron which finally predicts the sentiment rating class.

6 Results

After a sufficient amount of training the network learns to generate some realistic looking reviews. The additional loss term seems to force the review to not be repetitive and not to use generic words besides ensuring that the generated review adheres to the expected rating. For evaluation of the generated sentence quality, we use BLEU score which measures the precision of n-gram match-

ing by comparing the generated results with references, and penalizes length using a brevity penalty term. Here we use BLEU-1 (unigram) and BLEU-4 (upto 4 grams) to evaluate our models. The results for the same and comparison with some other works on the same task are shown in Table 2. We also perform some human evaluation of the polarity of the generated reviews against input polarity. The results for the same are shown in Table 3.

We also notice that the baseline sentiment analysis rating system which was trained directly on the Amazon reviews dataset attained an accuracy of 70.1% which improves to 72.4% when fine-tuned using this end to end framework. Some of the reviews generated by the system and their corresponding ratings are demonstrated in the Table 1

References

S. Bird, L. Edward, and K. Ewan. 2009. Natural language processing with python. *O'Reilly Media Inc.*

Junyoung Chung, Çaglar Gülçehre, KyungHyun Cho, and Yoshua Bengio. 2014. Empirical evaluation of gated recurrent neural networks on sequence modeling. *CoRR*, abs/1412.3555.

Li Dong, Shaohan Huang, Furu Wei, Mirella Lapata, Ming Zhou, and Ke Xu. 2017. Learning to generate product reviews from attributes. *Proceedings of the 15th Conference of the European Chapter of the Association for Computational Linguistics*, 1.

Michael U. Gutmann and Aapo Hyvärinen. 2012. Noise-contrastive estimation of unnormalized statistical models, with applications to natural image statistics. *J. Mach. Learn. Res.*, 13(1):307–361.

Sepp Hochreiter and Jürgen Schmidhuber. 1997. Long short-term memory. *Neural Comput.*, 9(8):1735–1780.

Diederik P. Kingma and Jimmy Ba. 2014. Adam: A method for stochastic optimization. *CoRR*, abs/1412.6980.

A. Maas, R. Daly, Peter Pham, D. Huang, A. Ng, and C. Potts. 2011. Learning word vectors for sentiment analysis. *In Proceedings of the 49th Annual Meeting of the Association for Computational Linguistics.*

J. McAuley and J. Leskovec. 2013. Hidden factors and hidden topics: Understanding rating dimensions with review text. *In Conference on Recommender Systems, RecSys*, pages 165–172.

Bryan McCann, James Bradbury, Caiming Xiong, and Richard Socher. 2017. Learned in translation: Contextualized word vectors. *Advances in Neural Information Processing Systems 30 (NIPS 2017).*

Tomas Mikolov, Kai Chen, Greg Corrado, and Jeffrey Dean. 2013. Efficient estimation of word representations in vector space. *CoRR*, abs/1301.3781.

Jeffrey Pennington, Richard Socher, and Christopher D. Manning. 2014. Glove: Global vectors for word representation.

S. Wang and C. Manning. 2012. Baselines and bigrams: Simple, good sentiment and text classification. *In Proceedings of the 50th Annual Meeting of the Association for Computational Linguistics.*

A   Details of Baseline Systems

We describe the comparison methods as follows. Note that the comparison baselines are same as used in (Dong et al., 2017):

- **Rand**: The predicted results are randomly sampled from all the reviews in the TRAIN set. This baseline method suggests the expected lower bound for this task.

- **MELM**: Maximum Entropy Language Model uses n-gram (up to trigram) features, and the feature template attribute n-gram (up to bigram). The feature hashing technique is employed to reduce memory usage in each feature group. Noise contrastive estimation (Gutmann and Hyvärinen, 2012) is used to accelerate the training by dropping the normalization term, with 20 contrastive samples in training.

- **NN-pr**: This Nearest Neighbor based method retrieves the reviews that have the same product ID and rating as the input attributes in the TRAIN set. Then we randomly choose a review from them, and use it as the prediction.

- **NN-ur**: The same method as NN-pr but uses both user ID and rating to retrieve candidate reviews

- **Att2seq**: The basic LSTM encoder decoder model without any attention mechanism.

- **Att2seq+A**: The present state of the art model on this task as explained in (Dong et al., 2017)

Neural Transition-based Syntactic Linearization

Linfeng Song[1], **Yue Zhang**[2] and **Daniel Gildea**[1]
[1]Department of Computer Science, University of Rochester, Rochester, NY 14627
[2]School of Engineering, Westlake University, China

Abstract

The task of linearization is to find a grammatical order given a set of words. Traditional models use statistical methods. Syntactic linearization systems, which generate a sentence along with its syntactic tree, have shown state-of-the-art performance. Recent work shows that a multilayer LSTM language model outperforms competitive statistical syntactic linearization systems without using syntax. In this paper, we study neural syntactic linearization, building a transition-based syntactic linearizer leveraging a feed forward neural network, observing significantly better results compared to LSTM language models on this task.

1 Introduction

Linearization is the task of finding the grammatical order for a given set of words. Syntactic linearization systems generate output sentences along with their syntactic trees. Depending on how much syntactic information is available during decoding, recent work on syntactic linearization can be classified into abstract word ordering (Wan et al., 2009; Zhang et al., 2012; de Gispert et al., 2014), where no syntactic information is available during decoding, full tree linearization (He et al., 2009; Bohnet et al., 2010; Song et al., 2014), where full tree information is available, and partial tree linearization (Zhang, 2013), where partial syntactic information is given as input. Linearization has been adapted to tasks such as machine translation (Zhang et al., 2014), and is potentially helpful for many NLG applications, such as cooking recipe generation (Kiddon et al., 2016), dialogue response generation (Wen et al., 2015), and question generation (Serban et al., 2016).

Previous work (Wan et al., 2009; Liu et al., 2015) has shown that jointly predicting the syntactic tree and the surface string gives better results by allowing syntactic information to guide statistical linearization. On the other hand, most such methods employ statistical models with discriminative features. Recently, Schmaltz et al. (2016) report new state-of-the-art results by leveraging a neural language model *without* using syntactic information. In their experiments, the neural language model, which is less sparse and captures long-range dependencies, outperforms previous discrete syntactic systems.

A research question that naturally arises from this result is whether syntactic information is helpful for a *neural* linearization system. We empirically answer this question by comparing a neural transition-based syntactic linearizer with the neural language model of Schmaltz et al. (2016). Following Liu et al. (2015), our linearizer works incrementally given a set of words, using a stack to store partially built dependency trees, and a set to maintain *unordered* incoming words. At each step, it either *shifts* a word onto the stack, or *reduces* the top two partial trees on the stack. We leverage a feed forward neural network, which takes stack features as input and predicts the next action (such as SHIFT, LEFTARC and RIGHTARC). Hence our method can be regarded as an extension of the parser of Chen and Manning (2014), adding word ordering functionalities.

In addition, we investigate two methods for integrating neural language models: interpolating the log probabilities of both models and integrating the neural language model as a feature. On standard benchmarks, our syntactic linearizer gives results that are higher than the LSTM language model of Schmaltz et al. (2016) by 7 BLEU points (Papineni et al., 2002) using greedy search,

Proceedings of The 11th International Natural Language Generation Conference, pages 431–440,
Tilburg, The Netherlands, November 5-8, 2018. ©2018 Association for Computational Linguistics

and the gap can go up to 11 BLEU points by integrating the LSTM language model as features. The integrated system also outperforms the LSTM language model by 1 BLEU point using beam search, which shows that syntactic information is useful for a neural linearization system.

2 Related work

Previous work (White, 2005; White and Rajkumar, 2009; Zhang and Clark, 2011; Zhang, 2013) on syntactic linearization uses best-first search, which adopts a priority queue to store partial hypotheses and a chart to store input words. At each step, it pops the highest-scored hypothesis from the priority queue, expanding it by combination with the words in the chart, before finally putting all new hypotheses back into the priority queue. As the search space is huge, a timeout threshold is set, beyond which the search terminates and the current best hypothesis is taken as the result.

Liu et al. (2015) adapt the transition-based dependency parsing algorithm for the linearization task by allowing the transition-based system to shift any word in the given set, rather than the first word in the buffer as in dependency parsing. Their results show much lower search times and higher performance compared to Zhang (2013). Following this line, Liu and Zhang (2015) further improve the performance by incorporating an n-gram language model. Our work takes the transition-based framework, but is different in two main aspects: first, we train a feed-forward neural network for making decisions, while they all use perceptron-like models. Second, we investigate a light version of the system, which only uses word features, while previous works all rely on POS tags and arc labels, limiting their usability on low-resource domains and languages.

Schmaltz et al. (2016) are the first to adopt neural networks on this task, while only using *surface* features. To our knowledge, we are the first to leverage both neural networks and *syntactic* features. The contrast between our method and the method of Chen and Manning (2014) is reminiscent of the contrast between the method of Liu et al. (2015) and the dependency parser of Zhang and Nivre (2011). Comparing with the dependency parsing task, which assumes that POS tags are available as input, the search space of syntactic linearization is much larger.

Recent work (Zhang, 2013; Song et al., 2014;

Liu et al., 2015; Liu and Zhang, 2015) on syntactic linearization uses dependency grammar. We follow this line of works. On the other hand, linearization with other syntactic grammars, such as context free grammar (de Gispert et al., 2014) and combinatory categorial grammar (White and Rajkumar, 2009; Zhang and Clark, 2011), has also been studied.

3 Task

Given an input bag-of-words $x = \{x_1, x_2, ..., x_n\}$, the goal is to output the correct permutation y, which recovers the original sentence, from the set of all possible permutations $\mathcal{Y}$. A linearizer can be seen as a scoring function f over $\mathcal{Y}$, which is trained to output its highest scoring permutation $\hat{y} = \mathrm{argmax}_{y' \in \mathcal{Y}} f(x, y')$ as close as possible to the correct permutation y.

3.1 Baseline: an LSTM language model

The LSTM language model of Schmaltz et al. (2016) is similar to the medium LSTM setup of Zaremba et al. (2014). It contains two LSTM layers, each of which has 650 hidden units and is followed by a dropout layer during training. The multi-layer LSTM language model can be represented as:

$$\mathbf{h}_{t,i}, \mathbf{c}_{t,i} = \mathrm{LSTM}(\mathbf{h}_{t,i-1}, \mathbf{h}_{t-1,i}, \mathbf{c}_{t-1,i}) \quad (1)$$

$$p(w_{t,j}|w_{t-1}, ..., w_1) = \frac{\exp(\mathbf{v}_j^\mathsf{T} \mathbf{h}_{t,I})}{\sum_{j'} \exp(\mathbf{v}_{j'}^\mathsf{T} \mathbf{h}_{t,I})}, \quad (2)$$

where $\mathbf{h}_{t,i}$ and $\mathbf{c}_{t,i}$ are the output and cell memory of the i-th layer at step t, respectively, $\mathbf{h}_{t,0} = \mathbf{x}_t$ is the input of the network at step t, I is the number of layers, $w_{t,j}$ represents outputting w_j at t step, $\mathbf{v}_j$ is the embedding of w_j, and the LSTM function is defined as:

$$\begin{pmatrix} \mathbf{i} \\ \mathbf{f} \\ \mathbf{o} \\ \mathbf{g} \end{pmatrix} = \begin{pmatrix} \sigma \\ \sigma \\ \sigma \\ \tanh \end{pmatrix} \mathbf{W}_{4n,2n} \begin{pmatrix} \mathbf{h}_{t,i-1} \\ \mathbf{h}_{t-1,i} \end{pmatrix}$$

$$(3)$$

$$\mathbf{c}_{t,i} = \mathbf{f} \odot \mathbf{c}_{t-1,i} + \mathbf{i} \odot \mathbf{g} \quad (4)$$

$$\mathbf{h}_{t,i} = \mathbf{o} \odot \tanh(\mathbf{c}_{t,i}), \quad (5)$$

where σ is the sigmoid function, $\mathbf{W}_{4n,2n}$ is the weights of LSTM cells, and $\odot$ is the element-wise product operator.

Figure 1 shows the linearization procedure of the baseline system, when taking the bag-of-words

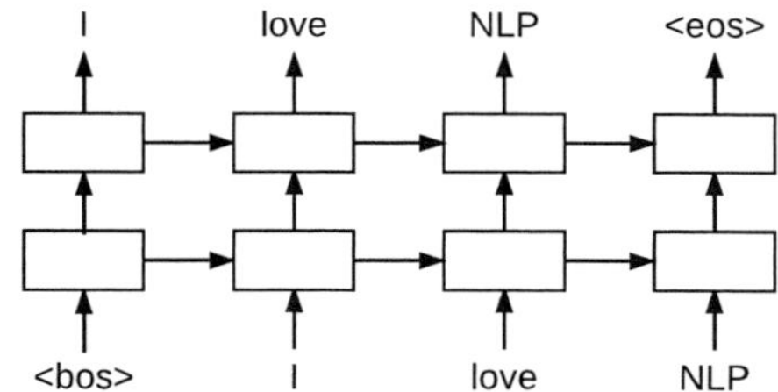

Figure 1: Linearization procedure of the baseline.

{"NLP","love","I"} as input. At each step, it takes the output word from the previous step as input and predicts the current word, which is chosen from the remaining input bag-of-words rather than from the entire vocabulary. Therefore it takes n steps to linearize a input consisting of n words.

4 Neural transition-based syntactic linearization

Transition-based syntactic linearization can be considered as an extension to transition-based dependency parsing (Liu et al., 2015), with the main difference being that the word order is not given in the input, so that any word can be shifted at each step. This leads to a much larger search space. In addition, under our setting, *extra* dependency relations or POS on input words are not available.

The output building process is modeled as a state-transition process. As shown in Figure 2, each state s is defined as (σ, ρ, A), where σ is a stack that maintains a partial derivation, ρ is an *unordered* set of incoming input words and A is the set of dependency relations that have been built. Initially, the stack σ is empty, while the set ρ contains all the input words, and the set of dependency relations A is empty. At the end, the set ρ is empty, while A contains all dependency relations for the predicted dependency tree. At a certain state, a SHIFT action chooses one word from the set ρ and pushes it onto the stack σ, a LEFT-ARC action makes a new arc $\{j \leftarrow i\}$ from the stack's top two items (i and j), while a RIGHTARC action makes a new arc $\{j \rightarrow i\}$ from i and j. Using these possible actions, the unordered word set $\{$"NLP$_0$","love$_1$","I$_2$"$\}$ is linearized as shown in Table 1, and the result is "I$_2 \leftarrow$ love$_1 \rightarrow$ NLP$_0$".[1]

---

[1]For a clearer introduction to our state-transition process, we omit the POS-p actions, which are introduced in Section 4.2. In our implementation, each SHIFT-w is followed by exact one POS-p action.

Initial State $([], [1...n], \varnothing)$

Final State $([], [], A)$

Induction Rules:

Shift $\quad \dfrac{(\sigma, [i|\beta], A)}{([\sigma|i], \beta, A)}$

LeftArc $\quad \dfrac{([\sigma|j\ i], \beta, A)}{([\sigma|i], \beta, A \cup \{j \leftarrow i\})}$

RightArc $\quad \dfrac{([\sigma|j\ i], \beta, A)}{([\sigma|j], \beta, A \cup \{j \rightarrow i\})}$

Figure 2: Deduction system of transition-based syntactic linearization

step	action	σ	ρ	A
init		[]	(1 2 3)	$\varnothing$
0	Shift-I	[1]	(2 3)	
1	Shift-love	[1 2]	(3)	
2	Shift-NLP	[1 2 3]	()	
3	RArc-dobj	[1 2]	()	$A \cup \{2 \rightarrow 3\}$
4	LArc-nsubj	[2]	()	$A \cup \{1 \leftarrow 2\}$
5	End	[]	()	A

Table 1: Transition-based syntactic linearization for ordering $\{$"NLP$_3$","love$_2$","I$_1$"$\}$, where *RArc* and *LArc* are the abbreviations for RightArc and LeftArc, respectively. More details on actions are in Section 4.2.

4.1 Model

To predict the next transition action for a given state, our linearizer makes use of a feed-forward neural network to score the actions as shown in Figure 3. The network takes a set of word, POS tag, and arc label features from the stack as input and outputs the probability distribution of the next actions. In particular, we represent each word as a d-dimensional vector $e_i^w \in \mathbb{R}^d$ using a word embedding matrix is $\mathbf{E}^w \in \mathbb{R}^{d \times N_w}$, where N_w is the vocabulary size. Similarly each POS tag and arc label are also mapped to a d-dimensional vector, where $e_j^t, e_k^l \in \mathbb{R}^d$ are the representations of the j-th POS tag and k-th arc label, respectively. The embedding matrices of POS tags and arc labels are $\mathbf{E}^t \in \mathbb{R}^{d \times N_t}$ and $\mathbf{E}^l \in \mathbb{R}^{d \times N_l}$, where N_t and N_l correspond to the number of POS tags and arc labels, respectively. We choose a set of feature words, POS tags, and arc labels from the stack context, using their embeddings as input to our neural network. Next, we map the input layer to the hidden layer via:

$$h = g(\mathbf{W}_1^w \mathbf{x}^w + \mathbf{W}_1^t \mathbf{x}^t + \mathbf{W}_1^l \mathbf{x}^l + \mathbf{b_1}), \quad (6)$$

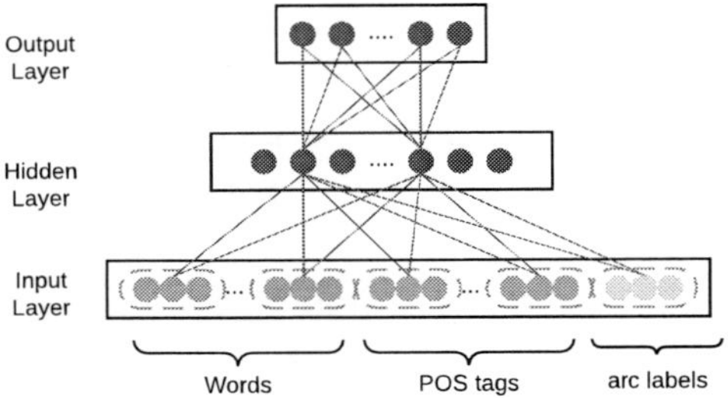

Figure 3: Neural syntactic linearization model

(1)	$S_1.w;\ S_1.t;\ S_2.w;\ S_2.t;\ S_3.w;\ S_3.t;$
(2)	$i = 1, 2$ $lc_1(S_i).w;\ lc_1(S_i).t;\ lc_1(S_i).l;$ $lc_2(S_i).w;\ lc_2(S_i).t;\ lc_2(S_i).l;$ $rc_1(S_i).w;\ rc_1(S_i).t;\ rc_1(S_i).l;$ $rc_2(S_i).w;\ rc_2(S_i).t;\ rc_2(S_i).l;$
(3)	$i = 1, 2$ $lc_1(lc_1(S_i)).w;\ lc_1(lc_1(S_i)).t;$ $lc_1(lc_1(S_i)).l;\ rc_1(rc_1(S_i)).w;$ $rc_1(rc_1(S_i)).t;\ rc_1(rc_1(S_i)).l;$

Table 2: Feature templates, where S_i denotes the ith item on the stack, w, t and l denotes the word, POS tag and arc label, respectively.

where $\mathbf{x}^w$, $\mathbf{x}^t$, and $\mathbf{x}^l$ are the concatenated feature word embeddings, POS tag embeddings, and arc label embeddings, respectively, $\mathbf{W}_1^w$, $\mathbf{W}_1^t$, and $\mathbf{W}_1^l$ are the corresponding weight matrices, $\mathbf{b}_1$ is the bias term and $g()$ is the activation function of the hidden layer. The word, POS tag and arc label features are described in Section 4.3.

Finally, the hidden vector $\mathbf{h}$ is mapped to an output layer, which uses a softmax activation function for modeling multi-class action probabilities:

$$p(a|s, \theta) = \text{softmax}(\mathbf{W}_2\mathbf{h}), \qquad (7)$$

where $p(a|s, \theta)$ represents the probability distribution of the next action. There is no bias term in this layer and the model parameter $\mathbf{W}_2$ can also be seen as the embedding matrix of all actions.

4.2 Actions

We use 5 types of actions:

- SHIFT-w pushes a word w onto the stack.

- POS-p assigns a POS tag p to the newly shifted word.

- LEFTARC-l pops the top two items i and j off stack and pushes $\{j \xleftarrow{l} i\}$ onto the stack.

- RIGHTARC-l pops the top two items i and j off stack and pushes $\{j \xrightarrow{l} i\}$ onto the stack.

- END ends the decoding procedure.

Given a set of n words as input, the linearizer takes $3n$ steps to synthesize the sentence. The number of actions is large, making it computationally inefficient to do softmax over all actions. Here for each set of words S we only consider all possible actions for linearizing the set, which constraints SHIFT-w_i to all words in the set.

4.3 Features

The feature templates our model uses are shown in Table 2. We pick (1) the words and POS tags of the top 3 items on the stack, (2) the words, POS tags, and arc labels of the first and the second leftmost / rightmost children of the top 2 items on the stack and (3) the words, POS tags and arc labels of the leftmost of leftmost / rightmost of rightmost children of the top two items on the stack. Under certain states, some features may not exist, and we use special tokens NULL^w, NULL^t and NULL^l to represent non-existent word, POS tag, and arc label features, respectively. Our feature templates are similar to that of Chen and Manning (2014), except that we do not leverage features from the set, because the words inside the set are unordered.

4.4 The light version

We also consider a light version of our linearizer that only leverages words and unlabeled dependency relations. Similar to Section 4.1, the system also uses a feed-forward neural network with 1 hidden layer, but only takes word features as input. It uses 4 types of actions: SHIFT-w, LEFTARC, RIGHTARC, and END. All actions are same as described in Section 4.2, except that LEFTARC and RIGHTARC are not associated with arc labels. Given a set of n words as input, the system takes $2n$ steps to synthesize the sentence, which is faster and less vulnerable to error propagation.

5 Integrating an LSTM language model

Our model can be integrated with the baseline multi-layer LSTM language model. Existing work (Zhang et al., 2012; Liu and Zhang, 2015) has shown that a syntactic linearizer can benefit from a surface language model by taking its scores as features. Here we investigate two methods for the integration: (1) joint decoding by interpolating the conditional probabilities and (2) feature-level integration by taking the output vector ($\mathbf{h}_I$) of the LSTM language model as features to the linearizer.

5.1 Joint decoding

To perform joint decoding, the conditional action probability distributions of both models given the current state are interpolated, and the best action under the interpolated probability distribution is chosen, before both systems advancing to a new state using the action. The interpolated conditional probability is:

$$p(a|s_i, h_i; \theta_1, \theta_2) = \log p(a|s_i; \theta_1)$$
$$+ \alpha \log p(a|h_i; \theta_2), \quad (8)$$

where s_i and θ_1 are the state and parameters of the linearizer, h_i and θ_2 are the state and parameters of the LSTM language model, and α is the interpolation hyper parameter.

The action spaces of the two systems are different because the actions of the LSTM language model correspond only to the shift actions of the linearizer. To match the probability distributions, we expand the distribution of the LSTM language model as shown in Equation 9, where w_a is the associated word of a shift action a. Generally, the probabilities of non-shift actions are 1.0, and those of shift actions are from the LSTM language model with respect to w_a:

$$p(a|h_i; \theta_2) = \begin{cases} p(w_a|h_i; \theta_2), & \text{if } a \text{ is shift} \\ 1.0, & \text{otherwise} \end{cases} \quad (9)$$

We do not normalize the interpolated probability distribution, because our experiments show that normalization only gives around 0.3 BLEU score gains, while significantly decreasing the speed. When a shift action is chosen, both systems advance to a new state; otherwise only the linearizer advances to a new state.

5.2 Feature level integration

To take the output of an LSTM language model as a feature in our model, we first train the LSTM language model independently. During the training of our model, we take $\mathbf{h}_I$, the output of the top LSTM layer after consuming all words on the stack, as a feature in the input layer of Figure 3, before finally advancing both the linearizer and the LSTM language model using the predicted action. This is analogous to adding a separately-trained n-gram language model as a feature to a discriminative linearizer (Liu and Zhang, 2015). Compared with joint decoding (Section 5.1), $p(a|s_i, h_i; \theta_1, \theta_2)$ is calculated by one model, and thus there is no need to tune the hyper-parameter α. The state update remains the same: the language model advances to a new state only when a shift action is taken.

6 Training

Following Chen and Manning (2014), we set the training objective as maximizing the log-likelihood of each successive action conditioned on the dependency tree, which can be gold or automatically parsed. To train our linearizer, we first generate training examples $\{(s_i, t_i)\}_{i=1}^{m}$ from the training sentences and their gold parse trees, where s_i is a state, and $t_i \in T$ is the corresponding oracle transition. We use the "arc standard" oracle (Nivre, 2008), which always prefers SHIFT over LEFTARC. The final training objective is to minimize the cross-entropy loss, plus an L2-regularization term:

$$L(\theta) = -\sum_i \log p_{t_i} + \frac{\lambda}{2}\|\theta\|^2,$$

where θ represents all the trainable parameters: $\mathbf{W}_1, \mathbf{b}_1, \mathbf{W}_2, \mathbf{E}^w, \mathbf{E}^t, \mathbf{E}^l$. A slight variation is that the softmax probabilities are computed only among the feasible transitions in practice. As described in Section 4.2, for an input set of words, the feasible transitions are: SHIFT-w, where w is a word in the set, POS-p for all POS tags, LEFTARC-l and RIGHTARC-l for all arc labels, and END.

To train a linearizer that takes an LSTM language model as features, we first train the LSTM language model on the same training data, then train the linearizer with the parameters of the LSTM language model unchanged.

7 Experiments

7.1 Setup

We follow previous work and conduct experiments on the Penn Treebank, using Wall Street Journal sections 2-21 for training, 22 for development and 23 for final testing. Gold-standard dependency trees are derived from bracketed sentences in the treebank using Penn2Malt.[2] In order to study the influence of parsing accuracy of the training data,

---

[2]https://stp.lingfil.uu.se/~nivre/research/Penn2Malt.html

System	BeamSize=1		BeamSize=10		BeamSize=64		BeamSize=512	
	BLEU	Time	BLEU	Time	BLEU	Time	BLEU	Time
LSTM	14.01	6m26s	26.83	13m	33.05	54m41s	37.08	405m10s
Syn	20.97	11m39s	27.72	26m40s	30.01	113m19s	31.12	891m39s
Syn+LSTM	21.17	18m15s	30.43	37m15s	34.35	157m16s	36.84	1058m
Syn×LSTM	**24.91**	18m12s	32.75	37m12s	35.88	156m50s	36.96	1070m
Syn_l×LSTM	24.55	9m50s	**32.84**	23m7s	**36.11**	77m6s	**37.99**	624m39s

Table 3: Main results and decoding times.

ID	#training sent	#iter	F1
syn90	all	30	90.28
syn85	all	1	85.38
syn79	9000	1	79.68
syn54	900	1	54.86

Table 4: Parsing accuracy settings, the F1 scores are measured on the training set.

we use ten-fold jackknifing to construct WSJ training data with different accuracies. More specifically, the data is first randomly split into ten equal-size subsets, and then each subset is automatically parsed with a constituent parser trained on the other subsets, before the results are finally converted to dependency trees using Penn2Malt. In order to obtain datasets with different parsing accuracies, we randomly sample a small number of sentences from each training subset and choose different training iterations, as shown in Table 4. In our experiments, we use ZPar[3] (Zhu et al., 2013) for automatic constituent parsing.

Our syntactic linearizer is implemented with Keras.[4] We randomly initialize $\mathbf{E}^w$, $\mathbf{E}^t$, $\mathbf{E}^l$, $\mathbf{W}^1$ and $\mathbf{W}^2$ within $(-0.01, 0.01)$, and use default setting for other parameters. The hyper-parameters and parameters which achieve the best performance on the development set are chosen for final evaluation. Our vocabulary comes from SENNA[5], which has 130,000 words. The activation functions $\tanh$ and softmax are added on top of the hidden and output layers, respectively. We use Adagrad (Duchi et al., 2011) with an initial learning rate of 0.01, regularization parameter $\lambda = 10^{-8}$, and dropout rate 0.3 for training. The interpolation coefficient α for joint decoding is set 0.4. During decoding, simple pruning methods are applied, such as a constraint that Pos-p actions always follow Shift-w actions.

We evaluate our linearizer (Syn) and its variances, where the subscript "l" denotes the light

version, "+LSTM" represents joint decoding with an LSTM language model, and "×LSTM" represents taking an LSTM language model as features in our model. We compare results with the current state-of-the-art: an LSTM (LSTM) language model from Schmaltz et al. (2016), which is similar in size and architecture to the medium LSTM setup of Zaremba et al. (2014). None of the systems use future cost heuristic. All experiments are conducted using Tesla K20Xm.

7.2 Tuning

We show some development results in this section. First, using the cube activation function (Chen and Manning, 2014) does not yield a good performance on our task. We tried other activations including Linear, $\tanh$ and ReLU (Nair and Hinton, 2010), and $\tanh$ gives the best results. In addition, we tried pretrained embeddings from SENNA, which does not yield better results compared to random initialization. Further, dropout rates from 0.3 to 0.8 give good training results. Finally, we tried different values from 0.1 to 1.0 for the interpolation coefficient α, finding that values between 0.3 and 0.7 give the best performances, while values larger than 1.5 yield poor performances.

7.3 Main results

The main results on the test set are shown in Table 3. Compared with previous work, our linearizers achieve the best results under all beam sizes, especially under the greedy search scenario (BeamSize=1), where Syn and Syn×LSTM outperform the baseline of LSTM by 7 and 11 BLEU points, respectively. This demonstrates that syntactic information is extremely important when beam size is small. In addition, our syntactic systems are still better than the baseline under very large beam sizes (such as, BeamSize=512), which lead to slow performance and are less useful practically. On the other hand, the baseline (LSTM) benefits more from beam size increases.

---

[3]https://github.com/frcchang/zpar
[4]https://keras.io/
[5]http://ronan.collobert.com/senna/

System	sentences
LSTM-512	the bush administration , known as 31 , 1992 , earlier this year said it would extend voluntary restraint agreements steel quotas until march .
$\text{SYN}_l\times$LSTM-512	earlier this year , the bush administration said it would extend steel agreements until march 31 , 1992 , known as voluntary restraint quotas .
REF	the bush administration earlier this year said it would extend steel quotas , known as voluntary restraint agreements , until march 31 , 1992 .
LSTM-512	shearson lehman hutton inc. said , however , that it is " going to set back with the customers , " because of friday 's plunge , president of jeffrey b. lane concern " reinforces volatility relations .
$\text{SYN}_l\times$LSTM-512	however , jeffrey b. lane , president of shearson lehman hutton inc. , said that friday 's plunge is " going to set back with customers because it reinforces the volatility of " concern , " relations .
REF	however , jeffrey b. lane , president of shearson lehman hutton inc. , said that friday 's plunge is " going to set back " relations with customers , " because it reinforces the concern of volatility .
LSTM-512	the debate between the stock and futures markets is prepared for wall street will cause another situation about whether de-linkage crash undoubtedly properly renewed friday .
$\text{SYN}_l\times$LSTM-512	the wall street futures markets undoubtedly will cause renewed debate about whether the stock situation is properly prepared for an other crash between friday and de-linkage .
REF	the de-linkage between the stock and futures markets friday will undoubtedly cause renewed debate about whether wall street is prope rly prepared for another crash situation .

Table 5: Output samples.

The results are consistent with (Ma et al., 2014) in that both increasing beam size and using richer features are solutions for error propagation.

$\text{SYN}\times$LSTM is better than $\text{SYN}+$LSTM. In fact, $\text{SYN}\times$LSTM can be considered as interpolation with α being automatically calculated under different states. Finally, $\text{SYN}_l\times$LSTM is better than $\text{SYN}\times$LSTM except under greedy search, showing that word-to-word dependency features may be sufficient for this task.

As for the decoding times, $\text{SYN}_l\times$LSTM shows a moderate time growth along increasing beam size, which is roughly 1.5 times slower than LSTM. In addition, $\text{SYN}+$LSTM and $\text{SYN}\times$LSTM are the slowest for each beam size (roughly 3 times slower than LSTM), because of the large number of features they use and the large number of decoding steps they take. SYN is roughly 2 times slower than LSTM.

Previous work, such as Schmaltz et al. (2016), adopts future cost and the information of base noun phrase (BNP) and shows further improvement on performance. However, these are highly task specific. Future cost is based on the assumption that all words are available at the beginning, which is not true for other tasks. On the other hand, our model does not rely on this assumption, thus can be better applicable on other tasks. BNPs are the phrases that correspond to leaf NP nodes in constituent trees. Assuming BNPs being available is not practical either.

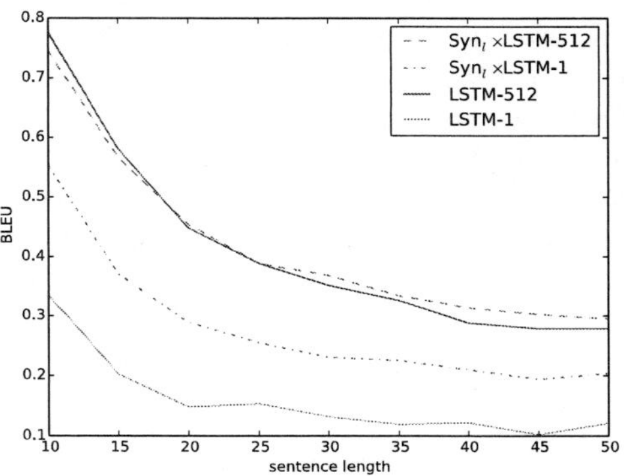

Figure 4: Performance on different lengths.

7.4 Influence of sentence length

We show the performances on different sentence lengths in Figure 4. The results are from LSTM and $\text{SYN}_l\times$LSTM using beam size 1 and 512. Sentences belonging to the same length range (such as 1–10 or 11–15) are grouped together, and corpus BLEU is calculated on each group. First of all, $\text{SYN}_l\times$LSTM-1 is significantly better than LSTM-1 on all sentence lengths, explaining the usefulness of syntactic features. In addition, $\text{SYN}_l\times$LSTM-512 is notably better than LSTM-512 on sentences that are longer than 25, and the difference is even larger on sentences that have more than 35 words. This is an evidence that $\text{SYN}_l\times$LSTM is better at modeling long-distance dependencies. On the other hand, LSTM-512 is better than $\text{SYN}_l\times$LSTM-512 on short sentences (length ≤ 10). The reason may be that LSTM is

Data	$\textsc{Syn}\times\textsc{LSTM}$	$\textsc{Syn}_l\times\textsc{LSTM}$
Gold	36.03	36.41
syn90	35.91	36.31
syn85	35.84	36.22
syn79	35.40	35.96
syn54	33.32	34.98

Table 6: Results of various parsing accuracy.

Actions	Top similar actions
S-wednesday	S-tuesday S-friday S-thursday S-monday
S-huge	S-strong S-serious S-good S-large
S-taxes	S-bills S-expenses S-loans S-payments
S-secretary	S-department S-officials S-director
S-largely	S-partly S-primarily S-mostly S-entirely

Table 7: Top similar actions for shift actions

good at modeling relatively shorter dependencies without syntactic guidance, while $\textsc{Syn}_l\times\textsc{LSTM}$, which takes more steps for synthesizing the same sentence, suffers from error propagation. Overall, this figure can be regarded as empirical evidence that syntactic systems are better choices for generating long sentences (Wan et al., 2009; Zhang and Clark, 2011), while surface systems may be better choices for generating short sentences.

Table 5 shows some linearization results of long sentences from LSTM and $\textsc{Syn}_l\times\textsc{LSTM}$ using beam size 512. The outputs of $\textsc{Syn}_l\times\textsc{LSTM}$ are notably more grammatical than those of LSTM. For example, in the last group, the output of $\textsc{Syn}_l\times\textsc{LSTM}$ means "the market will cause another debate about whether the situation now is prepared for another crash", while the output of LSTM is obviously less fluent, especially for the parts "... markets is prepared for wall street will cause ..." and "... crash undoubtedly properly renewed ..".

In addition, LSTM makes locally grammatical outputs, while suffering more mistakes in the global level. Taking the second group as an example, LSTM generates grammatical phrases, such as "going to set back with the customers" and "because of friday 's plunge", while misplacing "president of", which should be in the very front of the sentence. On the other hand, $\textsc{Syn}_l\times\textsc{LSTM}$ can capture patterns such as "president of some inc." and "someone, president of someplace said" to make the right choices. Finally, $\textsc{Syn}_l\times\textsc{LSTM}$ can makes grammatical sentences with different meanings. For example in the first group, the result of $\textsc{Syn}_l\times\textsc{LSTM}$ means "the bush administration will extend the steel agreement", while the true meaning is "the bush administration will extend the steel quotas". For syntactic linearization, such semantic variation is tolerable.

7.5 Results with auto-parsed data

There is no syntactically annotated data in many domains. As a result, performing syntactic linearization in these domains requires automatically

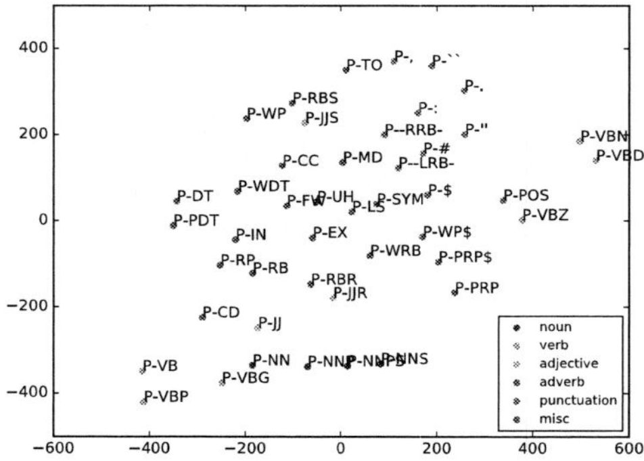

Figure 5: t-SNE visualization of POS embeddings

parsed training data, which may affect the performance of our syntactic linearizer. We study this effect by training both $\textsc{Syn}\times\textsc{LSTM}$ and $\textsc{Syn}_l\times\textsc{LSTM}$ with automatically parsed training data of different parsing accuracies, and show the results, which are generated with beamsize 64 on the devset, in Table 6. Generally, a higher parsing accuracy can lead to a better linearization result for both systems. It conforms to the intuition that syntactic quality affects the fluency of surface texts. On the other hand, the influence is not large, the BLEU scores of $\textsc{Syn}_l\times\textsc{LSTM}$ and $\textsc{Syn}\times\textsc{LSTM}$ drop by 1.5 and 2.8 BLEU points, respectively, as the parsing accuracy decreases from gold to 54%. Both observations are consistent with that of Liu and Zhang (2015) for discrete syntactic linearization. Finally, $\textsc{Syn}_l\times\textsc{LSTM}$ shows less BLEU score decreases than $\textsc{Syn}\times\textsc{LSTM}$. The reason is that $\textsc{Syn}_l\times\textsc{LSTM}$ only takes word features, and is less vulnerable to parsing accuracy decrease.

7.6 Embedding similarity

One main advantage of neural systems is that they use vectorized features, which are less sparse than discriminative features. Taking $\mathbf{W}_2$ as the embedding matrix of actions, we calculate the top similar actions for the $\textsc{Shift}\text{-}w$ actions by cosine distance and show examples in Table 7. In addition, Figure 5 presents the t-SNE visualization (Maaten and Hinton, 2008) of the embeddings for the POS-p

actions. Generally, the embeddings of similar actions are closer than these of other actions. From both results, we can see that our model learns reasonable embeddings from the Penn Treebank, a small-scale corpus, which shows the effectiveness of our system from another perspective.

8 Conclusion

We studied neural transition-based syntactic linearization, which combines the advantages of both neural networks and syntactic information. In addition, we compared two ways of integrating a neural language model into our system. Experimental results show that our system achieves improved results comparing with a state-of-the-art multi-layer LSTM language model. To our knowledge, we are the first to investigate neural syntactic linearization.

In the future work, we will investigate LSTM on this task. In particular, an LSTM decoder, taking features form the already-built subtrees as part of its inputs, is taken to model the sequences of shift-reduce actions. Another possible direction is creating complete graphs with their nodes being the input words, before encoding them with self-attention networks (Vaswani et al., 2017) or graph neural networks (Kipf and Welling, 2016; Beck et al., 2018; Zhang et al., 2018; Song et al., 2018). This approach can be better at capturing word-to-word dependencies than simply summing word embeddings up.

References

Daniel Beck, Gholamreza Haffari, and Trevor Cohn. 2018. Graph-to-sequence learning using gated graph neural networks. In *Proceedings of the 56th Annual Meeting of the Association for Computational Linguistics (ACL-18)*.

Bernd Bohnet, Leo Wanner, Simon Mill, and Alicia Burga. 2010. Broad coverage multilingual deep sentence generation with a stochastic multi-level realizer. In *Proceedings of the 23rd International Conference on Computational Linguistics (COLING-10)*. Beijing, China, pages 98–106.

Danqi Chen and Christopher Manning. 2014. A fast and accurate dependency parser using neural networks. In *Conference on Empirical Methods in Natural Language Processing (EMNLP-14)*. Doha, Qatar, pages 740–750.

Adrià de Gispert, Marcus Tomalin, and Bill Byrne. 2014. Word ordering with phrase-based grammars. In *Proceedings of the 14th Conference of the European Chapter of the ACL (EACL-14)*. Gothenburg, Sweden, pages 259–268.

John Duchi, Elad Hazan, and Yoram Singer. 2011. Adaptive subgradient methods for online learning and stochastic optimization. *Journal of Machine Learning Research* 12(Jul):2121–2159.

Wei He, Haifeng Wang, Yuqing Guo, and Ting Liu. 2009. Dependency based chinese sentence realization. In *Proceedings of the 47th Annual Meeting of the Association for Computational Linguistics (ACL-09)*. Suntec, Singapore, pages 809–816.

Chloé Kiddon, Luke Zettlemoyer, and Yejin Choi. 2016. Globally coherent text generation with neural checklist models. In *Conference on Empirical Methods in Natural Language Processing (EMNLP-16)*. Austin, Texas, pages 329–339.

Thomas N Kipf and Max Welling. 2016. Semi-supervised classification with graph convolutional networks. *arXiv preprint arXiv:1609.02907* .

Jiangming Liu and Yue Zhang. 2015. An empirical comparison between n-gram and syntactic language models for word ordering. In *Conference on Empirical Methods in Natural Language Processing (EMNLP-15)*. Lisbon, Portugal, pages 369–378.

Yijia Liu, Yue Zhang, Wanxiang Che, and Bing Qin. 2015. Transition-based syntactic linearization. In *Conference on Empirical Methods in Natural Language Processing (EMNLP-15)*. Denver, Colorado, pages 113–122.

Ji Ma, Yue Zhang, and Jingbo Zhu. 2014. Punctuation processing for projective dependency parsing. In *Proceedings of the 52nd Annual Meeting of the Association for Computational Linguistics (ACL-14)*. Baltimore, Maryland, pages 791–796.

Laurens van der Maaten and Geoffrey Hinton. 2008. Visualizing data using t-sne. *Journal of Machine Learning Research* 9(Nov):2579–2605.

Vinod Nair and Geoffrey E Hinton. 2010. Rectified linear units improve restricted Boltzmann machines. In *Proceedings of the 27th international conference on machine learning (ICML-10)*. pages 807–814.

Joakim Nivre. 2008. Algorithms for deterministic incremental dependency parsing. *Computational Linguistics* 34(4):513–553.

Kishore Papineni, Salim Roukos, Todd Ward, and Wei-Jing Zhu. 2002. Bleu: a method for automatic evaluation of machine translation. In *Proceedings of the 40th Annual Conference of the Association for Computational Linguistics (ACL-02)*. Philadelphia, Pennsylvania, USA, pages 311–318.

Allen Schmaltz, Alexander M. Rush, and Stuart Shieber. 2016. Word ordering without syntax. In *Conference on Empirical Methods in Natural*

Language Processing (EMNLP-16). Austin, Texas, pages 2319–2324.

Iulian Vlad Serban, Alberto García-Durán, Caglar Gulcehre, Sungjin Ahn, Sarath Chandar, Aaron Courville, and Yoshua Bengio. 2016. Generating factoid questions with recurrent neural networks: The 30m factoid question-answer corpus. In *Proceedings of the 54th Annual Meeting of the Association for Computational Linguistics (ACL-16)*. Berlin, Germany, pages 588–598.

Linfeng Song, Yue Zhang, Kai Song, and Qun Liu. 2014. Joint morphological generation and syntactic linearization. In *Proceedings of the National Conference on Artificial Intelligence (AAAI-14)*. pages 1522–1528.

Linfeng Song, Yue Zhang, Zhiguo Wang, and Daniel Gildea. 2018. A graph-to-sequence model for amr-to-text generation. In *Proceedings of the 56th Annual Meeting of the Association for Computational Linguistics (ACL-18)*.

Ashish Vaswani, Noam Shazeer, Niki Parmar, Jakob Uszkoreit, Llion Jones, Aidan N Gomez, Łukasz Kaiser, and Illia Polosukhin. 2017. Attention is all you need. In *Advances in Neural Information Processing Systems*. pages 5998–6008.

Stephen Wan, Mark Dras, Robert Dale, and Cécile Paris. 2009. Improving grammaticality in statistical sentence generation: Introducing a dependency spanning tree algorithm with an argument satisfaction model. In *Proceedings of the 12th Conference of the European Chapter of the ACL (EACL-09)*. Athens, Greece, pages 852–860.

Tsung-Hsien Wen, Milica Gasic, Nikola Mrkšić, Pei-Hao Su, David Vandyke, and Steve Young. 2015. Semantically conditioned LSTM-based natural language generation for spoken dialogue systems. In *Conference on Empirical Methods in Natural Language Processing (EMNLP-15)*. Lisbon, Portugal, pages 1711–1721.

Michael White. 2005. Designing an extensible api for integrating language modeling and realization. In *Proceedings of the ACL Workshop on Software*. Ann Arbor, Michigan, pages 47–64.

Michael White and Rajakrishnan Rajkumar. 2009. Perceptron reranking for CCG realization. In *Conference on Empirical Methods in Natural Language Processing (EMNLP-09)*. Singapore, pages 410–419.

Wojciech Zaremba, Ilya Sutskever, and Oriol Vinyals. 2014. Recurrent neural network regularization. *arXiv preprint arXiv:1409.2329* .

Yue Zhang. 2013. Partial-tree linearization: Generalized word ordering for text synthesis. In *Proceedings of the International Joint Conference on Artificial Intelligence (IJCAI-13)*.

Yue Zhang, Graeme Blackwood, and Stephen Clark. 2012. Syntax-based word ordering incorporating a large-scale language model. In *Proceedings of the 13th Conference of the European Chapter of the ACL (EACL-12)*. Avignon, France, pages 736–746.

Yue Zhang and Stephen Clark. 2011. Syntax-based grammaticality improvement using CCG and guided search. In *Conference on Empirical Methods in Natural Language Processing (EMNLP-11)*. Edinburgh, Scotland, UK., pages 1147–1157.

Yue Zhang, Qi Liu, and Linfeng Song. 2018. Sentence-state lstm for text representation. In *Proceedings of the 56th Annual Meeting of the Association for Computational Linguistics (ACL-18)*.

Yue Zhang and Joakim Nivre. 2011. Transition-based dependency parsing with rich non-local features. In *Proceedings of the 49th Annual Meeting of the Association for Computational Linguistics (ACL-11)*. Portland, Oregon, USA, pages 188–193.

Yue Zhang, Kai Song, Linfeng Song, Jingbo Zhu, and Qun Liu. 2014. Syntactic SMT using a discriminative text generation model. In *Conference on Empirical Methods in Natural Language Processing (EMNLP-14)*. Doha, Qatar, pages 177–182.

Muhua Zhu, Yue Zhang, Wenliang Chen, Min Zhang, and Jingbo Zhu. 2013. Fast and accurate shift-reduce constituent parsing. In *Proceedings of the 51st Annual Meeting of the Association for Computational Linguistics (ACL-13)*. Sofia, Bulgaria, pages 434–443.

Characterizing Variation in Crowd-Sourced Data for Training Neural Language Generators to Produce Stylistically Varied Outputs

Juraj Juraska and **Marilyn Walker**
Natural Language and Dialogue Systems Lab
University of California, Santa Cruz
{jjuraska,mawalker}@ucsc.edu

Abstract

One of the biggest challenges of end-to-end language generation from meaning representations in dialogue systems is making the outputs more natural and varied. Here we take a large corpus of 50K crowd-sourced utterances in the restaurant domain and develop text analysis methods that systematically characterize types of sentences in the training data. We then automatically label the training data to allow us to conduct two kinds of experiments with a neural generator. First, we test the effect of training the system with different stylistic partitions and quantify the effect of smaller, but more stylistically controlled training data. Second, we propose a method of labeling the style variants during training, and show that we can modify the style of the generated utterances using our stylistic labels. We contrast and compare these methods that can be used with any existing large corpus, showing how they vary in terms of semantic quality and stylistic control.

1 Introduction

Dialogue systems have become one of the key applications in natural language processing, but there are still many ways in which these systems can be improved. One obvious possible improvement is in the system's language generation to make it more natural and more varied. Both a benefit and a challenge of neural natural language generation (NLG) models is that they are very good at reducing noise in the training data. When they are trained on a sufficiently large dataset, they learn to generalize and become capable of applying the acquired knowledge to unseen inputs. The more data the models are trained on, the more robust they become, which minimizes the effect of noise in the data on their learning. However, the higher amount of training data can also drown out interesting stylistic features and variations that may not be very frequent in the data. In other words, the model, being statistical, will prefer producing the most common sentence structures, i.e. those which it observed most frequently in the training data and is thus most confident about.

In our work, we consider language generators whose inputs are structured *meaning representations* (MRs) describing a list of key concepts to be conveyed to the human user during the dialogue. Each piece of information is represented by a slot-value pair, where the *slot* identifies the type of information and the *value* is the corresponding content. A language generator must produce a syntactically and semantically correct utterance from a given MR. The *utterance* should express all the information contained in the MR, in a natural and conversational way. Table 1 shows an example MR for a restaurant called "The Waterman" paired with two (out of many) possible output utterances, the first of which might be considered stylistically interesting, since the name of the restaurant follows some aspects of the description and contains a concession, while the second example might be considered as more stylistically conventional.

Recently, the size of training corpora for NLG has become larger, and these same corpora have begun to manifest interesting stylistic variations. Here we start from the recently released E2E dataset (Novikova et al., 2017b) with nearly 50K samples of crowd-sourced utterances in the restaurant domain provided as part of the E2E NLG Challenge.[1] We first develop text analysis methods that systematically characterize types of sen-

----

[1] http://www.macs.hw.ac.uk/InteractionLab/E2E/

441

Proceedings of The 11th International Natural Language Generation Conference, pages 441–450,
Tilburg, The Netherlands, November 5-8, 2018. ©2018 Association for Computational Linguistics

MR	name [**The Waterman**], food [**English**], priceRange [**cheap**], customer rating [**low**], area [**city centre**], familyFriendly [**yes**]
Utt. #1	There is a **cheap**, **family-friendly** restaurant in the **city centre**, called **The Waterman**. It serves **English** food, but received a **low** rating by customers.
Utt. #2	**The Waterman** is a **family-friendly** restaurant in the **city centre**. It serves **English** food at a **cheap** price. It has a **low** customer rating.

Table 1: Example of a meaning representation and two corresponding utterances of different styles.

tences in the training data. We then automatically label the training data – with the help of a heuristic slot aligner and a handful of domain-independent rules for discourse marker extraction – in order to allow us to conduct two kinds of experiments with a neural language generator: (1) we test the effect of training the system with different stylistic partitions and quantify the effect of smaller, but more stylistically controlled training data; (2) we propose a method of labeling the style variants during training, and show that we can modify the style of the output using our stylistic labels. We contrast these methods, showing how they vary in terms of semantic quality and stylistic control. These methods promise to be usable with any sufficiently large corpus as a simple way of producing stylistic variation.

2 Related Work

The restaurant domain has always been the domain of choice for NLG tasks in dialogue systems (Stent et al., 2004; Gašić et al., 2008; Mairesse et al., 2010; Howcroft et al., 2013), as it offers a good combination of structured information availability, expression complexity, and ease of incorporation into conversation. Hence, even the more recent neural models for NLG continue to be tested primarily on data in this domain (Wen et al., 2015; Dušek and Jurčíček, 2016; Nayak et al., 2017). These tend to focus solely on syntactic and semantic correctness of the generated utterances, nevertheless, there have also been re-

cent efforts to collect training data for NLG with emphasis on stylistic variation (Nayak et al., 2017; Novikova et al., 2017a; Oraby et al., 2017).

While there is previous work on stylistic variation in NLG (Paiva and Evans, 2004; Mairesse and Walker, 2007), this work did not use crowdsourced utterances for training. More recent work in neural NLG that explores stylistic control has not needed to control semantic correctness, or examined the interaction between semantic correctness and stylistic variation (Sennrich et al., 2016; Ficler and Goldberg, 2017). Also related is the work of Niu and Carpuat (2017) that analyzes how dense word embeddings capture style variations, Kabbara and Cheung (2016) who explore the ability of neural NLG systems to transfer style without the need for parallel corpora, which are difficult to collect (Rao and Tetreault, 2018), while Li et al. (2018) use a simple delete-and-retrieve method also without alignment to outperform adversarial methods in style transfer. Finally, Oraby et al. (2018) propose two different methods that give neural generators control over the language style, corresponding to the Big Five personalities, while maintaining semantic fidelity of the generated utterances.

To our knowledge, there is no previous work exploring the use of and utility of stylistic selection for controlling stylistic variation in NLG from structured MRs. This may be either because there have not been sufficiently large corpora in a particular domain, or because it is surprising, as we show, that relatively small corpora (2000 samples) whose style is controlled can be used to train a neural generator to achieve high semantic correctness while producing stylistic variation.

3 Dataset

We perform the stylistic selection on the E2E dataset (Novikova et al., 2017b). It is by far the largest dataset available for task-oriented language generation in the restaurant domain. It offers almost 10 times more data than the San Francisco restaurant dataset (Wen et al., 2015), which had frequently been used for NLG benchmarks. This significant increase in size allows successful training of neural models on smaller subsets of the dataset. Careful selection of the training subset can be used to influence the style of the utterances produced by the model, as we show in this paper.

A portion of the human reference utterances

	Samples	Unique MRs
Training	42,061	4,862
Validation	4,672	547
Test	630	630
Total	47,363	6,039

Table 2: Number of samples vs. unique meaning representations in the training, validation and test set of the E2E dataset.

Slots	3	4	5	6	7	8
Sentences	1.09	1.23	1.41	1.65	1.84	1.92
Proportion	5%	18%	32%	28%	14%	3%

Table 3: Average number of sentences in the reference utterance for a given number of slots in the corresponding MR, along with the proportion of MRs with specific slot counts.

Domain	Utterance
TV	You might like the Dionysus 44 television that has an a+ eco rating and 720p resolution, *while* only using 32 watts in power consumption. (Wen et al., 2016)
Laptop	*For the price of 449 dollars*, you could purchase the Satellite Hypnos 38 laptop. (Wen et al., 2016)
People	*Born in the London Borough of Havering,* Alex Day started performing in 2006. (Gardent et al., 2017)
Food	Sago is the main ingredient in binignit, *but* sweet potatoes are also used in it. (Gardent et al., 2017)

Table 4: Examples of utterances in different datasets/domains, also exhibiting interesting discourse phenomena.

was collected using pictures as the source of information, which was shown to inspire more natural utterances compared to textual MRs (Novikova et al., 2016). The reference utterances in the E2E dataset exhibit superior lexical richness and syntactic variation, including more complex discourse phenomena. It aims to provide higher-quality training data for end-to-end NLG systems to learn to produce better phrased and more naturally sounding utterances.

Although the E2E dataset contains a large number of samples, each MR is associated on average with more than 8 different reference utterances, effectively supplying almost 5K unique MRs in the training set (Table 2). It thus offers multiple alternative ways of expressing the same information in an utterance, which the model can learn. We take advantage of this aspect of the dataset when selecting the subset of samples for training with a particular purpose of stylistic variation.

The dataset contains 8 different slot types, which are fairly equally distributed in the dataset. Each MR comprises 3 to 8 slots, whereas the majority of MRs consist of 5 and 6 slots. Even though most of the MRs contain many slots, the majority of the corresponding human utterances consist of one or two sentences only (Table 3), suggesting a reasonably high level of sentence complexity in the references.

4 Stylistic Selection

We note that the E2E dataset is significantly larger than what is needed for a neural model to learn to produce correct utterances in this domain. Thus, we seek a way to help the model learn more than just to be correct. We strive to achieve higher stylistic diversity of the utterances generated by the model through stylistic selection of the training samples. We start by characterizing variation in the crowd-sourced dataset and detect what opportunities it offers for the model to learn more advanced sentence structures. Table 5 illustrates some of the stylistic variation that we observe, which we describe in more detail below. We then judge the level of desirability of specific discourse phenomena in our context, and devise rules based on the parse tree to extract the samples that manifest those stylistic phenomena. This gives us the ability to create subsets of the samples with an arbitrary combination of stylistic features that we are interested in. We then explore the extent to which we can make the model's output demonstrate these stylistic features.

4.1 Stylistic Variation in the Dataset

This section gives an overview of different discourse phenomena in the E2E dataset that we consider relevant in the context of a task-oriented dialogue in the restaurant domain. The majority of

Category	Utterance
Aggregation	Located in the city centre is a family-friendly coffee shop called Fitzbillies. It is **both inexpensive and highly rated**.
Contrast	The Rice Boat is a Chinese restaurant in the riverside area. It has a customer rating of 5 out of 5 **but** is not family friendly.
Fronting	**With a 1 out of 5 rating** Midsummer House serves Italian cuisine in the high price range, found not far from All Bar One.
Subordination	Wildwood pub is serving 5 star food **while keeping their prices low**.
Exist. clause	In the city center, **there** is an average priced, non-family-friendly, Japanese restaurant called Alimentum.
Imperative/modal	In Riverside, **you'll** find Fitzbillies. It is a passable, affordable coffee shop which interestingly serves Chinese food. **Don't bring** your family though.

Table 5: Examples of the categories of discourse phenomena extracted from the utterances in the E2E dataset.

these would, however, generalize to other domains too, since they appear not only in summaries of restaurants, but, for example, in those of TVs, laptops (Wen et al., 2016), people and food (Gardent et al., 2017) too (see examples in Table 4). The extraction rules we have implemented can thus be widely used in task-oriented data-to-text language generators. We split the sentence features in the following six categories. An example of each is given in Table 5:

- **Aggregation:** Discourse phenomena grouping information together in a more concise way. This includes specifiers such as "both" or "also", as well as apposition and gerunds. Another type of aggregation uses the same quantitative adjective for characterizing multiple different qualities (such as "It has a *low customer rating and price range*.").

  Note that some of the following categories contain other markers that also represent aggregation.

- **Contrast:** Connectors and adverbs expressing concession or contrast between two or more qualities, such as "but", "despite", "however", or "yet".

- **Fronting:** Fronted adjective, verb and prepositional phrases, typically highlighting qualities of the eatery before its name is given.

  In this category we also include specificational copular constructions, which are formulations with inverted predication around a copula, bringing a particular quality of the eatery in the front (e.g. "*A family friendly option is* The Rice Boat.").

- **Subordination:** Clauses introduced by a subordinating conjunction (such as "if" or "while"), or by a relative pronoun (such as "whose" or "that").

- **Existential clause:** Sentences formulated using the expletive "there".

- **Imperative and modal verb:** Sentences involving a verb in the imperative form or a modal verb, making the utterance sound more personal and interactive.

4.2 Discourse Marker Weighting

Many human-produced utterances, naturally, contain multiple of the discourse phenomena described in Section 4.1. Such utterances are preferred to those only containing a single discourse phenomenon of interest, especially if it is a common one, such as the existential clause. We therefore devise a weighting schema for different groups of discourse markers, whose purpose is to represent the markers' general desirability in the output utterances, as well as to counteract the sparsity of some of the markers compared to others. In other words, the weighting is supposed to ensure all the most desirable utterances are picked from the training set during the selection, but some that only contain less interesting (and typically more prevalent) discourse phenomena would be omitted in favor of the more complex ones. Our reasoning behind that is that the greater the proportion of the most desirable discourse phenomena in the stylistically selected training set, the more confidently the model is expected to generate utterances in which they are present.

For an illustration, let us assume there are eight different reference utterances for an MR. All of them will be scored based on the discourse markers they contain, but only those that score above a certain threshold will be selected, while the rest will be ignored. The purpose of that is to encourage the model to learn to use, say, a contrastive phrase if there is an opportunity for it in the MR, and not be distracted by other possible realizations of the same MR, which are not as elegant (such as the example utterance #1 vs. #2 in Table 1). Thus, we can set the weighting schema in such a way that sentences containing only, for example, "which" or an existential clause, will not be picked. However, if there is no high scoring utterance for an MR, the utterance with the highest score is picked so that the model would not miss an opportunity to learn from any MR samples.

Our final weighting schema is specified in Table 6. When there are discourse markers from multiple subsets present in the utterance, the weights are accumulated. It is then the total weight that is used to determine whether the utterance satisfies the stylistic threshold or should be eliminated.

The weights have been determined through a combination of the discourse markers' frequency in the dataset, their intra-category variation, as well as their general desirability in the particular domain of our task. The weights can be easily adjusted for any new domain according to the above, or any other factors. As an example, another such factor could be the length of the utterance. We have experimented with a length penalty, i.e. giving an utterance that contains a verb in gerund form as the only advanced construct, but that is composed of three sentences, a lower score than a short one-sentence utterance with a gerund verb. However, we did not find the use of this extra coefficient helpful in our domain, as it resulted in eliminating a significant proportion of desirable utterances too.

5   Data Annotation

5.1   Contrastive Relation

One of the discourse phenomena whose actualization could benefit from explicit indication of when it should be applied, is the contrastive relation between two (or more) slot realizations in the utterance. There are several reasons why such a comparison of specific slots would be desired in the restaurant domain. One of them is to provide emphasis that one attribute is positive, whereas the other is negative. Another natural reason in dialogue systems could be to indicate that the closest match to the user's query that was found is a restaurant that does not satisfy one of the requested criteria. A third instance is when the value of one attribute creates the expectation of a particular value of another attribute, but the latter has in reality the opposite value.

Some of the above could presumably be learned by the model if sufficient training data was available. However, they involve fairly complex sentence constructs with various potentially confusing rules for the neural network. The slightly more than 2K samples with a contrasting relation can be drowned among the thousands of other samples in the E2E dataset, meaning that it is difficult for the learned model to produce them.

Hence, we augment the input given to the model with the information about which slots should be put into a contrastive relation. We hypothesize that this explicit indication will help the model to learn to apply contrasting significantly more easily despite the small proportion of training samples exhibiting the property.

In order to extract the information as exactly as possible from the training utterance, we use a heuristic slot aligner (Juraska et al., 2018) to identify two slots that are in a contrastive relation. For the relation we only consider the two scalar slots (*price range* and *customer rating*), plus the boolean slot *family friendly*. Whenever a contrastive relation appears to the aligner to involve a slot other than the above three, we discard it as an undesirable utterance formulation. Depending on the values of the two identified slots, we assign the sample either of the following labels:

- **Contrast:** If the slots have different values on the 3-level positivity scale that they can be mapped to (the *family friendly* slot is only mapped to levels $\{1, 3\}$). An example would

Category	Subset of markers	Proportion	Weight
Aggregation	"also, both, neither,...", quantitative adjectives	1.8%	3
	apposition	4.6%	2
	gerund	11.2%	2
Contrast	"but, however, despite, although,..."	5.4%	3
Fronting	fronted adjective/prepositional/verb clause	14.5%	2
Subordination	subordinating conj.	2.9%	2
	relative pronouns	19.3%	1
Existential clause	expletive "there"	10.0%	1
Imperative/modal	imperative	1.0%	2
	modal verb	4.1%	2

Table 6: The weighting schema for different discourse markers for each introduced category of discourse phenomena. For each set of markers we indicate the heuristically determined proportion of reference utterances in the training set they appear in.

be *customer rating* being "low" ($\to$ 1) and *family friendly* having value "yes" ($\to$ 3).

- **Concession:** If the slots have an equivalent value. For instance, *customer rating* being "5 out of 5" ($\to$ 3) and *price range* having value "cheap" ($\to$ 3).

The label is added in the form of a new auxiliary slot in the MR, containing the names of the two corresponding slots as its value, such as <contrast> [priceRange customer_rating].

We observed instances in the dataset that, semantically, can be classified neither as contrast nor as concession, but using our above rules, they would be considered a concession. An example of such a reference utterance is: "Strada is a low price restaurant located near Rainbow Vegetarian Café serving English food with a *low customer rating but not family-friendly.*" Notice that the emphasized part of the utterance contains a questionable use of the word "but", as both of the attributes of the restaurant (customer rating and family-friendliness) are negative. Such utterances were, however, scarce, and thus we considered them as an acceptable noise.

5.2 Emphasis

Another utterance property that might in practice be desired to be indicated explicitly and, in that way, enforced in the output utterance, is emphasis. Through fronting discourse phenomena, such as specificational copular constructions or fronted

User query	Is there a family-friendly Indian restaurant nearby?
Response with no emphasis	*The Rice Boat* in city centre near Express by Holiday Inn is serving Indian food at a high price. It is **family-friendly** and received a customer rating of 1 out of 5.
Response with emphasis	A **family-friendly** option is *The Rice Boat*. This Indian cuisine is priced on the higher end and has a rating of 1 out of 5. They are located near Express by Holiday Inn in the city centre.

Table 7: Example of emphasizing the information about family-friendliness in an utterance conveying the same content.

prepositional phrases, certain information about the subject can be emphasized at the beginning of the utterance.

This could be used to make the dialogue system's responses sound more context-aware and thus natural. Consider the following example in the restaurant domain. Assume the user asks the agent for a recommendation of a family-friendly Indian restaurant (see Table 7). Considering they have explicitly specified the "family-friendly" requirement in the query, it is arguably more natural for the response utterance to be in the form of the second response example in the table rather than

MR	name [Wildwood], *eatType [coffee shop], food [English],* priceRange [moderate], customer rating [1 out of 5], *near [Ranch]*
Reference	A low rated English style coffee shop around Ranch called Wildwood has moderately priced food.
No emph.	Wildwood is a coffee shop providing English food in the moderate price range. It is located near Ranch.
With emph.	There is an English coffee shop near Ranch called Wildwood. It has a moderate price range and a customer rating of 1 out of 5.

Table 8: Examples of generated utterances with or without an explicit emphasis annotation.

the first.

We argue that the order of the information given in the response matters and should not be entirely random. That motivated us to identify instances in the training set where some information about the restaurant is provided in the utterance before its name. In order to do so, and to extract the information about which slot(s) the segment of the utterance represents, we employ the heuristic slot aligner once again. Subsequently, we augment the corresponding input to the model with additional <emph> tokens before the slots that should be emphasized in the output utterance. This additional indication will give the model an incentive to learn to realize such slots at the beginning of the utterance when desired. From the perspective of the dialogue manager in a dialogue system, it simply needs to indicate slots to emphasize along with the generated MR whenever applicable.

6 Evaluation

6.1 Experimental Setup

For our sequence-to-sequence NLG model we use the standard encoder-decoder (Cho et al., 2014) architecture equipped with an attention mechanism as defined in Bahdanau et al. (2015). The samples are delexicalized before being fed into the model as input, so as to enhance the ability of the model to generalize the learned concepts to unseen MRs. We only delexicalize categorical slots whose values always propagate verbatim from the MR to the utterance. The corresponding values in the input MR get thus replaced with placeholder tokens for which the values from the original MR are eventually substituted in the output utterance as a part of post-processing.

We use a 4-layer bidirectional LSTM (Hochreiter and Schmidhuber, 1997) encoder and a 4-layer LSTM decoder, both with 512 cells per layer. During inference time, we use beam search with the beam width of 10 and length normalization of the beams as defined in Wu et al. (2016). The length penalty that we determined was providing the best results on the E2E dataset was 0.6. The beam search candidates are reranked using a heuristic slot aligner as described in Juraska et al. (2018), and the top candidate is returned as the final utterance.

6.2 Style Subsets

In the initial experiments, we trained the model on the reduced training set, which only contains the utterances filtered out based on the weighting schema defined in Table 6. Setting the threshold to 2, we obtained a training set of 17.5K samples, which is approximately 40% of the original training set. Although this reduced training set had a higher concentration of more desirable reference utterances, the dataset turned out to be still too general with most of the rare discourse phenomena drowned out. However, many of them, including contrast, apposition and fronting, appeared multiple times in the generated utterances in the test set, which was not the case for a model trained on the full training set.

Therefore, our next step was to verify whether our model is capable of learning all the concepts of the discourse phenomena individually and apply them in generated utterances. To that end, we repeatedly trained the model on subsets of the E2E dataset, each containing only samples with a specific group of discourse markers, as listed in the second column of Table 6.[2] We then evaluated the outputs on the correspondingly reduced

---

[2] The samples did not necessarily contain the respective discourse marker exclusively, and many exhibited additional markers.

test set, using the same method we used for identifying samples with specific discourse markers, as described in Section 4.1. In other words, we identified what proportion of the generated utterances did exhibit the desired discourse phenomenon.

The results show that the model is indeed able to learn how to produce various advanced sentence structures that are, moreover, syntactically correct despite being trained on a rather small training set (in certain cases less than 2K samples). In all of the experiments, 97–100% of the generated utterances conformed to the style the model was trained to produce. Any occasional incoherence that we observed (e.g. "It has a high customer rating, but *are* not kid friendly.") was actually picked up from poor reference utterances in the training set. The only exception in the syntactic correctness was the *Imperative/modal* category. Since this is one of the least represented categories among the six, and due to the particularly high complexity and diversity of the utterances, the model trained exclusively on the samples in this category generated a significant proportion of slightly incoherent utterances.

6.3 Data Annotation

The first set of experiments we performed with the data annotation involved explicit indication of emphasis in the input (see Section 5.2). As the results in Table 9 show, the model trained on data with emphasis annotation reached an almost 98% success rate of generating an utterance with the desired slots emphasized.[3] In order to get a better idea of the impact of the annotation, notice that the same model trained on non-annotated data does not produce a single utterance with emphasis. The latter model defaults to producing utterances in a rigid style, which always starts with the name of the restaurant (see Table 8).

We notice that the error rate of the slot realization rises (from 3.45% to 5.82%) when the annotation is introduced. Nevertheless, it is still lower than the error rate among the reference utterances in the test set, in which over 8% of slots have missing mentions. Thus we find it acceptable considering the desired stylistic improvement of the output utterances.

The experiments with contrastive relation annotation also show a significant impact of the added

---

[3]There were 3,309 slots across all the test MRs that were labeled as to-be-emphasized.

	Emph. realiz.	Slot error rate
Reference	100.00%	8.48%
No emph.	0.00%	3.45%
With emph.	97.85%	5.82%

Table 9: Comparison of the emphasis realization success rate (precision) and the slot realization error rate in the generated outputs using data annotation against the reference utterances, as well as the outputs of the same model trained on non-annotated data.

labels on the style of the output utterances produced by our model. However, the success rate of the realization of a contrast/concession formulation was only 49.12%, and the slot realization error rate jumped up to 8.34%. The contrast and concession discourse phenomena being syntactically more complex, and at the same time being less prevalent among the training utterances, it is understandable that it was more difficult for the model to learn how to use them properly.

6.4 Aggregation

One of the aggregation discourse markers that we identified in Section 4.1 as contributing to the stylistic variation in an interesting way is, unfortunately, very sparsely represented in the E2E dataset. It is the last aggregation type described in the category overview in Section 4.1. Its scarcity in the training set would not make it feasible to train a successful neural model on the subset of the corresponding samples only.

Nevertheless, we analyze the potential for this aggregation in the training set. Since there are only two scalar slots in this dataset – *price range* and *customer rating* – we obtain the frequencies of their value combinations. Both of these take on values on a scale of 3, however, the values are different for each of the slots. Moreover, there are two sets of values for both slots throughout the dataset. We have observed, however, that the values between the two sets are used somewhat interchangeably in the utterances, e.g. "low" seems to be a valid expression of the "less than £20" value of the *price range* slot, and vice versa.

As can be seen in Table 10, the potential for the aggregation is rather limited. Although the 6,604 samples in which a feasible value combination can be found corresponds to over 15% of the training set, due to the values not matching ex-

Price range	Customer rating	Frequency
less than £20	low	2,153
£20-25	3 out of 5	919
moderate	3 out of 5	1,282
more than £30	high	1,329
more than £30	5 out of 5	921

Table 10: Combinations of the slot values for which aggregation would be feasible. Note that only the combinations with a non-zero frequency are listed.

actly between the two slots, aggregation was not elicited in the utterances. Moreover, a high value in the *customer rating* means it is a positive attribute, while a high value in the *price range* slot indicates a negative attribute. We conjecture this might have also deterred the crowd-source workers who produced the utterances from aggregating the values together.

7 Conclusion

In this paper we have presented two different methods of giving a neural language generation system greater stylistic control. Our results indicate that the data annotation method has a significant impact on the model being able to learn how to use a specific style and sentence structures, without an unreasonable impact on the error rate. As our future work, we plan to utilize transfer learning in the style-subset method to improve the model's ability to apply various different styles at the same time, wherein we would also make further use of the weighting schema. Finally, these methods are a convenient way for achieving the goal of stylistic control when training a neural model with an arbitrary existing large corpus.

References

Dzmitry Bahdanau, Kyunghyun Cho, and Yoshua Bengio. 2015. Neural machine translation by jointly learning to align and translate. *ICLR*.

Merrienboer Cho, Bougares Gulcehre, and Bengio Schwenk. 2014. Learning phrase representations using RNN encoder-decoder for statistical machine translation. *EMNLP*.

Ondřej Dušek and Filip Jurčíček. 2016. Sequence-to-sequence generation for spoken dialogue via deep syntax trees and strings. *ACL*.

Jessica Ficler and Yoav Goldberg. 2017. Controlling linguistic style aspects in neural language generation. In *Proceedings of the Workshop on Stylistic Variation*, pages 94–104.

Claire Gardent, Anastasia Shimorina, Shashi Narayan, and Laura Perez-Beltrachini. 2017. Creating training corpora for micro-planners. In *Proceedings of the 55th Annual Meeting of the Association for Computational Linguistics (Volume 1: Long Papers)*, Vancouver, Canada. Association for Computational Linguistics.

Milica Gašić, Simon Keizer, Francois Mairesse, Jost Schatzmann, Blaise Thomson, Kai Yu, and Steve Young. 2008. Training and evaluation of the HIS POMDP dialogue system in noise. In *Proceedings of the 9th SIGDIAL Workshop on Discourse and Dialogue*, pages 112–119. Association for Computational Linguistics.

Sepp Hochreiter and Jürgen Schmidhuber. 1997. Long short-term memory. *Neural computation*, 9(8):1735–1780.

David Howcroft, Crystal Nakatsu, and Michael White. 2013. Enhancing the expression of contrast in the SPaRKy restaurant corpus. In *Proceedings of the 14th European Workshop on Natural Language Generation*, pages 30–39.

Juraj Juraska, Panagiotis Karagiannis, Kevin K. Bowden, and Marilyn A. Walker. 2018. A deep ensemble model with slot alignment for sequence-to-sequence natural language generation. *NAACL*.

Jad Kabbara and Jackie Chi Kit Cheung. 2016. Stylistic transfer in natural language generation systems using recurrent neural networks. In *Proceedings of the Workshop on Uphill Battles in Language Processing: Scaling Early Achievements to Robust Methods*, pages 43–47.

Juncen Li, Robin Jia, He He, and Percy Liang. 2018. Delete, retrieve, generate: A simple approach to sentiment and style transfer. In *Proceedings of the 2018 Conference of the North American Chapter of the Association for Computational Linguistics: Human Language Technologies*.

François Mairesse, Milica Gašić, Filip Jurčíček, Simon Keizer, Blaise Thomson, Kai Yu, and Steve Young. 2010. Phrase-based statistical language generation using graphical models and active learning. In *Proceedings of the 48th Annual Meeting of the Association for Computational Linguistics*, pages 1552–1561. Association for Computational Linguistics.

François Mairesse and Marilyn Walker. 2007. Personage: Personality generation for dialogue. In *Proceedings of the 45th Annual Meeting of the Association of Computational Linguistics*, pages 496–503.

Neha Nayak, Dilek Hakkani-Tur, Marilyn Walker, and Larry Heck. 2017. To plan or not to plan? discourse planning in slot-value informed sequence to sequence models for language generation. In *INTERSPEECH*.

Xing Niu and Marine Carpuat. 2017. Discovering stylistic variations in distributional vector space models via lexical paraphrases. In *Proceedings of the Workshop on Stylistic Variation*, pages 20–27.

Jekaterina Novikova, Ondřej Dušek, and Verena Rieser. 2017a. The E2E dataset: New challenges for end-to-end generation. *arXiv preprint arXiv:1706.09254*.

Jekaterina Novikova, Ondřej Dušek, and Verena Rieser. 2017b. The E2E NLG shared task. In *SIGDIAL: Conference of the Special Interest Group on Discourse and Dialogue*.

Jekaterina Novikova, Oliver Lemon, and Verena Rieser. 2016. Crowd-sourcing NLG data: Pictures elicit better data. In *International Conference on Natural Language Generation*.

Shereen Oraby, Sheideh Homayon, and Marilyn Walker. 2017. Harvesting creative templates for generating stylistically varied restaurant reviews. In *Proceedings of the Workshop on Stylistic Variation*, pages 28–36. Association for Computational Linguistics.

Shereen Oraby, Lena Reed, Shubhangi Tandon, TS Sharath, Stephanie Lukin, and Marilyn Walker. 2018. Controlling personality-based stylistic variation with neural natural language generators. *CoRR*.

Daniel S Paiva and Roger Evans. 2004. A framework for stylistically controlled generation. In *Natural Language Generation*, pages 120–129. Springer.

Sudha Rao and Joel Tetreault. 2018. Dear Sir or Madam, may I introduce the GYAFC dataset: Corpus, benchmarks and metrics for formality style transfer. In *Proceedings of the 2018 Conference of the North American Chapter of the Association for Computational Linguistics: Human Language Technologies*, volume 1, pages 129–140.

Rico Sennrich, Barry Haddow, and Alexandra Birch. 2016. Controlling politeness in neural machine translation via side constraints. In *Proceedings of the 2016 Conference of the North American Chapter of the Association for Computational Lingui stics: Human Language Technologies*, pages 35–40.

Amanda Stent, Rashmi Prasad, and Marilyn Walker. 2004. Trainable sentence planning for complex information presentation in spoken dialog systems. In *Proceedings of the 42nd annual meeting on association for computational linguistics*, page 79. Association for Computational Linguistics.

Tsung-Hsien Wen, Milica Gašić, Nikola Mrkšić, Lina M. Rojas-Barahona, Pei-Hao Su, David Vandyke, and Steve Young. 2016. Multi-domain neural network language generation for spoken dialogue systems. In *Proceedings of the 2016 Conference on North American Chapter of the Association for*

Computational Linguistics (NAACL). Association for Computational Linguistics.

Tsung-Hsien Wen, Milica Gašić, Nikola Mrkšić, Pei-Hao Su, David Vandyke, and Steve Young. 2015. Semantically conditioned LSTM-based natural language generation for spoken dialogue systems. In *Proceedings of the 2015 Conference on Empirical Methods in Natural Language Processing (EMNLP)*. Association for Computational Linguistics.

Yonghui Wu, Mike Schuster, Zhifeng Chen, Quoc V Le, Mohammad Norouzi, Wolfgang Macherey, Maxim Krikun, Yuan Cao, Qin Gao, Klaus Macherey, et al. 2016. Google's neural machine translation system: Bridging the gap between human and machine translation. *CoRR*.

Char2char Generation with Reranking for the E2E NLG Challenge

Shubham Agarwal
Heriot-Watt University *
Edinburgh, UK
sa201@hw.ac.uk

Marc Dymetman
NAVER Labs Europe[†]
Grenoble, France
marc.dymetman@naverlabs.com

Éric Gaussier
Université Grenoble Alpes
Grenoble, France
Eric.Gaussier@imag.fr

Abstract

This paper describes our submission to the E2E NLG Challenge. Recently, neural seq2seq approaches have become mainstream in NLG, often resorting to pre- (respectively post-) processing *delexicalization* (relexicalization) steps at the word-level to handle rare words. By contrast, we train a simple character level seq2seq model, which requires no pre/post-processing (delexicalization, tokenization or even lowercasing), with surprisingly good results. For further improvement, we explore two re-ranking approaches for scoring candidates. We also introduce a synthetic dataset creation procedure, which opens up a new way of creating artificial datasets for Natural Language Generation.

1 Introduction

Natural Language Generation from Dialogue Acts involves generating human understandable utterances from slot-value pairs in a Meaning Representation (MR). This is a component in Spoken Dialogue Systems, where recent advances in Deep Learning are stimulating interest towards using end-to-end models. Traditionally, the Natural Language Generation (NLG) component in Spoken Dialogue Systems has been rule-based, involving a two stage pipeline: 'sentence planning' (deciding the overall structure of the sentence) and 'surface realization' (which renders actual utterances using this structure). The resulting utterances using these rule-based systems tend

to be rigid, repetitive and limited in scope. Recent approaches in dialogue generation tend to directly learn the utterances from data (Mei et al., 2015; Lampouras and Vlachos, 2016; Dušek and Jurčíček, 2016; Wen et al., 2015).

Recurrent Neural Networks with gated cell variants such as LSTMs and GRUs (Hochreiter and Schmidhuber, 1997; Cho et al., 2014) are now extensively used to model sequential data. This class of neural networks when integrated in a Sequence to Sequence (Cho et al., 2014; Sutskever et al., 2014) framework have produced state-of-art results in Machine Translation (Cho et al., 2014; Sutskever et al., 2014; Bahdanau et al., 2015), Conversational Modeling (Vinyals and Le, 2015), Semantic Parsing (Xiao et al., 2016) and Natural Language Generation (Wen et al., 2015; Mei et al., 2015). While these models were initially developed to be used at word level in NLP related tasks, there has been a recent interest to use character level sequences, as in Machine Translation (Chung et al., 2016; Zhao and Zhang, 2016; Ling et al., 2016).

Neural seq2seq approaches to Natural Language Generation (NLG) are typically word-based, and resort to delexicalization (a process in which named entities (slot values) are replaced with special 'placeholders' (Wen et al., 2015)) to handle rare or unknown words (out-of-vocabulary (OOV) words, even with a large vocabulary). It can be argued that this de-lexicalization is unable to account for phenomena such as morphological agreement (gender, numbers) in the generated text (Sharma et al., 2016; Nayak et al., 2017).

However, Goyal et al. (2016) and Agarwal and Dymetman (2017) employ a char-based seq2seq model where the input MR is simply represented as a character sequence, and the output is also generated char-by-char; avoiding the rare word problem, as the character vocabulary is very small.

---

*Work done during internship at Naver Labs (Previously *Xerox Research Centre Europe*.)

[†] Previously *Xerox Research Centre Europe*.

Proceedings of The 11th International Natural Language Generation Conference, pages 451–456,
Tilburg, The Netherlands, November 5-8, 2018. ©2018 Association for Computational Linguistics

This work builds on top of the formulation of Agarwal and Dymetman (2017) and describes our submission for the E2E NLG challenge (Novikova et al., 2017). We further explore re-ranking techniques in order to identify the perfect 'oracle prediction' utterance. One of the strategies for re-ranking uses an approach similar to the 'inverted generation' technique of (Chisholm et al., 2017). Sennrich et al. (2015), Li et al. (2015) and Konstas et al. (2017) have also trained a reverse model for back translation in Machine Translation and NLG. A synthetic data creation technique is used by Dušek et al. (2017) and Logacheva and Specia (2015) but as far as we know, our protocol is novel. Our contributions in this paper and challenge can, thus, be summarized as:

1. We show how a vanilla character-based sequence-to-sequence model performs successfully on the challenge test dataset in terms of BLEU score, while having a tendency to omit semantic material. As far as we know, we are the only team using character based seq2seq for the challenge.

2. We propose a novel data augmentation technique in Natural Language Generation (NLG) which consists of 'editing' the Meaning Representation (MR) and using the original ReFerences (RF). This fabricated dataset helps us in extracting features (to detect errors), used for re-ranking the generated candidates (Section 2.2).

3. We introduce two different re-ranking strategies corresponding to our primary and secondary submission (in the challenge), defined in Section 2.3.[1]

2 Model

In the sequel, we will refer to our vanilla char2char model with the term Forward Model.

2.1 Forward Model

We use a Character-based Sequence-to-Sequence RNN model (Sutskever et al., 2014; Cho et al., 2014) with attention mechanism (Bahdanau et al., 2015). We feed a sequence of embeddings of the individual characters composing the source Meaning Representation (MR) -seen as a string- to the

---

[1]Due to space limitations, our description here omits a number of aspects. For a more extensive description, analysis and examples, please refer to http://www.macs.hw.ac.uk/InteractionLab/E2E/final_papers/E2E-NLE.pdf.

Encoder RNN and try to predict the character sequence of the corresponding utterances (RF) in the generation stage with the Decoder RNN.

Coupled with the attention mechanism, seq2seq models have become de-facto standard in generation tasks. The encoder RNN embeds each of the source characters into vectors exploiting the hidden states computed by the RNN. The decoder RNN predicts the next character based on its current hidden state, previous character, and also the "context" vector c_i, computed by the attention model.

While several strategies have been proposed to improve results using Beam Search in Machine Translation (Freitag and Al-Onaizan, 2017), we used the length normalization (aka length penalty) approach Wu et al. (2016) for our task. A heuristically derived length penalty term is added to the scoring function which ranks the probable candidates used to generate the best prediction.

2.2 Protocol for synthetic dataset creation

We artificially create a training set for the classifier (defined in Section 2.3.2) to detect errors (primarily omission of content) in generated utterances, by a data augmentation technique. The systematic structure of the slots in MR gives us freedom to naturally augment data for our use case. To the best of our knowledge, this is the first approach of using data augmentation in the proposed fashion and opens up new directions to create artificial datasets for NLG. We first define the procedure for creating a dataset to detect omission and then show how a similar approach can be used to create a synthetic dataset to detect additions.

Detecting omissions. This approach assumes that originally there are no omissions in RF for a given MR (in the training dataset). These can be considered as positive pairs when detecting omissions. Now if we artificially add another slot to the original MR and use the same RF for this new (constructed) MR, naturally the original RF tends to show omission of this added slot.

$$MR_{original} \xrightarrow{\text{+ Added slot}} MR_{new}$$
$$MR_{original} \xrightarrow{\text{- Removed slot}} MR_{new} \tag{1}$$

This is a two stage procedure: (a) Select a slot to add. (b) Select a corresponding slot value. Instead of sampling a particular slot in step (a), we add all the slots one by one (that could be augmented in MR apart from currently present slots).

Having chosen the slot type to be added, we add the slot value according to probability distribution of the slot values for that slot type. The original ($MR_{original}$,RF) pair is assigned a class label of 1 and the new artificial pairs (MR_{new},RF) a label of 0, denoting a case of omission (first line of (1)). Thus, these triplets (MR, RF, Class Label) allow us to treat this as a classification task.

Detecting additions. In order to create a dataset which can be used for training our model to detect additions, we proceed in a similar way. The difference is that now we systematically remove one slot in the original MR to create the new MRs (second line of (1)).

In both cases, we control the procedure by manipulating MRs instead of the Natural Language RF. This kind of augmented dataset opens up the possibility of using any classifier to detect the above mentioned errors.

2.3   Re-ranking Models

In this section, we define two techniques to re-rank the n-best list and these serve as primary and secondary submissions to the challenge.

2.3.1   Reverse Model

We generated a list of top-k predictions (using Beam Search) for each MR in what we call the *forward* phase of the model. In parallel, we trained a *reverse* model which tries to reconstruct the MR given the target RF, similar to the autoencoder model by Chisholm et al. (2017). This is guided by an intuition that if our prediction omits some information, the reverse reconstruction of MR would also tend to omit slot-value pairs for the omitted slot values in the prediction. We then score and re-rank the top-k predictions based on a distance metric, namely the edit distance between the original MR and the MR generated by the reverse model, starting from the utterance predicted in the forward direction.

To avoid defining the weights when combining edit distance with the log probability of the model, we used a simplified mechanism. At the time of re-ranking, we choose the first output in our n-best list with zero edit distance as our prediction. If no such prediction can be found, we rely upon the first prediction in our (probabilistically) sorted n-best list. Figure 1 illustrates our pipeline approach.

2.3.2   Classifier as a re-ranker

To treat omission (or more generally any kind of *semantic adequacy* mis-representation such as repetition or addition of content) in the predictions as a classification task, we developed a dataset (consisting of triplets) using the protocol defined earlier. However, to train the classifier we relied on hand-crafted features based on string matching in the prediction (with corresponding slot value in the MR). In total, there were 7 features, corresponding to each slot (except 'name' slot). To maintain the class balance, we replicated the original (MR,RF) pair (with a class label of 1) for each artificially generated (MR,RF) pair (with a class label of 0, corresponding to omissions).

We used a logistic regression classifier to detect omissions following a similar re-ranking strategy as defined for the reverse model. For each probable candidate by the forward model, we first extracted these features and predicted the label by this logistic regression classifier. The first output in our n-best list with a class label 1 is then chosen as the resulting utterance. As a fallback mechanism, we rely on the best prediction by the forward model (similar to the reverse model). We chose the primary submission to the challenge as the pipeline model with classifier as re-ranker. Our second submission was based on re-ranking using the reverse model while the vanilla forward char2char model was our third submission.

3   Experiments

The updated challenge dataset comprises 50K canonically ordered and systematically structured (MR,RF) pairs, collected following the crowdsourcing protocol explained in Novikova et al. (2016). Consisting of 8 different slots (and their respective different values), note that the statistics in the test set differ significantly from the training set. We used the open source *tf-seq2seq* framework[2], built over TensorFlow (Abadi et al., 2016) and provided along with (Britz et al., 2017), with some standard configurations. We experimented with different numbers of layers in the encoder and decoder as well as different beam widths, while using the bi-directional encoder with an "additive" attention mechanism. In terms of BLEU, our best performing model had the following configuration: encoder 1 layer, decoder 2 layers, GRU cell, beam-width 20, length penalty 1.

---

[2]https://github.com/google/seq2seq.

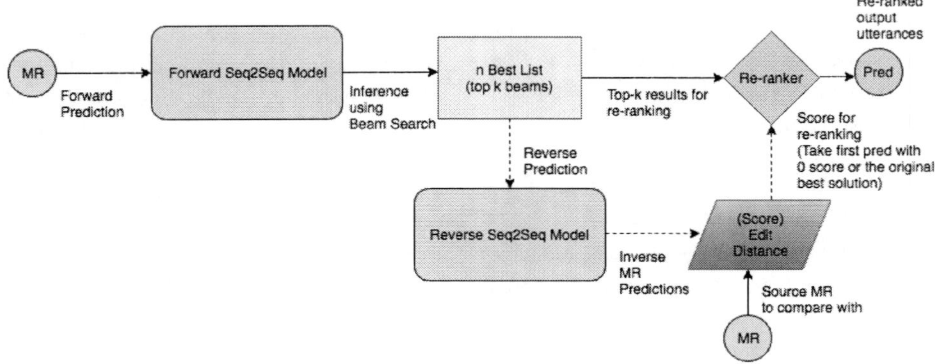

Figure 1: Illustration of the pipeline for the re-ranking approach (based on inverse reconstructions using reverse model) as described in Section 2.3. Apart from Forward and Reverse seq2seq models, we have a re-ranker based on the edit distance of the actual MR and the inverse reconstructed MR.

4 Evaluation

We chose our primary system to be the re-ranker using the classifier. Table 1 summarizes our ranking among all the 60+ submissions (primary as well as additional) on the test set. In terms of BLEU, two of our systems were in the top 5 among all 60+ submissions to the challenge.

Submission	BLEU	Overall Rank
Re-ranking using classifier (Primary)	0.653	18
Re-ranking using reverse (Secondary)	0.666	5
Forward (Third)	0.667	4
Baseline	0.659	10

Table 1: Automatic BLEU evaluations released by organizers on the final challenge submission. We had 3 submissions as described in Section 2. Two of our systems were in the top 5 among all 60+ submissions.

Metric	TrueSkill	Range	Cluster
Quality	0.048	(8-12)	2
Naturalness	0.105	(4-8)	2

Table 2: Human evaluation was crowd-sourced on the primary system according to the TrueSkill algorithm (Sakaguchi et al., 2014)

Results for human evaluation, as released by the challenge organizers, are summarized in Table 2 of (Dušek et al., 2018). They followed the TrueSkill algorithm (Sakaguchi et al., 2014) judging all the primary systems on *Quality* and *Naturalness*. We obtained competitive results in terms of both metrics, our system being in the 2nd clus-

ter out of 5 (for both evaluations). On the other hand, most systems ranked high on quality tended to have lower ranks for naturalness and vice versa.

5 Analysis

We found that the presence of an 'oracle prediction' (perfect utterance) was dependent on the number of slots in the MR. When the number of slots was 7 or 8, the presence of an oracle in the top-20 predictions decreased significantly, as opposed to the case when the number of slots was less than 7. However, the most prominent issue was that of omissions, among the utterances produced in first position (by forward model). There were no additions or non-words. We observed a similar issue of omissions in human references (target for our model) as well. Our two different strategies, thus, improved the semantic adequacy by re-ranking the probable candidates and successfully finding the 'oracle' prediction in the top-20 list. However, in terms of automatic evaluation, the BLEU score showed an inverse relationship with adequacy. Nevertheless, we chose our primary system to be the re-ranker with a classifier over the forward model.

We did not find any issues while "copying" the restaurant 'name' or 'near' slots on the dev set. However, on the test set, as the statistics of the data changed in terms of both slots, we found a tendency of the model to generate the more frequent slot values (corresponding to both slots in the training dataset), instead of copying the actual slot value.

6 Conclusion

We show how a char2char model can be employed for the task of NLG and show competitive results in this challenge. Our vanilla character based model, building on Agarwal and Dymetman (2017), requires minimal effort in terms of any processing of dataset while also producing great diversity in the generated utterances. We then propose two re-ranking strategies for further improvements. Even though re-ranking methods show improvements in terms of semantic adequacy, we find a reversal of trend in terms of BLEU.

Our synthetic data creation technique could be adapted for augmenting NLG datasets and the classifier-based score could also be used as a reward in a Reinforcement Learning paradigm.

Acknowledgements

We like to thank Chunyang Xiao and Matthias Gallé for their useful suggestions and comments.

References

Martín Abadi, Ashish Agarwal, Paul Barham, Eugene Brevdo, Zhifeng Chen, Craig Citro, Greg S Corrado, Andy Davis, Jeffrey Dean, Matthieu Devin, Sanjay Ghemawat, Ian Goodfellow, Andrew Harp, Geoffrey Irving, Michael Isard, Yangqing Jia, Rafal Jozefowicz, Lukasz Kaiser, Manjunath Kudlur, Josh Levenberg, Dan Mane, Rajat Monga, Sherry Moore, Derek Murray, Chris Olah, Mike Schuster, Jonathon Shlens, Benoit Steiner, Ilya Sutskever, Kunal Talwar, Paul Tucker, Vincent Vanhoucke, Vijay Vasudevan, Fernanda Viegas, Oriol Vinyals, Pete Warden, Martin Wattenberg, Martin Wicke, Yuan Yu, and Xiaoqiang Zheng. 2016. Tensorflow: Large-scale machine learning on heterogeneous distributed systems. *CoRR abs/1603.04467*.

Shubham Agarwal and Marc Dymetman. 2017. A surprisingly effective out-of-the-box char2char model on the E2E NLG challenge dataset. In *Proc. SIGdial*. ACL.

Dzmitry Bahdanau, Kyunghyun Cho, and Yoshua Bengio. 2015. Neural machine translation by jointly learning to align and translate. In *Proc. ICLR*.

Denny Britz, Anna Goldie, Thang Luong, and Quoc Le. 2017. Massive exploration of neural machine translation architectures. *CoRR abs/1703.03906*.

Andrew Chisholm, Will Radford, and Ben Hachey. 2017. Learning to generate one-sentence biographies from wikidata. *CoRR abs/1702.06235*.

Kyunghyun Cho, Bart Van Merriënboer, Caglar Gulcehre, Dzmitry Bahdanau, Fethi Bougares, Holger Schwenk, and Yoshua Bengio. 2014. Learning phrase representations using RNN encoder-decoder for statistical machine translation. In *Proc. EMNLP*.

Junyoung Chung, Kyunghyun Cho, and Yoshua Bengio. 2016. A character-level decoder without explicit segmentation for neural machine translation. *CoRR abs/1603.06147*.

Ondřej Dušek and Filip Jurčíček. 2016. Sequence-to-sequence generation for spoken dialogue via deep syntax trees and strings. *CoRR abs/1606.05491*.

Ondřej Dušek, Jekaterina Novikova, and Verena Rieser. 2017. Referenceless quality estimation for natural language generation. *arXiv preprint arXiv:1708.01759*.

Ondrej Dušek, Jekaterina Novikova, and Verena Rieser. 2018. Findings of the E2E NLG challenge. In *(in prep.)*.

Markus Freitag and Yaser Al-Onaizan. 2017. Beam search strategies for neural machine translation. *CoRR abs/1702.01806*.

Raghav Goyal, Marc Dymetman, and Eric Gaussier. 2016. Natural Language Generation through Character-based RNNs with Finite-State Prior Knowledge. In *Proc. COLING*, Osaka, Japan.

Sepp Hochreiter and Jürgen Schmidhuber. 1997. Long short-term memory. *Neural computation*, 9(8):1735–1780.

Ioannis Konstas, Srinivasan Iyer, Mark Yatskar, Yejin Choi, and Luke Zettlemoyer. 2017. Neural amr: Sequence-to-sequence models for parsing and generation. *CoRR abs/1704.08381*.

Gerasimos Lampouras and Andreas Vlachos. 2016. Imitation learning for language generation from unaligned data. In *Proc. COLING*, pages 1101–1112.

Jiwei Li, Michel Galley, Chris Brockett, Jianfeng Gao, and Bill Dolan. 2015. A diversity-promoting objective function for neural conversation models. *CoRR abs/1510.03055*.

Wang Ling, Isabel Trancoso, Chris Dyer, and Alan W Black. 2016. Character-based neural machine translation. In *Proc. ICLR*, pages 1–11.

Varvara Logacheva and Lucia Specia. 2015. The role of artificially generated negative data for quality estimation of machine translation. In *Proceedings of the 18th Annual Conference of the European Association for Machine Translation*.

Hongyuan Mei, Mohit Bansal, and Matthew R Walter. 2015. What to talk about and how? selective generation using LSTMs with coarse-to-fine alignment. *CoRR abs/1509.00838*.

Neha Nayak, Dilek Hakkani-Tur, Marilyn Walker, and Larry Heck. 2017. To plan or not to plan? sequence to sequence generation for language generation in dialogue systems.

Jekaterina Novikova, Ondrej Dušek, and Verena Rieser. 2017. The E2E dataset: New challenges for end-to-end generation. In *Proc. SIGdial, ACL*, Saarbrücken, Germany.

Jekaterina Novikova, Oliver Lemon, and Verena Rieser. 2016. Crowd-sourcing NLG Data: Pictures Elicit Better Data. *CoRR abs/1608.00339*.

Keisuke Sakaguchi, Matt Post, and Benjamin Van Durme. 2014. Efficient elicitation of annotations for human evaluation of machine translation. In *Proc. Statistical Machine Translation*, pages 1–11, Baltimore, Maryland, USA. ACL.

Rico Sennrich, Barry Haddow, and Alexandra Birch. 2015. Improving neural machine translation models with monolingual data. *CoRR abs/1511.06709*.

Shikhar Sharma, Jing He, Kaheer Suleman, Hannes Schulz, and Philip Bachman. 2016. Natural language generation in dialogue using lexicalized and delexicalized data. *arXiv preprint arXiv:1606.03632*.

Ilya Sutskever, Oriol Vinyals, and Quoc V Le. 2014. Sequence to sequence learning with neural networks. In *Proc. NIPS*, pages 3104–3112.

Oriol Vinyals and Quoc Le. 2015. A neural conversational model. *CoRR abs/1506.05869*.

Tsung-Hsien Wen, Milica Gasic, Nikola Mrksic, Pei-Hao Su, David Vandyke, and Steve Young. 2015. Semantically conditioned lstm-based natural language generation for spoken dialogue systems. In *Proc. EMNLP*.

Yonghui Wu, Mike Schuster, Zhifeng Chen, Quoc V Le, Mohammad Norouzi, Wolfgang Macherey, Maxim Krikun, Yuan Cao, Qin Gao, Klaus Macherey, Jeff Klinger, Apurva Shah, Melvin Johnson, Xiaobing Liu, Lukasz Kaiser, Stephan Gouws, Yoshikiyo Kato, Taku Kudo, Hideto Kazawa, Keith Stevens, George Kurian, Nishant Patil, Wei Wang, Cliff Young, Jason Smith, Jason Riesa, Alex Rudnick, Oriol Vinyals, Greg Corrado, Macduff Hughes, and Jeffrey Dean. 2016. Google's neural machine translation system: Bridging the gap between human and machine translation. *CoRR abs/1609.08144*.

Chunyang Xiao, Marc Dymetman, and Claire Gardent. 2016. Sequence-based structured prediction for semantic parsing. *Proc. ACL*.

Shenjian Zhao and Zhihua Zhang. 2016. An efficient character-level neural machine translation. *CoRR abs/1608.04738*.

E2E NLG Challenge Submission: Towards Controllable Generation of Diverse Natural Language

Henry Elder
Adapt Centre / DCU
`henry.elder@adaptcentre.ie`

Sebastian Gehrmann
Harvard NLP
`gehrmann@g.harvard.edu`

Alexander O'Connor
Pivotus Ventures Inc.
`alexander@pivotusventures.com`

Qun Liu
Adapt Centre / DCU
`qun.liu@adaptcentre.ie`

Abstract

In natural language generation (NLG), the task is to generate utterances from a more abstract input, such as structured data. An added challenge is to generate utterances that contain an accurate representation of the input, while reflecting the fluency and variety of human-generated text. In this paper, we report experiments with NLG models that can be used in task oriented dialogue systems. We explore the use of additional input to the model to encourage diversity and control of outputs. While our submission does not rank highly using automated metrics, qualitative investigation of generated utterances suggests the use of additional information in neural network NLG systems to be a promising research direction.

Meaning Representation
name[The Wrestlers]
eatType[restaurant]
food[Japanese]
priceRange[more than £30]
area[riverside]
familyFriendly[no]
near[Raja Indian Cuisine]
additionalWords[*looking adults offerings really try good prices situated*]
Generated utterance
If you're *looking* for an *adults* only Japanese restaurant, *try* The Wrestlers. It is *really good* and *situated* near Raja Indian Cuisine. The *prices* are more than £30.

Table 1: Utterance generated with a novel dialogue act containing additional words

1 Introduction

Natural Language Generation (NLG) is a broad field, ranging from text-to-text translation to experiments in computational poetry (Gatt and Krahmer, 2018). Whether the task is to summarize, translate, or entertain, a core challenge is doing so in a manner that is compatible with human needs and preferences.

Formally, NLG systems aim to create utterances from a set of abstract inputs. These inputs can be closely aligned, e.g. machine translation (Sutskever et al., 2014), or require significant abstractive reasoning, as in summarization or data-to-text tasks (See and Manning, 2017; Wiseman et al., 2017). Traditionally NLG systems have followed a rule-based approach (Reiter and Dale, 2000). While robust, these systems are noted to generate repetitive and stilted output, which can make interacting with rule based systems a tedious experience (Wen et al., 2015).

Data driven models using deep neural networks have achieved state-of-the-art results in many NLG tasks/datasets such as RoboCup, Weathergov, SF Hotels/Restaurants and AMR-to-text (Mei et al., 2016; Wen et al., 2016; Konstas et al., 2017). However Sharma et al. (2017) notes that high performance on datasets such as Wen et al. (2015)'s SF Restaurant indicates they no longer pose a sufficient challenge and that the community ought to progress to using larger and more complex datasets.

Two new crowd sourced datasets, each containing tens of thousands of examples and focusing on complex sentence structures, have been recently released; WebNLG and E2E (Colin et al., 2016; Novikova et al., 2017). This paper focuses on the E2E dataset which was created using a new

457

Proceedings of The 11th International Natural Language Generation Conference, pages 457–462,
Tilburg, The Netherlands, November 5-8, 2018. ©2018 Association for Computational Linguistics

methodology to maximize both the quality of collected utterances as well as their naturalness and variety (Novikova et al., 2016).

Wei et al. (2017) note that neural networks learning from highly unaligned datasets have trouble choosing between equally plausible outputs and tend towards short and less meaningful outputs. They suggest that the number of plausible outputs can be decreased by providing additional information to the model. In Table 1 we augment the meaning representation (MR) with a novel dialogue act (DA) containing additional words to be included in the generated utterance. By conditioning the output on these words the model has managed to generate an utterance with a complex sentence structure and wide vocabulary.

Our contribution is to propose a pipeline system. Additional words are sampled from a secondary model which uses DAs from a given MR as inputs. These additional words are put into a new DA and added to the existing MR, as shown in Table 1. The augmented MR is then used as input to a model which generates the final utterance.

The approach of augmenting the source sequence takes inspiration from recent work in paraphrase generation (Guu et al., 2017) and generating structured queries from natural language (Zhong et al., 2017). As noted by Sharma et al. (2016) delexicalization can often lead to grammatically incorrect sentences. We opt instead to use a pointer network (Vinyals et al., 2015) which allows the model to copy tokens directly from the source sequence into the generated utterance. The model does not perform well relative to the baseline and this is possibly due to the failure of the secondary model to generate appropriate additional words. Improving upon the pipeline system remains an area of active research for us.

2 System Description

Here we present details of the pipeline system. First we describe how the training data for the pointer network with additional words model is constructed. This is followed by an explanation of the additional word generator which uses DAs from a given MR as input.

Typical approaches to generating diverse outputs focus on objective functions that affect the decoding step (Li et al., 2015). Our approach of augmenting the input sequence is similar to previous work on common sense dialogue models (Young

et al., 2017) and content-introducing text generation (Mou et al., 2016). Other approaches to controllable text generation have focused on more abstract inputs. Language models which generate text about a specific topic, product, person, sentiment (Li et al., 2016; Tang et al., 2016; Fan et al., 2017; Dong et al., 2017).

2.1 Additional words model

We augment the MR with an extra DA containing additional words to be included in the generated sentence. To obtain the data for this we looked at each target sentence and, using a set of rules, determined what words the model would learn to include. These selected words were added to the source sequence inside a custom DA. This ability of the model to accept additional words ensured that we would have both diversity of outputs and fine grained control over those outputs at test time.

For our additional words model we extracted tokens from the target sequence that adhered to the following set of rules:

- Not part of a list of stopwords

- Does not appear in the source sequence or meaning representation

- Does not contain punctuation or numbers

After the original list was compiled we removed the most frequently appearing token *located* and any tokens which occurred less than 6 times.

Table 2 contains an example of an augmented MR and utterance pair used for training.

Source sequence
name[The Vaults]
eatType[pub]
priceRange[more than £30]
customer rating[5 out of 5]
near[Café Adriatic]
additionalWords[*star Prices start*]
Target sequence
The Vaults pub near Café Adriatic has a 5 *star* rating. *Prices start* at £30.

Table 2:   Example from the additional words model training set

2.1.1 Generating additional words

The unique contents of each DA in the MR are treated as a single token. We omit the *name* and *near* DAs as they were observed to have little correlation with the semantics of the additional words chosen. The model attempts to correlate specific DAs with the additional words that appear in target sentences. An example of the source and target sequences used for training are shown in Table 3. We use a sequence-to-sequence network with attention as the model.

Additional words are sampled from the model. We scale the final output layer of the model before applying softmax and sampling tokens for the generated utterance. The value used for scaling is known as *temperature*. Higher values of temperature lead to more diverse outputs. Temperature values close to 0 lead to the model choosing more conservative outputs. We use values of 0.9 to 1.1, to encourage the generation of a more diverse set of additional words.

Source sequence
pub
more_than_£30
5_out_of_5
Target sequence
star Prices start

Table 3: Example pair used for training the additional word generator

3 Experiments

The data set was tokenized using the NLTK port of the moses tokenizer with aggressive hyphen splitting. For each DA a custom start and stop token was added to the source sequence; e.g. _name_start_ The Vaults _name_end_

The models used were from the OpenNMT-py library (Klein et al., 2017). Our model architecture contains 2 layers of bidirectional recurrent neural networks (RNN) with long short-term memory (LSTM) cells (Hochreiter and Schmidhuber, 1997). We use 500 hidden units for the encoder and decoder layer, and 500 units for the word vectors which are learned jointly across the whole model. We add dropout of 0.3 applied between the LSTM stacks.

The models are trained using Adam (Kingma and Ba, 2014) with learning rate 0.001 and learning rate decay of 0.5 applied after 8 epochs. The models were trained for 10 epochs and the best performing checkpoint on the development set was chosen.

The exploration and choice of hyperparameters was aided by the use of Bayesian hyperparameter optimization platform SigOpt (2014).

4 Results & Discussion

We report results using automated evaluation metrics; BLEU (Papineni et al., 2002), NIST (Przybocki et al., 2009), METEOR (Lavie and Agarwal, 2007), and ROUGE-L (Lin, 2004). Table 4 shows the performance of the baseline relative to our models using both sample additional words and those extracted from target sentences, these are the gold standard additional words. The baseline model is TGen, a sequence-to-sequence model with attention (Dušek and Jurčíček, 2016).

The model using extracted additional words performs better in almost all metrics. The poor performance of models using sampled words versus gold standard words highlights an issue with the generation of additional words. These results maintain their relative ranking in the test set as shown in Table 5.

Human evaluation was carried out on the primary systems. The two metrics used were Quality; which measures grammatical correctness and overall adequacy in the context of the MR, and Naturalness; could the utterance have been produced by a native speaker. Crowd workers were used to collect pairwise comparisons for each system. Systems were ranked using the TrueSkill algorithm (Sakaguchi et al., 2014). Our model ranked 4th, below the baseline which came in 2nd, as shown in Table 4 (Dušek et al., 2018)

Automated evaluation and subsequent human evaluation results show our additional words model performs poorly relative to the baseline. A manual observation of the model's outputs reveal many errors such as repeated phrases and occasionally absent or incorrect information. We include a collection of generated utterances from the test set in table 7 to highlight areas where the model performs both well and poorly relative to the baseline.

Utterances from the baseline model tend to be more consistent but when viewed over many hundreds of samples this can be dry and repetitive. In most cases the baseline model appears to have

Model	BLEU	NIST	METEOR	ROUGE-L	CIDEr
Additional words - temperature 1.1	0.5307	7.1738	0.4108	0.6112	1.5658
Additional words - temperature 1.0	0.5574	7.4078	0.4171	0.6308	1.6380
Additional words - temperature 0.9	0.5659	7.5196	0.4209	0.6327	1.7652
Baseline	0.6925	8.4781	0.4703	0.7257	**2.3987**
Additional words - extracted from target	**0.7381**	**9.9435**	**0.4726**	**0.7508**	2.2858

Table 4: Dev set results

Model	BLEU	NIST	METEOR	ROUGE-L	CIDEr
Additional words - temperature 1.1	0.5092	7.1954	0.4025	0.5872	1.5039
Additional words - temperature 1.0	0.5265	7.3991	0.4095	0.5992	1.6488
Additional words - temperature 0.9	0.5573	7.7013	0.4154	0.6130	1.8110
Baseline	**0.6593**	**8.6094**	**0.4483**	**0.6850**	**2.2338**

Table 5: Test set results

Model	Naturalness	Quality
Baseline	2nd	2nd
Additional words - temperature 1.1	4th	4th

Table 6: True skill clusters

learned its own simple templates for generating utterances from an MR. The following is an example of the template-like output the baseline produces if provided with all 8 possible DAs; *"[name]* is a *[food] [eatType]* near *[near]* in the *[area]*. It has a *[customer rating]* and a price range of *[price range]*. It is *[family friendly]*."* While the baseline model outperformed rule based systems in the E2E challenge, its generated utterances do not appear to fully reflect the diversity of the dataset which has been collected.

5 Future Work

Many verbalization issues in the additional word model arise due to a conflict between an additional word and the existing DAs in the MR. This can be seen in some of the examples in Table 7. The model used for generating additional words could be improved substantially. Increasing the minimum frequency of occurrence for additional words in the training data may give the model more examples from which to better learn correct syntax. The pointer network with additional words model also suffers from an issue, common with pointer networks, in which source tokens are incorrectly repeated in the generated utterance. One way to handle this would be to have a second stage of training with a coverage loss as in See and Manning (2017).

6 Conclusion

We proposed the use of an additional DA to improve the diversity and level of control over utterances. Results show both the underlying network and the method used for generating additional words could be improved. Observation of generated samples show this approach has the potential to yield high quality and varied responses.

References

Emilie Colin, Claire Gardent, M Yassine, and Shashi Narayan. 2016. The WebNLG Challenge : Generating Text from DBPedia Data. *The 9th International Conference on Natural Language Generation.*

Li Dong, Shaohan Huang, Furu Wei, Mirella Lapata, Ming Zhou, and Ke Xu. 2017. Learning to Generate Product Reviews from Attributes.

Ondrej Dušek, Jekaterina Novikova, and Verena Rieser. 2018. Findings of the E2E NLG challenge.

Ondej Dušek and Filip Jurčíček. 2016. Sequence-to-Sequence Generation for Spoken Dialogue via Deep Syntax Trees and Strings.

Angela Fan, David Grangier, and Michael Auli. 2017. Controllable Abstractive Summarization.

Albert Gatt and Emiel Krahmer. 2018. Survey of the state of the art in natural language generation: Core tasks, applications and evaluation. *Journal of Artificial Intelligence Research*, 61(c):1–64.

Kelvin Guu, Tatsunori B Hashimoto, Yonatan Oren, and Percy Liang. 2017. Generating Sentences by Editing Prototypes. 2.

MR	name[The Cricketers] eatType[coffee shop] customerrating[low] familyFriendly[no] near[Express by Holiday Inn]
Additional words DA	additionalWords[satisfaction considered Join]
Additional words model	The Cricketers is a coffee shop near Express by Holiday Inn. It has a low customer satisfaction rating and is not considered family-friendly. Join Us.
Baseline	The Cricketers is a coffee shop near Express by Holiday Inn. It has a low customer rating and is not family-friendly.
MR	name[Zizzi] eatType[coffee shop] area[riverside]
Additional words DA	additionalWords[Located along river side offering snacks]
Additional words model	Located along the river side , Zizzi is a coffee shop offering snacks .
Baseline	Zizzi is a coffee shop in the riverside area with a price range of less than 20.
MR	name[The Mill] eatType[restaurant] food[English] priceRange[high] customerrating[average] area[riverside] familyFriendly[yes] near[Café Rouge]
Additional words DA	additionalWords[offers fare higher bracket]
Additional words model	The Mill is a family friendly restaurant that offers English fare in the higher price bracket . It is located near Café Rouge in the riverside area .
Baseline	The Mill is an english restaurant near Café Rouge in the riverside area. It is children friendly and has a high price range and an average customer rating.
MR	name[Strada] eatType[coffee shop] customerrating[1 out of 5] near[All Bar One]
Additional words DA	additionalWords[try perfect however]
Additional words model	For a coffee shop near All Bar One, try Strada. It has a perfect customer rating of 1 out of 5 however .
Baseline	Strada is a coffee shop near All Bar One with a customer rating of 1 out of 5.
MR	name[Blue Spice] eatType[coffee shop] customerrating[average] near[Burger King]
Additional words DA	additionalWords[neat]
Additional words model	Blue Spice is a coffee shop located neat Burger King.
Baseline	Blue Spice is a coffee shop near Burger King. It has an average customer rating.
MR	name[Wildwood] eatType[pub] area[riverside]
Additional words DA	additionalWords[Located river serving]
Additional words model	Located near the river , Wildwood is a pub serving pub .
Baseline	Wildwood is a pub by the riverside.

Table 7: Example generated utterances using MRs from the test set

Sepp Hochreiter and J Schmidhuber. 1997. Long Short-Term Memory. *Neural Computation*, 9(8):1735–1780.

Diederik P. Kingma and Jimmy Ba. 2014. Adam: A Method for Stochastic Optimization.

Guillaume Klein, Yoon Kim, Yuntian Deng, Josep Crego, Jean Senellart, and Alexander M. Rush. 2017. OpenNMT: Open-source Toolkit for Neural Machine Translation. pages 67–72.

Ioannis Konstas, Srinivasan Iyer, Mark Yatskar, Yejin Choi, and Luke Zettlemoyer. 2017. Neural AMR: Sequence-to-Sequence Models for Parsing and Generation. pages 146–157.

Alon Lavie and Abhaya Agarwal. 2007. Meteor: An Automatic Metric for MT Evaluation with High Levels of Correlation with Human Judgments. In *Proceedings of the Second Workshop on Statistical Machine Translation*, StatMT '07, pages 228–231, Stroudsburg, PA, USA. Association for Computational Linguistics.

Jiwei Li, Michel Galley, Chris Brockett, Jianfeng Gao, and Bill Dolan. 2015. A Diversity-Promoting Objective Function for Neural Conversation Models.

Jiwei Li, Michel Galley, Chris Brockett, Georgios P Spithourakis, Jianfeng Gao, and Bill Dolan. 2016. A Persona-Based Neural Conversation Model. pages 994–1003.

C Y Lin. 2004. Rouge: A package for automatic evaluation of summaries. *Proceedings of the workshop* on text summarization branches out (WAS 2004), (1):25–26.

Hongyuan Mei, Mohit Bansal, and Matthew R. Walter. 2016. What to talk about and how? Selective Generation using LSTMs with Coarse-to-Fine Alignment. *Proceedings of the 15th Annual Conference of the North American Chapter of the Association for Computational Linguistics: Human Language Technologies (NAACL-HLT'16(*, pages 1–11.

Lili Mou, Yiping Song, Rui Yan, Ge Li, Lu Zhang, and Zhi Jin. 2016. Sequence to Backward and Forward Sequences: A Content-Introducing Approach to Generative Short-Text Conversation.

Jekaterina Novikova, Ondrej Dušek, and Verena Rieser. 2017. The E2E dataset: New challenges for end-to-end generation. ArXiv:1706.09254.

Jekaterina Novikova, Oliver Lemon, and Verena Rieser. 2016. Crowd-sourcing NLG Data: Pictures Elicit Better Data. (1).

Kishore Papineni, Salim Roukos, Todd Ward, and Wei-Jing Zhu. 2002. BLEU: A Method for Automatic Evaluation of Machine Translation. In *Proceedings of the 40th Annual Meeting on Association for Computational Linguistics*, ACL '02, pages 311–318, Stroudsburg, PA, USA. Association for Computational Linguistics.

Franois Portet, Ehud Reiter, Albert Gatt, Jim Hunter, Somayajulu Sripada, Yvonne Freer, and Cindy Sykes. 2009. Automatic generation of textual summaries from neonatal intensive care data. *Artificial Intelligence*, 173(7-8):789–816.

Mark Przybocki, Kay Peterson, Sbastien Bronsart, and Gregory Sanders. 2009. The NIST 2008 Metrics for machine translation challenge—overview, methodology, metrics, and results. *Machine Translation*, 23(2):71–103.

Ehud Reiter and Robert Dale. 2000. *Building Natural Language Generation Systems*. Cambridge University Press, New York, NY, USA.

Keisuke Sakaguchi, Matt Post, and Benjamin Van Durme. 2014. Efficient Elicitation of Annotations for Human Evaluation of Machine Translation. *Proceedings of the Ninth Workshop on Statistical Machine Translation (WMT '14)*, pages 1–11.

Abigail See and Christopher D. Manning. 2017. Get To The Point : Summarization with Pointer-Generator Networks. *Association for Computational Linguistics*, pages 1–18.

Shikhar Sharma, Layla El Asri, Hannes Schulz, and Jeremie Zumer. 2017. Relevance of Unsupervised Metrics in Task-Oriented Dialogue for Evaluating Natural Language Generation.

Shikhar Sharma, Microsoft Maluuba, Jing He, Adeptmind Kaheer Suleman, Hannes Schulz, and Philip Bachman. 2016. Natural Language Generation in Dialogue using Lexicalized and Delexicalized Data.

Inc. SigOpt. 2014. Sigopt reference manual.

Ilya Sutskever, Oriol Vinyals, and Quoc V. Le. 2014. Sequence to Sequence Learning with Neural Networks. pages 1–9.

Jian Tang, Yifan Yang, Sam Carton, Ming Zhang, and Qiaozhu Mei. 2016. Context-aware Natural Language Generation with Recurrent Neural Networks.

Oriol Vinyals, Meire Fortunato, and Navdeep Jaitly. 2015. Pointer Networks.

Bolin Wei, Shuai Lu, Lili Mou, Hao Zhou, Pascal Poupart, Ge Li, and Zhi Jin. 2017. Why Do Neural Dialog Systems Generate Short and Meaningless Replies? A Comparison between Dialog and Translation.

Tsung-Hsien Wen, Milica Gaši, Nikola Mrkši, Pei-Hao Su, David Vandyke, and Steve Young. 2015. Semantically Conditioned LSTM-based Natural Language Generation for Spoken Dialogue Systems. pages 1711–1721.

Tsung-Hsien Wen, David Vandyke, Nikola Mrksic, Milica Gasic, Lina M. Rojas-Barahona, Pei-Hao Su, Stefan Ultes, and Steve Young. 2016. A Network-based End-to-End Trainable Task-oriented Dialogue System. 1:438–449.

Sam Wiseman, Stuart M Shieber, and Alexander M Rush. 2017. Challenges in Data-to-Document Generation.

Chen Xing, Wei Wu, Yu Wu, Jie Liu, Yalou Huang, Ming Zhou, and Wei-Ying Ma. 2016. Topic Augmented Neural Response Generation with a Joint Attention Mechanism. pages 1–9.

Tom Young, Erik Cambria, Iti Chaturvedi, Minlie Huang, Hao Zhou, and Subham Biswas. 2017. Augmenting End-to-End Dialog Systems with Commonsense Knowledge.

Victor Zhong, Caiming Xiong, and Richard Socher. 2017. Seq2SQL: Generating Structured Queries from Natural Language using Reinforcement Learning.

E2E NLG Challenge: Neural Models vs. Templates

Yevgeniy Puzikov and **Iryna Gurevych**
Ubiquitous Knowledge Processing Lab (UKP-TUDA)
Department of Computer Science, Technische Universität Darmstadt
Research Training Group AIPHES
www.ukp.tu-darmstadt.de

Abstract

E2E NLG Challenge is a shared task on
generating restaurant descriptions from sets
of key-value pairs. This paper describes the
results of our participation in the challenge.
We develop a simple, yet effective neural
encoder-decoder model [1] which produces
fluent restaurant descriptions and outperforms a strong baseline. We further analyze
the data provided by the organizers and conclude that the task can also be approached
with a template-based model developed in
just a few hours.

1 Introduction

Natural Language Generation (NLG) is the task of
generating natural language utterances from structured data representations. The E2E NLG Challenge[2] is a shared task which focuses on end-to-
end data-driven NLG methods. These approaches
attract a lot of attention, because they perform joint
learning of textual structure and surface realization
patterns from non-aligned data, which allows for a
significant reduction of the amount of human annotation effort needed for NLG corpus creation (Wen
et al., 2015; Mei et al., 2016; Dušek and Jurcicek,
2016; Lampouras and Vlachos, 2016).

The contribution of our submission to the challenge can be summarized as follows: (1) we show
how exploiting data properties allows us to design
more accurate neural architectures; (2) we develop
a simple template-based system which achieves
performance comparable to neural approaches.

---

[1] https://github.com/UKPLab/e2e-nlg-
challenge-2017
[2] http://www.macs.hw.ac.uk/
InteractionLab/E2E

MR:

name[The Eagle]	*eatType[coffee shop]*
food[French]	*priceRange[moderate]*
customerRating[3/5]	*area[riverside]*
kidsFriendly[yes]	*near[Burger King]*

Human Natural Language Reference:

*"The three star coffee shop, The Eagle, gives families a mid-
priced dining experience featuring a variety of wines and
cheeses. Find The Eagle near Burger King."*

Figure 1: E2E NLG Challenge data specification.

1.1 Task Definition

The organizers of the shared task provided a crowd-
sourced data set of 50k instances in the restaurant
domain (Novikova et al., 2017b). Each training
instance consists of a dialogue act-based meaning
representation (MR) and up to 16 references in
natural language (Figure 1).

The data was collected using pictorial representations as stimuli, with the intention of creating
more natural, informative and diverse human references compared to the ones one might generate
from textual inputs.

The task is to generate an utterance from a given
MR, which is both similar to human-generated reference texts and highly rated by humans. Similarity is assessed using standard evaluation metrics: BLEU (Papineni et al., 2002), NIST (Doddington, 2002), METEOR (Lavie and Agarwal, 2007),
ROUGE-L (Lin, 2004), CIDEr (Vedantam et al.,
2015). However, the final assessment is done via
human ratings obtained using a mixture of crowd-
sourcing and expert annotations.

To facilitate a better assessment of the proposed
approaches, the organizing team used TGen (Dušek
and Jurcicek, 2016), one of the recent E2E data-
driven systems, as a baseline. It is a sequence-to-
sequence neural system with attention (Bahdanau
et al., 2014). TGen uses beam search for decod-

Proceedings of The 11th International Natural Language Generation Conference, pages 463–471,
Tilburg, The Netherlands, November 5-8, 2018. ©2018 Association for Computational Linguistics

ing, incorporates a reranker over the top k outputs, penalizing the candidates that do not verbalize all attributes from the input MR. TGen also includes a delexicalization module which deals with sparsely occurring MR attributes (*name*, *near*) by mapping such values to placeholder tokens when preprocessing the input data, and substituting the placeholders with actual values as a post-processing step.

2   Our Approach

This section describes two different approaches we developed for the shared task.

The first one (Model-D, for "data-driven") is an encoder-decoder neural system which is similar to TGen, but uses a more efficient encoder module. The second approach is a simple template-based model (Model-T, for "template-based") which we developed based on the results of the data analysis.

2.1   Model-D

Model-D was motivated by two important properties of the E2E NLG Challenge data:

- fixed number of unique MR attributes

- low diversity of the lexical instantiations of the MR attribute values

Each input MR contains a fixed number of unique attributes (between three and eight), which allows us to associate a positional id with each attribute and omit the corresponding attribute names (or keys) from the encoding procedure. This shortens the encoded sequence, presumably making the learning procedure easier for the encoder. This also unifies the lengths of input MRs and thus allows us to use simpler and more efficient neural networks which are not sequential and process input sequences in one step (e.g. multilayer perceptron (MLP) networks).

One might argue that using an MLP would be complicated by the fact that neither the number of active (non-null value) input MR keys nor the number of tokens constituting the corresponding values is fixed. For example, an MR key *price* may have a one-token value of "low" or a more lengthy "less than £10". However, realizations of the MR attribute values exhibit low variability: six out of eight keys have less than seven unique values, while the remaining two keys (*name*, *near*) denote named entities and thus are easy to delexicalize. This allows us to treat each value as a single token,

posID	Key	Value
1	area	PAD
2	customerRating	high
3	eatType	PAD
4	familyFriendly	yes
5	food	PAD
6	name	Wrestlers
7	near	PAD
8	priceRange	PAD

Table 1: Input representation of the running example using positional ids.

even if it consists of multiple words (e.g. "more than £30", "Fast food").

Each predicted output is a textual description of a restaurant. As reported by Novikova et al. (2017b), the average number of words per reference is 20.1. We used the value of 50 as a cut-off threshold, filtering out training instances with long restaurant descriptions.

The overall architecture of our model is shown in Figure 2. The system is an encoder-decoder model (Cho et al., 2014b; Sutskever et al., 2014) consisting of three main modules: an embedding matrix, one dense hidden layer as an encoder and a RNN-based decoder with gated recurrent units (GRU) (Cho et al., 2014a).

Let us first describe the input specifications of the model. We will use the following MR instance as a running example:

> *name[Wrestlers]   customerRating[high]*
> *familyFriendly[yes]*

Considering the alphabetic ordering of the MR key names, we can assign positional ids to the keys as shown in Table 1. The remaining five keys are assigned dummy *PAD* values.

Given an instance of a *(MR, text)* pair, we decompose the MR into eight components (mr_j in Figure 2), each corresponding to a value for a unique MR key, and add an end-of-sentence symbol (*EOS*) to denote the end of the encoded sequence. Each component is represented as a high-dimensional embedding vector. Each embedding vector is further mapped to a dense hidden representation via an affine transformation followed by a ReLu (Nair and Hinton, 2010) function. These hidden representations are further used by the decoder network, which in our case is a unidirectional GRU-based RNN with an attention module (Bahdanau et al., 2014). The decoder is initialized with an average of the encoder outputs.

The decoder generates a sequence of tokens, one

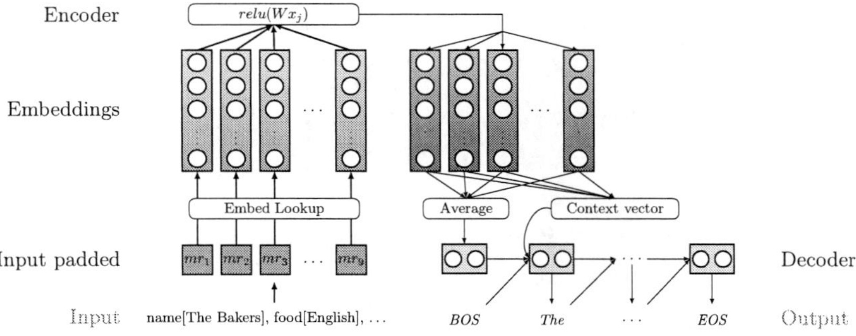

Figure 2: Schematic view of the neural network architecture (Model-D).

token at a time, until it predicts the *EOS* token. Our model employs the greedy search decoding strategy and does not use any reranker module.

2.2 Model-T

Taking into consideration low lexical variation of the MR attribute values, one might be interested in whether it is possible to design a deterministic NLG system to tackle the task. We examined the ways MR attribute keys and values are verbalized in the training data and discovered that the majority of textual descriptions follow a similar ordering of MR attribute verbalizations:

```
[name] is a [familyFriendly] [eatType]
which serves [food] food in the [price]
price range. It has a [customerRating]
customer rating. It is located in the
[area] area, near [near].
```

Here [X] denotes the value of the MR key X. This pattern became a central template of Model-T. Not all MR attribute verbalizations fit into this schema. For example, a key-value pair *customerRating[3 out of 5]* would be verbalized as "... has a 3 out of 5 customer rating", which is not the best phrasing one can come up with. A better way to describe it is "... has a customer rating of 3 out of 5". We incorporate such variations into Model-T with a set of simple rules which modify the general template depending on a specific value of an MR attribute.

As mentioned in Section 2.1, each instance's input can have up to eight MR attributes. In order to account for this fact, we decomposed the general template into smaller components, each corresponding to a specific MR attribute mentioned in the input. We further developed a set of rules which activate each component depending on whether an MR attribute is part of the input. For example, if

Metric	TGen	Model-D	Model-T
BLEU	0.6925	**0.7128** ± 0.013	0.6051
NIST	8.4781	**8.5020** ± 0.092	7.5257
CIDEr	2.3987	**2.4432** ± 0.088	1.6997
ROUGE-L	0.7257	**0.7378** ± 0.015	0.6890
METEOR	0.4703	**0.4770** ± 0.012	0.4678

Table 2: Evaluation results according to automatic metrics (development set).

price is not in the set of input MR attributes, then the general template becomes:

```
[name] is a [familyFriendly] [eatType]
which serves [food] food. It has a
[customerRating] customer rating.
It is located in the [area] area,
near [near].
```

Finally, we also add a simple post-processing step to handle specific punctuation and article choices.

3 Metric Evaluation

Table 2 shows the results of metric evaluation of the systems. Since we were provided with only one TGen prediction file and a single performance score, comparing score distributions is not possible and statistical significance tests are not meaningful due to the non-deterministic nature of the approaches based on neural networks and randomized training procedures (Reimers and Gurevych, 2017). In order to facilitate a fair comparison with other competing systems, we report the mean development score of Model-D (averaged across twenty runs with different random seeds) and performance variance for each automatic metric. Model-T is a deterministic system, so it is sufficient to report the results of a single run.

The results show that Model-D outperforms

Error type	TGen	Model-D	Model-T
dropped contents	9	**49**	0
punctuation errors	1	**12**	0
modified contents	4	4	0
bad grammar	4	1	0

Table 3: Common errors made by the compared models (100 randomly sampled development instances).

TGen as measured by all five metrics, albeit the performance variance is quite large. Model-T clearly scores below both TGen and Model-D. This is expected, since Model-T is not data-driven, and hence the texts it generates might be different from the reference outputs.

Previous studies have shown that widely used automatic metrics (including the ones used in our competition) lack strong correlation with human judgments (Scott and Moore, 2007; Reiter and Belz, 2009; Novikova et al., 2017a). We decided to examine the predictions made by the compared systems on one hundred randomly sampled input instances, focusing on generic errors, which make sense to look out for in many NLG scenarios. Table 3 shows the error types and the number of mistakes found in each of the prediction files. The error types should be self-explanatory (sample predictions are given in Appendix A.2).

As far as the (subjective) manual analysis goes, Model-T outputs descriptions with the best linguistic quality. Table 3 shows that the predictions of the template-based system contain no errors – this is because we incorporated our notion of grammaticality into the templates' definition, which allowed Model-T to avoid the errors found in predictions of the other two approaches.

The majority of errors made by Model-D are either wrong verbalizations of the input MR values or punctuation mistakes. The latter ones are limited to the cases of missing a comma between clauses or not finishing a sentence with a full stop. An easy solution to this problem is adding a postprocessing step which fixes punctuation mistakes before outputting the text.

Crucially, Model-D often drops or modifies some MR attribute values. According to the organizers, 40% of the data by design contain either additional or omitted information on the output side (Novikova et al., 2017b): crowd workers were allowed to not lexicalize attribute values which they deemed unimportant. We decided to examine the

training data and find out if the discrepancies of Model-D were learned from the data.

4 Training Data Analysis

The E2E NLG Challenge is based on noisy data, but the organizers provided multiple instances to account for this noise. In order to better understand the behaviour of Model-D and determine if it took advantage of having multiple references per training instance, we have randomly sampled a hundred training instances and manually checked their linguistic quality. Table 4 shows the most common errors we encountered.

Most mistakes come from ungrammatical constructions, e.g. incorrect phrase attachment decisions ("The price of the food is high and is located ..."), incorrect usage of articles ("located in riverside"), repetitive constructions ("Cotto, an Indian coffee shop located in ..., is an Indian coffee shop ..."). Some restaurant descriptions follow a tweet-style narration pattern which is understandable, but ungrammatical ("The Golden Palace Italian riverside coffee shop price range moderate and customer rating 1 out of 5").

A considerable number of instances have restaurant descriptions which contain information that does not entirely follow from the given input MR. These are cases in which input content elements are modified or dropped, which goes in line with what we observed in the outputs of Model-D.

Some instances (10%) contained descriptions which we marked as questionable due to pragmatic and/or stylistic considerations. For example, restaurants which have *familyFriendly[no]* as part of the input MR are often described by crowd workers as "adults-only" establishments, which has an undesirable connotation. Finally, it is necessary to mention that some crowd workers followed inconsistent spelling and punctuation rules when hyphenating compound modifiers ("family friendly restaurant", "the restaurant is family friendly") or capitalizing MR attributes ("Riverside", "Fast food"). Punctuation errors were mainly restricted to missing a full stop at the end of a restaurant description or failing to delimit sentence clauses with commas.

The results of manual data analysis show that Model-D indeed generates texts that are similar to the restaurant descriptions in the provided data set. Unfortunately, our data-driven approach is not flexible enough to make use of multiple references; it cannot cancel out the noise present in some train-

Error type	Example	%
bad grammar	"it's French food falls within a high price range"	15
modified contents	*area[riverside]* → "city centre"	12
dropped contents	*priceRange[high]* → ∅	10
questionable lexicalization	"Adult-only Chinese restaurant, The Waterman, offers top-rated food in the city centre"	9
punctuation errors	"X is a coffee shop and also a Japanese restaurant great for family and close to Crowne Plaza Hotel"	6

Table 4: Data annotation discrepancies (100 randomly sampled training instances).

	Model-T	Best result
Metric evaluation		
BLEU	0.5657	0.6805
NIST	7.4544	8.7777
METEOR	0.4529	0.4571
ROUGE-L	0.6614	0.7084
CIDEr	1.8206	2.3371
Human evaluation		
Quality	0.228/(2.0, 4.0)/2	0.300/(1.0, 1.0)/1
Naturalness	0.077/(5.0, 10.0)/2	0.211/(1.0, 1.0)/1

Table 5: Final evaluation results on the test set. Human evaluation results have the following format: *score/(range)/cluster*.

ing instances. One way of alleviating this problem could be reformulating the loss function to inform the system about the existence of multiple ways of generating a good restaurant description. Given a training instance, Model-D would generate a corresponding candidate text which could be compared to all human references. Each comparison results in computing a certain cost; the gradients could be then computed on the minimal cost among all comparisons.

4.1 Final Evaluation

For the final submission we have chosen Model-T's predictions – despite lower metric scores, they contained most grammatical outputs and kept all input information in the generated text.

The results of the final evaluation on the test data are presented in Table 5. They were produced by the TrueSkill algorithm (Sakaguchi et al., 2014), which performs pairwise system comparisons and clusters them into groups. For completeness, we include the highest reported scores among all the participants (rightmost column). Note, however, that the numerical scores are not directly interpretable, but the relative ranking of a system in terms of its range and cluster is important – systems within one cluster are considered tied.

Model-T was assigned to the second best cluster both in terms of quality and naturalness, despite the much lower metric scores. Retrospectively, this justifies our decision to choose Model-T instead of Model-D for the final submission. The E2E NLG Challenge focuses on end-to-end data-driven NLG methods, which is why systems like Model-T might not exactly fit into the task setup. Nevertheless, we view such a system as a necessary candidate for comparison, since the E2E NLG Challenge data was designed to learn models that produce "more natural, varied and less template-like system utterances" (Novikova et al., 2017b).

5   Conclusion

In this paper we have presented the results of our participation in the E2E NLG Challenge. We have developed two conceptually different approaches and analyzed their performance, both in quantity and in quality. We have shown that sometimes the costs of developing complex data-driven models are not justified and one is better off approaching the problem with simpler techniques. We hope that our observations and conclusions shed some light on the limitations of modern NLG approaches and possible ways of overcoming them.

Acknowledgments

This work was supported by the German Research Foundation (DFG) under grant No. GU 798/17-1 and the DFG-funded research training group "Adaptive Preparation of Information form Heterogeneous Sources" (AIPHES, GRK 1994/1). The first author of the paper is supported by the FAZIT Foundation scholarship. We thank the anonymous reviewers and our colleagues Michael Bugert, Tristan Miller, Maxime Peyrard, Nils Reimers and Markus Zopf who provided insightful comments and suggestions that greatly assisted our research.

References

Dzmitry Bahdanau, Kyunghyun Cho, and Yoshua Bengio. 2014. Neural Machine Translation by Jointly Learning to Align and Translate. *CoRR*, abs/1409.0473.

Kyunghyun Cho, Bart van Merrienboer, Dzmitry Bahdanau, and Yoshua Bengio. 2014a. On the Properties of Neural Machine Translation: Encoder–Decoder Approaches. In *Proceedings of SSST-8, Eighth Workshop on Syntax, Semantics and Structure in Statistical Translation*, pages 103–111, Doha, Qatar. Association for Computational Linguistics.

Kyunghyun Cho, Bart van Merrienboer, Caglar Gulcehre, Dzmitry Bahdanau, Fethi Bougares, Holger Schwenk, and Yoshua Bengio. 2014b. Learning Phrase Representations Using RNN Encoder–decoder for Statistical Machine Translation. In *Proceedings of the 2014 Conference on Empirical Methods in Natural Language Processing (EMNLP)*, pages 1724–1734, Doha, Qatar. Association for Computational Linguistics.

George Doddington. 2002. Automatic Evaluation of Machine Translation Quality Using N-gram Co-occurrence Statistics. In *Proceedings of the Second International Conference on Human Language Technology Research*, pages 138–145, San Francisco, CA, USA. Morgan Kaufmann Publishers Inc.

Ondřej Dušek and Filip Jurcicek. 2016. Sequence-to-sequence Generation for Spoken Dialogue via Deep Syntax Trees and Strings. In *Proceedings of the 54th Annual Meeting of the Association for Computational Linguistics (Volume 2: Short Papers)*, pages 45–51, Berlin, Germany. Association for Computational Linguistics.

Gerasimos Lampouras and Andreas Vlachos. 2016. Imitation Learning for Language Generation from Unaligned Data. In *Proceedings of COLING 2016, the 26th International Conference on Computational Linguistics: Technical Papers*, pages 1101–1112, Osaka, Japan. The COLING 2016 Organizing Committee.

Alon Lavie and Abhaya Agarwal. 2007. METEOR: An Automatic Metric for MT Evaluation with High Levels of Correlation with Human Judgments. In *Proceedings of the Second Workshop on Statistical Machine Translation*, pages 228–231, Prague, Czech Republic. Association for Computational Linguistics.

Chin-Yew Lin. 2004. ROUGE: a Package for Automatic Evaluation of Summaries. In *Text Summarization Branches Out: Proceedings of the ACL-04 Workshop*, pages 74–81, Barcelona, Spain. Association for Computational Linguistics.

Hongyuan Mei, Mohit Bansal, and Matthew R. Walter. 2016. What to Talk About and How? Selective Generation Using LSTMs with Coarse-to-fine Alignment. In *Proceedings of the 2016 Conference of the North American Chapter of the Association for Computational Linguistics: Human Language Technologies*, pages 720–730, San Diego, California. Association for Computational Linguistics.

Vinod Nair and Geoffrey E. Hinton. 2010. Rectified Linear Units Improve Restricted Boltzmann Machines. In *Proceedings of the 27th International Conference on Machine Learning (ICML)*, pages 807–814, USA. Omnipress.

Jekaterina Novikova, Ondřej Dušek, Amanda Cercas Curry, and Verena Rieser. 2017a. Why We Need New Evaluation Metrics for NLG. In *Proceedings of the 2017 Conference on Empirical Methods in Natural Language Processing*, pages 2231–2242, Copenhagen, Denmark. Association for Computational Linguistics.

Jekaterina Novikova, Ondřej Dušek, and Verena Rieser. 2017b. The E2E Dataset: New Challenges for End-to-end Generation. In *Proceedings of the 18th Annual SIGdial Meeting on Discourse and Dialogue*, pages 201–206, Saarbrücken, Germany. Association for Computational Linguistics.

Kishore Papineni, Salim Roukos, Todd Ward, and Wei-Jing Zhu. 2002. BLEU: a Method for Automatic Evaluation of Machine Translation. In *Proceedings of 40th Annual Meeting of the Association for Computational Linguistics*, pages 311–318, Philadelphia, Pennsylvania, USA. Association for Computational Linguistics.

Nils Reimers and Iryna Gurevych. 2017. Reporting Score Distributions Makes a Difference: Performance Study of LSTM-networks for Sequence Tagging. In *Proceedings of the 2017 Conference on Empirical Methods in Natural Language Processing (EMNLP)*, pages 338–348, Copenhagen, Denmark. Association for Computational Linguistics.

Ehud Reiter and Anja Belz. 2009. An Investigation into the Validity of Some Metrics for Automatically Evaluating Natural Language Generation Systems. *Computational Linguistics*, 35(4):529–558.

Keisuke Sakaguchi, Matt Post, and Benjamin Van Durme. 2014. Efficient Elicitation of Annotations for Human Evaluation of Machine Translation. In *Proceedings of the Ninth Workshop on Statistical Machine Translation*, pages 1–11, Baltimore, Maryland, USA. Association for Computational Linguistics.

Donia Scott and Johanna Moore. 2007. An NLG Evaluation Competition? Eight Reasons to Be Cautious. In *Proceedings of the NSF Workshop on Shared Tasks and Comparative Evaluation in Natural Language Generation*, pages 22–23. National Science Foundation.

Ilya Sutskever, Oriol Vinyals, and Quoc V Le. 2014. Sequence to Sequence Learning with Neural Networks. In Z. Ghahramani, M. Welling, C. Cortes,

N. D. Lawrence, and K. Q. Weinberger, editors, *Advances in Neural Information Processing Systems 27*, pages 3104–3112. Curran Associates, Inc.

Ramakrishna Vedantam, C. Lawrence Zitnick, and Devi Parikh. 2015. Cider: Consensus-based image description evaluation. In *2015 IEEE Conference on Computer Vision and Pattern Recognition (CVPR)*, pages 4566–4575. IEEE Computer Society.

Tsung-Hsien Wen, Milica Gasic, Nikola Mrkšić, Pei-Hao Su, David Vandyke, and Steve Young. 2015. Semantically Conditioned LSTM-based Natural Language Generation for Spoken Dialogue Systems. In *Proceedings of the 2015 Conference on Empirical Methods in Natural Language Processing*, pages 1711–1721, Lisbon, Portugal. Association for Computational Linguistics.

A Supplemental Material

A.1 Manual Data Analysis Results

As mentioned in Section 4, manual analysis of the training data revealed certain annotation problems. Below we provide sentence IDs of the instances which we considered as containing errors:

- modified contents: 4136, 34141, 32915, 35936, 6152, 2005, 1463, 14529, 14339, 21804, 25779, 11049;

- dropped contents: 4136 (price and food), 17455 (familyFriendly), 38742 (area), 1463 (customerRating), 27664 (food, priceRange), 19882 (priceRange), 25779 (customerRating, area), 40293 (food), 807 (familyFriendly), 15216 (familyFriendly);

- ungrammatical: 39810, 1904, 36233, 33671, 28698;
    - tweet-style descriptions: 19425, 38875, 14873;
    - word attachment problems, bad phrasing: 15276, 30950, 31973, 36468, 12442, 18623, 25773;

- punctuation errors: 6152, 14993, 38742, 14339, 35967, 25795;

- questionable realization: customerRating (8806, 24983, 29189), familyFriendly (20220, 10729), priceRange (29189), style (14993, 28362, 32494).

A.2 Example Predictions

The majority of predictions from all three systems are grammatically correct. Here is a random sample:

- **Input:** name[Cocum], eatType[coffee shop], food[English], priceRange[moderate], customerRating[3 out of 5], familyFriendly[no]

- **TGen:** Cocum is a moderately priced coffee shop serving english food. It has a customer rating of 3 out of 5 and is not kid friendly.

- **Model-D:** Cocum is a moderately priced coffee shop serving English food . It is not kid friendly and has a customer rating of 3 out of 5 .

- **Model-T:** Cocum is a coffee shop which serves English food in the moderate price range. It has a customer rating of 3 out of 5. It is not family friendly.

To illustrate common prediction mistakes (regardless of the system), we have hand-picked some samples. Full predictions by all models can be found in the GitHub repository.

A.2.1 Bad Grammar

- **Input:** name[The Wrestlers], eatType[coffee shop], food[Chinese], priceRange[less than £20], area[riverside], familyFriendly[no], near[Raja Indian Cuisine]

- **TGen:** The Wrestlers is a coffee shop providing chinese food in the less than £20 price range. It is located in the riverside. It is near Raja Indian Cuisine. <u>Its no children feel allowed.</u>

- **Model-D:** The Wrestlers is a coffee shop providing Chinese food in the less than £20 price range . It is located in the riverside . It is near Raja Indian Cuisine .

- **Model-T:** The Wrestlers is a coffee shop which serves Chinese food in the price range of less than £20. It is located in the riverside area, near Raja Indian Cuisine. It is not family friendly.

- **Input:** name[Wildwood], eatType[coffee shop], food[English], priceRange[high], customerRating[1 out of 5], near[Ranch]

- **TGen:** Wildwood is a high priced coffee shop that serves english food. It is located near Ranch and has a customer rating of 1 out of 5.

- **Model-D:** Wildwood <u>is</u> a coffee shop near Ranch , serving English food , <u>has</u> a high price range and a customer rating of 1 out of 5 .

- **Model-T:** Wildwood is a coffee shop which serves English food in the high price range. It has a customer rating of 1 out of 5 and is located near Ranch.

A.2.2   Modified and/or Dropped Contents

- **Input:** name[The Golden Palace], eatType[coffee shop], food[English], priceRange[high], customerRating[average], area[riverside]

- **TGen:** The Golden Palace is a high priced coffee shop serving english food in the riverside area. It has an average customer rating.

- **Model-D:** The Golden Palace is a high priced coffee shop located in the city centre .

- **Model-T:** The Golden Palace is a coffee shop which serves English food in the high price range. It has an average customer rating and is located in the riverside area.

A.2.3   Dropped Contents

- **Input:** name[The Eagle], eatType[coffee shop], food[English], priceRange[moderate], customerRating[1 out of 5], area[riverside], familyFriendly[yes], near[Burger King]

- **TGen:** The Eagle is a moderately priced coffee shop that serves english food. It is located in the riverside area near Burger King. It is kid friendly and has a customer rating of 1 out of 5.

- **Model-D:** The Eagle is a moderately priced coffee shop located near Burger King .

- **Model-T:** The Eagle is a family-friendly coffee shop which serves English food in the moderate price range. It has a customer rating of 1 out of 5 and is located in the riverside area, near Burger King.

The E2E NLG Challenge: A Tale of Two Systems

Charese Smiley[1], Elnaz Davoodi [2], Dezhao Song[1], Frank Schilder[1]
[1] Research & Development, Thomson Reuters, 610 Opperman Drive, Eagan, MN, USA
[2] Center for Cognitive Computing, Thomson Reuters, 120 Bremner Blvd, Toronto, ON, M5J 3A8, CA
firstname.lastname@thomsonreuters.com

Abstract

This paper presents the two systems we entered into the 2017 E2E NLG Challenge: TemplGen, a templated-based system and SeqGen, a neural network-based system. Through the automatic evaluation, SeqGen achieved competitive results compared to the template-based approach and to other participating systems as well. In addition to the automatic evaluation, in this paper we present and discuss the human evaluation results of our two systems.

1 Introduction

This paper describes our two primary systems for the 2017 E2E NLG Challenge (Novikova et al., 2017): (1) TemplGen, a template-based system that automatically mined templates and (Smiley et al., 2018) (2) SeqGen, a neural network system based on the encoder-decoder architecture (Davoodi et al., 2018).

This NLG challenge involves taking a meaning representation (MR) as input and generating natural language output from it. Many existing NLG systems are template-based because it is easier to control the correctness and the grammaticality of the generated text. For this competition, we explored two approaches, i.e., template-based and neural network-based, in order to examine whether a sequence-to-sequence model based on neural networks would produce better results than a template-based system.

We first briefly introduce the challenge and its dataset in Section 2. We then present the details of our two systems in Section 3. We demonstrate and discuss the results of our systems in Section 4 and conclude in Section 5.

2 The E2E NLG Challenge

The E2E NLG challenge is concerned with the restaurant domain and the dataset was crowd-sourced via CrowdFlower (Novikova et al., 2016). The crowdsourced dataset consists of 50,602 instances derived from 5,751 unique MRs (Novikova et al., 2017), and it is larger than previous end-to-end datasets, such as BAGEL (Mairesse et al., 2010) and SF Hotels/Restaurants (Wen et al., 2015).

While creating this dataset, crowd workers were asked to create a verbalization based on a given MR. They were allowed to omit information that they did not find useful. Each MR could contain three to eight different attributes selected from all available attributes: *name, eat type, food, price range, customer rating, area, family friendly*, and *near*. In 40% of the instances, verbalizations contain either omissions or additional information. The dataset is split in a 76.5/8.5/15 ratio into training, development, and test.

The following sample shows a MR and its corresponding natural language (NL) output:

MR:
name [Alimentum],
area [city centre],
familyFriendly [no]

NL:
There is a place in the city centre, Alimentum, that is not family-friendly.

3 Our Two Participating Systems

Many NLG systems are based on templates because the system developers can relatively easily control the system to ensure both grammatical and semantic correctness. However, due to the lack of variability of the used templates, such systems

Proceedings of The 11th International Natural Language Generation Conference, pages 472–477,
Tilburg, The Netherlands, November 5-8, 2018. ©2018 Association for Computational Linguistics

may produce language that does not sound natural and is often perceived as repetitive.

Another type of NLG system is based on neural networks. Although such systems have shown promising results, training such models/systems requires a large amount of training data. Furthermore, neural network-based systems may produce ungrammatical text often with repetitions in the same sentences. There is also no guarantee that the generated text is actually factually correct.

3.1 TemplGen : a Template-based System

First, we delexicalized the data using string match to automatically replace the attribute values contained in the MR with the attribute name (Oraby et al., 2017). The attribute values were largely consistent, but for additional coverage we added a few fuzzy matching rules to account for variants such as *Crown* vs. *Crowne*. We did this for all attributes except for *family friendly* which has a wide range of potential realizations (e.g., positive: *children are welcome, kid friendly*, or negative: *adult only, not for kids*). Therefore, we use a binary yes/no value for that attribute. For each delexicalized sentence, we check to see whether all attributes in the MR were captured during the delexicalization process. If there is a difference between the number of attributes in the MR and the number that were successfully delexicalized, we discard that instance. In total, we discarded roughly 45% of the training sentences. This is slightly more than the 40% of instances in the data that contained omissions or additions. We then use the delexicalized templates to create a dictionary look-up of the MRs.

With the templates now identified, we identify templates that are composed of multiple sentences and split along sentence boundaries. The individual sentences are then stored as partial templates along with the attributes reverse engineered from the templates. Table 1 shows the original template containing 2 sentences and the derived partial templates containing one sentence each. Through this process we collect templates containing all 8 of the attributes individually as well as combinations from 2-8. By extracting individual templates for each attribute alone, we guarantee that we can cover any combination of attributes by generating up to 8 separate sentences although this would not sound very natural.

In the testing phase, we are supplied with an MR which may consist of an unseen combination of attributes. We treat the attributes of the MR as a set, filling the templates using an algorithm that selects the best fitting template.

All templates in the candidate set are relexicalized with the current MR. From there we filter candidates by performing basic sentiment analysis using the NLTK[1] implementation of the VADER sentiment analysis tool (Gilbert, 2014) and removing sentences whose sentiment is incongruent (e.g., great restaurant described as having low rating). To determine this, we look for sentences with non-neutral scores for both positive and negative polarities but no word indicating a reversal such as *however*. The final output from the candidate set is selected at random.

3.2 The sequence-to-sequence system

Our sequence-to-sequence system consists of three main components: Delexicalization, Seq-to-Seq model, and Relexicalization.

Delexicalization. One of the challenges in NLG is generating both semantically and grammatically accurate texts. In order to train a satisfying seq-to-seq model, it is often required to have a large amount of parallel texts. However, among the attributes of the E2E data, most of the non-categorical attributes are very sparse which makes the learning process difficult. Thus, in order to generate accurate sentences based on the meaning representations, we delexicalized the values of some of the attributes to avoid data sparsity (Mairesse et al., 2010; Wen et al., 2015).

The delexicalization process involves replacing the values of the attributes with placeholders. Among the E2E attributes, we delexicalized the values of the attributes which seem to take a value from an open set of values. These include *name*, *price range*, *customer rating* and *near*. We delexicalized both the meaning representations and their corresponding natural language sentences. Delexicalizing *price range* and *customer rating* is more challenging than the others because both attributes have more value variations in the meaning representations and the natural language texts than the other attributes do. Hence, the learning task is between a MR template and a NL template.

Table 2 shows an example of a delexicalized meaning representation and its corresponding delexicalized natural language sentence. The

---

[1]http://www.nltk.org

	Attributes	**Template**
Original	customer rating, name, eat-Type, food, near, area	With a rating of _CUSTOMER RATING_, _NAME_ _EATTYPE_ serves _FOOD_ food. It is located near _NEAR_ and _AREA_.
Partial 1	customer rating, name, eat-Type, food	With a rating of _CUSTOMER RATING_, _NAME_ _EATTYPE_ serves _FOOD_ food.
Partial 2	near, area	It is located near _NEAR_ and _AREA_.

Table 1: Partial templates extracted from training data.

delexicalized meaning representations are used as input of our Sequence-to-Sequence model, in which the delexicalized natural language sentences are the model target output.

Seq-to-Seq Model. Neural Machine Translation (Kalchbrenner and Blunsom, 2013; Sutskever et al., 2014; Cho et al., 2014) is an end-to-end approach for machine translation. Sequence-to-Sequence models adopt the encoder-decoder architecture, in which an input sequence is encoded by the encoder and the output sequence is generated by the decoder (Jean et al., 2014; Luong et al., 2014; Sennrich et al., 2016).

In this challenge, we considered the task as a translation problem which takes a sequence of tokens (i.e., delexicalized meaning representations) as input, and generates a sequence of tokens (i.e., delexicalized natural language sentences) in the same language. In our current implementation, we used the state-of-the-art neural machine translation model (Britz et al., 2017). Table 3 shows the parameters of SeqGen model.

Relexicalization. As a last step, the placeholders in the automatically generated delexicalized sentences should be replaced by their actual values. Thus, for the training and development set, we kept the values of the attributes as they appeared in the original sentences and relexicalized the placeholders with these values. Since there is no corresponding sentence for meaning representations of the test sets, we used the value of the placeholders as they appeared in the original meaning representation. This may have a negative impact on the quality and naturalness.

4 Results and Discussion

4.1 Results

Evaluation for the E2E was conducted using both automatic metrics and human scoring. These results are given in Table 4 with the automatic scoring described in Section 4.2 and the human evalu-

ation in Section 4.3.

4.2 Automatic Scoring

Table 4 shows the results comparing the baseline system with the results from our systems. Systems were evaluated automatically using BLEU (Papineni et al., 2002), NIST (Doddington, 2002), METEOR (Denkowski and Lavie, 2014), ROUGE_L (Lin, 2004), and CIDEr (Vedantam et al., 2015). The first column contains the results for the BASELINE system – a sequence-to-sequence model with attention (Dušek et al., 2018). The other two columns in the table contain the automatic scores for our system where the results for TemplGen is composed of both the training and development data and SeqGen which is the sequence-to-sequence model with beam search decoder with beam size of 5. We tried a beam search decoder with various beam sizes and observed that the search decoder with beam size of 5 achieved the best results compared to the search decoder with larger beam sizes as well as the decoder with no beam search.

For the automatic metrics, none of our systems outperformed the baseline system. However, the SeqGen system outperforms TemplGen and exhibits similar performance to the baseline model which is also sequence-to-sequence based.

4.3 Human Evaluation

For the human evaluation metric (Dušek et al., 2018), raters were shown the reference sentence along with 5 generations from various competing systems. They were asked to rank the generations for *quality* and *naturalness*. For *quality*, raters were given the MR along with the system reference output. They were asked to rank the output based on grammatical correctness, fluency, adequacy, and so on. *Naturalness* measures whether the utterance could have been written by a native speaker. Raters were not given the MR for the

Original Meaning Representation	Original Natural Language Sentences
name [The Rice Boat], food [Indian], area [city centre], near [Express by Holiday Inn]	The Rice Boat is an Indian restaurant in the city centre near the Express by Holiday Inn

Delexicalized Meaning Representation	Delexicalized Natural Language Sentences
name [*name_x*], food [Indian], area [city centre], near [*near_x*]	*name_x* is an Indian restaurant in the city centre near *near_x*

Table 2: An example of the delexicalized MR and its corresponding natural language sentence.

Hyper-parameter	Parameter value
Batch size	16
# of hidden units	256
# of encoder layers	3
# of decoder layers	1
RNN cell	GRU
Optimizer	Adam
Input Dropout	1.0
Output Dropout	0.5

Table 3: The list of hyper-parameters tuned for SeqGen model.

Metric	Baseline	TemplGen	SeqGen
BLEU	0.6593	0.4202	0.6336
NIST	8.6094	6.7686	8.1848
METEOR	0.4483	0.3968	0.4322
ROUGE_L	0.6850	0.5481	0.6828
CIDEr	2.2338	1.4389	2.1425
Quality	1 of 5	3 of 5	4 of 5
Naturalness	1 of 5	5 of 5	3 of 5

Table 4: The results of automatic and human evaluation on the test set.

naturalness evaluation. Thus, this metric does not take into account faithfulness to the MR. The results of the human evaluation are based on the system's inferred TrueSkill score (Sakaguchi et al., 2014) which is computed based on pairwise comparisons between systems. For quality, TemplGen out scored SeqGen ranking 3rd and 4th, respectively, out of 5 clusters of systems. The results are reversed for naturalness, with SeqGen performing better than TemplGen ranking 3rd and 5th, respectively, out of 5 clusters. Systems within each cluster are considered statistically indistinguishable.

4.4 Discussion

For the human evaluations, we scored in the third cluster of groups. For a production NLG sys-tem, quality of generations would be the most important metric as users would expect faithfulness to the underlying data along with other standards such as grammaticality. Because a variety of features are encompassed within the metric of *quality* (e.g., fluency and adequacy), it is difficult to determine where our algorithm succeeds and fails. To help determine this, we took a closer look at 25 sentences generated by our SeqGen and TemplGen models.

Although SeqGen is an end-to-end approach, there are some limitations. First, we do not have control of the decoder to make it generate all the attributes that appeared in the meaning representations. Thus, the model may suffer from not generating all the attributes or generating extra attributes. In both cases, the relexicalization component either cannot relexicalize all the placeholders or there are extra placeholders that cannot be relexicalized. The first row in Table 5 shows an example of SeqGen generated sentence in which it does not generate text corresponding to all the attributes in the MR. Another issue that we noticed in the generated sentences by SeqGen model is related to the quality of the natural language sentences in terms of grammatically correctness. This issue may be due to the delexicalization. The scond row in Table 5 shows an example where the sentence is grammatically incorrect. In this example, the issue is caused by *less than £20ly priced*.

As for TemplGen, overall, we find that it did not perform well when evaluated on the automatic metrics. This is not particularly surprising as we did not make any attempts to optimize TemplGen for these metrics.

On the other hand, our analysis of the sentences generated by the TemplGen model shows that every generation contained all of the attributes from the MR while one contained additional information. However, we noticed a few issues with fluency that may have contributed to lowering the

<table>
<tr><td colspan="3" align="center">Examples generated by SeqGen model</td></tr>
<tr><td>#</td><td>MR</td><td>NL</td></tr>
<tr><td>1</td><td>name[The Phoenix], eatType[restaurant], food[French], priceRange[cheap], area[riverside], familyFriendly[yes], near[Raja Indian Cuisine]</td><td>The Phoenix is a family friendly restaurant located near Raja Indian Cuisine.</td></tr>
<tr><td>2</td><td>name[The Phoenix], eatType[restaurant], food[Fast food], priceRange[less than £20], area[city centre], familyFriendly[no], near[Raja Indian Cuisine]</td><td>The phoenix is a less than £20ly priced fast food restaurant located in the city centre near Raja Indian Cuisine. It is not child friendly.</td></tr>
<tr><td colspan="3" align="center">Examples generated by TempGen model</td></tr>
<tr><td>1</td><td>name[The Waterman], eatType[restaurant], food[Indian], priceRange[moderate], area[city centre], familyFriendly[yes], near[Raja Indian Cuisine]</td><td>The Waterman is a child friendly restaurant which serves moderately priced Indian food. It is near Raja Indian Cuisine in the city centre area.</td></tr>
<tr><td>2</td><td>name[The Plough], eatType[pub], food[Chinese], priceRange[high], area[riverside], familyFriendly[yes], near[Raja Indian Cuisine],</td><td>The Plough, a Chinese pub near Raja Indian Cuisine, offers family friendly riverside dining for high.</td></tr>
</table>

Table 5: Sample natural language output of MRs generated by both models.

scores for *quality*. Of the suboptimal generations, some were perhaps less fluent due to being composed of multiple sentences as a result of our strategy of randomly selecting a partition of attributes that satisfies the MR. Prioritizing partitions that encompass more attributes may be a simple solution. Finally, other generations sound disfluent due to issues with word choice such as the selection of the partial template containing just an adjective to insert *high* from the MR where a noun phrase such as *a high price* would have sounded more natural (cf. last row in Table 5).

For future work, we will put some restrictions on the decoder such that it would not generate repetitive tokens (including placeholders) and also push the model to generate all the attributes mentioned in the corresponding meaning representation.We also plan to use the released data set for generating semantically similar sentences for the meaning representations.

5 Conclusions

In this paper, we described our two systems for the 2017 E2E challenge: a rule-based system and a sequence-to-sequence neural network system. Although our rule-based system did not score well by automatic metrics, it was able to deliver sentences which are faithful to their underlying MR. On the other hand, our sequence-to-sequence system was also able to achieve decent performance compared to other participating systems.

References

D. Britz, A. Goldie, T. Luong, and Q. Le. 2017. Massive Exploration of Neural Machine Translation Architectures. *arXiv preprint arXiv:1703.03906*.

Kyunghyun Cho, Bart Van Merriënboer, Caglar Gulcehre, Dzmitry Bahdanau, Fethi Bougares, Holger Schwenk, and Yoshua Bengio. 2014. Learning phrase representations using RNN encoder-decoder for statistical machine translation. *arXiv preprint arXiv:1406.1078*.

Elnaz Davoodi, Charese Smiley, Dezhao Song, and Frank Schilder. 2018. The E2E NLG Challenge: Training a Sequence-to-Sequence Approach for Meaning Representation to Natural Language Sentences. In *(in prep. for INLG conference)*.

Michael Denkowski and Alon Lavie. 2014. Meteor universal: Language specific translation evaluation for any target language. In *Proceedings of the ninth workshop on statistical machine translation*, pages 376–380.

George Doddington. 2002. Automatic evaluation of machine translation quality using n-gram co-occurrence statistics. In *Proceedings of the second international conference on Human Language Technology Research*, pages 138–145. Morgan Kaufmann Publishers Inc.

Ondrej Dušek, Jekaterina Novikova, and Verena Rieser. 2018. Findings of the E2E NLG challenge. In *(in prep.)*.

CJ Hutto Eric Gilbert. 2014. Vader: A parsimonious rule-based model for sentiment analysis of social media text. In *Eighth International Conference on Weblogs and Social Media (ICWSM-14). Available at (20/04/16) http://comp. social. gatech. edu/papers/icwsm14. vader. hutto. pdf.*

Sébastien Jean, Kyunghyun Cho, Roland Memisevic, and Yoshua Bengio. 2014. On using very large target vocabulary for neural machine translation. *arXiv preprint arXiv:1412.2007*.

Nal Kalchbrenner and Phil Blunsom. 2013. Recurrent continuous translation models. In *Proceedings of the 2013 Conference on Empirical Methods in Natural Language Processing, EMNLP 2013, 18-21 October 2013, Grand Hyatt Seattle, Seattle, Washington, USA, A meeting of SIGDAT, a Special Interest Group of the ACL*, pages 1700–1709.

Chin-Yew Lin. 2004. Rouge: A package for automatic evaluation of summaries. *Text Summarization Branches Out*.

Minh-Thang Luong, Ilya Sutskever, Quoc V Le, Oriol Vinyals, and Wojciech Zaremba. 2014. Addressing the rare word problem in neural machine translation. *arXiv preprint arXiv:1410.8206*.

François Mairesse, Milica Gašić, Filip Jurčíček, Simon Keizer, Blaise Thomson, Kai Yu, and Steve Young. 2010. Phrase-based statistical language generation using graphical models and active learning. In *Proceedings of the 48th Annual Meeting of the Association for Computational Linguistics*, pages 1552–1561. Association for Computational Linguistics.

Jekaterina Novikova, Ondrej Dušek, and Verena Rieser. 2017. The E2E dataset: New challenges for end-to-end generation. In *Proceedings of the 18th Annual Meeting of the Special Interest Group on Discourse and Dialogue*, Saarbrücken, Germany. ArXiv:1706.09254.

Jekaterina Novikova, Oliver Lemon, and Verena Rieser. 2016. Crowd-sourcing nlg data: Pictures elicit better data. *arXiv preprint arXiv:1608.00339*.

Shereen Oraby, Sheideh Homayon, and Marilyn Walker. 2017. Harvesting creative templates for generating stylistically varied restaurant reviews. In *Proceedings of the Workshop on Stylistic Variation*, pages 28–36.

Kishore Papineni, Salim Roukos, Todd Ward, and Wei-Jing Zhu. 2002. Bleu: a method for automatic evaluation of machine translation. In *Proceedings of the 40th annual meeting on association for computational linguistics*, pages 311–318. Association for Computational Linguistics.

Keisuke Sakaguchi, Matt Post, and Benjamin Van Durme. 2014. Efficient elicitation of annotations for human evaluation of machine translation. In *WMT@ ACL*, pages 1–11.

Rico Sennrich, Barry Haddow, and Alexandra Birch. 2016. Edinburgh neural machine translation systems for wmt 16. *arXiv preprint arXiv:1606.02891*.

Charese Smiley, Elnaz Davoodi, Dezhao Song, and Frank Schilder. 2018. The E2E NLG Challenge: End-to-End Generation through Partial Template Mining. In *(in prep.)*.

Ilya Sutskever, Oriol Vinyals, and Quoc V Le. 2014. Sequence to sequence learning with neural networks. In *Advances in neural information processing systems*, pages 3104–3112.

Ramakrishna Vedantam, C Lawrence Zitnick, and Devi Parikh. 2015. Cider: Consensus-based image description evaluation. In *Proceedings of the IEEE conference on computer vision and pattern recognition*, pages 4566–4575.

Tsung-Hsien Wen, Milica Gasic, Nikola Mrksic, Pei-Hao Su, David Vandyke, and Steve Young. 2015. Semantically conditioned lstm-based natural language generation for spoken dialogue systems. *arXiv preprint arXiv:1508.01745*.

Interactive health insight miner: an adaptive, semantic-based approach

Isabel Funke
isabel.funke@gmail.com

Rim Helaoui and **Aki Härmä**
Philips Research
High Tech Campus 34
5656 AE Eindhoven
The Netherlands
rim.helaoui@philips.com
aki.harma@philips.com

Abstract

E-health applications aim to support the user in adopting healthy habits. An important feature is to provide insights into the user's lifestyle. To actively engage the user in the insight mining process, we propose an ontology-based framework with a Controlled Natural Language interface, which enables the user to ask for specific insights and to customize personal information.

1 Introduction

E-health services based on wearable sensors, such as smart watches, need methods to discover insights from the sensor data. *Insights* describe user-specific behavior patterns, or habits, that are relevant for guiding the user towards a healthy lifestyle. For example, an insight might reveal that the user is especially sedentary at the weekend.

Blind discovery of significant insights is essentially a search problem and requires a lot of data. If the discovery of insights took place in dialogue with the user, the search problem could be restricted to areas that interest the user the most. Also, the user could provide complementary information that cannot be inferred from the data.

In this paper, we propose a description logics-based approach towards an interactive system for the discovery of insights. Concretely, we describe an ontological framework implemented on top of a statistical insight miner (Härmä and Helaoui, 2016) that enables the natural language-based retrieval and customization of insights from wearable sensor data.

2 Proposed framework

Our framework consists of five layers, see Fig. 1. Data is acquired in the *data layer* and further processed in the *information extraction layer*. The *information & knowledge integration layer* abstracts

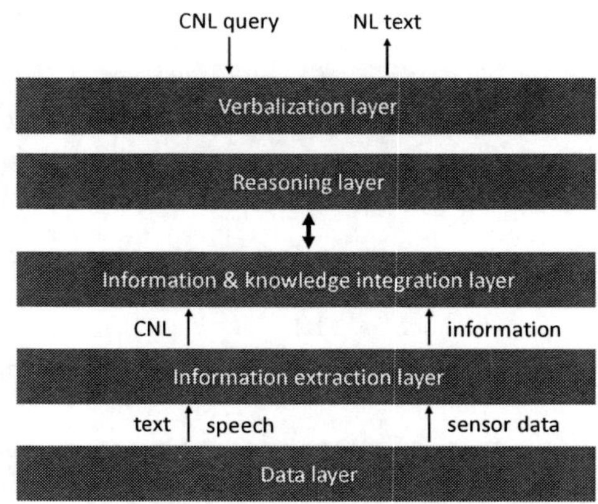

Figure 1: Proposed framework for the interactive health insight miner.

the extracted information into formal *facts*. The resulting knowledge base can include user- and situation-specific information as well as common sense knowledge. The *reasoning layer* leverages logic-based algorithms that reason with the available knowledge. The *verbalization layer* transforms the facts into coherent and comprehensible natural language (NL) messages. Similar systems for *data-to-text* summarization have been proposed in the literature (e.g. Portet et al., 2009).

We additionally introduce a *Controlled Natural Language (CNL)*. It is a formal language that can be translated unambiguously into knowledge base facts, but is also understandable by humans. By adopting the CNL, the user can interact with the system, i.e., add and query facts from the knowledge base. Natural language or spoken text can be fed into the system after translation into CNL.

3 Representing, summarizing and verbalizing insights

The user's lifestyle is described by an *ontology* that contains the routines, habits, and targets of the

Proceedings of The 11th International Natural Language Generation Conference, pages 478–479,
Tilburg, The Netherlands, November 5-8, 2018. ©2018 Association for Computational Linguistics

user. These concepts are leveraged to represent insights as knowledge base facts.

Inspired by NaturalOWL (Galanis and Androutsopoulos, 2007), we include *lexical annotations* in the ontology, which specify how ontology concepts are to be translated into natural text. This way, the ontology also acts as a lexicon. We include the lexical categories (e.g., noun, determiner, preposition, or verb) in the annotations to facilitate the use of standard *Natural Language Generation (NLG)* techniques, such as adapting verb conjugations, adapting the verb tense, or aggregating sentence parts.

To enable user interaction, we specify a CNL based on the vocabulary defined in the ontology. The CNL plays the role of a human and machine understandable interface which allows to directly map the user's input to the formal concepts of the ontology. This way, the user can add personal information to the system, e.g., "On Monday at work, I play tennis". This statement will be formalized as a fact and added to the knowledge base. The CNL also provides the basis for verbalizing the system's responses to the user's queries, such as "What are insights about Sunday afternoon?" We use the *Backus-Naur* form to specify the CNL as a context-free grammar.

To create an NL summary of a number of insights, we implement the following NLG steps (Bouayad-Agha et al., 2014): (1) *Content selection*: We let the user ask for specific insights, for example insights about their step count on Sunday. (2) *Discourse planning*: We group those insights together that are semantically related. The insights are first grouped by the measurement to which they refer (e.g. step count) and then ordered within each group from more general to more specific. For the grouping and ordering steps, we leverage our semantic model (ontology) and apply reasoning algorithms to determine which relationships hold between which insights. (3) *Lexicalization*: We follow a template-based approach using the lexical annotations in the ontology. (4) *Aggregation*: We verbalize each group of equally specific insights using an aggregation template. Finally, for (5) *realization*, we use the realization engine SimpleNLG (Gatt and Reiter, 2009).

4   Implementation

We demonstrate the viability of our framework by implementing one use case related to lifestyle insight mining. The ontology is implemented in OWL using the Protégé[1] editor. We use OWL API[2] 4.1.3 together with the reasoner HermiT[3] 1.3.8 to implement our system in Java. To implement the verbalization functionality, we build upon the library SimpleNLG[4].

5   Example run

> What are insights about my sedentary time on Sunday?
> *On Sunday your sedentary time is lower than on Tuesday, Friday, Wednesday or Thursday.*
On Sunday in the afternoon your sedentary time is lower than on Friday, Wednesday, Thursday or Tuesday in the afternoon.
> What are insights about when I go running?
> *Could not find any insights about this.*
> On Sunday in the afternoon, I go running.
> What are insights about when I go running?
> *On Sunday in the afternoon when you go running your sedentary time is lower than on Tuesday, Friday, Thursday or Wednesday in the afternoon.*

References

Nadjet Bouayad-Agha, Gerard Casamayor, and Leo Wanner. 2014. Natural language generation in the context of the semantic web. *Semantic Web*, 5(6):493–513.

Dimitrios Galanis and Ion Androutsopoulos. 2007. Generating multilingual descriptions from linguistically annotated OWL ontologies: the NaturalOWL system. In *Proceedings of the 11th European Workshop on Natural Language Generation*, pages 143–146.

Albert Gatt and Ehud Reiter. 2009. SimpleNLG: A realisation engine for practical applications. In *Proceedings of the 12th European Workshop on Natural Language Generation*, pages 90–93.

Aki Härmä and Rim Helaoui. 2016. Probabilistic scoring of validated insights for personal health services. In *2016 IEEE Symposium Series on Computational Intelligence (SSCI)*, pages 1–6.

François Portet, Ehud Reiter, Albert Gatt, Jim Hunter, Somayajulu Sripada, Yvonne Freer, and Cindy Sykes. 2009. Automatic generation of textual summaries from neonatal intensive care data. *Artificial Intelligence*, 173(7-8):789–816.

---

[1] http://protege.stanford.edu/
[2] https://github.com/owlcs/owlapi
[3] http://www.hermit-reasoner.com/
[4] https://github.com/simplenlg/ simplenlg

Multi-Language Surface Realisation as REST API based NLG Microservice

Andreas Madsack, Johanna Heininger, Nyamsuren Davaasambuu,
Vitaliia Voronik, Michael Käufl and Robert Weißgraeber

AX Semantics, Stuttgart, Germany
`{firstname.lastname}@ax-semantics.com`

Abstract

We present a readily available API that solves the morphology component for surface realizers in 10 languages (e.g., English, German and Finnish) for any topic and is available as REST API. This can be used to add morphology to any kind of NLG application (e.g., a multi-language chatbot), without requiring computational linguistic knowledge by the integrator.

1 Introduction

The proliferation of chatbots changed the way we see user interfaces. Alexa, Siri or Cortana want to draw us into a conversation, causing two challenges from a "natural" language perspective: grammar and context. Services like RASA or Google's Dialogflow, only provide the use of templates for the responses. In languages where the grammatical agreement is mostly represented by a variation for singular or plural this is fairly easy. However, for a language like German, French, or even Russian you have to write a large set of templates – or simplify your answers, consequently restricting your creativity and eliminating the naturalness of the responses.

Having implemented a few successful projects building chatbots using our NLG system (Weiß-graeber and Madsack, 2017), we saw the need to open up some underlying parts of our system to enable deeply integrated and componentized approaches. Using existing complete NLG systems for projects like chatbots works, but demands learning to use a system designed not to generate dialogues but complete articles. Instead of using our NLG system you may want a simpler way for story building, and possible integrations with the chatbot-serving app and data, for adding context from data signals while rendering your text response.

Whatever you are using to generate context, response interference and response context – for example from results given based on the parse of the Natural Language Understanding system you are using – your response has to be enriched with grammatical agreement.

2 Example: Dialogue interface for an e-commerce system

As an example, we will use a fictional order status update from an e-commerce system sent to the customer. The system should respond to the customer by using a fully grammatical sentence – and not only a list of products – in the customer's language. These messages can be personalized and used with mixed (unknown) languages and products where a templating approach can not guarantee to be grammatically accurate.

In English a potential response message could be: "We confirm your order of two new black TVs and an Amazon Echo".

3 Solution

In this paper we describe an approach that offers an intermediate solution for this problem, that is neither about writing simple templates, nor using a complete NLG system. Instead it uses a "Grammar API" microservice for the morphology components of the surface realiser and otherwise uses openly available software tools in the application chain.

This API offers three endpoints to allow granular access to morphological components.

The first one is *verb*. Given *tense, number, person*, and *gender* the inflected verb is returned. For example in Finnish providing *lemma=sanoa, tense=present, number=s*, and *person=1st* returns *sanon (to say → I say)*.

Proceedings of The 11th International Natural Language Generation Conference, pages 480–481,
Tilburg, The Netherlands, November 5-8, 2018. ©2018 Association for Computational Linguistics

language	lemma	parameters				result
en-us	TV	`adjs=[new, black]`	`prep=of`	`conj=' '`	`num=2`	of two new black TVs
		`num_type=cardinal`				
nl-nl	televisie	`adjs=[nieuw, zwart]`	`prep=van`		`num=2`	van twee nieuwe, zwarte televisies
		`num_type=cardinal`				
fi-fi	televisio	`adjs=[uusi, musta]`	`case=ela`		`num=2`	kahdesta uudesta, mustasta televisiosta
		`num_type=cardinal`				
ru-ru	телевизор	`adjs=[новый,чёрный]`	`num=2`		`case=gen`	двух новых, чёрных телевизоров
		`num_type=cardinal`				

Table 1: Examples for API parameters with resulting nounphrases

The second api endpoint is *quantifier*. The numeral_type parameter sets ordinal or cardinal and also the value of the numeral needs to be set: e.g., in Dutch providing *num_type=ordinal, num=3*, and *gender=f* returns *derde* (*third*).

The third and most interesting endpoint is *nounphrase*. A nounphrase consists of a noun and optionally also of one or more adjectives, a determiner, a quantifier, and/or a preposition. The need for case, gender, or animacy depends on the language. See table 1 for some examples.

3.1 API backend

The inflection is based on grammatical algorithms that run through a decision chain for each request, where all grammatical features of the language are implemented.

Corner-cases are covered by using lexicon entries. Grammatical features are implemented globally in a general way, and then added in each language by its individual configuration.

Languages covered by the first release of the Grammar API include English, German, French, Dutch, Spanish, Portuguese, Italian, Czech, Russian, and Finnish.

4 Related Work

Especially in academic works, the reference system to embed a surface realizer into one's own projects is *SimpleNLG* (Gatt and Reiter, 2009), mostly because it is the only openly accessible component.

Having to add a local library into your system does not follow modern software architecture methodologies, where cloud based services are readily available to cover all tasks of your toolchain and only need to be plugged in together with glue code, e.g. Dialogflow.

5 Availability

The Grammar API is available as a commercial web service for industrial applications, with English offered for free. Academic institutions and researchers however can get access to the API for all languages at no cost. For more information see `https://301.ax/grammar-api/`.

6 Conclusion and Future Work

By providing access to the grammar subcomponents from our integrated NLG systems, emerging use cases where NLG is integrated into other systems can be supported, allowing to build NLG-enabled applications faster than ever by lowering the barrier-to-entry on computational linguistics know how for software developers.

In our current work we concentrate on two main aspects that will be released into the API:

(1) Backend optimisations inside the algorithms, replacing some of the rule-based methods with statistics-based components.

(2) Providing expanded API endpoints, e.g. making it possible to render complete parts of a sentence from POS-Tag information.

Additionally, our microservice can be used as a surface realizer for NLG tasks in other applications.

References

Albert Gatt and Ehud Reiter. 2009. SimpleNLG: A realisation engine for practical applications. In *Proceedings of the 12th European Workshop on Natural Language Generation (ENLG 2009)*, pages 90–93, Athens, Greece. Association for Computational Linguistics.

Robert Weißgraeber and Andreas Madsack. 2017. A working, non-trivial, topically indifferent nlg system for 17 languages. In *Proceedings of the 10th International Conference on Natural Language Generation*, pages 156–157. Association for Computational Linguistics.

Statistical NLG for Generating the Content and Form of Referring Expressions

Xiao Li and **Kees van Deemter** and **Chenghua Lin**
Computing Science department
University of Aberdeen
Aberdeen, UK
{xiao.li, k.vdeemter, chenghua.lin}@abdn.ac.uk

Abstract

This paper argues that a new generic approach to statistical NLG can be made to perform Referring Expression Generation (REG) successfully. The model does not only select attributes and values for referring to a target referent, but also performs Linguistic Realisation, generating an actual Noun Phrase. Our evaluations suggest that the attribute selection aspect of the algorithm exceeds classic REG algorithms, while the Noun Phrases generated are as similar to those in a previously developed corpus as were Noun Phrases produced by a new set of human speakers.

1 Introduction

Referring Expressions Generation (REG) is a subtask of Natural Language Generation (NLG) that decides how to distinguish a target referent from its distractors, as when we say "the sofa", "the red sofa", and so on, to distinguish the referent from other furniture. Most current REG algorithms are rule-based (Gatt and Krahmer, 2018), though Machine Learning is also starting to be used (e.g. Di Fabbrizio et al., 2008).

REG is usually treated as an independent stage or component of NLG pipelines (e.g. Reiter and Dale, 2000; Reiter, 2007; Gatt and Krahmer, 2018; Di Fabbrizio et al., 2008). The present paper changes the relationship between NLG and REG: it regards REG as a special case of usual NLG, and proposes a vector-based algorithm to transform REG tasks into a generic NLG tasks. The paper adopts the NLG algorithm of our previous work (which is also vector-based; Li, 2019), but certain adaptations needed to be made to allow the algorithm to perform the traditional REG attribute selection task.

Our REG algorithm produces referring expressions (REs) by learning from a data-text corpus of REs. In a nutshell, the algorithm splits the textual expressions in the training corpus into small spans according to their meaning, and reassembles these spans into new expressions when it refers to a referent. We evaluate the performance of the REG function on the Tuna corpus (Gatt et al., 2007) against 3 strong baselines. Experimental results show that our algorithm outperforms the baselines in terms of Dice scores. An additional experiment also shows positive results for our algorithm on an experts-based evaluation based on a BLEU-based comparison between algorithm-generated and human-produced referring expressions.

2 Related Work

The main REG algorithms have often focussed on the semantic core of the REG task, which is to select semantic attributes for a referring expression (e.g., sofa, red), disregarding the expression of these attributes in words (e.g., "the red sofa") (Krahmer and Van Deemter, 2012). The term REG is sometimes restricted to "one-shot" references, where it is the task of one single NP to identify the referent. We will use the term REG in this restricted sense. Consequently, linguistic context is irrelevant, so pronouns and other anaphoric NPs (as in the GREC challenge, for instance (Gatt et al., 2009)) will not be taken into account.

Early REG approaches sought to find a *minimum* set of attributes that jointly single out the referent, this is called the Full Brevity (FB) approach (Dale, 1989), or to "greedily" add maximally discriminatory attributes one by one, that is, adding attributes one at a time, choosing always the one that removes the largest number of distractors, until the referent has been uniquely identified; this is

Proceedings of The 11th International Natural Language Generation Conference, pages 482–491,
Tilburg, The Netherlands, November 5-8, 2018. ©2018 Association for Computational Linguistics

called the Greedy algorithm (GR).

The approach that is often thought to be most suitable for relatively simple referential situations (cf. §6 below), known as the Incremental Algorithm (IA), resembles GR to the extent that it adds attributes one by one until the referent has been singled out. However, the order in which the IA selects attributes is not based on their discriminatory power (as was the case with GR), but on their place in what is known as the Preference Order (PO). The PO is a list that works like an oracle that tells us in what order Attributes should be selected and, although efforts have been made to determine the PO on independent grounds, in practice it is nontrivial to find the best PO for a given REG task. Thus each PO defines another IA. Therefore, when we evaluate our own REG approach in §4.3, we will not only compare it with FB and GR, but with a number of different IAs, with different POs.

Statistical methods have come to REG relatively late. The hybrid approach of Di Fabbrizio et al. (2008) used statistical methods to determine the PO of the IA. The Bayesian approach of Frank and Goodman (2012) went further, but although it has some attractive features, it does not yet perform at the same level as IA. Other statistical approaches have focussed specifically on the logical structure of complex REs (FitzGerald et al., 2013) and on collaborative aspects of referring (Garoufi and Koller, 2014), among other issues.

REG algorithms have typically focussed on Content Selection (i.e., selection of semantic attributes). For example, when the usefulness of REs for readers was addressed in the *Shared Task Evaluation Challenges* (STECs; Gatt and Belz, 2010), the sets of properties produced by each of the algorithms submitted to the STECs were converted into actual Noun Phrases (by one and the same simple Linguistic Realisation algorithm) before they were shown to readers.

3 Summary of the Text-Reassembling Generation Model

We are developing a new approach to NLG (Li, 2019), which we call the *Text-Reassembling Generation* (TRG) model. Earlier experiments with this method have focussed on the SUMTIME corpus (Sripada et al., 2002), and more specifically on Lexical Choice and the generation of SUMTIME-style sentences such as "MAINLY W-NW 10 OR LESS" (a brief weather prediction about the

Table 1: A simplified training corpus for training the Vector-Based Approach to NLG. Wind speed (ws) are expressed in Knots and wind direction (dir) is presented by Compass points.

Text	Data
W 10-12	$\{ws=10, dir=265\}$
WS 22-24	$\{ws=22, dir=130\}$
MAINLY 10 OR LESS	$\{ws=9, dir=10\}$
...	...

strength and direction of wind). In the present paper, we show how this approach can be adapted to perform the REG task (a task not previously considered in this work). Here we sketch the outlines of TRG; the next section applies these ideas to REG.

TRG uses a generation strategy that we call "splitting-and-reassembling". It splits the training sentences into text fragments (i.e. the strings consist of words, numbers, punctuations, and so on) during training; then, it reuses (reassembles) the fragments to generate new sentences. The training process aims to extract sentence fragments. From a training corpus, the approach learns what fragment express what non-linguistic data by inspecting what non-linguistic data most likely co-occurs with what fragment.

Vector-based Knowledge Representation (KR) is often used in deep learning-based and other Machine Learning approaches (Ramachandram and Taylor, 2017). TRG adopts *attribute-value* pairs for representing non-linguistic data (see §4.1 for details), and the attribute-value pairs are further represented by vectors. Table 1 presents a simplified training corpus of SUMTIME sentences about wind. For example, the fragment "10-12" co-occurs with $ws=10$ (i.e., the first data record). If this pattern was observed frequently in the training set, our model can learn that the fragment "10-12" expresses $ws=10$.

Another part of our approach is schema extraction, in which each text fragment is replaced by a placeholder that leaves out everything except the type of attribute expressed. After the replacement, the text becomes a sequence of placeholders, and we call the sequence the *schema*. For example, revisiting the example of Figure 1, the three corpus texts are transformed into two schemas:

W 10-12 $\Rightarrow$ [direction] [speed]
WS 22-24 $\Rightarrow$ [direction] [speed]

MAINLY 10 OR LESS $\Rightarrow$ [speed]

The two schemas are:

  schema 1: [direction] [speed]
  schema 2: [speed]

where the placeholders are denoted by square brackets.

Generation is a two-step process: given a set of non-linguistic data as input, TRG firstly selects a schema. It then replaces each placeholder in the schema with a text fragment which expresses the non-linguistic data (i.e., the input). Note that this approach can generate texts which do not appear in the training corpus. Because TRG represents input data by vectors, both schema selection and text fragment selection are based on vector comparison between the input data vector and corpus data vectors. Unlike most of its predecessors, it is *purely* statistical in that it does not use a hand-crafted grammar or other hand-crafted rules.

4 The Vector-Based REG Algorithm

In this section we show how the TRG algorithm was made to apply to REG, which generates expressions that distinguish a target from its distractors. A RE typically expresses only a subset of the features of the target referent. For example, although in the Tuna corpus, furniture has 4 properties including `type`, `colour`, `size`, and `orientation`. Speakers referring to a large red frontal chair (in the presence of other large frontal chairs) may only say "the red chair", because this suffices to distinguish the referent from all the other objects in the domain (called the distractors). The choice of features tells us something about the referent, but also about the differences between the target(s) and distractors.

To generate an appropriate referring expression, information of both the target and the distractors needs to be considered. To bring REG within the scope of TRG, we therefore combine the features of the target referent with the differences between the target and distractors, treating this as a new group of features. Then we generate a RE as well as a description of the new group, and this description is the textual RE for the target. The resulting algorithm is called the Vector-Based approach to REG (VB-REG).

In the following sections, we first introduce how we represent a domain object (i.e., a target or a distractor) and the differences between the target

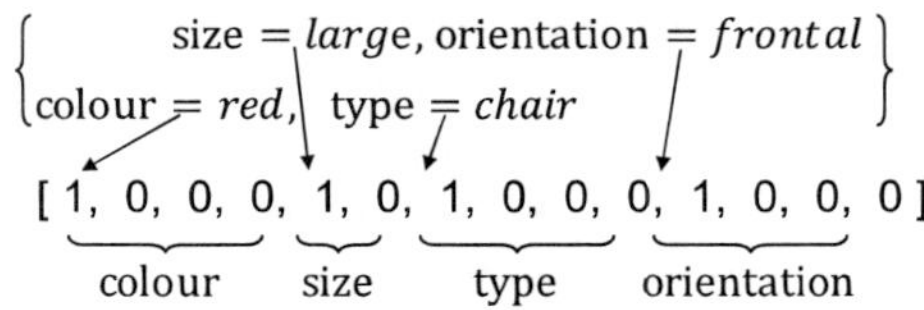

$$[\ 1,\ 0,\ 0,\ 0,\ 1,\ 0,\ 1,\ 0,\ 0,\ 0,\ 1,\ 0,\ 0,\ 0\ ]$$

   colour size type orientation

Figure 1: An example of vector representation for a domain object with the feature set `{colour=red, size=large, type=chair, orientation=frontal}`.

and distractors (§4.1). We then discuss our strategy for generating REs for a target referent (§4.2 and §4.3). Finally, we explain how to generate an actual referential noun phrase (§4.4).

4.1 Representing a Reference Problem as a Fixed-Length Vector

We represent a target or a distractor with features which are represented as *attribute-value* pairs, e.g., `colour=red` and `type=chair`. Here `colour` and `type` are attributes and *red* and *chair* are the values. A chair whose colour is red, size is large, and orientation is frontal can be represented by the feature set: `{colour=red, size=large, type=chair, orientation=frontal}`.

In order to apply our model, we need to represent feature sets in a vector. Recall that there are in total 14 features in the Tuna corpus (Gatt et al., 2007); they are:

`colour=`*red*	`type=`*chair*
`colour=`*blue*	`type=`*desk*
`colour=`*green*	`type=`*fan*
`colour=`*grey*	`type=`*sofa*
`orientation=`*front*	`size=`*large*
`orientation=`*back*	`size=`*small*
`orientation=`*left*	
`orientation=`*right*	

We therefore use a 14-dimension vector to represent an arbitrary feature set, with each dimension corresponding to an attribute-value pair. Also, each dimension is a binary variable (i.e., 1 or 0), with 1 indicating that the corresponding feature appears in the feature set, and 0 otherwise. In this way, the feature set `{colour=red, size=large, type=chair, orientation=frontal}` of the expression "a large red frontal chair" can be converted to a vector $[1, 0, 0, 0, 1, 0, 1, 0, 0, 0, 1, 0, 0, 0]$, that we

Table 2: An example of a simplified REG case from the Tuna corpus.

Target:	{colour=grey,size=large,...}
Distractor 1:	{colour=blue,size=small,...}
Distractor 2:	{colour=red,size=large,...}
Distractor 3:	{colour=blue,size=large,...}
Distractor 4:	{colour=red,size=large,...}

call the target vector (namely $\mathbf{t}$). Two objects are indistinguishable if their vector representations are the same.

Since the words that are used for referring to an object depend not just on that object (i.e., the referent), but on other objects as well (i.e., the distractors), we model the difference between a target and its distractors with an additional vector, which we call the difference vector ($\mathbf{d}$). In contrast to the feature set vector, here, the difference vector has only 4 dimensions, with each dimension corresponding to one of the attribute types of the Tuna corpus, i.e., colour, size, type, and orientation. The value of the dimensions indicates the degree to which the target differs from the distractors for a corresponding attribute.

Let $attr$ be an attribute, P_{attr} the probability that the value of $attr$ of the target matches the same attribute value of any of the distractors.

$$P_{attr} = \frac{count(attr_{target} = attr_{distractor})}{count(distractor)} \quad (1)$$

We show how to compute the difference vector d with the example in Table 2.

In Table 2, the value of the colour attribute of the target is grey. However, no distractor has the same value for the colour attribute, meaning that $P_{colour} = 0$. Thus, we have

$$\mathbf{d}^{(colour)} = 1 - P_{colour} = 1 \quad (2)$$

This means that target's colour is very different from the distractors, i.e., an outlier among the colour of the distractors. For the size attribute, target's size feature (i.e., size=large) occurs three times among the four distractors. Thus, we have

$$P_{size} = \frac{3}{4}$$

$$\mathbf{d}^{(size)} = 1 - P_{size} = \frac{1}{4}$$

That indicates that the size of the target is unlikely to be an outlier to the distractors. Finally, the difference vector $\mathbf{d}$ is given as

$$\mathbf{d} = [\mathbf{d}^{(colour)}, \mathbf{d}^{(size)}, \mathbf{d}^{(type)}, \mathbf{d}^{(orien)}] = [1, \frac{1}{4}, ...]$$

As we described, the referring expression generation considers both the target information (presented by $\mathbf{t}$) and the differential (presented by $\mathbf{d}$) between the target and distractors. We join the two vectors as a big vector (namely *knowledge vector* or $\mathbf{k}$) for combining the two parts of information. In this case, $\mathbf{k}$ is:

$$\mathbf{k} = [\,\mathbf{t} \vdots \mathbf{d}\,] = [1, 0, 0, 0, ..., 1, \frac{1}{4}, ...]$$

In this way, the two parts of information are merged together, and the length of $\mathbf{k}$ is fixed, even though the number of distractors varies. A traditional REG task is, therefore, represented by a fixed-length vector, the REG processing can be performed by our NLG algorithm. The following steps sketch the process for doing this.

4.2 Extracting Schemas From a Corpus

So far, we represented REG tasks as knowledge vectors; this section extracts from the corpus a set of what we call expression schemas, or *schemas* for short. Both the knowledge vectors and schemas will be used to train the REG model. A schema represents the overall structure of an RE. For example, from an occurrence of "the red chair" in the corpus, we extract the schema

"the" [colour] [type]

Similarly, "the old man wearing glasses" derives the schema

"the" [age] "man" [hasGlasses]

The words are replaced according to the alignment labels in the training corpus. For example, in Tuna corpus, the words "red", "chair", "old", and "wearing glasses" are labelled with colour=red, type=chair, age=old, and hasGlasses=true respectively in the two sample expressions (Figure 2). In this way, we extract a schema from each corpus expression.

4.3 Schema Selection

This step uses schema selection to perform traditional REG attribute selection, among other

```
<description> the red chair </description>
<alignment>
  <word> the </word>
  <word attr="colour" value="red"> red </word>
  <word attr="type" value ="chair"> chair </word>
</alignment>
...
<description> the old man wearing glasses </description>
<alignment>
  <word> the </word>
  <word attr="age" value="old"> old </word>
  <word> man </word>
  <word attr="hasGlasses" value="true"> wearing glasses
  </word>
</alignment>
...
```

Figure 2: The (simplified) alignment examples for human-produced expressions in Tuna corpus in XML format.

things. It focusses on how to obtain a schema for a given REG task (represented by a knowledge vector i.e. our vectorised KR), focussing on what attributes should be expressed. Instead of creating new schemas, we reuse the existing schemas extracted from the training corpus. Because the schemas omit the specific attribute values, multiple expressions share the same schema (and multiple schemas share the same set of placeholders). To select a schema for a given RE task, we adopt the lexical selector of Li et al. (2016) as schema selector, which is fully statistical, and which accepts the knowledge vector.

To train the schema selector, we represent each unique schema i extracted from the training corpus as a column vector (denoted by $\mathbf{s}_i^T$), whose dimension is equal to the total number of data records in the training set $\mathcal{M}$. If the schema of the j-th data record of the corpus is same as schema i, then the j-th element of $\mathbf{s}_i^T$ equals 1, and 0 otherwise. In addition, we also need to construct a matrix (namely $\mathbf{K}$) which encodes the information of all the data records of the corpus. $\mathbf{K}$ consists of knowledge vectors of each feature group of the training data, with each row corresponding to a knowledge vector $\mathbf{k}$ of a data record. Suppose the training corpus includes m records and n features in total, then $\mathbf{K}$ is a $m - by - n$ matrix. Based on $\mathbf{K}$ and $\mathbf{s}_i^T$, our model training process finds a projection vector (i.e., the column vector $\mathbf{p}_i^T$) of

Equation 3 by Least Square (Li et al., 2016).

$$\mathbf{K} \cdot \mathbf{p}_i^T = \mathbf{s}_i^T \tag{3}$$
$$\mathbf{p}_i^T = pinv(\mathbf{K}) \cdot \mathbf{s}_i^T \tag{4}$$

The projection vector $\mathbf{p}_i^T$ indicates how the information of a knowledge vector $\mathbf{k}_r$ projects on the use of the schema i. Therefore, a weight (w_r) that i should be adopted for expressing r is estimated by Equation 5.

$$w_r = \mathbf{k}_r \cdot \mathbf{p}_i^T \tag{5}$$

When every $\mathbf{p}_i^T$ is found, given an unseen knowledge vector ($\mathbf{k}^*$), we select the schema (denoted by x) for $\mathbf{k}^*$ such that x maximises $\mathbf{k}^* \cdot \mathbf{p}_{i=x}^T$ (Li et al., 2016):

$$x = \arg\max_x (\mathbf{k}^* \cdot \mathbf{p}_{i=x}^T) \tag{6}$$

When a schema is selected, we pick up and output the attributes of all the placeholders within the schema as the outcome for the REG task. Note that in the Tuna corpus, a given referent can never be described using two different values of the same attribute (e.g., a sofa cannot be both red and blue). Therefore, selecting attributes suffices for this part of the REG task.

In the above we have focussed on attribute selection. However, when a schema is selected, we do not only select attributes, we also fix the overall syntactic pattern of the RE. Thus, schema selection performs an important part of Linguistic Realisation as well.

4.4 Generating Complete Referential Noun Phrases

Expression schemas contain a lot of information about a referential Noun Phrase – including its syntactic structure and the use of function words – but they still contains placeholders for attributes. This section focuses on generating textual REs. The remaining generation task is to replace placeholders by actual words, after schema selection.

Analogous to schema selection, we adopt the selector of (i.e., Li et al., 2016) to do this. Placeholders are classified according to their corresponding attributes (e.g. `colour` or `type`). Two placeholders belong to the same class if they express the same attribute (whatever they are in the same or different REs), and we train an individual lexical selector for each class of placeholders.

For each placeholder class, we first build up a small training corpus that consists of all the words (or multi-word phrases) corresponding to the placeholder, with the features that the word (or the multi-word phrase) expresses.

Looking through the Tuna corpus, from the expressions, for example, "the red sofa" and "the blue chair", we find that the placeholder [colour] can be described by words "red" and "blue". So the extracted small corpus for [colour] contains the two words, which is shown in Table 3

Table 3: The extracted small corpus for placeholder [colour] from Tuna corpus

Text	Data
red	{colour=red}
blue	{colour=blue}
...	...

Then, for each class of placeholder (e.g. for [colour]), we train a lexical selector with the corresponding small corpus (e.g. Table 3). The training and word selecting processes are the same as in Schema Selection (§4.3). First, the words (and phrases) and corpus data in the small group are represented by vectors and a matrix; then they are used to find the projecting vectors through Equation 3; finally, words (or word phrases) are selected through Equation 6 for the placeholders of the class according to the given knowledge vector (that used to select the schema). Therefore, after selecting a schema, we replace its placeholders by the selected words (or word phrases) to transform the schema into a textual expression.

To summarise our approach to REG, we generate a textual RE (i.e., a Noun Phrase) for a REG task by adopting a three-step generation strategy: Given a REG task, we first represent the task as a knowledge vector which includes the knowledge of both target and distractor. Secondly, we select a schema, and finally, select words for each placeholder in the schema. If the process stops just after the schema selection, we still achieve the traditional RE task by picking up the attributes of the placeholder in the schema as the selected attribute set.

5 Evaluating the VB-REG Algorithm

We evaluated both Attribute Selection and Linguistic Realisation by making use of the Tuna corpus (Gatt et al., 2007), which contains two domains: Furniture and People. The Tuna corpus consists of corpus records; each record consists of a REG trail (i.e. one or two targets and some distractors) and a Noun Phrase produced by a participant to express the target. The Noun Phrases were collected in two conditions: the participants were either allowed to use location descriptions (e.g. "in the top left") or not (van der Sluis et al., 2006).

Here we focus on those corpus records which have one singular target object (rather than a set of two) and where the locational descriptions were not allowed to use. There are 210 corpus records in Furniture domain, and 180 records in People domain. We also discarded the records in which the locational descriptions were still used.

Our evaluation assumes a type of Knowledge Representation based on an attribute-value schema. Corpora such as ReferIt (Kazemzadeh et al., 2014), which do not use this type of KR, are not directly amenable to this approach.

5.1 Evaluating Attribute Selection in the VB-REG Algorithm

We evaluate the quality of our attribute selection using Dice score and PRP (Perfect Recall Percentage) scores, which are the most often used REG evaluation metrics (Van Deemter, 2016). Dice calculates the degree of similarity between sets: in our case, the set of properties expressed by the REs in the corpus versus the set of properties expressed by the REs generated by our algorithm; PRP gives the percentage of cases in which a generated RE expresses exactly the same properties as an RE in the corpus.

For each domain, we randomly divided the trials into two parts of the same size, for training and testing respectively. We repeated the experiment 10 times with different division of the trails to perform 10-fold cross-validation. We trained our model as explained in §4; then, we selected attributes for the testing data, and calculated the Dice and PRP scores based on the expressions of test data and the attributes generated. The scores of 10-fold cross-validation are shown in Table 4. The average Dice score (Mean) of the 10-fold experiments of Furniture domain is 0.916 with PRP being 61.6; for People domain, the average Dice score is 0.848 with PRP being 46.0.

To compare with other REG algorithms, we

Table 4: REG evaluation results, showing Dice scores, standard deviation (SD), PRP scores

	Furniture			People		
	Dice	SD	PRP	Dice	SD	PRP
fold 0	.930	.11	66.2	.828	.19	40.0
fold 1	.907	.13	60.3	.813	.22	44.8
fold 2	.917	.11	59.5	.854	.18	48.5
fold 3	.915	.12	60.6	.852	.18	46.6
fold 4	.914	.11	58.3	.885	.16	58.9
fold 5	.932	.12	69.2	.838	.17	44.8
fold 6	.924	.11	64.9	.832	.15	34.9
fold 7	.905	.13	60.3	.815	.17	36.4
fold 8	.923	.10	60.0	.892	.14	56.3
fold 9	.894	.14	56.6	.871	.15	49.2
Mean	.916	.12	61.6	.848	.17	46.0

Table 5: The performance comparison of our algorithm (VB-REG) with the Incremental Algorithms, Full Brevity algorithm, and Greedy Algorithm on Furniture domain.

	Dice	SD	PRP
IA-COS	.917	.12	6.9
IA-CSO	.917	.12	6.9
IA-RAND	.840	.15	31.4
IA-OCS	.829	.14	25.0
IA-SCO	.815	.14	19.2
IA-OSC	.803	.16	22.4
IA-SOC	.780	.16	18.6
FB	.841	.17	39.1
GR	.829	.17	37.2
VB-REG	.916	.12	61.6

Table 6: Performance comparison of our algorithm (VB-REG) with the Incremental Algorithms, Full Brevity algorithm, and Greedy Algorithm on the People domain.

	Dice	SD	PRP
IA-GBHOATSS	.844	.17	44.7
IA-BGHOATSS	.822	.17	36.4
IA-GHBOATSS	.776	.21	29.5
IA-BHGOATSS	.728	.19	15.9
IA-HGBOATSS	.688	.18	3.8
IA-HBGOATSS	.658	.20	4.5
IA-RAND	.598	.23	11.4
IA-SSTAOHBG	.344	.11	0.0
FB	.764	.23	34.1
GR	.693	.20	8.3
VB-REG	.848	.17	46.0

show the tables from Van Deemter (2016, see Table 5 and Table 6) which shows the performance of the classic REG algorithms on the part of the Tuna corpus on which we focus (i.e., excluding location and references to sets): Full Brevity algorithm (FB), Greedy Algorithm (GR), and Incremental Algorithms (IA-xxx), the IA-xxx suffixes denote different Preference Orders. For example, IA-COS is the version for the furniture corpus that had colour (C), orientation (O), and size (S) as its first-most, second-most, and third-most preferred attribute; IA-GBHOATSS was the version of IA for the people corpus that used the Preference Order has_Glasses, has_Beards, Hair, etc.

Our approach, which is statistical and domain independent (hence does not distinguish between the furniture and people domain), preforms extremely well compared to the classic algorithms.

Although our Mean Dice Score of Furniture domain (i.e. 0.916) is slightly lower than the champion, our algorithm beats the others in all other columns (Mean Dice scores of People domain and PRP for both domains).

5.2 Evaluating the fluency of NPs generated by the VB-REG algorithm

We also evaluate the fluency of the Noun Phrases generated by the VB-REG algorithm. We decided to use BLEU as a metric, with Noun Phrases produced by human experts as our baseline, using the same Tuna records and the same experimental settings as before. For each domain, the Tuna corpus was, once again, randomly divided into two parts: the training corpus and testing corpus.

The training corpus is only used to train the VB-REG model. After training, the model selects attributes and generates textual REs for each testing corpus data. The selected attributes are shown to 2 experts who are familiar with NLG but not with the Tuna corpus. The experts were also provided with relevant corpus texts. Then they were asked to produce referring expressions (i.e., Noun Phrases) for the attributes. They were asked to work individually, then discuss and produce only one answer sheet that both of them agreed on. The experts thus worked as a human Surface Realiser.

For each data in the testing corpus, we obtained three Noun Phrases: one generated by VB-REG algorithm, one produced by human experts; the third one was the original expression in the testing corpus. We calculated the BLEU scores of

Table 7: 10 fold REG evaluation results of BLEU scores

	Furniture		People	
	VB-REG	expert	VB-REG	expert
fold 0	.837	.889	.964	.923
fold 1	.751	.844	.910	.904
fold 2	.864	.815	.973	.923
fold 3	.873	.834	.931	.899
fold 4	.840	.844	.963	.888
fold 5	.822	.745	.979	.948
fold 6	.960	.793	.949	.977
fold 7	.853	.807	.883	.900
fold 8	.781	.901	.968	.897
fold 9	.840	.928	.983	.958
Mean	.842	.840	.950	.922
p-value	.943		.026	

the generated expression and expert expression by using the testing corpus (the corpus expression) as the reference for BLEU. Finally, we calculated the mean scores of every testing record. We performed 10-fold cross-validation; outcomes are shown in Table 7. The high BLEU scores suggest that our model achieves high fluency levels. In the furniture domain, our model performs at a similar level as the experts (no significant difference); in the people domain, our model "outperforms" our experts ($p = 0.026$). The p-values are calculated by a paired sample t-test.

6 Discussion

We have proposed a statistical model for automatically selecting attributes for REG and expressing these in an actual noun phrase. Our evaluation shows that the method performs well in terms of both attribute selection and text fluency.

Unlike previous approaches to REG (see e.g., §2), the VB-REG algorithm does not contain the idea of unique identification in any shape or form. Instead of singling out the referent from the distractors, our approach simply learns how human speakers refer. This approach has interesting consequences, not least for the dual phenomena of over- and under-specification, on which much work on REG has focussed. In a nutshell, our approach generates over- and under-specified REs to the extent that they occur in the data. Thus, if a corpus contains many underspecified REs (as may be the case if the corpus is based on children's speech, e.g., (Matthews et al., 2012)), then our

REG algorithm will loyally reproduce these. If our corpus contains many highly over-specified REs (e.g. if the domain is complicated (Paraboni et al., 2007) or contains a lot of clutter (Koolen, 2013)), then so will our algorithm.

Referring Expressions Generation is more than the relatively simple reference task on which we have focussed here. For example, reference can use logical operators such as negation; reference can be to sets (including e.g. geographic regions (Turner et al., 2010)); it can involve gradable attributes; it can involve guesses about the hearer's knowledge (R.Kutlak et al., 2016); it can involve collaboration between speaker and hearer (Garoufi and Koller, 2014), and so on (Van Deemter, 2016). Although our evaluation has focussed on the singular part of the Tuna corpus only, we believe that the VB-REG approach is suitable for dealing with the above complications, provided some adaptations are made to our KR method (e.g. allowing us to represent how a *set* of target referents differs from all other domain elements). We hope to test this hypothesis in future.

VB-REG generates textual REs through schema selection and word selection. This generation strategy suffices for generating the type of REs found in the TUNA corpus, as we have seen, but syntactically complex REs can pose a problem. Consider the expression "the old man carrying a young dog", whose schema is

"the" [age] "man carrying a" [age] [animal]

, containing two placeholders for age. When VB-REG selects words for [age] (as in §3) above, it lacks the information that the [age] is for the man or the dog. In this case, VB-REG would select the same word for the two [age] placeholders. This limitation stems from the NLG approach in which VB-REG is embedded; if VB-REG is embedded into an NLG approach that does not have this limitation (e.g., providing a mechanism to distinguish the two [age] placeholders), the resulting algorithm will not suffer from this limitation.

In addition, VB-REG adopts the strategy that all the schema shares the same set of placeholders to adapt to small-scale corpus (e.g. Tuna), but the strategy may cause a syntactically error. Selection of lexicalisations for placeholders is done without taking the context of the schema into account. However, it is not guaranteed that all lexicalisation always fits into all placeholder (of different schemas). For example, we could have the following two textual descriptions:

> "the man wearing glasses"
> "the bespectacled man"

They would lead to the schemas:

> "the" "man" [hasGlasses]
> "the" [hasGlasses] "man"

where both "wearing glasses" and "bespectacled" present the candidate phrases for the placeholder [hasGlasses]. Thus the generated textual REs could be "the man bespectacled" or "the wearing glasses man", which are not syntactically correct. Although the strategy works well in our evaluation, it would be safe if a restrictive strategy is adopted. If the scale of training corpus allows, we can let each schema use an unique set of placeholder (i.e. placeholders are no longer shared by schemas). Because usually multiple corpus texts derive the same schema, the frequent schemas still obtain enough training data under the restrictive strategy.

7   Conclusion and Future Work

This paper has presented REG as a special case of NLG. It is important to note that the key strategy that we employed for representing an REG task – which separates properties of the referent from differences between the referent and the distractors – can be applied to any vector-based NLG approach, for example the neural-network-based NLG approaches (e.g. Wen et al., 2015) and Concept-based NLG approaches (e.g. Belz, 2008; Konstas and Lapata, 2013). In this way, these NLG approaches can perform REG by adopting our knowledge representation as their input. Neural-network-based approaches adopt fixed-length vectors as their input, and generate texts word by word, so our knowledge vectors and the corresponding corpus texts can be used to train them. Concept-text generation models can likewise adopt vectorised inputs. These approaches usually adopt concept sets (i.e. sets of pairs of attributes and values) as their input. Vector-based KR can be transformed into concept sets by regarding the vector entries as pairs of an entry index and an entry value. Thus our knowledge vectors can be adopted by these approaches.

One important item for future work is further evaluation. Although the model performs very well on the Tuna reference task, further experimental evidence on more challenging reference tasks is required in order to assess the generality of the proposed approach. It would be interesting, for instance, to apply the method to the ReferIt corpus (Kazemzadeh et al., 2014).

Acknowledgments

We gratefully acknowledge the anonymous reviewers for their very helpful comments.

References

Anja Belz. 2008. Automatic generation of weather forecast texts using comprehensive probabilistic generation-space models. *Natural Language Engineering*, 14(4):431–455.

Robert Dale. 1989. Cooking up referring expressions. In *Proceedings of the 27th annual meeting on Association for Computational Linguistics*, pages 68–75. Association for Computational Linguistics.

Giuseppe Di Fabbrizio, Amanda J Stent, and Srinivas Bangalore. 2008. Referring expression generation using speaker-based attribute selection and trainable realization (attr). In *Proceedings of the Fifth International Natural Language Generation Conference*, pages 211–214. Association for Computational Linguistics.

Nicholas FitzGerald, Yoav Artzi, and Luke Zettlemoyer. 2013. Learning distributions over logical forms for referring expression generation. In *Proceedings of the 2013 Conference on Empirical Methods in Natural Language Processing (EMNLP)*, pages 1914–1925, Seattle, Washington.

Michael C Frank and Noah D Goodman. 2012. Predicting pragmatic reasoning in language games. *Science*, 336(6084):998–998.

Konstantina Garoufi and Alexander Koller. 2014. Generation of effective referring expressions in situated context. *Language, Cognition and Neuroscience*, 29(8):986–1001.

Albert Gatt and Anja Belz. 2010. Introducing shared tasks to nlg: The tuna shared task evaluation challenges. In *Empirical methods in natural language generation*, pages 264–293. Springer.

Albert Gatt, Anja Belz, and Eric Kow. 2009. The tuna-reg challenge 2009: Overview and evaluation results. In *Proceedings of the 12th European Workshop on Natural Language Generation*, pages 174–182. Association for Computational Linguistics.

Albert Gatt and Emiel Krahmer. 2018. Survey of the state of the art in natural language generation: Core tasks, applications and evaluation. *Journal of Artificial Intelligence Research*, 61:65–170.

Albert Gatt, Ielka Van Der Sluis, and Kees Van Deemter. 2007. Evaluating algorithms for the generation of referring expressions using a balanced corpus. In *Proceedings of the Eleventh European Workshop on Natural Language Generation*, pages 49–56. Association for Computational Linguistics.

Sahar Kazemzadeh, Vicente Ordonez, Mark Matten, and Tamara Berg. 2014. Referitgame: Referring to objects in photographs of natural scenes. In *Proceedings of the 2014 conference on empirical methods in natural language processing (EMNLP)*, pages 787–798.

Ioannis Konstas and Mirella Lapata. 2013. A global model for concept-to-text generation. *Journal of Artificial Intelligence Research*, 48:305–346.

Ruud Martinus Franciscus Koolen. 2013. Need i say more? on overspecification in definite reference.

Emiel Krahmer and Kees Van Deemter. 2012. Computational generation of referring expressions: A survey. *Computational Linguistics*, 38(1):173–218.

Xiao Li. 2019. A fully statistical approach to natural language generation.

Xiao Li, Kees van Deemter, and Chenghua Lin. 2016. Statistics-based lexical choice for nlg from quantitative information. In *Proceedings of the 9th International Natural Language Generation conference*, pages 104–108.

Danielle Matthews, Jessica Butcher, Elena Lieven, and Michael Tomasello. 2012. Two-and four-year-olds learn to adapt referring expressions to context: effects of distracters and feedback on referential communication. *Topics in cognitive science*, 4(2):184–210.

Ivandré Paraboni, Kees Van Deemter, and Judith Masthoff. 2007. Generating referring expressions: Making referents easy to identify. *Computational linguistics*, 33(2):229–254.

Dhanesh Ramachandram and Graham W Taylor. 2017. Deep multimodal learning: A survey on recent advances and trends. *IEEE Signal Processing Magazine*, 34(6):96–108.

Ehud Reiter. 2007. An architecture for data-to-text systems. In *Proceedings of the Eleventh European Workshop on Natural Language Generation*, pages 97–104. Association for Computational Linguistics.

Ehud Reiter and Robert Dale. 2000. *Building natural language generation systems*. Cambridge university press.

R.Kutlak, K. van Deemter, and C.Mellish. 2016. Production of referring expressions for an unknown audience: A computational model of communal common ground. *Frontiers in Psychology*, 7.

Ielka van der Sluis, Albert Gatt, and Kees van Deemter. 2006. Manual for tuna corpus: Referring expressions in two domains.

Somayajulu Sripada, Ehud Reiter, Jim Hunter, and Jin Yu. 2002. Sumtime-meteo: Parallel corpus of naturally occurring forecast texts and weather data. *Computing Science Department, University of Aberdeen, Aberdeen, Scotland, Tech. Rep. AUCS/TR0201*.

Ross Turner, Somayajulu Sripada, and Ehud Reiter. 2010. Generating approximate geographic descriptions. In *Empirical methods in natural language generation*, pages 121–140. Springer.

Kees Van Deemter. 2016. *Computational models of referring: a study in cognitive science*. MIT Press.

Tsung-hsien Wen, Pei-hao Su, V David, and Steve Young. 2015. Semantically conditioned lstm-based natural language generation for spoken dialogue systems. In *In Proceedings of EMNLP. Association for Computational Linguistics*. Citeseer.

Specificity measures and reference

Albert Gatt
Inst. of Linguistics & Language Technology
University of Malta
albert.gatt@um.edu.mt

Nicolás Marín
Dept. of Computer Science & AI
University of Granada
nicm@decsai.ugr.es

Gustavo Rivas-Gervilla
Dept. of Computer Science & AI
University of Granada
griger@decsai.ugr.es

Daniel Sánchez
Dept. of Computer Science & AI
University of Granada
daniel@decsai.ugr.es

Abstract

In this paper we study empirically the validity of measures of referential success for referring expressions involving gradual properties. More specifically, we study the ability of several measures of referential success to predict the success of a user in choosing the right object, given a referring expression. Experimental results indicate that certain fuzzy measures of success are able to predict human accuracy in reference resolution. Such measures are therefore suitable for the estimation of the success or otherwise of a referring expression produced by a generation algorithm, especially in case the properties in a domain cannot be assumed to have crisp denotations.

1 Introduction

Referring expression generation (REG) is one of the subtasks of Natural Language Generation (NLG) systems. Given a context comprised of a set of objects and a collection of properties that can be predicated of those objects, the REG problem is to find referring expressions – that is, subsets of those properties – that allow a user to locate a specific object and distinguish it from its distractors (Dale and Reiter, 1995; Krahmer and van Deemter, 2012; van Deemter, 2016).

The task definition given above corresponds to the *content determination* part of REG; in standard accounts, REG also involves a realisation step in which the form of a referring expression needs to be determined (Castro Ferreira, 2018).

From a general point of view, the REG problem intends to emulate through automatic means the process carried out by a human being whose purpose is to identify a certain object in a specific context, using natural language, so that another receiving user is able to precisely and univocally identify it.

One source of complexity for REG is context-dependence and graduality. This has become increasingly evident in work that has sought solutions to the REG problem in naturalistic scenes, as part of a broader research focus on the vision-language interface (Kazemzadeh et al., 2014; Mao et al., 2016; Yu et al., 2016). However, context dependence is also a central concern for approaches to REG that assume a more structured input representation where entities and their properties are available, but the extent to which a property applies to a referent is not necessarily an all-or-none decision (Horacek, 2005; van Deemter, 2006; Turner et al., 2008; Williams and Scheutz, 2017). Under these conditions, it is no longer possible to assume that properties are crisp or Boolean, or even that both sender and receiver necessarily assume the same semantics for those properties. For example, it may not be realistic to assume that all objects are red to the same degree, or that both sender and receiver have the same model of what counts as 'red'. Furthermore, the utility of the term 'red' in identifying the referent will depend in part on context, that is, whether there are any other red entities, and whether they are red to the same extent.

The above issues affect how referential success is to be defined, that is, what criteria an algorithm should use to determine whether a candidate referring expression is likely to succeed in helping a receiver identify the intended referent. There are three questions that arise in this connection: 1) How to model the semantics of gradual properties, 2) how to compute the degree of success of a candidate referring expression based on those semantics; and 3) whether such a measure of the degree of success is valid, in the sense that it indeed

Proceedings of The 11th International Natural Language Generation Conference, pages 492–502,
Tilburg, The Netherlands, November 5-8, 2018. ©2018 Association for Computational Linguistics

correlates with the ease and success with which a receiver in fact resolves the reference.

In this work we present the results of an empirical study of these issues, using geometric objects and basic properties such as color, size and position, all of which can be viewed as gradual. As we shall see, in relation to question number 1, we take results from the theory of fuzzy sets for the modeling of properties. In relation to question 2, the use of eight gradual measures related to referential success, which derive from the well-known concept of specificity of possibility distributions, is proposed. In relation to the third, an experimental study is made to validate these measures, as well as to gain a better understanding of the factors influencing referential success in the presence of gradual properties. The results are encouraging, in that they show that specificity measures do predict behavioural outcomes and hence that the framework proposed here provides a plausible account of success that can be incorporated in existing REG algorithms.

The rest of this paper is organized as follows: Section 2 introduces the problem of referential success of referring expressions with gradual properties, and the role specificity measures can play in this setting. In the same section we describe the set of measures that will be employed in the study. Section 3 describes an experiment to evaluate whether such specificity measures are useful in predicting the success of a referring expression. The results of the experiment are presented in Section 4. Finally, Section 5 is devoted to some discussion and conclusions.

2   Background

A referring expression $re = \{p_1, \ldots, p_n\}$ is said to have referential success for a certain object o when the object is the only one satisfying all the properties in the expression re. Formally:

$$\bigcap_{p \in re} [\![p]\!] = \{o\} \tag{1}$$

where $[\![p]\!]$ is the set of objects satisfying p.

When the properties are Boolean the above expression is both Boolean and easy to compute. Many REG algorithms are in fact couched as search procedures, where the process of searching for a combination of properties terminates as soon as the criterion in (1) is fulfilled (Dale and Reiter, 1995; Krahmer and van Deemter, 2012).

Additionally, since it is assumed that both sender and receiver have identical interpretations of the semantics of the relevant properties, it is accepted that when Eq. (1) holds, the receiver should be able to identify the target object, at least in principle. In practice, the ease and/or speed with which references are both produced and resolved by humans depends also on whether the choice of properties conforms to preferences, salient characteristics of objects, etc (Pechmann, 1989; Tarenskeen et al., 2015; Rubio-Fernandez, 2016).

However, in many application domains we work with gradual properties instead of Boolean ones (Gatt et al., 2016; van Deemter, 2006; Turner et al., 2008). This means that the success criterion in 1) no longer applies, unless the properties in question are transformed into crisp ones, as is done for example in the conversion of numerical properties to inequalities by van Deemter (2006). This, however, is not easily applicable to properties that are not typically modelled as numeric, but which are still gradual. Examples include colour (to what extent is the object red?) or location (how far towards the top or the left is the object?).

2.1   Properties as fuzzy sets

In this paper, the theoretical starting point for a treatment of referential success as gradual is a set of insights developed within the field of Fuzzy Set Theory and used to determine the core properties that measures of referential success need to satisfy (Marín et al., 2016).

In Fuzzy Set Theory, gradual properties (i.e. properties in which objects have varying degrees of membership) are modelled using possibility distributions and associated with linguistic terms through tools such as linguistic variables or, more broadly, the results of the Computational Theory of Perceptions (Zadeh, 1999).

Possibility distributions are fuzzy sets that represent the available information about the actual (unique) value of a given variable. In the context that concerns us, these types of functions can be used to represent the available information about what object a given expression refers to, whereby degrees of possibility indicate that some values are more plausible than others.

Thus, in order to analyze the referential success of the expression, it is useful to determine how difficult it is to find out the actual value (i.e. the object referred to) among those that belong to the associated possibility distribution to a greater or lesser degree. As a particular case, crisp sets can be employed for such purpose, all values being equally and completely plausible. For instance, one may say that the value of a variable X is in $\{3, 5, 6\}$, but we don't know which value in the set is the actual value of X.

2.2 The concept of specificity

For general (fuzzy) possibility distributions, the well-known measures of specificity (Yager, 1982) allow to determine how easy it is to determine the real value in view of the possibility distribution (that is, to which extent the distribution *specifies* the value). This can be interpreted in some contexts as the extent to which a possibility distribution is a singleton (i.e. the possibility distribution clearly indicates a unique value). There are infinitely many specificity measures, that can be classified into different families (linear, product, etc.). They serve to assess the amount of uncertainty about the value of the variable. As an example in the crisp case, the set $\{3, 5, 6\}$ is less specific than the set $\{3, 5\}$, and hence $X \in \{3, 5, 6\}$ is a more uncertain statement than $X \in \{3, 5\}$. Several additional theoretical results have been adduced based on this core insight (Dubois and Prade, 1987; Yager, 1990, 1992; Garmendia et al., 2003; Marín et al., 2017b).

The definition of specificity measures suggests a clear connection with the concept of referential success that is particularly useful when fuzzy properties are involved: A referring expression re has referential success to the extent that 1) the (fuzzy) set of objects satisfying re, denoted by O_{re}, viewed as a possibility distribution, is 'specific' (in the sense explained above), and ii) O_{re} contains the object intended to be referred.

Hence, the referential success of an expression re is upper-bounded by the specificity of the associated fuzzy set and the fulfillment of re by the intended object. In recent theoretical work, it has been shown that specificity measures can be used to derive measures of referential success for expressions containing gradual properties (Marín et al., 2016), and conversely, that referential success measures can derive specificity measures (Marín et al., 2018).

2.3 Spsecificity measures

In view of the previous discussion, as indicated by Marín et al. (2017a), given a fuzzy set associated with a referring expression and a set of objects in a given domain of discourse, the specificity of the fuzzy set indicates to what extent there is some single object of which the expression is true, that is, to what extent this expression has referential success in the set for some (unknown) object. Since there is an infinity of possible specificity measures, an important question is which family of measures is useful and empirically valid in the context of REG. We shall restrict our experimental study to the validity of a few measures that have been shown to be the most suitable for our purposes from a theoretical perspective (Marín et al., 2017b).

Let $\mathcal{O}$ be the universe of objects in a given context. Let $A \in [0, 1]^{\mathcal{O}}$ with $|\mathcal{O}| = m$ be the possibility distribution associated with a given referring expression. Let us consider that memberships of objects in A are ranked as $a_1 \geq a_2 \geq \cdots \geq a_m$.

Taking into account the previous framework, the specificity measures considered in this work are shown in table 1a. All these measures satisfy an important property for our purposes: when there are two objects that comply with the referring expression to degree 1 (that is, when $a_2 = 1$), the measures yield 0, which is a desirable result in terms of referential success (since it indicates that the expression is applicable to at least two objects, rather than just the target). Intuitively, this implies that if a target referent with property p has a similar distractor with p, a referring expression that uses p will be less successful.

The value computed by these measures can be thought of as reflecting the distance between a_2 and a_1, that is the distance, in terms of their membership in re, between the second-ranked and the highest-ranked entity in re of the second-ranked entity a_2, from the This is due to the fact that in all the cases, specificity is upper bounded by the value of a_1. As a consequence, in the particular case that the fuzzy set A is not normalized (that is, when $a_1 < 1$), the measure can yield the same value for different situations. For instance, m_1 in Table 1, yields the same value in case $a_1 = 1$, $a_2 = 0.5$ and in case $a_1 = 0.5$, $a_2 = 0$.

In order to distinguish these two cases, we propose to use measures that work as indices of the relation between the measures in Table 1, and the value of a_1. These are shown in table 1b, and are defined as follows: m_i in Table 1b is obtained from m_{i-1} in Table 1a as m_{i-1}/a_1, assuming by

Name	Definition
m_1	$a_1 - a_2$
m_3	$a_1 * (a_1 - a_2)$
m_5	$a_1 * (1 - a_2)$
m_7	$min\{1, 1 - a2\}$

(a) Specificity measures

Name	Definition
m_2	$(a_1 - a_2)/a_1$
m_4	$a_1 * (a_1 - a_2)/a_1$
m_6	$a_1 * (1 - a_2)/a_1$
m_8	$min\{1, 1 - a2\}/a_1$

(b) Normalised versions of measures in Table 1a.

Table 1: Specificity measures and their normalised counterparts

convention that $a_1 = 0$ implies $m_i = 0$ for all measures in Table 1b. All measures in Table 1b are in $[0, 1]$. Note that in case $a_1 = 1$, that is, when there is at least one object that fully complies with the referring expression, measures m_i in Table 1b coincide with the corresponding measures m_{i-1} in Table 1a. As a final remark, note that $m_1 = m_4$.

3 Validating the specificity measures: An experiment

We conducted an empirical study with a view to addressing the third question highlighted in the introduction, that is, to assess the validity of the specificity measures introduced in the previous section. The study took the form of an experiment in which the task was to identify a referent in a visual domain given a referring expression. This yielded two behavioural measures, identification time (id-time) and accuracy, both of which have been previously used in task-based REG evaluations (Gatt and Belz, 2010). Our aims were twofold: on the one hand, the experiment was intended as an empirical investigation of the impact of certain variables, notably gradability of properties, on the success of referring expressions; on the other, the data serves as a testbed to see whether the variance in id-time and (probability of) accuracy could be predicted by the measures in Table 1.

3.1 Participants

Twenty-one participants (17 male, age range 21–54; median age 26), with different academic profiles (mostly staff of the University of Granada), took part in the study. Participation was voluntary.

3.2 Materials and design

Each experimental item consisted of a visual display consisting of 5 geometric shapes (triangles, circles and/or squares), one of which was the target referent, which was accompanied by a referring expression which mentioned one property in addition to the head noun. There were four pos-sible properties, for each of which 5 degrees of membership distinct from 0 were defined:

1. Colour: Using the HSB colour space, all colours had constant hue and brightness, with membership defined in terms of saturation.

2. Size: Three different size intervals (small, medium and large) were defined. An object's maximum membership in a given size was defined in terms of whether the object fell towards lower (resp. higher) extremes of the interval in the case of small (resp. large), or towards the middle of the interval in the case of medium size.

3. Vertical location: The screen height was divided into three equal-sized intervals, corresponding to bottom, middle and top. Once again, membership was highest for objects close to the extremes of the intervals in the case of bottom and top, and towards the middle of the interval otherwise.

4. Horizontal location: Treated as above, by dividing the width of the screen into three equal intervals.

A further factor was *similarity*, which referred to whether there was one distractor in the display which was similar to the target on the identifying property. Let m be the degree of membership of some referent o in some identifying property p, and let d be one of the distractors in the visual domain, with membership m' in p. Then, o and d were defined as *similar* if $|m - m'| \leq \alpha$ for some threshold α, and *dissimilar* otherwise. Thresholds were set differently for the four properties.

The above is a 4 (property) $\times$ 2 (similarity) $\times$ 5 (membership) within-subjects design. We created 40 different target items with different shapes and colour/size/vertical/horizontal combinations. Items were rotated through a latin square so that different participants saw different items in different conditions.

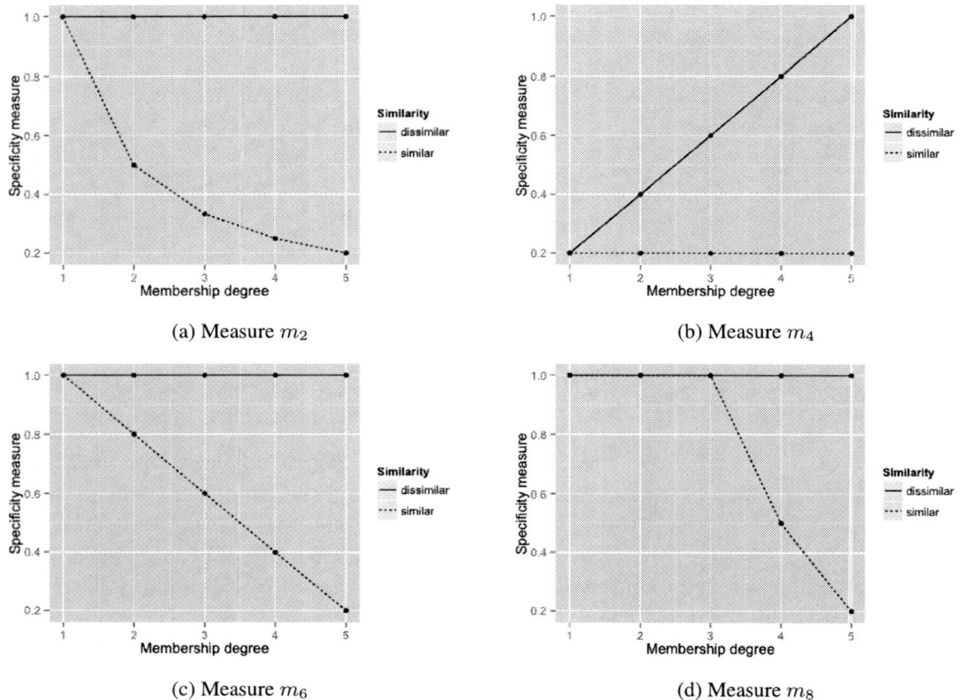

(a) Measure m_2

(b) Measure m_4

(c) Measure m_6

(d) Measure m_8

Figure 1: Specificity measures for the property Colour, by similarity and membership degree

3.3 Relationship to specificity measures

For a given experimental item involving a referring expression containing property p, it is possible to compute the specificity of the expression based on the degree of membership of the target referent in p. As an example, Figure 1 plots the normalised measures in Table 1b against membership degree for the two different values of similarity, for the property colour (the plots are in fact identical for all properties). Note that in the dissimilar case, where no distractors are present that are close to the referent, the specificity is either maximal or linearly increasing with membership. The opposite is true for the similar condition.

3.4 Procedure

The experiment was implemented as part of an Android application called Refer4Learning (Marín et al., 2017a), originally designed to help teachers in the early stages of child education to work on basic concepts such as color, size, or position of simple geometric objects. For the purposes of the present experiment, a version of the app was created for use with adult participants to administer experimental trials.

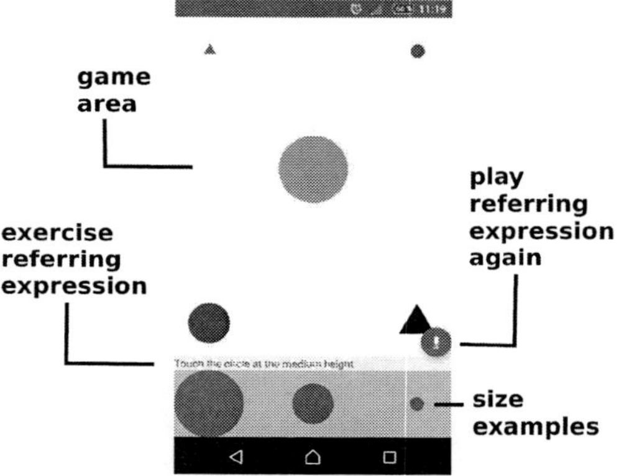

Figure 2: Screenshot of the experiment app. The referring expression in this case is *the circle at the medium height*.

As shown in Figure 2, trials consisted of a visual display with an instruction of the form *touch the NP*, where *NP* described the intended referent, which contained the identifying property (e.g. *the circle at the middle height*). The instruction was also played as an audio file.

Of the four properties used, size required special treatment. While the degree of membership

496

in a colour or location property can usually be determined based on the visual configuration or the user's knowledge (e.g. an object in a shade of pink has less membership in red than a stereotypically red object), for size, one typically requires reference points to determine what counts as stereotypically large, small etc, or else there is complete reliance on a comparison to other objects in the domain (van Deemter, 2006).

In the present case, this would result in a potential confusion between membership degree (to what extent is this object large?) and similarity (how much larger is it than others?). Hence, a standard of comparison was provided for expressions using size, showing three representative sizes for the target shape. An example is shown at the bottom of Figure 2, involving circles (since the target referent and distractors happen to be circles in this instance).

The app recorded the object a participant identified as well as the time taken to identify it. Each participant saw the 40 trials in random order.

4 Results

The analysis proceeds in two stages. First, we investigate the impact of the fixed effects of property, similarity and membership on participant responses as reflected in their id-time and accuracy. Second, we analyse the relationship between the primary measures of specificity and indexes presented in Section 2 and the results.

4.1 Effects of membership degree, similarity and property

Figure 3a summarises the frequency of correct responses, according to the identifying property, the similarity condition, and the target's degree of membership in the identifying property. The same is shown for mean reaction time in Figure 3b.

These figures suggest that similarity and membership degree had an impact on both accuracy and id-time. However, the picture varies considerably from one property to another. For example, accuracy goes down with increasing membership when the identifying property is colour and there is a similar distractor, while id-time is faster for size as membership increases, particularly in the dissimilar condition.

Figure 4 shows the impact of membership and similarity more clearly, by aggregating over all the four levels of the property fixed effect. Figure 4a shows that accuracy of identification is lower when there is a similar distractor to the target. In the case of id-time (Figure 4b), participants took longer to identify the target in the presence of a similar distractor. While membership degree does not appear to exert a clear impact on time in the similar case, in the dissimilar case, there is a downward trend in id-time as membership degree increases. This suggests that, in the absence of a similar distractor, people resolved references faster the more clearly the target belonged to the identifying property.

In the remainder of this part of the analysis, we use hierarchical mixed models, conducting an analysis separately for accuracy (modelled as a binomial variable) and time. In each case, we first build a separate model with each of the three factors as fixed effect, and establish whether the fixed effect helps to predict the dependent by comparing this model's goodness-of-fit to that of a null model consisting of only an intercept. We then construct a full model combining all fixed effects and their interactions and report the outcomes of a significance test. Models for accuracy are logit mixed models; those for id-time are linear mixed models. All models include by-subject and by-item random intercepts. Models are compared using log likelihood and the Bayesian Information Criterion (BIC; lower values indicate better fit). Membership is modelled as a continuous predictor; similarity and property are centered around a mean of zero to facilitate interpretation of main effects. Models are built using the `lme4` package in R (Bates et al., 2015); significance testing is conducted with `lmerTest` (Kuznetsova et al., 2014).

Table 2 shows the simple model comparisons for both accuracy and time. These suggest that of all the single predictors, it is similarity that has the highest explanatory value. The likelihood of participants identifying the correct target can to some extent be predicted from the membership degree of the target in the identifying property, though this model fits the data only marginally better than the null model. The role of membership degree is more clear in the case of id-time. There is no obvious impact of the type of property used to identify the target referent.

Next, we combine all fixed effects and their interactions in a single model to predict accuracy and time. The breakdown of the models is shown in Table 3. In both models, the effect of similarity

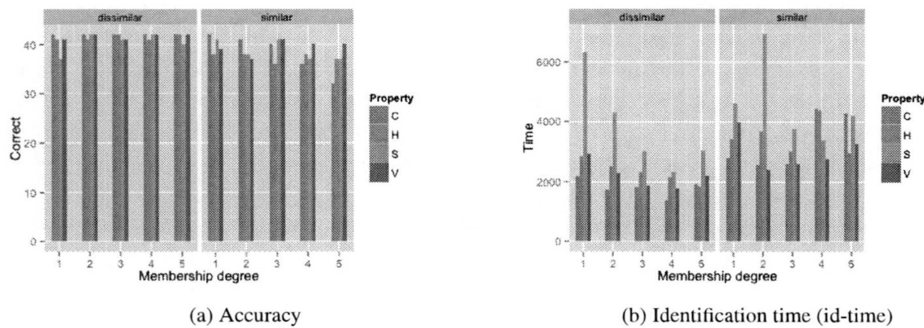

(a) Accuracy   (b) Identification time (id-time)

Figure 3: Time and accuracy as a function of property, similarity and membership (best viewed in colour).

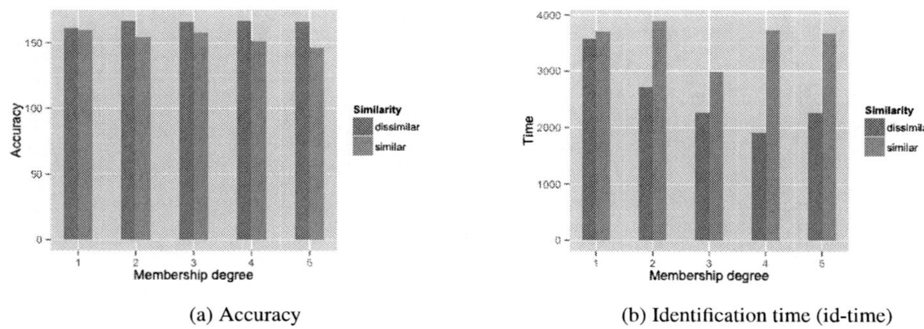

(a) Accuracy   (b) Identification time (id-time)

Figure 4: Time and accuracy as a function of similarity and membership (best viewed in colour).

Model	BIC	LL	χ^2
0. Intercept	546.74	-263.27	
1. Similarity	502.31	-237.69	51.159***
2. Membership	550.34	-261.7	3.134.
3. Property	552.88	-262.97	0.5939

(a) Accuracy

Model	BIC	LL	χ^2
0. Intercept	16019	-7996.1	
1. Similarity	16003	-7984.5	23.313***
2. Membership	16020	-7993.4	5.4181*
3. Property	16024	-7995	2.2904

(b) Identification time

Table 2: Single-factor model comparisons. All comparisons are to Model 0, the null model with no fixed effects. BIC: Bayesian Information Criterion; LL: Log Likelihood. ***: significant at $p < .001$; *: significant at $p < .05$; ·: marginally significant at $p \geq .05$.

turns out to be due to its interaction with membership degree. This corresponds to observations made above in connection with Figure 4: As membership degree increases, participants were more likely to identify the wrong target, and were slower in responding, in case there was a similar distractor.

On the other hand, a main effect of property is also evident. The nature of this main effect can be interpreted with reference to Figure 3 where, as noted above, the impact of membership degree and similarity differs between properties. In the case of id-time, membership interacts significantly with property type. This is likely due to the tendency for participants to respond faster as membership increases, when size or horizontal location is the identifying property (cf. Figure 3b).

4.2 Validation of specificity measures

In order to validate the specificity measures, we address two questions: 1) to what extent does the specificity of a referring expression, computed using one of the measures in Table 1, predict the accuracy and speed with which participants resolve references?; 2) do the specificity measures

498

Fixed Effects	Estimate	Std. Error	z-value
(Intercept)	2.88	0.45	6.39***
S	0.07	0.74	0.09
M	0.07	0.13	0.53
P	-0.66	0.33	-2.01*
S × M	-0.73	0.26	-2.77**
S × P	-0.42	0.66	-0.64
M × P	0.18	0.12	1.58
S × M × P	0.29	0.23	1.26

(a) Accuracy

Fixed Effects	Estimate	Std. Error	t-value
(Intercept)	3620.53	329.01	11***
S	119.29	508.24	0.24
M	-182.07	76.62	-2.38*
P	585.02	232.54	2.52*
S × M	314.26	153.24	2.05*
S × P	102.32	454.59	0.23
M × P	-142.17	69.58	-2.04*
S × M × P	-125.16	137.06	-0.91

(b) Identification time (id-time)

Table 3: Full models incorporating all fixed effects and interactions. Legend: *** significant at $p < .001$; ** significant at $p < .01$; * significant at $p < .05$.

correlate negatively with id-time, as would be expected?

	BIC	LL	z−test
m1	508.54	-240.81	4.871**
m2	500.68	-236.87	6.92**
m3	532.98	-253.02	3.809**
m4	508.54	-240.81	4.871**
m5	517.13	-245.1	4.934**
m6	504.32	-238.69	6.851**
m7	528.52	-250.79	4.621**
m8	516.73	-244.9	6.191**

(a) Dependent: Accuracy (binomial)

	BIC	LL	t−test
m1	15994	-7980.4	-5.662**
m2	16013	-7989.8	-3.581**
m3	16002	-7984.4	-4.883**
m4	15994	-7980.4	-5.662**
m5	15996	-7981	-5.555**
m6	16015	-7990.9	-3.25*
m7	15998	-7982.4	-5.277**
m8	16018	-7992.4	-2.738*

(b) Dependent: Response time

Table 4: Models with each of the eight success measures as predictor. BIC: Bayesian Information Criterion; LL: Log-likelihood. **$p < .01$; *$p < .01$.

	X_{corr}	X_{incorr}	$X_{corr} - X_{incorr}$
m1	0.418	0.238	0.180
m2	0.756	0.476	0.280
m3	0.293	0.161	0.132
m4	0.418	0.238	0.180
m5	0.455	0.301	0.154
m6	0.824	0.588	0.235
m7	0.493	0.360	0.134
m8	0.890	0.689	0.201

Table 5: Accuracy: Means and differences for the 8 specificity measures. $\bar{X}_{in/corr}$: mean measure of specificity for in/correctly identified referents.

	Pearson's r	Spearman's ρ
m1	-0.184	-0.258
m2	-0.117	-0.202
m3	-0.159	-0.239
m4	-0.184	-0.258
m5	-0.181	-0.293
m6	-0.107	-0.202
m7	-0.172	-0.265
m8	-0.091	-0.163

Table 6: Correlation coefficients between time and each referential success measure

In order to check whether the specificity measures have predictive power, we conducted two sets of mixed-models analysis, one on accuracy and one on id-time. In each case, constructed models contain one of the measures as the sole predictor. The outcomes are summarised in Table 4. All measures emerge as significant predictors of the likelihood with which a participant identifies a target referent accurately, and of the variance in id-time.

Accuracy To investigate the role of different measures in predicting accuracy, Table 5 divides the experimental data into instances on which a participant correctly identified the target referent and those where they did not. For each, we con-

sider the mean of each specificity measure and the difference in means. The latter can be thought of as a measure of 'sensitivity': The greater the difference between means of correct vs. incorrect trials, the more a measure is able to differentiate between the two. On these grounds, we obtain an ordering of the measures as follows: m3 < m7 < m5 < m1 < m4 < m8 < m6 < m2.

Identification time We further investigated the correlation between id-time and each specificity measure using both Pearson and Spearman correlations. These are summarised in Table 6. The correlations go in the predicted direction (i.e. they are negative), though they are generally on the low side. The low coefficients suggest that the relationship between time and specificity is nonlinear; in the case of Pearson's r, a further assumption that is probably violated in our data is that of monotonicity.

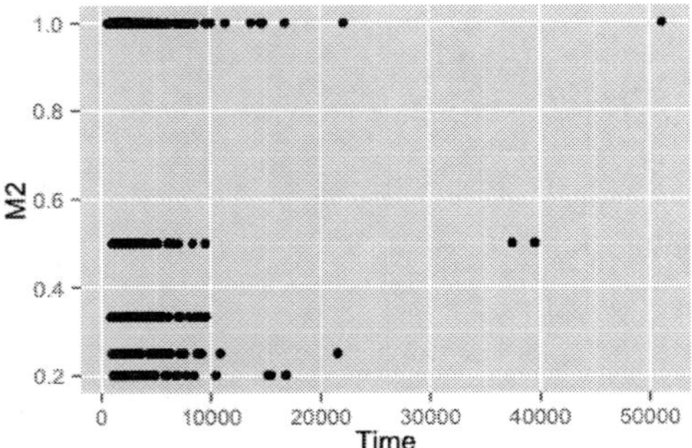

Figure 5: Relationship between $m2$ and id-time

As one example, Figure 5 plots id-time against measure $m2$ (similar patterns obtain for all measures). What the figure suggests is a tendency for the measure to divide cases into classes which do not linearly correspond with time. This is in spite of the evidence in Table 4, that specficity measures are good predictors of the variance in reaction time, as well as accuracy.

Ranking the measures according to the Spearman correlation coefficient yields a different ordering from the one obtained for accuracy: m5 < m7 < m1 < m4 < m3 < m2 < m6 < m8.

In summary, the results indicate that referential success measures can reliably predict human performance in resolving referring expressions. Crucially, however, the relationship is strongest with respect to accuracy, rather than id-time. This is to be expected: our measures of referential success are after all intended as measures of how likely it is that a referring expression singles out a particular object.

5 Discussion and Conclusions

This paper addressed the notion of referential success, arguing that predicting the success of a referring expression generated by a REG algorithm needs to take into account the graduality of the available properties and contextual factors, including the degree of membership in a property of a target's distractors.

While gradable properties have been addressed in the REG literature (van Deemter, 2006), the implications of graduality for referential success remain under-explored and the complex interactions between the evaluation of the properties of an entity and the visual context it is in have only recently begun to benefit from principled accounts (Yu et al., 2016; Williams and Scheutz, 2017).

The account of referential success given here is based on the concept of specificity, a measure of the identifiability of an entity based on the possibility distribution associated with its properties. Hence, we do not consider any property as necessarily crisp. Rather, by taking fuzzy membership degrees into account, we are able to quantify to what extent an entity is a member of the fuzzy set representing a property, and how close to it its distractors in their membership of that property. We identified a number of measures of specificity with desirable formal properties (including that they induce a ranking on membership degrees) and addressed the validity of this theoretical framework through an experiment. The results show that the theoretical assumptions are on the right track: Specificity measures are able to predict a significant proportion of the variance in identification time during referential tasks. Furthermore, they are able to account for the odds of selecting the correct referent given a referring expression. From a behavioural perspective, our experiments also confirm that reference resolution by humans is affected by similarity and property membership.

From the perspective of REG, the work presented here serves at least two important purposes: First, it provides a principle revision of the criterion that is typically used by algorithms to determine when a referent has been successfully identified by a description. Second, measures of referential success are also useful to evaluate the output of algorithms. This is especially the case for identification accuracy, where we find a strong relationship between referential success measures and the probability that a referring expression allows a receiver to identify the intended object.

This work also opens a number of avenues for future work. We are interested in extending our empirical validaiton of specificity measures to more complex scenarios, including descriptions in which a referent is identified by more than one property. Second, we are studying how current REG algorithms can be modified to use fuzzy measures of referential success as a stopping criterion, i.e. to determine when a referring expression is likely to provide sufficient information for a user to resolve it successfully.

Acknowledgments

This work has been partially supported by the Spanish Government and the European Regional Development Fund - ERDF (Fondo Europeo de Desarrollo Regional - FEDER) under project TIN2014-58227-P *Descripción lingüística de información visual mediante técnicas de minería de datos y computación flexible.*

References

D. Bates, M. Mchler, B. Bolker, and S. Walker. 2015. Fitting linear mixed-effects models using lme4. *Journal of Statistical Software, Articles*, 67(1):1–48.

T. Castro Ferreira. 2018. *Advances in Natural Language Generation: Generating varied outputs from semantic inputs.* Ph.D. thesis, Tilburg University, The Netherlands.

R. Dale and E. Reiter. 1995. Computational Interpretations of the Gricean Maxims in the Generation of Referring Expressions. *Cognitive Science*, 19(2):233–263.

K. van Deemter. 2006. Generating referring expressions that involve gradable properties. *Computational Linguistics*, 32(2):195–222.

K. van Deemter. 2016. *Computational Models of Referring: A Study in Cognitive Science.* MIT Press, Cambridge, MA.

D. Dubois and H. Prade. 1987. Properties of measures of information in evidence and possibility theories. *Fuzzy Sets and Systems*, 24:161–182.

L. Garmendia, R. R. Yager, E. Trillas, and A. Salvador. 2003. On t-norms based specificity measures. *Fuzzy Sets and Systems*, 133(2):237–248.

A. Gatt and A. Belz. 2010. Introducing shared task evaluation to NLG: The TUNA shared task evaluation challenges. In E. Krahmer and M. Theune, editors, *Empirical methods in natural language generation*. Springer, Berlin and Heidelberg.

A. Gatt, N. Marín, F. Portet, and D. Sánchez. 2016. The role of graduality for referring expression generation in visual scenes. In *Proc. IPMU 2016, Part I, CCIS 610*.

H Horacek. 2005. Generating referential descriptions under conditions of uncertainty. In *Proc. 10th European Workshop on Natural Language Generation (ENLG'05)*.

S. Kazemzadeh, V. Ordonez, M. Matten, and T.L. Berg. 2014. ReferItGame: Referring to Objects in Photographs of Natural Scenes. In *Proc. 2014 Conf. on Empirical Methods in Natural Language Processing (EMNLP'14)*.

E. Krahmer and K. van Deemter. 2012. Computational generation of referring expressions: A survey. *Computational Linguistics*, 38(1):173–218.

A. Kuznetsova, P.B. Brockhoff, and R.H.B. Christensen. 2014. lmerTest: Tests for random and fixed effects for linear mixed effect models.

J. Mao, J. Huang, A. Toshev, O. Camburu, A. Yuille, and K. Murphy. 2016. Generation and Comprehension of Unambiguous Object Descriptions. In *Proc. 2016 Conf. on Computer Vision and Pattern Recognition (CVPR'16)*.

N. Marín, G. Rivas-Gervilla, and D. Sánchez. 2016. Using specificity to measure referential success in referring expressions with fuzzy properties. In *Proc. IEEE Int. Conf. on Fuzzy Systems (FUZZ-IEEE'16)*.

N. Marín, G. Rivas-Gervilla, and D. Sánchez. 2017a. Scene selection for teaching basic visual concepts in the Refer4Learning app. In *Proc. IEEE Int. Conf. on Fuzzy Systems (FUZZ-IEEE'17)*.

N. Marín, G. Rivas-Gervilla, D. Sánchez, and R. R. Yager. 2017b. On families of bounded specificity measures. In *Proc. IEEE Int. Conf. on Fuzzy Systems (FUZZ-IEEE'17)*.

N. Marín, G. Rivas-Gervilla, D. Sánchez, and R. R. Yager. 2018. Specificity measures and referential success. *IEEE Trans. on Fuzzy Systems*, 26(2):859–868.

T. Pechmann. 1989. Incremental speech production and referential overspecification. *Linguistics*, 27(1):89–110.

P. Rubio-Fernandez. 2016. How redundant are redundant color adjectives? An efficiency-based analysis of color overspecification. *Frontiers in Psychology*, 7(153):1–15.

S. Tarenskeen, M. Broersma, and B. Geurts. 2015. Overspecification of color, pattern, and size: salience, absoluteness, and consistency. *Frontiers in Psychology*, 6(1703).

R. Turner, S. Sripada, E. Reiter, and I.P Davy. 2008. Selecting the Content of Textual Descriptions of Geographically Located Events in Spatio-Temporal Weather Data. In *Applications and Innovations in Intelligent Systems XV*, pages 75–88.

T. Williams and M. Scheutz. 2017. Referring Expression Generation under Uncertainty: Algorithm and Evaluation Framework. In *Proc. 10th Int. Conf. on Natural Language Generation (INLG'17)*.

R. R. Yager. 1982. Measuring tranquility and anxiety in decision-making: An application of fuzzy sets. *Internat. J. Gen. Systems*, 8:139–146.

R. R. Yager. 1990. Ordinal measures of specificity. *Internat. J. Gen. Systems*, 17:57–72.

R. R. Yager. 1992. On the specificity of a possibility distribution. *Fuzzy Sets and Systems*, 50:279–292.

L. Yu, P. Poirson, S. Yang, A.C. Berg, and T.L. Berg. 2016. Modeling Context in Referring Expressions. *arXiv*, 1608.00272.

L. A. Zadeh. 1999. From computing with numbers to computing with words. from manipulation of measurements to manipulation of perceptions. *IEEE Trans. on Circuits and Systems I: Fundamental Theory and Applications*, 46(1):105–119.

Decoding Strategies for Neural Referring Expression Generation

Sina Zarrieß and **David Schlangen**
Dialogue Systems Group // CITEC // Faculty of Linguistics and Literary Studies
Bielefeld University, Germany
{sina.zarriess,david.schlangen}@uni-bielefeld.de

Abstract

RNN-based sequence generation is now widely used in NLP and NLG (natural language generation). Most work focusses on how to train RNNs, even though also decoding is not necessarily straightforward: previous work on neural MT found seq2seq models to radically prefer short candidates, and has proposed a number of beam search heuristics to deal with this. In this work, we assess decoding strategies for referring expression generation with neural models. Here, expression length is crucial: output should neither contain too much or too little information, in order to be pragmatically adequate. We find that most beam search heuristics developed for MT do not generalize well to referring expression generation (REG), and do not generally outperform greedy decoding. We observe that beam search heuristics for termination seem to override the model's knowledge of what a good stopping point is. Therefore, we also explore a recent approach called trainable decoding, which uses a small network to modify the RNN's hidden state for better decoding results. We find this approach to consistently outperform greedy decoding for REG.

1 Introduction

Recently, many NLP problems that involve some form of natural language generation have been modeled with encoder-decoder architectures based on recurrent neural networks, e.g. in machine translation (Bahdanau et al., 2014), summarization (Ranzato et al., 2016), conversation modeling (Vinyals and Le, 2015), image captioning

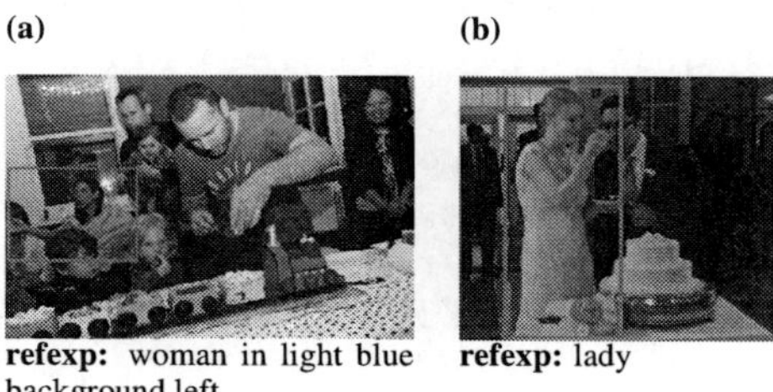

Figure 1: RefCOCO (Yu et al., 2016) examples for referring expressions to targets (red box) in images

(Xu et al., 2015), etc. A simple and efficient way to apply the decoder model during testing is to generate the most likely word at each time step, until an end symbol has been generated or the maximal number of time steps has been reached. However, this greedy search method does not generally produce optimal generation output, and has been shown to produce repetitive or invariable sentences in certain tasks, e.g. (Li et al., 2016). Thus, a common practice (particularly in MT) is to use beam search where a fixed number of hypotheses are considered (and expanded) at each time step. Unfortunately, beam search is a heuristic algorithm that can be defined and parametrized in different ways, and brings with it further modeling decisions that need to be explored. A particularly tricky issue in neural MT, for instance, is to define a good stopping criterion for search, as neural models tend to radically prefer short hypotheses (Graves, 2012). To the best of our knowledge, it has not yet been systematically investigated whether beam search heuristics developed for MT carry over to other generation tasks, in particular, to tasks in the area of language and vision.

In this paper, we investigate decoding strategies for neural referring expression generation (REG) applied to objects in real-world images. This task is closely related to image captioning in the sense

Proceedings of The 11th International Natural Language Generation Conference, pages 503–512,
Tilburg, The Netherlands, November 5-8, 2018. ©2018 Association for Computational Linguistics

that a visual entity has to be described by a verbal, semantically adequate expression. But beyond semantic adequacy, REG also requires pragmatic reasoning: referring expressions typically do not only depend on the object they refer to, but also on the visual context of that object, as human speakers tend to tailor their utterances such that a listener can easily understand them in the current context. For instance, a short RE that simply names the object (e.g. *lady* in Figure 1(b)) is unlikely to be produced than in a scene that contains more objects of the same category, see Figure 1(a). Thus, previous work on neural REG has investigated techniques of incorporating contextual knowledge into the model during training, looking at different visual representations and optimization techniques (Mao et al., 2015; Yu et al., 2016). Somewhat surprisingly, however, relatively complex architectural set-ups are needed to improve over simple, context-agnostic baselines that generate descriptions for the objects as captioning models do for entire images (Yu et al., 2017).

In this paper, we take a closer look at the decoding step in neural REG. As referring expressions tend to be much shorter than full sentences in MT, for instance, it is not guaranteed that heuristics developed for beam search in MT are equally successful. More importantly even, the problem of determining the appropriate length of a referring expression, i.e. terminating beam search, is conceptually different than determining the length of a good translation: a translation is complete when it covers the *meaning* of the words in the source sentence, and indeed, the length of the source is used as criterion in beam search for MT (see Section 2.3). A referring expression, on the other hand, is complete when it describes the visual target in a *pragmatically* adequate way, i.e. when it neither provides too little nor too much information.

We explore a range of different variants of beam search that have been proposed for MT and, interestingly, find that most of them *decrease* performance as compared to simple greedy decoding in REG. Whereas greedy decoding leads to referring expressions that, on average, have an adequate length, beam search produces REs that are markedly shorter and various heuristics can only partially remedy for this problem. Therefore, we look at *trainable decoding*, a method proposed by Gu et al. (2017), that offers a principled solution for obtaining a decoder that maximizes a given objective (e.g. BLEU scores). This method has been shown to outperform greedy decoding and to be computationally more efficient than beam search in MT (Gu et al., 2017; Chen et al., 2018). We find that it qualitatively outperforms both greedy and beam search in the case of neural REG.

2 Related Work

2.1 Symbolic formalizations of REG

Traditionally, research on NLG has conceived of REG as a multi-stage process that involves the tasks of lexicalization, content selection and surface realization (Reiter and Dale, 2000; Krahmer and Van Deemter, 2012). But foundational work in REG has mostly focused on algorithms for attribute selection (Dale and Reiter, 1995). In this paradigm, the task is to generate a distinguishing referring expression for an object in a visual scene, which is defined as a target object, a set of distractor objects and a set of symbolic attributes (e.g. type, position, size, color, ...), see Krahmer and Van Deemter (2012). In this setting, an attribute is said to *rule out* a distractor object, if the target and distractor have different values. Dale and Reiter (1995)'s well-known *Incremental Algorithm* (IA) iterates over the attribute set in a pre-defined order, selects an attribute if it rules out objects from the set of distractors and terminates when the set is empty. In the context of our work, this algorithm can be seen as a decoding procedure over a symbolically specified input for REG that heuristically defines the stopping criterion, i.e. when to terminate the expansion of the RE. A lot of subsequent work has looked at refining and extending this algorithm, testing it on human-generated expressions (Krahmer et al., 2003; Mitchell et al., 2010; van Deemter et al., 2012; Clarke et al., 2013).

2.2 Neural REG from real-world images

More recently, research on REG has started to investigate set-ups based on real-world images (Kazemzadeh et al., 2014; Gkatzia et al., 2015; Mao et al., 2015; Zarrieß and Schlangen, 2016), representing scenes with many different types of real-world objects. Here, the input to the REG system is defined as a low-level visual representation such that various aspects of the task have to be addressed, including lexicalization and content selection. Inspired by research on image captioning, Mao et al. (2015) proposed the first neural end-to-end model for REG that uses a CNN to represent the image, followed by an LSTM to generate the referring expression. Yu et al. (2016, 2017) investigate a number of ways to incorporate pragmatic reasoning into a CNN-LSTM architecture for REG, and also collected two datasets of referring expressions for objects in the MSCOCO corpus in the ReferItGame setup (Kazemzadeh et al., 2014). All these authors state that they use beam search during decoding, but do not investigate the effect of this search method (nor do they state exactly which variant of beam search was used). Our work suggests that the effectiveness of contextual features interacts with the decoding procedure.

2.3 Decoding for neural MT

We now turn to (neural) MT, where decoding algorithms for sequence generation have been investigated in detail. Here, beam search is the standard method for syntax- and phrase-based models (Rush et al., 2013), as well as for neural encoder-decoders (Freitag and Al-Onaizan, 2017). However, an important difference between the two is that candidates in phrase-based MT are completed in the same number of steps, whereas neural models generate hypotheses of different length and are biased for shorter output (Huang et al., 2017). To counteract this bias, OpenNMT (Klein et al., 2017) adopts three metrics for normalizing the coverage, length and end of sentence of candidate translations. Unfortunately, two of these metrics (coverage and end of sentence normalization) are based on the length of the source sentence, which is not available in REG. Another common NMT framework (Bahdanau et al., 2014) uses a shrinking beam where beam size is reduced each time a completed hypothesis is found, and search terminates when the beam size has reached 0.

Another shortcoming of beam search observed in previous work is that the beam tends to contain many candidates that share the same (most likely) prefix (Freitag and Al-Onaizan, 2017). This means that a relatively high value for beam size is needed to ensure that more diverse hypotheses that could potentially lead to more probable output are not excluded too early. A range of works have looked at modifying the objective of beam search such that more diverse candidates are considered during search (Li et al., 2016; Freitag and Al-Onaizan, 2017). See Section 4 for an overview of the beam search heuristics we use in this paper.

To overcome the limitations of heuristically defined beam search, Gu et al. (2017) introduce the notion of trainable decoding that takes a pre-trained neural MT system and optimizes the decoder for any objective. They treat the decoder as a small actor network that learns to manipulate the hidden state of the underlying trained MT system. Whereas Gu et al. (2017) train the decoder actor network with a policy gradient method, Chen et al. (2018) present a supervised method to train the decoder. We will follow the latter approach, as described in Section 4.

3 REG Models

As the focus of this work is on the decoding step for neural REG models, we adopt a standard model architecture in language and vision: we use the pre-softmax layer of a pre-trained CNN to represent the image and the image region that a given target expression refers to. We train a standard LSTM to generate a word at each time step, conditioned on the visual vector and the previous words. Our LSTM mainly follows the implementation of (Xu et al., 2015)[1], one of the most widely known models for image captioning, but does not use attention over the image.

We note that Xu et al. (2015) use a deep decoding layer that computes the output word probability given the LSTM state, the context vector and the previous word including dropout and non-linear (tanh) activation functions, similar to Yu et al. (2017) who also use dropout in the decoding layer, but only linear activation functions. Mao et al. (2015), on the other hand, adopt a simple linear layer for decoding the LSTM. In the following, we will investigate how these modeling decisions affect the performance, and how they interact with different search methods during inference.[2] We distinguish two variants of our model according to their decoding layer:

Linear decoding layer:

$$p = softmax(W_h h + b_h) \qquad (1)$$

where p is the distribution over the vocabulary, W_h is the weight matrix, b_h is the bias term, and h is the hidden state of the LSTM.

---

[1]`https://github.com/yunjey/show-attend-and-tell`

[2]Please note that there are two aspects of decoding in our set-up: the decoding layer of the LSTM, and the decoding inference procedure applied during testing.

Deep decoding layer:

$$
\begin{aligned}
h_1 &= dropout(h_0) \\
h_2 &= tanh((W_h h_1 + b_h) + (W_z z + b_z) + x_{prev}) \\
h_3 &= dropout(h_2) \\
p &= softmax(W_{out} h_3 + b_{out})
\end{aligned}
\tag{2}
$$

where h_0 is the hidden state, z is the visual vector and x_{prev} the embedding of the previous word.

Finally, we also vary the input visual representation that the LSTM is conditioned on. Whereas Mao et al. (2015) extract visual representations of the region representing the target referent and the global image, Yu et al. (2016) report a slightly detrimental effect of including these global context features. Thus, we distinguish two variants of the model according to its visual representation:

Target: 4103-dimensional vector, obtained by cropping the image to the target region, resizing to 224×224, extracting its CNN pre-softmax features with VGG19 (Simonyan and Zisserman, 2014) and concatenating 7 spatial features of the region (see Schlangen et al. (2016) for these)

Global+target: 8119-dimensional vector, obtained by extracting the CNN pre-softmax features with VGG19 (Simonyan and Zisserman, 2014) for the entire image, and concatenating it with **target-only**

Training We set the word embedding layer size to 512, and the hidden state to 1024. We optimized with ADAM (with $\alpha = 0.001$), and the batch size set to 50. The word embedding layer is initialized with random weights. The number of training epochs was tuned for each model on the validation set.

4 Decoding Strategies

We now explain the different decoding strategies that will be combined with the REG models.

4.1 Greedy decoding

This is the simplest way to apply an LSTM based generator for testing: at each time step, the most likely word is selected and added to the generation history. Greedy decoding terminates when the end symbol is generated.

4.2 Beam search

Beam search generalizes greedy decoding and keeps a fixed number K of generation candidates

that are expanded at each time step (greedy decoding corresponds to beam search with $K = 1$). This is computationally less efficient than greedy search, but often yields better results in NLP (see Section 2). A definition of a standard beam search algorithm that a lot of previous work has followed can be found in Graves (2012).

As discussed in Section 2.3, the general skeleton of the beam search algorithm allows for a number of modifications, that concern the following criteria: (i) pruning: which candidates are added to the beam for the next time step, (ii) termination: when does search stop, (iii) normalization: how to treat candidates of different length, (iv) beam size: constant or dynamic value for K. The summary of search strategies we will test is shown in Table 1.

In the simple beam search version, the decoder checks after each iteration, whether the top-most candidate is complete. If this is not the case, all current candidates remain for the next iteration, including complete hypotheses that have a rank > 1. During development, we noticed that this causes short, lower ranked complete hypotheses to climb up the beam too quickly and win over long hypotheses (see results in Section 6.3). Therefore, we also introduce a new variation of simple beam, called **same-len** in Table 1. The **same-len** variant excludes complete hypotheses on the beam that have a rank > 1, whereas in the standard version these would remain on the beam. In the **same-len** version a complete hypothesis either wins (when it is on top) or is pruned, which means that all candidates on the beam are of the same length (when counting the end symbol).

When candidates of different length are kept on the beam, we can normalize according to the following scores taken from Klein et al. (2017):

$$
lp(y) = \frac{(5 + |Y|)^\alpha}{(5 + 1)^\alpha}
\tag{3}
$$

where $|Y|$ is the length of the candidate output and α is usually set to a value between 0.6 and 0.8 (Wu et al., 2016). We could not find an explanation for the constant being set to 5 in the literature. This length penalty is then used to boost probabilities of longer sequences in the following way:

$$
score(y, x) = \frac{log P(y|x)}{lp(y)}
\tag{4}
$$

where $P(y|x)$ corresponds to the probability assigned to the candidate y at the given time step.

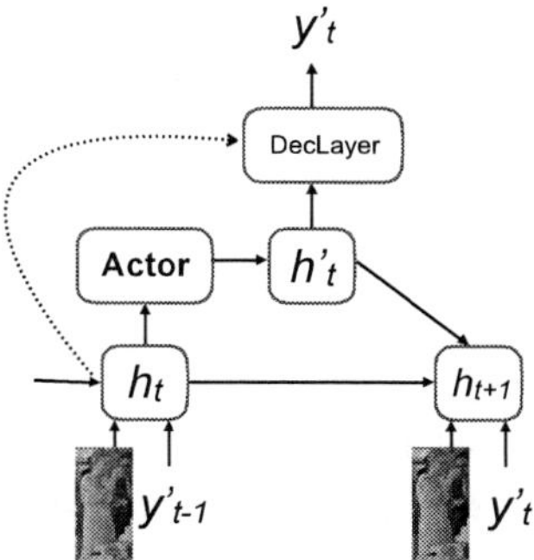

Figure 2: Illustration of neural REG architecture including an actor network that manipulates the hidden state; the dotted line indicates the information flow in the standard model where the hidden state is directly passed to the decoding layer

4.3 Trainable decoding

Finally, we set up a trainable decoder as in Chen et al. (2018) that adds a new *actor* module to the trained REG model. As illustrated in Figure 2, the actor learns to manipulate the hidden state that is then passed to the decoding layer. When training the actor, the weights of the underlying REG system are fixed. Thus, instead of optimizing the entire architecture in one stage, we adopt a procedure that first learns an REG model as usual, and then learns to decode this model in a second step.

For training the decoding actor in a supervised way, we need an 'artificial' corpus of referring expressions paired with objects in images that are both considered to be likely by the model and achieve a good BLEU score when compared to the original human expression. Thus, for an object x we use the REG model and beam search to produce a set of referring expressions $Y = y_1, y_2, ..., y_n$ that correspond to all completed hypotheses from all time steps, with a certain beam size K. But in contrast to the methods explained in Section 4.2, we do not need to define a heuristic stopping criterion. Instead, we use an oracle that selects y from the set Y that achieves the highest BLEU score given the human references. Of course, this oracle is only needed at training time. The actor itself is a simple feedforward layer that updates the hidden state as follows:

$$h' = h + relu(W_h h) \qquad (5)$$

This is a slightly simpler definition than the one used in Chen et al. (2018) where the actor is also conditioned on the original input vector. We experimented with their version, but found a simple

layer with ReLU activation to yield the best performance. When applying the actor at test time, it is possible to combine it with beam search (Gu et al., 2017). However, we only use it in a greedy fashion, as beam search did not lead to clear improvements in our experiments.

Training The main parameters to configure for training concern the definition of the oracle for compiling the new training data. We set K (beam size of the oracle) to 10, and use $BLEU_1$ (restricted to unigrams) as objective. We train the actor for 10 epochs, with ADAM.

5 Data

We conduct experiments on the RefCOCO(+) datasets, same as (Yu et al., 2016), which contain referring expressions to objects in MSCOCO (Lin et al., 2014) images. The data was collected via crowdsourcing with the ReferIt Game (Kazemzadeh et al., 2014) where two players were paired and a director needed to refer to a predetermined object to a matcher, who then selected it. Note that (Mao et al., 2015) performed experiments on a different data set for MSCOCO images in a non-interactive set-up. Thus, our evaluation set-up largely follows Yu et al. (2016, 2017).

RefCOCO and RefCOCO+ contain 3 referring expressions on average per object, and overall 150K expressions for 50K objects. The two datasets have been collected for an (almost) identical set of objects, but in RefCOCO+, players were asked not to use location words (*on the left*, etc.). See Yu et al. (2016) for more details. We use the predefined training and test splits. The respective test sets are divided into two subsets: **testA** is restricted to objects of the category human, **testB** consists of all other object types.

6 Experiments

6.1 Evaluation

Since we compare a whole range of REG models and decoding strategies, we opt for automatic evaluation measures, even though these might not fully reflect the performance that would be achieved in interaction with human users, cf. (Zarrieß and Schlangen, 2016). Unfortunately, different measures have been used in Yu et al. (2016) ($BLEU_1$, Meteor, ROUGE), and (Yu et al., 2017) (CIDEr, Meteor), which makes comparison less straightforward. Also note that Yu et al. (2017) state that they collected additional expressions for the test-sets, resulting in 10 expressions per objects. As we did not have access to these additional expressions at the time of writing, we follow Yu et al. (2016) and evaluate on the original RefCOCO collections with 3 expressions on average per object.

In the experiments below, we look at three measures: **BLEU$_1$** for unigrams (Papineni et al., 2002), **CIDEr** (Vedantam et al., 2015) and **lenr** (length ratio) as provided by the MSCOCO evaluation server (Chen et al., 2015). We are interested in the length ratio as a simple approximation of traditionally used measures in REG (Gatt and Belz, 2010), reflecting whether the generation output contains too much or too little information (attributes or words). **BLEU$_1$** gives us an indication of the lexical overlap between output and target, whereas **CIDEr** operates on the level of n-grams.

6.2 Simple beam search

In Table 2, we present results for the different configurations of our REG model, tested with greedy decoding and the simple variant of beam search, with $K = 3$ and $K = 10$. Our results for greedy decoding are comparable in BLEU$_1$ to the baseline results reported by Yu et al. (2016), with lower performance on RefCOCO+. This is likely due to different hyperparameter settings. The model comparison also shows that the combination of global context features and a deep decoding layer is clearly disadvantageous, especially for RefCOCO+. However, for the region model, the linear decoder outperforms the deep one on Ref-COCO+, but underperforms it on RefCOCO.

When analyzing the effect of beam size on performance for 16 model-test set combinations in Table 2, some clear patterns can be observed:

- a wider beam always leads to shorter expressions as shown be the average length ratio, the effect is drastic on the RefCOCO+ data (e.g. the av. ratio on testB is 0.92 for greedy decoding and 0.45 for beam search with $K = 3$)

- a wider beam leads to lower BLEU$_1$ scores for most models and test sets, except for 1 out of 16 model-test set combinations

- a wider beam sometimes leads to better CIDEr scores, BLEU$_1$ and CIDEr disagree in 7 out of 16 model-test set combinations

These results clearly suggest that the stopping criterion defined in standard beam search is not appropriate for neural REG models. The greedy decoding can estimate the appropriate expression length surprisingly well, even in the region model that does not have access to global context. In contrast, the standard beam search that keeps candidates of different length seems clearly biased towards output that is too short. However, the fact that CIDEr scores still improve in some cases suggests that beam search leads to linguistically more well-formed expressions (expressions with a lot of repetitions are avoided, e.g. *the blue blue shirt*).

6.3 Modified beam search

In Table 3, we report performance of the region and global model with the linear decoder and investigate the effect of different beam search variants on performance (for reasons of space, we omit the models with a deep decoder, as these were more unstable on RefCOCO+).

- a shrinking beam has a clearly detrimental effect on performance in all cases

- the other beam search variants consistently improve over simple beam search on all metrics

- there is no clear improvement of the beam search variants over greedy decoding

- len-norm and same-len achieve better length ratios than simple beam, but not better than greedy decoding

These results support our initial hypothesis that knowing when to terminate is an essential aspect of REG, and this aspect is learnt relatively well by the LSTM. Beam search heuristics for termination seem to override the model's knowledge of what a good stopping point is. The heuristics for length normalization and stopping have some positive effect over simple beam search, but are not fully effective, and might need more extensive tuning. But overall, this suggests that a more principled decoding solution for neural REG is needed as greedy decoding also leads to undesired output patterns (repeated words, for instance).

6.4 Trainable decoding

Table 4 compares the results for the greedy decoder against a decoder trained to optimize BLEU$_1$ scores, as explained in Section 4. Some interesting observations can be made:

- the trained decoder improves over the greedy decoder on all test sets, models and measures

method	filtering	termination	normalization	beam size
simple	–	when top y is complete	–	constant
len-norm	–	when top y is complete	length (eq. 3, 4)	constant
same-len	discard y if complete, but not top	when top y is complete	–	constant
pruning (Freitag and Al-Onaizan, 2017)	discard y if complete, but not top; discard y if m candidates with same history are in beam	when top y is complete	–	constant
shrinking (Bahdanau et al., 2014)	–	when beam size is 0, select top y that is complete	length (eq. 3, 4)	-1 for each complete y

Table 1: Beam search variants, y refers to generation candidates

model	K	testA Bleu1	testA CIDEr	testA lenr	testB Bleu1	testB CIDEr	testB lenr	testA+ Bleu1	testA+ CIDEr	testA+ lenr	testB+ Bleu1	testB+ CIDEr	testB+ lenr
Yu et al. (2016)'s BL	-	0.477	-	-	0.553	-	-	0.391	-	-	0.331	-	-
target,deep	1	**0.484**	**0.625**	**0.89**	**0.516**	**1.096**	**0.77**	**0.361**	**0.436**	1.04	**0.264**	0.552	**0.85**
target,deep	3	0.452	0.604	0.77	0.471	1.088	0.63	0.304	0.412	0.67	0.180	**0.587**	0.43
target,deep	10	0.430	0.592	0.70	0.454	1.093	0.60	0.208	0.379	0.50	0.148	0.582	0.38
target,lin	1	**0.445**	0.555	**0.85**	**0.513**	**1.078**	**0.85**	**0.378**	**0.443**	**1.00**	**0.296**	0.506	**0.99**
target,lin	3	0.420	**0.568**	0.70	0.480	**1.077**	0.69	0.302	0.415	0.65	0.252	**0.604**	0.57
target,lin	10	0.369	0.535	0.62	0.464	1.065	0.66	0.222	0.393	0.51	0.212	0.601	0.48
target+global,deep	1	0.400	**0.602**	**1.12**	**0.464**	1.011	**0.86**	**0.329**	**0.387**	1.04	**0.231**	0.525	**0.95**
target+global,deep	3	**0.440**	0.597	0.72	0.399	**1.014**	0.56	0.231	0.337	0.57	0.140	**0.567**	0.36
target+global,deep	10	0.387	0.569	0.62	0.371	1.003	0.53	0.147	0.326	0.41	0.150	0.576	0.37
target+global,lin	1	**0.461**	**0.593**	**0.89**	**0.497**	**1.043**	**0.78**	**0.357**	**0.382**	**0.91**	**0.281**	0.558	**0.92**
target+global,lin	3	0.426	0.588	0.72	0.443	**1.046**	0.61	0.267	0.350	0.61	0.192	**0.590**	0.45
target+global,lin	10	0.370	0.546	0.61	0.420	1.028	0.58	0.186	0.327	0.47	0.154	0.586	0.39

Table 2: Effect of beam size K on generation performance (beam with $K = 1$ corresponds to greedy decoding); comparing models with region and global features, and a deep vs. linear decoding layer.

model	decoder,K	testA Bleu1	testA CIDEr	testA lenr	testB Bleu1	testB CIDEr	testB lenr	testA+ Bleu1	testA+ CIDEr	testA+ lenr	testB+ Bleu1	testB+ CIDEr	testB+ lenr
target	greedy,1	0.445	0.555	**0.85**	**0.513**	1.078	**0.85**	**0.378**	**0.443**	**1.00**	**0.296**	0.506	**0.99**
target	simple,3	0.420	0.568	0.70	0.480	**1.077**	0.69	0.302	0.415	0.65	0.252	**0.604**	0.57
target	len-norm,3	0.454	0.598	0.77	0.504	**1.097**	0.75	0.314	0.417	0.71	0.275	0.616	0.64
target	len-norm,10	0.444	0.595	0.74	0.502	1.090	0.75	0.279	0.409	0.65	0.275	**0.622**	0.64
target	same-len,3	**0.464**	**0.601**	0.81	0.507	1.100	0.77	0.337	0.417	0.82	0.294	0.615	0.72
target	same-len,10	0.451	0.598	0.77	0.505	1.092	0.75	0.302	0.403	0.73	0.283	0.624	0.68
target	pruning,10	0.461	**0.602**	0.80	0.506	1.099	0.76	0.324	0.410	0.80	0.285	0.610	0.70
target	shrinking,3	0.237	0.317	2.48	0.272	0.600	2.06	0.254	0.319	1.45	0.230	0.460	1.34
target	shrinking,10	0.361	0.462	1.11	0.400	0.792	1.19	0.299	0.382	0.81	0.277	0.501	1.03
target+global	greedy,1	**0.461**	0.593	**0.89**	**0.497**	1.043	0.78	**0.357**	**0.382**	**0.91**	**0.281**	0.558	**0.92**
target+global	simple,3	0.426	0.588	0.72	0.443	**1.046**	0.61	0.267	0.350	0.61	0.192	**0.590**	0.45
target+global	len-norm,3	0.456	**0.613**	0.79	0.480	1.073	0.68	0.282	0.359	0.64	0.221	0.589	0.51
target+global	len-norm,10	0.441	0.601	0.76	0.484	1.073	0.69	0.237	0.355	0.57	0.218	**0.593**	0.50
target+global	same-len,3	**0.462**	**0.616**	0.84	0.490	**1.079**	0.71	0.328	0.380	0.79	0.264	0.588	0.64
target+global	same-len,10	0.447	0.606	0.79	0.490	1.072	0.71	0.269	0.357	0.66	0.255	0.582	0.60
target+global	pruning,10	0.459	0.617	0.83	0.488	1.068	0.70	0.302	0.366	0.74	0.258	0.588	0.61
target+global	shrinking,3	0.240	0.368	2.21	0.282	0.731	1.73	0.179	0.226	1.89	0.167	0.429	1.79
target+global	shrinking,10	0.379	0.469	0.89	0.436	0.843	**1.00**	0.275	0.314	0.75	0.233	0.545	0.62

Table 3: Model with linear decoding layer, different ways of normalizing/parametrizing beam search

model	decoder	testA Bleu1	testA CIDEr	testA lenr	testB Bleu1	testB CIDEr	testB lenr	testA+ Bleu1	testA+ CIDEr	testA+ lenr	testB+ Bleu1	testB+ CIDEr	testB+ lenr
target,deep	greedy	0.484	0.625	0.89	0.516	1.096	0.77	0.361	**0.436**	1.04	0.264	**0.552**	0.85
target,deep	bleu-actor	**0.507**	**0.658**	**0.95**	**0.534**	**1.112**	**0.82**	**0.377**	0.4	**1.02**	**0.269**	0.527	**0.75**
target,lin	greedy	0.445	0.555	0.85	0.513	1.078	0.85	**0.378**	0.443	**1.00**	0.296	0.506	**0.99**
target,lin	bleu-actor	**0.487**	**0.625**	**0.99**	**0.535**	**1.089**	**0.94**	**0.377**	**0.452**	1.09	**0.320**	**0.579**	0.97
target+global,lin	greedy	0.461	0.593	0.89	0.497	1.043	0.78	0.357	0.382	0.91	0.281	0.558	0.92
target+global,lin	bleu-actor	**0.498**	**0.655**	**1.02**	**0.549**	**1.083**	**0.93**	**0.375**	**0.419**	**1.02**	**0.315**	**0.587**	**0.93**

Table 4: Results for trainable decoding (actor model)

greedy: left vase
actor: left glass
(a2)

greedy: man on left
actor: girl on left

greedy: left
actor: left dog
(b2)

greedy: bottom right
actor: stove bottom right

greedy: guy on left
actor: person on far left
(c2)

greedy: person on left
actor: person in blue shirt on left

greedy: right bike
actor: bike on the right
(e) avoid rare words

greedy: bride
actor: woman in white dress

Figure 3: Examples from the RefCOCO validation set for strategies learned by the trained decoder

with only few exceptions (CIDEr scores on testA+ and testB+ for the deep region model)

- the improvements are substantial in many cases (between 2 and 8 points for $BLEU_1$, and up to 7 points for CIDEr)

- given the trained decoder, the global model now improves over the region model in the case of testB (BLEU, CIDEr, lenr) and testB+ (CIDEr)

These results demonstrate the importance of applying the right decoding procedure when generating with neural REG models. Interestingly, the qualitative improvements in performance we obtain clearly exceed the effects found with the same methods for MT (Chen et al., 2018), but generally support previous findings on positive effects when optimizing a sequence model for external evaluation metrics (Ranzato et al., 2016). A possible explanation is that our REG models benefit from a two-stage optimization procedure, similar to curriculum learning (Bengio et al., 2009). Another important question is whether $BLEU_1$, the objective we used to train the decoder, is conceptually appropriate for REG or whether we simply tune the model to our final evaluation measure. The fact that the actor model also improves the CIDEr scores and length ratios is a first positive indication that the $BLEU_1$-actor does not just fit to the metric in a superficial way. The qualitative analysis in Section 6.6 will shed more light on this.

6.5 Global context

Besides the effect of different decoding strategies on the performance of our neural REG model, an interesting and somewhat counterintuitive observation is that the models that incorporate global context features do not generally outperform the local models which only 'look' at the target referent. This finding seems to contradict some very basic assumptions that have been formulated in the REG literature, namely that the content of a referring expression (e.g. its attributes) depend on the distractors, cf. (Krahmer and Van Deemter, 2012). At the same time, a lot of theoretical and computational work on referring expressions has observed that human speakers tend to overspecify, i.e. use attributes even though they are not strictly needed to discriminate the target referent from its distractors (Koolen et al., 2011). Moreover, our findings seem to corroborate previous work on RefCOCO that even observed a detrimental effect of including global context features in a neural REG model.

Unfortunately, the RefCOCO corpora lack a ground truth annotation for attributes, hence, is it is hard to analyze whether the (missing) effect of global context is due to shortcomings of existing neural models for REG or due to inherent patterns in the data (such as e.g. overspecification). We believe that a more systematic approach to assessing the effect of distractors on content of referring expressions in real-world image corpora is a very promising direction for future research.

6.6 Analysis: Strategies learned via BLEU

We manually go through examples in the RefCOCO validation set, and broadly categorize the cases where the actor model improves over the greedy decoder. Figure 3 illustrates some frequent patterns we discovered with representative examples for each. Our analysis suggests that the actor has indeed automatically discovered strategies that lead to contextually more appropriate expressions: it learns to (a) fine-tune its lexicon and use object names in a sematically more adequate way, (b) include object names more often making expressions more pragmatically adequate, and (c) use more precise attributes also leading to more pragmatically adequate output. At the same time, the decoder also learns a strategy that can be considered as 'metric fitting', namely to (d) use more function words (articles, prepositions) which is a rather cheap strategy to increase BLEU scores. Finally, we find that the actor sometimes prevents the model from using short expressions containing rare words, as e.g. 'bride' in Figure 3(e).

These findings support the interpretation that a two-stage optimization set-up can help an REG model to pragmatically fine-tune its generation output. Vedantam et al. (2017) have recently adopted a similar approach, tuning a context-agnostic captioning system to produce discriminative captions at the stage of decoding (Yu et al., 2016).

7   Conclusion

We have investigated decoding strategies for neural REG, finding a clear advantage of trainable decoding optimized for BLEU over standard beam search methods. We think that this two-stage optimization set-up offers interesting directions for future work and can possibly be applied, for instance, in interactive learning scenarios and be tuned to more explicit communicative objectives.

References

Dzmitry Bahdanau, Kyunghyun Cho, and Yoshua Bengio. 2014. Neural machine translation by jointly learning to align and translate. *arXiv preprint arXiv:1409.0473*.

Yoshua Bengio, Jérôme Louradour, Ronan Collobert, and Jason Weston. 2009. Curriculum learning. In *Proceedings of the 26th annual international conference on machine learning*, pages 41–48. ACM.

Xinlei Chen, Hao Fang, Tsung-Yi Lin, Ramakrishna Vedantam, Saurabh Gupta, Piotr Dollár, and C Lawrence Zitnick. 2015. Microsoft coco captions: Data collection and evaluation server. *arXiv preprint arXiv:1504.00325*.

Yun Chen, Kyunghyun Cho, Samuel R Bowman, and Victor OK Li. 2018. Stable and effective trainable greedy decoding for sequence to sequence learning. In *ICLR 2018, Workshop Track*, Vancouver, Canada.

Alasdair DF Clarke, Micha Elsner, and Hannah Rohde. 2013. Where's wally: the influence of visual salience on referring expression generation. *Frontiers in psychology*, 4.

Robert Dale and Ehud Reiter. 1995. Computational interpretations of the gricean maxims in the generation of referring expressions. *Cognitive Science*, 19(2):233–263.

Kees van Deemter, Albert Gatt, Ielka van der Sluis, and Richard Power. 2012. Generation of referring expressions: Assessing the incremental algorithm. *Cognitive Science*, 36(5):799–836.

Markus Freitag and Yaser Al-Onaizan. 2017. Beam search strategies for neural machine translation. In *Proceedings of the First Workshop on Neural Machine Translation*, pages 56–60, Vancouver. Association for Computational Linguistics.

Albert Gatt and Anja Belz. 2010. Introducing shared tasks to nlg: The tuna shared task evaluation challenges. In *Empirical methods in natural language generation*, pages 264–293. Springer.

Dimitra Gkatzia, Verena Rieser, Phil Bartie, and William Mackaness. 2015. From the virtual to the real world: Referring to objects in real-world spatial scenes. In *Proceedings of EMNLP 2015*. Association for Computational Linguistics.

Alex Graves. 2012. Sequence transduction with recurrent neural networks. In *Representation Learning Worksop, ICML 2012*, Edinburgh, Scotland.

Jiatao Gu, Kyunghyun Cho, and Victor O.K. Li. 2017. Trainable greedy decoding for neural machine translation. In *Proceedings of the 2017 Conference on Empirical Methods in Natural Language Processing*, pages 1968–1978, Copenhagen, Denmark. Association for Computational Linguistics.

Liang Huang, Kai Zhao, and Mingbo Ma. 2017. When to finish? optimal beam search for neural text generation (modulo beam size). In *Proceedings of the 2017 Conference on Empirical Methods in Natural Language Processing*, pages 2134–2139, Copenhagen, Denmark. Association for Computational Linguistics.

Sahar Kazemzadeh, Vicente Ordonez, Mark Matten, and Tamara L Berg. 2014. ReferItGame: Referring to Objects in Photographs of Natural Scenes. In *Proceedings of the Conference on Empirical Methods in Natural Language Processing (EMNLP 2014)*, pages 787–798, Doha, Qatar.

Guillaume Klein, Yoon Kim, Yuntian Deng, Jean Senellart, and Alexander M. Rush. 2017. Opennmt: Open-source toolkit for neural machine translation. In *Proc. ACL*.

Ruud Koolen, Albert Gatt, Martijn Goudbeek, and Emiel Krahmer. 2011. Factors causing overspecification in definite descriptions. *Journal of Pragmatics*, 43(13):3231–3250.

Emiel Krahmer, Sebastiaan van Erk, and André Verleg. 2003. Graph-based generation of referring expressions. *Computational Linguistics*, 29(1):53–72.

Emiel Krahmer and Kees Van Deemter. 2012. Computational generation of referring expressions: A survey. *Computational Linguistics*, 38(1):173–218.

Jiwei Li, Will Monroe, and Dan Jurafsky. 2016. A simple, fast diverse decoding algorithm for neural generation. *CoRR*, abs/1611.08562.

Tsung-Yi Lin, Michael Maire, Serge Belongie, James Hays, Pietro Perona, Deva Ramanan, Piotr Dollr, and C.Lawrence Zitnick. 2014. Microsoft coco: Common objects in context. In *Computer Vision ECCV 2014*, volume 8693, pages 740–755. Springer International Publishing.

Junhua Mao, Jonathan Huang, Alexander Toshev, Oana Camburu, Alan L. Yuille, and Kevin Murphy. 2015. Generation and comprehension of unambiguous object descriptions. *ArXiv / CoRR*, abs/1511.02283.

Margaret Mitchell, Kees van Deemter, and Ehud Reiter. 2010. Natural reference to objects in a visual domain. In *Proceedings of the 6th international natural language generation conference*, pages 95–104. Association for Computational Linguistics.

Kishore Papineni, Salim Roukos, Todd Ward, and Wei-Jing Zhu. 2002. Bleu: a method for automatic evaluation of machine translation. In *Proceedings of the 40th annual meeting on association for computational linguistics*, pages 311–318. Association for Computational Linguistics.

Marc'Aurelio Ranzato, Sumit Chopra, Michael Auli, and Wojciech Zaremba. 2016. Sequence level training with recurrent neural networks. In *Proceedings of ICLR*.

Ehud Reiter and Robert Dale. 2000. *Building natural language generation systems*. Cambridge university press.

Alexander Rush, Yin-Wen Chang, and Michael Collins. 2013. Optimal beam search for machine translation. In *Proceedings of the 2013 Conference on Empirical Methods in Natural Language Processing*, pages 210–221.

David Schlangen, Sina Zarriess, and Casey Kennington. 2016. Resolving references to objects in photographs using the words-as-classifiers model. In *Proceedings of the 54rd Annual Meeting of the Association for Computational Linguistics (ACL 2016)*.

Karen Simonyan and Andrew Zisserman. 2014. Very deep convolutional networks for large-scale image recognition. *arXiv preprint arXiv:1409.1556*.

Ramakrishna Vedantam, Samy Bengio, Kevin Murphy, Devi Parikh, and Gal Chechik. 2017. Context-aware captions from context-agnostic supervision. In *Computer Vision and Pattern Recognition (CVPR)*, volume 3.

Ramakrishna Vedantam, C Lawrence Zitnick, and Devi Parikh. 2015. Cider: Consensus-based image description evaluation. In *Proceedings of the IEEE conference on computer vision and pattern recognition*, pages 4566–4575.

Oriol Vinyals and Quoc Le. 2015. A neural conversational model. *arXiv preprint arXiv:1506.05869*.

Yonghui Wu, Mike Schuster, Zhifeng Chen, Quoc V Le, Mohammad Norouzi, Wolfgang Macherey, Maxim Krikun, Yuan Cao, Qin Gao, Klaus Macherey, et al. 2016. Google's neural machine translation system: Bridging the gap between human and machine translation. *arXiv preprint arXiv:1609.08144*.

Kelvin Xu, Jimmy Ba, Ryan Kiros, Kyunghyun Cho, Aaron Courville, Ruslan Salakhudinov, Rich Zemel, and Yoshua Bengio. 2015. Show, attend and tell: Neural image caption generation with visual attention. In *International Conference on Machine Learning*, pages 2048–2057.

Licheng Yu, Patrick Poirson, Shan Yang, Alexander C. Berg, and Tamara L. Berg. 2016. *Modeling Context in Referring Expressions*. Springer International Publishing, Cham.

Licheng Yu, Hao Tan, Mohit Bansal, and Tamara L Berg. 2017. A joint speakerlistener-reinforcer model for referring expressions. In *Computer Vision and Pattern Recognition (CVPR)*, volume 2.

Sina Zarrieß and David Schlangen. 2016. Easy things first: Installments improve referring expression generation for objects in photographs. In *Proceedings of the 54th Annual Meeting of the Association for Computational Linguistics (Volume 1: Long Papers)*, pages 610–620, Berlin, Germany. Association for Computational Linguistics.

Author Index